ECONOMICS

Get Ahead of the Curve

With your purchase of a copy of this textbook, you received a Student Access Kit for MyEconLab for Parkin, Powell and Matthews, Seventh Edition

Don't throw it away!

The Power of Practice

MyEconLab puts you in control of your study, providing extensive practice exactly where and when you need it.

MyEconLab gives you unrivalled resources:

- Sample tests for each chapter to see how much you have learned.
- A personalized Study Plan, which constantly adapts to your strengths and weaknesses.
- An advanced Graphing Tool integrated into the exercises enables you to make and manipulate graphs to get a better understanding of how concepts, numbers and graphs connect.
- Animated figures from the textbook.
- Guided Solutions which break the problem into its component steps and guide you through with hints.
- E-text.
- An Online Glossary defines key terms and provides examples.
- Economics in the News – news links updated weekly during the academic year.
- Ask the Authors – extra help from the authors via email.

See the Guided Tour on page xxxi for more details.

To activate your pre-paid subscription go to **www.myeconlab.com/europarkin** and follow the instructions on-screen to register as a new user, and see your marks improve.

We work with leading authors to develop the strongest educational materials in economics bringing cutting-edge thinking and best learning practice to a global market.

Under a range of well-known imprints, including Addison Wesley, we craft high-quality print and electronic publications which help readers to understand and apply their content, whether studying or at work.

To find out more about the complete range of our publishing, please visit us on the World Wide Web at: www.pearsoned.co.uk.

SEVENTH EDITION

ECONOMICS

PARKIN POWELL MATTHEWS

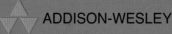

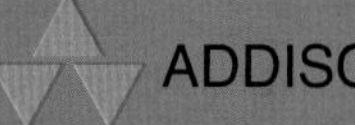
ADDISON-WESLEY

An imprint of Pearson Education

Harlow, England • London • New York • Boston • San Francisco • Toronto
Sydney • Tokyo • Singapore • Hong Kong • Seoul • Taipei • New Delhi
Cape Town • Madrid • Mexico City • Amsterdam • Munich • Paris • Milan

Pearson Education Limited
Edinburgh Gate
Harlow
Essex CM20 2JE
England

and Associated Companies throughout the world

Visit us on the World Wide Web at:
www.pearsoned.co.uk

Original edition entitled *Economics* published by Addison-Wesley Publishing Company, Inc. – A Pearson Education company

This edition published by Pearson Education Limited 2008

ISBN 978-0-13-204122-5

British Library Cataloguing-in-Publication Data
A catalogue record for this book is available from the British Library

10 9 8 7 6 5 4 3 2 1
11 10 09 08 07

Typeset in 10/12.5 Times by 35
Printed and bound by Mateu Cromo Artes Graficas, Spain

The publisher's policy is to use paper manufactured from sustainable forests.

About the Authors

Michael Parkin is Professor Emeritus in the Department of Economics at the University of Western Ontario, Canada, where he teaches the principles course to around 900 students each year. He studied economics at the University of Leicester but received his real training in the subject from an extraordinary group of economists at the University of Essex during the early 1970s. Professor Parkin has held faculty appointments at the Universities of Sheffield, Leicester, Essex and Manchester and visiting appointments at Brown University, Bond University, the Reserve Bank of Australia and the Bank of Japan. He is a past president of the Canadian Economics Association and has served on the editorial boards of the *American Economic Review* and the *Journal of Monetary Economics* and as managing editor of the *Manchester School* and the *Canadian Journal of Economics*. Professor Parkin's economic research has resulted in over 160 publications in journals and edited volumes, including the *American Economic Review*, the *Journal of Political Economy*, the *Review of Economic Studies*, the *Economic Journal*, *Economica*, the *Manchester School*, the *Journal of Monetary Economics* and the *Journal of Money, Credit and Banking*, and edited volumes. He became visible to the public through his work on inflation that discredited the use of prices and incomes policies.

Melanie Powell took her first degree at Kingston University and her MSc in economics at Birkbeck College, London University. She has been a research fellow in health economics at York University, a principal lecturer in economics at Leeds Metropolitan University, and the director of economic studies and part-time MBAs at the Leeds University Business School. She is now a Reader at the University of Derby, Derbyshire Business School. Her main interests as a microeconomist are in applied welfare economics, and she has many publications in the area of health economics and decision making. Her current research uses the experimental techniques of psychology applied to economic decision making.

Kent Matthews received his training as an economist at the London School of Economics, Birkbeck College University of London and the University of Liverpool. He is currently the Sir Julian Hodge Professor of Banking and Finance at the Cardiff Business School. He has held research appointments at the London School of Economics, the National Institute of Economic and Social Research, the Bank of England and Lombard Street Research Ltd, and faculty positions at the Universities of Liverpool, Western Ontario, Leuven, Liverpool John Moores and Humbolt Berlin. He is the author of eight books and over 60 papers in scholarly journals and edited volumes. His research interest is in applied macroeconomics and the economics of banking.

To Our Students

Brief Contents

Contents

**Summary (Key Points, Key Figures and Tables and Key Terms), Problems, Critical Thinking, and Web Activities appear at the end of each chapter.*

Guided Tour for Students

Setting the Scene

PART 2

How Markets Work

The Amazing Market

The five chapters that you will study in this part explain how markets work. A market is an amazing instrument. It enables people who have never met and who know nothing about each other to interact and do business. It also enables us to allocate our scarce resources to the uses that we value most highly.

You will begin in Chapter 3 by learning about the laws of demand and supply. You will discover the forces that make prices adjust to coordinate buyers' plans and sellers' plans.

In Chapter 4, you will meet the handy concept of elasticity and learn how to calculate, interpret and use it to predict how prices and quantities respond to changes in supply and demand.

In Chapter 5, you will discover what Adam Smith called "the invisible hand". You will see that when people pursue their self-interest in competitive markets, the outcome is in the social interest – resources go to their most highly valued uses.

In Chapter 6, you will learn about markets in action when governments intervene to fix the minimum price or the maximum price, impose taxes or quotas, or make some goods illegal.

Finally, in Chapter 7, you will study global markets in action. There, you will see how globalization brings gains from international trade and why restrictions on international trade benefit producers but damage the interest of consumers and are not in the social interest.

The book is divided into six parts. **Part Openers** clearly explain why a group of chapters are linked and how they relate to the previous and following parts, ensuring that you understand the connections among topics.

CHAPTER 3

Demand and Supply

After studying this chapter you will be able to:

- Describe a competitive market and think about a price as an opportunity cost
- Explain the influences on demand
- Explain the influences on supply
- Explain how demand and supply determine prices and quantities bought and sold
- Use demand and supply to make predictions about changes in prices and quantities

Energy Drinks Market Sparkles!

The market for energy drinks has exploded over the past few years and in 2007, Europeans spent almost €4 billion on these drinks. Despite this huge increase in consumption, the prices of energy drinks have been remarkably stable as dozens of new producers have entered the market.

Not all prices have been stable. Some, such as the price of a PC have tumbled whereas others such as the prices of houses and the prices commodities such as copper have rocketed.

Find out in this chapter what determines prices. And in *Reading Between the Lines* at the end of the chapter, put what you learn to work by explaining why the world price of copper jumped in 2006.

Learning Objectives enable you to see exactly where the chapter is going and to set your goals before you begin the chapter. We link these goals directly to the chapter's major headings.

Chapter Introductions motivate the topic and set the scene. We carry the introductory story into the main body of the chapter and return to it in the *Reading Between the Lines* or the *Business Case Study* at the end of the chapter.

Using the Study Tools

A **price ceiling** is a government regulation of the maximum price that may be legally charged. Trading at a price that exceeds the price ceiling is illegal and subject to penalties. Price ceilings have been many goods and services but most market for petrol and rental housing.

Highlighted **Key Terms** within the text simplify your task of learning the vocabulary of economics. Each term appears in a list of **Key Terms** at the end of the chapter and in the **Glossary** at the end of the book. The terms are also highlighted in the index and can be found online in the MyEconLab glossary and Flashcards.

Key Terms

Black market, 123
Minimum wage, 125
Price ceiling, 122
Price floor, 125
Price support, 134
Production quota, 134
Rent ceiling, 122
Search activity, 123
Subsidy, 133
Tax incidence, 127

Price ceiling A government regulation that sets the maximum price that may legally be charged. (p. 122)

Price discrimination The practice of selling different units of a good or service for different prices or of charging one customer different prices for different quantities bought. (p. 265)

Figure 3.6 myeconlab

A Change in the Quantity Supplied versus a Change in Supply

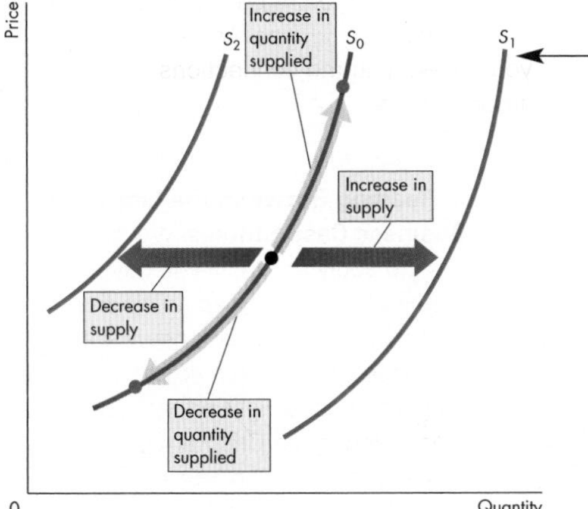

When the price of the good changes, there is a movement along the supply curve and *a change in the quantity supplied,* shown by the blue arrows on supply curve S_0.

When any other influence on selling plans changes, there is a shift of the supply curve and a *change in supply.* An increase in supply shifts the supply curve rightward (from S_0 *to* S_1), and a decrease in supply shifts the supply curve leftward (from S_0 *to* S_2).

Diagrams show where the economic action is! Graphical analysis is the most powerful tool available for teaching and learning economics. We have developed the diagrams with the study and review needs of students in mind. Our diagrams feature:

- Original curves consistently shown in blue
- Shifted curves consistently shown in red
- Colour-blended arrows to suggest movement
- Other important features highlighted in red
- Graphs often paired with data tables
- Graphs labelled with boxed notes
- Extended captions that make each diagram and its caption a self-contained object for study and review
- Every diagram can be found with a step-by-step animation in MyEconLab.

A **Review Quiz** at the end of every major section is tied to the chapter's learning objectives and enables you to go over the material again to reinforce your understanding of a topic before moving on. More practice on the topics can be found in the **MyEconLab Study Plan**.

Review Quiz

Study Plan 3.2

1 Define the quantity demanded of a good or service.
2 What is the law of demand and how do we illustrate it?
3 What does the demand curve tell us about the price that consumers are willing to pay?
4 List all the influences on buying plans that change demand and for each influence say whether it increases or decreases demand.
5 Distinguish between the quantity demanded of a good and demand for the good.
6 Why does the demand not change when the price of a good changes with no change in the other influences on buying plans?

Connecting with Reality

A series of **Boxes** show you the connections between theory and real-world data or events. Tables and figures put the real-world flesh on the bones of the models and help you learn how to apply your newly gained knowledge of economic principles to the economic world around you.

Box 9.1

European Firms' Size and Profitability

There are approximately 3 million firms in the United Kingdom and more than 90 per cent of them are very small businesses, which employ fewer than 10 workers. Small firms comprise a similarly high percentage of firms in most EU countries.

Table 1 shows the relative importance of the sizes of firms in 20 European countries (EU15 plus Iceland, Liechtenstein, Norway and Switzerland). Micro size firms (with fewer than 10 employees) comprise 93 per cent of all firms and they employ 34 per cent of all workers. Large firms (with 250 or more employees) comprise only 0.2 per cent of all firms but also employ 34 per cent of all workers.

Figure 1 shows the relationship between the profitability and firm size in the same 20 countries. The average profit rate across all firms is 39 per cent. Large and medium firms have profit rates that exceed the average, and small and micro size firms have profit rates below the average. The advantages of large scale in dealing with the principal–agent problem may exceed the benefits of small size in Europe's competitive economies.

Table 1

Firm Size and Employment

Number of employees	Size	Percentage of all firms	Percentage of firms' employment
< 10	Micro	93.0	34
10 < 50	Small	6.0	19
50 < 250	Medium	0.8	13
≥ 250	Large	0.2	34

Figure 1

Profitability by Firm Size

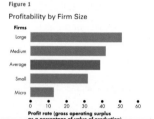

Firms: Large, Medium, Average, Small, Micro

0 10 20 30 40 50 60

Profit rate (gross operating surplus as a percentage of value of production)

Source of data: European Commission, *Observatory of European SMEs*, No. 2, 2002.

74 CHAPTER 3 DEMAND AND SUPPLY

Reading Between the Lines

Demand and Supply: Copper Prices Rise

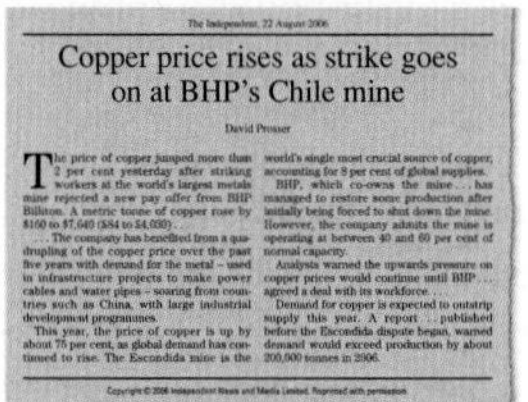

The Independent, 22 August 2006

Copper price rises as strike goes on at BHP's Chile mine

David Prosser

Copyright © 2006 Independent News and Media Limited. Reprinted with permission.

The Essence of the Story

- The world's largest copper mine in Chile was shut down when workers went on strike during a pay dispute.
- When production restarted it was only 40–60 per cent of normal output.
- The price of copper increased by £84 a tonne during the dispute.
- The price of copper has quadrupled over the past five years as a result of increased demand for copper in countries such as China.
- Analysts expect the price of copper to keep rising even if the dispute is settled.

READING BETWEEN THE LINES 75

Economic Analysis

- Figure 1 shows the world market for copper in August 2006, before the strike at the BHP Chile copper mine. The supply curve is S_0 and the demand curve is D_0. The equilibrium price is £3,946 per tonne and the equilibrium quantity is Q_0.
- The strike at the Chile copper mine decreased world supply. The supply curve in Figure 1 shifted leftward from S_0 to S_1.
- The world demand curve was constant at D in Figure 1 during the week of the strike.
- The equilibrium price of copper during the strike increased from £3,946 to £4,030 a tonne and the equilibrium quantity fell from Q_0 to Q_1.
- If the mine returns to full capacity, the supply curve in Figure 1 will shift back from S_1 to S_0 and the price will fall back to £3,046, other things remaining the same.
- The world demand for copper has been increasing each year as countries such as China expand industrial production.
- Figure 2 shows the world market for copper between 2005 and 2007. Without the effect of the strike, world supply is constant at S_0.
- In December 2005, the world demand for copper was D_{05}. During 2006, demand increased and by August 2006, the demand curve had shifted rightward to D_{06}. The equilibrium price had risen by 75 per cent from £2,255 to £3,946 and the equilibrium quantity had increased from Q_0 to Q_1.
- World demand increased in 2007 and the demand curve shifted rightward from D_{06} to D_{07}.
- By the start of 2007, and with no price change, demand was expected to exceed supply by 200,000 tones. Figure 2 shows this shortage as $(Q_2 - Q_1)$ at a price of £3,946 per tonne.
- A shortage raises the price. The copper price could rise a further 75 per cent to £6,906 per tonne.

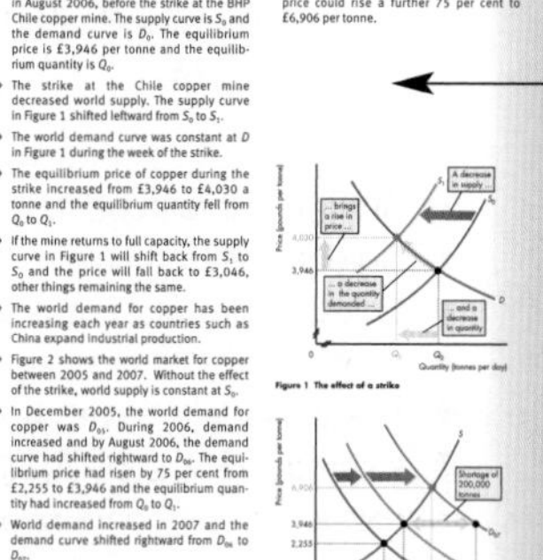

Figure 1 The effect of a strike

Figure 2 The effect of rising world demand

In **Reading Between the Lines** and **Business Case Studies**, we show you how to apply the tools you have learned by analyzing an article from a newspaper or an online news source. We have chosen each article so that it sheds additional light on the questions first raised in the Chapter Opener. Questions about the article appear in Critical Thinking exercises at the end of the chapter.

Each chapter closes with a concise **Summary** organized by major topics, a list of **Key Terms** (with page references), **Problems**, **Critical Thinking** exercises, and **Web Activities**. You can find solutions to odd-numbered problems on MyEconLab. Even-numbered problems are left for you to solve on your own.

78 CHAPTER 3 DEMAND AND SUPPLY

Summary

Key Points

Markets and Prices (p. 58)

Demand (pp. 59–63)

Supply (pp. 64–67)

Market Equilibrium (pp. 68–69)

Predicting Changes in Price and Quantity (pp. 70–73)

Key Figures

Key Terms

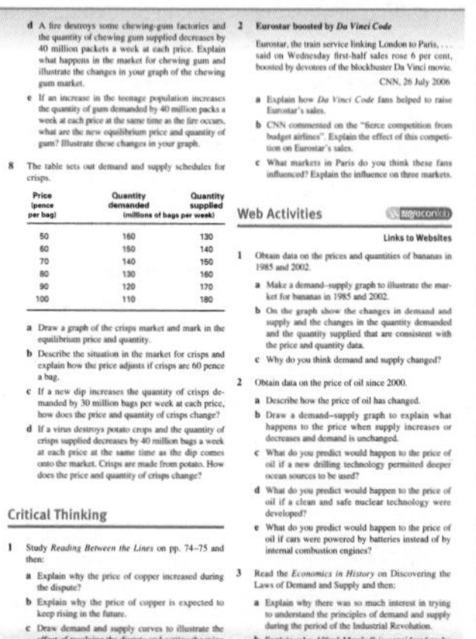

80 CHAPTER 3 DEMAND AND SUPPLY

Web Activities

Critical Thinking

Using MyEconLab

Packaged with every copy of the new, seventh edition of Parkin, Powell and Matthews, **MyEconLab** puts you in control of your study. To register as a new user, go to **www.myeconlab.com/europarkin** and follow the instructions on-screen using the code in your Student Access Kit.

By using MyEconLab, you *test* your understanding and *practise* what you have learned.

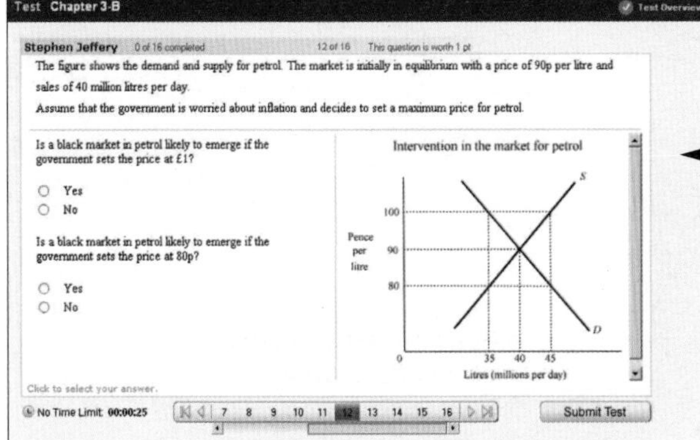

Sample Tests (two for each chapter) are preloaded in MyEconLab and enable you to test your understanding and identify the areas in which you need to do further work. Your lecturer might also create custom tests or quizzes.

MyEconLab creates a personal **Study Plan** for you based on your performance on tests. The Study Plan diagnoses weaknesses and consists of a series of additional exercises with detailed feedback and Guided Solutions for topics in which you need further help. The Study Plan is also linked to other study tools.

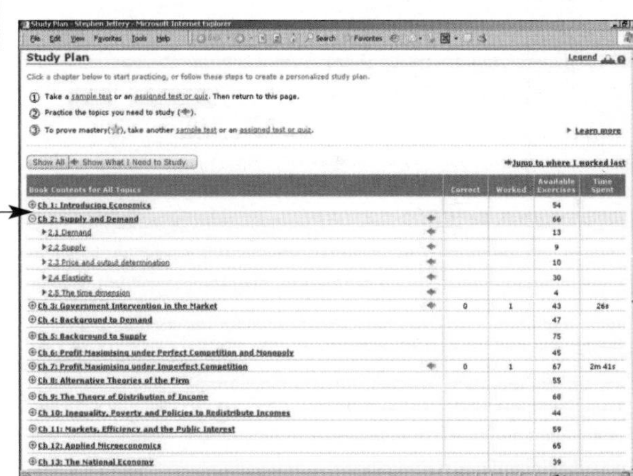

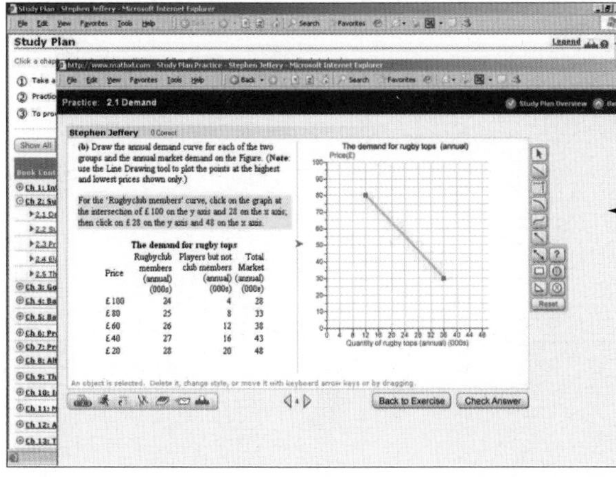

From the Study Plan exercises, you can link to **Guided Solutions** (step-by-step explanations) and an **electronic version of your textbook** with all the **figures animated**.

Note on MyEconLab for Lecturers

Why MyEconLab?

MyEconLab:

- Provides your students with practice tailored to their strengths and weaknesses.
- Provides you with a low-cost means of monitoring and testing your students.

How Do my Students Access MyEconLab?

Your students receive their prepaid Student Access Kit for MyEconlab when they buy a new copy of this text book. (They can alternatively buy an Access Kit.)

Each student individually registers online at **www.myeconlab.com/europarkin**, following the instructions on the Access Kit card, and can then make full use of the resources.

What Do I Need to Do?

Nothing! Your students automatically have access to MyEconLab's Sample Tests, Study Plan, and other resources. But you may choose to do any of the following:

- Monitor your students
- Set assignments
- Self-author exercises

Monitor Your Students

MyEconLab's gradebook automatically records each student's time spent and performance on the Tests and Study Plan and generates reports that you can organize either by student or by chapter. You can easily copy and paste data from the Gradebook into a spreadsheet for combining with your exam and paper test marks.

Set Assignments

You can use MyEconLab to build your own tests, quizzes, or homework assignments from the question base provided. The questions include multiple choice, graph drawing and free response. Many of the questions are generated algorithmically so that they present differently each time they are used.

If you set assignments, you need to be aware of the distinction between a Test, Quiz and Homework.

A Test and a Quiz play like an examination with no help and no feedback. Use this format when you want to test your students and give credit for their performance.

Homework plays like exercises in the Study Plan and gives the student detailed feedback and links to help in the form of guided solutions, the glossary, the electronic textbook and animated figures. Use this format when you want your students to do some practice and you want to know that they've done it.

Self-author Exercises

If you want to devote the time, you can create your own exercises by using the Econ Exercise Builder.

Special Versions of MyEconLab

MyEconLab with CourseCompass places the resources inside a course management system. To find out more about CourseCompass go to **www.coursecompass.com**.

MyEconLab Institutional Site licence is also available.

Please contact your local Academic Sales Representative at **www.pearsoned.co.uk/replocator** for further details of these options.

Lecturer Support

You can use MyEconLab in a wide variety of ways and spend no time or invest a great deal of time in tailoring it to your personal needs.

Pearson Education offers you personalized support for MyEconLab through its dedicated team of Technology Specialists. Their job is to support you in your use of all Pearson Education's media products, including MyEconLab.

To contact your Technology Specialist please go to **www.pearsoned.co.uk/replocator**.

Preface

To change the way students see the world – that has been our aim throughout the seven editions of this book.

The cover is a metaphor for this aim. It depicts scene in the economic world viewed through a geometric icon. The icon represents the clarity that economic science brings to our view and understanding of the economic world. When we view the world without the economic lens, we see questions but not answers. The lens provides answers by enabling us to focus on the unseen structures that shape our world. It is a tool that enables us to see the invisible forces.

This book equips students with the economic lens, shows them how to use it and enables them to gain their own informed and structured view of the economic world. It presents economics as a serious, lively and evolving science. Its goal is to open students' eyes to the "economic way of thinking" and to help them gain insights into how the economy works and how it might be made to work better.

We provide a thorough and complete coverage of the subject, using a straightforward, precise and clear writing style.

We are conscious that many students find economics hard, so we place the student at centre stage and write for the student. We use language that doesn't intimidate and that allows the student to concentrate on the substance.

We open each chapter with a clear statement of learning objectives, a brief student-friendly vignette and an illustration to grab attention. We illustrate principles with examples that are selected to hold the student's interest and to make the subject lively. And we put principles to work by using them to illuminate current real-world problems and issues.

Whether we're explaining traditional topics or more advanced ones such as oligopoly games, the principal–agent problem, public choices, uncertainty, asymmetric information, rational expectations, new growth theory and real business cycle theory, we repeatedly use the familiar core ideas and tools that unify economics.

Today's introductory economics course springs from today's issues – the information revolution and the new economy, the expansion of global trade and investment, the economics of climate change, the economic shockwaves of global terrorism and corporate scandals. But the principles that we use to understand these issues remain the core principles of our science.

Governments and international agencies place continued emphasis on long-term fundamentals as they seek to promote economic growth. This book reflects this emphasis.

To help promote a rich, active learning experience, we have developed a comprehensive online learning environment, MyEconLab, which features a personal study plan, dynamic e-book, quizzes and tests and weekly news updates.

The Seventh Edition Revision

Economics, Seventh Edition, retains all of the improvements achieved in its predecessor with its thorough and detailed presentation of modern economics, emphasis on real-world examples and critical thinking skills, diagrams renowned for pedagogy and precision and path-breaking technology. Every chapter has been critically reviewed and thoroughly updated. Beyond these widespread revisions, this new edition contains seven major revisions. They are:

- A new chapter on global markets in action
- A new treatment of consumer theory
- A revised treatment of factor markets
- A new chapter on uncertainty and information
- An expanded coverage of loanable funds markets
- A reorganized account of the monetary system
- An updated explanation of current monetary policy
- New *Reading Between the Lines*.

Global Markets in Action

A new Chapter 7 explains how global markets work, who gains and who loses from international trade and why globalization is in the social interest. The chapter applies the core ideas of comparative advantage

(Chapter 2), demand and supply (Chapter 3), and consumer surplus, producer surplus and deadweight loss (Chapter 5). By covering this topic early in the course, students are able to engage intelligently in the contemporary debate on globalization.

Consumer Theory

We have consolidated our coverage of consumer theory into a single chapter and appendix. The chapter presents the mainstream indifference curve analysis and the appendix presents the older, but still insightful, marginal utility analysis as well as explaining the links between the two approaches.

Factor Markets

We now cover unions and other non-competitive elements of factor markets in the body of the chapter and have moved the technicalities of discounting and present value calculation to an appendix.

Uncertainty and Information

New to this edition, Chapter 19 explains decisions in the face of risk and uncertainty and in the presence of asymmetric information. We explain how insurance markets and portfolio diversification limit risk. And we explain how signals and efficient contracts help markets cope with moral hazard and adverse selection. These topics are explained in clear non-technical language.

Loanable Funds Market

Chapter 24, "In the Long Run: The Classical Model", provides a comprehensive account of the factors that determine potential GDP, employment and the real wage rate at full employment. This chapter also explains how investment, saving and the real interest rate are determined in the long run in the loanable funds market.

The Monetary System

We have achieved some streamlining and avoidance of duplication in our coverage of the monetary system and money creation process by reorganizing the chapters on this topic. Chapter 27, "The Monetary System", now includes a section on central banking, explains how the banking system creates money by making loans and explains the money multiplier – the relationship between the monetary base and the quantity of money.

Monetary Policy

Our monetary policy chapter (Chapter 28) is essentially a new chapter. Its goal is to enable the student to read and understand news reports on the Bank of England's interest rate decisions and the Bank's *Inflation Report*. The chapter describes the objectives and framework of monetary policy and how the Bank of England makes its interest rate decision. The chapter also explains the transmission channels through which monetary policy influences real economic activity and ultimately, the inflation rate. The chapter closes with a comparison of alternative monetary policy strategies.

This new monetary policy chapter combines material found in monetary policy and macro policy challenges chapters of the previous edition.

Reading Between the Lines

All of the *Reading Between the Lines* (except for one classic) have been replaced with new news articles and economic analysis.

For the Lecturer

This book enables you to achieve three objectives in your principles course:

- Focus on the economic way of thinking
- Explain the issues and problems of our time
- Choose your own course structure.

Focus on the Economic Way of Thinking

You know how hard it is to encourage a student to think like an economist. But that is your goal. Consistent with this goal, the text focuses on and repeatedly uses the central ideas: choice; trade-off; opportunity cost; the margin; incentives; the gains from voluntary exchange; the forces of demand, supply, and equilibrium; the pursuit of economic rent; the tension between self-interest and the social interest; and the scope and limitations of government actions.

Explain the Issues and Problems of Our Time

Students must *use* the central ideas and tools if they are to begin to *understand* them. There is no better way to motivate students than by using the tools of economics to explain the issues that confront today's world. Issues such as globalization and the emergence of China as a major economic force; the new economy with new near-monopolies such as eBay and the widening income gap between rich and poor; the post 9/11 economy and the reallocation of resources towards counter-terrorism and the defence that it entails; corporate scandals and the principal–agent problems and incentives faced by corporate managers; HIV/AIDS and the enormous cost of drugs for treating it; the disappearing tropical rainforests and the challenge that this tragedy of the commons creates; the challenge of managing the world's water resources; and the persistent unemployment.

Choose Your Own Course Structure

You want to teach your own course. We have organized this book to enable you to do so. We demonstrate the book's flexibility in the flexibility chart and alternative sequences table that appear on pp. xl–xliii. You can use this book to teach a traditional course that blends theory and policy or a current policy issues course. Your micro course can emphasize theory or policy. You can structure your macro course to emphasize long-term growth and supply-side fundamentals. Or you can follow a traditional macro sequence and emphasize short-term fluctuations. The choices are yours.

Lecturer's Manual

Melanie Powell, working with Derek Fry and Eugen Mihaita of the University of Derby, has created a Lecturer's Manual. Each chapter contains an outline, what's new in the Seventh Edition, teaching suggestions, a look at where we have been and where we are going, a description of the electronic supplements, additional discussion questions, answers to the Review Quizzes and solutions to end-of-chapter problems.

Test Banks

Andrew Hunt of Durham University and Dimitrios Pontikakis of the National University of Ireland, Galway, have reviewed and edited all our Test Bank questions and created many new questions to ensure their clarity and consistency with the Seventh Edition.

An electronic Test Bank provides 3,500 multiple-choice questions. This Test Bank is available in Test Generator Software (TestGen with QuizMaster). Fully networkable, it is available for Windows and Macintosh. TestGen's graphical interface enables lecturers to view, edit and add questions; transfer questions to tests; and print different forms of tests. Tests can be formatted with varying fonts and styles, margins and headers and footers, as in any word-processing document. Search and sort features let the lecturer quickly locate questions and arrange them in a preferred order. QuizMaster, working with your university's computer network, automatically marks the exams, stores the results on disk and allows the lecturer to view or print a variety of reports.

A PDF Test Bank provides a further 1,500 true-false and numerical questions.

Both the electronic Test Bank and the PDF Test Bank are available online to download from **www.pearsoned.co.uk/parkin** and in the lecturers' resources section of MyEconbLab.

PowerPoint Lecture Notes

Robin Bade and Michael Parkin have developed a Microsoft PowerPoint lecture presentation for each chapter that includes all the figures from the text, animated graphs, and brief speaking notes. The slide outlines are based on the chapter outlines in the Lecturer's Manual, and the speaking notes are based on the Lecturer's Manual teaching suggestions. The presentations can be used electronically in the classroom or can be printed to create hard-copy transparency masters.

Clicker Questions

Andrew Hunt and Dimitrios Pontikakis have created a set of 10 multiple-choice Clicker Questions per chapter that encapsulate the chapter and are based on Test Bank questions. Clicker Questions enable students to use a group and audience response system and the wireless response technology enables lecturers to gather instant feedback from students and respond to it during the lecture. The system also enables student responses to be captured in a gradebook.

The Clicker Questions are embedded in PowerPoint sides and are available in both Turning Point and PRS, the two main types of personal response system software in use today.

MyEconLab

MyEconLab is an online resource for your economics course. Its central features are a powerful graphing engine and large bank of questions for study (with Guided Solutions) and testing. Lecturers can create and assign tests, quizzes or homework assignments that incorporate graphing questions. MyEconLab saves lecturers time by automatically marking all questions and tracking results in an online gradebook.

Questions include multiple choice, free response (usually numerical) and draw-graph. Many questions are generated algorithmically, so there lots of variety and practice opportunity.

The complete Test Bank is also preloaded into MyEconLab, giving lecturers ample material from which they can create assignments.

Once registered for MyEconLab, lecturers have access to downloadable supplements such as the Lecturer's Manual, PowerPoint lecture notes, Clicker questions and Test Banks. Lecturers also have access to a "Consult the Author" feature that allows them to ask questions of and make suggestions to authors via e-mail and receive a response within 24 hours.

Every week, we post a news headline and a link to a news article. We provide links to Web sites for students to use as sources of further information about the topic in the article. We also provide a number of questions that can be assigned as topics for either essays or classroom discussion.

You can see a Note on MyEconLab for Lecturers on p. xxxiii.

For more information about MyEconLab, or to request an Instructor Access Code, visit **http://www.myeconlab.com/europarkin**.

For the Student

Three outstanding support tools for the student are:

- MyEconLab
- Student PowerPoint Lecture Notes
- Podcast Study Help.

MyEconLab

MyEconLab is an online resource that students can use to self-test and practise. Sample Tests for each chapter enable students to test their ability and identify the areas in which they need further work. Based on a student's performance on a practice test, a personal Study Plan shows where further study needs to focus. Once students have received their Study Plan, additional practice exercises, keyed to the textbook, provide extensive practice. The Study Plan also has links directly to the e-text with animated graphs and other resources.

The powerful graphing tool integrated into both the practice tests and practice exercises enables students to draw and label graphs and test their understanding of the connections among concepts, numbers, and graphs. For more details on how to use MyEconLab, see the Guided Tour for Students on p. xxviii.

PowerPoint Lecture Notes

Robin Bade and Michael Parkin have prepared a set of Microsoft PowerPoint lecture notes especially for students. These notes contain an outline of each chapter with the textbook figures animated. Students can download these lecture notes from MyEconLab, print them and bring them to class or use them to create their own set of notes for use when preparing for tests or exams.

Podcast Study Help

We are sensitive to the fact that many students like to get information through their iPods or MP3 players. To respond to this important technological trend, we intend to deliver audio guides to chapters. For the current edition, Melanie Powell and Kent Matthews plan to make podcasts for two sample chapters. If the system works well, more chapters will be added during the life of the seventh edition. Students can download the files from MyEconLab.

Acknowledgements

We extend our gratitude and thanks to the many people who have contributed to this new edition of our text and to all those who made such important contributions to the previous editions on which this one is based. So many people have provided help and encouragement either directly or indirectly that it is impossible to name them all.

We particularly thank our colleagues, present and past, who have helped to shape our understanding of economics and who have provided help in the creation of this new edition. We thank our reviewers who have read and commented on our work and provided countless good ideas that we have eagerly accepted. We also thank our families for their input and patience.

We especially acknowledge and express our deep gratitude to Robin Bade whose innovative work on the most recent Canadian edition has been invaluable to us. We also thank Robin for her meticulous reading of this edition and for the uncountable, some detailed and some major, improvements she has brought to it.

We thank Richard Parkin for his work on the graphics, both in the text and on MyEconLab.

We thank Derek Fry and Eugen Mihaita of the University of Derby for their work (with Melanie) on the Lecturer's Manual and Andrew Hunt of Durham University and Dimitrios Pontikakis of the National University of Ireland, Galway, for their work on the Test Banks and Clicker Questions.

We thank Jeannie Gillmore and Laurel Davies for their work on MyEconLab test questions.

We could not have produced this book without the help of the people for whom it is written, our students. We thank the several thousand students we have been privileged to teach over many years. Their comments on previous editions (and on our teaching) whether in complaint or praise have been invaluable.

Nor could we have produced this book without the help of our publisher. We thank the many outstanding editors, media specialists, and others at Pearson Education who contributed to the concerted publishing effort that brought this edition to completion. They are: Julian Partridge, Editorial Director; Ellen Morgan, Acquisitions Editor; Hetty Reid, Development Editor; Stephen Jeffery, Content Systems Manager; Joe Vella, Senior Editor; Anita Atkinson, Senior Editor; Kevin Ancient, Design Manager; Angela Hawksbee, Senior Project Controller; Sylvia Edvinsson Marketing Manager; and Katherine Hyde, Marketing Executive. Michelle Neil, Executive Media Producer, managed the development of MyEconLab.

Finally, we want to thank our reviewers. A good textbook is the distillation of the collective wisdom of a generation of dedicated teachers. We have been privileged to tap into this wisdom. We extend our thanks to Douglas Chalmers, Glasgow Caledonian University; Steve Cook, Swansea University; Valerie Dickie, Heriot-Watt University; Maria Gil Molto, Loughborough University; Karen Jackson, University of Bradford; Gorm Jacobsen, Agder University, Norway; M. J. McCrostie, University of Buckingham; Chris Reid, University of Portsmouth; Cillian Ryan, University of Birmingham; Jen Snowball, Rhodes University, South Africa; and Phil Tomlinson, University of Bath. We also thank other reviewers who have asked to remain anonymous.

As always, the proof of the pudding is in the eating! The value of this book will be decided by its users and whether you are a student or a teacher, we encourage you to send us your comments and suggestions.

Michael Parkin,
University of Western Ontario,
michael.parkin@uwo.ca

Melanie Powell
University of Derby,
m.j.powell@derby.ac.uk

Kent Matthews,
Cardiff University,
MatthewsK@Cardiff.ac.uk

Flexibility Chart

Core	Policy	Optional
1 What Is Economics? 2 The Economic Problem 3 Demand and Supply 4 Elasticity		1 Appendix: Graphs in Economics Useful for students with a fear of graphs. 1 Mathematical Note: Equations to Straight Lines
5 Efficiency and Equity A chapter that provides a non-technical explanation of efficiency and equity that unifies the micro material and permits early coverage of policy issues in Chapters 14–16.	6 Markets in Action A chapter that gives extensive applications of demand and supply, elasticity, and efficiency and equity to the issues of price floors and ceilings, taxes, agriculture markets and markets for illegal goods.	3 Mathematical Note: Demand, Supply and Equilibrium
	7 Global Markets in Action A chapter that explains the gains from international trade and provides an application of the *PPF* model as well as extensive applications of demand and supply and efficiency to explain the distribution of gains and losses from international trade.	8 Households' Choices An unusual full chapter on indifference curves ensures that if you want to cover this material, you can do so with confidence. (Other texts condense this topic to render it indigestable.) This chapter presents marginal utility theory and the connections between indifference curves and marginal utility in an appendix. 9 Organizing Production This chapter may be skipped or assigned as reading.
10 Output and Costs 11 Perfect Competition 12 Monopoly		10 Appendix: Producing at Least Cost
13 Monopolistic Competition and Oligopoly	14 Government Regulation and Competition Policy Introduces the public choice theory of government and sets the scene for the following policy chapters. The first part of this chapter along with Chapters 15 and 16 can be covered any time after Chapter 5. 15 Externalities 16 Public Goods and Common Resources	
17 The Demand for Factors of Production	18 Economic Inequality and Redistribution	19 Uncertainty and Information

Flexibility Chart

Core	Policy	Optional
20 A First Look at Macroeconomics		
21 Measuring GDP and Economic Growth		
22 Monitoring Jobs and the Price Level		
23 Aggregate Supply and Aggregate Demand		24 In the Long Run: The Classical Model Strongly recommended in the light of the Kydland-Prescott 2004 Nobel Prize. You may wish to study this material before aggregate supply in Chapter 23.
		25 In the Short Run: The Keynesian Model If you cover fiscal policy multipliers in Chapter 26, you need this chapter. You may wish to study this material before aggregate demand in Chapter 23.
		25 Mathematical Note: The Algebra of the Multiplier
	26 Fiscal Policy	26 Mathematical Note: The Algebra of Fiscal Policy Multipliers
27 The Monetary System A newly organized chapter that describes the monetary system, including the central bank, and explains how the banking system creates money and how the quantity of money and the monetary base are connected.	28 Monetary Policy A thoroughly revised chapter that explains the objectives, implementation, and effects of the Bank of England's monetary policy as well as an account of alternative approaches to monetary policy	
	29 Fiscal and Monetary Policy Interactions	29 Appendix: The *IS–LM* Model of Aggregate Demand
30 Inflation		
31 Economic Growth		32 The Business Cycle Cycles and policy are covered throughout the macro chapters and Chapter 32 provides a deeper and more unified coverage of these topics.
		33 International Finance This international finance chapter may be covered at any time after Chapter 3 (with a minor omission of material on the national accounts).

Three Alternative Sequences for Microeconomics

Traditional Theory and Policy

1 What Is Economics?
2 The Economic Problem
3 Demand and Supply
4 Elasticity
5 Efficiency and Equity
6 Markets in Action
7 Global Markets in Action
8 Households' Choices
9 Organizing Production
10 Output and Costs
11 Perfect Competition
12 Monopoly
13 Monopolistic Competition and Oligopoly
14 Government Regulation and Competition Policy
15 Externalities
16 Public Goods and Common Resources
17 The Demand for Factors of Production
18 Economic Inequality and Redistribution
19 Uncertainty and Information

Microeconomics with a Business Emphasis

1 What Is Economics?
2 The Economic Problem
3 Demand and Supply
4 Elasticity
5 Efficiency and Equity
6 Markets in Action
7 Global Markets in Action
9 Organizing Production
10 Output and Costs
11 Perfect Competition
12 Monopoly
13 Monopolistic Competition and Oligopoly

Microeconomics with a Policy Emphasis

1 What Is Economics?
2 The Economic Problem
3 Demand and Supply
4 Elasticity
5 Efficiency and Equity
6 Markets in Action
7 Global Markets in Action
14 Government Regulation and Competition Policy
15 Externalities
16 Public Goods and Common Resources
17 The Demand for Factors of Production
18 Economic Inequality and Redistribution

Four Alternative Sequences for Macroeconomics

Traditional Theory and Policy	Classical Perspective	Keynesian Perspective	Monetarist Perspective
20 A First Look at Macroeconomics	20 A First Look at Macroeconomics	20 A First Look at Macroeconomics	20 A First Look at Macroeconomics
21 Measuring GDP and Economic Growth	21 Measuring GDP and Economic Growth	21 Measuring GDP and Economic Growth	21 Measuring GDP and Economic Growth
22 Monitoring Jobs and the Price Level	22 Monitoring Jobs and the Price Level	22 Monitoring Jobs and the Price Level	22 Monitoring Jobs and the Price Level
23 Aggregate Supply and Aggregate Demand	24 In the Long Run: The Classical Model	25 In the Short Run: The Keynesian Model	24 In the Long Run: The Classical Model
24 In the Long Run: The Classical Model	31 Economic Growth	26 Fiscal Policy [omit supply-side sections]	22 Aggregate Supply and Aggregate Demand
25 In the Short Run: The Keynesian Model	32 The Business Cycle [sections on real business cycle theory]	27 The Monetary System	27 The Monetary System
26 Fiscal Policy	27 The Monetary System	28 Monetary Policy	28 Monetary Policy
27 The Monetary System	28 Monetary Policy	29 Fiscal and Monetary Policy Interactions	30 Inflation
28 Monetary Policy	30 Inflation	30 Inflation	32 The Business Cycle
29 Fiscal and Monetary Policy Interactions	26 Fiscal Policy [sections on supply-side fiscal policy]	32 The Business Cycle [omit real business cycle theory]	29 Fiscal and Monetary Policy Interactions
30 Inflation	33 International Finance	31 Economic Growth	31 Economic Growth
31 Economic Growth		33 International Finance	33 International Finance
32 The Business Cycle			
33 International Finance			

Four Alternative Sequences for Macroeconomics

[illegible]	Classical Emphasis	Keynesian Emphasis	[illegible]
21. Measuring GDP and Economic Growth	21. Measuring GDP and Economic Growth	21. Measuring GDP and Economic Growth	21. Measuring GDP and Economic Growth
[illegible]	[illegible]	[illegible]	[illegible]

PART 1

The Scope of Economics

Talking with Xavier Sala-i-Martin

Xavier Sala-i-Martin is Professor of Economics at Columbia University. He is also Senior Economic Advisor to the World Economic Forum, Associate Editor of the Journal of Economic Growth, *founder and CEO of Umbele Foundation: A Future for Africa, and President of the Economic Commission of the Barcelona football club. Professor Sala-i-Martin was an undergraduate at Universitat Autonoma de Barcelona and a graduate student at Harvard University, where he obtained his PhD in 1990. In 2004, he was awarded the Premio Juan Carlos I de Economía, a biannual prize given by the Bank of Spain to the best economist in Spain and Latin America.*

Michael Parkin talked with Xavier Sala-i-Martin about his research and the challenges of lifting people from poverty.

What attracted you to economics?

It was a random event. I wanted to be rich, so I asked my mom, "In my family, who is the richest guy?" She said, "Your uncle John." And I asked, "What did he study?" And she said, "Economics." So I went into economics! In Spain, there are no liberal arts colleges where you can study lots of things. At age 18, you must decide what career you will follow. If you choose economics, you go to economics school and take economics five years in a row. So you have to make a decision in a crazy way, like I did.

We hear a lot about the rich getting richer and the poor getting poorer. But you say that poverty is going down. What is happening to the global distribution of income?

There are two issues: poverty and inequality. When in 2001 I said poverty is going down, everyone said I was crazy. The United Nations Development Report, which uses World Bank data, was saying the exact opposite. I said the World Bank methodology was flawed. After a big public argument that you can read in *The Economist*, the World Bank revised its poverty numbers and now agrees with me that poverty rates are falling.

Now, why is poverty falling? In 1970, 80 per cent of the world's poor were in Asia – in China, India, Bangladesh and Indonesia. China's "Great Leap Forward" was a great leap backward. People were starving to death. Now, the growth of these countries has been spectacular and the global poverty rate has fallen. Yet, if you look at Africa, Africa is going backwards. But Africa has 700 million people. China has 1.3 billion. India has 1.1 billion. Indonesia has 300 million. Asia has 4 billion of the world's 6 billion people.

These big guys are growing. It's impossible that global poverty is not going down.

But what we care about is poverty in different regions of the world. Asia has been doing very well, but Africa has not. Unfortunately, Africa is still going in the wrong direction.

You've made a big personal commitment to Africa. What is the Africa problem? Why does this continent lag behind Asia? Why, as you've just put it, is Africa going in the wrong direction?

Number one, Africa is a very violent continent. There are 22 wars in Africa as we speak. Two, nobody will invest in Africa. Three, we in the rich world – the United States, Europe and Japan – won't let them trade. Because we have agricultural subsidies, trade barriers and tariffs for their products, they can't sell to us.

Africans should globalize themselves. They should open, and we should let them open. They should introduce markets. But to get markets, you need legal systems, police, transparency, less red tape. You need a lot of the things we have now. They have corrupt economies, very bureaucratic, with no property rights, the judiciary is corrupt. All of that has to change. They need female education. One of the biggest rates of return that we have is educating girls. To educate girls, we'll need to build schools, we need to pay teachers, we need to buy uniforms, we need to provide the incentives for girls to go to school, which usually is like a string. You pull it, you don't push it. Pushing education doesn't work. What you need is: let the girls know that the rate of return on education is very high by providing jobs after they leave school. So you need to change the incentives of the girls to go to school and educate themselves. That's going to increase the national product, but it will also increase health, and it will also reduce fertility.

Returning to the problems of poverty and inequality, how can inequality be increasing within countries but decreasing globally – across countries?

Because most inequality comes from the fact that some people live in rich countries and some people live in poor countries. The big difference across people is not that there are rich Americans and poor Americans. Americans are very close to each other relative to the difference between Americans and people from Senegal. What is closing today is the gap across countries – and for the first time in history. Before the Industrial Revolution, everybody was equal. Equal and poor. Equally poor. People were living at subsistence levels, which means you eat, you're clothed, you have a house, you die. No movies, no travel, no music, no toothbrush. Just subsist. And if the weather is not good, one third of the population dies. That was the history of the world between 10,000 BC and today.

Yes, there was a king, there was Caesar, but the majority of the population were peasants.

All of a sudden, the Industrial Revolution means that one small country, England, takes off and there is 2 per cent growth every year. The living standard of the workers of England goes up and up and up. Then the United States, then France, then the rest of Europe, then Canada all begin to grow.

In terms of today's population, one billion people become rich and five billion remain poor. Now for the first time in history, these five billion people are growing more rapidly than the rich guys. They're catching up quickly. The incomes of the majority of poor citizens of the world are growing faster than those of Americans.

Question!
Question everything!

What advice do you have for someone who is just beginning to study economics?

Question! Question everything! Take some courses in history and math. And read my latest favorite book, Bill Easterly's *The White Man's Burden.** It shows why we have not been doing the right thing in the aid business. I'm a little bit less dramatic than he is. He says that nothing has worked. I think some things have worked, and we have to take advantage of what has worked to build on it. But I agree with the general principle that being nice, being good, doesn't necessarily mean doing good. Lots of people with good intentions do harm. Economic science teaches us that incentives are the key.

* William Easterly, *The White Man's Burden: Why the West's Efforts to Aid the Rest Have Done So Much Ill and So Little Good*, New York, Penguin Books, 2006.

What Is Economics?

CHAPTER 1

After studying this chapter you will be able to:

- Define economics and distinguish between microeconomics and macroeconomics
- Explain the big questions of economics
- Explain the key ideas that define the economic way of thinking
- Describe how economists go about their work as social scientists

Choice, Change, Opportunity and Challenge

You are studying economics, the science of choice, at a time of enormous change, opportunity and challenge. Mobile phones with TV, wireless connections, podcasting and other new technologies are making our lives easier and more fun. Global terrorism and other new challenges are making our lives more difficult when we travel. How will the choices we make respond to the changing opportunities and challenges we face? What are the principles that guide our choices? Find out in this chapter.

A Definition of Economics

All economic questions arise because we want more than we can get. We want a peaceful and secure world. We want clean air and rivers. We want long and healthy lives. We want good schools and universities. We want space and comfort in our homes. We want a huge range of sports and recreational gear from running shoes to motor bikes. We want the time to enjoy sports and games, reading books and magazines, seeing films, listening to music, travelling and so on.

What each one of us can get is limited by time, by the income we earn and by the prices we must pay. Everyone ends up with some unsatisfied wants. As a society, what we can get is limited by our productive resources. These resources include the gifts of nature, human labour and ingenuity, and tools and equipment that we have produced.

Our inability to satisfy all our wants is called **scarcity**. The poor and the rich alike face scarcity. A child in Tanzania is hungry and thirsty because her parents can't afford food and the well in her village is dirty and almost empty. The scarcity that she faces is clear and disturbing. But even David Beckham, a millionaire, faces scarcity. He wants to spend the weekend playing football *and* filming an advert, but he can't do both. We face scarcity as a society. We want to provide better healthcare *and* better education *and* a cleaner environment and so on. Scarcity is everywhere. Even parrots face scarcity!

Faced with scarcity, we must *choose* among the available alternatives. The child in Tanzania must *choose* dirty water and scraps of bread or go thirsty and hungry. David Beckham must *choose* the football *or* the filming. As a society, we must *choose* among healthcare, education and the environment.

The choices that we make depend on the incentives that we face. An **incentive** is a reward that encourages or a penalty that discourages an action. If heavy rain fills the well, the child in Tanzania has an *incentive* to choose more water. If the fee for filming is £1 million, David Beckham has an incentive to skip the football and make the advert. If computer prices tumble, we have an *incentive* as a society to connect more schools to the Internet.

Economics is the social science that studies the *choices* that individuals, businesses, governments and entire societies make as they cope with *scarcity* and the *incentives* that influence and reconcile those choices. The subject divides into two main parts:

- Microeconomics
- Macroeconomics

Microeconomics

Microeconomics is the study of the choices that individuals and businesses make, the way these choices interact in markets and the influence of governments. Some examples of microeconomic questions are: Why are people buying more mobile phones? How would a tax on downloading music affect the sales of CDs?

Macroeconomics

Macroeconomics is the study of the performance of the national economy and the global economy. Some examples of macroeconomic questions are: Why did production and jobs expand in 2006? Why did Japan's economy stagnate during the 1990s? Can the Bank of England bring prosperity by keeping interest rates low?

Not only do I want a cracker—we all want a cracker!

Review Quiz

Study Plan 1.1

1. List some examples of scarcity in Europe today.
2. Find stories in today's newspaper to illustrate the definition of economics with examples of scarcity, incentives and choices in the United Kingdom and around the world.
3. Find stories in today's newspaper that illustrate the distinction between microeconomics and macroeconomics.

Two Big Economic Questions

Two big questions summarize the scope of economics:

- How do choices end up determining *what*, *how* and *for whom* goods and services get produced?
- When do choices made in the pursuit of *self-interest* also promote the *social interest*?

What, How and For Whom?

Goods and services are the objects that people value and produce to satisfy wants. Goods are physical objects such as golf balls. Services are actions performed such as cutting hair and filling teeth. By far the largest part of what people in the rich industrial countries produce today are services such as retail and wholesale services, health services and education. Goods are a small and decreasing part of what we produce.

Figure 1.1 myeconlab

Changes in What We Produce

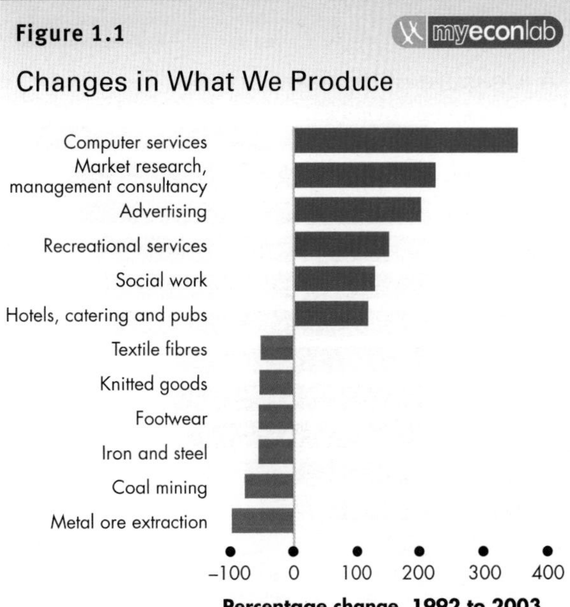

The production of many services has expanded, and mining and manufacture have shrunk.

Source of data: Office for National Statistics, *Change in Gross Value Added by Industry*.

What?

What we produce changes over time. Every year, new technologies allow us to build better equipped homes, more powerful sporting equipment and even deliver a more pleasant experience in the dentist's chair. And technological advance makes us incredibly more productive at producing food and manufactures.

Figure 1.1 shows some trends in what we produce. It highlights six items that have expanded and six that have shrunk during the 1990s and early 2000s. What are the forces that bring these changes in what we produce? Why are we producing more computer services, advertising and catering in hotels and pubs? And why are we producing less coal, iron and steel and clothing?

How?

Goods and services get produced by using productive resources that economists call **factors of production**. Factors of production are grouped into four categories:

- Land
- Labour
- Capital
- Entrepreneurship

Land

The "gifts of nature" that we use to produce goods and services are called **land**. In economics, land is what in everyday language we call *natural resources*. It includes land in the everyday sense together with metal ores, oil, gas and coal, water, air, wind and sunshine.

Our land surface and water resources are renewable and some of our mineral resources can be recycled. But the resources that we use to create energy are non-renewable – they can be used only once.

Labour

The work time and work effort that people devote to producing goods and services is called **labour**. Labour includes the physical and the mental efforts of all the people who work on farms and construction sites and in factories, shops and offices.

The *quality* of labour depends on **human capital**, which is the knowledge and skill that people obtain from education, on-the-job training and work experience. You are building your own human capital today as you work on your economics course, and your human capital will continue to grow as you become better at your job.

Human capital expands over time and varies between countries. Figure 1.2 shows the proportion of young people entering higher education as a measure of human capital in 12 countries.

Figure 1.2 myeconlab

A Measure of Human Capital

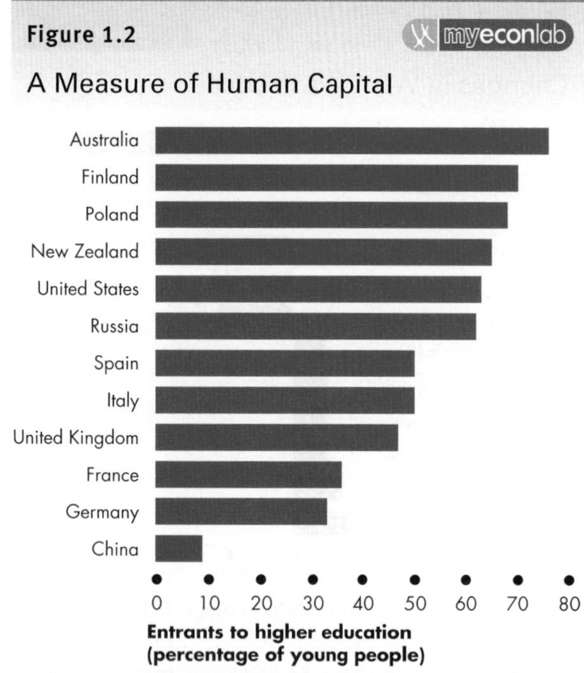

University education is a major source of human capital and one measure of the growth of human capital is the percentage of young people who attend university. This figure shows this measure of the growth of human capital in 12 countries and shows huge variation from more than 70 per cent entering university in Australia to less than 10 per cent in China.

Source of data: OECD, *Education at a Glance: OECD Indicators 2005.*

Capital

The tools, instruments, machines, buildings and other constructions that businesses now use to produce goods and services are called **capital**.

In everyday language, we talk about money, shares and bonds as being capital. These items are *financial capital*. Financial capital plays an important role in enabling businesses to borrow the funds that they use to buy capital. But financial capital is not used to produce goods and services – it is not a factor of production.

Entrepreneurship

The human resource that organizes labour, land and capital is called **entrepreneurship**. Entrepreneurs come up with new ideas about what and how to produce, make business decisions and bear the risks that arise from these decisions.

How do the quantities of factors of production that get used to produce the many different goods and services get determined?

For Whom?

Who gets the goods and services that are produced depends on the incomes that people earn. A large income enables a person to buy large quantities of goods and services. A small income leaves a person with few options and small quantities of goods and services.

People earn their incomes by selling the services of the factors of production they own:

1 Land earns **rent**.
2 Labour earns **wages**.
3 Capital earns **interest**.
4 Entrepreneurship earns **profit**.

Which factor of production earns the most income? The answer is labour. Wages and fringe benefits are around 70 per cent of total income. Land, capital and entrepreneurship share the rest. These percentages have been remarkably constant over time.

Knowing how income is shared among the factors of production doesn't tell us how it is shared among individuals. You know of lots of people who earn very large incomes. J. K. Rowling earns more than £20 million a year and David Beckham will make $US250 million over five years.

You know of even more people who earn very small incomes. People who serve fast food earn £5 an hour.

Some differences in income are persistent. On average, men earn more than women and whites earn more than ethnic minorities. Europeans earn more on average than Asians who in turn earn more than Africans. A typical annual income in the poorest countries of the world is just a few hundred pounds, less than the equivalent of a typical weekly wage in the richest countries of the world.

Why is the distribution of income so unequal? Why do women earn less than men? Why do J. K. Rowling and David Beckham earn such huge incomes? Why do university graduates earn more than people with only a few GCSEs? Why do Europeans earn more than Africans? Why are the incomes of Asians rising so rapidly?

Economics provides answers to all these questions about what, how and for whom goods and services get produced. And you will discover these answers as you progress with your study of the subject.

The second big question of economics that we'll now examine is a harder question both to appreciate and to answer.

When Is the Pursuit of Self-interest in the Social Interest?

Every day, you and 462 million other EU citizens, along with 6.6 billion people in the rest of the world, make economic choices that result in *What*, *How* and *For Whom* goods and services get produced.

Are the goods and services produced, and the quantities in which they are produced, the right ones? Do the factors of production employed get used in the best possible way? Do the goods and services that we produce go to the people who benefit most from them?

Self-interest

You know that your own choices are the best ones for you – or at least you think they're the best at the time that you make them. You use your time and other resources in the way that makes most sense to you. But you don't think much about how your choices affect other people. You order a home delivery pizza because you're hungry. You don't order it thinking that the delivery person or the cook needs an income. You make choices that are in your **self-interest** – choices that you think are best for you.

When you act on your choices, you come into contact with thousands of others who produce and deliver the things that you decide to buy or who buy the things that you sell. These people have made their own choices – what to produce and how to produce it, whom to hire or whom to work for and so on. Like you, everyone else makes choices that they think are best for them. When the pizza delivery person shows up at your home, he's not doing you a favour.

Social Interest

Could it be possible that when each one of us makes choices that are in our own best interest, it turns out that these choices are also the best for society as a whole? Choices that are the best for society as a whole are said to be in the **social interest**.

Economists have been trying to find the answer to this question since 1776, the year of American independence and the year in which Adam Smith's monumental book, *The Nature and the Causes of the Wealth of Nations*, was published. The question is a hard one to answer but a lot of progress has been made. Much of the rest of this book helps you to learn what we know about this question and its answer. To help you start thinking about the question, we're going to illustrate it with 10 topics that generate heated discussion in today's world. You're already at least a little bit familiar with each one of them. They are:

- Privatization
- Globalization
- The new economy
- Terrorism
- Corporate scandals
- HIV/AIDS
- Disappearing tropical rainforests
- Water shortages
- Unemployment
- Deficits and debts

Privatization

On 9 November 1989 the Berlin Wall tumbled, and with its destruction, two Germanys embarked on a path towards unity.

West Germany was a nation designed on the model of the rest of Western Europe. In these nations, people own property and operate businesses. Privately owned businesses produce goods and services and trade them freely with their customers in shops and markets. All this economic activity is conducted by people who pursue their own self-interest.

East Germany was a nation designed on the model of the Soviet Union – a communist state. In such a state, people are not free to operate businesses and trade freely. The government owns the factories, shops and offices, and it decides what to produce, how to produce it and for whom to produce. Economic life is managed in detail by a government central economic planning agency, and each individual follows instructions. The entire economy is operated like one giant company.

The Soviet Union collapsed soon after the fall of the Berlin Wall and splintered into a number of independent states, each of which embarked on a process of privatization. China, another communist state, began to encourage private enterprise and to move away from its sole reliance on public ownership and central economic planning during the 1980s.

Today, only Cuba and North Korea remain communist states. Do their economic systems serve the social interest better than private businesses trading in free markets? Or would an economic system on the European model do a better job?

Globalization

Globalization – the expansion of international trade and investment – has been going on for centuries, but during the 1990s, advances in microchip, satellite and fibre-optic technologies brought a dramatic fall in the cost of communication and accelerated the process. A phone call or even a video conference with people who live 10,000 miles apart has become an everyday and easily affordable event. Every day, 25,000 people travel by air between Europe and America and another 18,000 between Europe and Asia and the South Pacific.

The result of this explosion of communication is a globalization of production decisions. When Nike decides to increase the production of sports shoes, people who live in China, Indonesia or Malaysia get more work. When Sony wants to create a new game for PlayStation 3, programmers in India write the code. And when China Airlines wants some new aeroplanes, it is most likely that Europeans who work for Airbus or Americans who work for Boeing will build them.

As part of the process of globalization, Europe produces more services and fewer manufactured goods. And China and the small economies in East Asia produce an expanding volume of manufactures.

The economies of Asia are also growing more rapidly than are those of Europe and the United States. China is already the world's second largest economy in terms of production and, on current trends, by 2013 China will be the world's largest economy. This rapid economic expansion in Asia will bring further changes to the global economy as the wealthier Chinese and other Asians begin to travel and buy more of the goods and services that are produced in Europe and other parts of the world. Globalization will proceed at an accelerated pace.

But globalization is leaving some behind. European coal miners, steel makers, clothing and textile workers and workers in other manufacturing industries are losing their jobs and facing a tough search for a new job. Even when they find a new job, they must take a pay cut. Also, most of the nations of Africa and parts of South America are not sharing in the prosperity that globalization is bringing to other parts of the world.

Is globalization a good thing? Whom does it benefit? Globalization is clearly in the interest of the owners of multinational companies that profit by producing in low-cost regions and selling in high-price regions. But is globalization in your interest and the interest of the young worker in Malaysia who sews your new running shoes? Is it in the social interest?

The New Economy

The 1980s and 1990s were years of extraordinary economic change that have been called the *Information Revolution*. Economic revolutions don't happen very often. The previous one, the *Industrial Revolution*, occurred between 1760 and 1830 and saw the transformation from rural farm life to urban industrial life for most people. The revolution before that, the *Agrarian Revolution*, occurred around 12,000 years ago and saw the transformation from a life of hunting and gathering to a life of settled farming.

Placing the events of the past 25 years on the status of those two previous revolutions might be a stretch. But the changes that occurred during those 25 years were incredible. They were based on one major technology – the microprocessor or computer chip. Gordon Moore of Intel predicted in 1965 that the number of transistors that could be placed on one integrated chip would double every 18 months (Moore's Law). This prediction turned out to be remarkably accurate. In 1980, a PC chip had 60,000 transistors. By 2000, laptop computers had chips with more than 40 million transistors.

The spin-offs from faster and cheaper computing were widespread. Telecommunications became much faster and cheaper, music and movie recording become more realistic and cheaper, millions of routine tasks that previously required human decision and action were automated. You encounter these automated tasks every day when you check out at the supermarket or call a government department or large business.

All the new products and processes and the low-cost computing power that made them possible were produced by people who made choices in the pursuit of self-interest. They did not result from any grand design or government economic plan.

When Gordon Moore set up Intel and started making chips, no one had told him to do so and he wasn't thinking how much easier it would be for you to hand in your essay on time if you had a faster PC. When Bill Gates dropped out of Harvard to set up Microsoft, he wasn't trying to create an operating system to improve people's computing experience. These and the thousands of other entrepreneurs were in hot pursuit of the big payoff that many of them achieved. Yet their actions did make everyone else better off. They did advance the social interest.

But were resources used in the best possible way during the information revolution? Did Intel make the right quality of chips and sell them in the right quantities for the right prices? Or was the quality of chips too low and the price too high? And what about Microsoft? Did Bill Gates have to be paid $30 billion to produce the successive generations of Windows? Was this program developed in the social interest?

Terrorism

The awful events of 11 September 2001 in New York (9/11) and of 7 July 2005 in London created economic shockwaves that will last for decades and change *What*, *How* and *For Whom* goods and services are produced.

The biggest changes in production have occurred in travel, accommodation and security. Much business travel was replaced by teleconferencing. Initially, after 9/11, much holiday travel left the air and went onto the motorways and highways. Foreign trips were cut back. Airlines lost business and cut back on their own orders for new aeroplanes. Banks that had lent money to airlines incurred enormous losses.

Sales of recreational vehicles increased. And airports, although operating at lower capacity, beefed up their security services. Tens of thousands of new security agents were hired and state-of-the-art scanners were installed.

Thousands of people made choices in pursuit of their self-interest that led to these changes in production. But were these changes also in the social interest?

Corporate Scandals

In 2000, the names Enron and WorldCom meant corporate integrity and spectacular success. But today, they are tainted with scandal.

Founded in 1985, Enron expanded to become America's seventh largest business by 2001. But its expansion was built on an elaborate web of lies, deceit and fraud. In October 2001, after revelations by one of its former executives, Enron's directors acknowledged that by inflating reported income and by hiding debts, they had made the company appear to be worth considerably more than it was actually worth. Enron executives Jeffery Skilling and Kenneth Lay were convicted of fraud that made them millions of dollars but wiped out the shareholders' wealth.

Scott Sullivan, a highly respected financial officer, joined WorldCom in 1992 and helped turn it into one of the world's telecommunications giants. In his last year with the company, Sullivan's salary was $700,000 and his bonus (in stock options) $10 million. But just ten years after joining the company, Sullivan was fired and arrested for allegedly falsifying the company's accounts, inflating its book profits by almost $4 billion and inflating his own bonus in the process. Shortly after these events, WorldCom filed for bankruptcy protection in the largest bankruptcy filing in US history, laid off 17,000 workers and wiped out its shareholders' wealth.

These cases illustrate the fact that sometimes, in the pursuit of self-interest, people break the law. Such behaviour is not in the social interest. Indeed, the law was established precisely to limit such behaviour.

But some corporate behaviour is legal yet regarded by some as inappropriate. For example, many people think that top executive salaries are out of control. In some cases, executives who have received huge incomes have brought ruin to the companies that they manage.

The people who hired the executives acted in their own self-interest and appointed the best people they could find. The executives acted in their own self-interest. But what became of the self-interest of the shareholders and the customers of these companies. Didn't they suffer? Aren't these glaring examples of conflict between self-interest and the social interest?

HIV/AIDS

The World Health Organization and the United Nations estimate that 40 million people were suffering from HIV/AIDS in 2005. During that year, 3 million died from the disease and there were 4 million new cases. Most of the HIV/AIDS cases – 25 million of them in 2005 – are in Africa, where incomes average around £3 a day. The most effective available treatment for HIV/AIDS is an antiretroviral drug made by the large multinational drug companies. The cost of this treatment is around £1,200 a year – more than the £3 a day the average person earns.

Developing new drugs is a high-cost and high-risk activity. And if the activity were not in the self-interest of the drug companies, they would stop the effort. But once developed, the cost of producing a drug is just a few pence a dose. Would it be in the social interest for drugs to be made available at the low cost of producing them?

Disappearing Tropical Rainforests

Tropical rainforests in South America, Africa and Asia support the lives of 30 million species of plants, animals and insects – approaching 50 per cent of all species on the planet. These rainforests provides us with the ingredients for many goods including soaps, mouthwashes, shampoos, food preservatives, rubber, nuts and fruits. The Amazon rainforest alone converts about 1 trillion pounds of carbon dioxide into oxygen each year.

Yet tropical rainforests cover less than 2 per cent of the earth's surface and are heading for extinction. Logging, cattle ranching, mining, oil extraction, hydro-electric dams and subsistence farming are destroying an area the size of two football fields of forest every second. At the current rate of destruction, most tropical rainforest ecosystems will be gone by 2030.

Each one of us makes economic choices that are in our self-interest to consume products, some of which are destroying this natural resource. Are our choices damaging the social interest? And if they are, what can be done to change the incentives we face and change our behaviour?

Water Shortages

The world is awash with water – it is our most abundant resource. But 97 per cent of it is seawater. Another 2 per cent is frozen in glaciers and ice. The 1 per cent of the earth's water that is available for human consumption would be sufficient if only it were in the right places. Finland, Canada and a few other places have more water than they can use, but Australia, Africa and California (and many other places) could use much more water than they can get.

Some people pay less for water than others. Some of the highest prices for water are faced by people in the poorest countries who must either buy water from a water-dealer's truck or carry water in buckets over many miles.

In England, water is provided by private water companies. In Wales, Scotland, the United States and many other countries, public enterprises deliver water.

In India and Bangladesh, plenty of rain falls, but it falls during a short wet season and the rest of the year is dry. Dams could help, but not enough have been built in those countries.

Are national and global water resources being managed properly? Are the decisions that we each make in our self-interest to use, conserve and transport water also in the social interest?

Unemployment

During the 1930s, in a period called the *Great Depression*, more than 20 per cent of the workforce was unemployed. Even today, approaching 40 per cent of teenagers are unemployed in many countries. Why can't everyone who wants a job find one? If economic choices arise from scarcity, how can resources be left unused?

People get jobs because other people think they can earn a profit by employing them. And people accept a job when they think the pay and other conditions are good enough. So the number of people with jobs is determined by the self-interest of employers and workers. But is the number of jobs also in the social interest?

Deficits and Debts

Today, a massive imbalance exists in the global economy. The United States, the world's largest economy, is running a deficit with the rest of the world. And China, the world's second largest economy, is piling up US dollars.

The United States has had a deficit with the rest of the world every year since 1992 and by 2006, Americans had borrowed more than $4 trillion to spend more on goods and services from the rest of the world and in excess of what foreigners had bought from them. This enormous deficit and the debt it creates cannot persist indefinitely and will somehow have to end. Are these global debts and deficits in the social interest?

We've just looked at 10 topics that illustrate the big question: Do choices made in the pursuit of self-interest also promote the social interest?

You'll discover, as you work through this book, that much of what we do in the pursuit of our self-interest does indeed further the social interest. But there are areas in which social interest and self-interest come into conflict. You'll discover the principles that help economists to figure out when the social interest is being served, when it is not and what might be done when it is not.

Review Quiz

Study Plan 1.2

1. Describe the broad facts about *what, how* and *for whom* goods and services are produced.
2. Provide examples of goods or services that you think have high value or low value. Explain why you care about the quantity of these goods produced, how they are produced and who gets them.
3. Distinguish between self-interest and social interest.
4. Use headlines from the recent news stories to illustrate the potential for conflict between self-interest and social interest.

The Economic Way of Thinking

The definition of economics and the questions that economics tries to answer tell us about the *scope of economics*. But they don't tell you how economists *think* about these questions and go about seeking answers to them.

You're now going to begin to see how economists approach economic questions. In this section, we'll look at the ideas that define the *economic way of thinking*. This way of thinking needs practice, but it is powerful and as you become more familiar with it, you'll begin to see the world around you with a new and sharp focus.

Choices and Trade-offs

Because we face scarcity, we must make choices. And when we make a choice, we select from the available alternatives. For example, you can spend the weekend studying for your next economics test or having fun with your friends, but you can't do both of these activities at the same time. You must choose how much time to devote to each. Whatever choice you make, you could have chosen something else instead.

You can think about your choice as a trade-off. A **trade-off** is an exchange – giving up one thing to get something else. When you choose how to spend your weekend, you face a trade-off between studying and going out with your friends.

Guns versus Butter

The classic trade-off is between "guns" and "butter" that stand for any pair of goods. They might actually be guns and butter. Or they might be broader categories such as defence goods and food. Or they might be any pair of specific goods or services such as orange juice and bottled water, footballs and cricket balls, schools and hospitals, haircuts and career advice.

Regardless of the specific objects that guns and butter represent, the guns-versus-butter trade-off captures a hard fact of life: if we want more of one thing, we must trade something else in exchange for it.

The idea of a trade-off is central to the whole of economics. We'll look at some examples, beginning with three of the big questions: what, how and for whom? We can view each of these questions about the goods and services that are produced in terms of trade-offs.

What, *How* and *For Whom* Trade-offs

Each of the questions what, how and for whom goods and services get produced involves a trade-off that is similar to that between guns and butter.

What Trade-offs

What goods and services get produced depends on choices made by each one of us, by our government and by the businesses that produce the things we buy.

Each of these choices involves a trade-off. Each one of us faces a trade-off when we choose how to spend our income. You go to the pictures this week, but you forgo a few cups of coffee to buy the ticket. You trade off coffee for seeing a film.

The government faces a *what* trade-off when it chooses how to spend our taxes. Parliament votes for more defence goods but cuts back on student grants – Parliament trades off education for defence.

Businesses face a *what* trade-off when they decide which goods and services to produce and in what quantities. Gillette hires David Beckham and allocates resources to designing and marketing a new five-blade shaver but cuts back on its development of a new toothbrush. Gillette trades off toothbrushes for shavers.

How Trade-offs

How goods and services get produced depends on choices made by the businesses that produce the things we buy. These choices involve a trade-off. For example, Blockbuster opens a new video store with automated vending machines and closes an older store with traditional manual service. Blockbuster trades off labour for capital.

For Whom Trade-offs

For whom goods and services are produced depends on the distribution of buying power. Buying power can be redistributed – transferred from one person to another – in three ways: by voluntary payments, by theft, or through taxes and benefits organized by government. Redistribution brings a trade-off.

Each of us faces a *for whom* trade-off when we choose how much to contribute to an Oxfam appeal. You donate £5 and cut your spending. You trade off your own spending for a small increase in economic equality.

We face a *for whom* trade-off when we vote to make theft illegal and devote resources to law enforcement. We trade off goods and services for an increase in the security of our property.

We also face a *for whom* trade-off when we vote for taxes and welfare arrangements that redistribute buying power from the rich to the poor. Government redistribution confronts society with what has been called the **big trade-off** – the trade-off between equality and efficiency. Taxing the rich and making transfers to the poor bring greater economic equality. But taxing productive activities such as running a business, working hard and saving and investing in capital discourages these activities. So taxing productive activities means producing less. A more equal distribution means there is less to share.

Think of how to share a pie that everyone contributes to baking. If each person receives a share of the pie that reflects the size of her or his effort, everyone will work hard and the pie will be as large as possible. But if the pie is shared equally, regardless of contribution, some talented bakers will slacken off and the pie will shrink. The big trade-off is one between the size of the pie and how equally it is shared. We trade off some production for increased equality.

Choices Bring Change

What, how and for whom goods and services are produced changes over time. And choices bring change. The quantity and range of goods and services available today in Europe is much greater than that in Africa. And the economic condition of Europeans today is much better than it was a generation ago. But the quality of economic life (and its rate of improvement) doesn't depend purely on nature and on luck. It depends on the choices made by each one of us, by governments and by businesses. And these choices involve trade-offs.

One choice is that of how much of our income to consume and how much to save. Our saving can be channelled through the financial system to finance businesses and to pay for new capital that increases production. The more we save and invest, the more goods and services we'll be able to produce in the future. When you decide to save an extra £1,000 and forgo a holiday in Spain, you trade off the holiday for a higher future income. If everyone saves an extra £1,000 and businesses invest in more equipment that increases production, the average consumption per person rises. As a society, we trade off current consumption for economic growth and higher future consumption.

A second choice is how much effort to devote to education and training. By becoming better educated and more highly skilled, we become more productive and are able to produce more goods and services. When you decide to remain in university for another two years to complete a post-graduate degree and forgo a huge chunk of leisure time, you trade off leisure today for a higher future income. If everyone becomes better educated, production increases and income per person rises. As a society, we trade off current consumption and leisure time for economic growth and higher future consumption.

A third choice, usually made by businesses, is how much effort to devote to research and the development of new products and production methods. Airbus can divert production engineers into research on a new aircraft or leave them producing existing types of aircraft. More research brings greater production in the future but means smaller current production – a trade-off of current production for greater future production.

Seeing choices as trade-offs emphasizes the idea that to get something, we must give up something.

Opportunity Cost

"There's no such thing as a free lunch" is not just a clever one-liner. It expresses the central idea of economics: every choice involves a cost. The **opportunity cost** of something is the highest-valued alternative that we give up to get it.

You can drop out of university, or you can keep studying. If you drop out and take a job at McDonald's, you earn enough to buy a new iPod, go to the pictures and spend lots of free time with your friends. If you remain in university, you can't afford these things. You will be able to buy these things when you graduate, and that is one of the payoffs from being in university. But for now, when you've bought your books, you have nothing left for a new iPod and the cinema. And doing homework leaves little time to spend with your friends. The opportunity cost of being in university is the highest-valued alternative that you would have done if you had dropped out.

All the *what*, *how* and *for whom* trade-offs that we've just considered involve opportunity cost. The opportunity cost of some guns is the butter forgone; the opportunity cost of a cinema ticket is the number of cups of coffee forgone.

And the choices that bring change also involve opportunity cost. The opportunity cost of more goods and services in the future is less consumption today.

Choosing at the Margin

You can allocate the next hour between studying and e-mailing your friends. But the choice is not all or nothing. You must decide how many minutes to allocate to each activity. To make this decision, you compare the benefit of a little bit more study time with its cost – you make your choice at the **margin**.

The benefit that arises from an increase in an activity is called **marginal benefit**. For example, suppose that you're spending four nights a week studying and your average mark is 60 per cent. You decide that you want a higher mark and decide to study an extra night each week. Your mark now rises to 70 per cent. The marginal benefit from studying for one additional night a week is the 10 point increase in your mark. It is *not* the 70 per cent. The reason is that you already have the benefit from studying for four nights a week, so we don't count this benefit as resulting from the decision you are now making.

The cost of an increase in an activity is called **marginal cost**. For you, the marginal cost of increasing your study time by one night a week is the cost of the additional night not spent with your friends (if that is your best alternative use of the time). It does not include the cost of the four nights you are already studying.

To make your decision, you compare the marginal benefit from an extra night of study with its marginal cost. If the marginal benefit exceeds the marginal cost, you study the extra night. If the marginal cost exceeds the marginal benefit, you do not study the extra night.

By evaluating marginal benefits and marginal costs and choosing only those actions that bring greater benefit than cost, we use our scarce resources in the way that makes us as well off as possible.

Responding to Incentives

Our choices respond to incentives. A change in marginal cost or a change in marginal benefit changes the incentives that we face and leads us to change our choice.

For example, suppose your economics lecturer gives you some homework and tells you that all the questions will be on the next exam. The marginal benefit from working these questions is large, so you diligently work them all. In contrast, suppose that your maths lecturer sets some homework and tells you that none of the questions will be on the next exam. The marginal benefit from working these questions is lower, so you skip some of them.

A central idea of economics is that we can predict how choices will change by looking at changes in incentives. More of an activity is undertaken when its marginal cost falls or its marginal benefit rises; less of an activity is undertaken when its marginal cost rises or its marginal benefit falls.

Incentives are also the key to reconciling self-interest and the social interest. When our choices are *not* in the social interest, it is because of the incentives we face. One of the challenges for economists is to discover the incentive systems that result in self-interested choices leading to the social interest.

Human Nature, Incentives and Institutions

Economists take human nature as given and view people as acting in their self-interest. All people – consumers, producers, politicians and civil servants – pursue their self-interest.

Self-interested actions are not necessarily *selfish* actions. You might decide to use your resources in ways that bring pleasure to others as well as to yourself. But a self-interested act gets the most value for *you* based on *your* view about value.

If human nature is given and if people act in their self-interest, how can we take care of the social interest? Economists answer this question by emphasizing the crucial role that institutions play in influencing the incentives that people face as they pursue their self-interest.

Private property protected by a system of laws and markets that enable voluntary exchange are the fundamental institutions. You will learn as you progress with your study of economics that where these institutions exist, self-interest can indeed promote the social interest.

Review Quiz

Study Plan 1.3

1 Provide three everyday examples of trade-offs and describe the opportunity cost involved in each.
2 Provide three everyday examples to illustrate what we mean by choosing at the margin.
3 What are the marginal benefits and marginal costs that you've encountered in the choices you've made today?
4 How do economists predict changes in choices?
5 What do economists say about the role of institutions in promoting the social interest?

Economics: A Social Science

Economics is a social science and, like all scientists, economists distinguish two types of statement:

1 What *is*

2 What *ought to be*

Statements about what *is* are called *positive* statements and they might be right or wrong. We test a positive statement by checking it against the facts. When a chemist does an experiment in her laboratory, she is testing a positive statement.

Statements about what *ought to be* are called *normative* statements and they cannot be tested. When the European Parliament debates a motion, it is ultimately deciding what ought to be and making a normative statement.

To see the distinction between positive and normative statements, consider the following statements about global warming. Some scientists believe that centuries of burning of coal and oil are increasing the carbon dioxide content of the earth's atmosphere and leading to higher temperatures that eventually will have devastating consequences for life on this planet. "Our planet is warming because of an increased carbon dioxide build-up in the atmosphere" is a positive statement. It can (in principle and with sufficient data) be tested. "We ought to cut back on our use of carbon-based fuels such as coal and oil" is a normative statement. You can agree or disagree with this statement, but you can't test it. It is based on values.

Healthcare provides another example. "Universal healthcare cuts the amount of work time lost to illness" is a positive statement. "Every European should have equal access to healthcare" is a normative statement.

The task of economic science is to discover positive statements that are consistent with what we observe in the economic world. This task breaks into three steps:

- ◆ Observation and measurement
- ◆ Model building
- ◆ Testing models

Observation and Measurement

Economists observe and measure data on such things as the quantities of natural and human resources, wages and work hours, the prices and quantities of the goods and services, taxes and government spending and the items bought from and sold to other countries.

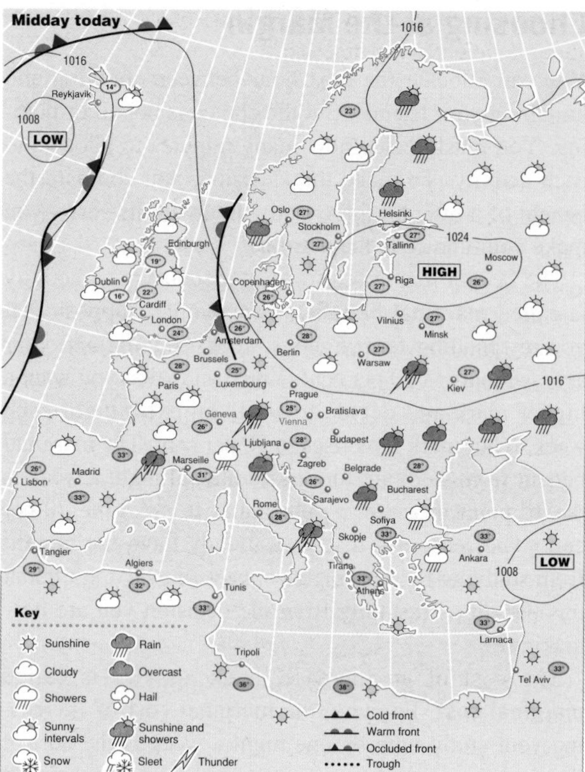

Map supplied by PA WeatherCentre Ltd

Model Building

The second step towards understanding how the economic world works is to build a model. An **economic model** is a description of some aspect of the economic world that includes only those features of the world that are needed for the purpose at hand. A model is simpler than the reality it represents. What a model includes and what it leaves out result from assumptions about what is essential and what are inessential details.

You can see how ignoring details is useful – even essential – to our understanding by thinking about a model that you see every day: the TV weather map. The weather map is a model that helps to predict the temperature, wind speed and direction and rainfall over the next few days. The weather map shows lines called isobars – lines of equal barometric pressure. It doesn't show the motorways because we assume that the pattern of air pressure, not the location of the motorways, determines the weather.

An economic model is similar to a weather map. For example, an economic model of a mobile phone network will include items such as the cost of using a mobile phone but it will ignore such details as the tunes people use for ring tones.

Testing Models

The third step is testing the model. A model's predictions may correspond, or be in conflict, with the facts. By comparing the model's predictions with the facts, we are able to test a model and develop an economic theory. An **economic theory** is a generalization that summarizes what we think we understand about the economic choices that people make and the performance of industries and entire economies. It is a bridge between an economic model and the real economy.

The process of building and testing models creates theories. For example, meteorologists have a theory that if the isobars form a particular pattern (a model), then it will rain (reality). They have developed this theory by repeated observation and testing of models.

Economics is a young science. It was born in 1776 with the publication of Adam Smith's *Wealth of Nations*. Since then, economists have discovered some useful theories. But in many areas economists are still looking for answers. Let's look at some of the obstacles to progress in economics.

Obstacles and Pitfalls in Economics

We cannot easily do economic experiments and most economic behaviour has many simultaneous causes. For these two reasons, it is difficult to unscramble cause and effect in economics.

Unscrambling Cause and Effect

By changing one factor at a time and holding all the other relevant factors constant, we isolate the factor of interest and investigate its effects in the clearest possible way. This logical device, which all scientists use to identify cause and effect, is called *ceteris paribus*. ***Ceteris paribus*** is a Latin term that means "other things being equal" or "if all other relevant things remain the same". Ensuring that other things are equal is crucial in many activities, including athletic events, and all successful attempts to make scientific progress use this device.

Economic models (like the models in all other sciences) enable the influence of one factor at a time to be isolated in the imaginary world of the model. When we use a model, we are able to imagine what would happen if only one factor changed. But *ceteris paribus* can be a problem in economics when we try to test a model.

Laboratory scientists, such as chemists and physicists, perform experiments by actually holding all the relevant factors constant except for the one under investigation. In the non-experimental sciences such as economics (and meteorology), we usually observe the outcomes of the simultaneous operation of many factors. Consequently, it is hard to sort out the effects of each individual factor and to compare the effects with what a model predicts. To cope with this problem, economists take three complementary approaches.

First, they look for pairs of events in which other things are equal (or similar). Data from different European countries might be used, for example, to study the effects of unemployment benefits on the unemployment rate. Second, economists use statistical tools called econometrics. Third, when economists can, they perform experiments. This relatively new approach puts real subjects (usually students) in a decision-making situation and varies their incentives in some way to discover how the subjects respond to a change in one factor at a time.

Economists try to avoid fallacies – errors of reasoning that lead to a wrong conclusion. Two fallacies are common and you need to be on your guard to avoid them. They are the:

- Fallacy of composition
- *Post hoc* fallacy

Fallacy of Composition

The fallacy of composition is the (false) statement that what is true of the parts is true of the whole or that what is true of the whole is true of the parts. Think of the statement, "Stand up at the football match to get a better view." If one person stands and the rest remain seated, the statement is true. If everyone stands, the statement is false. What is true for a part of the crowd isn't true for the whole crowd.

For an economic example, suppose a business fires some workers to cut costs and improve its profits. If all businesses take similar actions, people have less to spend, businesses sell less and profits don't improve.

Post Hoc Fallacy

Another Latin phrase – *post hoc ergo propter hoc* – means "after this, therefore because of this". The *post hoc* fallacy is the error of reasoning that a first event causes a second event because the first occurred before the second. Suppose you are a visitor from a far-off world. You observe lots of people shopping in early

December and then you see them opening gifts and partying on Christmas Day. "Does the shopping cause Christmas?", you wonder. After a deeper study, you discover that Christmas causes the shopping. A later event causes an earlier event.

Unravelling cause and effect is difficult in economics. Just looking at the timing of events often doesn't help. For example, does a stock market boom cause the economy to expand or does the anticipation of an expanding economy cause the stock market to boom? To disentangle cause and effect, economists use economic models and data and, to the extent that they can, perform experiments.

Economics is a challenging science. Does the difficulty of getting answers in economics mean that anything goes and that economists disagree on most questions? Perhaps you've heard the joke: "If you laid all the economists in the world end to end, they still wouldn't reach agreement." Surprisingly, perhaps, the joke does not describe reality.

Agreement and Disagreement

Economists agree on a remarkably wide range of questions. And often the agreed-upon view of economists disagrees with the popular and sometimes politically correct view. When Bank of England Governor Mervin King explains the Bank's latest interest rate decision, his words are rarely controversial among economists, even if they generate endless debate in the media.

Here are 10 propositions[1] with which at least two-thirds of economists broadly agree:

- Tariffs and import restrictions are not in the social interest.
- A large budget deficit has adverse effects.
- Flexible and floating exchange rates offer an effective international monetary arrangement.
- A minimum wage increases unemployment among young workers and low-skilled workers.
- Pollution taxes or marketable pollution permits are more efficient than pollution limits and standards.
- Rent ceilings decrease the availability of housing.
- When the economy is in a recession, a tax cut can lower the unemployment rate.
- Cash payments to welfare recipients make them better off than do transfers-in-kind of equal cash value.
- Inflation is primarily caused by a rapid rate of money creation.
- If the government budget is to be balanced, it should be balanced on the average over the course of the business cycle rather than every year.

Some of the above propositions are microeconomic and some are macroeconomic. Can you say which falls into each category? Some are positive and some are normative. Again, can you sort them into these two groups?

Notice that economists share personal opinions on normative issues as well as reach professional consensus on positive issues.

Review Quiz

Study Plan 1.4

1. What is the distinction between a positive statement and a normative statement? Provide an example (different from those in the chapter) of each type of statement.
2. What is a model? Think of a model that you might use (probably without thinking of it as a model) in your everyday life?
3. What is a theory? What is wrong with the statement "It might work in theory but it doesn't work in practice"? (Hint: Think about what a theory is and how it is used.)
4. What is the *ceteris paribus* assumption and how is it used? Provide three examples.
5. Provide some everyday examples of the fallacy of composition.
6. Provide some everyday examples of the *post hoc* fallacy.

Economics makes extensive use of graphs, as you will quickly discover. If you are comfortable with graphs, jump right into Chapter 2. But if you find graphs hard to work with, spend a bit of time becoming familiar with the basics of making and using graphs in the appendix to this chapter that begins on p. 19.

[1] For greater detail and qualification, see Richard M. Alston, J. R. Kearl and Michael B. Vaughan, "Is There a Consensus Among Economists?" *American Economic Review*, May 1992, 82, 203–209, and Dan Fuller and Doris Geide-Stevenson, "Consensus Among Economists: Revisited?" *Journal of Economics Education*, Fall 2003, 369–387.

Summary

Key Points

A Definition of Economics (p. 4)

- ◆ All economic questions arise from scarcity – from the fact that wants exceed the resources available to satisfy them.
- ◆ Economics is the social science that studies the choices people make as they cope with scarcity.
- ◆ The subject divides into microeconomics and macroeconomics.

Two Big Economic Questions

(pp. 5–10)

- ◆ Two big questions summarize the scope of economics:
  1. How do choices end up determining *what, how* and *for whom* goods and services get produced?
  2. When do choices made in the pursuit of *self-interest* also promote the *social interest*?

The Economic Way of Thinking

(pp. 11–13)

- ◆ Every choice is a trade-off – exchanging more of something for less of something else.
- ◆ The classic guns-versus-butter trade-off represents all trade-offs.
- ◆ There are trade-offs about what, how and for whom goods and services get produced.
- ◆ The big social trade-off is between equality and efficiency.
- ◆ The highest-valued alternative forgone is the opportunity cost of what is chosen.
- ◆ Choices are made at the margin and respond to incentives.

Economics: A Social Science

(pp. 14–16)

- ◆ Economists distinguish between positive statements – what is – and normative statements – what ought to be.
- ◆ Economists develop theories to explain the economic world by building and testing economic models.
- ◆ Economists use the *ceteris paribus* assumption to disentangle cause and effect and are careful to avoid the fallacy of composition and the *post hoc* fallacy.
- ◆ Economists agree on a wide range of questions about how the economy works.

Key Terms

Big trade-off, 12
Capital, 6
Ceteris paribus, 15
Economic model, 14
Economic theory, 15
Economics, 4
Entrepreneurship, 6
Factors of production, 5
Globalization, 8
Goods and services, 5
Human capital, 5
Incentive, 4
Interest, 6
Labour, 5
Land, 5
Macroeconomics, 4
Margin, 13
Marginal benefit, 13
Marginal cost, 13
Microeconomics, 4
Opportunity cost, 12
Profit, 6
Rent, 6
Scarcity, 4
Self-interest, 7
Social interest, 7
Trade-off, 11
Wages, 6

Problems

Tests, Study Plan and Solutions* 

1 Apple Computer Inc. decides to make iTunes freely available in unlimited quantities.

a Does Apple's decision mean that tunes are no longer scarce?

b Does Apple's decision change the incentives that people face?

c Is Apple's decision an example of a microeconomic or a macroeconomic issue?

d How does Apple's decision change the opportunity cost of a tune?

2 Which of the following pairs does not match?

a Labour and wages

b Land and rent

c Entreprenuership and profit

d Capital and profit

3 Explain how the following news headlines concern self-interest and the social interest:

a Tesco Expands in Europe

b Wal-Mart Opens in India

c McDonald's Moves into Salads

d Food Must Be Labelled with Nutrition Information

4 The night before an economics exam, you decide to go to the cinema instead of working your MyEconLab study plan. You get 50 per cent on your exam compared with the 70 per cent that you normally score.

a Did you face a trade-off?

b What was the opportunity cost of your evening at the cinema?

5 Which of the following statements is positive, which is normative and which can be tested?

a The European Union should cut its imports.

b China is the European Union's largest trading partner.

c If the price of antiretroviral drugs increases, HIV/AIDS sufferers will decrease their consumption of the drug.

6 Which statement illustrates the fallacy of composition and which the *post hoc* fallacy?

a Everyone can avoid the rush hour traffic by leaving home an hour earlier.

b The Internet came in the 1990s and terrorism increased in the 2000s, therefore the Internet caused terrorism.

* Solutions to odd-numbered problems are provided.

Critical Thinking

1 As London prepares to host the 2012 Olympic Games, concern about the cost of the event increases. For example:

Costs Soar for London Olympics – The regeneration of East London is set to add extra £1.5 billion to taxpayers' bill.

The Times, London, 6 July 2006

Is the cost of regenerating East London an opportunity cost of hosting the 2012 Olympic Games? Explain.

2 **Germans put price on protesting**

They refuse to rally for neo-Nazis, but as long as the price is right a new type of German mercenary will take to the streets and protest for you. . . . [F]or around 150 euros (£100), more than 300 would-be protesters are marketing themselves on a German rental website.

BBC, 23 January 2007

a Are these protesters acting in the social interest or their self-interest? Explain your answer.

b Would the protests that hire them be in the social interest or self-interest? Explain your answer.

Web Activities

Links to Websites

1 Visit the *Financial Times* website.

a Which big economic questions are in today's news?

b Which of the ideas that define the economic way of thinking are relevant to understanding today's news?

c Write a summary of a news item using the economic vocabulary that you have learned in this chapter and which is in the key terms list on p. 17.

2 Visit *Resources for Economists on the Internet.* This site is a good place from which to search for economic information on the Internet. Click on "Blogs, Commentaries and Podcasts."

a Click on the Becker-Posner Blog and read the latest blog by these two outstanding economists.

b As you read this blog, think about what it is saying about *what*, *how* and *for whom* questions.

c As you read this blog, think about what it is saying about self-interest and the social interest.

Chapter 1 Appendix

Graphs in Economics

After studying this appendix, you will be able to:

- **Make and interpret a time-series graph, a cross-section graph and a scatter diagram**
- **Distinguish between linear and non-linear relationships and between relationships that have a maximum and a minimum**
- **Define and calculate the slope of a line**
- **Graph relationships among more than two variables**

Graphing Data

A graph represents a quantity as a distance. Figure A1.1 shows two examples. A distance on the horizontal line represents temperature. A movement from left to right shows an increase in temperature. The point marked 0 represents zero degrees. To the right of 0, the temperature is positive. To the left of 0, the temperature is negative. A distance on the vertical line represents height. The point marked 0 represents sea level. Points above 0 represent metres above sea level. Points below 0 (indicated by a minus sign) represent metres below sea level.

By setting two scales perpendicular to each other, as in Figure A1.1, we can visualize the relationship between two variables. The scale lines are called *axes*. The vertical line is the y-axis, and the horizontal line is the x-axis. Each axis has a zero point, which is shared by the two axes. This common zero point is called the *origin*.

To show something in a two-variable graph, we need two pieces of information: the value of the x variable and the value of the y variable. For example, off the coast of Norway on a winter's day, the temperature is 0 degrees – the value of x. A fishing boat is located 0 metres above sea level – the value of y. This information appears at the origin at point A in Figure A1.1. In the heated cabin of the boat, the temperature is a comfortable 24 degrees. Point B represents this information. The same 24 degrees in the cabin of an airliner 9,000 metres above sea level is at point C.

Finally, the temperature of the ice cube in the drink of the airline passenger is shown by the point marked D.

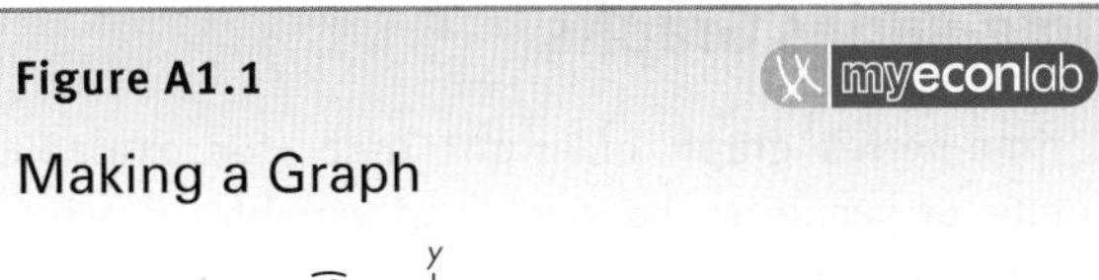

Figure A1.1

Making a Graph

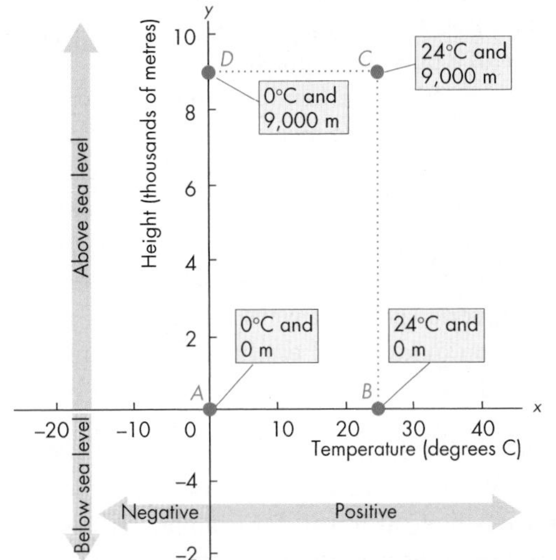

Graphs have axes that measure quantities as distances. Here, the horizontal axis (x-axis) measures temperature, and the vertical axis (y-axis) measures height.

Point A represents a fishing boat at sea level (0 on the y-axis) on a day when the temperature is 0°C. Point B represents inside the cabin of the boat at a temperature of 24°C.

Point C represents inside the cabin of an airliner 9,000 metres above sea level at a temperature of 24°C. Point D represents an ice cube in an airliner 9,000 metres above sea level.

This point represents 9,000 metres above sea level at a temperature of 0 degrees.

We can draw two lines, called *coordinates*, from point C. One, called the y-coordinate, runs from C to the horizontal axis. Its length is the same as the value marked off on the y-axis. The other, called the x-coordinate, runs from C to the vertical axis. Its length is the same as the value marked off on the x-axis. We describe a point in a graph by the values of its x-coordinate and its y-coordinate.

Graphs like that in Figure A1.1 can show any type of quantitative data on two variables. Economists use three types of graphs based on the principles in Figure A1.1 to reveal and describe the relationships among variables. They are:

- Time-series graphs
- Cross-section graphs
- Scatter diagrams

Time-series Graphs

A **time-series graph** measures time (for example, months or years) on the x-axis and variables in which we are interested on the y-axis. Figure A1.2 is an example of a time-series graph.

In Figure A1.2, we measure time in years running from 1976 to 2006. We measure the price of coffee (the variable that we are interested in) on the y-axis.

The point of a time-series graph is to enable us to visualize how a variable has changed over time and how its value in one period relates to its value in another period.

A time-series graph conveys an enormous amount of information quickly and easily, as this example illustrates. It shows:

1 The *level* of the price of coffee – when it is *high* and *low*. When the line is a long way from the x-axis, the price is high, as it was, for example, in 1986. When the line is close to the x-axis, the price is low, as it was, for example, in 2001.

2 How the price *changes* – whether it *rises* or *falls*. When the line slopes upward, as from 1992 to 1994, the price is rising. When the line slopes downward, as from 1977 to 1978, the price is falling.

3 The *speed* with which the price changes – whether it rises or falls *quickly* or *slowly*. If the line is very steep, then the price rises or falls quickly. If the line is not steep, the price rises or falls slowly. For example, the price rose quickly during 1994 and slowly during 1995. The price fell quickly during 1978 and slowly during 1984.

Figure A1.2

A Time-series Graph

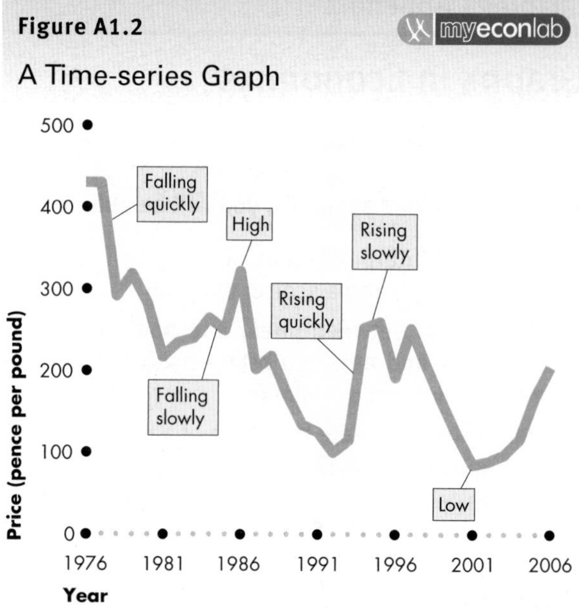

A time-series graph plots the level of a variable on the y-axis against time (day, week, month or year) on the x-axis. This graph shows the price of coffee (in pence per pound) each year from 1976 to 2006. It shows us when the price of coffee was *high* and when it was *low*, when the price *increased* and when it *decreased*, and when it changed *quickly* and when it changed *slowly*.

A time-series graph also reveals whether the variable has a trend. A **trend** is a general tendency for a variable to move in one direction. A trend might be upward or downward. In Figure A1.2, you can see a downward trend in the price of coffee. That is, although the price rose and fell, the general tendency was for the price of coffee to fall.

A time-series graph also helps us to detect cycles in variables. In Figure A1.2, you can see some clear cycles in the price of coffee. The price rises and falls in a series of cycles with peaks in 1986 and 1995 – almost exactly 10-year intervals. The cycles have troughs in 1981, 1992 and 2001, again, almost 10-year intervals.

Finally, a time-series graph lets us compare the variable in different periods quickly. Figure A1.2 shows that the average price of coffee was higher in the 1980s than in the 2000s. When we graph data at monthly intervals, we discover seasonal variations.

You can see that a time-series graph conveys a wealth of information. And it does so in much less space than we have used to describe only some of its features. But you do have to "read" the graph to obtain all this information.

Cross-section Graphs

A **cross-section graph** shows the values of an economic variable for different groups in a population at a point in time. Figure A1.3 shows an example. This graph is called a *bar chart*.

The bar chart in Figure A1.3 shows the percentage of young males who participate in various sporting activities. This figure enables you to compare the popularity of different activities. And you can do so much more quickly and clearly than by looking at a list of numbers. For example, you can quickly see that football is twice as popular as tennis or cricket and that very few young males do aerobics.

Figure A1.3

A Cross-section Graph

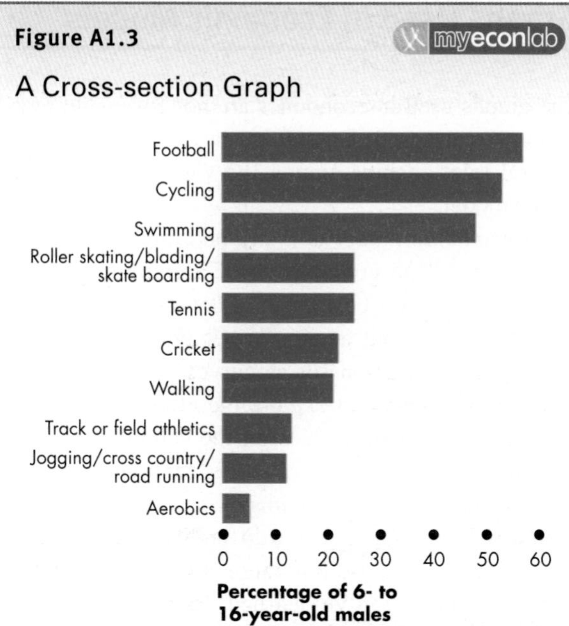

A cross-section graph shows the level of a variable across the members of a population. This bar chart shows the percentage of young males who participate in various sporting activities.

Scatter Diagrams

A **scatter diagram** plots the value of one variable against the value of another variable. Such a graph reveals whether a relationship exists between two variables and describes their relationship. Figure A1.4(a) shows the relationship between consumption expenditure and income. Each dot shows expenditure per person and income per person in a given year from 1992 to 2006. The dots are "scattered" within the graph. The dot labelled *A* tells us that in 1997, income per person was £9,670 and consumption expenditure per person was £9,000. The dots in this graph form a pattern, which reveals that as income increases, expenditure increases.

Figure A1.4(b) shows the relationship between the number of international phone calls and the price of a call. This graph shows that as the price per minute falls, the number of calls increases.

Figure A1.4(c) shows a scatter diagram of inflation and unemployment in the United Kingdom. Here, the dots show no clear relationship between these two variables. The dots reveal that there is no simple relationship between these two variables.

Figure A1.4

Scatter Diagrams

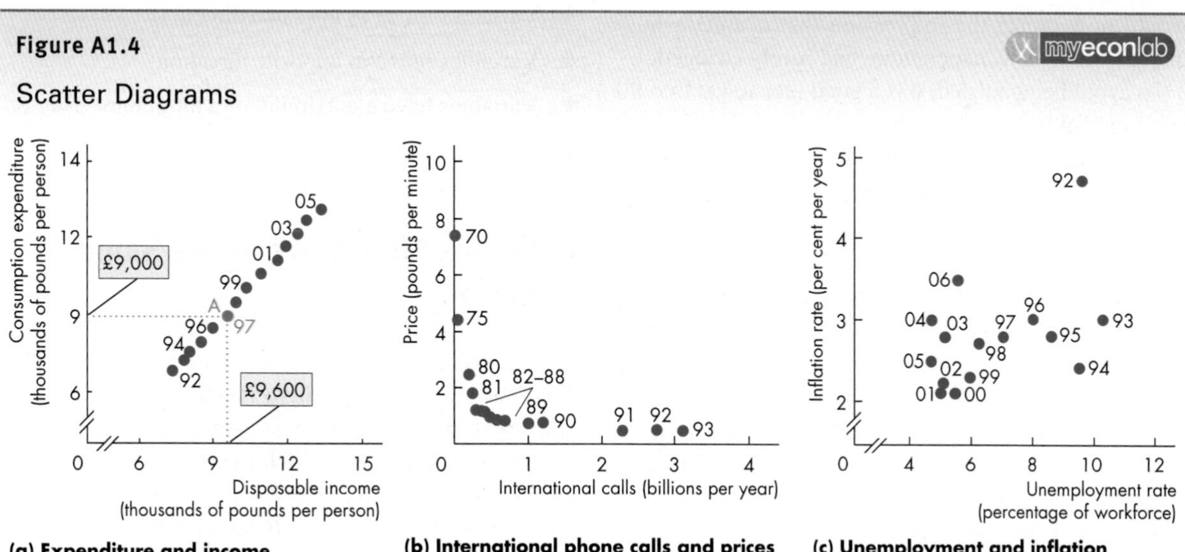

A scatter diagram reveals the relationship between two variables. Part (a) shows the relationship between expenditure and income. Each point shows the values of the two variables in a specific year. For example, point *A* shows that in 1997, average income was £9,600 and average expenditure was £9,000. The dots form a pattern that shows that as income increases, expenditure increases.

Part (b) shows the relationship between the price of an international phone call and the number of calls made. This graph shows that as the price of a phone call falls, the number of international calls made increases.

Part (c) shows a scatter diagram of the inflation rate and unemployment rate in the United Kingdom. This graph shows that inflation and unemployment are not closely related.

Breaks in the Axes

Figure A1.4(a) and Figure A1.4(c) have breaks in their axes, as shown by the small gaps. The breaks indicate that there are jumps from the origin, 0, to the first values recorded.

In Figure A1.4(a), the breaks are used because the lowest values exceed £6,000. With no breaks in the axes, there would be a lot of empty space, all the points would be crowded into the top right corner and it would be hard to see the relationship between these two variables. By breaking the axes, we bring the relationship into view.

Putting a break in the axes is like using a zoom lens to bring the relationship into the centre of the graph and magnify it so that it fills the graph.

Misleading Graphs

Breaks can be used to highlight a relationship. But they can also be used to mislead – to make a graph that lies. The most common way of making a graph lie is to use axis breaks and either to stretch or compress a scale. For example, suppose that in Figure A1.4(a), the *y*-axis that measures expenditure ran from zero to £45,000 while the *x*-axis was the same as the one shown. The graph would now create the impression that despite a huge increase in income, expenditure had barely changed.

To avoid being misled, it is a good idea to get into the habit of looking closely at the values and the labels on the axes of a graph before you start trying to interpret it.

Correlation and Causation

A scatter diagram that shows a clear relationship between two variables, such as Figure A1.4(a) or Figure A1.4(b), tells us that the two variables have a high correlation. When a high correlation is present, we can predict the value of one variable from the value of the other variable. But correlation does not imply causation.

Sometimes a high correlation is a coincidence, but sometimes it does arise from a causal relationship. It is likely, for example, that rising income causes rising expenditure (Figure A1.4a) and that the falling price of a phone call causes more calls to be made (Figure A1.4b).

You've now seen how we can use graphs in economics to show economic data and to reveal relationships between variables. Next, we'll learn how economists use graphs to construct and display economic models.

Graphs Used in Economic Models

The graphs used in economics are not always designed to show real-world data. Often they are used to show general relationships among the variables in an economic model.

An *economic model* is a stripped down, simplified description of an economy or of a component of an economy such as a business or a household. It consists of statements about economic behaviour that can be expressed as equations or as curves in a graph. Economists use models to explore the effects of different policies or other influences on the economy in ways that are similar to the use of model aeroplanes in wind tunnels and models of the climate.

You will encounter many different kinds of graphs in economic models, but there are some repeating patterns. Once you've learned to recognize these patterns, you will instantly understand the meaning of a graph. Here, we'll look at the different types of curves that are used in economic models, and we'll see some everyday examples of each type of curve. The patterns to look for in graphs are the four cases in which:

- Variables move in the same direction
- Variables move in opposite directions
- Variables have a maximum or a minimum
- Variables are unrelated

Variables That Move in the Same Direction

A relationship in which two variables move in the same direction is called a **positive relationship** or a **direct relationship**. Figure A1.5 shows some examples of positive relationships. Notice that the line that shows such a relationship slopes upward.

Figure A1.5 shows three types of relationships, one that has a straight line and two that have curved lines. But all the lines in these three graphs are called curves. Any line on a graph – no matter whether it is straight or curved – is called a *curve*.

A relationship shown by a straight line is called a **linear relationship**. Figure A1.5(a) shows a linear relationship between the number of miles travelled in 5 hours and speed. For example, point *A* shows that

Figure A1.5

Positive (Direct) Relationships

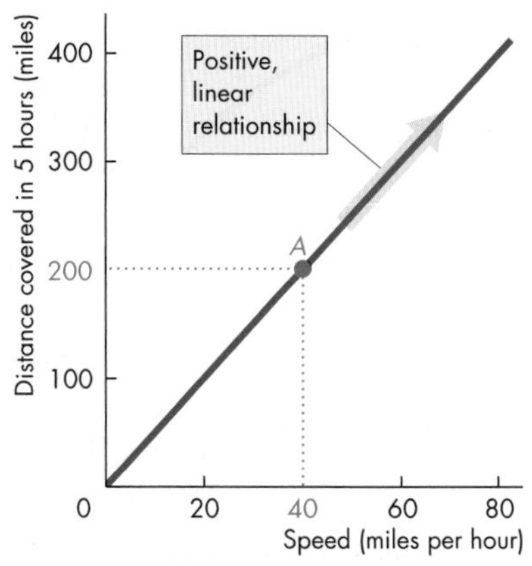

(a) Positive, linear relationship

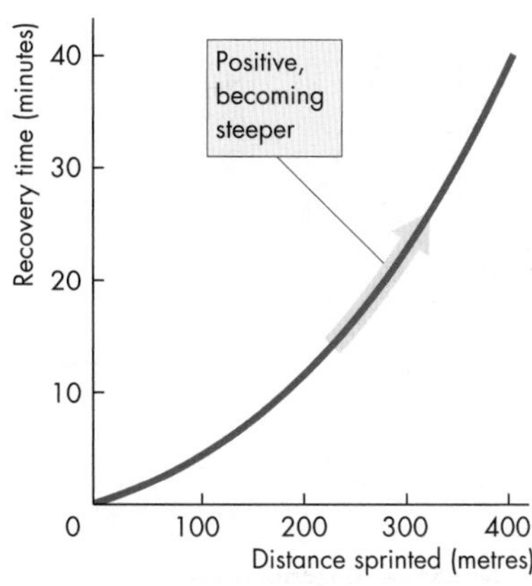

(b) Positive, becoming steeper

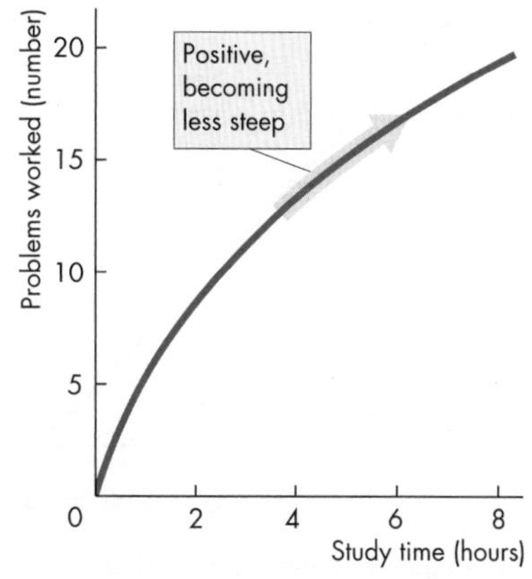

(c) Positive, becoming less steep

Each part of this figure shows a positive (direct) relationship between two variables. That is, as the value of the variable measured on the *x*-axis increases, so does the value of the variable measured on the *y*-axis. Part (a) shows a linear relationship – as the two variables increase together, we move along a straight line.

Part (b) shows a positive relationship such that as the two variables increase together, we move along a curve that becomes steeper.

Part (c) shows a positive relationship such that as the two variables increase together, we move along a curve that becomes less steep.

we will travel 200 miles in 5 hours if our speed is 40 miles an hour. If we double our speed to 80 miles an hour, we will travel 400 miles in 5 hours.

Figure A1.5(b) shows the relationship between distance sprinted and recovery time (the time it takes the heart rate to return to its normal resting rate). This relationship is an upward-sloping one that starts out quite flat but then becomes steeper as we move along the curve away from the origin. The reason this curve slopes upward and becomes steeper is because the additional recovery time needed from sprinting an additional 100 metres increases. It takes less than 5 minutes to recover from the first 100 metres but more than 10 minutes to recover from the third 100 metres.

Figure A1.5(c) shows the relationship between the number of problems worked by a student and the amount of study time. This relationship is an upward-sloping one that starts out quite steep and becomes flatter as we move away from the origin. Study time becomes less productive as you increase the hours spent studying and become more tired.

Variables That Move in Opposite Directions

A relationship between variables that move in opposite directions is called a **negative relationship** or an **inverse relationship**. Figure A1.6 shows some examples. Figure A1.6(a) shows the relationship between the number of hours available for playing squash and for playing tennis when the total is 5 hours. One extra hour spent playing tennis means one hour less playing squash and vice versa. This relationship is negative and linear.

Figure A1.6(b) shows the relationship between the cost per mile travelled and the length of a journey. The longer the journey, the lower is the cost per mile. But as the journey length increases, the cost per mile decreases, and the fall in the cost is smaller, the longer the journey. This feature of the relationship is shown by the fact that the curve slopes downward, starting out steep at a short journey length and then becoming flatter as the journey length increases. This relationship arises because some of the costs are fixed.

Figure A1.6

Negative (Inverse) Relationships

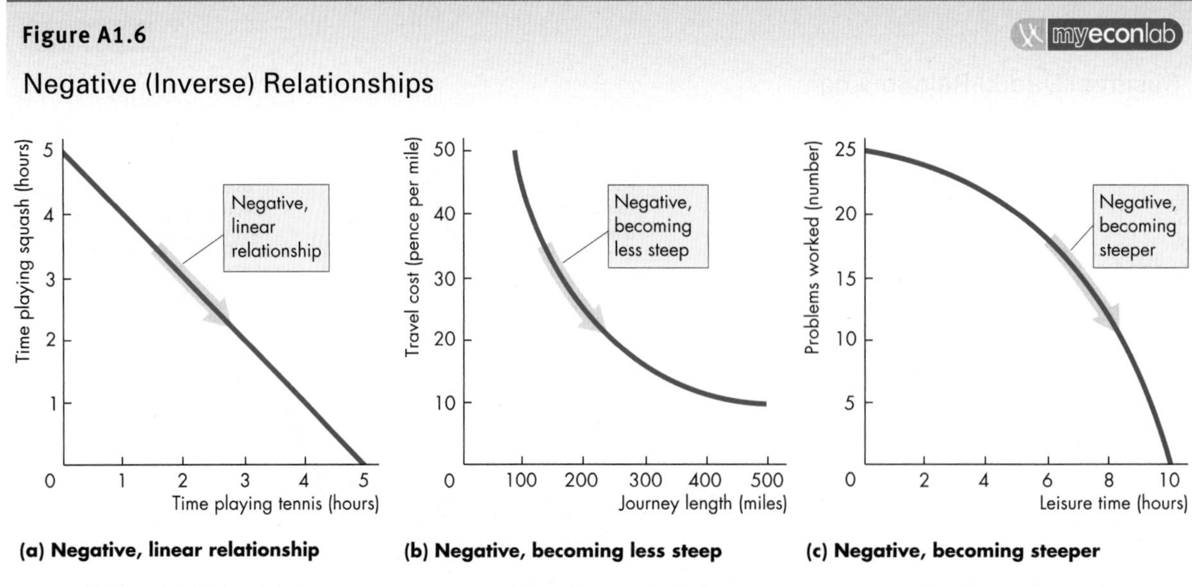

(a) Negative, linear relationship **(b) Negative, becoming less steep** **(c) Negative, becoming steeper**

Each part of this figure shows a negative (inverse) relationship between two variables. That is, as the value of the variable measured on the *x*-axis increases and the value of the variable measured on the *y*-axis decreases.

Part (a) shows a linear relationship. The total time spent playing tennis and squash is 5 hours. As the time spent playing tennis increases, the time spent playing squash decreases and we move along a straight line.

Part (b) shows a negative relationship such that as the journey length increases, the travel cost decreases as we move along a curve that becomes less steep.

Part (c) shows a negative relationship such that as leisure time increases, the number of problems worked decreases as we move along a curve that becomes steeper.

Figure A1.6(c) shows the relationship between the amount of leisure time and the number of problems worked by a student. Increasing leisure time produces an increasingly large reduction in the number of problems worked. This relationship is a negative one that starts out with a gentle slope at a small number of leisure hours and becomes steeper as the number of leisure hours increases. This relationship is a different view of the idea shown in Figure A1.5(c).

Variables That Have a Maximum or a Minimum

Many relationships in economic models have a maximum or a minimum. For example, firms try to make the largest possible profit and to produce at the lowest possible cost. Figure A1.7 shows relationships that have a maximum or a minimum.

Figure A1.7(a) shows the relationship between rainfall and wheat yield. When there is no rainfall, wheat will not grow, so the yield is zero. As the rainfall increases up to 10 days a month, the wheat yield increases. With 10 rainy days each month, the wheat yield reaches its maximum at 40 tonnes per hectare (point *A*). Rain in excess of 10 days a month starts to lower the yield of wheat. If every day is rainy, the wheat suffers from a lack of sunshine and the yield decreases to zero. This relationship is one that starts out sloping upward, reaches a maximum, and then slopes downward.

Figure A1.7(b) shows the reverse case – a relationship that begins sloping downward, falls to a minimum, and then slopes upward. Most economic costs are like this relationship. An example is the relationship between the travel cost per mile and speed for a car trip. At low speeds, the car is creeping in a traffic jam. The number of miles per gallon is low, so the cost per mile is high. At high speeds, the car is travelling faster than its efficient speed, using a large quantity of petrol, and again the number of miles per gallon is low and the cost per mile is high. At a speed of 55 miles an hour, the cost per mile is at its minimum (point *B*). This relationship is one that starts out sloping downward, reaches a minimum, and then slopes upward.

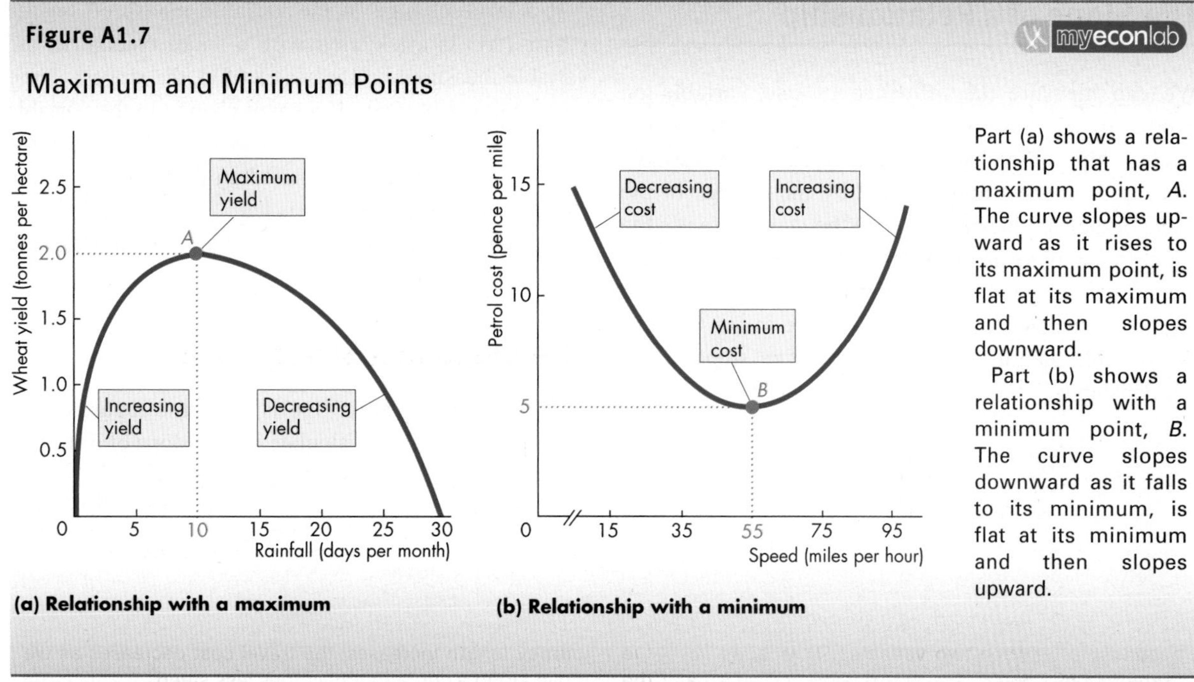

(a) Relationship with a maximum

(b) Relationship with a minimum

Part (a) shows a relationship that has a maximum point, *A*. The curve slopes upward as it rises to its maximum point, is flat at its maximum and then slopes downward.

Part (b) shows a relationship with a minimum point, *B*. The curve slopes downward as it falls to its minimum, is flat at its minimum and then slopes upward.

Variables That Are Unrelated

There are many situations in which no matter what happens to the value of one variable, the other variable remains constant. Sometimes we want to show the independence between two variables in a graph, and Figure A1.8 shows two ways of achieving this.

In describing the graphs in Figures A1.5 to Figure A1.7, we have talked about curves that slope upward or slope downward and curves that become steeper and less steep. Let's spend a little time discussing exactly what we mean by slope and how we measure the slope of a curve.

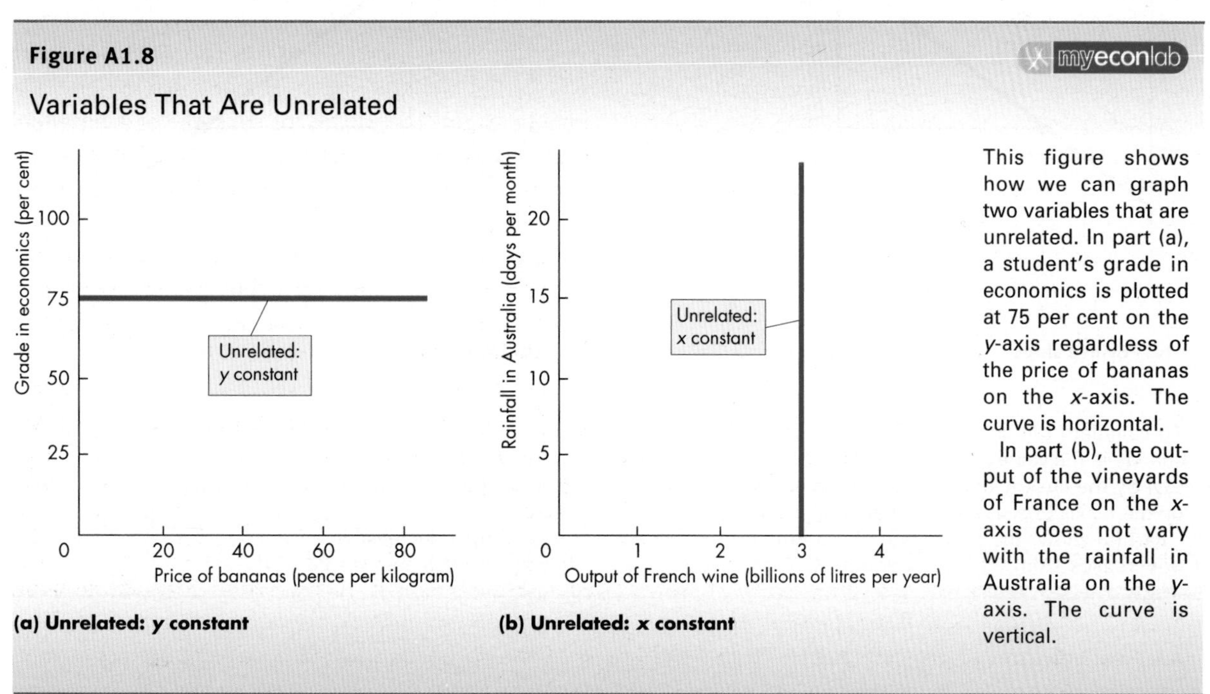

(a) Unrelated: *y* constant

(b) Unrelated: *x* constant

This figure shows how we can graph two variables that are unrelated. In part (a), a student's grade in economics is plotted at 75 per cent on the *y*-axis regardless of the price of bananas on the *x*-axis. The curve is horizontal.

In part (b), the output of the vineyards of France on the *x*-axis does not vary with the rainfall in Australia on the *y*-axis. The curve is vertical.

The Slope of a Relationship

We can measure the influence of one variable on another by the slope of the relationship. The **slope** of a relationship is the change in the value of the variable measured on the y-axis divided by the change in the value of the variable measured on the x-axis. We use the Greek letter Δ (*delta*) to represent "change in". So Δy means the change in the value of the variable measured on the y-axis, and Δx means the change in the value of the variable measured on the x-axis. The slope of the relationship is:

$$\frac{\Delta y}{\Delta x}$$

If a large change in the variable measured on the y-axis (Δy) is associated with a small change in the variable measured on the x-axis (Δx), the slope is large and the curve is steep. If a small change in the variable measured on the y-axis (Δy) is associated with a large change in the variable measured on the x-axis (Δx), the slope is small and the curve is flat.

We can make the idea of slope sharper by doing some calculations.

The Slope of a Straight Line

The slope of a straight line is the same regardless of where on the line you calculate it. The slope of a straight line is constant.

Figure A1.9

myeconlab

The Slope of a Straight Line

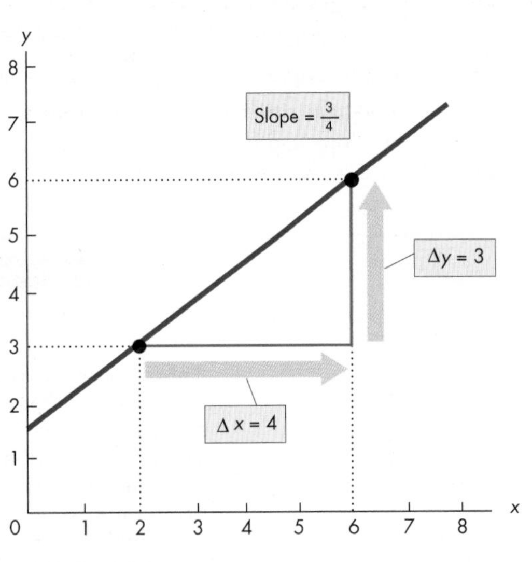

(a) Positive slope

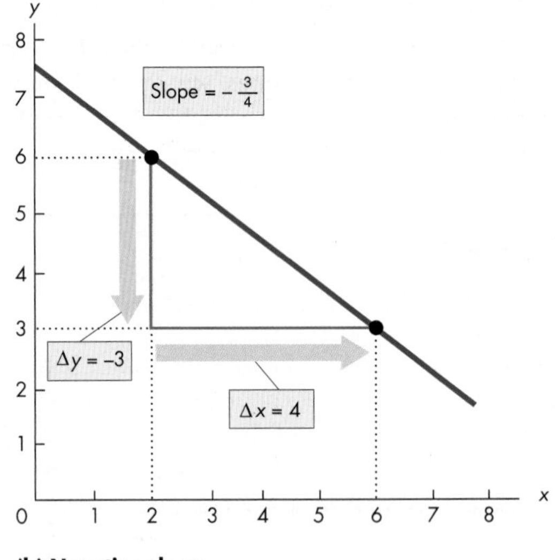

(b) Negative slope

To calculate the slope of a straight line, we divide the change in the value of the variable measured on the y-axis (Δy) by the change in the value of the variable measured on the x-axis (Δx), as we move along the curve.

Part (a) shows the calculation of a positive slope. When x increases from 2 to 6, Δx equals 4. That change in x brings about an increase in y from 3 to 6, so Δy equals 3. The slope ($\Delta y/\Delta x$) equals 3/4.

Part (b) shows the calculation of a negative slope. When x increases from 2 to 6, Δx equals 4. That increase in x brings about a decrease in y from 6 to 3, so Δy equals –3. The slope ($\Delta y/\Delta x$) equals –3/4.

Let's calculate the slopes of the lines in Figure A1.9. In part (a), when x increases from 2 to 6, y increases from 3 to 6. The change in x is +4: that is, Δx is 4. The change in y is +3: that is, Δy is 3. The slope of that line is:

$$\frac{\Delta y}{\Delta x} = \frac{3}{4}$$

In part (b), when x increases from 2 to 6, y decreases from 6 to 3. The change in y is *minus* 3: that is, Δy is –3. The change in x is *plus* 4: that is, Δx is 4. The slope of the curve is:

$$\frac{\Delta y}{\Delta x} = \frac{-3}{4}$$

Notice that the two slopes have the same magnitude (3/4), but the slope of the line in part (a) is positive (3/4), while the slope in part (b) is negative (–3/4). The slope of a positive relationship is positive; the slope of a negative relationship is negative.

Figure A1.10 myeconlab

Slope at a Point

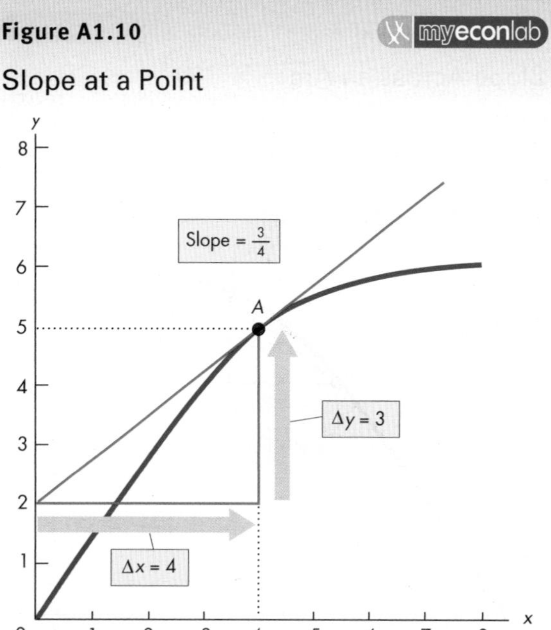

To calculate the slope of the curve at point A, draw the red line that just touches the curve at A – the tangent. The slope of this straight line is calculated by dividing the change in y by the change in x along the line. When x increases from 0 to 4, Δx equals 4. That change in x is associated with an increase in y from 2 to 5, so Δy equals 3. The slope of the red line is 3/4. So the slope of the curve at point A is 3/4.

The Slope of a Curved Line

The slope of a curved line is trickier. The slope of a curved line is not constant. Its slope depends on where on the line we calculate it. There are two ways to calculate the slope of a curved line: you can calculate the slope at a point, or you can calculate the slope across an arc of the curve. Let's look at the two alternatives.

Slope at a Point

To calculate the slope at a point on a curve, you need to construct a straight line that has the same slope as the curve at the point in question. Figure A1.10 shows how this is done. Suppose you want to calculate the slope of the curve at point A. Place a ruler on the graph so that it touches point A and no other point on the curve, then draw a straight line along the edge of the ruler. The straight red line is this line, and it is the *tangent* to the curve at point A. If the ruler touches the curve only at point A, then the slope of the curve at point A must be the same as the slope of the edge of the ruler. If the curve and the ruler do not have the same slope, the line along the edge of the ruler will cut the curve instead of just touching it.

Now that you have found a straight line with the same slope as the curve at point A, you can calculate the slope of the curve at point A by calculating the slope of the straight line. Along the straight line, as x increases from 0 to 4 ($\Delta x = 4$) y increases from 2 to 5 ($\Delta y = 3$). The slope of the line is:

$$\frac{\Delta y}{\Delta x} = \frac{3}{4}$$

So the slope of the curve at point A is 3/4.

Slope Across an Arc

An arc of a curve is a piece of a curve. In Figure A1.11, you are looking at the same curve as in Figure A1.10. But instead of calculating the slope at point A, we are going to calculate the slope across the arc from B to C. You can see that the slope is greater at B than at C. When we calculate the slope across an arc, we are calculating the average slope between two points. As we move along the arc from B to C, x increases from 3 to 5 and y increases from 4 to 5.5. The change in x is 2 ($\Delta x = 2$), and the change in y is 1.5 ($\Delta y = 1.5$).

Figure A1.11

Slope Across an Arc

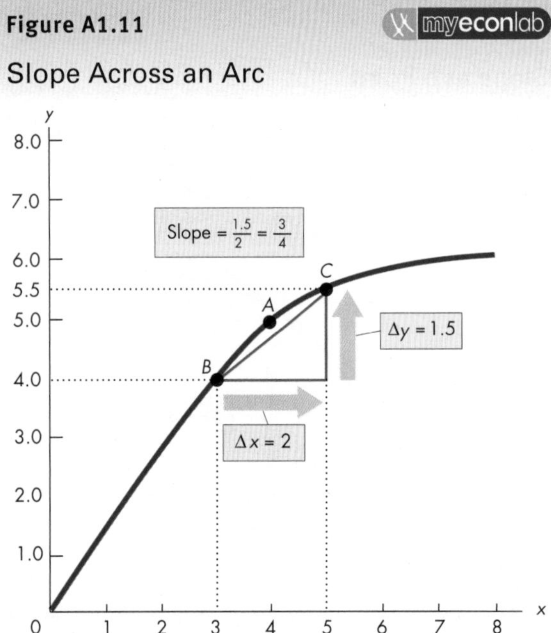

To calculate the average slope of the curve along the arc *BC*, draw a straight line from point *B* to point *C*. The slope of the line *BC* is calculated by dividing the change in *y* by the change in *x*. In moving from *B* to *C*, Δx equals 2 and Δy equals 1.5. The slope of the line *BC* is 1.5 divided by 2, or 3/4. So the slope of the curve across the arc *BC* is 3/4.

The slope of the red line *BC* is:

$$\frac{\Delta y}{\Delta x} = \frac{1.5}{2} = \frac{3}{4}$$

So the slope of the curve across the arc *BC* is 3/4.

This calculation gives us the slope of the curve between points *B* and *C*. The actual slope calculated is the slope of the straight line from *B* to *C*. This slope approximates the average slope of the curve along the arc *BC*. In this particular example, the slope across the arc *BC* is identical to the slope of the curve at point *A*. But the calculation of the slope of a curve does not always work out so neatly. You might have some fun constructing some more examples and some counter examples.

You now know how to make and interpret a graph. But so far, we've limited our attention to graphs of two variables. We're now going to learn how to graph more than two variables.

Graphing Relationships Among More Than Two Variables

We have seen that we can graph the relationship between two variables as a point formed by the *x*- and *y*-coordinates in a two-dimensional graph. You may be thinking that although a two-dimensional graph is informative, most of the things in which you are likely to be interested involve relationships among many variables, not just two. For example, the amount of ice cream consumed depends on the price of ice cream and the temperature. If ice cream is expensive and the temperature is low, people eat a lot less ice cream than when ice cream is inexpensive and the temperature is high. For any given price of ice cream, the quantity consumed varies with the temperature; and for any given temperature, the quantity of ice cream consumed varies with its price.

Figure A1.12 shows a relationship among three variables. The table shows the number of litres of ice cream consumed each day at various temperatures and ice cream prices. How can we graph these numbers?

To graph a relationship that involves more than two variables, we use the *ceteris paribus* assumption.

Ceteris Paribus

We noted in the chapter (see p. 15) that every laboratory experiment is an attempt to create *ceteris paribus* and isolate the relationship of interest. We use the same method to make a graph when more than two variables are involved.

Figure A1.12(a) shows an example. There, you can see what happens to the quantity of ice cream consumed as the price of ice cream varies when the temperature is held constant. The line labelled 20°C shows the relationship between ice cream consumption and the price of ice cream if the temperature remains at 20°C. The numbers used to plot that line are those in the third column of the table in Figure A1.12. For example, if the temperature is 20°C, 10 litres are consumed when the price is 30 pence a scoop and 52 litres are consumed when the price is 10 pence a scoop. The curve labelled 25°C shows consumption as the price varies if the temperature remains at 25°C.

We can also show the relationship between ice cream consumption and temperature when the price of ice cream remains constant, as shown in Figure A1.12(b). The curve labelled 30 pence shows how the consumption of ice cream varies with the temperature

Figure A1.12

myeconlab

Graphing a Relationship Among Three Variables

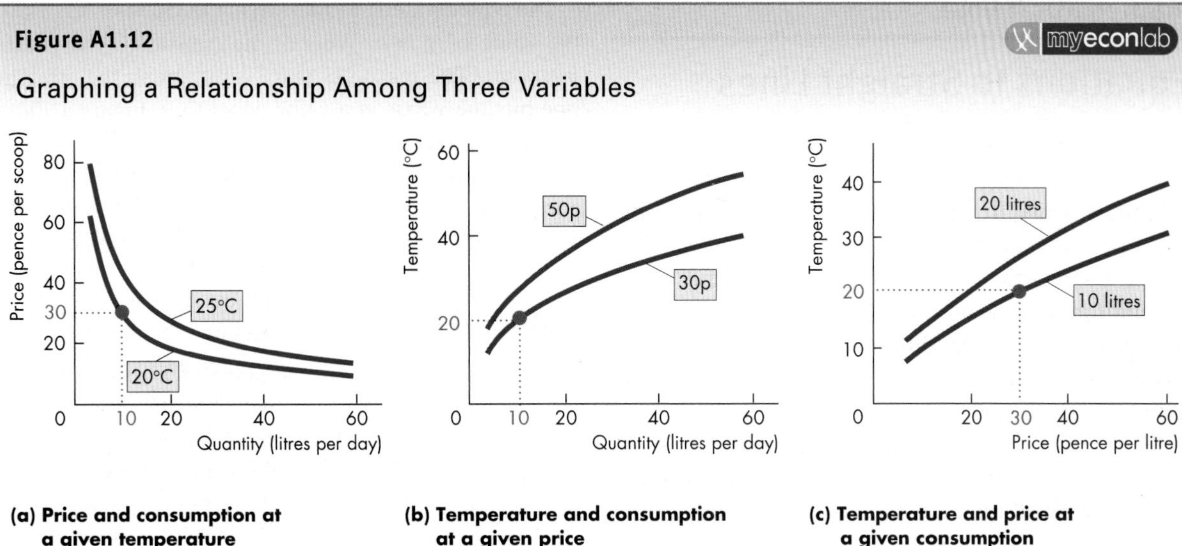

(a) Price and consumption at a given temperature

(b) Temperature and consumption at a given price

(c) Temperature and price at a given consumption

Price (pence per scoop)	Ice cream consumption (litres per day)			
	5°C	**10°C**	**20°C**	**25°C**
10	2	10	52	91
20	1	3	18	32
30	0	2	**10**	17
40	0	1	6	10
50	0	1	5	8
60	0	1	4	6

The quantity of ice cream consumed depends on its price and the temperature. The table gives some hypothetical numbers that tell us how many litres of ice cream are consumed each day at different prices and different temperatures. For example, if the price is 30 pence a scoop and the temperature is 20°C, 10 litres of ice cream are consumed. This set of values is highlighted in the table and each part of the figure.

To graph a relationship among three variables, the value of one variable is held constant. Part (a) shows the relationship between price and consumption when temperature is held constant. One curve holds temperature at 20°C and the other at 25°C. Part (b) shows the relationship between temperature and consumption when price is held constant. One curve holds the price at 30 pence a scoop and the other at 50 pence a scoop. Part (c) shows the relationship between temperature and price when consumption is held constant. One curve holds consumption at 10 litres and the other at 20 litres.

when ice cream costs 30 pence a scoop. On that curve, 10 litres are consumed when the temperature is 20°C. A second curve shows the relationship when ice cream costs 50 pence a scoop.

Figure A1.12(c) shows the combinations of temperature and price that result in a constant consumption of ice cream. One curve shows the combination that results in 10 litres a day being consumed, and the other shows the combination that result in 20 litres a day being consumed. A high price and a high temperature lead to the same consumption as a lower price and a lower temperature. For example, 10 litres of ice cream are consumed at 20°C and 30 pence a scoop, at 25°C and 40 pence a scoop, and at 10°C and 10 pence a scoop.

You can think of the curve in the graph as shifting when one of the factors on which its position depends changes. A change in temperature shifts the curve in part (a); a change in price shifts the curve in part (b); and a change in the quantity consumed shifts the curve in part (c). You will encounter graphs like the ones in Figure A1.12 at several points in your study of economics.

With what you have learned about graphs, you can move forward with your study of economics. There are no graphs in this book that are more complicated than those that have been explained in this appendix. Use this appendix as a refresher if you find that you're having difficulty interpreting or making a graph.

Mathematical Note

Equations to Straight Lines

If a straight line in a graph describes the relationship between two variables, we call it a *linear relationship*. Figure 1 shows the linear relationship between Cathy's expenditure and income. Cathy spends £100 a week (by borrowing or spending her past savings) when income is zero. And out of each pound earned, Cathy spends 50 pence (and saves 50 pence).

All linear relationships are described by the same general equation. We call the quantity that is measured on the horizontal (or x-axis) x and we call the quantity that is measured on the vertical (or y-axis) y. In the case of Figure 1, x is income and y is expenditure.

A Linear Equation

The equation that describes a linear relationship between x and y is:

$$y = a + bx$$

In this equation, a and b are fixed numbers and they are called constants. The values of x and y vary so these numbers are called variables. Because the equation describes a straight line, it is called a *linear equation*.

The equation tells us that when the value of x is zero, the value of y is a. We call the constant a the *y-axis intercept*. The reason is that on the graph the straight line hits the y-axis at a value equal to a. Figure 1 illustrates the y-axis intercept.

For positive values of x, the value of y exceeds a. The constant b tells us by how much y increases above a as x increases. The constant b is the slope of the line.

Slope of a Line

As we explain on p. 26, the slope of a relationship is the change in the value of y divided by the change in the value of x. We use the Greek letter Δ (delta) to represent "change in". So Δy means the change in the value of the variable measured on the y-axis, and Δx means the change in the value of the variable measured on the x-axis. Therefore the slope of the relationship is:

$$\Delta y/\Delta x$$

To see why the slope is b, suppose that initially the value of x is x_1, or £200 in Figure 2. The corresponding value of y is y_1, also £200 in Figure 2. The equation of the line tells us that:

$$y_1 = a + bx_1 \quad (1)$$

Now the value of x increases by Δx to $x_1 + \Delta x$ (or £400 in Figure 2). And the value of y increases by Δy to $y_1 + \Delta y$ (or £300 in Figure 2).

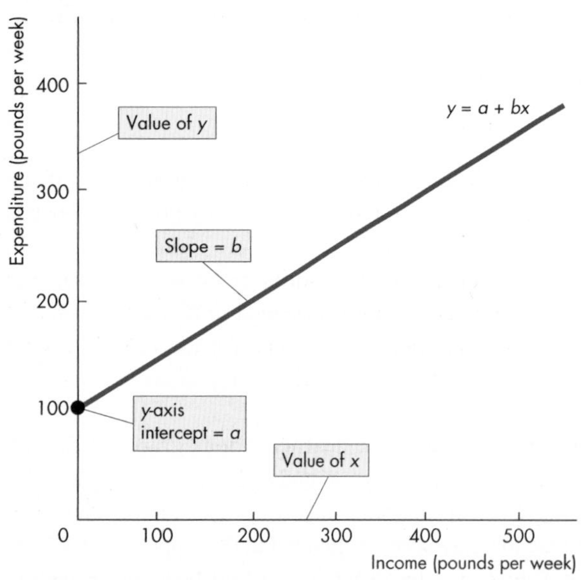

Figure 1 Linear relationship

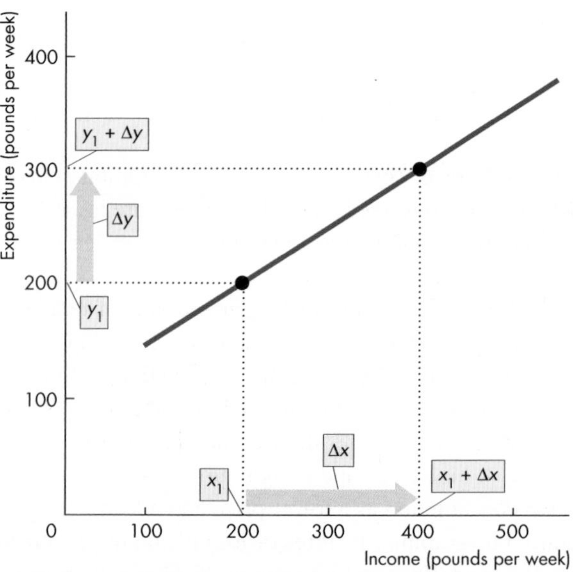

Figure 2 Calculating slope

The equation of the line now tells us that:

$$y_1 + \Delta y = a + b(x_1 + \Delta x) \qquad (2)$$

To calculate the slope of the line, subtract equation (1) from equation (2) to obtain:

$$\Delta y = b\Delta x \qquad (3)$$

and now divide equation (3) by Δx to obtain:

$$\Delta y/\Delta x = b$$

So the slope of the line is b.

We can calculate the slope of the line in Figure 2. When x increases from 200 to 400, y increases from 200 to 300, so Δx is 200 and Δy is 100. The slope, b, equals:

$$\Delta y/\Delta x = 100/200 = 0.5$$

Position of the Line

The y-axis intercept determines the position of the line on the graph. Figure 3 illustrates the relationship between the y-axis intercept and the position of the line on the graph. In this graph, the y-axis measures saving and the x-axis measures income.

When the y-axis intercept, a, is positive, the line hits the y-axis at a positive value of y – as the blue line does. Its y-axis intercept is 100.

When the y-axis intercept, a, is zero, the line hits the y-axis at the origin – as the purple line does. Its y-axis intercept is 0.

When the y-axis intercept, a, is negative, the line hits the y-axis at a negative value of y – as the red line does. Its y-axis intercept is –100.

As the equations of the three lines show, the value of the y-axis intercept does *not* influence the slope of the line. All three lines have a slope equal to 0.5.

Positive Relationships

Figures 1 and 2 show a positive relationship – the two variables x and y move in the same direction. All positive relationships have a slope that is *positive*. In the equation of the line, the constant b is positive.

In the example in Figure 2, the y-axis intercept, a, is 100. The slope b equals 0.5. The equation to the line is:

$$y = 100 + 0.5x$$

Negative Relationships

Figure 4 shows a negative relationship – the variables x and y move in the opposite direction. All negative relationships have a slope that is *negative*. In the equation to the line, the constant b is negative.

In the example in Figure 4, the y-axis intercept, a, is 30. The slope, b, equals $\Delta y/\Delta x$ as we move along the line. When x increases from 0 to 2, y decreases from 30 to 10, so Δx is 2 and Δy is –20. The slope equals $\Delta y/\Delta x$, which is –20/2 or –10. The equation to the line is:

$$y = 30 + (-10)x$$

or

$$y = 30 - 10x$$

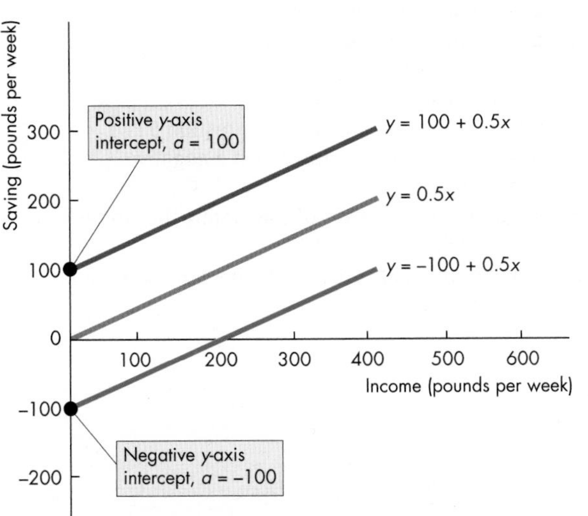

Figure 3 The *y*-axis intercept

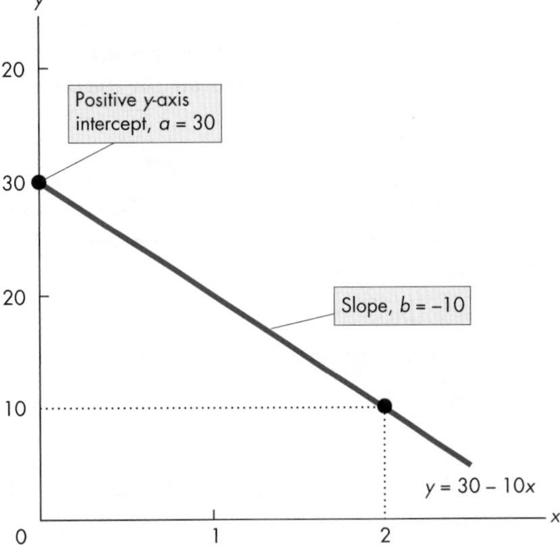

Figure 4 Negative relationship

Summary

Key Points

Graphing Data (pp. 19–22)

- A time-series graph shows the trend and fluctuations in a variable over time.
- A cross-section graph shows how variables change across the members of a population.
- A scatter diagram shows the relationship between two variables. It shows whether two variables are positively related, negatively related, or unrelated.

Graphs Used in Economic Models (pp. 22–25)

- Graphs are used to show relationships among variables in economic models.
- Relationships can be positive (an upward-sloping curve), negative (a downward-sloping curve), positive and then negative (have a maximum point), negative and then positive (have a minimum point), or unrelated (a horizontal or vertical curve).

The Slope of a Relationship (pp. 26–28)

- The slope of a relationship is calculated as the change in the value of the variable measured on the *y*-axis divided by the change in the value of the variable measured on the *x*-axis, that is, $\Delta y/\Delta x$.
- A straight line has a constant slope.
- A curved line has a varying slope. To calculate the slope of a curved line, we calculate the slope at a point or across an arc.

Graphing Relationships Among More Than Two Variables (pp. 28–29)

- To graph a relationship among more than two variables, we hold constant the values of all the variables except two.
- We then plot the value of one of the variables against the value of another.

Key Terms

Cross-section graph, 20
Direct relationship, 22
Inverse relationship, 23
Linear relationship, 22
Negative relationship, 23
Positive relationship, 22
Scatter diagram, 21
Slope, 26
Time-series graph, 20
Trend, 20

Review Quiz

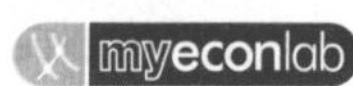

Study Plan 1.A

1. What are the three types of graphs used to show economic data?
2. Give an example of a time-series graph.
3. List three things that a time-series graph shows quickly and easily.
4. Give three examples, different from those in the chapter, of scatter diagrams that show a positive relationship, a negative relationship and no relationship.
5. Draw some graphs to show the relationships between two variables:
   a. That move in the same direction.
   b. That move in opposite directions.
   c. That have a maximum.
   d. That have a minimum.
6. Which of the relationships in question 5 is a positive relationship and which a negative relationship?
7. What are the two ways of calculating the slope of a curved line?
8. How do we graph a relationship among more than two variables?

Problems

Tests, Study Plan and Solutions* 

The spreadsheet provides data on the US economy: column A is the year, column B is the inflation rate, column C is the interest rate, column D is the growth rate and column E is the unemployment rate. Use this spreadsheet to answer problems 1, 2, 3 and 4.

	A	B	C	D	E
1	1995	2.8	7.6	2.5	5.6
2	1996	2.9	7.4	3.7	5.4
3	1997	2.3	7.3	4.5	4.9
4	1998	1.6	6.5	4.2	4.5
5	1999	2.2	7.0	4.4	4.2
6	2000	3.4	7.6	3.7	4.0
7	2001	2.8	7.1	0.8	4.7
8	2002	1.6	6.5	1.6	5.8
9	2003	2.3	5.7	2.7	6.0
10	2004	2.7	5.6	4.2	5.5
11	2005	3.4	5.2	3.5	5.1

1 **a** Draw a times-series graph of the inflation rate.

b In which year(s) (i) was inflation highest, (ii) was inflation lowest, (iii) did it increase, (iv) did it decrease, (v) did it increase most, and (vi) did it decrease most?

c What was the main trend in inflation?

2 **a** Draw a time-series graph of the interest rate.

b In which year(s) (i) was the interest rate highest, (ii) was the interest rate lowest, (iii) did it increase, (iv) did it decrease, (v) did it increase most, and (vi) did it decrease most?

c What was the main trend in the interest rate?

3 Draw a scatter diagram to show the relationship between the inflation rate and the interest rate. Describe the relationship.

4 Draw a scatter diagram to show the relationship between the growth rate and the unemployment rate. Describe the relationship.

5 Draw a graph to show the relationship between the two variables x and y:

x	0	1	2	3	4	5	6	7	8
y	0	1	4	9	16	25	36	49	64

a Is the relationship positive or negative?

b Does the slope of the relationship increase or decrease as the value of x increases?

c Think of some economic relationships that might be similar to this one.

6 Draw a graph that shows the relationship between the two variables x and y:

x	0	1	2	3	4	5
y	25	24	21	16	9	0

a Is the relationship positive or negative?

b Does the slope of the relationship increase or decrease as the value of x increases?

c Think of some economic relationships that might be similar to this one.

7 In problem 5, calculate the slope of the relationship between x and y when x equals 4.

8 In problem 6, calculate the slope of the relationship between x and y when x equals 3.

9 In problem 5, calculate the slope of the relationship across the arc when x increases from 3 to 4.

10 In problem 6, calculate the slope of the relationship across the arc when x increases from 3 to 4.

11 Calculate the slope of the relationship shown at point A in the following figure.

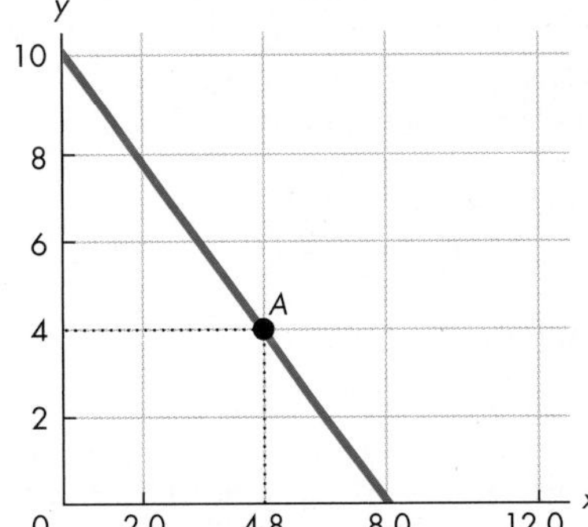

12 Calculate the slope of the relationship shown at point A in the following figure.

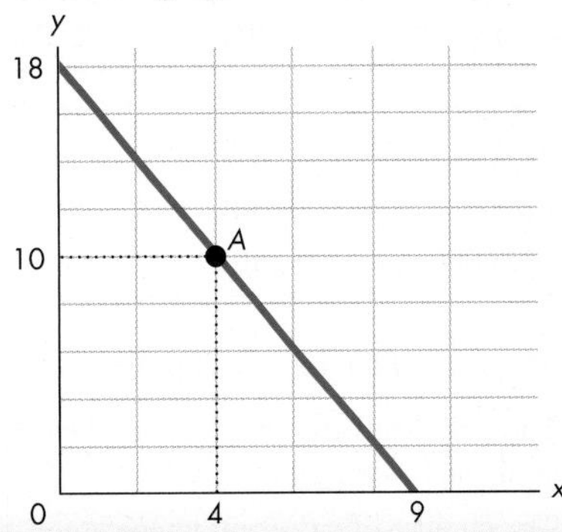

* Solutions to odd-numbered problems are provided.

13 Use the following figure to calculate the slope of the relationship.

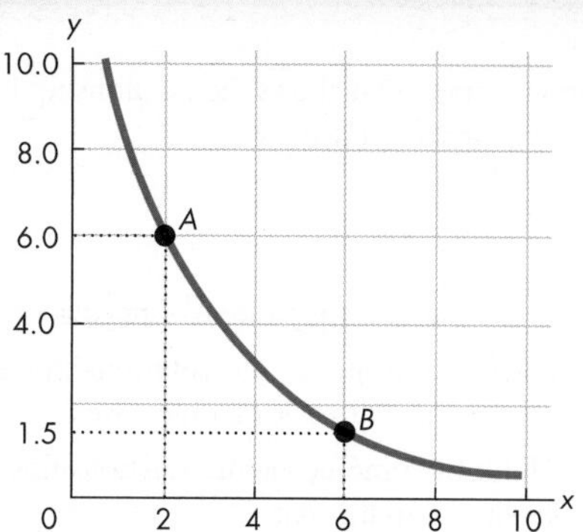

a At points *A* and *B*.

b Across the arc *AB*.

14 Use the following figure to calculate the slope of the relationship.

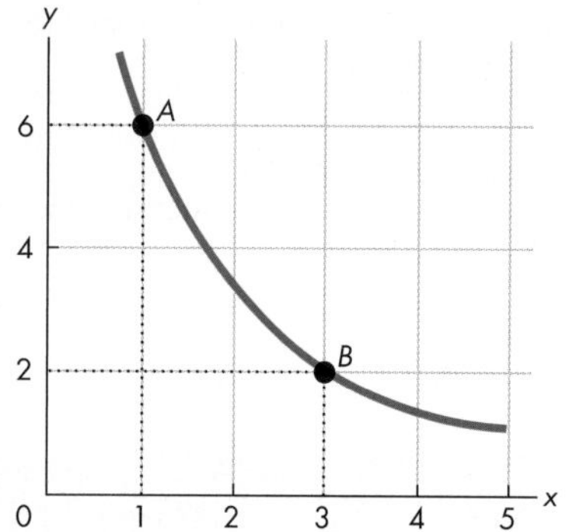

a At points *A* and *B*.

b Across the arc *AB*.

15 The table gives the price of a balloon ride, the temperature, and the number of rides a day.

Price (pounds per ride)	Balloon rides (number per day) 10°C	20°C	30°C
5.00	32	40	50
10.00	27	32	40
15.00	18	27	32
20.00	10	18	27

Draw graphs of the relationships between:

a The price and the number of rides, holding the temperature constant.

b The number of rides and temperature, holding the price constant.

c Temperature and price, holding the number of rides constant.

16 The table gives the price of an umbrella, the amount of rainfall, and the number of umbrellas purchased.

Price (pounds per umbrella)	Umbrellas (number per day) 0	2 (mm of rainfall)	12
5.00	7	8	12
10.00	4	7	8
15.00	2	4	7
20.00	1	2	4

Draw graphs of the relationships between:

a The price and the number of umbrellas purchased, holding the amount of rainfall constant.

b The number of umbrellas purchased and the amount of rainfall, holding the price constant.

c The amount of rainfall and the price, holding the number of umbrellas purchased constant.

Web Activities

Links to Websites

1 Find the Consumer Price Index (CPI) for the latest 12 months and make a graph of the CPI. During the most recent month:

a Did the CPI rise or fall?

b Was the rate of rise or fall increasing or decreasing?

2 Find the unemployment rate for the latest 12 months and make a graph of the unemployment rate. During the most recent month:

a Was it rising or falling?

b Was the rate of rise or fall increasing or decreasing?

3 Use the data that you obtained in questions 1 and 2. Make a graph to show whether the CPI and the unemployment rate are related to each other.

4 Use the data that you obtained in questions 1 and 2.

a Calculate the percentage change in the CPI each month.

b Make a graph to show whether the percentage change in the CPI and the unemployment rate are related to each other.

The Economic Problem

CHAPTER 2

After studying this chapter you will be able to:

- Define the production possibilities frontier and calculate opportunity cost
- Distinguish between production possibilities and preferences and describe an efficient allocation of resources
- Explain how current production choices expand future production possibilities
- Explain how specialization and trade expand our production possibilities
- Describe the economic institutions that coordinate decisions

Good, Better, Best!

What places limits on our ability to produce the goods and services we want? What must we do to use our limited resources efficiently? How can we expand our capacity to produce? How do we benefit by trading with others? Does everyone gain in a market exchange, or does only the seller gain? Why have social institutions such as firms, markets and private property rights evolved? Find the answers in this chapter. Also find out about the costs and benefits of your university education in *Reading Between the Lines* at the end of the chapter.

Production Possibilities and Opportunity Cost

Every working day, in mines and factories, shops and offices, on farms and construction sites, 200 million European workers produce a vast variety of goods and services valued at €50 billion. But the quantities of goods and services that we can produce are limited by both our available resources and technology. And if we want to increase our production of one good, we must decrease our production of something else – we face trade-offs.

You are going to learn about the production possibilities frontier, which describes the limit to what we can produce and provides a neat way of thinking about and illustrating the idea of a trade-off.

The **production possibilities frontier** (*PPF*) is the boundary between those combinations of goods and services that can be produced and those that cannot. To illustrate the *PPF*, we focus on two goods at a time and hold the quantities produced of all the other goods and services constant. That is, we look at a *model* economy in which everything remains the same (*ceteris paribus*) except for the production of the two goods we are considering.

Let's look at the production possibilities frontier for CDs and pizza, which stand for *any* pair of goods or services.

Production Possibilities Frontier

The *production possibilities frontier* for CDs and pizza shows the limits to the production of these two goods, given the total resources available to produce them. Figure 2.1 shows this production possibilities frontier. The table lists some combinations of the quantities of pizzas and CDs that can be produced in a month given the resources available. The figure graphs these combinations. The x-axis shows the quantity of pizzas produced and the y-axis shows the quantity of CDs produced.

The *PPF* illustrates *scarcity* because we cannot attain the points outside the frontier. They are points that describe wants that can't be satisfied. We can produce at all the points *inside* the *PPF* and *on* the *PPF*. These points are attainable. Suppose that in a typical month, we produce 4 million pizzas and 5 million CDs. Figure 2.1 shows this combination as point *E* and as possibility *E* in the table. The figure also shows other production possibilities.

Figure 2.1

The Production Possibilities Frontier

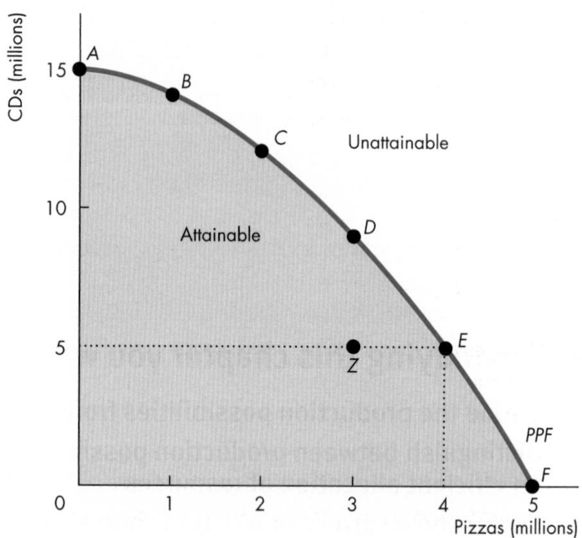

Possibility	Pizzas (millions)		CDs (millions)
A	0	and	15
B	1	and	14
C	2	and	12
D	3	and	9
E	4	and	5
F	5	and	0

The table lists six points on the production possibilities frontier for CDs and pizza. Row *A* tells us that if we produce no pizza, the maximum quantity of CDs we can produce is 15 million. Points *A, B, C, D, E* and *F* in the figure represent the rows of the table. The line passing through these points is the production possibilities frontier (*PPF*).

The *PPF* separates the attainable from the unattainable. Production is possible at any point *inside* the orange area or *on* the frontier. Points outside the frontier are unattainable. Points inside the frontier such as point *Z* are inefficient because resources are either wasted or misallocated. At such points, it is possible to use the available resources to produce more of either or both goods.

For example, we might stop producing pizza and move all the people who produce it into producing CDs. Point *A* in Figure 2.1 and possibility *A* in the table show this case. The quantity of CDs produced increases to 15 million, and pizza production dries up. Alternatively, we might close the CD factories and switch all the resources into producing pizza. In this situation, we produce 5 million pizzas. Point *F* in the figure and possibility *F* in the table show this case.

Production Efficiency

We achieve **production efficiency** if we cannot produce more of one good without producing less of some other good. When production is efficient, we are at a point *on* the *PPF*. If we are at a point *inside* the *PPF*, such as point Z, production is *inefficient* because we have some *unused* resources or we have some *misallocated* resources or both.

Resources are unused when they are idle but could be working. For example, we might leave some of the factories idle or some workers unemployed.

Resources are *misallocated* when they are assigned to tasks for which they are not the best match. For example, we might assign skilled pizza makers to work in a CD factory and skilled CD makers to work in a pizza shop. We could get more pizza *and* more CDs from these same workers if we reassigned them to the tasks that more closely match their skills.

If we produce at a point inside the *PPF* such as Z in Figure 2.1, we can use our resources more efficiently to produce more pizzas, more CDs, or more of *both* pizzas and CDs. But if we produce at a point *on* the *PPF*, we are using our resources efficiently and we can produce more of one good only if we produce less of the other. That is, along the *PPF*, we face a *trade-off*.

Trade-off Along the *PPF*

Every choice *along* the *PPF* involves a *trade-off* – we must give up something to get something else. On the *PPF* in Figure 2.1, we must give up some CDs to get more pizza or give up some pizza to get more CDs.

Trade-offs arise in every imaginable real-world situation, and you reviewed several of them in Chapter 1. At any given point in time, we have a fixed amount of labour, land, capital and entrepreneurship. By using our available technologies, we can employ these resources to produce goods and services. But we are limited in what we can produce. This limit defines a boundary between what we can attain and what we cannot attain. This boundary is the real world's production possibilities frontier, and it defines the trade-offs that we must make. On our real-world *PPF*, we can produce more of any one good or service only if we produce less of some other goods or services.

When doctors say that we must spend more on AIDS and cancer research, they are suggesting a trade-off: more medical research for less of some other things. When a politician says that she wants to spend more on education and healthcare, she is suggesting a trade-off: more education and healthcare for less defence expenditure or less private spending (because of higher taxes). When an environmental group argues for less logging in tropical rainforests, it is suggesting a trade-off: greater conservation of endangered wildlife for less hardwood. When your parents say that you should study more, they are suggesting a trade-off: more study time for less leisure or sleep.

All trade-offs involve a cost – an opportunity cost.

Opportunity Cost

The *opportunity cost* of an action is the highest-valued alternative forgone. The *PPF* helps us to make the concept of opportunity cost precise and enables us to calculate it. Along the *PPF*, there are only two goods, so there is only one alternative forgone: some quantity of the other good. Given our current resources and technology, we can produce more pizzas only if we produce fewer CDs. The opportunity cost of producing an additional pizza is the number of CDs we *must* forgo. Similarly, the opportunity cost of producing an additional CD is the quantity of pizzas we *must* forgo.

For example, at point *C* in Figure 2.1, we produce fewer pizzas and more CDs than at point *D*. If we choose point *D* over point *C*, the additional 1 million pizzas *cost* 3 million CDs. One pizza costs 3 CDs.

We can also work out the opportunity cost of choosing point *C* over point *D* in Figure 2.1. If we move from point *D* to point *C*, the quantity of CDs produced increases by 3 million and the quantity of pizzas produced decreases by 1 million. So if we choose point *C* over point *D*, the additional 3 million CDs *cost* 1 million pizzas. So 1 CD costs 1/3 of a pizza.

Opportunity Cost Is a Ratio

Opportunity cost is a ratio. It is the decrease in the quantity produced of one good divided by the increase in the quantity produced of another good as we move along the production possibilities frontier.

Because opportunity cost is a ratio, the opportunity cost of producing an additional CD is equal to the *inverse* of the opportunity cost of producing an additional pizza. Check this proposition by returning to the calculations we've just worked through. When we move along the *PPF* from *C* to *D*, the opportunity cost of a pizza is 3 CDs. The inverse of 3 is 1/3, so if we decrease the production of pizzas and increase the production of CDs by moving from *D* to *C*, the opportunity cost of a CD must be 1/3 of a pizza. You can check that this number is correct. If we move from *D* to *C*, we produce 3 million more CDs and 1 million fewer pizzas. Because 3 million CDs cost 1 million pizzas, the opportunity cost of 1 CD is 1/3 of a pizza.

Increasing Opportunity Cost

The opportunity cost of a pizza increases as the quantity of pizzas produced increases. Also, the opportunity cost of a CD increases as the quantity of CDs produced increases. This phenomenon of increasing opportunity cost is reflected in the shape of the *PPF* – it is bowed outward.

When a large quantity of CDs and a small quantity of pizzas are produced – between points *A* and *B* in Figure 2.1 – the frontier has a gentle slope. A given increase in the quantity of pizzas *costs* a small decrease in the quantity of CDs, so the opportunity cost of a pizza is a small quantity of CDs.

When a large quantity of pizzas and a small quantity of CDs are produced – between points *E* and *F* in Figure 2.1 – the frontier is steep. A given increase in the quantity of pizzas *costs* a large decrease in the quantity of CDs, so the opportunity cost of a pizza is a large quantity of CDs.

The *PPF* is bowed outward because resources are not all equally productive in all activities. People with several years of experience working for Philips are good at producing CDs but not very good at making pizzas. So if we move some of these people from Philips to Domino's, we get a small increase in the quantity of pizzas but a large decrease in the quantity of CDs. Similarly, people who have spent years working at Domino's are good at producing pizzas, but they have no idea how to produce CDs. So if we move some of these people from Domino's to Philips, we get a small increase in the quantity of CDs but a large decrease in the quantity of pizzas. The more of either good we try to produce, the less productive are the additional resources we use to produce that good and the larger is the opportunity cost of a unit of that good.

Increasing Opportunity Costs Are Everywhere

Just about every activity that you can think of is one with an increasing opportunity cost. We allocate the most skilful farmers and the most fertile land to the production of food. And we allocate the best doctors and the least fertile land to the production of healthcare services. If we shift fertile land and tractors away from farming to hospitals and ambulances and ask farmers to become hospital porters, the production of food drops drastically and the increase in the production of healthcare services is small. The opportunity cost of a unit of healthcare services rises. Similarly, if we shift our resources away from healthcare towards farming, we must use more doctors and nurses as farmers and more hospitals as hydroponic tomato factories. The decrease in the production of healthcare services is large, but the increase in food production is small. The opportunity cost of a unit of food rises. This example is extreme and unlikely, but these same considerations apply to most pairs of goods.

There may be some rare situations in which opportunity cost is constant. Switching resources from bottling ketchup to bottling mayonnaise is a possible example. But in general, when resources are reallocated, they must be assigned to tasks for which they are an increasingly poor match. Increasing opportunity costs are a general fact of life.

Review Quiz

Study Plan 2.1

1 How does the production possibilities frontier illustrate scarcity?
2 How does the production possibilities frontier illustrate production efficiency?
3 How does the production possibilities frontier show that every choice involves a trade-off?
4 How does the production possibilities frontier illustrate opportunity cost?
5 Why is opportunity cost a ratio?
6 Why does the *PPF* for most goods bow outward, so that opportunity cost of a good increases as the quantity produced increases?

We've seen that what we can produce is limited by the production possibilities frontier. We've also seen that production on the *PPF* is efficient. But we can produce many different quantities on the *PPF*. How do we choose among them? How do we know which point on the *PPF* is the best one?

Using Resources Efficiently

You've seen that we can achieve production efficiency at every point *on* the *PPF*. But which point is best? What quantities of CDs and pizzas best serve the social interest?

This question is an example of real-world questions of enormous consequence such as: how much should we spend on treating AIDS and how much on cancer research? Should we expand education and healthcare programmes or cut taxes? Should we spend more on the preservation of rainforests and the conservation of endangered wildlife?

To answer these questions, we must find a way of measuring and comparing costs and benefits.

The *PPF* and Marginal Cost

Marginal cost is the opportunity cost of producing *one more unit*. We can calculate marginal cost from the slope of the *PPF*. As the quantity of pizzas produced increases, the *PPF* gets steeper and marginal cost of a pizza increases. Figure 2.2 illustrates the calculation of the marginal cost of a pizza.

Begin by finding the opportunity cost of pizza in blocks of 1 million pizzas. The first million pizzas cost 1 million CDs, the second million pizzas cost 2 million CDs, the third million pizzas cost 3 million CDs, and so on. The bars in part (a) illustrate these calculations.

The bars in part (b) show the cost of an average pizza in each of the 1 million pizza blocks. Focus on the third million pizzas – the move from *C* to *D* in part (a). Over this range, because the 1 million pizzas cost 3 million CDs, one of these pizzas, on the average, costs 3 CDs – the height of the bar in part (b).

Next, find the opportunity cost of each additional pizza – the marginal cost of a pizza. The marginal cost of a pizza increases as the quantity of pizzas produced increases. The marginal cost at point *C* is less than it is at point *D*. On the average over the range from *C* to *D*, the marginal cost of a pizza is 3 CDs. But it exactly equals 3 CDs only in the middle of the range between *C* and *D*.

The red dot in part (b) indicates that the marginal cost of a pizza is 3 CDs when 2.5 million pizzas are produced. Each black dot in part (b) is interpreted in the same way. The red curve that passes through these dots, labelled *MC*, is the marginal cost curve. It shows the marginal cost of a pizza at each quantity of pizza as we move along the *PPF*.

Figure 2.2 myeconlab

The *PPF* and Marginal Cost

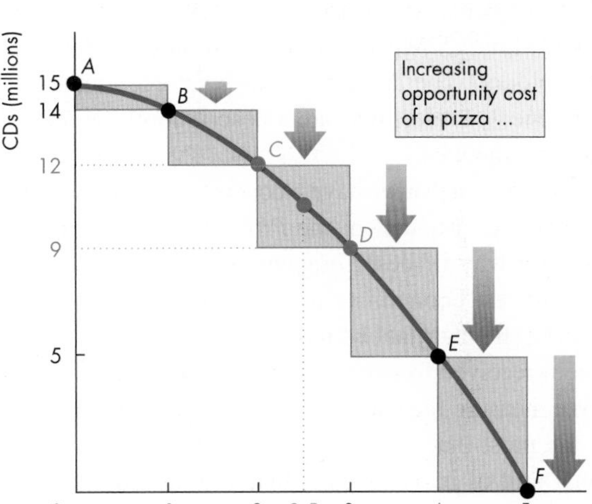

(a) *PPF* and opportunity cost

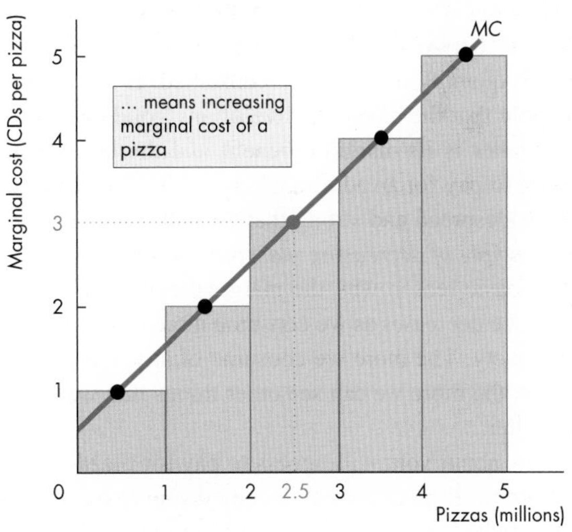

(b) Marginal cost

Marginal cost is calculated from the slope of the *PPF* in part (a). As the quantity of pizzas produced increases, the *PPF* gets steeper and the marginal cost of a pizza increases. The bars in part (a) show the opportunity cost of pizza in blocks of 1 million pizzas. The bars in part (b) show the cost of an average pizza in each of these 1 million blocks. The red curve, *MC*, shows the marginal cost of a pizza at each point along the *PPF*. This curve passes through the centre of each of the bars in part (b).

Preferences and Marginal Benefit

Look around your classroom and notice the wide variety of shirts, caps, trousers and shoes that you and your fellow students are wearing today. Why is there such a huge variety? Why don't you all wear the same styles and colours? The answer lies in what economists call preferences. **Preferences** are a description of a person's likes and dislikes.

You've seen that we have a concrete way of describing the limits to production: the *PPF*. We need a similarly concrete way of describing preferences. To describe preferences, economists use the concept of marginal benefit. The **marginal benefit** of a good or service is the benefit received from consuming one more unit of it.

We measure the marginal benefit of a good or service by the most that people are *willing to pay* for an additional unit of it. The idea is that you are not willing to pay more for a good than it is worth to you. But you are willing to pay an amount up to what it is worth. So the willingness to pay for something measures its marginal benefit.

Economists use the marginal benefit curve to illustrate preferences. The **marginal benefit curve** shows the relationship between the marginal benefit of a good and the quantity of that good consumed. It is a general principle that the more we have of any good or service, the smaller is its marginal benefit and the less we are willing to pay for an additional unit of it. This tendency is so widespread and strong that we call it a principle – the *principle of decreasing marginal benefit.*

The basic reason why the marginal benefit of a good or service decreases as we consume more of it is that we like variety. The more we consume of any one good or service, the more we can see other things that we would like better.

Think about your willingness to pay for pizza (or any other item). If pizza is hard to come by and you can buy only a few slices a year, you might be willing to pay a high price to get an additional slice. But if pizza is all you've eaten for the past few days, you are willing to pay almost nothing for another slice.

In everyday life, we think of what we pay for goods and services as the money that we give up – pounds or euros. But you've learned to think about cost as other goods or services forgone, not a money cost. So you can think about willingness to pay in the same terms. The price you are willing to pay for something is the quantity of other goods and services that you are willing to forgo. Let's continue with the example of CDs and pizzas and illustrate preferences this way.

Figure 2.3 myeconlab

Preferences and the Marginal Benefit Curve

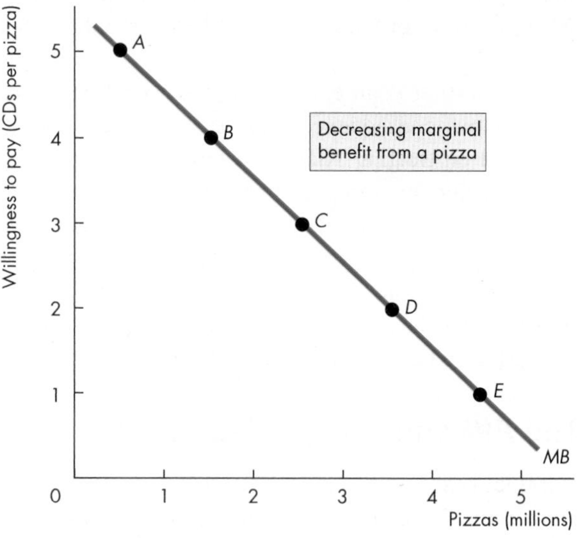

Possibility	Pizzas (millions)	Willingness to pay (CDs per pizza)
A	0.5	5
B	1.5	4
C	2.5	3
D	3.5	2
E	4.5	1

The smaller the quantity of pizzas produced, the more CDs people are willing to give up for an additional pizza. If pizza production is 0.5 million, people are willing to pay 5 CDs per pizza. But if pizza production is 4.5 million, people are willing to pay only 1 CD per pizza. Willingness to pay measures marginal benefit. And decreasing marginal benefit is a universal feature of people's preferences.

Figure 2.3 illustrates preferences as the willingness to pay for pizza in terms of CDs. In row *A*, pizza production is 0.5 million, and at that quantity, people are willing to pay 5 CDs per pizza. As the quantity of pizzas produced increases, the amount that people are willing to pay for a pizza falls. When pizza production is 4.5 million, people are willing to pay only 1 CD per pizza.

Let's now use the concepts of marginal cost and marginal benefit to describe the efficient quantity of pizzas to produce.

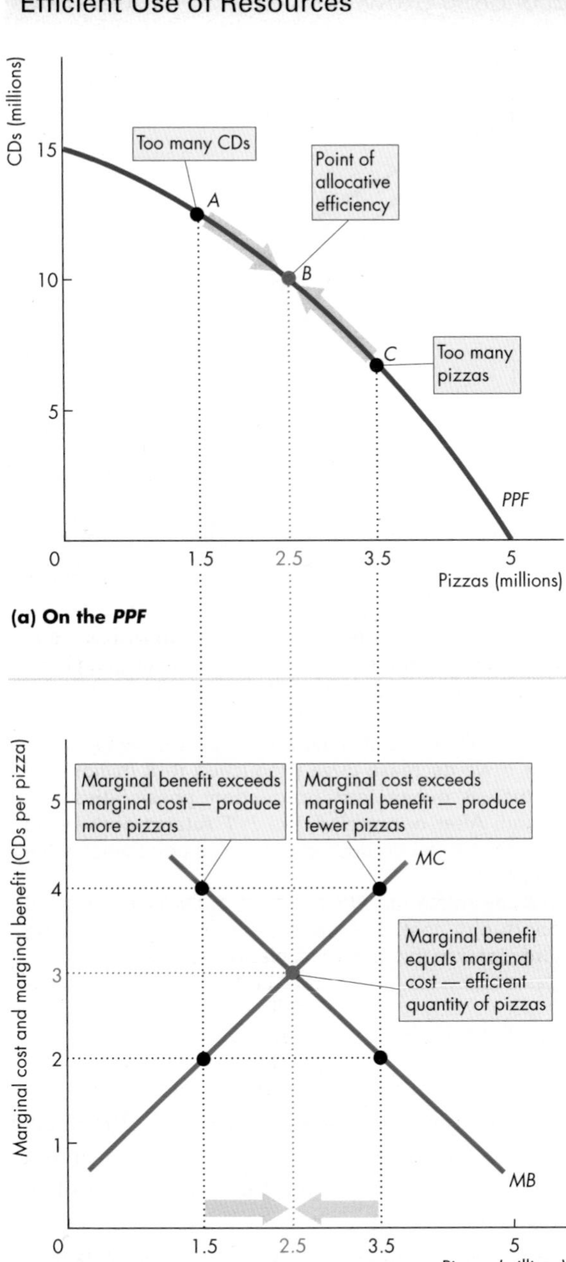

The greater the quantity of pizzas produced, the smaller is the marginal benefit (*MB*) from pizza – the fewer CDs people are willing to give up to get an additional pizza. But the greater the quantity of pizzas produced, the greater is the marginal cost (*MC*) of pizza – the more CDs people must give up to get an additional pizza. When marginal benefit equals marginal cost, resources are being used efficiently.

Efficient Use of Resources

When we cannot produce more of any one good without giving up some other good, we have achieved *production efficiency*, and we're producing at a point on the *PPF*. When we cannot produce more of any good without giving up some other good that we *value more highly*, we have achieved **allocative efficiency** and we are producing at the point on the *PPF* that we prefer above all other points.

Suppose in Figure 2.4, we produce 1.5 million pizzas. The marginal cost of a pizza is 2 CDs and the marginal benefit from a pizza is 4 CDs. Because someone values an additional pizza more highly than it costs to produce, we can get more value from our resources by moving some of them out of producing CDs and into producing pizzas.

Now suppose we produce 3.5 million pizzas. The marginal cost of a pizza is now 4 CDs, but the marginal benefit from a pizza is only 2 CDs. Because the additional pizza costs more to produce than anyone thinks it is worth, we can get more value from our resources by moving some of them away from producing pizzas and into producing CDs.

But suppose we produce 2.5 million pizzas. Marginal cost and marginal benefit are now equal at 3 CDs. This allocation of resources between pizzas and CDs is efficient. If more pizzas are produced, the forgone CDs are worth more than the additional pizzas. If fewer pizzas are produced, the forgone pizzas are worth more than the additional CDs.

Review Quiz

Study Plan 2.2

1 What is marginal cost? How is it measured?
2 How does the marginal cost of producing a good change as the quantity produced of that good increases?
3 What is marginal benefit? How is it measured?
4 How does the marginal benefit from a good change as the quantity of that good increases?
5 What is allocative efficiency and how does it relate to the production possibilites frontier?
6 What conditions must be satisfied if resources are used efficiently.

You now understand the limits to production and the conditions under which resources are used efficiently. Your next task is to study the expansion of production possibilities.

Economic Growth

In 2005, production per person in the four major European economies (France, Germany, Italy and the United Kingdom) was twice its 1970 level. In Hong Kong it was more than four times its 1970 level (see Box 2.1), and in the rest of China, it was almost seven times its 1970 level.

An expansion of production is called **economic growth**. Economic growth increases our *standard of living*. But it does not overcome scarcity. Nor does it avoid opportunity cost. To make our economy grow, we face a trade-off – we must forgo consuming everything that we produce and devote some resources to creating growth.

The Cost of Economic Growth

Economic growth comes from technological change and capital accumulation. **Technological change** is the development of new goods and of better ways of producing goods and services. **Capital accumulation** is the growth of capital resources, which includes *human capital*.

Because of technological change and capital accumulation, we have an enormous quantity of cars that enable us to produce more transportation than was available when we had only horses and carriages; we have satellites that make global communications possible on a scale that is much larger than that produced by the earlier cable technology. But if we use our resources to develop new technologies and to produce new capital, we must decrease our production of consumption goods and services. New technologies and new capital have an opportunity cost. Let's look at this opportunity cost.

Instead of studying the *PPF* of pizzas and CDs, we'll hold the quantity of CDs produced constant and examine the *PPF* for pizzas and pizza ovens. Figure 2.5 shows this *PPF* as the blue curve *ABC*. If we devote no resources to producing pizza ovens, we produce at point *A*. If we produce 3 million pizzas, we can produce 6 pizza ovens at point *B*. If we produce no pizza, we can produce 10 ovens at point *C*.

The amount by which our production possibilities expand depends on the resources we devote to technological change and capital accumulation. If we devote no resources to this activity (point *A*), our *PPF* remains at *ABC* – the blue curve in Figure 2.5. If we cut the current production of pizza and produce 6 ovens (point *B*), then in the future, we'll have more capital and our *PPF* will rotate outward to the position shown by the red curve. The fewer resources we devote to producing pizza and the more resources we devote to producing ovens, the greater is the future expansion of our production possibilities.

Economic growth is not free. To make it happen, we devote resources to producing new ovens and less to producing pizza. In Figure 2.5, we move from *A* to *B*. There is no free lunch. The opportunity cost of more pizzas in the future is fewer pizzas today. Also, economic growth is no magic formula for abolishing scarcity. On the new production possibilities frontier, we continue to face a trade-off and opportunity cost.

The ideas about economic growth that we have explored in the setting of the pizza industry also apply to nations as you can see in Box 2.1.

Figure 2.5 myeconlab

Economic Growth

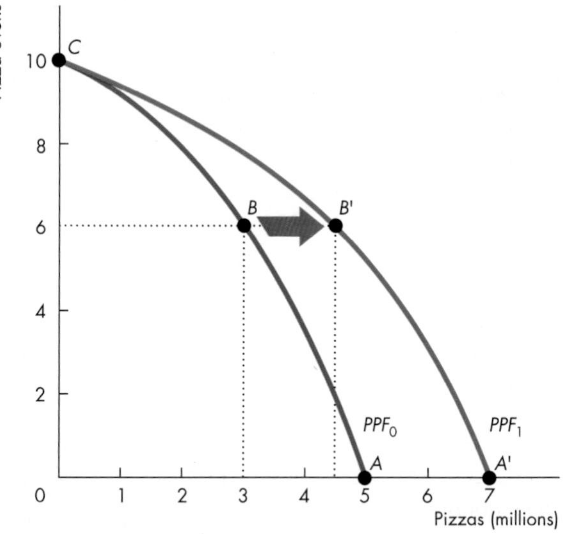

PPF_0 shows the limits to the production of pizza and pizza ovens, with the production of all other goods and services remaining the same. If we allocate no resources to producing pizza ovens and produce 5 million pizzas, our production possibilities will remain the same, PPF_0.

But if we decrease pizza production to 3 million and produce 6 ovens, our production possibilities will expand. After one period, the *PPF* rotates outward to PPF_1 and we can produce at point *B'*, a point outside the original PPF_0.

We can rotate the *PPF* outward, but we cannot avoid opportunity cost. The opportunity cost of producing more pizzas in the future is fewer pizzas today.

Box 2.1
Economic Growth in the European Union and Hong Kong

If a country devotes all its resources to producing consumption goods and none to research and capital accumulation, its production possibilities in the future will be the same as they are today. To expand our production possibilities in the future, we must devote fewer resources to producing consumption goods today and some resources to accumulating capital and developing technologies so that we can produce more consumption goods in the future. The decrease in today's consumption is the opportunity cost of an increase in future consumption.

The experiences of the European Union and some East Asian economies such as Hong Kong make a striking example of the effects of our choices on the rate of economic growth. In 1970, the production possibilities per person in the European Union were more than double those in Hong Kong.

On average since 1970, the European Union has devoted one-fifth of it resources to accumulating capital and the other four-fifths to consumption. In 1970, the European Union was at point *A* on its *PPF* in Figure 1. Hong Kong has devoted one-third of its resources to accumulating capital and two-thirds to consumption. In 1970, Hong Kong was at point *A* on its *PPF*.

Both economies experienced economic growth, but Hong Kong has grown more rapidly than the European Union. Because Hong Kong devoted a bigger fraction of its resources to accumulating capital, its production possibilities expanded more quickly.

By 2006, the production possibilities per person in Hong Kong had reached a similar level to those in the European Union. If Hong Kong continues to devote more resources to accumulating capital than the European Union does (at point *B* on its 2006 *PPF*), Hong Kong will continue to grow more rapidly. But if Hong Kong increases consumption and decreases capital accumulation (moving to point *C* on its 2006 *PPF*), then its economic growth rate will slow.

Figure 1

Economic Growth in the European Union and Hong Kong

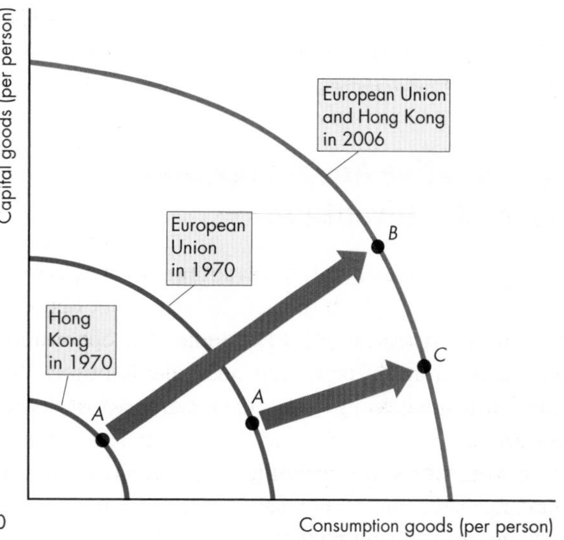

The European Union is typical of the rich industrial countries, which include the United States, Canada and Japan. Hong Kong is typical of the fast-growing Asian economies, which include Taiwan, Thailand, South Korea and China. Growth in these countries slowed during a financial crisis of 1998 but quickly rebounded. Production possibilities expand in these countries by between 5 and almost 10 per cent a year. If such high growth rates are maintained, these other Asian countries will eventually close the gap between themselves and the European Union, as Hong Kong has done.

Review Quiz

Study Plan 2.3

1. What are the two key factors that generate economic growth?
2. How does economic growth influence the *PPF*?
3. What is the opportunity cost of economic growth?
4. Why has Hong Kong experienced faster economic growth than the European Union has?

We have seen that we can increase our production possibilities by accumulating capital and developing new technology. Next, we'll study another way in which we can expand our production possibilities – the amazing fact that *both* buyers and sellers gain from specialization and trade.

Gains from Trade

People can produce for themselves all the goods that that they consume, or they can concentrate on producing one good (or perhaps a few goods) and then trade with others – exchange some of their own goods for those of others. Concentrating on the production of only one good or a few goods is called *specialization*.

We are going to discover how people gain by specializing in the production of the good in which they have a *comparative advantage* and trading with each other.

Comparative Advantage and Absolute Advantage

A person has a **comparative advantage** in an activity if that person can perform the activity at a lower opportunity cost than anyone else. Differences in opportunity costs arise from differences in individual abilities and from differences in the characteristics of other resources.

No one excels at everything. One person is an outstanding batter but a poor catcher; another person is a brilliant lawyer but a poor teacher. In almost all human endeavours, what one person does easily, someone else finds difficult. The same applies to land and capital. One plot of land is fertile but has no mineral deposits; another plot of land has outstanding views but is infertile. One machine has great precision but is difficult to operate; another is fast but often breaks down.

Although no one excels at everything, some people excel and can outperform others in many activities – perhaps all activities. A person who is more productive than others has an **absolute advantage**.

Absolute advantage involves comparing productivities – production per hour – whereas comparative advantage involves comparing opportunity cost.

Notice that a person who has an absolute advantage does not have a *comparative* advantage in every activity. Maria Sharapova can run faster and play tennis better than most people. She has an absolute advantage in these two activities. But compared with other people, she is a better tennis player than runner, so her *comparative* advantage is in playing tennis.

Because people's abilities and the quality of their resources differ, they have different opportunity costs of producing various goods and services. Such differences give rise to comparative advantage.

To explore the idea of comparative advantage, and its astonishing implications, we'll look at the production process in two smoothie bars: one operated by Erin and the other operated by Jack.

Erin's Smoothie Bar

Erin produces smoothies and salads. In Erin's high-tech bar, she can turn out either a smoothie or a salad every 90 seconds – see Table 2.1. If Erin spends all her time making smoothies, she can produce 40 an hour. And if she spends all her time making salads, she can also produce 40 an hour. If she splits her time equally between the two, she can produce 20 smoothies and 20 salads an hour.

For each additional smoothie Erin produces, she must decrease her production of salads by one, and for each additional salad she produces, she must decrease her production of smoothies by one. So

> **Erin's opportunity cost of producing 1 smoothie is 1 salad,**

and

> **Erin's opportunity cost of producing 1 salad is 1 smoothie.**

Erin's customers buy smoothies and salads in equal quantities, so she splits her time equally between the two items and produces 20 smoothies and 20 salads an hour.

Jack's Smoothie Bar

Jack also produces both smoothies and salads. But Jack's bar is smaller than Erin's. Also, Jack has only one blender, and it's a slow old machine. Even if Jack uses all his resources to produce smoothies, he can produce only 6 an hour – see Table 2.2. But Jack is good in the salad department, so if he uses all his resources to make salads, he can produce 30 an hour.

Jack's ability to make smoothies and salads is the same regardless of how he splits an hour between the

Table 2.1

Erin's Production Possibilities

Item	Minutes to produce 1	Quantity per hour
Smoothies	1.5	40
Salads	1.5	40

Table 2.2

Jack's Production Possibilities

Item	Minutes to produce 1	Quantity per hour
Smoothies	10	6
Salads	2	30

two tasks. He can make a salad in 2 minutes or a smoothie in 10 minutes. For each additional smoothie Jack produces, he must decrease his production of salads by 5. And for each additional salad he produces, he must decrease his production of smoothies by 1/5 of a smoothie. So

Jack's opportunity cost of producing 1 smoothie is 3 salads,

and

Jack's opportunity cost of producing 1 salad is 1/5 of a smoothie.

Jack's customers, like Erin's, buy smoothies and salads in equal quantities. So Jack spends 50 minutes of each hour making smoothies and 10 minutes of each hour making salads. With this division of his time, Jack produces 5 smoothies and 5 salads an hour.

Erin's Absolute Advantage

You can see from the numbers that describe the two smoothie bars that Erin is four times as productive as Jack – her 20 smoothies and salads an hour are four times Jack's 5. Erin has an absolute advantage – she is more productive than Jack in producing both smoothies and salads. But Erin has a comparative advantage in only one of the activities.

Erin's Comparative Advantage

In which of the two activities does Erin have a comparative advantage? Recall that comparative advantage is a situation in which one person's opportunity cost of producing a good is lower than another person's opportunity cost of producing that same good. Erin has a comparative advantage in producing smoothies. Her opportunity cost of a smoothie is 1 salad, whereas Jack's opportunity cost of a smoothie is 5 salads.

Jack's Comparative Advantage

If Erin has a comparative advantage in producing smoothies, Jack must have a comparative advantage in producing salads. His opportunity cost of a salad is 1/5 of a smoothie, whereas Erin's opportunity cost of a salad is 1 smoothie.

Achieving the Gains from Trade

Erin and Jack run into each other one evening in a singles bar. After a few minutes of getting acquainted, Erin tells Jack about her amazingly profitable smoothie business that is selling 20 smoothies and 20 salads an hour. Her only problem, she tells Jack, is that she wishes she could produce more because potential customers leave when the queue gets too long.

Jack isn't sure whether to risk spoiling his chances by telling Erin about his own struggling business. But he takes the risk. When he explains to Erin that he spends 50 minutes of every hour making 5 smoothies and 10 minutes making 5 salads, Erin's eyes pop. "Have I got a deal for you!" she exclaims.

Here's the deal that Erin sketches on a serviette. Jack stops making smoothies and allocates all his time to producing salads. And Erin increases her production of smoothies to 35 an hour and cuts her production of salads to 5 an hour – see Table 2.3(a).

Table 2.3

Erin and Jack Gain from Trade

	Erin	Jack
(a) Production		
Smoothies	35	0
Salads	5	30
(b) Trade		
Smoothies	sell 10	buy 10
Salads	buy 20	sell 20
(c) After trade		
Smoothies	25	10
Salads	25	10
(d) Gains from trade		
Smoothies	+5	+5
Salads	+5	+5

They then trade. Erin sells Jack 10 smoothies and Jack sells Erin 20 salads – the price of a smoothie is 2 salads – see Table 2.3(b).

After the trade, Jack has 10 salads – the 30 he produces minus the 20 he sells to Erin. And he has the 10 smoothies that he buys from Erin. So Jack doubles the quantities of smoothies and salads he can sell – see Table 2.3(c).

Erin has 25 smoothies – the 35 she produces minus the 10 she sells to Jack. And she has 25 salads – the 5 she produces plus the 20 she buys from Jack – see Table 2.3(c). Both Erin and Jack gain 5 smoothies and 5 salads – see Table 2.3(d).

Erin draws a graph (Figure 2.6) to illustrate her suggestion. The blue *PPF* in part (a) shows Jack's production possibilities. He is producing 5 smoothies and 5 salads an hour at point *A*. The blue *PPF* in part (b) shows Erin's production possibilities. She is producing 20 smoothies and 20 salads an hour at point *A*.

Erin's proposal is that they each produce more of the good in which they have a comparative advantage. Jack produces 30 salads and no smoothies at point *B* on his *PPF*. Erin produces 35 smoothies and 5 salads at point *B* on her *PPF*.

Erin and Jack then trade – exchange – smoothies and salads at a price of 2 salads per smoothie or 1/2 of a smoothie per salad. Jack buys smoothies from Erin for 2 salads each, which is less than the 5 salads it costs him to produce them. And Erin buys salads from Jack for 1/2 a smoothie each, which is less than the 1 smoothie that it costs her to produce them.

With trade, Jack has 10 smoothies and 10 salads at point *C* – a gain of 5 smoothies and 5 salads. Jack moves to a point *outside* his *PPF*.

With trade, Erin has 25 smoothies and 25 salads at point *C* – a gain of 5 smoothies and 5 salads. Erin moves to a point *outside* her *PPF*.

Figure 2.6

The Gains from Trade

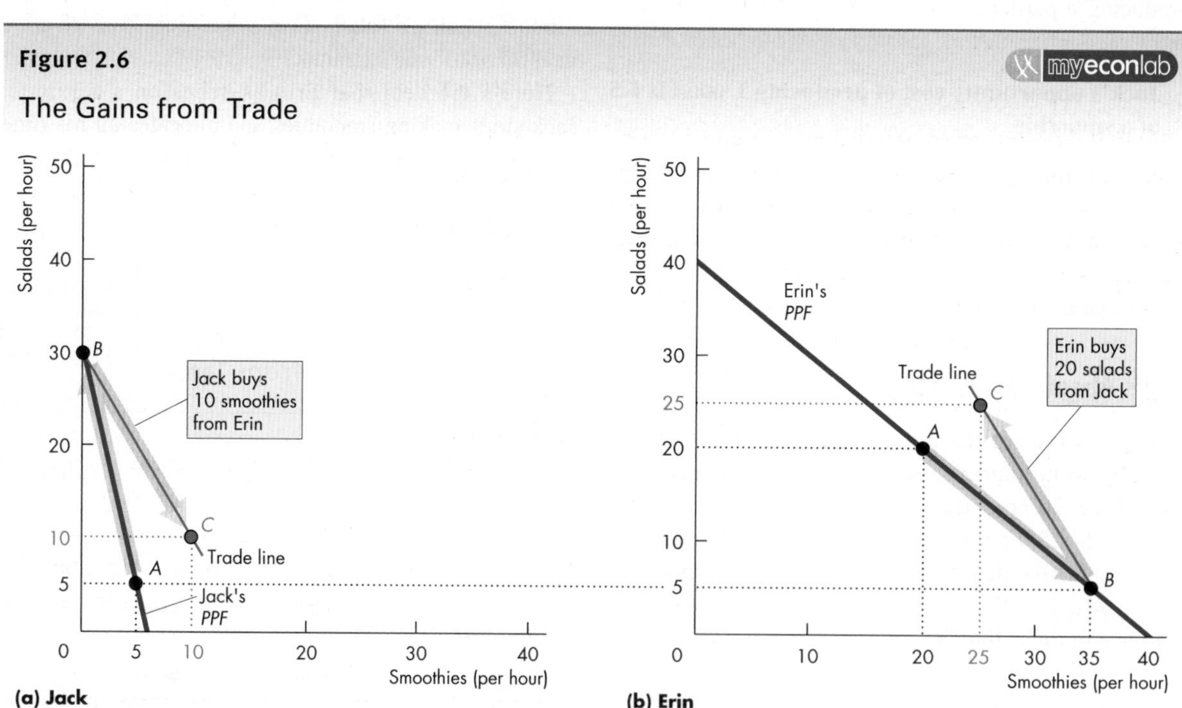

Jack initially produces at point *A* on his *PPF* in part (a), and Erin initially produces at point *A* on her *PPF* in part (b). Jack's opportunity cost of producing a salad is less than Erin's, so Jack has a comparative advantage in producing salads. Erin's opportunity cost of producing a smoothie is less than Jack's, so Erin has a comparative advantage in producing smoothies.

If Jack specializes in salad, he produces 30 salads and no smoothies at point *B* on his *PPF*. If Erin produces 35 smoothies and 5 salads, she produces at point *B* on her *PPF*.

They exchange salads for smoothies along the red "Trade line". Erin buys salads from Jack for less than her opportunity cost of producing them. And Jack buys smoothies from Erin for less than his opportunity cost of producing them. Each goes to point *C* – a point outside his or her *PPF*. Both Jack and Erin increase production by 5 smoothies and 5 salads with no change in resources.

Despite Erin's absolute advantage in producing smoothies and salads, both Erin and Jack gain from producing more of the good in which they have a comparative advantage and trading.

The gains that we achieve from international trade are similar to those achieved by Jack and Erin. When Europeans buy T-shirts from China and China buys Airbus aircraft from the European Union, both countries gain. China has a comparative advantage in producing T-shirts and the European Union has a comparative advantage in producing aircraft. Europe get its shirts at a lower cost than that at which it can produce them, and China gets its aircraft at a lower cost than that at which it can produce them.

Dynamic Comparative Advantage

At any given point in time, the resources and technologies available determine the comparative advantages that individuals and nations have. But just by repeatedly producing a particular good or service, people become more productive in that activity, a phenomenon called **learning-by-doing**. Learning-by-doing is the basis of *dynamic* comparative advantage.

Dynamic comparative advantage is a comparative advantage that a person (or a business or a country) possesses as a result of having specialized in a particular activity and, as a result of learning-by-doing, having become the producer with the lowest opportunity cost.

Hong Kong and Singapore are examples of countries that have pursued dynamic comparative advantage vigorously. They have developed industries such as biotechnology in which initially they did not have a comparative advantage but, through learning-by-doing, became low opportunity cost producers in those industries.

Review Quiz

Study Plan 2.4

1 What gives a person or a country a comparative advantage?
2 Distinguish between comparative advantage and absolute advantage.
3 Is production efficient when people specialize?
4 Why do people specialize and trade?
5 What are the gains from specialization and trade?
6 What is the source of the gains from trade?
7 How does dynamic comparative advantage arise?

Economic Coordination

People gain by specializing in the production of those goods and services in which they have a comparative advantage and trading with each other. Erin and Jack, whose production of salads and smoothies we studied earlier in this chapter, can get together and make a deal that enables them to enjoy the gains from specialization and trade. But for billions of individuals to specialize and produce millions of different goods and services, their choices must somehow be coordinated.

Two competing economic coordination systems have been used: central economic planning and decentralized markets.

Central economic planning might appear to be the best system because it can express national priorities. But when this system was tried, as it was for 60 years in Russia and for 30 years in China, it was a miserable failure. Today, these and most other previously planned economies are adopting a decentralized market system.

To make decentralized coordination work, four complementary social institutions that have evolved over many centuries are needed. They are:

- Firms
- Markets
- Property rights
- Money

Firms

A **firm** is an economic unit that employs factors of production and organizes them to produce and sell goods and services. Tesco and Virgin Atlantic are examples of firms.

Firms coordinate a huge amount of economic activity. A Starbucks coffee shop, for example, might buy the machines and labour services of Erin and Jack and start to produce salads and smoothies at all its outlets.

But if a firm gets too big, it can't keep track of all the information that is needed to coordinate its activities. For this reason, firms themselves specialize and trade with each other. For example, Tesco could produce all the things that it sells in its stores. And it could produce all the raw materials that are used to produce the things that it sells. But Tesco would not remain Britain's largest retailer for long if it followed that path. Instead, Tesco buys from other firms that specialize in the production of a narrow range of items. And this trade takes place in markets.

Markets

In ordinary speech, the word *market* means a place where people buy and sell goods such as fish, meat, fruits and vegetables. In economics, a *market* has a more general meaning. A **market** is any arrangement that enables buyers and sellers to get information and to do business with each other. An example is the market in which oil is bought and sold – the world oil market. The world oil market is not a place. It is the network of oil producers, oil users, wholesalers and brokers who buy and sell oil. In the world oil market, decision makers do not meet physically. They make deals throughout the world by telephone, fax and direct computer link.

Markets have evolved because they facilitate trade. Without organized markets, we would miss out on a substantial part of the potential gains from trade. Enterprising individuals and firms, each pursuing their own self-interest, have profited from making markets – standing ready to buy or sell the items in which they specialize. But markets can work only when property rights exist.

Property Rights

The social arrangements that govern the ownership use, and disposal of anything that people value are called **property rights**. *Real property* includes land and buildings – the things we call property in ordinary speech – and durable goods such as plant and equipment. *Financial property* includes shares and bonds and money in the bank. *Intellectual property* is the intangible product of creative effort. This type of property includes books, music, computer programs, and inventions of all kinds and is protected by copyrights and patents.

Where property rights are enforced, people have the incentive to specialize and produce the goods and services in which they have a comparative advantage. Where people can steal the production of others, resources are devoted not to production but to protecting possessions. Without property rights, we would still be hunting and gathering like our Stone Age ancestors.

Money

Money is any commodity or token that is generally acceptable as a means of payment. Erin and Jack didn't use money in the example above. They exchanged salads and smoothies. In principle, trade in markets can exchange any item for any other item. But you can perhaps imagine how complicated life would be if we exchanged goods for other goods. The "invention" of money makes trading in markets much more efficient.

Circular Flows Through Markets

Figure 2.7 shows the flows that result from the choices that households and firms make. Households specialize and choose the quantities of labour, land, capital and entrepreneurship to sell or rent to firms. Firms choose the quantities of factors of production to hire. These (red) flows go through the *factor markets*.

Households choose the quantities of goods and services to buy, and firms choose the quantities to produce. These (red) flows go through the *goods markets*.

Households receive incomes from firms and make expenditures on goods and services (the green flows). The red flows are real flows and the green flows are money flows. The money flows go in the opposite to the real flows.

How do markets coordinate all these decisions?

Coordinating Decisions

Markets coordinate decisions through price adjustments. To see how, think about your local market for fresh-baked bread.

Suppose that some people who want to buy fresh-baked bread are not able to do so. To make the choices of buyers and sellers compatible, buyers must switch to prepackaged bread or more fresh-baked bread must be offered for sale (or both must happen). A rise in the price of fresh-baked bread produces this outcome. A higher price encourages bakers to offer more fresh-baked bread for sale. It also encourages some people to change the bread that they plan to buy. Fewer people buy fresh-baked bread, and more buy prepackaged bread. More fresh-baked bread (and more prepackaged bread) are offered for sale.

Alternatively, suppose that more fresh-baked bread is available than people want to buy. In this case, to make the choices of buyers and sellers compatible, more fresh-baked bread must be bought or less fresh-baked bread must be offered for sale (or both). A fall in the price of fresh-baked bread achieves this outcome. A lower price encourages bakers to produce a smaller quantity of fresh-baked bread. It also encourages people to buy more fresh-baked bread.

Figure 2.7

Circular Flows in the Market Economy

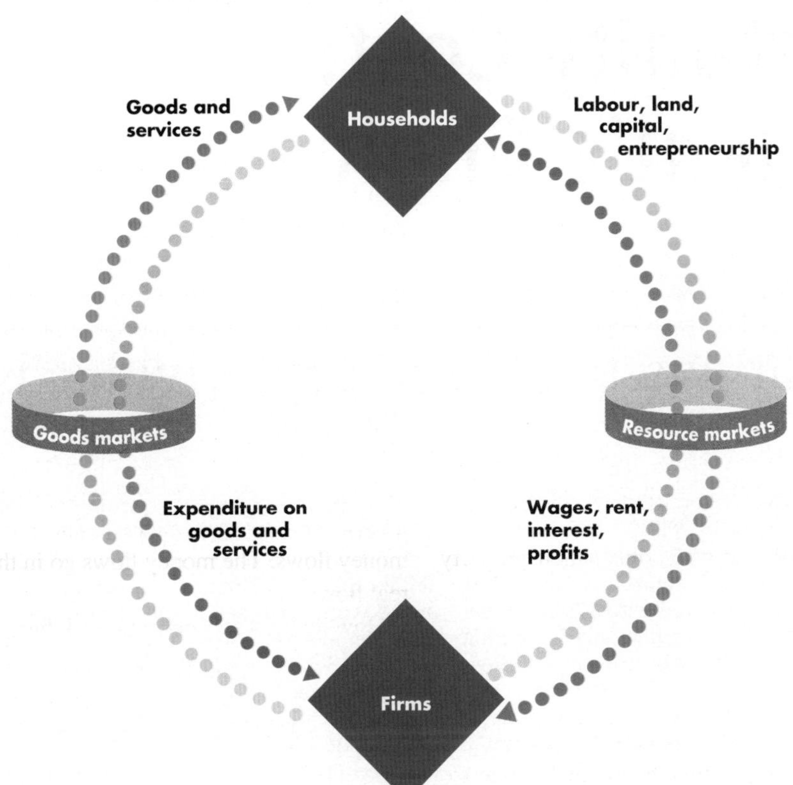

Households and firms make economic choices and markets coordinate these choices.

Households choose the quantities of labour, land, capital and entrepreneurship to sell or rent to firms in exchange for wages, rent, interest and profit. Households also choose how to spend their incomes on the various types of goods and services available.

Firms choose the quantities of factors of production to hire and the quantities of the various goods and services to produce.

Goods markets and factor markets coordinate these choices of households and firms.

The clockwise red flows are real flows – the flow of factors of production from households to firms and the flow of goods and services from firms to households.

The counterclockwise green flows are the payments for the red flows. They are the flow of incomes from firms to households and the flow of expenditure on goods and services from households to firms.

Review Quiz

Study Plan 2.5

1. Why are social institutions such as firms, markets, property rights and money necessary?
2. What are the main functions of markets?
3. What are the flows in the market economy that go from firms to households and from households to firms?
4. In the circular flows of the market economy, which flows are real flows? Which flows are money flows?

You have now begun to see how economists approach economic questions. Scarcity, choice and divergent opportunity costs explain why we specialize and trade and why firms, markets, property rights and money have developed. You can see all around you the lessons you've learned in this chapter. *Reading Between the Lines* on pp. 50–51 gives an example. It explores the *PPF* of a student like you and the choices that students must make that influence their own economic growth – the growth of their incomes.

Reading Between the Lines

Opportunity Cost: A Student's Choice

The Sunday Times, 11 March 2007

Returning to college pays dividends

Barbara McCarthy

. . . An HEA [Irish Higher Education Authority] survey in 2005 . . . showed that 49% of respondents with a bachelor's degree reported an annual salary of less than €21,000. This is compared with 34% for those with a master's degree, while only 5% of PhD graduates were in this lower earnings bracket.

It also showed that postgraduate students were earning at the higher end of the salary scale: 32% of those with master's degrees and 66% of PhD graduates earned more than €29,000, while only 11% of those with primary degrees earned more than this.

The HEA report shows those who may be daunted at taking on further study that degree costs and living costs can be made up in a short space of time.

For those in business postgraduate degrees, the numbers are even better. Graduates of a master's in business administration can earn up to three times their annual salary before their degree, according to the *Financial Times*'s MBA 2007 rankings.

A student who completed an MBA at Trinity College Dublin, which is ranked 70th in the world, will see a 90% salary increase upon completion, the survey says. A Smurfit Business School graduate can expect a 72% salary increase.

Fees for MBAs are among the highest of any postgraduate course, but taking the course here can save you a lot of money. Trinity College is ranked second in the world for value for money, although the full-time MBA costs €23,000, according to the FT.

An MBA at Insead in Fontainebleau, France, will cost more than €45,000, while living expenses there average out at €22,500 per year. In return, an Insead student will enjoy a salary increase of about 94%, only four percentage points more than if that student went to Trinity College. . . .

The Essence of the Story

- An Irish survey reports that, on the average, people with a bachelor's degree earn less than those with a master's degree, who in turn earn less that those with a PhD.
- The report shows that the cost of a higher degree is easily covered by higher earnings.
- MBA graduates can earn up to three times the pre-MBA salaries.
- A Trinity College MBA costs less and brings almost the same earnings increase as an Insead (Frances top business school) MBA.

Economic Analysis

- The opportunity cost of a university education is forgone consumption.
- But a university education increases human capital, which expands lifetime production possibilities and increases future consumption.
- Figure 1 illustrates the choices facing a school leaver who can consume education goods and services and consumption goods and services along the blue *PPF*.
- By working full time, the school leaver can consume at point *A* on the blue *PPF* in Figure 1.
- By attending university, the student moves from point *A* to point *B* along the blue *PPF*. The student incurs an opportunity cost (forgone current consumption) to increase consumption of educational goods and services.
- A university graduate's production possibilities are greater than those of a school leaver.
- Figure 2 shows a university graduate's choices. The blue curve is the same *PPF* as the red *PPF* in Figure 1.
- Working full time, a graduate consumes at point *C* on the blue *PPF* in Figure 2.
- To continue in university and obtain a post-graduate degree, the student forgoes current consumption (the opportunity cost of post-graduate study) for educational goods and services in a move along the *PPF* from point *C* to point *D*.
- With a post-graduate degree, earnings jump and the student's *PPF* shifts outward to the red curve in Figure 2.

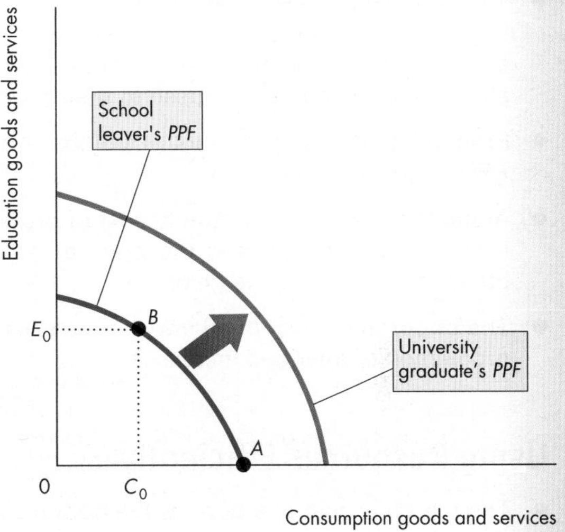

Figure 1 School leaver's choices

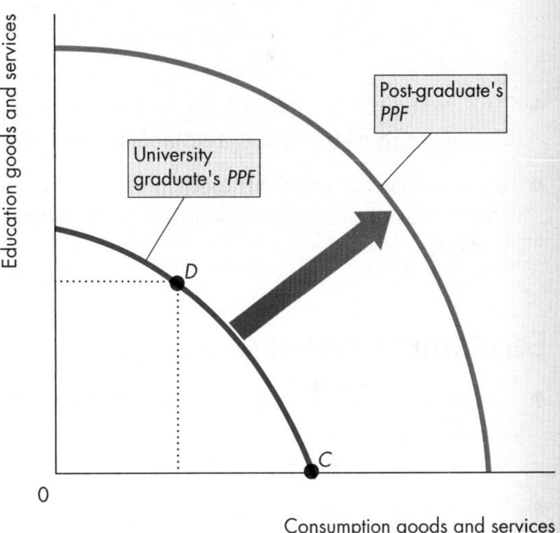

Figure 2 University graduate's choices

Summary

Key Points

Production Possibilities and Opportunity Cost (pp. 36–38)

- The production possibilities frontier, *PPF*, is the boundary between production levels that are attainable and those that are unattainable when all available resources are used to their limit.
- Production efficiency occurs at points on the *PPF*.
- Along the *PPF*, the opportunity cost of producing more of one good is the amount of the other good that must be given up.
- The opportunity cost of all goods increases as production of the good increases.

Using Resources Efficiently (pp. 39–41)

- The marginal cost of a good is the opportunity cost of producing one more unit.
- The marginal benefit from a good is the maximum amount of another good that a person is willing to forgo to obtain more of the first good.
- The marginal benefit of a good decreases as the amount of the good available increases.
- Resources are used efficiently when the marginal cost of each good is equal to its marginal benefit.

Economic Growth (pp. 42–43)

- Economic growth, which is the expansion of production possibilities, results from capital accumulation and technological change.
- The opportunity cost of economic growth is forgone current consumption.

Gains from Trade (pp. 44–47)

- A person has a comparative advantage in producing a good if that person can produce the good at a lower opportunity cost than everyone else.
- People gain by specializing in the activity in which they have a comparative advantage and trading.
- Dynamic comparative advantage arises from learning-by-doing.

Economic Coordination (pp. 47–49)

- Firms coordinate a large amount of economic activity, but there is a limit to the efficient size of a firm.
- Markets coordinate the economic choices of people and firms.
- Markets can work efficiently only when property rights exist.
- Money makes trading in markets more efficient.

Key Figures

Key Terms

Problems

Tests, Study Plan and Solutions*

1 Use the graph below to calculate Peter's opportunity cost of an hour of tennis when he increases the time he plays tennis from:

a 4 to 6 hours a week.

b 6 to 8 hours a week.

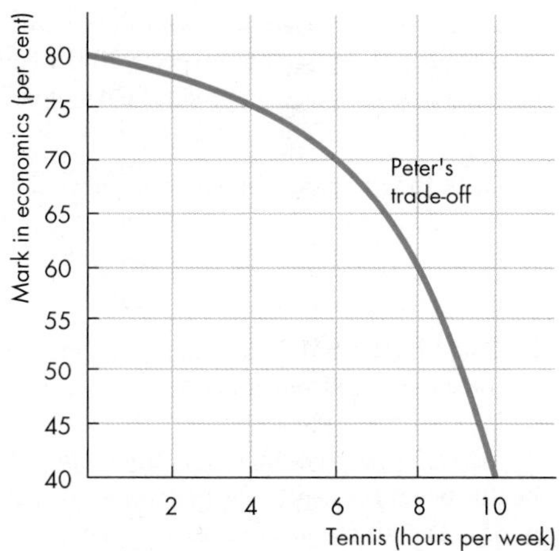

2 Peter, whose *PPF* is shown in problem 1, has the following marginal benefit curve.

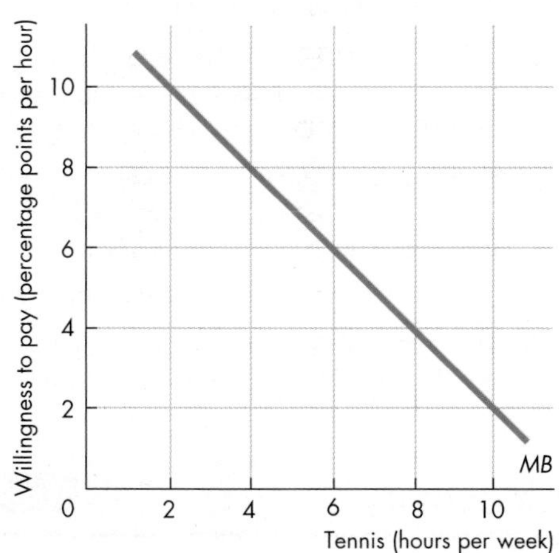

a If Peter uses his time efficiently, what is his mark and how many hours of tennis does he play?

b Explain why Peter would be worse off getting a higher mark?

3 Sunland's production possibilities are set our in the table at the top of the next column.

a Draw a graph of Sunland's production possibilities frontier.

Food (kilograms per month)		Sunscreen (litres per month)
300	and	0
200	and	50
100	and	100
0	and	150

b What are Sunland's opportunity costs of producing 1 kilogram of food?

c What are Sunland's opportunity costs of producing 1 litre of sunscreen?

4 In Sunland, which has the production possibilities shown in the table in problem 3, preferences are described by the following table.

Sunscreen (litres per month)		Willingness to pay (kilograms per litre)
25	and	3
75	and	2
125	and	1

a Draw a graph of Sunland's marginal benefit from sunscreen.

b What is the quantity of sunscreen produced in Sunland if it achieves allocative efficiency?

5 A farm grows wheat and produces pork. The marginal cost of producing each of these products increases as more of it is produced.

a Make a graph to illustrate the farm's *PPF*.

b The farm adopts a new technology that allows it to use fewer resources to fatten pigs. Use your graph to illustrate the impact of the new technology on the farm's *PPF*.

c With the farm using the new technology described in part (b), has the opportunity cost of producing a tonne of wheat increased, decreased or remained the same? Explain your answer.

d Is the farm more efficient with the new technology than it was with the old one?

6 Tom can produce 40 balls an hour or 4 bats an hour. Tessa can produce 80 balls an hour or 4 bats an hour.

a Calculate Tom's opportunity cost of producing a ball.

* Solutions to odd-numbered problems are provided.

b Calculate Tessa's opportunity cost of producing a ball.

c Who has a comparative advantage in producing balls?

d If Tom and Tessa specialize in producing the good in which each of them has a comparative advantage, and they trade 1 bat for 15 balls, who gains from specialization and trade? Explain your answer.

Suppose that Tessa buys a new machine for making bats that enables her to make 20 bats an hour. (She can still make only 80 balls an hour.)

e Who now has a comparative advantage in producing bats?

f Can Tom and Tessa still gain from trade?

g Would Tom and Tessa still be willing to trade 1 bat for 15 balls? Explain your answer.

Critical Thinking

1 Study the *Reading Between the Lines* news article about student choices on pp. 50–51 and answer the following questions:

a Why is the *PPF* for education goods and services and consumption goods and services bowed outward?

b Students are facing rising tuition fees. How does the higher tuition fee change the opportunity cost of education and how does it change the student's *PPF*s in Figures 1 and 2 on p. 51?

c Students are facing a falling earnings premium. Does the falling earnings premium make the opportunity cost of education increase, decrease or remain unchanged?

d Do you think that people obtain an efficient quantity of education? Explain why or why not.

2 "Britain's music stores are being squeezed off the high street," says *The Economist* (20 January 2007, p. 65). The article describes trends in music retailing: Sony Music and Amazon selling online, supermarkets selling at low prices, and traditional high street music retailers HMV, Music Zone, and Virgin Megastores all struggling. To explain these trends:

a Draw the *PPF* and marginal cost and marginal benefit curves for high street music retailers and online music retailers before the Internet became available.

b Draw the *PPF* and marginal cost and marginal benefit curves for high street music retailers and online music retailers after the Internet became available.

c Explain how changes in production possibilities and/or preferences have changed the way in which recorded music is retailed.

3 Ethanol can be produced from either sugar or corn. A gallon of ethanol costs 90¢ to produce from Brazilian sugarcane and $1 to produce from US corn. The US Department of Agriculture expects 20 per cent of the corn harvest to be used to produce ethanol in 2007, an increase of 34 per cent from 2006.

a Does Brazil or the United States have a comparative advantage in producing ethanol?

b Will the opportunity cost of producing ethanol in the United States increase in 2007?

c Could the United States gain by importing ethanol (or sugarcane) from Brazil?

4 "America's baby-boomers are embracing tea for its health benefits," said *The Economist* (8 July 2005, p. 65). The article went on to say: "Even though the climate is suitable, tea-growing [in the United States] is simply too costly, since the process is labour-intensive and resists automation."

Using the information provided:

a Sketch two *PPF*s for the production of tea and other goods and services: one in the United States and the other in India.

b Sketch the marginal benefit curve for tea in the United States before and after the baby-boomers appreciated the health benefits of tea.

c Does the United States produce tea or import it?

d Does the change in preferences towards tea have any effect on the opportunity cost of producing tea?

Web Activity

Links to Websites

1 Read about the costs to working mothers and the female poverty trap and then answer the following questions:

a Why have the opportunity costs to working mothers fallen over time?

b Why are the opportunity costs lower for highly educated women?

PART

2

How Markets Work

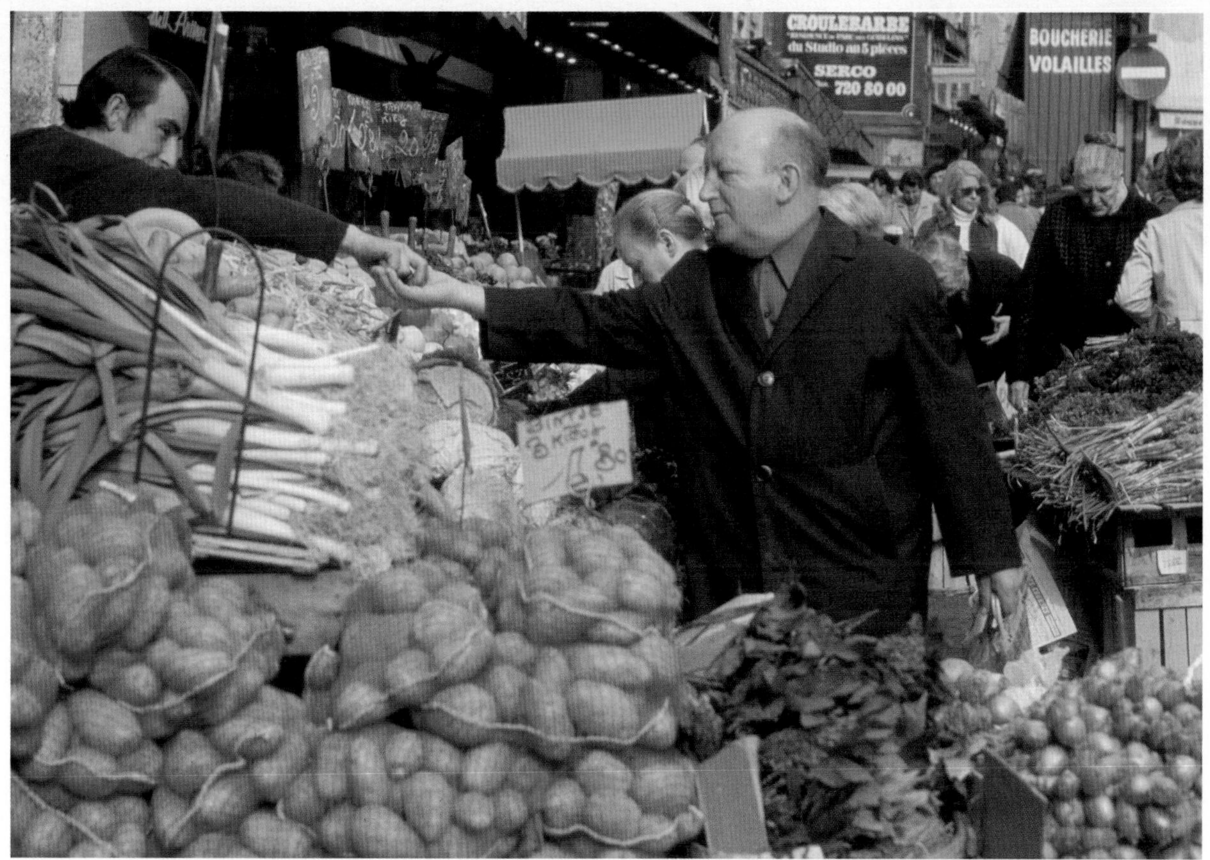

The Amazing Market

The five chapters that you will study in this part explain how markets work. A market is an amazing instrument. It enables people who have never met and who know nothing about each other to interact and do business. It also enables us to allocate our scarce resources to the uses that we value most highly.

You will begin in Chapter 3 by learning about the laws of demand and supply. You will discover the forces that make prices adjust to coordinate buyers' plans and sellers' plans.

In Chapter 4, you will meet the handy concept of elasticity and learn how to calculate, interpret and use it to predict how prices and quantities respond to changes in supply and demand.

In Chapter 5, you will discover what Adam Smith called "the invisible hand". You will see that when people pursue their self-interest in competitive markets, the outcome is in the social interest – resources go to their most highly valued uses.

In Chapter 6, you will learn about markets in action when governments intervene to fix the minimum price or the maximum price, impose taxes or quotas, or make some goods illegal.

Finally, in Chapter 7, you will study global markets in action. There, you will see how globalization brings gains from international trade and why restrictions on international trade benefit producers but damage the interest of consumers and are not in the social interest.

CHAPTER 3

Demand and Supply

After studying this chapter you will be able to:

- Describe a competitive market and think about a price as an opportunity cost
- Explain the influences on demand
- Explain the influences on supply
- Explain how demand and supply determine prices and quantities bought and sold
- Use demand and supply to make predictions about changes in prices and quantities

Energy Drinks Market Sparkles!

The market for energy drinks has exploded over the past few years and in 2007, Europeans spent almost €4 billion on these drinks. Despite this huge increase in consumption, the prices of energy drinks have been remarkably stable as dozens of new producers have entered the market.

Not all prices have been stable. Some, such as the price of a PC have tumbled whereas others such as the prices of houses and the prices of commodities such as copper have rocketed.

Find out in this chapter what determines prices. And in *Reading Between the Lines* at the end of the chapter, put what you learn to work by explaining why the world price of copper jumped in 2006.

Markets and Prices

When you want to buy a new pair of running shoes, or a sandwich, or an energy drink, or a bottle of water, or decide to upgrade your CD player, you must find a place where people sell those items. The place in which you find them is a *market*. You learned in Chapter 2 (p. 48) that a market is any arrangement that enables buyers and sellers to get information and to do business with each other.

A market has two sides: buyers and sellers. There are markets for *goods* such as apples and hiking boots, for *services* such as haircuts and tennis lessons, for *resources* such as computer programmers and earth-movers, and for other manufactured *inputs* such as memory chips and car parts. There are also markets for money such as the euro and the dollar and for financial securities such as BP shares and Yahoo! shares. Only our imagination limits what can be traded in markets.

Some markets are physical places where buyers and sellers meet and where an auctioneer or a broker helps to determine the prices. Examples of this type of market are the London Stock Exchange and the Billingsgate fish market.

Some markets are groups of people spread around the world who never meet and know little about each other but are connected through the Internet or by telephone and fax. Examples are the e-commerce markets and currency markets.

But most markets are unorganized collections of buyers and sellers. You do most of your trading in this type of market. An example is the market for football boots. The buyers in this multi-million pound a year market are the several million people who play football (or who want to make an exotic fashion statement). The sellers are the tens of thousands of retail sports equipment and footwear stores. Each buyer can visit several different stores, and each seller knows that the buyer has a choice of stores.

A Competitive Market

Markets vary in the intensity of competition that buyers and sellers face. In this chapter, we're going to study a **competitive market** – a market that has many buyers and many sellers, so no single buyer or seller can influence the price.

Producers offer items for sale only if the price is high enough to cover their opportunity cost. And consumers respond to changing opportunity cost by seeking cheaper alternatives to expensive items.

We are going to study the way people respond to *prices* and the forces that determine prices. But to pursue these tasks, we need to understand the relationship between a price and an opportunity cost.

In everyday life, the *price* of an object is the number of pounds or euros that must be given up in exchange for it. Economists refer to this price as the **money price**.

The *opportunity cost* of an action is the highest-valued alternative forgone. If, when you buy a coffee, the highest-valued thing you forgo is some chocolate, then the opportunity cost of the coffee is the *quantity* of chocolate forgone. We can calculate the quantity of chocolate forgone from the money prices of coffee and chocolate.

If the money price of coffee is £3 a cup and the money price of a chocolate bar is £1, then the opportunity cost of one cup of coffee is three chocolate bars. To calculate this opportunity cost, we divide the price of a cup of coffee by the price of a chocolate bar and find the *ratio* of one price to the other. The ratio of one price to another is called a **relative price**, and a *relative price is an opportunity cost.*

We can express the relative price of coffee in terms of chocolate or any other good. The normal way of expressing a relative price is in terms of a "basket" of all goods and services. To calculate this relative price, we divide the money price of a good by the money price of a "basket" of all goods (called a *price index*). The resulting relative price tells us the opportunity cost of the good in terms of how much of the "basket" we must give up to buy it.

The theory of demand and supply that we are about to study determines *relative prices*, and the word "price" means *relative* price. When we predict that a price will fall, we do not mean that its *money* price will fall – although it might. We mean that its *relative* price will fall. That is, its price will fall *relative* to the average price of other goods and services.

Review Quiz

Study Plan 3.1

1 What is the distinction between a money price and a relative price?
2 Explain why a relative price is an opportunity cost.
3 Think of examples of goods whose relative price have risen and have fallen by a large amount.

Let's begin our study of demand and supply, starting with demand.

Demand

If you demand something, then you

1 Want it,
2 Can afford it, and
3 Plan to buy it.

Wants are the unlimited desires or wishes that people have for goods and services. How many times have you thought that you would like something "if only you could afford it" or "if it weren't so expensive"? Scarcity guarantees that many – perhaps most – of our wants will never be satisfied. Demand reflects a decision about which wants to satisfy.

The **quantity demanded** of a good or service is the amount that consumers plan to buy during a given time period at a particular price. The quantity demanded is not necessarily the same as the quantity actually bought. Sometimes the quantity demanded exceeds the amount of goods available, so the quantity bought is less than the quantity demanded.

The quantity demanded is measured as an amount per unit of time. For example, suppose that you buy one cup of coffee a day. The quantity of coffee that you demand can be expressed as 1 cup per day, 7 cups per week, or 365 cups per year.

Many factors influence buying plans and one of them is price. We look first at the relationship between the quantity demanded of a good and its price. To study this relationship, we make a *ceteris paribus* assumption. That is, we keep all other influences on buying plans the same and we ask: How, other things remaining the same, does the quantity demanded of a good change as its price changes?

The law of demand provides the answer.

The Law of Demand

The **law of demand** states:

> **Other things remaining the same, the higher the price of a good, the smaller is the quantity demanded; and the lower the price of a good, the greater is the quantity demanded.**

Why does a higher price reduce the quantity demanded? For two reasons:

- Substitution effect
- Income effect

Substitution Effect

When the price of a good rises, other things remaining the same, its *relative* price – its opportunity cost – rises. Although each good is unique, it has *substitutes* – other goods that can be used in its place. As the opportunity cost of a good rises, people buy less of that good and more of its substitutes.

Income Effect

When the price of a good rises and other influences on buying plans remain unchanged, the price rises *relative* to incomes. Faced with a higher price and unchanged income, people cannot afford to buy all the things they previously bought. They must decrease the quantities demanded of at least some goods and services, and normally the good whose price has increased will be one of the goods that people buy less of.

To see the substitution effect and the income effect at work, think about the effects of a change in the price of an energy drink. Many goods are substitutes for an energy drink. For example, an energy bar or an energy gel could be consumed in place of an energy drink.

Suppose that an energy drink initially sells for £3 and then its price falls to £1.50. People now substitute energy bars for energy drinks – the substitution effect. And with a budget that now has some slack from the lower price of an energy drink, people buy more energy drinks – the income effect. The quantity of energy drinks demanded increases for these two reasons.

Now suppose that an energy drink initially sells for £3 and then the price rises to £4. People now substitute energy bars for energy drinks – the substitution effect. Faced with a tighter budget, people buy even fewer energy drinks – the income effect. The quantity of energy drinks demanded decreases for these two reasons.

Demand Curve and Demand Schedule

You are now about to study one of the two most used curves in economics: the demand curve. And you are going to encounter one of the most critical distinctions: the distinction between *demand* and *quantity demanded.*

The term **demand** refers to the entire relationship between the price of the good and the quantity demanded of the good. Demand is illustrated by the demand curve and the demand schedule. The term *quantity demanded* refers to a point on a demand curve – the quantity demanded at a particular price.

Figure 3.1 shows the demand curve for energy drinks. A **demand curve** shows the relationship between the quantity demanded of a good and its price when all other influences on consumers' planned purchases remain the same.

The table in Figure 3.1 is the *demand schedule*, which lists the quantities demanded at each price when all the other influences on consumers' planned purchases remain the same. For example, if the price of an energy drink is 50 pence, the quantity demanded is 9 million a week. If the price is £2.50, the quantity demanded is 2 million a week. The other rows of the table show the quantities demanded at prices of £1.00, £1.50 and £2.00.

We graph the demand schedule as a demand curve with the quantity demanded on the *x*-axis and the price on the *y*-axis. The points on the demand curve labelled *A* through *E* correspond to the rows of the demand schedule. For example, point *A* on the graph shows a quantity demanded of 9 million energy drinks a week at a price of 50 pence a drink.

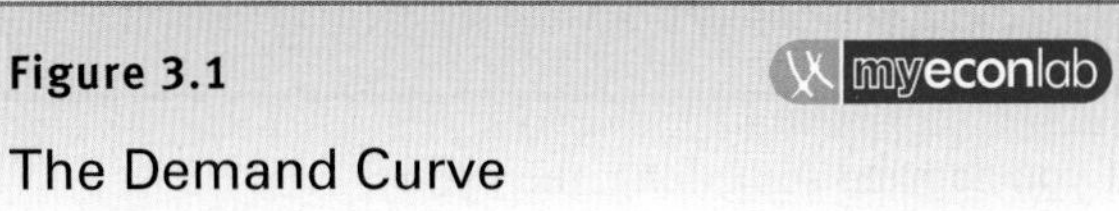

The Demand Curve

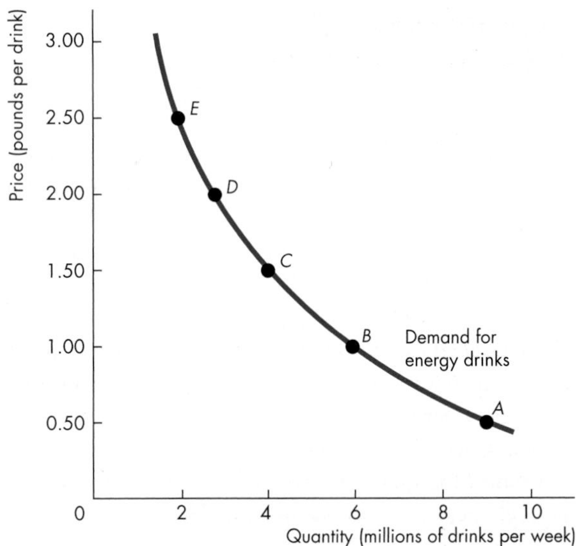

	Price (pounds per drink)	Quantity demanded (millions of energy drinks per week)
A	0.50	9
B	1.00	6
C	1.50	4
D	2.00	3
E	2.50	2

The table shows a demand schedule for energy drinks. At a price of 50 pence an energy drink, 9 million a week are demanded; at a price of £1.50 an energy drink, 4 million a week are demanded. The demand curve shows the relationship between quantity demanded and price, everything else remaining the same. The demand curve slopes downward: as price decreases, the quantity demanded increases.

The demand curve can be read in two ways. For a given price, the demand curve tells us the quantity that people plan to buy. For example, at a price of £1.50 an energy drink, the quantity demanded is 4 million energy drinks a week. For a given quantity, the demand curve tells us the maximum price that consumers are willing and able to pay for the last energy drink available. For example, the maximum price that consumers will pay for the 6 millionth drink is £1.00.

Willingness and Ability to Pay

We can also view a demand curve as a willingness-and-ability-to-pay curve. And the willingness and ability to pay is a measure of *marginal benefit*.

If a small quantity is available, the highest price that someone is willing and able to pay for one more unit is high. As the quantity available increases, the marginal benefit falls and the highest price that someone is willing and able to pay falls along the demand curve.

In Figure 3.1, if only 2 million energy drinks are available each week, the highest price that someone is willing to pay for the 2 millionth drink is £2.50. But if 9 million energy drinks are available each week, someone is willing to pay 50 pence for the last drink bought.

A Change in Demand

When any factor that influences buying plans other than the price of the good changes, there is a **change in demand**. Figure 3.2 illustrates an increase in demand. When demand increases, the demand curve shifts rightward and the quantity demanded is greater at each and every price. For example, at a price of £2.50, on the original (blue) demand curve, the quantity demanded is 2 million energy drinks a week. On the new (red) demand curve, the quantity demanded is 6 million energy drinks a week. Look closely at the numbers in the table in Figure 3.2 and check that the quantity demanded at each price is greater.

Six main factors bring changes in demand. They are changes in:

- Income
- Prices of related goods
- Expected future income
- Expected future prices
- Population
- Preferences

Income

Consumers' income influences demand. When income increases, consumers buy more of most goods, and when income decreases, consumers buy less of most goods. Although an increase in income leads to an increase in the demand for *most* goods, it does not lead to an increase in the demand for *all* goods.

A **normal good** is one for which demand increases as income increases. An **inferior good** is one for which demand decreases as income increases. Long-distance transport has examples of both normal goods and inferior goods. As income increases, the demand for air travel (a normal good) increases and the demand for long-distance bus trips (an inferior good) decreases.

Prices of Related Goods

The quantity of energy drinks that consumers plan to buy depends in part on the prices of its substitutes. A **substitute** is a good that can be used in place of another good. For example, a bus ride is a substitute for a train ride and an energy bar is a substitute for an energy drink. If the price of an energy bar rises, people buy fewer energy bars and more energy drinks. The demand for energy drinks increases.

The quantity of a good that people plan to buy also depends on the prices of its complements. A **complement** is a good that is used in conjunction with another good. For example, fish and chips are complements and so are energy drinks and exercise. If the price of an hour at the gym falls, people buy more gym time *and more* energy drinks.

Expected Future Income

When expected future income increases, demand might increase. For example, a sales person gets the news that she will receive a big bonus at the end of the year, so she decides to buy a new car right now.

Figure 3.2 myeconlab

An Increase in Demand

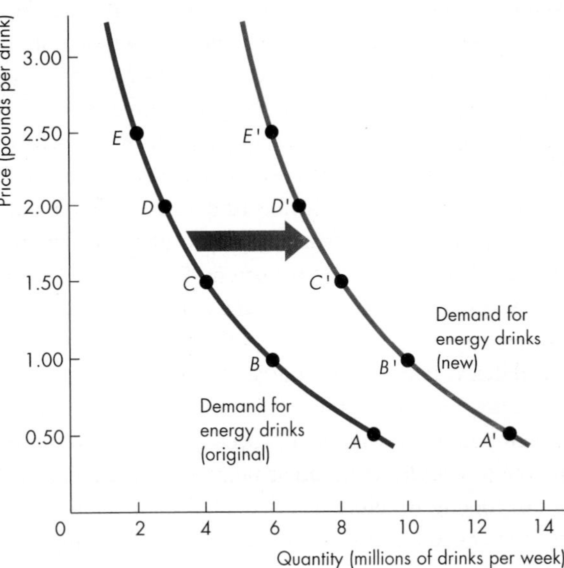

	Original demand schedule Original income			New demand schedule New income	
	Price (pounds per drink)	Quantity demanded (millions of drinks per week)		Price (pounds per drink)	Quantity demanded (millions of drinks per week)
A	0.50	9	*A'*	0.50	13
B	1.00	6	*B'*	1.00	10
C	1.50	4	*C'*	1.50	8
D	2.00	3	*D'*	2.00	7
E	2.50	2	*E'*	2.50	6

A change in any influence on buyers' plans other than the price of the good itself results in a new demand schedule and a shift of the demand curve. A change in income changes the demand for energy drinks.

At a price of £1.50 an energy drink, 4 million drinks a week are demanded at the original income (row C of the table) and 8 million energy drinks a week are demanded at the new higher income. A rise in income increases the demand for energy drinks. The demand curve shifts rightward, as shown by the shift arrow and the resulting red curve.

Expected Future Prices

If the price of a good is expected to rise in the future and if the good can be stored, the opportunity cost of obtaining the good for future use is lower today than it will be when the price has increased. So people retime their purchases – they substitute over time. They buy more of the good now before its price is expected to rise (and less later), so the demand for the good increases.

For example, suppose that Spain is hit by a frost that damages the season's orange crop. You expect the price of orange juice to rise in the future. So you fill your freezer with enough frozen juice to get you through the next six months. Your current demand for frozen orange juice has increased, and your future demand has decreased.

Similarly, if the price of a good is expected to fall in the future, the opportunity cost of buying the good today is high relative to what it is expected to be in the future. So again, people retime their purchases. They buy less of the good now before its price falls, so the demand for the good decreases today and increases in the future.

Computer prices are constantly falling, and this fact poses a dilemma. Will you buy a new computer now, in time for the start of the academic year, or will you wait until the price has fallen some more?

Because people expect computer prices to keep falling, the current demand for computers is less (the future demand is greater) than it otherwise would be.

Table 3.1

The Demand for Energy Drinks

The Law of Demand

The quantity of energy drinks demanded

Decreases if:	*Increases if:*
◆ The price of an energy drink rises	◆ The price of an energy drink falls

Changes in Demand

The demand for energy drinks

Decreases if:	*Increases if:*
◆ Income falls*	◆ Income rises*
◆ The price of a substitute falls	◆ The price of a substitute rises
◆ The price of a complement rises	◆ The price of a complement falls
◆ Expected future income falls	◆ Expected future income rises
◆ The price of an energy drink is expected to fall in the future	◆ The price of an energy drink is expected to rise in the future
◆ The population decreases	◆ The population increases

*An energy drink is a normal good.

Population

Demand also depends on the size and the age structure of the population. The larger the population, the greater is the demand for all goods and services; the smaller the population, the smaller is the demand.

For example, the demand for parking spaces or cinema seats or energy drinks or just about anything that you can imagine is much greater in London than it is in Lands End.

Also, the larger the proportion of the population in a given age group, the greater is the demand for the goods and services used by that age group. For example, the number of older people is increasing relative to the number of babies. As a result, the demand for walking frames and nursing home services is increasing at a faster pace than that at which the demand for prams and nappies is increasing.

Preferences

Demand depends on preferences. *Preferences* are an individual's attitudes towards goods and services. Preferences depend on such things as the weather, information and fashion. For example, greater health and fitness awareness has shifted preferences in favour of energy drinks, so the demand for energy drinks has increased.

Table 3.1 summarizes the influences on demand and the direction of those influences.

A Change in the Quantity Demanded versus a Change in Demand

Changes in the factors that influence buyers' plans cause either a change in the quantity demanded or a change in demand. Equivalently, they cause either a movement along the demand curve or a shift of the demand curve. The distinction between a change in the quantity demanded and a change in demand is the same as that between a movement along the demand curve and a shift of the demand curve.

A point on the demand curve shows the quantity demanded at a given price. So a movement along the demand curve shows a **change in the quantity demanded**. The entire demand curve shows demand. So a shift of the demand curve shows a *change in demand*. Figure 3.3 illustrates and summarizes these distinctions.

Movement Along the Demand Curve

If the price of a good changes but everything else remains the same, there is a movement along the demand curve. Because the demand curve slopes downward, a fall in the price of a good increases the quantity demanded of it and a rise in the price of the good decreases the quantity demanded of it – the law of demand.

In Figure 3.3, if the price of a good falls when everything else remains the same, the quantity demanded of that good increases and there is a movement down the demand curve D_0. If the price rises when everything else remains the same, the quantity demanded of that good decreases and there is a movement up the demand curve D_0.

A Shift of the Demand Curve

If the price of a good remains constant but some other influence on buyers' plans changes, there is a change in demand for that good. We illustrate a change in demand as a shift of the demand curve. For example, if more people work out at the gym, consumers buy more energy drinks regardless of the price of a drink. That is what a rightward shift of the demand curve – more energy drinks are bought at each and every price.

In Figure 3.3, when any influence on buyers' planned purchases changes, other than the price of the good, there is a *change in demand* and the demand curve shifts. Demand *increases* and the demand curve *shifts rightward* (to the red demand curve D_1) if income increases (for a normal good), the price of a substitute rises, the price of a complement falls, expected future income increases, the expected future price of the good rises, or the population increases.

Demand *decreases* and the demand curve *shifts leftward* (to the red demand curve D_2) if income decreases (for a normal good), the price of a substitute falls, the price of a complement rises, expected future income decreases, the expected future price of the good falls, or the population decreases. (For an inferior good, the effects of changes in income are in the direction opposite to those described above.)

Figure 3.3 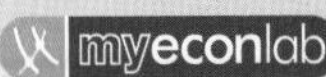

A Change in the Quantity Demanded versus a Change in Demand

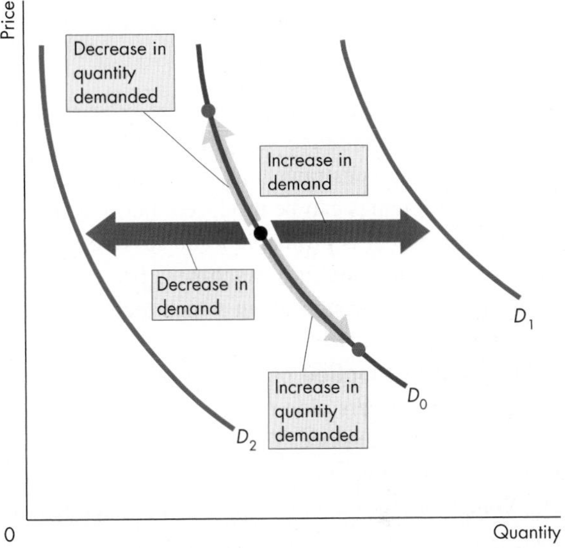

When the price of the good changes, there is a movement along the demand curve and *a change in the quantity demanded,* shown by the blue arrows on demand curve D_0.

When any other influence on buyers' plans changes, there is a shift of the demand curve and a *change in demand.* An increase in demand shifts the demand curve rightward (from D_0 to D_1). A decrease in demand shifts the demand curve leftward (from D_0 to D_2).

Review Quiz

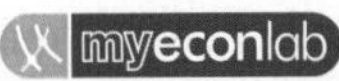

Study Plan 3.2

1. Define the quantity demanded of a good or service.
2. What is the law of demand and how do we illustrate it?
3. What does the demand curve tell us about the price that consumers are willing to pay?
4. List all the influences on buying plans that change demand and for each influence say whether it increases or decreases demand.
5. Distinguish between the quantity demanded of a good and demand for the good.
6. Why does the demand not change when the price of a good changes with no change in the other influences on buying plans?

Supply

If a firm supplies a good or a service, the firm

1 Has the resources and technology to produce it,

2 Can profit from producing it, and

3 Plans to produce it and sell it.

A supply is more than just having the *resources* and the *technology* to produce something. *Resources and technology* are the constraints that limit what is possible.

Many useful things can be produced, but they are not produced because it is profitable to do so. (No one produces electric bed-making machines, for example!) Supply reflects a decision about which technologically feasible items to produce.

The **quantity supplied** of a good or service is the amount that producers plan to sell during a given time period at a particular price. The quantity supplied is not necessarily the same amount as the quantity actually sold. Sometimes the quantity supplied is greater than the quantity demanded, so the quantity bought is less than the quantity supplied.

Like the quantity demanded, the quantity supplied is measured as an amount per unit of time. For example, suppose that Ford produces 1,000 cars a day. The quantity of cars supplied by Ford can be expressed as 1,000 a day, 7,000 a week, or 365,000 a year. Without the time dimension, we cannot tell whether a particular number is large or small.

Many factors influence selling plans and again, one of them is price. We look first at the relationship between the quantity supplied of a good and its price. And again, as we did when we studied demand, to isolate this relationship, we keep all other influences on selling plans the same and we ask: How, other things remaining the same, does the quantity supplied of a good change as its price changes?

The law of supply provides the answer.

The Law of Supply

The **law of supply** states:

> **Other things remaining the same, the higher the price of a good, the greater is the quantity supplied; and the lower the price of a good, the smaller is the quantity supplied.**

Why does a higher price increase the quantity supplied? It is because *marginal cost increases*. As the quantity produced of any good increases, the marginal cost of producing the good increases. (You can refresh your memory of increasing marginal cost in Chapter 2, p. 39.)

It is never worth producing a good if the price received for it does not at least cover the marginal cost of producing it. So when the price of a good rises, other things remaining the same, producers are willing to incur a higher marginal cost and increase production. The higher price brings forth an increase in the quantity supplied.

Let's now illustrate the law of supply with a supply curve and a supply schedule.

Supply Curve and Supply Schedule

You are now going to study the second of the two most used curves in economics: the supply curve. And you're going to learn about the critical distinction between *supply* and *quantity supplied.*

The term **supply** refers to the entire relationship between the quantity supplied and the price of a good. Supply is illustrated by the supply curve and the supply schedule. The term *quantity supplied* refers to a point on a supply curve – the quantity supplied at a particular price.

Figure 3.4 shows the supply curve of energy drinks. A **supply curve** shows the relationship between the quantity supplied of a good and its price when all other influences on producers' planned sales remain the same. The supply curve is a graph of a supply schedule.

The table in Figure 3.4 sets out the supply schedule for energy drinks. A *supply schedule* lists the quantities supplied at each price when all the other influences on producers' planned sales remain the same. For example, if the price of an energy drink is 50 pence, the quantity supplied is zero – in row *A* of the table. If the price of an energy drink is £1.00, the quantity supplied is 3 million drinks a week – in row *B*. The other rows of the table show the quantities supplied at prices of £1.50, £2.00 and £2.50.

To make a supply curve, we graph the quantity supplied on the *x*-axis and the price on the *y*-axis, just as in the case of the demand curve. The points on the supply curve labelled *A* through *E* correspond to the rows of the supply schedule. For example, point *A* on the graph shows a quantity supplied of zero at a price of 50 pence an energy drink.

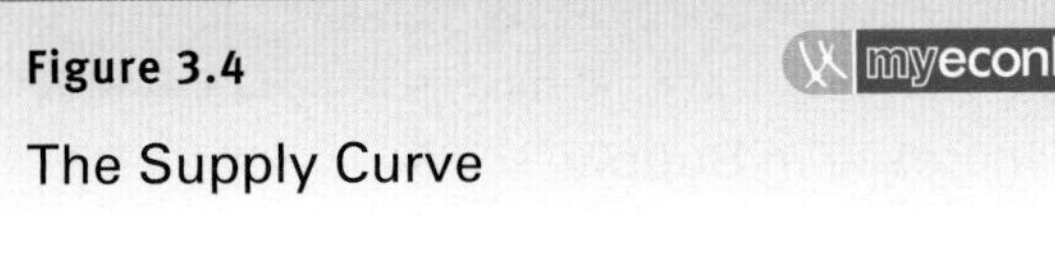

Figure 3.4

The Supply Curve

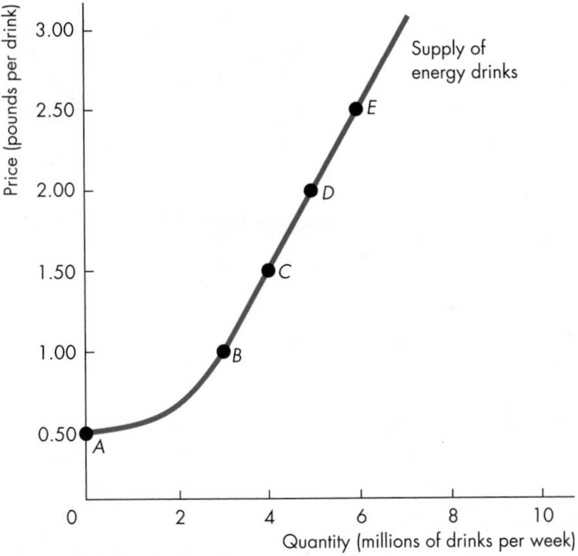

	Price (pounds per energy drink)	Quantity supplied (millions of energy drinks per week)
A	0.50	0
B	1.00	3
C	1.50	4
D	2.00	5
E	2.50	6

The table shows the supply schedule of energy drinks. For example, at a price of £1.00, 3 million energy drinks a week are supplied; at a price of £2.50, 6 million energy drinks a week are supplied. The supply curve shows the relationship between the quantity supplied and price, other things remaining the same. The supply curve usually slopes upward. As the price of a good increases, the quantity supplied increases.

A supply curve can be read in two ways. For a given price, it tells us the quantity that producers plan to sell at that price. For example, at a price of £1.50 a drink, producers are willing to supply 10 million drinks a week. For a given quantity, the supply curve tells us the minimum price at which producers are willing to sell one more drink. For example, if 5 million drinks are produced each week, the lowest price at which someone is willing to sell the 5 millionth drink is £2.50.

Minimum Supply Price

The supply curve, like the demand curve, has two interpretations. It is the minimum-supply-price curve. It tells us the lowest price at which someone is willing to sell another unit. This lowest price is *marginal cost.*

If a small quantity is produced, the lowest price at which someone is willing to sell one more unit is low. But as the quantity produced increases, the lowest price at which someone is willing to sell one more unit rises along the supply curve.

In Figure 3.4, if 6 million energy drinks are produced each week, the lowest price that a producer is willing to accept for the 6 millionth drink is £2.50. But if only 4 million energy drinks are produced each week, a producer is willing to accept £1.50 for the last drink sold.

A Change in Supply

When any factor that influences selling plans other than the price of the good changes, there is a **change in supply**. Five main factors bring changes in supply. They are changes in:

- Prices of factors of production
- Prices of related goods produced
- Expected future prices
- Number of suppliers
- Technology

Prices of Factors of Production

The prices of factors of production used to produce a good influence the supply of the good. The easiest way to see this influence is to think about the supply curve as a minimum-supply-price curve. If the price of a factor of production rises, the lowest price a producer is willing to accept rises, so supply decreases. For example, during 2006, as the price of jet fuel increased, the supply of air transportation decreased. Similarly, rise in the minimum wage decreases the supply of energy drinks.

Prices of Related Goods Produced

The prices of related goods and services that firms produce influence supply. For example, if the price of soft drinks rises, the supply of energy drinks decreases. Energy drinks and soft drinks are *substitutes in production* – goods that can be produced by using the same resources. If the price of beef rises, the supply of leather increases. Beef and leather are *complements in production* – goods that must be produced together.

Expected Future Prices

If the price of a good is expected to rise, the return from selling the good in the future is higher than it is today. So supply decreases today and increases in the future.

Number of Suppliers

The larger the number of firms that produce a good, the greater is the supply of the good. And as firms enter an industry, the supply in that industry increases. As firms leave an industry, the supply in that industry decreases.

Technology

The term "technology" is used broadly to mean the way that factors of production are used to produce a good. Technology changes both positively and negatively. A positive technology change occurs when a new method is discovered that lowers the cost of producing a good. An example is new methods used in the factories that produce computer chips. A negative technology change occurs when an event such as extreme weather or natural disaster increases the cost of producing a good. A positive technology change increases supply, and a negative technology change decreases supply.

Figure 3.5 illustrates an increase in supply. When supply increases, the supply curve shifts *rightward* and the quantity supplied is larger at each and every price. For example, at a price of £1.00, on the original (blue) supply curve, the quantity supplied is 3 million energy drinks a week. On the new (red) supply curve, the quantity supplied is 6 million energy drinks a week. Look closely at the numbers in the table in Figure 3.5 and check that the quantity supplied at each price is larger.

Table 3.2 summarizes the influences on supply and the directions of those influences.

A Change in the Quantity Supplied versus a Change in Supply

Changes in the factors that influence producers' planned sales cause either a change in the quantity supplied or a change in supply. Equivalently, they cause either a movement along the supply curve or a shift of the supply curve.

Figure 3.5 myeconlab

An Increase in Supply

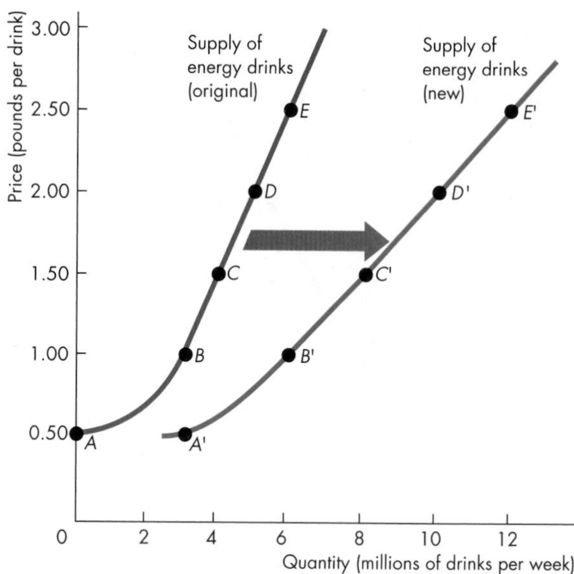

	Original supply schedule Original technology			New supply schedule New technology	
	Price (pounds per drink)	Quantity supplied (millions of drinks per week)		Price (pounds per drink)	Quantity supplied (millions of drinks per week)
A	0.50	0	*A'*	0.50	3
B	1.00	3	*B'*	1.00	6
C	1.50	4	*C'*	1.50	8
D	2.00	5	*D'*	2.00	10
E	2.50	6	*E'*	2.50	12

A change in any influence on sellers' plans other than the price of the good itself results in a new supply schedule and a shift of the supply curve. For example, with a new cost-saving technology for producing energy drinks, the supply of energy drinks changes.

At a price of £1.50 a drink, 4 million energy drinks a week are supplied when producers use the old technology (row *C* of the table) and 8 million energy drinks a week are supplied when producers use the new technology. An advance in technology *increases* the supply of energy drinks. The supply curve shifts *rightward*, as shown by the shift arrow and the resulting red curve.

A point on the supply curve shows the quantity supplied at a given price. A movement along the supply curve shows a **change in the quantity supplied**. The entire supply curve shows supply. A shift of the supply curve shows a *change in supply*.

Figure 3.6 illustrates and summarizes these distinctions. If the price of a good falls and other things remain the same, the quantity supplied of that good decreases and there is a movement down the supply curve S_0. If the price of a good rises and other things remain the same, the quantity supplied increases and there is a movement up the supply curve S_0. When any other influence on selling plans changes, the supply curve shifts and there is a *change in supply*. If the supply curve is S_0 and if production costs fall, supply increases and the supply curve shifts to the red supply curve S_1. If production costs rise, supply decreases and the supply curve shifts to the red supply curve S_2.

Figure 3.6 

A Change in the Quantity Supplied versus a Change in Supply

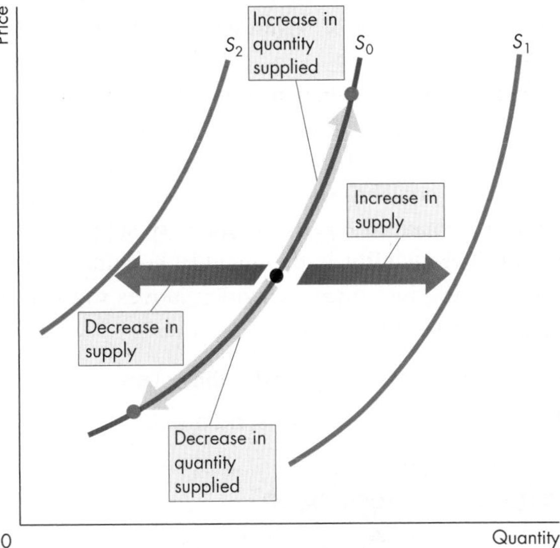

When the price of the good changes, there is a movement along the supply curve and *a change in the quantity supplied,* shown by the blue arrows on supply curve S_0.

When any other influence on selling plans changes, there is a shift of the supply curve and a *change in supply*. An increase in supply shifts the supply curve rightward (from S_0 *to* S_1), and a decrease in supply shifts the supply curve leftward (from S_0 *to* S_2).

Table 3.2

The Supply of Energy Drinks

The Law of Supply

The quantity of energy drinks supplied

Decreases if:	*Increases if:*
◆ The price of an energy drink falls	◆ The price of an energy drink rises

Changes in Supply

The supply of energy drinks

Decreases if:	*Increases if:*
◆ The price of a factor of production used to produce energy drinks rises	◆ The price of a factor of production used to produce energy drinks falls
◆ The price of a substitute in production rises	◆ The price of a substitute in production falls
◆ The price of a complement in production falls	◆ The price of a complement in production rises
◆ The price of an energy drink is expected to rise in the future	◆ The price of an energy drink is expected to fall in the future
◆ The number of energy drink producers decreases	◆ The number of energy drink producers increases
◆ A negative technology change in energy drink production occurs	◆ A positive technology change in energy drink production occurs

Review Quiz

Study Plan 3.3

1. Define the quantity supplied of a good or service.
2. What is the law of supply and how do we illustrate it?
3. What does the supply curve tell us about the price at which firms will supply a given quantity of a good?
4. List all the influences on selling plans, and for each influence say whether it changes supply.
5. What happens to the quantity of Palm Pilots supplied and the supply of Palm Pilots if the price of a Palm Pilot falls?

Your next task is to use what you've learned about demand and supply and see how prices and quantities are determined.

Market Equilibrium

We have seen that when the price of a good rises, the quantity demanded *decreases* and the quantity supplied *increases*. We are now going to see how prices coordinate the plans of buyers and sellers and achieve equilibrium.

Equilibrium is a situation in which opposing forces balance each other. Equilibrium in a market occurs when the price balances the plans of buyers and sellers. The **equilibrium price** is the price at which the quantity demanded equals the quantity supplied. The **equilibrium quantity** is the quantity bought and sold at the equilibrium price. A market moves towards its equilibrium because:

- Price regulates buying and selling plans.
- Price adjusts when plans don't match.

Price as a Regulator

The price of a good regulates the quantities demanded and supplied. If the price is too high, the quantity supplied exceeds the quantity demanded. If the price is too low, the quantity demanded exceeds the quantity supplied. There is one price at which the quantity demanded equals the quantity supplied. Let's work out what that price is.

Figure 3.7 shows the market for energy drinks. The table shows the demand schedule (from Figure 3.1) and the supply schedule (from Figure 3.4). If the price of an energy drink is 50 pence, the quantity demanded is 9 million drinks a week, but no drinks are supplied. There is a shortage of 9 million drinks a week. This shortage is shown in the final column of the table. At a price of £1.00 an energy drink, there is still a shortage, but only of 3 million drinks a week. If the price of an energy drink is £2.50, the quantity supplied is 6 million drinks a week, but the quantity demanded is only 2 million. There is a surplus of 4 million drinks a week. The one price at which there is neither a shortage nor a surplus is £1.50 an energy drink. At that price, the quantity demanded equals the quantity supplied: 4 million drinks a week. The equilibrium price is £1.50 an energy drink, and the equilibrium quantity is 4 million drinks a week.

Figure 3.7 shows that the demand curve and the supply curve intersect at the equilibrium price of £1.50 an energy drink. At each price *above* £1.50 an energy drink, there is a surplus. For example, at £2.00 an energy drink, the surplus is 2 million drinks a week, as

Figure 3.7

Equilibrium

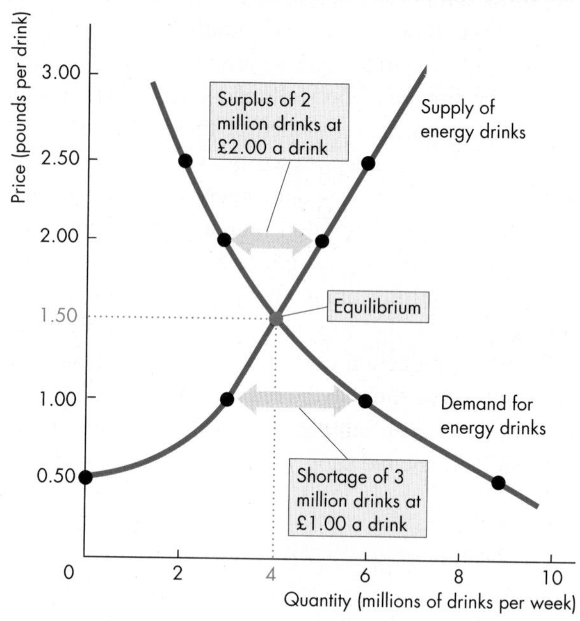

Price (pounds per drink)	Quantity demanded	Quantity supplied	Shortage (–) or surplus (+)
	(millions of drinks per week)		
0.50	9	0	–9
1.00	6	3	–3
1.50	**4**	**4**	**0**
2.00	3	5	+2
2.50	2	6	+4

The table lists the quantities demanded and quantities supplied as well as the shortage or surplus of drinks at each price. If the price is £1.00 an energy drink, 6 million drinks a week are demanded and 3 million are supplied. There is a shortage of 3 million drinks a week, and the price rises.

If the price is £2.00 an energy drink, 3 million drinks a week are demanded and 5 million are supplied. There is a surplus of 2 million drinks a week, and the price falls.

If the price is £1.50 an energy drink, 4 million drinks a week are demanded and 4 million are supplied. There is neither a shortage nor a surplus. Neither buyers nor sellers have any incentive to change the price. The price at which the quantity demanded equals the quantity supplied is the equilibrium price. The equilibrium quantity is 4 million drinks a week.

shown by the blue arrow. At each price *below* £1.50 an energy drink, there is a shortage of drinks. For example, at £1.00 an energy drink, the shortage is 3 million drinks a week, as shown by the red arrow.

Price Adjustments

You've seen that if the price is below equilibrium, there is a shortage and that if the price is above equilibrium, there is a surplus. But can we count on the price to change and eliminate a shortage or surplus? We can, because such price changes are beneficial to both buyers and sellers. Let's see why the price changes when there is a shortage or a surplus.

A Shortage Forces the Price Up

Suppose the price of an energy drink is £1. Consumers plan to buy 6 million drinks a week, and producers plan to sell 3 million drinks a week. Consumers can't force producers to sell more than they plan, so the quantity that is actually offered for sale is 3 million drinks a week. In this situation, powerful forces operate to increase the price and move it towards the equilibrium price. Some producers, noticing many unsatisfied consumers, raise the price. Some producers increase their output. As producers push the price up, the price rises towards its equilibrium. The rising price reduces the shortage because it decreases the quantity demanded and increases the quantity supplied. When the price has increased to the point at which there is no longer a shortage, the forces moving the price stop operating and the price comes to rest at its equilibrium.

A Surplus Forces the Price Down

Suppose the price of an energy drink is £2. Producers plan to sell 5 million drinks a week, and consumers plan to buy 3 million drinks a week. Producers cannot force consumers to buy more than they plan, so the quantity that is actually bought is 3 million drinks a week. In this situation, powerful forces operate to lower the price and move it towards the equilibrium price. Some producers, unable to sell the quantities of drinks they planned to sell, cut their prices. In addition, some producers scale back production. As producers cut the price, the price falls towards its equilibrium. The falling price decreases the surplus because it increases the quantity demanded and decreases the quantity supplied. When the price has fallen to the point at which there is no longer a surplus, the forces moving the price stop operating and the price comes to rest at its equilibrium.

The Best Deal Available for Buyers and Sellers

When the price is below equilibrium, it is forced up towards the equilibrium. Why don't buyers resist the increase and refuse to buy at the higher price? Because they value the good more highly than the current price and they cannot satisfy all their demands at the current price. In some markets – for example, the auction markets that operate on eBay – the buyers might even be the ones who force the price up by offering to pay higher prices.

When the price is above equilibrium, it is bid down towards the equilibrium. Why don't sellers resist this decrease and refuse to sell at the lower price? Because their minimum supply price is below the current price and they cannot sell all they would like to at the current price. Normally, it is the sellers who force the price down by offering lower prices to gain market share.

At the price at which the quantity demanded equals the quantity supplied neither buyers nor sellers can do business at a better price. Buyers pay the highest price they are willing to pay for the last unit bought, and sellers receive the lowest price at which they are willing to supply the last unit sold.

When people freely make offers to buy and sell and when buyers try to buy at the lowest possible price and sellers try to sell at the highest possible price, the price at which trade takes place is the equilibrium price – the price at which the quantity demanded equals the quantity supplied. The price coordinates the plans of buyers and sellers, and no one has an incentive to change it.

Review Quiz

Study Plan 3.4

1. What is the equilibrium price of a good or service?
2. Over what range of prices does a shortage arise?
3. Over what range of prices does a surplus arise?
4. What happens to the price when there is a shortage?
5. What happens to the price when there is a surplus?
6. Why is the price at which the quantity demanded equals the quantity supplied the equilibrium price?
7. Why is the equilibrium price the best deal available for both buyers and sellers?

Predicting Changes in Price and Quantity

The demand and supply theory that we have just studied provides us with a powerful way of analyzing influences on prices and the quantities bought and sold. According to the theory, a change in price stems from a change in demand, a change in supply, or a change in both demand and supply. Let's look first at the effects of a change in demand.

An Increase in Demand

When more and more people join health clubs, the demand for energy drinks increases. The table in Figure 3.8 shows the original and new demand schedules for energy drinks (the same as those in Figure 3.2) as well as the supply schedule of energy drinks.

When demand increases, there is a shortage at the original equilibrium price of £1.50 an energy drink. To eliminate the shortage, the price must rise. The price that makes the quantity demanded and quantity supplied equal again is £2.50 an energy drink. At this price, 6 million drinks are bought and sold each week. When demand increases, both the price and the quantity increase.

Figure 3.8 shows these changes. The figure shows the original demand for and supply of energy drinks. The original equilibrium price is £1.50 an energy drink, and the quantity is 4 million drinks a week. When demand increases, the demand curve shifts rightward. The equilibrium price rises to £2.50 an energy drink, and the quantity supplied increases to 6 million drinks a week, as highlighted in the figure. There is an *increase in the quantity supplied* but *no change in supply* – a movement along, but no shift of, the supply curve.

A Decrease in Demand

We can reverse this change in demand. Start at a price of £2.50 an energy drink with 6 million drinks a week, and then work out what happens if demand decreases to its original level. Such a decrease in demand might arise from a fall in the price of an energy bar (a substitute for energy drinks).

The decrease in demand shifts the demand curve *leftward*. The equilibrium price falls to £1.50 an energy drink, and the equilibrium quantity decreases to 4 million drinks a week.

Figure 3.8 myeconlab

The Effects of a Change in Demand

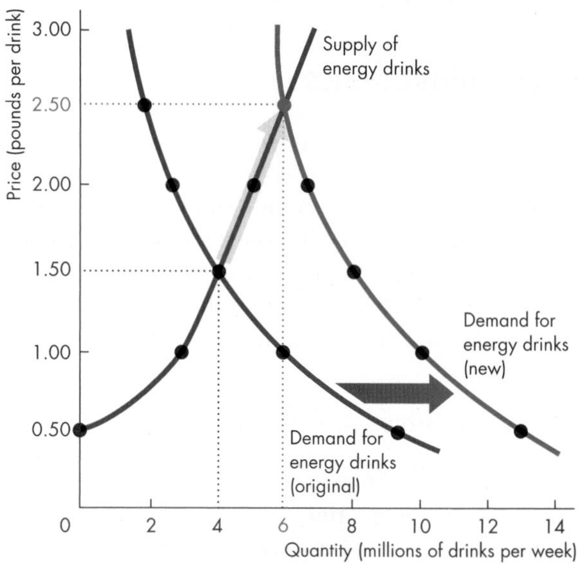

Price (pounds per drink)	Quantity demanded (millions of drinks per week) Original	New	Quantity supplied (millions of drinks per week)
0.50	9	13	0
1.00	6	10	3
1.50	**4**	8	**4**
2.00	3	7	5
2.50	2	**6**	**6**

Initially, the demand for energy drinks is the blue demand curve. The equilibrium price is £1.50 an energy drink, and the equilibrium quantity is 4 million drinks a week. With more health-conscious people doing more exercise, the demand for energy drinks increases and the demand curve shifts rightward to become the red curve.

At £1.50 an energy drink, there is now a shortage of 4 million drinks a week. The price of an energy drink rises to a new equilibrium of £2.50. As the price rises to £2.50, the quantity supplied increases – shown by the blue arrow on the supply curve – to the new equilibrium quantity of 6 million drinks a week. Following an increase in demand, the quantity supplied increases but supply does not change – the supply curve does not shift.

We can now make our first two predictions:

1 **When demand increases, both the price and the quantity increase.**

2 **When demand decreases, both the price and the quantity decrease.**

An Increase in Supply

When the producers of energy drinks switch to new cost-saving technology, the supply of energy drinks increases. The table in Figure 3.9 shows the new supply schedule (the same as that in Figure 3.5). What are the new equilibrium price and quantity? The answer is highlighted in the table: the price falls to £1.00 an energy drink, and the quantity increases to 6 million a week. You can see why by looking at the quantities demanded and supplied at the original price of £1.50 an energy drink. The quantity supplied at that price is 8 million drinks a week, and there is a surplus of drinks. The price falls. Only when the price is £1.00 an energy drink does the quantity supplied equal the quantity demanded.

Figure 3.9 illustrates the effect of an increase in supply. It shows the demand curve and the original and new supply curves. The equilibrium price is £1.50 a drink, and the quantity is 4 million drinks a week. When the supply increases, the supply curve shifts rightward. The equilibrium price falls to £1.00 a drink, and the quantity demanded increases to 6 million drinks a week, highlighted in the figure. There is an *increase in the quantity demanded* but *no change in demand* – a movement along, but no shift of, the demand curve.

A Decrease in Supply

Start out at a price of £1.00 an energy drink with 6 million drinks a week being bought and sold. Then suppose that the cost of labour or raw materials rises and the supply of energy drinks decreases. The decrease in supply shifts the supply curve *leftward*. The equilibrium price rises to £1.50 an energy drink, and the equilibrium quantity decreases to 4 million drinks a week.

We can now make two more predictions:

1 **When supply increases, the quantity increases and the price falls.**

2 **When supply decreases, the quantity decreases and the price rises.**

Figure 3.9 myeconlab

The Effects of a Change in Supply

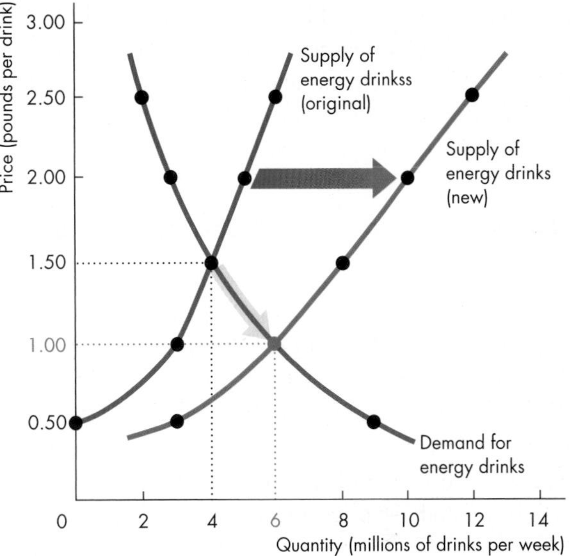

Price (pounds per drink)	Quantity demanded (millions of drinks per week)	Quantity supplied (millions of drinks per week)	
		Original	New
0.50	9	0	3
1.00	**6**	3	**6**
1.50	**4**	**4**	8
2.00	3	5	10
2.50	2	6	12

Initially, the supply of energy drinks is shown by the blue supply curve. The equilibrium price is £1.50 a drink, and the equilibrium quantity is 4 million drinks a week. When the new cost-saving technology is adopted, the supply of energy drinks increases and the supply curve shifts *rightward* to become the red curve.

At £1.50 an energy drink, there is now a surplus of 4 million drinks a week. The price of an energy drink falls to a new equilibrium of £1.00 a drink. As the price falls to £1.00 a drink, the quantity demanded increases – shown by the blue arrow on the demand curve – to the new equilibrium quantity of 6 million drinks a week. Following an increase in supply, the quantity demanded increases but demand does not change – the demand curve does not shift.

All Possible Changes in Demand and Supply

You can now predict the effects of a change in either demand or supply on the price and the quantity. And with what you've learned, you can also predict what happens if both demand and supply change together. To see what happens when both demand and supply change, let's summarize what you already know.

Change in Demand with No Change in Supply

The first row of Figure 3.10, parts (a), (b) and (c), summarizes the effects of a change in demand with no change in supply. In part (a), with no change in either demand or supply, neither the price nor the quantity changes. With an increase in demand and no change in supply in part (b), both the price and quantity increase. And with a decrease in demand and no change in supply in part (c), both the price and the quantity decrease.

Change in Supply with No Change in Demand

The first column of Figure 3.10, parts (a), (d) and (g), summarizes the effects of a change in supply with no change in demand. With an increase in supply and no change in demand in part (d), the price falls and quantity increases. And with a decrease in supply and no change in demand in part (g), the price rises and the quantity decreases.

Increase in Both Demand and Supply

You've seen that an increase in demand raises the price and increases the quantity. And you've seen that an increase in supply lowers the price and increases the quantity. Figure 3.10(e) combines these two changes. Because either an increase in demand or an increase in supply increases the quantity, the quantity also increases when both demand and supply increase. But the effect on the price is uncertain. An increase in demand raises the price and an increase in supply lowers the price, so we can't say whether the price will rise or fall when both demand and supply increase. We need to know the magnitudes of the changes in demand and supply to predict the effects on price. In the example in Figure 3.10(e), the price does not change. But notice that if demand increases by slightly more than the amount shown in the figure, the price will rise. And if supply increases by slightly more than the amount shown in the figure, the price will fall.

Decrease in Both Demand and Supply

Figure 3.10(i) shows the case in which demand and supply both decrease. For the same reasons as those we've just reviewed, when both demand and supply decrease, the quantity decreases, and again the direction of the price change is uncertain.

Decrease in Demand and Increase in Supply

You've seen that a decrease in demand lowers the price and decreases the quantity. And you've seen that an increase in supply lowers the price and increases the quantity. Figure 3.10(f) combines these two changes. Both the decrease in demand and the increase in supply lower the price. So the price falls. But a decrease in demand decreases the quantity and an increase in supply increases the quantity, so we can't predict the direction in which the quantity will change unless we know the magnitudes of the changes in demand and supply. In the example in Figure 3.10(f), the quantity does not change. But notice that if demand decreases by slightly more than the amount shown in the figure, the quantity will decrease. And if supply increases by slightly more than the amount shown in the figure, the quantity will increase.

Increase in Demand and Decrease in Supply

Figure 3.10(h) shows the case in which demand increases and supply decreases. Now, the price rises, and again the direction of the quantity change is uncertain.

Review Quiz

Study Plan 3.5

1 What is the effect on the price of an MP3 player (such as the iPod) and the quantity of MP3 players if (a) the price of a PC falls or (b) the price of an MP3 download rises or (c) more firms produce MP3 players or (d) electronics workers' wages rise or (e) any two of these events occur together? (Draw the diagrams!)

Now that you understand the demand and supply model and the predictions that it makes, try to get into the habit of using the model in your everyday life. To see how you might use the model, take a look at *Reading Between the Lines* on pp. 74–75, which uses the tools of demand and supply to explain the rising price of copper in 2006.

Figure 3.10

The Effects of All the Possible Changes in Demand and Supply

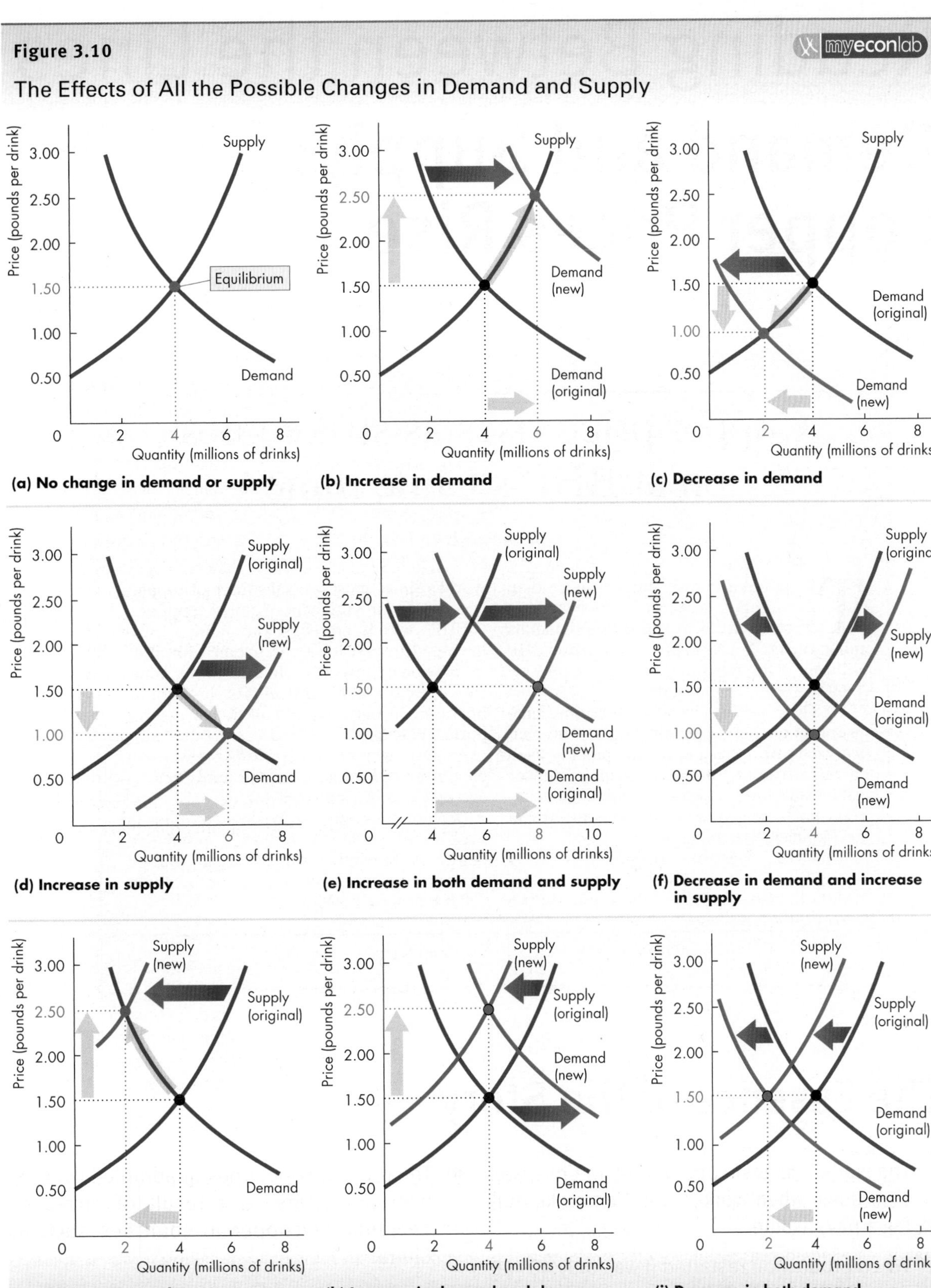

Reading Between the Lines

Demand and Supply: Copper Prices Rise

The Independent, 22 August 2006

Copper price rises as strike goes on at BHP's Chile mine

David Prosser

The price of copper jumped more than 2 per cent yesterday after striking workers at the world's largest metals mine rejected a new pay offer from BHP Billiton. A metric tonne of copper rose by $160 to $7,640 (£84 to £4,030) . . .

. . . The company has benefited from a quadrupling of the copper price over the past five years with demand for the metal – used in infrastructure projects to make power cables and water pipes – soaring from countries such as China, with large industrial development programmes.

This year, the price of copper is up by about 75 per cent, as global demand has continued to rise. The Escondida mine is the world's single most crucial source of copper; accounting for 8 per cent of global supplies.

BHP, which co-owns the mine . . . has managed to restore some production after initially being forced to shut down the mine. However, the company admits the mine is operating at between 40 and 60 per cent of normal capacity.

Analysts warned the upwards pressure on copper prices would continue until BHP . . . agreed a deal with its workforce. . . .

Demand for copper is expected to outstrip supply this year. A report . . . published before the Escondida dispute began, warned demand would exceed production by about 200,000 tonnes in 2006.

The Essence of the Story

- The world's largest copper mine in Chile was shut down when workers went on strike during a pay dispute.
- When production restarted it was only 40–60 per cent of normal output.
- The price of copper increased by £84 a tonne during the dispute.
- The price of copper has quadrupled over the past five years as a result of increased demand for copper in countries such as China.
- Analysts expect the price of copper to keep rising even if the dispute is settled.

Economic Analysis

- Figure 1 shows the world market for copper in August 2006, before the strike at the BHP Chile copper mine. The supply curve is S_0 and the demand curve is D_0. The equilibrium price is £3,946 per tonne and the equilibrium quantity is Q_0.
- The strike at the Chile copper mine decreased world supply. The supply curve in Figure 1 shifted leftward from S_0 to S_1.
- The world demand curve was constant at D in Figure 1 during the week of the strike.
- The equilibrium price of copper during the strike increased from £3,946 to £4,030 a tonne and the equilibrium quantity fell from Q_0 to Q_1.
- If the mine returns to full capacity, the supply curve in Figure 1 will shift back from S_1 to S_0 and the price will fall back to £3,046, other things remaining the same.
- The world demand for copper has been increasing each year as countries such as China expand industrial production.
- Figure 2 shows the world market for copper between 2005 and 2007. Without the effect of the strike, world supply is constant at S_0.
- In December 2005, the world demand for copper was D_{05}. During 2006, demand increased and by August 2006, the demand curve had shifted rightward to D_{06}. The equilibrium price had risen by 75 per cent from £2,255 to £3,946 and the equilibrium quantity had increased from Q_0 to Q_1.
- World demand increased in 2007 and the demand curve shifted rightward from D_{06} to D_{07}.
- By the start of 2007, and with no price change, demand was expected to exceed supply by 200,000 tones. Figure 2 shows this shortage as $(Q_2 - Q_1)$ at a price of £3,946 per tonne.
- A shortage raises the price. The copper price could rise a further 75 per cent to £6,906 per tonne.

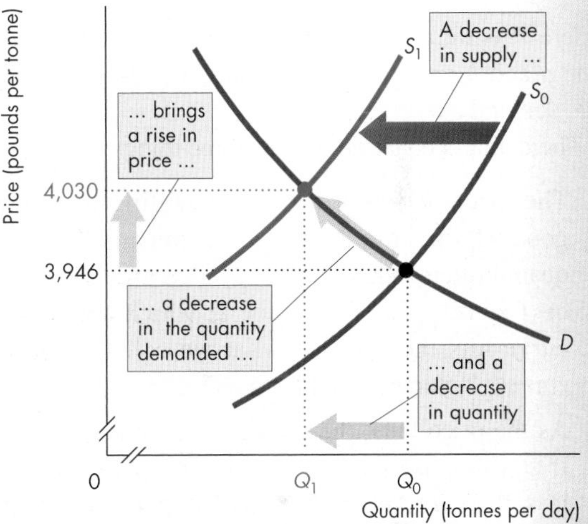

Figure 1 The effect of a strike

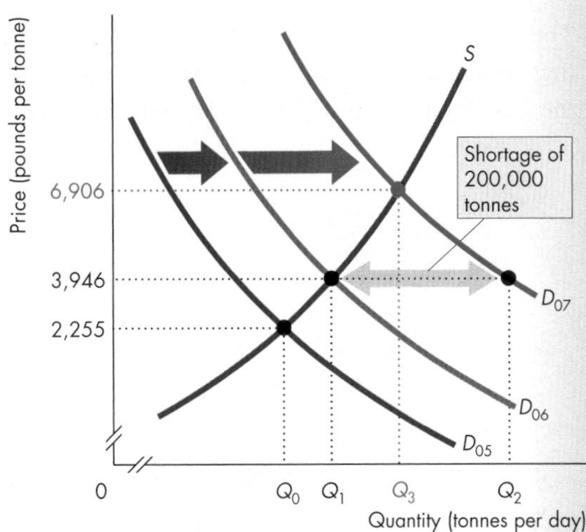

Figure 2 The effect of rising world demand

Mathematical Note

Demand, Supply and Equilibrium

Demand Curve

The law of demand states that as the price of a good or service falls, the quantity demanded of it increases. We illustrate the law of demand by setting out a demand schedule, drawing a graph of the demand curve, or writing down an equation. When the demand curve is a straight line, the following linear equation describes it:

$$P = a - bQ_D$$

where P is the price and Q_D is the quantity demanded. The a and b are positive constants. Figure 1 illustrates this demand curve.

The demand equation tells us three things:

1 The price at which no one is willing to buy the good (Q_D is zero). That is, if the price is a, then the quantity demanded is zero. You can see the price a on Figure 1. It is the price at which the demand curve hits the y-axis – what we call the demand curve's "intercept on the y-axis".

2 As the price falls, the quantity demanded increases. If Q_D is a positive number, then the price P must be less than a. And as Q_D gets larger, the price P becomes smaller. That is, as the quantity increases, the maximum price that buyers are willing to pay for the good falls.

3 The constant b tells us how fast the maximum price that someone is willing to pay for the good falls as the quantity increases. That is, the constant b tells us about the steepness of the demand curve. The equation tells us that the slope of the demand curve is $-b$.

Supply Curve

The law of supply states that as the price of a good or service rises, the quantity supplied of it increases. We illustrate the law of supply by setting out a supply schedule, drawing a graph of the supply curve, or writing down an equation. When the supply curve is a straight line, the following linear equation describes it:

$$P = c + dQ_S$$

where P is the price and Q_S the quantity supplied. The c and d are positive constants. Figure 2 illustrates this supply curve.

The supply equation tells us three things:

1 The price at which no one is willing to sell the good (Q_S is zero). If the price is c, then the quantity supplied is zero. You can see the price c on Figure 2. It is the price at which the supply curve hits the y-axis – what we call the supply curve's "intercept on the y-axis".

2 As the price rises, the quantity supplied increases. If Q_S is a positive number, then the price P must be greater than c. And as Q_S increases, the price P gets larger. That is, as the quantity increases, the minimum price that sellers are willing to accept rises.

3 The constant d tells us how fast the minimum price at which someone is willing to sell the good rises as the quantity increases. That is, the constant d tells us about the steepness of the supply curve. The equation tells us that the slope of the supply curve is d.

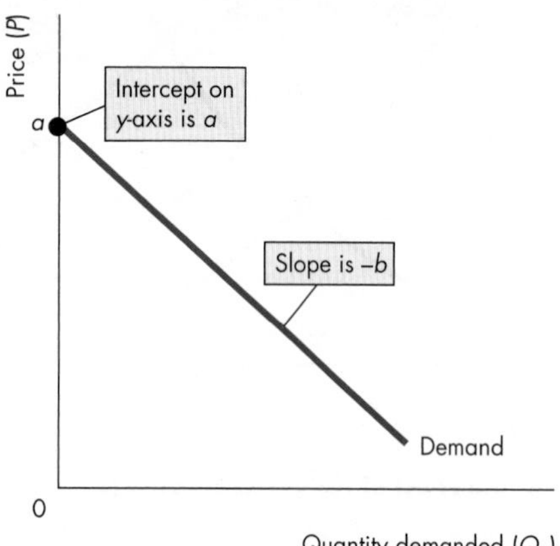

Figure 1 The demand curve

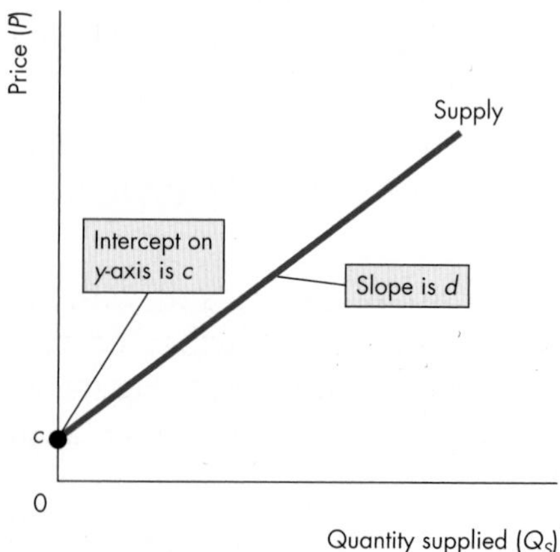

Figure 2 The supply curve

Market Equilibrium

Demand and supply determine market equilibrium. Figure 3 shows the equilibrium price (P^*) and equilibrium quantity (Q^*) at the intersection of the demand curve and the supply curve.

We can use the equations to find the equilibrium price and equilibrium quantity. The price of a good will adjust until the quantity demanded equals the quantity supplied. That is:

$$Q_D = Q_S$$

So at the equilibrium price (P^*) and equilibrium quantity (Q^*):

$$Q_D = Q_S = Q^*$$

To find the equilibrium price and equilibrium quantity: first substitute Q^* for Q_D in the demand equation and Q^* for Q_S in the supply equation. Then the price is the equilibrium price (P^*), which gives:

$$P^* = a - bQ^*$$

$$P^* = c + dQ^*$$

Notice that:

$$a - bQ^* = c + dQ^*$$

Now solve for Q^*:

$$a - c = bQ^* + dQ^*$$

$$a - c = (b + d)Q^*$$

$$Q^* = \frac{a - c}{b + d}$$

To find the equilibrium price (P^*) substitute for Q^* in either the demand equation or the supply equation.

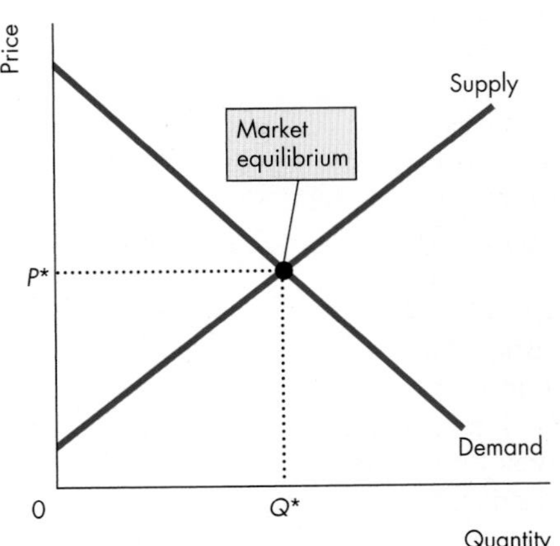

Figure 3 Market equilibrium

Using the demand equation:

$$P^* = a - b\left(\frac{a - c}{b + d}\right)$$

$$P^* = \frac{a(b + d) - b(a - c)}{b + d}$$

$$P^* = \frac{ad + bc}{b + d}$$

Alternatively, using the supply equation:

$$P^* = c + d\left(\frac{a - c}{b + d}\right)$$

$$P^* = \frac{c(b + d) + d(a - c)}{b + d}$$

$$P^* = \frac{ad + bc}{b + d}$$

An Example

The demand for ice cream is:

$$P = 400 - 2Q_D$$

The supply of ice cream is:

$$P = 100 + 1Q_S$$

The price of an ice cream is expressed in pence and the quantities are expressed in ice creams per day.

To find the equilibrium price (P^*) and equilibrium quantity (Q^*), substitute Q^* for Q_D and Q_S and substitute P^* for P.

That is:

$$P^* = 400 - 2Q^*$$

$$P^* = 100 + 1Q^*$$

Now solve for Q^*:

$$400 - 2Q^* = 100 + 1Q^*$$

$$300 = 3Q^*$$

$$Q^* = 100$$

And:

$$P^* = 400 - 2(100) = 200$$

The equilibrium price is £2 an ice cream, and the equilibrium quantity is 100 ice creams per day.

Summary

Key Points

Markets and Prices (p. 58)

- A competitive market is one that has so many buyers and sellers that no one can influence the price.
- Opportunity cost is a relative price.
- Demand and supply determine relative prices.

Demand (pp. 59–63)

- Demand is the relationship between the quantity demanded of a good and its price when all other influences on buying plans remain the same.
- The higher the price of a good, other things remaining the same, the smaller is the quantity demanded – the law of demand.
- Demand depends on income, the prices of substitutes and complements, expected future income, expected future prices, population, and preferences.

Supply (pp. 64–67)

- Supply is the relationship between the quantity supplied of a good and its price when all other influences on selling plans remain the same.
- The higher the price of a good, other things remaining the same, the greater is the quantity supplied – the law of supply.
- Supply depends on the prices of factors of production used to produce a good, the prices of related goods produced, expected future prices, the number of suppliers, and technology.

Market Equilibrium (pp. 68–69)

- At the equilibrium price, the quantity demanded equals the quantity supplied.
- At prices above equilibrium, there is a surplus and the price falls.
- At prices below equilibrium, there is a shortage and the price rises.

Predicting Changes in Price and Quantity (pp. 70–73)

- An increase in demand brings a rise in the price and an increase in the quantity supplied. A decrease in demand brings a fall in the price and a decrease in the quantity supplied.
- An increase in supply brings a fall in the price and an increase in the quantity demanded. A decrease in supply brings a rise in the price and a decrease in the quantity demanded.
- An increase in demand and an increase in supply bring an increased quantity but an uncertain price change. An increase in demand and a decrease in supply bring a higher price but an uncertain change in quantity.

Key Figures

Figure 3.1 The Demand Curve, 60
Figure 3.3 A Change in the Quantity Demanded versus a Change in Demand, 63
Figure 3.4 The Supply Curve, 65
Figure 3.6 A Change in the Quantity Supplied versus a Change in Supply, 67
Figure 3.7 Equilibrium, 68
Figure 3.10 The Effects of All Possible Changes in Demand and Supply, 73

Key Terms

Change in demand, 60
Change in supply, 65
Change in the quantity demanded, 63
Change in the quantity supplied, 67
Competitive market, 58
Complement, 61
Demand, 59
Demand curve, 60
Equilibrium price, 68
Equilibrium quantity, 68
Inferior good, 61
Law of demand, 59
Law of supply, 64
Money price, 58
Normal good, 61
Quantity demanded, 59
Quantity supplied, 64
Relative price, 58
Substitute, 61
Supply, 64
Supply curve, 64

Problems

Tests, Study Plan and Solutions* 

1 A notice in the *Edgehill Advertiser* in 1862 offered the following exchanges:

1 yard of cloth for 1 pound of bacon
2 yards of cloth for 1 pound of butter
4 yards of cloth for 1 pound of wool
8 yards of cloth for 1 bushel of salt

a What is the price of butter in terms of wool?

b If the price of bacon was 20 pence per pound, what do you predict was the price of butter?

c If the price of bacon was 20 pence per pound and the price of salt was £2.00 per bushel, do you think anyone would be willing to trade cloth for salt on the terms advertised above?

2 Classify the following pairs of goods and services as substitutes, complements, substitutes in production, or complements in production.

a Bottled water and health club memberships

b Chips and baked potatoes

c Leather purses and leather shoes

d Vans and trucks

e Diet coke and regular coke

f Low-fat milk and full-fat cream

3 "As more people buy computers, the demand for Internet service increases and the price of Internet service decreases. The fall in the price of Internet service decreases the supply of Internet service." Is this statement true or false? Explain your answer.

4 What is the effect on the price of a recordable CD and the quantity of recordable CDs sold if:

a The price of an MP3 download rises?

b The price of an iPod falls?

c The supply of CD players increases?

d Consumers' incomes increase?

e Workers who make CDs get a pay raise?

f The events in (a) and (e) occur together?

5 The following events occur one at a time:

(i) The price of crude oil rises.

(ii) The price of a car rises.

(iii) All speed limits on motorways are abolished.

(iv) Robots cut car production costs.

Which of these events will increase or decrease and state which occurs?

a The demand for gasoline

b The supply of gasoline

c The quantity of gasoline demanded

d The quantity of gasoline supplied

6 The figure illustrates the market for pizza.

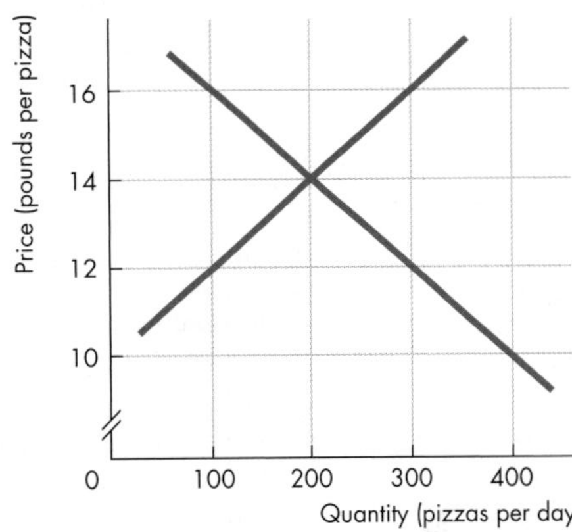

Label the curves in the figure and explain what happens if the price is:

a £16 a pizza

b £12 a pizza

7 The table sets out the demand and supply schedules for chewing gum.

Price (pence per packet)	Quantity demanded (millions of packets a week)	Quantity supplied (millions of packets a week)
20	180	60
30	160	80
40	140	100
50	120	120
60	100	140
70	80	160
80	60	180

a Draw a graph of the chewing gum market and mark in the equilibrium price and quantity.

b Suppose that chewing gum is 70 pence a packet. Describe the situation in the chewing gum market and explain how the price of chewing gum adjusts.

c Suppose that the price of chewing gum is 30 pence a packet. Describe the situation in the chewing gum market and explain how the price adjusts.

* Solutions to odd-numbered problems are provided.

d A fire destroys some chewing-gum factories and the quantity of chewing gum supplied decreases by 40 million packets a week at each price. Explain what happens in the market for chewing gum and illustrate the changes in your graph of the chewing gum market.

e If an increase in the teenage population increases the quantity of gum demanded by 40 million packs a week at each price at the same time as the fire occurs, what are the new equilibrium price and quantity of gum? Illustrate these changes in your graph.

8 The table sets out demand and supply schedules for crisps.

Price (pence per bag)	Quantity demanded	Quantity supplied
	(millions of bags per week)	
50	160	130
60	150	140
70	140	150
80	130	160
90	120	170
100	110	180

a Draw a graph of the crisps market and mark in the equilibrium price and quantity.

b Describe the situation in the market for crisps and explain how the price adjusts if crisps are 60 pence a bag.

c If a new dip increases the quantity of crisps demanded by 30 million bags per week at each price, how does the price and quantity of crisps change?

d If a virus destroys potato crops and the quantity of crisps supplied decreases by 40 million bags a week at each price at the same time as the dip comes onto the market. Crisps are made from potato. How does the price and quantity of crisps change?

Critical Thinking

1 Study *Reading Between the Lines* on pp. 74–75 and then:

a Explain why the price of copper increased during the dispute?

b Explain why the price of copper is expected to keep rising in the future.

c Draw demand and supply curves to illustrate the effect of resolving the dispute and getting the mine back to full capacity.

2 **Eurostar boosted by *Da Vinci Code***

Eurostar, the train service linking London to Paris, . . . said on Wednesday first-half sales rose 6 per cent, boosted by devotees of the blockbuster Da Vinci movie.

CNN, 26 July 2006

a Explain how *Da Vinci Code* fans helped to raise Eurostar's sales.

b CNN commented on the "fierce competition from budget airlines". Explain the effect of this competition on Eurostar's sales.

c What markets in Paris do you think these fans influenced? Explain the influence on three markets.

Web Activities

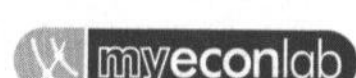

Links to Websites

1 Obtain data on the prices and quantities of bananas in 1985 and 2002.

a Make a demand–supply graph to illustrate the market for bananas in 1985 and 2002.

b On the graph show the changes in demand and supply and the changes in the quantity demanded and the quantity supplied that are consistent with the price and quantity data.

c Why do you think demand and supply changed?

2 Obtain data on the price of oil since 2000.

a Describe how the price of oil has changed.

b Draw a demand–supply graph to explain what happens to the price when supply increases or decreases and demand is unchanged.

c What do you predict would happen to the price of oil if a new drilling technology permitted deeper ocean sources to be used?

d What do you predict would happen to the price of oil if a clean and safe nuclear technology were developed?

e What do you predict would happen to the price of oil if cars were powered by batteries instead of by internal combustion engines?

3 Read the *Economics in History* on Discovering the Laws of Demand and Supply and then:

a Explain why there was so much interest in trying to understand the principles of demand and supply during the period of the Industrial Revolution.

b Explain why Alfred Marshall is considered to be the "father" of modern economics.

CHAPTER

4

Elasticity

After studying this chapter you will be able to:

- Define, calculate and explain the factors that influence the price elasticity of demand
- Define, calculate and explain the factors that influence the cross elasticity of demand and the income elasticity of demand
- Define, calculate and explain the factors that influence the elasticity of supply

Squeezing Out Revenue

A new juice bar opens and offers low-price smoothies that attract lots of customers. But is that a smart decision? Could the firm generate more revenue with higher prices and fewer customers? If a café opens next door, by how much will the price of a smoothie have to fall to avoid losing customers to the new rival? This chapter introduces tools that help to answer questions like these. And *Reading Between the Lines* at the end of the chapter shows you how these same tools enable us to interpret trends in the market for recorded music.

Price Elasticity of Demand

You know that when supply increases, the equilibrium price falls and the equilibrium quantity increases. But does the price fall by a large amount and the quantity increase by a little? Or will the price barely fall and the quantity increase by a large amount?

The answer depends on the responsiveness of the quantity demanded to a change in price. You can see why by studying Figure 4.1, which shows two possible scenarios in a local smoothie market. Figure 4.1(a) shows one scenario and Figure 4.1(b) shows the other.

In both cases, supply is initially S_0. In part (a), the demand for smoothies is shown by the demand curve D_A. In part (b), the demand for smoothies is shown by the demand curve D_B. Initially, in both cases, the price is £3 a smoothie and the quantity of smoothie produced and consumed is 10 smoothies an hour.

Now three new juice bars open and the supply of smoothies increases. The supply curve shifts rightward to S_1. In case (a), the price falls by £2 to £1 a smoothie, and the quantity increases by only 5 to 15 smoothies an hour. In contrast, in case (b), the price falls by only £1 to £2 a smoothie and the quantity doubles to 20 smoothies an hour.

The different outcomes arise from differing degrees of responsiveness of the quantity demanded to a change in price. But what do we mean by responsiveness? One answer is slope. The slope of demand curve D_A is steeper than the slope of demand curve D_B.

In this example, we can compare the slopes of the two demand curves. But we can't always do so. The reason is that the slope of a demand curve depends on the units in which we measure the price and quantity. And we often must compare the demand curves for different goods and services that are measured in unrelated units. For example, a juice bar operator might want to compare the demand for smoothies with the demand for sandwiches. Which quantity demanded is more responsive to a price change?

This question can't be answered by comparing the slopes of two demand curves. The units of measurement of smoothies and sandwiches are unrelated. But the question *can* be answered with a measure of responsiveness that is independent of units of measurement. Elasticity is such a measure.

The **price elasticity of demand** is a units-free measure of the responsiveness of the quantity demanded of a good to a change in its price, when all other influences on buyers' plans remain the same.

Figure 4.1

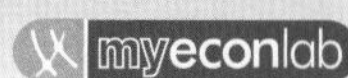

How a Change in Supply Changes Price and Quantity

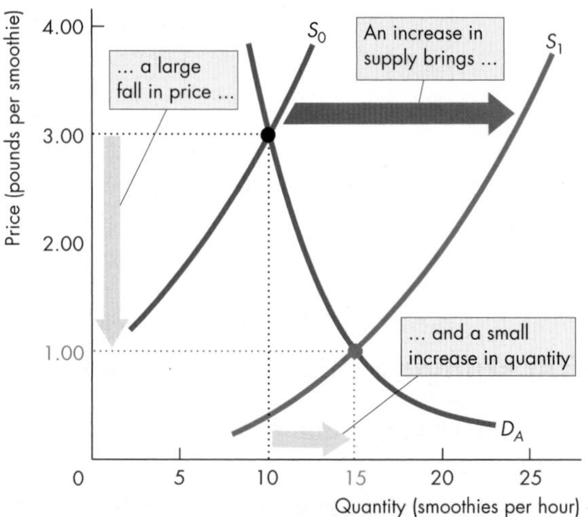

(a) Large price change and small quantity change

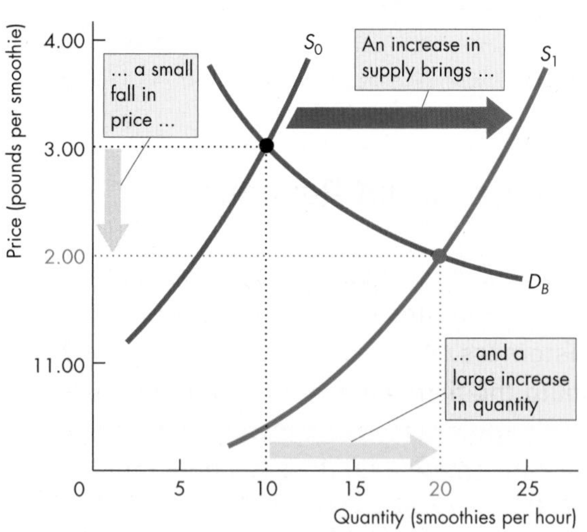

(b) Small price change and large quantity change

Initially, the price is £3 a smoothie and the quantity sold is 10 smoothies an hour. Then supply increases from S_0 to S_1. In part (a), the price falls by £2 to £1 a smoothie, and the quantity increases by 5 to 15 smoothies an hour.

In part (b), the price falls by only £1 to £2 a smoothie, and the quantity increases by 10 to 20 smoothies an hour. The price change is smaller and the quantity change is larger in case (b) than in case (a). The quantity demanded is more responsive to the price change in case (b) than in case (a).

Calculating Price Elasticity of Demand

We calculate the *price elasticity of demand* by using the formula:

$$\text{Price elasticity of demand} = \frac{\text{Percentage change in quantity demanded}}{\text{Percentage change in price}}$$

To use this formula, we need to know the quantities demanded at different prices, other things remaining the same. Suppose we have the data on prices and quantities demanded of smoothies and we calculate the price elasticity of demand for smoothies.

Figure 4.2 zooms in on the demand curve for smoothies and shows how the quantity demanded responds to a small change in price. Initially, the price is £3.10 a smoothie and 9 smoothies an hour are sold – the original point in the figure. The price then falls to £2.90 a smoothie, and the quantity demanded increases to 11 smoothies an hour – the new point in the figure. When the price falls by 20 pence a smoothie, the quantity demanded increases by 2 smoothies an hour.

To calculate the price elasticity of demand, we express the changes in price and quantity as percentages of the *average price* and *average quantity*. By using the average price and average quantity, we calculate the elasticity at a point on the demand curve midway between the original point and the new point.

The original price is £3.10 and the new price is £2.90, so the average price is £3. The 20 pence price decrease is 6.67 per cent of the average price. That is:

$$\Delta P/P_{AVE} = (£0.20/£3.00) \times 100 = 6.67\%$$

The original quantity demanded is 9 smoothies and the new quantity demanded is 11 smoothies, so the average quantity demanded is 10 smoothies. The increase in the quantity demanded of 2 smoothies is 20 per cent of the average quantity. That is:

$$\Delta Q/Q_{AVE} = (2/10) \times 100 = 20\%$$

So the price elasticity of demand, which is the percentage change in the quantity demanded (20 per cent) divided by the percentage change in price (6.67 per cent) is 3. That is:

$$\text{Price elasticity of demand} = \frac{\%\Delta Q}{\%\Delta P} = \frac{20\%}{6.67\%} = 3$$

Figure 4.2 myeconlab

Calculating the Elasticity of Demand

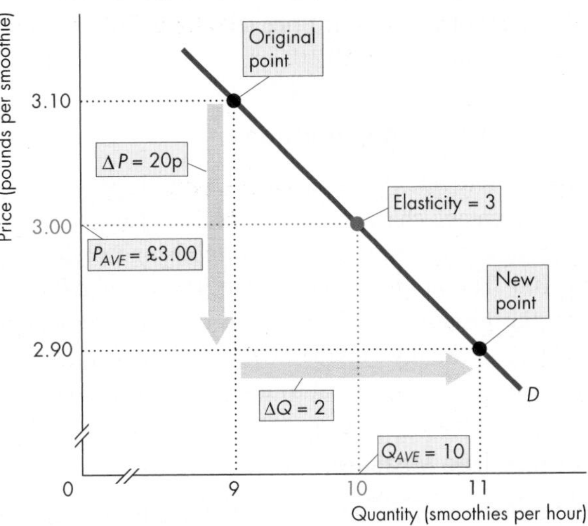

The elasticity of demand is calculated by using the formula:*

$$\text{Price elasticity of demand} = \frac{\text{Percentage change in quantity demanded}}{\text{Percentage change in price}} = \frac{\%\Delta Q}{\%\Delta P} = \frac{\Delta Q/Q_{AVE}}{\Delta P/P_{AVE}} = \frac{2/10}{0.20/3.00} = 3$$

This calculation measures the elasticity at an average price of £3.00 a smoothie and an average quantity of 10 smoothies an hour.

* In the formula, the Greek letter delta (Δ) stands for "change in" and %Δ stands for "percentage change in".

Average Price and Quantity

We use the *average* price and *average* quantity because it gives the most precise measurement of elasticity – midway between the original and new point. If the price falls from £3.10 to £2.90, the 20 pence price change is 6.45 per cent of £3.10. The 2 smoothies change in quantity is 22.2 per cent of 9 smoothies, the original quantity. So if we use these numbers, the price elasticity of demand is 22.2 divided by 6.45, which equals 3.44. If the price *rises* from £2.90 to £3.10, the 20 pence price change is 6.9 per cent of £2.90. The 2 smoothies change in quantity is 18.2 per cent of 11 smoothies, the original quantity. If we use these numbers, the price elasticity of demand is 18.2 divided by 6.9, which equals 2.64.

By using percentages of the *average* price and *average* quantity, we get the same value for the elasticity regardless of whether the price falls from £3.10 to £2.90 or rises from £2.90 to £3.10.

Percentages and Proportions

When we divide the percentage change in quantity by the percentage change in price, the 100s cancel. A percentage change is a *proportionate* change multiplied by 100. The proportionate change in price is $\Delta P/P_{AVE}$, and the proportionate change in quantity demanded is $\Delta Q/Q_{AVE}$. So if we divide $\Delta Q/Q_{AVE}$ by $\Delta P/P_{AVE}$, we get the same answer as we get by using percentage changes.

A Units-free Measure

Elasticity is a *units-free measure* because the percentage change in each variable is independent of the units in which the variable is measured. And the ratio of the two percentages is a number without units.

Minus Sign and Elasticity

When the price of a good *rises*, the quantity demanded *decreases* along the demand curve. Because a *positive* change in price brings a *negative* change in the quantity demanded, the price elasticity of demand is a negative number. But it is the magnitude, or *absolute value*, of the price elasticity of demand that tells us how responsive – how elastic – demand is. To compare price elasticities of demand, we use the magnitude of the elasticity and ignore the minus sign.

Inelastic and Elastic Demand

Figure 4.3 shows three demand curves that cover the entire range of possible elasticities of demand. In Figure 4.3(a), the quantity demanded is constant regardless of the price. If the quantity demanded remains constant when the price changes, then the price elasticity of demand is zero and the good is said to have a **perfectly inelastic demand**. One good that has a very low price elasticity of demand (perhaps zero over some price range) is insulin. Insulin is of such importance to some diabetics that if the price rises or falls, they do not change the quantity they buy.

If the percentage change in the quantity demanded equals the percentage change in price, then the price elasticity equals 1 and the good is said to have a **unit elastic demand**. The demand in Figure 4.3(b) is an example of unit elastic demand.

Between the cases shown in Figure 4.3(a) and Figure 4.3(b) is the general case in which the percentage change in the quantity demanded is less than the percentage change in price. In this case, the price elasticity of demand is between zero and 1 and the

Figure 4.3

Inelastic and Elastic Demand

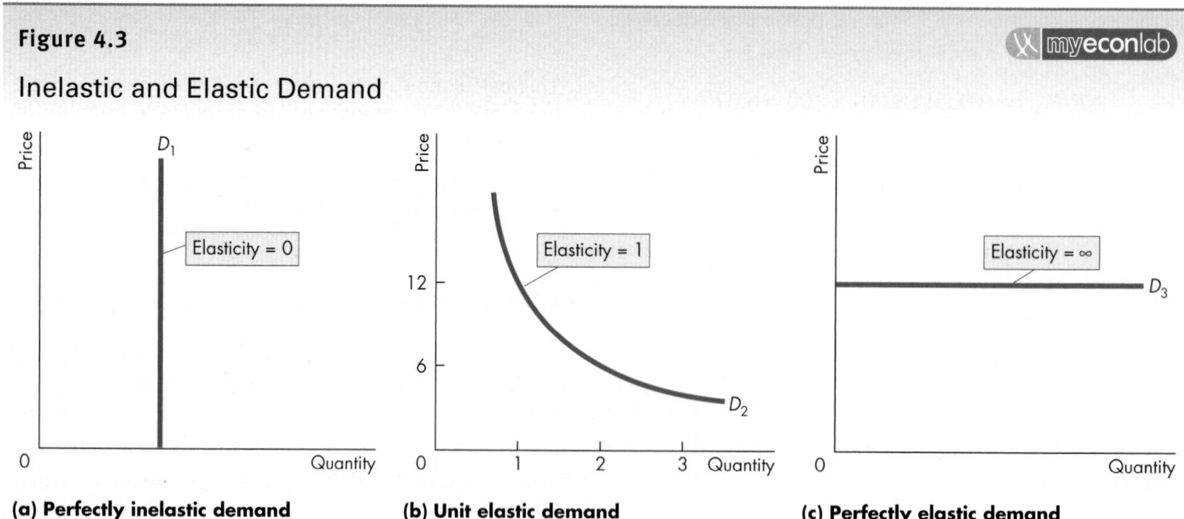

(a) Perfectly inelastic demand **(b) Unit elastic demand** **(c) Perfectly elastic demand**

Each demand illustrated here has a constant elasticity. The demand curve in part (a) illustrates the demand for a good that has a zero price elasticity of demand. The demand curve in part (b) illustrates the demand for a good with a unit price elasticity of demand. And the demand curve in part (c) illustrates the demand for a good with an infinite price elasticity of demand.

good is said to have an **inelastic demand**. Food and housing are examples of goods with inelastic demand.

If the quantity demanded changes by an infinitely large percentage in response to a tiny price change, then the price elasticity of demand is infinity and the good is said to have a **perfectly elastic demand**. Figure 4.3(c) shows a perfectly elastic demand. An example of a good that has a very high elasticity of demand (almost infinite) is a salad from two campus machines located side by side. If the two machines offer the same salads for the same price, some people buy from one machine and some from the other. But if one machine's price is higher than the other's, by even a small amount, no one will buy from the machine with the higher price. Salads from the two machines are perfect substitutes.

Between the cases in Figure 4.3(b) and Figure 4.3(c) is the general case in which the percentage change in the quantity demanded exceeds the percentage change in price. In this case, the price elasticity of demand is greater than 1 and the good is said to have an **elastic demand**. Cars and furniture are examples of goods that have elastic demand.

Elasticity Along a Linear Demand Curve

Elasticity and slope are not the same, but they are related. To understand how they are related, let's look at elasticity along a straight-line demand curve – a demand curve that has a constant slope.

Figure 4.4 illustrates the calculation of elasticity along a straight-line demand curve. First, suppose the price falls from £5 to £3 a smoothie. The quantity demanded increases from zero to 10 smoothies an hour. The average price is £4 a smoothie, and the average quantity is 5 smoothies. So:

$$\text{Price elasticity of demand} = \frac{\Delta Q/Q_{AVE}}{\Delta P/P_{AVE}} = \frac{10/5}{2/4} = 4$$

That is, the price elasticity of demand at an average price of £4 a smoothie is 4.

Next, suppose that the price falls from £3 to £2 a smoothie. The quantity demanded increases from 10 to 15 smoothies an hour. The average price is now £2.50 a smoothie, and the average quantity is 12.5 smoothies an hour.

So:

$$\text{Price elasticity of demand} = \frac{5/12.5}{1/2.5} = 1$$

That is, the price elasticity of demand at an average price of £2.50 a smoothie is 1.

Finally, suppose that the price falls from £2 to zero. The quantity demanded increases from 15 to 25 smoothies an hour. The average price is now £1 and the average quantity is 20 smoothies an hour. So:

$$\text{Price elasticity of demand} = \frac{10/20}{2/1} = 1/4$$

That is, the price elasticity of demand at an average price of £1 a smoothie is 1/4.

You've now seen how elasticity changes along a straight-line demand curve. At the mid-point of the curve, demand is unit elastic. At prices above the mid-point, demand is elastic. At prices below the mid-point, demand is inelastic.

Figure 4.4 myeconlab

Elasticity Along a Linear Demand Curve

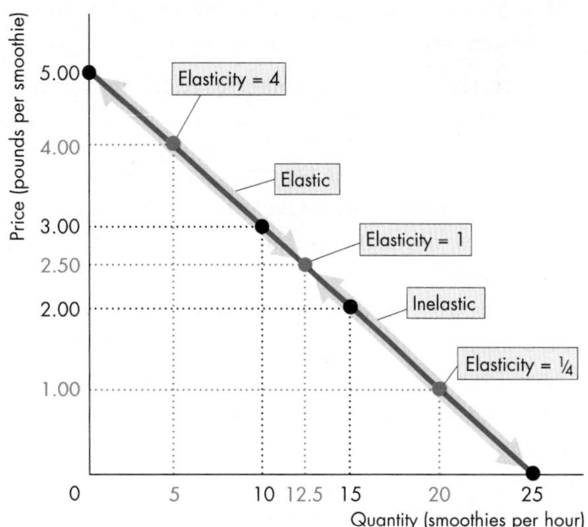

On a linear demand curve, elasticity decreases as the price falls and the quantity demanded increases. Demand is unit elastic at the mid-point of the demand curve (elasticity is 1). At prices above the mid-point, demand is elastic; at prices below the mid-point, demand is inelastic.

Total Revenue and Elasticity

The **total revenue** from the sale of a good equals the price of the good multiplied by the quantity sold. When a price changes, total revenue also changes. But a rise in the price does not always increase total revenue. The change in total revenue depends on the elasticity of demand in the following way:

1 If demand is elastic, a 1 per cent price cut increases the quantity sold by more than 1 per cent and total revenue increases.

2 If demand is inelastic, a 1 per cent price cut increases the quantity sold by less than 1 per cent and total revenue decreases.

3 If demand is unit elastic, a 1 per cent price cut increases the quantity sold by 1 per cent and so total revenue does not change.

Figure 4.5 shows how we can use this relationship between elasticity and total revenue to estimate elasticity using the total revenue test. The **total revenue test** is a method of estimating the price elasticity of demand by observing the change in total revenue that results from a change in the price, when all other influences on the quantity sold remain the same.

1 If a price cut increases total revenue, demand is elastic.

2 If a price cut decreases total revenue, demand is inelastic.

3 If a price cut leaves total revenue unchanged, demand is unit elastic.

In Figure 4.5(a), over the price range from £5 to £2.50, demand is elastic. Over the price range from £2.50 to zero, demand is inelastic. At a price of £2.50, demand is unit elastic.

Figure 4.5(b) shows total revenue. At a price of £5, the quantity sold is zero (part a), so total revenue is zero (part b). At a price of zero, the quantity demanded is 25 smoothies an hour and total revenue is again zero.

A price cut in the elastic range brings an increase in total revenue – the percentage increase in the quantity demanded is greater than the percentage decrease in price.

A price cut in the inelastic range brings a decrease in total revenue – the percentage increase in the quantity demanded is less than the percentage decrease in price. When demand is unit elastic, total revenue is at a maximum.

Figure 4.5 myeconlab

Elasticity and Total Revenue

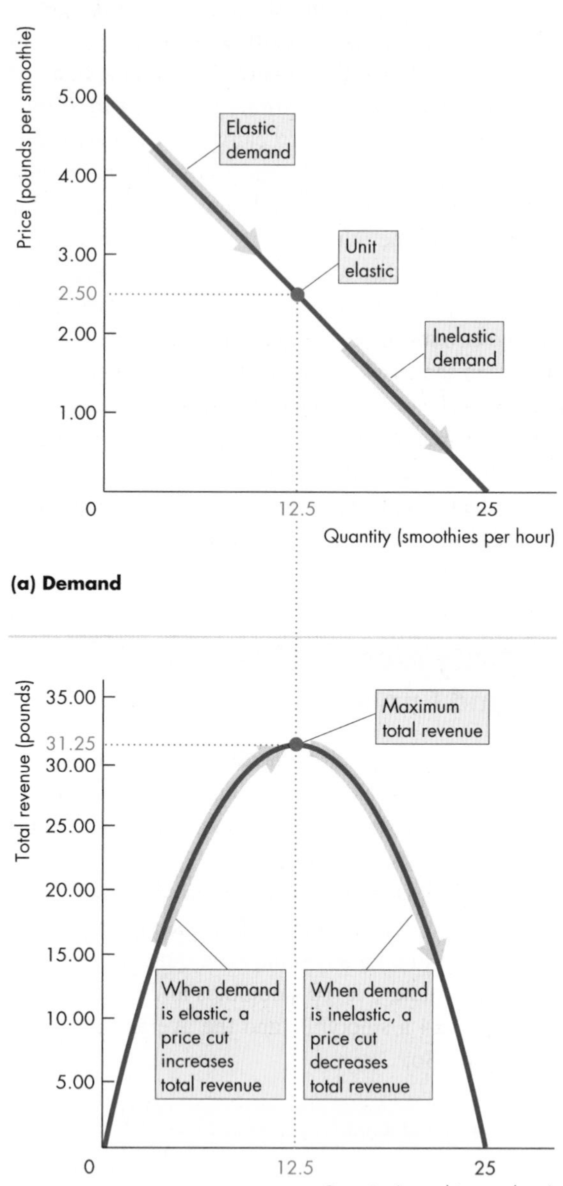

When demand is elastic, in the price range from £5 to £2.50, a decrease in price in part (a) brings an increase in total revenue in part (b). When demand is inelastic, in the price range from £2.50 to zero, a decrease in price in part (a) brings a decrease in total revenue in part (b). When demand is unit elastic, at a price of £2.50 in part (a), total revenue is at a maximum in part (b).

Your Expenditure and Your Elasticity

When a price changes, the change in your expenditure on the good depends on *your* elasticity of demand.

1 If your demand is elastic, a 1 per cent price cut increases the quantity you buy by more than 1 per cent and your expenditure on the item increases.
2 If your demand is inelastic, a 1 per cent price cut increases the quantity you buy by less than 1 per cent and your expenditure on the item decreases.
3 If your demand is unit elastic, a 1 per cent price cut increases the quantity you buy by 1 per cent and your expenditure on the item does not change.

So if you spend more on an item when its price falls, your demand for that item is elastic; if you spend the same amount, your demand is unit elastic; and if you spend less, your demand is inelastic.

The Factors That Influence the Elasticity of Demand

What makes the demand for some goods elastic and the demand for others inelastic? The magnitude of the elasticity of demand depends on:

- Closeness of substitutes
- Proportion of income spent on the good
- Time elapsed since a price change

Closeness of Substitutes

The closer the substitutes for a good or service, the more elastic is the demand for it. For example, oil has substitutes but none that are currently very close (imagine a steam-driven, coal-fuelled aircraft). So the demand for oil is inelastic.

The degree of substitutability between two goods also depends on how narrowly (or broadly) we define them. For example, a personal computer has no really close substitutes, but a Dell PC is a close substitute for a Gateway PC. So the elasticity of demand for personal computers is lower than that for a Dell or a Gateway.

In everyday language we call some goods, such as food and housing, *necessities* and other goods, such as exotic vacations, *luxuries*. A necessity is a good that has poor substitutes and that is crucial for our well-being, so a necessity has an inelastic demand. A luxury is a good that usually has many substitutes, so a luxury has an elastic demand. Box 4.1 lists and discusses some UK price elasticities of demand.

Box 4.1

Some Real-world Price Elasticities of Demand

The table shows some estimates of price elasticities of demand in the United Kingdom. These values range from 1.4 for fresh meat, the most elastic in the table, to zero for bread, the least elastic in the table. Fresh meat has many substitutes such as frozen meat and fish, so the demand for fresh meat is elastic. Green vegetables don't have many substitutes, so the demand for green vegetables is inelastic. But a particular green vegetable such as green beans has close substitutes such as green peas and broccoli. The elasticity of demand for green vegetables is lower than the elasticity of demand for green beans.

You can see that the items with an elastic demand include luxuries (wine and spirits) while items with an inelastic demand include necessities (bread and green vegetables).

The unit elasticity of demand for services is an average of the elasticities for many different services and hides wide variation across them.

Table 1

UK Price Elasticities of Demand

Good or service	Elasticity
Elastic demand	
Fresh meat	1.4
Spirits	1.3
Wine	1.2
Unit elasticity	
Services	1.0
Cereals	1.0
Inelastic demand	
Durable goods	0.9
Fruit juice	0.8
Green vegetables	0.6
Tobacco	0.5
Beer	0.5
Bread	0.0

Sources of data: Ministry of Agriculture, Food and Fisheries, *Household Food Consumption and Expenditure*, 1992, London, HMSO; C. Godfrey, "Modelling Demand", *Preventing Alcohol and Tobacco Problems*, Vol. 1, (A. Maynard and P. Tether, eds), Avebury, 1990; J. Muellbauer, "Testing the Barten Model of Household Composition Effects and the Cost of Children", *Economic Journal*, September 1977.

Proportion of Income Spent on the Good

Other things remaining the same, the greater the proportion of income spent on a good, the more elastic is the demand for it.

Think about your own demand for toothpaste and housing. If the price of toothpaste doubles, you consume almost as much as before. Your demand for toothpaste is inelastic. If the rent you pay doubles, you shriek and look for more students to share your accommodation. Your demand for housing is elastic. Why the difference? Housing takes a large proportion of your budget, and toothpaste takes only a tiny proportion. You don't like either price increase, but you hardly notice the higher price of toothpaste, while the higher rent puts your budget under severe strain.

Time Elapsed Since Price Change

The longer the time that has elapsed since a price change, the more elastic is demand. When the price of oil increased by 400 per cent during the 1970s, people barely changed the quantity of oil and petrol they bought. But gradually, as more efficient car and aeroplane engines were developed, the quantity used decreased. The demand for oil has become more elastic as more time has elapsed since that huge price hike. Similarly, when the price of a PC fell, the quantity of PCs demanded increased only slightly at first. But as more people have become better informed about the variety of ways of using a PC, the quantity of PCs bought has increased sharply. The demand for PCs has become more elastic.

Box 4.2
Price Elasticity of Demand for Food

Figure 1 shows the proportion of income spent on food and the price elasticity of demand for food in 10 countries. This figure confirms the general tendency that the larger the proportion of income spent on food, the more price elastic is the demand for food.

In a very poor country like Tanzania, where 62 per cent of income is spent on food, the price elasticity of demand for food is 0.77. In contrast, in Germany where 15 per cent of income is spent on food, the elasticity of demand for food is just 0.23. In a country that spends a large proportion of its income on food, an increase in the price of food forces people to make a bigger adjustment to the quantity of food they buy than in a country in which only a small proportion of income is spent on food.

Figure 1

Price Elasticities in 10 Countries

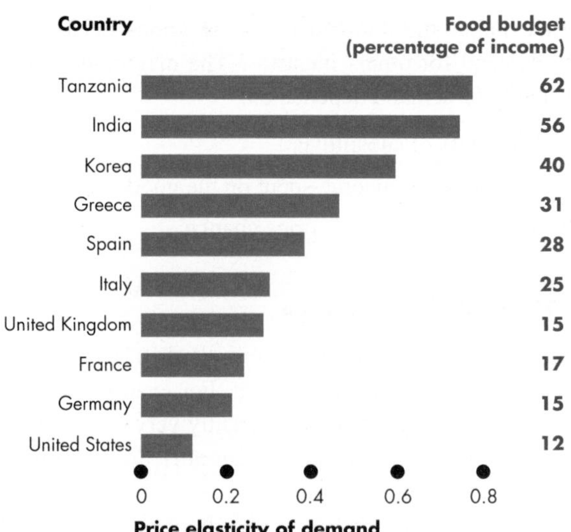

As income increases and the proportion of income spent on food decreases, the demand for food becomes less elastic.

Source of data: Henri Theil, Ching-Fan Chung and James L. Seale Jr, *Advances in Econometrics, Supplement 1, International Evidence on Consumption Patterns*. Greenwich, Connecticut, JAI Press Inc., 1989.

Review Quiz

Study Plan 4.1

1. Why do we need a units-free measure of the responsiveness of the quantity demanded of a good or service to a change in its price?
2. Can you define and calculate the price elasticity of demand?
3. Why, when we calculate the price elasticity of demand, do we express the change in price as a percentage of the *average* price and the change in quantity as a percentage of the *average* quantity?
4. What is the total revenue test and why does it work?
5. What are the main influences on the elasticity of demand that make the demand for some goods elastic and the demand for other goods inelastic?
6. Why is the demand for a luxury generally more elastic than the demand for a necessity?

You've now completed your study of the *price* elasticity of demand. Two other elasticity concepts tell us about the effects of other influences on demand. Let's look at these other elasticities of demand.

More Elasticities of Demand

Andy, who operates a juice bar, wants to know how a rise in the price of coffee at the café next door will affect the demand for his smoothies. He knows that smoothies and coffee are substitutes and that when the price of coffee rises, the demand for smoothies increases. But by how much?

Andy also wants to know how a rise in the price of his salads will affect the demand for his smoothies. He knows that smoothies and salads are complements and that when the price of a complement of smoothies rises, the demand for smoothies decreases. But again, by how much?

To answer these questions, Andy uses the cross elasticity of demand. Let's examine this elasticity measure.

Cross Elasticity of Demand

We measure the influence of a change in the price of a substitute or complement by using the concept of the cross elasticity of demand. The **cross elasticity of demand** is a measure of the responsiveness of the demand for a good to a change in the price of a substitute or complement, other things remaining the same. We calculate the *cross elasticity of demand* by using the formula:

$$\text{Cross elasticity of demand} = \frac{\text{Percentage change in quantity demanded}}{\text{Percentage change in price of substitute or complement}}$$

The cross elasticity of demand can be positive or negative. It is *positive* for a *substitute* and *negative* for a *complement*.

Substitutes

Suppose when the price of a coffee is £1.50, Andy sells 9 smoothies an hour. Now the price of a coffee rises to £2.50. With no change in the price of a smoothie or any other influence on buying plans, the quantity of smoothies sold increases to 11 an hour.

We use the same method that you learned when you studied the price elasticity of demand (p. 83). The change in the quantity demanded is +2 smoothies and the average quantity is 10 smoothies. So the quantity of smoothies demanded changes by 20 per cent. That is:

$$\Delta Q/Q_{AVE} = (+2/10) \times 100 = +20\%$$

The change in the price of a coffee, a substitute for a smoothie, is £1 – the new price, £2.50, minus the original price, £1.50. The average price is £2. So the price of a coffee rises by 50 per cent. That is:

$$\Delta P/P_{AVE} = (1/2) \times 100 = +50\%$$

So the cross elasticity of demand for smoothies with respect to the price of a coffee is:

$$\frac{+20\%}{+50\%} = 0.4$$

Because a *rise* in the price of coffee brings a *increase* in the demand for smoothies, the cross elasticity of demand for smoothies with respect to the price of coffee is *positive*. Both the price of the substitute and the quantity of the good change in the same direction. Figure 4.6 illustrates the cross elasticity of demand. Smoothies and coffees are substitutes. Because they are substitutes, when the price of a coffee *rises*, the demand for smoothies *increases*. The demand curve for smoothie shifts rightward from D_0 to D_1.

Figure 4.6 myeconlab

Cross Elasticity of Demand

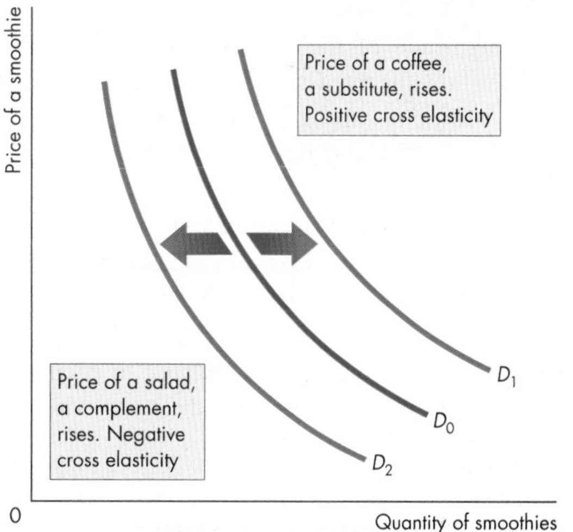

A coffee is a *substitute* for a smoothie. When the price of a coffee rises, the demand for smoothies increases and the demand curve for smoothie shifts rightward from D_0 to D_1. The cross elasticity of the demand is *positive*.

A salad is a *complement* of a smoothie. When the price of a salad rises, the demand for smoothies decreases and the demand curve for smoothies shifts leftward from D_0 to D_2. The cross elasticity of the demand is *negative*.

Complements

Now suppose that the price of smoothie is constant and 11 smoothies an hour are sold. Then the price of a salad rises from £1.50 to £2.50. No other influence on buying plans changes and the quantity of smoothies sold decreases to 9 an hour.

The change in the quantity demanded is the opposite of what we've just calculated (again as percentages of the average quantity and average price): the quantity of smoothies demanded decreases by 20 per cent (–20%).

The change in the price of a salad, a complement of smoothie, is the same as the percentage change in the price of a coffee that we've just calculated: the price of a salad rises by 50 per cent (+50%). So the cross elasticity of demand for smoothies with respect to the price of a salad is:

$$\frac{-20\%}{+50\%} = -0.4$$

Because smoothies and salads are complements, when the price of a salad *rises*, the demand for smoothies *decreases*. The demand curve for smoothie shifts leftward from D_0 to D_2. Because a *rise* in the price of a salad brings an *decrease* in the demand for smoothies, the cross elasticity of demand for smoothies with respect to the price of a salad is *negative*. The price and quantity change in *opposite* directions.

The magnitude of the cross elasticity of demand determines how far the demand curve shifts. The larger the cross elasticity (absolute value), the greater is the change in demand and the larger is the shift in the demand curve.

If two items are close substitutes, such as two brands of spring water, the cross elasticity is large. If two items are close complements, such as fish and chips, the cross elasticity is large.

If two items are somewhat unrelated to each other, such as newspapers and smoothies, the cross elasticity is small – perhaps even zero.

Income Elasticity of Demand

Suppose that the economy is expanding and people are enjoying rising incomes. This prosperity is bringing an increase in the demand for most types of goods and services. But by how much will the demand for smoothies increase? The answer depends on the **income elasticity of demand**, which is a measure of the responsiveness of the demand for a good or service to a change in income, other things remaining the same.

The income elasticity of demand is calculated by using the formula:

$$\text{Income elasticity of demand} = \frac{\text{Percentage change in quantity demanded}}{\text{Percentage change in income}}$$

Income elasticities of demand can be positive or negative and fall into three interesting ranges:

- Greater than 1 (*normal* good, income elastic)
- Positive and less than 1 (*normal* good, income inelastic)
- Negative (*inferior* good)

Income Elastic Demand

Suppose that the price of smoothie is constant and 9 smoothies an hour are sold. Then incomes rise from £475 to £525 a week and the quantity of smoothies sold increases to 11 an hour. The change in the quantity demanded is 2 smoothies. The average quantity is 10 smoothies, so the quantity demanded increases by 20 per cent. The change in income is £50 and the average income is £500, so incomes increase by 10 per cent. The income elasticity of demand for smoothies is:

$$\frac{20\%}{10\%} = 2$$

Because the income elasticity of demand is greater than 1, the demand for smoothies is income elastic. *When the demand for a good is income elastic, as income increases, the percentage of income spent on that good increases.*

Income Inelastic Demand

If the percentage increase in the quantity demanded is positive and less than the percentage increase in income, demand is income inelastic. *When the demand for a good is income inelastic, as income increases, the percentage of income spent on that good decreases.*

Inferior Goods

If the quantity demanded decreases as income increases, the income elasticity of demand is negative, and the good is an inferior good. The amount spent on an inferior good decreases as income increases. Goods in this category include small motorcycles, potatoes and rice. Low-income consumers buy most of these goods.

Box 4.3
Real-world Income Elasticities of Demand

Table 1 shows some estimates of the income elasticities of demand in the United Kingdom. The demand for a necessity such as fresh meat and green vegetables is income inelastic, while the demand for luxury goods such as wines and spirits is income elastic. The demand for some goods such as tobacco and bread have negative income elasticities, so they are classified as inferior goods.

What is a necessity or a luxury depends on the level of income. For people with low income, food and clothing can be luxuries. So the *level* of income has a big effect on income elasticities of demand.

Figure 1 shows this effect on the income elasticity of demand for food in 10 countries. In countries with low incomes, such as Tanzania and India, the income elasticity of demand for food is high, while in the high-income countries of Europe and North America, the income elasticity of demand for food is much lower.

The numbers in the figure tell us that a 10 per cent increase in income leads to about a 7.5 per cent increase in demand for food of in India, a 3 per cent increase in France, and a less than 2 per cent increase in the United States.

Table 1

Some UK Income Elasticities

Good or service	Elasticity
Income elastic demand	
Wine	2.6
Services	1.8
Spirits	1.7
Durable goods	1.5
Income inelastic demand	
Fruit juice	0.9
Beer	0.6
Green vegetables	0.1
Fresh meat	0.0
Cereals	0.0
Inferior goods	
Tobacco	−0.1
Bread	−0.3

Sources of data: Ministry of Agriculture, Food and Fisheries, *Household Food Consumption and Expenditure*, 1992, London, HMSO; C. Godfrey, "Modelling Demand", *Preventing Alcohol and Tobacco Problems*, Vol. 1, (A. Maynard and P. Tether, eds), Avebury, 1990; J. Muellbauer "Testing the Barten Model of Household Composition Effects and the Cost of Children", *Economic Journal*, September 1977.

Figure 1

Income Elasticities in 10 Countries

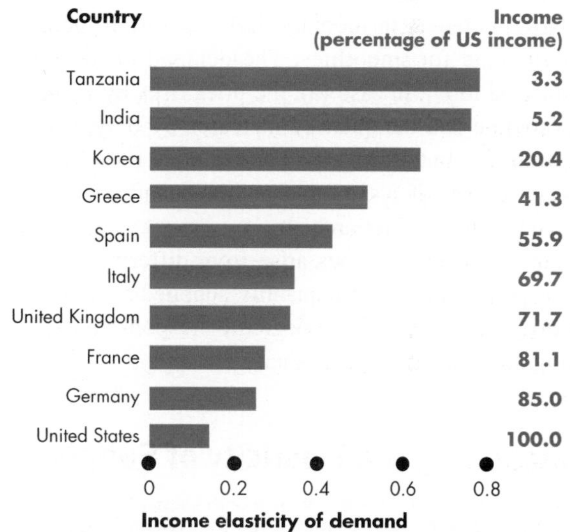

Source of data: See Box 4.2.

Review Quiz

Study Plan 4.2

1. What does the cross elasticity of demand measure?
2. What does the sign (positive versus negative) of the cross elasticity of demand tell us about the relationship between two goods?
3. What does the income elasticity of demand measure?
4. What does the sign (positive versus negative) of the income elasticity of demand tell us about a good?

You've now completed your study of the *price elasticity* of demand, the *cross elasticity* of demand and the *income elasticity* of demand. Let's now look at the other side of a market and examine the elasticity of supply.

Elasticity of Supply

You know that when demand increases, the equilibrium price rises and the equilibrium quantity increases. But does the price rise by a large amount and the quantity increase by a little? Or does the price barely rise and the quantity increase by a large amount?

The answer depends on the responsiveness of the quantity supplied to a change in price. You can see why by studying Figure 4.7, which shows two possible scenarios in a local smoothie market. Figure 4.7(a) shows one scenario, and Figure 4.7(b) shows the other.

In both cases, demand is initially D_0. In part (a), the supply of smoothie is shown by the supply curve S_A. In part (b), the supply of smoothie is shown by the supply curve S_B. Initially, in both cases, the price is £3 a smoothie and the quantity produced and consumed is 10 smoothies an hour.

Now increases in incomes and population increase the demand for smoothies. The demand curve shifts rightward to D_1. In case (a), the price rises by £2 to £5 a smoothie and the quantity increases by only 5 to 15 an hour. In contrast, in case (b), the price rises by only 20 pence to £3.20 a smoothie and the quantity increases by 10 to 20 smoothies an hour.

The different outcomes arise from differing degrees of responsiveness of the quantity supplied to a change in price. We measure the degree of responsiveness by using the concept of the elasticity of supply.

Calculating the Elasticity of Supply

The **elasticity of supply** measures the responsiveness of the quantity supplied to a change in the price of a good when all other influences on selling plans remain the same. It is calculated by using the formula:

$$\text{Price elasticity of supply} = \frac{\text{Percentage change in quantity supplied}}{\text{Percentage change in price}}$$

We again use the same method that you learned when you studied the elasticity of demand. (Refer back to p. 83 to check this method.) Let's calculate the elasticity of supply along the supply curves in Figure 4.7.

In Figure 4.7(a), when the price rises from £3 to £5, the price rise is £2 and the average price is £4, so the price rises by 50 per cent of the average price.

Figure 4.7 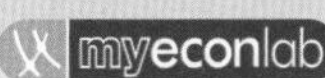

How a Change in Demand Changes Price and Quantity

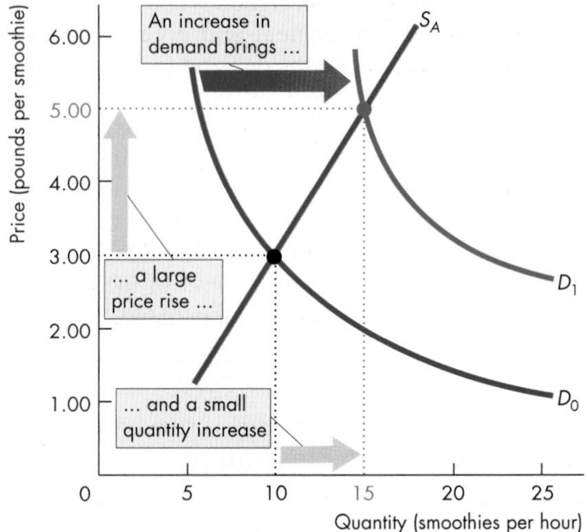

(a) Large price change and small quantity change

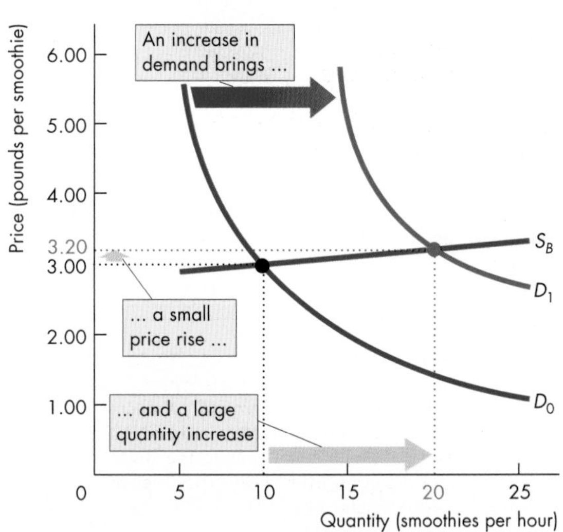

(b) Small price change and large quantity change

Initially, the price is £3 a smoothie and the quantity sold is 10 smoothies an hour. Then increases in incomes and population increase the demand for smoothies. The demand curve shifts rightward to D_1. In part (a) the price rises by £2 to £5 a smoothie, and the quantity increases by 5 to 14 smoothies an hour. In part (b), the price rises by only 20 pence to £3.20 a smoothie and the quantity increases by 10 to 20 smoothies an hour. The price change is smaller and the quantity change is larger in case (b) than in case (a). The quantity supplied is more responsive to a price change in case (b) than in case (a).

The quantity increases from 10 to 15 smoothies an hour, so the increase is 5 smoothies, the average quantity is 12.5 smoothies an hour, and the quantity increases by 40 per cent.

The elasticity of supply is equal to 40 per cent divided by 50 per cent, which equals 0.8.

In Figure 4.7(b), when the price rises from £3 to £3.20, the price rise is 20 pence and the average price is £3.10, so the price rises by 6.45 per cent of the average price. The quantity increases from 10 to 20 smoothies an hour, so the increase is 10 smoothies, the average quantity is 15 smoothies, and the quantity increases by 66.67 per cent. The elasticity of supply equals 66.67 per cent divided by 6.45 per cent, which equals 10.34.

Figure 4.8 shows the range of elasticities of supply. If the quantity supplied is fixed regardless of the price, the supply curve is vertical and the elasticity of supply is zero. Supply is perfectly inelastic. This case is shown in Figure 4.8(a). A special intermediate case is when the percentage change in price equals the percentage change in quantity. Supply is then unit elastic. This case is shown in Figure 4.8(b). No matter how steep the supply curve is, if it is linear and passes through the origin, supply is unit elastic. If there is a price at which sellers are willing to offer any quantity for sale, the supply curve is horizontal and the elasticity of supply is infinite. Supply is perfectly elastic. This case is shown in Figure 4.8(c).

The Factors That Influence the Elasticity of Supply

The magnitude of the elasticity of supply depends on:

- Resource substitution possibilities
- Time frame for the supply decision

Resource Substitution Possibilities

Some goods and services can be produced only by using unique or rare productive resources. These items have a low, even perhaps a zero, elasticity of supply. Other goods and services can be produced by using commonly available resources that could be allocated to a wide variety of alternative tasks. Such items have a high elasticity of supply.

A Van Gogh painting is an example of a good with a vertical supply curve and a zero elasticity of supply. At the other extreme, wheat can be grown on land that is almost equally good for growing corn. So it is just as easy to grow wheat as corn, and the opportunity cost of wheat in terms of forgone corn is almost constant. As a result, the supply curve of wheat is almost horizontal and its elasticity of supply is very large. Similarly, when a good is produced in many different countries (for example, wheat, sugar and beef), the supply of the good is highly elastic.

Figure 4.8 myeconlab

Inelastic and Elastic Supply

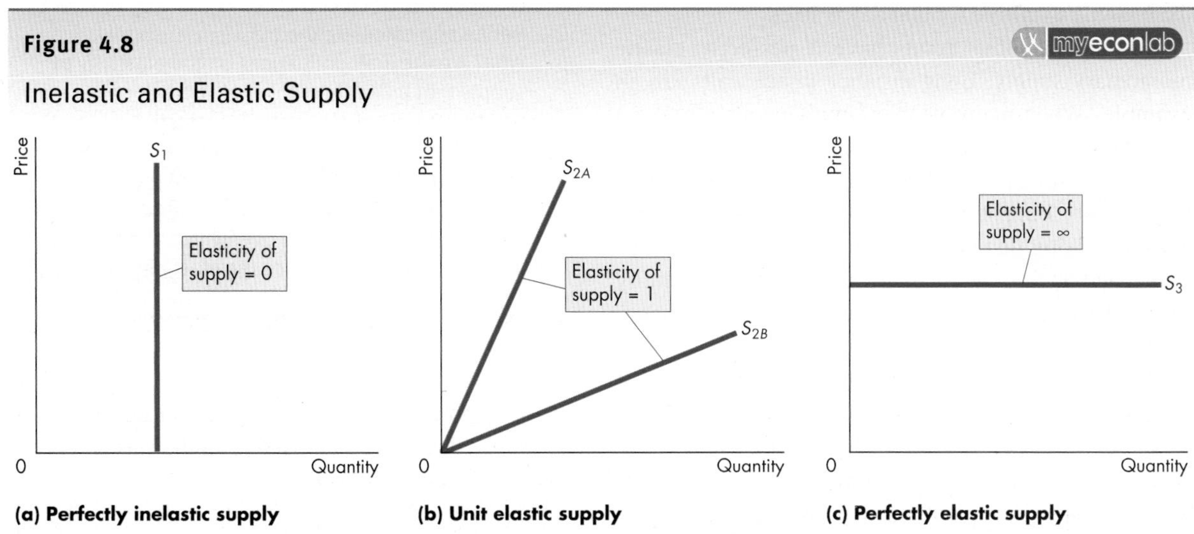

Each supply illustrated here has a constant elasticity. The supply curve in part (a) illustrates the supply of a good that has a zero elasticity of supply. The supply curve in part (b) illustrates the supply of a good with a unit elasticity of supply. All linear supply curves that pass through the origin illustrate supplies that are unit elastic. The supply curve in part (c) illustrates the supply of a good with an infinite elasticity of supply.

The supply of most goods and services lies between these two extremes. The quantity produced can be increased but only by incurring a higher cost. If a higher price is offered, the quantity supplied increases. Such goods and services have an elasticity of supply between zero and infinity.

Time Frame for Supply Decisions

To study the influence of the length of time elapsed since a price change we distinguish three time frames of supply:

1 Momentary supply
2 Long-run supply
3 Short-run supply

When the price of a good rises or falls, the *momentary supply curve* shows the response of the quantity supplied immediately following a price change.

Some goods, such as fruits and vegetables, have a perfectly inelastic momentary supply – a vertical supply curve. The quantities supplied depend on crop planting decisions made earlier. In the case of oranges, for example, planting decisions have to be made many years in advance of the crop being available.

The momentary supply curve is vertical because, on a given day, no matter what the price of oranges, producers cannot change their output. They have picked, packed and shipped their crop to market, and the quantity available for that day is fixed.

In contrast, some goods have a perfectly elastic momentary supply. Long-distance phone calls are an example. When many people simultaneously make a call, there is a big surge in the demand for telephone cables, computer switching and satellite time, and the quantity bought increases. But the price remains constant. Long-distance carriers monitor fluctuations in demand and reroute calls to ensure that the quantity supplied equals the quantity demanded without changing the price.

The *long-run supply curve* shows the response of the quantity supplied to a change in price after all the technologically possible ways of adjusting supply have been exploited. In the case of oranges, the long run is the time it takes new plantings to grow to full maturity – about 15 years. In some cases, the long-run adjustment occurs only after a completely new production plant has been built and workers have been trained to operate it – typically a process that might take several years.

The *short-run supply curve* shows how the quantity supplied responds to a price change when only *some* of the technologically possible adjustments to production have been made. The short-run response to a price change is a sequence of adjustments. The first adjustment that is usually made is in the amount of labour employed. To increase output in the short run, firms work their labour force overtime and perhaps hire additional workers. To decrease their output in the short run, firms either lay off workers or reduce their hours of work. With the passage of time, firms can make additional adjustments, perhaps training additional workers or buying additional tools and other equipment.

The short-run supply curve slopes upward because producers can take actions quite quickly to change the quantity supplied in response to a price change. For example, if the price of oranges falls, growers can stop picking and leave oranges to rot on the trees. Or if the price rises, they can use more fertilizer and improved irrigation to increase the yields of their existing trees. In the long run, they can plant more trees and increase the quantity supplied even more in response to a given price rise.

Review Quiz

Study Plan 4.3

1 Why do we need to measure the responsiveness of the quantity supplied of a good or service to a change in its price?
2 Define and calculate the elasticity of supply.
3 What are the main influences on the elasticity of supply that make the supply of some goods elastic and the supply of other goods inelastic?
4 Provide examples of goods or services whose elasticities of supply are (a) zero, (b) greater than zero but less than infinity and (c) infinity.
5 How does the time frame over which a supply decision is made influence the elasticity of supply? Explain your answer.

You have now learned about the elasticities of demand and supply. Table 4.1 summarizes all the elasticities that you've met in this chapter.

In the next chapter, we study the efficiency of competitive markets. But before leaving elasticity, *Reading Between the Lines* on pp. 96–97 puts the elasticity of demand to work interpreting trends in the market for album CDs.

Table 4.1

A Compact Glossary of Elasticities

Price Elasticity of Demand

A relationship is described as	When its magnitude is	Which means that
Perfectly elastic	Infinity	The smallest possible increase in price causes an infinitely elastic large decrease in the quantity demanded*
Elastic	Less than infinity but greater than 1	The percentage decrease in the quantity demanded exceeds the percentage increase in price
Unit elastic	1	The percentage decrease in the quantity demanded equals the percentage increase in price
Inelastic	Greater than zero but less than 1	The percentage decrease in the quantity demanded is less than the percentage increase in price
Perfectly inelastic	Zero	The quantity demanded is the same at all prices

Cross Elasticity of Demand

A relationship is described as	When its magnitude is	Which means that
Perfect substitutes	Infinity	The smallest possible increase in the price of one good causes an infinitely large increase in the quantity demanded of the other good
Substitutes	Positive, less than infinity	If the price of one good increases the quantity demanded of the other good also increases
Independent	Zero	The quantity demanded of one good remains constant regardless of the price of the other good
Complements	Less than zero	The quantity demanded of one good decreases when the price of the other good increases

Income Elasticity of Demand

A relationship is described as	When its magnitude is	Which means that
Income elastic (normal good)	Greater than 1	The percentage increase in the quantity demanded is greater than the percentage increase in income
Income inelastic (normal good)	Less than 1 but greater than zero	The percentage increase in the quantity demanded is less than the percentage increase in income
Negative income elastic (inferior good)	Less than zero	When income increases, quantity demanded decreases

Price Elasticity of Supply

A relationship is described as	When its magnitude is	Which means that
Perfectly elastic	Infinity	The smallest possible increase in price causes an infinitely large increase in the quantity supplied
Elastic	Less than infinity but greater than 1	The percentage increase in the quantity supplied exceeds the percentage increase in the price
Inelastic	Greater than zero but less than 1	The percentage increase in the quantity supplied is less than the percentage increase in the price
Perfectly inelastic	Zero	The quantity supplied is the same at all prices

* In each description, the directions of change may be reversed. For example, in this case: the smallest possible decrease in the price causes an infinitely large increase in the quantity demanded.

Reading Between the Lines

Elasticity: Demand for CDs

The Independent, 18 August 2003

Album sales hit all time high – but profits slide

Andrew Clennell

The record industry was enjoying some rare but welcome good news today as figures showed album sales had reached an all-time high.

Despite the relentless advance of CD burners and MP3 downloaders, between June 2002 and June 2003, 228 million albums were sold in the UK. This is a rise of nearly 3 per cent on the previous year. It is the biggest annual figure in terms of "units" moved yet recorded, the British Phonographic Industry (BPI) announced, and means that album sales have been over the 200 million mark since 1999.

Cheaper CDs and a declining singles market have fuelled the record sales figures. But more discs coming off the shelves has not meant more money going into the record companies' coffers. Overall, the value of all record sales is down 4.1 per cent annually. Cheaper CDs have meant profits for album sales fell by 2 per cent over the period from June to June. . . .

The BPI said: "It is clear that cheap retail prices combined with strong new-release titles are sustaining the UK album market at a high level."

Earlier this year, it was revealed that the average price for an album is now £9.79, the cheapest it has been in the UK.

The Essence of the Story

- The quantity of album CDs sold in the United Kingdom increased by 3 per cent to 228 million in the year ended 30 June 2003.
- The average price of records fell, so the total revenue from all record sales fell by 4.1 per cent.
- Despite an increase in the quantity of album CDs sold, total revenue from album sales fell by 2 per cent.
- The average price of a CD fell to £9.79.

Economic Analysis

- The news stories are about the UK market for album CDs and how total revenue is falling despite the fall in price and increase in the quantity of album CDs sold.
- The total revenue test predicts that a price fall leads to a fall in total revenue for goods with inelastic demand.
- The news story gives enough information for us to calculate the price elasticity of demand for album CDs and check the prediction.
- To calculate price elasticity of demand, we need two points on the demand curve.
- One point is for 2003, when the quantity of of album CDs sold was 228 million and the average price of an album was £9.79.
- A second point can be found for 2002 (other things remaining the same).
- The quantity of album CDs sold in 2003 was 3 per cent higher than in 2002. So the quantity in 2002 was 221 million albums. (Check that 3 per cent of 221 is 7 and note that 221 plus 7 equals 228.)
- We know that total revenue fell by 2 per cent between 2002 and 2003. Total revenue in 2003 was £9.79 × 228 million = £2,232 million. So total revenue in 2002 must have been £2,278 million. (Check that 2 per cent of £2,278 is £46 and note that £2,278 minus £46 equals £2,232.)
- With total revenue of £2,278 and a quantity of 221 million, we can calculate the average price as £10.31. (Total revenue = price × quantity, so price = total revenue ÷ quantity.)
- So the second point on the demand curve is a quantity of 221 million and an average price of £10.31.
- Figure 1 shows the demand curve for album CDs based on the numbers we've calculated from the information in the news articles.
- The price elasticity of demand equals the percentage change in the quantity demanded divided by the percentage change in price, using the *average* quantity and *average* price.
- In Figure 1, the quantity demanded increases by 7 million albums and the average quantity is 224.5 million albums.
- The price falls by £0.52 and the average price is £10.05.
- Price elasticity of demand equals

$$(7/224.5) \div (0.52/10.05) = 0.6$$

- The demand for album CDs is inelastic.
- In 2003, there were limited substitutes for album CDs, making demand inelastic. More widespread purchase of downloadable albums may make the demand for album CDs more elastic in future.

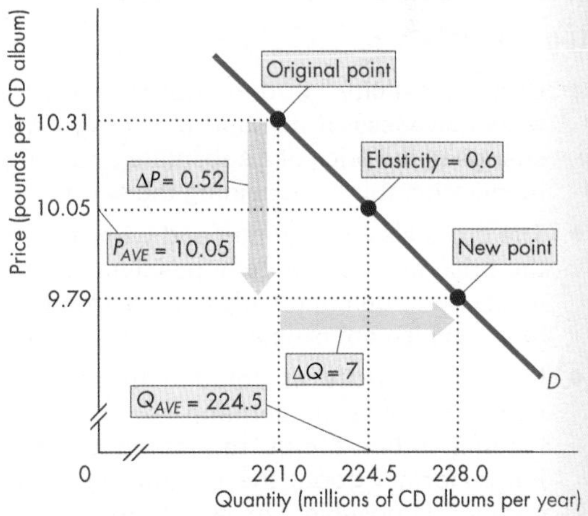

Figure 1 Price elasticity of demand

Summary

Key Points

Price Elasticity of Demand (pp. 82–88)

- Elasticity is a measure of the responsiveness of the quantity demanded of a good to a change in its price, other things remaining the same.
- Price elasticity of demand equals the percentage change in the quantity demanded divided by the percentage change in price.
- The larger the magnitude of the price elasticity of demand, the greater is the responsiveness of the quantity demanded to a given change in price.
- Price elasticity of demand depends on how easily one good serves as a substitute for another, the proportion of income spent on the good and the length of time elapsed since the price change.
- If demand is elastic, a decrease in price leads to an increase in total revenue. If demand is unit elastic, a decrease in price leaves total revenue unchanged. If demand is inelastic, a decrease in price leads to a decrease in total revenue.

More Elasticities of Demand (pp. 89–91)

- Cross elasticity of demand measures the responsiveness of demand for one good to a change in the price of a substitute or a complement, other things remaining the same.
- The cross elasticity of demand with respect to the price of a substitute is positive. The cross elasticity of demand with respect to the price of a complement is negative.
- Income elasticity of demand measures the responsiveness of demand to a change in income, other things remaining the same. For a normal good, the income elasticity of demand is positive. For an inferior good, the income elasticity of demand is negative.
- When the income elasticity of demand is greater than 1 (income elastic), the percentage of income spent on the good increases as income increases.
- When the income elasticity of demand is less than 1 but greater than zero (income elastic and inferior), the percentage of income spent on the good decreases as income increases.

Elasticity of Supply (pp. 92–95)

- Elasticity of supply measures the responsiveness of the quantity supplied of a good to a change in its price.
- The elasticity of supply is usually positive and ranges between zero (vertical supply curve) and infinity (horizontal supply curve).
- Supply decisions have three time frames: momentary, long run and short run.
- Momentary supply refers to the response of sellers to a price change at the instant that the price changes.
- Long-run supply refers to the response of sellers to a price change when all the technologically feasible adjustments in production have been made.
- Short-run supply refers to the response of sellers to a price change after some of the technologically feasible adjustments in production have been made.

Key Figures and Table

Key Terms

Problems

Tests, Study Plan and Solutions* 

1 Rain spoils the strawberry crop. As a result, the price rises from £2 to £3 a box and the quantity demanded decreases from 1,000 to 600 boxes a week. Over this price range:

a What is the price elasticity of demand?

b Describe the demand for strawberries.

2 The figure shows the demand for DVD rentals.

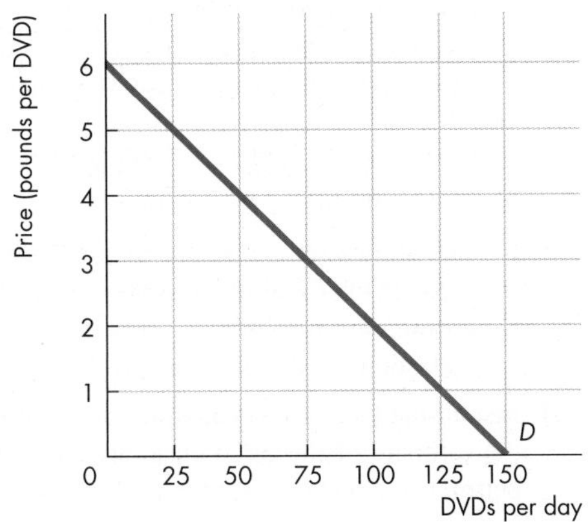

a Calculate the elasticity of demand when the price rises from £3 to £5 a DVD rental.

b At what price is the elasticity of demand equal to 1?

3 If the quantity of dental services demanded increases by 10 per cent when the price of dental services falls by 10 per cent, is the demand for dental service inelastic, elastic, or unit elastic?

4 The demand schedule for computer chips is

Price (euros per chip)	Quantity demanded (millions of chips per year)
200	50
250	45
300	40
350	35
400	30
450	25
500	20

a What happens to total revenue if the price falls from €400 to €350 a chip?

b What happens to total revenue if the price falls from €350 to €300 a chip?

c At what price is total revenue at a maximum? Use the total revenue test to answer this question.

d At an average price of €350, is the demand for chips elastic or inelastic?

5 In problem 4, at €250 a chip, is the demand for chips elastic or inelastic? Use the total revenue test to answer this question.

6 Your price elasticity of demand for bananas is 4. If the price of bananas rises by 5 per cent, what is the percentage change in:

a Your expenditure on bananas?

b The quantity of bananas you buy?

7 If a 12 per cent rise in the price of an orange juice decreases the quantity of orange juice demanded by 22 per cent and increases the quantity of apple juice demanded by 14 per cent, calculate the cross elasticity of demand between orange juice and apple juice.

8 When Alex's income increased from £3,000 to £5,000, he increased his consumption of bagels from 4 to 8 a month and decreased his consumption of doughnuts from 12 to 6 a month. Calculate Alex's income elasticity of demand for:

a Bagels.

b Doughnuts.

9 In 2003, when music downloading first took off, Universal Music slashed the prices of CDs from an average of $21 to an average of $15. The company said that it expected the price cut to boost the quantity of CDs sold by 30 per cent.

a What was Universal Music's estimate of the price elasticity of demand for CDs?

b Given your answer to part (a), if you were making the pricing decision at Universal Music, would you cut the price, raise the price, or leave the price unchanged? Explain your decision.

10 The table gives the supply schedule for long-distance phone calls.

Price (cents per minute)	Quantity supplied (millions of minutes per day)
10	200
20	400
30	600
40	800
50	900

Calculate the elasticity of supply when:

a The price falls from 40 cents to 30 cents a minute.

b The average price is 20 cents a minute.

* Solutions to odd-numbered problems are provided.

11 If a 10 per cent rise in the price of bread increases the quantity of bread supplied by 20 per cent, calculate the elasticity of supply of bread.

12 The elasticity of supply of blue jeans is 4. If the price of a pair of jeans rises by 5 per cent, what is the percentage change in quantity of jeans supplied.

Critical Thinking

1 Read the news article in *Reading Between the Lines* on p. 96 on the elasticity of demand for album CDs and then answer the following questions.

a Explain what the calculated value of the price elasticity of demand for album CDs in the story means in words.

b If the price of downloadable albums were to fall, what would be the likely immediate effect on the demand for album CDs?

c Would you expect the cross elasticity of album CDs with respect to downloadable albums to be positive or negative. Explain your answer.

d Why might the price elasticity of demand for album CDs change over time?

2 The demand for illegal drugs is inelastic. Much of the expenditure on illegal drugs comes from crime. Assuming these statements to be correct,

a How will a successful campaign that decreases the supply of illegal drugs influence the price of illegal drugs and the amount spent on them?

b What will happen to the amount of crime?

c What is the most effective way of decreasing the quantity of illegal drugs consumed and decreasing the amount of drug-related crime?

3 Alan Krueger, an economist at Princeton University, writing about the US market for petrol says that in the short run (a period of about a year), a 10 per cent rise in the price of petrol brings a 1 to 2 per cent decrease in the quantity of petrol purchased. He also observes that from September 2004 to September 2005, the average retail price of petrol increased from $1.87 a gallon to $2.90 a gallon. During the same period, the quantity of petrol consumed decreased by only 3.5 per cent.

a What is the price elasticity of demand for petrol implied by what most studies have found?

b If other things remained the same, what would the data for the year to September 2005 imply about the price elasticity of demand for petrol?

c How does your answer to part (a) compare with your answer to part (b) and what do you think might account for the difference?

4 Alan Krueger (again writing about the US market for petrol) says that in the long run (a period of several years) a 10 per cent rise in the price of petrol brings a 5 to 10 per cent decrease in the quantity of petrol consumption, other things remaining the same. He observes that the US average price of petrol increased by 53 per cent from 1998 to 2004, after adjusting for inflation. The quantity of petrol consumption increased by 10 per cent during this period. Incomes grew by 19 per cent, which, other things remaining the same, would increase the quantity of petrol consumed by about 20 per cent.

a What does the above information about estimates of the long-run response to price movements imply about the long-run price elasticity of demand for petrol?

b What is the income elasticity of demand for petrol implied by the above information?

c If other things remained the same except for the increase in income and the rise in price, what would the data for 1998 to 2004 imply about the price elasticity of demand for petrol?

d List all the factors you can think of that might bias the estimate of the price elasticity of demand for petrol, using just the data for 1998 to 2004.

Web Activities

Links to Websites

1 Obtain information on the price of petrol during the past year and then:

a Use the concepts of demand, supply and elasticity to explain the change in the price of petrol from one year ago.

b Find the latest price of crude oil.

c Use the concepts of demand, supply and elasticity to explain the change in the price of crude oil from one year ago.

2 Use the Web to obtain information you need to answer the following questions.

a How many gallons are in a barrel and what is the cost of the crude oil in a gallon of petrol.

b What other costs make up the total cost of a gallon of petrol?

c If the price of crude oil falls by 10 per cent, by what percentage would you expect the price of petrol to change, other things remaining the same?

d In light of your answer to part (c), which demand is more elastic: that for crude oil or for petrol? Why?

Efficiency and Equity

CHAPTER

5

After studying this chapter you will be able to:

- Describe the alternative methods of allocating scarce resources
- Explain the connection between demand and marginal benefit and define consumer surplus
- Explain the connection between supply and marginal cost and define producer surplus
- Explain the conditions under which markets move resources to their highest-valued uses and the sources of inefficiency in our economy
- Explain the main ideas about fairness and evaluate claims that markets result in unfair outcomes

Self-interest and Social Interest

When you buy goods and services, you try to get the most out of your scarce resources, you further your self-interest. With everyone pursuing self-interest in markets, what happens to the social interest? Do markets do a good job and allocate resources efficiently? Do markets deliver an outcome that is best or even fair for everyone?

Find some answers in this chapter. Then apply what you learn to the severe problem of allocating India's water resources in *Reading Between the Lines* at the end of the chapter.

Resource Allocation Methods

The goal of this chapter is to evaluate the ability of markets to allocate resources efficiently and fairly. But to see whether the market does a good job, we must compare it with its alternatives. Resources are scarce, so they must be allocated somehow. And trading in markets is just one of several alternative methods.

Resources might be allocated by

- Market price
- Command
- Majority rule
- Contest
- First-come, first-served
- Lottery
- Personal characteristics
- Force

Let's briefly examine each method.

Market Price

When a market price allocates a scarce resource, the people who are willing and able to pay that price get the resource. Two kinds of people decide not to pay the market price: those who can afford to pay but choose not to buy and those who are too poor and simply can't afford to buy.

For many goods and services, distinguishing between those who choose not to buy and those who can't afford to buy does not matter. But for some goods and services, it does matter. For example, poor people can't afford to pay school fees, pay for healthcare, or save to provide a pension when they retire. Because poor people can't afford these items that most people consider to be essential, in most societies, they are allocated by one of the other methods.

Command

A **command system** allocates resources by the order (command) of someone in authority. A command system is used extensively inside firms, public organizations and government departments. For example, if you have a job, most likely someone tells you what to do. Your labour is allocated to specific tasks by a command.

Command systems work well in organizations in with clearly defined lines of authority and responsibility when it is easy to monitor the activities being performed. But a command system works badly when the range of activities to be monitored is large and when these activities are difficult to monitor.

A manager might be able to monitor several employees but a government department cannot monitor every firm in the economy. The system works so badly in North Korea, where it is used in place of markets, that it fails even to deliver an adequate supply of food.

Majority Rule

Majority rule allocates resources in the way that a majority of voters choose. Societies use majority rule to elect representative governments that make some of the biggest decisions. For example, majority rule in each member state of the European Union determines the tax rates that eventually allocate scarce resources between private use and public use. Majority rule also determines how tax revenues are allocated among competing uses such as education and healthcare.

Majority rule works well when the decisions being made affect large numbers of people and self-interest must be suppressed to use resources most effectively.

Contest

A contest allocates resources to a winner (or a group of winners). Sporting events use this method.

Manchester United competes with Chelsea to end up at the top of the Premier League, and the winner gets the biggest payoff. Andy Murray competes to win tennis matches and get the biggest prize. But contests are more general than those in a sports arena, though we don't normally call them contests. For example, there is a contest among Nokia, Motorola and Sony Ericsson in the mobile phone market. Managers often create contests inside their firms among employees for special bonuses.

Contests work well when the efforts of the "players" are hard to monitor and reward directly. If everyone is offered the same wage, there is no incentive for anyone to make a special effort. But if a manager offers everyone in the company the opportunity to win a big prize, people are motivated to work hard and try to become the winner. Only a few people win the prize, but many people work harder in the process of trying to win. So total output produced by the workers of the firms is much greater than it would be without the contest.

First-come, First-served

A first-come, first-served method allocates resources to those who are first in line. Many restaurants won't accept reservations. They use first-come, first-served to allocate their scarce tables. Scarce space on congested motorways is allocated in this way too: the first to arrive on the slip-road gets the road space. If too many vehicles enter the motorway, the speed slows and people wait on the slip-road for space to become available.

First-come, first-served works best when a scarce resource can serve just one user at a time in a sequence. By serving the user who arrives first, this method minimizes the time spent waiting for the resource to become available.

Lottery

Lotteries allocate resources to those who pick the winning number, draw the lucky cards, or who pick the winning ticket in a gamble. National lotteries throughout Europe reallocate millions of euros worth of goods and services every year.

But lotteries are more widespread than jackpots and roulette wheels in casinos. Lotteries are used to allocate licensed taxi permits, landing slots to airlines at some airports, fishing rights and the electromagnetic spectrum used by mobile phones.

Lotteries work best when there is no effective way to distinguish among potential users of a scarce resource.

Personal Characteristics

When resources are allocated on the basis of personal characteristics, people with the "right" characteristics get the resources. Some of the resources that matter most to you are allocated in this way. For example, you will choose a marriage partner on the basis of personal characteristics. But this method is also used in unfair ways. For example, allocating the best jobs to white, able-bodied males and discriminating against minorities, older people, people with disabilities and females.

Force

Force plays a crucial role, for both good and ill, in allocating scarce resources. Let's start with the ill.

War, the use of military force by one nation against another, has played an enormous role historically in allocating resources. The economic supremacy of European settlers in the Americas and Australia owes much to the use of this method.

Theft, the taking of the property of others without their consent, also plays a large role. Local crime and international crime throughout Europe allocate billions of euros worth of resources annually.

But force plays a crucial positive role in allocating resources. It provides the state with an effective method of transferring wealth from the rich to the poor. It also provides the legal framework in which voluntary exchange in markets can take place.

A legal system is the foundation on which our market economy functions. Without courts to enforce contracts, it would not be possible to do business. But the courts could not enforce contracts without the ability to apply force if necessary. The state provides the ultimate force that enables the courts to do their work.

More broadly, the force of the state is essential to uphold the principle of the rule of law. This principle is the bedrock of civilized economic (and social and political) life. With the rule of law upheld, people can go about their daily economic lives with the assurance that their property will be protected – that they can sue for violations against their property (and be sued if they violate the property of others).

Free from the burden of protecting their property and confident in the knowledge that those with whom they trade will honour their agreements, people can get on with focusing on the activity at which they have a comparative advantage and trading for mutual gain.

Review Quiz

Study Plan 5.1

1. Why do we need methods of allocating scarce resources?
2. Describe the alternative methods of allocating scarce resources.
3. Provide an example of each allocation method that illustrates when it works well.
4. Provide an example of each allocation method that illustrates when it works badly.

In the next sections, we're going to see how a market can achieve an efficient use of resources and serve the social interest. We will also examine the obstacles to efficiency and see how sometimes an alternative method might improve on the market. After looking at efficiency, we'll turn our attention to the more difficult issue of fairness.

Demand and Marginal Benefit

Resources are allocated efficiently when they are used in the ways that people value most highly. This outcome occurs when marginal benefit equals marginal cost (Chapter 2, pp. 39–41). So to determine whether a competitive market is efficient, we need to see whether, at the market equilibrium quantity, marginal benefit equals marginal cost. We begin by seeing how market demand reflects marginal benefit.

Demand, Willingness to Pay and Value

In everyday life, we talk about "getting value for money". When we use this expression, we are distinguishing between *value* and *price*. Value is what we get, and the price is what we pay.

The value of one more unit of a good or service is its marginal benefit. And we measure marginal benefit by the maximum price that is willingly paid for another unit of the good or service. But willingness to pay determines demand. *A demand curve is a marginal benefit curve.*

In Figure 5.1(a), Lisa is willing to pay €1 for the 30th slice of pizza and €1 is her marginal benefit from that slice. In Figure 5.1(b), Nick is willing to pay €1 for the 10th slice and €1 is his marginal benefit from that slice. But for what quantity is the economy willing to pay €1. The answer is provided by the market demand curve.

Individual Demand and Market Demand

The relationship between the price of a good and the quantity demanded by one person is called *individual demand*. And the relationship between the price of a good and the quantity demanded by all buyers is called *market demand*.

The market demand curve is the horizontal sum of the individual demand curves and is formed by adding the quantities demanded by all the individuals at each price.

Figure 5.1(c) illustrates the market demand for pizza if Lisa and Nick are the only people. Lisa's demand curve in part (a) and Nick's demand curve in part (b) sum horizontally to the market demand curve in part (c).

Figure 5.1

Individual Demand, Market Demand and Marginal Social Benefit

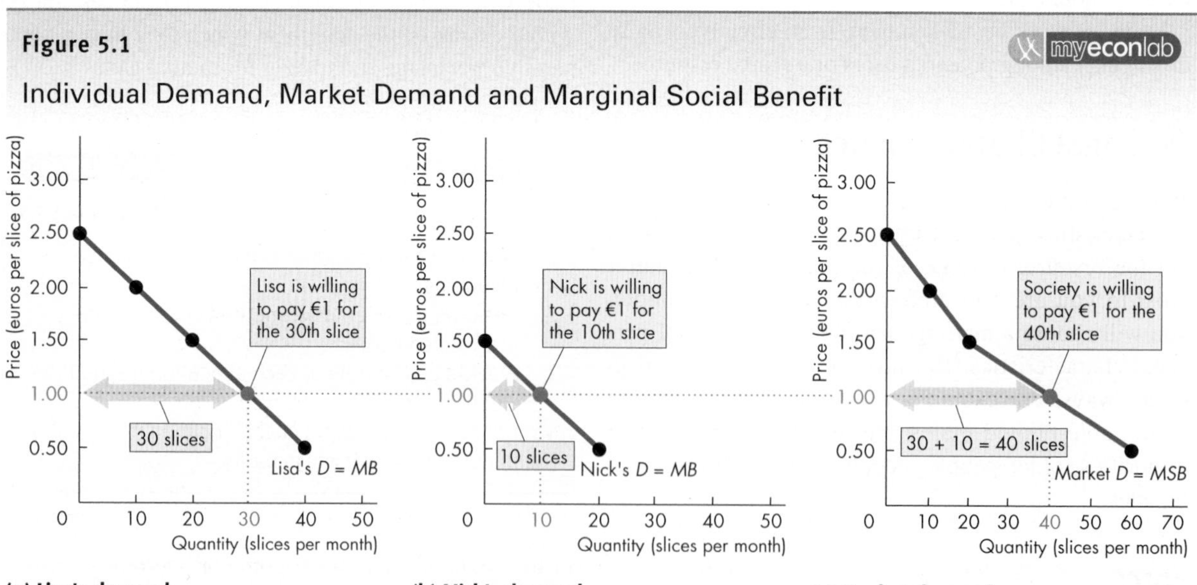

At a price of €1 a slice, the quantity demanded by Lisa is 30 slices and the quantity demanded by Nick is 10 slices, so the quantity demanded by the market is 40 slices.

Lisa's demand curve in part (a) and Nick's demand curve in part (b) sum *horizontally* to the market demand curve in part (c).

The market demand curve is the marginal social benefit (*MSB*) curve.

At a price of €1 a slice, Lisa demands 30 slices and Nick demands 10 slices, so the quantity demanded by the market at €1 a slice is 40 slices.

So from the market demand curve, we see that the economy (or society) is willing to pay €1 for 40 slices a month. The *market demand curve is the economy's marginal social benefit (MSB) curve*.

Although we're measuring the price in euros, think of the price as telling us the number of *euros' worth of other goods and services willingly forgone* to obtain one more slice of pizza.

Consumer Surplus

We don't always have to pay what we are willing to pay – we get a bargain. When people buy something for less than it is worth to them, they receive a consumer surplus. A **consumer surplus** is the value (or marginal benefit) of a good minus the price paid for it, summed over the quantity bought.

Figure 5.2(a) shows Lisa's consumer surplus from pizza when the price is €1 a slice. At this price, she buys 30 slices a month because the 30th slice is worth only €1 to her. But Lisa is willing to pay €2 for the 10th slice, so her marginal benefit from this slice is €1 more than she pays for it – she receives a *consumer surplus* of €1 on the 10th slice.

Lisa's consumer surplus is the sum of the surpluses on *all of the slices she buys*. This sum is the area of the green triangle – the area below the demand curve and above the market price line. The area of this triangle is equal to its base (30 slices) multiplied by its height (€1.50) divided by 2, which is €22.50. The area of the blue rectangle in Figure 5.2(a) shows what Lisa pays for 30 slices of pizza.

Figure 5.2(b) shows Nick's consumer surplus. Part (c) shows the consumer surplus for the economy, which is the sum of the consumer surpluses of Lisa and Nick.

All goods and services, like pizza, have decreasing marginal benefit. So people receive more benefit from consumption than the amount they pay.

Review Quiz

Study Plan 5.2

1. How do we measure the value or marginal benefit of a good or service?
2. What is consumer surplus? How is it measured?

Figure 5.2

Demand and Consumer Surplus

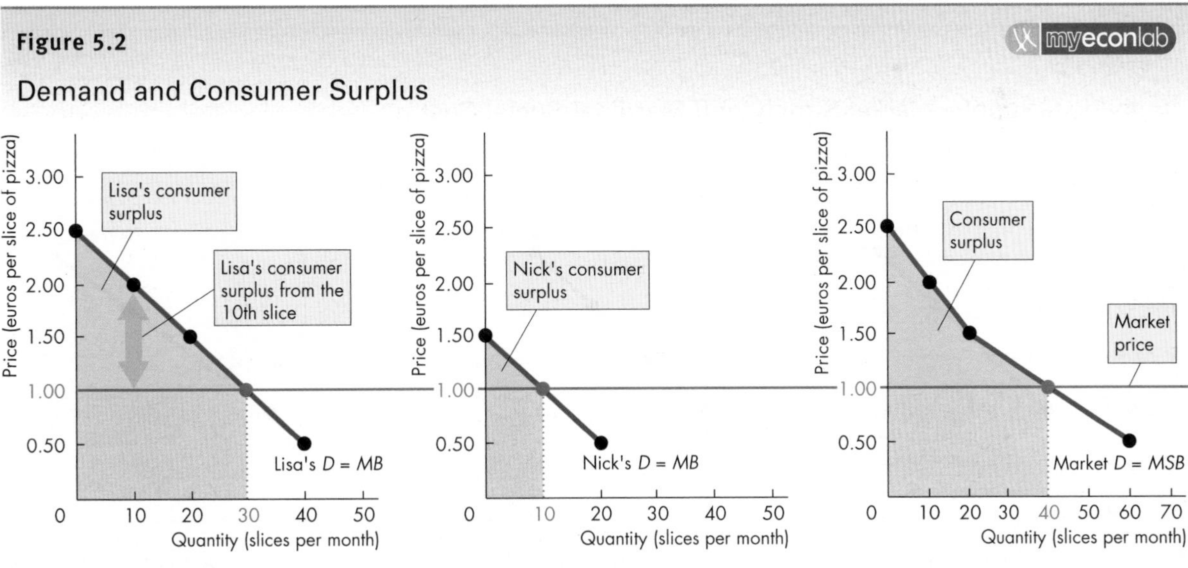

(a) Lisa's consumer surplus **(b) Nick's consumer surplus** **(c) Market consumer surplus**

Lisa is willing to pay €2.00 for her 10th slice of pizza (part a). At a market price of €1 a slice, Lisa receives a consumer surplus of €1 on the 10th slice. The green triangle shows her consumer surplus on the 30 slices she buys at €1 a slice.

The green triangle in part (b) shows Nick's consumer surplus on the 10 slices he buys at €1 a slice. The green area in part (c) shows the consumer surplus for the economy. The blue rectangles show the amounts spent on pizza.

Supply and Marginal Cost

We are now going to see how market supply reflects marginal cost. This section closely parallels the related ideas about market demand and marginal benefit that you've just studied. Firms are in business to make a profit. To do so, they must sell their output for a price that exceeds the cost of production. Let's investigate the relationship between cost and price.

Supply, Cost and Minimum Supply-price

Making a profit means receiving more from the sale of a good or service than the cost of producing it. Just as consumers distinguish between *value* and *price*, so producers distinguish between cost and price. Cost is what a producer gives up, and the price is what a producer receives.

The cost of producing one more unit of a good or service is its marginal cost. And marginal cost is the minimum price that producers must receive to induce them to offer to sell another unit of the good or service. But the minimum supply-price determines supply. *A supply curve is a marginal cost curve.*

In Figure 5.3(a), Max is willing to produce the 100th pizza for €15, his marginal cost of that pizza. In Figure 5.3(b), Mario is willing to produce the 50th pizza for €15, his marginal cost of that pizza. But what quantity is the economy willing to produce for €15 a pizza? The answer is provided by the *market supply curve.*

Individual Supply and Market Supply

The relationship between the price of a good and the quantity supplied by one producer is called *individual supply*. And the relationship between the price of a good and the quantity supplied by all producers is called *market supply*.

The market supply curve is the horizontal sum of the individual supply curves and is formed by adding the quantities supplied by all the producers at each price.

Figure 5.3(c) illustrates the market supply if Max and Mario are the only producers. Max's supply curve in part (a) and Mario's supply curve in part (b) sum horizontally to the market supply curve in part (c).

At a price of €15 a pizza, Max supplies 100 pizzas and Mario supplies 50 pizzas, so the quantity supplied by the market at €15 a pizza is 150 pizzas.

Figure 5.3

Individual Supply, Market Supply and Marginal Social Cost

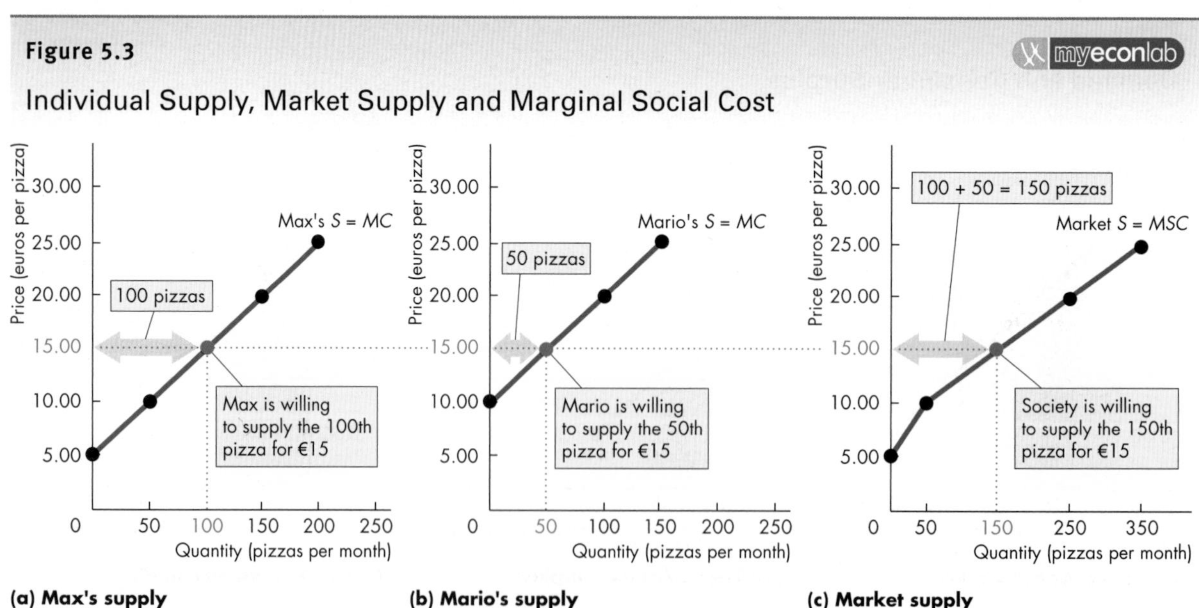

At a price of €15 a pizza, the quantity supplied by Max is 100 pizzas and the quantity supplied by Mario is 50 pizzas, so the quantity supplied by the market is 150 pizzas

Max's supply curve in part (a) and Mario's supply curve in part (b) sum horizontally to the market supply curve in part (c).

The market supply curve is the marginal social cost (*MSC*) curve.

So from the market supply curve, we see that the economy (or society) is willing to produce 150 pizzas a month for €15 each. *The market supply curve is the economy's marginal social cost (MSC) curve.*

Again, although we're measuring price in euros, think of the price as telling us the number of euros' worth of other goods and services that must be forgone to obtain one more pizza.

Producer Surplus

When price exceeds marginal cost, the firm receives a producer surplus. A **producer surplus** is the price received for a good minus its minimum supply-price (or marginal cost), summed over the quantity sold.

Figure 5.4(a) shows Max's producer surplus from pizza when the price is €15 a pizza. At this price, he sells 100 pizzas a month because the 100th pizza costs him €15 to produce. But Max is willing to produce the 50th pizza for his marginal cost, which is €10. So he receives a *producer surplus* of €5 on this pizza.

Max's producer surplus is the sum of the surpluses on each pizza he sells. This sum is the area of the blue triangle – the area below the market price and above the supply curve. The area of this triangle is equal to its base (100) multiplied by its height (€10) divided by 2, which is €500. The red area in Figure 5.4(a) below the supply curve shows what it costs Max to produce 100 pizzas.

Figure 5.4(b) shows Mario's producer surplus and part (c) shows the producer surplus for the economy. The producer surplus for the economy is the sum of the producer surpluses of Max and Mario.

Review Quiz

Study Plan 5.3

1. What is the relationship between the marginal cost, minimum supply-price, and supply?
2. What is producer surplus? How is it measured?

Consumer surplus and producer surplus can be used to measure the efficiency of a market. Let's see how we can use these concepts to study the efficiency of a competitive market.

Figure 5.4

Supply and Producer Surplus

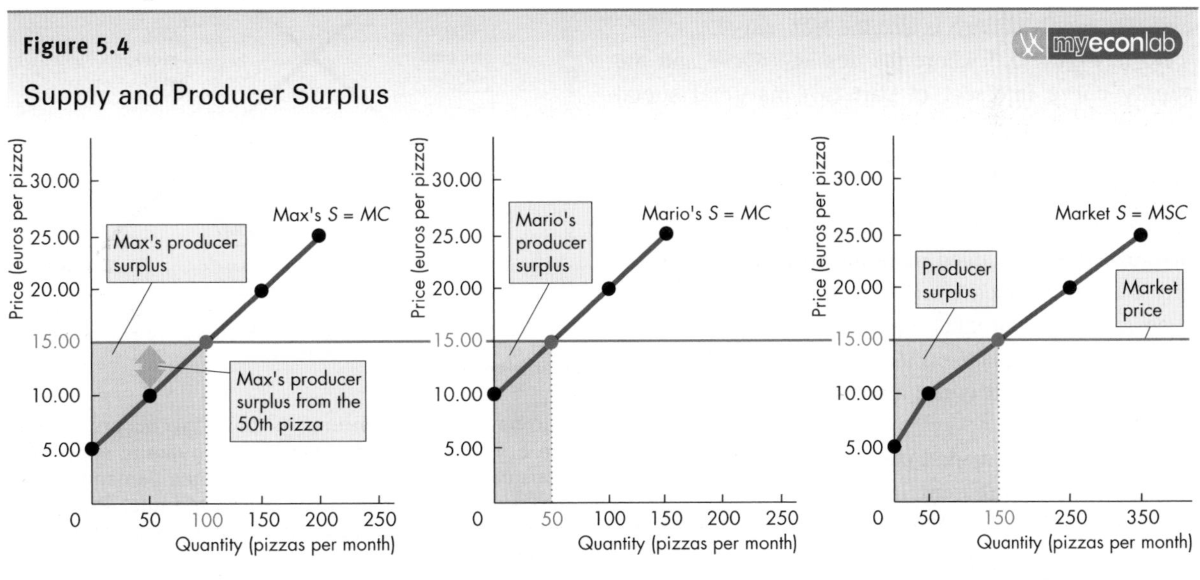

(a) Max's producer surplus

(b) Mario's producer surplus

(c) Market producer surplus

Max is willing to produce the 50th pizza for €10 (part a). At a market price of €15 a pizza, Max gets a producer surplus of €5 on the 50th pizza. The blue triangle shows his producer surplus on the 100 pizzas he sells at €15 each.

The blue triangle in part (b) shows Mario's producer surplus on the 50 pizzas that he sells at €15 each. The blue area in part (c) shows producer surplus for the economy. The red areas show the cost of producing the pizzas sold.

Is the Competitive Market Efficient?

Figure 5.5 shows the market for pizza. The market forces that you studied in Chapter 3 (pp. 68–69) will pull the pizza market to its equilibrium price of €15 a pizza and equilibrium quantity of 10,000 pizzas a day. Buyers enjoy a consumer surplus (green area) and sellers enjoy a producer surplus (blue area). But is this competitive equilibrium efficient?

Efficiency of Competitive Equilibrium

The demand curve tells us the marginal benefit from pizza. If the only people who benefit from pizza are the people who buy it, then the demand curve for pizza measures the marginal benefit to the entire society from pizza. We call the marginal benefit to the entire society, marginal *social* benefit, *MSB*. In this case, the demand curve *D* is also the *MSB* curve.

You've also seen that the supply curve tells us the marginal cost of pizza. If the only people who bear the cost of pizza are the people who produce it, then the supply curve of pizza measures the marginal cost to the entire society of pizza. We call the marginal cost to the entire society, marginal *social* cost, *MSC*. In this case, the supply curve *S* is also the *MSC* curve.

So in Figure 5.5 where the demand curve and the supply curve intersect in part (a), marginal social benefit equals marginal social cost in part (b). This condition delivers an efficient use of resources for the society.

If production is less than 10,000 pizzas a day, the marginal pizza is valued more highly than its opportunity cost. If production exceeds 10,000 pizzas a day, it costs more to produce the marginal pizza than the value consumers place on it. Only when 10,000 pizzas a day are produced is the marginal pizza worth what it costs.

The competitive market pushes the quantity of pizza produced to its efficient level of 10,000 a day. If production is less than 10,000 pizzas a day, a shortage raises the price, which increases production. If production exceeds 10,000 pizzas a day, a surplus lowers the price, which decreases production. So, a competitive pizza market is efficient.

When the efficient quantity is produced, **total surplus** – the sum of consumer surplus and producer surplus – is maximized. Buyers and sellers acting in their self-interest end up promoting the social interest.

Figure 5.5 myeconlab

An Efficient Market for Pizza

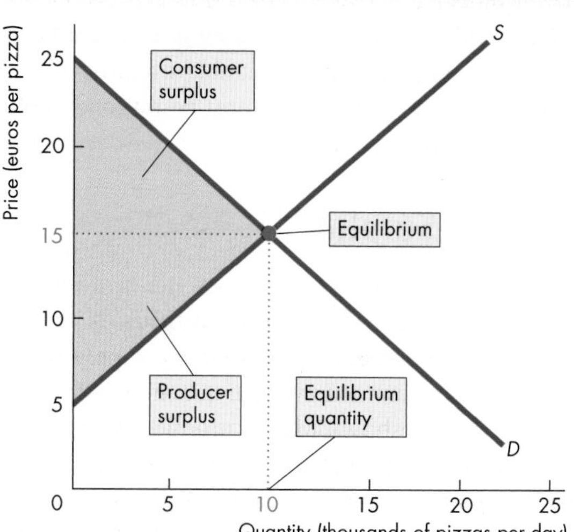

(a) Equilibrium and surpluses

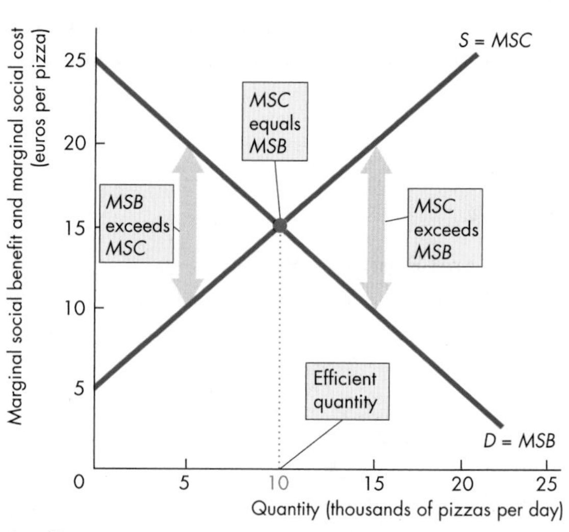

(b) Efficiency

Competitive equilibrium in part (a) occurs when the quantity demanded equals the quantity supplied. Consumer surplus is the area under the demand curve and above the price – the green triangle. Producer surplus is the area above the supply curve and below the price – the blue triangle.

Resources are used efficiently in part (b) when marginal social benefit, *MSB*, equals marginal social cost, *MSC*.

The efficient quantity in part (b) is the same as the equilibrium quantity in part (a). The competitive pizza market produces the efficient quantity of pizza. At the competitive equilibrium, total surplus – the sum of the consumer surplus and the producer surplus – is maximized.

The Invisible Hand

Writing in his book, *The Wealth of Nations*, in 1776, Adam Smith was the first to suggest that competitive markets send resources to the uses in which they have the highest value. Smith believed that each participant in a competitive market is "led by an invisible hand to promote an end [the efficient use of resources] which was no part of his intention."

You can see the invisible hand at work in the cartoon. The cold drinks vendor has both cold drinks and shade. He has an opportunity cost of each and a minimum supply-price of each. The reader on the park bench has a marginal benefit from a cold drink and from shade.

You can see that the marginal benefit from shade exceeds the price but the price of a cold drink exceeds its marginal benefit. The transaction that occurs creates a producer surplus and a consumer surplus. The vendor obtains a producer surplus from selling the shade for more than its opportunity cost, and the reader obtains a consumer surplus from buying the shade for less than its marginal benefit.

In the third frame of the cartoon, both the consumer and the producer are better off than they were in the first frame. The umbrella has moved to its highest-valued use.

The Invisible Hand at Work Today

The market economy relentlessly performs the activity illustrated in the cartoon and in Figure 5.5 to achieve an efficient allocation of resources. And rarely has the market been working as hard as it is today. Think about a few of the changes taking place in our economy that the market is guiding towards an efficient allocation of resources.

New technologies have cut the cost of producing computers. As these advances have occurred, supply has increased and the price has fallen. Lower prices have encouraged an increase in the quantity demanded of this now less costly tool. The marginal social benefit from computers is brought to equality with their marginal social cost.

An early frost cuts the supply of grapes. With fewer grapes available, the marginal social benefit increases. A shortage of grapes raises their price, so the market allocates the smaller quantity available to the people who value them most highly.

Market forces persistently bring marginal social cost and marginal social benefit to equality and maximize total surplus.

Underproduction and Overproduction

Inefficiency can occur because either too little of an item is produced – underproduction – or too much is produced – overproduction.

Underproduction

Figure 5.6(a) shows that at this quantity, consumers are willing to pay €20 for a pizza that costs only €10 to produce. The quantity produced is inefficient – there is underproduction.

The scale of the inefficiency is measured by **deadweight loss**, which is the decrease in total surplus (the sum of consumer surplus and producer surplus) that results from an inefficient level of production. The grey triangle in Figure 5.6(a) shows the deadweight loss.

Figure 5.6

myeconlab

Underproduction and Overproduction

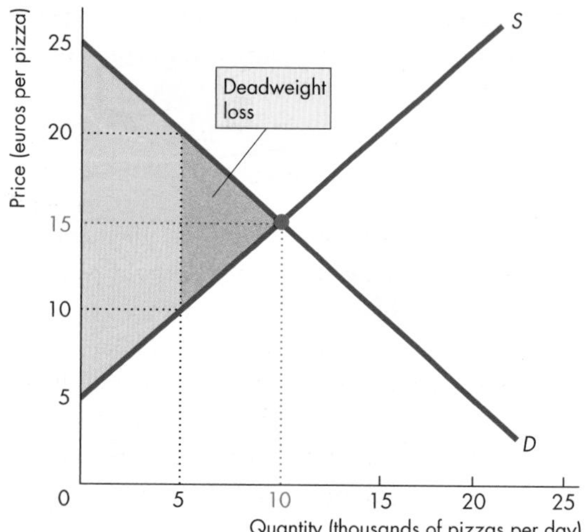

(a) Underproduction

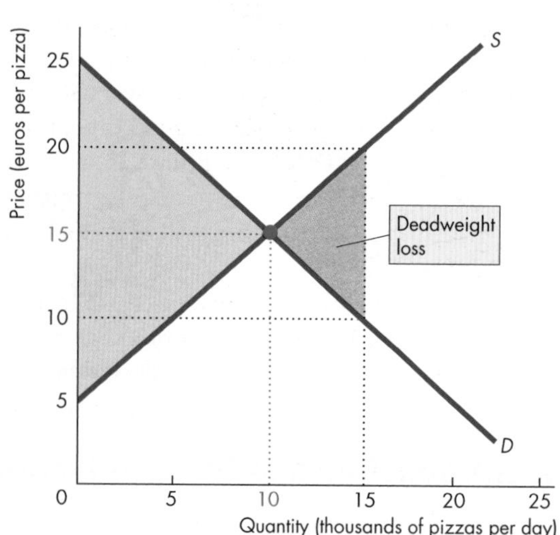

(b) Overproduction

If pizza production is cut to only 5,000 a day, a deadweight loss (the grey triangle) arises in part (a). Consumer surplus and producer surplus (the green and blue areas) are reduced. At 5,000 pizzas, the benefit of one more pizza exceeds its cost. The same is true for all levels of production up to 10,000 pizzas a day.

If production increases to 15,000 pizzas a day, a deadweight loss arises in part (b). At 15,000 pizzas a day, the cost of the 15,000th pizza exceeds its benefit. The cost of each pizza above 10,000 exceeds its benefit. Consumer surplus plus producer surplus equals the sum of the green and blue areas minus the deadweight loss triangle.

Overproduction

In Figure 5.6(b), the quantity of pizzas produced is 15,000 a day. At this quantity, consumers are willing to pay only €10 for a pizza that costs €20 to produce. By producing the 15,000th pizza, €10 of resources are wasted. Again, the grey triangle shows the deadweight loss. The total surplus (the sum of consumer surplus and producer surplus) is smaller than its maximum by the amount of the deadweight loss. The deadweight loss is borne by the entire society. It is not a loss for the consumers and a gain for the producer. It is a *social* loss.

Obstacles to Efficiency

Although markets generally do a good job at sending resources to where they are most highly valued, they do not always get it right. Sometimes, markets produce too much of a good or service, and sometimes they produce too little. The most significant obstacles to achieving an efficient allocation of resources in a market economy are:

- Price and quantity regulations
- Taxes and subsidies
- Externalities
- Public goods and common resources
- Monopoly
- High transaction costs

Price and Quantity Regulations

Price regulations that put a cap on the rent a landlord can charge and laws that require employers to pay a minimum wage sometimes block the price adjustments that balance the quantity demanded and the quantity supplied and lead to underproduction. *Quantity regulations* that limit the amount that a farm is permitted to produce also lead to underproduction.

Taxes and Subsidies

Taxes increase the prices paid by buyers and lower the prices received by sellers. So taxes decrease the quantity produced and lead to underproduction. *Subsidies*, which are payments by the government to producers, decrease the prices paid by buyers and increase the prices received by sellers. So subsidies increase the quantity produced and lead to overproduction.

Externalities

An *externality* is a cost or a benefit that affects someone other than the seller or the buyer of a good or service. An electric power utility creates an external cost by burning coal that brings acid rain and crop damage. The utility doesn't consider the cost of pollution when it decides how much power to produce. The result is overproduction. An apartment owner would provide an *external benefit* if she installed a smoke detector. But she doesn't consider her neighbour's marginal benefit when she is deciding whether to install a smoke detector. There is underproduction.

Public Goods and Common Resources

A *public good* is a good or service that is consumed simultaneously by everyone even if they don't pay for it. Examples are national defence and law enforcement. Competitive markets would underproduce a public good because of the *free-rider problem*: it is in each person's interest to free ride on everyone else and avoid paying for her or his share of a public good.

A *common resource* is owned by no one but used by everyone. Atlantic cod is an example. It is in everyone's self-interest to ignore the costs of their own use of a common resource that fall on others (called the *tragedy of the commons*), which leads to overproduction.

Monopoly

A *monopoly* is a firm that is the sole provider of a good or service. Local water supply and cable television are supplied by firms that are monopolies. The self-interest of a monopoly is to maximize its profit. The monopoly has no competitors, so it can set the price to achieve its self-interested goal. To achieve its goal, a monopoly produces too little and charges too high a price. It leads to underproduction.

High Transactions Costs

Retail markets employ enormous quantities of scarce labour and capital resources. It is costly to operate any market. Economists call the opportunity costs of making trades in a market **transactions costs**.

To use market price to allocate scarce resources, it must be worth bearing the opportunity cost of establishing a market. Some markets are just too costly to operate. For example, when you want to play tennis on your local "free" court, you don't pay a market price for use of the court. You wait until the court becomes vacant, and you "pay" with your waiting time. When transactions costs are high, the market might underproduce.

You now know the conditions under which resource allocation is efficient. You've seen how a competitive market can be efficient, and you've seen some impediments to efficiency.

Alternatives to the Market

When a market is inefficient, can one of the alternative non-market methods that we described at the beginning of this chapter do a better job? Sometimes it can.

Often, majority rule might be used but majority rule has its own shortcomings. A group that pursues the self-interest of its members can become the majority. For example, a price or quantity regulation that creates a deadweight loss is almost always the result of a self-interested group becoming the majority and imposing costs on the minority. Also, with majority rule, votes must be translated into actions by bureaucrats who have their own agendas based on their self-interest.

Managers in firms issue commands and avoid the transactions costs which would incur if they went to a market every time they needed a job done. First-come, first-served saves a lot of hassle. A queue could have markets in which people trade their place in the queue – but someone would have to enforce the agreements. Can you imagine the hassle at a busy ATM if you had to buy your spot at the head of the queue?

There is no one efficient mechanism for allocating resources efficiently. But markets, when supplemented by majority rule, command systems inside firms and occasionally by first-come, first-served work well.

Review Quiz

Study Plan 5.4

1. Do competitive markets use resources efficiently? Explain why or why not.
2. What is deadweight loss and when does it occur?
3. What are the obstacles to achieving an efficient allocation of resources in the market economy?

Is an efficient allocation of resources also a fair allocation? Does the competitive market provide people with fair incomes and do people always pay a fair price? Don't we need the government to step into some competitive markets to prevent the price from falling too low or rising too high? Let's now study these questions.

Is the Competitive Market Fair?

When a natural disaster strikes, such as a severe winter storm or a major flood, the prices of many essential items jump. The reason the prices jump is that some people have a greater demand and greater willingness to pay when the items are in limited supply. So the higher prices achieve an efficient allocation of scarce resources. News reports of these price hikes almost never talk about efficiency. Instead, they talk about **equity** or fairness. The claim often made is that it is unfair for profit-seeking dealers to cheat the victims of natural disaster.

Similarly, when low-skilled people work for a wage that is below what most would regard as a "living wage", the media and politicians talk of employers taking unfair advantage of their workers.

How do we decide whether something is fair or unfair? You know when *you* think something is unfair. But how do you know? What are the *principles* of fairness?

Philosophers have tried for centuries to answer this question. Economists have offered their answers too. But before we look at the proposed answers, you should know that there is no universally agreed upon answer.

Economists agree about efficiency. That is, they agree that it makes sense to make the economic pie as large as possible and to bake it at the lowest possible cost. But they do not agree about equity. That is, they do not agree about what are fair shares of the economic pie for all the people who make it. The reason is that ideas about fairness are not exclusively economic ideas. They touch on politics, ethics and religion. Nevertheless, economists have thought about these issues and have a contribution to make. So let's examine the views of economists on this topic.

To think about fairness, think of economic life as a game – a serious game. All ideas about fairness can be divided into two broad groups. They are:

- It's not fair if the *result* isn't fair.
- It's not fair if the *rules* aren't fair.

It's Not Fair if the *Result* Isn't Fair

The earliest efforts to establish a principle of fairness were based on the view that the result is what matters. The general idea was that it is unfair if people's incomes are too unequal. It is unfair that bank presidents earn millions of pounds a year while bank tellers earn only thousands of pounds a year. It is unfair that a shop owner enjoys a large profit and her customers pay higher prices in the aftermath of a flood.

There was a lot of excitement during the nineteenth century when economists thought they had made the incredible discovery that efficiency requires equality of incomes. To make the economic pie as large as possible, it must be cut into equal pieces, one for each person. This idea turns out to be wrong, but there is a lesson in the reason that it is wrong. So this nineteenth century idea is worth a closer look.

Utilitarianism

The nineteenth century idea that only equality brings efficiency is called *utilitarianism*. **Utilitarianism** is a principle that states that we should strive to achieve "the greatest happiness for the greatest number". The people who developed this idea were known as utilitarians. They included some famous thinkers, such as Jeremy Bentham and John Stuart Mill.

Utilitarianism argues that to achieve "the greatest happiness for the greatest number", income must be transferred from the rich to the poor up to the point of complete equality – to the point that there are no rich and no poor.

They reasoned in the following way: first, everyone has the same basic wants and are similar in their capacity to enjoy life. Second, the greater a person's income, the smaller is the marginal benefit of a pound. The millionth pound spent by a rich person brings a smaller marginal benefit to that person than the marginal benefit of the thousandth pound spent by a poorer person. So by transferring a pound from the millionaire to the poorer person, more is gained than is lost and the two people added together are better off.

Figure 5.7 illustrates this utilitarian idea. Tom and Jerry have the same marginal benefit curve, *MB*. (Marginal benefit is measured on the same scale of 1 to 3 for both Tom and Jerry.) Tom is at point *A*. He earns €5,000 a year, and his marginal benefit of a pound is 3. Jerry is at point *B*. He earns €45,000 a year, and his marginal benefit of a pound is 1. If a euro is transferred from Jerry to Tom, Jerry loses 1 unit of marginal benefit and Tom gains 3 units. So together, Tom and Jerry are better off. They are sharing the economic pie more efficiently. If a second euro is transferred, the same thing happens: Tom gains more than Jerry loses. And the same is true for every euro transferred until they both reach point *C*. At point *C*, Tom and Jerry have €25,000 each, and each has a marginal benefit of 2 units. Now they are sharing the economic pie in the most efficient way. It is bringing the greatest attainable happiness to Tom and Jerry.

Figure 5.7

myeconlab

Utilitarian Fairness

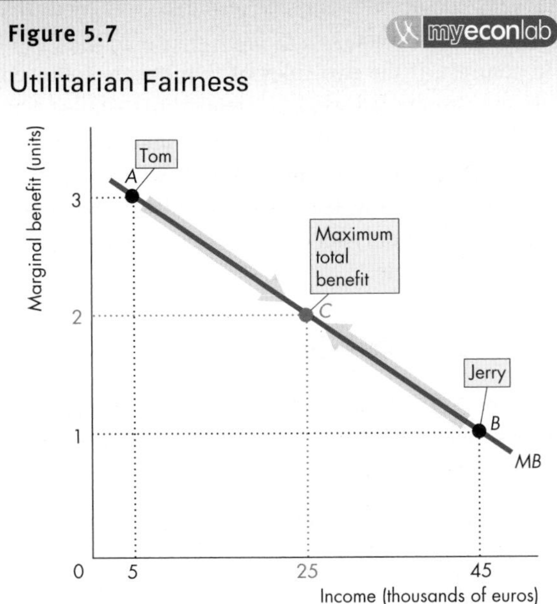

Tom earns €5,000 and has 3 units of marginal benefit at point *A*. Jerry earns €45,000 and has 1 unit of marginal benefit at point *B*. If income is transferred from Jerry to Tom, Jerry's loss is less than Tom's gain. Only when they have €25,000 each and 2 units of marginal benefit (at point *C*) can the sum of their total benefits increase no further.

The Big Trade-off

One big problem with the utilitarian ideal of complete equality is that it ignores the costs of making income transfers. The economist, Arthur Okun, in his book *Equality and Efficiency: The Big Tradeoff*, described the process of redistributing income as like trying to transfer water from one barrel to another with a leaky bucket. The more we try to increase equity by redistributing income, the more we reduce efficiency. Recognizing the cost of making income transfers leads to what is called the **big trade-off** – a trade-off between efficiency and fairness.

The big trade-off is based on the following facts. Income can be transferred from people with high incomes to people with low incomes only by taxing the high incomes. Taxing people's income from employment makes them work less. It results in the quantity of labour being less than the efficient quantity. Taxing people's income from capital makes them save less. It results in the quantity of capital being less than the efficient quantity. With smaller quantities of both labour and capital, the quantity of goods and services produced is less than the efficient quantity. The economic pie shrinks.

The trade-off is between the size of the economy and the degree of equality with which its produce is shared. The greater the amount of income redistribution through income taxes, the greater the inefficiency – the smaller is the economic pie.

A second source of inefficiency arises because a euro taken from a rich person does not end up as a euro in the hands of a poorer person. Some of it is spent on administration of the tax and transfer system. The cost of the tax-collection agency, Revenue & Customs, and the welfare administering agency, Department of Work and Pensions, must be paid with some of the taxes collected.

Also, taxpayers hire accountants, auditors and lawyers to help ensure that they pay the correct amount of taxes. These activities use skilled labour and capital resources that could otherwise be used to produce goods and services that people value.

You can see that when all these costs are taken into account, taking a euro from a rich person does not give a euro to a poor person. It is even possible that with high taxes, those with low incomes end up being worse off. Suppose, for example, that highly taxed entrepreneurs decide to work less hard and shut down some of their businesses. Low-income workers get fired and must seek other, perhaps even lower-paid, work.

Because of the big trade-off, those who say that fairness is equality propose a modified version of utilitarianism.

Make the Poorest as Well Off as Possible

A Harvard philosopher, John Rawls, proposed a modified version of utilitarianism in a classic book entitled *A Theory of Justice*, published in 1971. Rawls says that, taking all the costs of income transfers into account, the fair distribution of the economic pie is the one that makes the poorest person as well off as possible.

The incomes of rich people should be taxed and, after paying the costs of administering the tax and transfer system, what is left should be transferred to the poor. But the taxes must not be so high that they make the economic pie shrink to the point that the poorest person ends up with a smaller piece. A bigger share of a smaller pie can be less than a smaller share of a bigger pie. The goal is to make the piece enjoyed by the poorest person as big as possible. Most likely this piece will not be an equal share.

The "fair results" idea requires a change in the results after the game is over. Some economists say these changes are themselves unfair and they propose a different way of thinking about fairness.

It's Not Fair if the *Rules* Aren't Fair

The idea that it's not fair if the rules aren't fair is based on a fundamental principle that seems to be hard-wired into the human brain. It is the **symmetry principle**. The symmetry principle is the requirement that people in similar situations be treated similarly. It is the moral principle that lies at the centre of all the big religions. It says, in some form or other, "behave towards others in the way you expect them to behave towards you".

In economic life, this principle translates into *equality of opportunity*. But equality of opportunity to do what? This question is answered by the Harvard philosopher, Robert Nozick, in a book entitled *Anarchy, State, and Utopia*, published in 1974. Nozick argues that the idea of fairness as an outcome or result cannot work and that fairness must be based on the fairness of the rules. He suggests that fairness obeys two rules:

1 The state must enforce laws that establish and protect private property.

2 Private property may be transferred from one person to another only by voluntary exchange.

The first rule says that everything that is valuable must be owned by individuals and that the state must ensure that theft is prevented. The second rule says that the only legitimate way a person can acquire property is to buy it in exchange for something else that the person owns. If these rules, which are fair rules, are followed, then the result is fair. It doesn't matter how unequally the economic pie is shared, provided that the pie is baked by people, each one of whom voluntarily provides services in exchange for a share of the pie offered in compensation.

These rules satisfy the symmetry principle. And if these rules are not followed, the symmetry principle is broken. You can see these facts by imagining a world in which the laws are not followed.

First, suppose that some resources or goods are not owned. They are common property. Then everyone is free to participate in a grab to use these resources or goods. The strongest will prevail. But when the strongest prevails, the strongest effectively *owns* the resources or goods in question and prevents others from enjoying them.

Second, suppose that we do not insist on voluntary exchange for transferring ownership of resources from one person to another. The alternative is *involuntary* transfer. In simple language, the alternative is theft.

Both of these situations violate the symmetry principle. Only the strong get to acquire what they want. The weak end up with only the resources and goods that the strong don't want.

In contrast, if the two rules of fairness are followed, everyone, strong and weak, is treated in a similar way. Everyone is free to use their resources and human skills to create things that are valued by themselves and others and to exchange the fruits of their efforts with each other. This is the only set of arrangements that obeys the symmetry principle.

Fairness and Efficiency

If private property rights are enforced and if voluntary exchange takes place in a competitive market, resources will be allocated efficiently if there are no:

1 Price and quantity regulations

2 Taxes and subsidies

3 Externalities

4 Public goods and common resource

5 Monopolies

6 High transactions costs

And according to the Nozick rules, the resulting distribution of income and wealth will be fair. Let's study a concrete example to examine the claim that if resources are allocated efficiently, they are also allocated fairly.

Case Study: A Water Shortage in a Natural Disaster

A severe winter storm has broken the pipes that deliver drinking water to a city. Bottled water is available, but there is no tap water. What is the fair way to allocate the bottled water?

Market Price

Suppose that if the water is allocated by market price, the price jumps to €8 a bottle – five times its normal price. At this price, the people who own water can make a large profit by selling it. People who are willing and able to pay €8 a bottle get the water. And because most people can't afford the €8 price, they end up either without water or consuming just a few drops a day.

You can see that the water is being used efficiently. There is a fixed amount available, some people are willing to pay €8 to get a bottle, and the water goes to those people. The people who own and sell water receive a large producer surplus. Total surplus (the sum of consumer surplus and producer surplus) is maximized.

In the rules view, the outcome is also fair. No one is denied the water they are willing to pay for. In the results view, the outcome would most likely be regarded as unfair. The lucky owners of water make a killing, and the poorest end up the thirstiest.

Non-market Methods

Suppose that by a majority vote, the citizens decide that the government will buy all the water, pay for it with a tax, and use one of the non-market methods to allocate the water to the citizens. The possibilities now are:

Command
Someone decides who is the most deserving and needy. Perhaps everyone is given an equal share or perhaps government officials and their families get most water.

Contest
Bottles of water are prizes that go to those who are best at a particular contest.

First-come, First-served
Water goes to the first off the mark or to those who place the lowest value on their time and can afford to queue for it.

Lottery
Water goes to those in luck.

Personal characteristics
Water goes to those with the "right" characteristics. For example, the old, the young or pregnant mothers.

Except by chance, none of these methods delivers an allocation of water that is either fair or efficient. It is unfair in the rules view because the tax involves involuntary transfers of resources among citizens. It is unfair in the results view because the poorest don't end up being made as well off as possible.

The allocation is inefficient for two reasons. First, resources are used to operate the allocation scheme. Second, some people are willing to pay for more water than they have been allocated and others have been allocated more water than they are willing to pay for.

The second source of inefficiency can be overcome if, after the non-market allocation, people are permitted to trade water at its market price. Those who value water below the market price will sell, and those who are willing to pay the market price will buy. Those who value the water most highly are the ones who consume it.

Market Price with Taxes

Another approach is to allocate the scarce water using the market price but after the redistribution of buying power by taxing the sellers of water and providing benefits to the poor.

Suppose water owners are taxed on each bottle sold and the revenue from these taxes is given to the poorest people. People are then free, starting from this new distribution of buying power, to trade water at the market price. Because the owners of water are taxed on what they sell, they have a weaker incentive to offer water for sale and the supply decreases. The equilibrium price rises to more than €8 a bottle. There is now a deadweight loss in the market for water – similar to the loss that arises from underproduction on p. 109. (We study the effects of a tax and show its inefficiency in Chapter 6 on pp. 130–134.)

So the tax is inefficient. In the rules view, the tax is also unfair because it forces the owners of water to make a transfer to others. In the results view, the outcome might be regarded as being fair.

This brief case study illustrates the complexity of ideas about fairness. Economists have a clear criterion of efficiency but no comparably clear criterion of fairness. Most economists regard Nozick as being too extreme and want a fair tax in the rules. But there is no consensus about what would be a fair tax.

Review Quiz

Study Plan 5.5

1. What are the two big approaches to fairness?
2. Explain the utilitarian idea of fairness and what is wrong with it.
3. Explain the big trade-off and the idea of fairness developed to deal with it.
4. What is the main idea of fairness based on fair rules? Explain your answer.

You've now studied the two biggest issues that run right through the whole of economics: efficiency and equity, or fairness. In the next chapter, we study some sources of inefficiency and unfairness. And at many points throughout this book – and in your life – you will return to and use the ideas about efficiency and fairness that you've learned in this chapter. *Reading Between the Lines* on pp. 116–117 looks an example of inefficiency in India's allocation of scarce water resources.

Reading Between the Lines

Inefficiency in Water Use

The New York Times, 30 September 2006

India digs deeper, but wells are drying up, and farming crisis looms

Somini Sengupta

Across India, where most people still live off the land, the chief source of irrigation is groundwater, at least for those who can afford to pump it.

Indian law has virtually no restrictions on who can pump groundwater, how much and for what purpose. Anyone, it seems, can – and does – extract water as long as it is under his or her patch of land. That could apply to homeowner, farmer or industry. . . .

"We forgot that water is a costly item," lamented K. P. Singh, regional director of the Central Groundwater Board, in his office in the city of Jaipur. "Our feeling about proper, judicious use of water vanished."

. . . On a parched, hot morning . . . a train pulled into the railway station at a village called Peeplee Ka Bas. Here, the wells have run dry and the water table fallen so low that it is too salty even to irrigate the fields.

The train came bearing precious cargo: 15 tankers loaded with nearly 120,000 gallons of clean, sweet drinking water.

The water regularly travels more than 150 miles, taking nearly two days, by pipeline and then by rail, so that the residents of a small neighboring town can fill their buckets with water for 15 minutes every 48 hours.

It is a logistically complicated, absurdly expensive proposition. Bringing the water here costs the state about a penny a gallon; the state charges the consumer a monthly flat rate of 58 cents for about 5,300 gallons, absorbing the loss. . . .

The Essence of the Story

- In India, groundwater is the chief source of irrigation.
- Indian law has few restrictions on who can pump groundwater.
- A regional director of the Central Groundwater Board laments that Indians are behaving as if water were a free resource.
- Where the wells have run dry, water is delivered by pipeline and then by train.
- Water is rationed by permitting residents to fill their buckets with water for 15 minutes every 48 hours.
- Transporting water costs 1 cent per gallon, but consumers pay about 11 cents per 1,000 gallons.

Economic Analysis

- Water is one of the world's most vital resources, and it is used inefficiently.
- Markets in water are not competitive. They are controlled by governments or private producers, and they do not work like the competitive markets that deliver an efficient use of resources.
- The major problem in achieving an efficient use of water is to get it from the places where it is most abundant to the places in which it has the most valuable uses.
- Some places have too little water, and some have too much.
- The news article tells us that the owners of land that has groundwater under it pump the water and sell it and pay little attention to the fact that they will pump the well dry.
- Figure 1 illustrates this situation. The curve *D* shows the demand for water and its marginal social benefit *MSB*. The curve *S* shows the supply of water and its marginal social cost *MSC*.
- Ignoring the high marginal social cost, land owners produce W_A gallons a day, which is greater than the efficient quantity. Farmers are willing to pay *B*, which is less than the marginal social cost *C* but enough to earn the land owner a profit.
- A deadweight loss arises from overproduction.
- Figure 2 shows the situation in places where the wells have run dry.
- A limited quantity of water, W_B, is transported in, and each consumer is restricted to the quantity that can be put into a bucket in 15 minutes every 48 hours.
- Consumers are willing to pay *B* per gallon, which is much more than the marginal social cost *C*.
- The green area shows the consumer surplus, and the red rectangle shows the cost of the water, which is paid by the government and borne by the taxpayers.
- A deadweight loss arises from underproduction.
- The situation in India is replicated in thousands of places around the world.

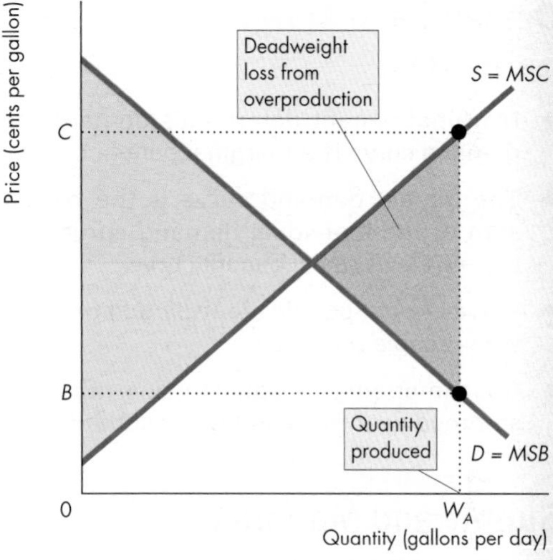

Figure 1 Overproduction where wells are not dry

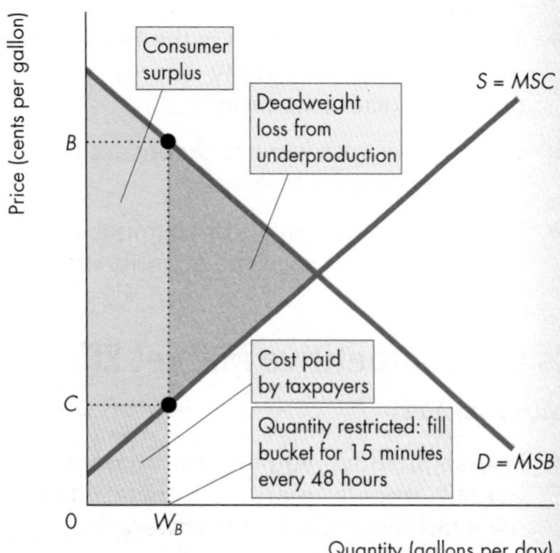

Figure 2 Underproduction where wells run dry

Summary

Key Points

Resource Allocation Methods

(pp. 102–103)

- Because resources are scarce, some mechanism must allocate them.
- The alternative allocation methods are market price; command; majority rule; contest; first-comer, first-served; lottery; personal characteristics; and force.

Demand and Marginal Benefit

(pp. 104–105)

- Marginal benefit determines demand, and a demand curve is a marginal benefit curve.
- The market demand curve is the horizontal sum of the individual demand curves and is the marginal social benefit curve.
- Value is what people are *willing to* pay; price is what people *must* pay.
- Consumer surplus equals value minus price, summed over the quantity consumed.

Supply and Marginal Cost

(pp. 106–107)

- The minimum supply-price determines supply, and the supply curve is the marginal cost curve.
- The market supply curve is the horizontal sum of the individual supply curves and is the marginal social cost curve.
- Opportunity cost is what producers pay; price is what producers receive.
- Producer surplus equals price minus opportunity cost, summed over the quantity produced.

Is the Competitive Market Efficient?

(pp. 108–111)

- In a competitive equilibrium, marginal social benefit equals marginal social cost and resource allocation is efficient.
- Buyers and sellers acting in their self-interest end up promoting the social interest.
- The sum of consumer surplus and producer surplus is maximized. Producing less than or more than the efficient quantity creates deadweight loss.
- Price and quantity regulations; taxes and subsidies; externalities; public goods and common resources; monopoly; and high transactions costs can create inefficiency and deadweight loss.

Is the Competitive Market Fair?

(pp. 112–115)

- Ideas about fairness divide into two groups: fair *results* and fair *rules*.
- Fair-results ideas require income transfers from the rich to the poor.
- Fair-rules ideas require property rights and voluntary exchange.

Key Figures

Key Terms

Big trade-off, 113
Command system, 102
Consumer surplus, 105
Deadweight loss, 109
Equity, 112
Producer surplus, 107
Symmetry principle, 114
Total surplus, 108
Transactions costs, 111
Utilitarianism, 112

Problems

Tests, Study Plan and Solutions*

1 The table gives the demand and supply schedules for train travel for Ben, Beth and Bill.

Price (euros per mile)	Quantity demanded (miles)		
	Ben	Beth	Bill
3	30	25	30
4	25	20	20
5	20	15	10
6	15	10	0
7	10	5	0
8	5	0	0
9	0	0	0

a Construct the market demand schedule if Ben, Beth and Bill are the only people in the market.

b What is marginal social benefit when the quantity is 50 miles? Why?

c What is each traveller's consumer surplus when the price is €4 a mile?

d What is the economy consumer surplus when the price is €4 a mile?

2 The table gives the supply schedules for jetski rides by three owners: Ann, Arthur and Abby.

Price (pounds per ride)	Quantity supplied (rides)		
	Ann	Arthur	Abby
10.00	0	0	0
12.50	5	0	0
15.00	10	5	0
17.50	15	10	5
20.00	20	15	10

a What is each owner's minimum supply-price of 10 rides a day?

b Which owner has the largest producer surplus when the price of a ride is £17.50? Explain why.

c What is the marginal social cost of producing 45 rides a day?

d Construct the market supply schedule if Ann, Arthur and Abby are the only suppliers of jetski rides.

3 The figure shows the demand for and supply of CDs.

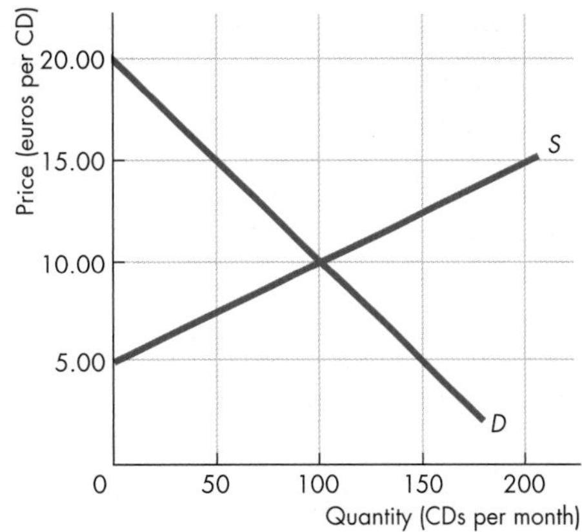

a What are the equilibrium price and equilibrium quantity of CDs?

b Shade in the consumer surplus (and label it) and shade in the producer surplus (and label it).

c Shade in the cost of producing the CDs sold.

d Calculate total surplus.

e What is the efficient quantity of CDs?

4 The table gives the demand and supply schedules for sandwiches.

Price (pounds per sandwich)	Quantity demanded (sandwiches per hour)	Quantity supplied (sandwiches per hour)
0	300	0
1	250	50
2	200	100
3	150	150
4	100	200
5	50	250
6	0	300

a What is the maximum price that consumers are willing to pay for the 200th sandwich?

b What is the minimum price that producers are willing to accept for the 200th sandwich?

c Are 200 sandwiches a day less than or greater than the efficient quantity?

d If the sandwich market is efficient, what is the consumer surplus?

e If the sandwich market is efficient, what is the producer surplus?

f If sandwich makers produce 200 a day, what is the deadweight loss?

g If the demand for sandwiches increases and the sandwich makers continue to produce 200 a day, describe the change in consumer surplus, producer surplus and the deadweight loss.

* Solutions to odd-numbered problems are provided.

5 The table gives the demand and supply schedules for sunscreen.

Price (euros per bottle)	Quantity demanded (bottles per day)	Quantity supplied (bottles per day)
0	800	0
5	700	100
10	600	200
15	500	300
20	400	400
25	300	500
30	200	600

a What is the maximum price that consumers are willing to pay for the 300th bottle?

b What is the minimum price that producers are willing to accept for the 300th bottle?

c Describe the situation in the market for sunscreen.

d How can the 300 bottles be allocated to beach goers? Which possible methods would be fair and which would be unfair?

Critical Thinking

1 Study Reading *Between the Lines* on pp. 116–117 and then answer the following questions:

a What is the major problem in achieving an efficient use of the world's water?

b If there were a global market in water, like there is in oil, how do you think the market would work?

c Would a free world market in water achieve an efficient use of the world's water resources? Explain why or why not.

d Would a free world market in water achieve a fair use of the world's water resources? Explain why or why not and be clear about the concept of fairness that you are using.

2 Explain how you would calculate your consumer surplus on an item that you buy regularly.

3 Write a short description of how you would determine whether the allocation of your time between studying different subjects is efficient. In what units would you measure marginal benefit and marginal cost? Use the concepts of marginal benefit, marginal cost, price, consumer surplus and producer surplus in your answer.

4 In 2001, the European Commission investigated why the prices of DVDs in the European Union were higher than those in the United States. The price differential was maintained because regional tagging of DVDs made the US DVDs unreadable on European players. Consider the impact of regional tagging and then answer the following questions:

a Does regional tagging lead to underproduction or overproduction of DVDs? Use the concepts of marginal benefit, marginal cost, price, consumer surplus and producer surplus to explain why.

b As DVD rewriting technology becomes cheaper, more pirate copies will be made and they will sell at very low prices. How will piracy change consumer surplus and producer surplus of legitimate EU DVD producers? Will the DVD market be more efficient? Explain your answer.

c If EU producers are correct when they say that the tagging system raises their cost above those of US producers, what will be the impact of removing regional tagging on the producer surplus in Europe?

Web Activities

Links to Websites

1 Obtain information about DRM and its use by Apple Computer to restrict the playing of iTunes to the iPod. Then think about the economic aspects of Apple's behaviour.

a What is the marginal social benefit of a tune downloaded from the iTunes Music Store?

b How would the marginal social benefit of a tune downloaded from the iTunes Music Store change if the file could be played on any MP3 player?

c What is the marginal cost to you of downloading an iTune?

d What is the marginal *social* cost of downloading an iTune?

e How would the marginal social cost of a tune downloaded from iTunes Music Store change if the file could be played on any MP3 player?

f Is the quantity of iTunes downloaded the efficient quantity? If it isn't the efficient quantity, is there underproduction or overproduction of iTunes?

g If an iTune file could be played on any MP3 player, would the quantity of iTunes downloaded increase, decrease, or remain the same?

h If an iTune file could be played on any MP3 player, would the quantity of iTunes downloaded be the efficient quantity? If it wouldn't be the efficient quantity, would there be underproduction or overproduction of iTunes?

i Write an executive summary of your answers to the above questions for Steve Jobs, the CEO of Apple Computer, explaining your view on the social interest aspects of restricting iTunes to the iPod.

Markets in Action

CHAPTER 6

After studying this chapter you will be able to:

- Explain what a price ceiling is and how a rent ceiling creates a housing shortage and inefficiency
- Explain what a price floor is and how a minimum wage creates unemployment and inefficiency
- Explain the effects of a tax on price, quantity, government revenue and efficiency
- Explain why farm prices and revenues fluctuate and how subsidies, production quotas and price supports influence farm production, costs and prices
- Explain how markets for illegal goods work

Turbulent Times

With rocketing house prices, it costs a pretty packet to rent an apartment in one of Britain's cities! Should the government cap the rents that landlords can charge? Or what about increasing the minimum wage? Wouldn't that help the low paid?

Almost everything we buy is taxed, but who really pays a tax: the buyer or the seller? In markets for many food items producers receive a subsidy. Who benefits from the subsidy: the farmer or the consumer? Some goods are illegal, yet they are still traded. How do markets for illegal goods work? This chapter answers these questions. And in *Reading Between the Lines* at the end of the chapter, we look at sugar subsidies in the European Union.

Price Ceilings

A **price ceiling** is a government regulation of the maximum price that may be legally charged. Trading at a price that exceeds the price ceiling is illegal and subject to penalties. Price ceilings have been used in markets for many goods and services but most prominently in the market for petrol and rental housing.

To see how a price ceiling works, we'll examine its effects in a market for rental housing, when it is called a **rent ceiling**.

A Rental Housing Market

The demand for and supply of rental housing determine the equilibrium rent and the equilibrium quantity of rental housing available. A rent ceiling tries to change the rent. The effects of a rent ceiling depend crucially on whether the ceiling is *binding* or *not binding*.

A rent ceiling is *not binding* if it is set *above* the equilibrium rent. In such a case, no one wants to charge or pay a rent that exceeds the ceiling. The force of the law and the market forces are not in conflict.

A rent ceiling is *binding* if it is set *below* the equilibrium rent. In this case, the rent ceiling prevents the price from allocating scarce housing resources. The force of the rent ceiling law and market forces are in conflict. With a binding rent ceiling, rent adjustments are blocked and the market is prevented from allocating scarce housing resources.

Figure 6.1 illustrates a rental housing market. In this market, the demand for housing, D, and the supply of housing, S, determine the equilibrium rent at €1,100 a month and the equilibrium quantity at 7,400 housing units.

The red line shows the rent ceiling and divides the price between the white legal region and the grey illegal region.

In part (a), the rent ceiling is €1,200 a month, which is *above* the equilibrium rent, so it is *not binding*. The rent ceiling has no effect in this market.

But in part (b), the rent ceiling is €1,000 a month, which is *below* the equilibrium rent. The equilibrium rent is now illegal. At the rent ceiling of €1,000 a month, 4,400 units of housing are supplied and 10,000 units are demanded. There is a shortage of 5,600 units – the

Figure 6.1

A Rent Ceiling

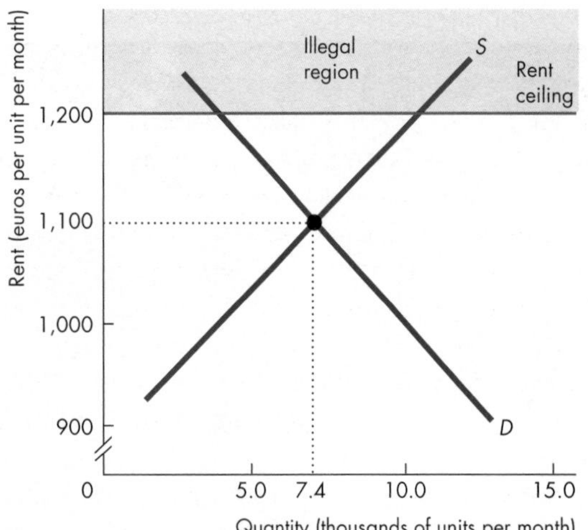

(a) Non-binding rent ceiling

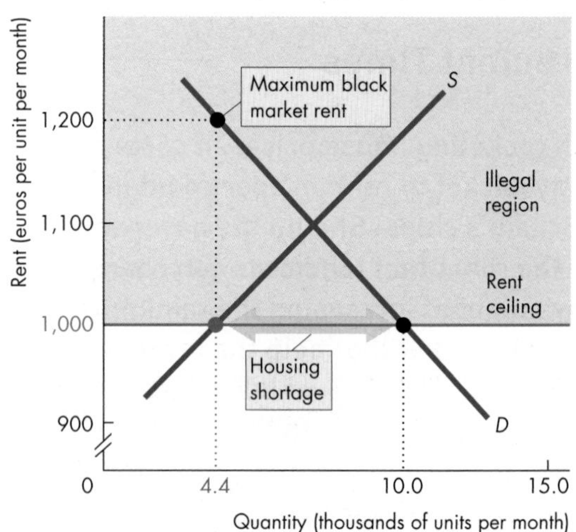

(b) Binding rent ceiling

The government imposes a rent ceiling and rents in the grey-shaded region are illegal.

In part (a), the rent ceiling is €1,200 a month which is *above* the equilibrium rent of €1,100 a month. The rent ceiling is not binding and has no effect – the equilibrium rent is already below the rent ceiling.

In part (b), the rent ceiling is €1,000 a month which is *below* the equilibrium rent of €1,100 a month. This rent ceiling is binding and has powerful effects. At a rent of €1,000 a month, the quantity of housing supplied is 4,400 units. Someone would be willingly to pay €1,200 a month for the 4,400th unit. Frustrated renters spend time searching for housing and frustrated renters and landlords make deals in a black market.

quantity demanded exceeds the quantity supplied by 5,600 units. The 4,400 units of available housing must somehow be allocated among the people who demand 10,000 units.

When the rent is not legally permitted to allocate scarce housing, other mechanisms must operate. You saw in Chapter 5 (pp. 102–103) that the market price is just one of the methods available for allocating scarce resources. Of the other mechanisms, those most likely to operate in a rental housing market are a lottery, a queue and discrimination. Also, the market price is likely to be used, but illegally, in a black market.

Let's see how scarce housing resources get allocated in the face of a binding rent ceiling by examining two groups of mechanisms:

- Lottery, queue and discrimination
- Black market

Lottery, Queue and Discrimination

The lottery that allocates scarce housing in the face of a rent ceiling isn't a formal lottery like the National Lottery. It is informal. Some people are lucky and find a house quickly and others are left out in the cold for a longer time.

The queue that allocates scarce housing in the face of a rent ceiling takes the form a waiting list. People express their interest in renting in a particular place and hope that their name rises to the top of the list in a reasonable amount of time.

Discrimination takes the form of landlords doing business with the people who most appeal to them, for whatever reason.

Faced with a lottery, queue and discrimination, would-be renters must spend an increasing amount of time looking for a place to rent.

The time spent looking for someone with whom to do business is called **search activity**. We spend some time in search activity almost every time we buy something. You want the latest hot mobile phone, and you know four shops that stock it. But which shop has the best deal? You need to spend a few minutes on the Internet or the telephone finding out. In some markets, we spend a lot of time searching. An example is the used car market. People spend a lot of time checking out alternative dealers and cars.

But when a price is regulated and there is a shortage, search activity increases. In the case of a rent-controlled housing market, frustrated would-be renters scan the newspapers, not only for housing ads but also for death notices! Any information about newly available housing is useful. And they race to be first on the scene when news of possible housing breaks.

The *opportunity cost* of a good is equal not only to its price but also to the value of the time spent searching the good. So the opportunity cost of housing is equal to the rent (a regulated price) plus the time and other resources spent searching for the restricted quantity available. Search activity is costly. It uses time and other resources, such as telephones, cars and petrol that could have been used in other productive ways. A rent ceiling controls the rent portion of the cost of housing but it does not control the opportunity cost, which might even be *higher* than the rent would be if the market were unregulated.

Black Market

A **black market** is an illegal market in which the price exceeds the legally imposed price ceiling. Black markets occur in rent-controlled housing markets. They also occur in the market for tickets to big sporting events and rock concerts, where "ticket touts" (or "scalpers") operate.

When a rent ceiling is in force, frustrated renters and landlords constantly seek ways of increasing rents. One common way is for a new tenant to pay a high price for worthless fittings, such as charging €2,000 for threadbare curtains. Another is for the tenant to pay an exorbitant price for new locks and keys called "key money". The level of a black market rent depends on how tightly the rent ceiling is enforced. With loose enforcement, the black market rent is close to the unregulated rent. But with strict enforcement, the black market rent is equal to the maximum price that renters are willing to pay for the available housing.

With strict enforcement of the rent ceiling in the example shown in Figure 6.1(b), the quantity of housing available remains at 4,400 units. A small number of people offer housing for rent at €1,200 a month – the highest rent that someone is willing to pay – and the government detects and punishes some of these black market traders.

Inefficiency of Rent Ceilings

Without a rent ceiling, the market determines the equilibrium rent and equilibrium quantity of housing. In this situation, scarce housing resources are allocated efficiently. *Marginal social benefit* equals *marginal social cost* (see Chapter 5, p. 108).

With a rent ceiling, the efficient outcome is blocked. Figure 6.2 shows the inefficiency of a rent ceiling. With the rent is fixed at €1,000 a month, 4,400 units are supplied. Marginal social benefit is €1,200 a month. The blue triangle above the supply curve and below the rent ceiling line shows producer surplus. Because the quantity of housing is less than the competitive quantity, there is a deadweight loss, shown by the grey triangle. This loss is borne by the consumers who can't find housing and by producers who can't supply housing at the new lower price. Consumers who do find housing at the controlled rent gain. If no one incurs search cost, consumer surplus is shown by the sum of the green triangle and the red rectangle. But search costs might eat up part of the consumer surplus, possibly as much as the entire amount that consumers are willing to pay for the available housing, (the red rectangle).

Are Rent Ceilings Fair?

Do rent ceilings achieve a fairer allocation of scarce housing? Chapter 5 (pp. 112–114) explores the complex ideas about fairness. According to the *fair rules* view, anything that blocks voluntary exchange is unfair, so rent ceilings are unfair. But according to the *fair result* view, a fair outcome is one that benefits the less well off. So according to this view, the fairest outcome is the one that allocates scarce housing to the poorest.

The mechanisms that operate in the face of a binding rent ceiling don't seem likely to achieve this outcome. A lottery allocates housing to the lucky, not the poor. A queue (a method used to allocate housing in England after the Second World War) allocates housing to those with the foresight to get their names on a list first, not to the poorest. Discrimination allocates scarce housing based on the views and self-interest of owners.

It is hard, then, to make a case for rent ceilings on the basis of fairness.

Figure 6.2 myeconlab

The Inefficiency of a Rent Ceiling

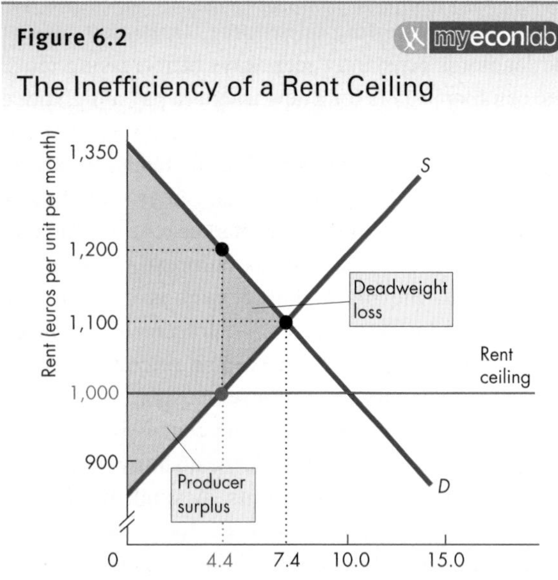

A rent ceiling of €1,000 a month decreases the quantity of housing supplied to 4,400 units. Producer surplus shrinks to the blue triangle and a deadweight loss (the grey triangle) arises. If people use no resources in search activity, consumer surplus is the green triangle plus the red rectangle. But if people use resources in search activity equal to the amount they are willing to pay for available housing (red rectangle), the consumer surplus shrinks to the green triangle.

If Rent Ceilings Are so Bad, Why Do We Have Them?

The economic case against rent ceilings is now widely accepted, so new rent ceiling laws are rare. But when governments try to repeal rent control laws, current renters lobby politicians to maintain the ceilings. Also, other people would be happy if they were lucky enough to find a rent-controlled apartment. So there is plenty of political support for rent ceilings.

Apartment owners who oppose rent ceilings are a minority. Because more people support rent ceilings than oppose them, politicians are sometimes willing to support them too.

Review Quiz

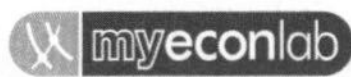

Study Plan 6.1

1. How does a rental housing market allocate scarce housing resources?
2. Describe and distinguish between a rent ceiling that is binding and one that is not binding.
3. What are the effects of a binding rent ceiling on the quantity of housing demanded and supplied?
4. How do scarce housing resources get allocated when a binding rent ceiling is in place?
5. What are the effects of a binding rent ceiling on producer surplus, consumer surplus and deadweight loss?
6. Does a binding rent ceiling achieve a fair outcome?

Next, we'll learn about the effects of price floors.

Price Floors

A **price floor** is a regulation that makes it illegal to trade at a price lower than the specified level. Price floors are used in many markets. But when a price floor is applied to labour markets, it is called a **minimum wage**.

A Labour Market

In the labour market, employers are on the demand side and workers are on the supply side. Firms decide how much labour to demand, and the lower the wage rate, the greater is the quantity of labour demanded. Households decide how much labour to supply, and the higher the wage rate, the greater is the quantity of labour supplied. The demand for and supply of labour determine the equilibrium wage rate and the equilibrium quantity of labour employed.

A minimum wage law tries to change the wage rate. The effects of a minimum wage, like those of a rent ceiling, depend crucially on whether the minimum is *binding* or *not binding*.

A minimum wage is *not binding* if it is set *below* the equilibrium wage rate. In such a case, no one wants to pay or work for a wage that is below the minimum. The force of the law and the market forces are not in conflict.

A minimum wage is *binding* if it is set *above* the equilibrium wage. In this case, the force of the minimum wage law and market forces are in conflict. With a binding minimum, wage adjustments are blocked and the market is prevented from allocating labour resources.

Figure 6.3 illustrates a labour market. The demand for labour, *D*, and the supply of labour, *S*, determine the equilibrium wage rate at €6 an hour and the equilibrium quantity at 21 million hours of labour. The red line shows the minimum wage rate and divides the wage between the white legal region and the grey illegal region.

In part (a), the minimum wage is €4 an hour, which is *below* the equilibrium wage, so it is *not binding*. The minimum wage has no effect in this market.

But in part (b), the minimum wage is €6 an hour, which is *above* the equilibrium wage. The equilibrium wage is now illegal. At the minimum wage of €6 an hour, 20 million hours of labour are demanded and

Figure 6.3

A Minimum Wage

myeconlab

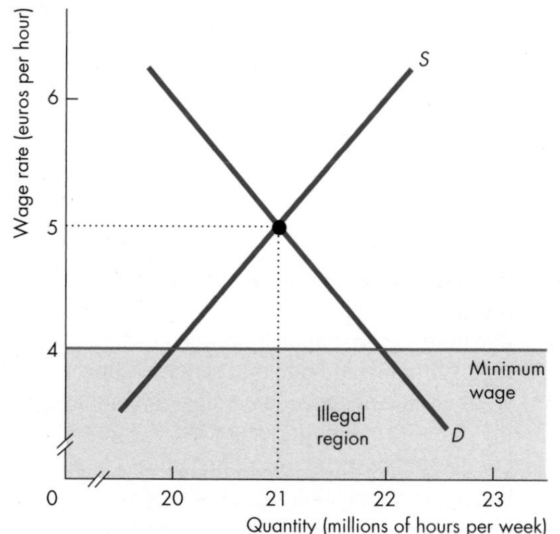

(a) Non-binding minimum wage

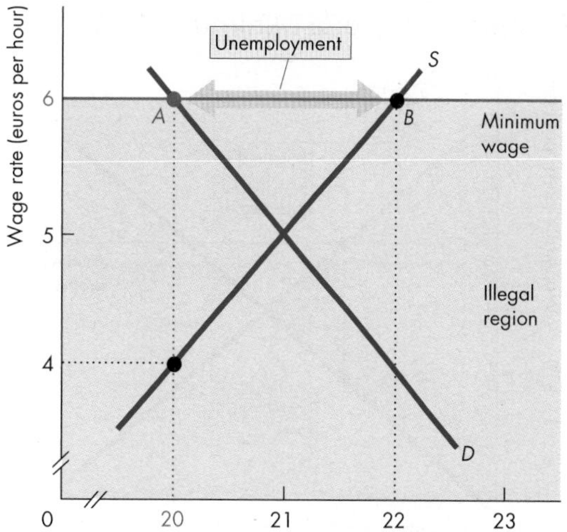

(b) Binding minimum wage

The government imposes a minimum wage and wages in the grey-shaded region are illegal.

In part (a), the minimum wage is *below* the equilibrium wage rate and is not binding. The equilibrium wage rate is legal so this minimum wage has no effect.

In part (b), the minimum wage is *above* the equilibrium wage rate and is binding. A wage rate of €5 an hour is illegal (in the grey-shaded illegal region). At a minimum wage of €6 an hour, 20 million hours are hired but 22 million hours are available. Unemployment *AB* of 2 million hours a year is created.

22 million hours are supplied. Frustrated unemployed workers who are willing to supply the 20 millionth hour for €4 spend time and other resources searching for hard-to-find jobs.

Inefficiency and the Minimum Wage

The minimum wage results in unemployment – wasted labour resources – and an inefficient amount of job search. Figure 6.4 illustrates the inefficiency of the minimum wage. There is a deadweight loss because at the quantity of labour employed, 20 million hours, the value to the firm of the marginal worker exceeds that wage rate for which that person is willing to work.

But the total loss exceeds the deadweight loss. At the equilibrium level of employment, unemployed people have a big incentive to spend time and effort looking for work. The red rectangle shows the potential loss from this extra job search. This loss arises because someone who finds a job earns €6 an hour (from the demand curve) but would have been willing to work for €4 an hour (from the supply curve). So everyone who is unemployed has an incentive to search hard and use resources that are worth the €2-an-hour surplus to find a job.

Figure 6.4 myeconlab

The Inefficiency of a Minimum Wage

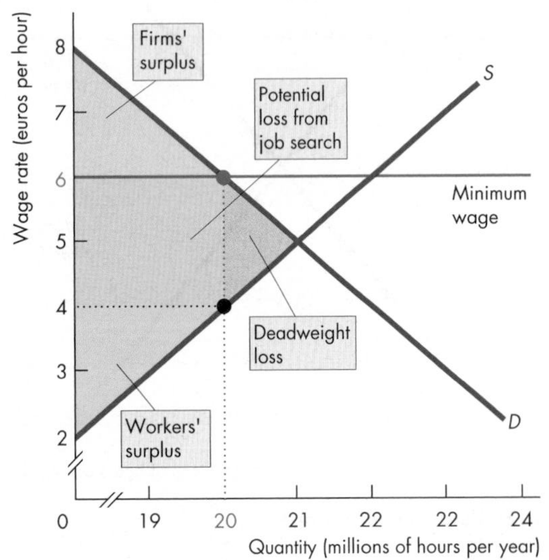

A minimum wage shrinks the firms' surplus (blue) and workers' surplus (green) and creates a deadweight loss (grey). If people use resources in job search equal to the amount they are able to gain by finding a job, the red rectangle is also lost.

Is the Minimum Wage Fair?

The minimum wage is unfair on both views of fairness – it delivers an unfair result and imposes unfair rules. The result is unfair because only those people who find jobs benefit. The unemployed end up worse off than with no minimum wage. And those who get jobs are probably not those who are least well off. When the wage rate doesn't allocate jobs, discrimination, another source of unfairness, increases.

The minimum wage imposes unfair rules because it blocks voluntary exchange. Firms are willing to hire more labour and people are willing to work more. But the minimum wage law does not permit them to do so.

If the Minimum Wage Is so Bad, Why Do We Have It?

Although the minimum wage is inefficient, not everyone loses from it. The people who find jobs at the minimum wage rate are better off. Other supporters of the minimum wage believe that the elasticities of demand and supply in the labour market are low, so not much unemployment results. Labour unions support the minimum wage because it puts upward pressure on all wage rates, including those of union workers. Non-union labour is a substitute for union labour, so when the minimum wage rises, the demand for union labour increases.

Review Quiz

Study Plan 6.2

1. How does a labour market allocate scarce labour resources?
2. Describe and distinguish between a minimum wage that is binding and one that is not binding.
3. What are the effects of a binding minimum wage on the quantity of labour demanded, the quantity of labour supplied and unemployment?
4. Why does a minimum wage create inefficiency?

Next we're going to study taxes. We'll see how taxes change the prices and quantities of the things taxed. You will discover the surprising fact that while the government can impose a tax on either the buyer or the seller of a good or service, the government can't decide who will pay the tax!

Taxes

Everything you earn and almost everything you buy is taxed. The income tax and a National Insurance contribution are deducted from your earnings. The prices of most of the things you buy include VAT and the prices of a few goods such as cigarettes, alcoholic drinks and petrol include a heavy excise tax. Firms also pay some taxes, one of which is a National Insurance contribution for every person they employ.

Who *really* pays these taxes? Because the income tax and National Insurance contribution are deducted from your pay, isn't it obvious that *you* pay these taxes? And isn't it equally obvious that you pay the VAT, that smokers pay the tax on cigarettes and that your employer pays the employer's contribution to the National Insurance?

You're going to discover that it isn't obvious who *really* pays a tax and that lawmakers don't make that decision. We begin with a definition of tax incidence.

Tax Incidence

Tax incidence is the division of the burden of a tax between the buyer and the seller. When the government imposes a tax on the sale of a good,[1] the price paid by the buyer might rise by the full amount of the tax, by a lesser amount, or not at all. If the price paid by the buyer rises by the full amount of the tax, then the burden of the tax falls entirely on the buyer – the buyer pays the tax. If the price paid by the buyer rises by a lesser amount than the tax, then the burden of the tax falls partly on the buyer and partly on the seller. And if the price paid by the buyer doesn't change at all, then the burden of the tax falls entirely on the seller.

Tax incidence does not depend on the tax law. The law might impose a tax on sellers or on buyers, but the outcome is the same in either case. To see why, let's look at the tax on cigarettes.

A Tax on Sellers

During 2003, the government of France increased the tax on the sale of cigarettes three times. We'll assume that the percentage tax increase over the year is equivalent to €1.50 a pack. To work out the effects of this tax on the sellers of cigarettes, we begin by examining the effects on demand and supply in the market for cigarettes.

In Figure 6.5, the demand curve is *D*, and the supply curve is *S*. With no tax, the equilibrium price is €3 per pack and 350 million packs a year are bought and sold. A tax on sellers is like an increase in cost, so it decreases the supply of cigarettes. To determine the position of the new supply curve, we add the tax to the minimum price that sellers are willing to accept for each quantity sold. You can see that without the tax, sellers are willing to offer 350 million packs a year for €3 a pack. So with a €1.50 tax, they will offer 350 million packs a year only if the price is €4.50 a pack. The supply curve shifts to the red curve labelled *S* + *tax on sellers*.

Equilibrium occurs where the new supply curve intersects the demand curve at 325 million packs a year. The price paid by buyers rises by €1 to €4 a pack. And the price received by sellers falls by 50 cents to €2.50 a pack. So buyers pay €1 of the tax and sellers pay the other 50 cents.

Figure 6.5 myeconlab

A Tax on Sellers

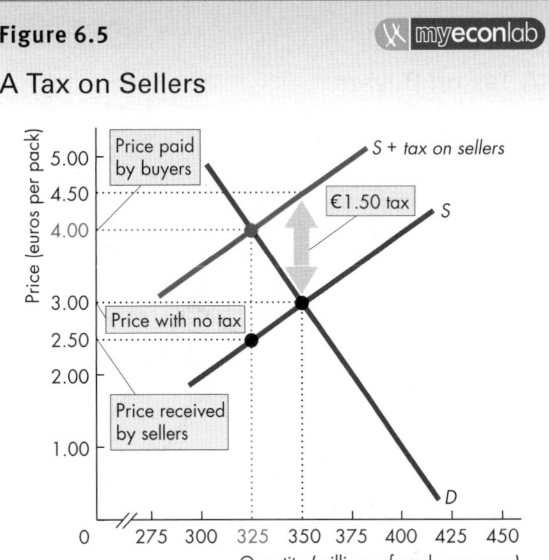

With no tax, 350 million packs a year are bought and sold at €3 a pack. A tax on sellers of €1.50 a pack decreases the supply of cigarettes and shifts the supply curve leftward to *S* + *tax on sellers*.

The equilibrium quantity decreases to 325 million packs a year, the price paid by buyers rises to €4 a pack, and the price received by sellers falls to €2.50 a pack. The tax raises the price paid by buyers by less than the tax and lowers the price received by sellers, so buyers and sellers share the burden of the tax.

[1] These propositions also apply to services and factors of production (land, labour and capital).

A Tax on Buyers

Suppose that instead of taxing sellers, the French government taxes cigarette buyers €1.50 a pack. A tax on buyers lowers the amount they are willing to pay the seller, so it decreases demand and shifts the demand curve leftward. To determine the position of this new demand curve, we subtract the tax from the maximum price that buyers are willing to pay for each quantity bought.

You can see in Figure 6.6 that with no tax, buyers are willing to buy 350 million packs a year for €3 a pack. So with a €1.50 tax, they will buy 350 packs a year only if the price including the tax is €3 a pack, which means that they're willing to pay the seller only €1.50 a pack. The demand curve shifts to become the red curve labelled *D – tax on buyers.*

Equilibrium occurs where the new demand curve intersects the supply curve at a quantity of 325 million packs a year. The price received by sellers is €2.50 a pack, and the price paid by buyers is €4 a pack.

Figure 6.6

myeconlab

A Tax on Buyers

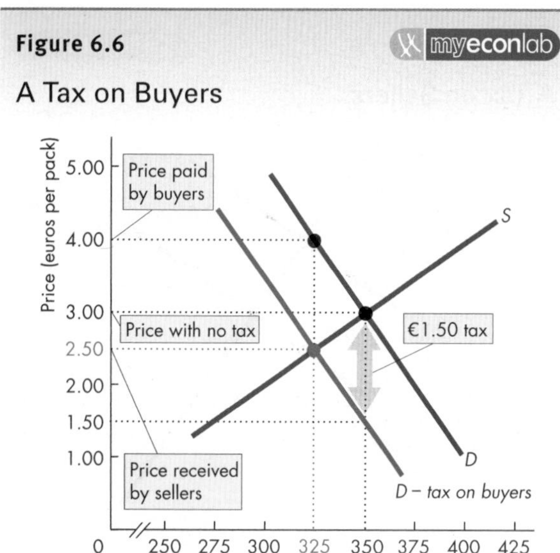

With no tax, 350 million packs a year are bought and sold at €3 a pack. A tax on buyers of €1.50 a pack decreases the demand for cigarettes and shifts the demand curve leftward to *D – tax on buyers.*

The equilibrium quantity decreases to 325 million packs year. The price paid by buyers rises to €4 a pack and the price received by sellers falls to €2.50 a pack. The tax raises the price paid by buyers by less than the tax and lowers the price received by sellers, so buyers and sellers share the burden of the tax.

Equivalence of Tax on Buyers and Sellers

You can see that the tax on buyers in Figure 6.6 has the same effects as the tax on sellers in Figure 6.5. The quantity decreases to 325 million packs a year, the price paid by buyers rises to €4 a pack and the price received by sellers falls to €2.50 a pack. Buyers pay €1 of the €1.50 tax. Sellers pay the other 50 cents of the tax.

Can We Share the Burden Equally?

Suppose that the government wants the burden of the cigarette tax to fall equally on buyers and sellers and declares that a 75 cents tax be imposed on each. Is the burden of the tax then shared equally?

You can see that it is not. The tax is still €1.50 a pack. You've seen that the tax has the same effect regardless of whether it is imposed on sellers or buyers. So imposing half the tax on one and half on the other is like an average of the two cases you've examined. In this case, the demand curve shifts downward by 75 cents and the supply curve shifts upward by 75 cents. The equilibrium quantity is still 325 million packs. Buyers pay €4 a pack, of which 75 cents is tax. Sellers receive €2.50 a pack (€3.25 from buyers minus the 75 cents tax).

The key point is that when a transaction is taxed, there are two prices: the price paid by buyers, which includes the tax; and the price received by sellers, which excludes the tax. Buyers respond only to the price that includes the tax because that is the price they pay. Sellers respond only to the price that excludes the tax because that is the price they receive. A tax is like a wedge between the buying price and the selling price. It is the size of the wedge, not the side of the market – demand side or supply side – on which the tax is imposed that determines the effects of the tax.

Payroll Taxes

In some countries, governments impose a payroll tax and share the tax equally between both employers (buyers) and workers (sellers). But the principles you've just learned apply to this tax too. The market for labour, not the government, decides how the burden of a payroll tax is divided by firms and workers.

In the cigarette tax examples, the buyers end up bearing twice the burden of the tax borne by sellers. In general, the division of the burden of a tax between buyers and sellers depends on the elasticities of demand and supply, as you will now see.

Tax Division and Elasticity of Demand

The division of the total tax between buyers and sellers depends partly on the elasticity of demand. There are two extreme cases:

- Perfectly inelastic demand – buyers pay
- Perfectly elastic demand – sellers pay

Perfectly Inelastic Demand

Figure 6.7(a) shows the UK market for insulin. Demand is perfectly inelastic at 100,000 bottles a day, regardless of the price, as shown by the vertical curve *D*. That is, a diabetic would sacrifice all other goods and services rather than not consume the quantity of insulin that provides good health. The supply curve of insulin is *S*. With no tax, the price is £2 a bottle and the quantity is 100,000 bottles a day.

If insulin is taxed at 20 pence a bottle, we must add the tax to the minimum price at which drug companies are willing to sell insulin. The result is the new supply curve *S* + *tax*. The price rises to £2.20 a bottle, but the quantity does not change. Buyers pay the entire sales tax of 20 pence a bottle.

Perfectly Elastic Demand

Figure 6.7(b) illustrates the UK market for pink marker pens. Demand is perfectly elastic at £1 a pen, as shown by the horizontal curve *D*. If pink markers are less expensive than the other pens, everyone uses pink. If pink pens are more expensive than the others, no one uses pink. The supply curve is *S*. With no tax, the price of a pink marker is £1 and the quantity is 4,000 a week.

If a tax of 20 pence is imposed on pink marker pens but not on other colours, we add the tax to the minimum price at which sellers are willing to offer pink pens for sale. The new supply curve is *S* + *tax*. The price remains at £1 a pen and the quantity decreases to 1,000 a week. The tax leaves the price paid by buyers unchanged but lowers the amount received by sellers by the full amount of the tax. Sellers pay the entire tax on a pink marker pen.

We've seen that when demand is perfectly inelastic, buyers pay the entire tax and when demand is perfectly elastic, sellers pay the entire tax. In the usual case, demand is neither perfectly inelastic nor perfectly elastic and the tax is split between buyers and sellers. The division depends on the elasticity of demand. The more inelastic the demand, the larger is the amount of the tax paid by buyers.

Figure 6.7 myeconlab

Tax and the Elasticity of Demand

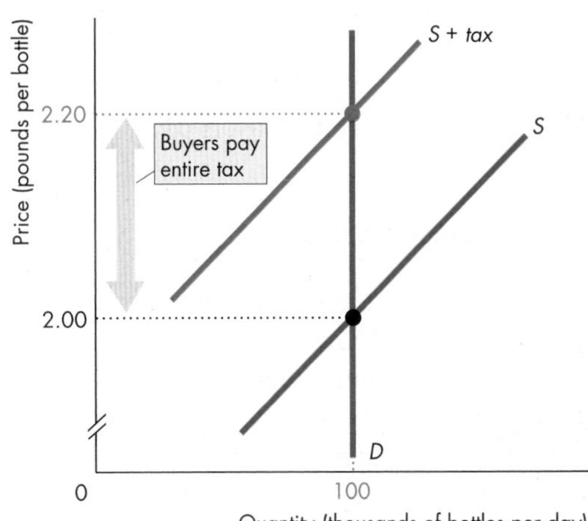

(a) Inelastic demand

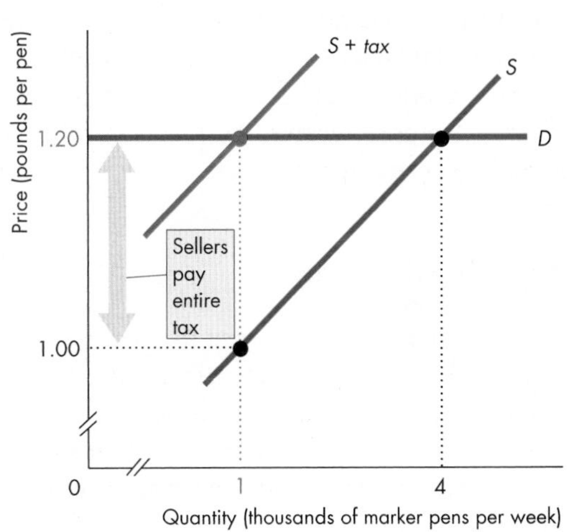

(b) Elastic demand

Part (a) shows the market for insulin, where demand is perfectly inelastic. With no tax, the price is £2 a bottle and the quantity is 100,000 bottles a day. A sales tax of 20 pence a bottle decreases supply and shifts the supply curve to *S* + *tax*. The price rises to £2.20 a bottle, but the quantity bought does not change. Buyers pay the entire tax.

Part (b) shows the market for pink marker pens. The demand for pink pens is perfectly elastic. With no tax, the price of a pen is £1 and the quantity is 4,000 pens a week. A sales tax of 20 pence a pink pen decreases supply and shifts the supply curve to *S* + *tax*. The price remains at £1 a pen, and the quantity of pink pens sold decreases to 1,000 a week. The sellers pay the entire tax.

Tax Division and Elasticity of Supply

The division of the tax between buyers and sellers depends, in part, on the elasticity of supply. There are two extreme cases:

- Perfectly inelastic supply – sellers pay
- Perfectly elastic supply – buyers pay

Perfectly Inelastic Supply

Figure 6.8(a) shows the market for water from a UK mineral spring which flows at a constant rate that can't be controlled. The quantity supplied is 100,000 bottles a week, as shown by the supply curve *S*. The demand curve for the water from this spring is *D*. With no tax, the price is 50 pence a bottle and the 100,000 bottles that flow from the spring are bought.

Suppose this spring water is taxed at 5 pence a bottle. The supply curve does not change because the spring owners still produce 100,000 bottles a week even though the price has fallen. But buyers are willing to buy the 100,000 bottles only if the price is 50 pence a bottle. So the price remains at 50 pence a bottle. The tax reduces the price received by sellers to 45 pence a bottle and sellers pay the entire tax.

Perfectly Elastic Supply

Figure 6.8(b) illustrates the market for sand from which computer-chip makers extract silicon. The supply of this sand is perfectly elastic at 10 pence a kilogram. The supply curve is *S*. The demand curve for sand is *D*. With no tax, the price is 10 pence a kilogram and 5,000 kilograms a week are bought.

If sand is taxed at 1 penny a kilogram, we add the tax to the minimum supply-price. Sellers are now willing to offer any quantity at 11 pence a kilogram along the curve *S + tax*. The price rises to 11 pence a kilogram and 3,000 kilograms a week are bought. The price paid by buyers has increased by the full amount of the tax. Buyers pay the entire tax.

We've seen that when supply is perfectly inelastic, sellers pay the entire tax and when supply is perfectly elastic, buyers pay the entire tax. In the usual case, supply is neither perfectly inelastic nor perfectly elastic and the tax is split between sellers and buyers. But how the tax is split depends on the elasticity of supply. The more elastic the supply, the larger is the amount of the tax paid by buyers.

Figure 6.8

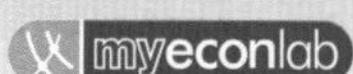

Tax and the Elasticity of Supply

(a) Inelastic supply

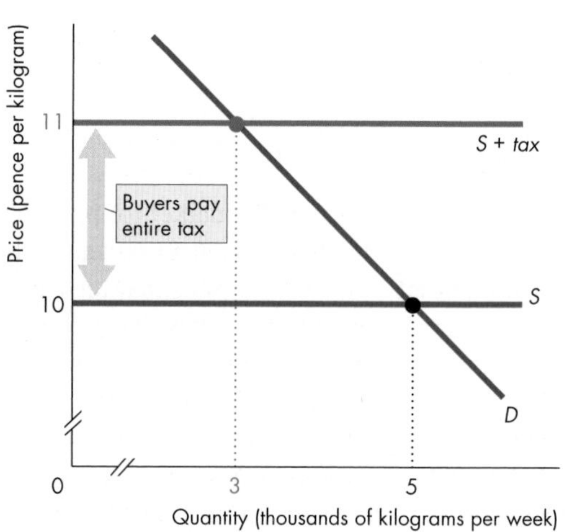

(b) Elastic supply

Part (a) shows the market for water from a mineral spring. Supply is perfectly inelastic. With no tax, the price is 50 pence a bottle. With a tax of 5 pence a bottle, the price remains at 50 pence a bottle. The number of bottles bought remains the same, but the price received by sellers decreases to 45 pence a bottle. Sellers pay the entire tax.

Part (b) shows the market for sand. Supply is perfectly elastic. With no tax, the price of sand is 10 pence a kilogram. A tax of 1 penny a kilogram increases the minimum supply-price to 11 pence a kilogram. The supply curve shifts to *S + tax*. The price increases to 11 pence a kilogram. Buyers pay the entire tax.

Taxes in Practice

Supply and demand are rarely perfectly elastic or perfectly inelastic. But some items tend towards one of the extremes. For example, alcohol, tobacco and petrol have low elasticities of demand and high elasticities of supply. So the burden of these taxes falls more heavily on buyers than on sellers. Labour has a low elasticity of supply and a high elasticity of demand. So despite the government's desire to split the National Insurance contribution equally between workers and employers, the burden of this tax falls mainly on workers.

The most heavily taxed items are those that have either a low elasticity of demand or a low elasticity of supply. For these items, the equilibrium quantity doesn't decrease much when a tax is imposed. So the government collects a large tax revenue and the deadweight loss from the tax is small.

It is unusual to tax an item heavily if neither its demand nor its supply is inelastic. With an elastic supply *and* demand, a tax brings a large decrease in the equilibrium quantity and a small tax revenue.

Taxes and Efficiency

We've seen that a tax can place a wedge between the price buyers pay and the price sellers receive. The price buyers pay is also the buyers' willingness to pay or marginal benefit. The price sellers receive is also the sellers' minimum supply price, which equals marginal cost.

So because a tax puts a wedge between the buyers' price and the sellers' price, it also puts a wedge between marginal benefit and marginal cost and creates inefficiency. With a higher buyers' price and a lower sellers' price, the tax decreases the quantity produced and consumed and a deadweight loss arises. Figure 6.9 shows the inefficiency of a tax. With a tax, both consumer surplus and producer surplus shrink. Part of each surplus goes to the government in tax revenue – the purple area in the figure. And part of each surplus becomes a deadweight loss – the grey area.

In the extreme cases of perfectly inelastic demand and perfectly inelastic supply, the tax does not change the quantity bought and sold and there is no deadweight loss. The more inelastic is either demand or supply, the smaller is the decrease in quantity and the smaller is the deadweight loss.

In a market in which there is overproduction, a tax can help to achieve a more efficient use of resources. We will examine this case in Chapter 15 where we study externalities.

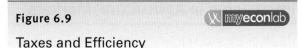

Figure 6.9 myeconlab

Taxes and Efficiency

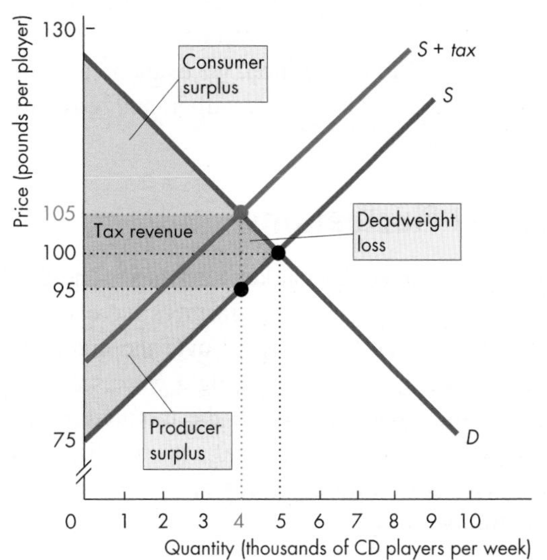

With no tax on CD players, 5,000 a week are bought and sold at £100 each. With a tax of £10 a CD player, the buyers' price rises to £105 a player, the sellers' price falls to £95 a player, and the quantity decreases to 4,000 CD players a week.

With the tax, consumer surplus shrinks to the green area and the producer surplus shrinks to the blue area. Part of the loss of consumer surplus and producer surplus goes to the government as tax revenue, which is shown as the purple area. A deadweight loss arises, which is shown by the grey area.

Review Quiz

Study Plan 6.3

1. How does the elasticity of demand influence the effect of a tax on the price paid by buyers, the price received by sellers, the quantity, the tax revenue and the deadweight loss?
2. How does the elasticity of supply influence the effect of a tax on the price paid by buyers, the price received by sellers, the quantity, the tax revenue and the deadweight loss?
3. Why does a tax create a deadweight loss?

Next, we look at agricultural markets and see how governments intervene in these markets to try to stabilize and boost farm revenues.

Intervening in Agricultural Markets

Farmers' lives are filled with uncertainty, fluctuating output, and fluctuating prices and revenues. Can governments help farmers by intervening in the markets for farm products? In this section, we examine agricultural markets and see how the weather and government policies influence them.

Harvest Fluctuations

Figure 6.10 shows the market for wheat. The demand curve for wheat is *D*. Once farmers have harvested their crop, they have no control over the quantity supplied and supply is inelastic along a *momentary supply curve*. With a normal harvest, the momentary supply curve is MS_0, the price is €160 a tonne, the quantity produced is 4 million tonnes and farm revenue is €640 million.

Poor Harvest

In Figure 6.10(a), a poor harvest decreases the quantity produced to 3 million tonnes. The momentary supply curve shifts leftward to MS_1, the price rises to €240 a tonne, and farm revenue increases to €720 million. A *decrease* in supply brings a rise in price and an *increase* in farm revenue.

Bumper Harvest

In Figure 6.10(b), a bumper harvest increases the quantity produced to 5 million tonnes. The momentary supply curve shifts rightward to MS_2, the price falls to €80 a tonne and farm revenue decreases to €400 million. An *increase* in supply brings a fall in price and a *decrease* in farm revenue.

Elasticity of Demand

Farm revenue and the quantity produced move in opposite directions because the demand for wheat is *inelastic*. The percentage change in price exceeds the change in the quantity demanded. In Figure 6.10(a), the increase in revenue from the higher price (€240 million the light blue area) exceeds the decrease in revenue from the smaller quantity (€160 million the red area). In Figure 6.10(b), the decrease in revenue from the lower price (€320 million the red area) exceeds the increase in revenue from the increase in the quantity sold (€80 million the light blue area).

Figure 6.10

Harvests, Farm Prices and Farm Revenues

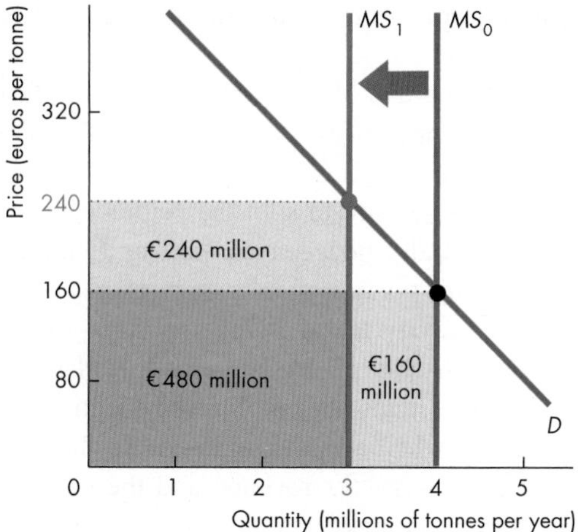

(a) Poor harvest: revenue increases

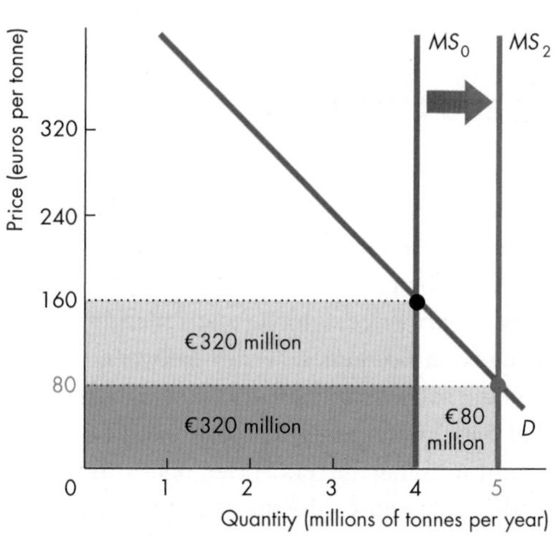

(b) Bumper harvest: revenue decreases

The demand curve for wheat is *D*. In normal times, the supply curve is MS_0, and 4 million tonnes are sold for €160 a tonne.

In part (a), a poor growing season decreases supply, shifting the supply curve to MS_1. The price increases to €240 a tonne and farm revenue *increases* from €640 million to €720 million – the increase in revenue from the higher price (light blue area) exceeds the decrease in revenue from the smaller quantity (red area).

In part (b), a bumper harvest increases supply, shifting the supply curve to MS_2. The price decreases to €80 a tonne and farm revenue *decreases* to €400 million – the decrease in revenue from the lower price (red area) exceeds the increase in revenue from the increase in the quantity sold (light blue area).

If demand is *elastic*, farm revenue and the quantity produced fluctuate in the same direction. Bumper harvests increase revenue and poor harvests decrease it. But the demand for most agricultural products is inelastic, so the case we've studied is the relevant one.

Avoiding a Fallacy of Composition

Although *total* farm revenue increases when there is a poor harvest, the revenue of those *individual* farmers whose entire crop is wiped out decreases. Those whose crop is unaffected gain. So a poor harvest is not good news for all farmers.

Government Intervention

Because the markets for farm products often confront farmers with low incomes, government intervention occurs in these markets. Three methods of intervention are used in markets for farm products, often in combination. They are:

- Subsidies
- Production quotas
- Price supports

Subsidies

The producers of peanuts, sugar beet, milk, wheat and many other farm products receive subsidies. A **subsidy** is a payment made by the government to a producer. To discover the effects of a subsidy, we'll look at a market for peanuts. Figure 6.11 shows this market. The demand for peanuts is *D* and the supply of peanuts is *S*. With no subsidy, equilibrium occurs at a price of €40 a tonne and a quantity of 40 million tonnes of peanuts per year.

Suppose that the government introduces a subsidy on peanuts of €20 a tonne. A subsidy is like a negative tax. You've seen earlier in this chapter that a tax is equivalent to an increase in cost. A subsidy is equivalent to a decrease in cost. And a decrease in cost brings an increase in supply.

To determine the position of the new supply curve, we subtract the subsidy from farmers' minimum supply-price. Without a subsidy, farmers are willing to offer 40 million tonnes a year for €40 a tonne. So with a subsidy of €20 a tonne, they will offer 40 million tonnes a year if the price is as low as €20 a tonne. The supply curve shifts to the red curve labelled *S* – *subsidy*.

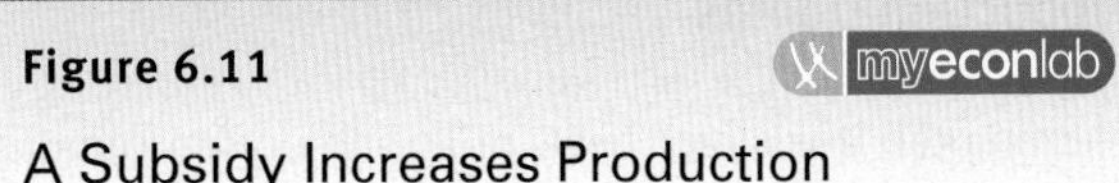

Figure 6.11 myeconlab

A Subsidy Increases Production

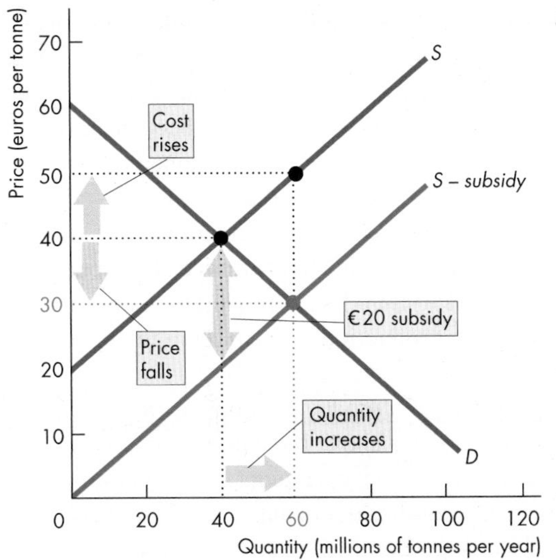

With no subsidy, 40 million tonnes a year are produced at €40 a tonne. A subsidy of €20 a tonne shifts the supply curve rightward to *S* – *subsidy*. The equilibrium quantity increases to 60 million tonnes a year, the price falls to €30 a tonne, and the price plus subsidy received by farmers rises to €50 a tonne. In the new equilibrium, marginal cost (on the blue supply curve) exceeds marginal benefit (on the demand curve) and a deadweight loss arises from overproduction.

Equilibrium occurs where the new supply curve intersects the demand curve at 60 million tonnes a year. The price falls by €10 to €30 a tonne. But the price plus subsidy received by farmers rises by €10 to €50 a tonne.

Because the supply curve is the marginal cost curve, and the demand curve is the marginal benefit curve, a subsidy raises marginal cost above marginal benefit and creates a deadweight loss from overproduction.

Subsidies spill over to the rest of the world. Because they lower the price, subsidized farmers offer some of their output for sale on the world market, which lowers the price in the rest of the world. Faced with lower prices, farmers in other countries decrease production and receive smaller revenues.

Farm subsidies are a major obstacle to achieving an efficient use of resources in the global markets for farm products and are a source of tension between Europe, the United States and poorer developing nations.

Production Quotas

The markets for sugar beet, milk and cotton (among others) have, from time to time, been regulated with production quotas. A **production quota** is an upper limit to the quantity of a good that may be produced in a specified period. To discover the effects of quotas, we'll look at a market for sugar beet in Figure 6.12. With no quota, the price is €30 a tonne and 60 million tonnes of sugar beet per year are produced.

Suppose that the sugar beet growers want to limit total production to get a higher price. They persuade the government to introduce a production quota that limits sugar beet production to a maximum of 40 million tonnes a year.

The effect of a production quota depends on whether it is set below or above the equilibrium quantity. If the government introduced a quota above 60 million tonnes a year, the equilibrium quantity in Figure 6.12, nothing would change because sugar beet growers are already producing less than the quota. But a quota of 40 million tonnes is less than the equilibrium quantity. Figure 6.12 shows the effects of this quota.

To implement the quota, each grower is assigned a production limit and the total of the production limits equals 40 million tonnes. Production that in total exceeds 40 million tonnes is illegal, so we've shaded the illegal region with the quantity above the quota. Growers are no longer permitted to produce the equilibrium quantity because it is in the illegal region. As in the case of price ceilings and price floors, market forces and political forces are in conflict.

When the government sets a production quota, it does not regulate the price. Market forces determine it. In the example in Figure 6.12, with production limited to 40 million tonnes a year, the market price rises to €50 a tonne.

The quota not only raises the price but also *lowers* the marginal cost of producing the quota because the sugar beet growers slide down their supply (and marginal cost) curves.

A production quota is inefficient because it results in underproduction. At the quota quantity, marginal benefit is equal to the market price and marginal cost is less than the market price, so marginal benefit exceeds marginal cost.

Because of these effects of a quota, such arrangements are often popular with producers and in some cases, producers, not governments, attempt to implement them. But it is hard for quotas to work when they are voluntary. The reason is that each producer has an incentive to cheat and produce a little bit more than the allotted quota. You can see why by comparing the market price and marginal cost. If one producer could get away with a tiny increase in production, her or his profit would increase. But if all producers cheat by producing more than the quota, the market moves back towards the unregulated equilibrium and the gain for producers disappears.

Figure 6.12

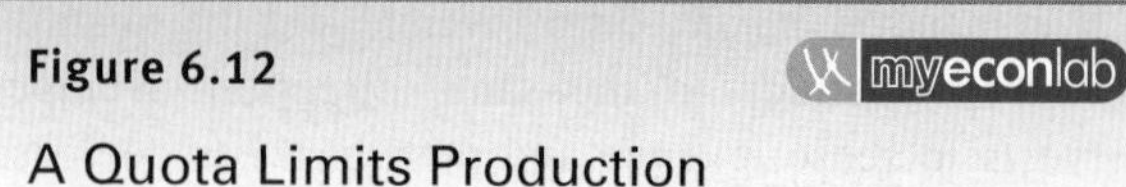

A Quota Limits Production

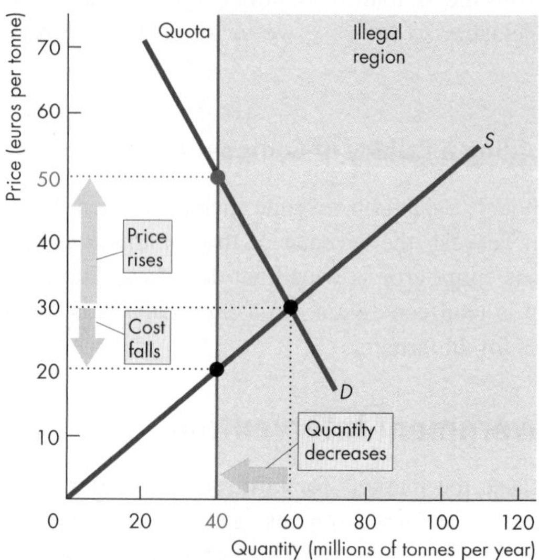

With no quota, 60 million tonnes a year are produced at €30 a tonne. A quota of 40 million tonnes a year restricts total production to that amount. The equilibrium quantity decreases to 40 million tonnes a year, the price rises to €40 a tonne, and the farmers' marginal cost falls to €20 a tonne. In the new equilibrium, marginal cost (on the supply curve) is less than marginal benefit (on the demand curve) and a deadweight loss arises from underproduction.

Price Supports

A **price support** is the government guaranteed minimum price of a good. A price support in an agricultural market operates in a similar way to a *price floor* in other markets. It creates a surplus. But there is a crucial difference between a price floor and a price support. With a price support, the government buys the surplus and ends up with unwanted inventories.

Figure 6.13 shows how a price support works in the market for wheat. The competitive equilibrium price of wheat is €130 a tonne, and 4 million tonnes are

Figure 6.13

A Price Support

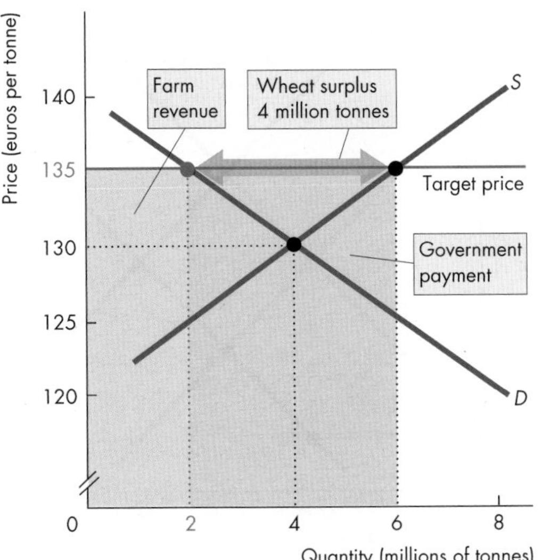

With no price support, 4 million tonnes are produced at €130 a tonne. A price support of €135 a tonne raises the price to €135 a tonne, decreases the quantity sold to 2 million tonnes, and increases the quantity produced to 6 million tonnes. The price support creates a surplus of 4 million tonnes. To maintain the price support, the government buys the surplus for €540 million a year. If the government does not buy the surplus, the price returns to €130 a tonne.

produced and bought. If the government sets a price support of €135 a tonne, then the price increases to €135 a tonne and the quantity demanded decreases to 2 million tonnes.

The quantity supplied increases to 6 million tonnes. Farmers produce a surplus of 4 million tonnes. This method of stabilizing farm revenue would fail without a method of taking up the surplus produced. If farmers are left to find a market for their surplus, then the price will fall below the price support to the competitive price of €130 a tonne.

If, on the other hand, the government buys the surplus at the support price, then the price will remain at the price support. If the government systematically buys more than it sells, it will end up with a large inventory or stockpile.

Such has been the outcome in the European Union (see Box 6.1), which has mountains of butter and lakes of wine! The cost of buying and storing the inventory falls on taxpayers and the winners from a price support are large, efficient farms.

Box 6.1

The EU Common Agricultural Policy

The EU Common Agricultural Policy (CAP) is the world's most extensive farm support programme. The CAP was set up in 1957 to make sure the bad experiences of wartime shortages and low farm incomes would not be repeated.

The centrepiece of the programme is a price support system that works in a similar way to the one described in Figure 6.13. (A complicating factor arises from EU imports from the rest of the world, but the basic story is the same.)

If the CAP target price is consistently higher than the world price, the European Union will always buy more agricultural produce than it sells. Such a policy creates surpluses in the form of mountains of grain, beef and butter. Payments for buying and storing the EU surpluses take 50 per cent of the EU budget!

Table 1 shows the rising cost of these payments.

Table 1

The Cost of the CAP Price Supports

Year	Price support costs (billions of euros)
1980	11
1990	27
2000	41
2005	49

Source of data: European Commission, *Eurostat*, 2007.

Review Quiz

Study Plan 6.4

1. How do poor harvests and bumper harvests influence farm prices and farm revenues?
2. Explain how a subsidy influences farm prices and output. How does a subsidy affect farm revenues?
3. Explain how a production quota influences farm prices and output. How does a production quota affect farm revenues?
4. Explain how a price support influences farm prices and output. How does a price support affect farm revenues?

Governments intervene in some markets by making it illegal to trade in a good. Let's now see how these markets work.

Markets for Illegal Goods

The markets for many goods and services are regulated, and buying and selling some goods is illegal. The best known examples of illegal goods are drugs, such as cannabis, Ecstasy, cocaine and heroin.

Despite the fact that these drugs are illegal, trade in them is a multi-billion pound business. This trade can be understood by using the same economic model and principles that explain trade in legal goods. To study the market for illegal goods, we're first going to examine the prices and quantities that would prevail if these goods were not illegal. Second we'll see how prohibition works. Then we'll how a tax might be used to limit the consumption of these goods.

A Free Market for a Drug

Figure 6.14 shows a market for a drug. The demand curve, *D*, shows that, other things remaining the same, the lower the price of the drug, the larger is the quantity demanded. The supply curve, *S*, shows that, other things remaining the same, the lower the price of the drug, the smaller is the quantity supplied. If drugs are not illegal, the quantity bought and sold would be Q_C and the price would be P_C.

A Market for an Illegal Drug

When a good is illegal, the cost of trading in the good increases. By how much the cost increases and on whom the cost falls depend on the penalties for breaking the law and the effectiveness with which the law is enforced. The larger the penalties and the more effective the policing, the higher are the costs of trading the drug. Penalties might be imposed on sellers or buyers or both sellers and buyers.

Penalties on Sellers

If selling drugs is illegal, sellers will face fines and prison sentences if their activities are detected. Penalties for selling illegal drugs are part of the cost of supplying those drugs. These penalties lead to a decrease in supply and shift the supply curve of the drug leftward. To determine the new supply curve, we add the cost of breaking the law to the minimum price that drug dealers are willing to accept. In Figure 6.14, the cost of breaking the law by selling drugs (*CBL*) is added to the minimum price that dealers will accept and the supply curve shifts leftward to *S* + *CBL*. If penalties are imposed only on sellers, the market moves from point *E* to point *F*. The price rises and the quantity bought decreases.

Figure 6.14

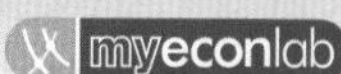

A Market for an Illegal Good

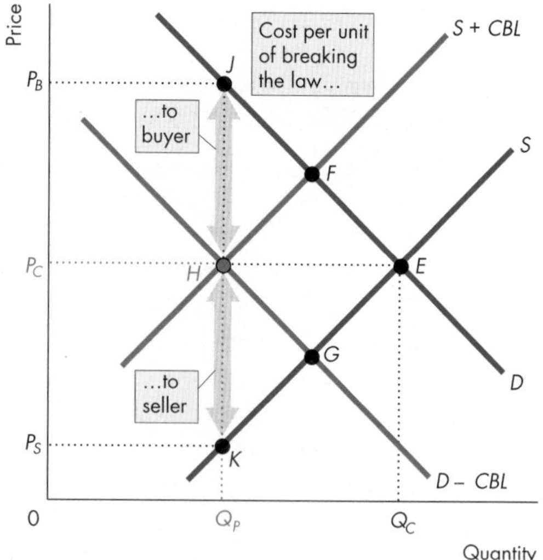

The demand curve for drugs is *D* and the supply curve is *S*. If drugs are not illegal, the quantity bought and sold is Q_C at a price of P_C at point *E*.

If selling drugs is illegal, the cost of breaking the law by selling drugs (*CBL*) is added to the minimum supply-price and supply decreases to *S* + *CBL*. The market moves to point *F*.

If buying drugs is illegal, the cost of breaking the law is subtracted from the maximum price that buyers are willing to pay, and demand decreases to *D* – *CBL*. The market moves to point *G*.

With both buying and selling illegal, the supply curve and the demand curve shift and the market moves to point *H*. The market price remains at P_C, but the market price plus the penalty for buying rises to P_B (point *J*) and the market price minus the penalty for sellers falls to P_S (point *K*).

Penalties on Buyers

If buying drugs is illegal, buyers face fines and prison sentences if their activities are detected. Penalties for buying the illegal drugs fall on buyers and the cost of breaking the law must be subtracted from the value of the good to determine the maximum price that buyers are willing to pay. Demand decreases and the demand curve shifts leftward. In Figure 6.14, the demand curve shifts to *D* – *CBL*. If penalties are imposed only on buyers, the market moves from point *E* to point *G*. The market price falls and the quantity bought decreases.

Penalties on Both Sellers and Buyers

If penalties are imposed on sellers *and* buyers, both supply and demand decrease. In Figure 6.14, the costs of breaking the law are the same for both buyers and sellers, so the demand and supply curves shift leftward by the same amounts. The market moves to point H. The market price remains at the competitive market price, but the quantity bought decreases to Q_P. The buyer pays P_C plus the cost of breaking the law, which is P_B. And the seller receives P_C minus the cost of breaking the law, which is P_S.

The larger the penalty and the greater the degree of law enforcement, the larger is the decrease in demand and/or supply and the greater is the shift of the demand and/or supply curve. If the penalties are heavier on sellers, the supply curve shifts further than the demand curve and the market price rises above P_C. If the penalties are heavier on buyers, the demand curve shifts further than the supply curve and the price falls below P_C. In many European countries, the penalties on sellers of illegal drugs are larger than those on buyers. As a result, the decrease in supply is much larger than the decrease in demand. The quantity of drugs traded decreases and the price is higher than in a free market.

With high enough penalties and effective law enforcement, it is possible to decrease demand and/or supply so that the quantity bought is zero. But in reality, such an outcome is unusual. The key reason is the high cost of law enforcement and insufficient resources for the police to achieve effective enforcement. Because of this situation, some people suggest that drugs (and other illegal goods) should be legalized and sold openly but should also be taxed at a high rate in the same way that legal drugs such as alcohol are taxed. How would such an arrangement work?

Legalizing and Taxing Drugs

From your study of the effects of taxes, it is easy to see that the quantity of drugs bought could be decreased if drugs were legalized and taxed. A sufficiently high tax could be imposed to decrease supply, raise the price and achieve the same decrease in the quantity bought as with a prohibition on drugs. The government would collect a large tax revenue. Such a debate in the United Kingdom concerning cannabis led the government to reduce penalties on the illegal trade in 2003 but not to legalize the trade. We'll look at some of the issues that influenced this decision now.

Illegal Trading to Evade the Tax

It is likely that an extremely high tax rate would be needed to cut the quantity of drugs bought to the level prevailing with a prohibition. It is also likely that many drug dealers and consumers would try to cover up their activities to evade the tax. If they did act in this way, they would face the cost of breaking the law – the tax law. If the penalty for tax law violation is as severe and as effectively policed as drug-dealing laws, the analysis we've already conducted applies also to this case. The quantity of drugs bought would depend on the penalties for law breaking and on the way in which the penalties are assigned to buyers and sellers.

Taxes versus Prohibition: Some Pros and Cons

Which is more effective: prohibition or taxes? In favour of taxes and against prohibition is the fact that the tax revenue can be used to make law enforcement more effective. It can also be used to run a more effective education campaign against illegal drug use. In favour of prohibition and against taxes is the fact that prohibition sends a signal that might influence preferences, decreasing the demand for illegal drugs. Also, some people intensely dislike the idea of the government profiting from trade in harmful substances.

Review Quiz

Study Plan 6.5

1 How does imposing a penalty on buying a drug influence demand and the quantity consumed?
2 How does imposing the penalty on selling a drug influence supply and the quantity consumed?
3 Is there an economic case for legalizing drugs?
4 Is there any case for legalizing drugs?

You now know how to use the demand and supply model to study government interventions in markets. You've seen how price ceilings, minimum wages, taxes, subsidies, quotas and price supports create inefficient resource use. You've also seen how in a market for an illegal good, the quantity can be decreased by imposing penalties or by legalizing and taxing the good.

Before you leave this topic, take a look at *Reading Between the Lines* on pp. 138–139 to see why the European Union is reforming its Common Agricultural Policy.

Reading Between the Lines

Price Supports: EU Sugar Reforms

The Times, 23 June 2005

EU sugar shake-up threatens £40m hole in profits

. . . The European Commission plans to cut guaranteed prices to European [sugar] producers by 39 per cent over the next four years. It will also offer financial sweeteners to farmers and sugar factories to move out of the sector in an attempt to end surplus production.

The moves are part of a wider programme in the European Union to modernise the Common Agricultural Policy (CAP). They are also necessary to bring the policy into line with international trade rules after Australia, Brazil and Thailand challenged successfully the present practice of generous subsidies at the World Trade Organization.

. . .

The changes are expected to hit sugar producers but could lead to substantial benefits for big sugar users such as Cadbury Schweppes, the confectionary group, and soft-drink producers such as Coca-Cola.

Marian Fischer Boel, the European Agriculture Commissioner, said: "There is no alternative to a profound reform. The easy option would be to sit on my hands but that would mean a slow and painful death for the European sugar sector. I am convinced that EU sugar producers have a competitive future but only if we act now and act decisively."

The reforms are designed to end the situation whereby EU sugar prices, protected by high import tariffs, are three times higher than the world market rate and huge export subsidies are paid every year to dispose of millions of tonnes of excess sugar. Britain will press for the package to be agreed by national governments this year during its EU presidency.

The Essence of the Story

- In 2005, the EC proposed to cut the guaranteed price for sugar in the Common Agricultural Policy (CAP) by 39 per cent.
- The moves are part of a programme to bring the EU CAP into line with international trade rules.
- Farmers and sugar factories will receive compensation to encourage them to stop producing sugar.
- The changes will bring losses for sugar producers but gains for sugar users such as producers of confectionary and soft drinks.

Economic Analysis

- Figure 1 shows the EU market for sugar in 2004 – the data for the figure are from EU sources.
- The EU demand curve for sugar is D_{04} and the EU supply curve of sugar is S_{04}.
- With no intervention, the price would be €150 per tonne and the quantity produced would be 15.5 million tonnes.
- The EU sets the target price at €500 per tonne. At this price, the quantity of sugar supplied increases to 17 million tonnes
- The quantity demanded at the target price is 14.3 million tonnes so a surplus of 2.7 million tonnes of sugar is created.
- The EU buys the surplus at €500 a tonne, paying out €1.34 billion to sugar farmers and processors (the red area). Revenue for farmers and processors is the blue area received from the market plus the red area received as a subsidy.
- Figure 2 shows the impact of cutting the target price to €300 a tonne by 2008 with no change in the demand for or supply of sugar.
- The sugar surplus is reduced to 1.2 million tonnes and the subsidy falls to €0.36 billion.
- Revenue for farmers and processors – the blue area received from the market plus the red area received as a subsidy – falls.
- Cutting the target price improves the efficiency of the EU sugar market.
- Compensation payments to farmers equivalent to 60 per cent of the former subsidy, will not increase the quantity supplied because these payments are independent of the quantity produced.
- You can see why reform of sugar subsidies is hard to achieve.

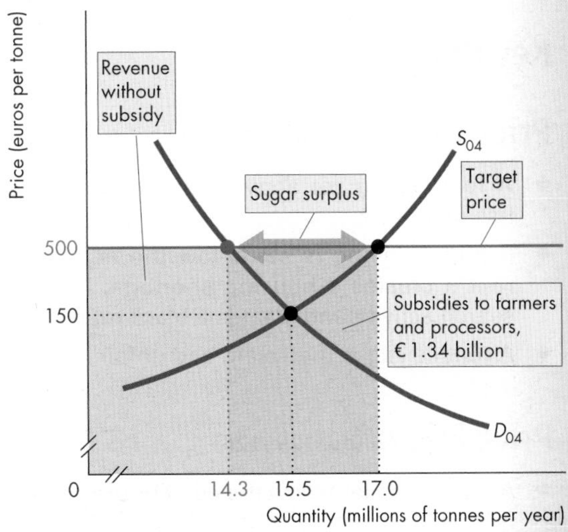

Figure 1 EU sugar market in 2004

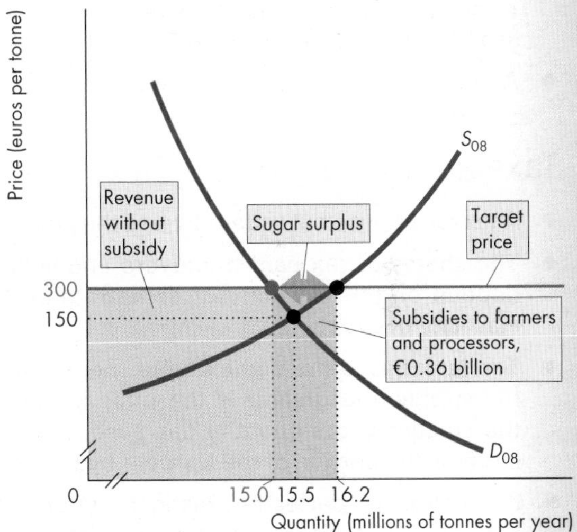

Figure 2 EU sugar market in 2008

- EU sugar farmers and processors have a lot to lose from reform and organize to oppose it. And they must be compensated for accepting reform.

Summary

Key Points

Price Ceilings (pp. 122–124)

- A rent ceiling set above the equilibrium rent has no effects.
- If a rent ceiling is set below the equilibrium rent it creates a housing shortage, increases search activity and creates a black market.
- A rent ceiling is inefficient and unfair.

Price Floors (pp. 125–126)

- A price floor set below the equilibrium price has no effect.
- The minimum wage is an example of a price floor.
- A minimum wage set above the equilibrium wage rate creates unemployment and increases search activity and illegal trading.
- A price floor is inefficient and unfair.

Taxes (pp. 127–131)

- A tax raises price but usually by less than the tax.
- The shares of tax paid by buyers and sellers depend on the elasticity of demand and the elasticity of supply.
- The less elastic the demand and more elastic the supply, the greater is the price increase, the smaller is the quantity decrease, and the larger is the portion of the tax paid by buyers.
- If demand is perfectly elastic or supply is perfectly inelastic, sellers pay the entire tax. And if demand is perfectly inelastic or supply is perfectly elastic, buyers pay the entire tax.

Intervening in Agricultural Markets (pp. 132–135)

- Farm revenues fluctuate because supply fluctuates. Because the demand for most farm products is inelastic, a decrease in supply increases farm revenue while an increase in supply decreases farm revenue.
- A subsidy is like a negative tax. It lowers the price and leads to inefficient overproduction.
- A quota leads to inefficient underproduction, which raises price.
- A price support leads to inefficient overproduction.
- The Common Agricultural Policy uses costly price supports.

Markets for Illegal Goods (pp. 136–137)

- Penalties on sellers of an illegal good increase the cost of selling the good and decrease its supply. Penalties on buyers decrease their willingness to pay and decrease demand for the good.
- The higher the penalties and the more effective the law enforcement, the smaller is the quantity bought.
- A tax that is set at a sufficiently high rate will decrease the quantity of a drug consumed, but there will be a tendency for the tax to be evaded.

Key Figures

Key Terms

Problems

Tests, Study Plan and Solutions* 

1 The figures shows the demand for and supply of rental housing in Townsville.

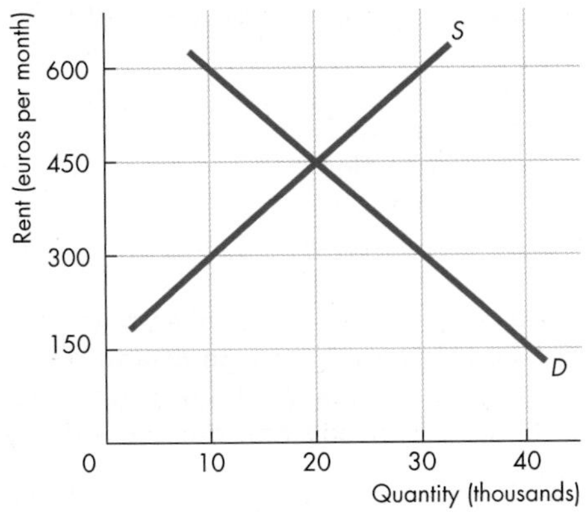

a What are the equilibrium rent and equilibrium quantity of rented housing?

If a rent ceiling is set at €300 a month, what is:

b The quantity of housing rented?

c The shortage of housing?

d The maximum price that someone is willing to pay for the last unit available?

If a rent ceiling is set at €600 a month, what is:

e The quantity of housing rented?

f The shortage of housing?

g The maximum price that someone is willing to pay for the last unit available?

2 The table gives the demand and supply schedules of teenage labour.

Wage rate (pounds per hour)	Quantity demanded (hours per month)	Quantity supplied
4	3,000	1,000
5	2,500	1,500
6	2,000	2,000
7	1,500	2,500
8	1,000	3,000

a What are the equilibrium wage rate and level of employment?

b What is the quantity of unemployment?

c If a minimum wage for teenagers is £5 an hour, how many hours do they work?

d If a minimum wage for teenagers is £5 an hour, how many hours are unemployed?

e If a minimum wage for teenagers is £7 an hour, how many hours are employed and unemployed?

3 The table shows the demand and supply schedules for chocolate brownies in the United Kingdom.

Price (pence per brownie)	Quantity demanded (millions per day)	Quantity supplied
50	5	3
60	4	4
70	3	5
80	2	6
90	1	7

a If brownies are not taxed, what is the price of a brownie and how many are consumed?

b If sellers are taxed at 20 pence a brownie, what is the price and how many brownies are consumed? Who pays the tax?

c If buyers are taxed at 20 pence a brownie, what is the price and how many brownies are consumed? Who pays the tax?

4 The demand and supply schedules for roses are:

Price (pounds per bunch)	Quantity demanded (bunches per week)	Quantity supplied
10	100	40
12	90	60
14	80	80
16	70	100
18	60	120

a If there is no tax on roses, what is the price and how many bunches of roses are bought?

b If a tax of £6 a bunch is introduced, what is the price, how many bunches of roses are bought? Who pays the tax?

5 The demand and supply schedules for rice are:

Price (pounds per box)	Quantity demanded (boxes per week)	Quantity supplied
1.00	3,500	500
1.10	3,250	1,000
1.20	3,000	1,500
1.30	2,750	2,000
1.40	2,500	2,500
1.50	2,250	3,000
1.60	2,000	3,500

* Solutions to odd-numbered problems are provided.

What are the price, the marginal cost of producing rice, and the quantity produced if the government:

a Introduces a subsidy of £0.30 a box on rice?

b Sets a quota of 2,000 boxes a week instead of a subsidy?

6 The figure shows the market for a banned substance.

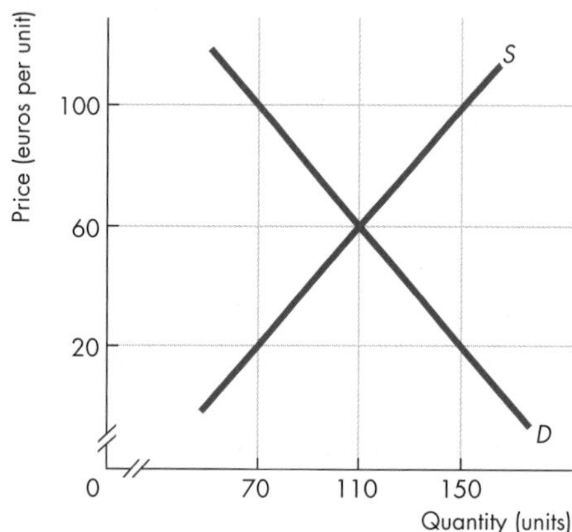

What are the equilibrium price and quantity if there is a penalty of €20 a unit on:

a Sellers only?

b Buyers only?

c Both sellers and buyers?

Critical Thinking

1 Read the article in *Reading Between the Lines* on pp. 138–139 about EU sugar subsidies:

a Explain how the CAP uses a target price for sugar to maintain EU farm incomes.

b New developments in sugar substitutes and fears about rising obesity may decrease the demand for sugar. How would this change in demand affect farm incomes and sugar subsidies?

c Explain how cutting the link between production and subsidies affects the efficiency of the sugar market.

2 **Why Rent Control Won't Go Away**

Once in place, rent control usually proves extremely difficult to undo. London and Paris still have rent controls adopted as temporary measures during World War I. "Nelson's Third Law" – the contention by the late economist Arthur Nelson that the worse a government regulation is, the more difficult it is to get rid of – seems to apply here. . . .

William Tucker, Heartland Institute
1 September 1997

a Who are the people who gain from rent controls?

b Why are rent controls inefficient?

c Are the rent controls in London that remain from the First World War fair?

d Explain "Nelson's Third law". Why does it seem to apply to the rental market in London?

3 Minimum wage setting has been seen by many as a barrier to needed flexibility in the labour market and to job creation. However, . . . a policy based on severe wage restraint does not necessarily create employment, and may possibly increase poverty at the household level. While wage flexibility may indeed increase jobs, if the associated employment elasticity proves to be low, then household poverty will rise.

Poverty and Inequality in South Africa
13 May 1998

a Explain the above quotation and in particular assess what is meant by "employment elasticity".

b How might poverty arise from a flexible wage policy?

c Explain why a minimum wage set above the market equilibrium wage is inefficient and unfair, even in a low-income, developing country.

d How would you design a policy to reduce the poverty of low-income workers?

Web Activities

Links to Websites

1 Read the Web page on the Irish tax on carrier bags:

a Why does the Irish government tax carrier bags?

b What is the opportunity cost of a carrier bag and who bears that cost, the shopper or the shop?

c Do you think that the market produces the efficient quantity of carrier bags or does it underproduce or overproduce them? Explain your answer.

d How do you think the tax on carriers bags will influence efficiency in the market for carrier bags?

2 Obtain information about cigarette smuggling in the European Union.

a Why are cigarettes smuggled in the European Union?

b Who are the gainers and the losers?

c What are the measures being used to stop cigarette smuggling?

d How would you improve on current policy?

Global Markets in Action

CHAPTER

7

After studying this chapter you will be able to:

- Explain how a country can gain from international trade
- Explain how markets enable us to reap the gains from international trade and identify its winners and losers
- Explain the effects of international trade barriers
- Explain the arguments used to justify international trade barriers and show how they are incorrect but also why some barriers are hard to remove

Silk Routes and Cargo Jets

Scania trucks, call centres in Delhi, Chinese-made shoes and American TV programmes are all examples of the fruits of the process of globalization. Today, cargo jets and container ships carry billions of pounds worth of goods around the globe and technology allows us to sell UK services through call centres in Delhi. Why do people go to such lengths to trade with others in far away places? How can we compete with people whose wages are much lower than our own? Why do some people want to restrict international trade so that people will buy local products? You can find the answers in this chapter. And you can see in *Reading Between the Lines* at the end of the chapter how by raising the tariff on shoes produced in China and Vietnam, we shoot ourselves in the foot!

The Gains from International Trade

The goods and services that we buy from people in other countries are our **imports**. The goods and services that we sell to people in other countries are our **exports**.

UK International Trade

About 70 per cent of UK international trade is trade in goods and 30 per cent is trade in services.

Trade in Goods

Manufactures are by far the largest category of goods traded by the United Kingdom. The United Kingdom is also a net importer (imports exceed exports) of manufactures, textile fibres, metals and agricultural products and a net exporter (exports exceed imports) of chemical goods, pharmaceuticals and oil.

Trade in Services

International trade in these services is growing rapidly and the United Kingdom is a net exporter of services. Your hotel bill for a holiday in France and the purchase by a UK company of Greek shipping services are examples of UK service imports. And the hotel bill for a Spanish student's UK holiday and the purchase by a Greek shipping company of cargo insurance from a London insurer, are examples of UK service exports.

Net Exports and Intertemporal Trade

The value of exports minus the value of imports is **net exports**. In 2006, UK net exports were a negative £40 billion – UK imports exceeded exports by £40 billion. Net exports result from our aggregate saving and spending decisions – our intertemporal allocation of resources. When net exports are negative, we borrow from foreigners or sell some of our assets to them. When net exports are positive, we lend to foreigners or buy some of their assets. When we borrow and lend, we engage in intertemporal trade. We trade *today's imports* for *future exports* when we borrow from the rest of the world; and we trade *today's exports* for *future imports* when we lend to the rest of the world. When intertemporal trade is taken into account, trade is always balanced. Your task in this chapter is to explain the *volume* of trade, not its balance. (Chapter 32 explains the balance of international trade).

What Drives International Trade?

The fundamental force that determines international trade is *comparative advantage*. And the basis of comparative advantage is divergent opportunity costs. You met these ideas in Chapter 2, when we learned about the gains from specialization and exchange between Erin and Jack.

Jack specializes in producing just one good but most nations, like Erin, do not go to the extreme of specializing in a single good and importing everything else. Like Erin and Jack, nations can increase the consumption of all goods if they redirect their scarce resources towards the production of those goods and services in which they have a comparative advantage.

To see how this outcome occurs, we'll apply the same basic ideas that we learned in the case of Erin and Jack to trade among nations. We'll begin by recalling how we can use the production possibilities frontier to measure opportunity cost. Then we'll see how divergent opportunity costs bring comparative advantage and gains from trade for countries as well as for individuals even though no country completely specializes in the production of just one good.

The UK *PPF*

The United Kingdom can produce chemicals (fertilizers, pesticide, pharmaceuticals) and cars at any point inside or along the production possibilities frontier, *PPF*, in Figure 7.1. (We're holding constant the output of all the other goods and services that the United Kingdom produces.)

Imagine that international trade is prohibited and that UK citizens must consume all the chemicals and cars that they produce. Suppose that the United Kingdom, is operating at point *A* on its *PPF* in Figure 7.1. That is, the United Kingdom produces and consumes 100 million tonnes of chemicals and 1 million cars each year.

What is the opportunity cost of a car in the United Kingdom?

The Opportunity Cost of a Car

The opportunity cost of a UK car is the number of tonnes of chemicals forgone to produce a car. You learned in Chapter 2 that the production possibilities frontier (*PPF*) measures the opportunity cost of producing one more unit of a good. We can calculate the opportunity cost of a car as the slope of the *PPF* at point *A* in Figure 7.1.

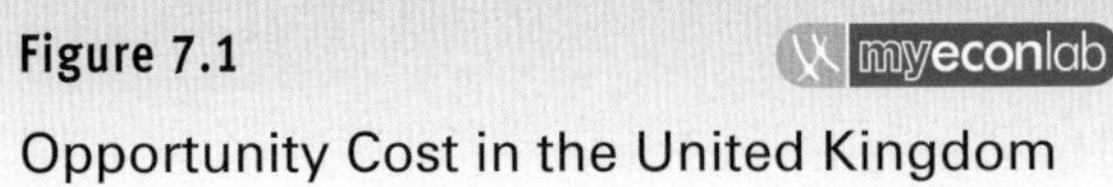

Figure 7.1

Opportunity Cost in the United Kingdom

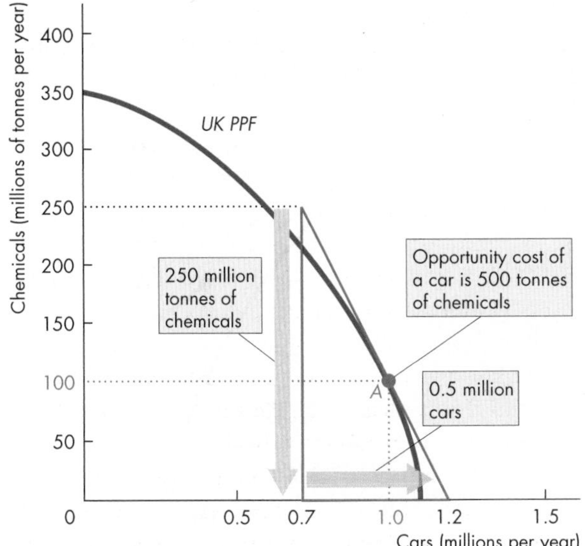

The United Kingdom produces and consumes 1 million cars and 100 million tonnes of chemicals a year. That is, the United Kingdom produces and consumes at point *A* on its production possibilities frontier (*PPF*).

Opportunity cost is equal to the magnitude of the slope of the *PPF*. The slope of the red line tangential to the *PPF* at point *A* measures the opportunity cost of a car at that point. That slope is 250 million tonnes of chemicals divided by 0.5 million cars, which is 500 tonnes of chemicals per car. That is, at point *A*, a car costs 500 tonnes of chemicals. Equivalently, 500 tonnes of chemicals cost 1 car.

To measure the slope of the frontier at point *A*, place a straight line tangential to the frontier at point *A* and calculate the slope of that straight line. Recall that the formula for the slope of a line is the change in the value of the variable measured on the *y*-axis divided by the change in the value of the variable measured on the *x*-axis as we move along the line.

Here, the variable measured on the *y*-axis is millions of tonnes of chemicals and the variable measured on the *x*-axis is millions of cars. So the slope is the change in the number of tonnes of chemicals divided by the change in the number of cars.

As you can see from the red triangle at point *A* in Figure 7.1, if the number of cars produced increases by 0.5 million, chemicals production decreases by 250 million tonnes. Therefore the magnitude of the slope is 250 million tonnes divided by 0.5 million cars, which equals 500 tonnes per car.

To produce one more car, the UK producers must give up 500 tonnes of chemicals. So the opportunity cost of 1 car is 500 tonnes of chemicals.

The Opportunity Cost of Chemicals

The opportunity cost of chemicals is the inverse of the opportunity cost of a car (see Chapter 2, pp. 37–38). So because the opportunity cost of 1 car is 500 tonnes of chemicals, the opportunity cost of 500 tonnes of chemicals is 1 car.

Money Prices and Opportunity Cost

You learned in Chapter 3, (p. 58) about the relationship between *money price*, *relative price* and *opportunity cost*.

The *opportunity costs* that we've just calculated are the relative prices faced by UK producers and consumers of cars and chemicals. The relative price of a car is 500 tonnes of chemicals and the relative price of 500 tonnes of chemicals is 1 car.

We can also calculate these relative prices if we know the money prices of the two goods.

Suppose that the money prices are £40 a tonne for chemicals and £20,000 for a car. The relative price of a car is its money price divided by the money price of chemicals. You can see that £20,000 per car divided by £40 per tonne is 500 tonnes per car. This number is the same as the slope of the *PPF* at point *A*.

Opportunity Cost in the Rest of the World

Cars and chemicals are produced in the rest of the world. And the opportunity cost of a car produced outside the United Kingdom is determined by the rest of the world's *PPF*.

We'll assume that in the rest of the world, the opportunity cost of producing a car is 200 tonnes of chemicals. Equivalently, the opportunity cost of 200 tonnes of chemicals is 1 car.

Comparative Advantage

A country has a comparative advantage in producing a good if it can produce that good at a lower opportunity cost than any other country. Cars cost less to produce in the rest of the world than in the United Kingdom. One car costs 500 tonnes of chemicals in the United Kingdom but only 200 tonnes of chemicals in the rest of the world.

But chemicals cost less to produce in the United Kingdom than in the rest of the world – 500 tonnes of chemicals cost only 1 car in the United Kingdom whereas that same amount of chemicals costs 2.5 cars in the rest of the world.

So the United Kingdom has a comparative advantage in producing chemicals and the rest of the world has a comparative advantage in producing cars.

Let's see how these opportunity cost differences and comparative advantage generate gains from international trade.

Figure 7.2

The Gains from Trade

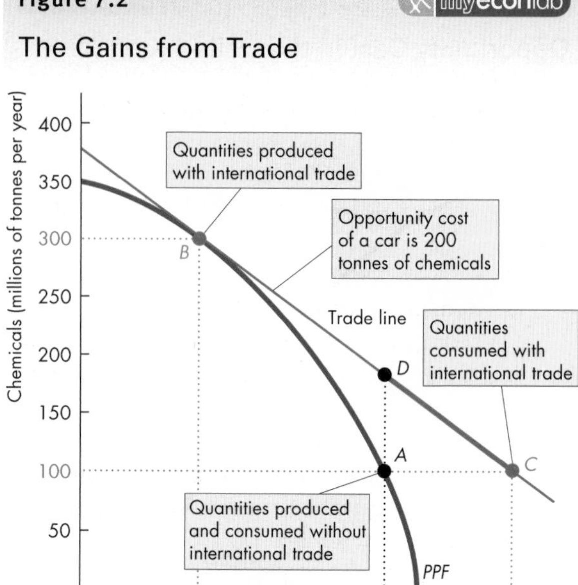

With no international trade, the United Kingdom produces and consumes at point *A* and the opportunity cost of a car is 500 tonnes of chemicals. Goods can be exchanged internationally at the world price of 200 tonnes of chemicals for 1 car. If the United Kingdom decreases its production of cars and increases its production of chemicals, moving from *A* to *B*, it can exchange chemicals for cars along the red *trade line*. By exporting 200 million tonnes of chemicals, the United Kingdom can import 1 million cars and consume at point *C*. At this point, UK citizens have 0.4 million more cars and the same quantity of chemicals as when they produce all their own consumption goods – at point *A*.

Cheaper to Buy Than to Produce

If the rest of the world bought chemicals for what it costs the United Kingdom to produce it, then the rest of the world could buy 500 tonnes of chemicals for 1 car. That is much lower than the cost of producing chemicals in the rest of the world, because there it costs 2.5 cars to produce 500 tonnes of chemicals. If the the rest of the world can buy chemicals at the low UK price, it will reap some gains.

If UK citizens can buy cars for what they cost to produce in the rest of the world, they can get a car for 200 tonnes of chemicals. Because it costs 500 tonnes of chemicals to produce a car in the United Kingdom, the UK citizens gain from such an opportunity.

In this situation, it makes sense for the rest of the world to buy chemicals from the United Kingdom and for UK citizens to buy cars from the rest of the world.

Consumption Possibilities

A country's *consumption possibilities frontier* is the limit to what its citizens can consume. Like a *PPF*, a consumption possibilities frontier is a boundary that separates attainable consumption levels from unattainable consumption levels.

Without international trade, an economy can consume only what it produces – its consumption possibilities frontier is the same as its *PPF*.

But with international trade, an economy can consume quantities of goods and services that differ from those that it produces. The *PPF* describes the limit of what a country can produce, but it does not describe the limits to what it can consume. It is not a consumption possibilities frontier.

Figure 7.2 illustrates the distinction between production possibilities and consumption possibilities when a country trades with other countries.

The red line labelled *trade line* shows the UK consumption possibilities frontier with international trade. The world opportunity cost of a car in terms of chemicals determines the slope of this line – 200 tonnes of chemicals per car. And the UK production possibilities and quantities produced determines the position of the consumption possibilities frontier.

The United Kingdom can't produce *outside* its *PPF*, so its consumption possibilities line must touch its *PPF*. To maximize its consumption possibilities, the United Kingdom produces at the point on its *PPF* at which its opportunity cost of producing a car equals the world opportunity cost.

In Figure 7.2, that point is *B*, where the United Kingdom produces 0.4 million (400,000) cars and 300 million tonnes of chemicals. By producing at point *B*, and engaging in international trade, the United Kingdom can consume at *any* point along the red trade line.

In particular, the United Kingdom can consume at any point along the thicker segment of the trade line that runs from *C* to *D*. This range of possibilities is significant because it enables people to consume at least as much of one good and more of the other good than without international trade.

But the point on the trade line to which the economy moves depends on *preferences* – on *marginal benefit* and *demand.*

Let's assume that UK consumers decide that they would like to maintain chemical consumption at 100 million tonnes and take the gains from international trade in the form of more cars.

In this case, UK citizens consume at point *C*. With production at point *B*, the United Kingdom exports 200 million tonnes of chemicals and imports 1 million cars. Chemical production of 300 million tonnes minus chemical exports of 200 million tonnes equals chemical consumption of 100 million tonnes. And car consumption of 1.4 million cars equals car production 0.4 million plus car imports of 1 million.

The additional 0.4 million cars (400,000 cars) that UK citizens consume are the gains from international trade.

Gains from Trade in Reality

The gains from trade that we have just studied between the United Kingdom and the rest of the world in chemicals and cars occur in a model economy – in an economy that we have imagined. But these same phenomena occur every day in our real economy.

Comparative Advantage Today

We buy cars made in Japan, clothing and household goods from China, TV sets from South Korea and mobile phones from Finland. In exchange, we sell chemicals (pharmaceuticals, fertilizers and pesticides), energy and services to those countries. We make some kinds of machines, and Europeans and Japanese make other kinds, and we trade one type of manufactured good for another.

These examples of international trade are generated by comparative advantage, just like that between the United Kingdom and the rest of the world in our model economy. All international trade arises from comparative advantage, even when it is trade in similar goods such as tools and machines. At first, it seems puzzling that countries exchange manufactured goods. Why doesn't each developed country produce all the manufactured goods its citizens want to buy? Let's look a bit more closely at this question.

Trade in Similar Goods

The United Kingdom imports a big range of cars but it also produces and exports cars to the rest of the world. Why does it make sense for a country to produce cars for export and at the same time to import cars from the rest of the world? From what you have learned, the answer must be that the United Kingdom has a comparative advantage in some types of cars and the rest of the world has a comparative advantage in other types of cars. What generates these differences?

Diversity of Taste and Economies of Scale

The answer is that people have a large diversity of taste and there are economies from producing a large quantity of each variety of a good.

Let's stick with cars. The tremendous diversity in tastes for cars means that people would be dissatisfied if they were forced to buy from a limited range of standardized cars. People value variety and are willing to pay for it in the marketplace. But variety is costly to produce. With small production runs, costs are high. International trade enables each car producer to access the whole world market. Each producer can specialize in a limited range of products and then sell its output to the world market.

Review Quiz

Study Plan 7.1

1. What is the fundamental source of the gains from international trade?
2. What determines the goods and services that a country exports?
3. What determines the goods and services that a country imports?
4. What is comparative advantage and what role does it play in determining the amount and type of international trade that occurs?
5. How can it be that all countries gain from international trade and that no country loses?
6. Provide some examples of comparative advantage in today's world.

Markets and the Distribution of Gains and Losses

You've seen that a country can gain by exporting a good in which it has a comparative advantage, and importing a good in which other countries have a comparative advantage. But how do markets achieve this gains? And who gets the gains? The consumers, producers of exports, producers of imports, or all of these?

We're now going to answer these questions. We'll continue to use the same examples of cars and chemicals.

An Import

To see how the market generates international trade, we'll first study the market for cars, in which the United Kingdom is an importer. To identify the gains and losses of the various economic actors, we'll begin by imagining that car imports are banned.

The Market without International Trade

Figure 7.3(a) shows the market for cars without international trade. The supply of UK car producers is S_{UK} and the demand of UK consumers is D_{UK}. The equilibrium price is £20,000 a car and 1 million cars a year are produced and consumed in the United Kingdom.

If the price of a car in the rest of the world is less than £20,000, other countries have a comparative advantage in producing cars. The opportunity cost of a car is less in the rest of the world than it is in the United Kingdom.

The Market with International Trade

Now suppose that the ban on car imports is lifted. Figure 7.3(b) illustrates what happens. The price of a car in the world market is determined by demand and supply in the world market. In this figure, the world price of a car is £15,000. The United Kingdom is a small car consumer and producer and we will assume

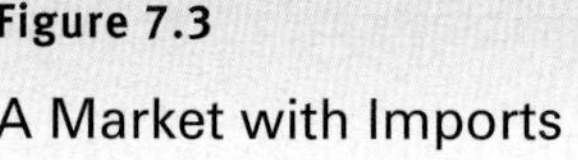

Figure 7.3

A Market with Imports

myeconlab

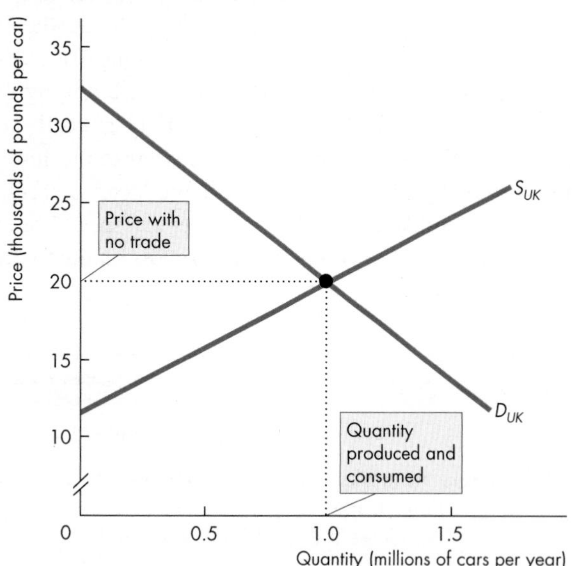

(a) Equilibrium without international trade

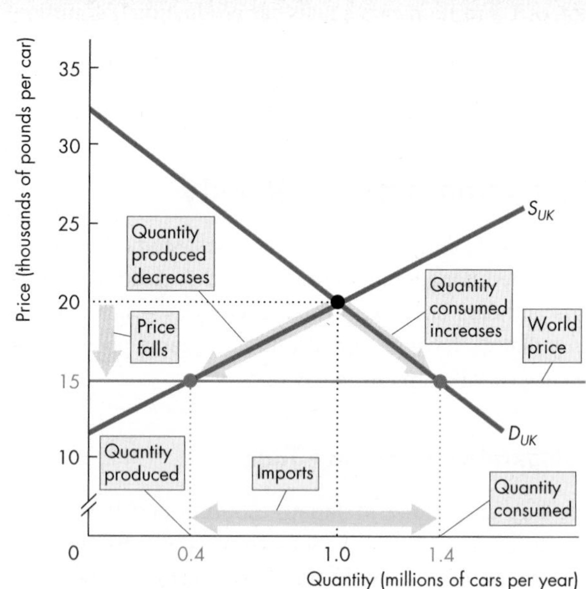

(b) Equilibrium in a market with imports

The supply of cars of UK producers is S_{UK} and the demand for cars by UK consumers is D_{UK}. With no international trade, in part (a), the equilibrium price of a car in the United Kingdom is £20,000 and 1 million cars a year are produced and consumed.

In part (b), the world price of a car is £15,000 and the rest of the world has a comparative advantage in producing cars. With international trade, the price of a car in the United Kingdom falls to the world price.

The quantity of cars bought in the United Kingdom increases, the quantity produced in the United Kingdom decreases and the quantity imported equals the quantity bought minus the quantity produced in the United Kingdom.

that no individual UK car producer can influence the world price.

With free international trade, the supply of cars to UK citizens is perfectly elastic at £15,000 per car. Car buyers are not willing to pay domestic producers more than that price. So UK consumers buy cars from the rest of the world, the United Kingdom imports cars and the domestic price of a car falls to the world price. At the lower domestic price, the quantity of cars produced in the United Kingdom decreases.

In Figure 7.3(b), purchases increase to 1.4 million cars, UK production decreases to 0.4 million cars, and 1 million cars are imported.

Winners and Losers in an Import Market

By comparing the consumer surplus and producer surplus in Figure 7.4(a) without imports and Figure 7.4(b) with imports, you can see who gains and who loses. UK consumers gain and UK producers lose.

Producers receive a lower price, sell a smaller quantity and receive a smaller producer surplus. The blue producer surplus in part (b), labelled *C*, is smaller than the producer surplus in part (a). Consumers pay a lower price, buy a larger quantity and receive a larger consumer surplus. The green consumer surplus in part (b) labelled *A*, *B* and *D* is greater than in part (a).

Part of the increase in consumer surplus – the part labelled *B* in part (b) – is a transfer from producers to consumers but the area labelled *D* is an increase in total surplus and is a gain from trade.

When a country opens up to international trade and imports a good, domestic producers of the good lose and domestic consumers of the good gain.

The gains exceed the losses and total surplus increases.

An Export

Now we'll study the market for chemicals, some of which the United Kingdom exports. Again, to identify

Figure 7.4

myeconlab

Gains and Losses in a Market with Imports

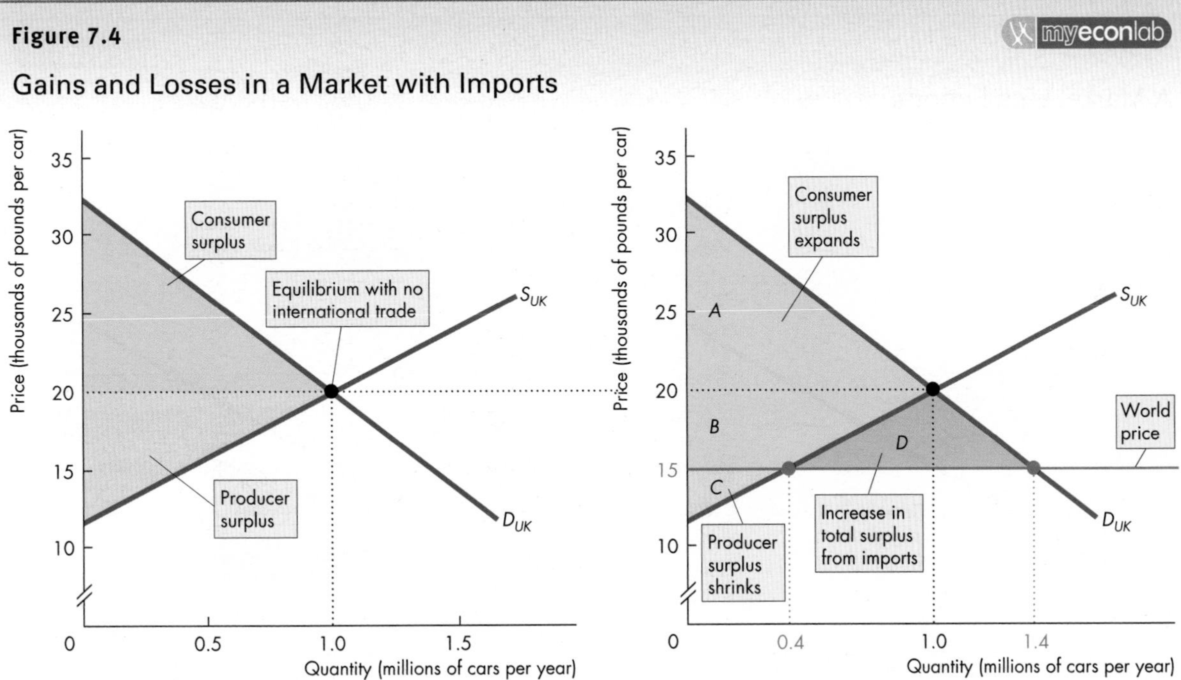

(a) Consumer and producer surplus without international trade

(b) The gains and losses from imports

Part (a) shows consumer surplus and producer surplus without imports. Part (b) shows the effects of imports on consumer surplus and producer surplus. When the United Kingdom imports cars, the price of a car in the United Kingdom falls, UK car producers lose and UK consumers gain. The loss of producer surplus is the green area *B*, which is transferred to consumers and becomes part of the expanded consumer surplus. Consumers also gain the dark green area labelled *D*, which is also the increase in total surplus.

the gains and losses of the various economic actors, we'll begin by imagining that chemical exports are banned.

The Market without International Trade

Figure 7.5(a) shows the market for chemicals if exports are banned. The supply of UK producers is S_{UK} and the demand of UK consumers is D_{UK}. The equilibrium price in the United Kingdom is £40 a tonne and 100 million tonnes a year are produced and consumed.

If the price of chemicals in the rest of the world exceeds £40 a tonne, the United Kingdom has a comparative advantage in producing chemicals. The opportunity cost of a tonne of chemicals is less in the United Kingdom than it is in the rest of the world.

The Market with International Trade

Now suppose that the ban on exports of chemicals is lifted. Figure 7.5(b) shows what happens. The price of chemicals in the world market is £75 a tonne. Demand and supply in the world as a whole determine this price. The United Kingdom is a big producer of chemicals but we will assume that no individual UK producer can influence the world price.

With a price of £75 a tonne in the rest of the world, UK producers increase production of chemicals and start exporting. Also, UK producers are not willing to sell to UK buyers below the price they can get from foreign buyers. So the UK price of chemicals rises to the world price.

The gains from international trade bring an increase in UK incomes. And with higher incomes, people are willing and able to pay more for chemicals, so the demand for chemicals increases and the demand curve shifts rightward to D'_{UK}.

Other things remaining the same, the rise in the price of chemicals would decrease the quantity of chemicals demanded. But the increase in income increases the demand for chemicals.

In Figure 7.5(b), production increases to 300 million tonnes, consumption remains at 100 million tonnes and 200 million tonnes are exported.

Figure 7.5

A Market with Exports

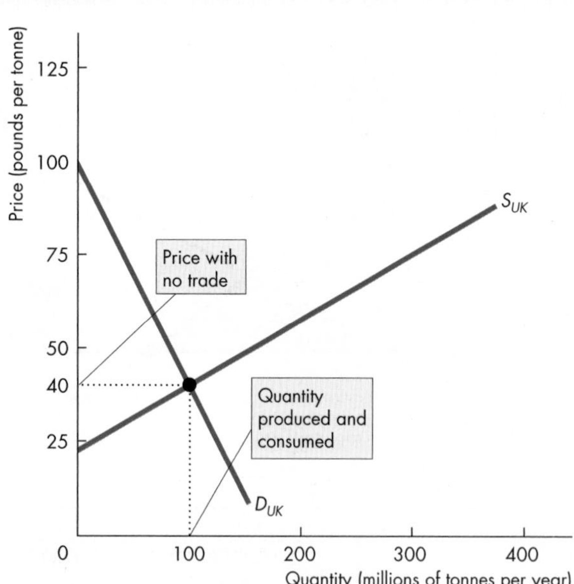

(a) Equilibrium without international trade

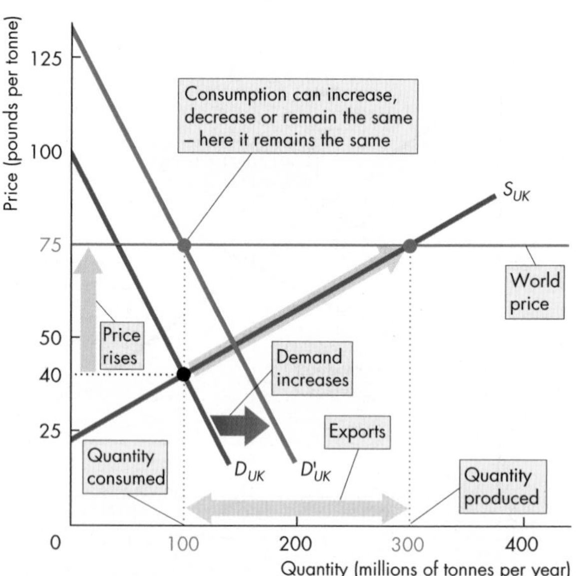

(b) Equilibrium in a market with exports

The supply of UK chemical producers is S_{UK} and the demand for chemicals of UK consumers is D_{UK}. Without international trade, in part (a), the equilibrium price in the United Kingdom is £40 a tonne and 100 million tonnes a year are produced and consumed.

In part (b), the world price is £75 a tonne and the United Kingdom has a comparative advantage in producing chemicals. The price in the United Kingdom rises to the world price, the quantity consumed decreases and the quantity produced increases. The quantity exported is the quantity produced in the United Kingdom minus the quantity consumed.

Winners and Losers in an Export Market

We can see who gains and who loses by looking at the changes in consumer surplus and producer surplus that exports generate. Figure 7.6(a) shows the consumer surplus and producer surplus without exports and Figure 7.6(b) shows the situation with exports. Consumer surplus remains the same and producer surplus increases.

Consumers lose because they pay a higher price but they gain the area labelled *F* because with higher incomes, they are willing and able to pay more. The consumer surplus from chemicals can increase, decrease, or remain the same. Here, it remains the same.

Producers gain because they receive the higher price, sell more and receive a larger producer surplus. You can see that the blue producer surplus – the sum of the blue areas labelled *B*, *C*, *D* and *E* in part (b) – is greater than that in part (a). Part of the increase in producer surplus – the area labelled *B* in part (b) – is a transfer from consumers to producers. But the part of the producer surplus labelled *D* and *E* is a net gain. Total surplus increases by the sum of the areas *D*, *E* and *F*.

When a country opens up to international trade and exports a good, domestic producers of the good gain and domestic consumers of the good can gain, lose or remain unaffected.

The gains exceed the losses and total surplus increases.

Review Quiz

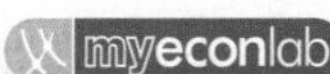

Study Plan 7.2

1. How are the gains from imports distributed between consumers and domestic producers?
2. How are the gains from exports distributed between consumers and domestic producers?

You've now seen how free international trade brings gains for all countries. But trade is not free in our world. We'll now look at trade restrictions and their effects.

Figure 7.6

myeconlab

Gains and Losses in a Market with Exports

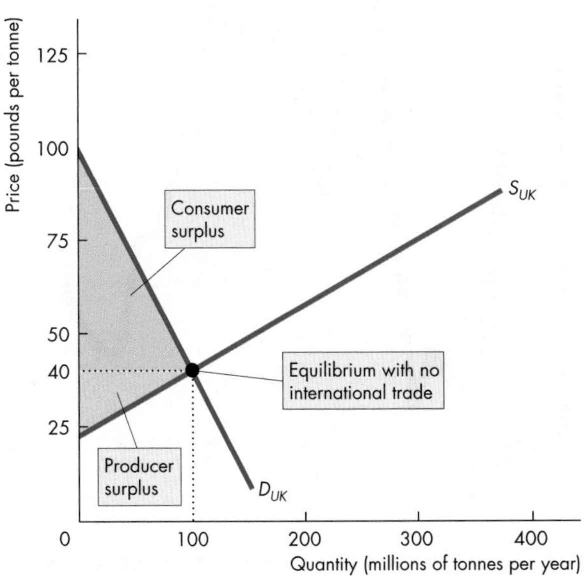

(a) Consumer and producer surplus without international trade

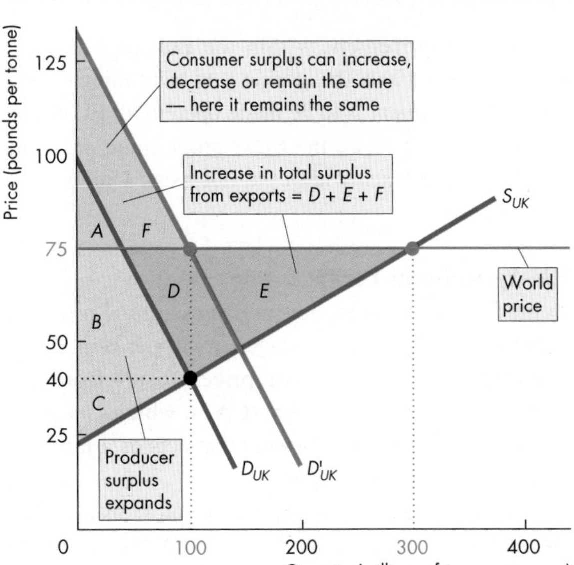

(b) The gains and losses from exports

Part (a) shows consumer surplus and producer surplus without exports.

Part (b) shows the effects of exports on consumer surplus and producer surplus. When the UK producers export chemicals, the price of chemicals in the United Kingdom rises, UK consumers lose and UK chemical producers gain. Consumer surplus decreases by area *B* but increases by area *F*. Producer surplus increases by the sum of areas *B*, *D* and *E*. Total surplus increases by the sum of areas *D*, *E* and *F*.

International Trade Restrictions

Governments restrict international trade to protect domestic industries from foreign competition by using three main tools:

1 Tariffs
2 Subsidies
3 Quotas

A **tariff** is a tax that is imposed by the importing country when an imported good crosses its international boundary.

A **subsidy** is a payment made by a government to a domestic producer based on the quantity produced. Examples of subsidies are the payments made by the European Union and the United States to domestic wheat producers.

A **quota** is a limit on the quantity of a good that may be imported. Most countries no longer use quotas. Voluntary export restraints (VERs) are agreements between two governments in which the exporting government agrees to limit its exports.

The History of Tariff

Tariffs have been used as a source of government revenue for centuries. As a means of protecting home markets from foreign competition, their use peaked during

Box 7.1
Free Trade and Tariffs in the European Union

EU Free Trade Area

The Single European Market (SEM) in the European Union has created the largest unified tariff-free market in the world. It has simplified border formalities for the movement of goods; capital and labour have complete freedom of movement within the European Union. Protectionism within the market is to be eliminated and public procurement is to be made open to all EU firms.

In the longer term, the SEM programme provides for all indirect taxes within the European Union to be harmonized.

EU Agricultural Tariffs

In the European Union, buyers of agricultural products face prices that, on the average, are 40 per cent above world prices. These higher prices result from the Common Agricultural Policy (CAP), which is a price support programme for farmers that acts as a tariff on non-EU agricultural products.

The meat, cheese and sugar that you consume cost significantly more because of EU tariffs than they would with free international trade.

Figure 1 shows the average tariff the CAP imposes on world agricultural goods. The implied average tariff varies because the world price of agricultural goods varies from year to year.

The OECD estimates the average percentage subsidy paid to EU farmers that would give them the same additional income as the actual CAP price supports. The graph shows an estimate of the percentage by which EU prices exceed world prices.

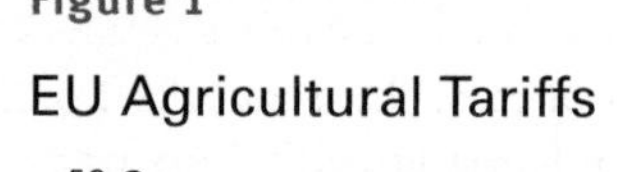

Figure 1

EU Agricultural Tariffs

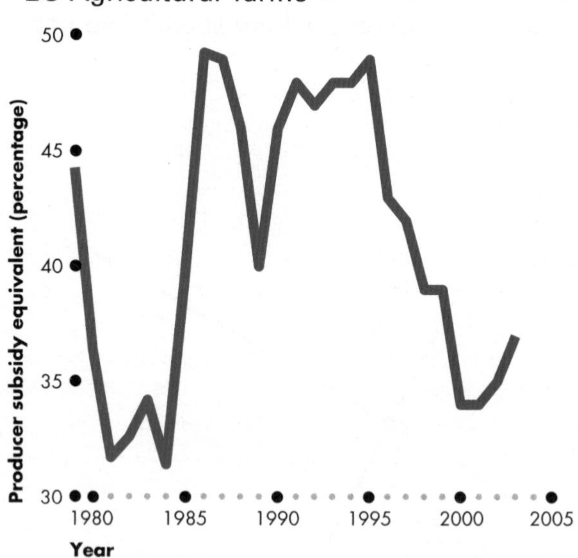

Source of data: OECD, *Agricultural Policies in OECD Countries: At a Glance*, 2006 Edition. Copyright © OECD 2006.

the 1930s. These enormous tariffs contributed to the severity of the Great Depression.

Determined to avoid the tariff wars of the 1920s and 1930s, the United States, Europe, and many other countries joined together in 1947 in a **General Agreement on Tariffs and Trade** (GATT). Since its formation, the GATT has organized several rounds of negotiations that have resulted in tariff reductions. One of these, the Kennedy Round that began in the early 1960s, resulted in large tariff cuts starting in 1967. Another, the Tokyo Round, resulted in further tariff cuts in 1979.

The Uruguay Round, which started in 1986 and was completed in 1994, was the most ambitious and comprehensive of the rounds and led to the creation of a new **World Trade Organization** (WTO). Membership of the WTO brings greater obligations on countries to observe the GATT rules. Tariff cuts agreed by the WTO apply to all members without discrimination.

The Doha Round that began in 2000 aims to liberalise trade in agriculture and services but has had only limited success.

In 1994, discussions among the Asia-Pacific Economic group (APEC) led to an agreement in principle to work towards a free trade area that embraces China, all the economies of East Asia and the South Pacific, and the United States and Canada. These countries include the fastest-growing economies and hold the promise of heralding a global free trade area. But the Asia crisis of 1997 and other problems with China make it unlikely that free trade will come to APEC in the near term.

Canada, the United States and Mexico form the North American Free Trade Agreement that has lowered tariffs among these countries. The European Union is also a free trade area covering 27 member states.

A consequence of this persistent movement towards lower tariffs is that UK tariffs today stand at less than 1 per cent of total imports and tariffs on trade with other members of the European Union have been eliminated completely. But despite the effort to achieve freer trade, most agricultural products are still subject to extremely high tariffs.

The temptation for governments to impose tariffs is a strong one. They do, of course, provide revenue to the government, but this is not particularly large compared with other sources. Their most important attribute is that they enable the government to satisfy special interest groups in import-competing industries. But, as we'll see, free international trade brings enormous benefits that are reduced when tariffs are imposed.

Let's see how tariffs work.

How Tariffs Work

To analyse how tariffs work, let's return to the UK market for cars. With free international trade, the world price of a car is £15,000 and the UK imports 0.4 million cars as in Figures 7.3(b) and 7.4(b).

Imagine the UK government is under pressure from car producers and it imposes a tariff of £4,000 on each car imported. What happens in the United Kingdom?

When the United Kingdom imposes a tariff on car imports:

- The price of a car rises
- Car imports decrease
- The government collects the tariff revenue
- Producer surplus increases
- Consumer surplus decreases
- Total surplus decreases – a deadweight loss

The Price of a Car Rises

Cars are no longer available at the world price of £15,000. The tariff of £4,000 a car must be added to that price, raising the UK car price to £19,000, which is the world price of £15,000 plus the tariff of £4,000.

Car Imports Decrease

Car imports decrease for two reasons. First, at the higher price, the quantity of cars demanded decreases. Second, at the higher price, the quantity of cars supplied by UK producers increases.

The Government Collects Tariff Revenue

When someone buys an imported car, the foreign producer receives the world price and the UK government receives the tariff revenue. The total tariff revenue collected by the government equals £4,000 multiplied by the number of cars imported.

Producer Surplus Increases

Consumers of cars respond to the full price of the car – the price paid to the seller plus the tariff. They don't care who gets what they spend.

Because the price of an imported car rises by the £4,000 tariff, UK car producers are now able to sell cars for an additional £4,000. And because the price of a car rises to £19,000, UK producers increase the quantity supplied. But the marginal cost of producing a car in the United Kingdom is less than £19,000 on all cars produced except for the marginal car. So producer surplus increases.

Consumer Surplus Decreases

Because the price of a car rises, the quantity of cars demanded decreases. The combination of a higher price and smaller quantity decreases consumer surplus.

Figure 7.7 illustrates the changes that we've just described. The price rises above the world price by the amount of the tariff. Imports shrink because the quantity of cars demanded decreases and the quantity supplied by UK producers increases. The government collects tariff revenue shown by the purple rectangle labelled *D*.

Figure 7.7

The Effects of a Tariff

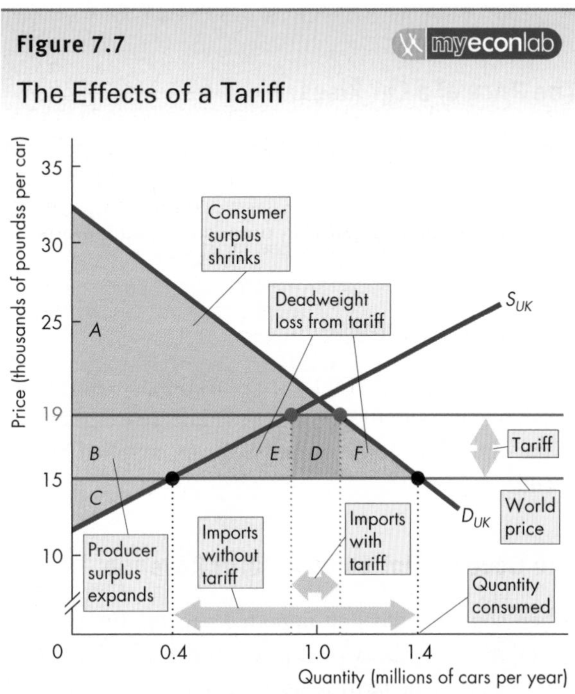

A tariff raises the price above the world price by the amount of the tariff. At the higher price, the quantity demanded decreases, the quantity supplied by domestic producers increases, and imports decrease.

Producer surplus increases by the area labelled *B*, domestic producers sell their cars at the world price plus the tariff and receive all the revenue. The government collects a tariff revenue shown by the purple area labelled *D*. Consumer surplus decreases by the increase in producer surplus (area *B*) and the tariff revenue (area *D*). Consumer surplus also decreases by the two grey areas labelled *E* and *F* and this loss of consumer surplus is a deadweight loss.

Producer surplus increases, shown by the blue area labelled *B* to become the areas *B* plus *C*. And consumer surplus decreases to the area labelled *A*.

Total Surplus Decreases – a Deadweight Loss

Figure 7.7 also shows that total surplus decreases so a tariff brings a deadweight loss. The two grey areas labelled *E* and *F* show this loss.

The deadweight loss is a loss of consumer surplus. Consumers lose area *B* to producers and area *D* to the government. So these losses of consumer surplus are gains to others. But the losses in the areas labelled *E* and *F* are no one's gain. They are a loss of total surplus – a deadweight loss.

How Subsidies Work

A subsidy works just like a tax except in the opposite direction. You saw in Chapter 6 (pp. 127–131) that a tax on a seller shifts the supply curve leftward, raises the price, decreases the quantity and creates a deadweight loss from underproduction.

A subsidy shifts the supply curve rightward, lowers the price, increases the quantity and creates a deadweight loss from overproduction. But when the item that receives a subsidy is an export or an import, the subsidy also changes the amount of international trade.

Subsidies in the World Today

The biggest subsidies in today's world are those paid by EU and US governments to farmers. These subsidies benefit EU and US farmers and are paid for by EU and US taxpayers and by farmers in the rest of the world.

These subsidies have devastating effects on farmers in the low-income countries of Africa, Asia and Central and South America, and we're now going to explain why.

We'll illustrate the effects of today's agricultural subsidies using Africa as our example. In Figure 7.8, the demand for sugar in Africa is D_A and the supply of sugar from African producers is S_A.

With no EU and US farm subsidies, African farmers take the world price of sugar, which we assume here to be €4 a kilogram. At this free-trade price of €4 a kilogram, African consumers buy 1 million tonnes a year and African producers sell 14 million tonnes a year. African sugar exports are 13 million tonnes a year. There is a thriving and healthy sugar industry in Africa that creates jobs and prosperity for African workers.

Figure 7.8

Effect of EU and US Farm Subsidies on the African Economy

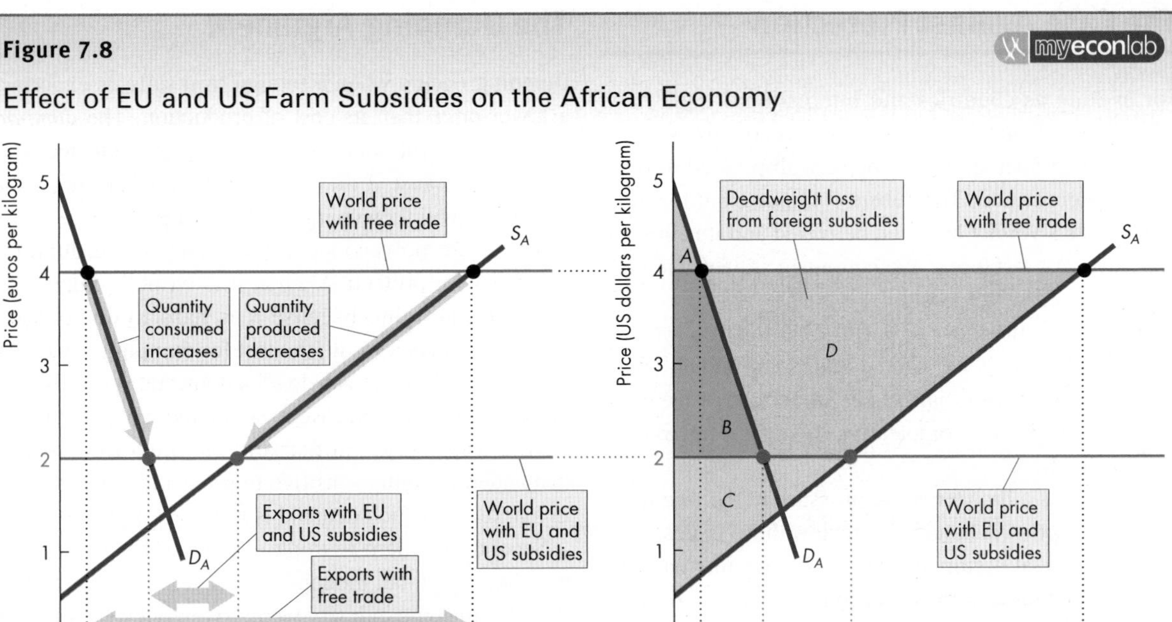

(a) Changes in production, consumption and exports

The demand for sugar in Africa is D_A and the supply of sugar by African producers is S_A. If there is free international trade, the world price is €4 per kilogram. Africa produces 14 million tonnes of sugar per year, consumes 1 million tonnes and exports 13 million tonnes.

(b) Inefficiency of foreign subsidies

EU and US subsidies lower the world price to €2 per kilogram. In part (a), African production and exports shrink and African consumption increases. In part (b), consumer surplus in Africa expands from *A* to *A* + *B*, producer surplus shrinks from *B* + *C* + *D* to *C*, and total surplus decreases (a deadweight loss) by *D*.

With EU and US sugar subsidies, growers in these countries increase production. The world supply increases and the price falls to €2 a kilogram. African production now shrinks to 6 million tonnes and consumption increases to 3 million tonnes. Sugar exports decrease to 3 million tonnes.

Figure 7.8(b) shows that consumer surplus in Africa increases from the green area *A* to *A* + *B*, producer surplus shrinks from the area *B* + *C* + *D* to *C*. And a deadweight loss, area *D*, arises.

The Realities of the Deadweight Loss

The deadweight losses created by EU and US farm subsides fall on the poor nations of Africa, Asia and Central and South America. These subsidies are a source of tension and disagreement among nations today and are the biggest single challenge facing the WTO.

Review Quiz

Study Plan 7.3

1. What are the tools that a country can use to restrict international trade?
2. Have tariffs and quotas been on the increase or the decrease? Why?
3. Explain the effects of tariffs on domestic output and price of the product on which a tariff is applied when the importer is a small country in world trade.
4. Who gains and who loses from a tariff?
5. What is the deadweight loss from a tariff?
6. How do EU and US farm subsidies affect farmers and consumers in poor countries?

Let's now look at some commonly heard arguments for restricting international trade and see why they are almost never correct.

The Case Against Protection

For as long as countries and international trade have existed, people have debated whether a country is better off with free international trade or with protection from foreign competition. The debate continues, but for most economists a verdict has been delivered and it is the one you have just explored. Protectionism is inefficient. It creates a deadweight losses.

We've seen the most powerful case for free trade in the example of how the United Kingdom (and all countries) benefit from specializing in production of the good in which they have a comparative advantage and trading with each other.

But there is a broader range of issues in the free trade versus protection debate. Let's review these issues.

Two classical arguments for restricting international trade are that protection is needed to:

- Establish an infant industry
- Counteract dumping

The Infant-industry Argument

An infant industry is a new industry. The **infant-industry argument** is that a new industry must be protected from foreign competition to enable it to grow into a mature industry and compete in world markets. The argument is based on the idea of *dynamic comparative advantage* which can arise from *learning-by-doing* (see Chapter 2, p. 47).

Learning-by-doing is a powerful engine of productivity growth and comparative advantage does evolve and change because of on-the-job experience. But these facts do not justify protection.

First, the infant-industry argument is valid only if the benefits of learning-by-doing not only accrue to the owners and workers of the firms in the infant industry but also spill over to other industries and parts of the economy. When the people making the decisions, bearing the risk and doing the work are the ones who benefit, they take the dynamic gains into account when they decide on the scale of their activities. In this case, almost no benefits spill over to other parts of the economy, so there is no need for government assistance to achieve an efficient outcome.

Second, even if the case is made for protecting an infant industry, it is more efficient to do so by a direct subsidy to the firms in the industry, with the subsidy financed out of taxes.

The Dumping Argument

Dumping occurs when a foreign firm sells its exports at a lower price than its cost of production. The *dumping argument* is that domestic firms must be protected from dumping because if they are driven out of business, foreign firms will then charge higher prices.

These are powerful reasons to resist the dumping argument for protection. First, it is virtually impossible to detect dumping because it is hard to determine a firm's costs. As a result, the test for dumping is whether a firm's export price is below its domestic price. But this test is a weak one because it can be rational for a firm to charge a low price in markets in which the quantity demanded is highly sensitive to price and a higher price in markets in which demand is less price-sensitive.

Second, it is hard to think of a good that is produced by a natural global monopoly. So even if all the domestic firms in some industry were driven out of business, it would always be possible to find many alternative foreign sources of supply and to buy at prices determined in competitive markets.

Third, if a good or service were produced by a truly global natural monopoly, the best way of dealing with it would be by regulation – just as in the case of domestic monopolies. Such regulation would require international cooperation.

The two main arguments for protection that you have just studied have an element of credibility but there are other arguments. You may read newspaper stories that mention the following arguments for protectionism:

- Saves jobs
- Allows us to compete with cheap foreign labour
- Penalizes lax environmental standards
- Prevents rich countries from exploiting developing countries

Let's look at these in more detail.

Saves Jobs

Free trade does cost some jobs, but it also creates other jobs. Free trade brings about a global rationalization of labour and allocates labour resources to their highest-value activities. As protection of the textile industry has decreased, many workers have lost jobs in the UK textile industry but many textile jobs have been created in other countries such as Turkey and Malaysia. And many of the UK workers who lost textile jobs now have better-paying jobs in other industries, which have expanded. In total, more jobs have been created than have been destroyed in the textile industry.

Second, imports create jobs. They create jobs for retailers which sell imported goods and for firms which service these goods. They also create jobs by creating incomes in the rest of the world, some of which are spent on UK-produced goods and services.

Protectionism doesn't save jobs. It changes the mix of jobs but at the cost of a deadweight loss. Removing protectionism does impose costs of adjustment on people who previously worked in the protected industry and can have political costs and policy-making implications.

Allows Us to Compete with Cheap Foreign Labour

The relatively high wages in the United Kingdom and other EU member states doesn't imply that European Union cannot compete. Wages are higher, other things the same, the higher is the productivity of labour. EU workers are more productive, on the average, than lower-paid workers in China or India. For example, the productivity of EU labour is higher in financial services, biotechnology products and business computer systems than in assembling cars or televisions. These activities are ones in which the European Union has a comparative advantage.

By engaging in free trade, the European Union can increase production and exports of the goods in which it has a comparative advantage, and increase the imports of goods in which our trading partners have a comparative advantage. We can make ourselves and our trading partners better off.

Penalizes Lax Environmental Standards

Another argument for protection is that many low-income countries keep costs low by having poor environmental standards. So we should put a tariff on the goods that we import from them.

In reply, it is not true that all poorer countries have significantly lower environmental standards than EU member states. Many poor countries do have a bad environmental record – including India and China – but some poorer countries have strict environmental laws and do enforce them. Also, the demand for higher environmental standards in poorer economies increases with income. Developing countries have the means to match environmental aspirations as their incomes rise. Rapid growth in income will most likely lead to rapid improvements in environmental standards. Free trade can generate rapid income growth and higher environmental standards in the long run.

Prevents Rich Countries from Exploiting Developing Countries

Another argument is that international trade must be restricted to prevent the people of the rich industrial world from exploiting the poorer people of the developing countries, forcing them to work for slave wages.

Wage rates in some developing countries are very low. But by trading with developing countries, we increase the demand for the goods that they produce and, more significantly, we increase the demand for their labour. When the demand for labour in developing countries increases, the wage rate also increases. So, far from exploiting people in developing countries, international trade improves their opportunities and increases their incomes.

The arguments for protection that we've reviewed leave free trade unscathed. But a new phenomenon is at work in our economy: offshore outsourcing. Surely this new source of foreign competition needs protection. Let's see if it does.

Offshoring and Outsourcing

BT, HSBC, Lloyds TSB, Burberry, Norwich Union and Tesco are just a few of the many UK firms have sent jobs that were previously done in the United Kingdom to countries such as India, Sri Lanka, China, Thailand and to Eastern European countries such as Romania. These firms are outsourcing and offshoring. What exactly are these activities?

What Are Offshoring and Outsourcing?

A UK company can source and produce its output in four main ways:

1 Hire UK labour and produce in the United Kingdom
2 Hire foreign labour and produce in other countries
3 Buy its output from other UK companies
4 Buy its output from foreign companies

Activities 3 and 4 are **outsourcing** and activities 2 and 4 are **offshoring**. Activity 4 is offshore outsourcing. Notice that offshoring includes activities that take place inside UK companies. If a UK company opens its own facilities in another country, then it is offshoring.

Offshoring has been going on for hundreds of years. But the activity expanded rapidly and became a source of concern during the 1990s when it began to cover activities that went beyond manufacturing to include information technology services and general office services such as finance, accounting and human resources management.

Why Did Offshoring Services Boom?

A dramatic fall in the cost of telecommunication generated the offshoring services boom of the 1990s. The gains from specialization and trade that you saw in the previous section must be large enough to make it worth incurring the costs of communication and transport. If the cost of producing a shirt in China isn't lower than the cost in the United Kingdom by an amount that exceeds the cost of transporting a shirt from China to the United Kingdom, then it is more efficient to produce shirts in the United Kingdom and avoid the transport costs.

If services are to be produced offshore, then the cost of delivering those services must be low enough to leave the buyer with an overall lower cost. Until the 1990s, the cost of communicating across large distances was too high to make the offshoring of business services efficient. But when satellites, fibre-optic cables and computers cut the cost of a phone call between the United Kingdom and India to less than a few pence an hour, a huge base of offshore resources became competitive with similar resources in the United Kingdom.

What Are the Benefits of Offshoring?

Offshoring brings gains from trade in the same way as any other type of international trade. A UK bank can export banking services to Indian companies and Indians might provide call centre services to UK companies. This trade benefits both UK citizens and Indian citizens provided the United Kingdom has a comparative advantage in banking services and India has a comparative advantage in call centre services.

Why Is Offshoring a Concern?

Despite the gains from trade that offshoring brings, some people believe that it also brings costs that outweigh the gains. Why?

The concerns arise because offshoring is taking jobs in services. The loss of manufacturing jobs to other countries has been going on for decades. But the UK service sector has always expanded by enough to create new jobs to replace the lost manufacturing jobs. Now that service sector jobs are going overseas, the fear is that there will not be enough jobs in the the United Kingdom. This fear is misplaced.

It is true that some service jobs are going overseas. But many service jobs are expanding. The United Kingdom imports call centre services, but it exports education, healthcare, legal, financial and a host of other types of services. Jobs in these sectors are expanding and will continue to expand. The numbers reinforce this view that the fear of job loss is misplaced. The exact number of jobs that have moved to lower-cost offshore locations is not known, and estimates vary. But the number is likely to be small compared with the normal rate of job creation.

Winners and Losers from Offshoring

The trade gains from offshoring do not bring benefits to every person.

People who export the outsourced offshore services are clearly among the winners. They face an increased demand for their services, receive a higher price for them and sell a greater quantity. Given that most of these people are among the world's poorest, this gain must be considered a very important positive outcome from outsourcing and offshoring.

People who import outsourced offshore services, such as the citizens of the United Kingdom and the European Union win *on the average* but some lose. The winners are the consumers of the many goods and services that become available at a lower price. The winners also include the owners and investors in the firms that enjoy lower costs and increased profits. The losers are those who have invested in human capital to do a specific job that has now gone offshore. finding a new job of any kind can be difficult. And finding a new job in a preferred location at a wage similar to that for the job that has gone abroad is often impossible.

Unemployment benefits provide short-term relief for these displaced workers. But this relief is not sufficient to fully compensate them for their loss.

The long-term solution to becoming redundant and losing a job is retraining and the acquisition of new skills. Providing educational facilities for repeated bouts of training and retraining is a task for governments that will become increasingly important as the 21st century progresses and technology advances.

Avoiding Trade Wars

There is one counter-argument to protection that is overwhelming. Protection invites retaliation and can trigger a trade war. The best example of a trade war occurred during the Great Depression of the 1930s when the United States raised its tariffs. Country after country retaliated with its own tariff, and in a short time world trade had almost disappeared. The costs to all countries were large and led to a renewed international resolve to avoid such self-defeating moves in future. They also led to the creation of the GATT and eventually of the WTO, the European Union and APEC.

Why Is International Trade Restricted?

Why, despite all the arguments against protection, is trade restricted? There are two key reasons.

First, government revenue is costly to collect and for some governments, especially those in developing countries, a tariff is easier to collect than other types of tax.

Second, and more important, tariffs benefit the domestic producers of import-competing goods and services. You saw in the example that we worked through earlier in this chapter that UK car producers lose from free trade (Figure 7.4(b), p. 149) and gain from a tariff (Figure 7.7, p. 154).

The number of people who stand to gain from protection is small but each one of them has a lot at stake. In contrast, the number of people who stand to lose from protection is large but each one of them has a small amount at stake. Think about the market for sugar. A small number of producers stand to gain a few million pounds each from protection. And a few million consumers stand to lose just a few pence a day. Add up all the losses and they exceed the gains. But each losing consumer barely notices the extra expenditure on sugar while the gain for each winning producer is a very big deal.

This lopsided balance between winners and losers has powerful political consequences. The winners are willing to spend substantial amounts to persuade politicians to support a protectionist policy. They have a strong, well-organized political voice. They never argue that protection is needed for their own benefit. They dress up their cause by finding arguments that appear to make protection serve the social interest, even though it clearly does not. The losers, who support free trade, are a weak, ill-organized group that is barely heard. So the political outcome favours the protectionists.

Compensating Losers

Given that the gains from free international trade exceed the losses, why don't the individuals who gain compensate those who lose so that everyone is in favour of free trade?

First, the cost of identifying the losers from free trade and of estimating the value of their losses would be enormous.

Second, it would never be clear whether a person who has fallen on hard times is suffering because of free trade or for other reasons, perhaps reasons that are largely under the control of the individual.

Third, some people who look like losers at one point in time may, in fact, end up gaining. The young textile worker who loses his job and becomes a Webmaster resents the loss of work and the need to move. But a year or two later, looking back on events, he counts himself fortunate. He's made a move that has increased his income and given him greater job security.

Because we do not explicitly compensate the losers from free international trade, protectionism remains a popular and permanent feature of our national economic and political life.

Review Quiz

Study Plan 7.4

1. What are the two classic arguments for protection and why are they wrong?
2. Review the arguments that protection saves jobs, compensates for low foreign wages, compensates for costly environmental policies and prevents developing countries from being exploited.
3. Does offshore outsourcing justify protection?
4. What is the most convincing argument against protection?
5. Does the UK government need a tariff to raise revenue?
6. Given that international trade restrictions are costly, why do we have them?

You've now seen how free international trade enables people to gain from increased specialization and trade and how barriers to international trade bring gains for some, but greater losses for all.

Reading Between the Lines on pp. 160–161 shows how the EU shoe market has adjusted to a recent increase in the tariff on shoes imported from China and Vietnam. You can see why the shoe industry is happier with the new tariff and why the consumer loses.

Reading Between the Lines
A Rise in the EU Shoe Tariff

The Guardian, 7 April 2006

EU–China tariff war hits shoes

Ros Davidson

Last year, it was a battle over bras. Now, it's "shoe wars", as the European Union imposes new tariffs on imported leather shoes from China and Vietnam, starting on Friday.

Retailers are warning that shoe prices in the UK may rise because of the duties, which will increase over the next five months to 19.4% on Chinese leather shoes and 16.8% on Vietnamese.

The European commission decided to impose the new duties after a probe suggested that shoe manufacturers in the Asian countries were receiving "disguised subsidies" from their governments and are exporting shoes at below cost price.

Peter Mandelson, the EU trade commissioner, has said that the two countries used cheap financing, tax breaks and land-rent incentives to compete unfairly. The tariffs are backed by the governments of EU members with large shoe industries, such as Italy. They say that such unfair trade practices could push their manufacturers out of business.

In other parts of the 25-member EU, especially in the Nordic countries, sentiment is far more mixed. China and Vietnam deny the allegation and say that the EU is merely engaging in protectionism. . . .

The battle over shoes is the latest chapter in a fight with the Far East over trade and globalisation. Earlier this month, the EU and the US filed a complaint against China at the World Trade Organisation for its "discriminatory" tariff on imported car parts. And last year, the EU imposed limits on Chinese clothing imports, including bras.

The Essence of the Story

- The European Union has decided to impose additional tariffs on shoes imported from China and Vietnam.
- The European commission says that China and Vietnam are subsidizing shoe production and exporting shoes below the cost of production.
- Some EU governments support the tariff increase because the Asian subsidies could put their shoe producers out of business.
- Other EU countries claim that the EU is engaging in protectionism to keep out more efficiently produced shoes.

Economic Analysis

- Figure 1 shows the EU market for shoes before the tariff increase. EU demand and supply of shoes are D_{EU} and S_{EU} but shoes can be imported from non-EU producers.
- The world price of shoes is €50 a pair and the EU tariff on shoe imports is 20 per cent.
- EU shoe makers produce a small proportion of world production and the EU faces a perfectly elastic supply of shoes at the world price. The EU price of shoes is €60 a pair – the world price plus the 20 per cent tariff.
- In Figure 1, the quantity of EU-produced shoes is Q_A and the quantity of shoe consumed is Q_B. Shoe imports are Q_B minus Q_A.
- Consumer surplus is the green area A, producer surplus is the blue area B, tariff revenue is the purple area C, and the deadweight loss from the tariff is the grey area, $D + E$.
- Later in 2006, the European Union increased the tariff on shoes imported from China and Vietnam to 30 per cent.
- Figure 2 shows the effects in the EU market for shoes.
- The EU price rises from €60 to €65. The quantity of EU-produced shoes increases from Q_A to Q'_A and the quantity consumed decreases to Q'_B. Imports decrease to Q'_B minus Q'_A.
- In Figure 2, EU consumer surplus shrinks, EU producer surplus expands, and the deadweight loss increases. The EU shoe market is less efficient.
- The increase in production for EU producers will be short lived as some producers move to other countries.
- The world price might even fall in two years' time if Chinese and Vietnamese producers become more efficient.

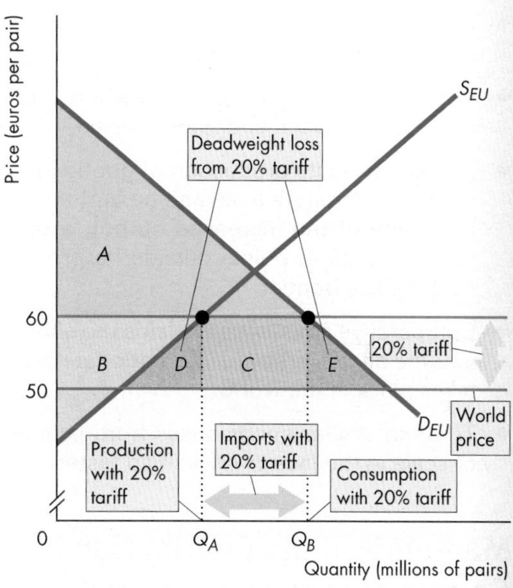

Figure 1 The EU shoe market with a 20 per cent tariff

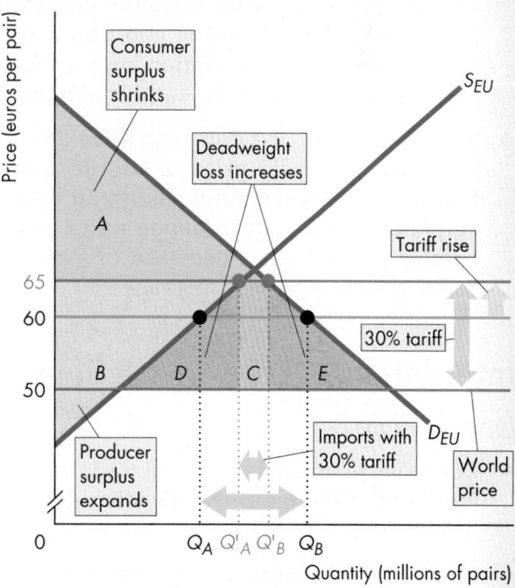

Figure 2 The EU shoe market with a 30 per cent tariff

Summary

Key Points

The Gains from International Trade (pp. 144–147)

- Comparative advantage is the fundamental source of the gains from trade.
- Comparative advantage exists when opportunity costs between countries diverge.
- By increasing its production of goods in which it has a comparative advantage and then trading some of the increased output, a country can consume at points outside its production possibilities frontier.
- Comparative advantage explains the enormous volume and diversity of international trade that takes place in the world.
- Trade in similar goods arises from economies of scale in the face of diversified tastes.

Markets and the Distribution of Gains and Losses (pp. 148–151)

- If, without trade, the domestic price of a good exceeds the world price, a country imports that good. Domestic production and producer surplus decrease, consumption and consumer surplus increase and total surplus increases.
- If, without trade, the domestic price of a good is below the world price, a country exports that good. Domestic production and producer surplus increase, consumption and consumer surplus can increase, decrease or remain the same, and total surplus increases.

International Trade Restrictions (pp. 152–155)

- Countries restrict international trade by imposing tariffs or quotas or by subsidising domestic production.
- A tariff on an imported good raises its domestic price, decreases the volume of imports, increases producer surplus for domestic producers, decreases consumer surplus and decreases total surplus.

The Case Against Protection (pp. 156–159)

- There are more efficient instruments to protect infant industries and prevent dumping than protection policy.
- Arguments that protection is necessary to save jobs, allow us to compete with cheap foreign labour, penalize lax environmental standards and prevent exploitation of developing countries are flawed.
- Offshore outsourcing is just a new way of reaping gains from trade and does not justify protection.
- Trade is restricted because tariffs raise government revenue and because protection brings a small loss to a large number of people and a large gain per person to a small number of people. The gainers have a stronger political voice than the losers.

Key Figures

Key Terms

Problems

Tests, Study Plan and Solutions* 

1 The table provides information about the production possibilities in a country called Virtual Reality.

TV sets (per day)		Computers (per day)
0	and	36
10	and	35
20	and	33
30	and	30
40	and	26
50	and	21
60	and	15
70	and	8
80	and	0

a Calculate Virtual Reality's opportunity cost of a TV set when it produces 10 sets a day.

b Calculate Virtual Reality's opportunity cost of a TV set when it produces 40 sets a day.

c Calculate Virtual Reality's opportunity cost of a TV set when it produces 70 sets a day.

d Using the answers to parts (a), (b) and (c), graph the relationship between the opportunity cost of a TV set and the quantity of TV sets produced in Virtual Reality.

2 The table provides information about the production possibilities in a country called Vital Signs.

TV sets (per day)		Computers (per day)
0	and	18.0
10	and	17.5
20	and	16.5
30	and	15.0
40	and	13.0
50	and	10.5
60	and	7.5
70	and	4.0
80	and	0

a Calculate Vital Signs' opportunity cost of a TV set when it produces 10 sets a day.

b Calculate Vital Signs' opportunity cost of a TV set when it produces 40 sets a day.

c Calculate Vital Signs' opportunity cost of a TV set when it produces 70 sets a day.

d Using the answers to parts (a), (b) and (c), sketch the relationship between the opportunity cost of a TV set and the quantity of TV sets produced in Vital Signs.

3 Suppose that, with no international trade, Virtual Reality in problem 1 produces and consumes 10 TV sets a day and Vital Signs in problem 2 produces and consumes 60 TV sets a day. Also suppose that the world price of a TV set is 1/4 of a computer. If the two countries begin to trade:

a Which country, if either, exports TV sets?

b Which country, if either, exports computers?

c What adjustments are made to the amount of each good produced by each country?

d Show on a graph how each country can consume beyond its production possibilities.

4 Suppose that, with no international trade, Virtual Reality in problem 1 produces and consumes 50 TV sets a day and Vital Signs in problem 2 produces and consumes 20 TV sets a day. Also suppose that the world price of a TV set is 1/3 of a computer. If the two countries begin to trade:

a Which country, if either, exports TV sets?

b Which country, if either, exports computers?

c What adjustments are made to the amount of each good produced by each country?

d Show on a graph how each country can consume beyond its production possibilities.

5 Compare the total quantities of each good produced in problems 1 and 2 with the total quantities of each good produced in problems 3 and 4.

a Does free trade increase or decrease the total quantities of TV sets and computers produced in both cases? Why or why not?

b What happens to the price of a TV set in Virtual Reality in the two cases? Why does it rise in one case and fall in the other?

c What happens to the price of a computer in Vital Signs in the two cases? Why does it rise in one case and fall in the other?

6 Compare the international trade in problem 3 with that in problem 4.

a Why does Virtual Reality export TV sets in one of the cases and import them in the other case?

b Do the TV producers or the computer producers gain in each case?

c Do consumers gain in each case?

---

* Solutions to odd-numbered problems are provided.

7 The figure illustrates the market for T-shirts in the United Kingdom. The demand for T-shirts is D_{UK} the supply by UK producers is S_{UK}. The world price of T-shirts is £5.

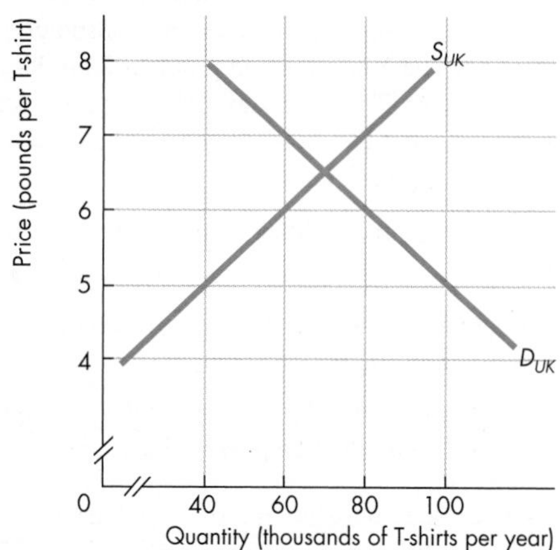

If the UK government levies a 10 per cent tariff on imported T-shirts, what is:

a The change in producer surplus?

b The tax revenue collected by the UK government?

c The change in consumer surplus?

d The deadweight loss created?

8 In problem 7, instead of imposing a tariff, suppose the government used a subsidy.

a Show on the figure the subsidy to UK producers that has the same effect on UK T-shirt production as the tariff has.

b Calculate the subsidy required.

c Identify the effect on consumers of the subsidy.

d Compare the quantity of imports under the subsidy with that under a tariff.

e Calculate the deadweight loss created by the subsidy and compare it with that of the tariff.

Critical Thinking

1 Study *Reading Between the Lines*, pp. 160–161 and then answer the following questions:

a Why is there a gap between the world price of shoes and the EU price of shoes?

b Who gains and who loses from an increased tariff on shoe imports into the European Union?

c Why do you think Italian producers wanted a higher tariff?

d What is the alleged problem with the Italian shoe making industry?

e Why might the protectionist effect of the increase in the shoe tariff be short lived?

2 **Gulf Louvre deal riles French art world**

The Louvre in Paris will benefit from the deal, officials insist. . . . A storm is raging in France over the government's decision to build a branch of the Louvre in Abu Dhabi – the first-ever foreign annex of the world-famous art gallery. The controversy is not over public spending on culture – French taxpayers think nothing of subsidising films to the tune of 500m euros a year ($700m; £350m). The row centres on the fact that France stands to make money from the deal . . .

BBC News, 6 March 2007

a Is the Louvre deal outsourcing, offshoring, both or neither?

b Who will gain from a branch of the Louvre located in Abu Dhabi?

c Who will lose from a branch of the Louvre located in Abu Dhabi?

d What other markets will be influenced by the decision to build a branch of the Louvre in Abu Dhabi?

e Do you think the Louvre would have decided to build a branch of its museum outside France if it was not expected not make money?

Web Activities

Links to Websites

1 Read the EU document on "Facts and Figures" about sugar policy and the Oxfam briefing paper, *Dumping on the World.*

a What are the main differences between the EU facts and figures document and the Oxfam report?

b What arguments are there for a sugar tariff?

c What arguments are there for a sugar export subsidy?

d The WTO has recently ruled that EU export subsidies must be removed by 2006. What effect will the elimination of these subsidies have on sugar producers and consumers in the European Union and the rest of the world?

e Do you support or oppose the EU sugar policy? Provide your reasons using the concepts of efficiency and equity.

PART

3

Households, Firms and Markets

Choices and the Pursuit of Profit

The powerful forces of demand and supply shape the fortunes of families, businesses and nations in the same unrelenting way that tides and winds shape rocks and coastlines.

You've seen in Chapters 3 through 7 how these forces raise and lower prices, increase and decrease quantities bought and sold and sometimes send resources to their most valuable uses.

These powerful market forces begin quietly and privately with the choices that each one of us makes. We choose how to allocate our budgets and our time to get the most we can out of our own scarce resources. Chapter 8 probes these choices and shows you the neat idea of mapping people's preferences and predicting how our choices respond to changing price incentives and affordable opportunities.

We make our choices against the backdrop of ever-changing technology. Every year, new goods appear and old ones disappear. New firms are born and old ones die. This process of change is managed by firms operating in markets.

We begin our study of firms in Chapter 9 by learning about their costs and the relationship between technology and cost. In Chapter 10, we study the relationship between output and the costs of production. Then we see how firms operate in various types of markets.

Some markets, like the ones we've studies so far, are competitive. The most extreme competition, called perfect competition, is the topic of Chapter 11.

At the other extreme is monopoly, a single firm with no competitors, which we study in Chapter 12.

Then, in Chapter 13 we look at a blend of competition and monopoly where we study the behaviour of the firms that produce the huge variety of brands and flavours that confront us.

Chapter 13 also explores situations in which firms, like armies, act strategically, guessing the effects of their choices on the choices of others.

CHAPTER 8

Households' Choices

After studying this chapter you will be able to:

- Describe a household's budget line and show how it changes when a price or income changes
- Make a map of preferences and explain the principle of diminishing marginal rate of substitution
- Predict the effects of changes in prices and income on consumption choices
- Predict the effect of changes of wage rates on work–leisure choices

Menus of Choice

We spend a lot of our time making choices. We choose how to spend our income. And when we've decided to spend some of it on ice cream, we sometimes take an incredible amount of time to ponder the flavour to go for. Our choices are not static: they change over time. What determines our choices and what makes our choices change? How do we choose the best affordable use of our limited income and time? Find out in this chapter. In *Reading Between the Lines* at the end of the chapter you can apply what you learn to predict the effects of a rise in train fares on our travel choices.

Consumption Possibilities

Consumption choices are limited by income and by prices. A household has a given amount of income to spend and cannot influence the prices of the goods and services it buys. It takes prices as given. A household's **budget line** describes the limits to a household's consumption choices. Let's look at Lisa's budget line.

The Budget Line

Lisa is the only person in her household and she has an income of £30 a month to spend. She buys two goods – films and cola. The price to see a film is £6 and the price of cola is £3 a six-pack. Figure 8.1 shows the alternative affordable ways for Lisa to see films and consume cola. Row *A* says that she can buy 10 six-packs of cola and see no films, a combination of films and cola that exhausts her monthly income of £30. Row *F* says that Lisa can see 5 films and drink no cola – another combination that exhausts the £30 available. Each of the other rows in the table also exhausts Lisa's income. (Check that each of the other rows costs exactly £30.) The numbers in the table define Lisa's consumption possibilities. We can graph these consumption possibilities as points *A* to *F* in Figure 8.1.

Divisible and Indivisible Goods

Some goods – called divisible goods – can be bought in any quantity desired. Examples are petrol and electricity. We can best understand the household choice we're about to study if we assume that all goods and services are divisible. For example, Lisa can see half a film a month *on average* by seeing one film every two months. When we think of goods as being divisible, the consumption possibilities are not just the points *A* to *F* shown in Figure 8.1, but these points plus all the intermediate points that form the line running from *A* to *F*. Such a line is a budget line.

Lisa's budget line is a constraint on her choices. It marks the boundary between what she can afford and what she cannot afford. Lisa can afford any point on the line and inside it. She cannot afford any point outside the budget line. The constraint on her consumption depends on the prices of the two goods (cinema tickets and six-packs) and her income. This constraint changes when either price or her income changes. Let's see how by studying an equation that describes her consumption possibilities.

Figure 8.1 myeconlab

The Budget Line

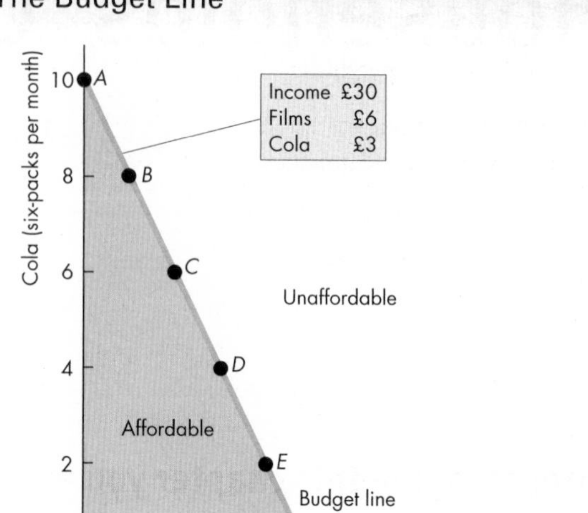

Consumption possibility	Films (per month)	Cola (six-packs per month)
A	0	10
B	1	8
C	2	6
D	3	4
E	4	2
F	5	0

Lisa's budget line is the boundary between what she can and cannot afford. The rows of the table are Lisa's affordable combinations of films and cola when her income is £30, the price of a cinema ticket is £6 and the price of cola is £3 a six-pack. For example, row *A* tells us that Lisa spends her £30 income when she buys 10 six-packs and sees no films.

The graph shows Lisa's budget line. Points *A* to *F* on the graph represent the rows of the table. For divisible goods, the budget line is the continuous line *AF*.

To calculate the equation of Lisa's budget line, start from the fact that expenditure equals income. If quantity of films that Lisa sees is Q_F and the quantity of cola she buys is Q_C, then:

$$(£3 \times Q_C) + (£6 \times Q_F) = £30$$

Divide by £3 to obtain:

$$Q_C + 2Q_F = 10$$

Subtract $2Q_F$ from both sides to obtain:

$$Q_C = 10 - 2Q_F$$

The Budget Equation

We can describe the budget line by using a *budget equation*. The budget equation starts with the fact that:

$$\text{Expenditure} = \text{Income}$$

Expenditure is equal to the sum of the price of each good multiplied by the quantity bought. For Lisa:

$$\text{Expenditure} = (\text{Price of cola} \times \text{Quantity of cola}) + (\text{Price to see a film} \times \text{Quantity of films})$$

Call the price of cola P_C, the quantity of cola Q_C, the price to see a film P_F, the quantity of films Q_F and income Y. We can write Lisa's budget equation as:

$$P_C Q_C + P_F Q_F = Y$$

Using the prices Lisa faces, £3 for a six-pack and £6 to see a film, and Lisa's income, £30, we get:

$$£3Q_C + £6Q_F = £30$$

Lisa can choose any quantities of cola (Q_C) and films (Q_F) that satisfy this equation. To find the relationship between these quantities, divide both sides of the equation by the price of cola (P_C) to get:

$$Q_C + \frac{P_F}{P_C} \times Q_F = \frac{Y}{P_C}$$

Now subtract the term $P_F/P_C \times Q_F$ from both sides of this equation to give:

$$Q_C = \frac{Y}{P_C} - \frac{P_F}{P_C} \times Q_F$$

For Lisa, income (Y) is £30, the price to see a film (P_F) is £6 and the price of cola (P_C) is £3 a six-pack. So Lisa must choose the quantities of films and cola to satisfy the equation:

$$Q_C = \frac{£30}{£3} - \frac{£6}{£3} \times Q_F$$

$$Q_C = 10 - 2 \times Q_F$$

To interpret the equation, look at the budget line in Figure 8.1 and check that the equation delivers that budget line. First, set Q_F equal to zero. The budget equation tells us that Q_C, the quantity of cola, equals Y/P_C, which is 10 six-packs. This combination of Q_F and Q_C is the one in row *A* of the table in Figure 8.1. Next, set Q_F equal to 5. Now Q_C equals zero (the combination in row *F*). Check that you can derive the other rows.

The budget equation contains two variables chosen by the household (Q_F and Q_C) and two variables (Y/P_C and P_F/P_C) that the household takes as given. Let's look more closely at these variables.

Real Income

A household's **real income** is its income expressed as the quantity of goods that the household can afford to buy. Lisa's real income in terms of cola is Y/P_C. This quantity is the maximum number of six-packs that Lisa can buy. It is equal to her money income divided by the price of cola. Lisa's income is £30 and the price of cola is £3 a six-pack, so her real income is 10 six-packs of cola. In Figure 8.1, real income is the point at which the budget line intersects the *y*-axis.

Relative Price

A **relative price** is the price of one good divided by the price of another good. In Lisa's budget equation, the variable (P_F/P_C) is the relative price of a film in terms of cola. For Lisa, P_F is £6 a film and P_C is £3 a six-pack, so P_F/P_C is equal to 2 six-packs per film. That is, to see one more film, Lisa must give up 2 six-packs.

You've just calculated Lisa's opportunity cost of seeing a film. Recall that the opportunity cost of an action is the best alternative forgone. For Lisa to see 1 more film a month, she must forgo 2 six-packs. You've also calculated Lisa's opportunity cost of cola. For Lisa to buy 2 more six-packs a month, she must give up seeing 1 film. So her opportunity cost of 2 six-packs is 1 film.

The relative price of a film in terms of cola is the magnitude of the slope of Lisa's budget line. To calculate the slope of the budget line, recall the formula (see the Chapter 1 Appendix): slope equals the change in the variable measured on the *y*-axis divided by the change in the variable measured on the *x*-axis as we move along the line. In Lisa's case (Figure 8.1), the variable measured on the *y*-axis is the quantity of cola and the variable measured on the *x*-axis is the quantity of films. Along Lisa's budget line, as cola decreases from 10 to 0 six-packs, films increase from 0 to 5. So the slope of the budget line is 10 six-packs divided by 5 films, or 2 six-packs per film. The magnitude of this slope is exactly the same as the relative price we've just calculated. It is also the opportunity cost of a film.

A Change in Prices

When prices change, so does the budget line. The lower the price of the good measured on the *x*-axis, other things remaining the same, the flatter is the budget

Figure 8.2

myeconlab

Changes in Prices and Income

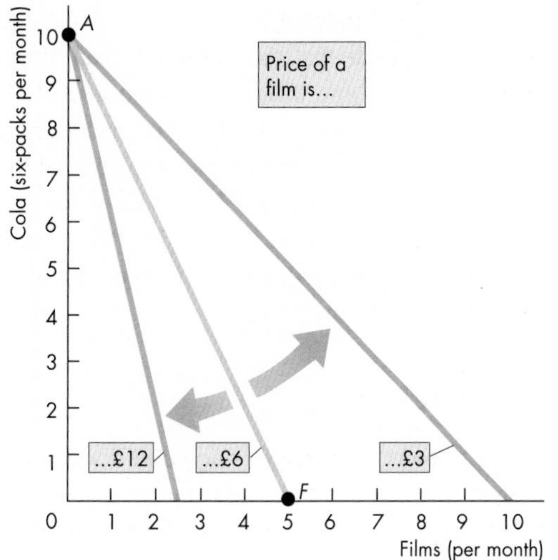

(a) A change in price

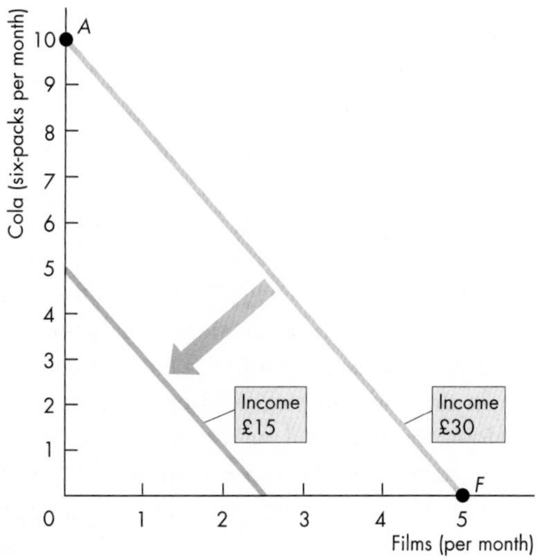

(b) A change in income

In part (a), the price to see a film changes. A fall in the price from £6 to £3 increases the number of films that Lisa can see for £30, so her budget line rotates outward and becomes flatter. A rise in the price from £6 to £12 rotates the budget line inward and makes it steeper.

In part (b), income falls from £30 to £15 while the prices of cola and seeing a film remain constant. The budget line shifts leftward but its slope does not change.

line. For example, if the price to see a film falls from £6 to £3, real income in terms of cola does not change but the relative price to see a film falls. The budget line rotates *outward* and becomes flatter as shown in Figure 8.2(a). The higher the price of the good measured on the *x*-axis, other things remaining the same, the steeper is the budget line. For example, if the price to see a film rises from £6 to £12, the relative price to see a film increases. The budget line rotates *inward* and becomes steeper as shown in Figure 8.2(a).

A Change in Income

A change in *money* income changes real income but does not change the relative price. The budget line shifts, but its slope does not change. The bigger a household's money income, the bigger is real income and the further to the right is the budget line. The smaller a household's money income, the smaller is real income and the further to the left is the budget line.

Figure 8.2(b) shows the effect of a change in income on Lisa's budget line. The initial budget line when Lisa's income is £30 is the same one that we began with in Figure 8.1. The new budget line shows how much Lisa can consume if her income falls to £15 a month. The two budget lines have the same slope – are parallel – because the relative price is the same. The new budget line is closer to the origin than the initial one because Lisa's real income has decreased.

Review Quiz

Study Plan 8.1

1. What does Lisa's budget line show?
2. How does the relative price and a household's real income influence its budget line?
3. If a European household has an income of €40 and consumes only bus rides at €4 each and magazines at €2 each, what is the equation that describes the household's budget line?
4. If the price of one good changes, what happens to the relative price and to the slope of the household's budget line?
5. If a household's money income changes and prices do not change, what happens to the household's real income and budget line?

We've studied the limits to what a household can consume. Let's now learn how we can describe the household's preferences and make a map that contains a lot of information about a household's preferences.

Preferences and Indifference Curves

Preferences are your likes and dislikes. You are going to discover a very neat idea: that of drawing a map of a person's preferences. A preference map is based on the intuitively appealing assumption that people can sort all the possible combinations of goods they might consume into three groups: preferred, not preferred and indifferent. To make this idea more concrete, we asked Lisa to rank various combinations of films and cola.

Figure 8.3(a) shows part of Lisa's answer. She tells us that she currently sees 2 films and consumes 6 six-packs a month at point *C*. She then lists all the combinations of films and cola that she thinks are just as good as her current consumption. When we plot these combinations of films and cola, we get the green curve shown in Figure 8.3(a). This curve is the key element in a map of preferences and is called an indifference curve.

An **indifference curve** is a line that shows combinations of goods among which a consumer is *indifferent*. The indifference curve in Figure 8.3(a) tells us that Lisa is just as happy to see 2 films and drink 6 six-packs a month at point *C* as she is to consume the combination of films and cola at point *G* or at any other point along the curve.

Lisa also says she prefers any of the combinations of films and cola above the indifference curve in Figure 8.3(a) – the yellow area – to any combination on the indifference curve. And she prefers any combination on the indifference curve to any combination in the grey area below the indifference curve.

The indifference curve in Figure 8.3(a) is just one of a whole family of such curves. This indifference curve appears again in Figure 8.3(b). It is labelled I_1 and it passes through points *C* and *G*. The curves labelled I_0 and I_2 are two other indifference curves. Lisa prefers any point on indifference curve I_2 to any point on indifference curve I_1 and she prefers any point on I_1 to any point on I_0. We refer to I_2 as being a higher indifference curve than I_1 and I_1 as being higher than I_0. Because Lisa prefers I_2 to I_1 and I_1 to I_0, these indifference curves do not intersect.

A *preference map* is a series of indifference curves that look like the contour lines on a map. By looking at a map, we can draw some conclusions about the terrain. Similarly, by looking at the shape of the indifference curves, we can draw conclusions about a person's preferences.

Let's see how to "read" a preference map.

Figure 8.3 myeconlab

A Preference Map

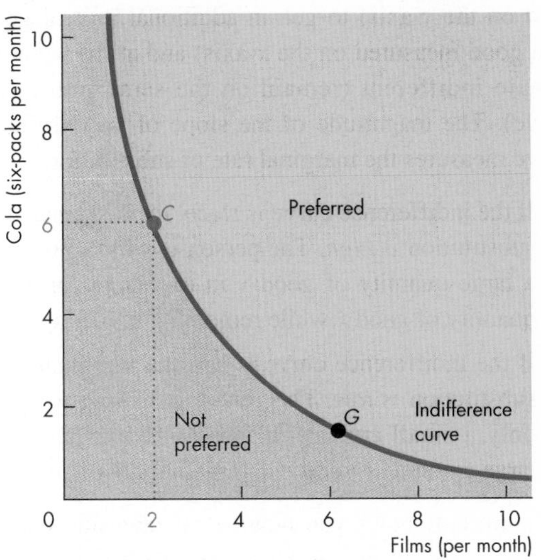

(a) An indifference curve

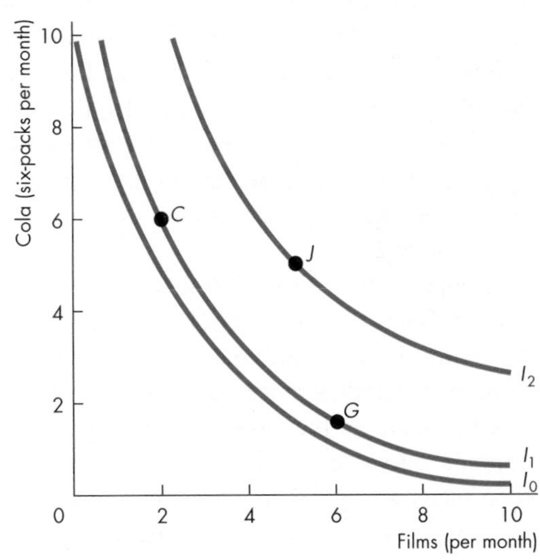

(b) Lisa's preference map

In part (a), Lisa consumes 6 six-packs of cola and sees 2 films a month at point *C*. She is indifferent between all the points on the green indifference curve such as *C* and *G*. She prefers any point above the indifference curve (yellow area) to any point on it, and she prefers any point on the indifference curve to any point below it (grey area).

Part (b) shows three indifference curves – I_0, I_1 and I_2 – that are part of Lisa's preference map. She prefers point *J* to point *C* or *G*, so she prefers any point on I_2 to any point on I_1.

Marginal Rate of Substitution

The **marginal rate of substitution** (or *MRS*) is the rate at which a person will give up good *y* (the good measured on the *y*-axis) to get an additional unit of good *x* (the good measured on the *x*-axis) and at the same time remain indifferent (remain on the same indifference curve). The magnitude of the slope of an indifference curve measures the marginal rate of substitution.

1 If the indifference curve is *steep*, the marginal rate of substitution is *high*. The person is willing to give up a large quantity of good *y* in exchange for a small quantity of good *x* while remaining indifferent

2 If the indifference curve is *flat*, the marginal rate of substitution is *low*. The person is willing to give up only a small amount of good *y* in exchange for a large amount of good *x* to remain indifferent

Figure 8.4 shows you how to calculate the marginal rate of substitution. Suppose that Lisa drinks 6 six-packs and sees 2 films at point *C* on indifference curve I_1. To calculate her marginal rate of substitution, we measure the absolute magnitude of the slope of the indifference curve at point *C*. To measure this magnitude, place a straight line against, or tangent to, the indifference curve at point *C*. Along that line, as the quantity of cola decreases by 10 six-packs, the number of films increases by 5 – an average of 2 six-packs per film. So at point *C*, Lisa is willing to give up cola for films at the rate of 2 six-packs per film – a marginal rate of substitution of 2.

Now, suppose that Lisa sees 6 films and drinks 1.5 six-packs at point *G* in Figure 8.4. Her marginal rate of substitution is now measured by the magnitude of the slope of the indifference curve at point *G*. That slope is the same as the slope of the tangent to the indifference curve at point *G*. Here, as cola consumption increases by 4.5 six-packs, film consumption decreases by 9 – an average of 1/2 six-packs per film. So at point *G*, Lisa is willing to give up cola for films at the rate of 1/2 six-packs per film – a marginal rate of substitution of 1/2.

As Lisa sees more films and drinks less cola, her marginal rate of substitution diminishes. Diminishing marginal rate of substitution is the key assumption of consumer theory. The assumption of **diminishing marginal rate of substitution** is a general tendency for the marginal rate of substitution to diminish as the consumer moves along an indifference curve, increasing consumption of the good on the *x*-axis and decreasing consumption of the good on the *y*-axis.

Figure 8.4 myeconlab

The Marginal Rate of Substitution

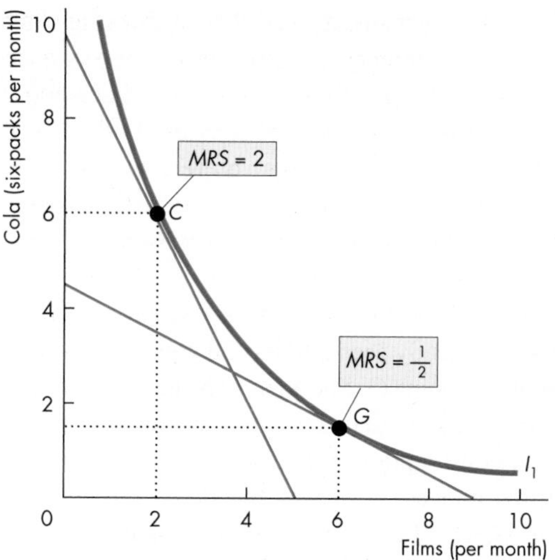

The magnitude of the slope of an indifference curve is called the marginal rate of substitution (*MRS*). The red line at point *C* tells us that Lisa is willing to give up 10 six-packs to see 5 films. Her marginal rate of substitution at point *C* is 10 divided by 5, which equals 2. The red line at point *G* tells us that Lisa is willing to give up 4.5 six-packs to see 9 films. Her marginal rate of substitution at point *G* is 4.5 divided by 9, which equals 1/2.

Your Own Diminishing Marginal Rate of Substitution

Think about your own diminishing marginal rate of substitution. Suppose that in one month you drink 10 six-packs of cola and see no films. You would probably be happy to give up lots of cans of cola just to see one film. But now suppose that in a month, you see 6 films and drink only 1 six-pack of cola. Most likely, you will probably not now be willing to give up a few cans of cola to see an extra film. As a general rule, the greater the number of films you see, the smaller is the quantity of cola you will give up to see an extra film.

The shape of the indifference curves incorporates the principle of the diminishing marginal rate of substitution because the curves are bowed towards the origin. The tightness of the bend of an indifference curve tells us how willing a person is to substitute one good for another while remaining indifferent. The examples that follow will make this point clear.

Degree of Substitutability

Most of us would not regard films and cola as being close substitutes for each other. Substitutes are goods that can be used in place of each other. But to some degree, we are willing to substitute between these two goods. No matter how enthusiastic you are for cola, there is surely some increase in the number of films you can see that will compensate you for being deprived of a can of cola. Similarly, no matter how addicted you are to films, surely some number of cans of cola will compensate you for being deprived of seeing one film. A person's indifference curves for films and cola might look something like those shown in Figure 8.5(a).

Close Substitutes

Some goods substitute so easily for each other that most of us do not even notice which we are consuming. The different brands of personal computers are an example. As long as it runs "Intel inside" and runs Windows, most of us don't care whether our PC is a Dell, an HP, an Elonex or any of a dozen other brands. The same holds true for marker pens. Most of us don't care whether we use a marker pen from the university bookshop or the local supermarket. When two goods are perfect substitutes, their indifference curves are straight lines that slope downward, as Figure 8.5(b) illustrates. The marginal rate of substitution between perfect substitutes is constant.

Complements

Some goods cannot substitute for each other at all. Instead, they are complements. The complements in Figure 8.5(c) are left and right running shoes. Indifference curves of perfect complements are L-shaped. For most of us, one left running shoe and one right running shoe are as good as one left running shoe and two right ones. Having two of each is preferred to having one of each, but two of one and one of the other is no better than one of each.

The extreme cases of perfect substitutes and perfect complements shown here don't often happen in reality. But they do illustrate that the shape of the indifference

Figure 8.5

The Degree of Substitutability

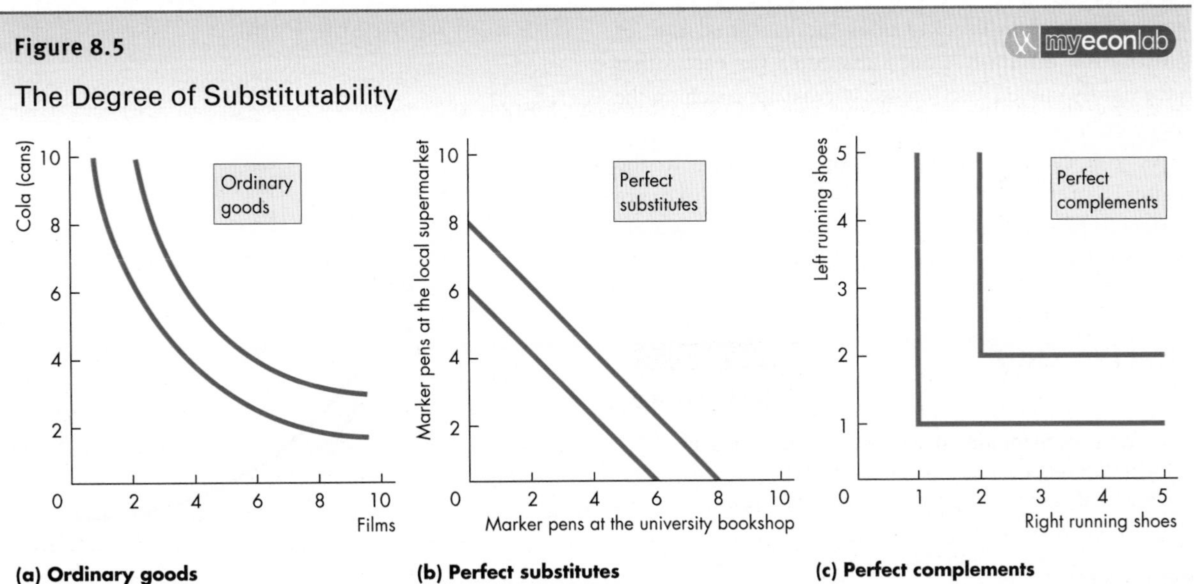

(a) Ordinary goods **(b) Perfect substitutes** **(c) Perfect complements**

The shape of the indifference curves reveals the degree of substitutability between two goods. Part (a) shows the indifference curves for two ordinary goods: films and cola. To consume less cola and remain indifferent, one must see more films. The number of films that compensates for a reduction in cola increases as less cola is consumed.

Part (b) shows the indifference curves for two perfect substitutes. For the consumer to remain indifferent, one fewer marker pen from the local supermarket must be replaced by one extra marker pen from the university bookshop.

Part (c) shows two perfect complements – goods that cannot be substituted for each other at all. One left running shoe with two right running shoes is no better than one of each. But having two of each is preferred to having one of each.

"With the pork I'd recommend an Alsatian white or a Coke."

curve shows the degree of substitutability between two goods. The more perfectly substitutable the two goods, the more nearly are their indifference curves straight lines and the less quickly does the marginal rate of substitution diminish. Poor substitutes for each other have tightly curved indifference curves, approaching the shape of those shown in Figure 8.5(c).

As you can see in the cartoon, according to the waiter's preferences, Alsatian white and Coke are perfect substitutes and each is a complement of pork. We hope the customers agree with him.

Review Quiz

Study Plan 8.2

1. What is an indifference curve and how does an indifference map show preferences?
2. Why does an indifference curve slope downward, and why is it bowed towards the origin?
3. What do we call the magnitude of the slope of an indifference curve?
4. What is the key assumption about a consumer's marginal rate of substitution?

The two components of the model of household choice are now in place: the budget line and the preference map. We will use these components to work out the consumer's choice and to predict how choices change when prices and income change.

Predicting Consumer Behaviour

We are now going to develop a model to predict the quantities of films and cola that Lisa *chooses* to buy. Figure 8.6 shows Lisa's budget line from Figure 8.1 and her indifference curves from Figure 8.3(b). We assume that Lisa consumes at her best affordable point, which is 2 films and 6 six-packs of cola – point *C*. Here Lisa:

1. Is on her budget line
2. Is on the highest attainable indifference curve
3. Has a marginal rate of substitution between films and cola equal to the relative price of films and cola

For every point inside the budget line, such as point *I* in Figure 8.6, there are points *on* the budget line that Lisa prefers. For example, she prefers all the points on the budget line between *F* and *H* to point *I*. So she chooses a point on the budget line.

Figure 8.6

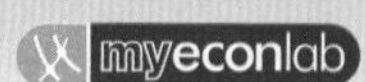

The Best Affordable Point

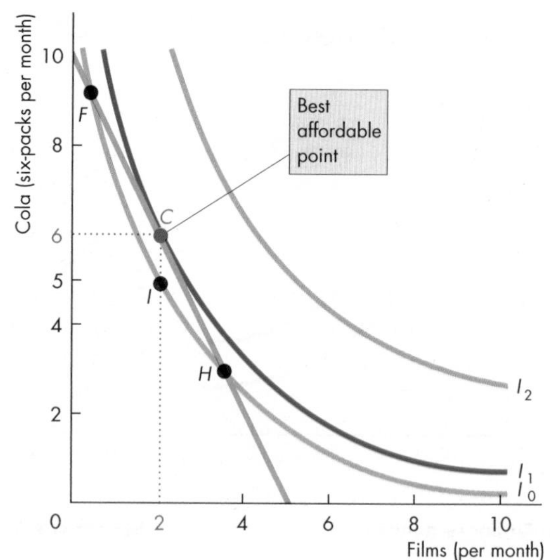

Lisa's best affordable point is *C*. At that point, she is on her budget line and also on the highest attainable indifference curve. At a point such as *H*, Lisa is willing to give up more films in exchange for cola than she has to. She can move to point *I*, which is just as good as point *H*, and have some unspent income. She can spend that income and move to *C*, a point that she prefers to point *I*.

Every point on the budget line lies on an indifference curve. For example, point H lies on the indifference curve I_0. At point H in Figure 8.6, Lisa's marginal rate of substitution is less than the relative price. Lisa is willing to give up more films in exchange for cola than the budget line says she must give up. So Lisa moves along her budget line towards point C.

As Lisa moves along her budget line from point H, she passes through a number of indifference curves (not shown in the figure) located between I_0 and I_1. All of these indifference curves are higher than I_0 and therefore Lisa prefers any point on them to point H. But when Lisa gets to point C, she is on the highest attainable indifference curve. If she keeps moving further along the budget line, she starts to encounter indifference curves that are lower than I_1. So Lisa chooses point C – her best affordable point.

At the best affordable point, the marginal rate of substitution (the magnitude of the slope of the indifference curve) equals the relative price (the magnitude of the slope of the budget line). That is, at the best affordable point, the budget line is tangential to the indifference curve.

You can now use this model of household choice to predict the effects on consumption of changes in prices and income. We'll begin by studying the effects of a price change.

A Change in Price

The effect of a change in price on the quantity of a good consumed is called the **price effect**. We will use Figure 8.7(a) to work out the price effect of a fall in the price of seeing a film. We start with the price at £6, the price of cola at £3 a six-pack and with Lisa's income at £30 a month. In this situation, Lisa chooses point C, where her budget line is tangent to her highest attainable indifference curve, I_1. She consumes 6 six-packs and sees 2 films a month.

Now suppose that the price of a film falls to £3. With a lower price of film, the budget line rotates outward and becomes flatter. (Check back with Figure 8.2(a) for a reminder on how a price change affects the budget line.) The new budget line is the darker orange line in Figure 8.7(a).

Lisa's best affordable point is J, where she sees 5 films and consumes 5 six-packs of cola. When the price of a film falls and the price of cola and her income remain constant, Lisa cuts her cola consumption from 6 to 5 six-packs and increases the number of films she sees from 2 to 5 a month. Lisa substitutes films for cola.

Figure 8.7

myeconlab

Price Effect and Demand Curve

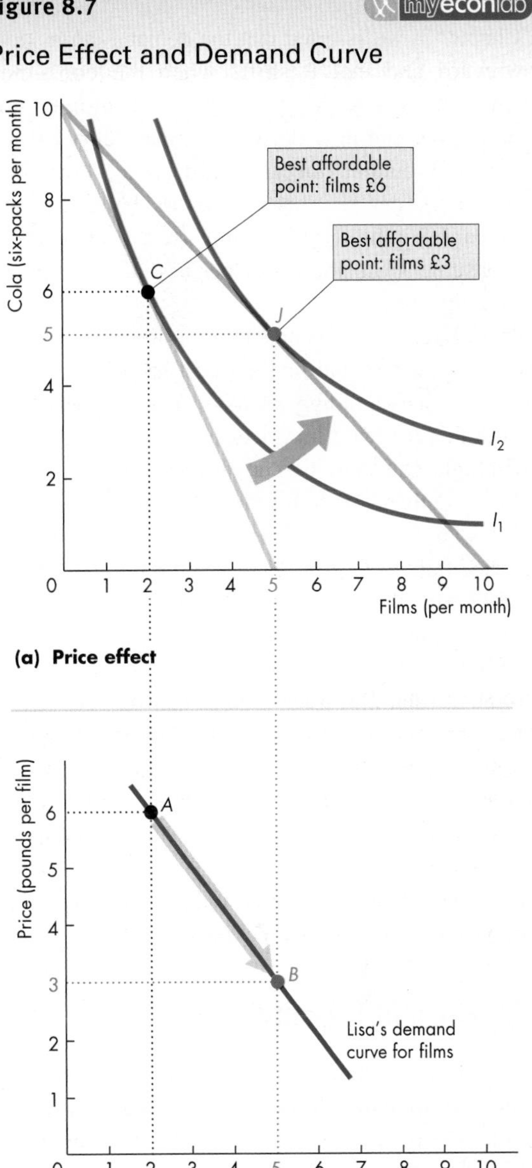

Initially, Lisa consumes at point *C* in part (a). If the price to see a film falls from £6 to £3, Lisa consumes at point *J*. Lisa increases the number of films she see from 2 to 5 a month and decreases the cola she drinks from 6 to 5 six-packs. The move from point *C* to point *J* is the *price effect*.

At a price of £6 a film, Lisa sees 2 films a month. This combination is shown as point *A* in part (b). At a price of £3 a film, Lisa sees 5 films a month. This combination is shown point *B* in part (b). Lisa's demand curve for films passes through points *A* and *B* and traces out her best affordable quantity of films as the price of a film varies.

The Demand Curve

In Chapter 3, we asserted that the demand curve slopes downward and that it shifts when the consumer's income changes or when the price of another good changes. We can now derive a demand curve from a consumer's budget line and indifference curves. By doing so, we can see that the law of demand and the downward-sloping demand curve are consequences of the consumer choosing his or her best affordable combination of goods.

To derive Lisa's demand curve for films, we lower the price to see a film and find her best affordable point at different prices, holding all other things constant. We just did this for two film prices in Figure 8.7(a). Figure 8.7(b) highlights these two prices and two points that lie on Lisa's demand curve for films. When the price to see a film is £6, Lisa sees 2 films a month at point *A*. When the price falls to £3, she increases the number of films she sees to 5 films a month at point *B*. Lisa's demand curve for films is made up of these two points plus all the other points of Lisa's best affordable consumption of films at each film price – more than £6, between £6 and £3 and less than £3 – given the price of cola and Lisa's income. As you can see, Lisa's demand curve for films slopes downward – the lower the price to see a film, the more films she sees each month. This is the law of demand.

Next, let's examine how Lisa adjusts her consumption of films and cola when her income changes.

A Change in Income

The effect of a change in income on consumption is called the **income effect**. Figure 8.8(a) shows the income effect when Lisa's income falls. With an income of £30, the price of a film £3 and the price of cola £3 a six-pack, she consumes at point *J* – 5 films and 5 six-packs. If her income falls to £21, she consumes at point *K* – 4 films and 3 six-packs. So when Lisa's income falls, she consumes less of both goods. Films and cola are normal goods.

The Demand Curve and the Income Effect

A change in income leads to a shift in the demand curve, as shown in Figure 8.8(b). With an income of £30, Lisa's demand curve is D_0, the same as in Figure 8.7. But when her income falls to £21, she plans to see fewer films at each price, so her demand curve shifts leftward to D_1.

Figure 8.8

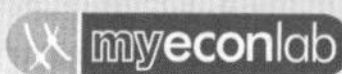

Income Effect and Change in Demand

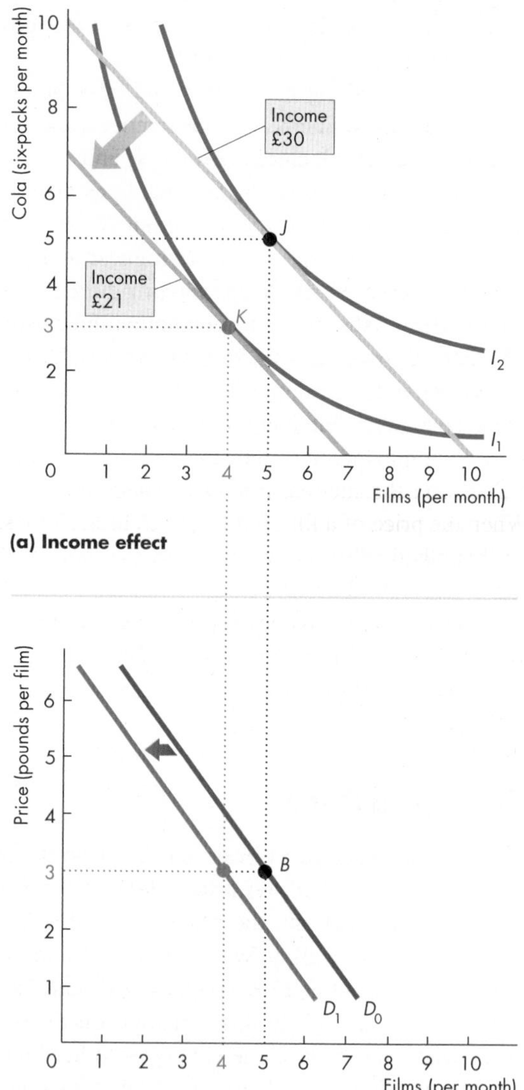

When Lisa's income is £30, the price of a film is £3 and the price of cola is £3 a six-pack, she consumes at point *J* in part (a) and her demand curve for films is D_0 in part (b).

A change in income shifts the budget line, changes the best affordable point and shifts the demand curve.

In part (a), when Lisa's income decreases from £30 to £21, she consumes at point *K*. Lisa sees fewer films and consumes less cola. In part (b), when Lisa's income decreases to £21, her demand curve for films shifts leftward to D_1. Lisa's demand for films decreases because she now sees fewer films at each price.

Substitution Effect and Income Effect

For a normal good, a fall in price *always* increases the quantity bought. We can prove this assertion by dividing the price effect into two parts:

- The substitution effect
- The income effect

Figure 8.9(a) shows the price effect and Figure 8.9(b) divides the price effect into its two parts.

Substitution Effect

The **substitution effect** is the effect of a change in price on the quantities bought when the consumer (hypothetically) remains indifferent between the original and the new combinations of goods consumed. To work out Lisa's substitution effect, when the price of a film falls, we cut her income by enough to leave her on the same indifference curve as before.

When the price of a film falls from £6 to £3, let's suppose (hypothetically) that we cut Lisa's income to £21. What's special about £21? It is the income that is just enough, at the new price of a film, to keep Lisa's best affordable point on the same indifference curve as her original consumption point *C*. Lisa's budget line is now the light orange line in Figure 8.9(b). With the lower price of a film and less income, Lisa's best affordable point is *K* on indifference curve I_1. The move from *C* to *K* is the substitution effect of the price change. The substitution effect of the fall in the price of a film is an increase in films she sees from 2 to 4 a month. The direction of the substitution effect never varies: when the relative price of a good falls, the consumer substitutes more of that good for the other good.

Income Effect

To calculate the substitution effect, we gave Lisa a £9 pay cut. Now let's give Lisa her £9 back. The £9 increase in income shifts Lisa's budget line outward, as shown in Figure 8.9(b). The slope of the budget line does not change because both prices remain constant. This change in Lisa's budget line is similar to the one illustrated in Figure 8.8. As Lisa's budget line shifts outward, her best affordable point becomes *J* on indifference curve I_2 in Figure 8.9(b). The move from *K* to *J* is the income effect of the price change: as Lisa's income increases, she increases the number of films she sees. For Lisa, films are a normal good. For a normal good, the income effect reinforces the substitution effect.

Figure 8.9 myeconlab

Substitution Effect and Income Effect

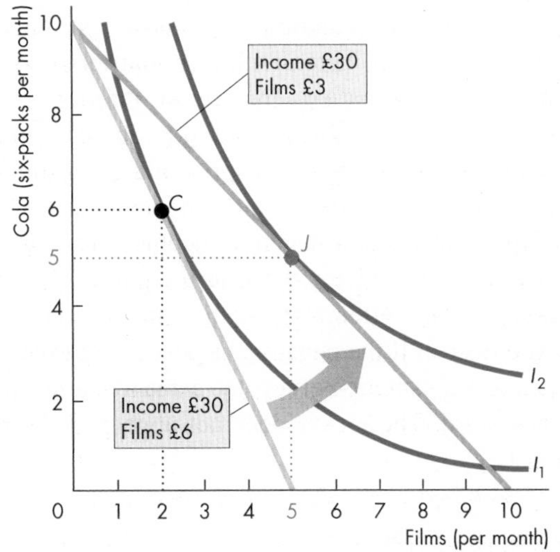

(a) Price effect

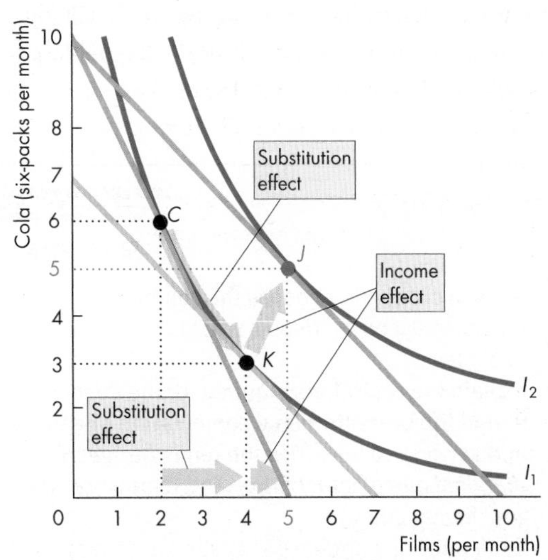

(b) Substitution effect and income effect

The price effect in part (a) can be separated into a substitution effect and an income effect in part (b).

To isolate the substitution effect, we confront Lisa with the new price but keep her on her original indifference curve, I_1. The substitution effect is the move from *C* to *K*.

To isolate the income effect, we confront Lisa with the new price of films but change her income so that she can move from the original indifference curve, I_1, to the new one, I_2. The income effect is the move from *K* to *J*.

Inferior Goods

The example that we have just studied is that of a change in the price of a normal good. The effect of a change in the price of an inferior good is different. Recall that an inferior good is one whose consumption decreases as income increases. For an inferior good, the income effect is negative. Thus for an inferior good a lower price does not always lead to an increase in the quantity demanded. The lower price has a substitution effect that increases the quantity demanded. But the lower price also has a negative income effect, which reduces the demand for the inferior good. Thus the negative income effect offsets the substitution effect to some degree. If the negative income effect exceeded the positive substitution effect, the demand curve would slope upward. These case does not appear in the real world.

Back to the Facts

We have used the indifference curve to explain how consumption patterns change over time. The best affordable choices determine spending patterns. Changes in prices and incomes change the best affordable choice and change consumption patterns.

Review Quiz

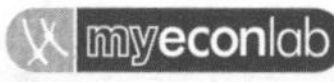

Study Plan 8.3

1. When a consumer chooses the combination of goods and services to buy, what is she or he trying to achieve?
2. Explain the conditions required for the consumer to find the best affordable combination of goods and services to buy. (Use the terms *budget line, marginal rate of substitution* and *relative price* in your explanation.)
3. If the price of a normal good falls, what happens to the quantity demanded of that good?
4. If the consumer's income falls, what happens to the demand for a normal good?
5. Into what two effects can we divide the effect of a price change?
6. For a normal good, does the income effect reinforce the substitution effect or does it partly offset the substitution?

The model of household choice can explain many other household choices. Let's look at one of them: the choice between work and leisure.

Work–Leisure Choices

Households make many choices other than those about how to spend their income on the various goods and services available. We can use the model of consumer choice to understand a wide range of other household choices. Here we'll study a key choice: how much labour to supply and how much time to spend on leisure rather than work.

Labour Supply

Every week we allocate hours between working – called *labour* – and all other activities – called *leisure*. We can use the theory of household choice to show how we allocate our time between labour and leisure.

The more hours we spend on leisure, the smaller is our income. The relationship between leisure and income is described by an *income–leisure budget line*. The orange lines in Figure 8.10(a) show Lisa's income–leisure budget lines. If Lisa devotes the entire week to leisure – 168 hours – she does no work and has no income. She is at point *Z*. By supplying labour in exchange for a wage, she can convert leisure into income along the income–leisure budget line.

The slope of the income–leisure budget line is determined by the hourly wage rate. If the wage rate is £2 an hour, Lisa faces the flattest budget line. If she worked for 68 hours a week, she would make an income of £136 a week. If the wage rate is £4 an hour, she faces the middle budget line. If the wage rate is £6 an hour, she faces the steepest budget line.

Lisa buys leisure by not supplying labour and by forgoing income. The opportunity cost of an hour of leisure is the hourly wage rate forgone.

Figure 8.10(a) also shows Lisa's indifference curves for income and leisure. Lisa chooses her best attainable point. This choice of income and time allocation is just like her choice of films and cola. She gets onto the highest possible indifference curve by making her marginal rate of substitution between income and leisure equal to her wage rate.

Lisa's choice depends on the wage rate she can earn. At a wage rate of £2 an hour, Lisa chooses point *A* and works 20 hours a week (168 minus 148) for an income of £40 a week. At a wage rate of £4 an hour, she chooses point *B* and works 35 hours a week (168 minus 133) for an income of £140 a week. At a wage rate of £6 an hour, she chooses point *C* and works 30 hours a week (168 minus 138) for an income of £180 a week.

Figure 8.10

The Supply of Labour

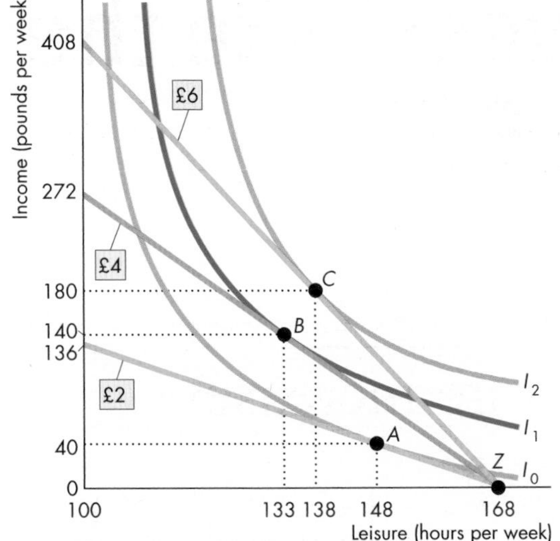

(a) Time allocation decision

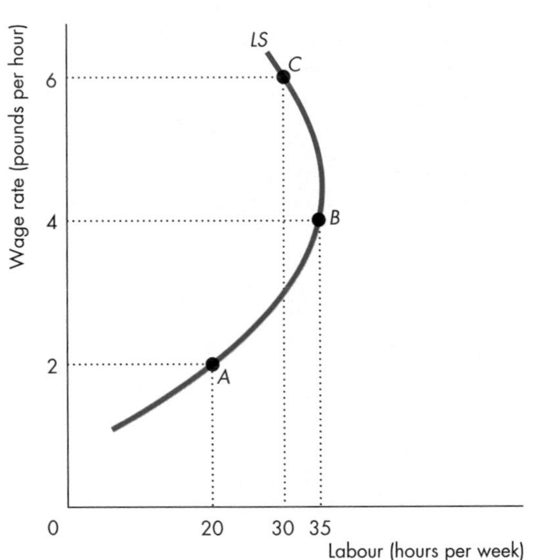

(b) Labour supply curve

In part (a), at a wage rate of £2 an hour, Lisa takes 148 hours of leisure and works 20 hours a week at point *A*. If the wage rate rises from £2 to £4 an hour, she decreases her leisure to 133 hours and increases her work to 35 hours a week at point *B*. But if the wage rises from £4 to £6 an hour, Lisa *increases* her leisure to 138 hours and *decreases* her work to 30 hours a week at point *C*.

Part (b) shows Lisa's labour supply curve. Points *A*, *B* and *C* on the supply curve correspond to Lisa's choices on her income–leisure budget line in part (a).

The Labour Supply Curve

Figure 8.10(b) shows Lisa's labour supply curve. This curve shows that as the wage rate increases from £2 an hour to £4 an hour, Lisa increases the quantity of labour supplied from 20 hours a week to 35 hours a week. But when the wage rate increases from £4 an hour to £6 an hour, she decreases her quantity of labour supplied to 30 hours a week.

Lisa's supply of labour is similar to that for the economy as a whole. As wage rates have increased, work hours have decreased. At first, this pattern seems puzzling. We've seen that the hourly wage rate is the opportunity cost of leisure. So a higher wage rate means a higher opportunity cost of leisure. This fact on its own leads to a decrease in leisure and an increase in work hours. But instead, we've cut our work hours. Why? Because our incomes have increased. As the wage rate increases, incomes increase, so people demand more of all normal goods. Leisure is a normal good, so as incomes increase, people demand more leisure.

The higher wage rate has both a *substitution effect* and an *income effect*. The higher wage rate increases the opportunity cost of leisure and so leads to a substitution effect away from leisure. The higher wage rate increases income and so leads to an income effect towards more leisure. This outcome of rational household choice explains why the average working week has fallen steadily from 70 hours a week in the nineteenth century to 35 hours a week today. Although people substitute work for leisure as wage rates increase, they also use their higher incomes to consume more leisure. The theory can also explain why more women now have jobs in the labour market. Increasing wage rates and improvements in their job opportunities have led to a substitution effect away from working at home and towards working in the labour market.

Review Quiz

myeconlab

Study Plan 8.4

1. What is the opportunity cost of leisure?
2. Why might a rise in the wage rate lead to an increase in leisure and a decrease in work hours?

You can apply what you've just learned in *Reading Between the Lines* on pp. 180–181, which examines the choice between bus and train travel. And in the appendix to this chapter, you can learn about a different way of studying choices that enables us to interpret indifference curves using the concept of utility.

Reading Between the Lines

Indifference Curves: Take the Train or Take the Bus?

Financial Times, 2 January 2007

FT

Above-inflation rail fare increases draw protests

Above-inflation fare increases on the railways . . . drew protests on Tuesday from groups representing businesses and passengers, but were described as essential by the service operators.

The cost of most regulated train fares such as season tickets and off-peak savers – around 40 per cent of tickets sold – rose by an average of 4.3 per cent, 1 per cent above inflation. Unregulated fares on cheap day returns, long distance open tickets and some advance purchase tickets increased by 4.7 per cent on average.

Some fares have risen by more, with regulated fares on Southeastern up 6.3 per cent and unregulated fares on the Heathrow and Gatwick Expresses up 7.3 per cent. Fares on Virgin West Coast rose 6.6 per cent, taking a standard open return from London to Manchester to £219 (£337 in first class). . . .

Sally Low of the British Chambers of Commerce said the cost of going to work was rising faster than inflation year after year without a corresponding increase in the quality of service offered to commuters.

"Train fare rises to the extent we are seeing are not justifiable and could well force commuters into their cars. The government is going to find it very difficult to win support for road pricing if the cost of public transport keeps rising like this." . . .

Passenger groups also attacked the inflation-beating increases. Anthony Smith of Passenger Focus, the rail consumer watchdog, said travellers who had no choice about when to travel or who needed flexibility in their tickets faced "off-putting prices" that were pricing them off the railways. . . .

The Essence of the Story

- Train fares increased by an average of 4.3 per cent in January 2007.
- Some fares increased by as much as 7.3 per cent.
- These train fare increases exceed the general rate of increase in prices and incomes.
- The rise in fares will put some people off using the trains.

Economic Analysis

- Charlotte, a university student, has a budget of £200 a year to spend on travelling home.
- The price of a train ticket is £20 and the price of a bus ticket is £10, so Charlotte can afford 10 train tickets or 20 bus tickets a year.
- Charlotte hates taking the bus and loves the train. But because of the price difference, she makes 8 trips a year by bus (spending £80) and 6 trips by train (spending £120).
- The price of a train ticket rises to £30 but the price of a bus ticket remains at £10. If Charlotte made 6 train trips at £30 a trip, she would only have enough left over for 2 bus trips.
- Although Charlotte hates taking the bus, she decides to continue taking 8 bus trips a year and cuts back her train trips to 4 a year. So she continues to spend £80 on bus trips and £120 on train trips.
- Figure 1 explains Charlotte's choices using her budget lines and indifference curves between train and bus travel, I_0 and I_1.
- Because Charlotte doesn't like the bus as much as the train, the two modes of travel are not close substitutes – her marginal rate of substitution diminishes strongly.
- At the initial price of train travel, Charlotte's best affordable point is *A* on I_1 and the higher budget line.
- When the price of train travel rises, the budget line rotates inward.
- At the higher price of train travel, Charlotte's best affordable point is *B* on I_0.
- Figure 2 shows Charlotte's demand curve for train tickets home.
- At a price of £20, Charlotte buys 6 tickets, but when the price rises to £30, she buys 4 tickets.
- The movement up Charlotte's demand curve and the fall in quantity demanded shows how she is "put off" train travel.

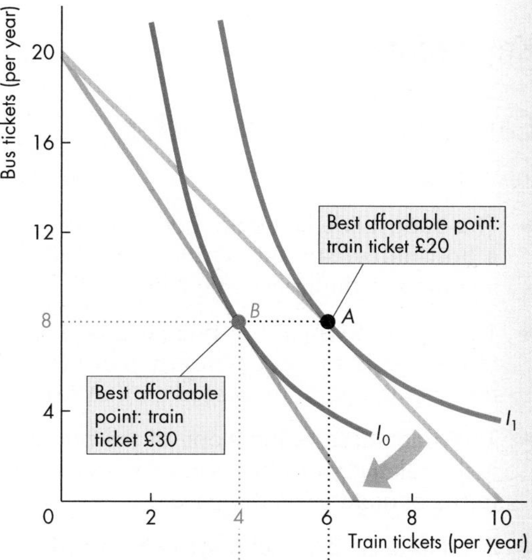

Figure 1 Best affordable travel home

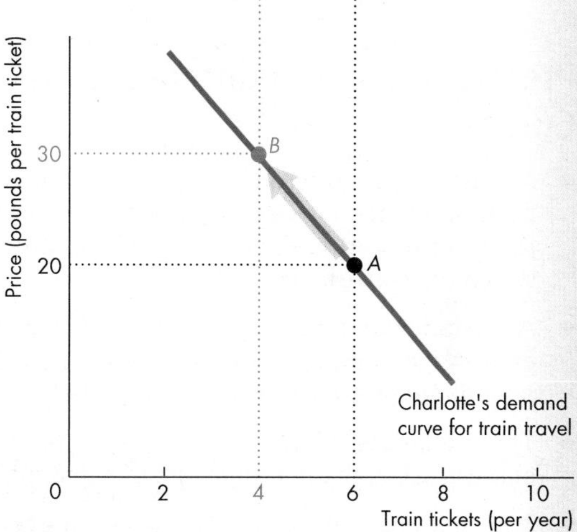

Figure 2 Charlotte's demand for train travel

- People who have less flexibility when they travel will have more inelastic demand for train travel. A similar price rise will lead to a smaller decrease in train travel.
- People who have more flexibility when they travel will have more elastic demand for train travel. A similar price rise will lead to a larger decrease in train travel.

Summary

Key Points

Consumption Possibilities

(pp. 168–170)

- The budget line is the boundary between what a household can and cannot afford given its income and the prices of goods.
- The point at which the budget line intersects the *y*-axis is the household's real income in terms of the good measured on that axis.
- The magnitude of the slope of the budget line is the relative price of good *x* (on the *x*-axis) in terms of good *y* (on the *y*-axis).
- A change in price changes the slope of the budget line. A change in income shifts the budget line but does not change its slope.

Preferences and Indifference Curves (pp. 171–174)

- A consumer's preferences can be represented by indifference curves. An indifference curve joins all the combinations of goods among which the consumer is indifferent.
- A consumer prefers any point above an indifference curve to any point on it and any point on an indifference curve to any point below it.
- The magnitude of the slope of an indifference curve is called the marginal rate of substitution.
- The marginal rate of substitution diminishes as consumption of the good measured on the *y*-axis decreases and consumption of the good measured on the *x*-axis increases.

Predicting Consumer Behaviour

(pp. 174–178)

- A household consumes at its best affordable point. This point is on the budget line and on the highest attainable indifference curve and has a marginal rate of substitution equal to the relative price.
- The effect of a price change (the price effect) can be divided into a substitution effect and an income effect.
- The change in quantity when the price changes but the consumer (hypothetically) remains on the initial indifference curve is the substitution effect.
- The substitution always results in an increase in consumption of the good whose relative price has decreased.
- The income effect is the effect of change in income on consumption.
- For a normal good, the income effect reinforces the substitution effect. For an inferior good, the income effect works in the opposite direction to the substitution effect.

Work–Leisure Choices

(pp. 178–179)

- The model of household choice enables us to understand how a household allocates its time between leisure and work.
- Work hours have decreased and leisure hours have increased because the income effect on the demand for leisure has been greater than the substitution effect.

Key Figures

Key Terms

Problems

Tests, Study Plan and Solutions* 

1 Sara has an income of €12 a week. The price of popcorn is €3 a bag, and the price of cola is €3 a can.

a What is Sara's real income in terms of cola?

b What is her real income in terms of popcorn?

c What is the relative price of cola in terms of popcorn?

d What is the opportunity cost of a can of cola?

e Calculate the equation for Sara's budget line (placing bags of popcorn on the left side).

f Draw a graph of Sara's budget line with cola on the x-axis.

g In part (f), what is the slope of Sara's budget line? What determines its value?

2 Sara's income falls from €12 a week to €9 a week. The price of popcorn remains at €3 a bag, and the price of cola remains at €3 a can.

a What is the effect of the fall in Sara's income on her real income in terms of cola?

b What is the effect of the decrease in Sara's income on her real income in terms of popcorn?

c What is the effect of the decrease in Sara's income on the relative price of cola in terms of popcorn?

d What is the slope of Sara's new budget line if it is drawn with cola on the x-axis?

3 Sara's income falls from €12 a week to €9 a week. The price of popcorn rises from €3 a bag to €6 a bag, and the price of cola remains at €3 a can.

a What is the effect of the rise in the price of popcorn on her real income in terms of cola?

b What is the effect of the rise in the price of popcorn on her real income in terms of popcorn?

c What is the effect of the rise in the price of popcorn on the relative price of cola in terms of popcorn?

d What is the slope of Sara's new budget line if it is drawn with cola on the x-axis?

4 Rashid buys only books and DVDs and the figure in the next column illustrates his preferences.

a When Rashid chooses the consumption point of 3 books and 2 DVDs, what is his marginal rate of substitution?

b When Rashid consumes 2 books and 6 DVDs, what is his marginal rate of substitution?

c Do Rashid's indifference curves display a diminishing marginal rate of substitution? Explain why or why not.

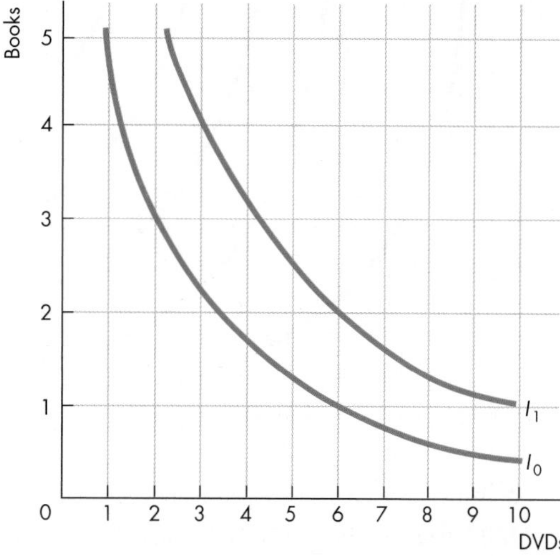

5 Draw figures that show your indifference curves for the following pairs of goods. For each pair, explain whether the goods are perfect substitutes, perfect complements or neither. If the goods are neither, discuss the shape of the indifference curve you have drawn and explain how your marginal rate of substitution changes as the quantities of the two goods change. The pairs of goods are:

a Right gloves and left gloves

b Coca-Cola and Pepsi

c Cricket balls and bats

d Neurofen and ibuprofen (the generic form of Neurofen)

e Eye glasses and contact lenses

f Desktop computers and laptop computers

g Skis and ski poles

6 Sara's income is €12 a week. The price of popcorn is €3 a bag, and the price of cola is €3 a can. The figure (on the next page) illustrates Sara's preferences for popcorn and cola.

a What are the quantities of popcorn and cola does Sara buys?

b What is Sara's marginal rate of substitution at the point at which she consumes?

7 Now suppose that in the situation described in problem 6, the price of cola falls to €1.50 per can but the price of popcorn and Sara's income remain constant.

* Solutions to odd-numbered problems are provided.

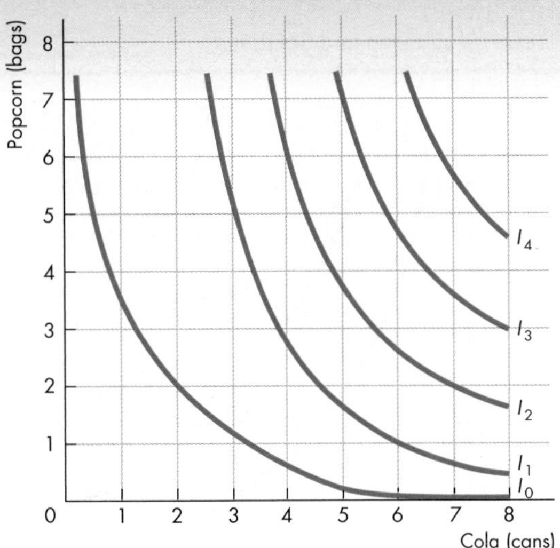

a How much cola and popcorn does Sara buys now?

b Find two points on Sara's demand curve for cola.

c Find the substitution effect of the price change.

d Find the income effect of the price change.

e Is cola a normal good or an inferior good for Sara?

f Is popcorn a normal good or an inferior good?

8 Pam buys slices of cake and books. The price of cake is €1 a slice and the price of a book is €2. Each month, Pam spends all of her income and buys 30 slices of cake and 5 books. Next month, the price of cake will fall to 50 cents a slice and the price of a book will rise to €5. Assume that Pam's preference map is similar to that in Figure 8.5(a). Use a graph to answer the following questions:

a Will Pam be able to buy 30 slices of cake and 5 books next month?

b Will Pam want to buy 30 slices of cake and 5 books?

c Which situation does Pam prefer: cake at €1 a slice and books at €2 each, or cake at 50 cents a slice and books at €3 each?

d If Pam changes the quantities that she buys next month, which good will she buy more of and which will she buy less of?

e When the prices change next month, will there be both an income effect and a substitution effect at work or just one of them?

9 Yangjie can earn €15 an hour and she chooses to work for 40 hours a week. Then Yangjie's wage rate increases to €25 an hour. If Yangjie now chooses to work for more than 40 hours a week, describe her indifference curves and explain her choice in terms of the income effect and the substitution effect.

Critical Thinking

1 Read the article in *Reading Between the Lines* on pp. 180–181 and then answer the following questions:

a Suppose that the price of a bus trip is halved but the price of a train trip remains at £20. (Charlotte is still a student.)

(i) What would happen to the slope of her budget line?

(ii) Would Charlotte buy more or fewer bus trips? Use an indifference curve drawing to explain your answer.

b Suppose that Charlotte's friend Dick finds bus travel almost as pleasant as train travel.

(i) How do Dick's indifference curves between bus trips and train trips differ from Charlotte's?

(ii) Use a graph to show whether Dick buys more or fewer bus trips than Charlotte.

(iii) What is Charlotte's elasticity of demand for train trips? Is Dick's demand for train trips more elastic or less elastic than Charlottes?

2 VAT is a tax on most goods and services. Until recently, no VAT was paid on newspapers and magazines in the United Kingdom. The European Union has made the United Kingdom impose VAT on newspapers and magazines. When this change occurred:

a What happened to the relative price of magazines and coffee?

b What happened to the budget line showing the quantities of magazines and coffee you can buy?

c How did your purchases of magazines and coffee change?

d Why did the European Union want to impose the tax on all goods and services and not allow some to be free of tax?

Web Activity

Links to Websites

1 Obtain information about the prices of mobile phone services and the postage rates on letters.

a Sketch the budget line for a consumer who spent £25 a month on these two goods in 2000 and 2006.

b Can you say whether the consumer was better off or worse off in 2006 than in 2000?

c Sketch some indifference curves for mobile phone calls and letters posted and show the income effect and the substitution effect of the changes in prices that occurred between 2000 and 2006.

Chapter 8 Appendix

The Marginal Utility Theory of Households' Choices

After studying this appendix, you will be able to:

- Describe preferences and choices using the concept of utility
- Explain the connection between indifference curves and utility and why choosing the best affordable point maximizes utility

Utility, Preferences and Choices

You've seen how economists describe preferences using an indifference map. Economists also describe preferences using an older idea, the concept of **utility**, which is the benefit or satisfaction that a person gets from the consumption of a good or service. Utility seems like an unobservable subjective concept. And for this reason, economists struggled to develop the objective indifference curve description of preferences. But it turns out that indifference curves and utility complement each other. We're going to explain the utility description of preferences and then show the equivalence of the utility and indifference curve methods and a remarkable insight – that we can measure utility.

Total Utility and Marginal Utility

Total utility is the *total* benefit that a person gets from the consumption of goods and services. Total utility depends on the level of consumption – more consumption generally gives more total utility. The units of utility are arbitrary. Suppose we tell Lisa that we want to measure her utility. We're going to call the utility from no consumption zero. And we are going to call the utility she gets from 1 film a month 50 units. We then ask her to tell us, on the same scale, how much she would like 2, 3 and more films up to 14 a month. We also ask her to tell us, on the same scale, how much she would like 1 six-pack of cola a month, 2 six-packs and more up to 14 six-packs a month. Table A8.1 shows Lisa's answers.

Marginal utility is the *change in total utility* that results from a one-unit increase in the quantity of a good consumed. When the number of six-packs Lisa buys increases from 4 to 5 a month, her total utility from cola increases from 181 units to 206 units. So for Lisa, the *marginal utility* from consuming a fifth six-pack each month is 25 units.

TABLE A8.1

Lisa's Total Utility from Films and Cola

Films		Cola	
Quantity (number per month)	Total utility	Quantity (six-packs per month)	Total utility
0	0	0	0
1	50	1	75
2	88	2	117
3	121	3	153
4	150	4	181
5	175	5	206
6	196	6	225
7	214	7	243
8	229	8	260
9	241	9	276
10	250	10	291
11	256	11	305
12	259	12	318
13	261	13	330
14	262	14	341

The table in Figure A8.1 shows Lisa's marginal utility from cola for the first 5 six-packs. Notice that marginal utility appears midway between the quantities of cola. It does so because it is the change in consumption from 4 to 5 six-packs that produces the marginal utility of 25 units. The table displays calculations of marginal utility for each number of six-packs that Lisa buys from 1 to 5.

Figure A8.1(a) illustrates Lisa's total utility from cola. The more cola Lisa drinks in a month, the more total utility she gets. Figure A8.1(b) illustrates her marginal utility. This graph tells us that as Lisa drinks more cola, her marginal utility from cola decreases. For example, her marginal utility decreases from 75 units from the first six-pack to 42 units from the second six-pack and to 36 units from the third.

Diminishing Marginal Utility

We call the decrease in marginal utility as the quantity of the good consumed increases the principle of **diminishing marginal utility**.

Figure A8.1

Total Utility and Marginal Utility

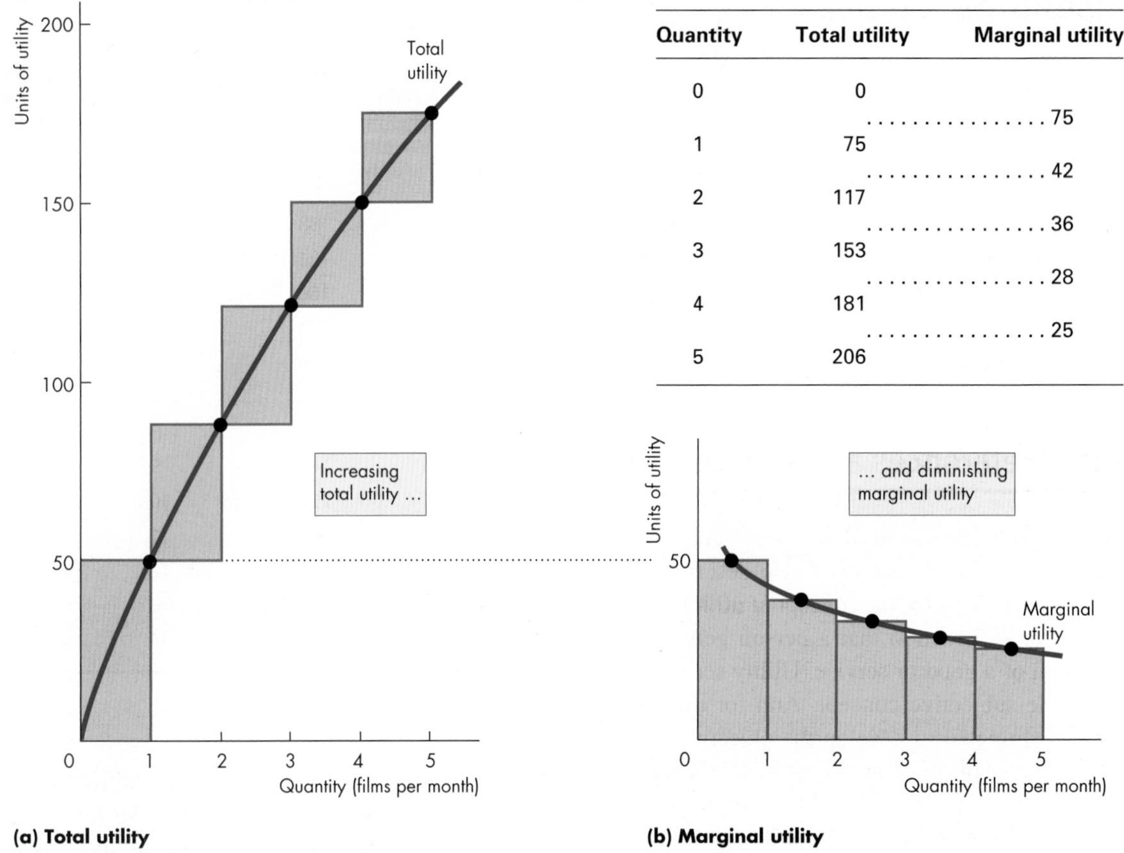

Quantity	Total utility	Marginal utility
0	0	
		75
1	75	
		42
2	117	
		36
3	153	
		28
4	181	
		25
5	206	

The table shows that as Lisa consumes more cola, her total utility from cola increases. The table also shows her marginal utility – the change in total utility resulting from the last six-pack she consumes. Marginal utility declines as consumption increases.

The figure graphs Lisa's total utility and marginal utility from cola. Part (a) shows her total utility. It also shows as a bar the extra total utility she gains from each additional six-pack – her marginal utility.

Part (b) shows how Lisa's marginal utility from cola diminishes by placing the bars shown in part (a) side by side as a series of declining steps.

Marginal utility is positive but diminishes as consumption of a good increases. Why does marginal utility have these two features? In Lisa's case, she likes cola, and the more she drinks the better. That's why marginal utility is positive. The benefit that Lisa gets from the last six-pack consumed is its marginal utility.

To see why marginal utility diminishes, think about the following two situations. In one, you've just been studying all through the day and evening and you've been too busy finishing an assignment to go shopping. A friend drops by with a six-pack of cola. The utility you get from that cola is the marginal utility from one six-pack. In the second situation, you've been on a cola binge. You've been working on an assignment all day but you've guzzled three six-packs while doing so. You are up to your eyeballs in cola. You are happy enough to have one more can. But the thrill that you get from it is not very large. It is the marginal utility of the nineteenth can in a day.

We've now described Lisa's preferences in terms of utility. Our next task is to see how Lisa's choice maximizes her total utility.

Maximizing Utility

A household's income and the prices that it faces limit the household's consumption choices, and the household's preferences determine the utility that it can obtain from each consumption possibility. The key assumption of marginal utility theory is that the household chooses the consumption possibility that maximizes its total utility. This assumption of utility maximization is a way of expressing the fundamental economic problem: scarcity. People's wants exceed the resources available to satisfy those wants, so they must make hard choices. In making choices, they try to get the maximum attainable benefit – that is, to maximize total utility.

Let's see how Lisa allocates £30 a month between films and cola to maximize her total utility. We'll continue to assume that the price of a film is £6 and the price of cola is £3 a six-pack.

Equalizing Marginal Utility per Pound

A **consumer equilibrium** is a situation in which a consumer has allocated all his or her available income in the way that, given the prices of goods and services, maximizes his or her total utility. A consumer's total utility is maximized by following the rule:

Spend all the available income and equalize the marginal utility per pound for all goods.

The **marginal utility per pound** is the marginal utility from a good divided by its price. For example, Lisa's marginal utility from seeing 1 film a month, MU_F, is 50 units of utility. The price of a film, P_F, is £6, which means that the marginal utility per pound from 1 film a month, MU_F/P_F, is 50 units divided by £6, or 8.33 units of marginal utility per pound.

You can see why following this rule maximizes total utility by thinking about a situation in which Lisa has spent all her income but the marginal utilities per pound are not equal. Suppose that Lisa's marginal utility per pound for cola, MU_C/P_C, exceeds that for films. By spending a pound more on cola and a pound less on films, her total utility from cola rises and her total utility from films falls. But her utility gain from cola exceeds her utility loss from films, so her total utility increases. Because she's consuming more cola, her marginal utility from cola has fallen. And because she sees fewer films, her marginal utility from films has risen. Lisa keeps increasing her consumption of cola and decreasing her consumption of films until the two marginal utilities per pound are equal.

That is:

$$\frac{MU_F}{P_F} = \frac{MU_C}{P_C}$$

Table A8.2

Equalizing Marginal Utilities per Pound

	Films (£6 each)			Cola (£3 per six-pack)		
	Quantity	Marginal utility	Marginal utility per pound	Six-packs	Marginal utility	Marginal utility per pound
A	0	0		10	15	5.00
B	1	50	8.33	8	17	5.67
C	2	38	6.33	6	19	6.33
D	3	33	5.50	4	28	9.33
E	4	29	4.83	2	42	14.00
F	5	25	4.17	0	0	

Table A8.2 calculates Lisa's marginal utility per pound for each good. Each row exhausts Lisa's income of £30. In row *B*, Lisa's marginal utility from films is 50 units. Because the price of a film is £6, Lisa's marginal utility per pound for films is 50 units divided by £6, which is 8.33. Marginal utility per pound for each good decreases as more of the good is consumed.

Lisa maximizes her total utility when the marginal utility per pound for films is equal to the marginal utility per pound for cola – possibility *C*. Lisa consumes 2 films and 6 six-packs.

Review Quiz

Study Plan 8.A1

1. What is utility and what is the distinction between total utility and marginal utility?
2. What is the key assumption about marginal utility?
3. What is Lisa's goal when choosing the quantities of films she sees and cola she drinks?
4. What are the two conditions that are met if a consumer like Lisa is maximizing utility?
5. Explain why equalizing the marginal utilities of all goods does *not* maximize utility.
6. Explain why equalizing the marginal utility per pound on each good *does* maximize utility.

You've now seen how we can describe preferences and predict choices using the concept of utility. Your next task is to discover the equivalence of the indifference curve and utility methods.

Indifference Curves and Utility

The indifference curve model describes preferences by using the concepts of preference and indifference to define a map of indifference curves. A higher indifference curve is preferred to a lower one. The marginal rate of substitution diminishes down along an indifference curve (see Figure 8.3, p. 171, and Figure 8.4, p. 172).

The marginal utility model describes preferences by using the concept of utility. An increase in the quantity consumed of a good brings an increase in the total utility derived from that good and a decrease in its marginal utility.

The indifference curve model doesn't need the concept of utility. In fact, it was developed precisely because economists wanted a more objective way of describing preferences. But we can interpret the indifference curve model by using the concept of utility. And there are some benefits from doing so.

Because a consumer is indifferent among the combinations of goods at all the points on an indifference curve, these combinations provide the same amount of total utility. An indifference curve is a constant utility curve.

You can see the connection between utility and an indifference map by looking at Figure A8.2. Part (a) provides information about the total utility from films and cola. It is based on Table A8.1, but instead of listing the quantities of the two goods and the total utility arising from each quantity consumed, the numbers are arranged with films across the bottom and cola down the side. With no cola, the total utility from 6 films is 196 units. And with no films, the total utility from 2 six-packs is 117 units.

Figure A8.2(a) also shows the total utility from some other combinations of films and cola. For example the total utility from 6 films and 2 six-packs is 313 units (196 plus 117). Part (a) shows another combination that delivers 313 units and three combinations that deliver 331 units of utility.

The figure shows the indifference curves associated with these two levels of total utility.

Figure A8.2

Total Utility and the Indifference Map

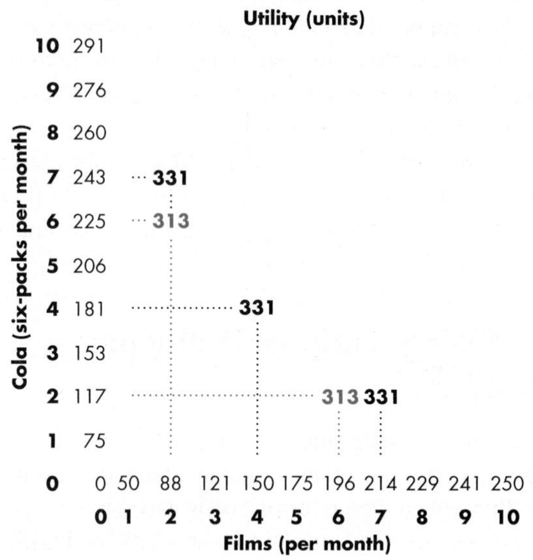

(a) Total utility

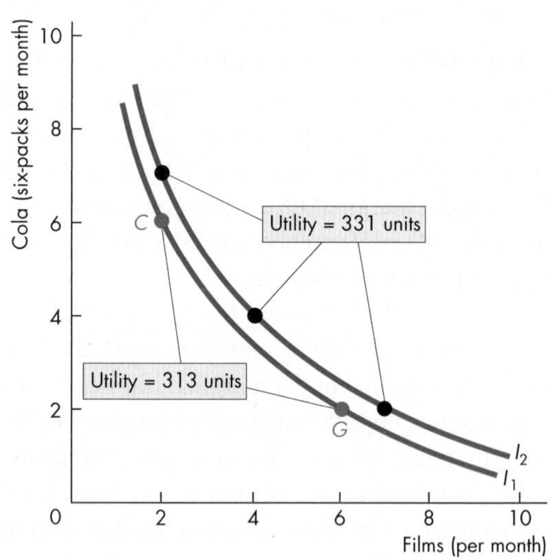

(b) Indifference curves

We can represent preferences by using the concept of utility or indifference curves. In the table, Lisa's total utility depends on the quantities of films and cola that she consumes. Different combinations can yield the same total utility. These combinations lie on the same indifference curve. The figure shows two indifference curves: one for 313 units of utility and one for 331 units of utility.

Choosing the Best Affordable Point Is Maximizing Utility

In the indifference curve model, Lisa chooses the best affordable point by spending her income on the combination of films and cola that makes the marginal rate of substitution (*MRS*) equal to the relative price of the two goods. That is:

$$MRS = P_F/P_C \qquad (1)$$

In the marginal utility model, Lisa maximizes total utility by spending her income on the combination of films and cola that makes the marginal utility per pound on films equal to the marginal utility per pound on cola. By observing the prices of goods and the quantities consumed, we can infer a consumer's marginal utilities at each quantity. That is:

$$MU_F/P_F = MU_C/P_C \qquad (2)$$

Choosing the best affordable point and maximizing total utility are the same. To see why, first multiply both sides of equation (2) by P_F and divide both sides by MU_C to obtain:

$$MU_F/MU_C = P_F/P_C \qquad (3)$$

This equation states that the ratio of the marginal utilities of the two goods is equal to the relative price of the two goods.

Inspect equations (1) and (3) and you can see that if the two ways of describing a consumer's choice are the same, then the marginal rate of substitution must equal the ratio of the marginal utilities of the two goods. That is:

$$MRS = MU_F/MU_C \qquad (4)$$

To establish that this proposition is true, note that total utility changes when the quantities consumed change in the following way:

$$\Delta U = MU_F \times \Delta Q_F + MU_C \times \Delta Q_C \qquad (5)$$

where Δ means "change in", Q_F is the quantity of films consumed, and Q_C is the quantity of cola consumed.

Recall that along an indifference curve, total utility is constant so the change in total utility is zero. Then, along an indifference curve, it must be the case that:

$$0 = MU_F \times \Delta Q_F + MU_C \times \Delta Q_C \qquad (6)$$

or

$$MU_F \times \Delta Q_F = -MU_C \times \Delta Q_C \qquad (7)$$

Divide both sides of equation (7) by MU_C and by ΔQ_F to obtain:

$$MU_F/MU_C = -\Delta Q_C/\Delta Q_F \qquad (8)$$

This equation tells us that along an indifference curve, the change in the quantity of cola consumed divided by the change in the quantity of films consumed equals the ratio of the marginal utilities of films and cola.

But $-\Delta Q_C/\Delta Q_F$ (rise over run) is the slope of the indifference curve. And, removing the minus sign, $\Delta Q_C/\Delta Q_F$ is the marginal rate of substitution of films for cola. So:

$$MRS = \Delta Q_C/\Delta Q_F = MU_F/MU_C \qquad (9)$$

You've now seen that the two models of consumer choice make identical predictions about the quantities that a consumer chooses.

Spending the available budget with the marginal rate of substitution between the two goods equal to their relative price is the same as spending the available budget with the marginal utility per pound the same for both goods.

Utility Exists and We Can Measure It!

The indifference curve model is powerful because its only assumptions are that people can rank alternative combinations of goods as preferred or indifferent and that the marginal rate of substitution diminishes. From these assumptions, we can derive the downward-sloping demand curve. We can also easily visualize the effects of changes in prices and income on a consumer's choice. The indifference curve model is also powerful because its assumptions imply the existence of utility and of (generally) diminishing marginal utility.

By observing prices of goods and the quantities consumed at those prices, we can infer a consumer's marginal rate of substitution. And from the marginal rate of substitution, we can infer a consumer's marginal utilities at each quantity. The scale of measurement of marginal utility is arbitrary, like the scale (or rather the scales) on which we measure temperature. But marginal utilities are proportional to prices.

Marginal utility theory helps us to deepen our understanding of the concept of efficiency and also helps us to see more clearly the distinction between value and price. Let's see how.

Consumer Efficiency and Marginal Benefit

When Lisa allocates her limited budget at her best affordable point, she is also maximizing her total utility and she is using her resources efficiently. Any other allocation of her budget would waste some resources.

But when Lisa has allocated her limited budget to maximize utility, she is *on* her demand curve for each good. A demand curve is a description of the quantity demanded at each price when utility is maximized. When we studied efficiency in Chapter 5, we learned that value equals marginal benefit and that a demand curve is also a willingness-to-pay curve. It tells us a consumer's *marginal benefit* – the benefit from consuming an additional unit of a good. You can now give the idea of marginal benefit a deeper meaning:

Marginal benefit is proportional to marginal utility and is the maximum price that a consumer is willing to pay for an extra unit of a good or service when utility is maximized.

Finally, marginal utility theory enables us to solve a very old puzzle called the paradox of value.

The Paradox of Value

Water is essential to life itself while diamonds are just inessential luxuries. So water is much more valuable than diamonds. Yet the price of water is a tiny fraction of the price of a diamond. Why? This question is the paradox of value that has puzzled philosophers for centuries. Adam Smith tried but failed to solve this paradox. Not until the theory of marginal utility had been developed could anyone give a satisfactory answer.

You can solve this puzzle by distinguishing between *total* utility and *marginal* utility. The total utility that we get from water is enormous. But remember, the more we consume of something, the smaller is its marginal utility. We use so much water that its marginal utility – the benefit we get from one more glass of water – diminishes to a small value. Diamonds, on the other hand, have a small total utility relative to water, but because we buy few diamonds, they have a high marginal utility. When a consumer has maximized her total utility, she has allocated her budget in the way that makes the marginal utility per pound equal for all goods. That is, the marginal utility from a good divided by its price is equal for all goods.

This equality of marginal utilities per pound holds true for diamonds and water: diamonds have a high price and a high marginal utility; water has a low price and a low marginal utility. When the high marginal utility of diamonds is divided by the high price of a diamond, the result is a number that equals the low marginal utility of water divided by the low price of water.

The marginal utility per pound is the same for diamonds as it is for water.

Two Theories, Same Predictions, Different Insights

You've seen that the two theories of households' choice make the same predictions about the allocation of scarce household resources. Choosing the best affordable point on the budget line is the same as choosing the utility-maximizing point. The highest attainable indifference curve gives the highest attainable total utility.

Marginal utility theory enables economists to predict prices and quantities using a model of demand and supply in which the principle of diminishing marginal utility accounts for the downward-sloping demand curve. The indifference curve theory uses the more objective idea of a diminishing marginal rate of substitution to reach the same conclusion about the demand curve.

But the two theories provide different insights into the distinction between value and price. And the marginal utility theory, although the older of the two theories, gets the higher marks for its neat resolution of the paradox of value and for clarifying the concept of marginal benefit.

We don't know what the next advance in understanding households' and individuals' choices will be. But advances in neuroscience are now being combined with economics to develop neuro-economics. The goal of this new branch of economics is to understand choices, and possibly even utility, at the deeper level of brain activity.

Review Quiz

Study Plan 8.A2

1. Explain why the indifference curve and utility descriptions of a consumer's preferences are equivalent.
2. Explain why choosing the best affordable point on a budget line and indifference curve is equivalent to maximizing total utility.
3. Explain the connection between the marginal rate of substitution and marginal utility.
4. How can we use data to infer a consumer's marginal utilities of different goods and services?
5. Why, along a demand curve, are a consumer's choices efficient?
6. What is the relationship between marginal utility and marginal benefit?
7. What is the paradox of value?
8. Is the marginal utility from water or from diamonds greater? Is the total utility from water or from diamonds greater? Is the consumer surplus from water or from diamonds greater?

Organizing Production

CHAPTER 9

After studying this chapter you will be able to:

- Explain what a firm is and describe the economic problems that *all* firms face
- Distinguish between technological efficiency and economic efficiency
- Define and explain the principal–agent problem and describe how different types of business organizations cope with this problem
- Describe and distinguish between the different markets in which firms operate
- Explain why firms coordinate some economic activities and markets coordinate others

Spinning a Web

When Tim Berners-Lee invented the World Wide Web in 1990, he paved the way for the creation of thousands of profitable businesses. One of these is SAP, Europe's biggest software producer. How does SAP and the other 20 million firms that operate in Europe make business decisions? How do businesses operate efficiently? Why do firms produce some things but outsource others? Find out in this chapter. And in the *Business Case Study* at the end of the chapter, examine the competition between SAP and another software giant, Oracle, in the market for business systems software.

The Firm and Its Economic Problem

The 20 million or so firms in the European Union differ in their size and in the scope of what they do. But they all perform the same basic economic functions. Each **firm** is an institution that hires productive resources and organizes those resources to produce and sell goods and services. Our goal is to predict firm behaviour. To do so, we need to know a firm's goals and the constraints it faces. We begin with the goals.

The Firm's Goal

Most firms make statements about their goals in their annual reports and accounts. If you read these reports you will see that some firms talk about making a quality product, others about business growth and market share, others about worker job satisfaction, and yet others about the environment. Firms might pursue all of these goals, but they are not the fundamental goal.

A firm's goal is to *maximize profit*. A firm that does not seek to maximize profit will either go out of business or be bought by a firm that does seek to maximize profit. What exactly is the profit that a firm seeks to maximize? To answer this question, we're going to look at a small firm called Neat Knits.

Measuring a Firm's Profit

Norma runs Neat Knits, a successful small business that makes jumpers. In 2007, Neat Knits receives £400,000 a year for the jumpers it sells. Its expenses are £80,000 a year for wool, £20,000 for utilities, £120,000 for wages, £5,000 for lease of a computer from Dell, Inc., and £5,000 in interest on a bank loan. With receipts of £400,000 and expenses of £230,000, Neat Knits' surplus in 2007 is £170,000.

Norma's accountant lowers this number by £20,000, which he says is the depreciation (fall in value) of the firm's buildings and knitting machines during the year. (Accountants use standard rules set by accounting professionals to calculate the depreciation.) So the accountant reports that Neat Knit's 2007 profit is £150,000.

The accountant measures cost and profit to ensure that a firm pays the correct amount of income tax and to show the bank how its loan has been used. But we want to predict the decisions that a firm makes. These decisions respond to *opportunity cost* and are made in the pursuit of *economic profit*.

Opportunity Cost

The *opportunity cost* of any action is the highest-valued alternative forgone. The action that you choose not to do – the highest-valued alternative forgone – is the cost of the action that you choose to do. For a firm, the opportunity cost of production is the value of the firm's best alternative use of its resources.

Opportunity cost is a real alternative forgone. But so that we can compare the cost of one action with that of another action, we express opportunity cost in money units. A firm's opportunity costs includes:

- Explicit costs
- Implicit costs

Explicit Costs

Explicit costs are paid in money. The amount paid for a resource could have been spent on something else, so it is the opportunity cost of using the resource. For Neat Knits, its expenditures on wool, utilities, wages and bank interest are explicit costs.

Firms often lease capital – computers photocopies, earth-moving equipment and so on. Neat Knits leases a computer and the payment it makes to Dell is also an explicit cost.

Implicit Costs

A firm incurs implicit costs when it forgoes an alternative action but does not make a payment. A firm incurs implicit costs when it:

1 Uses its own capital
2 Uses its owner's time or financial resources

The cost of using its own capital is an implicit cost – and an opportunity cost – because the firm could rent the capital to another firm. The rental income forgone is the firm's opportunity cost of using its own capital. This opportunity cost is called the **implicit rental rate** of capital.

If a firm uses the capital it owns, it incurs an *implicit* cost, which is made up of:

1 Economic depreciation
2 Interest forgone

Economic depreciation is change in the *market* value of capital over a given period. It is calculated as the market price of the capital at the beginning of the period minus its market price at the end of the period. For example, suppose that Neat Knits could have sold its buildings and knitting machines on 31 December 2006, for £400,000. If it can sell the same capital on 31 December 2007, for £375,000, its economic depreciation during 2007 is £25,000 – the fall in the market value of the buildings and machines. This £25,000 is an implicit cost of using the capital during 2007.

The funds used to buy capital could have been used for some other purpose. And in their next best use, they would have earned an interest income. This forgone interest is part of the opportunity cost of using the capital. For example, Neat Knits could have bought bonds instead of a knitting factory. The interest forgone on the bonds is an implicit cost of operating the knitting factory.

Cost of Owner's Resources

A firm's owner often supplies entrepreneurial ability – the factor of production that organizes the business, makes business decisions, innovates and bears the risk of running the business. The return to entrepreneurship is profit, and the return that an entrepreneur can expect to receive on the average is called **normal profit**.

The entrepreneur's normal profit is part of a firm's opportunity cost, because it is the cost of a forgone alternative – running another firm. If normal profit in the knitting business is £50,000 a year, this amount is Norma's normal profit and it is part of Neat Knits' opportunity costs.

As well as being the entrepreneur, the owner of a firm can supply labour, which earns a wage. The opportunity cost of the owner's labour is the wage income that the owner forgoes by not taking the best alternative job. Suppose that, in addition to being the entrepreneur, Norma could supply labour to another firm and earn £40,000 a year. By working for her own business, Norma forgoes £40,000 a year and this amount is part of Neat Knits' opportunity cost.

Economic Profit

What is the bottom line – the profit or loss of the firm? A firm's **economic profit** is equal to its total revenue minus its total cost. The firm's total cost is the sum of its explicit costs and implicit costs. And the implicit costs, remember, include *normal profit*. The return to entrepreneurial ability is greater than normal in a firm that makes a positive economic profit. And the return to entrepreneurial ability is less than normal in a firm that makes a negative economic profit – a firm that incurs an economic loss.

Economic Accounting: A Summary

Table 9.1 summarizes the economic accounting concepts that we've just reviewed. Neat Knits's total revenue is £400,000. Its explicit costs are £230,000 and its implicit costs are £135,000. Its total cost (the sum of explicit costs and implicit costs) is £365,000. So Neat Knits's economic profit is £35,000.

The Firm's Decisions

To achieve the objective of maximum profit – maximum *economic* profit – a firm must make five basic decisions:

1 What goods and services to produce and in what quantities.
2 What techniques of production to use – how to produce.
3 How to organize and compensate its managers and workers.
4 How to market and price its products.
5 What to produce itself and what to outsource – what to buy from other firms.

In all these decisions, a firm's actions are limited by the constraints that it faces. Our next task is to learn about these constraints.

Table 9.1
Economic Accounting

Item	Amount (pounds)	Amount (pounds)
Total revenue		**400,000**
Opportunity costs		
Wool	80,000	
Utilities	20,000	
Wages paid	120,000	
Bank interest paid	10,000	
Total explicit costs		**230,000**
Norma's wages forgone	40,000	
Norma's interest forgone	20,000	
Economic depreciation	25,000	
Normal profit	50,000	
Total implicit costs		**135,000**
Total cost		**365,000**
Economic profit		**35,000**

The Firm's Constraints

Three features of a firm's environment limit the maximum profit it can make. They are:

- Technology constraints
- Information constraints
- Market constraints

Technology Constraints

Economists define technology broadly. A **technology** is any method of producing a good or service. Technology includes the detailed designs of machines. It also includes the layout of the workplace and the organization of the firm. For example, the shopping centre is a technology for producing retail services. It is a different technology from catalogue shopping, which in turn is different from the high street stores.

It might seem surprising that a firm's profits are limited by technology. Every year we learn about the latest technological advances that will revolutionize future production and consumption. Technology is advancing, but to produce more output and gain more revenue with current technology, a firm must hire more resources and incur greater costs. At any point in time, the increase in profit that the firm can achieve is limited by the technology currently available. For example, using its current plant and workforce, BMW can produce some maximum number of cars per day. To produce more cars per day, BMW must hire more resources, which increases BMW's costs and limits the increase in profit that BMW can make by selling the additional cars.

Information Constraints

A business manager can never possess all the information needed to make decisions. Businesses lack information about the present and the future – uncertainty. For example, suppose you plan to buy a new computer for your business. When should you buy it? The answer depends on how the price is going to change in the future. Where should you buy it? The answer depends on the prices at many different suppliers. To get the best deal, you must compare the quality and price in all the different shops. The opportunity cost of actually getting all this information and making all these comparisons will exceed the cost of the computer!

Similarly, a firm is constrained by limited information about the quality and effort of its workforce, the current and future plans of its customers and the plans of its competitors. Workers may slacken off when managers believe they are working hard. Customers may switch to competing suppliers. Firms must face competition from new firms and the new products and services they offer.

Firms try to create incentive systems for workers to ensure they work hard even when no one is monitoring their efforts. Firms also spend billions every year on market research and product development. But none of these efforts and expenditures eliminates the problems of incomplete information and uncertainty. Again, the cost of coping with limited information and uncertainty itself limits profit.

Market Constraints

What each firm can sell and the price it can obtain is constrained by the willingness of customers to pay and by the prices and marketing efforts of other firms. Similarly, the resources that each firm can buy and the prices it must pay are limited by the willingness of people to work for and invest in the firm. Firms spend billions every year marketing and selling their products. Some of the most creative minds strive to find the right message that will produce a knockout television advertisement. Market constraints and the expenditures firms make to overcome them limit the profit a firm can make.

Review Quiz

Study Plan 9.1

1. Why do firms seek to maximize profit? What happens to firms that don't pursue this goal?
2. Why do accountants and economists calculate a firm's cost and profit in different ways?
3. What are the items that make opportunity cost different from the accountants' measure of cost?
4. Why is normal profit an opportunity cost?
5. What are the constraints that each firm faces? Explain how each constraint limits the profit that a firm can make.

In the rest of this chapter and in Chapters 10 to 13, we study the decisions that firms make. You will learn how to predict a firm's behaviour as the response to both the constraints that it faces and the changes in those constraints. We begin by taking a closer look at the technology constraints that firms face.

Technological and Economic Efficiency

Microsoft employs a large workforce and most Microsoft workers possess a large amount of human capital. But the firm uses a small amount of physical capital. In contrast, an oil extraction company employs a huge amount of drilling equipment (physical capital) and relatively little labour. Why? The answer lies in the concept of efficiency. There are two concepts of production efficiency: technological efficiency and economic efficiency. **Technological efficiency** occurs when the firm produces a given output by using the least amount of inputs. **Economic efficiency** occurs when the firm produces a given output at least cost. Let's explore the two concepts of efficiency by studying an example.

Suppose that there are four alternative techniques for making TV sets:

A *Robot production.* One person monitors the entire computer-driven process.

B *Production line.* Workers specialize in a small part of the job as the emerging TV set passes them on a production line.

C *Bench production.* Workers specialize in a small part of the job but walk from bench to bench to perform their tasks.

D *Hand-tool production.* A single worker uses a few hand tools to make a TV set.

Table 9.2 sets out the amounts of labour and capital required by each of these four methods to make 10 TV sets a day.

Which of these alternative methods are technologically efficient?

Table 9.2

Four Ways of Making 10 TV Sets a Day

	Quantities of inputs	
Method	**Labour**	**Capital**
A Robot production	1	1,000
B Production line	10	10
C Bench production	100	10
D Hand-tool production	1,000	1

Technological Efficiency

Recall that technological efficiency occurs when the firm produces a given output by using the least inputs. Inspect the numbers in Table 9.2 and notice that method *A* uses the most capital but the least labour. Method *D* uses the most labour but the least capital. Methods *B* and *C* use less capital but more labour than method *A* and less labour but more capital than method *D*. Compare methods *B* and *C*. Method *C* requires 100 workers and 10 units of capital to produce 10 TV sets. Those same 10 TV sets can be produced by method *B* with 10 workers and the same 10 units of capital. Because method *C* uses the same amount of capital and more labour than method *B*, method *C* is not technologically efficient.

Are any of the other methods not technologically efficient? The answer is no. Each of the other three methods is technologically efficient. Method *A* uses more capital but less labour than method *B*, and method *D* uses more labour but less capital than method *B*.

Which of the alternative methods are economically efficient?

Economic Efficiency

Recall that economic efficiency occurs when the firm produces a given output at least cost. Suppose that labour costs £75 per person-day and that capital costs £250 per machine-day. Table 9.3(a) calculates the costs of using the different methods. By inspecting the table, you can see that method *B* has the lowest cost. Although method *A* uses less labour, it uses too much expensive capital. And although method *D* uses less capital, it uses too much expensive labour.

Method *C*, which is technologically inefficient, is also economically inefficient. It uses the same amount of capital as method *B* but 10 times as much labour, so it costs more. A technologically inefficient method is never economically efficient.

Although method *B* is the economically efficient method in this example, method *A* or *D* could be economically efficient with different input prices.

First, suppose that labour costs £150 a person-day and capital costs only £1 a machine-day. Table 9.3(b) now shows the costs of making a TV set. In this case, method *A* is economically efficient. Capital is now so cheap relative to labour that the method that uses the most capital is the economically efficient method.

Table 9.3

Costs of Three Ways of Making 10 TV Sets a Day

(a) Four ways of making TV sets

Method	Labour cost (£75 per day)		Capital cost (£250 per day)		Total cost	Cost per TV set
A	£75	+	£250,000	=	£250,075	£115.00
B	750	+	2,500	=	3,250	325.00
C	7,500	+	2,500	=	10,000	1,000.00
D	75,000	+	250	=	75,250	7,525.00

(b) Three ways of making TV sets: high labour costs

Method	Labour cost (£150 per day)		Capital cost (£1 per day)		Total cost	Cost per TV set
A	£150	+	£1,000	=	£1,150	£115.00
B	1,500	+	10	=	1,510	151.00
D	150,000	+	1	=	150,001	15,000.10

(c) Three ways of making TV sets: high capital costs

Method	Labour cost (£1 per day)		Capital cost (1,000 per day)		Total cost	Cost per TV set
A	£1	+	£1,000,000	=	£1,000,001	£100,000.10
B	10	+	10,000	=	10,010	1,001.00
D	1,000	+	1,000	=	2,000	200.00

Second, suppose that labour costs only £1 a person-day while capital costs £1,000 a machine-day. Table 9.3(c) shows the costs in this case. Method *D*, which uses a lot of labour and little capital, is now the least-cost method and the economically efficient method.

From these example, you can see that while technological efficiency depends only on what is feasible; economic efficiency depends on the relative costs of resources. The economically efficient method is the one that uses the smaller amount of a more expensive resource and a larger amount of a less expensive resource.

A firm that is not economically efficient does not maximize profit. Natural selection favours efficient firms and opposes inefficient firms. Inefficient firms go out of business or are taken over by firms with lower costs.

Review Quiz

Study Plan 9.2

1. Define technological efficiency. Is a firm technologically efficient if it uses the latest technology? Why?
2. Define economic efficiency. Is a firm economically inefficient if it can cut costs by producing less? Why?
3. Explain the key distinction between technological efficiency and economic efficiency.
4. Why do some firms use lots of capital and not much labour, while others use not much capital and lots of labour?

Next we will study information constraints that firms face and the diversity of organizational structures they generate.

Information and Organizations

Each firm organizes the production of goods and services by combining and coordinating the productive resources it hires. But there is variety across firms in how they organize production. Firms use a mixture of two systems:

- Command systems
- Incentive systems

Command Systems

A **command system** is a method of organizing production that uses a managerial hierarchy. Commands pass downward through the managerial hierarchy and information passes upward. Managers collect and process information about the performance of the people under their control and make decisions about commands to issue and report to their own superiors.

The military uses the purest form of command system. Command systems in firms are less rigid than those in the military but share similar features. A chief executive officer (CEO) sits at the top of a firm's command system. Executives report to and receive commands from the CEO and pass their own commands down to middle managers who in turn supervise the day-to-day operations of the business.

Small-scale firms have one or two layers of managers while large-scale firms have several layers. As production processes have become ever more complex, management ranks have swollen. Today, more people have management jobs than ever before. But the information revolution of the 1990s slowed the growth of management and, in some industries, it decreased the number of layers of managers and brought a shake-out of middle managers.

Managers always have incomplete information about the efforts of those for whom they are responsible. It is for this reason that firms use incentive systems.

Incentive Systems

An **incentive system** is a method of organizing production that uses a market-like mechanism inside the firm. Instead of issuing commands, managers create compensation schemes that induce workers to perform in ways that maximize the firm's profit.

Selling organizations use incentive systems most extensively. Sales representatives who spend most of their working time alone and unsupervised are induced to work hard by being paid a small salary and a large performance-related bonus.

But incentive systems operate at all levels in a firm. CEOs share in the firm's profit, and factory floor workers receive wages based on the quantity they produce.

Mixed Systems

Firms will use both commands and incentives in a mixed system if it will help to maximize profit. They use commands when it is easy to monitor performance. They use incentives when monitoring performance is either not possible or too costly to be worth doing.

For example, it is easy and costs little to monitor the performance of workers on a production line. If one person works too slowly, the entire line slows. So a production line is organized with a command system.

In contrast, it is costly for shareholders to monitor the efforts of a CEO. So CEOs are rewarded with profit-related bonus payments.

Incentives systems are an attempt to cope with a general problem that we'll now examine.

The Principal–Agent Problem

The **principal–agent problem** is the problem of devising compensation rules that induce an *agent* to act in the best interest of a *principal*. The principal might be the firm's shareholders, in which case the managers are the *agents*. The shareholders (the principals) want to induce the managers (agents) to act in the shareholders' interest. Or the principals might be the managers, in which case, the agents are the workers below the managers. There is a chain of principal–agent relationships throughout a firm.

Agents pursue their own goals and often impose costs on a principal. For example, the goal of a shareholder of the HSBC Bank (a principal) is to maximize the bank's profit. But the bank's profit depends on the actions of its managers (agents) who have their own goals. A manager might want to expand the size of her workforce to gain status when this action is inefficient.

Issuing commands does not solve the principal–agent problem. In most firms, the shareholders can't monitor the managers and often the managers can't monitor workers. Each principal must create incentives that induce each agent to work in the interests of the principal.

Three ways of coping with the principal–agent problem are:

- ◆ Ownership
- ◆ Incentive pay
- ◆ Long-term contracts

Ownership

By assigning the part ownership of a business to a manager or a worker, the principal seeks to induce a better job performance that increases a firm's profit.

Share-ownership schemes for senior managers are common and firms increasingly award bonuses in the form of company shares. Share-ownership schemes for workers are less common but many employees are investing in the shares of their employer, either individually or through pension plans.

Ownership schemes work best when the firm's profit is directly influenced by the efforts of the agent. If a CEO or top manager does a poor job, the firm's profits will suffer. So providing CEOs and manager with compensation in the form of shares might be very effective. Share ownership schemes also encourage the more highly motivated people to join a firm. So for CEOs and senior managers, ownership schemes are useful ways of coping with the principal–agent problem.

Ownership schemes work badly when the efforts of the agent have a negligible impact on the firm's profit. With or without shares in the company, a lazy worker has the same incentive to shirk and be unproductive. In these cases, other methods of coping with the principal–agent problem must be found.

The cartoon is a comment on the use of share ownership to address the principal–agent problem. The employee says he is happy to be compensated with shares but that as a shareholder, he wouldn't employ himself!

Incentive Pay

Incentive pay schemes – pay related to performance – are very common. They are based on a variety of performance criteria such as profits, production or sales targets. Promoting an employee for good performance is another example of an incentive pay scheme. Like share ownership, incentive pay induces greater effort by an agent and increase the profit.

Long-term Contracts

Long-term contracts tie the long-term fortunes of managers and workers (agents) to the success of the principal(s) – the owner(s) of the firm. For example, a multi-year employment contract for a CEO encourages that person to take a long-term view and devise strategies that achieve maximum profit over a sustained period.

Types of Business Organization

The three main types of business organization are:

- ◆ Proprietorship
- ◆ Partnership
- ◆ Company

Proprietorship

A *proprietorship* is a firm with a single owner who has unlimited liability. *Unlimited liability* is the legal responsibility for all the debts of a firm up to an amount equal to the entire wealth of the owner including the personal property of the owner. The proprietor makes management decisions, receives the firm's profits and is responsible for its losses. Profits are taxed at the same rate as other sources of the proprietor's income.

Partnership

A *partnership* is a firm with two or more owners who have unlimited liability. Partners must agree on an appropriate management structure and on how to divide the firm's profits among themselves. The profits of a partnership are taxed as the personal income of the owners. But each partner is legally liable for all the debts of the partnership (limited only by the wealth of an individual partner). Liability for the full debts of the partnership is called *joint unlimited liability*.

Company

A *company* is a firm owned by one or more limited liability shareholders. *Limited liability* means that the owners have legal liability only for the value of their initial investment. This limitation of liability means that if the company becomes bankrupt, its owners are not required to use their personal wealth to pay the company's debts.

Company profits are taxed independently of shareholders' incomes. Because shareholders pay taxes on the income they receive as dividends on shares, corporate profits are taxed twice. The shareholders also pay capital gains tax on the profit they earn by selling a share for a higher price than they paid for it.

Company shares generate capital gains when a company retains some of its profit and reinvests it in profitable activities. So even retained earnings are taxed twice because the capital gains they generate are taxed.

Pros and Cons of Different Types of Firms

So why are there so many different types of business organization? The different types of business organization that you have looked at arise as different ways of trying to cope with the principal–agent problem. Each type of business has advantages in particular situations. Because of its special advantages, each type continues to exist. Each type also has its disadvantages, which explains why it has not driven out the other two types.

Table 9.4 sets out the pros and cons of the different types of firms.

Table 9.4

The Pros and Cons of Different Types of Firms

Type of firm	Pros	Cons
Proprietorship	◆ Easy to set up ◆ Simple decision making ◆ Profits taxed only once as owner's income	◆ Bad decisions not checked by need for consensus ◆ Owner's entire wealth at risk ◆ Firm dies with owner ◆ Capital is expensive ◆ Labour is expensive
Partnership	◆ Easy to set up ◆ Diversified decision making ◆ Can survive withdrawal of partner ◆ Profits taxed only once as owners' incomes	◆ Achieving consensus may be slow and expensive ◆ Owners' entire wealth at risk ◆ Withdrawal of a partner may create capital shortage ◆ Capital is expensive
Company	◆ Owners have limited liability ◆ Large-scale, low-cost capital available ◆ Professional management not restricted by ability of owners ◆ Perpetual life ◆ Long-term labour contracts cut labour costs	◆ Complex management structure can make decisions slow and expensive ◆ Profits taxed twice as company profit and as shareholders' income

Box 9.1

European Firms' Size and Profitability

There are approximately 3 million firms in the United Kingdom and more than 90 per cent of them are very small businesses, which employ fewer than 10 workers. Small firms comprise a similarly high percentage of firms in most EU countries.

Table 1 shows the relative importance of the sizes of firms in 20 European countries (EU15 plus Iceland, Liechtenstein, Norway and Switzerland). Micro size firms (with fewer than 10 employees) comprise 93 per cent of all firms and they employ 34 per cent of all workers. Large firms (with 250 or more employees) comprise only 0.2 per cent of all firms but also employ 34 per cent of all workers.

Table 1

Firm Size and Employment

Number of employees	Size	Percentage of all firms	Percentage of firms' employment
< 10	Micro	93.0	34
10 < 50	Small	6.0	19
50 < 250	Medium	0.8	13
≥ 250	Large	0.2	34

Figure 1 shows the relationship between the profitability and firm size in the same 20 countries. The average profit rate across all firms is 39 per cent. Large and medium firms have profit rates that exceed the average, and small and micro size firms have profit rates below the average. The advantages of large scale in dealing with the principal–agent problem may exceed the benefits of small size in Europe's competitive economies.

Figure 1

Profitability by Firm Size

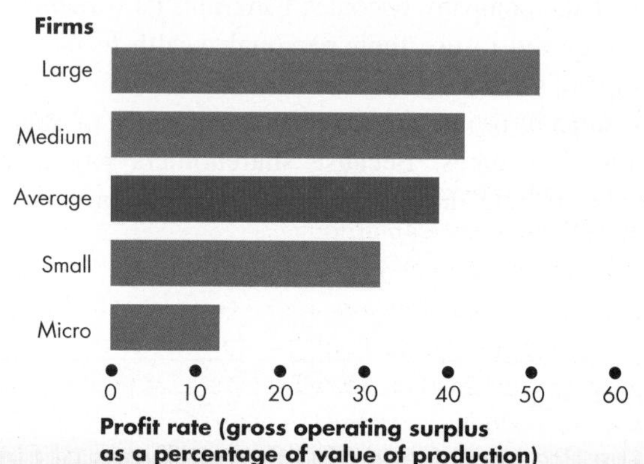

Source of data: European Commission, *Observatory of European SMEs*, No. 2, 2002.

Decision making in partnerships is relatively easy but production costs can be high. By contrast, companies can produce at low cost but decision making can be difficult because of their size and complexity. Because of the balance of advantages and disadvantages, each type continues to exist throughout Europe and the rest of the world. Companies dominate where they are the most profitable. This is usually when a large amount of capital is required. Proprietorships and partnerships dominate when they are most profitable, usually where flexibility in decision making is critical.

Partnerships are small-scale firms while companies are large-scale firms that employ many people. Box 9.1 examines the relationship between size and profitability of European firms.

Review Quiz

Study Plan 9.3

1. Explain the distinction between a command system and an incentive system in business organizations.
2. What is the principal–agent problem and what are the ways in which firms try to cope with it?
3. What are the three types of firm? Explain their advantages and disadvantages.
4. Why do all three types of firm survive and in which sectors is each type most prominent?

You've now seen how technological constraints and information constraints influence firms. We'll look at market constraints next to see how they influence the environment in which firms compete.

Markets and the Competitive Environment

The markets in which firms operate vary a great deal. Some markets are highly competitive and profits are hard to come by. Some appear to be almost free from competition and firms in these markets earn large profits. Some markets are dominated by fierce advertising campaigns in which each firm seeks to persuade buyers that it has the best products. Some markets display a war-like character.

Economists identify four market types:

- Perfect competition
- Monopolistic competition
- Oligopoly
- Monopoly

Perfect Competition

Perfect competition arises when there are many firms that sell an identical product, many buyers and no restrictions on the entry of new firms into the industry. The many firms and buyers are all well informed about the prices of the products of each firm in the industry. The worldwide markets for wheat, rice, and other grain crops are examples of perfect competition.

Monopolistic Competition

Monopolistic competition is a market structure in which a large number of firms compete by making similar but slightly different products. Making a product slightly different from the product of a competing firm is called **product differentiation**.

Firms in monopolistic competition are in fierce competition with each other. But production differentiation gives each monopolistically competitive firm an element of monopoly power. The firm is the sole producer of the particular version of the good in question.

For example, in the market for running shoes, Nike, Reebok, Fila, Asics, and many other firms compete, but all make their own version of the perfect shoe. Each of these firms is the sole producer of a particular brand and so has a monopoly on that particular brand of shoe.

Differentiated products need not be different products. What matters is that consumers perceive the products to be different. For example, different brands of ibuprofen tablets are chemically identical and differ only in their packaging.

Oligopoly

Oligopoly is a market structure in which a small number of firms compete. Aeroplane manufacture, international air transport, and computer software are examples of oligopolistic industries. Oligopolies might produce

almost identical products, such as the colas produced by Coca-Cola and Pepsi Co. Or they might produce differentiated products such as the Airbus A380 and the Boeing 747.

Monopoly

Monopoly arises when there is one firm which produces a good or service for which no close substitute exists and in which the firm is protected from competition by a barrier preventing the entry of new firms. In some places, the phone, gas, electricity and water suppliers are local monopolies – monopolies restricted to a given location. Microsoft, the software developer that created Windows, the operating system used by the vast majority of PCs, is an example of a global monopoly.

Perfect competition is the most extreme form of competition. Monopoly is the most extreme absence of competition. The other two market types fall between these extremes.

We've described the four types of market. But how do we recognize these market types? You would probably have little difficulty recognizing the difference between a perfectly competitive market and a monopoly market. But how would you distinguish between monopolistic competition and oligopoly?

Identifying a Market Structure

Many factors must be taken into account to determine which market structure describes a particular real-world market. One of these factors is the extent to which the market is dominated by a small number of firms. To measure this feature of markets, economists use indexes called measures of concentration.

Measures of Concentration

The most common measure of concentration uses total revenue and puts five firms in the group of largest firms. The result is the **five-firm concentration ratio**, which is the percentage of total revenue (or the value of sales) in an industry accounted for by the five firms with the largest value of sales. The range of the concentration ratio is from almost zero for perfect competition to 100 for monopoly.

Table 9.5 shows two hypothetical calculations of the five-firm concentration ratio, one for shoe manufacturing and one for egg farming. In this example, there are 15 firms in the shoe manufacturing industry. The largest five have 81 per cent of the sales, so the five-firm concentration ratio for that industry is 81 per cent. In the egg industry, with 1,005 firms, the top five firms account

Table 9.5

Concentration Ratio Calculations

Shoemakers		Egg farmers	
Firm	**Sales (millions of pounds)**	**Firm**	**Sales (millions of pounds)**
Lace-up plc	250	Bills's	0.9
Finefoot plc	200	Sue's	0.7
Easyfit plc	180	Jane's	0.5
Comfy plc	120	Tom's	0.4
Loafers plc	70	Jill's	0.2
Top 5 sales	820	Top 5 sales	2.8
Other 10 firms	190	Other 1,000 firms	349.2
Industry sales	1,010	Industry sales	352.0

Five-firm concentration ratios:

Shoemakers: $\frac{820}{1{,}010}$ = 81 per cent

Egg farmers: $\frac{2.80}{352}$ = 0.8 per cent

for only 0.8 per cent of total industry sales. In this case, the five-firm concentration ratio is 0.8 per cent.

The five-firm concentration ratio helps us measure the degree of competitiveness of a market. A low concentration ratio indicates a high degree of competition, and a high concentration ratio indicates an absence of competition. In the extreme case of monopoly, the concentration ratio is 100 per cent because the largest (and only) firm makes the entire industry sales. Between these extremes, the five-firm concentration ratio is regarded as being a useful indicator of the likelihood of collusion among firms in an oligopoly. If the concentration ratio exceeds 60 per cent, it is likely that firms have a high degree of market power and may collude and behave like a monopoly.

If the concentration ratio is less than 40 per cent, the industry is regarded as competitive. A concentration ratio between 40 and 60 per cent indicates that the market structure is oligopoly.

Limitations of Concentration Measures

Concentration ratios are useful, but they have some limitations. They must be supplemented by other information to determine the market structure of an industry and the degree of market power of firms in that industry. The three key problems are:

- The geographical scope of the market
- Barriers to entry and firm turnover
- Market and industry correspondence

Geographical Scope of Market

Concentration ratio data are based on a *national* view of the market. Many goods are sold on a national market, and for these goods, the concentration measures are useful.

But some goods are sold on a *regional* market. There are many national firms but few firms in each regional market. In this type of market, the national concentration ratios underestimate the true degree of concentration. The brewing industry is an example of good in which the local market is more relevant than the national market. So although the national concentration ratio for brewers is in the middle range, there is a high degree of concentration in the brewing industry in most regions.

Other industries operate in a *global* market. So although the largest five car producers in the United Kingdom account for 80 per cent of all cars sold by UK producers, they account for a smaller percentage of the total UK car market, which includes imports. In the global market for cars, UK producers account for an even smaller percentage of total sales. In this case, the national concentration ratios overestimate the true degree of concentration.

Barriers to Entry and Firm Turnover

Measures of concentration do not measure the severity of barriers to entry in a market. Some industries are highly concentrated but their markets have virtually free entry and a high turnover of firms. For example, many small towns have few restaurants, but there are few restrictions on opening the restaurant. Many firms enter and exit with great regularity.

Even if the turnover of new firms in a market is limited, an industry might be competitive because of *potential entry* – because a few firms in the market face competition from many firms that can easily enter the market and will do so if economic profits are available.

Market and Industry Correspondence

The classifications used to calculate concentration ratios allocate every firm in the economy to a particular industry. But markets for particular goods do not usually correspond to these industries for three reasons.

First, markets are often narrower than industries. For example, the pharmaceutical industry, which has a low concentration ratio, operates in many separate markets for individual products – for example, measles vaccine and AIDS-fighting drugs. These drugs do not compete with each other, so this industry, which looks competitive, includes firms that are monopolies (or near monopolies) in markets for individual drugs.

Second, most firms make many products. For example, the tobacco firms also operate in the food and insurance industries. The privatized water companies operate hotels and printing works. The value of sales for each firm show up in the industry to which the firm has been assigned. So their contribution to the industry to which they have been assigned might be overestimated.

Third, firms switch from one market to another depending on profit opportunities. Virgin, which today produces air transport services, train services and other products, has diversified from being a retail record shop and recording studio. Virgin no longer produces albums. Today, the Virgin group's products include credit cards and home loans, soft drinks, mobile phones, wines, balloon rides and more.

Publishers of newspapers, magazines and textbooks are today rapidly diversifying into Internet and multimedia products. These switches among industries show that there is much scope for entering and exiting an industry, and so measures of concentration have limited usefulness in describing the true degree of competition in a market.

Despite their limitations, when supplemented with other information about the geographical scope of a market, barriers to entry and the extent to which large, multi-product firms straddle a variety of markets, concentration measures do provide a basis for determining the degree of competition in a market they can provide a basis for classifying markets. The less concentrated an

Box 9.2
Concentration Ratios in the United Kingdom

Concentration ratios in the United Kingdom are derived from the Census of Production. This census is undertaken by the UK government and it provides information on the sales, employment and structure of every manufacturing firm in the United Kingdom.

Figure 1 shows some five-firm concentration ratios. Plastics, printing and publishing, hotels, catering and pubs, and jewellery have low concentration ratios, which indicates that they are competitive industries. Tobacco products, confectionary, soft drinks and mineral waters have high concentration ratios, which indicates that they are industries with a high degree of market power. Soap and toilet preparations, motor vehicles, leather goods and agricultural machinery have intermediate concentration ratios, which indicates limited market power.

Figure 1

Concentration Ratios

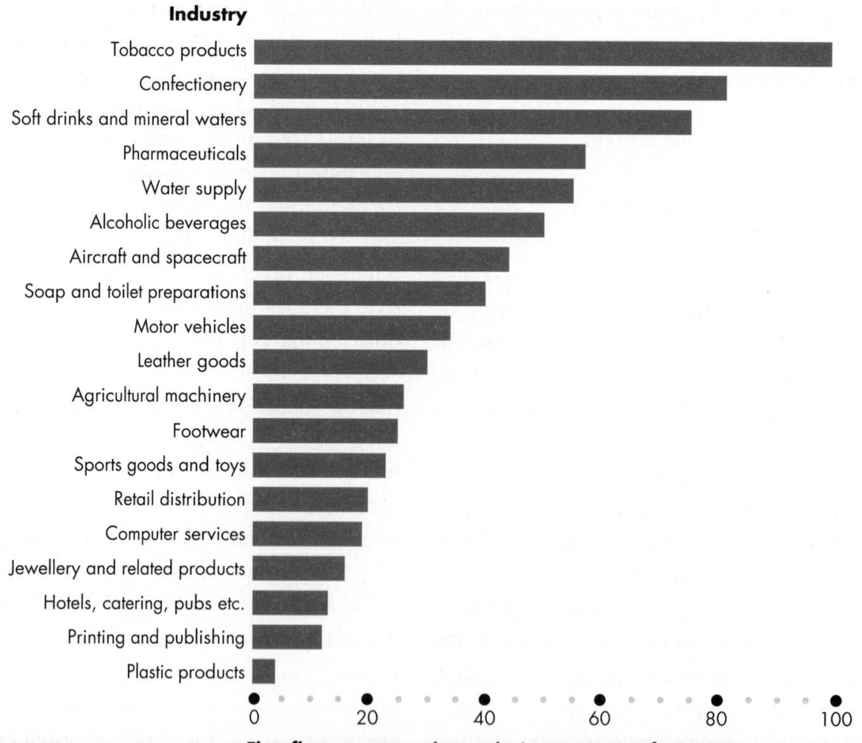

Source of data: Office for National Statistics, *Concentration Ratios for Business by Industry in 2004*.

Table 9.6

Market Structure

Characteristics	Perfect competition	Monopolistic competition	Oligopoly	Monopoly
Number of firms in industry	Many	Many	Few	One
Product	Identical	Differentiated	Either identical or differentiated	No close substitutes
Barriers to entry	None	None	Moderate	High
Firm's control over price	None	Some	Considerable	Considerable or regulated
Concentration ratio	0	Low	High	100
Examples	Agricultural products	Cosmetics, bread, clothing	Washing powders, cereals	Local water utility, postal letter service

industry and the lower its barriers to entry, the more closely it approximates the perfect competition case. The more concentrated an industry and the higher the barriers to entry, the more it approximates oligopoly or even monopoly.

Table 9.6 summarizes the characteristics of different market structures and their concentration ratios.

Market Structures in Europe

The majority of markets for goods and services in Europe are highly competitive and only a few markets are monopolies. For example, more than 70 per cent by value of goods and services bought and sold in the United Kingdom are traded in highly competitive markets. Where monopoly does arise, it is usually in the public services although with privatization, public services have become more competitive.

But market power can still be strong in markets when privatization attracts few new entrants such as in the telecommunications industry. Less than 6 per cent of goods and services traded in the UK markets are essentially uncompetitive. Oligopoly is more common in manufacturing than in the services sector, but more than 55 per cent of UK manufacturing industries have a concentration ratio of less than 40 per cent.

The overall level of concentration in an economy can be measured by the proportion of total output accounted for by the largest 100 firms. The UK aggregate concentration ratio in manufacturing increased in the post-war period, indicating an increase in market power, but it levelled off in the 1970s and 1980s and has fallen in recent years. The increase in concentration resulted from several waves of merger activity and the growth of transnational companies serving new global markets. But given the growth in world trade and advances in telecommunications and low-cost transport, many UK firms operate in global markets, which are highly competitive.

Review Quiz

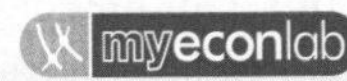

Study Plan 9.4

1. What are the four market types? Explain the distinguishing characteristics of each.
2. Describe and explain the main measures of market concentration.
3. Under what conditions do measures of concentration give a good indication of the degree of competition in the market?
4. Is our economy competitive? Is it becoming more competitive or less competitive?

You now know the variety of market types and the way we classify firms and industries into the different market types. Our final question in this chapter is what determines the items that firms decide to buy from other firms rather than produce for themselves?

Firms and Markets

At the beginning of this chapter, we defined a firm as an institution that hires factors of production and organizes them to produce and sell goods and services. To organize production, firms coordinate the economic decisions and activities of many individuals. But firms are not the only coordinators of economic decisions. You learned in Chapter 3 that markets also coordinate decisions. By adjusting prices, markets make the decisions of buyers and sellers consistent – make the quantities demanded equal to the quantities supplied of the many different goods and services.

Market Coordination

Markets can coordinate production. For example, markets might coordinate the production of a rock concert. A promoter hires a stadium, some stage equipment, audio and video recording engineers and technicians, some rock groups, a superstar, a publicity agent and a ticket agent – all market transactions – and sells tickets to thousands of rock fans, audio rights to a recording company and video and broadcasting rights to a television network – another set of market transactions. If rock concerts were produced like cornflakes, the firm producing them would own all the capital used (stadiums, stage, sound and video equipment) and would employ all the labour needed (singers, engineers, sales people and so on).

Outsourcing, buying parts or products from other firms, is another example of market coordination. The major car makers use outsourcing for windscreens and windows, gear boxes, tires, and many other parts. Apple Computer even outsources the production of the iPod.

What determines whether a firm or markets coordinate a particular set of activities? Why is the production of cornflakes coordinated by a firm and the production of a rock concert coordinated by markets? The answer is cost. Taking account of the opportunity cost of time as well as the costs of the other inputs, people use the method that costs least. In other words, they use the economically efficient method.

Firms coordinate economic activity when they can perform a task more efficiently than markets can. In such a situation, it is profitable to set up a firm. If markets can perform a task more efficiently than a firm can, firms will use markets and any attempt to set up a firm to replace such market coordination will be doomed to failure.

Why Firms?

Firms are often more efficient than markets as coordinators of economic activity because they can achieve:

- Lower transactions costs
- Economies of scale
- Economies of scope
- Economies of team production

Lower Transactions Costs

The idea that firms exist because there are activities in which firms are more efficient than markets was first suggested by University of Chicago economist and Nobel Laureate Ronald Coase.[1] Coase focused on the firm's ability to reduce or eliminate transactions costs. **Transactions costs** are the costs arising from finding someone with whom to do business, of reaching an agreement about the price and other aspects of the exchange, and of ensuring that the terms of the agreement are fulfilled. *Market* transactions require buyers and sellers to get together and to negotiate the terms and conditions of their trading. Sometimes lawyers have to be hired to draw up contracts. A broken contract leads to still more expenses. A *firm* can lower such transactions costs by reducing the number of individual transactions undertaken.

Consider, for example, two ways of getting your creaking car fixed:

1 *Firm coordination*. You take the car to the garage. Parts and tools as well as the mechanic's time are coordinated by the garage owner and your car gets fixed. You pay one bill for the entire job.

2 *Market coordination*. You hire a mechanic who diagnoses the problems and makes a list of the parts and tools needed to fix them. You buy the parts from the local breaker's yard and rent the tools from ABC Rentals. You hire the mechanic again to fix the problems. You return the tools and pay your bills – wages to the mechanic, rental to ABC and the cost of the parts used to the breaker.

What determines the method that you use? The answer is cost. Taking account of the opportunity cost of your own time as well as the costs of the other inputs that you would have to buy, you will use the method that costs least – the economically efficient method.

[1] Ronald H. Coase 'The Nature of the Firm', *Economica* (November 1937) pp. 386–405.

The first method requires that you undertake only one transaction with one firm. It's true that the firm has to undertake several transactions – hiring the labour and buying the parts and tools required to do the job. But the firm doesn't have to undertake those transactions simply to fix your car. One set of such transactions enables the firm to fix hundreds of cars. Thus there is an enormous reduction in the number of individual transactions that take place if people get their cars fixed at the garage rather than going through an elaborate sequence of market transactions.

Economies of Scale

When the cost of producing a unit of a good falls as its output rate increases, **economies of scale** exist. Many industries experience economies of scale; car manufacturing is an example. One firm can produce 4 million cars a year at a lower cost per car than 200 firms each producing 20,000 cars a year. Economies of scale arise from specialization and the division of labour that can be reaped more effectively by firm coordination rather than market coordination.

Economies of Scope

A firm experiences **economies of scope** when it uses its specialized and often expensive resources to produce a range of goods and services. For example, SAP hires specialist programmers, designers, marketing experts and sales representatives and uses their skills across an enormous range of software products. As a result, SAP coordinates the resources that produce software at a lower cost than the cost of producing each one of these products in a large number of small specialist firms.

Economies of Team Production

A production process in which a group of individuals each specializes in mutually supportive tasks is *team production*. The idea that firms arise as a consequence of the economies of team production was first suggested by Armen Alchian and Harold Demsetz, of the University of California at Los Angeles.[2] Sport provides the best example of team activity. Some team members specialize in striking and some in defending, some in speed and some in strength.

The production of goods and services offers many examples of team activity. For example, production lines in car plants and TV manufacturing plants work most efficiently when individual activity is organized in teams, each specializing in a small task. You can also think of an entire firm as being a team. The team has buyers of raw materials and other inputs, production workers and sales persons. There are even specialists within these various groups. Each individual member of the team specializes, but the value of the output of the team and the profit that it earns depend on the coordinated activities of all the team's members.

Because firms can economize on transactions costs, reap economies of scale and scope, and organize efficient team production, it is firms rather than markets that coordinate most of our economic activity. But there are limits to the economic efficiency of firms. If a firm becomes too big or too diversified in the things that it seeks to do, the cost of management and monitoring per unit of output begins to rise and, at some point, the market becomes more efficient at coordinating the use of resources. This explains why Ford restructured into a global transnational company, effectively creating a set of smaller, more independent national companies.

Sometimes firms enter into long-term alliances with each other that cut out market transactions and make it difficult to see where one firm ends and another begins. For example, long-term alliances are also common between supermarkets and manufacturers. Famous cereal manufacturers produce supermarket own-label brands as well as their own more established brands.

Review Quiz

Study Plan 9.5

1. Describe the main ways in which economic activity can be coordinated.
2. What determines whether a firm or markets coordinate production?
3. What are the main reasons why firms can often coordinate production at lower cost than markets?

In the *Business Case Study* on pp. 208–209, you can read how Europe's biggest software company, SAP, dealt with its technology, information and market constraints.

In the next chapter, you will learn about the relationship between a firm's cost and its output. These cost–output relationships are common to all types of firm in all types of markets.

---

[2] Armen Alchian and Harold Demsetz, 'Production, Information Costs, and Economic Organization', *American Economic Review* (December 1972) 57, 5, pp. 777–795.

Business Case Study

Constraints on Profit

Europe's biggest software company: SAP

The Company

SAP, a German company, is Europe's software giant. It became a public traded company in 1988 and now employs over 30,000 people in more than 50 countries. It runs 36,000 installations of its software serving 10 million users in 21,000 organizations across 120 countries. Its customers include other corporate giants such as Sony and Microsoft.

The Products

SAP specializes in writing and installing business software, particularly collaborative e-business systems for firms in all types of industries and markets. These Enterprise Resource Planning systems help companies to run their back-office functions such as distribution, accounting and manufacturing. SAP began to grow in the late 1990s with its provision of millennium bug products and services.

Competition and Market Constraints

SAP's main rivals are US companies like Oracle, Siebel Systems and PeopleSoft. The market for the services of these companies was severely cut in 2001 with the economic slowdown in the United States and limited growth potential in computer hardware. But SAP's sales and profits have rocketed since 1999 whilst competitors recorded losses. First quarter figures for 2004 are similar, with a 23 per cent rise in profits.

Information Constraints

SAP was founded in 1972 by five former IBM systems engineers. As it has grown, SAP has adopted a standard corporate structure. Its CEO is Mr Henning Kagermann, but three of its original founders still control 40 per cent of the shares.

Technology Constraints

In the late 1990s, SAP realized that its profit was limited by traditional software delivery systems. In 1999, the company launched a new Enterprise Resource Planning website called mySAP.com. The site supports all types of business software and allows employees, customers and business partners to work together more efficiently, by increasing information flows, raising supply chain efficiency and improving customer-to-business relationships.

SAP is now developing Internet partnerships with related organizations. In June 2001, SAP linked up with IBM and Compaq to gain access to new customers like Shell Oil. In 2003, SAP established links with Dell computers and in 2004, SAP began negotiations with Microsoft.

Economic Analysis

- SAP aims to maximize profit. It operates in a global oligopoly market where a few large firms compete worldwide for customers. Its profits are constrained by technology, information and market constraints.
- Tables 1 and 2 compare SAP's performance relative to its main competitor. SAP has steadily expanded employment, whereas Oracle cut employment before rapid expansion.
- In 1999, SAP lagged behind Oracle which had begun to develop Internet services. SAP was constrained by its existing technology. SAP launched its own Internet services in 1999 to raise efficiency by capturing economies of scale and scope.
- SAP's Internet strategy helped it to specialize in software management, cut transactions costs and capture economies of team production. Tables 1 and 2 shows the rise in SAP's profits compared to the fall in Oracle's profit up to 2003 as costs were cut.
- Oracle's sales were constrained by US market conditions in 2001. The slowdown in the US economy decreased demand for Oracles's software. Tables 1 and 2 show how Oracle's sales fell whilst SAP's sales rocketed.
- The figure compares share of ownership by the founder managers in SAP and Oracle. SAP's original founders have maintained greater control. This may reduce principal–agent problems for senior management to help cut costs and raise profit.
- But Oracle's latest strategy is to expand by taking over competitors. By 2006, Oracle achieved a sharp rise in sales, profits and size reaping economies of scale and scope. Oracle may have greater market power and SAP faces tighter market constraints.

Table 1

SAP's Position

Item	Dec 1999	Dec 2002	Dec 2005
Employment	24,480	30,251	34,500
(1-year growth)	13%	3.0%	1.7%
Profit ($million)	596	1,354	1,772
(1-year growth)	2%	53.5%	0.9%
Sales ($million)	5,881	8,831.3	10,082
(1-year growth)	14%	13.4%	1.7%

Table 2

Oracle's Position

Item	Dec 1999	Dec 2002	Dec 2005
Employment	42,927	40,650	56,133
(1-year growth)	4%	–3.2%	12.6%
Profit ($million)	2,561	2,301	3,381
(1-year growth)	59%	–3.7%	17.6%
Sales ($million)	10,860	9,475	14,380
(1-year growth)	7%	–2%	21.9%

Source of data: http://cobrands.hoovers.com/

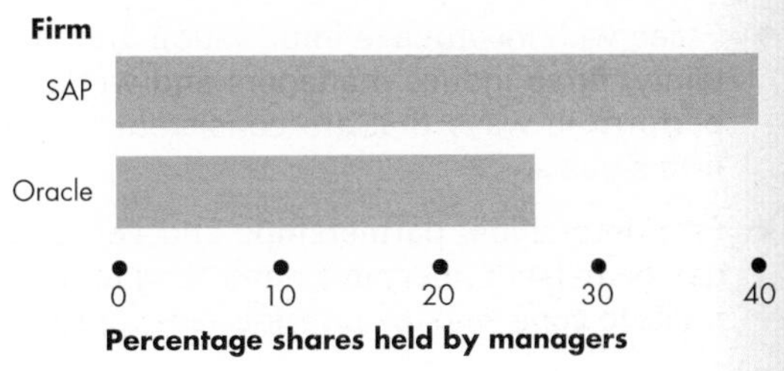

Figure 1 Share of ownership by founder members

Summary

Key Points

The Firm and Its Economic Problem (pp. 192–194)

- Firms hire and organize factors of production to produce and sell goods and services.
- Firms seek to maximize economic profit (total revenue minus total cost).
- A firm's total cost is the sum of explicit cost and implicit costs of using the firm's capital and owner's resources.
- Normal profit is the opportunity cost of entrepreneurship and is part of the firm's explicit costs.
- Technology, information and markets limit a firm's profit.

Technological and Economic Efficiency (pp. 195–196)

- A method of production is technologically efficient when a firm produces a given output by using the least amount of resources.
- A method of production is economically efficient when the cost of producing a given output is as low as possible.

Information and Organizations (pp. 197–200)

- Firms use a combination of command systems and incentive systems to organize production.
- Faced with incomplete information and uncertainty, firms induce managers and workers to perform in ways that are consistent with the firm's goals.
- Proprietorships, partnerships and companies use ownership, incentives and long-term contracts to cope with the principal–agent problem.

Markets and the Competitive Environment (pp. 201–205)

- In perfect competition, many buyers and sellers offer an identical product to many buyers.
- In monopolistic competition, many sellers offer slightly different products to many buyers and entry is free.
- In oligopoly, a small number of firms compete.
- In monopoly, one firm produces a good or services that has no close substitutes and the firm is protected by a barrier that prevents the entry of competitors.
- Concentration ratios measure the degree of competition in markets.

Firms and Markets (pp. 206–207)

- Firms coordinate economic activities when they can perform a task more efficiently – at lower cost – than markets can.
- Firms economize on transactions costs and achieve the benefits of economies of scale, economies of scope and of team production.

Key Tables

Key Terms

Problems

Tests, Study Plan and Solutions* 

1 One year ago, Jack and Jill set up a vinegar bottling firm (called JJVB). Use the following information to calculate JJVB's explicit costs and implicit costs during its first year of operation:

a Jack and Jill put €50,000 of their own money into the firm.

b They bought equipment for €30,000.

c They hired one employee to help them for an annual wage of €20,000.

d Jack gave up his previous job, at which he earned €30,000, and spent all his time working for JJVB.

e Jill kept her old job, which paid €30 an hour, but gave up 10 hours of leisure each week (for 50 weeks) to work for JJVB.

f JJVB bought €10,000 of goods and services from other firms.

g The market value of the equipment at the end of the year was €28,000.

h Jack and Jill have a €100,000 home loan on which they pay an interest rate of 6 per cent a year.

2 Four methods of completing a tax return are: a personal computer (PC), a pocket calculator, a pocket calculator with pencil and paper, a pencil and paper. With a PC, the job takes an hour; with a pocket calculator, it takes 12 hours; with a pocket calculator and pencil and paper, it takes 12 hours; and with a pencil and paper, it takes 16 hours. The PC and its software cost €1,000, the pocket calculator costs €10, and the pencil and paper cost €1.

a Which, if any, of the methods is technologically efficient?

b Which method is economically efficient if the wage rate is

(i) €5 an hour?
(ii) €50 an hour?
(iii) €500 an hour?

3 Alternative ways of laundering 100 shirts are:

Method	Labour (hours)	Capital (machines)
A	1	10
B	5	8
C	20	4
D	50	1

a Which methods are technologically efficient?

b Which method is economically efficient if the hourly wage rate and the implicit rental rate of capital are:

(i) Wage rate €1, rental rate €100?
(ii) Wage rate €5, rental rate €50?
(iii) Wage rate €50, rental rate €5?

4 Tesco plc has more than 2,700 stores, more than a quarter of a million employees, and total revenues of about £40 million a year. Sarah runs the family-owned Frey Farms and supplies Tesco plc with mushrooms and other fresh produce.

a How do you think Tesco plc coordinates its activities? Is it likely to use mainly a command system or also to use incentive systems?

b How do you think Sarah coordinates the activities of Frey Farms? Is she likely to use mainly a command system or also to use incentive systems? Why?

c Describe, compare and contrast the principal–agent problems faced by Tesco plc and Frey Farms. How might each firm cope with its principal–agent problems?

5 Sales of the firms in the tattoo industry are:

Firm	Sales (euros)
Bright Spots plc	450
Freckles plc	325
Love Galore plc	250
Native Birds plc	200
Tiny Tattoo plc	175
Other 15 firms	800

a Calculate the five-firm concentration ratio.

b What is the structure of the tattoo industry on the basis of just the concentration ratio data?

c What other information would you need to determine whether the tattoo industry is competitive?

6 In 2003 and 2004, Lego, the Danish toymaker that produces coloured plastic bricks, incurred economic losses. The firm faced competition from low-cost copies of its products and faced a fall in the number of 5- to 9-year-old boys (its main customers) in many rich countries. In 2004, Lego launched a plan to restore profits. It fired 3,500 of its 8,000 workers; closed factories in Switzerland and the United States; opened factories in Eastern Europe and Mexico; and introduced performance-based pay for its managers.

* Solutions to odd-numbered problems are provided.

Lego reported a return to profit in 2005. (Based on 'Picking up the pieces', *The Economist*, 28 October 2006.)

a Describe the problems that Lego faced in 2003 and 2004 using the concepts of the three types of constraint that all firms face.

b Which of the actions that Lego took to restore profits addressed an inefficiency? How did Lego seek to achieve economic efficiency?

c Which of the actions that Lego took to restore profits addressed an information and organization problem? How did Lego change the way in which it coped with the principal–agent problem?

d In what type of market does Lego operate?

7 Two leading design firms, Astro Studios of San Francisco and Hers Experimental Design Laboratory, Inc. of Osaka, Japan, worked with Microsoft to design the Xbox 360 video game console. IBM, ATI and SiS designed the Xbox 360's hardware. Two firms, Flextronics & Wistron and Celestica, manufacture the Xbox 360 at their plants in China.

a Describe the roles of market coordination and coordination by firms in the design, manufacture and marketing of the Xbox 360.

b Why do you think Microsoft works with a large number of other firms rather than performing all the tasks required to bring the Xbox to market at its headquarters in Seattle?

c What are the roles of transactions costs, economies of scale, economies of scope and economies of team production in the design, manufacture and marketing of the Xbox?

8 The iPod economy has many tentacles. An American company, PortalPlayer, makes the chips that power it. Another American company, Synaptics makes the interface for its clickwheel. Japanese companies Sony and Sanyo make its rechargeable batteries. Two other Japanese companies, Hitachi and Toshiba, make the iPod's tiny in size but large capacity hard drive that stores your songs. And a Taiwanese company Inventec manufactures it. Hewlett-Packard has done a deal with Apple, which allows HP to resell the iPod (as the Apple iPod by HP), saves HP the cost of developing its own MP3 player, and gives HP a competitive edge over Dell with its Jukebox MP3 player.

a For each firm mentioned in the above account, describe how they are coping with their own economic problem.

b Why doesn't Apple manufacture the iPod and keep exclusive marketing rights to itself?

Critical Thinking

1 Study the *Business Case Study* about the European software company, SAP, on pp. 208–209 and then:

a Describe the economic problem that SAP faced in the late 1990s.

b Compare and contrast how SAP achieves technological efficiency and economic efficiency.

c SAP and its competitors provide software services which help other companies to reduce their costs and become more efficient. Why might the demand for SAP's services buck the trend when the economy slows down?

2 By 2004, three of the 100 UK companies with the fastest growth had created share-option schemes to make employees part-owners of the business. These companies were Vivid Imaginations, LGC and RFIB Group. Their annual profits increased by 51, 46 and 40 per cent respectively.

a What internal problems might have led these firms to encourage employees to be part owners?

b How can such schemes affect the growth rate of profits?

Web Activities

Links to Websites

1 Obtain information about SAP's competitors and SAP's performance in the third quarter of 2001.

a What firms are SAP's main competitors?

b What are the main economic problems faced by SAP and its competitors?

c Why is SAP suggesting that it must cut labour costs in the United States?

2 Read James D. Miller's views on providing airport security services.

a Explain Mr. Miller's views using the principal–agent analysis. Who is the principal and who is the agent?

b What exactly is the principal–agent problem in providing airport security services?

c Why might a private provider offer better security than a public provider?

d Do you think that a private provider would operate at a lower cost than a public provider? Why or why not?

Output and Costs

CHAPTER 10

After studying this chapter you will be able to:

- Distinguish between the short run and the long run
- Explain the relationship between a firm's output and labour employed in the short run
- Explain the relationship between a firm's output and costs in the short run and derive a firm's short-run cost curves
- Explain the relationship between a firm's output and costs in the long run and derive a firm's long-run average cost curve

Survival of the Fittest

What does a firm have to do to be a survivor? Does size guarantee survival? Why do some very small firms survive? Why do some firms, such as car makers, have plenty of slack and wish they could sell more whereas others, such as Powergen, operate flat out with no spare capacity ?

This chapter answers these questions. And in the *Business Case Study* at the end of the chapter, you can see how the merger of two firms to create a mega-size firm influences costs.

Time Frames for Decisions

People who operate firms make many decisions. All of these decisions are aimed at one overriding objective: maximum attainable profit. But the decisions are not all equally critical. Some of the decisions are big ones. Once made, they are costly (or impossible) to reverse. If such a decision turns out to be incorrect, it might lead to the failure of the firm. Some of the decisions are small ones. They are easily changed. If one of these decisions turns out to be incorrect, the firm can change its actions and survive.

The biggest decision that any firm makes is what industry to enter. For most entrepreneurs, their background knowledge and interests drive this decision. But the decision also depends on profit prospects. No one sets up a firm without believing it will be profitable. And profit depends on total revenue and total cost (see Chapter 9, pp. 192–193).

The firm that we'll study has already chosen the industry in which to operate. It has also chosen its most effective method of organization. But it has not decided the quantity to produce, the quantities of factors of production to hire or the price at which to sell its output.

Decisions about the quantity to produce and the price to charge depend on the type of market in which the firm operates. Perfect competition, monopolistic competition, oligopoly and monopoly all confront the firm with their own special problems.

But decisions about *how* to produce a given output do not depend on the type of market in which the firm operates. These decisions are similar for *all* types of firms in *all* types of markets.

The actions that a firm can take to influence the relationship between output and cost depend on how soon the firm wants to act. A firm that plans to change its output rate tomorrow has fewer options than one that plans to change its output rate six months from now.

To study the relationship between a firm's output decision and its costs, we distinguish two decision time frames:

- The short run
- The long run

The Short Run

The **short run** is a time frame in which the quantity of at least one factor of production is fixed. For most firms, capital, land and entrepreneurship are fixed factors of production and labour is the variable factor of production. We call the fixed factors of production the firm's *plant*. So in the short run, a firm's plant is fixed.

For our firm, Neat Knits, the fixed plant is its factory building and its knitting machines. For an electric power utility, the fixed plant is its buildings, generators, computers and control systems.

To increase output in the short run, a firm must increase the quantity of a variable factor of production, which is usually labour. So to produce more output, Neat Knits must hire more labour and operate its knitting machines for more hours per day. Similarly, an electric power utility must hire more labour and operate its generators for more hours per day.

Short-run decisions are easily reversed. The firm can increase or decrease output in the short run by increasing or decreasing the labour it hires.

The Long Run

The **long run** is a time frame in which the quantities of *all* factors of production can be varied. That is, the long run is a period in which the firm can change its *plant*.

To increase output in the long run, a firm is able to choose whether to change its plant as well as whether to increase the quantity of labour it hires. Neat Knits can decide whether to install some additional knitting machines, use a new type of machine, reorganize its management or hire more labour. An electric power utility can decide whether to install more generators. And an airport can decide whether to build more runways, terminals and traffic-control facilities.

Long-run decisions are *not* easily reversed. Once a plant decision is made, the firm must live with it for some time. To emphasize this fact, we call the *past* expenditure on a plant that has no resale value a **sunk cost**. A sunk cost is irrelevant to the firm's current decisions. The only costs that influence its current decisions are the short-run cost of changing the quantity of labour and the long-run cost of changing its plant.

Review Quiz

Study Plan 10.1

1. Distinguish between the short run and the long run.
2. Why is a sunk cost irrelevant?

We're going to study costs in the short run and the long run. We begin with the short run and describe the technology constraint the firm faces.

Short-run Technology Constraint

To increase output in the short run, a firm must increase the quantity of labour employed. We describe the relationship between output and the quantity of labour employed by using three related concepts:

1 Total product
2 Marginal product
3 Average product

These product concepts can be illustrated either by product schedules or by product curves. We'll look first at the product schedules.

Product Schedules

Table 10.1 shows some data that describe Neat Knits' total product, marginal product and average product. The numbers tell us how Neat Knits' production changes as more workers are employed, for a fixed level of plant and machines. They also tell us about the productivity of Neat Knits' workforce.

Look first at the columns headed "Labour" and "Total product". **Total product** is the maximum output that a given quantity of labour can produce. The table shows how total product increases as Neat Knits employs more labour. For example, when Neat Knits employs 1 worker, total product is 4 jumpers a day and when Neat Knits employs 2 workers, total product is 10 jumpers a day. Each increase in employment brings an increase in total product.

The **marginal product** of labour is the increase in total product resulting from a one-unit increase in the quantity of labour employed with all other inputs remaining the same. For example, in Table 10.1, when Neat Knits increases employment from 2 to 3 workers and does not change its capital, the marginal product of the third worker is 3 jumpers – total product increases from 10 to 13 jumpers.

The average product tells how productive workers are on the average. The **average product** of labour is equal to total product divided by the quantity of labour employed. For example, in Table 10.1, 3 workers can knit 13 jumpers a day, so the average product of labour is 13 divided by 3, which is 4.33 jumpers per worker.

If you look closely at the numbers in Table 10.1, you can see some patterns. For example, as Neat Knits employs more workers, marginal product at first increases and then begins to decrease. For example, marginal product increases from 4 jumpers a day for the first worker to 6 jumpers a day for the second worker and then decreases to 3 jumpers a day for the third worker. Also average product at first increases and then decreases. You can see the relationships between the number of workers employed and the three product concepts more clearly by looking at the product curves.

Table 10.1

Total Product, Marginal Product and Average Product

	Labour (workers per day)	Total product (jumpers per day)	Marginal product (jumpers per worker)	Average product (jumpers per worker)
A	0	0		
			4	
B	1	4		4.00
			6	
C	2	10		5.00
			3	
D	3	13		4.33
			2	
E	4	15		3.75
			1	
F	5	16		3.20

Total product is the total amount produced. Marginal product is the change in total product resulting from a one-unit increase in labour. For example, when labour increases from 2 to 3 workers a day (row *C* to row *D*), total product increases from 10 to 13 jumpers a day. The marginal product of going from 2 to 3 workers is 3 jumpers. (Marginal product is shown between the rows because it is the result of a change in the quantity of labour.) Average product of labour is total product divided by the quantity of labour employed. For example, 3 workers produce 13 jumpers a day, so the average product of 3 workers is 4.33 jumpers per worker.

Product Curves

The product curves are graphs of the relationships between employment and the three product concepts you've just studied. They show how total product, marginal product and average product change as employment changes. They also show the relationships among the three concepts. Let's look at the three product curves.

Total Product Curve

Figure 10.1 shows Neat Knits' total product curve, *TP*. As employment increases, so does the number of jumpers knitted. Points *A* to *F* on the curve correspond to the same rows in Table 10.1. These points show total product as the quantity of labour changes by one day of labour. But labour is divisible into hours and even minutes. By varying the amount of labour in the smallest units possible, we can draw the total product curve shown in Figure 10.1.

Look carefully at the shape of the total product curve. As employment increases from zero to 1 worker a day, the curve becomes steeper. Then, as employment continues to increase to 3, 4 and 5 workers per day, the curve becomes less steep.

The total product curve is similar to the *production possibilities frontier* (explained in Chapter 2). It separates the attainable output levels from those that are unattainable. All the points that lie above the curve are unattainable. Points that lie below the curve, in the orange area, are attainable. But they are inefficient – they use more labour than is necessary to produce a given output. Only the points *on* the total product curve are technologically efficient.

Figure 10.1 myeconlab

Total Product Curve

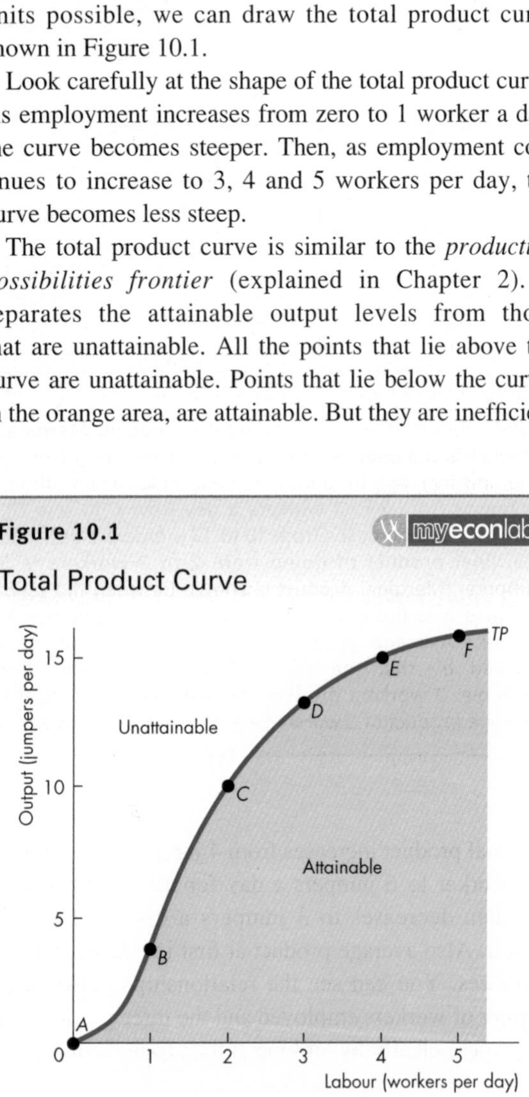

The total product curve (*TP*), is based on the data in Table 10.1. The total product curve shows how the quantity of jumpers changes as the quantity of labour employed changes. For example, using 1 knitting machine, 2 workers can produce 10 jumpers a day (row *C*). Points *A* to *F* on the curve correspond to the rows of Table 10.1. The total product curve separates the attainable output from the unattainable output. Points on the *TP* curve are efficient.

Marginal Product Curve

Figure 10.2 shows Neat Knits' marginal product of labour with 1 machine. Part (a) reproduces the total product curve from Figure 10.1. Part (b) shows the marginal product curve, *MP*.

In Figure 10.2(a), the orange bars illustrate the marginal product of labour. The height of each bar measures marginal product. Marginal product is also measured by the slope of the total product curve. Recall that the slope of a curve is the change in the value of the variable measured on the *y*-axis – output – divided by the change in the variable measured on the *x*-axis – labour – as we move along the curve. A one-unit increase in labour, from 2 to 3 workers, increases output from 10 to 13 jumpers, so the slope from point *C* to point *D* is 3 jumpers per worker, the same as the marginal product that we've just calculated.

By varying the amount of labour in the smallest imaginable units, we can draw the marginal product curve shown in Figure 10.2(b). The *height* of this curve measures the *slope* of the total product curve at a point. The total product curve in part (a) shows that an increase in employment from 2 to 3 workers increases output from 10 to 13 jumpers (an increase of 3). The increase in output of 3 jumpers appears on the vertical axis of part (b) as the marginal product of going from 2 to 3 workers. We plot that marginal product at the mid-point between 2 and 3 workers. Notice that marginal product in Figure 10.2(b) reaches a peak at 1.5 workers and at that point marginal product is 6 jumpers. The peak occurs at 1.5 workers because the total product curve is steepest when employment increases from 1 to 2 workers.

The total product and marginal product curves differ across firms and types of goods. BMW's product curves are different from those of your local supermarket, which in turn are different from those of Neat Knits. But the shapes of the product curves are similar because almost every production process has two features:

- Increasing marginal returns initially
- Diminishing marginal returns eventually

Increasing Marginal Returns

Increasing marginal returns occur when the marginal product of an additional worker exceeds the marginal product of the previous worker. Increasing marginal

Figure 10.2 myeconlab

Total Product and Marginal Product

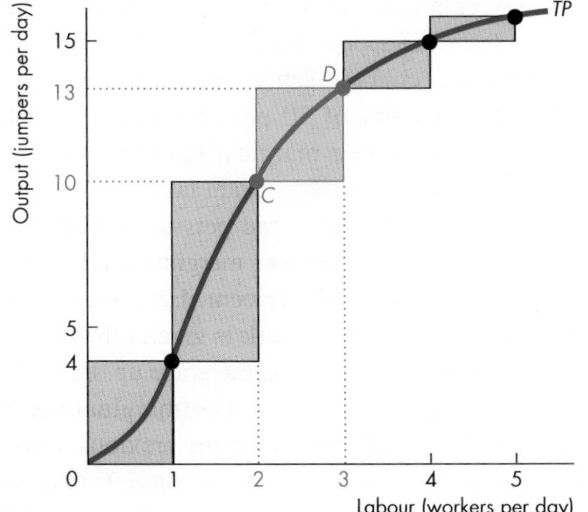

(a) Total product

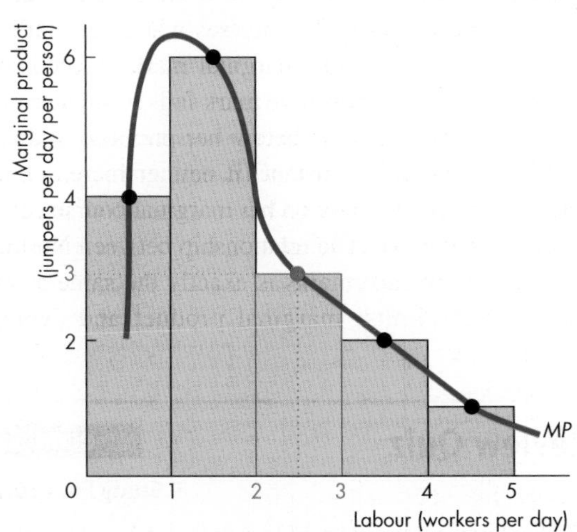

(b) Marginal product

Marginal product is illustrated in both parts of the figure by the orange bars. For example, when labour increases from 2 to 3 workers a day, marginal product is the orange bar whose height is 3 jumpers. (Marginal product is shown midway between the quantities of labour to emphasize that it is the result of *changing* the quantity of labour.)

The steeper the slope of the total product curve (*TP*) in part (a), the larger is marginal product (*MP*) in part (b). Marginal product increases to a maximum (in this example when the second worker is employed) and then declines – diminishing marginal product.

returns arise from increased specialization and division of labour in the production process.

For example, if Neat Knits employs just one worker, that person has to learn all the different aspects of jumper production: running the knitting machines, fixing breakdowns, packaging and mailing jumpers and buying and checking the type and colour of the wool. All of these tasks have to be done by that one person.

If Neat Knit employs a second person, the two workers can specialize in different parts of the production process. As a result, two workers produce more than twice as much as one. The marginal product of the second worker is greater than the marginal product of the first worker. Marginal returns are increasing.

Diminishing Marginal Returns

Most product processes experience increasing marginal returns initially. But all production processes eventually reach a point of *diminishing* marginal returns. **Diminishing marginal returns** occur when the marginal product of an additional worker is less than the marginal product of the previous worker.

Diminishing marginal returns arise from the fact that more and more workers are using the same capital and working in the same space. As more workers are added, there is less and less for the additional workers to do that is productive. For example, if Neat Knits employs a third worker, output increases but not by as much as it did when it added the second worker. In this case, after two workers are employed, all the gains from specialization and the division of labour have been exhausted. By employing a third worker, the factory produces more jumpers, but the equipment is being operated closer to its limits. There are even times when the third worker has nothing to do because the machine is running without the need for further attention. Adding more and more workers continues to increase output but by successively smaller amounts. Marginal returns are diminishing. This phenomenon is such a pervasive one that it is called 'the law of diminishing returns'. The **law of diminishing returns** states that:

> **As a firm uses more of a variable factor of production, with a given quantity of the fixed factor of production, the marginal product of the variable factor eventually diminishes.**

You will return to the law of diminishing returns when we study a firm's costs. But before we do, let's look at average product and the average product curve.

Average Product Curve

Figure 10.3 illustrates Neat Knits' average product of labour, *AP*, and the relationship between the average and marginal product. Points *B* to *F* on the average product curve correspond to those same rows in Table 10.1. Average product increases from 1 to 2 workers (its maximum value is at point *C*) but then decreases as yet more workers are employed. Also average product is largest when average product and marginal product are equal. That is, the marginal product curve cuts the average product curve at the point of maximum average product. For the number of workers at which the marginal product exceeds average product, average product is increasing. For the number of workers at which marginal product is less than average product, average product is decreasing.

The relationship between the average product and marginal product curves is a general feature of the relationship between the average and marginal values of any variable. Let's look at a familiar example.

Figure 10.3 myeconlab

Average Product

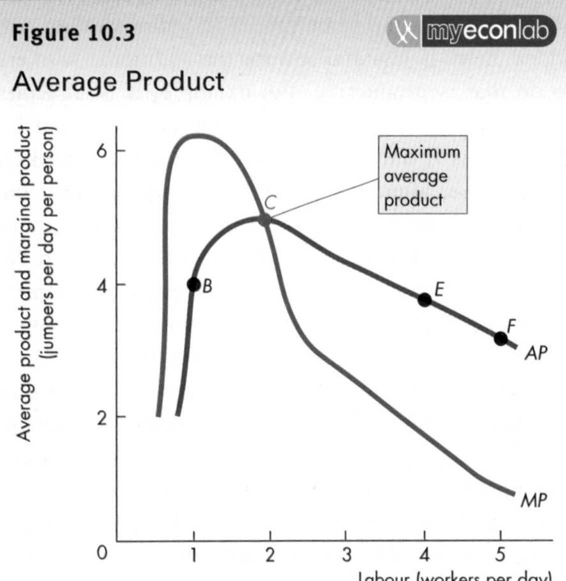

The figure shows the average product of labour and the connection between the average product and marginal product. With 1 worker a day, marginal product exceeds average product, so average product is increasing. With 2 workers a day, marginal product equals average product, so average product is at its maximum. With more than 2 workers a day, marginal product is less than average product, so average product is decreasing.

Marginal Marks and Average Marks

To see the relationship between average product and marginal product, think about the similar relationship between Norma's average mark and her marginal marks over five terms. (Suppose Norma is a part-time student who takes one course each term.) In the first term, Norma gains a mark of 50 per cent in her statistics exam. This mark is her marginal mark. It is also her average mark as it is the first exam taken. Norma takes French in the second term and gets 60 per cent. The French exam mark is now her marginal mark and her average mark rises to 55 per cent. Her average mark rises because her marginal mark is greater than his previous average mark – it pulls her average up. In the third term, Norma takes economics. Her marginal mark is 70 per cent, which is higher than his previous average. Her marginal mark pulls her average up to 60 per cent. In the fourth term, Norma takes accounting and her mark is 60 per cent. Her marginal mark is equal to her previous average, so her average does not change. In the fifth term, Norma takes management and her mark is 50 per cent. Her marginal mark is below her previous average, so it drags her average down to 58 per cent.

Norma's average mark increases when her mark on the last course taken, the marginal mark, exceeds her previous average. Her average mark falls when her mark on the marginal course is below her previous average. Her average mark is constant (it neither increases nor decreases) when her mark on her marginal course equals her previous average. The relationship between Norma's marginal and average marks is exactly the same as that between Neat Knits' marginal product and average product.

Review Quiz

Study Plan 10.2

1. Explain how the marginal product of labour and the average product of labour change as the quantity of labour employed increases (a) initially and (b) eventually.
2. What is the law of diminishing returns? Why does marginal product eventually diminish?
3. Explain the relationship between marginal product and average product. How does average product change when marginal product exceeds average product? How does average product change when average product exceeds marginal product? Why?

Norma cares about Neat Knits' product curves because they influence its costs. Let's look at Neat Knits' costs.

Short-run Cost

To produce more output in the short run, a firm must employ more labour, which means it must increase its costs. We describe the relationship between output and costs by using three concepts:

- Total cost
- Marginal cost
- Average cost

Total Cost

A firm's **total cost** (*TC*) is the cost of *all* the factors of production it uses. We separate total cost into total *fixed* cost and total *variable* cost.

Total fixed cost (*TFC*) is the cost of the firm's fixed factors. For Neat Knits, total fixed cost includes the cost of renting knitting machines and *normal profit*, which is the opportunity cost of Norma's entrepreneurship (see Chapter 9, p. 193). The quantities of a fixed factor don't change as output changes, so total fixed costs is the same at all outputs.

Total variable cost (*TVC*) is the cost of the firm's variable inputs. For Neat Knits, labour is the variable factor, so this component of costs is its wage bill. Total variable cost changes as total product changes.

Total cost is the sum of total fixed costs and total variable cost. That is:

$$TC = TFC + TVC$$

The table in Figure 10.4 shows Neat Knits' total costs. With one knitting machine that Neat Knits rents for £25 a day, *TFC* is £25 a day. To produce jumpers, Neat Knits hires labour, which costs £25 a day. *TVC* is the number of workers multiplied by £25. For example, to produce 13 jumpers a day, Neat Knits hires 3 workers and its *TVC* is £75. *TC* is the sum of *TFC* and *TVC*, so to produce 13 jumpers a day, Neat Knits' total cost, *TC*, is £100. Check the calculation in each row of the table.

Figure 10.4 shows Neat Knits' total cost curves, which graph total cost against output. The green total fixed cost curve (*TFC*) is horizontal because total fixed cost is constant at £25. It does not change when output changes. The purple total variable cost (*TVC*) and the blue total cost (*TC*) curve both slope upward because total variable cost increases as output increases. The arrows highlight total fixed cost as the vertical distance between the *TVC* and *TC* curves.

Figure 10.4 myeconlab

Short-run Total Cost

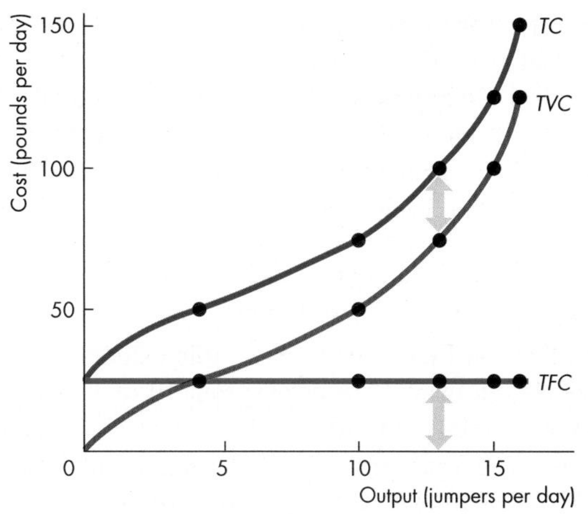

	Labour (workers per day)	Output (jumpers per day)	Total fixed cost (*TFC*)	Total variable cost (*TVC*)	Total cost (*TC*)
			(pounds per day)		
A	0	0	25	0	25
B	1	4	25	25	25
C	2	10	25	50	75
D	3	13	25	75	100
E	4	15	25	100	125
F	5	16	25	125	150

Neat Knits rents a knitting machine for £25 a day. This amount is Neat Knits' total fixed cost. Neat Knits hires workers at a wage rate of £25 a day, and this cost is Neat Knits' total variable cost. For example, if Neat Knits employs 3 workers, its total variable cost is (3 × £25), which equals £75.

Total cost is the sum of total fixed cost and total variable cost. For example, when Neat Knits employs 3 workers, its total cost is £100: total fixed cost of £25 plus total variable cost of £75. The graph shows Neat Knits' total cost curves.

Total fixed cost (*TFC*) is constant – it graphs as a horizontal line – and total variable cost (*TVC*) increases as output increases. Total cost (*TC*) also increases as output increases. The vertical distance between the total cost curve and the total variable cost curve is total fixed cost, as illustrated by the two arrows.

Marginal Cost

In Figure 10.4, total variable cost and total cost increase at a decreasing rate at small outputs and begin to increase at an increasing rate as output increases. To understand these patterns in the changes in total cost, we need to use the concept of *marginal cost*.

A firm's **marginal cost** is the change in total cost resulting from a one-unit increase in output. Marginal cost (MC) is calculated as the change in total cost (ΔTC) divided by the change in output (ΔQ). That is:

$$MC = \frac{\Delta TC}{\Delta Q}$$

The table in Figure 10.5 shows this calculation. For example, an increase in output from 10 to 13 jumpers increases total cost from £75 to £100. The change in output is 3 jumpers, and the change in total cost is £25. The marginal cost of one of those 3 jumpers is (£25 ÷ 3), which equals £8.33.

Figure 10.5 graphs the marginal cost as the red marginal cost curve, MC. This curve is U-shaped because when Neat Knits hires a second worker, marginal cost decreases, but when it hires a third, a fourth and a fifth worker, marginal cost successively increases.

Marginal cost decreases at low outputs because of economies from greater specialization. It eventually increases because of *the law of diminishing returns*. The law of diminishing returns means that each additional worker produces a successively smaller addition to output. So to get an additional unit of output, ever more workers are required. Because more workers are required to produce one additional unit of output, the cost of the additional output – marginal cost – must eventually increase.

Marginal cost tells us how total cost changes as output changes. The final cost concept tells us what it costs, on the average, to produce a unit of output. Let's now look at Neat Knits' average costs.

Average Cost

Average cost is cost per unit of output. There are three average costs:

1 Average fixed cost
2 Average variable cost
3 Average total cost

Average fixed cost (AFC) is total fixed cost per unit of output. **Average variable cost** (AVC) is total variable cost per unit of output. **Average total cost** (ATC) is total cost per unit of output. The average cost concepts are calculated from the total cost concepts as follows:

$$TC = TFC + TVC$$

Divide each total cost term by the quantity produced, Q, to give:

$$\frac{TC}{Q} = \frac{TFC}{Q} + \frac{TVC}{Q}$$

or:

$$ATC = AFC + AVC$$

The table in Figure 10.5 shows the calculation of average total costs. For example, in row C when output is 10 jumpers, average fixed cost is (£25 ÷ 10), which equals £2.50, average variable cost is (£50 ÷ 10), which equals £5.00, and average total cost is (£75 ÷ 10), which equals £7.50. Note average total cost is equal to average fixed cost (£2.50) plus average variable cost (£5.00).

Figure 10.5 shows the average cost curves. The green average fixed cost curve (AFC) slopes downward. As output increases, the same constant fixed cost is spread over a larger output. The blue average total cost curve (ATC) and the purple average variable cost curve (AVC) are U-shaped. The vertical distance between the average total cost and average variable cost curves is equal to average fixed cost – as indicated by the arrows. That distance between the ATC and AVC curves shrinks as output increases because average fixed cost declines with increasing output.

The red marginal cost curve (MC) intersects the average variable cost curve and the average total cost curve at their minimum point. That is, when marginal cost is less than average cost, average cost is decreasing, and when marginal cost exceeds average cost, average cost is increasing. This relationship holds for both the ATC and the AVC curves and is another example of the relationship you saw in Figure 10.3 between average product and marginal product and in Norma's exam marks.

Why the Average Total Cost Curve Is U-shaped

Average total cost, ATC, is the sum of average fixed cost, AFC, and average variable cost, AVC. So the shape of the ATC curve combines the shapes of the AFC and AVC curves. The U-shape of the average total

Figure 10.5

Marginal Cost and Average Costs

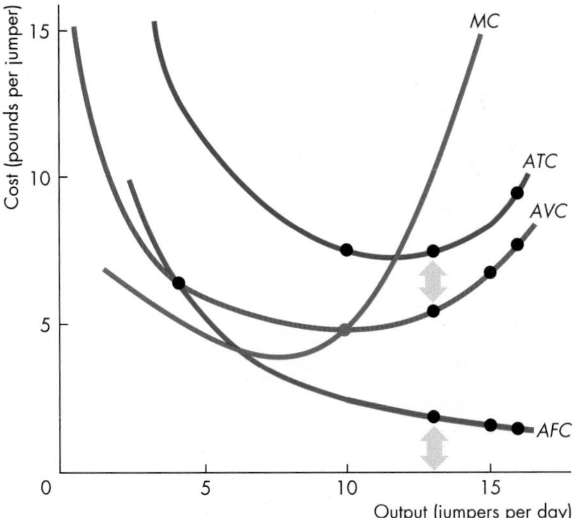

Marginal cost is calculated as the change in total cost divided by the change in output. When output increases from 4 to 10, an increase of 6, total cost increases by £25 and marginal cost is £25 ÷ 6, which equals £4.17. Each average cost concept is calculated by dividing the related total cost by output. When 10 jumpers are produced, *AFC* is £2.50 (£25 ÷ 10), *AVC* is £5 (£50 ÷ 10), and *ATC* is £7.50 (£75 ÷ 10).

The graph shows the marginal cost curve and the average cost curves. The marginal cost curve (*MC*) is U-shaped and intersects the average variable cost curve and the average total cost curve at their minimum points. Average fixed cost (*AFC*) decreases as output increases. The average total cost curve (*ATC*) and average variable cost curve (*AVC*) are U-shaped. The vertical distance between these two curves is equal to average fixed cost, as illustrated by the two arrows.

Labour (workers per day)	Output (jumpers per day)	Total fixed cost (*TFC*)	Total variable cost (*TVC*)	Total cost (*TC*)	Marginal cost (*MC*)	Average fixed cost (*AFC*)	Average variable cost (*AVC*)	Average total cost (*ATC*)
		(pounds per day)			(pounds per jumper)			
0	0	25		25				
					6.25			
1	4	25	25	50		6.25	6.25	12.50
					4.17			
2	10	25	50	75		2.50	5.00	7.50
					8.33			
3	13	25	75	100		1.92	5.77	7.69
					12.50			
4	15	25	100	125		1.67	6.00	8.33
					25.00			
5	16	25	125	150		1.56	7.81	9.38

cost curve arises from the influence of two opposing forces:

1 Spreading fixed cost over a larger output
2 Eventually diminishing returns

When output increases, the firm spreads its total fixed costs over a larger output and its average fixed cost decreases – its average fixed cost curve slopes downward.

Diminishing returns means that as output increases, ever-larger amounts of labour are needed to produce an additional unit of output. So average variable cost eventually increases and the firm's AVC curve eventually slopes upward.

The shape of the average total cost curve combines these two effects. Initially, as output increases, both average fixed cost and average variable cost decrease, so average total cost decreases and the *ATC* curve slopes downward. But as output increases further and diminishing returns set in, average variable cost begins to increase. Eventually, average variable cost increases more quickly than average fixed cost decreases, so average total cost increases and the *ATC* curve slopes upward.

Cost Curves and Product Curves

The technology that a firm uses determines its costs. Figure 10.6 shows the links between the firm's technology constraint (its product curves) and its cost curves. The upper part of the figure shows the average product curve and the marginal product curve – like those in Figure 10.3. The lower part of the figure shows the average variable cost curve and the marginal cost curve – like those in Figure 10.5.

The figure highlights the links between technology and costs. As labour increases initially, marginal product and average product rise and marginal cost and average variable cost fall. Then, at the point of maximum marginal product, marginal cost is a minimum. As labour increases further, marginal product diminishes and marginal cost increases. But average product continues to rise and average variable cost continues to fall. Then at the point of maximum average product, average variable cost is a minimum. As labour increases further, average product diminishes and average variable cost increases.

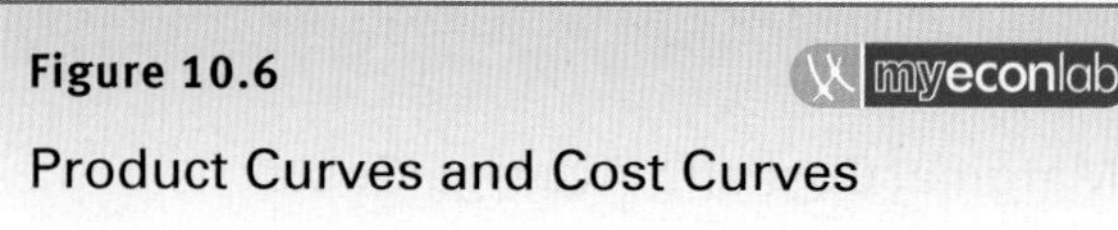

Figure 10.6

Product Curves and Cost Curves

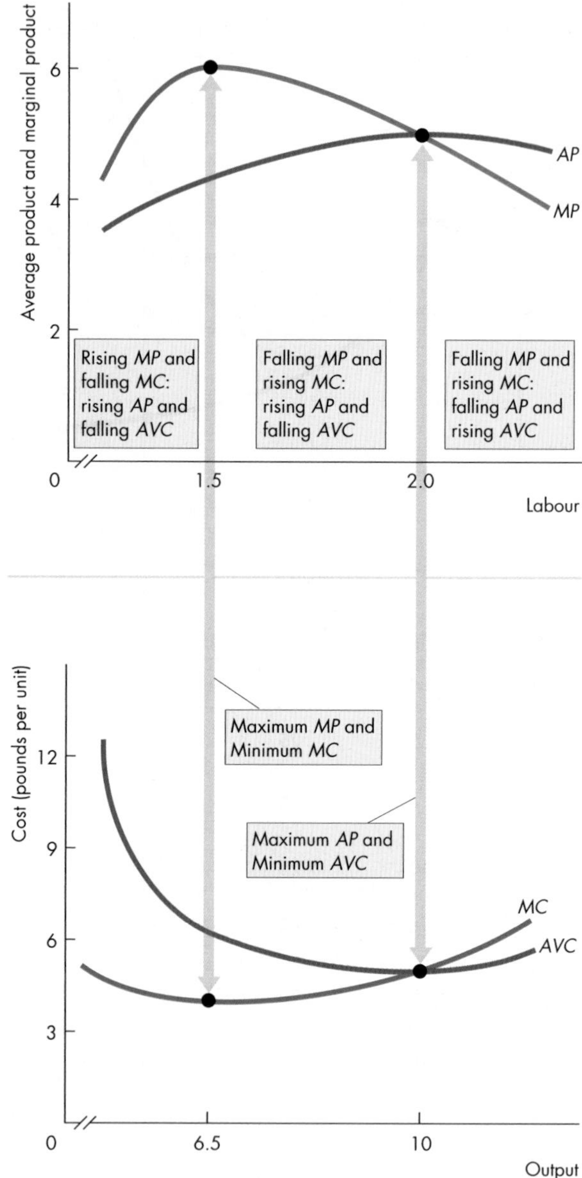

A firm's marginal product curve is linked to its marginal cost curve. If as the firm hires more labour its marginal product rises, its marginal cost falls. If marginal product is at a maximum, marginal cost is at a minimum. If, as the firm hires more labour, its marginal product diminishes, its marginal cost rises.

A firm's average product curve is linked to its average variable cost curve. If as the firm hires more labour its average product rises, its average variable cost falls. If its average product is a maximum, average variable cost is a minimum. If as the firm hires more labour its average product diminishes, its average variable cost rises.

Shifts in the Cost Curves

The position of a firm's short-run cost curves depends on two factors:

- Technology
- Prices of factors of production

Technology

A technological change that increases productivity shifts the total product curve upward. It also shifts the marginal product curve and the average product curve upward. With better technology, the same factors of production can produce more output. So technological change lowers cost and shifts the cost curves downward.

For example, advances in robotic production techniques have increased productivity in the car industry. As a result, the product curves of BMW, Renault and Volvo have shifted upward and their cost curves have shifted downward. But the relationships between their product curves and cost curves have not changed. The curves are still linked in the way shown in Figure 10.6.

Often, a technological advance results in a firm using more capital (a fixed factor) and less labour (a variable factor). For example, today the telephone companies use computers to provide directory assistance in place of the

Table 10.2

A Compact Glossary of Costs

Term	Symbol	Definition	Equation
Fixed cost		Cost that is independent of the output level; cost of a fixed factor	
Variable cost		Cost that varies with the output level; cost of a variable factor	
Total fixed cost	*TFC*	Cost of the fixed factors (equals their number times their unit price)	
Total variable cost	*TVC*	Cost of the variable factors (equals their number times their unit price)	
Total cost	*TC*	Cost of all factors of production	$TC = TFC + TVC$
Total product (output)	*TP*	Total quantity produced (*Q*)	
Marginal cost	*MC*	Change in total cost resulting from a one-unit increase in total product	$MC = \Delta TC \div \Delta Q$
Average fixed cost	*AFC*	Total fixed cost per unit of output	$AFC = TFC \div Q$
Average variable cost	*AVC*	Total variable cost per unit of output	$AVC = TVC \div Q$
Average total cost	*ATC*	Total cost per unit of output	$ATC = AFC + AVC$

human operators they used in the 1980s. When such a technological change occurs, total cost decreases, but fixed costs increase and variable costs decrease. This change in the mix of fixed cost and variable cost means that at low output levels, average total cost might increase, while at high output levels, average total cost decreases.

Prices of Factors of Production

An increase in the price of a factor of production increases costs and shifts the cost curves. But the way the curves shift depends on which factor price changes. An increase in rent or some other component of *fixed* cost shifts the fixed cost curves (*TFC* and *AFC*) upward and the total cost curve (*TC*) upward, but leaves the variable cost curves (*AVC* and *TVC*) and the marginal cost curve (*MC*) unchanged. An increase in the wage rate or some other component of *variable* cost shifts the variable curves (*TVC* and *AVC*) upward, the total cost curve (*TC*) and the marginal cost curve (*MC*) upward, but leaves the fixed cost curves (*AFC* and *TFC*) unchanged. So for example, if lorry drivers' wage rate increases, the variable cost and marginal cost of transportation services increase. If the interest expense paid by a trucking company increases, the fixed cost of transportation services increases.

You've now completed your study of short-run costs. All the concepts that you've met are summarized in a compact glossary in Table 10.2.

Review Quiz

Study Plan 10.3

1. What relationships do a firm's short-run cost curves show?
2. How does marginal cost change as output increases (a) initially, and (b) eventually?
3. What does the law of diminishing returns imply for the shape of the marginal cost curve?
4. What is the shape of the average fixed cost curve and why?
5. What are the shapes of the average variable cost curve and average total cost curve and why?

Long-run Cost

In the short run, a firm can vary the quantity of labour but the quantity of capital is fixed. So the firm has variable costs of labour and fixed costs of capital. In the long run, a firm can vary both the quantity of labour and the quantity of capital. So in the long run, all the firm's costs are variable. We are now going to study the firm's costs in the long run, when *all* costs are variable costs and when the quantity of labour and capital vary.

The behaviour of long-run costs depends on the firm's production function. The *production function* is the relationship between the maximum output attainable and the quantities of both labour and capital.

Table 10.3 

The Production Function

Labour (workers per day)	Output (jumpers per day)			
	Plant 1	Plant 2	Plant 3	Plant 4
1	4	10	13	15
2	10	15	18	21
3	13	18	22	24
4	15	20	24	26
5	16	21	25	27
Knitting machines (number)	1	2	3	4

The table shows the total product data for four quantities of capital – four plant sizes. The bigger the plant size, the larger is the total product for any given amount of labour employed. But for a given plant size, the marginal product of labour diminishes. For a given quantity of labour, the marginal product of capital diminishes.

The Production Function

Table 10.3 shows Neat Knits' production function. The table lists the total product for four different quantities of capital. The quantity of capital is defined as the plant size. Plant 1 represents a factory with 1 knitting machine – the case we have just studied. The other three plants have 2, 3 and 4 knitting machines. If Neat Knits doubles its plant size from 1 to 2 knitting machines, the various amounts of labour can produce the outputs shown in the column under Plant 2 of the table. The next two columns show the outputs of yet larger plants. Each column in the table could be graphed as a total product curve for each plant size.

Diminishing Returns

Diminishing returns occur in each of the four plants as the quantity of labour increases. You can check that fact by calculating the marginal product of labour in plants with 2, 3 and 4 knitting machines. At each plant size, as the quantity of labour increases, the marginal product of labour (eventually) decreases.

Diminishing Marginal Product of Capital

Diminishing returns also occur as the quantity of capital increases. You can check that fact by calculating the marginal product of capital at a given quantity of labour. The *marginal product of capital* is the change in total product divided by the change in capital employed when the amount of labour employed is constant. It is the change in output resulting from a one-unit increase in the quantity of capital employed.

For example, if Neat Knits employs 3 workers and increases its capital from 1 machine to 2 machines, output increases from 13 to 18 jumpers a day. The marginal product of capital is 5 jumpers a day. If with 3 workers, Neat Knits increases its capital from 2 machines to 3 machines, output increases from 18 to 22 jumpers a day. The marginal product of the third machine is 4 jumpers a day, down from 5 jumpers a day for the second machine.

We can now see what the production function implies for long-run costs.

Short-run Cost and Long-run Cost

Continue to assume that labour costs £25 per worker per day and capital costs £25 per machine per day. Using these factor prices and the data in Table 10.3, we can calculate and graph the average total cost curves for factories with 1, 2, 3 and 4 knitting machines. We've already studied the costs of a factory with 1 knitting machine in Figures 10.5 and 10.6. In Figure 10.7, the average total cost curve for that case is ATC_1. Figure 10.7 also shows the average total cost curve for a factory with 2 machines, ATC_2, with 3 machines, ATC_3, and with 4 machines, ATC_4.

Figure 10.7

Short-run Costs of Four Different Plants

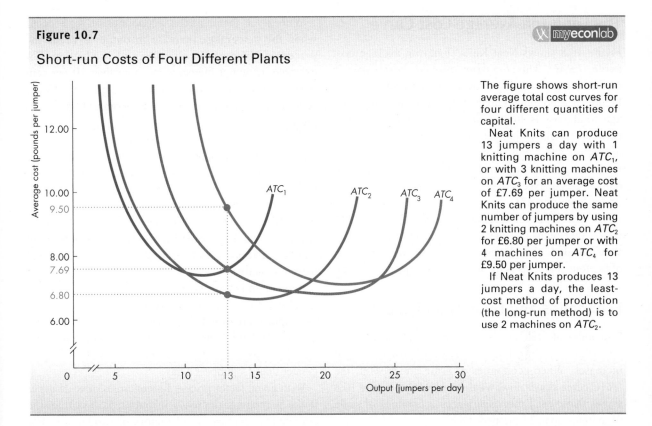

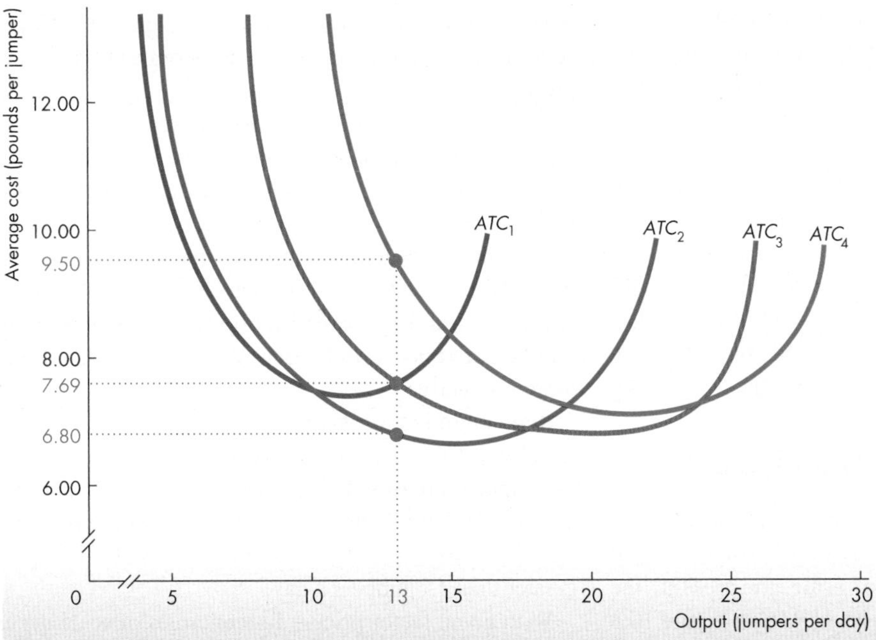

The figure shows short-run average total cost curves for four different quantities of capital.

Neat Knits can produce 13 jumpers a day with 1 knitting machine on ATC_1, or with 3 knitting machines on ATC_3 for an average cost of £7.69 per jumper. Neat Knits can produce the same number of jumpers by using 2 knitting machines on ATC_2 for £6.80 per jumper or with 4 machines on ATC_4 for £9.50 per jumper.

If Neat Knits produces 13 jumpers a day, the least-cost method of production (the long-run method) is to use 2 machines on ATC_2.

You can see, in Figure 10.7, that plant size has a big effect on the firm's average total cost. Two things stand out.

1 Each short-run *ATC* curve is U-shaped.

2 For each short-run *ATC* curve, the larger the plant, the greater is the output at which average total cost is a minimum.

Each short-run average total cost curve is U-shaped because, as the quantity of labour increases, its marginal product at first increases and then diminishes. This pattern in the marginal product of labour, which we examined in some detail for the plant with 1 knitting machine on pp. 216–217, occurs at all plant sizes.

The minimum average total cost for a larger plant occurs at a greater output than it does for a smaller plant because the larger plant has a higher fixed cost and therefore, for any given output level, a higher average fixed cost.

Which short-run average cost curves Neat Knits operates on depends on its plant size. But in the long run, Neat Knits chooses its plant size. Its choice of plant size depends on the output that it plans to produce. The reason is that the average total cost of producing a given output depends on the plant size.

To see why, suppose that Neat Knits plans to produce 13 jumpers a day. With 1 machine, the average total cost curve is ATC_1 (in Figure 10.7) and the average total cost of 13 jumpers a day is £7.69 per jumper. With 2 machines, on ATC_2, average total cost is £6.80 per jumper. With 3 machines on ATC_3, average total cost is £7.69 per jumper, the same as with 1 machine. Finally, with 4 machines, on ATC_4, average total cost is £9.50 per jumper.

The economically efficient plant size for producing a given output is the one that has the lowest average total cost. For Neat Knits, the economically efficient plant to use to produce 13 jumpers a day is the one with 2 machines. In the long run, Neat Knits chooses the plant size that minimizes average total cost. When a firm is producing a given output at the least possible cost, it is operating on its *long-run average cost curve*.

The **long-run average cost curve** is the relationship between the lowest attainable average total cost and output when both the plant size and labour are varied. The long-run average cost curve is a planning curve. It tells the firm the plant size and the quantity of labour to use at each output to minimize cost. Once the plant size is chosen, the firm operates on the short-run cost curves that apply to that plant size.

The Long-run Average Cost Curve

Figure 10.8 shows Neat Knits' long-run average cost curve, *LRAC*. This *long-run average cost curve* is derived from the short-run average total cost curves in Figure 10.7. For output up to 10 jumpers a day, the average total cost is lowest on ATC_1. For output rates between 10 and 18 jumpers a day, average total cost is lowest on ATC_2. For output rates between 18 and 24 jumpers a day, average total cost is lowest on ATC_3. For output rates in excess of 24 jumpers a day, average total cost is lowest on ATC_4.

In Figure 10.8, the segment of each *ATC* curve for which that plant has the lowest average total cost is shown as dark blue. The scallop-shaped curve made up of the four segments is the long-run average cost curve.

Economies and Diseconomies of Scale

Economies of scale are features of a firm's technology that lead to falling long-run average cost as output increases. When economies of scale are present, the *LRAC* curve slopes downward. The *LRAC* in Figure 10.8 shows that Neat Knits experiences economies of scale for outputs up to 15 jumpers a day.

With given factor prices, economies of scale occur when the percentage increase in output exceeds the percentage increase in all factors of production. For example, if output increases by more than 10 per cent when a firm increases its labour and capital by 10 per cent, its average total cost falls. Economies of scale are present.

The main source of economies of scale are the specialization of both labour and capital. For example, if BMW produces only 100 cars a week, each worker must be capable of performing many different tasks and the capital must be general-purpose machines and tools. But if BMW produces 10,000 cars a week, each worker specialized and becomes highly proficient in a small number of tasks. Capital can also be specialized and more productive.

Diseconomies of scale are features of a firm's technology that lead to rising long-run average costs as output increases. When diseconomies of scale are present, the *LRAC* curve slopes upward. In Figure 10.8, Neat Knits experiences diseconomies of scale at outputs greater than 15 jumpers a day.

With given factor prices, diseconomies of scale occur if the percentage increase in output is less than the percentage increase in all factors of production. For

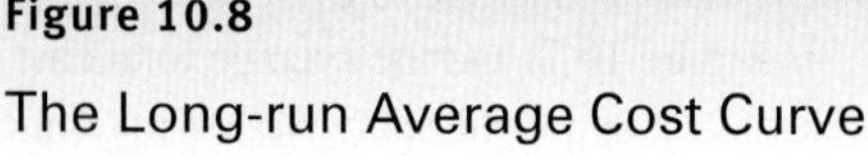
Figure 10.8
The Long-run Average Cost Curve

myeconlab

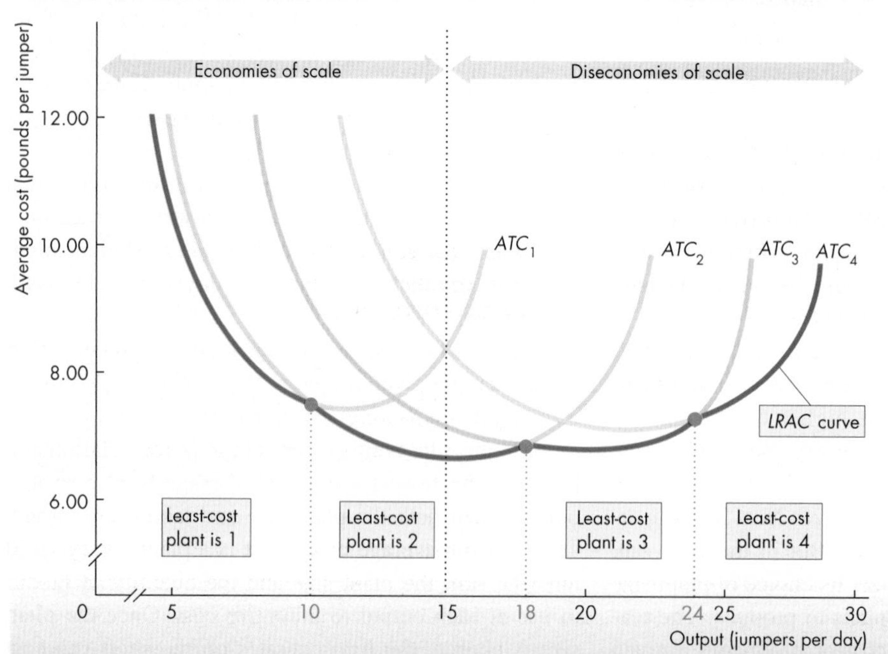

In the long run, Neat Knits can vary both its capital and labour. The long-run average cost curve traces the lowest attainable average total cost of production.

Neat Knits produces on its long-run average cost curve if it uses 1 machine to produce up to 10 jumpers a day, 2 machines to produce between 10 and 18 a day, 3 machines to produce between 18 and 24 a day, and 4 machines to produce more than 24 a day. Within these ranges, Neat Knits varies its output by varying its labour.

example, if output increases by less than 10 per cent when a firm increases all its labour and capital by 10 per cent, its average total cost rises. Diseconomies of scale are present.

The main source of diseconomies of scale is the difficulty of managing a very large enterprise. The larger the firm, the greater is the challenge of organizing it and the greater is the cost of communicating both up and down the management hierarchy and among managers. Eventually, management complexity brings rising average cost.

Diseconomies of scale occur in all production processes but perhaps only at a very large output rate.

Constant returns to scale are features of a firm's technology that lead to constant long-run average costs as output increases. When constant returns to scale are present, the *LRAC* curve is horizontal.

Constant returns to scale occur if the percentage increase in output equals the percentage increase in all factors of production. For example, if output increases by exactly 10 per cent when a firm increases its labour and capital by 10 per cent, then constant returns to scale are present. For example, BMW can double its output of its 5-series by doubling its production facility. BMW can build an identical production line and hire an identical number of workers. With two identical production facilities, BMW produces exactly twice as many cars.

Minimum Efficient Scale

A firm experiences economies of scale up to some output level. Beyond that level, it moves into constant returns to scale or diseconomies of scale. A firm's **minimum efficient scale** is the smallest quantity of output at which long-run average cost reaches its lowest level.

The minimum efficient scale plays a role in determining market structure, as you will learn in the next three chapters. The minimum efficient scale also helps to answer some questions about real businesses.

Economies of Scale at Neat Knits

The technology that Neat Knits used, shown in Table 10.3, illustrates economies of scale and diseconomies of scale. If Neat Knits decides to double its factors of production from 1 worker and 1 machine to 2 workers and 2 machines, a 100 per cent increase, output increases by more than 100 per cent from 4 jumpers to 15 jumpers a day. Neat Knits experiences economies of scale and the long-run average cost decreases. But if Neat Knits increases its factor of production to 3 machines and 3 workers, a 50 per cent increase, output increases by less than 50 per cent, from 15 to 22 jumpers a day. Now Neat Knits experiences diseconomies of scale, and its long-run average cost increases. Its minimum efficient scale is at 15 jumpers a day.

Producing Cars and Generating Electric Power

Why do car makers have expensive equipment lying around that isn't fully used? You can now answer this question. A car maker uses the plant that minimizes the average total cost of producing the output that it can sell. But it operates below the minimum efficient scale. Its short-run average total cost curve looks like ATC_1 in Figure 10.8. If it could sell more cars, it would produce more cars and its average total cost would fall.

Why do many electricity producers such as Powergen have too little production equipment to meet demand on the coldest and hottest days and so have to buy power from other producers? You can now see why this happens and why an electricity producer doesn't build a larger plant with more production capacity. A power producer uses the plant size that minimizes the average total cost of producing the output that it can sell on a normal day. But it produces above the minimum efficient scale and experiences diseconomies of scale. Its short-run average total cost curve looks like ATC_3 in Figure 10.8. With a larger plant size, its average total costs of producing its normal output would be higher.

Review Quiz

Study Plan 10.4

1 What does a firm's production function show and how is it related to a total product curve?
2 Does the law of diminishing returns apply to capital as well as labour? Explain why or why not.
3 What does a firm's long-run average cost curve show? How is it related to the firm's short-run average cost curve?
4 What are economies and diseconomies of scale? How do they arise? What do they imply for the shape of the long-run average cost curve?
5 What is a firm's minimum efficient scale?

You have now studied how a firm's costs vary as it changes its output. The appendix presents an alternative analysis of costs. The *Business Case Study* applies what you have learned about a firm's cost curves. It looks at the scale and costs of global steel producers.

Business Case Study
Mergers and Costs

Economies of scale in global steel production

World Steel Market Conditions

The global demand for steel has been increasing with the rapid expansion of the Chinese and Indian economies. World steel prices rose from $US360 per tonne in November, 2002 to $US651 in November, 2004, fell to $US559 in November 2005, and then rose again to $US716 by November 2006.

European Mergers

Global steel production runs at about 1,000 million tonnes per year. The table shows the output of the top ten steel producers in 2005. The UK producer, Corus, was formed in 1999 when British Steel and the Dutch group, Hoogovens, merged. Since then, other smaller European steel companies have merged. The biggest merger came in early 2006, when Mittal Steel, the Dutch based giant owned by the Indian, Lakshri Mittal, bought Arcelor, another European steel giant. The merged firm, Arcelor Mittal is now the world's biggest steel producer, accounting for 10 per cent of world steel production, with total sales of 55 billion euros and employing 320,000 employees.

International Mergers

More recently, European steel companies have merged across global boundaries. At the end of 2006, Corus accepted a takeover bid from Tata, India's largest conglomerate company, boosting Tata from 56th to fifth in the world steel-making rankings. Tata gains access to efficient new technology and lowers its administration, marketing and production costs. Corus gains access to India's fast-growing market and to low-cost labour and materials.

Global Steel Production in 2005

Production rank	Company	Production (millions of tonnes)
1	Mittal Steel (Netherlands)	50
2	Arcelor (Luxembourg)	47
3	Nippon Steel (Japan)	33
4	Posco (South Korea)	31
5	JFE Steel (Japan)	30
6	Shanghai Baosteel (China)	23
7	US Steel (United States)	19
8	Nucor (United States)	18
9	Corus (United Kingdom)	18
10	Riva (Italy)	18

Source of data: http://news.bbc.co.uk/2/hi/business/6069492.stm.

Economic Analysis

- A steel producer can increase production with fixed capital by increasing the quantity of labour employed along its short-run product curve. But short-run average total costs will rise because of diminishing returns.
- In the long-run, a steel producer can increase production by increasing the quantity of both labour and capital.
- The European firm, Mittal, chose to increase production by increasing its capital and labour. It did so by taking over its rival, Arcelor. Both firms had similar technology and operated on a similar short-run average total cost curve.
- Figure 1 shows the short-run average cost curve, ATC_0, on which both Mittal and Arcelor operated before the takeover. After the takeover, the merged steel producer, Mittal Arcelor can operate on average cost curve, ATC_1.
- On ATC_1 in Figure 1, Mittal Arcelor's combined output of 97 million tonnes can be produced at lower average total cost than in separate firms by reaping economies of scale.
- Tata also hopes to reap economies of scale from the Corus takeover by cutting average costs of factors of production, marketing and staff in the larger firm.
- While Tata is a small scale steel producer, it produces many other goods and has low-cost access to the wider Indian market. Corus will gain cheap access to the growing Indian steel market which it cannot have as a European producer.
- Most steel producers are producing below minimum efficient scale and are looking for international mergers to exploit economies of scale in the expanding global market.

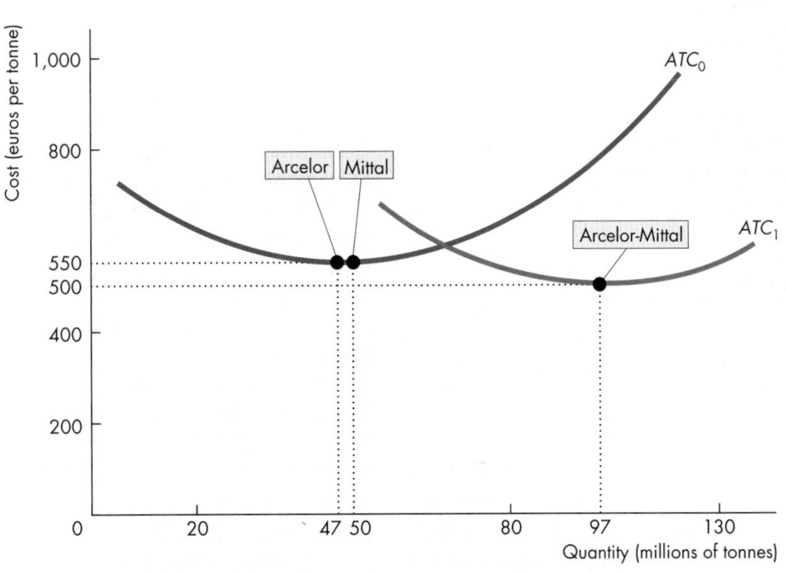

Figure 1 Average total cost of two firms and one merged firm

Summary

Key Points

Time Frames for Decisions (p. 214)

- In the short run, the quantity of at least one actor of production is fixed and the quantities of the other factors can be varied.
- In the long run, the quantities of all factors of production can be varied.

Short-run Technology Constraint (pp. 215–218)

- A total product curve shows the quantity of output that a firm can produce using a given quantity of capital and different quantities of labour.
- Initially, the marginal product of labour increases as the quantity of labour increases, but eventually, marginal product diminishes – the law of diminishing marginal returns.
- Average product increases initially and eventually diminishes.

Short-run Cost (pp. 219–223)

- As output increases, total fixed cost is constant, and total variable cost and total cost increase.
- As output increases, average variable cost, average total cost and marginal cost decrease at small outputs and increase at large outputs. These costs curves are U-shaped.

Long-run Cost (pp. 224–227)

- Long-run cost is the cost of production when all factors of production – labour as well as plant and equipment – have been adjusted to their economically efficient levels.
- There is a set of short-run cost curves for each different plant size. There is one least-cost plant for each output. The larger the output, the larger is the plant size that will minimize average total cost.
- The long-run average cost curve traces the relationship between the lowest attainable average total cost and output when both its capital and labour can be varied.
- With economies of scale, the long-run average cost curve slopes downward. With diseconomies of scale, the long-run average cost curve slopes upward.

Key Figures and Table

Key Terms

Average fixed cost, 220
Average product, 215
Average total cost, 220
Average variable cost, 220
Constant returns to scale, 227
Diminishing marginal returns, 217
Diseconomies of scale, 226
Economies of scale, 226
Law of diminishing returns, 217
Long run, 214
Long-run average cost curve, 225
Marginal cost, 220
Marginal product, 215
Minimum efficient scale, 227
Short run, 214
Sunk cost, 214
Total cost, 219
Total fixed cost, 219
Total product, 215
Total variable cost, 219

Problems

Tests, Study Plan and Solutions* 

1 Sue's Snowboards has the following total product schedule:

Labour (workers per week)	Output (snowboards per week)
1	30
2	70
3	120
4	160
5	190
6	210
7	220

a Draw the total product curve.

b Calculate the average product of labour and draw the average product curve.

c Calculate the marginal product of labour and draw the marginal product curve.

d Over what output range does the firm enjoy the benefits of increased specialization and division of labour?

e Over what output range does the firm experience diminishing marginal product of labour?

f Over what range of output does this firm experience an increasing average product of labour but a diminishing marginal product of labour?

g Explain how it is possible for a firm to experience simultaneously an increasing average product of labour but a diminishing marginal product of labour.

2 Sue's Snowboards has the total product schedule shown in problem 1. Each worker is paid €500 a week and the firm's total fixed cost is €1,000 a week.

a Calculate total cost, total variable cost, and total fixed cost for each output and draw the short-run total cost curves.

b Calculate average total cost, average fixed cost, average variable cost, and marginal cost at each output and draw the short-run average and marginal cost curves.

c Draw the *AP*, *MP*, *AVC*, and *MC* curves like those in Figure 10.6.

3 The owner of the building that Sue's Snowboards rents increases the rent by €200 a week. Everything else remains as described in problems 1 and 2. Explain what changes occur in Sue's Snowboards' short-run average cost curve and marginal cost curve.

4 The labour union that represents the workers at Sue's Snowboards negotiates a pay increase of €100 a week for each worker. Everything else remains as described in problems 1 and 2. Explain how Sue's Snowboards' short-run average cost curve and marginal cost curve change.

5 Bill's Bakery has a fire and Bill loses some of his cost data. The bits of paper that he recovers after the fire provide the data in the following table (all the cost numbers are euros).

TP	*AFC*	*AVC*	*ATC*	*MC*
10	120	100	220	
				80
20	*A*	*B*	150	
				90
30	40	90	130	
				130
40	30	*C*	*D*	
				E
50	24	108	132	

Bill asks you to come to his rescue and provide the missing data in the five spaces identified as *A*, *B*, *C*, *D* and *E*.

6 Sue's Snowboards, described in problems 1 and 2, buys a second plant and the total product of each quantity of labour increases by 50 per cent. The total fixed cost of operating each plant is €1,000 a week. Each worker is paid €500 a week.

a Set out the average total cost curve when Sue's Snowboards operates two plants.

b Draw the long-run average cost curve.

c Over what output ranges is it efficient to operate one plant and two plants?

7 The table shows the production function of Bonnie's Balloon Rides.

Labour (workers per day)	Output (rides per day)			
	Plant 1	Plant 2	Plant 3	Plant 4
1	4	10	13	15
2	10	15	18	21
3	13	18	22	24
4	15	20	24	26
5	16	21	25	27
Balloons (number)	1	2	3	4

* Solutions to odd-numbered problems are provided.

Bonnie pays €500 a day for each balloon she rents and €25 a day for each balloon operator she hires.

a Find and graph the average total cost curve for each plant size.

b Draw Bonnie's long-run average cost curve.

c What is Bonnie's minimum efficient scale?

d Explain how Bonnie uses her long-run average cost curve to decide how many balloons to rent.

8 A firm is producing at minimum average total cost with its current plant. Explain, using the concepts of economies of scale and diseconomies of scale, the circumstances in which the firm:

a Can lower its average total cost by increasing its plant size.

b Can lower its average total cost by decreasing its plant size.

c Cannot lower its average total cost.

Sketch the firm's short-run average total cost curve and long-run average cost curve for each of the three cases.

9 The cost of producing electricity using hydro power is about one-third of the cost of using coal, oil or nuclear power plants and is less than one quarter the cost of using gas turbine plants. Most of the cost differences comes from differences in fuel costs. But part of the cost difference comes from differences in plant costs. It costs less to build a hydroelectric plant than a coal, oil or nuclear plant. Gas turbine plants cost the least to build but are the most expensive to operate.

(Based on *Projected Costs of Generating Electricity*, International Energy Agency, 2005)

a Use the above information to sketch the average cost curves for electricity production (*AFC*, *AVC* and *ATC*) using three technologies:

(i) Hydro

(ii) Coal, oil or nuclear

(iii) Gas turbine

b Use the above information to sketch the marginal cost curves for electricity production using three technologies:

(i) Hydro

(ii) Coal, oil or nuclear

(iii) Gas turbine

c Given the cost differences among the different methods of generating electricity, why do we use more than one method? If we could use one method, which would it be?

Critical Thinking

1 Read the *Business Case Study* on pp. 228–229 and the original articles about the global steel market.

a Why do you think the world price of steel rose during 2003 and 2004, fell during 2005, and then rose again during 2006?

b Of the factors that you identify in your answer to part (a), which brought a movement along the steel producers short-run cost curves and which involved shifts in the cost curves?

c How does a merger influence a firm's cost curves? Why can a merged firm often produce the same output as the combined output of the pre-merged firms but at a lower average total cost?

d What factors would lead to a merged firm having higher costs than the pre-merged firms?

e Which do you think cuts costs most and why: the merger of two similar-size firms such as Mittal and Arcelor, or the merger of a very large and much smaller firm?

2 A telecommunication company is considering replacing human telephone operators with computers. Create your own example and graph:

a The average cost curves and the marginal cost curve when the firm uses human operators.

b The average cost curves and the marginal cost curve when the firm uses computers.

Web Activities

Links to Websites

1 Read about teleworking and then:

a What is the short-run impact of introducing teleworking on company costs?

b Why does teleworking involve investing in new technology?

c What is the long-run impact of introducing teleworking on company costs?

d What do you think are the advantages and disadvantages for employees of teleworking?

e Why did companies think that employees would take more time off when teleworking?

f Why might employees tend to work harder as a result of teleworking from home as opposed to working from an office or depot?

Chapter 10 Appendix

Producing at Least Cost

After studying this appendix, you will be able to:

- Make an isoquant map and explain the law of diminishing marginal rate of substitution
- Explain an isocost line and how a change in factor price shifts it
- Calculate the least-cost technique of production

Isoquants and Factor Substitution

A firm's long-run production function describes all the technically feasible combinations of labour and capital that can produce given output levels. Whatever goods it produces, a firm can choose between labour-intensive or capital-intensive production techniques. To move from one technique to another, a firm must change the combination of labour and capital it uses – a change called factor substitution.

In this appendix, you are going to use a new model to find the best combination of factors.

Figure A10.1 shows Neat Knits' production function. The figure shows that in the long run, Neat Knits can use three different combinations of labour and capital to produce 15 jumpers a day, and two different combinations to produce 10 and 21 jumpers a day. So to maximize profit, Neat Knits uses the least-cost combination of labour and capital that minimizes its total cost.

Figure A10.1

Neat Knits' Production Function

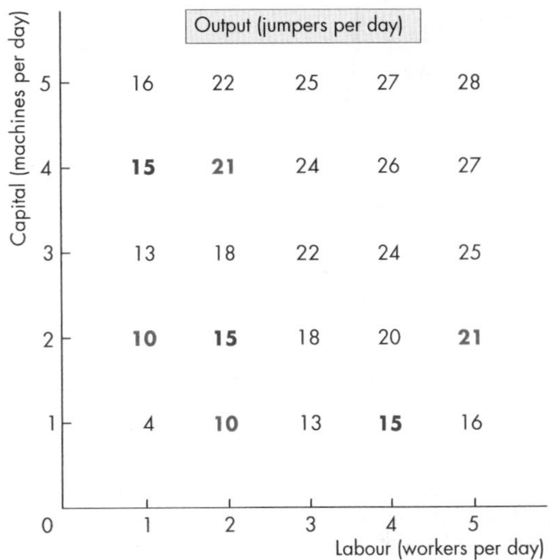

The figure shows how many jumpers can be produced each day using different combinations of labour and capital. For example, Neat Knits can produce 15 jumpers a day using 1 worker and 4 machines, or 2 workers and 2 machines, or 4 workers and 1 machine.

An Isoquant Map

An **isoquant** is a curve that shows the different combinations of labour and capital required to produce a given quantity of output. The word isoquant means "equal quantity". There is an isoquant for each output level. A series of isoquants is called an **isoquant map**. Figure A10.2 shows an isoquant map for Neat Knits with three isoquants: one for 10 jumpers a day, one for 15 jumpers a day and one for 21 jumpers a day. Each isoquant shown is based on the production function in Figure A10.1.

Although all goods and services can be produced using a variety of alternative production techniques, the ease with which labour and capital can be substituted for each other varies from industry to industry. The production function reflects the ease of factor substitution and can be used to calculate the degree of substitutability between factors. This calculation involves the marginal rate of substitution of labour for capital. The **marginal rate of substitution of labour for capital** is the increase in labour needed per unit decrease in capital to allow output to remain constant. Let's look at this in more detail.

The Marginal Rate of Substitution

The marginal rate of substitution is the magnitude of the slope of an isoquant. Figure A10.3 shows the isoquant for 13 jumpers a day. Pick any point on this isoquant and imagine decreasing capital by the smallest conceivable amount and increasing labour by the amount necessary to keep output constant at 13 jumpers. As we decrease the quantity of capital and increase the quantity of labour to keep output constant at 13 jumpers a day, we travel down along the isoquant.

Figure A10.2

An Isoquant Map

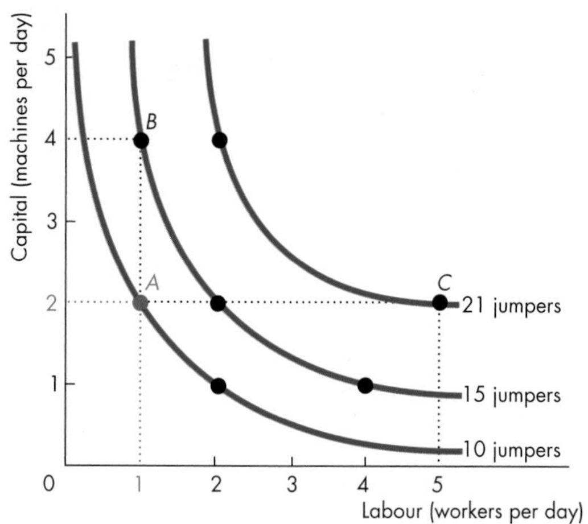

The figure shows three isoquants that are part of Neat Knits' isoquant map. Along each isoquant, the output produced by labour and capital is constant. These isoquants correspond to the production function for 10, 15 and 21 jumpers a day in Table A10.1.

If Neat Knits uses 2 machines and 1 worker (at point *A*), it produces 10 jumpers a day. If Neat Knits uses 4 machines and 1 worker (at point *B*), it produces 15 jumpers a day. If Neat Knits uses 2 machines and 5 workers (at point *C*), it produces 21 jumpers a day.

Figure A10.3

The Marginal Rate of Substitution

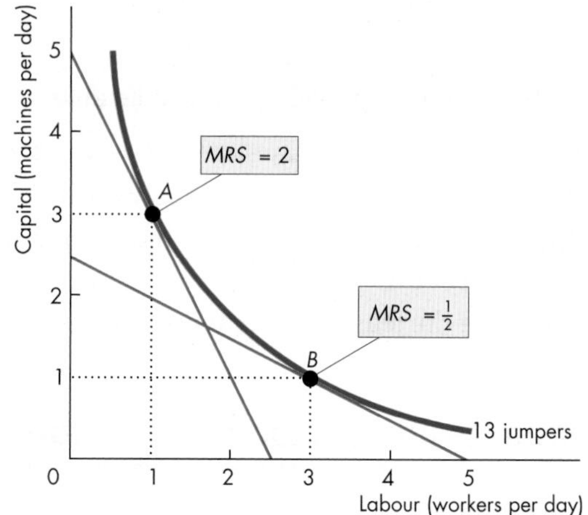

The marginal rate of substitution is measured by the magnitude of the slope of the isoquant. For example, to find the slope of the isoquant at point *A*, calculate the slope of the red line tangential to the isoquant at point *A*. The magnitude of the slope at point *A* is 2 (5 ÷ 2.5), so the marginal rate of substitution of labour for capital at point *A* is 2. Similarly, the marginal rate of substitution at point *B* equals the slope of the red line tangential and is 1/2. So the marginal rate of substitution of labour for capital at point *B* is 1/2.

In Figure A10.3, the marginal rate of substitution at point *A* is the magnitude of the slope of the red line tangential to the isoquant at point *A*. The slope of the isoquant at point *A* equals the slope of the line. To calculate the slope, move along the red line from 5 knitting machines and no workers to 2.5 workers and no knitting machines. Capital decreases by 5 knitting machines and labour increases by 2.5 workers. The magnitude of the slope is 5 divided by 2.5, which equals 2. So when using technique *A* to produce 13 jumpers a day, the marginal rate of substitution of labour for capital is 2.

The marginal rate of substitution at point *B* is the magnitude of the slope of the red line tangential to the isoquant at point *B*. Along this red line, if capital decreases by 2.5 knitting machines, labour increases by 5 workers. The magnitude of the slope is 2.5 knitting machines divided by 5, which equals 1/2. So when using technique *B* to produce 13 jumpers a day, the marginal rate of substitution of labour for capital is 1/2.

The marginal rates of substitution we have just calculated obey the **law of diminishing marginal rate of substitution** which states that:

> **The marginal rate of substitution of labour for capital diminishes as the amount of labour increases and the amount of capital decreases.**

The law of diminishing marginal rate of substitution determines the shape of the isoquant. When the quantity of capital is large and the quantity of labour is small, the isoquant is steep and the marginal rate of substitution of labour for capital is large. As the quantity of capital decreases and the quantity of labour increases, the isoquant becomes flatter and the marginal rate of substitution of labour for capital diminishes. Isoquants bow towards the origin.

We are going to use Neat Knits' isoquant map to work out the firm's least-cost technique of production, but first we must add the firm's costs to the model.

Isocost Lines

An **isocost line** shows the combinations of labour and capital that can be bought for a given total cost and given factor prices. Suppose that a knitting-machine worker can be hired for £25 a day and that a knitting machine can be rented for £25 a day. Figure A10.4 shows five possible combinations of labour and capital (A, B, C, D and E) that Neat Knits can employ for a total cost of £100 a day. For example, point B shows that Neat Knits can use 3 machines (for a cost of £75) and 1 worker (for a cost of £25). If neat Knits can employ workers and machines for fractions of a day, then any combination along the line AE will cost Neat Knits £100 a day. This line is Neat Knits' isocost line for a total cost of £100.

Figure A10.4

An Isocost Line

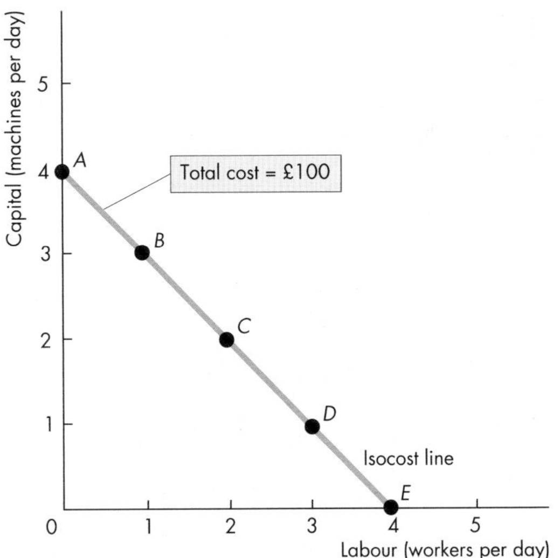

If labour is £25 a day and a knitting machine rents for £25 a day, Neat Knits can employ the combinations of labour and capital shown by points A to E for a total cost of £100. The line through these points is an isocost line. It shows all possible combinations of labour and capital that Neat Knits can hire for a total cost of £100 when labour is £25 a day and capital can be rented for £25 a day.

The Isocost Equation

An isocost equation describes an isocost line. The variables that affect a firm's total cost (TC) are the price of labour (P_L), the price of capital (P_K), the quantity of labour (L) and the quantity of capital (K).

The cost of the labour is ($P_L \times L$). The cost of capital is ($P_K \times K$). Total cost is the sum of these two costs.

Equation 1 shows a firm's total cost:

$$P_L L + P_K K = TC \qquad (1)$$

Equation 2 shows the total cost for Neat Knits using the numbers in our example. The wage rate is £25 a day and the capital rental rate is also £25 a day, so Neat Knits' total cost is:

$$£25L + £25K = £100 \qquad (2)$$

Now rearrange equation (1) by dividing by the price of capital and then subtract $(P_L/P_K)L$ from both sides of the equation. The resulting equation is the equation of the isocost line:

$$K = \frac{TC}{P_K} - \frac{P_L}{P_K} \times L \qquad (3)$$

Equation 3 tells us how the firm can vary the quantity of capital as it changes the quantity of labour, holding total cost constant. Neat Knits' isocost line is:

$$K = 4 - L \qquad (4)$$

Equation 4 corresponds to the isocost line in Figure A10.4.

The Isocost Map

An **isocost map** is a series of isocost lines, each one of which represents a different total cost but for given prices of labour and capital.

The larger the total cost, the greater are the quantities of labour and capital that can be employed. Figure A10.5 shows an isocost map. The middle isocost is the one you've seen before for a total cost of £100, when labour and capital cost £25 a day each. The other two isocost lines are for a total cost of £125 and £75, holding constant the factor prices at £25 a day each. The larger the total cost, the further is the isocost line from the origin.

The Effect of Factor Prices

The magnitude of the slope of the isocost lines shown in Figure A10.5 is 1. The slope tells us that 1 unit of labour costs 1 unit of capital. To decrease its capital by 1 unit and keep its total cost at £100 a day, Neat Knits must increase the quantity of labour by 1 unit.

Figure A10.5

An Isocost Map

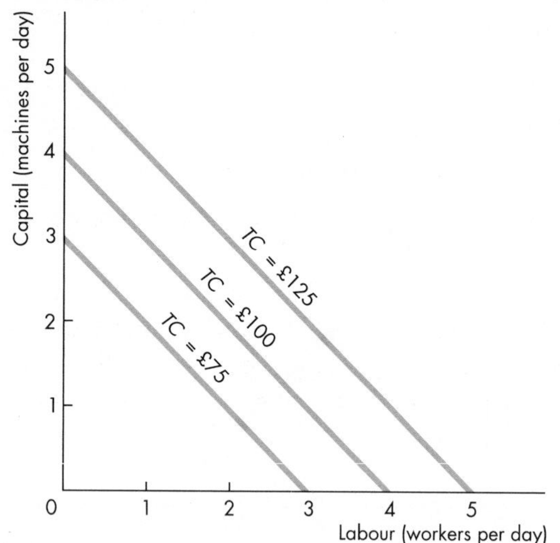

An isocost map shows the set of isocost lines, each for a different total cost. This isocost map shows three isocost lines, one for a total cost of £75 a day, one for £100 a day and one for £125 a day. Along the isocost lines, the prices of labour and capital are constant. For each isocost line shown here, the prices of labour and capital are £25 a day. The slope of an isocost line is equal to the relative price of labour to capital. The larger the total cost, the farther is the isocost line from the origin.

Figure A10.6

Factor Prices and the Isocost Line

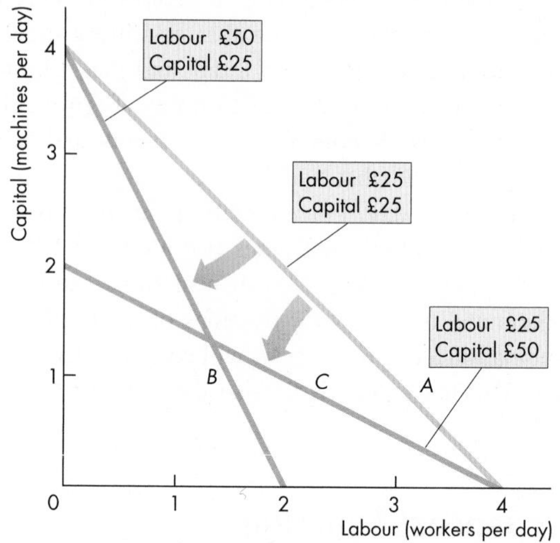

The slope of the isocost line depends on the relative factor price. Each of the isocost lines shown here have a total cost of £100 a day. If the prices of labour and capital are £25 a day, the isocost line is the line labelled *A*. If the price of labour rises to £50 a day but the price of capital remains at £25 a day, the isocost line becomes steeper and is the line labelled *B*. If the price of capital rises to £50 day and the price of labour remains at £25 a day, the isocost line becomes flatter and is the line labelled *C*.

If factor prices change, the slope of the isocost line changes. You can see the effect of factor prices on the slope of the isocost line start with the isocost equation:

$$K = \frac{TC}{P_K} - \frac{P_L}{P_K} \times L \qquad (3)$$

If the wage rate rises to £50 a day and the rental rate of a machine remains at £25 a day, then 1 unit of labour costs 2 units of capital. The relative price of labour to capital is £50/£25, which is 2. The isocost line becomes the steeper line *B* in Figure A10.6.

If the capital rental rate rises to £50 a day and the wage rate remains at £25 a day, then 1 unit of capital costs 2 units of labour. The relative price of labour to capital becomes £25/£50, which is 0.5. The isocost line becomes the flatter line *C* in Figure A10.6.

The higher the relative price of labour, the steeper is the isocost line. The magnitude of the slope of the isocost line measures the relative price of labour in terms of capital – the price of labour divided by the price of capital.

The Least-cost Technique

The **least-cost technique** is the combination of labour and capital that minimizes the total cost of producing a given level of output.

Suppose Neat Knits plans to produce 15 jumpers a day, given the prices of capital and labour at £25 a day. What is the least-cost technique that Neat Knits can use? Figure A10.7 shows the isoquant for an output of 15 jumpers and two isocost line. One isocost is for a total cost of £125 a day and the other for £100 a day.

At point *A* in Figure A10.7, Neat Knits can produce 15 jumpers using 1 worker and 4 machines. With this technique, the total cost is £125 a day. Point *C*, which uses 4 workers and 1 machine, is another technique that produces 15 jumpers for the same cost of £125 a day. At point *B*, Neat Knits can use 2 machines and 2 workers to produce 15 jumpers, but the cost is £100 a day. So point *B* is the least-cost technique or the economically efficient technique for producing 15 jumpers, when machines and workers cost £25 a day each.

Figure A10.7

The Least-Cost Technique of Production

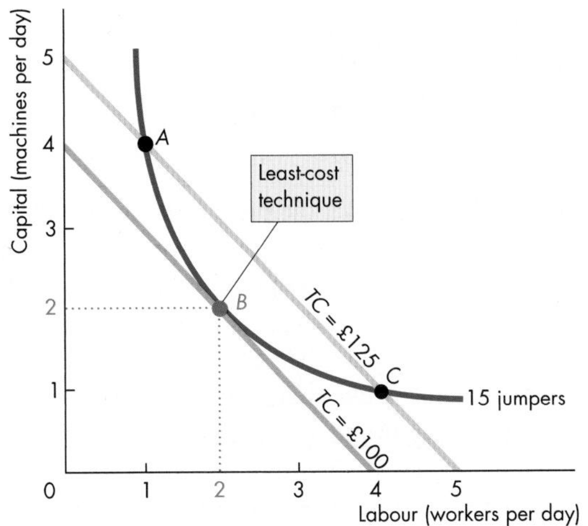

Neat Knits can produce 15 jumpers a day by using 4 machines and 1 worker at point *A* or 1 machine and 4 workers at point *C*. The total cost using either of these techniques has a total cost of £125 a day.

Neat Knits can also use 2 machines and 2 workers at point *B* to produce 15 jumpers a day. The total cost using this technique is £100 a day. Point *B* is the least-cost technique of producing 15 jumpers.

At point *B*, the isoquant for 15 jumpers is tangential to the isocost line. The slope of the isoquant (the marginal rate of substitution) and the slope of the isocost line (the relative price of the factors) are the same.

Figure A10.7 shows that there is only one way for Neat Knits to produce 15 jumpers for £100 a day, but several ways to produce 15 jumpers for more than £100 a day. Techniques shown by points *A*, *B* and *C* are just examples. The points between *A*, *B* and *C* are also possible ways of producing 15 jumpers but for a total cost between £100 and £125 a day. Isocost lines exist between those shown which cut the isoquant for 15 jumpers at points between *A*, *B* and *C*. Neat Knits could also produce 15 jumpers for a total cost of more than £125 a day by moving to a point on the isoquant outside the isocost line shown.

The least-cost technique for producing 15 jumpers day is at point *B* in Figure A10.7. Neat Knits cannot produce 15 jumpers for less than £100 a day. An isocost line for a total cost of less than £100 a day would not touch the isoquant for 15 jumpers because at the given prices of capital and labour, the total cost will not buy the factors needed to produce 15 jumpers.

Marginal Rate of Substitution and Marginal Products

The marginal rate of substitution and the marginal products are linked by an interesting formula:

> **The marginal rate of substitution of labour for capital equals the marginal product of labour divided by the marginal product of capital.**

A few steps of reasoning are needed to establish this proposition.

First, we know that output changes when a firm changes the quantities of labour and capital employed. The change in output that results from a change in one of the factors is determined by the marginal product of the factor. So:

$$\text{Change in output} = (MP_L \times \Delta L) + (MP_K \times \Delta K) \quad (4)$$

Equation 4 shows a change in output equals the marginal product of labour, MP_L, multiplied by the change in labour, ΔL, plus the marginal product of capital, MP_K, multiplied by the change in capital, ΔK.

Suppose that Neat Knits wants to change the quantities of labour and capital but continue to produce the same number of jumpers. That is, Neat Knits wants to stay on the same isoquant, so the change in output must be zero. We can make the change in output zero in equation (4) to give equation (5):

$$MP_L \times \Delta L = -(MP_K \times \Delta K) \quad (5)$$

To stay on an isoquant when labour increases, capital must decrease. That is, when labour increases by ΔL, capital must decrease by:

$$MP_L \times \Delta L = MP_K \times -\Delta K \quad (6)$$

Equation 6 states that the marginal product of labour multiplied by the increase in labour equals the marginal product of capital multiplied by the decrease in capital. Dividing both sides of equation 6 by the increase in labour, ΔL, and then dividing both sides by the marginal product of capital, MP_K, gives equation 7:

$$\frac{MP_L}{MP_K} = -\frac{\Delta K}{\Delta L} \quad (7)$$

Equation 7 shows that when Neat Knits remains on an isoquant, the decrease in its capital, $-\Delta K$, divided by the increase in its labour, ΔL, is equal to the marginal product of labour, MP_L, divided by the marginal product of capital, MP_K.

The decrease in capital divided by the increase in labour when the firm remains on a given isoquant is the *marginal rate of substitution of labour for capital*. What we have shown is that the marginal rate of substitution of labour for capital equals the ratio of the marginal product of labour to the marginal product of capital.

Marginal Cost

We can use the fact that the marginal rate of substitution of labour for capital equals the ratio of the marginal product of labour to the marginal product of capital to examine marginal cost.

We know that when the least-cost technique is used, the slope of the isoquant and the isocost line are equal as shown in equation 8:

$$\frac{MP_L}{MP_K} = \frac{P_L}{P_K} \qquad (8)$$

We can now show that the total cost is minimized when the marginal product of labour per pound spent on labour equals the marginal product of capital per pound spent on capital.

Rearrange equation 8 by multiplying both sides by the marginal product of capital and then dividing both sides by the price of labour, you get equation 9:

$$\frac{MP_L}{P_L} = \frac{MP_K}{P_K} \qquad (9)$$

Equation 9 says that the marginal product of labour per pound spent on labour is equal to the marginal product of capital per pound spent on capital. In other words, the extra output produced by the last pound spent on labour equals the extra output produced by the last pound spent on capital.

If the extra output produced by the last pound spent on labour exceeds the extra output produced by the last pound spent on capital, it pays a firm to use less capital and more labour. The firm can produce the same output at a lower total cost. Conversely, if the extra output produced by the last pound spent on capital exceeds the extra output produced by the last pound spend on labour, the firm can lower its cost of producing a given output by using less labour and more capital. A firm achieves the least-cost technique of production only when the extra output produced by the last pound spent on all the factors of production is the same.

Finally, we can show that the marginal cost of producing a unit of output with fixed capital and variable labour equals the marginal cost with fixed labour and variable capital. To see why, invert equation 9 to give:

$$\frac{P_L}{MP_L} = \frac{P_K}{MP_K} \qquad (10)$$

Equation 10 shows that the price of labour divided by its marginal product equals the price of capital divided by its marginal product. The price of labour divided by the marginal product of labour is marginal cost of producing a unit of output when the quantity of capital is constant. Remember that marginal cost is the change in total cost resulting from a unit increase in output.

If output increases when one more unit of labour is employed, total output increases by the marginal product of labour. So marginal cost is the price of labour divided by the marginal product of labour. For example, if labour costs £25 a day and the marginal product of labour is 2 jumpers, then the marginal cost of a jumper is £12.50 (£25 divided by 2).

The price of capital divided by the marginal product of capital has a similar interpretation. The price of capital divided by the marginal product of capital is marginal cost when the quantity of labour is constant.

You can see from equation 10 that with the least-cost technique, the marginal cost of producing a unit of output is the same regardless of whether the quantity of capital is constant and more labour is used or the quantity of labour is constant and more capital is used.

Making Connections

You're probably thinking that what you've learned in this Appendix looks a lot like what you learned in Chapter 8 about a consumer's decision. You are right. In a graph, an isoquant is like an indifference curve; an isocost line is like a budget line; and the least-cost production technique is like the consumer's best affordable point.

But there is an important difference between the two models. The consumer's problem is to get to the *highest* attainable indifference curve with a given budget. The firm's problem is to get to the *lowest* attainable isocost line for a given output. Nonetheless, the two models share similar techniques of analysis.

Perfect Competition

CHAPTER 11

After studying this chapter you will be able to:

- Define perfect competition
- Explain how firms make their supply decisions and why they sometimes shut down temporarily and lay off workers
- Explain how price and output in an industry are determined and why firms enter and leave the industry
- Predict the effects of a change in demand and of a technological advance
- Explain why perfect competition is efficient

Fierce Competition

You might be relaxing over a cup of coffee, but producing coffee is a fiercely competitive business with lean pickings for most of its producers. Competition is also fierce in other industries that affect your life such as personal computers and mobile phones where prices have tumbled. Agricultural markets, such as the market for strawberries that you will encounter in *Reading Between the Lines*, are also competitive. What determines prices and profits in a competitive industry? Why do firms enter or leave a competitive industry? Why do firms sometimes shut down and lay off their workers? Is fierce competition efficient? We answer these questions in this chapter.

What Is Perfect Competition?

The firms that you study in the chapter face the force of raw competition. This type of extreme competition is called perfect competition. **Perfect competition** is industry in which:

1 Many firms sell identical products to many buyers.
2 There are no restrictions on entry into the industry.
3 Existing firms have no advantage over new ones.
4 Sellers and buyers are well informed about prices.

Farming, fishing, wood pulping and paper milling, the manufacture of paper cups and plastic shopping bags, grocery retailing, plumbing and dry cleaning are examples of highly competitive industries.

How Perfect Competition Arises

Perfect competition arises if the firm's minimum efficient scale is small relative to the demand for the good. A firm's *minimum efficient scale* is the smallest quantity of output at which long-run average cost reaches its lowest level. (See Chapter 10, p. 227.) If the firm's minimum efficient scale is small relative to demand, there is room for many firms in the industry.

Perfect competition also arises if each firm is perceived to produce a good or service that has no unique characteristics so that consumers don't care which firm they buy from.

Price Takers

Firms in perfect competition are price takers. A **price taker** is a firm that cannot influence the market price and that sets its own price at the market price.

The key reason why a perfectly competitive firm is a price taker is that it produces a tiny fraction of the total output of a particular good and buyers are well informed about the prices of other firms.

Imagine you are a wheat farmer with a hundred hectares under cultivation, which sounds like a lot. But when compared to the millions of hectares in Ukraine, Canada, Australia, Argentina and the United States, your hundred hectares is a drop in the ocean. Nothing makes your wheat any better than any other farmer's and all the buyers of wheat know the price at which they can do business.

If the market price of wheat is £85 a tonne and you ask £90 a tonne, no one will buy from you. People can go to the next farmer and the next and the one after that and buy all they need for £85 a tonne. If you set your price at £84 a tonne, you'll have lots of buyers. But you can sell all your output for £85 a tonne, so you're just giving away £1 a tonne. You can do no better than sell for the market price – you are a *price taker*.

Economic Profit and Revenue

A firm's goal is to maximize *economic profit*, which is equal to total revenue minus total cost. Total cost is the *opportunity cost* of production, which includes *normal profit*, the return that the firm's entrepreneur can expect to receive on average in an alternative business (see Chapter 9, p. 193).

A firm's **total revenue** equals the price of its output multiplied by the number of units of output sold (price × quantity). **Marginal revenue** is the change in total revenue that results from a one-unit increase in the quantity sold. Marginal revenue is calculated by dividing the change in total revenue by the change in the quantity sold.

Figure 11.1 illustrates these concepts in the market for jumpers. In part (a), the market demand curve, *D*, and the supply curve, *S*, determine the market price. The market price remains at £25 a jumper regardless of the quantity that Neat Knits, one small firm, produces, and the best that it can do is to sell its jumpers at £25.

Total Revenue

Total revenue is equal to the price multiplied by the quantity sold. In the table in Figure 11.1, if Neat Knits sells 9 jumpers, the firm's total revenue is 9 × £25, which equals £225.

Figure 11.1(b) shows the firm's total revenue curve (*TR*), which graphs the relationship between total revenue and quantity sold. At point *A* on the *TR* curve, Neat Knits sells 9 jumpers and has total revenue of £225. Because each additional jumper sold brings in a constant amount – £25 – the total revenue curve is an upward-sloping straight line.

Marginal Revenue

Marginal revenue is the change in total revenue that results from a one-unit increase in quantity. In the table in Figure 11.1, when the quantity sold increases from 8 to 9 jumpers, total revenue increases from £200 to £225. Marginal revenue is £25. Marginal revenue is

Figure 11.1

Demand, Price and Revenue in Perfect Competition

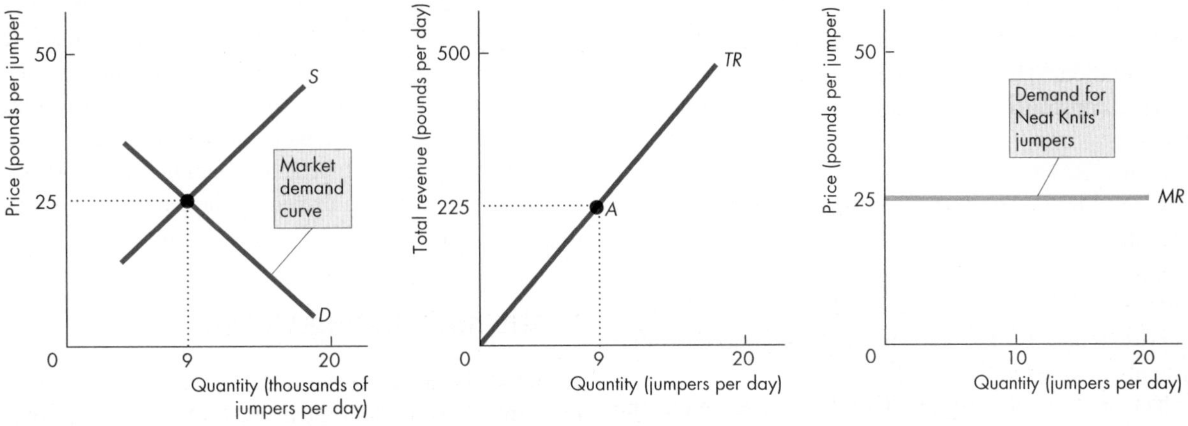

(a) Jumper industry

(b) Neat Knits' total revenue

(c) Neat Knits' marginal revenue

Quantity sold (*Q*) (jumpers per day)	Price (*P*) (pounds per jumper)	Total revenue (*TR* = *P* × *Q*) (pounds)	Marginal revenue (*MR* = Δ*TR*/Δ*Q*) (pounds per jumper)
8	25	200	
			25
9	25	225	
			25
10	25	250	

In part (a), market demand and supply determine the market price (and quantity). Part (b) shows Neat Knits' total revenue curve (*TR*). Point *A* corresponds to the second row of the table – Neat Knits sells 9 jumpers at £25 a jumper, so total revenue is £225. Part (c) shows Neat Knits' marginal revenue curve (*MR*). This curve is the demand curve for jumpers produced by Neat Knits. Neat Knits faces a perfectly elastic demand for its jumpers at the market price of £25 a jumper.

£25 a jumper. Because the price remains constant when the quantity sold changes, the change in total revenue that results from a one-unit increase in the quantity sold equals price. In perfect competition, marginal revenue equals price.

Figure 11.1(c) shows Neat Knits' marginal revenue curve (*MR*), which is a horizontal line at the going market price.

The firm can sell any quantity it chooses at the market price. So the demand curve for the firm's product is a horizontal line at the market price, the same as the firm's marginal revenue curve

Demand for Firm's Product and Market Demand

A horizontal demand curve is perfectly elastic. So the firm faces a perfectly elastic demand for its output. One of Neat Knits' jumpers is a perfect substitute for jumpers from the factory next door or from any other factory. Notice, though, that the *market* demand for jumpers in Figure 11.1(a) is not perfectly elastic. The market demand curve is downward-sloping, and its elasticity depends on the substitutability of jumpers for other goods and services.

Review Quiz

Study Plan 11.1

1. Why is a firm in perfect competition a price taker?
2. In perfect competition, what is the relationship between the demand for the firm's output and the market demand?
3. In perfect competition, why is a firm's marginal revenue curve also the demand curve for the firm's output?
4. Why is the total revenue curve in perfect competition an upward-sloping straight line?

The Firm's Decisions in Perfect Competition

Firms in a perfectly competitive industry face a given market price and have the revenue curves that you've just studied. These revenue curves summarize the market constraint that the firm in perfect competition faces.

Firms also face a technology constraint, which is described by the product curves (total product, average product and marginal product) that you studied in Chapter 10. The technology available to the firm determines its costs, which are described by the cost curves (total cost, average cost and marginal cost) that you also studied in Chapter 10.

The goal of the competitive firm is to make the maximum possible profit, given the market constraints and technology constraints it faces. To achieve this objective, a firm must make four key decisions: two in the short run and two in the long run.

Short-run Decisions

The short run is a time frame in which each firm has a given plant size and the number of firms in the industry is fixed. But many things change in the short run and the firm must react to these changes. For example, the price for which the firm can sell its output might change with the seasons or it might fluctuate with general business conditions. The firm must react to such short-run price fluctuations and decide:

1 Whether to produce or to temporarily shut down
2 If the decision is to produce, what quantity to produce

Long-run Decisions

The long run is a time frame in which each firm can change its plant size and decide whether to leave an industry or enter an industry. So in the long run, both the plant size of each firm and the number of firms in the industry can change. Also the constraints that the firm faces can change in the long run. For example, the demand for its good can permanently fall or a technological advance can change an industry's costs. The firm must react to such long-run changes and decide:

1 Whether to increase or decrease its plant size
2 Whether to remain in an industry or leave it

The Firm and the Industry in the Short Run and the Long Run

To study a competitive industry, we begin by looking at an individual firm's short-run decisions. We then see how the short-run decisions of all the firms in a competitive industry combine to determine the industry price, output and economic profit. We then turn to the long run and study the effects of long-run decisions on the industry price, output and economic profit. All the decisions we study are driven by the pursuit of a single objective: maximization of economic profit.

Profit-maximizing Output

A perfectly competitive firm maximizes economic profit by choosing its output level. One way of finding the profit-maximizing output is to study a firm's total revenue and total cost curves and to find the output level at which total revenue exceeds total cost by the largest amount.

Figure 11.2 shows you how to find the profit-maximizing output for Neat Knits. The table lists Neat Knits' total revenue and total cost at different outputs, and part (a) of the figure shows its total revenue and total cost curves. These curves are graphs of the numbers shown in the first three columns of the table. The total revenue curve (*TR*) is the same as that in Figure 11.1(b). The total cost curve (*TC*) is similar to the one that you met in Chapter 10. As output increases, so does total cost.

Economic Profit and Economic Loss

Economic profit equals total revenue minus total cost. The fourth column of the table in Figure 11.2 shows Neat Knits' economic profit and part (b) of the figure illustrates these numbers as Neat Knits' economic profit curve (*EP*). This curve shows that Neat Knits makes an economic profit at outputs between 4 and 12 jumpers a day. At outputs less than 4 jumpers a day, Neat Knits incurs an economic loss. It also incurs an economic loss if it produces more than 12 jumpers a day. If Neat Knits produces either 4 jumpers or 12 jumpers a day, its total cost equals its total revenue and its economic profit is zero.

An output at which total cost equals total revenue is called a *break-even point*. Normal profit is part of total cost, so at the break-even point, the entrepreneur makes normal profit.

Notice the relationship between the total revenue,

Figure 11.2

Total Revenue, Total Cost and Economic Profit

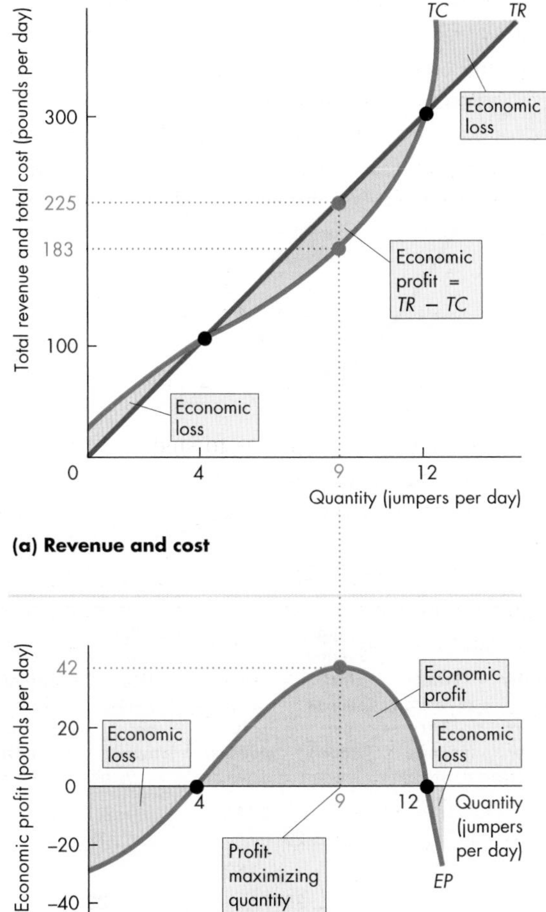

Quantity (Q) (jumpers per day)	Total revenue (TR) (pounds)	Total cost (TC) (pounds)	Economic profit ($TR - TC$) (pounds)
0	0	22	−22
1	25	45	−20
2	50	66	−16
3	75	85	−10
4	100	100	0
5	125	114	11
6	150	126	24
7	175	141	34
8	200	160	40
9	225	183	42
10	250	210	40
11	275	245	30
12	300	300	0
13	325	360	−35

The table lists Neat Knits' total revenue, total cost and economic profit. Part (a) graphs the total revenue and total cost curves. Economic profit, in part (a), is the height of the blue area between the total cost and total revenue curves. Neat Knits makes maximum economic profit, £42 a day (£225 − £183), when it produces 9 jumpers – the output at which the vertical distance between the total revenue and total cost curves is at its largest.

At outputs of 4 jumpers a day and 12 jumpers a day, Neat Knits makes zero economic profit – these are break-even points. At outputs less than 4 and greater than 12 jumpers a day, Neat Knits incurs an economic loss.

Part (b) shows Neat Knits' economic profit curve (*EP*). The economic profit curve is at its highest when economic profit is at a maximum and it cuts the *x*-axis at the break-even points.

total cost and economic profit curves. Economic profit is measured by the vertical distance between the total revenue and total cost curves. When the total revenue curve in Figure 11.2(a) is above the total cost curve, between 4 and 12 jumpers, the firm is making an economic profit and the profit curve in Figure 11.2(b) is above the horizontal axis. At the break-even point, where the total cost and total revenue curves intersect, the profit curve intersects the x-axis. The profit curve is at its highest when the distance between the total revenue and total cost curves is greatest. In this example, profit maximization occurs at an output of 9 jumpers a day. At this output, Neat Knits makes an economic profit of £42 a day.

Marginal Analysis

Another way of finding the profit-maximizing output is to use *marginal analysis*, by comparing marginal revenue, *MR*, with marginal cost, *MC*. As output increases, marginal revenue remains constant but marginal cost changes. At low output levels, marginal cost decreases as output increases but eventually marginal cost increases. So where the marginal cost curve intersects the marginal revenue curve, marginal cost is rising – the marginal cost curve is upward sloping.

If marginal revenue exceeds marginal cost (if $MR > MC$), then the extra revenue from selling one more unit exceeds the extra cost incurred to produce it. The firm makes an economic profit on the marginal unit, so economic profit increases if output *increases*.

If marginal revenue is less than marginal cost (if $MR < MC$), then the extra revenue from selling one more unit is less than the extra cost incurred to produce it. The firm incurs an economic loss on the marginal unit, so its economic profit decreases if output increases and its economic profit increases if output *decreases*.

If marginal revenue equals marginal cost ($MR = MC$), the firm makes maximum economic profit. The rule $MR = MC$ is an example of marginal analysis. Let's check that this rule works to find the profit-maximizing output, by returning to Neat Knits.

Look at Figure 11.3. The table records Neat Knits' marginal revenue and marginal cost. Marginal revenue is constant at £25 per jumper. Over the range of outputs shown in the table, marginal cost increases from £19 a jumper to £35 a jumper. The graph shows Neat Knits' marginal revenue and marginal cost curves.

Focus on the highlighted rows of the table. If output increases from 8 jumpers to 9 jumpers, marginal revenue is £25 and marginal cost is £23. Because marginal revenue exceeds marginal cost, economic profit increases. The last column of the table shows that economic profit increases from £40 to £42, an increase of £2. This economic profit from the ninth jumper is shown as the blue area in the figure.

If Neat Knits increases output from 9 jumpers to 10 jumpers, marginal revenue is still £25 but marginal cost is £27. Because marginal revenue is less than marginal cost, economic profit decreases. The last column of the table shows that economic profit decreases from £42 to £40. This loss from the tenth jumper is shown as the red area in the figure.

Neat Knits maximizes economic profit by producing 9 jumpers a day, the quantity at which marginal revenue equals marginal cost.

Figure 11.3 myeconlab

Profit-maximizing Output

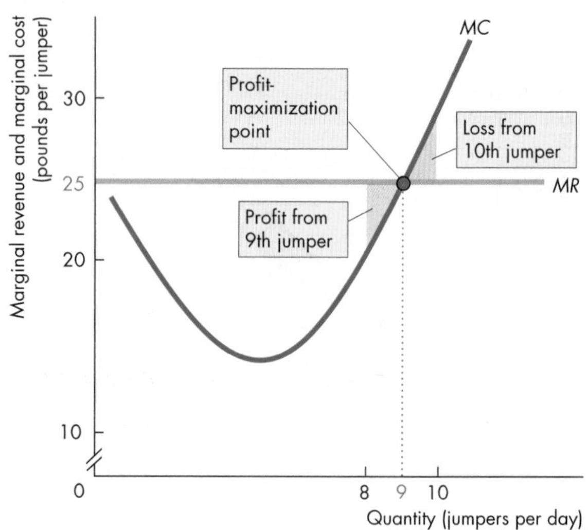

Quantity (Q) (jumpers per day)	Total revenue (TR) (pounds)	Marginal revenue (MR) (pounds per jumper)	Total cost (TC) (pounds)	Marginal cost (MC) (pounds per jumper)	Economic profit (TR – TC) (pounds)
7	175		141		34
		25		19	
8	200		160		40
		25		**23**	
9	**225**		**183**		**42**
		25		**27**	
10	250		210		40
		25		35	
11	275		245		30

Another way of finding the profit-maximizing output is to determine the output at which marginal revenue equals marginal cost. The table shows that if output increases from 8 to 9 jumpers, marginal cost is £23, which is less than the marginal revenue of £25. If output increases from 9 to 10 jumpers, marginal cost is £27, which exceeds the marginal revenue of £25.

The graph shows that marginal cost and marginal revenue are equal when Neat Knits produces 9 jumpers a day. If marginal revenue exceeds marginal cost, an increase in output increases economic profit. If marginal revenue is less than marginal cost, an increase in output decreases economic profit. If marginal revenue equals marginal cost, economic profit is maximized.

Profits and Losses in the Short Run

In the short run, although the firm produces the profit-maximizing output, it does not necessarily end up making an economic profit. It might do so, but it might alternatively break even (make zero economic profit) or incur an economic loss.

Economic profit (or loss) per jumper is price, P, minus average total cost, ATC. So economic profit is $(P - ATC) \times Q$. If price equals average total cost, a firm breaks even – makes zero economic profit. The entrepreneur makes normal profit. If price exceeds average total cost, a firm makes an economic profit. If price is less than average total cost, the firm incurs an economic loss.

Figure 11.4 shows these three possible short-run profit outcomes.

Three Possible Profit Outcomes

In Figure 11.4(a), the price of a jumper is £20. Neat Knits produces 8 jumpers a day. Average total cost is £20 a jumper. Price equals average total cost (*ATC*), so Neat Knits breaks even (makes zero economic profit) and Norma, the entrepreneur, makes normal profit.

In Figure 11.4(b), the price of a jumper is £25. Neat Knits maximizes profit by producing 9 jumpers a day. Here, price exceeds average total cost, so Neat Knits makes an economic profit. Economic profit is £42 a day. It is made up of £4.67 a jumper (£25.00 – £20.33), multiplied by the number of jumpers (£4.67 × 9), which is £42 a day. The blue rectangle in Figure 11.4(b) shows this economic profit. The height of the rectangle is profit per jumper, £4.67, and the length is the quantity of jumpers produced, 9 a day, so the area of the rectangle measures Neat Knits' economic profit of £42 a day.

In Figure 11.4(c), the price of a jumper is £17. Here, price is less than average total cost and Neat Knits incurs an economic loss. Price and marginal revenue are £17 a jumper, and the profit-maximizing (in this case, loss-minimizing) output is 7 jumpers a day. Neat Knits' average total cost is £20.14 a jumper, so its economic loss is £3.14 per jumper (£20.14 – £17.00). Neat Knits' economic loss equals this loss per jumper multiplied by the number of jumpers (£3.14 × 7), which equals £22 a day. The red rectangle shows this economic loss. The height of that rectangle is economic loss per jumper, £3.14, and the length is the quantity of jumpers produced, 7 a day, so the area of the rectangle is Neat Knits' economic loss of £22 a day.

Figure 11.4

myeconlab

Three Possible Profit Outcomes in the Short-Run

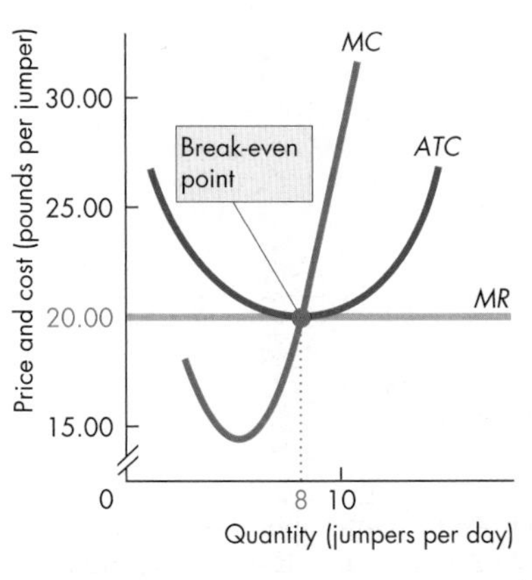

(a) Break even

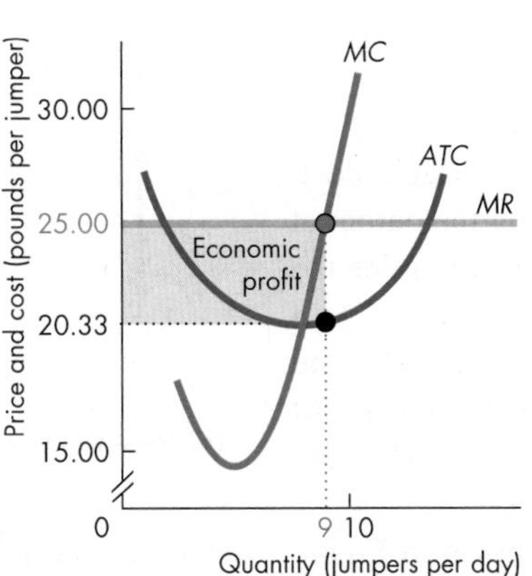

(b) Economic profit

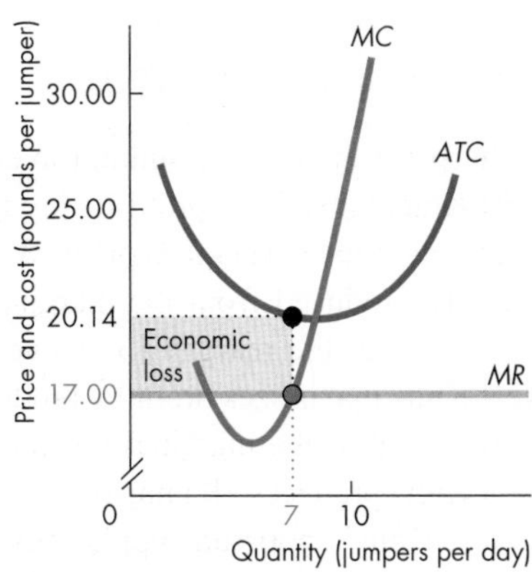

(c) Economic loss

In the short run, firms might break even (make zero economic profit), make an economic profit or incur an economic loss. If price equals minimum average total cost, the firm breaks even and makes zero economic profit in part (a). If the market price exceeds the average total cost of producing the profit-maximizing output, the firm makes an economic profit equal to the area of the blue rectangle in part (b). If the price is less than minimum average total cost, the firm incurs an economic loss equal to the area of the red rectangle in part (c).

The Firm's Short-run Supply Curve

A perfectly competitive firm's supply curve shows how the firm's profit-maximizing output varies as the market price varies, other things remaining the same. Figure 11.5 shows you how to derive Neat Knits' supply curve. Part (a) shows Neat Knits' marginal cost and average variable cost curves and part (b) shows its supply curve. There is a direct link between these cost curves and the supply curve. Let's see what that link is.

Temporary Plant Shutdown

In the short run, a firm cannot avoid its fixed costs. But it can avoid variable costs by temporarily laying off workers and shutting down. If a firm shuts down and produces no output, it incurs an economic loss equal to its total fixed cost. This loss is the largest that a firm need incur. A firm shuts down if the price falls below the minimum average variable cost. A firm's **shutdown point** is the output and price at which the firm just covers its total *variable* costs – point *T* in Figure 11.5(a). If the price is £17, the marginal revenue curve is MR_0, and the profit-maximizing output is 7 jumpers a day at point *T*. But both price and average variable cost equal £17, so Neat Knits' total revenue equals its total variable cost. Neat Knits incurs an economic loss equal to total fixed cost. If the price falls below £17, no matter what quantity Neat Knits produces, average *variable* cost exceeds price and its loss exceeds total fixed cost. So Neat Knits shuts down temporarily.

The Short-run Supply Curve

If the price is above minimum average variable cost, Neat Knits maximizes profit by producing the output at which marginal cost equals price. We can determine the quantity produced from the marginal cost curve. At a price of £25, the marginal revenue curve is MR_1 and Neat Knits maximizes profit by producing 9 jumpers. At a price of £31, the marginal revenue curve is MR_2 and Neat Knits produces 10 jumpers.

Neat Knits' short-run supply curve, shown in Figure 11.5(b), has two parts: at prices above minimum average variable cost, the supply curve is the same as the marginal cost curve above the shutdown point (*T*). At prices below minimum average variable cost, Neat Knits shuts down and produces nothing. Its supply curve runs along the *y*-axis. At a price of £17, Neat Knits is indifferent between shutting down and producing 7 jumpers a day. Either way, it incurs a loss of £25 a day.

Figure 11.5

myeconlab

A Firm's Supply Curve

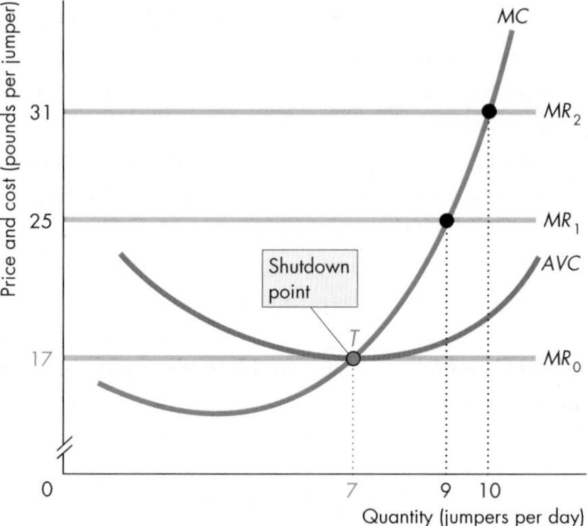

(a) Marginal cost and average variable cost

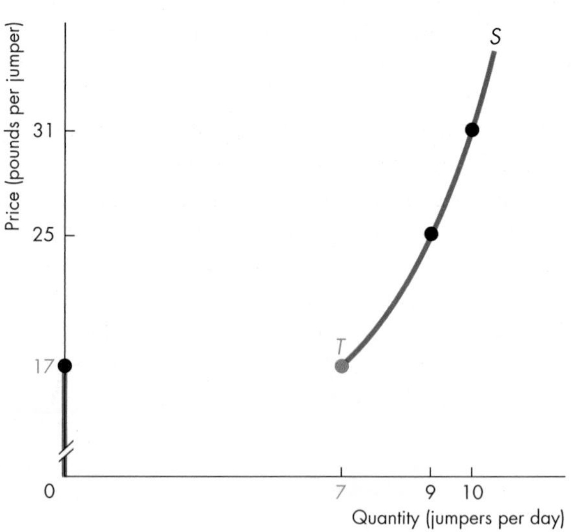

(b) Neat Knits' supply curve

Part (a) shows Neat Knits' profit-maximizing output at each market price. At £25 a jumper, Neat Knits produces 9 jumpers. At £17 a jumper, Neat Knits produces 7 jumpers. At any price below £17 a jumper, Neat Knits produces nothing. Neat Knits' shutdown point is *T*.

Part (b) shows Neat Knits' supply curve – the number of jumpers Neat Knits will produce at each price. It is made up of the marginal cost curve (part a) at all points above minimum average variable cost and the *y*-axis at all prices below minimum average variable cost.

Short-run Industry Supply Curve

The **short-run industry supply curve** shows how the quantity supplied by the industry varies as the market price varies when the plant size of each firm and the number of firms in the industry remain the same. The quantity supplied by the industry at a given price is the sum of the quantities supplied by all firms in the industry at that price.

Figure 11.6 shows the supply curve for the competitive jumper industry. In this example, the industry consists of 1,000 firms exactly like Neat Knits. At each price, the quantity supplied by the industry is 1,000 times the quantity supplied by a single firm.

The table in Figure 11.6 shows the firm's and the industry's supply schedule and how the industry supply curve is constructed. At prices below £17, every firm in the industry shuts down and produces nothing. The quantity supplied by the industry is zero. At a price of £17, each firm is indifferent between shutting down and producing nothing or producing 7 jumpers. Some firms will shut down and other will produce 7 jumpers a day. The quantity supplied by each firm is *either* 0 or 7 jumpers, but the quantity supplied by the industry is *between* 0 (all firms shut down) and 7,000 (all firms produce 7 jumpers a day each).

To construct the industry supply curve, we sum the quantities supplied by the individual firms at each price. Each of the 1,000 firms in the industry has a supply schedule like Neat Knits. At prices below £17, the industry supply curve runs along the *y*-axis. At a price of £17, the industry supply curve is horizontal – supply is perfectly elastic. As the price rises above £17, each firm increases its quantity supplied and the quantity supplied by the industry increases by 1,000 times that of an individual firm. Figure 11.6 shows the industry supply curve S_I.

Review Quiz

Study Plan 11.2

1. Why does a firm in perfect competition produce the quantity at which marginal cost equals price?
2. What is the lowest price at which a firm will produce an output? Explain why.
3. What is the largest economic loss that a firm will incur in the short run?
4. What is the relationship between a firm's supply curve, its marginal cost curve and its average variable cost curve?
5. Explain how we derive an industry supply curve?

Figure 11.6 myeconlab

Industry Supply Curve

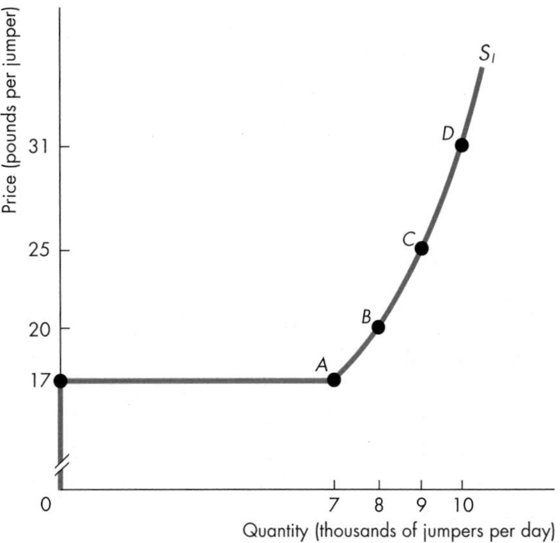

	Price (pounds per jumper)	Quantity supplied by Neat Knits (jumpers per day)	Quantity supplied by industry (jumpers per day)
A	17	0 or 7	0 to 7,000
B	20	8	8,000
C	25	9	9,000
D	31	10	10,000

The industry supply schedule is the sum of the supply schedules of all individual firms. An industry that consists of 1,000 identical firms has a supply schedule similar to that of the individual firm, but the quantity supplied by the industry is 1,000 times as large as that of the individual firm (see the table).

The curve labelled S_I is the industry supply curve. Points *A*, *B*, *C* and *D* correspond to the rows of the table. At the shutdown price of £17, each firm produces either 0 or 7 jumpers per day. The industry produces between 0 and 7,000 jumpers a day. The industry supply is perfectly elastic at the shutdown price.

So far, we have studied a single firm in isolation. We have seen that the firm's profit-maximizing actions depend on the market price, which the firm takes as given. But how is the market price determined? Let's find out.

Output, Price and Profit in Perfect Competition

To determine the market price and the quantity bought and sold in a perfectly competitive market, we need to study how market demand and the industry supply interact. We begin this process by studying a perfectly competitive market in the short run when the number of firms is fixed and each firm has a given plant size.

Short-run Equilibrium

Market demand and industry supply determine market price and industry output. Figure 11.7 shows the short-run equilibrium. The supply curve, *S*, is the same as S_I in Figure 11.6. If market demand is shown by the demand curve D_1, the equilibrium price is £20 a jumper. Each firm takes this price as given and produces its profit-maximizing output, which is 8 jumpers a day. Because the industry has 1,000 firms, industry output is 8,000 jumpers a day.

A Change in Demand

Changes in market demand bring changes to short-run industry equilibrium. Figure 11.7 shows these changes.

If the market demand increases and the demand curve shifts rightward to D_2, the price rises to £25. At this price, each firm maximizes profit by increasing its output. The new output is 9 jumpers a day for each firm and 9,000 jumpers a day for the industry.

If the market demand decreases and the demand curve shifts leftward to D_3, the price falls to £17. At this price, each firm maximizes profit by decreasing its output. The new output is 7 jumpers a day for each firm and 7,000 jumpers a day for the industry.

If the market demand curve shifts further leftward than D_3, the price remains constant at £17 because the industry supply curve is horizontal at that price. Some firms continue to produce 7 jumpers a day and others temporarily shut down. Firms are indifferent between these two activities, and whichever they choose, they incur an economic loss equal to total fixed cost. The number of firms continuing to produce is just enough to satisfy the market demand at a price of £17.

Figure 11.7

Short-run Equilibrium

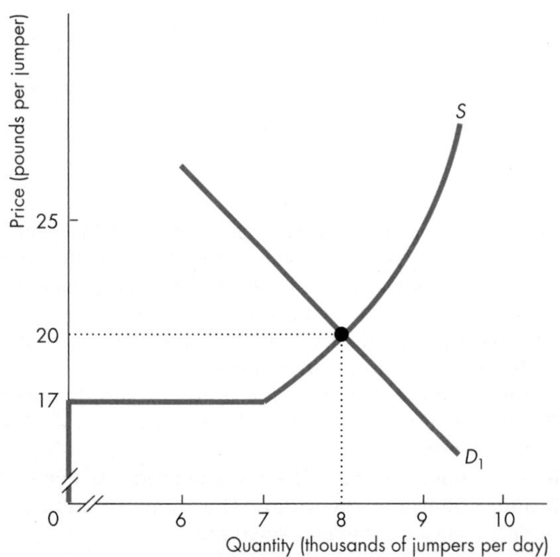

(a) Equilibrium

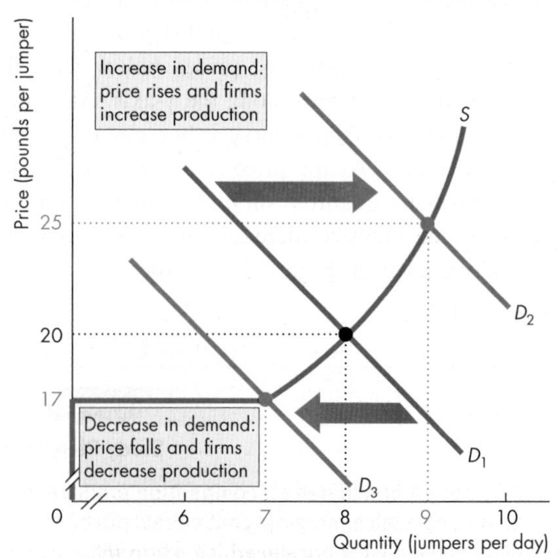

(b) Change in equilibrium

In part (a), the competitive jumper industry's supply curve is *S*, the market demand is D_1 and the price is £20 a jumper. At this price, each firm produces 8 jumpers a day and the industry produces 8,000 jumpers a day.

In part (b), when the market demand increases to D_2, the price rises to £25 and each firm increases its output to 9 jumpers a day. Industry produces 9,000 jumpers a day.

When demand decreases to D_3, the price falls to £17 and each firm decreases its output to 7 jumpers a day. Industry produces 7,000 jumpers a day.

Long-run Adjustments

In short-run equilibrium, a firm might make an economic profit, incur an economic loss or break even. Although each of these three situations is a short-run equilibrium, only one of them is a long-run equilibrium. To see why, we need to examine the forces at work in a competitive industry in the long run.

In the long run, an industry adjusts in two ways:

- Entry and exit
- Changes in plant size

We'll look first at entry and exit.

Entry and Exit

In the long run, firms respond to economic profit and economic loss by either entering or exiting an industry. Firms enter an industry in which firms are making an economic profit. Firms exit an industry in which firms are incurring an economic loss. Temporary economic profit and temporary economic loss do not trigger entry and exit. But the prospect of persistent economic profit or loss does.

Entry and exit influence the market price, the quantity produced and economic profit. The immediate effect of entry and exit is to shift the industry supply curve. If more firms enter an industry, supply increases and the industry supply curve shifts rightward. If firms exit an industry, supply decreases and the industry supply curve shifts leftward.

Let's see what happens when new firms enter an industry.

The Effects of Entry

Figure 11.8 shows the effects of entry. Suppose that all the firms in this industry have cost curves like those in Figure 11.4. At any price greater than £20 a jumper, firms make an economic profit. At any price less than £20 a jumper, firms incur an economic loss. And at a price of £20 a jumper, firms make zero economic profit. Also suppose that the demand curve for jumpers is *D*. If the industry supply curve is S_1, jumpers sell for £23 and 7,000 jumpers a day are produced. Firms in the industry make an economic profit. This economic profit is a signal for new firms to enter the industry. As these events unfold, supply increases and the industry supply curve shifts rightward to S_0. With the greater supply and unchanged demand, the market price falls from £23 to £20 a jumper and the quantity produced by the industry increases from 7,000 to 8,000 jumpers a day.

Industry output increases, but Neat Knits, like each other firm in the industry, *decreases* output! Because the price falls, each firm moves down along its supply curve and produces less. But because the number of firms in the industry increases, the industry as a whole produces more.

Because the price falls, each firm's economic profit decreases. When the price falls to £20 a jumper, each firm makes zero economic profit.

You have just discovered a key proposition:

As new firms enter an industry, the price falls and the economic profit of each existing firm decreases.

An example of this process occurred during the 1980s in the personal computer industry. When IBM introduced its first personal computer, there was little competition and the price of a PC gave IBM a big profit. But

Figure 11.8

Entry and Exit

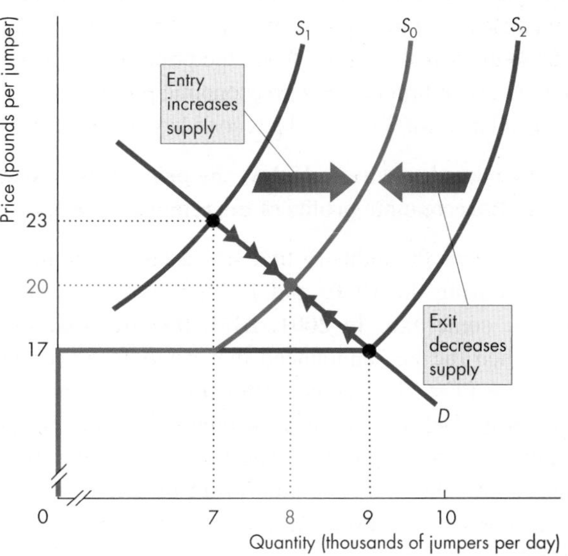

When new firms enter the jumper industry, the industry supply curve shifts rightward, from S_1 to S_0. The market price falls from £23 to £20 a jumper and the quantity produced increases from 7,000 to 8,000 jumpers.

When firms exit the jumper industry, the industry supply curve shifts leftward, from S_2 to S_0. The market price rises from £17 to £20 a jumper, and the quantity produced decreases from 9,000 to 8,000 jumpers.

new firms such as Amstrad, Dell, Elonex and a host of others soon entered the industry with machines technologically identical to IBM's. In fact, they were so similar that they came to be called "clones". The massive wave of entry into the personal computer industry shifted the supply curve rightward and lowered the price and the economic profit.

Let's now look at the effects of exit.

The Effects of Exit

Figure 11.8 shows the effects of exit. Suppose that firms' costs and the market demand are the same as before. But now suppose that the industry supply curve is S_2. The market price is £17 a jumper and 9,000 jumpers a day are produced. Firms in the industry are now incurring an economic loss. This economic loss is a signal for some firms to exit the industry. As firms exit, the industry supply curve shifts leftward to S_0. With the decrease in supply, industry output decreases from 9,000 to 8,000 jumpers and the price rises from £17 to £20 a jumper.

As the price rises, Neat Knits, like every other firm in the industry, moves up along its supply curve and increases output. That is, for each firm remaining in the industry, the profit-maximizing output increases. Because the price rises and each firm sells more, economic loss decreases. When the price rises to £20 a jumper, each firm makes zero economic profit.

You have just discovered a second key proposition:

As firms leave an industry, the price rises and so do the economic profits of the remaining firms.

The same PC industry that saw a large amount of entry during the 1980s and 1990s is now beginning to see some exit. In 2001, IBM, the firm that first launched the PC, announced that it would no longer produce PCs. The intense competition from Compaq, Gateway, Dell and the host of others that entered the industry following IBM's lead has lowered the price and eliminated the economic profit on PCs. So IBM will now concentrate on servers and other parts of the computer market.

IBM exited the PC market because it was incurring economic losses on that line of business. Its exit decreased supply and made it possible for the remaining firms in the industry to make zero economic profit.

You've now seen how economic profits induce entry, which in turn lowers economic profits. And you've seen how economic losses induce exit, which in turn eliminates economic losses. Let's now look at changes in plant size.

Changes in Plant Size

A firm changes its plant size if, by doing so, it can lower its costs and increase its economic profit. You can probably think of lots of examples of firms that have changed their plant size.

One example that has almost certainly happened near your university in recent years is a change in the plant size of copy shops. Another is the number of courier vans that you see on the streets and motorways. And another is the number of square feet of retail space devoted to selling computers, video games and DVDs. These are examples of firms increasing their plant size to seek larger profits.

There are also examples in recent years of firms that have decreased their plant size to avoid economic losses – a process called *downsizing*. European shoe makers, furniture factories and even car assembly lines have been cut back in the face of tough competition from Asian producers.

Figure 11.9 shows a situation in which Neat Knits can increase its profit by increasing its plant size. With its current plant, Neat Knits' marginal cost curve is MC_0 and its short-run average total cost curve is $SRAC_0$. The market price is £25 a jumper, so Neat Knits' marginal revenue curve is MR_0 and Neat Knits maximizes profit by producing 6 jumpers a day.

Neat Knits' long-run average cost curve is *LRAC*. By increasing its plant size – installing more knitting machines – Neat Knits can move along its long-run average cost curve. As Neat Knits increases its plant size, its short-run marginal cost curve shifts rightward.

Recall that a firm's short-run supply curve is linked to its marginal cost curve. As Neat Knits' marginal cost curve shifts rightward, so does its supply curve. If Neat Knits and the other firms in the industry increase their plant size, the short-run industry supply curve shifts rightward and the market price falls. The fall in the market price limits the extent to which Neat Knits can profit from increasing its plant size.

Figure 11.9 also shows Neat Knits in a long-run competitive equilibrium. This situation arises when the market price has fallen to £20 a jumper. Marginal revenue is MR_1, and Neat Knits maximizes profit by producing 8 jumpers a day. In this situation, Neat Knits cannot increase its profit by changing its plant size. Neat Knits is producing at minimum long-run average cost (point *M* on *LRAC*).

Because Neat Knits is producing at minimum long-run average cost, it has no incentive to change its

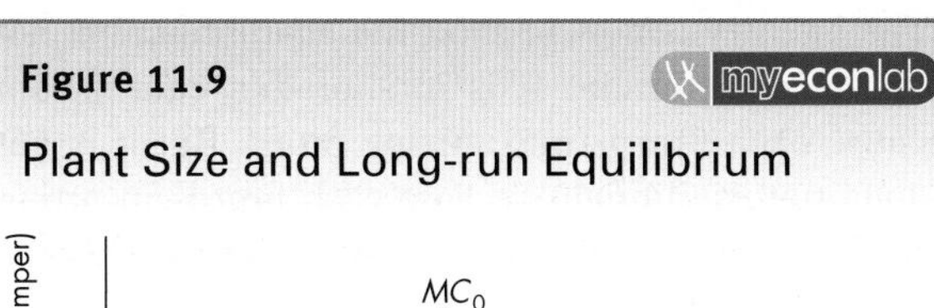

Figure 11.9

Plant Size and Long-run Equilibrium

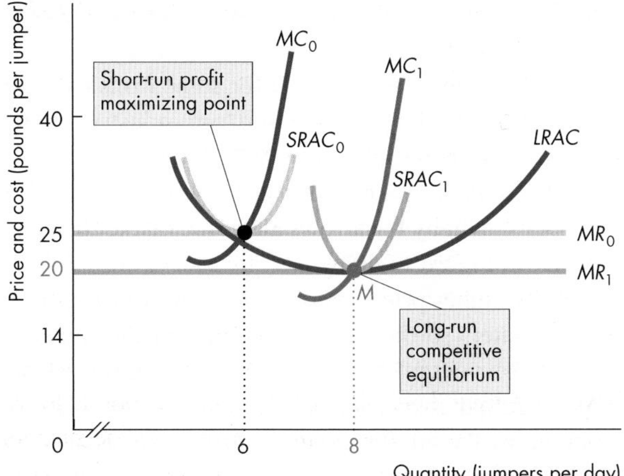

Initially, Neat Knits' plant has marginal cost curve MC_0 and short-run average total cost curve $SRAC_0$. The market price is £25 a jumper and Neat Knits' marginal revenue is MR_0. The short-run profit-maximizing quantity is 6 jumpers a day. Neat Knits can increase its profit by increasing its plant size. If all firms in the jumper industry increase their plant sizes, the short-run industry supply increases and the market price falls.

In long-run equilibrium, a firm operates with the plant size that minimizes its average total cost. Here, Neat Knits operates the plant with short-run marginal cost MC_1 and short-run average total cost $SRAC_1$. Neat Knits is also on its long-run average cost curve $LRAC$ and produces at point M. Its output is 8 jumpers a day and average total cost equals the price of a jumper at £20.

plant size. Either a bigger plant or a smaller plant has a higher long-run average cost. If Figure 11.9 describes the situation of all firms in the jumper industry, the industry is in long-run equilibrium. No firm has an incentive to change its plant size. Also, because each firm is making zero economic profit, no firm has an incentive to enter the industry or to leave it.

Long-run Equilibrium

Long-run equilibrium occurs in a competitive industry when firms make zero economic profit. If the firms in a competitive industry are making positive economic profit, new firms enter the industry. If firms can lower their costs by increasing their plant size, they expand. Each of these actions increases the industry supply, shifts the industry supply curve rightward, lowers the market price and decreases economic profit.

Firms continue to enter and economic profit continues to decrease as long as firms in the industry are making positive economic profits. When economic profit has been eliminated, firms stop entering the industry. And when firms are operating with the least-cost plant size, they stop expanding.

If the firms in a competitive industry are incurring economic losses, some firms exit the industry. If firms can lower their average cost by decreasing their plant size, they downsize. Each of these actions decreases the industry supply, shifts the industry supply curve leftward, raises the market price and economic loss falls.

Firms continue to leave and economic loss continues to decrease as long as firms in the industry are incurring economic losses. When the economic losses have been eliminated, firms stop exiting the industry. And when firms are operating with the least-cost plant size, they stop downsizing.

So in long-run equilibrium in a competitive industry, firms neither enter nor exit the industry and old firms neither expand nor downsize. Each firm makes zero economic profit.

Review Quiz

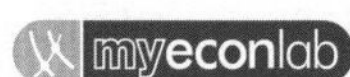

Study Plan 11.3

1. In perfect competition, when the market demand decreases, explain how the price of the good and the output of each firm changes in the short run.
2. If firms in a competitive industry are making a positive economic profit, what happens to the industry supply, the market price, the firm's output, the number of firms and economic profit in the long run?
3. If firms in a competitive industry are incurring an economic loss, what happens to the industry supply, the market price, the firm's output, the number of firms and economic profit in the long run?
4. Under what conditions would a firm choose to change its plant size?

You've seen how a competitive industry adjusts towards its long-run equilibrium. But a competitive industry is rarely in a state of long-run equilibrium. A competitive industry is constantly and restlessly evolving towards such an equilibrium. But the constraints that firms in the industry face are constantly changing. The two most persistent sources of change are in tastes and technology. Let's see how a competitive industry reacts to such changes.

Changing Tastes and Advancing Technology

Increased awareness of the health hazard of smoking has decreased the demand for cigarettes. The development of inexpensive cars and air travel has decreased the demand for long-distance trains and buses. Solid-state electronics have decreased the demand for TV and radio repair services. The development of good-quality inexpensive clothing has decreased the demand for sewing machines. What happens in a competitive industry when there is a permanent decrease in the market demand for its products?

Advances in video technology have brought a huge increase in the demand for flat panel TV sets. Advances in wireless communication have brought an explosion in the demand for mobile phones. Web services such as MySpace and YouTube have brought a big increase in the demand for Internet service. What happens in a competitive industry if the demand for its product increases?

Advances in technology are constantly lowering the costs of production. New biotechnologies have dramatically lowered the costs of producing many food and pharmaceutical products. New electronic technologies have lowered the cost of producing just about every good and service. What happens in a competitive industry when technological change lowers its production costs?

Let's use the theory of perfect competition to answer these questions.

A Permanent Change in Demand

Figure 11.10(a) shows an industry that initially is in long-run competitive equilibrium. The demand curve is D_0, the supply curve is S_0, the market price is P_0 and industry output is Q_0. Figure 11.10(b) shows a single firm in this initial long-run equilibrium. The firm produces q_0 and makes zero economic profit.

Now suppose that demand decreases and the demand curve shifts leftward to D_1, as shown in Figure 11.10(a). The market price falls to P_1 and the quantity supplied by the industry decreases from Q_0 to Q_1 as the industry slides down its short-run supply curve S_0.

Figure 11.10(b) shows the situation facing a firm. Price is now below minimum average total cost so the firm incurs an economic loss. But to keep its loss to a minimum, the firm adjusts its output to keep marginal cost equal to the market price. At a price of P_1, each firm produces an output of q_1.

The industry is now in short-run equilibrium but not long-run equilibrium. It is in short-run equilibrium because each firm is maximizing profit. But it is not in long-run equilibrium because each firm is incurring an economic loss – its average total cost exceeds the market price.

The economic loss is a signal for some firms to leave the industry. As they do so, short-run industry supply decreases and the supply curve shifts leftward.

As the industry supply decreases, the market price rises – as shown by the arrows along the market demand curve D_1 in Figure 11.10(a).

At each higher price, a firm's profit-maximizing output is greater, so the firms remaining in the industry increase their output as the price rises. Each firm slides up its marginal cost or supply curve in Figure 11.10(b), as shown by the arrows along the *MC* curve. That is, as some firms exit the industry, the output of the industry decreases but the output of each firm that remains in the industry increases.

Eventually, enough firms leave the industry for the industry supply curve to have shifted to S_1 in Figure 11.10(a). At this time, the price has returned to its original level, P_0. At this price, the firms remaining in the industry produce q_0 in part (b), the same quantity that they produced before the decrease in the market demand. Because firms are now making zero economic profit, no firm wants to enter or exit the industry. The industry supply curve remains at S_1, and the industry produces Q_2. The industry is again in long-run equilibrium.

The difference between the initial long-run equilibrium and the final long-run equilibrium is the number of firms in the industry. A permanent decrease in market demand has decreased the number of firms. Each remaining firm produces the same output in the new long-run equilibrium as it did initially and earns zero economic profit. In the process of moving from the initial equilibrium to the new one, firms that remain in the industry incur economic losses.

We've just worked out how a competitive industry responds to a permanent *decrease* in the market demand. A permanent increase in the market demand triggers a similar response, but in the opposite direction. The increase in demand brings a higher market price, increased economic profit and entry. As new firms enter, the industry supply increases and the market price starts to fall. And as the market price falls, firms' profits start to decrease. Eventually, the market price returns to its original level and economic profit falls. Each firm makes zero economic profit.

Figure 11.10

A Decrease in Demand

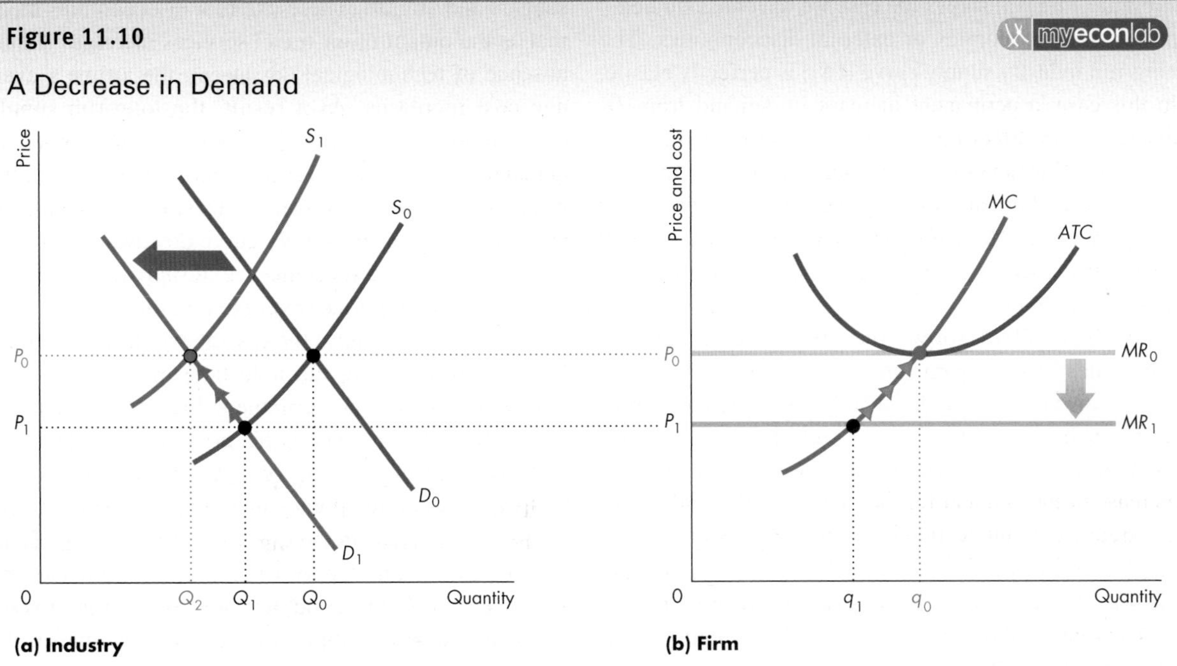

An industry starts in long-run competitive equilibrium. Part (a) shows the market demand curve D_0, the industry supply curve S_0, the equilibrium quantity Q_0 and the market price P_0. Each firm sells at the price P_0, so its marginal revenue curve is MR_0 in part (b). Each firm produces q_0 and makes zero economic profit.

Market demand decreases from D_0 to D_1 in part (a). The market price falls to P_1, each firm decreases its output to q_1 in part (b), and industry output decreases to Q_1 (part a).

In this situation, firms are incurring economic losses and some firms leave the industry. As they do so, the industry supply curve gradually shifts leftward, from S_0 to S_1. This shift gradually raises the market price from P_1 back to P_0. While the price is below P_0, firms continue to incur economic losses and more firms leave the industry. Once the price has returned to P_0, each firm makes zero economic profit. Firms have no further incentive to leave the industry. Each firm produces q_0 and industry output is Q_2.

The demand for Internet service increased permanently during the 1990s and huge profit opportunities arose in this industry. The result was a massive rate of entry of Internet service providers. The process of competition and change in the Internet service industry is similar to what we have just studied but with an increase in demand rather than a decrease in demand.

We've now studied the effects of a permanent change in demand for a good. In doing so, we began and ended in a long-run equilibrium and we examined the process that takes a market from one long-run equilibrium to another. It is this process, not the equilibrium points, that describes the real world.

One feature of the predictions that we have just generated seems odd. In the long run, regardless of whether the change in demand is a permanent increase or a permanent decrease, the market price returns to its original level. Is this outcome inevitable? In fact, it is not. It is possible for the market price in long-run equilibrium to remain the same, rise or fall.

External Economies and Diseconomies

The change in the long-run equilibrium price depends on external economies and external diseconomies. **External economies** are factors beyond the control of an individual firm that lower its costs as *industry* output increases. **External diseconomies** are factors outside the control of a firm that raise its costs as *industry* output increases. With no external economies or external diseconomies, a firm's costs remain constant as industry output changes.

Figure 11.11 illustrates these three cases and introduces a new supply concept, the long-run industry supply curve.

A **long-run industry supply curve** shows how the quantity supplied by an industry varies as the market price varies, after all the possible adjustments have been made, including changes in plant size and changes in the number of firms in the industry.

Figure 11.11(a) shows the case we have just studied – no external economies or external diseconomies. The long-run industry supply curve (LS_A) is perfectly elastic. In this case, a permanent increase in demand from D_0 to D_1 has no effect on the price in the long run. The increase in demand brings a temporary increase in price to P_S and a short-run quantity increase from Q_0 to Q_S. Entry increases short-run supply from S_0 to S_1, which lowers the price to its original level, P_0, and increases the quantity to Q_1.

Figure 11.11(b) shows the case of external diseconomies. The long-run industry supply curve (LS_B) slopes upward. A permanent increase in demand from D_0 to D_1 increases the price in both the short run and the long run. As in the previous case, the increase in demand brings a temporary increase in price to P_S, and a short-run quantity increase from Q_0 to Q_S. Entry increases short-run supply from S_0 to S_2, which lowers the price from P_S to P_2 and increases the quantity to Q_2.

One source of external diseconomies is congestion. The airline industry in recent years provides a good illustration. With bigger airline industry output, there is more congestion of both airports and airspace, which results in longer delays and extra waiting time for passengers and aircraft. These external diseconomies mean that as the output of air travel services increases (in the absence of technological advances), the airline's average cost increases. As a result, the long-run supply curve is upward-sloping. So a permanent increase in demand brings an increase in quantity and a rise in the price. Technological advances decrease average costs and *shift* the long-run supply curve downward. So even an industry that experiences external diseconomies might have falling prices over the long run.

Figure 11.11(c) shows the case of external economies. In this case, the long-run industry supply curve (LS_C) slopes downward. A permanent increase in demand from D_0 to D_1 increases the price in the short run and lowers it in the long run. Again, the increase in demand brings a temporary increase in price to P_S and a short-run increase in the quantity from Q_0 to Q_S. Entry increases short-run supply from S_0 to S_3, which lowers the price from P_S to P_3 and increases the quantity to Q_3.

One of the best examples of external economies is the growth of specialist support services for an industry as it expands. As farm output increased in the nineteenth and early twentieth centuries, the services available to farmers expanded and their costs fell. New firms

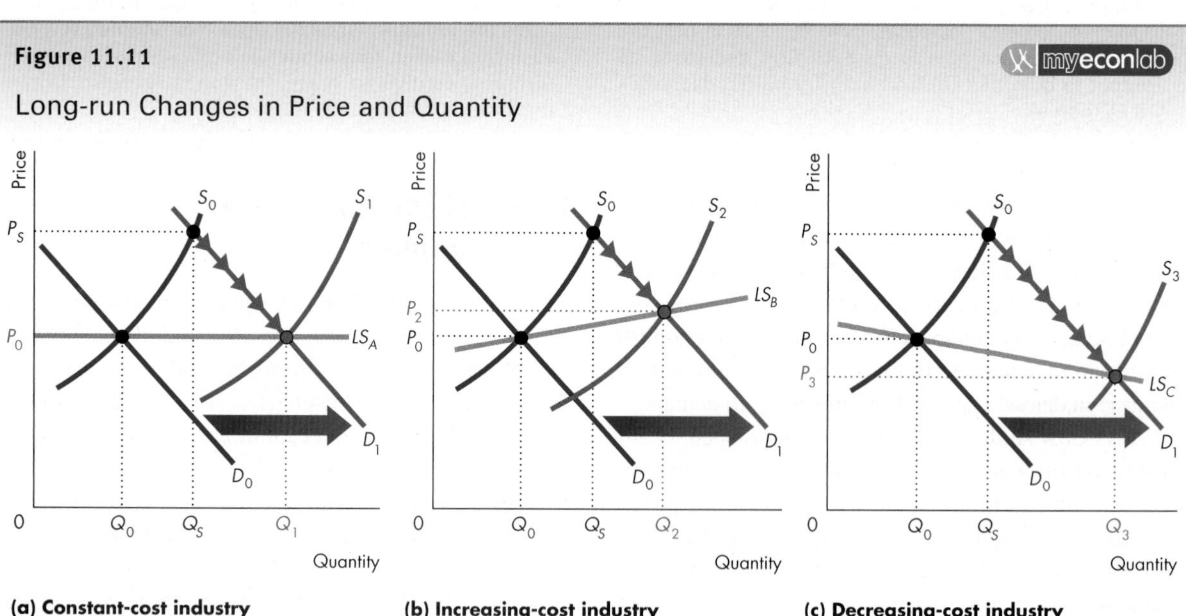

Figure 11.11

Long-run Changes in Price and Quantity

Three possible changes in price and quantity occur in the long run. When demand increases from D_0 to D_1, entry occurs and the industry supply curve shifts from S_0 to S_1. In part (a), the long-run supply curve LS_A is horizontal. The quantity increases from Q_0 to Q_1 and the price remains constant at P_0.

In part (b), the long-run supply curve is LS_B; the price increases to P_2 and the quantity increases to Q_2. This case occurs in industries with external diseconomies. In part (c), the long-run supply curve is LS_C; the price decreases to P_3 and the quantity increases to Q_3. This case occurs in an industry with external economies.

specialized in the development and marketing of farm machinery and fertilizers. As a result, average farm costs decreased. Farms enjoyed the benefits of external economies. As a consequence, as the demand for farm products increased, the output increased but the price fell.

Over the long term, the prices of many goods and services have fallen, not because of external economies but because of technological change. Let's now study this influence on a competitive market.

Technological Change

Industries are constantly discovering lower-cost techniques of production. Most cost-saving production techniques cannot be implemented, however, without investing in new plant and equipment. As a consequence, it takes time for a technological advance to spread through an industry. Some firms whose plants are on the verge of being replaced will be quick to adopt the new technology, while other firms whose plants have recently been replaced will continue to operate with an old technology until they can no longer cover their average variable cost. Once average variable cost cannot be covered, a firm will scrap even a relatively new plant (embodying an old technology) in favour of a plant with a new technology.

New technology allows firms to produce at a lower cost and to make a larger profit than does the existing technology. As a result, as firms adopt a new technology, their average total cost and marginal cost fall and the *ATC* and *MC* curves shift downward. With lower costs, firms are willing to supply a given quantity at a lower price or, equivalently, they are willing to supply a larger quantity at a given price. In other words, when a firm adopts a new technology it increases its supply and its supply curve shifts rightward. With a given demand, the quantity produced increases and the price falls.

Two forces are at work in an industry undergoing technological change:

1 Firms that adopt the new technology make an economic profit. So there is entry by new-technology firms.

2 Firms that stick with the old technology incur economic losses. They either exit the industry or switch to the new technology.

As old-technology firms disappear and new-technology firms enter, the price falls and the quantity produced increases. Eventually, the industry arrives at a long-run equilibrium in which all the firms use the new technology, produce at minimum long-run average cost and make zero economic profit. In the long run, competition eliminates economic profit, so technological change brings only temporary gains to producers. But the lower prices and better products that technological advances bring are permanent gains for consumers.

The process that we've just described is one in which some firms experience economic profits and others experience economic losses. It is a period of dynamic change for an industry. Some firms do well, and others do badly. Often, the process has a geographical dimension – the expanding new-technology firms bring prosperity to what was once a backwater and traditional industrial regions decline. Sometimes, the new-technology firms are in another country, while the old-technology firms are in the domestic economy.

The information revolution of the 1990s produced many examples of changes like these. Commercial banking, which was traditionally concentrated in large cities such as London and Frankfurt, has decentralized with data processing centres in small Yorkshire towns. Scotland's "silicon glen" has displaced traditional agricultural production.

Technological advances are not confined to the information industry. Even in the agricultural sector, biotechnological advances are revolutionizing milk and crop production.

Review Quiz

Study Plan 11.4

1 Describe the course of events in a competitive industry following a permanent decrease in the market demand. What happens to output, market price and economic profit in the short run and in the long run?
2 Describe the course of events in a competitive industry following a permanent increase in the market demand. What happens to output, market price and economic profit in the short run and in the long run?
3 Describe the course of events in a competitive industry following the adoption of a new technology. What happens to output, market price and economic profit in the short run and in the long run?

We've seen how a competitive industry works in the short run and the long run. But does a competitive industry achieve an efficient use of resources?

Competition and Efficiency

A competitive industry can achieve an efficient use of resources. You first studied efficiency in Chapter 2. Then in Chapter 5, using only the concepts of demand, supply, consumer surplus and producer surplus, you saw how a competitive market achieves efficiency. Now that you have learned what lies behind demand and supply curves in a competitive market, you can gain a deeper understanding of the efficiency of a competitive market.

Efficient Use of Resources

Resource use is efficient when we produce the goods and services that people value most highly (see Chapter 2, p. 41 and Chapter 5, p. 108). If someone can become better off without anyone else becoming worse off, resources are *not* being used efficiently. For example, suppose we produce a computer that no one wants and no one will ever use and, at the same time, some people are clamouring for more video games. If we produce one less computer and reallocate the unused resources to produce more video games, some people will become better off and no one will be worse off. So the initial resource allocation was inefficient.

In the more technical language that you have learned, resource use is efficient when marginal social benefit equals marginal social cost. In the computer and video games example, the marginal social benefit of a video game exceeds its marginal social cost. And the marginal social cost of a computer exceeds its marginal social benefit. So by producing fewer computers and more video games, we move resources towards a higher-valued use.

Choices, Equilibrium and Efficiency

We can use what you have learned about the decisions made by consumers and competitive firms and market equilibrium to describe an efficient use of resources.

Choices

Consumers allocate their budgets to get the most value possible out of them. And we derive a consumer's demand curve by finding how the best budget allocation changes as the price of a good changes. So consumers get the most value out of their resources at all points along their demand curves. If the people who consume a good or service are the only ones who benefit from it, there are no external benefits and the market demand curve is the marginal social benefit curve.

Competitive firms produce the quantity that maximizes profit. And we derive the firm's supply curve by finding the profit-maximizing quantity at each price. So firms get the most value out of their resources at all points along their supply curves. If the firms that produce a good or service bear all the costs of producing it, there are no external costs and the market supply curve is the marginal social cost curve.

Equilibrium and Efficiency

Resources are used efficiently when marginal social benefit equals marginal social cost. And competitive equilibrium achieves this efficient outcome because for consumers, price equals marginal social benefit and for producers, price equals marginal social cost.

The gains from trade are the consumer surplus plus the producer surplus. The gains from trade for consumers are measured by consumer surplus, which is the area below the demand curve and above the price paid (see Chapter 5, p. 105). The gains from trade for producers are measured by producer surplus, which is the area above the supply curve and below the price received (see Chapter 5, p. 107). The total gains from trade are the sum of consumer surplus and producer surplus. When the market for a good or service is in equilibrium, the gains from trade are maximized.

Illustrating an Efficient Allocation

Figure 11.12 illustrates an efficient allocation in perfect competition in long-run equilibrium. Part (a) shows the situation of an individual firm, and part (b) shows the market. The equilibrium market price is P^*. At that price, each firm makes zero economic profit. Each firm has a plant size that enables it to produce at the lowest possible average total cost. In this situation, consumers are as well off as possible because the good cannot be produced at a lower cost and the price equals that least possible cost.

In part (b), consumers are efficient at all points on the market demand curve, $D = MSB$. Producers are efficient at all points on the market supply curve, $S = MSC$. Resources are used efficiently at the quantity Q^* and price P^*. At this point, marginal social benefit equals marginal social cost, and the sum of producer surplus (blue area) and consumer surplus (green area) is maximized.

Figure 11.12

Efficiency of Perfect Competition

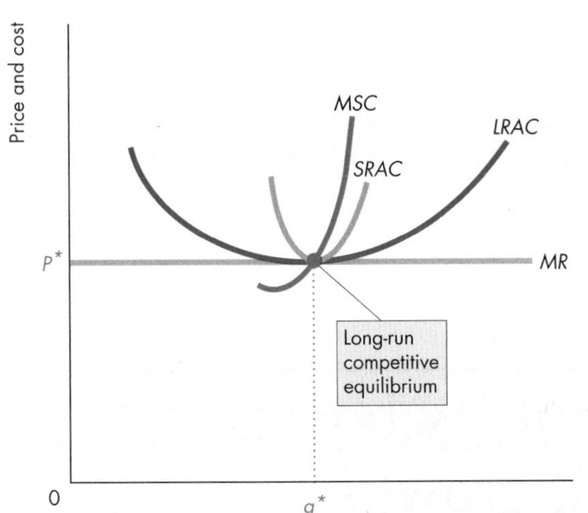

(a) A single firm

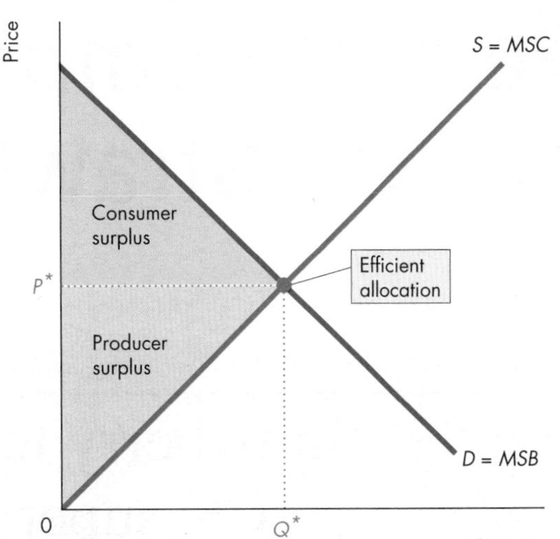

(b) A market

In part (a), a firm in perfect competition produces at the lowest possible long-run average total cost q^*. In part (b), consumers have made their best available choices and are on the market demand curve. Firms are producing at least cost and are on the market supply curve. With no external benefits or external costs, resources are used efficiently at the quantity Q^* and the price P^*. Perfect competition achieves an efficient allocation of resources.

When firms in perfect competition are away from long-run equilibrium, either entry into the industry or exit from the industry is taking place and the market is moving towards the situation depicted in Figure 11.12. But the competitive market is still efficient. As long as marginal social benefit (on the market demand curve) equals marginal social cost (on the market supply curve), the market is efficient. But it is only in long-run equilibrium that consumers pay the lowest possible price.

Review Quiz

Study Plan 11.5

1 State the conditions that must be met for resources to be allocated efficiently.
2 Describe the choices that consumers make and explain why consumers are efficient on the market demand curve.
3 Describe the choices that producers make and explain why producers are efficient on the market supply curve.
4 Explain why resources are used efficiently in a competitive market.

You've now completed your study of perfect competition. And *Reading Between the Lines* on pp. 258–259 gives you an opportunity to use what you have learned to understand recent events in the competitive UK market for strawberries.

Although many markets approximate the model of perfect competition, many do not. In Chapter 12, we study markets at the opposite extreme of market power: monopoly. Then, in Chapter 13, we'll study markets that lie between perfect competition and monopoly: monopolistic competition (competition with monopoly elements) and oligopoly (competition among a few producers).

When you have completed your study of Chapters 12 and 13, you'll have a tool kit that will enable you to understand the variety of real-world markets.

Reading Between the Lines

Perfect Competition: The UK Strawberry Market

www.foodnavigator.com, 30 May 2006

Strawberry technology boosts UK super fruit growth

Anthony Fletcher

The use of polytunnels has revolutionised soft fruit production in the UK, and the advantages vastly outweigh the drawbacks, according to the NFU [National Farmers' Union].

Since the introduction of polytunnels 13 years ago, UK soft fruit growers have been producing increasingly successful crops, partly because they prevent rain damage to the developing fruit.

In an average year 40 per cent of the crop can be damaged by rainfall.

"Polytunnels have allowed British fruit growers to make huge advances, both in saving the ripening fruit from rain damage and in extending the season which now lasts from May until October," said Anthony Snell, NFU horticultural board member.

The season used to last only six weeks but now it can last six months.

"British growers are now successfully competing with foreign imports from Egypt and Spain, extending the growing season has a big impact on the food miles that used to be attached to strawberries before June and after July."

Demand for strawberries, a rich source of vitamin C as well as antioxidants like ellagic acid, has increased in the UK, with many supermarkets marketing the fruit as one of nature's Superfoods. Strawberry sales in the UK are reported to have increased by 34 per cent during the last two years. . . .

Polytunnels are plastic structures developed from similar designs used by farmers in Spain to protect their winter salad crops. They consist of a tubular steel framework of hoops over which polythene is secured. . . .

The Essence of the Story

- Polytunnels — tubular steel hoops that hold polythene covers — have increased the productivity of strawberry farmers.
- Polytunnels have increased the growing season from six weeks to six months.
- The demand for strawberries has increased.
- The value of strawberries sold increased by 34 per cent during 2005 and 2006.

Economic Analysis

- UK-grown strawberries and foreign-grown strawberries are different products. Here we analyze the market for UK-grown strawberries. This market is highly competitive and an example of perfect competition.
- In 2004, the demand for strawberries was D_0 and the supply was S_0 in Figure 1. The equilibrium price was £3.00 per kilogram. We'll call the equilibrium quantity 100 (an index number.)
- Rising incomes and an increasing population increase the demand for strawberries. In Figure 1, demand increases from D_0 to D_1. The price rises to £3.40 per kilogram and the equilibrium quantity increases.
- Figure 2 shows the situation at one farm that does *not* use the polytunnel technology. At £3.00 a kilogram, the farm earns zero economic profit but at £3.40 a kilogram, the farm earns a positive economic profit (shown by the blue rectangle), which induces entry.
- Polytunnel technology has a higher fixed cost but lower variable and marginal cost. Figure 3 shows the situation at one farm that uses this technology. At £3.00 a kilogram, the farm earns zero economic profit (an assumption) but at £3.40 a kilogram, the farm earns a positive economic profit, which induces entry.
- The economic profit with the new polytunnel technology is greater than the economic profit without the new technology (the blue profit area in Figure 3 is bigger than that in Figure 2). This larger profit induces farms that use the old technology to adopt the polytunnel technology.
- Entry and the adoption of the polytunnel technology increase supply. The supply curve in Figure 1 shifts rightward and the price falls. Here the price returns to £3.00 per kilogram (an assumption).
- In Figures 2 and 3, strawberry farms decrease production and again earn zero economic profit in long-run equilibrium.

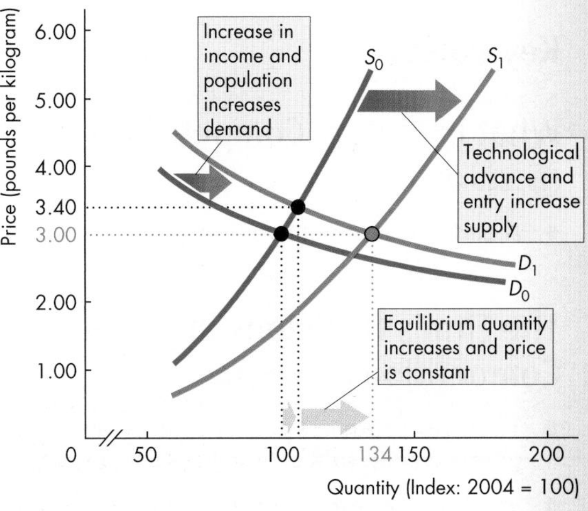

Figure 1 The market for UK strawberries

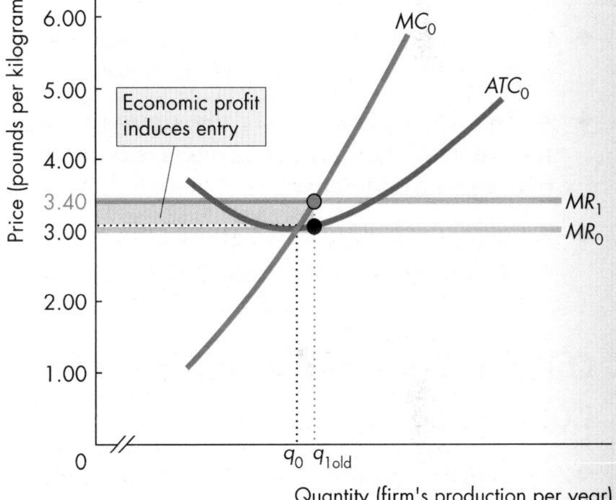

Figure 2 Strawberry grower with old technology

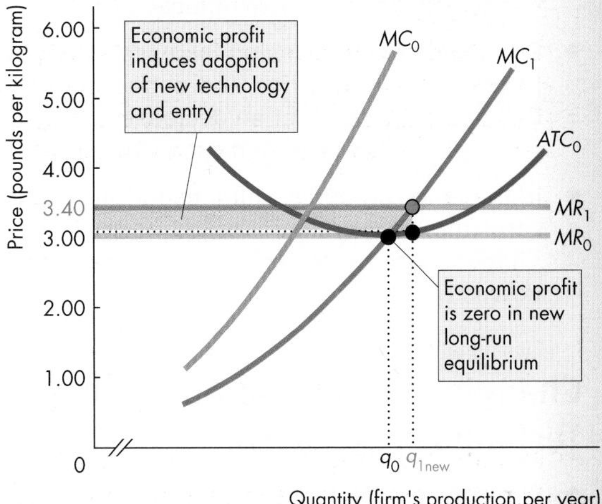

Figure 3 Strawberry grower with new technology

Summary

Key Points

What Is Perfect Competition? (pp. 240–241)

- A perfectly competitive firm is a price taker.

The Firm's Decisions in Perfect Competition (pp. 242–247)

- The firm produces the output at which marginal revenue (price) equals marginal cost.
- In short-run equilibrium, a firm can make an economic profit, incur an economic loss or break even.
- If price is less than minimum average variable cost, the firm temporarily shuts down.
- A firm's supply curve is the upward-sloping part of its marginal cost curve above minimum average variable cost.
- An industry supply curve shows the sum of the quantities supplied by each firm at each price.

Output, Price and Profit in Perfect Competition (pp. 248–251)

- Market demand and market supply determine price.
- Persistent economic profit induces entry. Persistent economic loss induces exit.
- Entry and plant expansion increase supply and lower the market price and economic profit. Exit and plant contraction decrease supply and raise the market price and economic profit.
- In the long-run equilibrium, economic profit is zero (the entrepreneur makes normal profit). There is no entry, exit, plant expansion or downsizing.

Changing Tastes and Advancing Technology (pp. 252–255)

- A permanent decrease in demand for the good leads to a smaller industry output and a smaller number of firms.
- A permanent increase in the demand for the good leads to a larger industry output and a larger number of firms.
- The long-run effect of a change in demand on market price depends on whether there are external economies (the price falls), external diseconomies (the price rises) or neither (the price remains constant).
- New technologies increase supply and in the long run the price falls and the quantity increases.

Competition and Efficiency (pp. 256–257)

- Resources are used efficiently when we produce goods and services in the quantities that everyone values most highly.
- When there are no external benefits or external costs, perfect competition achieves an efficient allocation. In long-run equilibrium, consumers pay the lowest possible price, marginal social benefit equals marginal social cost and the sum of consumer surplus and producer surplus is maximized.

Key Figures

Key Terms

External diseconomies, 253
External economies, 253
Long-run industry supply curve, 253
Marginal revenue, 240
Perfect competition, 240
Price taker, 240
Short-run industry supply curve, 247
Shutdown point, 246
Total revenue, 240

Problems

Tests, Study Plan and Solutions* 

1 Lin's fortune cookies are identical to those of dozens of other firms and there is free entry in the fortune cookie market. Buyers and sellers are well informed about prices.

a Based on the above information, in what type of market does Lin's fortune cookies operate?

b What determines the price of fortune cookies?

c What determines Lin's marginal revenue of fortune cookies?

d If fortune cookies sell for €10 a box and Lin offers his cookies for sale at €10.50 a box, how many boxes does he sell?

e If fortune cookies sell for €10 a box and Lin offers his cookies for sale at €9.50 a box, how many boxes does he sell?

f What is the elasticity of demand for Lin's fortune cookies and how does it differ from the elasticity of the market demand for fortune cookies?

2 Quick Copy is one of the many copy shops in London. The figure shows Quick Copy's cost curves.

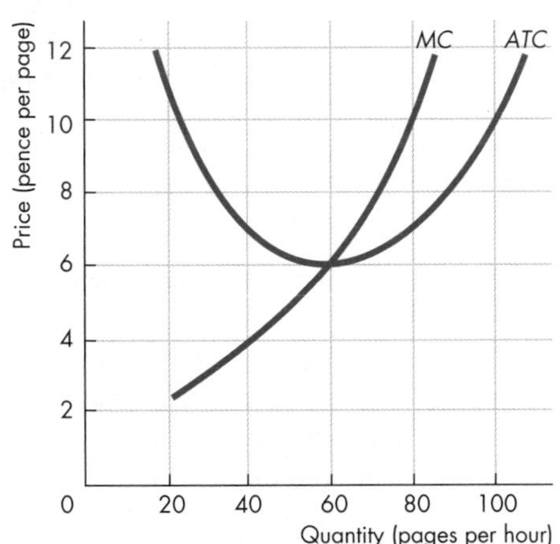

a If the market price of copying one page is 10 pence, what is Quick Copy's profit-maximizing output?

b Calculate Quick Copy's profit.

c With no change in demand or technology, how will the price change in the long run?

3 Pat's Pizza Restaurant is a price taker. The table in the next column sets out its hourly costs.

a What is Pat's profit-maximizing output and how much profit does Pat make if the market price is (i) €14 a pizza, (ii) €12 a pizza and (iii) €10 a pizza?

b What is Pat's shutdown point?

c Derive Pat's supply curve.

Output (pizza per hour)	Total cost (euros per hour)
0	10
1	21
2	30
3	41
4	54
5	69

d At what price will firms with costs the same as Pat's exit the pizza industry in the long run?

e At what price will firms with costs the same as Pat's enter the pizza industry in the long run?

4 The EU market demand schedule for paper is:

Price (euros per box)	Quantity demanded (thousands of boxes per week)
3.65	500
5.20	450
6.80	400
8.40	350
10.00	300
11.60	250
13.20	200

The market is perfectly competitive and each firm has the same cost structure described by the following table:

Output (boxes per week)	Marginal cost	Average variable cost	Average total cost
	(euros per box)		
200	4.60	7.80	11.80
250	7.00	7.00	11.00
300	7.65	7.10	10.43
350	8.40	7.20	10.06
400	10.00	7.50	10.00
450	12.40	8.00	10.22
500	20.70	9.00	11.00

There are 1,000 firms in the industry.

a What is the market price?

b What is the industry's output?

c What is the output produced by each firm?

d What is the economic profit made or economic loss incurred by each firm?

e Do firms enter or exit the industry in the long run?

f What is the number of firms in the long run?

* Solutions to odd-numbered problems are provided.

g What is the market price in the long run?

h What is the equilibrium quantity in the long run?

5 As the quality of computer monitors improves, more and more people stop printing documents and instead read them on the screen. In the market for paper, demand permanently decreases and the demand schedule becomes:

Price (euros per box)	Quantity demanded (thousands of boxes per week)
2.95	500
4.13	450
5.30	400
6.48	350
7.65	300
8.83	250
10.00	200
11.18	150

The costs remain the same as in the table on the previous page.

a What now are the market price, industry output and economic profit or loss of each firm?

b What now is the long-run equilibrium price, industry output and economic profit or loss of each firm?

c Does this industry experience external economies, external diseconomies or constant cost? Illustrate by drawing the long-run supply curve.

6 A perfectly competitive industry is in long-run equilibrium. Answer the following questions and give explanations.

a Can consumer surplus be increased?

b Can producer surplus be increased?

c Can a consumer become better off by making a substitution away from this industry?

d Can the good be produced for a lower average total cost?

Critical Thinking

1 Study the *Reading Between the Lines* on pp. 258–259 and then answer the following questions:

a What are the characteristics of strawberry production that makes the market for strawberries highly competitive?

b What are the two changes in the UK market for strawberries that have influenced the price and quantity? Provide a graphical illustration of these changes.

c If there had been no technological change in the production of strawberries, how would the market have been different today?

d How has the adoption of polytunnel technology changed the UK market for strawberries? Why does competition force all producers to adopt the new technology?

e Do you think the UK market for strawberries is efficient? Would it be efficient if producers had not adopted the polytunnel technology? Illustrate your answer with an appropriate graphical analysis.

2 What has been the effect of an increase in world population on the wheat market and the individual wheat farmer? Explain your answer.

3 Why have the prices of pocket calculators and DVD players fallen? What do you think has happened to the costs and economic profits of the firms that make these products?

Web Activities

Links to Websites

1 Read about "grey imports from Japan". Then answer the following questions:

a What is meant by a "grey import"?

b How do grey imports influence the UK car market in the short run?

c Do you think grey imports will increase the efficiency of the UK car market? Explain your answer.

d What effect will grey imports have on the UK car market in the long run?

2 Read about the EU decision to increase the quotas on imports of textiles from China.

a Why do you think the European Union limits imports of textiles from China?

b Draw a graph to illustrate the EU market for textiles and the situation facing an individual textile producer. In these graphs, show the equilibrium price, the equilibrium quantity, the quantity produced by a firm and its profit.

c On your graphs, show the effect of increasing the textiles import quota?

d Who benefits and who bears costs from the EU quotas on imports of textiles from China?

CHAPTER 12

Monopoly

After studying this chapter you will be able to:

- ◆ Explain how monopoly arises and distinguish between single-price monopoly and price-discriminating monopoly
- ◆ Explain how a single-price monopoly determines its output and price
- ◆ Compare the performance and efficiency of single-price monopoly and competition
- ◆ Explain how a price-discriminating monopoly increases profit
- ◆ Explain how monopoly regulation influences output, price, economic profit and efficiency

Dominating the Internet

eBay and Google are dominant players in the markets they serve. How do firms like these behave? How do they choose the quantities to produce and the prices to charge? Do they charge too much and produce too little? Would more competition among Internet auctioneers and search engines bring greater efficiency? Find out in this chapter. And in *Reading Between the Lines* at the end of the chapter, return to eBay and Google and see which one has the greater monopoly power.

Market Power

Market power and competition are the two forces that operate in markets. **Market power** is the ability to influence the market, and in particular the market price, by influencing the total quantity offered for sale.

The firms in perfect competition that you studied in Chapter 11 have no market power. They face the force of raw competition and are price takers. The firms that we study in this chapter operate at the opposite extreme. They face no competition and exercise raw market power. We call this extreme monopoly. A **monopoly** is a firm that produces a good or service for which no close substitute exists and which is protected by a barrier that prevents other firms from selling that good or service. In monopoly, the firm is the industry.

Examples of monopoly include the firms that operate the pipelines and cables that bring gas, water and electricity to your home. Microsoft Corporation, the software firm that created the Windows operating system, is close to being a monopoly.

How Monopoly Arises

Monopoly has two key features:

- No close substitutes
- Barriers to entry

No Close Substitutes

If a good has a close substitute, even though only one firm produces it, that firm effectively faces competition from the producers of substitutes. Water supplied by a local water board is an example of a good that does not have close substitutes. While it does have a close substitute for drinking – bottled spring water – it has no effective substitutes for showering or washing a car.

Monopolies are constantly under attack from new products and ideas that substitute for products produced by monopolies. For example, DHL, UPS, local couriers, the fax machine, texting, e-mail and direct debt have ended the monopoly of the Post Office.

Barriers to Entry

Legal or natural constraints that protect a firm from potential competitors are called **barriers to entry**. A firm can sometimes create its own barrier to entry by acquiring a significant portion of a key resource. For example, De Beers controls more than 80 per cent of the world's supply of natural diamonds. But most monopolies arise from two other types of barriers: legal barriers and natural barriers.

Legal Barriers to Entry

Legal barriers to entry create legal monopoly. A **legal monopoly** is a market in which competition and entry are restricted through ownership of a resource, by the granting of a monopoly franchise, a government licence, a patent or a copyright.

A *monopoly franchise* is an exclusive right granted to a firm to supply a good or service. An example is the exclusive right granted to the Post Office to carry first-class mail.

A *government licence* controls entry into particular occupations, professions and industries. Examples of this type of barrier to entry occur in medicine, law, dentistry and many other professional services. A government licence doesn't always create a monopoly, but it does restrict competition.

A *patent* is an exclusive right granted to the inventor of a product or service. A *copyright* is an exclusive right granted to the author or composer of a literary, musical, dramatic or artistic work. Patents and copyrights are valid for a limited time period that varies from country to country. In the United Kingdom, a patent is valid for 16 years. Patents encourage the *invention* of new products and production methods.

Patents also stimulate *innovation* – the use of new inventions – by encouraging inventors to publicize their discoveries and offer them for use under licence. Patents have stimulated innovations in areas as diverse as soya bean seeds, pharmaceuticals, memory chips and video games.

Natural Barriers to Entry

Natural barriers to entry create **natural monopoly**, an industry in which economies of scale enable one firm to supply the entire market at the lowest possible cost.

Figure 12.1 shows a natural monopoly in the distribution of electric power. Here, the market demand curve for electric power is D, and the long-run average cost curve is $LRAC$. Because long-run average cost decreases as output increases, economies of scale prevail over the entire length of the $LRAC$ curve. One firm can produce 4 million kilowatt-hours at 5 pence a kilowatt-hour. At this price, the quantity demanded is 4 million kilowatt-hours. So if the price were 5 pence, one firm could supply the entire market. If two firms shared the market, it would cost each of them 10 pence a kilowatt-hour to produce a total of 4 million kilowatt-hours. If four firms shared the market, it would cost each of them 15 pence a kilowatt-hour to produce a total of 4 million kilowatt-hours. So in conditions like those shown in Figure 12.1, one firm can supply the entire market at a lower cost than two or more firms can. The distribution of electric power, water and gas are examples of natural monopoly.

Most monopolies are regulated in some way by government agencies. We will study such regulation at the end of this chapter. But for two reasons, we'll begin by studying unregulated monopoly. First, we can better understand why governments regulate monopolies and the effects of regulation if we also know how an unregulated monopoly behaves.

Second, even in industries with more than one producer, firms often have a degree of monopoly power, and the theory of monopoly sheds light on the behaviour of such firms and industries.

Figure 12.1 myeconlab

Natural Monopoly

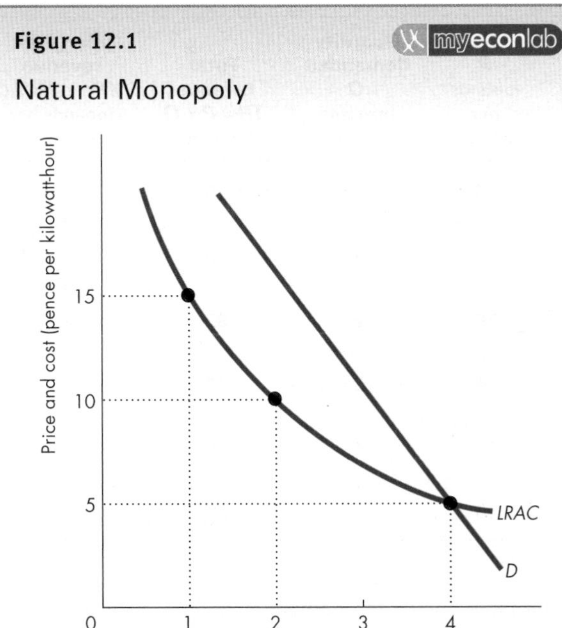

The market demand curve for electric power is *D*, and the long-run average cost curve is *LRAC*. Economies of scale exist over the entire *LRAC* curve. One firm can distribute 4 million kilowatt-hours at a cost of 5 pence a kilowatt-hour. This same total output costs 10 pence a kilowatt-hour with two firms and 15 pence a kilowatt-hour with four firms. So one firm can meet the market demand at a lower cost than two or more firms can, and the market is a natural monopoly.

A major difference between monopoly and competition is that a monopoly sets its own price. But in doing so, it faces a market constraint. Let's see how the market limits a monopoly's pricing choices.

Monopoly Price-setting Strategies

All monopolies face a trade-off between price and the quantity sold. To sell a larger quantity, the monopoly must charge a lower price. But there are two broad monopoly situations that create different trade-offs. They are:

- Single price
- Price discrimination

Single Price

De Beers sells diamonds (of a given size and quality) for the same price to all its customers. If it tried to sell at a low price to some customers and at a higher price to others, only the low-price customers would buy from De Beers. Others would buy from De Beers' low-price customers. De Beers is a *single-price* monopoly. A **single-price monopoly** is a monopoly that must sell each unit of its output for the same price to all its customers.

Price Discrimination

Airlines offer a dizzying array of different prices for the same trip so different passengers on the same flight end up paying different prices. Pizza producers often charge one price for a single pizza and almost give away a second pizza. These are all examples of *price discrimination*. **Price discrimination** is the practice of selling different units of a good or service for different prices.

When a firm price discriminates, it looks as though it is doing its customers a favour. In fact, it is charging the highest possible price for each unit that it sells and making the largest possible profit.

Review Quiz

Study Plan 12.1

1. How does monopoly arise?
2. How does a natural monopoly differ from a legal monopoly?
3. Distinguish between a price-discriminating monopoly and a single-price monopoly.

A Single-price Monopoly's Output and Price Decision

To understand how a single-price monopoly makes its output and price decision, we must first study the link between price and marginal revenue.

Price and Marginal Revenue

Because in a monopoly there is only one firm, the demand curve facing the firm is the market demand curve. Let's look at Gina's Cut and Dry, the only hairdressing salon within a 15 mile radius of a North Yorkshire town. The table in Figure 12.2 shows the market demand schedule. At a price of £20, she sells no haircuts. The lower the price, the more haircuts per hour Gina can sell. For example, at £12, consumers demand 4 haircuts per hour (row *E*).

Total revenue (*TR*) is the price (*P*) multiplied by the quantity sold (*Q*). For example, in row *D*, Gina sells 3 haircuts at £14 each, so total revenue is £42. *Marginal revenue* (*MR*) is the change in total revenue (ΔTR) resulting from a one-unit increase in the quantity sold. For example, if the price falls from £16 (row *C*) to £14 (row *D*), the quantity sold increases from 2 to 3 haircuts. Total revenue rises from £32 to £42, so the change in total revenue is £10. Because the quantity sold increases by 1 haircut, marginal revenue equals the change in total revenue and is £10. Marginal revenue is placed between the two rows to emphasize that marginal revenue relates to the *change* in the quantity sold.

Figure 12.2 shows the market demand curve and marginal revenue curve (*MR*) and also illustrates the calculation we've just made. Notice that at each level of output, marginal revenue is less than price – the marginal revenue curve lies below the demand curve.

Why is marginal revenue *less* than price? It is because when the price is lowered to sell one more unit, two opposing forces affect total revenue. The lower price results in a revenue loss and the increased quantity sold results in a revenue gain. For example, at a price of £16, Gina sells 2 haircuts (point *C*). If she lowers the price to £14, she sells 3 haircuts and has a revenue gain of £14 on the third haircut. But she now receives only £14 on the first two – £2 less than before. She loses £4 of revenue on the first 2 haircuts. To calculate marginal revenue, she must deduct this amount from the revenue gain of £14. So her marginal revenue is £10, which is less than the price.

Figure 12.2

Demand and Marginal Revenue

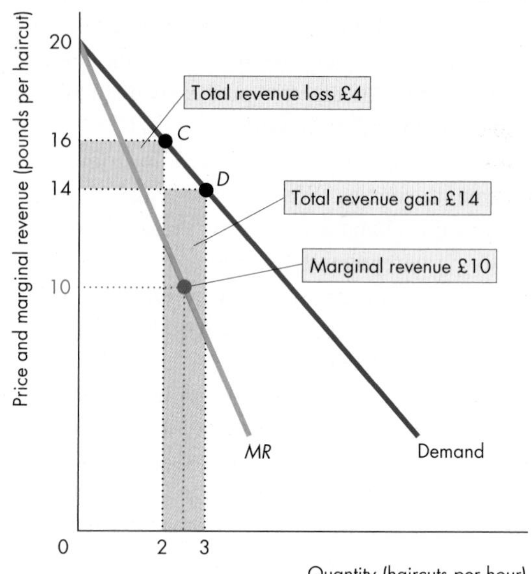

	Price *P* (pounds per haircut)	Quantity demanded *Q* (haircuts per hour)	Total revenue $TR = P \times Q$ (pounds)	Marginal revenue $MR = \Delta TR/\Delta Q$ (pounds per haircut)
A	20	0	0	
				18
B	18	1	18	
				14
C	**16**	**2**	**32**	
				10
D	**14**	**3**	**42**	
				6
E	12	4	48	
				2
F	10	5	50	

The table shows the demand schedule. Total revenue (*TR*) is price multiplied by quantity sold. For example, in row *C*, the price is £16 a haircut, Cut and Dry sells 2 haircuts and its total revenue is £32. Marginal revenue (*MR*) is the change in total revenue that results from a one-unit increase in the quantity sold. For example, when the price falls from £16 to £14 a haircut, the quantity sold increases by 1 haircut and total revenue increases by £10. Marginal revenue is £10. The demand curve and the marginal revenue curve, *MR*, are based on the numbers in the table and illustrate the calculation of marginal revenue when the price falls from £16 to £14 a haircut.

Marginal Revenue and Elasticity

A single-price monopoly's marginal revenue is related to the *elasticity of demand* for its good. The demand for a good can be *elastic* (the elasticity of demand is greater than 1), *inelastic* (the elasticity of demand is less than 1), or *unit elastic* (the elasticity of demand is equal to 1). Demand is *elastic* if a 1 per cent fall in price brings a greater than 1 per cent increase in the quantity demanded. Demand is *inelastic* if a 1 per cent fall in price brings a less than 1 per cent increase in the quantity demanded. And demand is *unit elastic* if a 1 per cent fall in price brings a 1 per cent increase in the quantity demanded. (See Chapter 4, pp. 84–85.)

If demand is elastic, a fall in price brings an increase in total revenue – the increase in revenue from the increase in quantity sold outweighs the decrease in revenue from the lower price – and marginal revenue is *positive*. If demand is inelastic, a fall in price brings a decrease in total revenue – the increase in revenue from the increase in quantity sold is outweighed by the decrease in revenue from the lower price – and marginal revenue is *negative*. If demand is unit elastic, total revenue does not change – the increase in revenue from the increase in quantity sold offsets the decrease in revenue from the lower price – and marginal revenue is *zero*. (The relationship between total revenue and elasticity is explained in Chapter 4, p. 84.)

Figure 12.3 illustrates the relationship between marginal revenue, total revenue and elasticity. As the price of a haircut gradually falls from £20 to £10, the quantity of haircuts demanded increases from 0 to 5 an hour, marginal revenue is positive in part (a), total revenue increases in part (b) and the demand for haircuts is elastic. As the price falls from £10 to £0, the quantity of haircuts demanded increases from 5 to 10 an hour, marginal revenue is negative in part (a), total revenue decreases in part (b) and the demand for haircuts is inelastic. When the price is £10 a haircut, marginal revenue is zero in part (a), total revenue is a maximum in part (b) and the demand for haircuts is unit elastic.

In Monopoly, Demand Is Always Elastic

The relationship between marginal revenue and elasticity that you've just discovered implies that a profit-maximizing monopoly never produces an output in the inelastic range of its demand curve. If it did so, it could produce a smaller quantity, charge a higher price and increase its economic profit. Let's now look at a monopoly's price and output decision.

Figure 12.3 myeconlab

Marginal Revenue and Elasticity

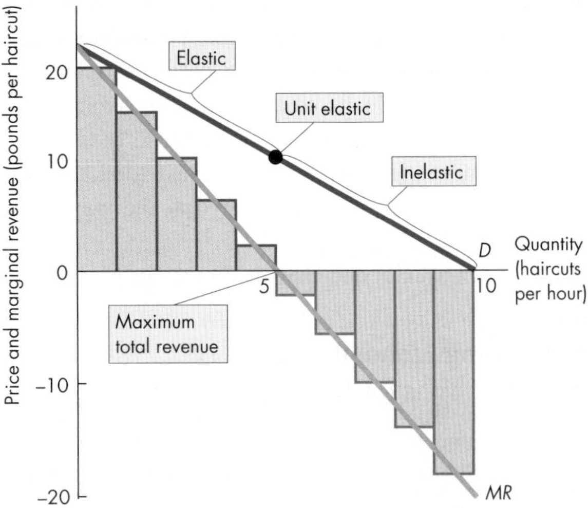

(a) Demand and marginal revenue curves

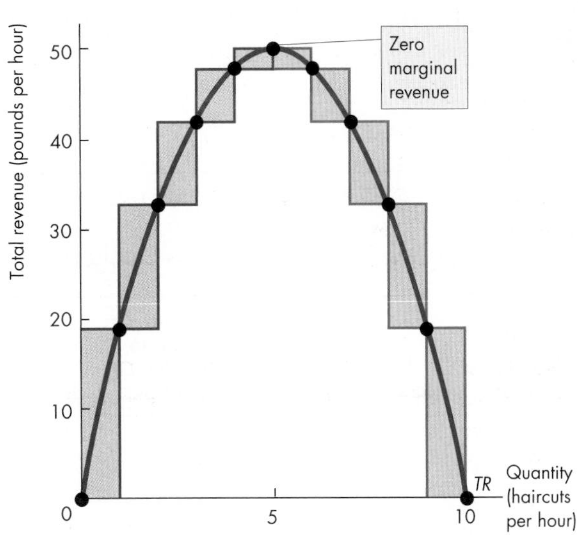

(b) Total revenue curve

In part (a), the demand curve is *D* and the marginal revenue curve is *MR*. In part (b), the total revenue curve is *TR*. Over the range from 0 to 5 haircuts an hour, a price cut increases total revenue, so marginal revenue is positive – as shown by the blue bars. Demand is elastic. Over the range from 5 to 10 haircuts an hour, a price cut decreases total revenue, so marginal revenue is negative – as shown by the red bars. Demand is inelastic. At 5 haircuts an hour, total revenue is maximized and marginal revenue is zero. Demand is unit elastic.

Price and Output Decision

A monopoly sets its price and output at the levels that maximize economic profit. To determine this price and output level, we need to study the behaviour of both cost and revenue as output varies. A monopoly faces the same types of technology and cost constraints as a competitive firm. So its costs (total cost, average cost and marginal cost) behave just like those of a firm in perfect competition. And its revenues (total revenue, price and marginal revenue) behave in the way we've just described.

Let's see how Cut and Dry maximizes its profit.

Maximizing Economic Profit

You can see in Table 12.1 and Figure 12.4(a) that total cost (*TC*) and total revenue (*TR*) both rise as output increases, but *TC* rises at an increasing rate and *TR* rises at a decreasing rate.

Economic profit, which equals *TR* minus *TC*, increases at small output levels, reaches a maximum and then decreases. The maximum profit (£12) occurs when Cut and Dry sells 3 haircuts for £14 each. If it sells 2 haircuts for £16 each or 4 haircuts for £12 each, Cut and Dry's economic profit will be only £8.

Marginal Revenue Equals Marginal Cost

You can see in Table 12.1 and Figure 12.4(b) Cut and Dry's marginal revenue (*MR*) and marginal cost (*MC*). When Cut and Dry increases output from 2 to 3 haircuts, *MR* is £10 and *MC* is £6. *MR* exceeds *MC* by £4 and Cut and Dry's profit increases by that amount. If Cut and Dry increases output yet further, from 3 to 4 haircuts, *MR* is £6 and *MC* is £10. In this case, *MC* exceeds *MR* by £4, so Cut and Dry's profit decreases by that amount.

When *MR* exceeds *MC*, profit increases if output increases. When *MC* exceeds *MR*, profit increases if output *decreases*. When *MC* equals *MR*, profit is maximized.

Figure 12.4(b) shows the maximum profit as price (on the demand curve *D*) minus average total cost (on the *ATC* curve) multiplied by the quantity produced – the blue rectangle.

Maximum Price the Market will Bear

Unlike a firm in perfect competition, a monopoly influences the price of what it sells. But a monopoly doesn't set the price at the maximum *possible* price. At the maximum possible price, the firm would be able to sell only one unit of output, which in general is less than the profit-maximizing quantity. Rather, a monopoly

Table 12.1

A Monopoly's Output and Price Decision

Price (*P*) (pounds per haircut)	Quantity demanded (*Q*) (haircuts per hour)	Total revenue ($TR = P \times Q$) (pounds)	Marginal revenue ($MR = \Delta TR/\Delta Q$) (pounds per haircut)	Total cost (*TC*) (pounds)	Marginal cost ($MC = \Delta TC/\Delta Q$) (pounds per haircut)	Profit ($TR - TC$) (pounds)
20	0	0		20		–20
			18		1	
18	1	18		21		–3
			14		3	
16	2	32		24		8
			10		6	
14	**3**	**42**		**30**		**+12**
			6		10	
12	4	48		40		+8
			2		15	
10	5	50		55		–5

Total revenue (*TR*) equals price (*P*) multiplied by the quantity sold (*Q*). Profit equals total revenue minus total cost (*TC*). Profit is maximized when the price is £14 a haircut and 3 haircuts are sold. Total revenue is £42 an hour, total cost is £30 an hour and economic profit is £12 an hour.

Figure 12.4

A Monopoly's Output and Price

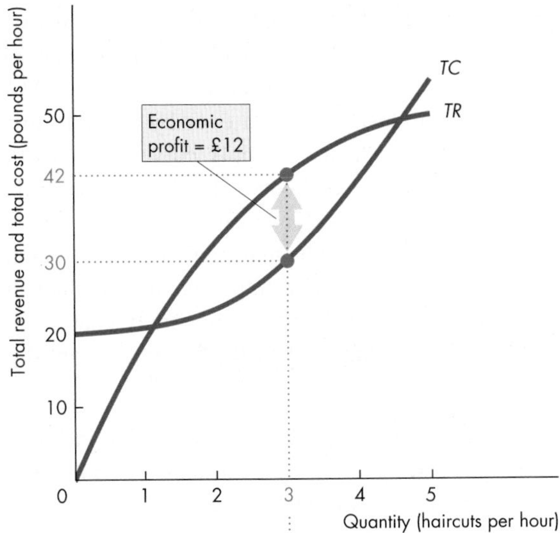

(a) Total revenue and total cost curves

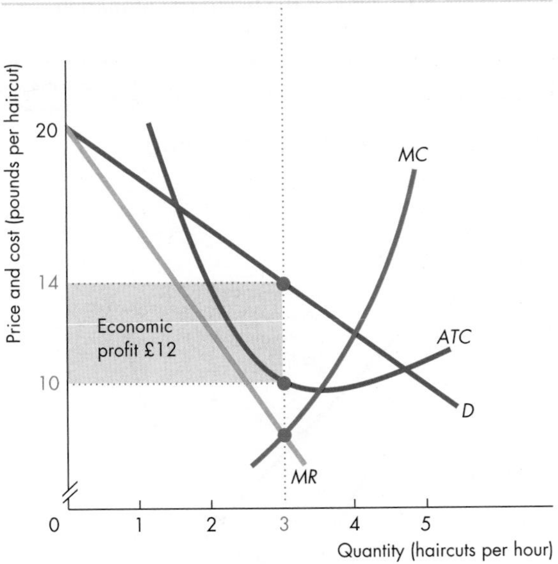

(b) Demand and marginal revenue and cost curves

In part (a), economic profit is the vertical distance equal to total revenue (*TR*) minus total cost (*TC*) and it is maximized at 3 haircuts an hour.

In part (b), economic profit is maximized when marginal cost (*MC*) equals marginal revenue (*MR*). The profit-maximizing output is 3 haircuts an hour. The price is determined by the demand curve (*D*) and is £14 a haircut. The average total cost is £10 a haircut, so economic profit, the blue rectangle, is £12, which equals the profit per haircut (£4) multiplied by 3 haircuts.

produces the profit-maximizing quantity and sells that quantity for the highest price it can get.

All firms maximize profit by producing the output at which marginal revenue equals marginal cost. For a competitive firm, price equals marginal revenue, so price also equals marginal cost. For a monopoly, price exceeds marginal revenue, so price also exceeds marginal cost.

A monopoly charges a price that exceeds marginal cost, but does it always make an economic profit? In Figure 12.4(a), Cut and Dry produces 3 haircuts an hour. Its average total cost is £10 (read from the *ATC* curve) and its price is £14 (read from the *D* curve). It makes a profit of £4 a haircut (£14 minus £10). Cut and Dry's economic profit is shown by the blue rectangle, which equals the profit per haircut (£4) multiplied by the number of haircuts (3), for a total of £12 an hour.

If firms in a perfectly competitive industry make a positive economic profit, new firms enter. That does *not* happen in monopoly. Barriers to entry prevent new firms from entering an industry in which there is a monopoly. So a monopoly can make a positive economic profit and might continue to do so indefinitely. Sometimes that profit is large, as in the international diamond business.

Cut and Dry makes a positive economic profit. But suppose that the owner of the shop that Gina rents increases Cut and Dry's rent. If Cut and Dry pays an additional £12 an hour, its fixed cost increases by £12 an hour. Its marginal cost and marginal revenue don't change, so its profit-maximizing output remains at 3 haircuts an hour. Economic profit decreases by £12 an hour to zero. If Cut and Dry pays more than an additional £12 an hour for its shop rent, it incurs an economic loss. If this situation were permanent, Cut and Dry would go out of business.

Review Quiz

Study Plan 12.2

1. What is the relationship between marginal cost and marginal revenue when a single-price monopoly maximizes profit?
2. How does a single-price monopoly determine the price it will charge its customers?
3. What is the relationship between price, marginal revenue and marginal cost when a single-price monopoly is maximizing profit?
4. Why can a monopoly make a positive economic profit even in the long run?

Single-price Monopoly and Competition Compared

Imagine an industry that is made up of many small firms operating in perfect competition. Then imagine that a single firm buys out all these small firms and creates a monopoly.

What will happen in this industry? Will the price rise or fall? Will the quantity produced increase or decrease? Will economic profit increase or decrease? Will either the original competitive situation or the new monopoly situation be efficient?

These are the questions we're now going to answer. First, we look at the effects of monopoly on the price and quantity produced. Then we turn to the questions about efficiency.

Comparing Output and Price

Figure 12.5 shows the market we'll study. The market demand curve is *D*. The demand curve is the same regardless of how the industry is organized. But the supply side and the equilibrium are different in monopoly and competition. First, let's look at the case of perfect competition.

Perfect Competition

Initially, with many small, perfectly competitive firms in the market, the market supply curve is *S*. This supply curve is obtained by summing the supply curves of all the individual firms in the market.

In perfect competition, equilibrium occurs where the market supply curve and market demand curve intersect. The quantity produced by the industry is Q_C and the price is P_C. Each firm takes the price P_C and maximizes its profit by producing the output at which its own marginal cost equals the price. Because each firm is a small part of the total industry, there is no incentive for any firm to try to manipulate the price by varying its output.

Monopoly

Now suppose that this industry is taken over by a single firm. Consumers do not change, so the market demand curve remains the same as in the case of perfect competition. But now the monopoly recognizes this demand curve as a constraint on the price at which it can sell its output. The monopoly's marginal revenue curve is *MR*.

The monopoly maximizes profit by producing the quantity at which marginal revenue equals marginal cost. To find the monopoly's marginal cost curve, first recall that in perfect competition the industry supply curve is the sum of the supply curves of the firms in the industry. Also recall that each firm's supply curve is its marginal cost curve (see Chapter 11, pp. 246–247). So when the industry is taken over by a single firm, the competitive industry's supply curve becomes the monopoly's marginal cost curve. To remind you of this fact, the supply curve is also labelled *MC*.

The output at which marginal revenue equals marginal cost is Q_M. This output is smaller than the competitive output Q_C. And the monopoly charges the price P_M, which is higher than P_C. We have established that:

Compared with a perfectly competitive industry, a single-price monopoly produces a smaller output and charges a higher price.

We've seen how the output and price of a monopoly compare with those in a competitive industry. Let's now compare the efficiency of the two types of market.

Figure 12.5 myeconlab

Monopoly's Smaller Output and Higher Price

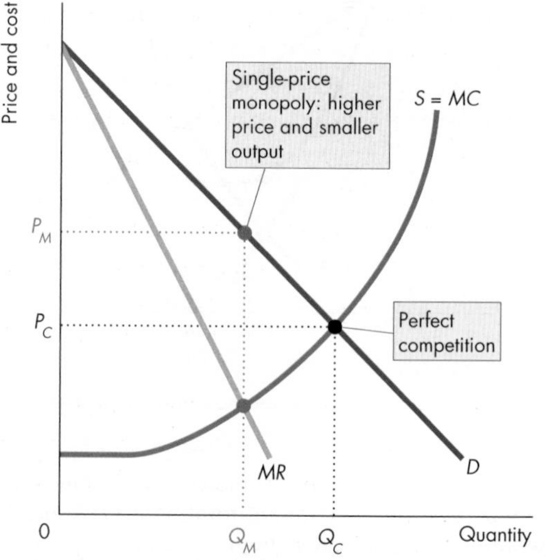

A competitive industry produces the quantity Q_C at price P_C. A single-price monopoly produces the quantity Q_M at which marginal revenue equals marginal cost and sells that quantity for the price P_M. Compared with perfect competition, a single-price monopoly produces a smaller output and charges a higher price.

Efficiency Comparison

You saw in Chapter 11 (pp. 256–257) that perfect competition (with no external costs and benefits) is efficient. Figure 12.6(a) illustrates the efficiency of perfect competition and serves as a benchmark against which to measure the inefficiency of monopoly.

Along the demand curve and marginal social benefit curve ($D = MSB$), consumers are efficient. Along the supply curve and marginal social cost curve ($S = MSC$), producers are efficient. In competitive equilibrium, the price is P_C, the quantity is Q_C and marginal social benefit equals marginal social cost.

Consumer surplus is the green triangle under the demand curve and above the equilibrium price (see Chapter 5, p. 105). *Producer surplus* is the blue area above the supply curve and below the equilibrium price (see Chapter 5, p. 107). The sum of the consumer surplus and producer surplus is maximized.

Also, in long-run competitive equilibrium, entry and exit ensure that each firm produces its output at the minimum possible long-run average cost.

To summarize: at the competitive equilibrium, marginal social benefit equals marginal social cost; the sum of consumer surplus and producer surplus is maximized; firms produce at the lowest possible long-run average cost; and resource use is efficient.

Figure 12.6(b) illustrates the inefficiency of monopoly and the sources of that inefficiency. A monopoly produces Q_M and charges P_M. The smaller output and higher price drive a wedge between marginal social benefit and marginal social cost and create a *deadweight loss*. The grey area shows the deadweight loss and its magnitude is a measure of the inefficiency of monopoly.

Consumer surplus shrinks for two reasons. First, consumers lose by having to pay more for the good. This loss to consumers is a gain for the producer and increases the producer surplus. Second, consumers lose by getting less of the good, and this loss is part of the deadweight loss.

Although the monopoly gains from a higher price, it loses some of the original producer surplus because it produces a smaller output. That loss is another part of the deadweight loss.

Because a monopoly restricts output below the level in perfect competition and faces no competitive threat, it does not produce at the minimum possible long-run average cost. As a result, monopoly damages the consumer interest in three ways: it produces less, it increases the cost of production, and it raises the price to above the increased cost of production.

Figure 12.6 myeconlab

Inefficiency of Monopoly

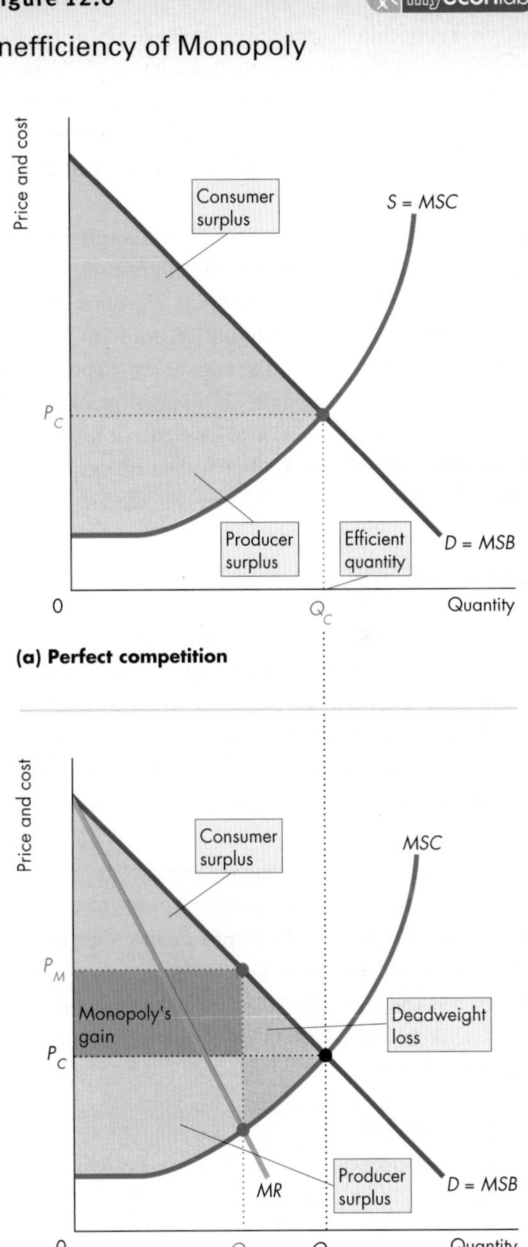

In perfect competition in part (a), output is Q_C and the price is P_C. Marginal social benefit (MSB) equals marginal social cost (MSC); consumer surplus (the green triangle) plus producer surplus (the blue area) is maximized; and in the long-run, firms produce at the lowest possible average cost.

A monopoly in part (b) restricts output to Q_M and raises the price to P_M. Consumer surplus shrinks, the monopoly gains and a deadweight loss (the grey area) arises.

Redistribution of Surpluses

You've seen that monopoly is inefficient because marginal social benefit exceeds marginal social cost and there is deadweight loss – a social loss. But monopoly also brings a *redistribution* of surpluses. And this redistribution is a further reason why monopoly might require regulation.

Some of the lost consumer surplus goes to the monopoly. In Figure 12.6(b), the monopoly gets the difference between the higher price, P_M, and the competitive price, P_C, on the quantity sold, Q_M. So the monopoly takes the part of the consumer surplus shown by the darker blue rectangle. This portion of the loss of consumer surplus is not a loss to society. It is a redistribution from consumers to the monopoly producer. This redistribution might be regarded as unfair.

Rent Seeking

You've seen that monopoly creates a deadweight loss and is inefficient. But the social cost of monopoly can exceed the deadweight loss because of an activity called rent seeking. Any surplus – consumer surplus, producer surplus or economic profit – is called **economic rent**. And **rent seeking** is the pursuit of wealth by capturing economic rent.

You've seen that a monopoly makes its economic profit by diverting part of consumer surplus to itself – by converting consumer surplus into economic profit. So the pursuit of economic profit by a monopoly is rent seeking. It is the attempt to capture consumer surplus.

Rent seekers pursue their goals in two main ways. They might:

- Buy a monopoly
- Create a monopoly

Buy a Monopoly

To rent seek by buying a monopoly, a person searches for a monopoly that is for sale at a lower price than the monopoly's economic profit. Trading of taxi licences is an example of this type of rent seeking. In some cities, taxis are regulated. The city restricts both the fares and the number of taxis that can operate so that operating a taxi results in economic profit or rent. A person who wants to operate a taxi must buy a licence from someone who already has one. People rationally devote time and effort to seeking out profitable monopoly businesses to buy. In the process, they use up scarce resources that could otherwise have been used to produce goods and services. The value of this lost production is part of the social cost of monopoly. The amount paid for a monopoly is not a social cost because the payment is just a transfer of an existing producer surplus from the buyer to the seller.

Create a Monopoly

Rent seeking by creating a monopoly is mainly a political activity. It takes the form of lobbying and seeking to influence the political process. Such influence is sometimes sought by making political contributions in exchange for legislative support or by indirectly seeking to influence political outcomes through publicity in the media or more direct contacts with politicians and bureaucrats. An example of this type of rent seeking would be the donations that alcohol and tobacco companies make to political parties in an attempt to avoid a tightening of legislation on activities such as advertising and licensing, which might affect their profits.

This type of rent seeking is a costly activity that uses up scarce resources. In aggregate, firms spend millions of pounds lobbying Parliament in the pursuit of licences and laws that create barriers to entry and establish a monopoly. Everyone has an incentive to rent seek, and because there are no barriers to entry into rent seeking, there is a great deal of competition in this activity. The winners of the competition become monopolies.

Rent-seeking Equilibrium

How much will a person be willing to give up to acquire a monopoly right? The answer is the entire value of a monopoly's economic profit. Barriers to entry create monopoly. But there is no barrier to entry into rent seeking. Rent seeking is like perfect competition. If an economic profit is available, a new rent seeker will try to get some of it. And competition among rent seekers pushes up the price that must be paid for a monopoly to the point at which the rent seeker makes zero economic profit by operating the monopoly.

Figure 12.7 shows a rent-seeking equilibrium. The cost of rent seeking is a fixed cost that must be added to a monopoly's other costs. Rent-seeking and rent-seeking costs increase to the point at which no economic profit is made. The average total cost curve, which includes the fixed cost of rent seeking, shifts upward until it just touches the demand curve. Economic profit is zero. It has been lost in rent seeking. Consumer surplus is unaffected. But the deadweight loss of monopoly

Figure 12.7 myeconlab

Rent-seeking Equilibrium

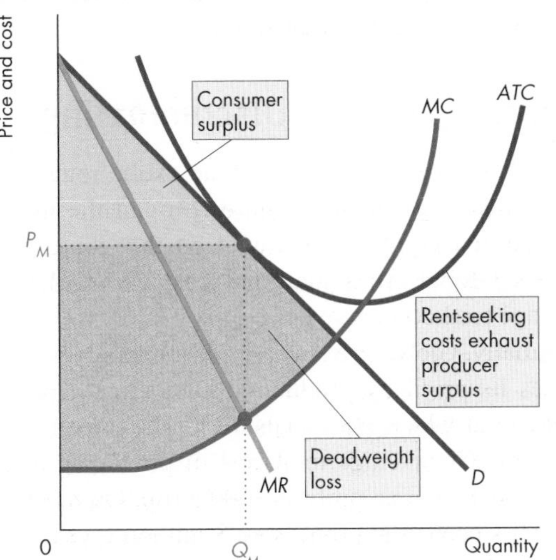

With competitive rent seeking, a monopoly uses all its economic profit to prevent another firm from taking its economic rent. The firm's rent-seeking costs are fixed costs. They add to total fixed cost and to average total cost. The *ATC* curve shifts upward until, at the profit-maximizing price, the firm breaks even.

now includes the original deadweight loss plus the lost producer surplus, shown by the enlarged grey area in the figure.

Review Quiz

Study Plan 12.3

1. Why does a single-price monopoly produce a smaller output and charge a higher price than what would prevail if the industry were perfectly competitive?
2. How does a monopoly transfer consumer surplus to itself?
3. Why is a single-price monopoly inefficient?
4. What is rent seeking and how does it influence the inefficiency of monopoly?

So far, we've considered only a single-price monopoly. But many monopolies do not operate with a single price. Instead, they price discriminate. Let's now see how price-discriminating monopoly works.

Price Discrimination

Price discrimination – selling a good or service at a number of different prices – is widespread. You encounter it when you travel, go to the cinema, go shopping or go out to eat. Most price discriminators are not monopolies, but monopolies price discriminate when they can do so.

To be able to price discriminate, a monopoly must:

1. Identify and separate different buyer types
2. Sell a product that cannot be resold

Price discrimination is charging different prices for a single good or service because of differences in buyers' willingness to pay and not because of differences in production costs. So not all price *differences* are price *discrimination*. Some goods that are similar but not identical have different prices because they have different production costs. For example, the cost of producing electricity depends on time of day. If an electric power company charges a higher price during the peak consumption periods from 7:00 to 9:00 in the morning and from 4:00 to 7:00 in the evening than it does at other times of the day, it is not price discriminating.

At first sight, it appears that price discrimination contradicts the assumption of profit maximization. Why would a railway company give a student discount? Why would a hairdresser charge students and senior citizens less? Aren't these producers losing profit by being so generous?

Deeper investigation shows that far from losing profit, price discriminators make a bigger profit than they would otherwise. So a monopoly has an incentive to find ways of discriminating and charging each buyer the highest possible price. Some people pay less with price discrimination, but others pay more.

Price Discrimination and Consumer Surplus

The key idea behind price discrimination is to convert consumer surplus into economic profit. Demand curves slope downward because the value that people place on any good decreases as the quantity consumed of that good increases. When all the units consumed are sold for a single price, consumers benefit. The benefit is the value the consumers get from each unit of the good minus the price actually paid for it. This benefit is *consumer surplus*. Price discrimination is an attempt by a monopoly to capture as much of the consumer surplus as possible for itself.

To extract every pound of consumer surplus from every buyer, the monopoly would have to offer each individual customer a separate price schedule based on that customer's own willingness to pay. Clearly, such price discrimination cannot be carried out in practice because a firm does not have enough information about each consumer's demand curve.

But firms try to extract as much consumer surplus as possible and to do so, they discriminate in two broad ways:

- Among units of a good
- Among groups of buyers

Discriminating Among Units of a Good

One method of price discrimination charges each buyer a different price on each unit of a good bought. A discount for bulk buying is an example of this type of discrimination. The larger the quantity bought, the larger is the discount – and the lower is the price. (Note that some discounts for bulk arise from lower costs of production for greater bulk. In these cases, such discounts are not price discrimination.)

Discriminating Among Groups of Buyers

Price discrimination often takes the form of discriminating among different groups of consumers on the basis of age, employment status or some other easily distinguished characteristic. This type of price discrimination works when each group has a different average willingness to pay for the good or service.

For example, a face-to-face sales meeting with a customer might bring in a large and profitable order. For sales people and other business travellers, the marginal benefit from a trip is large (or the opportunity cost of *not* taking the trip might be large) so a business traveller is willing to pay a high price for a trip. In contrast, for a holiday traveller, any of several different destinations and even no holiday trip, are options. So for holiday travellers, the marginal benefit of a trip is small and the price that such a traveller is willing to pay for a trip is low.

Because business travellers are willing to pay more than holiday travellers are, it is possible for an airline to profit by price discriminating between these two groups. Similarly, because students have a lower willingness to pay for a haircut than do working people, it is possible for a hairdresser to profit by price discriminating between these two groups.

Let's see how an airline exploits the differences in demand by business and holiday travellers and increases its profit by price discriminating.

Profiting by Price Discriminating

Global Air has a monopoly on an exotic route. Figure 12.8 shows the demand curve (*D*) and the marginal revenue curve (*MR*) for travel on this route. It also shows Global Air's marginal cost curve (*MC*) and average total cost curve (*ATC*).

Initially, Global is a single-price monopoly and maximizes its profit by producing 8,000 trips a year (the quantity at which *MR* equals *MC*). The price is €1,200 per trip. The average total cost of producing a trip is €600, so economic profit is €600 a trip. On 8,000 trips, Global's economic profit is €4.8 million a year, shown by the blue rectangle. Global's customers enjoy a consumer surplus shown by the green triangle.

Figure 12.8

A Single Price of Air Travel

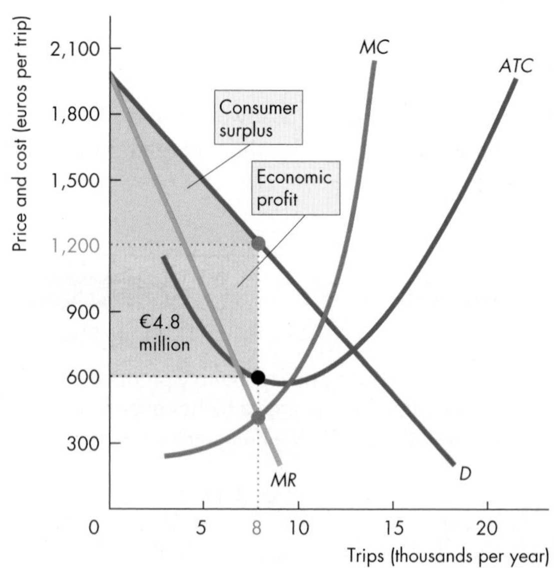

Global Air has a monopoly on an air route. The market demand curve is *D* and marginal revenue curve is *MR*. Global Air's marginal cost curve is *MC* and its average total cost curve is *ATC*. As a single-price monopoly, Global maximizes profit by selling 8,000 trips a year at €1,200 a trip. Its profit is €4.8 million a year – the blue rectangle. Global's customers enjoy a consumer surplus – the green triangle.

Global is struck by the fact that many of its customers are business travellers and it suspects they are willing to pay more than €1,200 a trip. So Global does some market research, which reveals that some business travellers are willing to pay as much as €1,800 a trip. Also, these customers frequently change their travel plans at the last moment. Another group of business travellers is willing to pay €1,600. These customers know a week ahead when they will travel and they never want to stay over a weekend. Yet another group would pay up to €1,400. These travellers know two weeks ahead when they will travel and also don't want to stay away over a weekend.

So Global announces a new fare schedule:

No restrictions, €1,800

7-day advance purchase, non-refundable, €1,600

14-day advance purchase, non-refundable, €1,400

14-day advance purchase, must stay over a weekend, €1,200.

Figure 12.9 shows the outcome with this new fare structure and also shows why Global is pleased with its new fares. Global sells 2,000 seats at each of its four prices. Global's economic profit increases by the blue steps in Figure 12.9. Its economic profit is now its original €4.8 million a year plus an additional €2.4 million from its new higher fares. Consumer surplus has shrunk to the smaller green area.

Figure 12.9

myeconlab

Price Discrimination

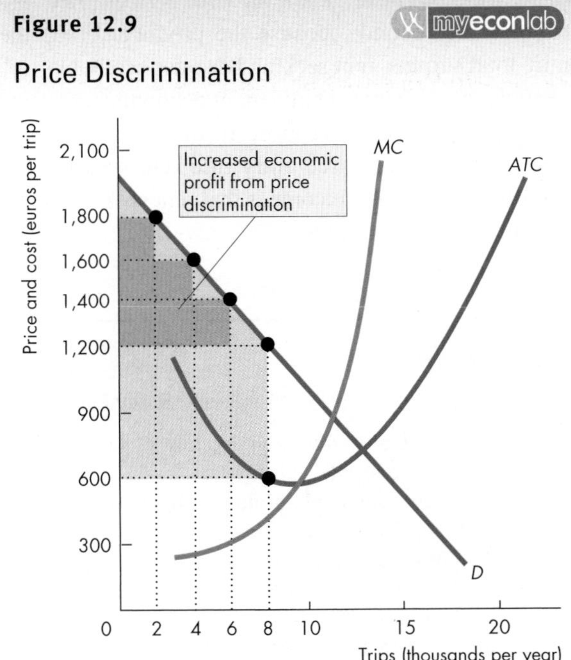

Global revises its fare structure: no restrictions at €1,800, 7-day advance purchase at €1,600, 14-day advance purchase at €1,400, and must stay over a weekend at €1,200. Global sells 2,000 trips at each of its four new fares. Its economic profit increases by €2.4 million a year to €7.2 million a year, which is shown by the original blue rectangle plus the blue steps. Global's customers' consumer surplus (total green area) shrinks.

Perfect Price Discrimination

Perfect price discrimination occurs if a firm is able to sell each unit of output for the highest price anyone is willing to pay for it. In such a case, the entire consumer surplus is eliminated and captured by the producer. To practise perfect price discrimination, a firm must be creative and come up with a host of prices and special conditions each one of which appeals to a tiny segment of the market.

With perfect price discrimination, something special happens to marginal revenue. For the perfect price discriminator, the market demand curve becomes the marginal revenue curve. The reason is that when the price is cut to sell a larger quantity, the firm sells only the marginal unit at the lower price. All the other units continue to be sold for the highest price that each buyer is willing to pay. So for the perfect price discriminator, marginal revenue *equals* price and the demand curve becomes the marginal revenue curve.

With marginal revenue equal to price, Global can obtain even greater profit by increasing output up to the point at which price (and marginal revenue) is equal to marginal cost.

So Global now seeks additional travellers who will not pay as much as €1,200 a trip but who will pay more than marginal cost. Global gets more creative and comes up with holiday specials and other fares that have combinations of advance reservation, minimum stay and other restrictions that make these fares unattractive to its existing customers but attractive to a different group of travellers. With all these fares and specials, Global increases sales, extracts the entire consumer surplus and maximizes economic profit.

Figure 12.10 shows the outcome with perfect price discrimination. The dozens of fares paid by the original 8,000 travellers who are willing to pay between €1,200 and €2,000 have extracted the entire consumer surplus from this group and converted it into economic profit for Global.

The new fares between €900 and €1,200 have attracted 3,000 additional travellers but taken their entire consumer surplus also. Global is earning an economic profit of more than €9 million.

Figure 12.10 myeconlab

Perfect Price Discrimination

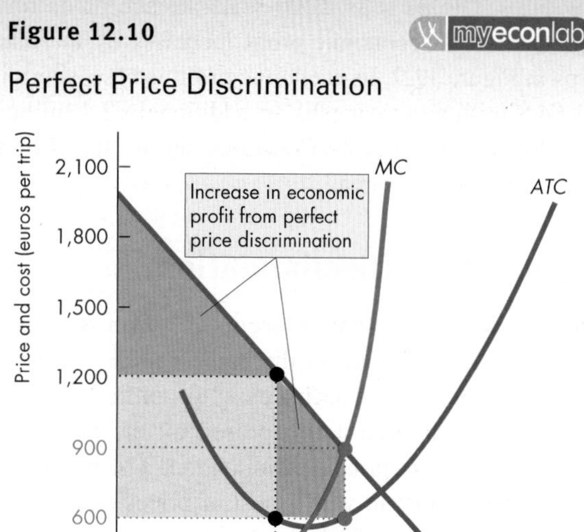

Dozens of fares discriminate among many different types of business travellers and many new low fares with restrictions appeal to holiday travellers. With perfect price discrimination, the market demand curve becomes Global's marginal revenue curve. Economic profit is maximized when the lowest price equals marginal cost. Here, Global sells 11,000 trips and makes an economic profit of €9.35 million a year.

Real-world airlines are just as creative as Global, as you can see in the cartoon!

Would it bother you to hear how little I paid for this flight?

From William Hamilton, "Voodoo Economics", © 1992 by The Chronicle Publishing Company, p. 3. Reprinted with permission of Chronicle Books.

Efficiency and Rent Seeking with Price Discrimination

With perfect price discrimination, output increases to the point at which price equals marginal cost – where the marginal cost curve intersects the market demand curve. This output is identical to that of perfect competition. Perfect price discrimination pushes consumer surplus to zero but increases producer surplus to equal the sum of consumer surplus and producer surplus in perfect competition. Deadweight loss with perfect price discrimination is zero. So perfect price discrimination achieves efficiency.

The more perfectly the monopoly can price discriminate, the closer its output gets to the competitive output and the more efficient is the outcome.

But there are two differences between perfect competition and perfect price discrimination. First, the distribution of the total surplus is different. It is shared by consumers and producers in perfect competition, whereas the producer gets it all with perfect price discrimination. Second, because the producer grabs the entire total surplus, rent seeking becomes profitable.

People use resources in pursuit of economic rents, and the bigger the rents, the more resources get used in pursuing them. With free entry into rent seeking, the long-run equilibrium outcome is that rent seekers use up the entire producer surplus.

Review Quiz

Study Plan 12.4

1. What is price discrimination and how is it used to increase a monopoly's profit?
2. Explain how consumer surplus changes when a monopoly price discriminates.
3. Explain how consumer surplus, economic profit and output change when a monopoly perfectly price discriminates.
4. What are some of the ways that real-world airlines use to price discriminate?

You've seen that monopoly is profitable for the monopoly but costly for consumers. Monopoly results in inefficiency. Because of these features of monopoly, it is subject to policy debate and regulation. We'll now study the key monopoly policy issues.

Monopoly Policy Issues

Monopoly looks bad when we compare it with competition. Monopoly is inefficient, and it captures consumer surplus and converts it into producer surplus or pure waste in the form of rent-seeking costs. If monopoly is so bad, why do we put up with it? Why don't we have laws that crack down on monopoly so hard that it never rears its head? We do indeed have laws that limit monopoly power and regulate the prices that monopolies are permitted to charge. But monopoly also brings some benefits. We begin this review of monopoly policy issues by looking at the benefits of monopoly. We then look at monopoly regulation.

Gains from Monopoly

The main reason why monopoly exists is that it has potential advantages over a competitive alternative. These advantages arise from:

- Incentives to innovation
- Economies of scale and economies of scope

Incentives to Innovation

Invention leads to a wave of innovation as new knowledge is applied to the production process. Innovation may take the form of developing a new product or a lower-cost way of making an existing product. Controversy has raged over whether large firms with market power or small competitive firms lacking such market power are the most innovative. It is clear that some temporary market power arises from innovation. A firm that develops a new product or process and patents it obtains an exclusive right to that product or process for the term of the patent.

But does the granting of a monopoly, even a temporary one, to an innovator increase the pace of innovation? One line of reasoning suggests that it does. Without protection, an innovator is not able to enjoy the profits from innovation for very long. Thus the incentive to innovate is weakened. A contrary argument is that monopolies can afford to be lazy whereas competitive firms cannot. Competitive firms must strive to innovate and cut costs even though they know that they cannot hang onto the benefits of their innovation for long. But that knowledge spurs them on to greater and faster innovation.

The evidence on whether monopoly leads to greater innovation than competition is mixed. Large firms do more research and development than do small firms. But research and development are inputs into the process of innovation. What matters is not input but output. Two measures of the output of research and development are the number of patents and the rate of productivity growth. On these measures, it is not clear that bigger is better. But as a new process or product spreads through an industry, the large firms adopt the new process or product more quickly than do small firms. So large firms help to speed the process of diffusion of technological change.

Economies of Scale and Scope

Economies of scale and economies of scope can lead to natural monopoly. And as you saw at the beginning of this chapter, in a natural monopoly, a single firm can produce at a lower average cost than a number of firms can.

A firm experiences *economies of scale* when an increase in its output of a good or service brings a decrease in the average total cost of producing it (see Chapter 10, p. 226). A firm experiences *economies of scope* when an increase in the *range of goods produced* brings a decrease in average total cost (see Chapter 9, p. 207). Economies of scope occur when different goods can share specialized (and usually costly) capital resources. For example, McDonald's can produce both hamburgers and chips at a lower average total cost than can two separate firms – a burger firm and a chips firm – because at McDonald's, hamburgers and chips share the use of specialized food storage and preparation facilities. A firm that produces a wide range of products can hire specialist computer programmers, designers and marketing experts whose skills can be used across the product range, thereby spreading their costs and lowering the average total cost of production of each of the goods.

There are many examples in which a combination of economies of scale and economies of scope arise, but not all of them lead to monopoly. Some examples are the brewing of beer, the manufacture of refrigerators and other household appliances, the manufacture of pharmaceuticals and the refining of petroleum.

Examples of industries in which economies of scale are so significant that they lead to a natural monopoly are becoming rare. Public utilities such as gas, electric power, local telephone service and waste collection once were natural monopolies. But technological advances now enable us to separate the *production* of electric power or gas from its *distribution*. The provision of water, though, remains a natural monopoly.

A large-scale firm that has control over supply and can influence price – and therefore behaves like the monopoly firm that you've studied in this chapter – can reap these economies of scale and scope. Small, competitive firms cannot. Consequently, there are situations in which the comparison of monopoly and competition that we made earlier in this chapter is not valid.

Recall that we imagined the takeover of a large number of competitive firms by a monopoly firm. But we also assumed that the monopoly would use exactly the same technology as the small firms and have the same costs. If one large firm can reap economies of scale and scope, its marginal cost curve will lie below the supply curve of a competitive industry made up of many small firms. It is possible for such economies of scale and scope to be so large as to result in a larger output and lower price under monopoly than a competitive industry would achieve.

Where significant economies of scale and scope exist, it is usually worth putting up with monopoly and regulating its price.

Regulating Natural Monopoly

Where demand and cost conditions create a natural monopoly, government at the EU, national or local level usually steps in to regulate the price of the monopoly. By regulating a monopoly, some of the worst aspects of monopoly can be avoided or at least moderated. Let's look at monopoly price regulation.

Figure 12.11 shows the demand curve *D*, the marginal revenue curve *MR*, the long-run average cost curve *ATC* and the marginal cost curve *MC* for a gas distribution company that is a natural monopoly.

The firm's marginal cost is constant at 10 cents per cubic metre. But average total cost decreases as output increases. The reason is that the gas company has a large investment in pipelines and so has high fixed costs. These fixed costs are part of the company's average total cost and appear in the *ATC* curve. The average total cost curve slopes downward because as the number of cubic metres sold increases, the fixed cost is spread over a larger number of units. (If you need to refresh your memory on how the average total cost curve is calculated, look back at Chapter 10, p. 220.)

This one firm can supply the entire market at a lower cost than two firms can because average cost is falling even when the entire market is supplied. (Refer back to pp. 264–265 if you need a quick refresher on natural monopoly.)

Profit Maximization

First, suppose the gas company is not regulated and instead maximizes profit. Figure 12.11 shows the outcome. The company produces 2 million cubic metres a day, the quantity at which marginal cost equals marginal revenue. It prices this gas at 20 cents a cubic metre and makes an economic profit of 2 cents a cubic metre, or €40,000 a day.

This outcome is fine for the gas company, but it is inefficient. Gas costs 20 cents a cubic metre when its marginal cost is only 10 cents a cubic metre. Also, the gas company is making a big profit. What can regulation do to improve this outcome?

The Efficient Regulation

If the monopoly regulator wants to achieve an efficient use of resources, it must require the gas monopoly to produce the quantity of gas that brings marginal social benefit into equality with marginal social cost. With no external benefits, marginal social benefit is what the consumer is willing to pay and is shown by the demand curve. With no external costs, marginal social cost is shown by the firm's marginal cost curve. You can see in Figure 12.11 that this outcome occurs if the price is regulated at 10 cents per cubic metre and if 4 million cubic metres per day are produced.

The regulation that produces this outcome is called a marginal cost pricing rule. A **marginal cost pricing rule** sets price equal to marginal cost. It maximizes total surplus in the regulated industry. In this example, that surplus is all consumer surplus and it equals the area of the triangle beneath the demand curve and above the marginal cost curve.

The marginal cost pricing rule is efficient. But it leaves the natural monopoly incurring an economic loss. Because average total cost is falling as output increases, marginal cost is below average total cost.

And because price equals marginal cost, price is below average total cost. Average total cost minus price is the loss per unit produced. It's pretty obvious that a gas company that is required to use a marginal cost pricing rule will not stay in business for long. How can a company cover its costs and, at the same time, obey a marginal cost pricing rule?

One possibility is price discrimination. The company might charge a higher price to some customers but marginal cost to the customers who pay least. If the conditions required for marginal cost pricing are met, that solution is attractive. Another possibility is to use a

Figure 12.11 

Regulating a Natural Monopoly

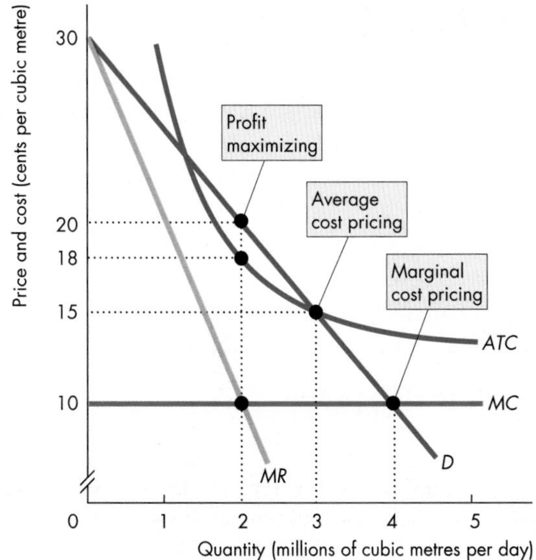

A natural monopoly is an industry in which average total cost is falling even when the entire market demand is satisfied. A gas producer faces the demand curve *D*. The firm's marginal cost is constant at 10 cents per cubic metre, as shown by the curve labelled *MC*. The average total cost curve is *ATC*.

A profit-maximizing monopoly produces 2 million cubic metres a day and charges a price of 20 cents per cubic metre.

An average cost pricing rule sets the price at 15 cents per cubic metre. The monopoly produces 3 million cubic metres per day and makes zero economic profit.

A marginal cost pricing rule sets the price at 10 cents per cubic metre. The monopoly produces 4 million cubic metres per day and incurs an economic loss.

two-part price (called two-part tariff). For example, the gas company might charge a monthly fixed fee that covers its fixed cost and then charge for gas consumed at marginal cost.

But a natural monopoly cannot always cover its costs in these ways. If a natural monopoly cannot cover its total cost from its customers, and if the government wants it to follow a marginal cost pricing rule, the government must give the firm a subsidy. In such a case, the government raises the revenue for the subsidy by taxing some other activity. But as we saw in Chapter 6, taxes themselves generate deadweight loss. Thus the deadweight loss resulting from additional taxes must be subtracted from the efficiency gained by forcing the natural monopoly to adopt a marginal cost pricing rule. When the deadweight loss from taxes is taken into account, it might turn out to be better to abandon marginal cost pricing.

Average Cost Pricing

Regulators almost never impose efficient pricing because of its consequences for the firm's economic profit. Instead, they compromise by permitting the firm to cover its costs and to break even (make zero economic profit). So pricing to cover total cost means setting price equal to average total cost – called an **average cost pricing rule**.

Figure 12.11 shows the average cost pricing outcome. The gas company charges 15 cents a cubic metre and sells 3 million cubic metres per day. This outcome is better for consumers than the unregulated profit-maximizing outcome. The price is 5 cents a cubic metre lower, and the quantity consumed is 1 million cubic metres per day more. And the outcome is better for the producer than the marginal cost pricing rule outcome. The firm breaks even (makes zero economic profit). The outcome is inefficient but less so than the unregulated profit-maximizing outcome.

Review Quiz

Study Plan 12.5

1 What are the two main reasons why monopoly is worth tolerating?
2 Provide some examples of economies of scale and economies of scope.
3 Why might the incentive to innovate be greater for a monopoly than for a small competitive firm?
4 What is the price that achieves an efficient outcome for a regulated monopoly? And what is the problem with this price?
5 Compare the consumer surplus, producer surplus and deadweight loss that arise from average cost pricing with those that arise from profit-maximization pricing and marginal cost pricing.

You've now have studied perfect competition and monopoly. *Reading Between the Lines* on pp. 280–281 looks at market power in the markets for Internet auctions and search. In the next chapter, we study markets that lie between the extremes of perfect competition and monopoly and that blend elements of the two.

Reading Between the Lines

eBay Is a Monopoly but Google Isn't!

The Economist, 30 October 2002

How good is Google

. . . As search engines go . . . Google has clearly been a runaway success. Not only is its own site the most popular for search on the web, but it also powers the search engines of major portals, such as Yahoo! and AOL. All told, 75% of referrals to websites now originate from Google's algorithms. That is power.

For some time now, Google's board . . . has been deliberating how to translate that power into money. They appear to have decided to bring Google to the stock market next spring. Bankers have been overheard estimating Google's value at $15 billion or more. That could make Google Silicon Valley's first hot IPO since the dotcom bust, and perhaps its biggest ever.

. . . To be worth the rumoured $15 billion for longer than it takes a bubble to burst, it will need to raise its profitability substantially. That means matching such internet stars as eBay (market capitalisation $37 billion), but without the natural-monopoly advantages that have made eBay so dominant – the classic network effect of buyers and sellers knowing they do best by all trading in one place. For Google to stay permanently ahead of other search-engine technologies is almost impossible, since it takes so little – only a bright idea by another set of geeks – to lose the lead. In contrast to a portal such as Yahoo!, which also offers customers free e-mail and other services, a pure search engine is always but a click away from losing users.

The Essence of the Story

- Google is the most popular search engine and 75 per cent of referrals to websites originate from its searches.
- Some bankers estimate Google's value at $15 billion or more.
- It is almost impossible for Google to stay permanently ahead of other search-engine technologies because it takes only a bright idea by another set of programmers to lose its lead.
- Google does not have the natural-monopoly advantages that have made eBay dominant – network effect of buyers and sellers knowing they do best by all trading in one place.

Economic Analysis

- Almost all the costs of eBay or Google are fixed costs. When all costs are fixed, average fixed cost equals average total cost, and average variable cost and marginal cost are zero. Figure 1 shows eBay's cost curves. (Google's cost curves look just like these.)
- A natural monopoly has two features:
  1. Economies of scale at the output that meet the entire market demand, and
  2. No close substitutes.
- Both eBay and Google have the first feature but only eBay has the second.
- If another firm developed a better search engine than Google, it would take the market for Internet search. But Google can prevent this outcome by constantly improving its search engine and keeping it the best available.
- Because it enjoys the benefit of a network externality, as the article says, "buyers and sellers knowing they do best by all trading in one place", eBay has no close substitute and is unlikely to be confronted with one.
- The demand for eBay's services is *D* in Figure 1. The firm maximizes profit by setting a price, *P*, that generates a quantity demanded, *Q*, where marginal revenue is zero and equal to the zero marginal cost.
- eBay users enjoy a consumer surplus, eBay earns a large economic profit (capital value at an estimated $37 billion), but there is a deadweight loss.
- Although, as a monopoly, eBay is inefficient and creates a deadweight loss, the world is better off with eBay than it would be without it. Figure 2 shows why.
- In the market for a rarely traded item such as carved bone fishes, the supply including the cost of finding a buyer was S_0 before eBay began to operate. The cost of finding a buyer was so large that none of these items were traded.
- Supply increases to S_1 when eBay lowers the cost of finding a buyer. Now the item is traded. The buyer pays *PB* and receives a consumer surplus, the seller receives *PS* and a seller's surplus and eBay makes an economic profit.
- A deadweight loss arises because eBay doesn't set the price equal to marginal cost. So the market is inefficient. But compared with the situation before eBay existed, a huge consumer surplus and a surplus for the seller arise.

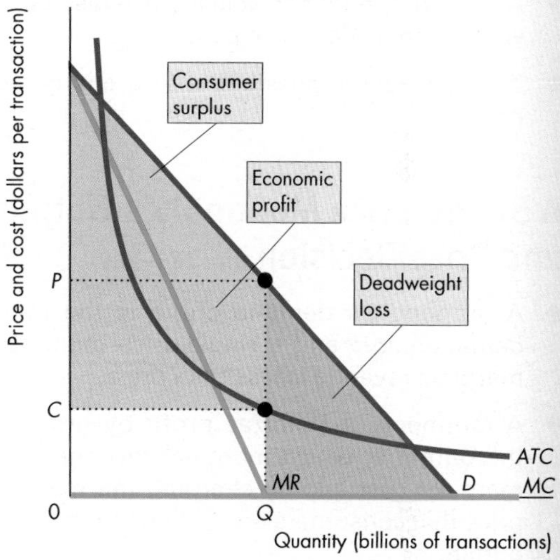

Figure 1 eBay's market for auction services

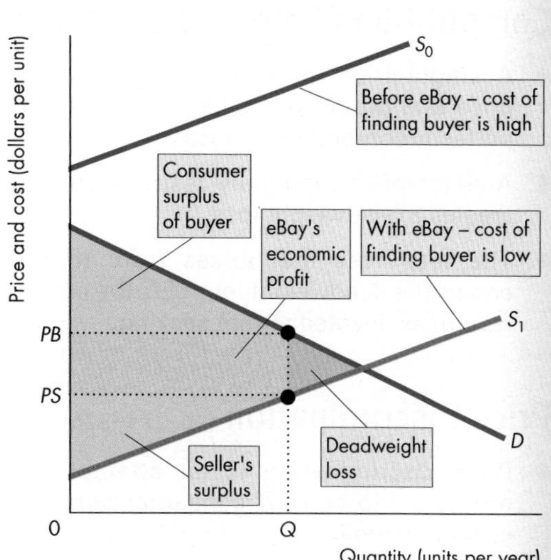

Figure 2 The view from the market for carved bone fishes

Summary

Key Points

Market Power (pp. 264–265)

- A monopoly is an industry with a single supplier of a good or service that has no close substitutes and in which barriers to entry prevent competition.
- Barriers to entry may be legal (public franchise, licence, patent, copyright, firm owns control of a resource) or natural (created by economies of scale).
- A monopoly might be able to price discriminate when there is no resale possibility.
- Where resale is possible, a firm charges one price.

A Single-price Monopoly's Output and Price Decision (pp. 266–269)

- A monopoly's demand curve is the market demand curve and a single-price monopoly's marginal revenue is less than price.
- A monopoly maximizes profit by producing the output at which marginal revenue equals marginal cost and by charging the maximum price that consumers are willing to pay for that output.

Single-price Monopoly and Competition Compared (pp. 270–273)

- A single-price monopoly charges a higher price and produces a smaller quantity than a perfectly competitive industry.
- A single-price monopoly restricts output and creates a deadweight loss.
- The total loss that arises from monopoly equals the deadweight loss plus the cost of the resources devoted to rent seeking.

Price Discrimination (pp. 273–276)

- Price discrimination is an attempt by the monopoly to convert consumer surplus into economic profit.
- Perfect price discrimination extracts the entire consumer surplus. Such a monopoly charges a different price for each unit sold and obtains the maximum price that each consumer is willing to pay for each unit bought.
- With perfect price discrimination, the monopoly produces the same output as would a perfectly competitive industry.
- Rent seeking with perfect price discrimination might eliminate the entire total surplus.

Monopoly Policy Issues (pp. 277–279)

- With large economies of scale and scope, monopoly can produce at a lower price and might be more innovative than firms in perfect competition.
- Efficient regulation requires a monopoly to charge a price equal to marginal cost, but for a natural monopoly, such a price is less than average cost.
- Average cost pricing is a compromise pricing rule that covers a firm's costs and allows the firm to break even but is not efficient.

Key Figures and Table

Key Terms

Problems

Tests, Study Plan and Solutions*

1 Sky is the sole provider of satellite television service in the United Kingdom. Pfizer Inc. makes LIPITOR, a prescription drug that lowers cholesterol. Yorkshire Water is the sole supplier of drinking water in parts of northern England.

a What are the substitutes, if any, for the goods and services described above?

b What are the barriers to entry, if any, that protect these three firms from competition?

c Which of these three firms, if any, is a natural monopoly? Explain your answer and illustrate it by drawing an appropriate figure.

d Which of these three firms, if any, is a legal monopoly? Explain your answer.

e Which of these three firms are most likely to be able to profit from price discrimination and which are most likely to sell their good or service for a single price?

2 Minnie's European Mineral Springs, a single-price monopoly, faces the market demand schedule:

Price (euros per bottle)	Quantity demanded (bottles)
10	0
8	1
6	2
4	3
2	4
0	5

a Calculate the total revenue schedule for Minnie's European Mineral Springs.

b Calculate the marginal revenue schedule.

c Draw a graph of market demand curve and Minnie's marginal revenue curve.

d Why is Minnie's marginal revenue less than the price?

e At what price is Minnie's total revenue maximized?

f Over what range of prices is the demand for water from Minnie's Mineral Springs elastic?

g Why will Minnie not produce a quantity at which the market demand for water is inelastic?

3 Minnie's European Mineral Springs faces the demand schedule in problem 2 and the table at the top of the next column sets out the firm's total cost.

a Calculate the marginal cost of producing each output listed in the table.

Quantity produced (bottles)	Total cost (euros)
0	1
1	3
2	7
3	13
4	21
5	31

b Calculate Minnie's profit-maximizing output and price.

c Calculate economic profit.

d Does Minnie's European Mineral Springs use resources efficiently? Explain your answer.

4 The figure illustrates the situation facing the publisher of the only newspaper containing local news in an isolated European community.

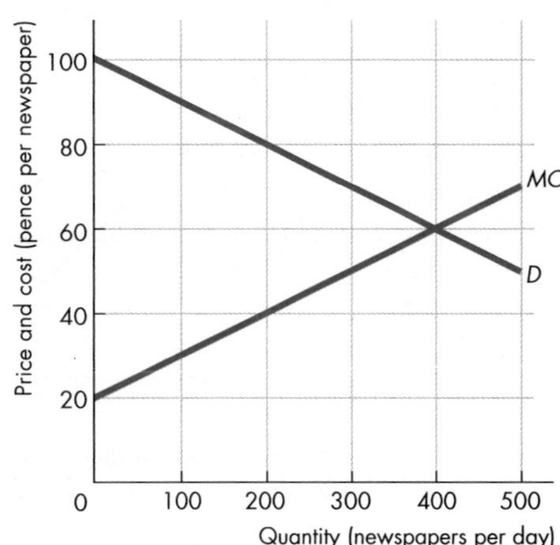

a On the graph, mark the profit-maximizing quantity and price.

b What is the publisher's daily total revenue?

c At the price charged, is the demand for this newspaper elastic or inelastic? Why?

d What are consumer surplus and deadweight loss? Mark each on your graph.

e Explain why this market might encourage rent seeking.

f If this market were perfectly competitive, what would be the quantity, price, consumer surplus and producer surplus? Mark each on your graph.

* Solutions to odd-numbered problems are provided.

5 La Bella Pizza can produce a pizza for a marginal cost of €2. Its standard price is €14.99 per pizza. It offers a second pizza for €4.99. It also distributes coupons that give a €5 rebate on a standard price pizza.

- **a** How can La Bella Pizza make a larger economic profit with this range of prices than it could if it sold every pizza for €14.99?
- **b** Draw a figure that illustrates your answer to part (a).
- **c** Can you think of a way of increasing La Bella Pizza's economic profit even more?
- **d** Is La Bella Pizza more efficient than it would be if it charged just one price?

6 The figure shows a situation similar to that facing Trans Europa Pipeline, a firm that operates a natural gas distribution system in Europe. Trans Europa is a natural monopoly that cannot price discriminate.

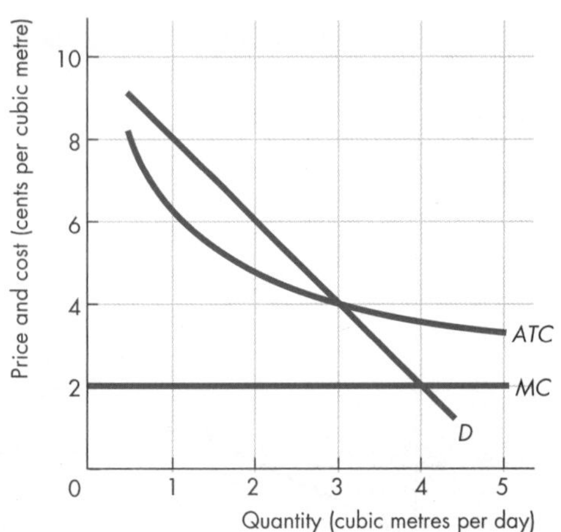

What quantity will Trans Europa produce and at what price if Trans Europa is:

- **a** An unregulated profit-maximizing firm?
- **b** Regulated to make zero economic profit?
- **c** Regulated to be efficient?

7 Given the information provided in the figure in problem 6, what is the producer surplus, consumer surplus and deadweight loss if the firm is:

- **a** An unregulated profit-maximizing firm?
- **b** Regulated to make zero economic profit?
- **c** Regulated to be efficient?

Critical Thinking

1 Study *Reading Between the Lines* on pp. 280–281 and then answer the following questions:

- **a** Why is eBay a monopoly but Google not a monopoly?
- **b** How would you regulate the Internet search engine business to ensure that resources are used efficiently?
- **c** How would you regulate the Internet auction business to ensure that resources are used efficiently?
- **d** "Anyone is free to buy stock in eBay, so everyone is free to share in eBay's economic profit, and the bigger that economic profit, the better for all." Evaluate this statement.

Web Activities

Links to Websites

1 Study the market for computer chips, then answer the following questions.

- **a** Is it correct to call Intel a monopoly? Explain why or why not.
- **b** How does Intel try to raise barriers to entry in this market?

2 Obtain information on Microsoft, then answer the following questions.

- **a** Is it correct to call Microsoft a monopoly? Explain why or why not.
- **b** How do you think Microsoft set the price of Vista and decided how many copies of the program to produce?
- **c** How is the expanding take-up of Linux, the main alternative operating system to Windows, affecting Microsoft?
- **d** How is the constant threat of virus attacks on Windows affecting Microsoft?
- **e** "Anyone is free to buy shares in Microsoft, so everyone is free to share in Microsoft's economic profit, and the bigger that economic profit, the better for all." Evaluate this statement.

CHAPTER 13

Monopolistic Competition and Oligopoly

After studying this chapter you will be able to:

- Define and identify monopolistic competition
- Explain how price and output are determined in a monopolistically competitive industry
- Explain why advertising and branding costs are high in monopolistic competition
- Define and identify oligopoly
- Explain two traditional models of oligopoly
- Use game theory to explain how price and output are determined in oligopoly
- Use game theory to explain other strategic decisions

Fliers and Brand Names

Every day, Europeans enjoy the huge variety of choice created by the globalized trade in brand name products. How do brand names change the competitive landscape? How does competition between just two or a few leading firms work? Do they operate like firms in perfect competition or do they restrict output to increase profit like a monopoly? Find out in this chapter. And in *Reading Between the Lines* at the end of the chapter, see how Apple hopes its video iPod will enable it to compete with the new generation of mobile phones.

What Is Monopolistic Competition?

You have studied two types of market structure: perfect competition and monopoly. In perfect competition, a large number of firms produce identical goods, there are no barriers to entry, and each firm is a price taker. In the long run, there is no economic profit and perfect competition is efficient. In monopoly, a single firm is protected from competition by barriers to entry and can make an economic profit, even in the long run.

Most real-world markets are competitive but not perfectly competitive because firms in these markets possess some market power to set their prices as monopolies do. We call this type of market *monopolistic competition*.

Monopolistic competition is a market structure in which:

- A large number of firms compete.
- Each firm produces a differentiated product.
- Firms compete on product quality, price, marketing and branding.
- Firms are free to enter and exit.

Large Number of Firms

In monopolistic competition, as in perfect competition, the industry consists of a large number of firms. The presence of a large number of firms has three implications for the firms in the industry.

Small Market Share

In monopolistic competition, each firm supplies a small part of the total industry output. Consequently, each firm has only limited market power to influence the price of its product. Each firm's price can deviate from the average price of other firms by a relatively small amount.

Ignore Other Firms

A firm in monopolistic competition must be sensitive to the average market price of the product, but each firm does not pay attention to any one individual competitor. Because all the firms are relatively small and each firm has only a small share of the total market, no one firm can dictate market conditions. So no one firm's actions directly affect the actions of the other firms.

Collusion Impossible

Firms in monopolistic competition would like to be able to conspire to fix a higher price – called collusion. But because there are many firms, collusion is not possible.

Product Differentiation

A firm practices **product differentiation** if it makes a product that is slightly different from the products of competing firms. A differentiated product is one that is a close substitute but not a perfect substitute for the products of the other firms. Some people will pay more for one variety of the product, so when its price rises, the quantity demanded falls but it does not (necessarily) fall to zero. For example, Adidas, Asics, Diadora, Etonic, Fila, New Balance, Nike, Puma and Reebok all make differentiated running shoes. Other things remaining the same, if the price of Adidas running shoes rises and the prices of the other shoes remain constant, Adidas sells fewer shoes and the other producers sell more. But Adidas shoes don't disappear unless the price rises by a large enough amount.

Competing on Quality, Price and Marketing

Product differentiation enables a firm to compete with other firms in three areas: product quality, price and marketing.

Quality

The quality of a product is the physical attributes that make it different from the products of other firms. Quality includes design, reliability, the service provided to the buyer and the buyer's ease of access to the product. Quality lies on a spectrum that runs from high to low. Some firms – such as Dell Computer Corp. – offer high-quality products. They are well designed and reliable, and the customer receives quick and efficient service. Other firms offer a lower-quality product that is less well designed, that might not work perfectly and that the buyer must travel some distance to obtain.

Price

Because of product differentiation, a firm in monopolistic competition faces a downward-sloping demand curve. So, like a monopoly, the firm can set both its price and its output. But there is a trade-off between the product's quality and price. A firm that makes a high-quality product can charge a higher price than a firm that makes a low-quality product.

Marketing

Because of product differentiation, a firm in monopolistic competition must market its product. Marketing takes two main forms: advertising and packaging. A firm that produces a high-quality product wants to sell it for a suitably high price. To be able to sell a high-quality product for a high price, a firm must advertise and package its product in a way that convinces buyers that they are getting the higher quality for which they are paying. For example, pharmaceutical companies advertise and package their brand-name drugs to persuade buyers that these items are superior to lower-priced generic alternatives. Similarly, a low-quality producer uses advertising and packaging to persuade buyers that although the quality is low, the low price more than compensates for this fact.

Entry and Exit

In monopolistic competition, there is free entry and free exit. Consequently, a firm cannot make an economic profit in the long run. When firms make economic profits, new firms enter the industry. This entry lowers prices and eventually eliminates economic profit. When firms incur economic losses, some firms leave the industry. This exit increases prices and eventually eliminates economic loss. In long-run equilibrium, firms neither enter nor leave the industry and the firms in the industry make zero economic profit.

Examples of Monopolistic Competition

Figure 13.1 shows ten examples of industries in the United Kingdom which are monopolistically competitive. These industries have a large number of firms, they produce differentiated products, they compete on quality, price and marketing. In the most concentrated of these industries, dairy products, the largest 5 firms produce 32 per cent of industry output and the largest 15 firms produce 57 per cent of industry output. In the least concentrated of these industries, furniture, the largest 5 firms produce only 5 per cent of industry output and the largest 15 firms produce 13 per cent of industry output.

Review Quiz

Study Plan 13.1

1 What are the distinguishing characteristics of monopolistic competition?
2 How do firms in monopolistic competition compete?
3 In addition to the examples in Figure 13.1, provide some examples of industries near your university that operate in monopolistic competition.

Figure 13.1

Examples of Monopolistic Competition

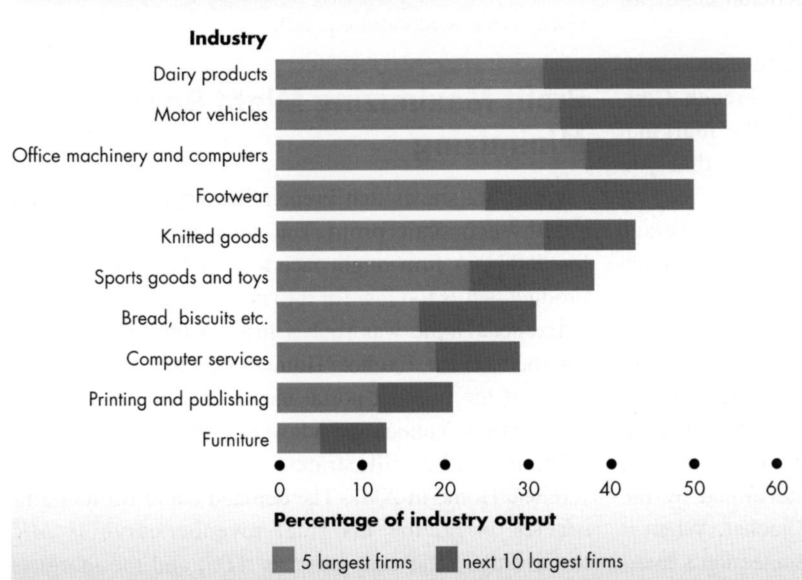

These industries operate in monopolistic competition. The red bar shows the percentage of industry output produced by the five largest firms and the blue bar shows the percentage of industry output produced by the next 10 largest firms. So the entire length of the bar shows the percentage of industry output produced by the largest 15 firms.

The industries shown have many firms that produce differentiated products and compete on quality, price and marketing.

Price and Output in Monopolistic Competition

Suppose you've been employed by French Connection to manage the production and marketing of jackets. Think about the decisions that you must make at French Connection. First, you must decide on the design and quality of jackets and on your marketing plan. Second, you must decide on the quantity of jackets to produce and the price at which to sell them.

We'll suppose that French Connection has already made its decisions about design, quality and marketing, and now we'll concentrate on the output and pricing decision. We'll study quality and marketing decisions in the next section.

For a given quality of jackets and marketing activity, French Connection faces given costs and market conditions. How, given its costs and the demand for its jackets, does French Connection decide the quantity of jackets to produce and the price at which to sell them?

Figure 13.2 myeconlab

Economic Profit in the Short Run

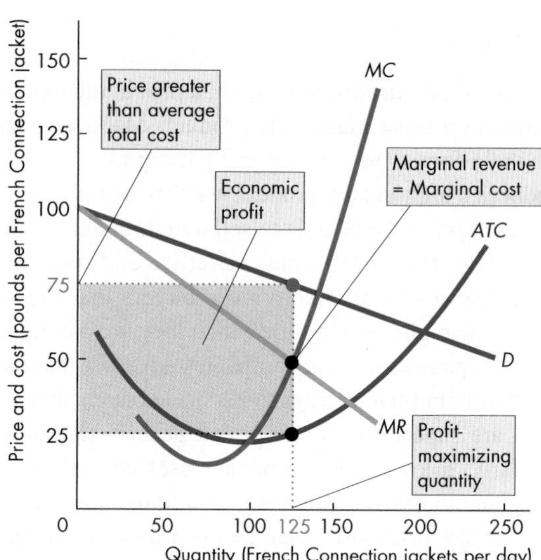

Profit is maximized where marginal revenue equals marginal cost. The profit-maximizing quantity is 125 jackets a day. The price of £75 a jacket exceeds the average total cost of £25 a jacket, so the firm makes an economic profit of £50 a jacket. The blue rectangle illustrates economic profit, which equals £6,250 a day (£50 a jacket multiplied by 125 jackets a day).

The Firm's Short-run Output and Price Decision

In the short run, a firm in monopolistic competition makes its output and price decision just like a monopoly firm does. Figure 13.2 illustrates this decision for French Connection jackets.

The demand curve for French Connection jackets is *D*. This demand curve tells us the quantity of French Connection jackets demanded at each price, given the prices of other jackets. It is not the demand curve for jackets in general.

The *MR* curve shows the marginal revenue curve associated with the demand curve for French Connection jackets. It is derived just like the marginal revenue curve of a single-price monopoly that you studied in Chapter 12.

The *ATC* curve and the *MC* curve show the average total cost and the marginal cost of producing French Connection jackets.

French Connection's goal is to maximize its economic profit. To do so, it will produce the output at which marginal revenue equals marginal cost. In Figure 13.2, this output is 125 jackets a day. French Connection charges the price that buyers are willing to pay for this quantity, which is determined by the demand curve. This price is £75 per jacket. When it produces 125 jackets a day, French Connection's average total cost is £25 per jacket and it makes an economic profit of £6,250 a day (£50 per jacket multiplied by 125 jackets a day). The blue rectangle shows French Connection's economic profit.

Profit Maximizing Might Be Loss Minimizing

Figure 13.2 shows that French Connection is making a healthy economic profit. But such an outcome is not inevitable. A firm might face a level of demand for its product that is too low for it to make an economic profit.

Excite@Home was such a firm. Offering high-speed Internet service, Excite@Home hoped to capture a large share of the Internet portal market in competition with AOL, MSN, Yahoo! and a host of other providers.

Figure 13.3 illustrates the situation facing Excite@Home in 2001. The demand curve for its portal service is *D*, the marginal revenue curve is *MR*, the average total cost curve is *ATC*, and the marginal cost curve is *MC*. Excite@Home maximized profit –

Figure 13.3

myeconlab

Economic Loss in the Short Run

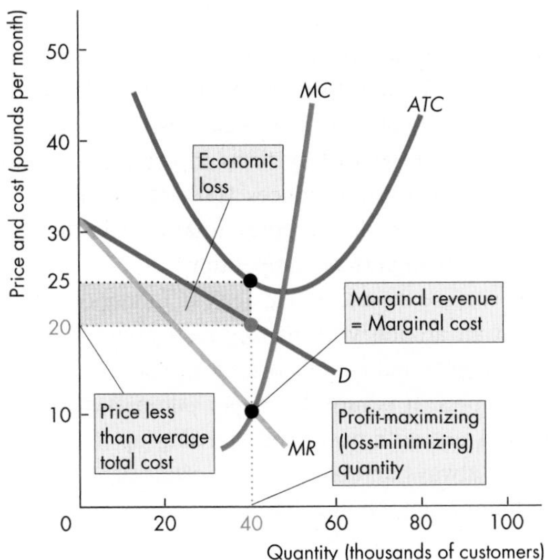

Profit is maximized where marginal revenue equals marginal cost. The loss-minimizing quantity is 40,000 customers. The price of £20 a month is less than the average total cost of £25 a month, so the firm incurs an economic loss of £5 a customer. The red rectangle illustrates economic loss, which equals £200,000 a month (£5 a customer multiplied by 40,000 customers).

equivalently, it minimized its loss – by producing the output at which marginal revenue equals marginal cost. In Figure 13.3, this output is 40,000 customers.

Excite@Home charged the price that buyers were willing to pay for this quantity, which was determined by the demand curve and which was £20 a month. With 40,000 customers, Excite@Home's average total cost was £25 per customer, so it incurred an economic loss of £200,000 a month (£5 a customer multiplied by 40,000 customers). The red rectangle shows Excite@Home's economic loss.

So far, the firm in monopolistic competition looks like a single-price monopoly. It produces the quantity at which marginal revenue equals marginal cost and then charges the price that buyers are willing to pay for that quantity, determined by the demand curve. The key difference between monopoly and monopolistic competition lies in what happens next when firms either make an economic profit or incur an economic loss.

Long Run: Zero Economic Profit

A firm like Excite@Home is not going to incur an economic loss for long. Eventually, it goes out of business. Also, there is no restriction on entry in monopolistic competition, so if firms in an industry are making an economic profit, other firms have an incentive to enter that industry.

As Burberry, Gap and other firms start to make jackets similar to those made by French Connection, the demand for French Connection jackets decreases. The demand curve for French Connection jackets and the marginal revenue curve shift leftward. And as these curves shift leftward, the profit-maximizing quantity and price fall.

Figure 13.4 shows the long-run equilibrium. The demand curve for French Connection jackets and the marginal revenue curve have shifted leftward. The firm produces 75 jackets a day and sells them for £50 each. At this output level, average total cost is also £50 per jacket.

Figure 13.4

myeconlab

Output and Price in the Long Run

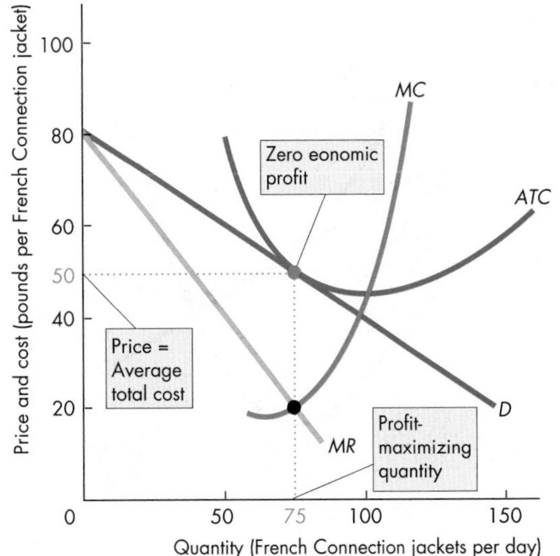

Economic profit encourages entry, which decreases the demand for each firm's product. When the demand curve touches the *ATC* curve at the quantity at which *MR* equals *MC*, the market is in long-run equilibrium. The output that maximizes profit is 75 jackets a day, and the price is £50 per jacket. Average total cost is also £50 per jacket, so economic profit is zero.

So French Connection is making zero economic profit on its jackets. When all the firms in the industry are making zero economic profit, there is no incentive for new firms to enter.

If demand is so low relative to costs that firms incur economic losses, exit will occur. As firms leave an industry, the demand for the products of the remaining firms increases and their demand curves shift rightward. The exit process ends when all the firms in the industry are making zero economic profit.

Monopolistic Competition and Perfect Competition

Figure 13.5 compares monopolistic competition and perfect competition and highlights two key differences between them:

- Excess capacity
- Mark up

Excess Capacity

A firm has excess capacity if it produces below its efficient scale, which is the quantity at which average total cost is a minimum – the quantity at the bottom of the U-shaped *ATC* curve. In Figure 13.4, the efficient scale is 100 jackets a day. French Connection in part (a) produces 75 French Connection jackets a day and has *excess capacity* of 25 jackets a day. But if all jackets are alike and are produced by firms in perfect competition in part (b) each firm produces 100 jackets a day, which is the efficient scale. Average total cost is the lowest possible only in *perfect* competition.

You can see the excess capacity in monopolistic competition all around you. Family restaurants (except for the truly outstanding ones) almost always have some empty tables. It is rare that every pump at a petrol station is in use with customers queuing up to be served. There is always an abundance of estate agents ready to help find or sell a home. These industries are examples

Figure 13.5

myeconlab

Excess Capacity and Mark up

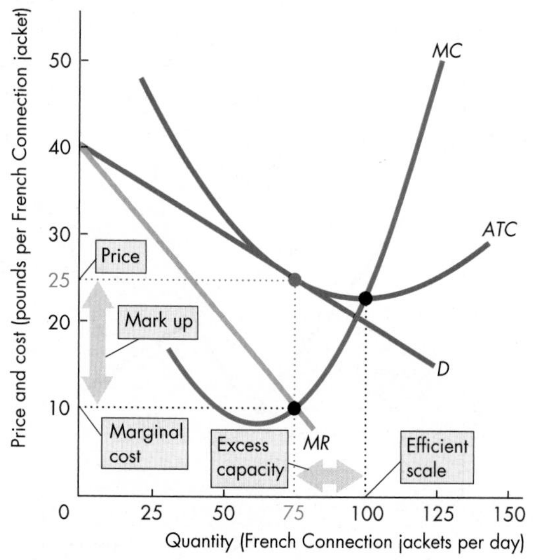

(a) Monopolistic competition

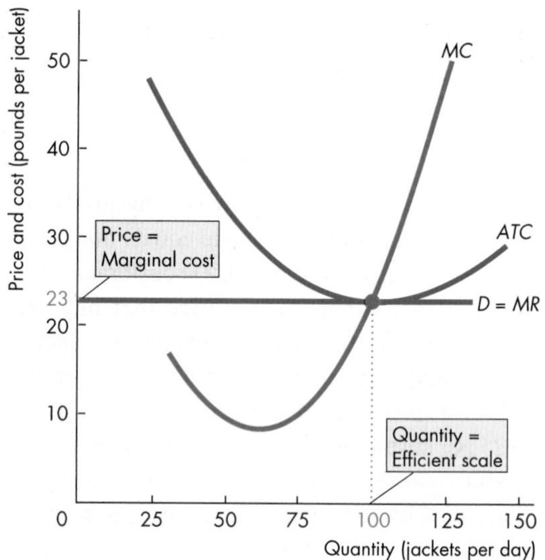

(b) Perfect competition

The efficient scale is 100 jackets a day. In monopolistic competition in the long run, because the demand curve for the firm's product is downward sloping, the quantity produced is less than the efficient scale and the firm has excess capacity. Price exceeds marginal cost and this gap is the firm's mark up.

In contrast, because in perfect competition the demand for each firm's product is perfectly elastic, the quantity produced equals the efficient scale and price equals marginal cost. The firm produces at the least possible cost and there is no mark up.

of monopolistic competition. The firms have excess capacity. They could sell more by cutting their prices, but they would then incur economic losses.

Mark Up

A firm's mark up is the amount by which the price exceeds marginal cost. Figure 13.5(a) shows French Connection's mark up. In perfect competition, price always equals marginal cost and there is no mark up. Figure 13.5(b) shows this case. In monopolistic competition, buyers pay a higher price than in perfect competition and also pay more than marginal cost.

Is Monopolistic Competition Efficient?

Resources are used efficiently when marginal social benefit equals marginal social cost. Price measures marginal social benefit and the firm's marginal cost equals marginal social cost (assuming there are no external benefits or costs). So if the price of a French Connection jacket exceeds the marginal cost of producing it, the quantity of French Connection jackets produced is less than the efficient quantity. And you've just seen that in long-run equilibrium in monopolistic competition, price *does* exceed marginal cost. So is the quantity produced in monopolistic competition less than the efficient quantity?

Making the Relevant Comparison

Two economists meet in the street, and one asks the other how her husband is. "Compared to what?" is the quick reply. This bit of economic wit illustrates a key point: before we can conclude that something needs fixing, we must check out the available alternatives.

The mark up that drives a gap between price and marginal cost in monopolistic competition arises from product differentiation. It is because French Connection jackets are not quite the same as jackets from Banana Republic, Diesel, DKNY, Earl Jackets, Gap or any of the other dozens of producers of jackets that the demand for French Connection jackets is not perfectly elastic. The only way in which the demand for jackets from French Connection might be perfectly elastic is if there is only one kind of jacket and all firms make it. In this situation, French Connection jackets are indistinguishable from all other jackets. They don't even have labels.

If there was only one kind of jacket, the total benefit of jackets would almost certainly be less than it is with variety. People value variety. And people value variety not only because it enables each person to select what he or she likes best but also because it provides an external benefit. Most of us enjoy seeing variety in the choices of others. Contrast a scene from the China of the 1960s, when everyone wore a Mao tunic, with the China of today, where everyone wears the clothes of their own choosing. Or contrast a scene from the Germany of the 1930s, when almost everyone who could afford a car owned a first-generation Volkswagen Beetle, with the world of today with its enormous variety of styles and types of cars.

If people value variety, why don't we see infinite variety? The answer is that variety is costly. Each different variety of any product must be designed, and then customers must be informed about it. These initial costs of design and marketing – called setup costs – mean that some varieties that are too close to others already available are just not worth creating.

The Bottom Line

Product variety is both valued and costly. The efficient degree of product variety is the one for which the marginal benefit of product variety equals its marginal cost. The loss that arises because the marginal benefit of one more unit of a given variety exceeds marginal cost is offset by a gain that arises from having an efficient degree of product variety. So compared to the alternative – complete product uniformity – monopolistic competition is probably efficient.

Review Quiz

Study Plan 13.2

1. How does a firm in monopolistic competition decide how much to produce and at what price to offer its product for sale?
2. Why can a firm in monopolistic competition make an economic profit only in the short run?
3. Why do firms in monopolistic competition operate with excess capacity?
4. Why is there a price mark up over marginal cost in monopolistic competition?
5. Is monopolistic competition efficient?

You've seen how the firm in monopolistic competition determines its output and price when it produces a given product and undertakes a *given* marketing effort. But how does the firm choose its product quality and marketing effort? We'll now study these decisions.

Product Development and Marketing

When we studied French Connection's price and output decision, we assumed that it had already made its product quality and marketing decisions. We're now going to study these decisions and the impact they have on the firm's output, price and economic profit.

Innovation and Product Development

The prospect of new firms entering the industry keeps firms in monopolistic competition on their toes!

To enjoy economic profits, firms in monopolistic competition must be continually seeking ways of keeping one step ahead of imitators – other firms who imitate the success of the economically profitable firms.

One major way of trying to maintain economic profit is for a firm to seek out new products that will provide it with a competitive edge, even if only temporarily. A firm that introduces a new and differentiated product faces a less elastic demand for its product and so the firm is able to increase its price and make an economic profit. But economic profit is an incentive for new firms to enter the market. So eventually, imitators will enter the market and make close substitutes for the innovative product and compete away the economic profit arising from an initial advantage. So to restore economic profit, the firm must again innovate.

Profit-maximizing Product Innovation

The decision to innovate and develop a new or improved product is based on the same type of profit-maximizing calculation that you've already studied.

Innovation and product development are costly activities, but they also bring in additional revenues. The firm must balance the marginal cost and marginal revenue. The marginal dollar spent on developing a new or improved product is the marginal cost of product development. The marginal pound that the new or improved product earns for the firm is the marginal revenue of product development.

At a low level of product development, the marginal revenue from a better product exceeds the marginal cost. At a high level of product development, the marginal cost of a better product exceeds the marginal revenue. When the marginal cost and the marginal revenue of product development are equal, the firm is undertaking the profit-maximizing amount of product development.

Efficiency and Product Innovation

Is the profit-maximizing amount of product innovation also the efficient amount? Efficiency is achieved if the marginal social benefit of a new and improved product equals its marginal social cost.

The marginal social benefit of an innovation is the increase in the price that consumers are willing to pay for it. The marginal social cost is the amount that the firm must pay to make the innovation. Profit is maximized when marginal *revenue* equals marginal cost. But in monopolistic competition, marginal revenue is less than the price, so product innovation is probably not pushed to its efficient level.

Monopolistic competition brings many product innovations that cost little to implement and are purely cosmetic such as new and improved packaging or a new scent in laundry powder. And even when there is a genuine improved product, it is never as good as what the consumer is willing to pay for. For example, "The Legend of Zelda: Twilight Princess" is regarded as an almost perfect and very cool game, but reviewers complain that it isn't quite perfect. It is a game with features whose marginal revenue equals the marginal cost of creating them.

Advertising

Designing and developing products that are actually different from those of its competitors helps a firm achieve some product differentiation. But firms also attempt to create a consumer perception of product differentiation even when actual differences are small. Advertising and packaging are the principal means firms use to achieve this end. A Canon PowerShot camera is a different product from a Kodak EasyShare. But the actual differences are not the main ones that Canon emphasizes in its marketing. The deeper message is that if you use a Canon, you can be like Maria Sharapova (or some other high-profile successful person).

Advertising Expenditures

Firms in monopolistic competition incur huge costs in order to persuade buyers to appreciate and value the differences between their own products and those of their competitors. So a large proportion of the prices that we pay cover the cost of selling a good. And this proportion is increasing.

Advertising in newspapers and magazines and on radio, television and the Internet is the main selling cost. But it is not the only one. Selling costs include the cost of shopping centres, glossy catalogues and brochures, and the salaries, airfares and hotel bills of sales staff.

The total scale of advertising costs is hard to estimate, but, on the average, probably 15 per cent of the price of an item is spent on advertising. Figure 13.6 shows estimates for some industries.

The proportion of the prices we pay that covers the cost of selling a good is not only large, it is also rising. Advertising expenditure in the United Kingdom topped £19 billion in 2005. Even after allowing for inflation, this level of spending is 36 per cent higher than it was in 1995 and 57 per cent higher than in 1990.

Advertising expenditures and other selling costs affect the profits of firms in two ways: they increase costs and they change demand. Let's look at these effects.

Selling Costs and Total Costs

Selling costs such as advertising expenditures increase the costs of a monopolistically competitive firm above those of a perfectly competitive firm or a monopoly. Advertising costs and other selling costs are fixed costs. They do not vary as total output varies. So, just like fixed production costs, advertising costs per unit decrease as production increases.

Figure 13.7 shows how selling costs and advertising expenditures change a firm's average total cost. The blue curve shows the average total cost of production. The red curve shows the firm's average total cost of production with advertising. The height of the shaded area between the two curves shows the average fixed cost of advertising. The *total* cost of advertising is fixed. But the *average* cost of advertising decreases as output increases.

Figure 13.7 shows that if advertising increases the quantity sold by a large enough amount, it can lower average total cost. For example, if the quantity sold increases from 25 jackets a day with no advertising to 100 jackets a day with advertising, average total cost falls from £60 to £40 a jacket. The reason is that although the *total* fixed cost has increased, the greater fixed cost is spread over a greater output, so average total cost decreases.

Figure 13.6 myeconlab

Advertising Expenditures

Industry

Newspapers
Television
Direct Mail
Internet
Directories
Business
Outdoor
Magazines
Radio
Cinema

0 1 2 3 4 5

Advertising expenditure (billions of pounds)

Most UK advertising expenditure is through television and various forms of newspapers, magazines and directories. However, direct mail and increasingly, the Internet are also important.

Source of data: Advertising Association, http://www.adassoc.org.uk.

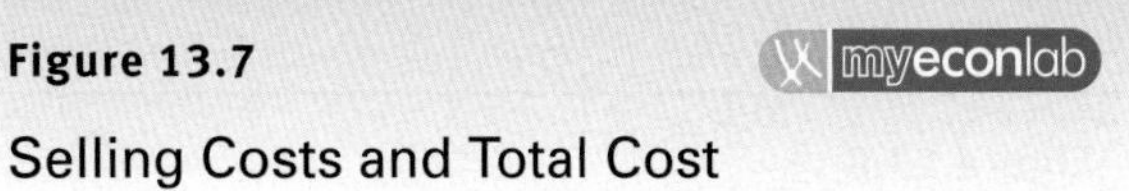

Figure 13.7
myeconlab
Selling Costs and Total Cost

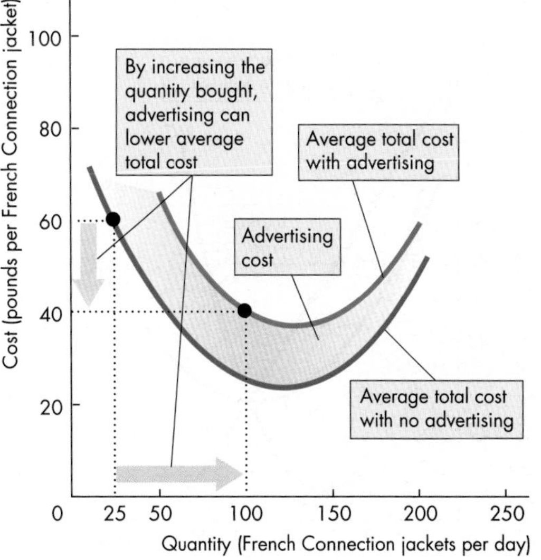

Selling costs such as the cost of advertising are fixed costs. When added to the average total cost of production, selling costs increase average total cost by a greater amount at small outputs than at large outputs. If advertising enables sales to increase from 25 jackets a day to 100 jackets a day, average total cost *falls* from £60 to £40 a jacket.

Selling Costs and Demand

Advertising and other selling efforts change the demand for a firm's product. But how? Does demand increase or does it decrease? The most natural answer is that advertising increases demand. By informing people about the quality of its products or by persuading people to switch from the products of other firms, a firm might expect to increase the demand for its own products.

But all firms in monopolistic competition advertise. And all seek to persuade customers that they have the best deal. If advertising enables a firm to survive, it might increase the number of firms in the market. And to the extent that the number of firms does increase, advertising *decreases* the demand faced by any one firm. Advertising by all the firms might also make the demand for any one firm's product more elastic. In this case, advertising ends up not only lowering average total cost but also lowering the mark up and the price.

Figure 13.8 illustrates this possible effect of advertising. In part (a), with no advertising, the demand for French Connection jackets is not very elastic. Profit is maximized at 75 jackets per day and the mark up is large. In part (b), advertising, which is a fixed cost, increases average total cost from ATC_0 to ATC_1 but leaves marginal cost unchanged at MC. Demand for the firm's product becomes much more elastic, the profit-maximizing quantity increases and the mark up shrinks.

Using Advertising to Signal Quality

Some advertising, like the David Beckham Gillette ads on television and in glossy magazines or the huge amounts that Coke and Pepsi spend, seems hard to understand. There doesn't seem to be any concrete information about a shaver in the smiling face of a footballer. And surely everyone knows about Coke and Pepsi. What is the gain from pouring millions of pounds a month into advertising these well-known colas?

One answer is that advertising is a signal to the consumer of a high-quality product. A **signal** is an action taken by an informed person (or firm) to send a message to uninformed people. Think about two shavers: Fusion

Figure 13.8

Advertising and the Mark Up

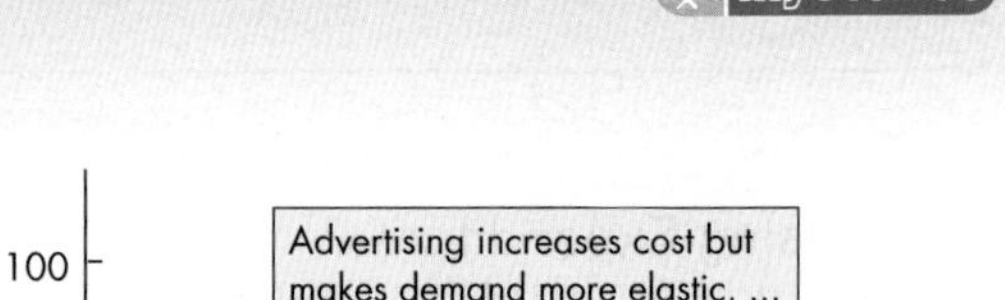

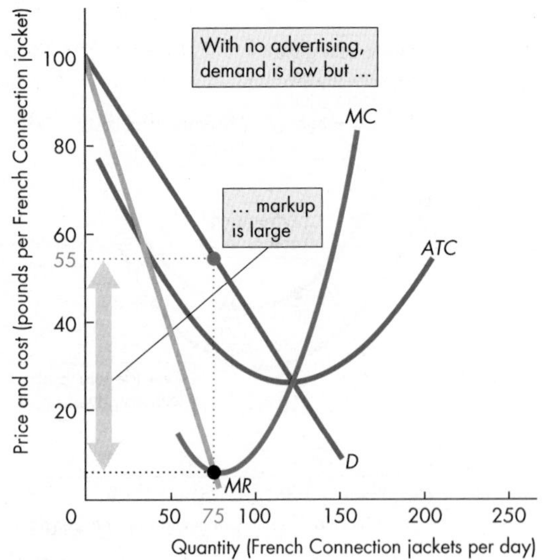

(a) No firms advertise

With no firms advertising, demand is low and not very elastic. The profit-maximizing output is small, the mark up is large and the price is high.

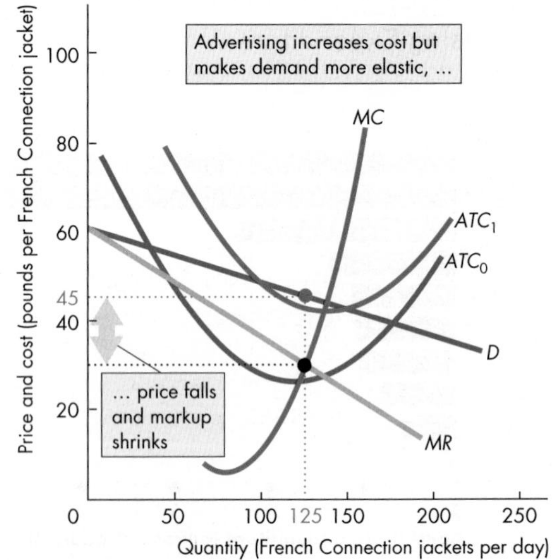

(b) All firms advertise

Advertising increases average total cost and shifts the ATC curve upward from ATC_0 to ATC_1. With all firms advertising, the demand for each firm's product becomes more elastic. Output increases, the mark up shrinks and the price falls.

and Bland. Bland knows that its blades are poor and of variable quality that depends on which cheap batch of unsold blades it happens to buy each week. So Bland knows that while it could get a lot of people to try Bland by advertising, they would all quickly discover what a poor product it is and switch back to the shaver they bought before. Gillette, in contrast, knows that its blade gives a high-quality consistent shave and that once consumers have tried it, there is a good chance they'll never use anything else. On the basis of this reasoning, Bland doesn't advertise but Gillette does.

And Gillette spends a lot of money to make a big splash. Fusion users who know that Gillette has done a $10 million deal with Beckham know that the firm would not spend so much money advertising if its product were not truly good. So consumers reason that a Gillette shaver is indeed a really good product. The flashy expensive ad has signalled that a Fusion shaver is really good without saying anything about the shaver.

Notice that if advertising is a signal, it doesn't need any specific product information. It just needs to be expensive and hard to miss. That's what a lot of advertising looks like. So the signalling theory of advertising predicts much of the advertising that we see.

Brand Names

Many firms create and spend a lot of money promoting a brand name. Why? What benefit does a brand name bring to justify the sometimes high cost of establishing it?

The basic answer is that a brand name provides information about the quality of a product to consumers and an incentive to the producer to achieve a high and consistent quality standard.

To see how a brand name helps the consumer, think about how you use brand names to get information about quality. You've decided to take a holiday in the sun and you're trying to decide where to go. You see advertisements for Club Med and Sheraton Resorts and for Joe's Beachside Shack and Annie's Dive.

You know about Club Med and Sheraton Resorts because although you've not stayed in them before, you've seen their advertisements and you've heard about them from others. You know what to expect from them.

You have no information at all about Joe's and Annie's. They might be better than the places you do know about, but without that knowledge, you're not going to chance them. You use the brand name as information and choose Club Med.

This same story explains why a brand name provides an incentive to achieve high and consistent quality. Because no one would know whether Joe's and Annie's were offering a high standard of service, they have no incentive to do so. But equally, because everyone expects a given standard of service from Club Med, a failure to meet a customer's expectation would almost surely lose that customer to a competitor. So Club Med has a strong incentive to deliver what it promises in the advertising that creates its brand name.

Efficiency of Advertising and Brand Names

To the extent that advertising and brand names provide consumers with information about the precise nature of product differences and about product quality, they benefit the consumer and enable a better product choice to be made. But the opportunity cost of the additional information must be weighed against the gain to the consumer.

The final verdict on the efficiency of monopolistic competition is ambiguous. In some cases, the gains from extra product variety unquestionably offset the selling costs and the extra cost arising from excess capacity. The tremendous varieties of books and magazines, clothing, food and drinks are examples of such gains. It is less easy to see the gains from being able to buy a brand-name drug that has a chemical composition identical to that of a generic alternative. But many people do willingly pay more for the brand-name alternative.

Review Quiz

Study Plan 13.3

1. What are the two main ways, other than by adjusting price, in which a firm in monopolistic competition competes with other firms?
2. Why might product innovation and development be efficient and why might it be inefficient?
3. How does a firm's advertising expenditure influence its cost curves? Does average total cost increase or decrease?
4. How does a firm's advertising expenditure influence the demand for its product? Does demand increase or decrease?
5. Why is it difficult to determine whether monopolistic competition is efficient or inefficient? What is your opinion about the bottom line and why?

What Is Oligopoly?

Oligopoly, like monopolistic competition, lies between perfect competition and monopoly. The firms in oligopoly might produce an identical product and compete only on price, or they might produce a differentiated product and compete on price, product quality and marketing. **Oligopoly** is a market structure in which:

- Natural or legal barriers prevent the entry of new firms
- A small number of firms compete

Barriers to Entry

Either natural or legal barriers to entry can create oligopoly. You saw in Chapter 12 how economies of scale and demand form a natural barrier to entry that can create a *natural monopoly*. These same factors can create a *natural oligopoly*.

Figure 13.9 illustrates two natural oligopolies. The demand curve, *D* (in both parts of the figure), shows the market demand for taxi rides in a town. If the average total cost curve of a taxi company is ATC_1 in part (a), the market is a natural **duopoly** – an oligopoly with two firms. You can probably see some examples of duopoly where you live. Some cities have only two suppliers of milk, two local newspapers, two taxi companies, two car rental firms, two copy centres or two bookshops.

The lowest price at which the firm would remain in business is £10 a ride. At that price, the quantity of rides demanded is 60 a day, the quantity that can be provided by just two firms. There is no room in this market for three firms. But if there were only one firm, it would make an economic profit and a second firm would enter to take some of the business and economic profit.

If the average total cost curve of a taxi company is ATC_2 in part (b), the efficient scale of one firm is 20 rides a day. This market is large enough for three firms.

A legal oligopoly arises when a legal barrier to entry protects the small number of firms in a market. A city might license two taxi firms or two bus companies, for example, even though the combination of market demand and economies of scale leaves room for more than two firms.

Figure 13.9

Natural Oligopoly

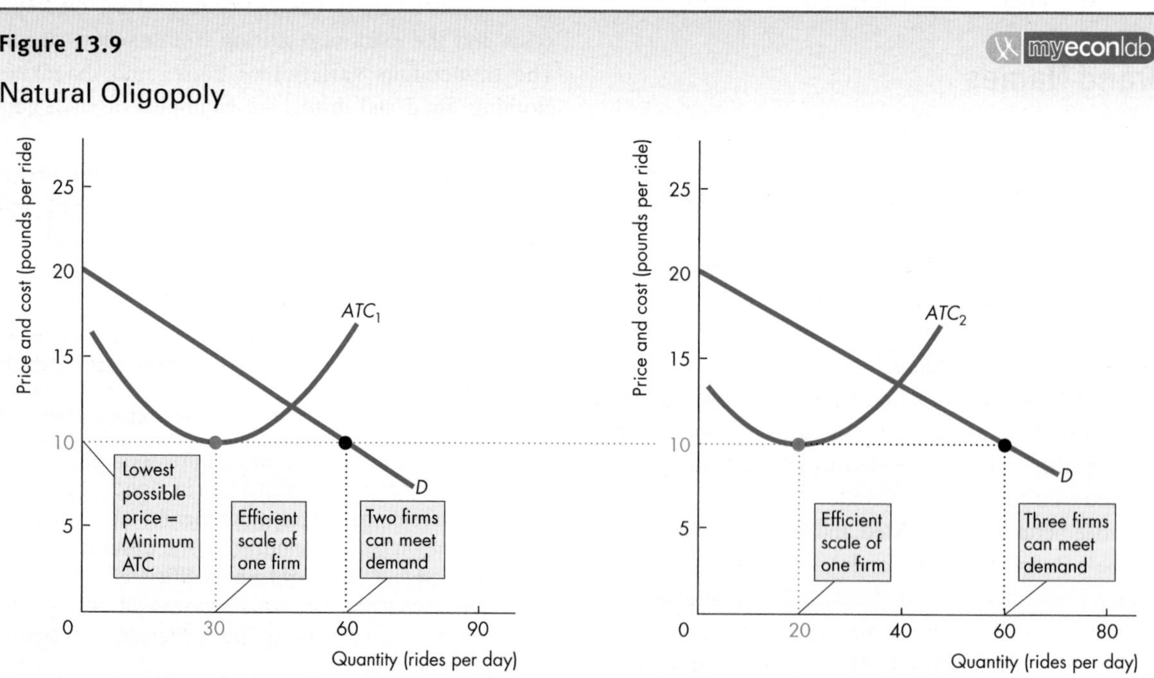

(a) Natural duopoly

(b) Natural oligopoly with three firms

The lowest possible price is £10 a ride, which is the minimum average total cost. When a firm produces 30 rides a day, the efficient scale, two firms can satisfy the market demand. This natural oligopoly has two firms – a natural duopoly.

When the efficient scale of one firm is 20 rides per day, three firms can satisfy the market demand at the lowest possible price. This natural oligopoly has three firms.

Small Number of Firms

Because barriers to entry exist, oligopoly consists of a small number of firms, each of which has a large share of the market. Such firms are interdependent and they face a temptation to cooperate to increase their joint economic profit.

Interdependence

With a small number of firms in a market, each firm's actions influence the profits of all the other firms. When Starbucks opened in Meadowhall Shopping Centre all the other coffee shops took a hit. Within days, Café Moda began to attract Starbucks' customers with enticing offers and lower prices. Eventually, Café Moda survived but others went out of business. The coffee shops in Meadowhall are interdependent.

Temptation to Cooperate

When a small number of firms share a market, they can increase their profits by forming a cartel and acting like a monopoly. A **cartel** is a group of firms acting together – colluding – to limit output, raise price and increase economic profit. Cartels are illegal, but they do operate in some markets. But for reasons you'll discover in this chapter, cartels tend to break down.

Examples of Oligopoly

Figure 13.10 shows some examples of oligopoly. The dividing line between oligopoly and monopolistic competition is hard to pin down. As a practical matter, we try to identify oligopoly by looking at the five-firm concentration ratio qualified with other information about the geographical scope of the market and barriers to entry. A concentration ratio that divides oligopoly from monopolistic competition is generally taken to be 60 per cent. An industry in which the concentration ratio exceeds 60 per cent is usually an example of oligopoly and an industry in which the concentration ratio is below 60 per cent is monopolistic competition.

Examples of oligopoly include tobacco products, man-made fibres, soft drinks and mineral waters, postal and courier services and pharmaceuticals.

Review Quiz

Study Plan 13.4

1. What are the distinguishing characteristics of oligopoly?
2. Why are firms in oligopoly interdependent?
3. What arrangement are firms in oligopoly tempted to try to make?
4. Think of some examples of firms in oligopoly that you buy from.

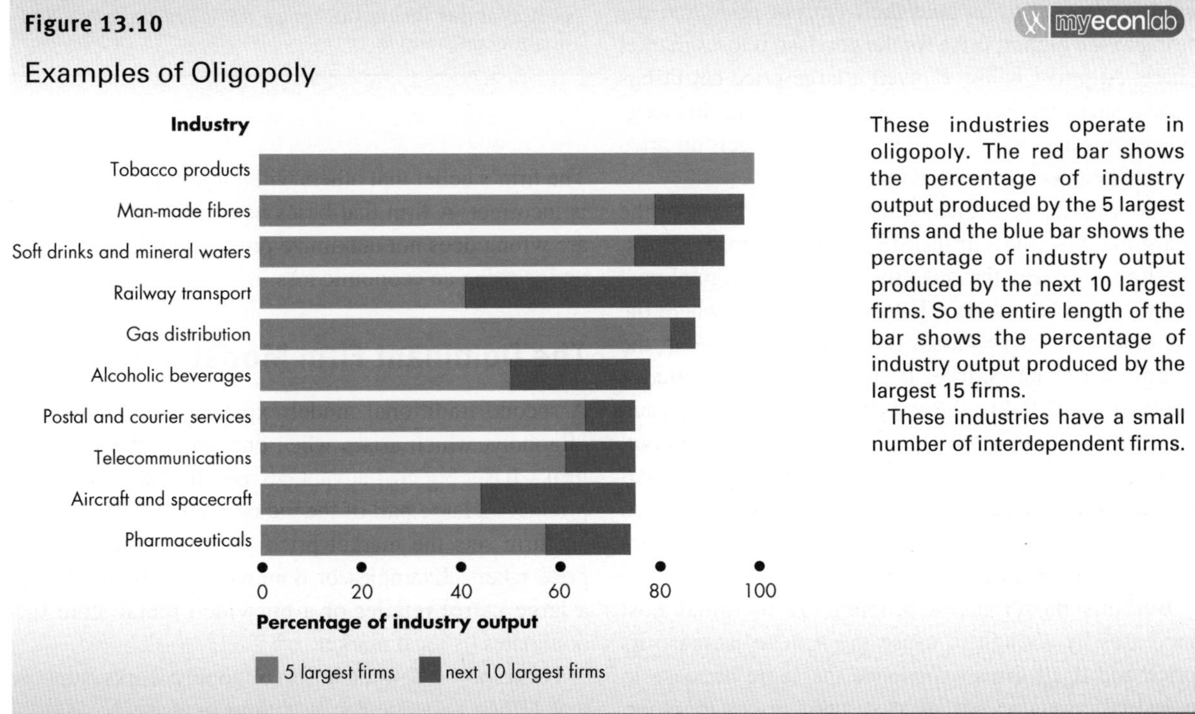

Figure 13.10

Examples of Oligopoly

These industries operate in oligopoly. The red bar shows the percentage of industry output produced by the 5 largest firms and the blue bar shows the percentage of industry output produced by the next 10 largest firms. So the entire length of the bar shows the percentage of industry output produced by the largest 15 firms.

These industries have a small number of interdependent firms.

Two Traditional Oligopoly Models

Suppose you run one of the three petrol stations in a small town. If you cut your price and your two competitors don't cut theirs, your sales increase and the sales of the other two firms decrease. With lower sales, the other firms most likely cut their prices too. If they do cut their prices, your sales and profits take a tumble. So before deciding to cut your price, you must predict how the other firms will react and attempt to calculate the effects of those reactions on your own profit.

Several models have been developed to explain the prices and quantities in oligopoly markets. But no one theory has been found that can explain all the different types of behaviour that we observe in such markets. The models fall into two broad groups: traditional models and game theory models. We'll look at examples of both types, starting with two traditional models.

The Kinked Demand Curve Model

The kinked demand curve model of oligopoly is based on the assumption that each firm believes that if it raises its price, others will not follow, but if it cuts its price, other firms will cut theirs.

Figure 13.11 shows the demand curve (D) that a firm believes it faces. The demand curve has a kink at the current price, P, and quantity, Q. At prices above P, a small price rise brings a big decrease in the quantity sold. The other firms hold their current price and the firm has the highest price for the good, so it loses market share. At prices below P, even a large price cut brings only a small increase in the quantity sold. In this case, other firms match the price cut, so the firm gets no price advantage over its competitors.

The kink in the demand curve creates a break in the marginal revenue curve (MR). To maximize profit, the firm produces the quantity at which marginal cost equals marginal revenue. That quantity, Q, is where the marginal cost curve passes through the gap AB in the marginal revenue curve. If marginal cost fluctuates between A and B, like the marginal cost curves MC_0 and MC_1, the firm does not change its price or its output. Only if marginal cost fluctuates outside the range AB does the firm change its price and output. So the kinked demand curve model predicts that price and quantity are insensitive to small cost changes.

But this model has a problem. If marginal cost increases by enough to cause the firm to increase its price and if all firms experience the same increase in marginal cost, they all increase their prices together.

Figure 13.11

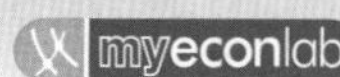

The Kinked Demand Curve Model

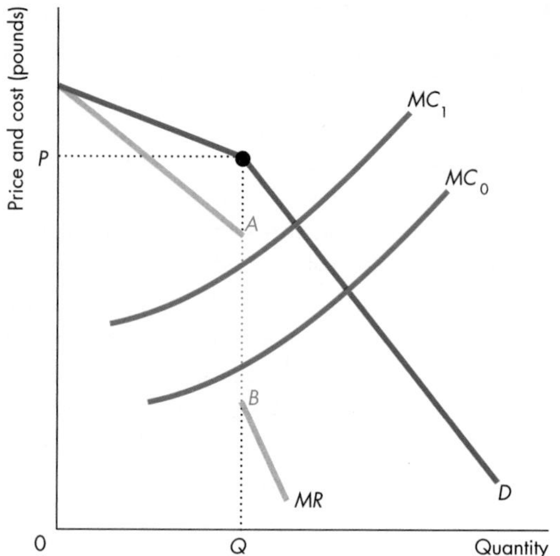

The market price is P. Each firm believes it faces the demand curve D. At prices above P, a small price rise brings a big decrease in the quantity sold because other firms do not raise their prices. At prices below P, even a big price cut brings only a small increase in the quantity sold because other firms also cut their prices.

Because the demand curve is kinked, the marginal revenue curve, MR, has a break AB at the quantity at which the demand curve is kinked. Profit is maximized by producing Q. The marginal cost curve passes through the break in the marginal revenue curve. Marginal cost changes inside the range AB leave the price and quantity unchanged.

The firm's belief that others will not join it in a price rise is incorrect. A firm that bases its actions on beliefs that are wrong does not maximize profit and might even end up incurring an economic loss.

The Dominant Firm Model

A second traditional model explains a dominant firm oligopoly, which arises when one firm – the dominant firm – has a big cost advantage over the other firms and produces a large part of the industry output. The dominant firm sets the market price and the other firms are price takers. Examples of dominant firm oligopoly are a large petrol retailer or a big video rental store that dominates its local market.

To see how a dominant firm oligopoly works, suppose that 11 firms operate petrol stations in a city.

Figure 13.12

A Dominant Firm Model

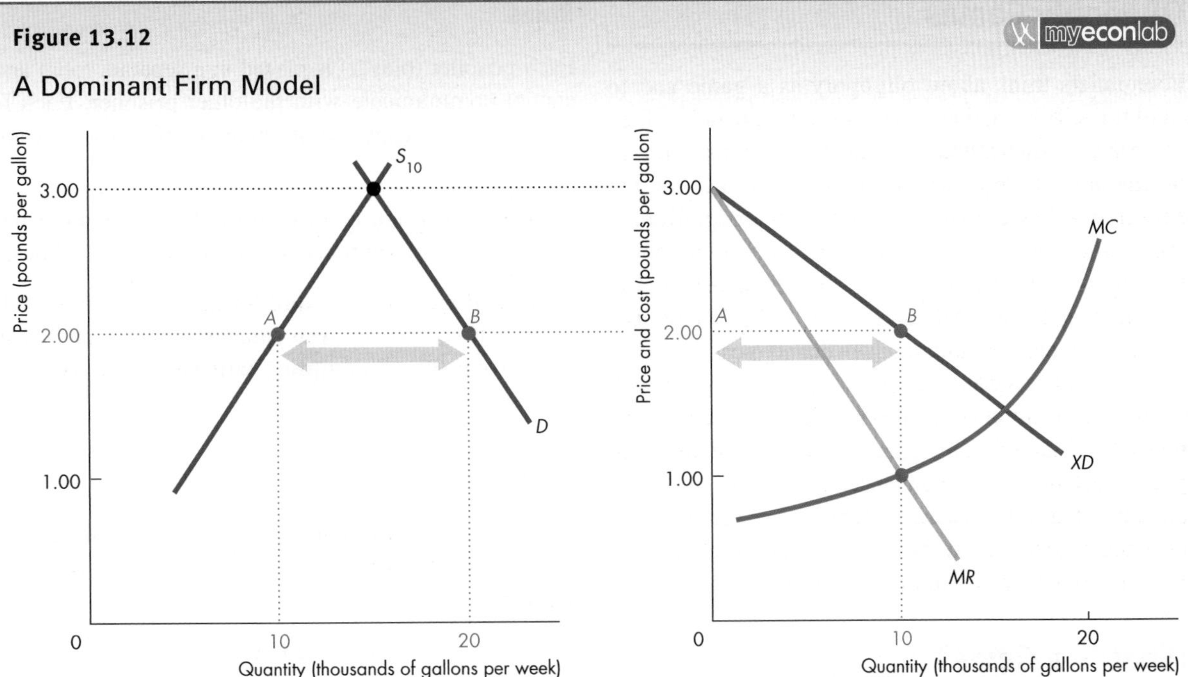

(a) Ten small firms and market demand

(b) Big-G's price and output decision

The demand curve for petrol in a city is *D* in part (a). There are 10 small competitive firms that together have a supply curve of S_{10}. In addition, there is 1 large firm, Big-G, shown in part (b). Big-G faces the demand curve *XD*, determined as the market demand *D* minus the supply of the 10 small firms S_{10} – the demand that is not satisfied by the small firms.

Big-G's marginal revenue is *MR* and marginal cost is *MC*. Big-G sets its output to maximize profit by equating marginal cost, *MC*, and marginal revenue, *MR*. This output is 10,000 gallons per week. The price at which Big-G can sell this quantity is £2 a gallon. The 10 small firms take this price and each firm sells 1,000 gallons per week, point *A* in part (a).

Big-G is the dominant firm. Figure 13.12 shows the market for petrol in this city. In part (a), the demand curve *D* tells us the total quantity of petrol demanded in the city at each price. The supply curve S_{10} is the supply curve of the 10 small suppliers. Part (b) shows the situation facing Big-G. Its marginal cost curve is *MC*. Big-G faces the demand curve *XD* and its marginal revenue curve is *MR*. The demand curve *XD* shows the excess demand not met by the 10 small firms. For example, at a price of £1 a gallon, the quantity demanded is 20,000 gallons, the quantity supplied by the 10 small firms is 10,000 gallons, and the excess quantity demanded is 10,000 gallons, measured by the distance *AB* in both parts of the figure.

To maximize profit, Big-G operates like a monopoly. It sells 10,000 gallons a week, where marginal revenue equals marginal cost, for a price of £2 a gallon. The 10 small firms take the price of £2 a gallon. They behave just like firms in perfect competition. The quantity of petrol demanded in the entire city at £2 a gallon is 20,000 gallons, as shown in part (a). Of this amount, Big-G sells 10,000 gallons and the 10 small firms each sell 1,000 gallons.

Review Quiz

Study Plan 13.5

1. What does the kinked demand curve model predict and why must it sometimes make a prediction that contradicts its basic assumption?
2. Do you think a market with a dominant firm is in long-run equilibrium? Explain why or why not.

The traditional models don't enable us to understand all oligopoly markets and we're now going to study some newer models based on game theory.

Oligopoly Games

Economists think about oligopoly as a game and to study oligopoly markets they use a set of tools called game theory. **Game theory** is a tool for studying *strategic behaviour* – behaviour that takes into account the expected behaviour of others and the recognition of mutual interdependence. Game theory was invented by John von Neumann in 1937 and extended by von Neumann and Oskar Morgenstern in 1944. Today, it is one of the major research fields in economics.

Game theory seeks to understand oligopoly as well as all other forms of economic, political, social and even biological rivalries, by using a method of analysis specifically designed to understand games of all types, including the familiar games of everyday life. We will begin our study of game theory and its application to the behaviour of firms by thinking about familiar games.

What Is a Game?

What is a game? At first thought, the question seems silly. After all, there are many different games. There are ball games and parlour games, games of chance and games of skill. But what is it about all these different activities that make them games? What do they have in common? We're going to answer these questions by looking at a game called "the prisoners' dilemma". This game captures some of the essential features of many games, including oligopoly, and gives a good illustration of how game theory works.

The Prisoners' Dilemma

Art and Bob have been caught red-handed, stealing a car. Facing airtight cases, they will receive a 2-year sentence each for their crime. During his interviews with the two prisoners, the police sergeant begins to suspect that he has stumbled on the two people who were responsible for a multimillion-pound bank robbery some months earlier. But this is just a suspicion. The police sergeant has no evidence on which he can convict them of the greater crime unless he can get them to confess. But how can he extract a confession? He makes the prisoners play a game, which we will now describe.

All games share four features:

- Rules
- Strategies
- Payoffs
- Outcome

Rules

Each prisoner (player) is placed in a separate room and cannot communicate with the other prisoner. Each is told that he is suspected of having carried out the bank robbery and that:

> **If both of them confess to the larger crime, each will receive a sentence of 3 years for both crimes.**
>
> **If he alone confesses and his accomplice does not, he will receive an even shorter sentence of 1-year whereas his accomplice will receive a 10-year sentence.**

Strategies

In game theory, **strategies** are all the possible actions of each player. Art and Bob each have two possible actions:

1 Confess to the bank robbery

2 Deny having committed the bank robbery

Because there are two players, each with two strategies, there are four possible outcomes:

1 Both confess

2 Both deny

3 Art confesses and Bob denies

4 Bob confesses and Art denies

Payoffs

Each prisoner can work out exactly what happens to him – his *payoff* – in each of these four situations. We can tabulate the four possible payoffs for each of the prisoners in what is called a payoff matrix for the game. A **payoff matrix** is a table that shows the payoffs for every possible action by each player for every possible action by each other player.

Table 13.1 shows a payoff matrix for Art and Bob. The squares show the payoffs for each prisoner – the red triangle in each square shows Art's and the blue triangle shows Bob's. If both confess (top left), each gets a prison term of 3 years. If Bob confesses but Art denies (top right), Art gets a 10-year sentence and Bob gets a 1-year sentence. If Art confesses and Bob denies (bottom left), Art gets a 1-year sentence and Bob gets a 10-year sentence. Finally, if both of them deny (bottom right), neither can be convicted of the bank robbery charge but both are sentenced for the car theft – a 2-year sentence.

Table 13.1

Prisoners' Dilemma Payoff Matrix

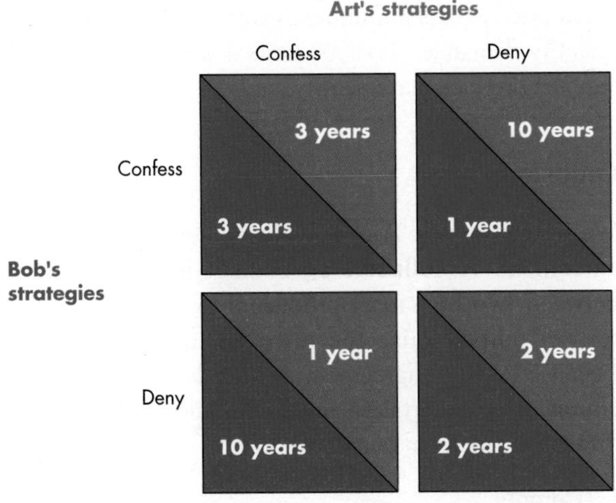

Each square shows the payoffs for the two players, Art and Bob, for each possible pair of actions. In each square, the red triangle shows Art's payoff and the blue triangle shows Bob's. For example, if both confess, the payoffs are in the top left square. The equilibrium of the game is for both players to confess and each gets a 3-year sentence.

Outcome

The choices of both players determine the outcome of the game. To predict that outcome, we use an equilibrium idea proposed by John Nash of Princeton University (who received the Nobel Prize for Economic Science in 1994 and was the subject of the 2001 film *A Beautiful Mind*). In a **Nash equilibrium**, player *A* takes the best possible action given the action of player *B* and player *B* takes the best possible action given the action of player *A*.

In the case of the prisoners' dilemma, the Nash equilibrium occurs when Art makes his best choice given Bob's choice and when Bob makes his best choice given Art's choice.

To find the Nash equilibrium, we compare all the possible outcomes associated with each choice and eliminate those that are dominated – that are not as good as some other choice. Let's find the Nash equilibrium for the prisoners' dilemma game.

Finding the Nash Equilibrium

Look at the situation from Art's point of view. If Bob confesses, Art's best action is to confess because in that case, he is sentenced to 3 years rather than 10 years. If Bob does not confess, Art's best action is still to confess because in that case he receives 1 year rather than 2 years. So Art's best action is to confess.

Now look at the situation from Bob's point of view. If Art confesses, Bob's best action is to confess because in that case, he is sentenced to 3 years rather than 10 years. If Art does not confess, Bob's best action is still to confess because in that case, he receives 1 year rather than 2 years. So Bob's best action is to confess.

Because each player's best action is to confess, each does confess, each gets a 3-year prison term, and the police sergeant has solved the bank robbery. This is the Nash equilibrium of the game.

The Dilemma

Now that you have found the solution to the prisoners' dilemma, you can better see the dilemma. The dilemma arises as each prisoner contemplates the consequences of denying. Each prisoner knows that if both of them deny, they will receive only a 2-year sentence for stealing the car. But neither has any way of knowing that his accomplice will deny.

Each poses the following questions: Should I deny and rely on my accomplice to deny so that we will both get only 2 years? Or should I confess in the hope of getting just 1 year (provided that my accomplice denies) knowing that if my accomplice does confess, we will both get 3 years in prison? The dilemma is resolved by finding the equilibrium of the game.

A Bad Outcome

For the prisoners, the equilibrium of the game, with each confessing, is not the best outcome. If neither of them confesses, each gets only 2 years for the lesser crime. Isn't there some way in which this better outcome can be achieved? It seems that there is not, because the players cannot communicate with each other. Each player can put himself in the other player's place, and so each player can figure out that there is a best strategy for each of them. The prisoners are indeed in a dilemma. Each knows that he can serve 2 years only if he can trust the other to deny. But each prisoner also knows that it is not in the best interest of the other to deny. So each prisoner knows that he must confess, thereby delivering a bad outcome for both.

The firms in an oligopoly are in a similar situation to Art and Bob in the prisoners' dilemma game. Let's see how we can use this game to understand oligopoly.

An Oligopoly Price-fixing Game

We can use game theory and a game like the prisoners' dilemma to understand price fixing, price wars and other aspects of the behaviour of firms in oligopoly.

We'll begin with a price-fixing game. To understand price fixing, we're going to study the special case of duopoly – an oligopoly with two firms. Duopoly is easier to study than oligopoly with three or more firms, and it captures the essence of all oligopoly situations. Somehow, the two firms must share the market. And how they share it depends on the actions of each. We're going to describe the costs of the two firms and the market demand for the item they produce. We're then going to see how game theory helps us to predict the prices charged and the quantities produced by the two firms in a duopoly.

Cost and Demand Conditions

Two firms, Trick and Gear, produce switchgears. They have identical costs. Figure 13.13(a) shows their average total cost curve (*ATC*) and marginal cost curve (*MC*). Figure 13.13(b) shows the market demand curve for switchgears (*D*).

The two firms produce identical switchgears, so one firm's switchgear is a perfect substitute for the other's. So the market price of each firm's product is identical. The quantity demanded depends on that price – the higher the price, the smaller is the quantity demanded.

This industry is a natural duopoly. Two firms can produce this good at a lower cost than either one firm or three firms can. For each firm, average total cost is at its minimum when production is 3,000 units a week. And when price equals minimum average total cost, the total quantity demanded is 6,000 units a week. So two firms can just produce that quantity.

Collusion

We'll suppose that Trick and Gear enter into a collusive agreement. A **collusive agreement** is an agreement between two (or more) producers to form a cartel to restrict output, raise the price and increase profits. Because such an agreement is illegal in the European Union, it is undertaken in secret. The strategies that firms in a cartel can pursue are to:

1 Comply
2 Cheat

A firm that complies carries out the agreement. A firm that cheats breaks the agreement to its own benefit and to the cost of the other firm.

Because each firm has two strategies, there are four possible combinations of actions for the firms:

1 Both firms comply
2 Both firms cheat
3 Trick complies and Gear cheats
4 Gear complies and Trick cheats

Figure 13.13

Costs and Demand

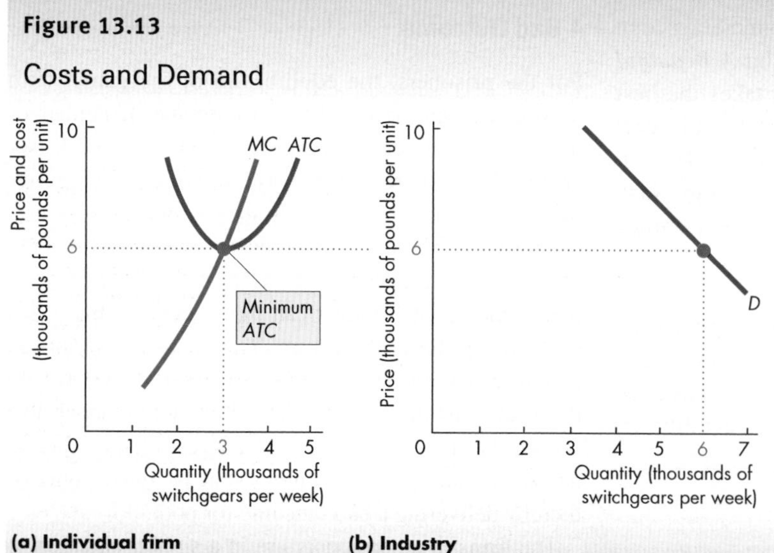

The average total cost curve for each firm is *ATC* and the marginal cost curve is *MC* (part a). Minimum average total cost is £6,000 a unit, and it occurs at a production of 3,000 units a week.

Part (b) shows the market demand curve. At a price of £6,000, the quantity demanded is 6,000 units per week. The two firms can produce this output at the lowest possible average cost. If the market had one firm, it would be profitable for another to enter. If the market had three firms, one would exit. There is room for only two firms in this industry. It is a natural duopoly.

Colluding to Maximize Profits

Let's work out the payoffs to the two firms if they collude to make the maximum profit for the cartel by acting like a monopoly. The calculations that the two firms perform are the same calculations that a monopoly performs. (You can refresh your memory of these calculations by looking at Chapter 12, pp. 268–269.)

The only thing that the duopolists must do beyond what a monopolist does is to agree on how much of the total output each of them will produce.

Figure 13.14 shows the price and quantity that maximize industry profit for the duopolists. Part (a) shows the situation for each firm and part (b) shows the situation for the industry as a whole. The curve labelled *MR* is the industry marginal revenue curve. This marginal revenue curve is like that of a single price monopoly (Chapter 12, p. 266). The curve labelled MC_I is the industry marginal cost curve if each firm produces the same level of output. That curve is constructed by adding together the outputs of the two firms at each level of marginal cost. That is, at each level of marginal cost, industry output is twice the output of each individual firm. So the curve MC_I in part (b) is twice as far to the right as the curve *MC* in part (a).

To maximize industry profit, the duopolists agree to restrict output to the rate that makes the industry marginal cost and marginal revenue equal. That output rate, as shown in part (b), is 4,000 units a week. The demand curve shows that the highest price for which the 4,000 switchgears can be sold is £9,000 each. Trick and Gear agree to charge this price.

To hold the price at £9,000 a unit, production must not exceed 4,000 units a week. So Trick and Gear must agree on production levels for each of them that total 4,000 units a week. Let's suppose that they agree to split the market equally so that each firm produces 2,000 switchgears a week. Because the firms are identical, this division is the most likely.

The average total cost of producing 2,000 switchgears a week is £8,000, so the profit per unit is £1,000 and economic profit is £2 million (2,000 units × £1,000 per unit). The economic profit of each firm is represented by the blue rectangle in Figure 13.14(a).

We have just described one possible outcome for a duopoly game: the two firms collude to produce the monopoly profit-maximizing output and divide that output equally between them. From the industry point of view, this solution is identical to a monopoly. A duopoly that operates in this way is indistinguishable from a monopoly. The economic profit that is made by a monopoly is the maximum total profit that can be made by the duopoly when the firms collude.

But with price greater than marginal cost, either firm might think of trying to increase its profit by cheating on the agreement and producing more than the agreed amount. Let's see what happens if one of the firms does cheat in this way.

Figure 13.14

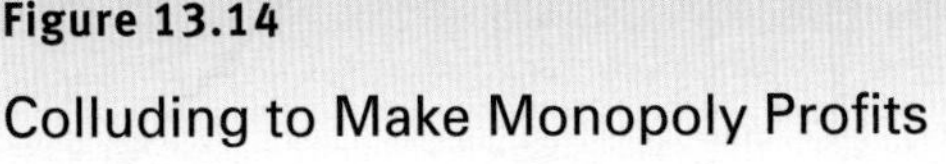

Colluding to Make Monopoly Profits

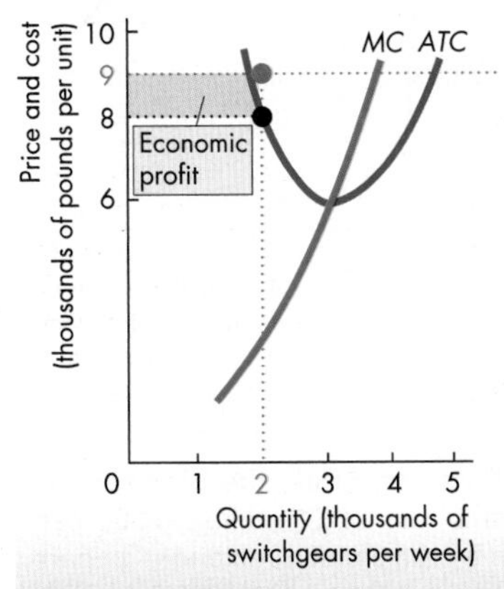

(a) Individual firm

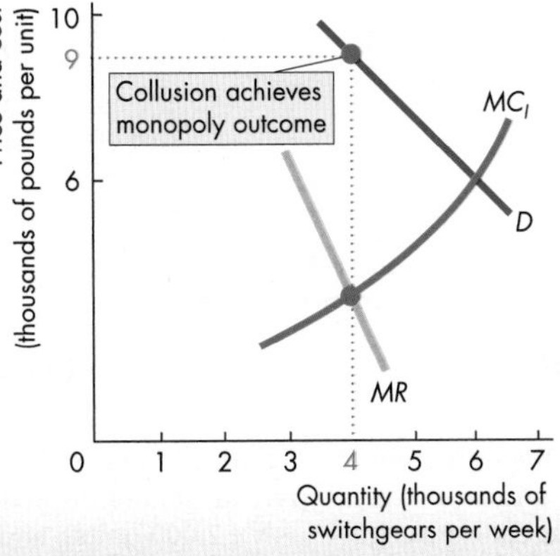

(b) Industry

The industry marginal cost curve, MC_I in part (b), is the horizontal sum of the two firms' marginal cost curves, *MC* in part (a). The industry marginal revenue curve is *MR*. To maximize profit, the firms produce 4,000 units a week (the quantity at which marginal revenue equals marginal cost). They sell that output for £9,000 a unit. Each firm produces 2,000 units a week. Average total cost is £8,000 a unit, so each firm makes an economic profit of £2 million (blue rectangle) – 2,000 units multiplied by £1,000 profit a unit.

One Firm Cheats on a Collusive Agreement

To set the stage for cheating on their agreement, Trick convinces Gear that demand has decreased and that it cannot sell 2,000 units a week. Trick tells Gear that it plans to cut its price in order to sell the agreed 2,000 units each week. Because the two firms produce an identical product, Gear matches Trick's price cut but still produces only 2,000 units a week.

In fact, there has been no decrease in demand. Trick plans to increase output, which it knows will lower the price, and Trick wants to ensure that Gear's output remains at the agreed level.

Figure 13.15 illustrates the consequences of Trick's cheating. Part (a) shows Gear (the complier); part (b) shows Trick (the cheat); and part (c) shows the industry as a whole. Suppose that Trick increases output to 3,000 units a week. If Gear sticks to the agreement to produce only 2,000 units a week, total output is 5,000 a week, and given demand in part (c), the price falls to £7,500 a unit.

Gear continues to produce 2,000 units a week at a cost of £8,000 a unit and incurs a loss of £500 a unit, or £1 million a week. This economic loss is represented by the shaded rectangle in part (a). Trick produces 3,000 units a week at an average total cost of £6,000 each.

With a price of £7,500, Trick makes a profit of £1,500 a unit and therefore an economic profit of £4.5 million. This economic profit is the blue rectangle in part (b).

We've now described a second possible outcome for the duopoly game: one of the firms cheats on the collusive agreement. In this case, the industry output is larger than the monopoly output and the industry price is lower than the monopoly price. The total economic profit made by the industry is also smaller than the monopoly's economic profit. Trick (the cheat) makes an economic profit of £4.5 million and Gear (the complier) incurs an economic loss of £1 million. The industry makes an economic profit of £3.5 million. Thus the industry profit is £0.5 million less than the economic profit a monopoly would make. But the profit is distributed unevenly. Trick makes a bigger economic profit than it would under the collusive agreement, while Gear incurs an economic loss.

A similar outcome would arise if Gear cheated and Trick complied with the agreement. The industry profit and price would be the same, but in this case, Gear (the cheat) would make an economic profit of £4.5 million and Trick (the complier) would incur an economic loss of £1 million.

Let's next see what happens if both firms cheat.

Figure 13.15

myeconlab

One Firm Cheats

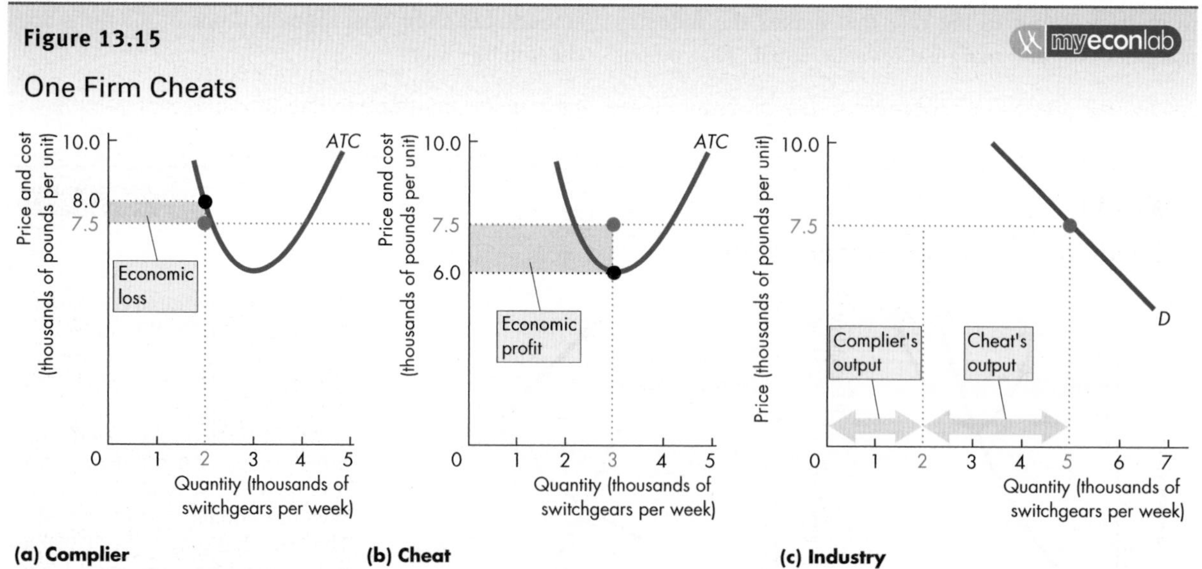

One firm, shown in part (a), complies with the agreement and produces 2,000 units. The other firm, shown in part (b), cheats on the agreement and increases its output to 3,000 units. Given the market demand curve, shown in part (c), and with a total production of 5,000 units a week, the price falls to £7,500. At this price, the complier in part (a) incurs an economic loss of £1 million (£500 per unit × 2,000 units), shown by the shaded rectangle. In part (b), the cheat makes an economic profit of £4.5 million (£1,500 per unit × 3,000 units), shown by the blue rectangle.

Both Firms Cheat

Suppose that both firms cheat and that each firm behaves like the cheating firm that we have just analyzed. Each tells the other that it is unable to sell its output at the going price and that it plans to cut its price. But because both firms cheat, each will propose a successively lower price. As long as price exceeds marginal cost, each firm has an incentive to increase its production – to cheat. Only when price equals marginal cost is there no further incentive to cheat. This situation arises when the price has reached £6,000. At this price, marginal cost equals price. Also, price equals minimum average total cost. At a price less than £6,000, each firm incurs an economic loss. At a price of £6,000, each firm covers all its costs and makes zero economic profit (makes normal profit). Also, at a price of £6,000, each firm wants to produce 3,000 units a week, so the industry output is 6,000 units a week. Given the demand conditions, 6,000 units can be sold at a price of £6,000 each.

Figure 13.16 illustrates the situation just described. Each firm, in part (a), produces 3,000 units a week, and its average total cost is a minimum (£6,000 per unit). The market as a whole, in part (b), operates at the point at which the market demand curve (*D*) intersects the industry marginal cost curve (MC_I). Each firm has lowered its price and increased its output to try to gain an advantage over the other firm. Each has pushed this process as far as it can without incurring an economic loss.

We have now described a third possible outcome of this duopoly game: both firms cheat. If both firms cheat on the collusive agreement, the output of each firm is 3,000 units a week and the price is £6,000. Each firm makes zero economic profit.

The Payoff Matrix

Now that we have described the strategies and payoffs in the duopoly game, we can summarize the strategies and the payoffs in the form of the game's payoff matrix. Then we can find the Nash equilibrium.

Table 13.2 sets out the payoff matrix for this game. It is constructed in the same way as the payoff matrix for the prisoners' dilemma in Table 13.1. The squares show the payoffs for the two firms – Gear and Trick. In this case, the payoffs are profits. (For the prisoners' dilemma, the payoffs were losses.)

The table shows that if both firms cheat (top left), they achieve the perfectly competitive outcome – each firm makes zero economic profit. If both firms comply (bottom right), the industry makes the monopoly profit and each firm makes an economic profit of £2 million. The top right and bottom left squares show what happens if one firm cheats while the other complies. The firm that cheats makes an economic profit of £4.5 million, and the one that complies incurs a loss of £1 million.

Nash Equilibrium in the Duopolists' Dilemma

The duopolists have a dilemma like the prisoners' dilemma. Do they comply or cheat? To answer this question, we must find the Nash equilibrium.

Figure 13.16

myeconlab

Both Firms Cheat

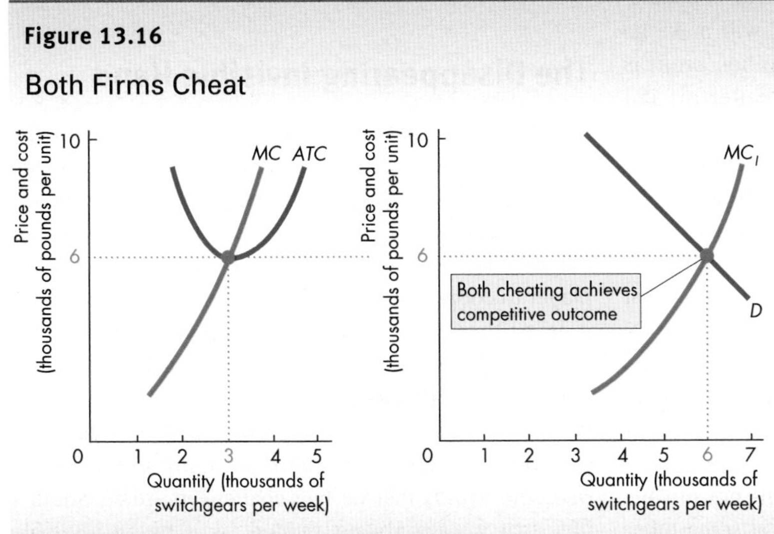

If both firms cheat by increasing production, the collusive agreement collapses. The limit to the collapse is the competitive equilibrium. Neither firm will cut the price below £6,000 (minimum average total cost) because to do so will result in losses.

In part (a), each firm produces 3,000 units a week at an average total cost of £6,000. In part (b), with a total production of 6,000 units, the price falls to £6,000. Each firm now makes zero economic profit. This output and price are the ones that would prevail in a competitive industry.

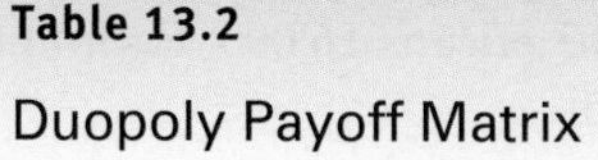

Table 13.2

Duopoly Payoff Matrix

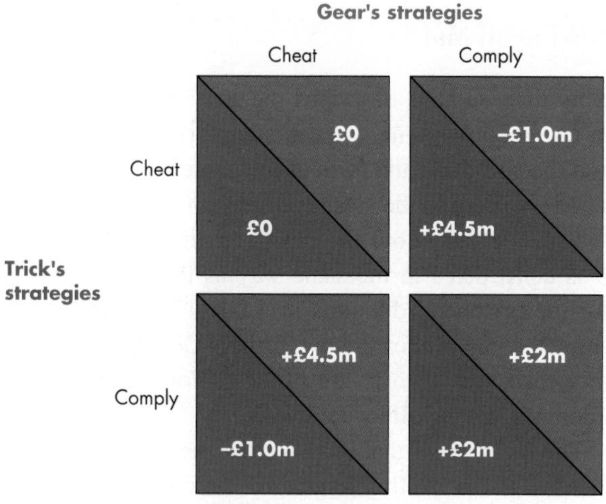

Each square shows the payoffs from a pair of actions. For example, if both firms comply with the collusive agreement, the payoffs are recorded in the bottom right square. The red triangle shows Gear's payoff, and the blue triangle shows Trick's. In the Nash equilibrium, both firms cheat.

Look at things from Gear's point of view. Gear reasons as follows. Suppose that Trick cheats. If I comply, I will incur an economic loss of £1 million. If I also cheat, I will make zero economic profit. Zero is better than *minus* £1 million, so I'm better off if I cheat. Now suppose Trick complies. If I cheat, I will make an economic profit of £4.5 million, and if I comply, I will make an economic profit of £2 million. A £4.5 million profit is better than a £2 million profit, so I'm better off if I cheat.

So regardless of whether Trick cheats or complies, it pays Gear to cheat. Cheating is Gear's best strategy.

Trick comes to the same conclusion as Gear because the two firms face an identical situation. So both firms cheat. The Nash equilibrium of the duopoly game is that both firms cheat. And, although the industry has only two firms, they charge the same price and produce the same quantity as those in a competitive industry. Also, as in perfect competition, each firm makes zero economic profit.

This conclusion is not general and will not always arise. We'll see why not first by looking at some other games that are like the prisoners' dilemma. Then we'll broaden the types of games we consider.

Other Oligopoly Games

Firms in oligopoly must decide whether to mount expensive advertising campaigns; whether to modify their product; whether to make their product more reliable and more durable; whether to price discriminate and, if so, among which groups of customers and to what degree; whether to undertake a large research and development (R&D) effort aimed at lowering production costs; and whether to enter or leave an industry.

All of these choices can be analysed as games that are similar to the one that we've just studied. For example, in a duopoly R&D game, the success of the firm depends on its ability to create a product that people value highly relative to the cost of producing it. The firm that creates the most highly valued product at least-cost can undercut the rest of the market, increase its market share and increase its profit. But the R&D that achieves product improvements and cost reductions is costly. So the cost of R&D must be deducted from the profit resulting from the increased market share. If neither firm undertakes R&D, both firms might be better off, but if one firm does R&D, the other must follow.

Another game is the retail strategic game that is playing out in the UK supermarket sector. This industry is dominated by three companies – Tesco, Asda and Sainsbury's – that share 63 per cent of the market. Morrisons has the next largest share at 11 per cent and the remainder is taken by small independent chains. In 1997, Sainsbury's was the market leader and Tesco was in second position. In 2006, Tesco was market leader and Sainsbury's was in third position behind Asda. Box 13.1 looks at this retail strategic game.

The Disappearing Invisible Hand

All the games that we've studied are versions of the prisoners' dilemma. The essence of that game lies in the structure of its payoffs. The worst possible outcome for each player arises from cooperating when the other player cheats. The best possible outcome, for each player to cooperate, is not a Nash equilibrium because it is in neither player's *self-interest* to cooperate if the other one cooperates. It is this failure to achieve the best outcome for both players – the best social outcome if the two players are the entire economy – that led John Nash to claim (as he was portrayed as doing in the film *A Beautiful Mind*) that he had challenged Adam Smith's idea that we are always guided, as if by an invisible hand, to promote the social interest when we are pursuing our self-interest.

Box 13.1
A Prisoners' Dilemma in Supermarket Strategy

Tesco and Asda have expanded rapidly and Sainsbury's has stagnated. Table 1 shows sales data and Figure 1 shows market shares in recent years.

The battle for market share was fought and won on strategic marketing decisions. Three main strategies were used: loyalty cards to encourage repeat buying, expanding non-food retailing, and overseas expansion to capture new markets and economies of scale.

Tesco introduced its customer loyalty card in 1997 but Sainsbury's did not follow immediately. Tesco increased floor space and expanded into non-food retailing in 2000. Asda followed Tesco but again, Sainsbury's did not. Tesco expanded overseas trading in 2006 and yet again Sainsbury's did not follow.

Tesco's marketing strategies were designed to increase sales and market share at the expense of its competitors, and they worked. With each strategy, Tesco increased market share and Sainsbury's market share shrank.

Table 1

UK Supermarket Sales

	Annual revenue (millions of pounds)		
	2000	2005	2006
Tesco	18,550	33,866	39,454
Sainsbury's	16,187	16,573	16,058
Asda	8,875	14,707	15,163

Figure 1

UK Supermarket Shares

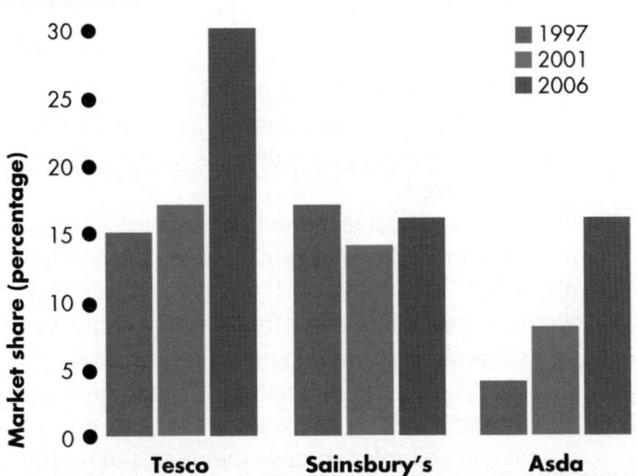

Source of data: TNS (www.tns-global.com) Worldpanel grocery market press reports.

The Game the Supermarkets Play

Table 2 represents the competition between Tesco and Sainsbury's as a strategic game. The payoffs in the table are changes in profit. If neither supermarket expanded non-food retailing, both save marketing and development costs, market shares are similar and profits increase for both companies by 8 per cent (bottom right). Marketing and product development costs lower profits, so if both companies expand non-food retailing, market shares are similar and economic profits are cut by 4 per cent (top left).

The Nash equilibrium is for both firms to expand non-food retailing. But Sainsbury's did not play its Nash equilibrium strategy and lost market share. Profit increased by 12 per cent for Tesco and fell by 4 per cent for Sainsbury's (bottom left of table).

Sainsbury's paid a high price for not following Tesco's marketing lead in 1997, 2000 and 2006. It slipped to third place behind the fast-growing Asda.

Table 2

A Strategic Game

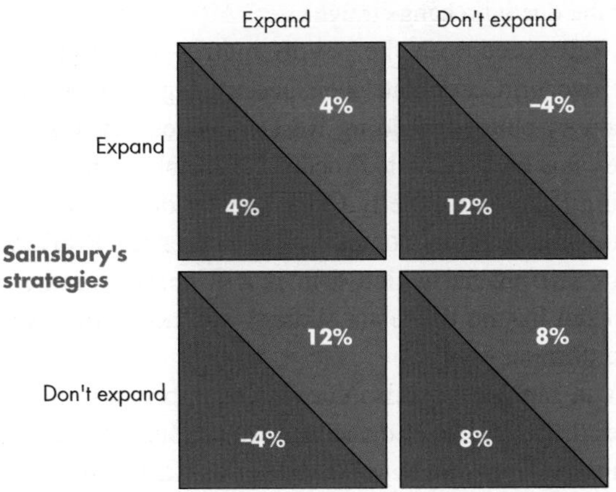

Today, Tesco and Asda are locked in a similar strategic game to that played previously by Tesco and Sainsbury's. So far, Tesco and Asda have matched each others' moves but Tesco has the first mover advantage and will be hard to catch.

A Game of Chicken

The Nash equilibrium for the prisoners' dilemma is called a **dominant strategy equilibrium**, which is an equilibrium in which the best strategy of each player is to cheat (deny) *regardless of the strategy of the other player*. Not all games have such an equilibrium, and one that doesn't is a game called "chicken".

In a graphic, if disturbing, version of this game, two cars race towards each other. The first driver to swerve and avoid a crash is "chicken". The payoffs are a big loss for both if no one "chickens", zero for the chicken and a gain for the player who hangs tough.

If player 1 chickens, player 2's best strategy is to hang tough. And if player 1 hangs tough, player 2's best strategy is to chicken.

For an economic form of this game, suppose the R&D that creates a new nappy technology results in information that cannot be kept secret or patented, so both firms benefit from the R&D of either firm. The chicken in this case is the firm that does the R&D.

Table 13.3 illustrates a payoff matrix for an R&D game of chicken between Kimberly-Clark and Procter & Gamble. Each firm has two strategies: do the R&D (and "chicken") or don't do the R&D (and hang tough).

If neither "chickens", there is no R&D and each firm makes zero additional profit. If each firm conducts R&D – each "chickens" – each firm makes £5 million (the profit from the new technology minus the cost of the research). If one of the firms does the R&D, the payoffs are £1 million for the chicken and £10 million for the one who hangs tough.

Confronted with the payoff matrix in Table 13.3, the two firms calculate their best strategies. Kimberly-Clark is better off doing R&D if Procter & Gamble does not undertake it. Procter & Gamble is better off doing R&D if Kimberly-Clark doesn't do it. There are two equilibrium outcomes: one firm does the R&D, but we can't predict which firm it will be. The game of chicken has no dominant strategy and no unique Nash equilibrium.

You can see that it isn't a Nash equilibrium if no firm does the R&D because one firm would then be better off doing it. And you can see that it isn't a Nash equilibrium if both firms do the R&D because then one firm would be better off not doing it.

The firms could toss a coin or use some other random device to make a decision in this game. In some circumstances, such a strategy – called a mixed strategy – is actually better for both firms than choosing any of the strategies we've considered.

Table 13.3

An R&D Game of Chicken

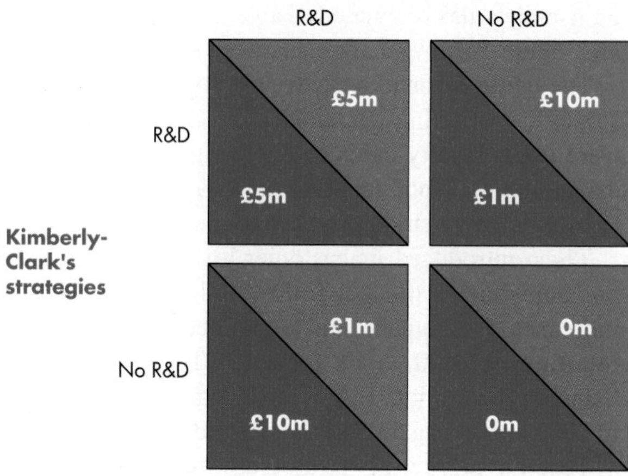

If both firms undertake R&D, their payoffs are those shown in the top left square. If neither firm undertakes R&D, their payoffs are in the bottom right square. When one firm undertakes R&D and the other one does not, their payoffs are in the top right and bottom left squares. The red triangle shows Procter & Gamble's payoff, and the blue triangle shows Kimberly-Clark's.

The Nash equilibrium for this R&D game of chicken is for only one firm to undertake R&D. We cannot tell which firm will do the R&D and which will not.

Review Quiz

Study Plan 13.6

1. What are the common features of all games?
2. Describe the prisoners' dilemma game and explain why the Nash equilibrium delivers a bad outcome for both players.
3. Why does a collusive agreement to restrict output and raise price create a game like the prisoners' dilemma?
4. What creates an incentive for firms in a collusive agreement to cheat and increase production?
5. What is the equilibrium strategy for each firm in a duopolists' dilemma and why do the firms not succeed in colluding to raise the price and profits?
6. Describe two structures of payoffs for an R&D game and contrast the prisoners' dilemma and chicken game.

Repeated Games and Sequential Games

The games that we've studied are played just once. In contrast, many real-world games are played repeatedly. This feature of games turns out to enable real-world duopolists to cooperate, collude and make a monopoly profit.

Another feature of the game that we've studied is that the players move simultaneously. But in many real-world situations, one player moves first and then the other moves – the play is sequential rather than simultaneous. This feature of real-world games creates a large number of possible outcomes.

We're now going to examine these two aspects of strategic decision making.

A Repeated Duopoly Game

If two firms play a game repeatedly, one firm has the opportunity to penalize the other for previous "bad" behaviour. If Gear cheats this week, perhaps Trick will cheat next week. Before Gear cheats this week, won't it consider the possibility that Trick will cheat next week? What is the equilibrium of this game?

Actually, there is more than one possibility. One is the Nash equilibrium that we have just analyzed. Both players cheat, and each makes zero economic profit forever. In such a situation, it will never pay one of the players to start complying unilaterally because to do so would result in a loss for that player and a profit for the other. But a **cooperative equilibrium** in which the players make and share the monopoly profit is possible.

A cooperative equilibrium might occur if cheating is punished. There are two extremes of punishment. The smallest penalty is called "tit for tat". A *tit-for-tat strategy* is one in which a player cooperates in the current period if the other player cooperated in the previous period but cheats in the current period if the other player cheated in the previous period. The most severe form of punishment is called a trigger strategy. A *trigger strategy* is one in which a player cooperates if the other player cooperates but plays the Nash equilibrium strategy forever thereafter if the other player cheats.

In the duopoly game between Gear and Trick, a tit-for-tat strategy keeps both players cooperating and making monopoly profits. Let's see why with an example.

Table 13.4 shows the economic profit that Trick and Gear will make over a number of periods under two alternative sequences of events: colluding and cheating with a tit-for-tat response by the other firm.

If both firms stick to the collusive agreement in period 1, each makes an economic profit of £2 million. Suppose that Trick contemplates cheating in period 1. The cheating produces a quick £4.5 million economic profit and inflicts a £1 million economic loss on Gear.

But a cheat in period 1 produces a response from Gear in period 2. If Trick wants to get back into a profit-making situation, it must return to the agreement in period 2 even though it knows that Gear will punish it for cheating in period 1. So in period 2, Gear punishes Trick and Trick cooperates. Gear now makes an economic profit of £4.5 million, and Trick incurs an economic loss of £1 million.

Adding up the profits over two periods of play, Trick would have made more profit by cooperating – £4 million compared with £3.5 million.

What is true for Trick is also true for Gear. Because each firm makes a larger profit by sticking with the collusive agreement, both firms do so and the monopoly price, quantity and profit prevail.

In reality, whether a cartel works like a one-play game or a repeated game depends primarily on the number

Table 13.4

Cheating with Punishment

	Collude		Cheat with tit-for-tat	
Period of play	Trick's profit (millions of pounds)	Gear's profit (millions of pounds)	Trick's profit (millions of pounds)	Gear's profit (millions of pounds)
1	2	2	4.5	−1.0
2	2	2	−1.0	4.5
3	2	2	2.0	2.0
4	.	.	.	.

If duopolists repeatedly collude, each makes an economic profit of £2 million per period of play. If one player cheats in period 1, the other player plays a tit-for-tat strategy and cheats in period 2. The profit from cheating can be made for only one period and must be paid for in the next period by incurring a loss. Over two periods of play, the best that a duopolist can achieve by cheating is an economic profit of £3.5 million, compared to an economic profit of £4 million by colluding.

of players and the ease of detecting and punishing cheating. The larger the number of players, the harder it is to maintain a cartel.

Games and Price Wars

A repeated duopoly game can help us understand real-world behaviour and, in particular, price wars. Some price wars can be interpreted as the implementation of a tit-for-tat strategy. But the game is a bit more complicated than the one we've looked at because the players are uncertain about the demand for the product.

Playing a tit-for-tat strategy, firms have an incentive to stick to the monopoly price. But fluctuations in demand lead to fluctuations in the monopoly price, and sometimes, when the price changes, it might seem to one of the firms that the price has fallen because the other has cheated. In this case, a price war will break out. The price war will end only when each firm is satisfied that the other is ready to cooperate again. There will be cycles of price wars and the restoration of collusive agreements. Fluctuations in the world price of oil might be interpreted in this way.

Some price wars arise from the entry of a small number of firms into an industry that had previously been a monopoly. Although the industry has a small number of firms, the firms are in a prisoners' dilemma and they cannot impose effective penalties for price cutting.

A Computer Chip Price War

The prices of computer chips during 1995 and 1996 can be explained by the game you've just examined. Until 1995, the market for chips for IBM-compatible computers was dominated by Intel Corporation. Intel was able to make maximum economic profit by producing the quantity of chips at which marginal cost equalled marginal revenue. The price of Intel's chips was set to ensure that the quantity demanded equalled the quantity produced. Then in 1995 and 1996, with the entry of a small number of new firms, the industry became an oligopoly. If the firms had maintained Intel's price and shared the market, together they could have made economic profits equal to Intel's profit. But the firms were in a prisoners' dilemma. So prices fell toward the competitive level.

Let's now study a sequential game. There are many such games, and the one we'll examine is among the simplest. It has an interesting implication and it will give you the flavour of this type of game. We'll study an entry game in a contestable market.

A Sequential Entry Game in a Contestable Market

If two firms play a sequential game, one firm makes a decision at the first stage of the game and the other makes a decision at the second stage.

We're going to study a sequential game in a **contestable market** – a market in which firms can enter and leave so easily that firms in the market face competition from *potential* entrants. Examples of contestable markets are routes served by airlines and by barge companies that operate on Europe's major waterways.

These markets are contestable because firms could enter if an opportunity for economic profit arose and could exit with no penalty if the opportunity for economic profit disappeared.

If the five-firm concentration ratio (see Chapter 9, p. 202) is used to determine the degree of competition, a contestable market appears to be uncompetitive. But a contestable market can behave as if it were perfectly competitive. To see why, let's look at an entry game for a contestable air route.

A Contestable Air Route

Agile Air is the only firm operating on a particular route. Demand and cost conditions are such that there is room for only one airline to operate. Wanabe, Inc. is another airline that could offer services on the route.

We describe the structure of a sequential game by using a *game tree* like that in Figure 13.17. At the first stage, Agile Air must set a price. Once the price is set and advertised, Agile can't change it. That is, once set, Agile's price is fixed and Agile can't react to Wanabe's entry decision. Agile can set its price at either the monopoly level or the competitive level.

At the second stage, Wanabe must decide whether to enter or to stay out. Customers have no loyalty (there are no frequent flyer programmes) and they buy from the lowest-price firm. So if Wanabe enters, it sets a price just below Agile's and takes all the business.

Figure 13.17 shows the payoffs from the various decisions (Agile's in the red triangles and Wanabe's in the blue triangles).

To decide on its price, Agile's CEO reasons as follows. Suppose that Agile sets the monopoly price. If Wanabe enters, it earns 90 (think of all payoff numbers as thousands of pounds). If Wanabe stays out, it earns nothing. So Wanabe will enter. In this case Agile will lose 50.

Figure 13.17

myeconlab

Agile versus Wanabe: A Sequential Entry Game in a Contestable Market

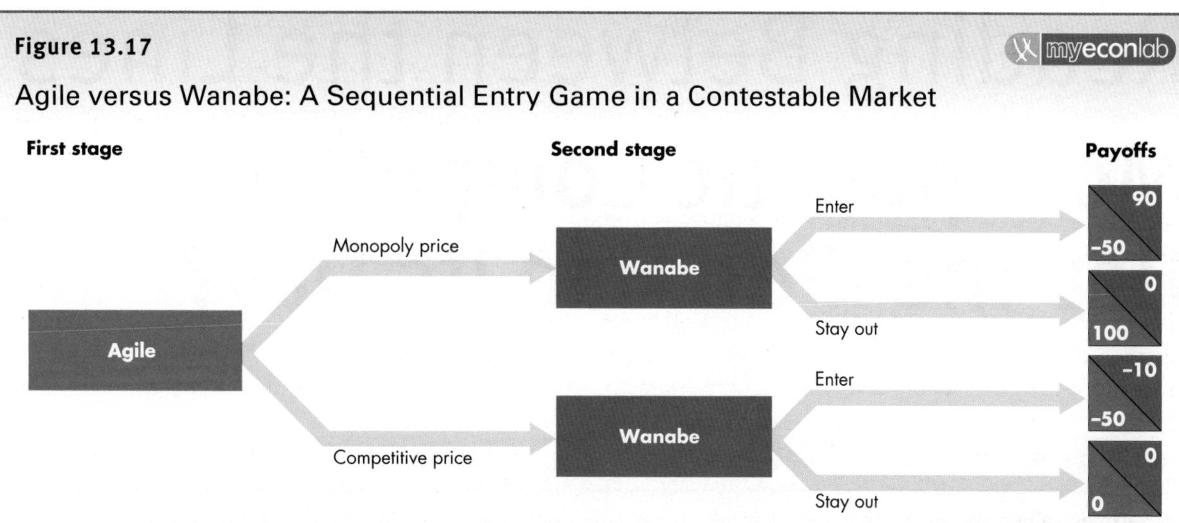

If Agile sets the monopoly price, Wanabe makes 90 (thousand pounds) by entering and earns nothing by staying out. So if Agile sets the monopoly price, Wanabe enters.

If Agile sets the competitive price, Wanabe earns nothing if it stays out and incurs a loss if it enters. So if Agile sets the competitive price, Wanabe stays out.

Now suppose that Agile sets the competitive price. If Wanabe stays out, it earns nothing and if it enters, it loses 10, so Wanabe will stay out. In this case, Agile will make zero economic profit.

Agile's best strategy is to set its price at the competitive level and make zero economic profit. The option of earning 100 by setting the monopoly price with Wanabe staying out is not available to Agile. If Agile sets the monopoly price, Wanabe enters, undercuts Agile, and takes all the business.

In this example, Agile sets its price at the competitive level and makes zero economic profit. A less costly strategy, called **limit pricing**, sets the price at the highest level that inflicts a loss on the entrant. Any loss is big enough to deter entry, so it is not always necessary to set the price as low as the competitive price. In the example of Agile and Wanabe, at the competitive price, Wanabe incurs a loss of 10 if it enters. A smaller loss would still keep Wanabe out.

This game is interesting because it points to the possibility of a monopoly behaving like a competitive industry and serving the consumer interest without regulation. But the result is not general and depends on one crucial feature of the setup of the game: at the second stage, Agile is locked into the price set at the first stage.

If Agile could change its price in the second stage, it would want to set the monopoly price if Wanabe stayed out – 100 with the monopoly price beats zero with the competitive price. But Wanabe can figure out what Agile would do, so the price set at the first stage has no effect on Wanabe. Agile sets the monopoly price and Wanabe might either stay out or enter.

We've looked at two of the many possible repeated and sequential games, and you've seen how these types of game can provide insights into the complex forces that determine prices and profits.

Review Quiz

Study Plan 13.7

1. If a prisoners' dilemma game is played repeatedly, what punishment strategies might the players employ and how does playing the game repeatedly change the equilibrium?
2. If a market is contestable, how does the equilibrium differ from that of a monopoly?

Monopolistic competition and oligopoly are the most common market structures that you encounter in your daily life. *Reading Between the Lines* on pp. 312–313 looks which examines monopolistic competition in the MP3 players market.

So far, except for a brief look at monopoly policy issues at the end of Chapter 12, we have studied unregulated market power. Your next task is to see how government regulation influences market power.

Reading Between the Lines

Monopolistic Competition: Has the iPod Had Its Day?

The Business, 17–18 September 2006

Over here, over priced, over the hill

It's only five years old, . . . but in its short life it has revolutionised the music industry . . . and shaped the world's youth culture. The Apple iPod has been the zippiest product to hit the music market since the Sony Walkman. But analysts are beginning to ask "for how long". . . .

An astonishing 60 million iPods have been sold around the world since the first version was put on sale in November 2001. It has gone through several design upgrades since. . . .

Seventy-five per cent of all MP3 music players sold are iPods. . . . For the first time sales have gone into reverse and imitators have appeared on the market offering cheaper models.

So last week, Steve Jobs, Apple's chief executive, unveiled yet another incarnation of the ubiquitous musical device. This one will play full-length films on 2.5 inch colour screens, . . . downloaded from Apple's iTunes website. . . .

Although Apple has blown away all competitors in the MP3 player market over the first five years, it is today facing new competition that it might not beat, . . .

This year Apple's iPod sales fell for the first time. They dropped to 8.5m in the first quarter and 8.1m in the second. Competition from mobile phones with MP3 players appears to be the culprit, outselling them six times. Microsoft, too, will introduce a portable media player called Zune . . . It has a special new wireless feature that will allow users nearby to transmit songs, pictures or videos to each other.

The Essence of the Story

- Apple introduced its iPod MP3 player in 2001. By 2006, Apple had sold over 60 million iPods and dominated the market.
- Apple have constantly updated the iPod, keeping competition at bay.
- Strong new competitors including Microsoft and mobile phone operators entered the MP3 market in 2006.
- In the first two quarters of 2006, iPod sales fell for the first time.

Economic Analysis

- The market for MP3 players is an example of monopolistic competition.
- Figure 1 shows the situation facing Apple in 2005, when the iPod had kept competition at bay.
- Apple's average total cost curve for producing the iPod as *ATC* and its marginal cost curve as *MC*.
- The demand curve for the iPod is D_0 and the marginal revenue curve is MR_0.
- To maximize profit, Apple produces the quantity of iPods at which marginal revenue equals marginal cost and sells them at the highest price the market will pay for the profit-maximizing quantity.
- The profit maximizing quantity is 12 million iPods per quarter and the profit-maximizing price is £200 per iPod. The blue rectangle shows Apple's economic profit from iPods.
- Since 2006, many new competitors, including mobile phone producers, have successfully entered the market for MP3 players.
- Each competitor produces a slightly different type of MP3 player. The firms compete on quality, price and marketing.
- New entrants decrease demand for iPods and make iPod demand more elastic.
- Figure 2 shows Apple's situation after new firms successfully enter the market. Apple's average total cost is still *ATC* and its marginal cost curve is *MC*. But the demand curve has shifted demand curve to D_1 and the marginal revenue curve has shifted to MR_1.
- Now Apple maximizes profit by selling 8 million iPods a quarter at £150 each.
- Apple earns zero economic profit on iPods because price is equal to average total cost.
- But Apple is not willing to remain in the situation shown in Figure 2. It innovates again, and introduces iPod video.

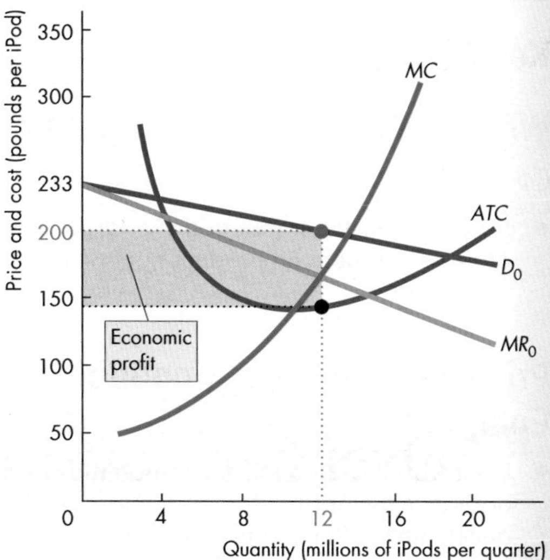

Figure 1 Before entry

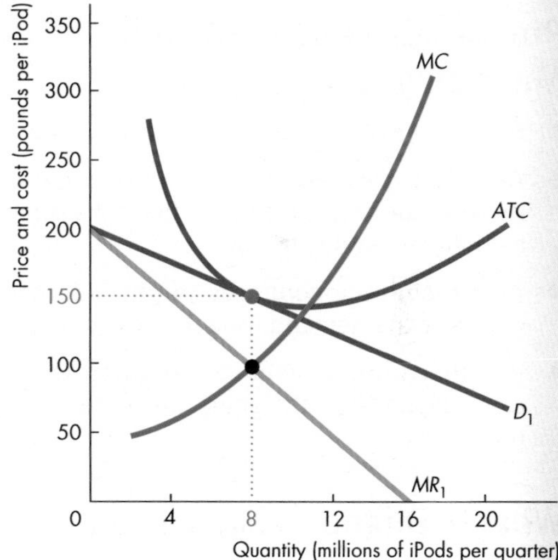

Figure 2 After entry

- If the iPod video is as successful as the original iPod, Apple returns to a situation like the one shown in Figure 1.
- But again, economic profit induces entry. Mobile phone producers begin to offer video-capable phones and the market moves relentlessly to a situation like that in Figure 2.
- The cycle keeps repeating with ever-better products for consumers.

Summary

Key Points

What Is Monopolistic Competition?
(pp. 286–287)

- In monopolistic competition, a large number of firms compete on product quality, price and marketing.

Price and Output in Monopolistic Competition (pp. 288–291)

- Each firm in monopolistic competition faces a downward-sloping demand curve and produces the profit-maximizing quantity.
- Entry and exit result in zero economic profit and excess capacity in long-run equilibrium.

Product Development and Marketing (pp. 292–295)

- Firms innovate and develop new products.
- Advertising expenditures increase total cost, but average total cost might fall if the quantity sold increases by enough.
- Advertising expenditures might increase or decrease the demand for a firm's product.
- Whether monopolistic competition is inefficient depends on the value we place on product variety.

What Is Oligopoly? (pp. 296–297)

- Oligopoly is a market in which a small number of firms compete.

Two Traditional Oligopoly Models
(pp. 298–299)

- If rivals match price cuts but do not match price hikes, they face a kinked demand curve.
- If one firm dominates, it acts like a monopoly and the small firms act as price takers.

Oligopoly Games (pp. 300–308)

- Game theory is used to analyze strategic behaviour in oligopoly.
- In a prisoners' dilemma game, two prisoners acting in their own self-interest harm their joint interest.
- An oligopoly (duopoly) price-fixing game is a prisoners' dilemma.

Repeated Games and Sequential Games (pp. 309–311)

- In a repeated oligopoly game, punishment can produce a cooperative equilibrium in which price and output are the same as in monopoly.
- In a sequential contestable market game, a small number of firms can behave like firms in perfect competition.

Key Figures and Tables

Key Terms

Cartel, 297
Collusive agreement, 302
Contestable market, 310
Cooperative equilibrium, 309
Dominant strategy equilibrium, 308
Duopoly, 296
Game theory, 300
Limit pricing, 311
Monopolistic competition, 286
Nash equilibrium, 301
Oligopoly, 296
Payoff matrix, 300
Product differentiation, 286
Signal, 294
Strategies, 300

Problems

Tests, Study Plan and Solutions* 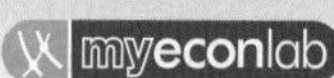

1 The figure shows the situation facing Liter and Kook plc, a European producer of running shoes.

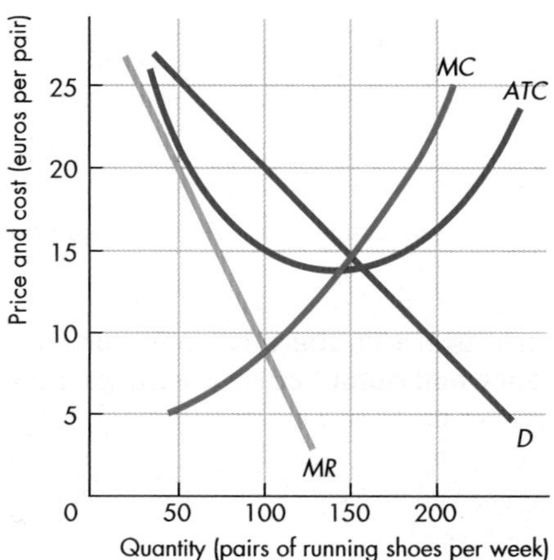

a What quantity does Liter and Kook produce?

b What does it charge?

c How much profit does Liter and Kook make?

2 In the market for running shoes all the firms face a similar demand curve and have similar cost curves to those of Liter and Kook in problem 1.

a What happens to the price of running shoes in the long run?

b What happens to the quantity of running shoes produced by Liter and Kook in the long run?

c What happens to the quantity of running shoes in the entire market in the long run?

d Does Liter and Kook produce at minimum average total cost in the long run? Explain your answer.

e What is the relationship between Liter and Kook's price and marginal cost?

3 Suppose that Hugo Boss's marginal cost of a jacket is €100 and at one of the firm's shops, total fixed cost is €2,000 a day. The profit-maximizing number of jackets sold in this shop is 20 a day. Then the shops nearby start to advertise. The Hugo Boss shop spends €2,000 a day advertising its jackets, and its profit-maximizing number of jackets sold jumps to 50 a day.

a What is this shop's average total cost of a jacket sold before the advertising begins?

b What is this shop's average total cost of a jacket sold after the advertising begins?

c Can you say what happens to the price of a Hugo Boss jacket? Why or why not?

d Can you say what happens to Hugo Boss's mark up? Why or why not?

e Can you say what happens to Hugo Boss's economic profit?

4 Two firms make most of the chips that power a PC: Intel and Advanced Micro Devices. What makes the market for PC chips a duopoly? Sketch the market demand curve and cost curves that describe the situation in this market and that prevent other firms from entering the industry.

5 The price at which Wald-Mart can buy flat panel TVs has fallen, and the firm is making a decision about whether to lower its selling price. It believes that if it lowers its price, all its competitors will lower their prices too. Wald-Mart also believes that if it raises its price, none of its competitors would raise theirs.

a Draw a figure to illustrate the situation that Wald-Mart believes it faces in the market for flat panel TVs.

b Do you predict that Wald-Mart will lower its flat-panel TV prices? Explain and illustrate your answer.

6 Big Joe's Trucking has lower costs than the other 20 small truckers in the market. The market operates like a dominant firm oligopoly and is initially in equilibrium. Then the demand for trucking services increases. Explain the effects of the increase in demand on the price, output and economic profit of:

a Big Joe's.

b A typical small firm.

7 Consider a game with two players and in which each player is asked a question. The players can answer the question honestly or lie. If both answer honestly, each receives €100. If one answers honestly and the other lies, the liar receives €500 and the honest player gets nothing. If both lie, then each receives €50.

a Describe strategies and payoffs of this game.

b Construct the payoff matrix.

c What is the equilibrium of this game?

d Compare this game to the prisoners' dilemma. Are the two games similar or different? Explain your answer.

8 Two firms, Soapy plc and Suddsies plc, are the only producers of soap powder. They collude and agree to share the market equally. If neither firm cheats on the agreement, each makes €1 million economic profit. If

* Solutions to odd-numbered problems are provided.

either firm cheats, the cheater increases its economic profit to €1.5 million while the firm that abides by the agreement incurs an economic loss of €0.5 million. Neither firm has any way of policing the other's actions.

a Describe the best strategy for each firm in a game that is played once.

b What is the economic profit for each firm if both cheat?

c Construct the payoff matrix of a game that is played just once.

d What is the equilibrium if the game is played once?

e If this duopoly game can be played many times, describe some of the strategies that each firm might adopt.

9 If Soapy plc and Suddies plc repeatedly play the duopoly game that has the payoffs described in problem 8 on each round of play,

a What now are the strategies that each firm might adopt?

b Does the game now have a cooperative equilibrium?

c If the payoffs from one firm cheating changed to a profit of €1.4 million for the cheat and a loss of €0.5 million for the complier, would the game have a cooperative equilibrium?

Critical Thinking

1 Read the *Reading Between the Lines* on pp. 312–313 and answer the following questions:

a Why is the global market for MP3 players and example of monopolistic competition?

b Why did it become harder for Apple to sell its iPod during 2006?

c What did Apple do before 2006 to limit the effect of new competition in the MP3 market?

d How do successful competitors in the MP3 market try to earn an economic profit?

e What must Apple do to keep earning an economic profit from the iPod?

2 Read Box 13.1 about the supermarket strategy game on p. 307 and then answer the following questions:

a Why do you think Sainsbury's did not follow Tesco's innovative lead to introduce customer loyalty cards, expand into non-food retailing and expand overseas?

b What impact did Sainsbury's decisions have on market shares?

3 Why do Coca-Cola and PepsiCo spend huge amounts on advertising? Do they benefit? Does the consumer benefit? Explain your answer.

4 Think about the strategic interactions of Airbus and Boeing in the market for very large aircraft – the Airbus A380 and the Boeing 747.

a Describe the competition between these two firms in the market for very large aircraft.

b What are the strategies in this game concerning design, marketing and price?

c What do you predict will be the equilibrium of the game and why?

5 Microsoft with Xbox 360, Nintendo with Wii, and Sony with PlayStation 3 are slugging it out in the market for the latest generation of video games consoles. Xbox 360 was the first to market; Wii has the lowest price; PS3 uses the most advanced technology and has the highest price.

a Describe the competition among these firms in the market for consoles as a game.

b What are the strategies in this game concerning design, marketing and price?

c What turned out to be the equilibrium of the game?

d Can you think of reasons why the three consoles are so different?

Web Activities

Links to Websites

1 Obtain information about the market for vitamins.

a In what type of market are vitamins sold?

b What illegal act occurred in the vitamins market during the 1990s?

c Describe the actions of BASF and Roche as a game and set out a hypothetical payoff matrix for the game.

d Is the game played by BASF and Roche a one-shot game or a repeated game? How do you know which type of game it is?

2 Obtain information about the market for art and antiques.

a What illegal act occurred in the art and antiques auction market during the 1990s?

b Describe the game played by Sotheby's and Christie's and set out a payoff matrix.

PART 4

Government, Income Distribution and Uncertainty

Constitutions, Government, Laws and Regulations

Valery Giscard d'Estaing knows better than most people the hazards of trying to define the rules by which governments play. As Chairman of the Convention that drafted the new EU constitution, he struggled to craft a set of arrangements that would enable a large and still growing number of national European governments to work together and achieve better economic outcomes for their people.

A constitution that makes despotic and tyrannical rule impossible is relatively easy. The constitutions of Australia, France, Germany, Japan, Switzerland and the United States are all examples of political arrangements based on sound economics. They are sophisticated systems of incentives – of carrots and sticks – designed to make the government responsive to public opinion and to limit the ability of individual self-interests to gain at the expense of the majority. But no one has yet managed to design a constitution that effectively blocks the ability of special-interest groups to capture the consumer and producer surpluses that result from specialization and trade.

We face four economic problems that cannot be solved by self-interested individual action in markets and a fifth problem that presents special challenges for the market economy.

The four problems that the market economy cannot solve are:

1 Markets dominated by monopolies produce too small a quantity and charge too high a price;
2 Markets produce too small a quantity of those goods and services that we must consume together, such as security and public health;
3 Markets produce too large a quantity of those goods and services that create pollution and degrade our environment and too small a quantity of the the goods and services that bring external benefits, such as education and research; and
4 Markets generate a distribution of income and wealth that most people believe is unfair because it is too unequal.

To deal with these four problems, we need mechanisms that enable us to make *public choices*. Government tries to provide such mechanisms. But as the drafters of all constitutions know, when governments get involved in the economic life, people try to steer the government's actions in directions that serve self-interest at the expense of the social interest.

The first three chapters in this part explain the first three problems we've just reviewed. Chapter 14 overviews the entire range of problems and studies the first of them: monopoly and the role of competition law and regulation to steer monopolies toward acting in the social interest.

Chapter 15 deals with externalities. It focuses on pollution and an example of a source of external cost education and research as examples of activities that bring external benefits. The chapter describes some of the ways in which externalities can be dealt with. It also explains that one way of coping with externalities is to strengthen the market and "internalize" the externalities rather than to intervene in the market.

Chapter 16 studies the "free-rider" problem created by public goods and services – items enjoyed by all but paid for directly by none – and the "tragedy of the commons" – a tragic situation that arises when resources are owned by no one but used by everyone and get overexploited.

Chapters 17 and 18 study economic inequality. Chapter 17 presents an overview of all factor markets. It explains how the demand for factors of production results from the profit-maximizing decisions of firms, how the supply of factors of production results from decisions made by households, and how equilibrium in factor markets determines factor prices and the incomes of owners of factors of production. Chapter 17 uses labour resources and the labour market as its main example. But it also looks at some special features of capital markets and natural resource markets.

Chapter 18 studies the distribution of income. This chapter takes you back to the fundamentals of economics and answers one of the big economic questions: who consumes the goods and services produced?

Chapter 19 studies the challenges thrown at the market economy by the problems of risk, uncertainty and private information and explains how markets handle these problems.

CHAPTER 14

Government Regulation and Competition Policy

After studying this chapter you will be able to:

- Explain the economic theory of governments and how government activity arises from market failure and redistribution
- Explain how regulation and deregulation affects prices, outputs, profits and the distribution of the gains
- Explain how monopoly control laws are applied in Europe
- Explain how public ownership and privatization affect prices, output and allocative efficiency

Social Interest or Self-interest?

Why are the firms that produce our drinking water, electric power, natural gas and telephone services regulated? Why are European railways and pharmaceutical companies subject to anti-monopoly laws? Do regulations and anti-monopoly laws serve the social interest – the interest of all consumers and producers – or do they serve the self-interest of the regulated firms? Find the answers in this chapter. And in the *Business Case Study* at the end of the chapter, find out how EU regulators seek to make Europe's electricity and gas markets more competitive and better able to serve the social interest.

The Economic Theory of Government

The economic theory of government explains why governments exist, the economic roles of government, the economic choices they make and the consequences of those choices.

Why Governments Exist

Governments exist for three major reasons. First, they establish and maintain property rights. Second, they provide mechanisms for allocating scarce resources. Third, they implement arrangements that redistribute income and wealth.

Property rights are the fundamental foundation of the market economy. By establishing property rights and the legal system that enforces them, governments enable markets to function. In many situations, markets function well and help us to allocate our scarce resources efficiently.

But the market economy sometimes results in inefficiency – a situation called **market failure**. When market failure occurs, too many of some things and too few of some other things are produced. Choices made in the pursuit of self-interest have not served the social interest. By reallocating resources, it is possible to make some people better off while making no one worse off.

Also the market economy delivers a distribution of income and wealth that most people regard as being unfair. Equity requires some redistribution.

The Economic Roles of Government

In this chapter and in Chapters 15, 16 and 18, we're going to study the economic roles of government in five areas. They are:

- Monopoly and oligopoly regulation
- Externalities regulation
- Provision of public goods
- Use of common resources
- Income redistribution

Monopoly and Oligopoly Regulation

Monopoly and oligopoly can prevent resources from being allocated efficiently. Every business tries to maximize profit, and when monopoly or oligopoly exists, firms try to increase profit by restricting output and keeping the price high.

For example, until a few years ago, most European national telecommunication companies had a monopoly on telephone services and the price of business and domestic telephone services was higher and the quality of service was lower than it is today.

Although some monopolies arise from *legal barriers to entry* – barriers to entry created by governments – a major activity of government is to regulate monopoly and to enforce laws that prevent cartels and other restrictions on competition.

We'll study competition law and monopoly regulations in this chapter.

Externalities regulation

When a chemical factory (perhaps legally) dumps its waste into a river and kills the fish, it imposes a cost – called an *external cost* – on the members of a fishing club who fish downstream. When a homeowner fills her garden with spring bulbs, she generates an external benefit for all the passers-by.

External costs and external benefits are not usually taken into account by the people whose actions create them. The chemical factory does not take the fishing club's wishes into account when it decides whether to dump waste into the river. The homeowner does not take her neighbours' views into account when she decides to fill her garden with flowers.

Because self-interested choices ignore or place a low weight on the wishes of others, externalities can result in the overprovision or underprovision of some goods and services. Government actions can try to overcome these sources of market failure. We study externalities in Chapter 15.

Provision of Public Goods

Some goods and services are consumed by everyone and no one can be excluded from the benefits that arise from their provision. Examples are national defence, law and order and sewage and waste disposal services. A national defence system can't isolate individuals and refuse to protect them. Airborne diseases from untreated sewage don't favour some people and hit others. A good or service that is consumed by everyone is called a *public good.*

The market economy fails to deliver the efficient quantity of public goods because of a *free-rider problem.*

Everyone tries to free ride on everyone else because the good is available to all whether they pay for it or not.

We'll provide a more thorough description of public goods and the free-rider problem in Chapter 16. We'll also study the factors that influence the scale of provision of public goods in that chapter.

Use of Common Resources

Some resources are owned by no one and used by everyone. Examples are the Pennine Way, public parks and fish in the North Sea. Every week, hundreds of boats scoop up tonnes of fish from the North Sea. The consequence is that the stocks of some species – cod is one of them – are dangerously depleted.

The market economy fails to use common resources efficiently because no one has an incentive to conserve what everyone else is free to use.

We'll describe this problem more thoroughly in Chapter 16, where we'll also review some ideas for coping with the problem.

Income Redistribution

The market economy delivers an unequal distribution of income and wealth. Most people regard the market outcome as being unfair – it creates too much inequality. (We reviewed ideas about fairness in Chapter 5, pp. 112–115.)

Governments redistribute income by using income support systems and progressive income taxes. You've already seen, in Chapter 6, how taxes affect markets and create deadweight losses. We'll look at the role of taxes in redistributing income in Chapter 18 after learning how factor markets operate in Chapter 17.

Before we begin to study these problems from which government activity arises, let's look at the arena in which governments operate: the "political marketplace".

Public Choice and the Political Marketplace

Government is a complex organization made up of many individuals, each with his or her own economic objectives. Government policy is the outcome of the choices made by these individuals. To analyze these choices, economists have developed a *public choice theory* of the political marketplace.

Figure 14.1 shows the actors in and the anatomy of the political marketplace.

The actors are:

- Voters
- Firms
- Politicians
- Civil servants

Voters

Voters are the consumers of the political process. In the political marketplace, voters express their demands by voting, campaigning, lobbying and making financial contributions. Public choice theory assumes that people support policies that they believe will make them better off and oppose policies that they believe will make them worse off. They neither oppose nor support policies that

Figure 14.1 myeconlab

The Political Marketplace

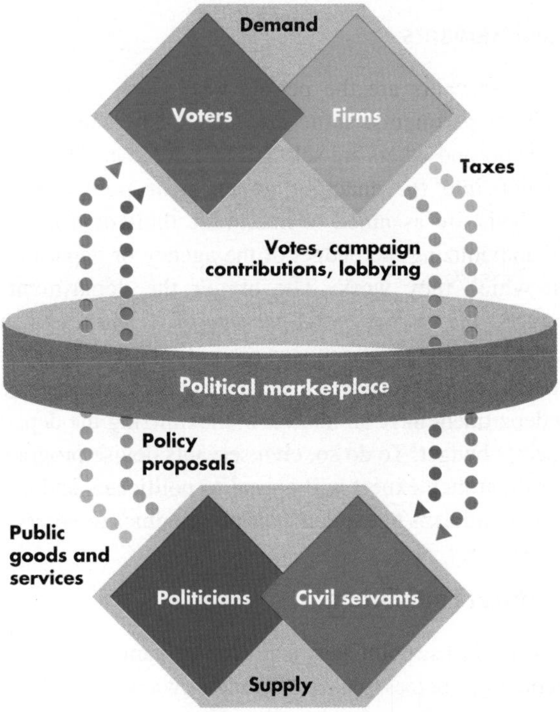

Voters express their demands for policies with their votes, and voters and firms express demands by making campaign contributions and lobbying. Politicians propose policies that appeal to a majority of voters and to firms whose campaign contributions they seek. Civil servants try to maximize the budgets of their departments. A political equilibrium is a situation in which no group can improve its position by making a different choice.

they believe have no effect on them. Voters' *perceptions* of policy outcomes are what guide their choices.

Firms

Firms are also consumers in the political marketplace. They are the main source of campaign contributions and lobbying activity. Public choice theory assumes that entrepreneurs support the policies that increase their profits and oppose those that impose losses.

Politicians

Politicians are the elected administrators and legislators at all levels of government. Economic models of public choice assume that the objective of a politician is to get elected and to remain in office. Votes, to a politician, are like profits to a firm. To get enough votes, politicians form political parties to develop policy proposals, which they expect will appeal to a majority of voters.

Civil Servants

Civil servants are the people who work in government departments: some are selected by senior civil servants and others are selected by politicians. They are responsible for enacting government policy. Civil servants are assumed to maximize their own utility, by maximizing the budget of the agency or department in which they work. The bigger the department's budget, the greater is the prestige of its chief and the larger is the opportunity for promotion for people farther down the bureaucratic ladder. So all the members of a department have an interest in maximizing the department's budget. To do so, civil servants devise programmes that they expect will appeal to politicians and they help politicians to explain their programmes to voters.

Political Equilibrium

Voters, firms, politicians and civil servants make their economic choices to maximize their own objectives. But each group is constrained by the preferences of the other groups and by what is technologically feasible. The outcome of the choices of voters, politicians and civil servants is the **political equilibrium**, which is a situation in which the choices of voters, firms, politicians and civil servants are all compatible and in which no group can improve its position by making a different choice.

The rest of this chapter looks at the public choices that we make in regulating monopoly and oligopoly.

Monopoly and Oligopoly Regulation

The economic theory of monopoly and oligopoly regulation is an application of the broader theory of public choice theory. In the political marketplace, there is a demand for regulation, a supply of regulation and the political equilibrium amount and type of regulation.

The Demand for Regulation

People and firms demand the regulation that makes them better off and they express this demand through political activity: voting, lobbying and making campaign contributions. Consumers demand regulation that increases consumer surplus and firms demand regulation that increases producer surplus. The greater the number of people or firms that can benefit from a regulation, the greater is the demand for it. But numbers alone do not always translate into an effective political force because it is costly to organize for political action. A more powerful influence on the demand for regulation is the gain per person or per firm that results from it.

The Supply of Regulation

Politicians supply the regulations that increase their campaign funds and that get them enough votes to achieve and maintain office. If a regulation benefits a large number of people and by enough for it to be noticed, that regulation appeals to politicians and is supplied. If a regulation benefits a large number of people but by too small an amount per person to be noticed, that regulation does not appeal to politicians and is not supplied. If a regulation benefits a *small* number of people but by a large amount per person, that regulation also appeals to politicians because it helps them to get campaign funds from those who gain.

Equilibrium Regulation

In political equilibrium, regulation might be in the social interest or in the self-interest of producers. The **social interest theory** of regulation is that politicians supply the regulation that achieves an efficient allocation of resources.

According to this view, the political process works well, relentlessly seeks out deadweight loss and introduces regulations that eliminate it. For example, where monopoly practices exist, the political process introduces price regulations to ensure that outputs increase and prices fall to their competitive levels.

The **capture theory** of regulation is that regulation is in the self-interest of producers. The key idea of capture theory is that the cost of political organization is high and the political process will supply only those regulations that increase the surplus of small, easily identified groups that have low organization costs. Such regulations are supplied even if they impose costs on others, provided that those costs are spread thinly and widely enough that they do not decrease votes.

People who stand from the centre to the left of the political spectrum (socialists and social democrats) tend to believe that regulation is in the social interest and that when it is not, sufficient goodwill and hard work can ensure that it is changed. People who stand from the centre to the right of the political spectrum (conservatives and libertarians) tend to believe that most regulation is in the self-interest of producers and that no regulation is better for the social interest than the regulation that we have.

The predictions of the capture theory are less clear cut than those of the social interest theory. According to capture theory, regulations benefit cohesive interest groups by large and visible amounts and impose small costs on everyone else. Because these costs per person are small, no one feels it is worthwhile to incur the cost of organizing an interest group to avoid them.

Alternative Intervention Methods

Governments intervene in monopoly and oligopoly markets to influence prices, quantities produced and the distribution of the gains from economic activity – the distribution of consumer surplus and producer surplus – in three main ways:

- Regulation
- Monopoly control laws
- Public ownership

Regulation

Regulation consists of rules administered by a government agency to influence economic activity by determining prices, product standards and types and the conditions under which new firms may enter an industry. Price and entry condition regulations are typically applied at the industry level and product regulation is more often applied at the firm level. **Deregulation** is the process of removing previously imposed regulation.

Monopoly Control Laws

Monopoly control laws are laws that regulate and prohibit monopoly and monopolistic practices. These laws cover practices such as the creation of barriers to entry, collusion over prices, restriction of consumer choice and mergers to enhance market power.

Public Ownership

Public ownership is the ownership (and sometimes operation) of a firm or industry by a government or a government controlled agency. Public ownership was popular during the 1940s and 1950s when much of what was called the "commanding heights" of industry was placed in public ownership in much of Europe.

Today, the opposite process is more common – **privatization** – the sale of a government-owned enterprise to private owners. Most European governments are in the process of selling firms and industries to private owners.

To understand why governments intervene in markets and to examine the impact of this intervention, we need to identify the gains and losses that these actions create. These gains and losses are the consumer and producer surpluses associated with different levels of output and prices. We'll start with the economic theory of regulation.

Review Quiz

Study Plan 14.1

1. What are the three main reasons why governments exist?
2. Describe five areas in which government choices influence economic life.
3. Describe the political marketplace. Who are the demanders and who are the suppliers? How do the demanders "pay" the suppliers?
4. How do consumers and producers express their demand for economic regulation? What are their objectives? What are the costs of expressing a demand for regulation?
5. When politicians and civil servants supply regulation, what are they trying to achieve? Do politicians and civil servants have the same objectives? Explain your answer.
6. What is a political equilibrium? When does the political equilibrium achieve economic efficiency?

We're now going to look at the regulation of monopoly and oligopoly today and see how they try to serve the social interest but might serve self-interest.

Regulating and Deregulating Monopoly and Oligopoly

The past 20 years have seen dramatic changes in the way in which European economies are regulated by government. We're going to examine some of these changes. To begin we'll look at what is regulated and also at the scope of regulation. Then we'll turn to the regulatory process itself and examine how regulators control prices and other aspects of market behaviour. Finally, we'll tackle the more difficult and controversial questions: Why do we regulate some things but not others? Who benefits from this regulation – consumers or producers?

The Scope of Regulation

Table 14.1 shows some of the main regulatory agencies that operate in the United Kingdom. At the top are institutions created by agreement among countries. These institutions regulate firms indirectly by restricting government protection of domestic industry. The World Trade Organization oversees and monitors international trade agreements and aims to avoid trade wars among its 124 participating countries. Below this is the European Commission, responsible for ensuring its member states comply with EU-level regulation of industries and markets, based on its legal treaties. EU directives control many aspects of business activity both directly and indirectly. For example, EU directives determine standards of production and marketing, the pricing of agricultural products, employment practices, health and safety, industrial pollution, market power, collusive practices and mergers.

Firms are also subject to regulation by agencies at the national and local levels. Some regulatory agencies cover all industries, for example, the Health and Safety Executive and the Environment Agency. Other agencies regulate specific industries, such as the Office of Gas and Electricity Markets and the Office of Water Services. Local and regional governments also regulate firms, for example in relation to waste management and building planning regulations.

The Regulatory Process

Although regulatory agencies vary in size and scope and in the detailed aspects of economic life that they control, there are certain features common to all agencies.

Table 14.1

Regulatory Agencies

Level	Agency	Activity
Global	World Trade Organization	Monitors and enforces rules on international trade
European Union	European Commission	Monitors and enforces EU rules on member states
UK central government	Departments/Ministries	Monitor and control public provision of health, agriculture, industry, education, and so on
	Monopolies and Mergers Commission	Investigates monopoly and recommends action
	Health and Safety Executive	Investigates breaches of health and safety law
	Environment Agency	Monitors and enforces environmental law
	Finance and Securities Agency	Regulates financial investment firms and other financial agencies
	Bank of England	Regulates banks and building societies
	Civil Aviation Authority	Monitors and regulates airlines, airports and air-traffic control
	Office of Gas and Electricity Markets	Monitors and regulates gas and electricity markets
	Office of Water Services	Monitors and regulates water companies
UK local and regional government	Departments	Control and monitor planning, waste management, and so on

First, the civil servants, who are the key decision makers in the main regulatory agencies, are appointed by central and local governments. In addition, all agencies have a permanent bureaucracy made up of experts in the industry being regulated and often recruited from the regulated firms. Agencies are allocated financial resources by government to cover the costs of their operations.

Second, each agency adopts a set of practices or operating rules for controlling prices and other aspects of economic or professional performance. Regulation usually involves limiting the power of firms to determine one or more of the following: the price of output, the quantities sold, the quality of the product, or the markets served. The regulatory agency grants certification to a company to serve a particular market with a particular line of products, and it determines the level and structure of prices that will be charged. In some cases, the agency also determines the scale and quality of output permitted.

To analyze the way in which regulation works, we will focus on the regulation of natural monopoly and cartels. Let's begin with natural monopoly.

Natural Monopoly

Natural monopoly was defined in Chapter 12 (p. 264) as an industry in which one firm can supply the entire market at a lower price than can two or more firms. As a consequence, a natural monopoly experiences economies of scale, no matter how high an output rate it achieves. Examples of natural monopolies include telephone and cable TV companies, local electricity and water companies, and rail infrastructure. It is much more expensive to have two or more competing sets of wires, pipes and railway lines serving every area than it is to have a single set.

Let's consider the example of UK cable TV shown in Figure 14.2. The demand curve for cable TV is *D*. The cable TV company's marginal cost curve is *MC*. That marginal cost curve is (assumed to be) horizontal at £10 per household per month – that is, the cost of providing each additional household with a month of cable programming is £10. The cable TV company has a heavy investment in satellite receiving dishes, cables and control equipment and so has high fixed costs. These fixed costs are part of the company's average total cost curve, shown as *ATC*. The average total cost curve slopes downward because as the number of households served increases, the fixed cost is spread over a larger number of households.

Figure 14.2 myeconlab

Natural Monopoly: Marginal Cost Pricing

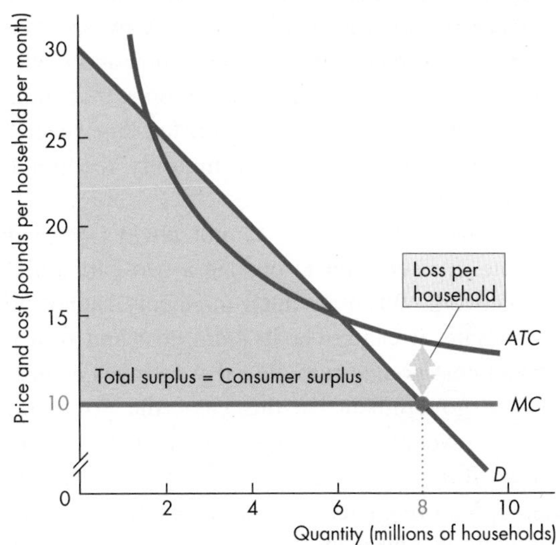

A cable TV company is a natural monopoly and it faces the demand curve *D*. The firm's marginal cost is constant at £10 per household per month, as shown by the curve *MC*. Fixed costs are large and the average total cost curve, which includes average fixed cost, is shown as *ATC*. A marginal cost pricing rule sets the price at £10 a month, with 8 million households being served. Consumer surplus is shown by the green area. The firm incurs a loss on each household, indicated by the red arrow. To remain in business, the cable TV company must either price discriminate or receive a subsidy.

Regulating Monopoly in the Social Interest

According to the social interest theory, the cable TV company will be regulated to maximize **total surplus** – the sum of consumer surplus and producer surplus. Regulation will be in the social interest if the price equals marginal cost. In Figure 14.2, this outcome occurs if the price is regulated at £10 per household per month and 8 million households are served. This regulation is called a marginal cost pricing rule. A **marginal cost pricing rule** sets price equal to marginal cost. It maximizes total surplus in the regulated industry.

Figure 14.2 shows the average total cost curve is always falling for a natural monopoly, so marginal cost is below average total cost. If the regulator sets price equal to marginal cost, price is below average total cost and the monopoly will incur an economic loss. Average total cost minus price is the loss per unit produced. This cable TV company will go out of business eventually if it cannot cover its costs.

One way to avoid this problem is to allow the monopoly to price discriminate. Some natural monopolies can price discriminate by using a two-part tariff that gives consumers a bill for connection and a bill for units used. A cable TV company can price discriminate by charging a one-time connection fee that covers its fixed cost and then charging a monthly fee equal to marginal cost.

But a natural monopoly cannot always price discriminate. It is difficult to operate a two-part tariff on a rail network. When a natural monopoly cannot price discriminate, it can cover its total cost and follow a marginal cost pricing rule only if it receives a subsidy from the government. In this case, the government raises the revenue for the subsidy by taxing some other activity. But we saw in Chapter 6, taxes themselves generate deadweight loss. The deadweight loss resulting from additional taxes must be offset against the allocative efficiency gained by forcing the natural monopoly to adopt a marginal cost pricing rule.

Figure 14.3 myeconlab

Natural Monopoly: Average Cost Pricing

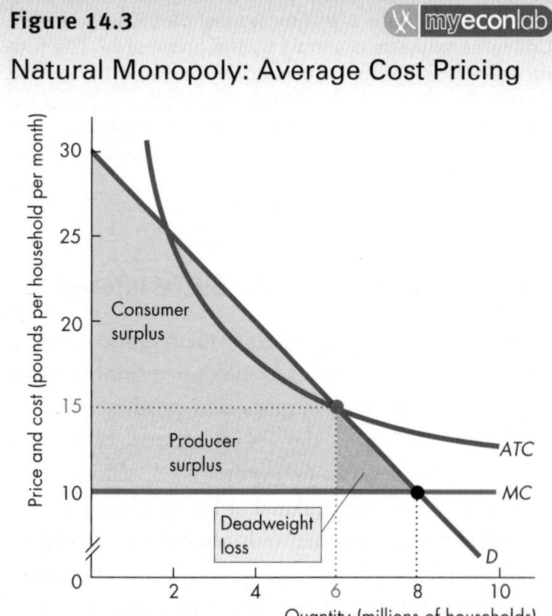

Average cost pricing sets price equal to average total cost. The cable TV company charges £15 a month and serves 6 million households. In this situation the firm breaks even – average total cost equals price. Deadweight loss, shown by the grey triangle, is generated. Consumer surplus is reduced to the green area.

The regulatory agency could also avoid the problem if it used an average cost pricing rule. An **average cost pricing rule** sets the price equal to average total cost. Figure 14.3 shows the average cost pricing solution. The cable TV company charges £15 a month and serves 6 million households. A deadweight loss arises, shown by the grey triangle in the figure, but consumer surplus is less than under marginal cost pricing regulation.

The major obstacle to implementing these pricing rules is that the regulator knows less than the regulated firm about the cost of production. The regulator does not directly observe the firm's costs and doesn't know how hard the firm is trying to minimize cost. For this reason, regulators use one of two practical rules:

- Rate of return regulation
- Price cap regulation

Let's see whether these rules deliver an outcome that is in the social interest or the private interest.

Rate of Return Regulation

Under **rate of return regulation**, a regulated firm must justify its price by showing that its percentage return on its capital is in line with what is normal in competitive industries. If the regulator could observe the firm's costs and also know that the firm had minimized total cost, it would accept only a price proposal from the firm that was equivalent to average cost pricing.

The outcome would be like that in Figure 14.3. But the managers of a regulated firm have an incentive to inflate costs and raise price. One way to inflate the firm's costs is to spend on inputs that are not strictly required for the production of the good. On-the-job luxury in the form of sumptuous office suites, big cars, Premier League football tickets (disguised as public relations expenses), company jets, lavish international travel and entertainment are all ways in which managers can inflate costs.

If the cable TV operator in our example manages to persuade the regulator that its true average total cost curve is that shown as *ATC* (*inflated*) in Figure 14.4, then the regulator, applying the normal rate of return principle, will accept the firm's proposed price of £20 a month. In this example, the price and quantity will be the same as those under unregulated monopoly.

Price Cap Regulation

For the reason we've just examined, rate of return regulation is increasingly being replaced by price cap

Figure 14.4

Natural Monopoly: Inflating Costs

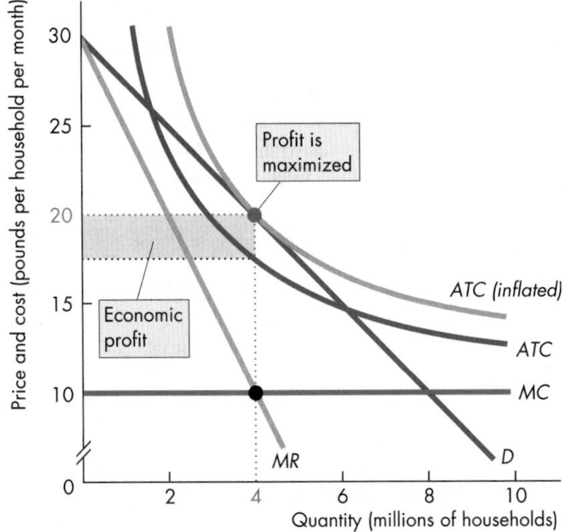

If the cable TV company is able to inflate its costs to *ATC (inflated)* and persuade the regulator that these are genuine minimum costs of production, rate of return regulation results in a price of £20 a month – the profit-maximizing price. To the extent that the producer can inflate costs above average total cost, the price rises, output decreases and deadweight loss increases. The profit is captured by the managers, not the shareholders (owners) of the firm.

Figure 14.5

Price Cap Regulation

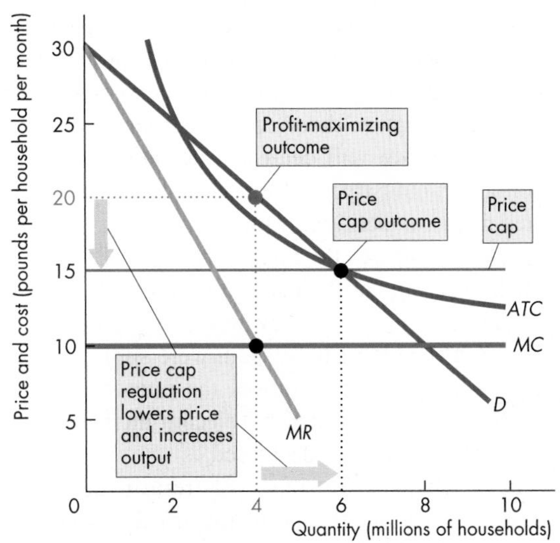

If the cable TV company is subject to a price cap regulation, the price cap limits the price that may be charged. At all quantities less than 6 million, the firm incurs a loss. At all quantities greater than 6 million, the firm also incurs a loss. Only at an output of 6 million can the firm break even and earn a normal rate of return. The firm has an incentive to keep costs as low as possible and to produce the quantity demanded at the price cap.

regulation. A **price cap regulation** is a price ceiling – a rule that specifies the highest price the firm is permitted to set. This type of regulation gives a firm an incentive to operate efficiently and keep costs under control. Price cap regulation has become common for the electricity and telecommunications industries and is replacing rate of return regulation.

To see how a price cap works, let's suppose that the cable TV company in our example is subject to this type of regulation. Figure 14.5 shows what happens.

Without regulation, the firm maximizes profit by serving 4 million households and charging a price of £20 a month. If a price cap is set at £15 a month, the firm is permitted to sell any quantity it chooses at that price or at a lower price. At 4 million households, the firm now incurs an economic loss. It can decrease the loss by *increasing* output to 6 million households. But at more than 6 million households, the firm incurs losses. So the profit-maximizing quantity is 6 million households – the same as with average cost pricing.

Notice that a price cap lowers the price and increases output. This outcome is in sharp contrast to the effect of a price ceiling in a competitive market – see Chapter 6 (pp. 122–124). The reason is that in an unregulated monopoly, the equilibrium output is less than the competitive equilibrium output and the price cap regulation replicates the conditions of a competitive market.

Social Interest or Capture?

We cannot be sure whether the regulator gets captured or whether regulation works to serve the social interest. But we can examine some of the implications of each theory. One test of the two theories is based on rates of return before and after privatization, which you can take a look at in Box 14.1 on the next page. After privatization, most government monopolies become industries with an oligopoly structure. Oligopoly is also regulated. So now we turn to regulation in oligopoly – the regulation of cartels.

Box 14.1

Regulation of UK Monopolies

The social interest theory predicts that because regulation is efficient, there will be no change in the rate of return in an industry if it is privatized and deregulated. In contrast, capture theory predicts that privatization and deregulation will decrease the rate of return by forcing the industry to compete rather than be protected from competition by the regulator.

Table 1 compares the rates of return of British Gas, British Telecom and British Airways before and after privatization. By 1992 they were all privatized, but British Gas and British Telecom were subject to price regulation. After privatization, the rates of return of both British Gas and British Telecom increased while that of British Airways decreased.

These changes in rates of return deliver an ambiguous verdict but point toward the conclusion that regulation has to some degree been in the social interest. Price caps were used, and this type of regulation is more likely to operate in the social interest than target rates of return.

Table 1

Regulated UK Monopolies

	British Gas	British Telecom	British Airways
Rate of return before privatization (1979)	5%	14%	14%
Rate of return after privatization (1992)	7%	21%	12%
Productivity increase (1979–1992)	71%	180%	11%

Source of data: D. Parker, "Privatization and Business Restructuring: Change and Continuity in the Privatized Industries", *The Review of Policy Issues*, 1994, 1(2).

Cartel Regulation

A *cartel* is a collusive agreement among a number of firms designed to restrict output and achieve a higher profit for the cartel's members. Cartels are illegal in the United Kingdom, the European Union and most other countries. International cartels can sometimes operate legally, such as the international cartel of oil producers known as OPEC (the Organization of Petroleum Exporting Countries).

Cartels can operate in oligopoly if firms agree to act like a monopoly to reap monopoly profit. So how is oligopoly regulated? Does regulation prevent monopoly practices or does it encourage those practices?

According to social interest theory, oligopoly is regulated to ensure a competitive outcome. Consider, for example, the market for road haulage of carrots from East Anglia to Yorkshire in the United Kingdom, illustrated in Figure 14.6. The demand curve for trips is D. The industry marginal cost curve – and the competitive supply curve – is MC. Social interest regulation will regulate the price of a trip at £20 and there will be 300 trips a week.

According to the capture theory, regulation of an oligopoly in the producer interest will maximize profit. In Figure 14.6, profit is maximized when the quantity produced is 200 trips a week (marginal cost, MC, equals marginal revenue, MR) and the price is set at £30 a trip. The regulator can achieve this outcome by placing an output limit on each firm in the industry. If there are 10 haulage companies, an output limit of 20 trips per company ensures that the total number of trips in a week is 200. Penalties can be imposed to ensure that no single producer exceeds its output limit.

All the firms in the industry would support this type of output regulation because it helps to prevent cheating and to maintain a monopoly outcome. Each firm knows that without the regulation, every firm has an incentive to increase output. (For each firm, price exceeds marginal cost so a greater output brings a larger profit.) So each firm wants a method of preventing output from increasing above the industry profit-maximizing level and the regulation achieves this. With this type of cartel regulation, the regulator enables a cartel to operate legally and in its own best interest.

What does cartel regulation do in practice? Although there is disagreement about the matter, the consensus view is that regulation tends to favour the producer. Regulating taxis (by local authorities) and airlines (by the Civil Aviation Authority) are specific examples in which profits of producers increased as a result of regulation.

Figure 14.6

Collusive Oligopoly

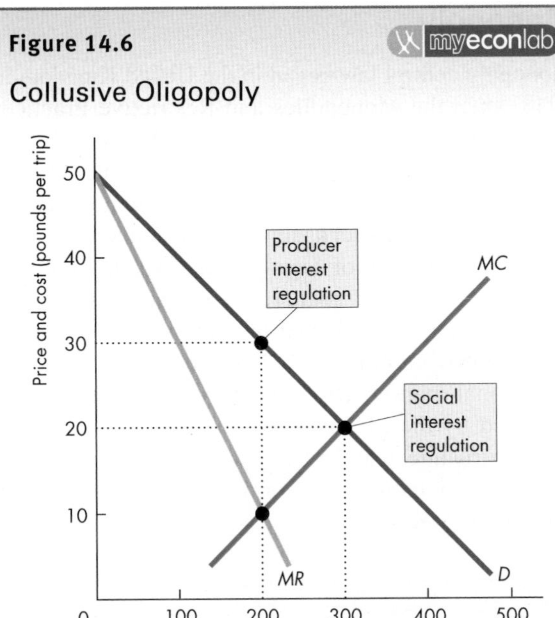

Ten firms transport carrots from East Anglia to Yorkshire. The demand curve is *D* and the industry marginal cost curve is *MC*. Under competition, the *MC* curve is the industry supply curve. If the industry is competitive, the price of a trip will be £20 and 300 trips will be made each week. The firms will demand regulation that restricts entry and limits output to 200 trips a week. This regulation raises the price to £30 a trip and results in each firm making maximum profit – as if it were a monopoly.

Making Predictions

Most industries have a few producers and many consumers. In these cases, public choice theory predicts that regulation will protect producer interests because a small number of people stand to gain a large amount and so they will be fairly easy to organize as a cohesive lobby. Under such circumstances, politicians will be rewarded with political contributions rather than votes. But there are situations in which the consumer interest is sufficiently strong and well-organized and thus able to prevail. There are also cases in which the balance switches from producer to consumer, as seen in the deregulation process that began in the late 1970s.

Deregulation raises some hard questions for economists seeking to understand and make predictions about regulation. Why were so many sectors deregulated across Europe in the 1980 and 1990s? If producers gained from regulation and if the producer lobby was strong enough to achieve regulation, what happened in the 1980s to change the equilibrium to one in which the consumer interest prevailed? We do not have a complete answer to this question at present. But regulation had become so costly to consumers, and the potential benefits to consumers from deregulation so great, that the cost of organizing the consumer voice became a price worth paying.

One factor that increased the cost of regulation borne by consumers in the airline sector, eventually bringing deregulation, was the large increase in energy prices in the 1970s. These price hikes made route regulation extremely costly and changed the balance in favour of consumers in the political equilibrium. Another factor was technological change, which affected the airline sector and many other sectors such as finance and telecommunications as well. Computerized accounts, automatic tellers, satellite communications and mobile phones enabled smaller producers to offer low-cost services, which forced deregulation.

In the case of EU airlines, most member states allowed only two airlines to operate each route and regulated fares and traffic in such a way that airlines could not compete. These restrictions were lifted in 1997 to encourage competition. Now, airlines from one European country can launch domestic services in another. Ryanair and EasyJet operate dramatic cut-price services, which make economic profits when the big flag-ship carriers incur economic losses. How is it done? These airlines use direct telephone sales technology, pick the cheapest airports to serve, cut red tape and adopt a 'no frills' service approach. Customers get what they pay for, but low quality is accepted on short haul flights. If rapid technological change continues, we could expect to see more consumer-oriented regulation in future.

Review Quiz

Study Plan 14.2

1. Why does a natural monopoly need to be regulated?
2. What pricing rule enables a natural monopoly to operate in the social interest?
3. Why is a marginal cost pricing rule difficult to implement?
4. What pricing rule is typically used to regulate a natural monopoly and what problems does it create?
5. Why is it necessary to regulate a cartel and how could cartels be regulated in the social interest?

We now turn to monopoly control laws.

Monopoly Control Laws

Monopoly control laws give powers to courts and to government agencies to investigate monopolies and ensure competitive practices. Like regulation, monopoly control law can operate in the social interest, maximizing total surplus, or in the private interest, maximizing the surpluses of particular interest groups such as producers.

European monopoly control laws cover three aspects of firm activity:

- Monopoly
- Mergers
- Restrictive practices

Monopoly

Monopoly control law began in the United Kingdom in 1948 when the Monopolies and Restrictive Practices Act created an agency called the Monopolies and Restrictive Practices Commission. Its role was to investigate the activities of reported monopolies to assess whether they act against the social interest.

The interpretation of social interest is still a political rather than a judicial matter. Several subsequent Acts of Parliament have adapted the law, and monopoly is now defined as a firm with a 25 per cent share of a local or national market. UK monopoly investigations are triggered by the existence of monopoly, defined as a market structure, and the UK government has the power to break up monopolies or impose restrictions on activities of UK firms.

Box 14.2
European Regulation in Action

Monopoly, Restrictive Practice and Mergers

Table 1 shows some examples of EU investigations and actions concerning monopoly, restrictive practices and mergers. It is rare for monopolies to be fined but Microsoft, an exception, was fined for illegal monopolistic practices. More commonly, the EU requires changes in monopolistic practice. For example, in 2001 the Italian government-owned rail monopoly was ordered to allow German rail operators to run trains on their tracks. Fines for companies operating in oligopoly markets who abuse market power through collusive agreements are more common. The record fine for cartel activity stands at €478 million for the EU-wide price agreement on plasterboard. Merger investigations are common, 212 in 2003, but it is rare for mergers to be blocked. The European Union usually negotiates a settlement with companies after raising objections.

Table 1

Examples of EU Regulation Cases

Regulation	Date	Fine or action	Main companies	Countries	Product
Monopoly	2004	€500 million	Microsoft	United States	Software
	2001	Required to remove restrictive practice	Ferrovie dello Stato	Italy	State-owned railway
	2001	Objections raised	BskyB	United Kingdom	Premier League Football TV
Restrictive practices	2003	€138.4 million	Hoechst and others	Germany, Japan	Food preservative
	2002	€478 million	Lafarge, BPB, Knauf	France, Germany United Kingdom	Plasterboard
	2002	€149 million	Nintendo	United States	Computer games
	2001	€462 million	Hoffman La Roche, BASF and others	Switzerland Germany	Vitamins
Mergers	2004	Merger agreed	Aventis and Sanofi-Synthelabo	France Germany	Pharmaceuticals
	2004	Merger objections	Sony and BMG	Japan, Germany	Music

Source of data: European Commission.

EU monopoly control laws define monopoly in a different way. Monopoly investigations, under EU law, are triggered by indications of abuse of power by a firm in a dominant position. Market power is illegal if it affects trade among member states by creating unfair trading conditions. Abuse includes imposing unfair price and purchase conditions, limiting production, applying different conditions in different countries and imposing restrictive contracts. The European Commission has wide-ranging powers to enforce its decisions with fines for the offending firms operating in the European Union.

Box 14.2 gives some recent examples of European regulation.

Mergers

A **merger** occurs when the assets of two or more firms are combined to form a single, new firm. In 1965, the UK Monopolies Commission became the Monopolies and Mergers Commission, which extended its powers to investigate any merger likely to create a monopoly or might lead to abuse of market power and would not be in "the social interest". According to the 1973 Fair Trading Act, "social interest" means any practice that maintains and promotes effective competition, which suggests that consumer surplus is given a higher weighting than producer surplus in evaluating merger proposals.

In contrast, the EU Merger Control Regulation of 1990 allows the European Commission to investigate mergers between firms that have dominant positions in European markets. The Commission only allows proposed mergers if any strengthening of a dominant position does not lead to a reduction in competition.

The number of mergers investigated by the European Union increased from just 12 in 1990 to a peak of 345 in 2000. Despite the large number of investigations, few EU mergers are ever blocked. Box 14.2 gives some recent examples of EU merger investigations.

Restrictive Practices

The UK 1973 Fair Trading Act defines **restrictive practices** as agreements between firms on prices, terms and conditions of sale and market share. Such practices are illegal unless the parties can prove to the Restrictive Practices Court that the agreements are in the social interest. The law sets out eight possible defences. Firms must prove at least one defence and that on balance, the benefits of the agreement to consumers outweigh the costs.

A restrictive practice under EU law is any agreement that affects trade among member states and reduces competition. Firms can but don't have to register their agreements. Restrictive practices are illegal unless they improve production and distribution or technical progress and do not reduce competition.

EU law is concerned with the *effect* of the agreement, while UK law is focused on its *form*. Focusing on the effect reduces the cost of investigation and increases the chance that anti-competitive agreements are identified. The European Commission has greater powers of enforcement than the UK Restrictive Practices Court and can impose fines of up to 10 per cent of a firm's worldwide annual turnover.

The European Union regularly fines companies operating in oligopoly markets for restrictive practices that raise prices. Box 14.2 European Regulation in Action gives some recent examples. In some cases, the restrictive practice is a simple cartel agreement; in others it is a distribution practice as in the case of Nintendo, which increased prices.

Social or Self-interest?

It appears that monopoly control law has evolved to protect the social interest and to restrain profit-seeking and the anti-competitive actions of producers. Although the interests of the producer can influence the way in which the national law is interpreted and applied, the overall thrust of EU law is towards achieving allocative efficiency and serving the social interest. The European Commission is now more proactive and forceful in its application of monopoly control laws in a drive to increase competition in the European single market.

Review Quiz

Study Plan 14.3

1. What main aspects of firms' activities do monopoly control laws cover?
2. What are the main differences between the UK and EU monopoly control laws?

Let's now look at the effects of public ownership and privatization on the social interest.

Public Ownership and Privatization

The main type of public ownership is in the form of nationalized companies. Nationalization involves the 100 per cent ownership of companies by governments, either through compulsory purchase or share purchase. Most European governments followed a continuous programme of nationalization and purchase after the Second World War. But during the 1980s and 1990s many nationalized companies throughout Europe were privatized. Governments also sold off the part-shares that they held in many private companies.

The UK case is an interesting example because it is extreme. The range of UK public companies in 1979 included the main utilities, transport systems, key industries such as coal and steel, and many firms from relatively competitive industries. Between 1979 and 1999, nearly all of the publicly owned companies were sold.

So why were so many UK firms nationalized and brought into public ownership and then sold again? Let's look at an economic model of public ownership to find out.

Efficient Public Ownership

Public ownership is another way in which government can influence the behaviour of a natural monopoly. Suppose that an industry under public ownership is operated in a manner that results in economic efficiency – maximization of total surplus.

Let's consider the example of a railway that offers a freight service. Figure 14.7(a) illustrates the demand for freight service and the railway's costs. The demand curve is *D*. The marginal cost curve, *MC*, is horizontal at £2 a tonne. The railway has large fixed costs that feature in the company's average total cost curve, *ATC*. The average total cost curve slopes downward because as the number of tonnes of freight carried increases, the fixed costs are spread over a larger number of tonnes. To be efficient, a publicly owned railway adopts the rule:

Produce an output such that price equals marginal cost.

Figure 14.7

Public Ownership

myeconlab

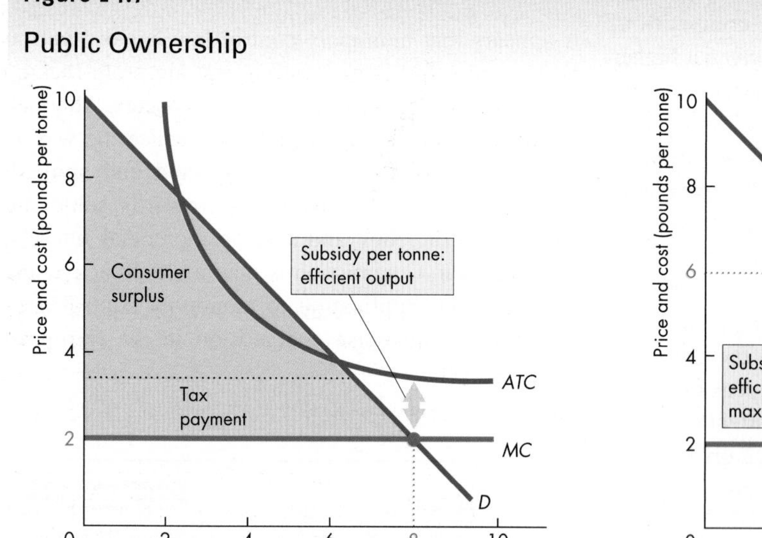

(a) Efficient outcome

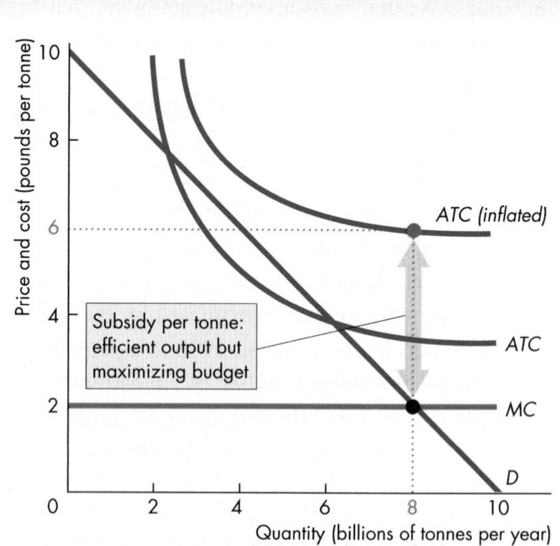

(b) Budget maximization

Part (a) shows a railway in public ownership that produces the output at which price equals marginal cost. Its output is 8 billion tonnes a year and the price is £2 a tonne. The railway receives a subsidy that enables it to cover its total cost and that cost is the minimum possible cost of providing the efficient quantity.

Part (b) shows what happens if the managers of the railway under public ownership pursue their own interest and maximize their budget by inflating costs. Average total cost now increases to *ATC* (*inflated*). If the railway is required to keep price equal to marginal cost, the quantity produced is efficient, but the managers divert the consumer surplus to themselves.

In this example, that output level is 8 billion tonnes of freight a year at a price – and marginal cost – of £2 a tonne. To be able to operate in this manner, a publicly owned railway has to be subsidized; and the subsidy on each unit of output must equal the difference between average total cost and marginal cost. So the subsidy must be collected through taxation rather than through the price of the good or service. If the government taxes each household by a fixed amount, the consumer surplus will shrink to the green triangle shown Figure 14.7(a), but consumer surplus will be at its maximum.

The situation depicted in Figure 14.7(a) achieves an efficient outcome because consumer surplus is maximized. But this outcome might not be in the interests of the managers of a publicly owned railway. The behaviour of managers in companies under public ownership can be predicted using the economic theory of bureaucracy. We'll look at this now.

A Bureaucratic Model of Public Ownership

The basic assumption of the economic theory of bureaucracy is that civil servants aim to maximize their departmental budgets. The equivalent assumption for managers in a company under public ownership is that they seek to maximize the company budget. The effect on the company under public ownership depends on the pricing constraints under which the managers operate. We will consider two alternative cases:

- Budget maximization with marginal cost pricing
- Budget maximization at a zero price

Budget Maximization with Marginal Cost Pricing

If managers maximize the budget but follow the marginal cost pricing rule, the outcome is efficient. In our case, the railway moves 8 billion tonnes of freight a year at a cost of £2 a tonne, as Figure 14.7(b) illustrates. But the railway managers do not minimize production costs because the internal control mechanisms that ensure efficiency in a private company are weak. So the railway pads its costs and becomes inefficient. The managers hire more workers than are required to move the efficient quantity and average total costs rise to *ATC* (*inflated*).

How far can the railway inflate its costs? The answer is the maximum that railway freight customers can be made to pay through taxation. That maximum is the total consumer surplus – the area beneath the demand curve and above the marginal cost curve. From Figure 14.7(b), this amount is £32 billion (1/2 × £8 billion × £8). This amount will be the upper limit that any government – in a political democracy – can extract from the taxpaying consumers of the output of the publicly owned company. Spread over 8 billion tonnes, £32 billion gives a subsidy of £4 a tonne, the amount shown in the figure.

Budget Maximization at Zero Price

What happens if a government provides goods or services free? Across Europe, for example, many governments provide or fund education and healthcare. Box 14.3 examines the costs of the UK National Health Service. As you saw in Chapter 15, governments provide goods and services in kind such as health and education, as a method of redistributing income. The goods and services are provided free at the point of demand to everyone, but they are not free. The government uses general taxation to pay for them. If the poor pay less tax on average and demand similar quantities of these goods and services, then redistribution occurs from the rich to the poor.

Of course, it is improbable that a publicly owned railway would be able to persuade politicians and taxpayers that its activities should be expanded to the point of providing its freight service free. But to maintain the comparison with Figure 14.7, we'll continue with the example of the railway.

If freight transport is provided free, consumers maximize their surplus by demanding the largest quantity, which is 10 billion tonnes a year. Their maximum consumer surplus is the whole area under the demand curve *D* in Figure 14.7(b). If the price is zero, the transport department increases output to the point at which the price that consumers are willing to pay for the last unit produced is zero and output increases to 10 billion tonnes a year.

Providing freight transport services is not without costs. If the price of freight transport is zero, a deadweight loss is created. Figure 14.7(b) shows that at an output of 10 billion tonnes, the marginal cost of production, £2 a tonne, is higher than the marginal benefit or willingness to pay, £0 per tonne. To provide the service free, the government will have to subsidize the railway.

There may also be additional bureaucratic inefficiency. The railway might inflate its costs so that its budget increases. The subsidy would increase with the inflated costs. The consumer surplus is the maximum subsidy that taxpayers are willing to pay.

Box 14.3

Budget Maximization in Action

UK Health Operation Costs

The National Health Service (NHS) in the United Kingdom provides healthcare free at the point of demand. But the cost of providing the service has been rising faster than the prices of goods and service on the average. The rising real cost of NHS provision is partly due to the rising cost of providing operations. Economic theory predicts that providing the NHS free at the point of demand may lead to budget maximization and the inflating of costs.

If some hospitals are inflating costs, we would expect to see large variation in the prices of similar operations across different hospitals. The figures in Table 1 show some of the range of prices charged by NHS hospitals for three common operations in 2003. Prices varied by up to 70 per cent for the same operation.

Table 1

NHS Average Costs

Operation	Price range (2003 pounds)	Fixed price (2006 pounds)
Heart bypass	2,540 to 6,911	9,049
Hip replacement	4,111 to 5,319	6,280
Cataracts	763 to 1,164	786

Source of data: UK Department of Health.

To reduce the burden of rising costs on the taxpayer, the UK government imposed strict budget controls. As a result, by 2001 UK healthcare spending per person was below the EU average and below that in some European private healthcare systems. But in that same year, the UK government announced plans to increase *real* expenditure on the NHS.

In 2004, to prevent cost increases that would raise the tax burden, the government required hospitals to charge the same fixed price for similar operations. Table 1 also shows the fixed prices in use in 2006.

Hospitals with a good reputation will attract more patients and hospitals with a poor reputation will lose patients. Efficient hospitals with costs below the fixed prices will enjoy higher profits. Inefficient hospitals with costs above the fixed prices will incur losses. Inefficient hospitals will either cut costs or close and efficient hospitals will expand patient services.

Privatization

The reasons for privatization are derived from the predictions of our bureaucracy model. According to this model, firms in public ownership tend to overproduce and to inflate costs, although realistically not to the extent suggested in Figure 14.7(b). As the subsidy increases, consumer interest shifts towards supporting privatization as a means of increasing efficiency.

Many publicly owned companies are not natural monopolies. Privatization exposes these companies to the forces of market competition, which forces average total costs down, reduces prices, and removes the need for subsidies and taxes.

Some economists have questioned the benefits of privatizing natural monopolies. Natural monopolies must be regulated even if they are privately owned. As you have seen, the capture theory of regulation means that regulation of private monopoly might not be more effective than public ownership. But as privatized monopolies have the extra monitoring of shareholders, they might be less likely to inflate costs.

Pressure from shareholders to cut costs might work in the social interest but it might work against other aspects of social interest such as safety and equity. This concern has been raised in debate about the provision of rail and health services in the United Kingdom. The UK government took the provision of the rail infrastructure out of the private sector and placed it under the control of a non-profit making organization in 2001, after a series of rail disasters highlighted safety concerns.

Other economists argue that competition following the privatization of natural monopolies can also be achieved by separating the service part of the business from the ownership of physical networks. For example, the retail supply of gas and electricity, telecommunications and rail services are retail activities. These services can be supplied by a number of privately owned companies and be highly competitive. The real natural monopoly lies in the network of pipes, lines and track.

Box 14.4 Privatization in Action gives an example of the problems that can arise when a government privatizes a natural monopoly. This box assesses the success of the privatization of gas and electricity markets in the United Kingdom and the impact of privatization on EU competitiveness. The European Union is pressing countries such as France and Italy to privatize and deregulate monopolies to promote competition.

Box 14.4
Privatization in Action

The UK Gas Market

British Gas (now Centrica) was the state-owned monopoly supplier of gas until 1997 when it was privatized. One company now owns the network of pipes and privatization promoted competition between gas suppliers. But by 2006, Centrica still supplied 60 per cent of domestic gas customers.

Since privatization, more than 20 million customers have switched their gas supplier. Domestic bills fell in real terms from £450 to £300 up to 2002, but then increased to £575 by 2006 as wholesale gas and oil prices rose. After wholesale gas prices fell by 50 per cent in early 2007, domestic gas prices fell by 17 per cent.

The UK Electricity Market

The UK electricity network and supply was privatized during 1997. Since privatization, 20 million customers have switched their electricity supplier. Domestic bills fell in real terms from £350 to £256 by 2003, but increased to £340 by 2006 as wholesale gas and coal prices rose. As wholesale gas prices fell in early 2007, domestic bills fell by 11 per cent.

The National Audit Office estimated that electricity consumers saved £750 million between 1997 and 2001 as a result of privatization.

In 2006, 4 million customers switched gas or electricity suppliers as firms offered new pricing packages and switching supplier became available on the Internet.

Comparing Competition Across Europe

The UK energy market is the most competitive in the European Union. Between 1990 and 2004, UK gas and electricity customers paid £75 billion less than they would have paid in Italy, £67 billion less than in Spain, £35 billion less than in France and £25 billion less than in Holland.

Table 1

European Competitiveness

	Competitiveness rank	
Country	**Europe**	**World Top 50**
Finland	1	2
Sweden	2	3
Denmark	3	4
Germany	4	8
Netherlands	5	9
United Kingdom	6	10
France	7	18
Belgium	8	20
Ireland	9	21
Luxembourg	10	22
Estonia	11	25
Spain	12	28
Slovenia	13	33
Portugal	14	34
Latvia	15	36
Malta	16	39
Lithuania	17	40
Hungry	18	41
Italy	19	42
Greece	20	47
Poland	21	48

Source of data: World Economic Forum, *Global Competitiveness Report 2006–2007.*

Table 1 shows European competitiveness using the rank calculated by the World Economic Fund. Countries with high levels of privatization and deregulation are those at the top of the table, including the United Kingdom. The countries with low levels of privatization and deregulation are at the bottom.

Review Quiz

Study Plan 14.4

1 How might a company under public ownership operate efficiently?
2 What are the effects of budget maximization by managers in publicly owned companies?
3 How can governments fight the padding of costs?
4 Why might governments want to privatize a publicly owned company?

In the next chapter, we will see how governments regulate markets in which externalities arise. But first read more about the reasons for privatizing the gas and electricity markets in the European Union in the *Business Case Study* on pp. 336–337.

Business Case Study
Regulation and Competition

Europe's Electricity and Gas Market

The European Industries

The electricity and gas industries in the European Union have traditionally been state-owned monopolies. During the 1990s, some countries, such as Sweden and the United Kingdom, privatized the whole of these industries and introduced price regulation to limit market power. Other countries, such as Greece and France, have maintained state ownership and allowed only limited competition.

Progress on EU Deregulation

Despite the EU directives to increase competition, less than 65 per cent of the EU electricity and gas markets are open to competition. The bar chart shows that electricity markets in the United Kingdom, Sweden, Finland and Germany were highly competitive markets whereas those in France, Greece and Ireland remain state owned and are the least competitive.[1]

The Impact of Limited Competition

When gas and electricity industries are state owned, the state can subsidize the cost of borrowing to aid cross-border mergers and can limit privatized suppliers' access to the gas and electricity supply networks. This limited access reduces the extent to which new entrants can put downward pressure on prices. As a result, privatized gas and electricity companies in the European Union are not competing on the same terms as those protected by state ownership.

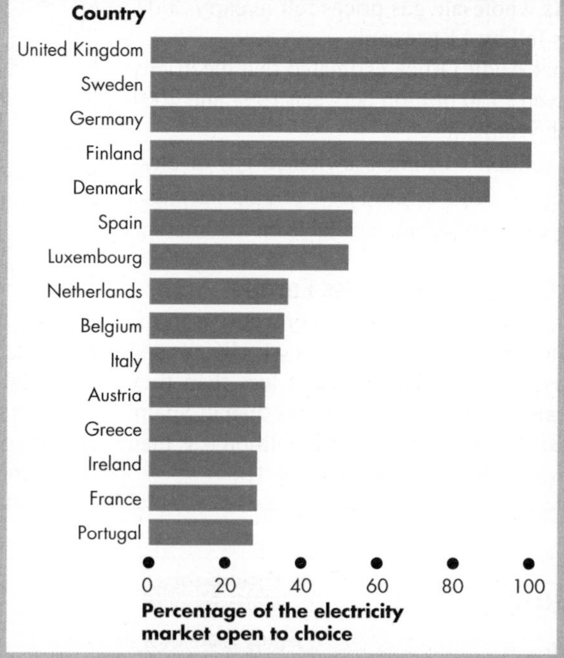

[1] D. Gow and M. Milner, "Hain plays national champion", *The Guardian*, 11 May 2001.

Economic Analysis

- Before privatization, the UK electricity market (and the gas market) was a monopoly market.
- Figure 1 shows this market. The demand curve for domestic electricity is *D* and the marginal revenue curve is *MR*. The marginal cost curve is *MC*.
- The UK monopoly maximizes profit by setting marginal revenue equal to marginal cost and supplying quantity Q_M at price P_M. The UK consumer surplus is the green area and the deadweight loss is the grey area.
- After privatization, the UK domestic electricity market is deregulated to remove barriers to entry. The market becomes competitive.
- Figure 2 shows the effect of deregulation if the market becomes perfectly competitive. The marginal cost curve, *MC*, becomes the supply curve. Market forces lower the price from P_M to P_C and the quantity increases from Q_M to Q_C. Consumer surplus increases and the deadweight loss is eliminated (in the absence of externalities, see Chapter 15).
- The French state monopoly (Electricité de France) is an example of a new entrant in the competitive UK market.
- In France, Electricité de France acts as a monopoly. It produces the quantity Q_F and charges the price P_F in Figure 3 and generates a deadweight loss similar to that in Figure 1.
- Figure 3 shows the impact on Electricité de France when it has access to the UK market but is subject to a price cap in that market. The firm maximizes profit by selling in France at P_F and selling in the United Kingdom at the capped price (assumed here to be the competitive price) of P_{UK}. The French consumer surplus in unchanged, but producer surplus increases and the deadweight loss decreases.

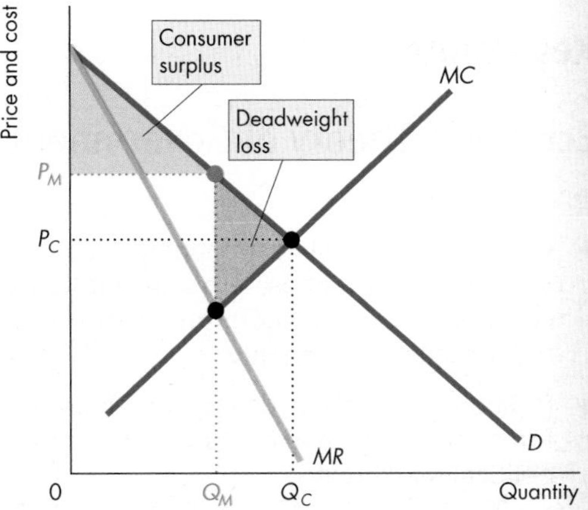

Figure 1 UK national monopoly

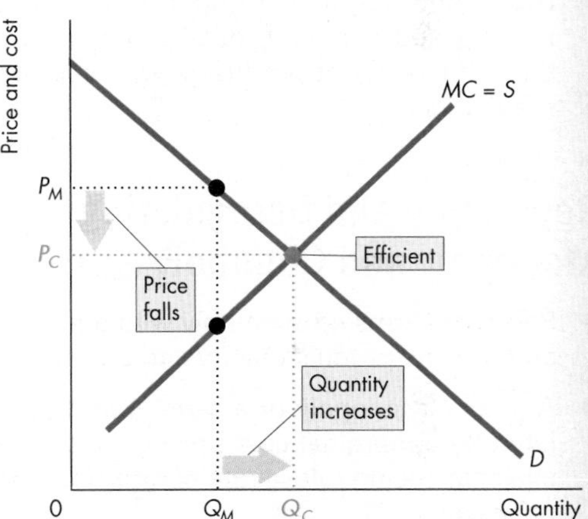

Figure 2 UK privatization and deregulation

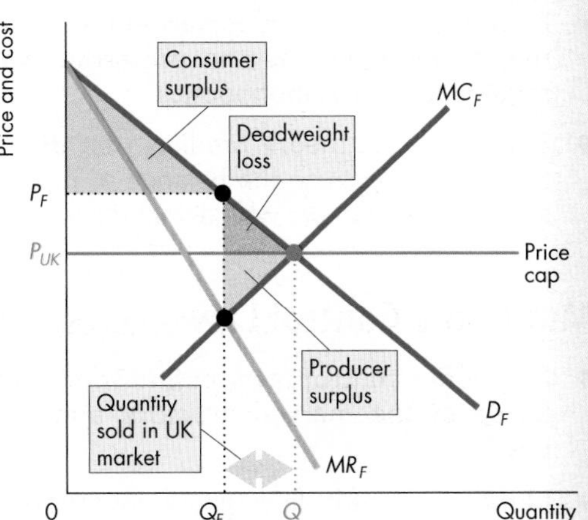

Figure 3 French monopoly sells in UK market

Summary

Key Points

Economic Theory of Government

(pp. 320–323)

- Governments regulate monopoly and oligopoly, regulate externalities, provide public goods, control the use of common resources and reduce income inequality.
- Public choice theory explains how voters, firms, politicians and civil servants interact in a political marketplace.
- Consumers demand regulation that increases consumer surplus and firms demand regulation that increases producer surplus.
- Equilibrium regulation might be in the social interest and eliminate deadweight loss or in the self-interest of producers who capture the regulators.

Regulating and Deregulating Monopoly and Oligopoly (pp. 324–329)

- Regulated firms must comply with agency rules about price, product quality and output levels.
- A natural monopoly or a cartel might be regulated by a marginal cost pricing rule, an average cost pricing rule, a rate of return target or a price cap.
- Regulation in the social interest would set price equal to marginal cost. In practice, price at best equals average cost.
- Price cap regulation is replacing target rate of return regulation as the preferred way of regulating natural monopoly.
- Social interest theory predicts that deregulation occurs because the balance of power has shifted to consumers who demand lower prices.

Monopoly Control Laws (pp. 330–331)

- Monopoly control laws define monopoly in terms of the market structure and market power.
- Monopoly control laws allow governments to control monopoly and monopolistic practices.
- The overall thrust of European monopoly control law is directed towards serving the social interest.

Public Ownership and Privatization

(pp. 332–335)

- European countries have a long history of public ownership of firms, but many of these firms have now been privatized – sold to private investors.
- Privatization is in the consumer interest if regulatory costs fall and firms are exposed to competition but against consumer interest if social interest factors such as equity and safety are compromised.

Key Figures

Key Terms

Problems

Tests, Study Plan and Solutions* 

1 Elixir Springs plc, is an unregulated European natural monopoly that bottles Elixir, a unique health product with no substitutes. The total fixed cost incurred by Elixir Springs is €150,000, and its marginal cost is 10 cents a bottle. The figure illustrates the demand for Elixir.

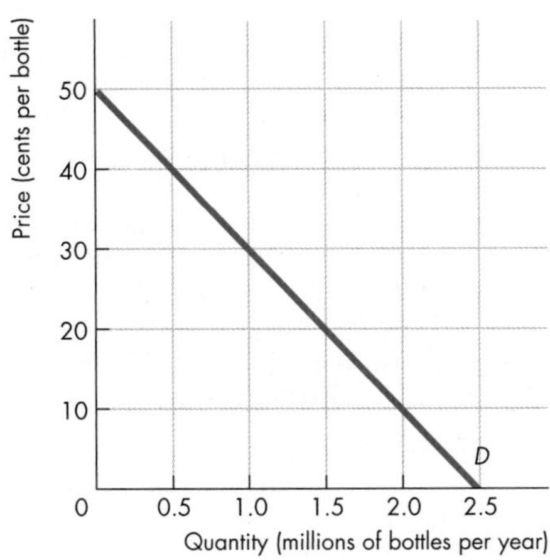

a What is the price of a bottle of Elixir?

b How many bottles does Elixir Springs sell?

c Does Elixir Springs maximize total surplus or producer surplus?

2 The EU Commission regulates Elixir Springs in problem 1 by imposing a marginal cost pricing rule.

a What is the price of a bottle of Elixir?

b How many bottles does Elixir Springs sell?

c What is Elixir Springs' producer surplus?

d What is the consumer surplus?

e Is the regulation in the social interest? Explain.

3 The EU Commission regulates Elixir Springs in problem 1 by imposing an average cost pricing rule.

a What is the price of a bottle of Elixir?

b How many bottles does Elixir Springs sell?

c What is Elixir Springs' producer surplus?

d What is the consumer surplus?

e Is the regulation in the social interest? Explain.

4 The government imposes rate of return regulation on Elixir Springs in problem 1. If Elixir Springs captures the regulator:

a What is the price of a bottle of Elixir?

b How many bottles does Elixir Springs sell?

c What is the inflated average total cost at the quantity produced?

5 Two airlines share an international route. The figure shows the demand curve for trips on this route and the marginal cost curve that each firm faces.

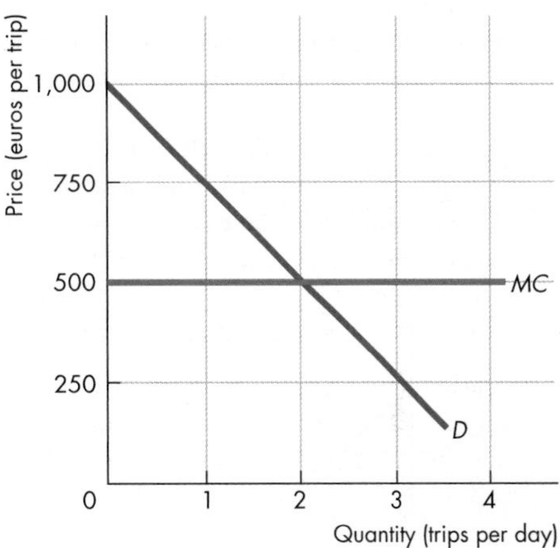

a What is the price of a trip and what is the number of trips per day if the regulation is in the social interest?

b What is the price of a trip and what is the number of trips per day if the airlines capture the regulator?

c What is the deadweight loss in part (b)?

d What do you need to know to predict whether the regulation will be in the social interest or the producer interest?

6 Suppose that in problem 5, the air route is unregulated. What is the price of a trip and what is the number of trips per day if the airlines can form an effective cartel?

7 Suppose that in problem 5, the air route is unregulated but the price of a trip has been driven down to the competitive level because the airlines are unable to form an effective cartel. One airline would like to drive the other airline off the route and considers practicing predatory pricing (pricing below cost). Could the airline succeed in eliminating competition in the short run and in the long run? Why or why not?

8 What charges, if any, might be brought by the EU Commission under the monopoly control laws in each of the following situations?

---

* Solutions to odd-numbered problems are provided.

a The owners of the only two taxi companies in a town are discovered holding secret meetings to fix their prices.

b Optical Express proposes to buy Vision Express and other major opticians in major UK cities.

c A producer of hair care products opens a chain of hair salons.

d A video rental store requires customers to rent a foreign-produced movie with every UK-produced movie they rent.

e Access to a cooking website is given only with the subscription to a monthly food magazine.

9 Two telephone companies offer local calls in an area. The figure shows the market demand curve for calls and the marginal cost curves of each firm. These firms are regulated.

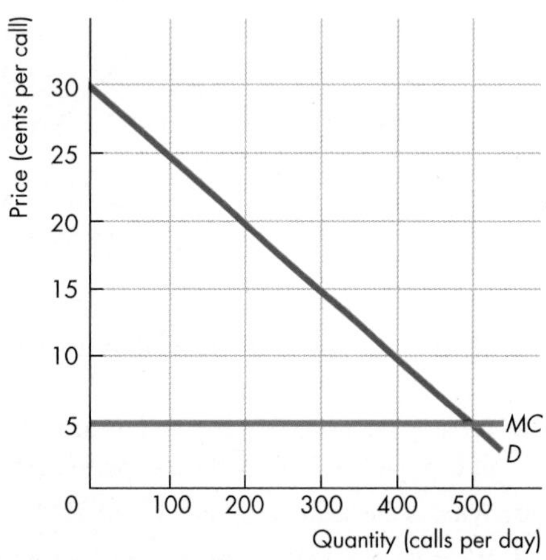

a What is the price of a call and what is the number of calls per day if the regulation is in the social interest?

b What is the price of a call and what is the number of calls per day if the telephone companies capture the regulator?

c What is the deadweight loss in part (b)?

d What do you need to know to predict whether the regulation will be in the social interest or the producer's interest?

10 Explain the main differences between regulation and monopoly law. In which situations does each apply? Provide examples of the use of each approach to regulating monopoly and oligopoly in Europe.

11 Explain the main differences between a regulated private monopoly and a monopoly in public ownership. Which do you think provides the best way of achieving an efficient use of resources and why.

Critical Thinking

1 Read the *Business Case Study* on pp. 336–337 and then answer the following questions.

a Why does the European Union want deregulation and liberalization in the electricity and gas markets?

b Why does the European Union want to convert the 15 national electricity markets into one integrated market?

c Would a fully integrated European electricity market still need regulation? If so, what type of regulation?

2 **Lufthansa settles price fix claim**

German airline Lufthansa has agreed to pay $85m (£45.6m; €67m) to settle legal action in the US surrounding allegations of price fixing. . . . Lufthansa was one . . . [of] more than a dozen airlines . . . drawn into an investigation into suspected collusion in the air cargo industry to fix prices on surcharges for fuel, security and insurance.

BBC News, 12 September 2006

a What is "collusion"?

b What did the airline attempt to gain by fixing the surcharges on fuel, security and insurance?

c Do you think a fine of €67 million is an appropriate penalty?

Web Activities

Links to Websites

1 Visit the *Financial Times* website and read the surveys on the telecoms sector and British Telecom's local loop monopoly. Then answer the following questions.

a How can British Telecom generate economic profit from charging for calls to the Internet?

b Why has British Telecom focused on developing its dominance in domestic calls to the Internet?

c What effect would "local loop unbundling" have on competition and price for local calls?

d What effect would "local loop unbundling" have on British Telecom's profits?

e Is it better to regulate price for calls or open access to new entrants into line supply? Explain your answer.

Externalities

CHAPTER 15

After studying this chapter you will be able to:

- Explain how externalities arise
- Explain why negative externalities lead to inefficient overproduction and how property rights, emission charges, marketable permits and taxes can be used to achieve a more efficient outcome
- Explain why positive externalities lead to inefficient underproduction and how public provision, subsidies, vouchers and patents can increase economic efficiency

Greener and Smarter

All of us contribute to pollution, but few of us have the incentive to stop it. What can we do to protect our environment? Can government action help us to take account of the damage that we cause others every time we turn on our heating or drive our cars? Knowledge and technology advances everyday, but do we devote enough resources to education, research and development? Can government policy provide the necessary incentives and guide us to use our educational and scientific resources efficiently? Find out in this chapter. In *Reading Between the Lines* at the end of the chapter, find out how consumers of electricity in the United Kingdom can help to save the tropical rain forests of Brazil.

Externalities in Our Lives

A cost or a benefit that arises from production and falls on someone other than the producer, or a cost or benefit that arises from consumption and falls on someone other than the consumer is called an **externality**. Let's review the range of externalities, classify them and look at some everyday examples.

An externality can arise from either *production* or *consumption* and it can be either a **negative externality**, which imposes an external cost, or a **positive externality**, which provides an external benefit. So there are four types of externalities:

- Negative production externalities
- Positive production externalities
- Negative consumption externalities
- Positive consumption externalities

Negative Production Externalities

During the Wimbledon tennis tournament, television viewers see players and spectators sharing a negative production externality that many Londoners experience every day: the noise of airplanes taking off from Heathrow Airport. Aircraft noise imposes a large cost on millions of people who live under the approach paths to airports in every major city.

When you use hot water, drive a car, or even take a bus or train, your action contributes to pollution of the atmosphere. Pollution is another example of a negative production externality.

Positive Production Externalities

If a honey farmer locates beehives beside an orange grower's orchard, two positive production externalities arise. The honey farmer gets a positive production externality from the orange grower because the bees collect pollen and nectar from orange blossoms. And the orange grower gets a positive production externality because the bees pollinate the blossoms.

Negative Consumption Externalities

Negative consumption externalities are a source of irritation for most of us. Smoking tobacco in a confined space creates fumes that many people find unpleasant and that pose a health risk. Smoking creates a negative consumption externality. To deal with this externality, in many places and in almost all public places, smoking is banned. But banning smoking imposes a negative consumption externality on smokers! The majority imposes a cost on the minority – the smokers who would prefer to consume tobacco while dining or taking a plane trip.

Noisy parties and outdoor rock concerts are other examples of negative consumption externalities. They are also examples of the fact that a simple ban on an activity is not a solution. Banning noisy parties avoids the external cost on sleep-seeking neighbours, but it results in the sleepers imposing an external cost on the fun-seeking partygoers.

Allowing a dog to bark loudly or to foul a neighbour's lawn are other sources of negative consumption externalities.

Positive Consumption Externalities

When you get a flu vaccination, you lower your risk of getting infected this winter. But if you avoid the flu, your neighbour who didn't get vaccinated has a better chance of avoiding it too. Flu vaccination generates positive consumption externalities.

When you walk around the streets of London, you enjoy the sight of beautiful buildings and bridges, some built many years ago and some built recently. Everything that you see was built for a purpose. But that purpose doesn't include giving you pleasure. The pleasure that you receive is an externality – an external consumption benefit.

By working hard in university, you are preparing yourself for an interesting and rewarding career. But you are also making yourself a more interesting person whose company others enjoy. You and your friends are generating consumption externalities for each other.

Review Quiz

Study Plan 15.1

1. What are the four types of externality?
2. Try to think of an example of each type of externality, different from the ones described above.
3. How are the externalities that you've described addressed, either by the market or by public policy?

Negative Externalities: Pollution

Pollution is not a new problem and is not restricted to rich industrial countries. Pre-industrial towns and cities in Europe had sewage disposal problems that created cholera epidemics and plagues that killed millions. London's air in the Middle Ages was dirtier than that of Mexico City today. Some of the worst pollution today is found in Russia and China. Nor is the desire to find solutions to pollution new. The development in the fourteenth century of garbage and sewage disposal is an example of early attempts to tackle pollution.

Popular discussions of pollution usually pay little attention to economics. They focus on physical aspects of the problem, not on the costs and benefits. A common assumption is that if people's actions cause *any* pollution, those actions must cease. In contrast, an economic study of pollution emphasizes costs and benefits. An economist talks about the efficient amount of pollution. This emphasis on costs and benefits does not mean that economists, as citizens, do not share the same goals as others and value a healthy environment. Nor does it mean that economists have the right answers and everyone else has the wrong ones (or vice versa). The starting point for an economic analysis of pollution is the demand for a pollution-free environment.

The Demand for a Pollution-free Environment

The demand for a pollution-free environment is greater today than it has ever been. We express this demand by joining organizations that lobby for antipollution regulations and policies. We vote for politicians who support the policies that we want to see implemented. We buy "green" products, even if we pay a bit more to do so. And we pay higher housing costs and commuting costs to live in pleasant villages.

The demand for a pollution-free environment has grown for two main reasons. First, as our incomes increase, we demand a larger range of goods and services, and one of these "goods" is a pollution-free environment. We value clean air, unspoiled natural scenery, and wildlife, and we are willing and able to pay for them.

Second, as our knowledge of the effects of pollution grows, we are able to take measures that reduce those effects. For example, now that we know how sulphur dioxide causes acid rain and how clearing rain forests destroys natural stores of carbon dioxide, we are able, in principle, to design measures that limit these problems.

Let's look at the range of pollution problems that have been identified and the actions that create those problems.

The Sources of Pollution

Economic activity pollutes air, water and land, and these individual areas of pollution interact through the *ecosystem*.

Air Pollution

More than two-thirds of air pollution in most European economies arises from road transport and industrial processes. The remainder arises mainly from electricity power generation and fuel combustion.

A common belief is that air pollution is getting worse. In many developing countries, air pollution *is* getting worse. But air pollution in Europe is getting less severe for most substances.

Figure 15.1 shows the emissions of carbon dioxide in the United Kingdom between 1990 and 2003. During this period, sulphur dioxide concentrations fell by 80 per cent and suspended particulates by 60 per cent. Nitrogen dioxide concentrations, which increased in the early 1990s, have now fallen. The ozone level concentrations vary substantially year by year and have only fallen a little during this period.

The general reductions of air pollution in the United Kingdom and Europe are impressive when compared with the growth of economic activity. Between 1990 and 2003, the real value of EU production increased by 20 per cent. During this same period, the population increased by 3.6 per cent and vehicle miles travelled also increased. The main problem has been greenhouse gas emissions which increased by 5.4 per cent despite a decrease in energy consumption of 9.4 per cent.

While the facts about the sources and trends in air pollution are not in doubt, there is disagreement about the *effects* of air pollution. The least controversial is *acid rain* caused by sulphur dioxide and nitrogen oxide emissions from coal and oil-fired generators of power stations. Acid rain begins with air pollution, leads to water pollution and damages vegetation.

More controversial are airborne substances (suspended particulates) such as lead from leaded petrol. Some scientists believe that in sufficiently large concentrations, these substances (189 of which have currently been identified) cause cancer and other life-threatening conditions.

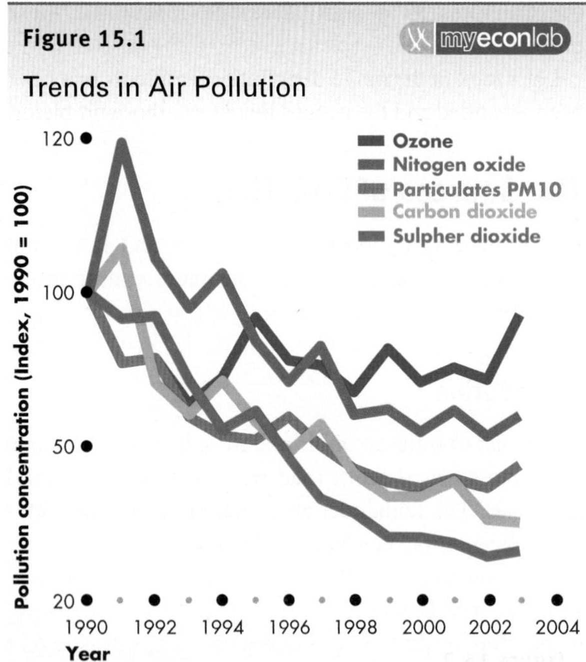

Figure 15.1

Trends in Air Pollution

Both sulphur dioxide and suspended particulate concentrations have fallen dramatically since 1990. Nitrogen dioxide concentrations have also fallen, but ozone concentrations vary annually.

Source of data: Environment Agency (www.environment-agency.gov.uk spreadsheeti2_airtrends_a2_dt_1158809.xls)

Even more controversial is *global warming*, which some scientists believe results from carbon dioxide emissions. The earth's average temperature has increased over the past 100 years, but most of the increase occurred *before* 1940. Determining what causes changes in the earth's temperature and isolating the effect of carbon dioxide from other factors are proving to be difficult.

Equally controversial is the problem of *ozone layer depletion*. There is no doubt that a hole in the ozone layer exists over Antarctica and that the ozone layer protects us from cancer-causing ultraviolet rays from the sun. But how our industrial activity influences the ozone layer is simply not understood at this time.

One air pollution problem has almost been eliminated: lead from gasoline. In part, this happened because the cost of living without leaded petrol, it turns out, is not high. But sulphur dioxide and the so-called greenhouse gases are a much tougher problem to tackle. Their alternatives are costly or have pollution problems of their own. The major sources of these pollutants are road vehicles and electric utilities. Road vehicles can be made "greener" in a variety of ways. One is with new fuels and some alternatives being investigated are alcohol, natural gas, propane and butane and hydrogen. Another way of making cars and trucks "greener" is to change the chemistry of gasoline. Refiners are working on reformulations of gasoline that reduce road vehicle emissions. Similarly, electric power can be generated in cleaner ways by harnessing solar power, tidal power or geothermal power. While technically possible, these methods are more costly than conventional carbon-fuelled generators. Another alternative is nuclear power. This method is good for air pollution but creates a potential long-term problem for land and water pollution because there is no known entirely safe method of disposing of spent nuclear fuel.

Water Pollution

The largest sources of water pollution are the dumping of industrial waste and treated sewage in lakes and rivers and the run-off from fertilizers. A more dramatic source is the accidental spilling of crude oil into the oceans such as the *Prestige* spill off Spain in 2002 and deliberate dumping of oil and nuclear waste at sea.

There are two main alternatives to polluting the waterways and oceans. One is the chemical processing of waste to render it inert or biodegradable. The other, in wide use for nuclear waste, is to use land sites for storage in secure containers.

Land Pollution

Land pollution arises from dumping toxic waste products. Ordinary household garbage does not pose a pollution problem unless contaminants from dumped garbage seep into the water supply. This possibility increases as landfills reach capacity and less suitable landfill sites are used. It is estimated that 80 per cent of existing landfills will be full by 2010. Some countries (the Netherlands and Japan) are seeking less costly alternatives to landfill, such as recycling and incineration. Recycling is attractive, but it requires an investment in new technologies. Incineration is a high-cost alternative to landfill, and it produces air pollution. Furthermore, these alternatives are not free, and they become efficient only when the cost of using landfill is high.

We've seen that the demand for a pollution-free environment has grown, and we've described the range of pollution problems. Let's now look at the economics of these problems. The starting point is the distinction between private costs and social costs.

Private Costs and Social Costs

A *private cost* of production is a cost that is borne by the producer of a good or service. *Marginal cost* is the cost of producing an *additional unit* of a good or service. So **marginal private cost** (*MC*) is the cost of producing an additional unit of a good or service that is borne by the producer of that good or service.

You've seen that an *external cost* is a cost of producing a good or service that is *not* borne by the producer but borne by other people. A **marginal external cost** is the cost of producing an additional unit of a good or service that falls on people other than the producer of the good or service.

Marginal social cost (*MSC*) is the marginal cost incurred by the entire society – by the producer and by everyone else on whom the cost falls – and is the sum of marginal private cost and marginal external cost. That is:

$$MSC = MC + \text{Marginal external cost}$$

We express costs in pounds. But we must always remember that a cost is an opportunity cost – what we give up to get something. A marginal external cost is what someone other than the producer of a good or service must give up when the producer makes one more unit of the item. Something real, such as a clean river or clean air, is given up.

Valuing an External Cost

Economists use market prices to put a pound value on the cost of pollution. For example, suppose that there are two similar rivers: one polluted and the other clean. Five hundred identical homes are built along the side of each river. The homes on the clean river rent for £2,500 a month, and those on the polluted river rent for £1,500 a month. If the pollution is the only detectable difference between the two rivers and the two locations, the decrease in the rent of £1,000 per month is the cost of the pollution. For the 500 homes on the polluted river, the external cost is £500,000 a month.

External Cost and Output

Figure 15.2 shows an example of the relationship between output and cost in a chemical industry that pollutes. The marginal cost curve, *MC*, describes the marginal private cost borne by the firms that produce the chemical. Marginal private cost increases as the quantity of chemical produced increases.

If the firms dump waste into a river, they impose an external cost that increases with the amount of the chemical produced. The marginal social cost curve, *MSC*, is the sum of marginal private cost and marginal external cost. For example, when output is 4,000 tonnes per month, marginal private cost is £100 a tonne, marginal external cost is £125 a tonne and marginal social cost is £225 a tonne.

In Figure 15.2, when the quantity of chemicals produced increases, the amount of pollution increases and the external cost of pollution increases.

Figure 15.2 shows the relationship between the quantity of chemicals produced and the amount of pollution created, but it doesn't tell us how much pollution gets created. That quantity depends on how the market for chemicals operates. First, we'll see what happens when the industry is free to pollute.

Figure 15.2

myeconlab

An External Cost

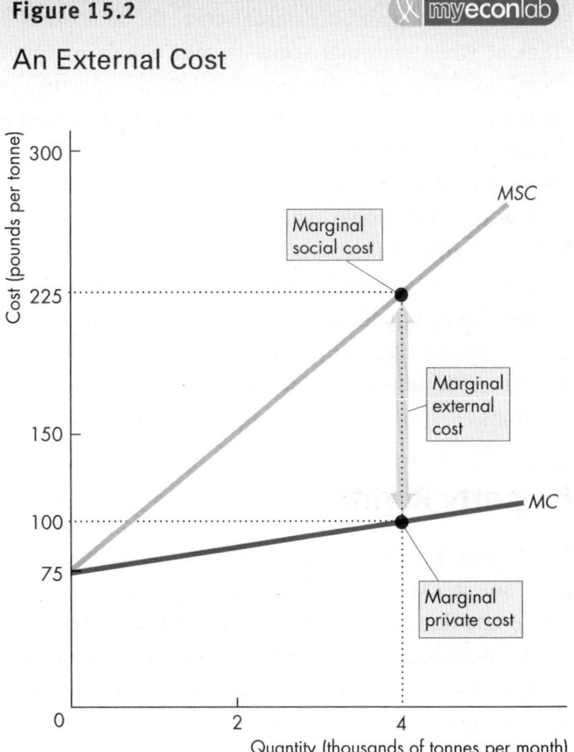

The *MC* curve shows the marginal private cost borne by the factories that produce a chemical. The *MSC* curve shows the sum of marginal private cost and marginal external cost. When output of the chemical is 4 tonnes a month, marginal private cost is £100 a tonne, marginal external cost is £125 a tonne and marginal social cost is £225 a tonne.

Production and Pollution: How Much?

When an industry is unregulated, the amount of pollution it creates depends on the market equilibrium price and quantity of the good produced. In Figure 15.3, the demand curve for a pollution-creating chemical is *D*. This curve also measures the marginal social benefit, *MSB*, of the chemical. The supply curve is *S*. This curve also measures the marginal private cost, *MC*. The supply curve is the marginal private cost curve because when firms make their production and supply decisions, they consider only the costs that they will bear. Market equilibrium occurs at a price of £100 a tonne and a quantity of 4,000 tonnes of chemical a month.

This equilibrium is inefficient. You learned in Chapter 5 that the allocation of resources is efficient when marginal social benefit equals marginal social cost. But we must count all the costs – private and external – when we compare marginal social benefit and marginal social cost. So with an external cost, the allocation is efficient when marginal social benefit equals marginal *social* cost. This outcome occurs when the quantity of chemical produced is 2,000 tonnes a month. The market equilibrium overproduces by 2,000 tonnes a month and creates a deadweight loss, the grey triangle.

How can the people who live by the polluted river get the chemical factories to decrease their output of chemicals and create less pollution? If some method can be found to achieve this outcome, everyone – the owners of the chemical factories and the residents of the riverside homes – can gain. Let's explore some solutions.

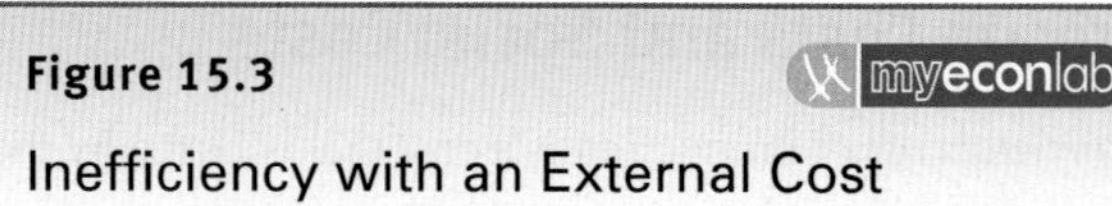

Inefficiency with an External Cost

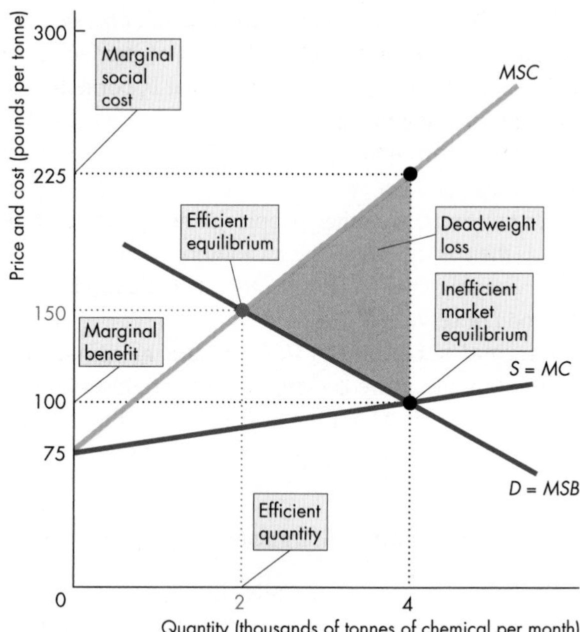

The market supply curve is the marginal private cost curve, *S* = *MC*. The demand curve is the marginal social benefit curve, *D* = *MSB*. Market equilibrium at a price of £100 a tonne and 4,000 tonnes a month is inefficient because the marginal social cost exceeds marginal social benefit. The efficient quantity is 2,000 tonnes a month. The grey triangle shows the deadweight loss created by the pollution externality.

Property Rights

Sometimes it is possible to reduce the inefficiency arising from an externality by establishing a property right where one does not currently exist. **Property rights** are legally established titles to the ownership, use and disposal of factors of production and goods and services that are enforceable in the courts.

Suppose that the chemical factories own the river and the 500 homes alongside it. The rent that people are willing to pay depends on the amount of pollution. Using the earlier example, people are willing to pay £2,500 a month to live alongside a pollution-free river but only £1,500 a month to live with the pollution created by 4,000 tonnes of chemical a month. If the factories produce this quantity, they lose £1,000 a month for each home – a total of £500,000 a month.

The chemical factories are now confronted with the cost of their pollution – forgone rent from the people who live by the river.

Figure 15.4 illustrates the outcome by using the same example as in Figure 15.3. With property rights in place, the *MC* curve no longer measures all the costs that the factories face in producing the chemical. It excludes the pollution costs that they must now bear. The *MSC* curve now becomes the marginal private cost curve *MC*. All the costs fall on the factories, so the market supply curve is based on all the marginal costs and is the curve labelled *S* = *MC* = *MSC*.

Market equilibrium now occurs at a price of £150 a tonne and a quantity of 2,000 tonnes of chemical a month. This outcome is efficient. The factories still produce some pollution, but it is the efficient quantity.

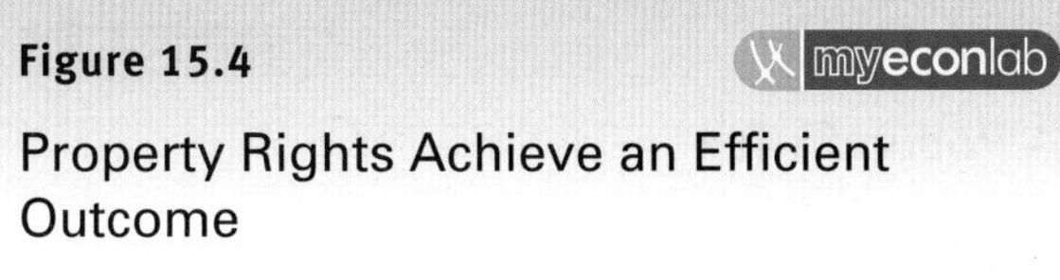

Figure 15.4

Property Rights Achieve an Efficient Outcome

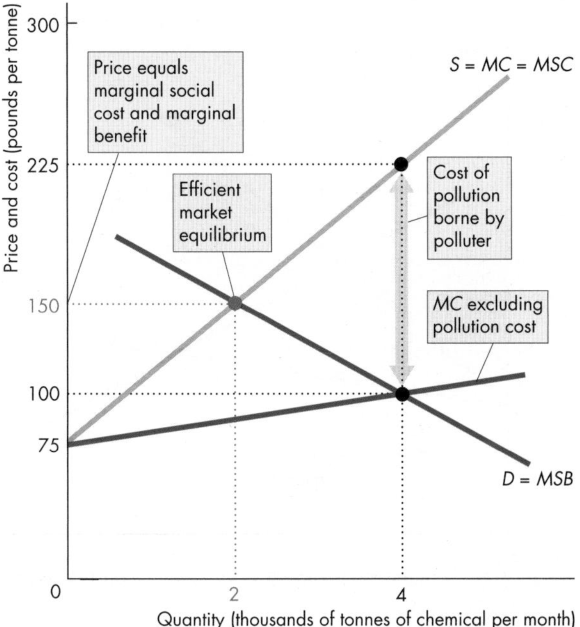

With property rights, the marginal cost curve that excludes pollution costs shows only part of the producers' marginal cost. The marginal private cost curve includes the cost of pollution, and the supply curve is $S = MC = MSC$. Market equilibrium is a price of £150 a tonne and a quantity of 2,000 tonnes of chemical a month. This equilibrium is efficient because marginal social cost equals marginal social benefit.

The Coase Theorem

Does it matter how property rights are assigned? Does it matter whether the polluter or the victim of the pollution owns the resource that might be polluted? Until 1960, everyone – including economists who had thought long and hard about the problem – thought that it did matter. But in 1960, Ronald Coase had a remarkable insight, now called the Coase theorem.

The **Coase theorem** is the proposition that if property rights exist, if only a small number of parties are involved and if transactions costs are low, then private transactions are efficient. There are no externalities because the transacting parties take all the costs and benefits into account. Furthermore, it doesn't matter who has the property rights.

Application of the Coase Theorem

In the example that we've just studied, the factories own the river and the homes. Suppose that instead, the residents own their homes and the river. Now the factories must pay a fee to the homeowners for the right to dump their waste. The greater the quantity of waste dumped into the river, the more the factories must pay. So again, the factories face the opportunity cost of the pollution they create. The quantity of chemical produced and the amount of waste dumped are the same whoever owns the homes and the river. If the factories own them, they bear the cost of pollution because they receive a lower income from home rents. And if the residents own the homes and the river, the factories bear the cost of pollution because they must pay a fee to the homeowners. In both cases, the factories bear the cost of their pollution and dump the efficient amount of waste into the river.

The Coase solution works only when transactions costs are low. **Transactions costs** are the opportunity costs of conducting a transaction. For example, when you buy a house, you incur a series of transactions costs. You might pay an estate agent to help you find the best place and a lawyer to run checks that assure you that the seller owns the property and that after you've paid for it, the ownership has been properly transferred to you.

In the example of the homes alongside a river, the transactions costs that are incurred by a small number of chemical factories and a few homeowners might be low enough to enable them to negotiate the deals that produce an efficient outcome. But in many situations, transactions costs are so high that it would be inefficient to incur them. In these situations, the Coase solution is not available.

Suppose, for example, that everyone owns the airspace above their homes up to, say, 10 miles. If someone pollutes your airspace, you can charge a fee. But to collect the fee, you must identify who is polluting your airspace and persuade them to pay you. Imagine the costs of negotiating and enforcing agreements with the more than 50 million people who live in the United Kingdom (and perhaps those that live in Europe) and the several thousand factories that emit sulphur dioxide and create acid rain that falls on your property! In this situation, we use public choices to cope with externalities. But the transactions costs that block a market solution are real costs, so attempts by the government to deal with externalities offer no easy solution. Let's look at some of these attempts.

Government Actions in the Face of External Costs

The three main methods that governments use to cope with externalities are:

- Taxes
- Emission charges
- Marketable permits

Taxes

The government can use taxes as an incentive for producers to cut back on pollution. Taxes used in this way are called **Pigovian taxes**, in honour of Arthur Cecil Pigou, the British economist who first worked out this method of dealing with externalities during the 1920s.

By setting the tax rate equal to the marginal external cost, firms can be made to behave in the same way as they would if they bore the cost of the externality directly. To see how government actions can change market outcomes in the face of externalities, let's return to the example of the chemical factories and the river.

Assume that the government has assessed the marginal external cost accurately and imposes a tax on the factories that exactly equals this marginal external cost. Figure 15.5 illustrates the effects of this tax.

The demand curve and marginal social benefit curve, *D* = *MSB*, and the firms' marginal private cost curve, *MC*, are the same as in Figure 15.3. The government sets the pollution tax equal to the marginal external cost of the pollution. We add this tax to the marginal private cost to find the market supply curve. This curve is the one labelled *S* = *MC* + *tax* = *MSC*. This curve is the market supply curve because it tells us the quantity of chemicals supplied at each price given the firms' marginal private cost and the tax they must pay.

The curve *S* = *MC* + *tax* = *MSC* is also the marginal social cost curve because the pollution tax has been set equal to the marginal external cost.

Demand and supply now determine the market equilibrium price at £150 a tonne and the equilibrium quantity at 2,000 tonnes of chemical a month. At this quantity of chemical production, the marginal social cost is £150 a tonne and the marginal social benefit is £150 a tonne, so the outcome is efficient. The firms incur a marginal private cost of £88 a tonne and pay a pollution tax of £62 a tonne. The government collects tax revenue of £124,000 a month, which is shown by the purple rectangle.

Figure 15.5

A Pollution Tax

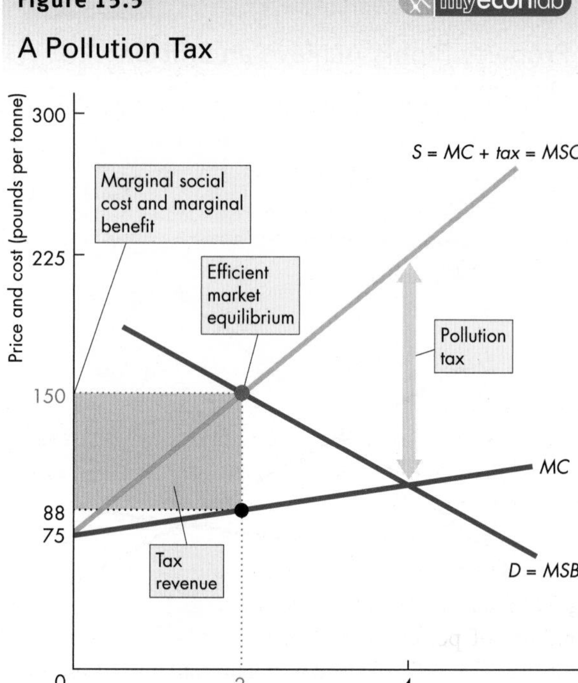

A pollution tax is imposed equal to the marginal external cost of pollution. The supply curve becomes the marginal private cost curve, *MC*, plus the tax: *S* = *MC* + *tax*. Market equilibrium is at a price of £150 a tonne and a quantity of 2,000 tonnes of chemical a month. This equilibrium is efficient because marginal social cost equals marginal social benefit. The government collects a tax revenue shown by the purple rectangle.

Emission Charges

Emission charges are an alternative to a tax for confronting a polluter with the external cost of pollution. The government sets a price per unit of pollution. The more pollution a firm creates, the more it pays in emission charges. This method of dealing with pollution externalities is common in Europe where, for example, France, Germany and the Netherlands make water polluters pay a waste disposal charge. But to work out the emission charge that achieves efficiency, the government needs a lot of information about the polluting industry that, in practice, is rarely available.

The European Union introduced the idea of a tax on carbon emissions as part of its sustainable environmental policy in 1992. The issue is still pressing. Today, annual carbon emissions worldwide are a staggering 6 billion tonnes. By 2050, with current policies, that annual total is predicted to be 24 billion tonnes. If the rich countries used carbon taxes to keep emissions to their 1990 level and the developing countries remove subsidies from coal and oil, total emissions in 2050 might be held at 14 billion tonnes. So why have the European Union and other rich countries worldwide failed to introduce taxes on carbon emissions?

Marketable Permits

Instead of taxing or imposing emission charges on polluters, each potential polluter might be assigned a permitted pollution limit. Each firm knows its own costs and benefits of pollution, and making pollution limits marketable is a clever way of using this private information that is unknown to the government. The government issues each firm a permit to emit a certain amount of pollution, and firms can buy and sell these permits. Firms that have a low marginal cost of reducing pollution sell their permits, and firms that have a high marginal cost of reducing pollution buy permits. The market in permits determines the price at which firms trade permits. And firms buy or sell permits until their marginal cost of pollution equals the market price.

This method of dealing with pollution provides an even stronger incentive than do emission charges to find technologies that pollute less because the price of a permit to pollute rises as the demand for permits increases.

Review Quiz

Study Plan 15.2

1. What is the distinction between private cost and social cost?
2. How does an externality prevent a competitive market from allocating resources efficiently?
3. How can a negative externality be eliminated by assigning property rights? How does this method of coping with an externality work?
4. How do taxes help us to cope with negative externalities? At what level must a pollution tax be set if it is to induce firms to produce the efficient quantity of pollution?
5. How do emission charges and marketable pollution permits work?

Positive Externalities: Knowledge

Knowledge comes from education and research. To study the economics of knowledge, we must distinguish between private benefits and social benefits.

Private Benefits and Social Benefits

A *private benefit* is a benefit that the consumer of a good or service receives. *Marginal benefit* is the benefit from an *additional unit* of a good or service. So a **marginal private benefit** (*MB*) is the benefit from an additional unit of a good or service that the consumer of that good or service receives.

The *external benefit* from a good or service is the benefit that someone other than the consumer of the good or service receives. A **marginal external benefit** is the benefit from an additional unit of a good or service that people other than the consumer enjoy.

Marginal social benefit (*MSB*) is the marginal benefit enjoyed by society – by the consumer of a good or service (marginal private benefit) plus the marginal benefit enjoyed by others (the marginal external benefit). That is:

$$MSB = MB + \text{Marginal external benefit}$$

Figure 15.6 shows an example of the relationship between marginal private benefit, marginal external benefit and marginal social benefit. The marginal benefit curve, *MB*, describes the marginal private benefit – such as expanded job opportunities and higher incomes – enjoyed by university graduates. Marginal private benefit decreases as the quantity of education increases.

But university graduates generate external benefits. On the average, they tend to be better citizens. Their crime rates are lower and they are more tolerant of the views of others. A society with a large number of graduates can support activities such as high-quality newspapers and television channels, music, theatre and other organized social activities.

In the example in Figure 15.6, the marginal external benefit is £15,000 per student per year when 15 million students attend university. The marginal social benefit is the sum of marginal private benefit and marginal external benefit. For example, when 15 million students a year attend university, the marginal private benefit is £10,000 per student and the marginal external benefit is £15,000 per student, so the marginal social benefit is

Figure 15.6 myeconlab

An External Benefit

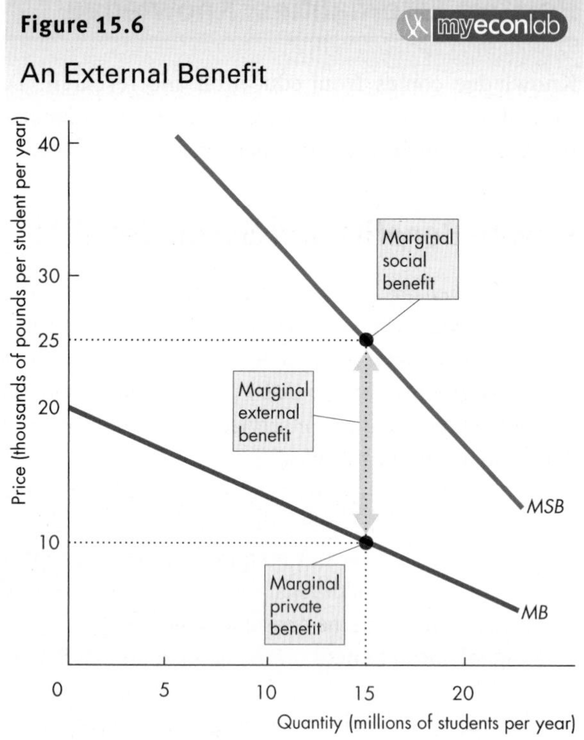

The *MB* curve shows the marginal private benefit enjoyed by the people who receive a university education. The *MSB* curve shows the sum of marginal private benefit and marginal external benefit. When 15 million students attend university, marginal private benefit is £10,000 per student, marginal external benefit is £15,000 per student and marginal social benefit is £25,000 per student.

Figure 15.7 myeconlab

Inefficiency with an External Benefit

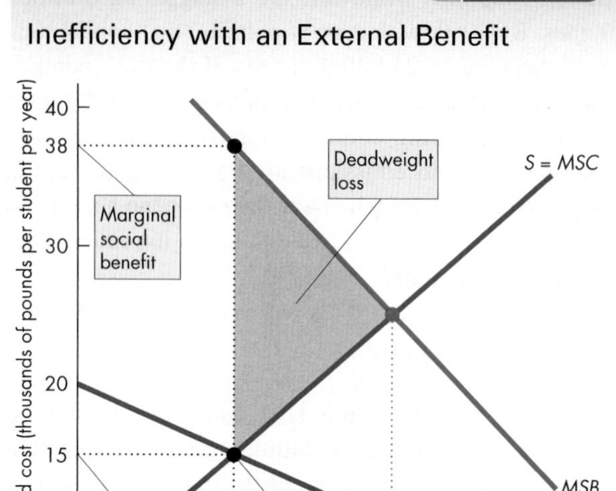

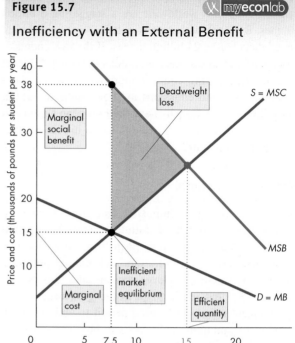

The market demand curve is the marginal private benefit curve, *D* = *MB*. The supply curve is the marginal social cost curve, *S* = *MSC*. Market equilibrium at a tuition fee of £15,000 a year and 7.5 million students is inefficient because marginal social benefit exceeds marginal cost. The efficient quantity is 15 million students. The grey triangle shows the deadweight loss created because too few students attend university.

£25,000 per student. The curve labelled *MSB is the* marginal social benefit curve.

When people make decisions about how much education to take, they ignore its external benefits and consider only the private benefits that education brings. So if education were provided by private universities that charged full-cost tuition, we would produce too few graduates.

Figure 15.7 illustrates the underproduction if the government left education to the private market. The supply curve is the marginal social cost curve, *S* = *MSC*. The demand curve is the marginal private benefit curve, *D* = *MB*. Market equilibrium occurs at a tuition fee of £15,000 per student per year and 7.5 million students per year. At this equilibrium, marginal social benefit is £38,000 per student, which exceeds marginal social cost by £23,000. There are too few students in university. The efficient number is 15 million, where marginal social benefit equals marginal social cost. The grey triangle shows the deadweight loss.

Underproduction similar to that in Figure 15.7 would occur in primary school and secondary school if an unregulated market produced it. When children learn basic reading, writing and number skills, they receive the private benefit of increased earning power. But even these basic skills bring the external benefit of developing better citizens.

External benefits also arise from the discovery of new knowledge. When Isaac Newton worked out the formulas for calculating the rate of response of one variable to another – calculus – everyone was free to use his method. When a spreadsheet program called VisiCalc was invented, Lotus Corporation and Microsoft were free to copy the basic idea and create 123 and Excel. When the first shopping mall was built and found to be a successful way of arranging retailing, everyone was free to copy the idea, and malls spread like mushrooms.

Once someone has discovered how to do something, others can copy the basic idea. They do have to work to copy an idea, so they face an opportunity cost. But they do not usually have to pay a fee to the person who made the discovery to use it. When people make decisions, they ignore the external benefits and consider only the private benefits.

When people make decisions about the quantity of education or the amount of research to undertake, they balance the marginal private cost against the marginal private benefit. They ignore the external benefit. As a result, if we left education and research to unregulated market forces, we would get too little of these activities.

To get closer to producing the efficient quantity of a good or service that generates an external benefit, we make public choices, through governments, to modify the market outcome.

Government Actions in the Face of External Benefits

Four devices that governments can use to achieve a more efficient allocation of resources in the presence of external benefits are:

- Public provision
- Private subsidies
- Vouchers
- Patents and copyrights

Public Provision

Under **public provision**, a public authority that receives its revenue from the government produces the good or service. The education services produced by the public universities and schools are examples of public provision.

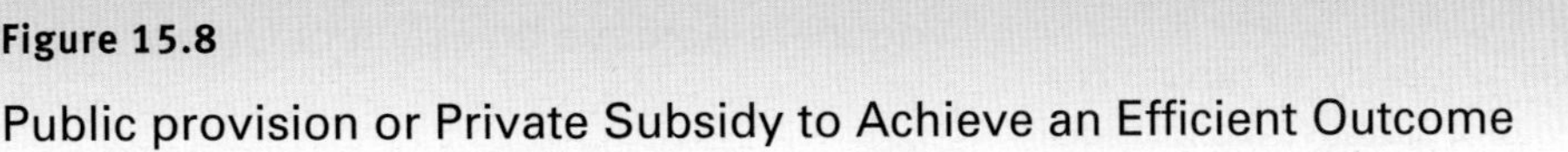

Figure 15.8

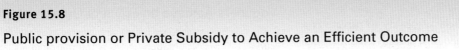

Public provision or Private Subsidy to Achieve an Efficient Outcome

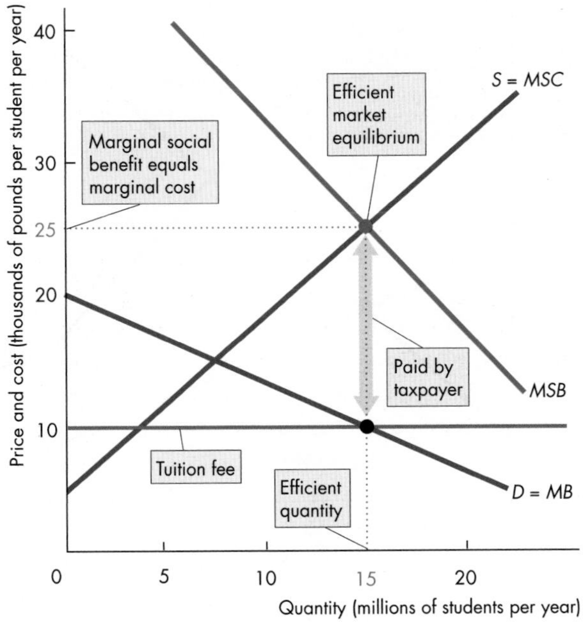

(a) Public provision

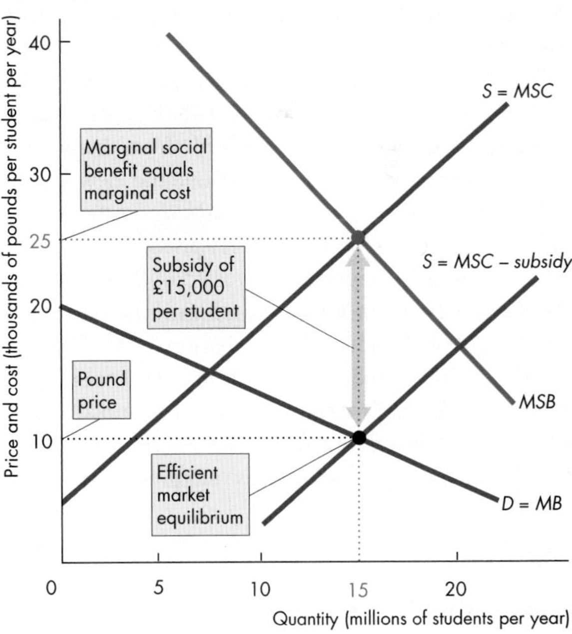

(b) Private subsidy

In part (a), marginal social benefit equals marginal social cost with 15 million students attending university, the efficient quantity. The tuition fee is set at £10,000 per student and the taxpayers cover the other at £15,000 of cost per student.

In part (b) with a subsidy of £15,000 per student, the supply curve is *S* = *MSC* – *subsidy*. The equilibrium price is £10,000 and the market equilibrium is efficient with 15 million students a year attending university. Marginal social benefit equals marginal social cost.

Figure 15.8(a) shows how public provision might overcome the underproduction that arises in Figure 15.7. Public provision cannot lower the cost of production, so marginal cost is the same as before. Marginal private benefit and marginal external benefit are also the same as before.

The efficient quantity occurs where marginal social benefit equals marginal social cost. In Figure 15.8(a), this quantity is 15 million students. The tuition fee is set to ensure that the efficient number of students attend. That is, tuition is set at the level that equals the marginal private benefit at the efficient quantity. In Figure 15.8(a), the tuition fee is £10,000 a year. The rest of the cost of the public university is borne by the taxpayers and, in this example, is £15,000 per student per year.

Private Subsidies

A **subsidy** is a payment that the government makes to private producers. By making the subsidy depend on the level of output, the government can induce private decision makers to consider external benefits when they make their choices.

Figure 15.8(b) shows how a subsidy to private colleges works. In the absence of a subsidy, the marginal cost curve is the market supply curve of private college education, $S = MSC$. The marginal benefit is the demand curve, $D = MB$. In this example, the government provides a subsidy to universities of £15,000 per student per year. We must subtract the subsidy from the universities' marginal cost of education to find the new supply curve. That curve is $S = MSC - subsidy$ in the figure. The equilibrium tuition fee (market price) is £10,000 a year, and the equilibrium quantity is 15 million students. The marginal cost of educating 15 million students a year is £25,000 a student and the marginal social benefit is also £25,000 a student. So with marginal social cost equal to marginal social benefit, the subsidy has achieved an efficient outcome. The tuition fee and the subsidy just cover the universities' marginal cost.

Vouchers

A **voucher** is a token that the government provides to households, which they can use to buy specified goods or services. Food stamps are examples of vouchers. The vouchers (stamps) can be spent only on food and are designed to improve the diet and health of extremely poor families. School vouchers have been advocated as a means of improving the quality of education.

A school voucher allows parents to choose the school their children will attend and to use the voucher to pay part of the cost. The school cashes the vouchers to pay its bills. A voucher could be provided to a university student in a similar way.

Because vouchers can be spent only on a specified item, they increase the willingness to pay for that item and so increase the demand for it. Figure 15.9 shows how a voucher system works. The government provides vouchers worth £15,000 per student per year. Parents (or students) use these vouchers to supplement the pounds they pay for university education. The marginal social benefit curve becomes the demand for university education, $D = MSB$. The market equilibrium occurs at a price of £25,000 per student per year, and 15 million students attend university. Each student pays £10,000 tuition fee, and universities collect an additional £15,000 per student from the voucher.

Figure 15.9 myeconlab

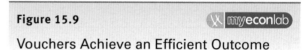

Vouchers Achieve an Efficient Outcome

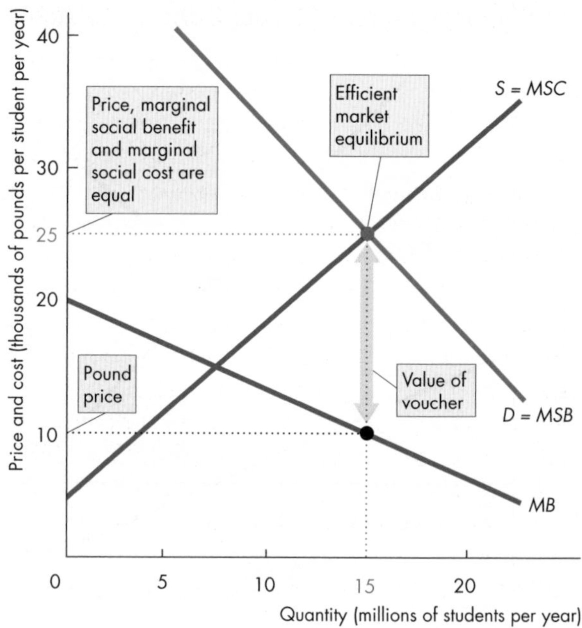

With vouchers, buyers are willing to pay MB plus the value of the voucher, so the demand curve becomes the marginal social benefit curve, $D = MSB$. Market equilibrium is efficient with 15 million students in university because price, marginal social benefit and marginal social cost are equal. The tuition fee consists of the pound price of £10,000 a year and a voucher valued at £15,000.

If the government estimates the value of the external benefit correctly and makes the value of the voucher equal the marginal external benefit, the outcome from the voucher scheme is efficient. Marginal social cost equals marginal social benefit, and the deadweight loss is eliminated.

Vouchers are similar to subsidies, but their advocates say that they are more efficient than subsidies because the consumer can monitor school performance more effectively than the government can.

Patents and Copyrights

Knowledge might be an exception to the principle of diminishing marginal benefit. Additional knowledge (about the right things) makes people more productive. And there seems to be no tendency for the additional productivity from additional knowledge to diminish.

For example, in just 15 years, advances in knowledge about microprocessors have given us a sequence of processor chips that has made our personal computers increasingly powerful. Each advance in knowledge about how to design and manufacture a processor chip has brought apparently ever larger increments in performance and productivity. Similarly, each advance in knowledge about how to design and build an airplane has brought apparently ever larger increments in performance. Orville and Wilbur Wright's 1903 Flyer was a one-seat plane that could hop a farmer's field. The Lockheed Constellation, designed in 1949, was an airplane that could fly 120 passengers from New York to London, but with two refuelling stops in Newfoundland and Ireland. Since June 2004, an Airbus 340 is transporting 200 people non-stop from Singapore to New York, a distance of 10,000 miles, in 18.5 hours. Similar examples can be found in agriculture, biogenetics, communications, engineering, entertainment and medicine.

One reason why the stock of knowledge increases without diminishing returns is the sheer number of different techniques that can in principle be tried. Paul Romer explains this fact. "Suppose that to make a finished good, 20 different parts have to be attached to a frame, one at a time. A worker could proceed in numerical order, attaching part one first, then part two . . . Or the worker could proceed in some other order, starting with part 10, then adding part seven . . . With 20 parts, . . . there are [more] different sequences . . . than the total number of seconds that have elapsed since the big bang created the universe, so we can be confident that in all activities, only a very small fraction of the possible sequences have ever been tried."[1]

Think about all the processes, all the products, and all the different bits and pieces that go into each, and you can see that we have only begun to scratch around the edges of what is possible.

Because knowledge is productive and generates external benefits, it is necessary to use public policies to ensure that those who develop new ideas have incentives to encourage an efficient level of effort. The main way of providing the right incentives uses the central idea of the Coase theorem and assigns property rights – called **intellectual property rights** – to creators. The legal device for establishing intellectual property rights is the patent or copyright. A **patent** or **copyright** is a government-sanctioned exclusive right granted to the inventor of a good, service or productive process to produce, use and sell the invention for a given number of years. A patent enables the developer of a new idea to prevent others from benefiting freely from an invention for a limited number of years.

Although patents encourage invention and innovation, they do so at an economic cost. While a patent is in place, its holder has a monopoly. And monopoly is another source of inefficiency (which is explained in Chapter 12). But without a patent, the effort to develop new goods, services or processes is diminished and the flow of new inventions is slowed. So the efficient outcome is a compromise that balances the benefits of more inventions against the cost of temporary monopoly in newly invented activities.

Review Quiz

Study Plan 15.3

1. What is special about knowledge that creates external benefits?
2. How might governments use public provision, private subsidies and vouchers to achieve an efficient amount of education?
3. How might governments use public provision, private subsidies, vouchers, and patents and copyrights to achieve an efficient amount of research and development?

Reading Between the Lines on pp. 354–355 looks at the negative externality that arises when tropical rain forests are cleared and the way in which UK consumers of electricity can help to overcome this externality.

[1] Paul Romer, "Ideas and Things", in *The Future Surveyed*, supplement to *The Economist*, 11 September 1993, pp. 71–72.

Reading Between the Lines

A Tropical Rainforest Externality

The Financial Times, 24 March 2007

FT

Call for aid to fight tropical deforestation

John Aglionby

Sir Nicholas Stern, the author of a significant British report on climate change, called yesterday for an additional \$15bn a year in aid for the developing world to combat tropical deforestation and its significant contribution to greenhouse gas emissions.

The new report, commissioned by the British government and the World Bank, found 83 per cent of Indonesia's annual emissions and 60 per cent of Brazil's come from the destruction of their forests. Together these account for almost 10 per cent of the world's total emissions.

An investment of \$15bn (€11.3bn, £7.7bn), . . . could halve the current destruction rate and reduce annual global greenhouse gas emissions by about 9 per cent . . . the aid should be replaced "as soon as possible" by a trading scheme whereby nations can earn money for not clearing forests, said Sir Nicholas.

Countries with extensive forests, such as Brazil, Cameroon and Indonesia, have been lobbying hard for such a scheme to be included in whatever replaces the Kyoto protocol. Under Kyoto carbon credits can be obtained for planting trees but not for preserving forests.

. . . Agus Sari, south-east Asia director of EcoSecurities, a company developing and trading carbon credits, believes a forest preservation incentive scheme must be in place within two years to make a significant difference. "Local governments see conservation as a burden," he said. "They want to cut the trees and develop the land."

If successful, the aid would work out to a cost of \$4 per tonne of carbon dioxide saved, according to current estimates on forest emissions. Western countries are currently paying up to \$9 per tonne of carbon dioxide saved in other sectors.

The Essence of the Story

- Clearing rainforests creates carbon dioxide and accounts for about 10 per cent of global greenhouse gas emissions each year.
- Under the Kyoto carbon credit scheme polluters can buy credits for planting trees but there is no credit for preserving forests.
- It currently costs polluters \$9 per tonne of carbon dioxide saved. It would cost an estimated \$4 per tonne if the Kyoto carbon credit system included forest preservation.

Economic Analysis

- We analyze this news article in the market for cleared land in Brazil and electricity in the United Kingdom.
- Figure 1 shows the market for cleared land in Brazil. The demand curve, which is also the marginal social benefit curve is $D = MSB$ and the supply curve, which is also the forest clearer's marginal cost curve is $S = MC$. In equilibrium, Q_0 hectares per year are cleared at a price and marginal cost of P_0 per hectare.
- Forest clearing creates carbon dioxide and imposes an external cost. The marginal *social* cost of forest clearing is *MSC* in Figure 1. The efficient amount of clearing is Q_1 hectares per year at a price and marginal social cost of P_1 per hectare. A deadweight loss arises.
- Figure 2 shows the market for electricity in the United Kingdom. The demand curve for electricity, which is also the marginal social benefit curve is $D = MSB$ and the power generator's marginal cost curve is *MC*.
- Power generators pay $9 per tonne of carbon dioxide (CO_2) and this cost must be added to the *MC* curve to find the supply curve.
- Assume that the $9 per tonne cost of carbon credits is equal to the marginal external cost of generating electricity. Adding this cost to *MC* means that the supply curve is $S_0 = MSC$.
- The market is in equilibrium with Q_0 megawatts per day produced at a price and marginal social cost of P_0 per megawatt. This equilibrium (we are assuming) is efficient.
- Now suppose that forest preservation is included in the Kyoto trading scheme and the equilibrium price of carbon credits falls to $4 per tonne of carbon saved, as reported in the news article.
- Also suppose that when forest clearers face the marginal social cost of clearing they cut back clearing to the efficient amount of Q_1 in Figure 1. The deadweight loss is eliminated and forest clearing is now generating its efficient amount of CO_2.

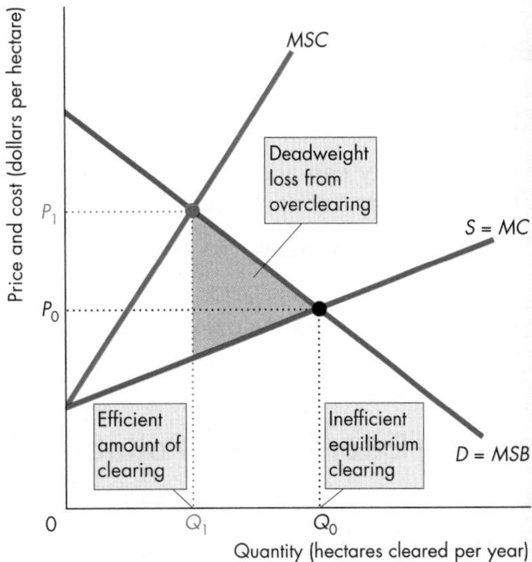

Figure 1 The market for cleared land in Brazil

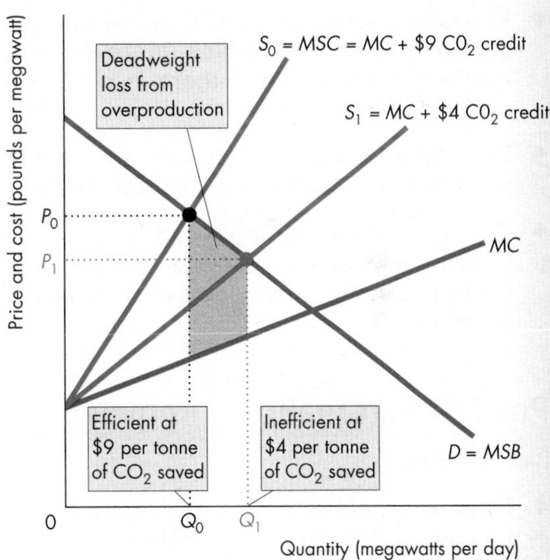

Figure 2 The market for electricity in the United Kingdom

- But at $4 per tonne of carbon saved, the supply of UK electricity increases to $S_1 = MC + \$4$ CO_2 credit, electricity production increases, and a deadweight loss arises.
- To avoid this deadweight loss, when carbon credits are extended to forest preservation, they must be decreased for tree planting.
- With an efficient market in carbon credits, the price will be greater than $4 per tonne of carbon saved.

Summary

Key Points

Externalities in Our Lives (p. 342)

- An externality can arise from either a production activity or a consumption activity.
- A negative externality imposes an external cost.
- A positive externality provides an external benefit.

Negative Externalities: Pollution (pp. 343–349)

- External costs are costs of production that fall on people other than the producer of a good or service. Marginal social cost equals marginal private cost plus marginal external cost.
- Producers take account only of marginal private cost and produce more than the efficient quantity when there is a marginal external cost.
- Sometimes it is possible to overcome a negative externality by assigning a property right.
- When property rights cannot be assigned, governments might overcome externalities by using taxes, emission charges or marketable permits.

Positive Externalities: Knowledge (pp. 349–353)

- External benefits are benefits that are received by people other than the consumer of a good or service. Marginal social benefit equals marginal private benefit plus marginal external benefit.
- External benefits from education arise because better-educated people tend to be better citizens, commit fewer crimes and support social activities.
- External benefits from research arise because once someone has worked out a basic idea, others can copy it.
- Vouchers or subsidies to schools or the provision of public education below cost can achieve a more efficient provision of education.
- Patents and copyrights create intellectual property rights and an incentive to innovate. But they do so by creating a temporary monopoly, the cost of which must be balanced against the benefit of more inventive activity.

Key Figures

Key Terms

Problems

Tests, Study Plan and Solutions* 

1 Classify each of the following items as creating a negative externality, a positive externality, an externality arising from production, an externality arising from consumption, or not an externality.

a Airplanes taking off from Heathrow Airport during the Wimbledon tennis tournament, which is located nearby

b A sunset over the Atlantic Ocean

c An increase in the number of people who are studying for post-graduate degrees

d A person wears perfume while attending an orchestral concert

e A homeowner plants an attractive garden in front of his house

f A person drives while drunk

g A bakery bakes bread

2 The table provides information about costs and benefits from the production of pesticide that pollutes a lake used by a trout farmer.

Total product of pesticide (tonnes per week)	Pesticide producer's *MC* (euros per tonne)	Marginal external cost (euros per tonne)	Marginal social benefit of pesticide (euros per tonne)
0	0	0	250
1	5	33	205
2	15	67	165
3	30	100	130
4	50	133	100
5	75	167	75
6	105	200	55
7	140	233	40

a If no one owns the lake and if there is no regulation of pollution, what is the quantity of pesticide produced per week and what is the marginal cost of pollution borne by the trout farmer?

b If the trout farm owns the lake, how much pesticide is produced per week and what does the pesticide producer pay the farmer per tonne?

c If the pesticide producer owns the lake, and if a pollution-free lake rents for €1,000 a week, how much pesticide is produced per week and how much rent per week does the farmer pay the pesticide producer for the use of the lake?

d Compare the quantities of pesticide produced in parts (b) and (c) and explain the relationship between them.

3 Back at the pesticide plant and trout farm described in problem 2, suppose that no one owns the lake and that the government introduces a pollution tax.

a What is the tax per tonne of pesticide produced that achieves an efficient outcome?

b Explain the connection between your answer to (a) and the answer to problem 1.

4 Using the information provided in problem 2, suppose that no one owns the lake and that the government issues two marketable pollution permits, one to the farmer and one to the factory. Each may pollute the lake by the same amount, and the total amount of pollution is the efficient amount.

a What is the quantity of pesticide produced?

b What is the market price of a pollution permit? Who buys and who sells a permit?

c What is the connection between your answer and the answers to problems 2 and 3?

5 Betty and Anna work at the same office in Manchester. They both must attend a meeting in Sheffield, and they have decided to drive to the meeting together. Betty is a cigarette smoker and her marginal benefit from smoking one package of cigarettes a day is £40. The price of a package of cigarettes is £6. Anna dislikes cigarette smoke and her marginal benefit from a smoke-free environment is £50 a day. What is the outcome if:

a Betty drives her car with Anna as a passenger?

b Anna drives her car with Betty as a passenger?

6 The figure shows the marginal private benefit from education.

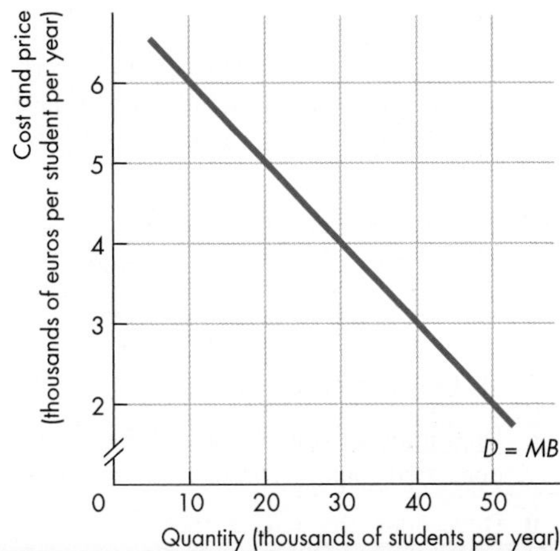

* Solutions to odd-numbered problems are provided.

The marginal cost of educating a student is €4,000 a year and is constant.

a With no government involvement and if the schools are competitive, how many students are enrolled and what is the tuition fee?

b The external benefit from education is €2,000 per student per year and is constant. If the government provides the efficient amount of education, how many school places does it offer and what is the tuition fee?

7 Online learning aids cuts the marginal cost of educating a student to €2,000 a year. The marginal private benefit is the same as that in problem 6. The external benefit from education increases to €4,000 per student per year.

a With no government involvement and if the schools are competitive, how many students are enrolled and what is the tuition fee?

b If the government provides the efficient amount of education, how many school places does it offer and what is the tuition fee?

c Compare the outcomes in problem 7 with those in problem 6. Explain the differences.

Critical Thinking

1 After you have studied *Reading Between the Lines* on pp. 354–355, answer the following questions:

a What are the alternative ways of addressing the overclearing of tropical forests discussed in the news article?

b If the rich countries paid $15 billion a year to Brazil and other developing countries, how would that payment influence the amount of forest clearing?

c Explain exactly how extending the carbon credit trading scheme to include forest preservation would lower the cost of the credit per tonne of carbon.

d Why must the credit per tree planted be decreased if credit is extended to forest preservation?

e Can you think of any other ways of making the markets for cleared land in Brazil and electricity in the United Kingdom efficient?

f Does it matter who pays for greenhouse gas reductions, rich countries or developing countries?

g How does the Coase theorem relate to your answers to the above questions?

2 **EU tackles aircraft CO_2 emissions**

Airlines operating in the EU should pay for any increase in their carbon emissions . . . Commissioners called on the industry to make a "fair contribution" to the fight against climate change. . . . The European Commission said it expected short-haul air tickets to rise by €1.8 (£1.20) to €9 each by 2020 – too little, environmentalists said, to deter people flying. . . . But the Association of European Airlines (AEA), . . . said the proposals would force its members to buy emission permits.

BBC News, 12 September 2006

a What is a "fair contribution"?

b Do you agree that the expected rise in ticket prices will reduce the number of flights?

c If people don't fly, will that reduce the number of people taking holidays "in the sun"?

d How would airlines use emission permits?

e What policy do you think environmentalists might prefer? Explain your answer.

Web Activities

Links to Websites

1 Obtain two viewpoints on global warming. Then answer the following questions:

a What are the benefits and costs of greenhouse gas emissions?

b Do you agree with environmentalists that greenhouse gas emissions must be cut or do you think the costs of reducing greenhouse gas emissions exceed the benefits? Explain your answer.

c If greenhouse gas emissions are to be reduced, what policy will achieve the reduction?

2 Visit the UK Environment Agency and then:

a Describe the trend in UK emissions of carbon dioxide and sulphur dioxide over the past 20 years.

b Describe the trend in UK nitrogen oxides and volatile organic compounds over the past 20 years.

c Do these figures give any indication of the success of environmental policies to control emissions?

3 Visit the UK government's Department of Education. Read about top-up fees for students in higher education and then answer the following questions.

a To what extent does higher education generate private benefits for graduate students?

b To what extent does higher education generate external benefits for society?

c Do you think top-up fees are efficient based on your answers to part (a) and (b)?

CHAPTER 16

Public Goods and Common Resources

After studying this chapter you will be able to:

- Distinguish among private goods, public goods and common resources
- Explain how the free-rider problem arises and how the quantity of public goods is determined
- Explain the tragedy of the commons and its possible solutions

Government: The Solution or the Problem?

Governments provide some goods and services but not all. What determines the proper scope and scale of government? Are our local, national and EU governments too bureaucratic? Do we need as much government as we've got? Or have governments grown too big? Find out in this chapter. Also find out what we can do about the overuse of resources that no one owns and to which everyone has access. In *Reading Between the Lines* at the end of the chapter, find out about the serious overuse of tropical rain forests.

Classifying Goods and Resources

Goods, services and resources differ in the extent to which people can be *excluded* from consuming them and in the extent to which one person's consumption *rivals* the consumption of others.

A good is **excludable** if it is possible to prevent someone from enjoying its benefits. Brinks's security services, East Coast's fish and a UB40's concert are examples. You must pay to consume them.

A good is **non-excludable** if everyone benefits from it regardless of whether they pay for it. The services of Scotland Yard, fish in the North Sea and a concert on network television are examples.

A good is **rival** if one person's use decreases the quantity available for someone else. A Brinks's truck can't deliver cash to two banks at the same time. A fish can be consumed only once. And one seat at a concert can hold only one person at a time. These items are rival.

A good is **non-rival** if one person's use does not decrease the quantity available for someone else. The services of Scotland Yard and a concert on television are non-rival.

A Four-fold Classification

Figure 16.1 classifies goods, services, and resources into four types.

Private Goods

A **private good** is both rival and excludable. A can of Coke and a fish on East Coast's farm are examples.

Public Goods

A **public good** is both non-rival and non-excludable. A public good can be consumed simultaneously by everyone and no one can be excluded from enjoying its benefits. National defence is the best example.

Common Resources

A **common resource** is rival and non-excludable. A unit of a common resource can be used only once, but no one can be prevented from using what is available. Ocean fish are a common resource. They are rival because a fish taken by one person isn't available for anyone else and they are non-excludable because it is difficult to prevent people from catching them.

Figure 16.1 myeconlab

Four-fold Classification of Goods

	Excludable	Non-excludable
Rival	**Private goods** Food and drink Car House	**Common resources** Fish in ocean Atmosphere City parks
Non-rival	**Natural monopolies** Internet Cable television Bridge or tunnel	**Public goods** National defence The law Air traffic control

A private good is one for which consumption is rival and from which consumers can be excluded. A public good is one for which consumption is non-rival and from which it is impossible to exclude a consumer. A common resource is one that is rival but non-excludable. And a good that is non-rival but excludable is produced by a natural monopoly.

Natural Monopolies

In a natural monopoly, economies of scale exist over the entire range of output for which there is a demand (see Chapter 12, p. 264). A special case of natural monopoly arises when the good or service can be produced at zero marginal cost. If it is also excludable, it is produced by a natural monopoly. The Internet and cable television are examples.

Two Problems

Public goods create a **free-rider problem** – the absence of an incentive for people to pay for what they consume. *Common resources* create a problem called the **tragedy of the commons** – the absence of incentives to prevent the overuse and depletion of a resource.

The rest of this chapter looks more closely at the free-rider problem and the tragedy of the commons and examines public choice solutions to them.

Review Quiz

Study Plan 16.1

1 Distinguish among public goods, private goods, common resources and natural monopolies.
2 Provide examples of goods (or services or resources) in each of the four categories that differ from the examples in this section.

Public Goods and the Free-rider Problem

Suppose that for its defence, a country must launch some surveillance satellites. The benefit provided by a satellite is the *value* of its services. The *value* of a *private* good is the maximum amount that a person is willing to pay for one more unit, which is shown by the person's demand curve. The *value* of a *public* good is the maximum amount that *all* the *people* are willing to pay for one more unit of it. To calculate the value placed on a public good, we use the concepts of total benefit and marginal benefit.

The Benefit of a Public Good

Total benefit is the euro value that a person places on a given quantity of a good. The greater the quantity of a good, the larger is a person's total benefit. *Marginal benefit* is the increase in total benefit that results from a one-unit increase in the quantity of a good.

Figure 16.2(a) and 16.2(b) show the marginal benefit that arises from defence satellites for a society with only two people, Lisa and Max, whose marginal benefits are graphed as MB_L and MB_M, respectively. The marginal benefit from a public good (like that from a private good) diminishes as the quantity of the good increases. For Lisa, the marginal benefit from the first satellite is €80 and that from the second is €60. By the time five satellites are deployed, Lisa's marginal benefit is zero. For Max, the marginal benefit from the first satellite is €50 and that from the second is €40. By the time five satellites are deployed, Max perceives only €10 worth of marginal benefit.

Figure 16.2(c) shows the economy's marginal social benefit curve, *MSB*. The economy's marginal social benefit curve for a *public* good is different from the market demand curve for a *private* good. To obtain the market demand curve for a private good, we sum the quantities demanded by all individuals at each *price* – we sum the individual demand curves *horizontally* (see Chapter 5, p. 104). But to find the economy's marginal benefit curve of a *public* good, we sum the marginal benefits of each individual at each *quantity* – we sum the individual marginal benefit curves *vertically*. So the curve *MSB* in part (c) is the marginal social benefit curve for the economy made up of Lisa and Max. Lisa's marginal benefit from each satellite gets added to Max's marginal benefit from each satellite because they *both* consume the services of each satellite.

Figure 16.2

Benefits of a Public Good

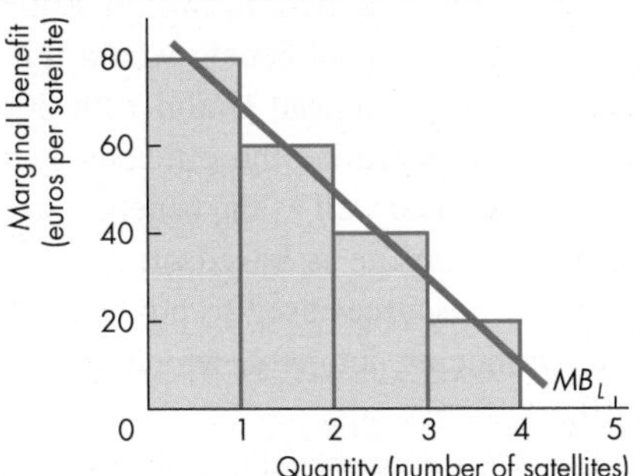

(a) Lisa's marginal benefit

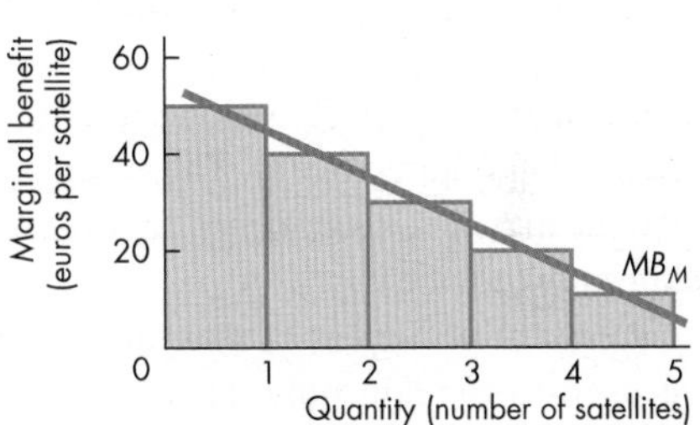

(b) Max's marginal benefit

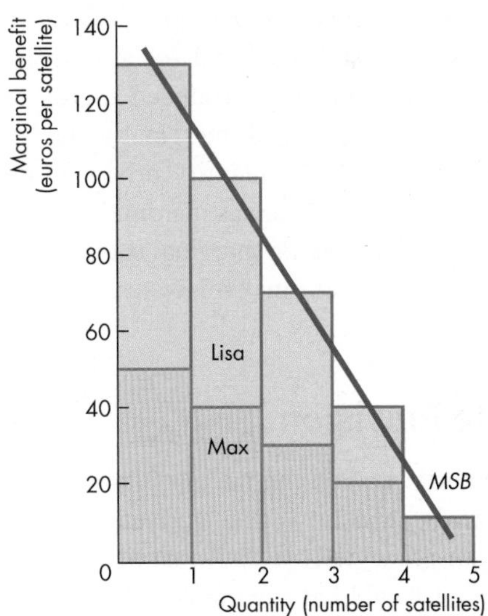

(c) Economy's marginal social benefit

The marginal social benefit at each quantity of the public good is the sum of the marginal benefits of all individuals. The marginal benefit curves are MB_L for Lisa and MB_M for Max. The economy's marginal social benefit curve is *MSB*.

The Efficient Quantity of a Public Good

An economy with two people would not buy any satellites – because the total benefit would fall far short of the cost. But the European Union with 300 million people might. To determine the efficient quantity, we need to take the cost as well as the benefit into account.

The cost of a satellite is based on technology and the prices of the resources used to produce it (just like the cost of producing jumpers, which you studied in Chapter 10).

Figure 16.3 sets out the benefits and costs. The second and third columns of the table show the total and marginal benefits. The next two columns show the total and marginal costs of producing satellites. The final column shows the net benefit – total benefit minus total cost.

The total benefit curve, *TB*, and the total cost curve, *TC*, are graphed in Figure 16.3(a). The efficient quantity is the one that maximizes *net benefit* and occurs when two satellites are provided.

The fundamental principles of marginal analysis that you have used to explain how consumers maximize utility and how firms maximize profit can also be used to calculate the efficient scale of provision of a public good. Figure 16.3(b) shows this alternative approach. The marginal social benefit curve is *MSB*, and the marginal social cost curve is *MSC*. When marginal social benefit exceeds marginal social cost, net benefit increases if the quantity produced increases. When marginal social cost exceeds marginal social benefit, net benefit increases if the quantity produced decreases. Marginal social benefit equals marginal social cost with two satellites. So making marginal social cost equal to marginal social benefit maximizes net benefit and uses resources efficiently.

Private Provision

We have now worked out the quantity of satellites that maximizes net benefit. Would a private firm – Eurozone Protection plc – deliver that quantity? It would not. To do so, it would have to collect €15 billion to cover its costs – or €50 from each of the 300 million people in the European Union. But no one would have an incentive to buy his or her "share" of the satellite system. Everyone would reason as follows. The number of satellites provided by Eurozone Protection is not affected by my €50. But my own private consumption is greater if I free ride and do not pay my share of the cost of the satellite system. If I do not pay, I enjoy the same level of security and I can buy more private goods. Therefore I will spend my €50 on other goods and free ride on the public good. This is the free-rider problem.

If everyone reasons the same way, Eurozone Protection has zero revenue and so provides no satellites. Because two satellites is the efficient level, private provision is inefficient.

Public Provision

Suppose there are two political parties, the Blues and the Greens, and they agree with each other on all issues except for the quantity of satellites. The Blues would like to provide 4 satellites. Figure 16.3(a) show that with 4 satellites, total cost is €50 billion, total benefit is €50 billion and net benefit is zero. The Greens would like to provide 1 satellite. Figure 16.3(a) shows that with 1 satellite, total cost is €5 billion, total benefit is €20 billion and net benefit is €15 billion.

Before deciding on their policy proposals, the two political parties do a "what-if" analysis. Each party reasons as follows. If each party offers the satellite programme it wants – the Blues 4 satellites and Greens 1 satellite – the voters will see that they will get a net benefit of €15 billion from the Greens and zero net benefit from the Blues. The Greens will win the election.

Contemplating this outcome, the Blues realize that they are too blue to get elected. They must scale back their proposal to 2 satellites. Figure 16.3(a) shows that with 2 satellites, total cost is €15 billion, total benefit is €35 billion, and net benefit is €20 billion. So if the Greens stick with 1 satellite, the Blues will win the election.

Contemplating this outcome, the Greens realize that they must match the Blues. They too propose to provide 2 satellites. If the two parties offer the same number of satellites, the voters are indifferent between the parties. They flip coins to decide their votes, and each party receives around 50 per cent of the vote.

The result of the politicians' "what-if" analysis is that each party offers 2 satellites, so regardless of who wins the election, this is the quantity of satellites installed. This quantity is efficient. It maximizes the perceived net benefit of the voters. In this example, competition in the political marketplace results in the efficient provision of a public good. But for the efficient outcome to occur, voters must be well informed and evaluate the alternatives. As you will see below, they do not always have an incentive to achieve this outcome.

Figure 16.3

The Efficient Quantity of a Public Good

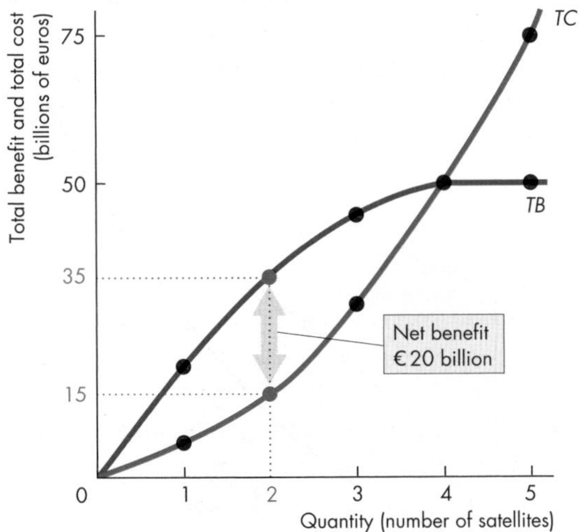

(a) Total benefit and total cost

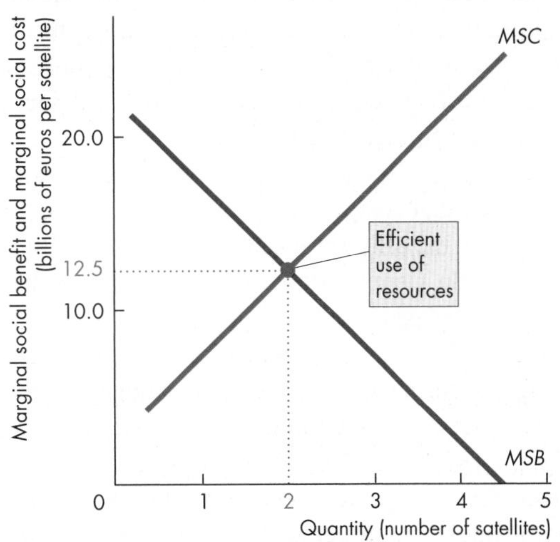

(b) Marginal social benefit and marginal social cost

Quantity (number of satellites)	Total benefit (billions of euros)	Marginal social benefit (billions of euros per satellite)	Total cost (billions of euros)	Marginal social cost (billions of euros per satellite)	Net benefit (billions of euros)
0	0		0		0
		20		5	
1	20		5		15
		15		10	
2	**35**		**15**		**20**
		10		15	
3	45		30		15
		5		20	
4	50		50		0
		0		25	
5	50		75		–25

Net benefit – the vertical distance between total benefit, *TB*, and total cost, *TC* – is maximized when 2 satellites are installed in part (a) and where marginal social benefit, *MSB*, equals marginal social cost, *MSC* in part (b).

The Greens would like 1 satellite, and the Blues would like 4. But each party recognizes that is its only hope of being elected is to provide 2 satellites – the quantity that maximizes net benefit.

The Principle of Minimum Differentiation

In the example we've just studied, both parties propose identical policies. This tendency towards identical policies is an example of the **principle of minimum differentiation**, which is the tendency for competitors to make themselves similar so as to appeal to the maximum number of clients or voters. This principle not only describes the behaviour of political parties, but also explains why fast-food restaurants cluster in the same block and even why new models of cars have similar features. If McDonald's opens a restaurant in a new location, it is likely that Burger King will open next door to McDonald's rather than a mile down the road. If Chrysler designs a new van with a sliding door on the driver's side, most likely Ford will too.

The Role of Civil Servants

We have analyzed the behaviour of politicians but not that of the civil servants who translate the choices of the politicians into programmes and who control the day-to-day activities that deliver public goods. Let's now see how the economic choices of civil servants influence the political equilibrium.

To do so, we'll stick with the previous example. We've seen that competition between two political parties delivers the efficient quantity of satellites. But will the European Commission's civil servants cooperate and accept this outcome?

Suppose the EU Directorate General for Defence's objective is to maximize the defence budget. With two satellites being provided at minimum cost, the defence budget is €15 billion (see Figure 16.3). To increase its budget, the Directorate General might do two things. First, it might try to persuade the politicians that two satellites cost more than €15 billion. As Figure 16.4 shows, if possible, the Directorate General would like to convince Parliament that two satellites cost €35 billion – the entire benefit. Second, and pressing its position even more strongly, the Directorate General might argue for more satellites. It might press for four satellites and a budget of €50 billion. In this situation, total benefit and total cost are equal and net benefit is zero.

The Directorate General wants to maximize its budget, but won't the politicians prevent it from doing so because the Directorate General's preferred outcome costs votes? They will if voters are well informed and know what is best for them. But voters might be rationally ignorant. In this case, well-informed interest groups might enable the Directorate General to achieve its objective.

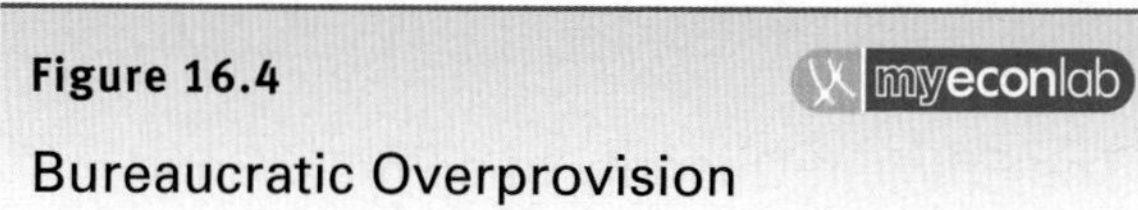

Figure 16.4

myeconlab

Bureaucratic Overprovision

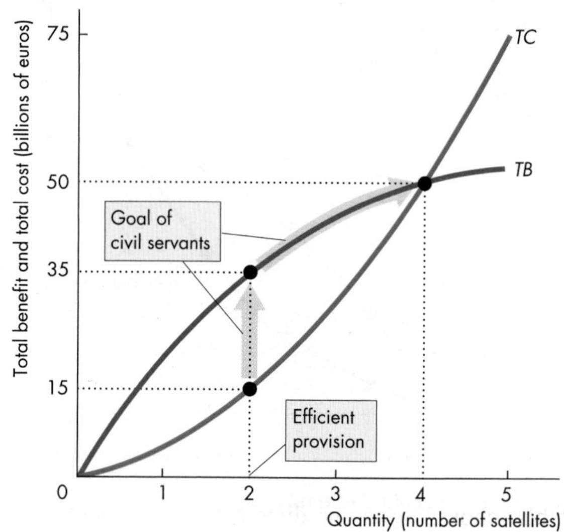

The goal of civil servants is to maximize the department's budget. A department that maximizes its budget will seek to increase its budget until its total cost equals total benefit. Then it will use its budget and expenditure. Here the EU Directorate General of Defence tries to get €35 billion to provide satellites. It would like to increase the quantity of satellites to four with a budget of €50 billion.

Rational Ignorance

A principle of public choice theory is that it is rational for a voter to be ignorant about an issue unless that issue has a perceptible effect on the voter's income. **Rational ignorance** is the decision *not* to acquire information because the cost of doing so exceeds the expected benefit. For example, each voter knows that he or she can make virtually no difference to the defence policy of the EU government. Each voter also knows that it would take an enormous amount of time and effort to become even moderately well informed about alternative defence technologies. So voters remain relatively uninformed about the technicalities of defence issues. (Though we are using defence policy as an example, the same applies to all aspects of government economic activity.)

All voters are consumers of national defence. But not all voters are producers of national defence. Only a small number are in this latter category. Voters who own or work for firms that produce satellites have a direct personal interest in defence because it affects their incomes. These voters have an incentive to become well informed about defence issues and to operate a political lobby aimed at furthering their own interests. In collaboration with the defence bureaucracy, these voters exert a larger influence than do the relatively uninformed voters who only consume this public good.

When the rationality of the uninformed voter and special interest groups are taken into account, the political equilibrium provides public goods in excess of the efficient quantity. So in the satellite example, three or four satellites might be installed rather than the efficient quantity, which is two satellites.

Two Types of Political Equilibrium

We've seen that two types of political equilibrium are possible: efficient and inefficient. These two types of political equilibrium correspond to two theories of government:

- Social interest theory
- Public choice theory

Social Interest Theory

Social interest theory predicts that governments make choices that achieve efficiency. This outcome occurs in a perfect political system in which voters are fully informed about the effects of policies and refuse to vote for outcomes that can be improved upon.

Public Choice Theory

Public choice theory predicts that governments make choices that result in inefficiency. This outcome occurs in political markets in which voters are rationally ignorant and base their votes only on issues that they know affect their own net benefit. Voters pay more attention to their interests as producers than their interests as consumers, and public officials also act in their own best interest. The result is *government failure* that parallels market failure.

Why Government Is Large and Grows

Now that we know how the quantity of public goods is determined, we can explain part of the reason for the growth of government. Government grows in part because the demand for some public goods increases at a faster rate than the demand for private goods. There are two possible reasons for this growth:

- Voter preferences
- Inefficient overprovision

Voter Preferences

The growth of government can be explained by voter preferences in the following way. As voters' incomes increase (as they do in most years), the demand for many public goods increases more quickly than income. (Technically, the *income elasticity of demand* for many public goods is greater than 1 – see Chapter 4, p. 90.) These goods include public health, education, national defence, highways and air-traffic control systems. If politicians did not support increases in expenditures on these items, they would not get elected.

Inefficient Overprovision

Inefficient overprovision might explain the size of government but not its growth rate. It (possibly) explains why government is larger than its efficient scale, but it does not explain why governments use an increasing proportion of total resources.

Voters Strike Back

If government grows too large relative to the value that voters place on public goods, there might be a voter backlash against government programmes and a large bureaucracy. Electoral success during the 1990s required politicians of all parties to embrace smaller, leaner and more efficient government. The September 11 attacks have led to a greater willingness to pay for security but have probably not lessened the desire for lean government.

Another way in which voters – and politicians – can try to counter the tendency of civil servants to expand their budgets is to privatize the production of public goods. Government *provision* of a public good does not automatically imply that a government-operated department must *produce* the good. Prisons are a public good and experiments are being conducted with private prisons in the United Kingdom. Garbage collection is often done by a private firm.

Review Quiz

Study Plan 16.2

1. What is the free-rider problem and why does it make the private provision of a public good inefficient?
2. Under what conditions will competition for votes among politicians result in an efficient quantity of a public good?
3. How do rationally ignorant voters and budget-maximizing civil servants prevent competition in the political marketplace from producing the efficient quantity of a public good? Do they result in too much or too little public provision of public goods?

You've seen how public goods create a free-rider problem that would result in the underprovision of such goods. We're now going to learn about common resources and see why they result in the opposite problem – the overuse of such resources.

Common Resources

North Sea cod stocks have been declining since the 1950s and some marine biologists fear that this species is in danger of becoming extinct in some regions. The whale population has been declining also and some groups are lobbying to establish a whale sanctuary in the waters south of Australia and New Zealand. Since the start of the Industrial Revolution in 1750, the concentration of carbon dioxide in the atmosphere has steadily increased and it is estimated to be about 30 per cent higher today than it was in 1750.

These situations involve common property, and the problem that we have identified is called the tragedy of the commons.

The Tragedy of the Commons

The *tragedy of the commons* is the absence of incentives to prevent the overuse and depletion of a commonly owned resource. If no one owns a resource, no one considers the effects of her or his use of the resource on others.

The Original Tragedy of the Commons

The term "tragedy of the commons" comes from fourteenth century England where areas of rough grassland surrounded villages. The commons were open to all and used for grazing cows and sheep owned by the villagers.

Because the commons were open to all, no one had an incentive to ensure that the land was not over grazed. The result was a severe over-grazing situation. Because the commons were over grazed, the quantity of cows and sheep that they could feed kept on falling.

During the sixteenth century, the price of wool increased and England became a wool exporter to the world. Sheep farming became profitable and sheep owners wanted to gain more effective control of the land they used. So the commons were gradually enclosed and privatized. Overgrazing ended and land use became more efficient.

A Tragedy of the Commons Today

One of today's pressing tragedies of the commons is overfishing. Several fish species have been seriously over fished, and one of them is Atlantic Cod.

To study the tragedy of the commons, we'll use the Atlantic Cod as an example.

Sustainable Production

Sustainable production is the rate of production that can be maintained indefinitely. In the case of ocean fish, the sustainable rate of production is the quantity of fish (of a given species) that can be caught each year into the indefinite future.

This production rate depends on the existing stock of fish and the number of boats that go fishing. For a given stock of fish, sending more boats to sea increases the quantity of fish caught. But sending too many boats to sea depletes the stock. So as the number of boats increases, the quantity of fish caught increases as long as the stock is maintained. But above some crucial level, as more boats go fishing, the stock of fish decreases and the number of fish caught also decreases.

Table 16.1 illustrates the relationship between the number of boats that go fishing and the quantity of fish caught. The numbers in this example are hypothetical.

Table 16.1

Sustainable Production: Total, Average and Marginal Catch

	Boats (thousands)	Total catch (thousands of tonnes)	Average catch (tonnes per boat)	Marginal catch (tonnes per boat)
A	0	0		
				90
B	1	90	90	
				70
C	2	160	80	
				50
D	3	210	70	
				30
E	4	240	60	
				10
F	5	250	50	
				−10
G	6	240	40	
				−30
H	7	210	30	
				−50
I	8	160	20	
				−70
J	9	90	10	
				−90
K	10	0	0	

As the number of fishing boats increases, the quantity of fish caught increases up to the maximum sustainable catch and then decreases. The average catch and marginal catch decrease as the number of boats increases.

Total Catch

The total catch is the sustainable rate of production. The numbers in the first two columns of Table 16.1 show the relationship between the number of fishing boats and the total catch, and Figure 16.5 illustrates this relationship.

You can see that as the number of boats increases from zero to 5,000, the sustainable catch increases to a maximum of 250,000 tonnes a month. As the number of boats increases above 5,000, the sustainable catch begins to decrease. By the time 10,000 boats are fishing, the fish stock is depleted to the point at which no fish can be caught.

With more than 5,000 boats, there is overfishing. Overfishing arises if the number of boats increases to the point at which the fish stock begins to fall and the remaining fish are harder to find and catch.

Average Catch

The average catch is the catch per boat and equals the total catch divided by the number of boats. The numbers in the third column of Table 16.1 show the average catch. With 1,000 boats, the total catch is 90,000 tonnes and the catch per boat is 90 tonnes. With 2,000 boats, the total catch is 160,000 tonnes, and the catch per boat 80 tonnes. As more boats take to the ocean, the catch per boat decreases. By the time 8,000 boats are fishing, each boat is catching just 20 tonnes a month.

The decreasing average catch is an example of the principle of diminishing returns.

Marginal Catch

The marginal catch is the change in the total catch that occurs when one more boat joins the existing number. It is calculated as the change in the total catch divided by the increase in the number of boats. The numbers in the fourth column of Table 16.1 show the marginal catch.

For example, in rows *C* and *D* of the table, when the number of boats increases by 1,000, the catch increases by 50,000 tonnes, so the increase in the catch per boat equals 50 tonnes. In the table, we place this amount mid-way between the two rows because it is the marginal catch at 2,500 boats, mid-way between the two levels that we used to calculate it.

Notice that the marginal catch, like the average catch, decreases as the number of boats increases and also that the marginal catch is always less than the average catch.

When the number of boats reaches that at which the sustainable catch is a maximum, the marginal catch is zero. At a larger number of boats, the marginal catch becomes negative – more boats decrease the total catch.

Figure 16.5 myeconlab

Sustainable Production of Fish

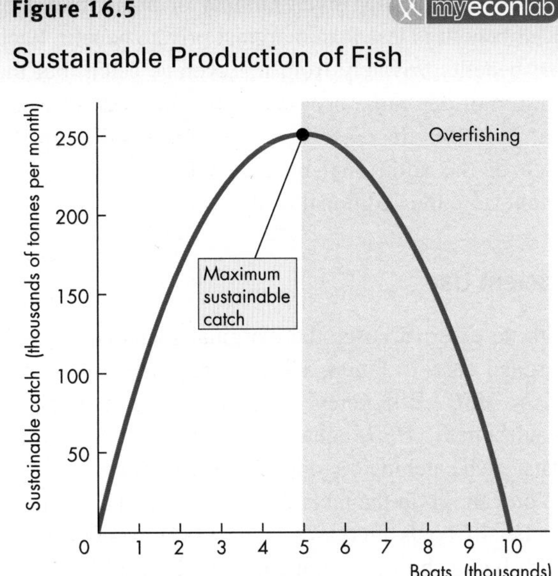

As the number of boats increases, the sustainable catch increases up to a maximum. Beyond that number, more boats will diminish the fish stock and the sustainable catch decreases. Overfishing occurs when the maximum sustainable catch decreases.

An Overfishing Equilibrium

The tragedy of the commons is that common resources are overused. Why might the fish stock be overused? Why might overfishing occur? Why isn't the maximum number of boats that take to the sea the number that maximizes the sustainable catch – 5,000 in this example?

To answer this question, we need to look at the marginal cost and marginal private benefit to an individual boat owner.

Suppose that the marginal cost of a fishing boat is the equivalent of 20 tonnes of fish a month. That is, to cover the opportunity cost of maintaining and operating a boat, the boat must catch 20 tonnes of fish a month. This quantity of fish also provides the boat owner with normal profit (part of the cost of operating the boat), so the boat owner is willing to go fishing.

The marginal private benefit of operating a boat is the quantity of fish that the boat can catch. This quantity is the average catch that we've just calculated.

The average catch is the marginal private benefit because that is the quantity of fish that the boat owner gets by taking the boat to sea.

The boat owner will go fishing as long as the average catch (marginal private benefit) exceeds the marginal cost. And the boat owner will maximize profit when marginal private benefit equals marginal cost.

Figure 16.6 shows the marginal cost curve, *MC*, and the marginal private benefit curve, *MB*. The marginal private benefit curve is based on the numbers for the average catch in Table 16.1.

You can see in Figure 16.6 that with fewer than 8,000 boats, each boat catches more fish than it costs to catch them. Because boat owners can gain from fishing, the number of boats is 8,000 and there is an overfishing equilibrium.

If one boat owner stopped fishing, the overfishing would be less severe. But that boat owner would be giving up an opportunity to make an economic profit.

The self-interest of the boat owner is to fish, but the social interest is to limit fishing. The quantity of fish caught by each boat decreases as additional boats go fishing. But when individual boat owners are deciding whether to fish, they ignore this decrease. They consider only the marginal *private* benefit. The result is an *inefficient* overuse of the resource.

Figure 16.6 myeconlab

Why Overfishing Occurs

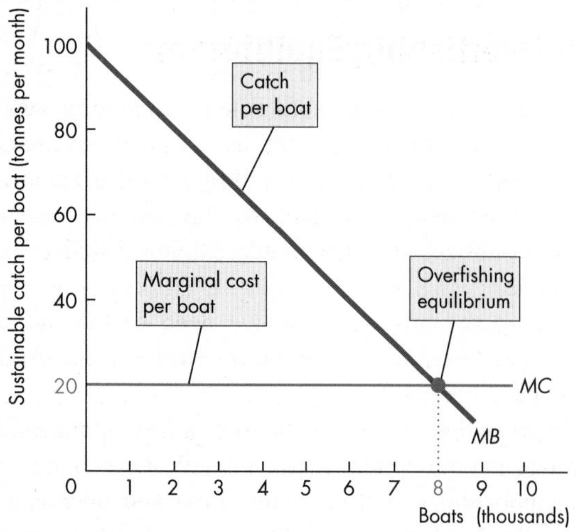

The average catch decreases as the number of boats increases. The average catch per boat is the marginal private benefit, *MB*, of a boat. The marginal cost of a boat is equivalent to 20 tonnes of fish, shown by the curve *MC*. The equivalent number of boats is 8,000 – an overfishing equilibrium.

The Efficient Use of the Commons

What is the efficient use of a common resource? It is the use of the resource that makes the marginal cost of using the resource equal to the marginal *social* benefit from its use.

Marginal Social Benefit

The marginal *social* benefit of a boat is the boat's marginal catch – the increase in the total catch that results from an additional boat. The reason is that when an additional boat puts to sea, it catches the average catch but it decreases the average catch for itself and for every other boat. The *marginal social benefit* is the *increase* in the quantity of fish caught, not the average number of fish caught.

We calculated the marginal catch in Table 16.1 and we repeat part of that table for convenience in Figure 16.7. This figure also shows the marginal private benefit curve, *MB*, and the marginal social benefit curve, *MSB*.

Notice that at any given number of boats, marginal social benefit is less than marginal private benefit. Each boat benefits privately from the average catch, but the addition of one more boat *decreases* the catch of every boat, and this decrease must be subtracted from the catch of the additional boat to determine the social benefit from the additional boat.

Efficient Use

With no external costs, the marginal social cost equals marginal cost. In Figure 16.7, the marginal cost curve, *MC* = *MSC*. Efficiency is achieved when marginal social benefit, *MSB*, equals marginal cost, *MC*: 4,000 boats, each catching 60 tonnes of fish a month.

You can see in the table in Figure 16.7 that when the number of boats increases from 3,000 to 4,000 (with 3,500 being the mid-point), marginal social benefit is 30 tonnes, which exceeds marginal social cost. When the number of boats increases from 4,000 to 5,000 (with 4,500 being the mid-point), marginal social benefit is 10 tonnes, which is less than marginal social cost. At 4,000 boats, marginal social benefit is 20 tonnes, which equals marginal social cost.

Figure 16.7

myeconlab

Efficient Use of a Common Resource

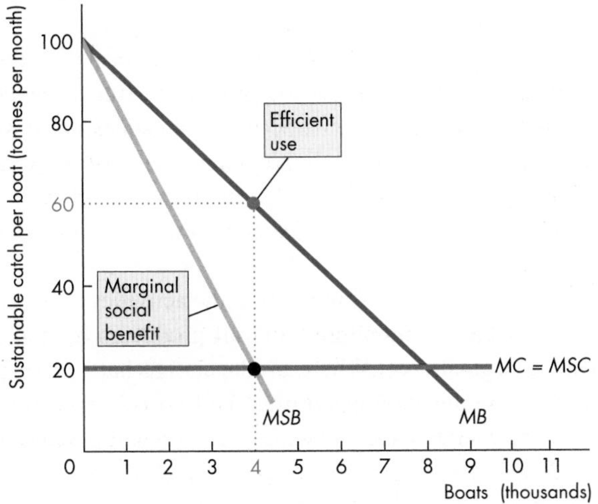

	Boats (thousands)	Total catch (thousands of tonnes)	Marginal private benefit (tonnes per boat)	Marginal social benefit (tonnes per boat)
A	0	0		
				90
B	1	90	90	
				70
C	2	160	80	
				5
D	3	210	70	
				30
E	4	240	60	
				10
F	5	250	50	

The marginal social benefit of a fishing boat is the change in total benefit that results from an additional boat. The table shows that when the number of boats increases from 2,000 to 3,000 (from row *C* to row *D*), the total catch increases from 160,000 to 210,000 tonnes a month and marginal catch and marginal social benefit is 50 tonnes.

The graph shows the marginal social benefit curve, *MSB*, and the marginal private benefit curve, *MB*. Marginal social benefit is less than marginal private benefit and decreases as the number of boats increases. The efficient quantity of boats is that at which marginal social benefit equals marginal social cost and is 4,000. The common resource is used efficiently.

Achieving an Efficient Outcome

Defining the conditions under which a common resource is used efficiently is easier than bringing those conditions about. To use a common resource efficiently, it is necessary to design an incentive mechanism that confronts users of the resource with the marginal social consequences of their actions. The same principles apply to common resources as those that you met when you studied externalities in Chapter 15.

Three main methods might be used to achieve the efficient use of a common resource. They are:

- Property rights
- Quotas
- Individual transferable quotas (ITQs)

Property Rights

A common resource that no one owns and that anyone is free to use contrasts with *private property*, which is a resource that *someone* owns and has an incentive to use in the way that maximizes its value. One way of overcoming the tragedy of the commons is to remove the commons and make the resource private property. By assigning private property rights, each owner faces the same conditions as society faces. The *MSB* curve of Figure 16.7 becomes the marginal *private* benefit curve, and the use of the resource is efficient.

The private property solution to the tragedy of the commons *is* available in some cases. It was the solution to the original tragedy of the commons in England's Middle Ages. It is also a solution that has been used to prevent the airwaves that we use to carry our mobile phone messages from being overused. The right to use this space – called the frequency spectrum – has been auctioned by governments to the highest bidders, and the owner of a particular part of the spectrum is the only one allowed to use it (or license someone else to use it).

But assigning private property rights is not always feasible. It would be difficult, for example, to assign private property rights to the oceans. It would not be impossible, but the cost of enforcing private property rights over thousands of square miles of ocean would be high. And it would be even harder to assign and protect property rights to the atmosphere.

In some cases, there is an emotional objection to assigning private property rights. When private property rights are too costly to assign and enforce, some form of government intervention is used and quotas are the simplest.

Quotas

You studied the effects of a quota in Chapter 6 (p. 134) and learned that a quota can drive a wedge between marginal social benefit and marginal social cost and create deadweight loss. But in that earlier example, the market was efficient without a quota. In the case of the use of common property, the market is inefficient and is overproducing. So a quota that limits production can bring a move towards a more efficient outcome.

Figure 16.8 shows a quota that achieves an efficient use of a common resource. A quota is set for total production at the quantity at which marginal social benefit equals marginal social cost. Here, that quantity is what 4,000 boats can catch. Individual boat owners are assigned their own share of the total permitted catch. If everyone sticks to the assigned quota, the outcome is efficient.

There are two problems in implementing a quota. First, it is in everyone's self-interest to cheat and use more of a common resource than the amount based on the assigned quota. The reason is that marginal private benefit exceeds marginal cost. So by catching more than the allocated quota, each boat owner gets a higher income. If everyone breaks the quota, overproduction returns and the tragedy of the commons remains.

Second, marginal cost is not, in general, the same for every producer. Some producers have a comparative advantage in using a resource.

Efficiency requires that the quotas are allocated to the producers with the lowest marginal cost. But the government department that allocates quotas does not possess information about individual marginal cost. Even if the government tried to get this information, producers would have an incentive to lie about their costs in order to get a bigger quota.

So a quota can work, but only if the activities of every producer can be monitored and all producers have the same marginal cost. Where producers are hard or very costly to monitor or where marginal costs vary across producers, a quota cannot achieve an efficient outcome.

Figure 16.8 myeconlab

Using a Quota to Use a Common Resource Efficiently

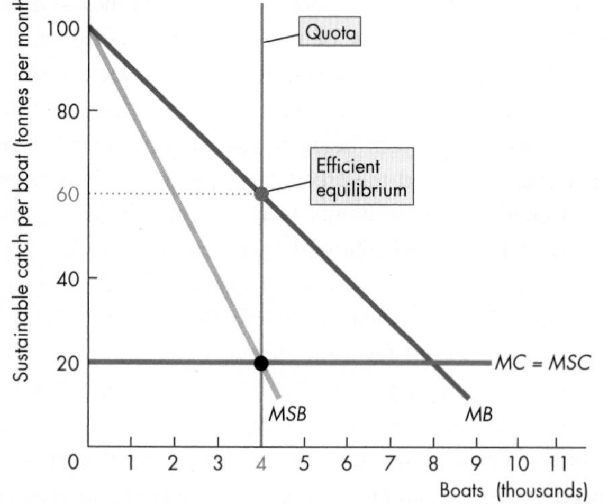

A quota is set at the efficient quantity, which makes the number of boats equal to the quantity at which marginal social benefit, *MSB*, equals marginal cost, *MC*. If the quota is enforced, the outcome is efficient.

Individual Transferable Quotas

Where producers are hard to monitor and where marginal costs differ across producers, a more sophisticated quota system can be used. An **individual transferable quota (ITQ)** is a production limit that is assigned to an individual who is free to transfer the quota to someone else. A market in ITQs emerges and ITQs are transferred at their market price.

Figure 16.9 shows how ITQs work. In the market for ITQs, the price is the highest price that an ITQ is worth. If the number of ITQs issued equals the efficient production level, then the price of an ITQ will equal the amount shown in the figure. This price equals the marginal private benefit at the quota quantity minus the private marginal cost of using a boat. The price rises to this level because people who don't have an ITQ would be willing to pay this amount to acquire the right to fish. And people who do own an ITQ could sell it for this price, so not to sell it is to incur an opportunity cost. The result is that the marginal cost, which now includes the price of the ITQ, rises from MC_1 to MC_2. The outcome is efficient.

Individual differences in marginal cost do not prevent an ITQ system from delivering the efficient outcome. Producers that have a low marginal cost are willing and able to pay more for a quota than are producers that have a high marginal cost. The market price of a quota will equal the marginal cost of the marginal producer at the efficient quantity. Producers with higher marginal costs will not produce.

Figure 16.9

Individual Transferable Quotas to Use a Common Resource Efficiently

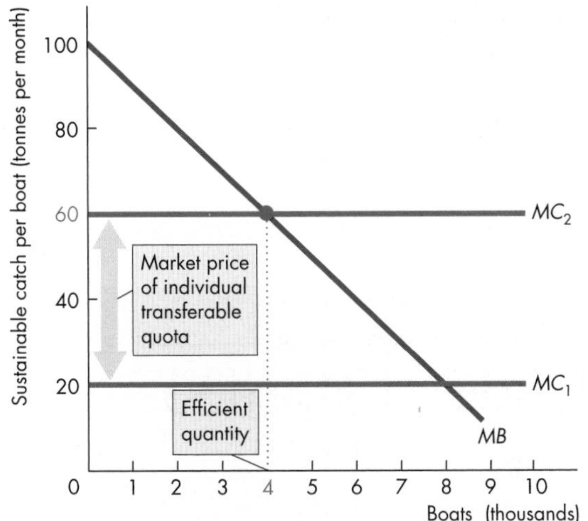

ITQs are issued on a scale that keeps output at the efficient level, the quantity of fish that 4,000 boats can catch. The market price of an ITQ equals the marginal private benefit minus marginal cost. With 4,000 boats, the marginal private benefit is 60 tonnes and the marginal cost is 20 tonnes of fish plus the price of the ITQ. So the price of an ITQ is 40 tonnes of fish. Because each user of the common resource faces the opportunity cost of using the resource, self-interest achieves the social interest.

Public Choice and the Political Equilibrium

You saw in the previous part of this chapter where we studied the provision of public goods that a political equilibrium might be inefficient – that there might be government failure.

This same political outcome might arise in the face of a tragedy of the commons. Defining an efficient allocation of resources and designing an ITQ system to achieve that allocation is not sufficient to ensure that the political process delivers the efficient outcome. In the case of the wild ocean fish stock, some countries have achieved an efficient political equilibrium, but not all have done so.

There is wide agreement among economists that ITQs offer the most effective tool for dealing with overfishing and achieving an efficient use of the stock of ocean fish. So a political commitment to ITQs is an efficient outcome and an unwillingness to use ITQs is an inefficient political outcome.

Australia and New Zealand have introduced ITQs to conserve fish stocks in the South Pacific Ocean. The evidence from these examples suggests that ITQs work well. Fishing boat operators have an incentive to cheat and produce more than the amount for which they have a quota. But such cheating seems to be relatively rare. And producers that have paid for a quota have an incentive to monitor and report on cheating by others who have not paid the market price for a quota.

So ITQs do the job they are designed to do: help to maintain fish stocks. But they also reduce the size of the fishing industry. This consequence of ITQs puts them against the self-interest of fishers.

In all countries, the fishing industry opposes restrictions on its activities. But in Australia and New Zealand, the opposition is not strong enough to block ITQs. In contrast, in the United States the opposition is so strong that the fishing industry has persuaded Congress to outlaw ITQs. In 1996, the US Congress passed the Sustainable Fishing Act that puts a moratorium on ITQs. The result of this act is that earlier attempts to introduce ITQs in the Gulf of Mexico and the Northern Pacific have been abandoned.

Review Quiz

Study Plan 16.3

1. What is the tragedy of the commons?
2. Provide two examples of the tragedy of the commons, including one from your own neighbourhood.
3. Describe the conditions under which a common resource is used efficiently.
4. Review three methods that might achieve the efficient use of a common resource and explain the obstacles to efficiency.

Reading Between the Lines on pp. 372–373 looks at the overuse of tropical rainforests.

The next chapter examines the third big question – for whom are goods and services produced? We examine the markets for factors of production and discover how wage rates and other incomes are determined.

Reading Between the Lines

Rainforests: A Tragedy of the Commons

The Times, 19 December 2006

Surprises in the wild side of Borneo

Lewis Smith and Lucy Alexander

. . . Borneo, the world's third largest island, has some of the richest animal habitats on the planet – and much of its inaccessible rainforest has yet to be explored.

Scientists expect that thousands more species are still to be identified and studied, according to a report published today by WWF [formerly known as the World Wildlife Fund], the world's largest independent conservation organisation.

From July 2005 to September 2006, 52 animals and plants were newly identified, according to WWF, many within a 136,000 square mile mountainous region known as the Heart of Borneo. . . .

WWF reported in April last year that at least 361 species had been newly identified on the island between 1994 and 2004, a rate of three animals and plants a month.

Conservationists are trying to protect the Heart of Borneo area from loggers who clear vast swaths of forest for rubber, oil palm and pulp production. The average rate of deforestation in Indonesia is 2 million hectares per year. Only half of Borneo's original forest cover remains today.

In March the three national Governments that split Borneo between them – Brunei Darussalam, Indonesia and Malaysia – promised to support conservation in the Heart of Borneo, but have yet to make a formal declaration. . . .

The Essence of the Story

- Clearing Borneo's rainforest to produce rubber, oil palm and pulp is destroying the planet's richest habitat for animals and plants.
- Newly identified animals and plants are being discovered at the rate of 3 per month.
- But only half of Borneo's original forest remains and it is disappearing at a rapid rate.

Economic Analysis

- The tropical rainforests of Borneo grow valuable rubber, palm oil and timber. These forests are also home to many rare species and provide a carbon-dioxide sink that helps maintain the earth's atmosphere.
- The forests are common property but their use is subject to the laws and international agreements.
- The private incentive to exploit these forest resources is strong. And because no one owns the forests, there is no incentive to conserve the resources and use them on a sustainable basis.
- The situation is worsened by the fact that three national governments are involved.
- The result is overuse, just like the overuse of the commons of England in the Middle Ages.
- The figures illustrate the tragedy of the commons in a tropical rainforest.
- Figure 1 shows the relationship between the sustainable production of wood from a rainforest and the number of lumber producers working the forest.
- Figure 2 shows the marginal benefit and marginal cost of a producer and the marginal social benefit and social cost.
- The marginal cost of felling a tree incurred by a producer is assumed to be zero.
- As a common resource, the marginal benefit received by a producer is *MB* and *LD* producers acting in their self-interest deplete the resource. Sustainable production falls to zero.
- As a privately owned resource, the marginal social benefit curve, *MSB*, becomes the marginal private benefit curve. Self-interest results in *LP* producers who maximize the sustainable output of the rainforest.
- If the only benefit from the rainforest were its timber, maximum sustainable timber output would be efficient.

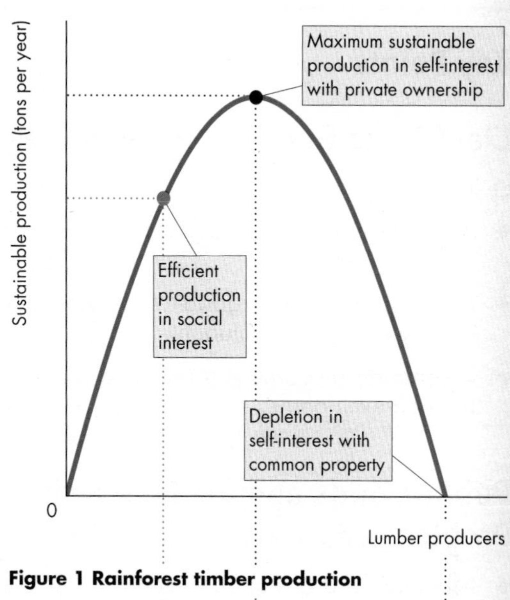

Figure 1 Rainforest timber production

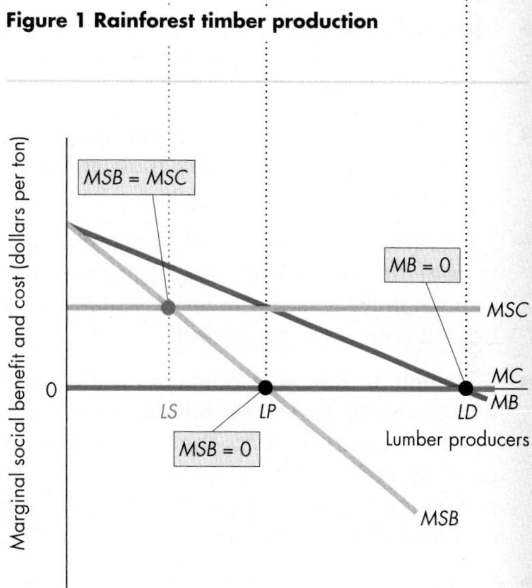

Figure 2 Marginal benefits and marginal costs

- But external benefits arise from the diversity of the wildlife supported by the forest, so marginal social cost exceeds the zero marginal private cost.
- Production in the social interest – the efficient level of production – is achieved with *LS* producers and is less than the maximum sustainable production.

Summary

Key Points

Classifying Goods and Resources (p. 360)

- A private good is a good or service that is rival and excludable.
- A public good is a good or service that is non-rival and non-excludable.
- A common resource is a resource that is rival but non-excludable.

Public Goods and the Free-Rider Problem (pp. 361–365)

- A public good is a good or service that is consumed by everyone and that is *non-rival* and *non-excludable*.
- A public good creates a *free-rider problem*: no one has an incentive to pay their share of the cost of providing a public good.
- The efficient level of provision of a public good is that at which net benefit is maximized. Equivalently, it is the level at which marginal benefit equals marginal cost.
- Competition between political parties, each of which tries to appeal to the maximum number of voters, can lead to the efficient scale of provision of a public good and to both parties proposing the same policies – the principle of minimum differentiation.
- Civil servants try to maximize the department's budget, and if voters are rationally ignorant, producer interests might result in voting to support taxes that provide public goods in quantities that exceed those that maximize net benefit.

Common Resources (pp. 366–371)

- Common resources create the *tragedy of the commons* – no one has a private incentive to conserve the resources and use them at an efficient rate.
- A common resource is used to the point at which the marginal private benefit equals the marginal cost.
- A common resource might be used efficiently by creating a private property right, setting a quota or issuing individual transferable quotas.

Key Figures

Key Terms

Problems

Tests, Study Plan and Solutions* 

1 Classify each of the following items as excludable, non-excludable, rival, non-rival, a public good, a private good, or a common resource.

a Tower of London

b A Big Mac

c Forth Road Bridge

d The Pennine Way

e Air

f Police protection

g Footpaths

h Royal Mail

i FedEx

j The MyEconLab website

2 For each of the following goods, explain whether there is a free-rider problem. If there is no such problem, how is it avoided?

a New Year fireworks display

b M1

c Wireless Internet access in hotels

d Sharing downloaded music

e The public library in your city

3 You are provided with the following information about a sewage disposal system that a city of 1 million people is considering installing.

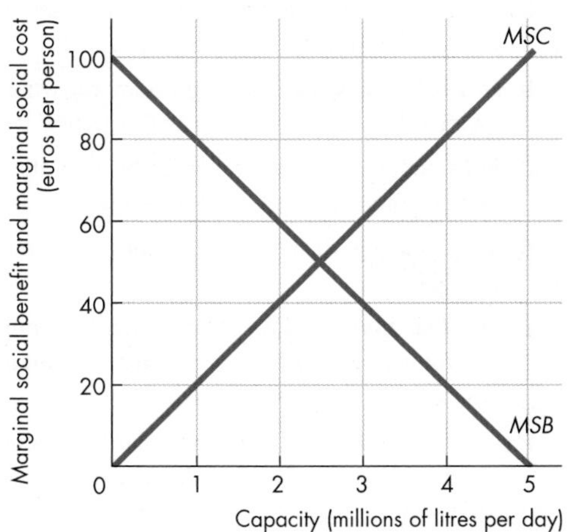

a What is the capacity that achieves maximum net benefit?

b How much will each person have to pay in taxes to pay for the efficient capacity level?

c What is the political equilibrium if voters are well informed?

d What is the political equilibrium if voters are rationally ignorant and civil servants achieve the highest attainable budget?

4 The table shows the value of cod caught in the North Atlantic Ocean by American and European fishing boats. It also shows the value that concerned citizens of America, Canada and Europe place on the Atlantic Cod stock. The marginal cost of operating a boat is €80,000 a month.

Number of boats	Value of cod caught (thousands of euros per month)
0	0
10	2,000
20	3,400
30	4,200
40	4,400
50	4,000
60	3,000
70	1,400

a What is the marginal private benefit of a fishing boat at each quantity of boats shown in the table?

b What is the marginal social benefit of a fishing boat at each quantity of boats shown in the table?

c With no regulation of cod fishing, what is the equilibrium number of boats and the value of cod caught?

d Is the equilibrium in part (c) an overfishing equilibrium?

e What is the efficient number of boats?

f What is the efficient value of the cod catch?

g Do you think that the consumers of fish and the fishing industry will agree about how much cod should be caught?

h If the European Union, the United States and Canada imposed a quota to limit the catch to the efficient quantity, what would be the total value of the catch under the quota?

i If the European Union, the United States and Canada issued ITQs to fishing boats to limit the catch to the efficient quantity, what would be the price of an ITQ?

* Solutions to odd-numbered problems are provided.

Critical Thinking

1 After you have studied *Reading Between the Lines* on pp. 372–373, answer the following questions:

a What is happening in the Heart of Borneo that is contributing to the depletion of the rainforest?

b How would the creation of private property rights in Borneo's rainforests change the way in which the forest resources are used?

c Would private ownership solve all the problems of resource overuse? If not, why not?

2 Your city council is contemplating upgrading its system for controlling traffic signals. The council believes that by installing computers, it can improve the speed of the traffic flow. The bigger the computer the council buys, the better job it can do. The mayor and the other elected officials who are working on the proposal want to determine the scale of the system that will win them the most votes. The city councillors want to maximize the budget. Suppose that you are an economist who is observing this public choice. Your job is to calculate the quantity of this public good that uses resources efficiently.

a What data would you need to reach your own conclusions?

b What does the public choice theory predict will be the quantity chosen?

c How could you, as an informed voter, attempt to influence the choice?

3 **Southern Africa bids for ivory sale**

. . . Five Southern African countries have launched a bid to be allowed to sell ivory, despite a ban . . . They are seeking permission to sell 80 tonnes of ivory, arguing that their game parks have too many elephants and [they] are not at risk of extinction . . . and say they should not be punished for their sound elephant-protection policies. . . . They argue that allowing elephants to "pay their way" by selling ivory is actually the best way of ensuring their survival in the long term.

BBC News, 9 October 2002

a When did the ban on ivory sales come into effect and why was it introduced?

b Will the sale of 80 tonnes of ivory encourage more or less poaching? Explain your answer.

c Explain what "elephants' paying their way" means.

d Do you agree that selling ivory is actually the best way of ensuring the survival of elephants in the long term? Explain why or why not.

Web Activities

Links to Websites

1 Visit Ed Clarke's Public Goods website and read his article on demand revealing processes.

a What is a demand revealing process and what is its purpose?

b Why might using a demand revealing process deliver a more efficient level of public goods than our current political system?

c Why might our current political system deliver a more efficient level of public goods than would a demand revealing process?

2 Visit the ITT Industries website and read the article on "The Rising Tide of Water Markets".

a What is the purpose of a water market?

b What do you think are the main advantages of the market mechanism as a means of allocating scarce water resources?

c What do you think are the main disadvantages of the market mechanism as a means of allocating scarce water resources?

d Why do you think we don't use the market mechanism more widely to allocate scarce water resources?

e Write a short executive summary of your view in using the market to allocate scarce water resources.

3 Visit the International Whaling Commission (IWC) website.

a What is the purpose of the IWC and when was the IWC established?

b In 1975, a new management policy for whales was adopted by the IWC. Describe this policy.

c How many countries are members of the IWC? Which countries as eligible to be come members?

d What was the disagreement among IWC members in 2007?

e Do you think the IWC is enhancing or hindering the long-term survival of whales? Explain your answer.

f Norway and Iceland are two European countries that have whaling fleets. What are their arguments in favour of whaling?

g Whale watching in South Africa is a great tourist attraction. Do you think this tourist activity is a danger to the whales or will it help the whale population to increase? Explain your answer.

h What is the IWC's policy on whale watching?

CHAPTER 17

The Markets for Factors of Production

After studying this chapter you will be able to:

- Explain the link between factor prices and factor incomes
- Explain what determines the wage rate and employment in a competitive labour market
- Explain how a trades union influences the wage rate and employment
- Explain what determines the interest rate and investment in the capital market
- Explain what determines the price and rate of use of a natural resource
- Explain the concept of economic rent and distinguish between economic rent and opportunity cost

Many Happy Returns

The returns we get from our work vary a lot. Julie Adams does vital work as a nurse for £16,000 a year, the Chief Executive of Xstrata earns £15 million a year and David Beckham earns £25 million playing football at LA Galaxy. Why are some jobs well paid and others not? How does a nurse who saves people's lives earn so much less than someone in business or entertainment? What determines the returns to other factors of production such as capital and natural resources? Find out in this chapter and learn about the price of oil in *Reading Between the Lines* at the end of the chapter.

Factor Prices and Incomes

Goods and services are produced by using the four factors of production – *labour*, *capital*, *land* and *entrepreneurship*. (These factors of production are defined in Chapter 1, pp. 5–6.) Incomes are determined by the quantities of the factors used and by factor prices. The factor prices are the *wage* rate earned by labour, the *interest* rate earned by capital, the *rental* rate earned by land and *the normal profit* rate earned by entrepreneurship.

In addition to the four factor incomes, a residual income *economic profit* (or *economic loss*) is earned (or borne) by the firm's owners, who might be the entrepreneur or the shareholders.

Factors of production, like goods and services, are traded in markets. Some factor markets are competitive and behave similarly to competitive markets for goods and services. Some labour market have non-competitive elements.

Demand and supply is the main tool used to understand a competitive factor market. Firms demand factors of production and households supply them.

The quantity demanded of a factor of production is the quantity that firms plan to employ during a given time period and at a given factor price. The law of demand applies to factors of production just as it does to goods and services. The lower the factor price, other things remaining the same, the greater is the quantity demanded of that factor. The demand for a factor of production is called a **derived demand** because it is *derived* from the demand for the goods and services produced by the factor.

The quantity supplied of a factor also depends on its price. With a possible exception that we'll identify later in this chapter, the law of supply applies to factors of production. The higher the price of a factor of production, other things remaining the same, the greater is the quantity supplied of the factor.

Figure 17.1 shows the market for a factor of production. The demand curve for the factor is the curve labelled *D*, and the supply curve of the factor is the curve labelled *S*. The equilibrium factor price is *PF*, and the equilibrium quantity is *QF*. The income earned by the factor is its price multiplied by the quantity used. In Figure 17.1, the factor income equals the area of the blue rectangle.

A change in demand or supply changes the equilibrium price, quantity and income. An increase in demand shifts the demand curve rightward and increases income. An increase in supply shifts the supply curve rightward and income might increase, decrease or remain constant depending on the elasticity of demand for the factor. If demand is elastic, income rises; if demand is inelastic, income falls; and if demand is unit elastic, income remains constant (see Chapter 4, p. 86).

Figure 17.1 myeconlab

Demand and Supply in a Factor Market

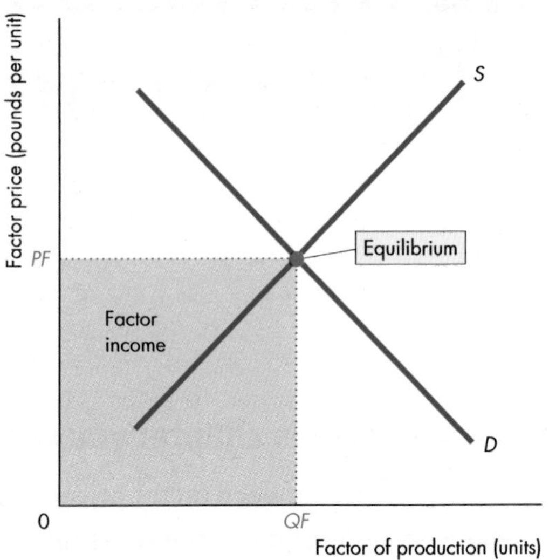

The demand curve for a factor of production (*D*) slopes downward, and the supply curve of a factor (*S*) slopes upward. Where the demand and supply curves intersect, the factor price (*PF*) and the quantity of a factor used (*QF*) are determined. The factor income is the product of the factor price and the quantity of the factor, as represented by the blue rectangle.

Review Quiz

Study Plan 17.1

1. Why do we call the demand for a factor of production a *derived demand*? From what is it derived?
2. Why does an increase in the supply of a factor of production have an ambiguous effect on the factor's income?

In the rest of this chapter, we explore the influences on the demand for and supply of factors of production. We begin with the market for labour.

Labour Markets

For most people, the labour market is the major source of income. And for many people, it is the only source of income. In a typical year, labour income represents around 55 per cent of total income in the United Kingdom.

Average weekly earnings of full-time employees before tax were £476 in 2003. Part-time employees earned £152 a week. These earnings average around £13 an hour.

The average earnings rate hides a lot of diversity across individual occupations. You can see some of that diversity in Box 17.1, which shows a sample of wage rates in the 10 highest paid and 10 lowest paid jobs in 2000. The numbers in the box don't contain any major surprises, but they do show some interesting facts, so spend a minute looking at them.

Earnings rise most years and bring rising living standards. In 2003, they rose by an average of around 2.5 per cent. Although the average wage rate rises, the distribution of wage rates around the average changes, and some wage rates rise rapidly while some even fall.

To understand what determines wage rates, why some are high and some are low, and why some rise and some fall, we must probe the forces that influence the demand for labour and the supply of labour.

We begin on the demand side of the labour market.

The Demand for Labour

There is a link between the quantity of labour that a firm employs and the quantity of output that it plans to produce. The *total product curve* shows that link (Chapter 10, p. 216). A consequence of this link is that a firm's demand for labour is the flip side of its supply of output. To produce more output in the short run, a firm must employ more labour. In the long run, a firm can increase its output by using more capital and does not necessarily have to employ more labour.

A firm tries to produce the quantity of output that maximizes profit. And the profit-maximizing output is that at which marginal revenue equals marginal cost. To produce the profit-maximizing output, a firm must employ the profit-maximizing quantity of labour.

What is the profit-maximizing quantity of labour? And how does it change as the wage rate changes? We can answer these questions by comparing the marginal revenue earned by employing one more worker with the marginal cost of that worker. Let's look first at the marginal revenue side of this comparison.

Box 17.1
The Diversity of UK Wage Rates

The most recent major survey of wage rates in the United Kingdom is for 2003. *Relative* wage rates don't change rapidly, so the 2003 data provide a good picture of the diversity of wage rates.

The lowest paid workers, a group that includes petrol pump attendants and hairdressers earned less than £6 an hour – less than half the average wage rate. At the other extreme, company financial officers and doctors earned £30 an hour. Figure 1 shows these and some other high-paid and low-paid jobs. Most people have jobs that lie between these groups. They include lorry drivers and school teachers. A few people earn incomes that are off the scale of the figure. The £38 million that J. K. Rowling earned in 2006, for example, translates to £19,000 an hour, assuming she worked a 40 hour week!

Figure 1

10 High-paid and 10 Low-paid Jobs

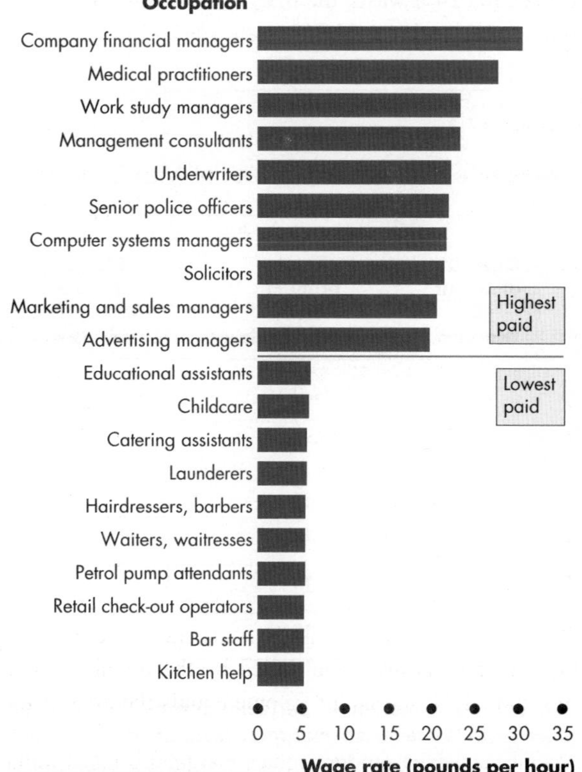

Source of data: Office for National Statistics, *New Earnings Survey*.

Marginal Revenue Product

The change in total revenue resulting from employing one worker, holding the quantity of all other factors constant, is called **marginal revenue product**. Table 17.1 shows you how to calculate marginal revenue product for a perfectly competitive firm.

The first two columns show the total product schedule for Max's Wash 'n' Wax car wash business. The numbers tell us how the number of car washes per hour varies as the quantity of labour increases. The third column shows the *marginal product of labour* – the change in total product that results from a one unit increase in the quantity labour employed. (Look back at Chapter 10, p. 215 for a quick refresher on this concept.)

The car wash market in which Max operates is perfectly competitive, and he can sell as many car washes as he chooses at £4 a wash, the (assumed) market price. So Max's *marginal revenue* is £4 a wash.

Given this information, we can calculate Max's *marginal revenue product* (fourth column). It equals marginal product multiplied by marginal revenue. For example, the marginal product of employing a second worker is 4 car washes an hour and because marginal revenue is £4 a wash, the marginal revenue product of the second worker is £16 (4 washes at £4 each).

The last two columns of Table 17.1 show an alternative way to calculate the marginal revenue product of labour. Total revenue is equal to total product multiplied by price. For example, two workers produce 9 washes per hour and generate a total revenue of £36 (9 washes at £4 each). One worker produces 5 washes per hour and generates a total revenue of £20 (5 washes at £4 each). Marginal revenue product, in the sixth column, is the change in the total revenue from employing one more worker. When the second worker is employed, total revenue increases from £20 to £36, an increase of £16. So the marginal revenue product of the second worker is £16, which agrees with the previous calculation.

Diminishing Marginal Revenue Product

As the quantity of labour rises, the marginal revenue product of labour diminishes. For a firm in perfect competition, marginal revenue product diminishes because marginal product diminishes. For a monopoly (or in monopolistic competition), marginal revenue product diminishes for a second reason. When more labour is employed and total product increases, the firm must cut its price to sell the extra product. So marginal product and marginal revenue decrease, both of which bring decreasing marginal revenue product.

Table 17.1

Marginal Revenue Product at Max's Wash 'n' Wax

	Quantity of labour (L) (workers)	Total product (TP) (car washes per hour)	Marginal product ($MP = \Delta TP/\Delta L$) (washes per worker)	Marginal revenue product ($MRP = MR \times MP$) (pounds per workers)	Total revenue ($TR = P \times TP$) (pounds)	Marginal revenue product ($MRP = \Delta TR/\Delta L$) (pounds per worker)
A	0	0			0	
			5	20		20
B	1	5			20	
			4	16		16
C	2	9			36	
			3	12		12
D	3	12			48	
			2	8		8
E	4	14			56	
			1	4		4
F	5	15			60	

The car wash market is perfectly competitive and the price is £4 a wash, so marginal revenue is £4 a wash. Marginal revenue product equals marginal product multiplied by marginal revenue. For example, the marginal product of the second worker is 4 washes, so the marginal revenue product of the second worker is £16. Alternatively, if Max employs 1 worker (row *B*), total product is 5 washes an hour and total revenue is £20. If he employs 2 workers (row *C*), total product is 9 washes an hour and total revenue is £36. By employing the second worker, total revenue rises by £16 – the marginal revenue product of labour is £16.

The Labour Demand Curve

Figure 17.2 shows how the labour demand curve is derived from the marginal revenue product curve. The *marginal revenue product curve* graphs the marginal revenue product of a factor at each quantity of the factor employed. Figure 17.2(a) illustrates the marginal revenue product curve for workers employed by Max. The horizontal axis measures the number of workers that Max employs and the vertical axis measures the marginal revenue product of labour. The blue bars show the marginal revenue product of labour as Max employs more workers. These bars correspond to the numbers in Table 17.1. The curve labelled *MRP* is Max's marginal revenue product curve.

A firm's marginal revenue product curve is also its demand for labour curve. Figure 17.2(b) shows Max's demand for labour curve (*D*). The horizontal axis measures the number of workers employed – the same as in part (a). The vertical axis measures the wage rate in pounds per hour. In Figure 17.2(a), when Max increases the quantity of labour employed from 2 workers an hour to 3 workers an hour, his marginal revenue product is £12 an hour. In Figure 17.2(b), at a wage rate of £12 an hour, Max employs 3 workers an hour.

The marginal revenue product curve is also the demand for labour curve because the firm employs the profit-maximizing quantity of labour. If the wage rate is *less* than marginal revenue product, the firm can increase its profit by employing one more worker. Conversely, if the wage rate is *greater* than marginal revenue product, the firm can increase its profit by employing one fewer worker. But if the wage rate *equals* marginal revenue product, the firm cannot increase its profit by changing the number of workers it employs – the firm is maximizing its profit. So the quantity of labour demanded by the firm is such that the wage rate equals the marginal revenue product.

Because the marginal revenue product curve is also the demand curve, and because marginal revenue product diminishes as the quantity of labour employed increases, the demand for labour curve slopes downward. The lower the wage rate, other things remaining the same, the more workers a firm employs.

When we studied firms' output decisions, we discovered that a condition for maximum profit is that marginal revenue equals marginal cost. We've now discovered another condition for maximum profit: marginal revenue product of a factor equals the factor's price. Let's study the connection between these two conditions.

Figure 17.2

The Demand for Labour at Max's Wash 'n' Wax

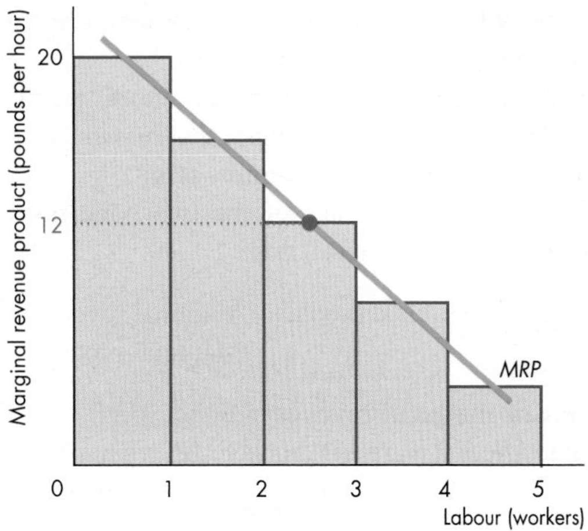

(a) Marginal revenue product

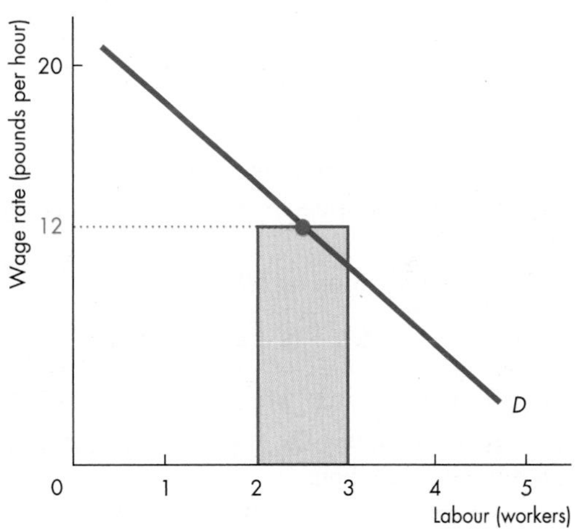

(b) Demand for labour

Max's Wash 'n' Wax operates in a perfectly competitive car wash market and can sell any quantity of washes at the market price of £4 a wash. The blue bars in part (a) represent the firm's marginal revenue product of labour. They are based on the numbers in Table 17.1. The orange line is the firm's marginal revenue product of labour curve.

Part (b) shows Max's demand for labour curve. This curve is identical to Max's marginal revenue product curve. Max demands the quantity of labour that makes the wage rate equal to the marginal revenue product of labour. The demand for labour curve slopes downward because marginal revenue product diminishes as the quantity of labour employed increases.

Equivalence of Two Conditions for Profit Maximization

Profit is maximized when at the quantity of labour employed, *marginal revenue product* equals the wage rate and when, at the quantity produced, *marginal revenue* equals *marginal cost*.

These two conditions for maximum profit are equivalent. The quantity of labour that maximizes profit produces the output that maximizes profit.

To see the equivalence of the two conditions for maximum profit, first recall that:

$$\text{Marginal revenue product} = \text{Marginal revenue} \times \text{Marginal product}$$

If we call marginal revenue product MRP, marginal revenue MR and marginal product MP, we have:

$$MRP = MR \times MP$$

If we call the wage rate W, the first condition for maximum profit is:

$$MRP = W$$

But $MRP = MR \times MP$, so:

$$MR \times MP = W$$

This equation tells us that when profit is maximized, marginal revenue multiplied by marginal product equals the wage rate.

Divide the last equation by MP to obtain:

$$MR = W \div MP$$

This equation states that when profit is maximized, marginal revenue equals the wage rate divided by the marginal product of labour.

The wage rate divided by the marginal product of labour equals marginal cost. It costs the firm W to employ one more hour of labour. But the labour produces MP units of output. So the cost of producing one of those units of output, which is marginal cost, is W divided by MP.

If we call marginal cost MC, then:

$$MR = MC$$

which is the second condition for maximum profit.

Because the first condition for maximum profit implies the second condition, these two conditions are equivalent. Table 17.2 summarizes the reasoning and calculations that show the equivalence between the two conditions for maximum profit.

Table 17.2

Two Conditions for Maximum Profit

Symbols

Marginal product	***MP***
Marginal revenue	***MR***
Marginal cost	***MC***
Marginal revenue product	***MRP***
Wage rate	***W***

Two Conditions for Maximum Profit

1 $MR = MC$ 2 $MRP = W$

Equivalence of Conditions

1 $MRP/MP = \mathbf{MR}$ = $\mathbf{MC} = W/MP$

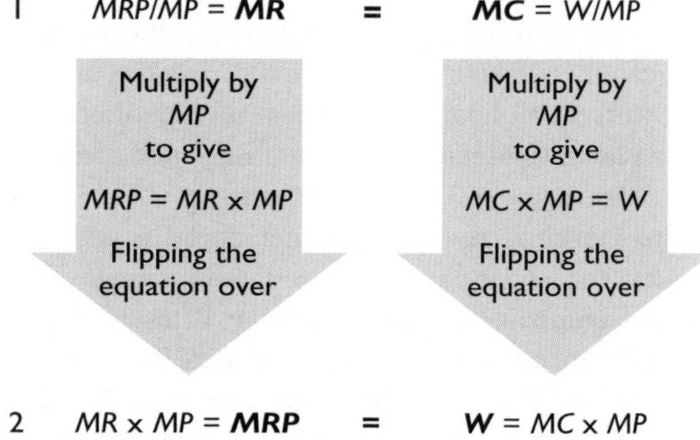

2 $MR \times MP = \mathbf{MRP}$ = $\mathbf{W} = MC \times MP$

The two conditions for maximum profit are that marginal revenue product (*MR*) equals marginal cost (*MC*) and marginal revenue product (*MRP*) equals the wage rate (*W*). These two conditions for maximum profit are equivalent because marginal revenue product (*MRP*) equals marginal revenue (*MR*) multiplied by marginal product (*MP*), and the wage rate (*W*) equals marginal cost (*MC*) multiplied by marginal product (*MP*).

Max's Numbers

Check that the numbers for Max's Wash 'n' Wax and confirm that the conditions you've just examined work. Max's profit-maximizing labour decision is to employ 3 workers if the wage rate is £12 an hour. When Max employs 3 hours of labour, marginal product is 3 washes per hour. Max sells the 3 washes an hour for a marginal revenue of £4 a wash. So marginal revenue product is 3 washes multiplied by £4 a wash, which equals £12 per hour. At a wage rate of £12 an hour, Max is maximizing profit.

Equivalently, Max's marginal cost is £12 an hour divided by 3 washes per hour, which equals £4 per wash. At a marginal revenue of £4 a wash, Max is maximizing profit.

You've just discovered that the law of demand applies to labour as it does to goods and services. Other things remaining the same, the lower the wage rate (the price of labour), the greater is the quantity of labour demanded.

Let's now study the influences that change the demand for labour and shift the demand for labour curve.

Changes in the Demand for Labour

The demand for labour changes and the demand curve for labour shifts when any of the following three factors change:

- The price of the firm's output
- Other factor prices
- Technology

The Price of the Firm's Output

The higher the price of a firm's output, the greater is the firm's demand for labour. The price of output affects the demand for labour through its influence on marginal revenue product. A higher price for the firm's output increases marginal revenue which, in turn, increases the marginal revenue product of labour. A change in the price of a firm's output leads to a shift in the firm's demand for labour curve. If the output price increases, the demand for labour curve shifts rightward.

Other Factor Prices

If the price of some other factor of production changes, the demand for labour changes, but only in the *long run* when all factors of production can be varied. The effect of a change in some other factor price depends on whether that factor is a *substitute* for or a *complement* of labour. For example, computers are substitutes for telephone operators but complements of word processor operators. So if computers become less costly to use, the demand for telephone operators decreases but the demand for word processor operators increases.

Technology

An advance in technology that changes the marginal product of labour changes the demand for labour. There is a general belief that advances in technology destroy jobs and therefore decrease the demand for labour. In fact, the opposite is true. Advances in technology destroy *some* jobs and create others. But the number of jobs created exceeds the number destroyed.

New technologies are substitutes for some types of labour and complements of other kinds. For example, the electronic telephone exchange is a substitute for telephone operators, so the arrival of this new technology has decreased the demand for telephone operators. This same new technology is a complement of systems managers, programmers and electronic engineers. So its arrival has increased the demand for these types of labour. Again, these effects on the demand for labour are long-run effects that occur when a firm adjusts all its resources and incorporates new technologies into its production process.

Table 17.3 summarizes the influences on a firm's demand for labour.

Table 17.3

A Firm's Demand for Labour

The Law of Demand
(Movements along the demand for labour curve)

The quantity of labour demanded by a firm

Decreases if:	*Increases if:*
◆ The wage rate increases	◆ The wage rate decreases

Changes in Demand
(Shifts in the demand for labour curve)

A firm's demand for labour

Decreases if:	*Increases if:*
◆ The price of the firm's output decreases	◆ The price of the firm's output increases
◆ The price of a substitute for labour falls	◆ The prices of a substitute for labour rises
◆ The price of a complement of labour rises	◆ The price of a complement of labour falls
◆ A new technology decreases the marginal product of labour	◆ A new technology increases the marginal product of labour

Market Demand

So far we have studied only the demand for labour by an individual firm. The market demand for labour is the total demand for labour by all firms in the market. The market demand for labour curve is found by adding together the quantities of labour demanded by all firms at each wage rate. Because each firm's demand for labour curve slopes downward, so does the market demand for labour curve.

Elasticity of Demand for Labour

This elasticity is important because it tells us how labour income changes when the supply of labour changes. An increase in supply (other things remaining the same) brings a lower wage rate. If demand is inelastic, it also brings lower labour income. But if demand is elastic, an increase in supply brings a lower wage rate and an increase in labour income. And if the demand for labour is unit elastic, a change in supply leaves labour income unchanged.

The demand for labour is less elastic in the short run, when only the quantity of labour can be varied, than in the long run, when the quantities of labour and other factors of production can be varied. The elasticity of demand for labour depends on:

- The labour intensity of the production process
- The elasticity of demand for the product
- The substitutability of capital for labour

The Labour Intensity of the Production Process

A labour-intensive production process is one that uses a lot of labour and little capital – a process that has a high ratio of labour to capital. Home building is an example. The larger the degree of labour intensity, the more elastic is the demand for labour, other things remaining the same. To see why, suppose wages are 90 per cent of total cost. A 10 per cent increase in the wage rate increases total cost by 9 per cent. Firms will be extremely sensitive to such a large change in total cost, so if the wage rate increases, firms will decrease the quantity of labour demanded by a relatively large amount. But if wages are 10 per cent of total cost, a 10 per cent increase in the wage rate increases total cost by only 1 per cent. Firms will be less sensitive to this increase in cost, so if the wage rate increases in this case, firms will decrease the quantity of labour demanded by a small amount.

The Elasticity of Demand for the Product

The greater the elasticity of demand for the good, the larger is the elasticity of demand for labour used to produce it. An increase in the wage rate increases marginal cost of producing the good and decreases the supply of it. The decrease in the supply of the good increases the price of the good and decreases the quantity demanded of the good and the factors of production used to produce it. The greater the elasticity of demand for the good, the larger is the decrease in the quantity demanded of the good and so the larger is the decrease in the quantities of the factors of production used to produce it.

The Substitutability of Capital for Labour

The more easily capital can be used instead of labour in production, the more elastic is the long-run demand for labour. For example, it is fairly easy to use robots rather than assembly-line workers in car factories and grape-picking machines rather than labour in vineyards. So the demand for these types of labour is elastic. At the other extreme, it is difficult (though not impossible) to substitute computers for newspaper reporters, bank loan officers and teachers. So the demand for these types of labour is inelastic. The more readily capital can be substituted for labour, the more elastic is the firm's demand for labour in the long run.

We can now turn from the demand side of the labour market to the supply side and examine the decisions people make about how to allocate their time between working and other activities.

Supply of Labour

People can allocate their time to two broad activities – labour supply and leisure. (Leisure is a term that includes all activities other than supplying labour.) For most people, leisure is more enjoyable than supplying labour. We'll look at the labour supply decision of Amy, who is like most people. She enjoys her leisure time, and she would be pleased if she didn't have to spend her weekends working in a supermarket.

But Amy has chosen to work weekends because she is offered a wage rate that exceeds her *reservation wage*. Amy's reservation wage is the lowest wage at which she is willing to supply labour. If the wage rate exceeds her reservation wage, she supplies some labour. But how much labour will she supply? The quantity of labour that Amy is willing to supply depends on the wage rate.

Substitution Effect

Other things remaining the same, the higher the wage rate Amy is offered, at least over a range, the greater is the quantity of labour that she supplies. The reason is that Amy's wage rate is her *opportunity cost of leisure*. If she takes an hour off work to go shopping, the cost of that extra hour of leisure is the wage forgone. The higher the wage rate, the less willing is Amy to forgo the income and take the extra leisure time. This tendency for a higher wage rate to induce Amy to work longer hours is a *substitution effect*.

But there is also an *income effect* that works in the opposite direction to the substitution effect.

Income Effect

The higher Amy's wage rate, the higher is her income. A higher income, other things remaining the same, induces Amy to increase her demand for most goods. Leisure is one of these goods. Because an increase in income creates an increase in the demand for leisure, it also creates a decrease in the quantity of labour supplied.

Backward-Bending Labour Supply Curve

As the wage rate rises, the substitution effect brings an increase in the quantity of labour supplied while the income effect brings a decrease in the quantity of labour supplied. At low wage rates, the substitution effect is larger than the income effect, so as the wage rate rises, people supply more labour. But as the wage rate continues to rise, the income effect eventually becomes larger than the substitution effect and the quantity of labour supplied decreases. The labour supply curve is *backward bending*.

Figure 17.3(a) shows the labour supply curves for Amy, and two friends, Jack and Lisa. Each labour supply curve is backward bending, but the three people have different reservation wage rates.

Market Supply

The market supply of labour curve is the sum of the individual supply curves. Figure 17.3(b) shows the market supply curve (S_M) derived from the supply curves of Amy, Jack and Lisa (S_A, S_B and S_C respectively). At wage rates of less than £1 an hour, no one supplies any labour. At a wage rate of £1 an hour, Amy works but Jack and Lisa don't. At £7 an hour, all three will work. The market supply curve S_M eventually bends backward, but it has a long upward-sloping section.

Changes in the Supply of Labour

The supply of labour changes when influences other

Figure 17.3

The Supply of Labour

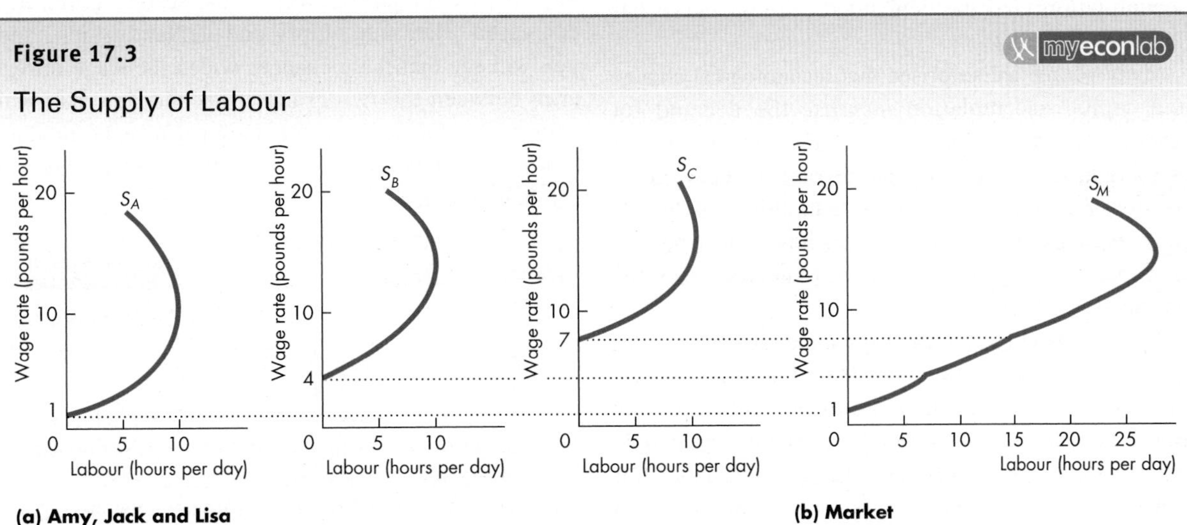

Part (a) shows the labour supply curves of Amy (S_A), Jack (S_B) and Lisa (S_C). Each person has a reservation wage below which he or she will supply no labour. As the wage rises, the quantity of labour supplied rises to a maximum. If the wage continues to rise, the quantity of labour supplied begins to decrease. Each person's supply curve eventually bends backward.

Part (b) shows how, by adding together the quantities of labour supplied by each person at each wage rate, we derive the market supply of labour curve (S_M).

than the wage rate change. The key factors that change the supply of labour and that have increased it are:

1 The size of the adult population
2 Technological change and capital accumulation

An increase in the adult population increases the supply of labour. So does a technological change or an increase in capital in home production (of meals, laundry and cleaning services). Factors that increase the supply of labour shift the labour supply curve rightward.

Let's now build on what we've learned about the demand for labour and the supply of labour and study labour market equilibrium.

Labour Market Equilibrium

Equilibrium in the labour market determines wage rates and employment. You saw, in Box 17.1 Figure 1 that both the wage rate and total hours of employment have increased. But this picture hides some important differences between different types of labour markets. Now you can see why.

Trends in the Demand for Labour

The demand for labour had *increased* in most European countries because of technological change and capital accumulation, and the demand for labour curve has shifted rightward.

Many people are surprised that technological change and capital accumulation *increase* the demand for labour. They see new technologies *destroying jobs*, not creating them. Downsizing has become a catchword as the use of computers has eliminated millions of "good" jobs, even those of managers. So how can it be that technological change *creates* jobs and increases the demand for labour?

Technological change destroys some jobs and creates others. But it creates more jobs than it destroys, and *on average*, the new jobs pay more than the old ones did. But to benefit from the advances in technology, people must acquire new skills and change their jobs. For example, during the past 20 years, the demand for typists has fallen almost to zero. But the demand for people who can type (on a computer rather than a typewriter) and do other tasks as well has increased. And the output of these people is worth more than that of a typist. So the demand for people with typing (and other) skills has increased.

Trends in the Supply of Labour

The supply of labour has increased because of population growth and technological change as well as capital accumulation in the home. The mechanization of home production of fast-food preparation services (the freezer and the microwave oven) and laundry services (the automatic washer and dryer and wrinkle-free fabrics) has decreased the time spent on activities that once were full-time jobs and have led to a large increase in the supply of labour. As a result, the supply labour curve has shifted steadily rightward, but at a slower pace than the shift in the demand curve.

Trends in Equilibrium

Because technological advances and capital accumulation have increased demand by more than population growth and technological change in home production have increased supply, both wage rates and employment have increased. But not everyone has shared in the increased prosperity. Some groups have been left behind, and seen their wage rates fall. Why?

Two key reasons can be identified. First, technological change affects the marginal productivity of different groups in different ways. High-skilled computer-literate workers have benefited from the information revolution while low-skilled workers have suffered. The demand for the services of the first group has increased, and the demand for the services of the second group has decreased. (Draw a supply and demand graph, and you will see that these changes widen the wage difference between the two groups.) Second, international competition has lowered the marginal revenue product of low-skilled workers and so has decreased the demand for their labour.

Review Quiz

Study Plan 17.2

1 What links the quantity that a firm produces and the quantity of labour it employs?
2 Distinguish between marginal revenue product and marginal revenue and illustrate the distinction with an example.
3 Why is it that when a firm's marginal revenue product equals the wage rate, marginal revenue also equals marginal cost?
4 What determines the amount of labour that households plan to supply?
5 Describe and explain the trends in wages and employment.

Labour Market Power

In some labour markets, workers organized by trades unions possess market power and are able to raise the wage rate above the competitive level. In some other labour markets, a large employer dominates the demand side of the market and can exert market power that lowers the wage rate below its competitive level. But an employer might also decide to pay more than the competitive wage rate to attract the best workers. Let's look at these cases.

Trades Unions

A **trades union** is an organized group of workers that aims to increase wages and influence other job conditions. The two types of unions are closed unions and open unions. A *closed union* is a group of workers who have a similar range of skills but work in many different industries. Examples are the National Union of Railwaymen and the National Union of Seamen. An *open union* is a group of workers who have a variety of skills and job types but work in the same industry. Examples are the National Union of Public Employees and the Amalgamated Engineering Union.

There are about 300 unions in the United Kingdom that represent 6.5 million or one in five workers. About a quarter of the unions, and all the large unions that together account for 90 per cent of union members, are affiliated to the Trades Union Congress (TUC), which acts as the voice of organized labour.

Unions vary greatly in size from many with fewer than 100 members to giants like Amicus and the Transport and General Workers Union with more than a million members. Union strength peaked in the 1950s, when 35 per cent of the labour force belonged to unions.

Unions negotiate with employers in a process called *collective bargaining*. A *strike*, a group decision to refuse to work under prevailing conditions, is the main weapon available to the union. A lockout, a firm's refusal to operate its plant and employ its workers, is the main weapon available to the employer. Each party uses the threat of a strike or a lockout to try to get an agreement in its own favour. Sometimes, when the two parties in the collective bargaining process cannot agree on the wage rate or other employment conditions, they agree to submit their disagreement to binding arbitration. *Binding arbitration* is a process in which a third party – an arbitrator – determines wages and other employment conditions on behalf of the negotiating parties.

Unions' Objectives and Constraints

A union has three broad objectives: It seeks to:

1 Increase compensation
2 Improve working conditions
3 Expand job opportunities

A union's ability to pursue its objectives is restricted by two sets of constraints, one on the supply side of the labour market and the other on the demand side. On the supply side, the union's activities are limited by how well it can restrict non-union workers from offering their labour in the same market as union labour. The larger the fraction of the workforce controlled by the union, the more effective the union can be in this regard. It is difficult for unions to operate in markets where there is an abundant supply of willing non-union labour. For example, the influx of labour from new EU member countries makes it harder for unions to organize because of a ready flow of non-union labour. At the other extreme, unions in the construction industry can better pursue their goals because they can influence the number of people who can obtain skills as electricians, plasterers and joiners. The professional associations of doctors, dentists and lawyers are best able to restrict the supply. These groups control the number of qualified workers by controlling either the examinations that new entrants must pass or entrance into professional degree courses.

On the demand side of the labour market, the union faces a trade-off that arises from firms' profit-maximizing decisions. Because labour demand curves slope downward, anything a union does that increases the wage rate or other employment costs decreases the quantity of labour demanded.

Let's see how unions operate in an otherwise competitive labour market.

A Union in a Competitive Labour Market

When a union enters a competitive labour market, it seeks to increase the wage rate and to increase the demand for the labour of its members. That is, the union tries to take actions that shift the demand curve for its members' labour rightward.

Figure 17.4 illustrates a competitive labour market that a union enters. The demand curve is D_C, and the supply curve is S_C. With no union, the wage rate is £7 an hour and 100 hours of labour are employed.

Now suppose that a union is formed to organize the workers in this market. The union can attempt to increase the wage rate in this market in two ways. It can try to restrict the supply of labour or it can try to stimulate the demand for labour. First, look at what happens if the union has sufficient control over the supply of labour to be able to artificially restrict that supply below its competitive level – to S_U. If that is all the union is able to do, employment falls to 85 hours of labour and the wage rate rises to £8 an hour. The union simply picks its preferred position along the demand curve that defines the trade-off it faces between employment and the wage rate. You can see that if the union can only restrict the supply of labour, it raises the wage rate but decreases the number of jobs available. Because of this outcome, unions try to increase the demand for labour and shift the demand curve rightward. Let's see what they might do to achieve this outcome.

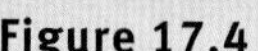

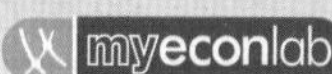

Figure 17.4

A Union Enters a Competitive Labour Market

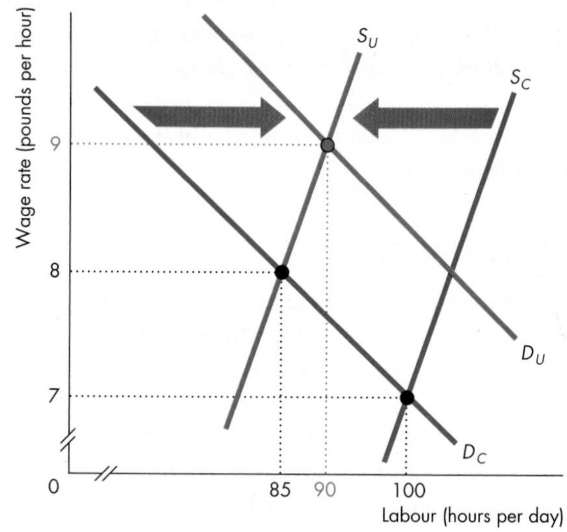

In a competitive labour market, the demand curve is D_C and the supply curve is S_C. Competitive equilibrium occurs at a wage rate of £7 an hour with 100 hours employed. By restricting employment below the competitive level, the union shifts the supply of labour to S_U. The wage rate will increase to £8 an hour but employment will fall to 85 hours.

If the union can also increase the demand for labour and shift the demand curve to D_U, then it can increase the wage rate still higher, to £9 an hour, and achieve employment of 90 hours.

How Unions Try to Change the Demand for Labour

A union tries to operate on the demand for labour in two ways. First, it tries to make the demand for union labour less elastic. Second, it tries to increase the demand for union labour. Making the demand for labour less elastic does not eliminate the trade-off between employment and the wage rate. But it does make the trade-off less unfavourable. If a union can make the demand for labour less elastic, it can increase the wage rate at a lower cost in terms of lost employment opportunities. But if the union can increase the demand for labour, it might even be able to increase both the wage rate and the employment opportunities of its members. Some of the methods used by the unions to change the demand for the labour of its members are to:

- Increase the marginal product of union members
- Encourage import restrictions
- Support minimum wage laws
- Support immigration restrictions
- Increase demand for the good produced

Unions try to increase the marginal product of their members, which in turn increases the demand for their labour, by organizing and sponsoring training schemes, by encouraging apprenticeship and other on-the-job training activities, and by professional certification.

Unions lobby to restrict imports and encourage people to buy goods made by unionized workers in the United Kingdom. For example, today, union workers in the United Kingdom and EU are seeking to restrict the imports of cheap textiles and other goods from China.

Unions support minimum wage laws to increase the cost of employing low-skilled labour. An increase in the wage rate of low-skilled labour leads to a decrease in the quantity demanded of low-skilled labour and to an increase in demand for high-skilled union labour, a substitute for low-skilled labour.

Restrictive immigration laws decrease the supply of low-skilled workers and increase their wage rate. As a result, the demand for high-skilled union labour increases.

Because the demand for labour is a derived demand, an increase in the demand for the good produced by union labour increases the demand for union labour.

Figure 17.4 illustrates the effects of an increase in the demand for the labour of a union's members. If the union can also take steps that increase the demand for labour to D_U, it can achieve an even bigger increase in the wage rate with a smaller fall in employment. By maintaining the restricted labour supply at S_U, the union increases the wage rate to £9 an hour and achieves an employment level of 90 hours of labour.

Because a union restricts the supply of labour in the market in which it operates, its actions increase the supply of labour in non-union markets. Workers who can't get union jobs must look elsewhere for work. This increase in the supply of labour in non-union markets lowers the wage rate in those markets and further widens the gap between union and non-union wages.

The Scale of Union–Non-union Wage Gap

How much of a difference to wage rates do unions make? To answer this question, we must look at the wages of unionized and non-unionized workers who do similar work. The evidence suggests that after allowing for skill differences, the union–non-union wage gap lies between 10 per cent and 25 per cent. For example, unionized airline pilots earn about 25 per cent more than non-union pilots with the same level of skill.

Let's now look at a labour market in which the employer possesses market power.

Monopsony in the Labour Market

A market in which there is a single buyer is called a **monopsony**. This market type is unusual, but it does exist. With the growth of large-scale production over the last century, large manufacturing plants such as coal mines, steel and textile mills and car production plants became the major employer in some regions, and in some places a single firm employed almost all the labour. Today, in some parts of the country, managed healthcare organizations are the major employer of healthcare professionals. These firms have market power.

In monopsony, the employer determines the wage rate and pays the lowest wage at which it can attract the labour it plans to employ. A monopsony makes a bigger profit than a group of firms that compete with each other for their labour. Let's find out how they achieve this outcome.

Like all firms, a monopsony has a downward-sloping marginal revenue product curve, which is *MRP* in Figure 17.5. This curve tells us the extra revenue the monopsony receives by selling the output produced by an extra hour of labour. The supply of labour curve is *S*. This curve tells us how many hours are supplied at each wage rate. It also tells us the minimum wage for which a given quantity of labour is willing to work.

A monopsony recognizes that to employ more labour, it must pay a higher wage; equivalently, by employing less labour, it can pay a lower wage. Because a monopsony controls the wage rate, the marginal cost of labour exceeds the wage rate. The marginal cost of labour is shown by the curve *MCL*. The relationship between the marginal cost of labour curve and the supply curve is similar to the relationship between the marginal cost and average cost curves that you studied in Chapter 10.

The supply curve is like the average cost of labour curve. In Figure 17.5, the firm can employ 49 hours of labour for a wage rate of just below £4.90 an hour. The firm's total labour cost is £240. But suppose that the firm employs 50 hours of labour. It can employ the 50th hour of labour for £5 an hour. The total cost of labour is now £250 an hour. So employing the 50th hour of labour increases the cost of labour from £240 to £250,

Figure 17.5

A Monopsony Labour Market

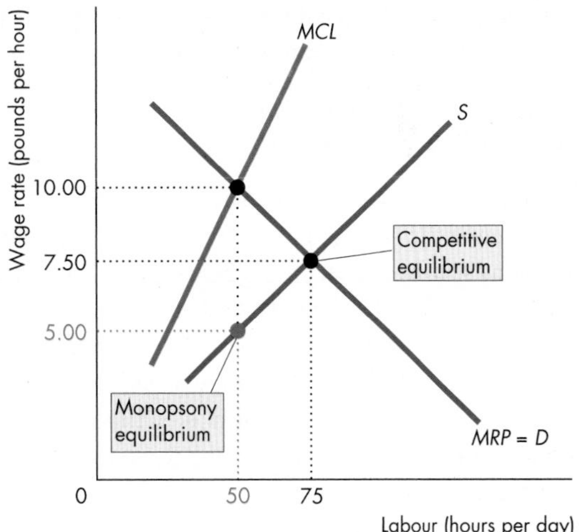

A monopsony is a market structure in which there is a single buyer. A monopsony in the labour market has value of marginal revenue product curve *MRP* and faces a labour supply curve *S*. The marginal cost of labour curve is *MCL*. The monopsony maximizes profit by making the marginal cost of labour equal to marginal revenue product. The monopsony employs 50 hours of labour and pays the lowest wage for which that labour will work, which is £5 an hour.

which is a £10 increase. The marginal cost of labour is £10 an hour. The curve *MCL* shows the £10 marginal cost of employing the 50th hour of labour.

To calculate the profit-maximizing quantity of labour to employ, the firm sets the marginal cost of labour equal to the marginal revenue product of labour. That is, the firm wants the cost of the last worker employed to equal the extra total revenue brought in. In Figure 17.5, this outcome occurs when the monopsony employs 50 hours of labour. What is the wage rate that the monopsony pays? To employ 50 hours of labour, the firm must pay £5 an hour, as shown by the supply of labour curve. So workers are paid £5 an hour. But the marginal revenue product of labour is £10 an hour, so the firm makes an economic profit of £5 on the last hour of labour that it employs. Compare this outcome with that in a competitive labour market.

If the labour market shown in Figure 17.5 were competitive, equilibrium would occur at the point of intersection of the demand curve and the supply curve. The wage rate would be £7.50 an hour, and 75 hours of labour a day would be employed. So compared with a competitive labour market, a monopsony decreases both the wage rate and employment.

The ability of a monopsony to cut the wage rate and employment and make an economic profit depends on the elasticity of labour supply. If the supply of labour is highly elastic, a monopsony has little power to cut the wage rate and employment to boost its profit.

A Union and a Monopsony

In Chapter 12, we discovered that in monopoly, a firm can determine the market price. We've now seen that in monopsony – a market with a single buyer – the buyer can determine the price. Suppose that a union operates in a monopsony labour market. A union is like a monopoly. If the union (monopoly seller) faces a monopsony buyer, the situation is called **bilateral monopoly**. In bilateral monopoly, the wage rate is determined by bargaining.

The Range of Bargaining Outcomes

In Figure 17.6, if the monopsony is free to determine the wage rate and the level of employment, it hires 50 hours of labour for a wage rate of £5 an hour. But suppose that a union represents the workers. The union agrees to maintain employment at 50 hours but seeks the highest wage rate the employer can be forced to pay. That wage rate is £10 an hour – the wage rate that equals the marginal revenue product of labour. The union might not be able to get the wage rate up to £10 an hour. But it won't accept £5 an hour. The monopsony firm and the union bargain over the wage rate, and the result is an outcome between £10 an hour and £5 an hour.

The outcome of the bargaining depends on the costs that each party can inflict on the other as a result of a failure to agree on the wage rate. The firm can shut down the plant and lock out its workers, and the workers can shut down the plant by striking. Each party knows the other's strength and knows what it will lose if it does not agree to the other's demands. If the two parties are equally strong and they realize it, they will split the gap between £5 and £10 and agree to a wage rate of £7.50 an hour. If one party is stronger than the other – and both parties know that – the agreed wage will favour the stronger party. Usually, an agreement is reached without a strike or a lockout. The threat is usually enough to bring the bargaining parties to an agreement. When a strike or lockout does occur, it is usually because one party has misjudged the costs each party can inflict on the other.

Minimum wage laws have interesting effects in monopsony labour markets. Let's study these effects.

Monopsony and the Minimum Wage

In a competitive labour market, a minimum wage that exceeds the equilibrium wage decreases employment (see Chapter 6, pp. 125–126). But this outcome does not occur in all types of labour market. In particular, it does not occur in monopsony. In a monopsony labour market, a minimum wage can end up increasing both the wage rate and employment. Let's see how.

Figure 17.7 shows a monopsony labour market in which the wage rate is £5 an hour and 50 hours of labour are employed. A minimum wage law is passed that requires employers to pay at least £7.50 an hour.

The monopsony in Figure 17.7 now faces a perfectly elastic supply of labour at £7.50 an hour up to 75 hours. Above 75 hours, a wage above £7.50 an hour must be paid to hire additional hours of labour. Because the wage rate is a fixed £7.50 an hour up to 75 hours, the marginal cost of labour is also constant at £7.50 up to 75 hours. Beyond 75 hours, the marginal cost of labour rises above £7.50 an hour. To maximize profit, the monopsony sets the marginal cost of labour equal to the marginal revenue product of labour. That is, the monopsony hires 75 hours of labour at £7.50 an hour. The minimum wage law has made the supply of labour perfectly elastic and made the marginal cost of labour the same as

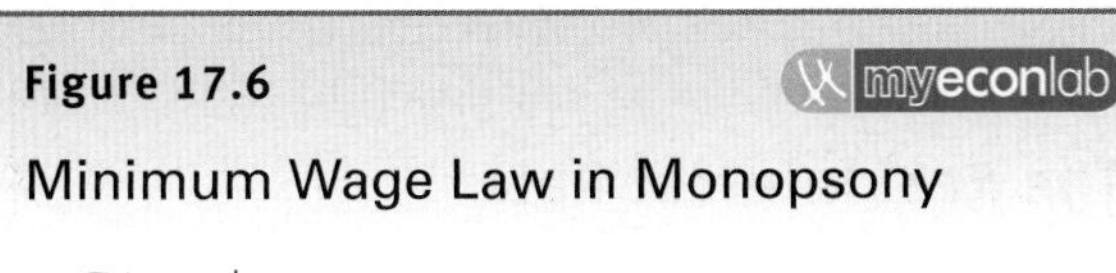

Figure 17.6

Minimum Wage Law in Monopsony

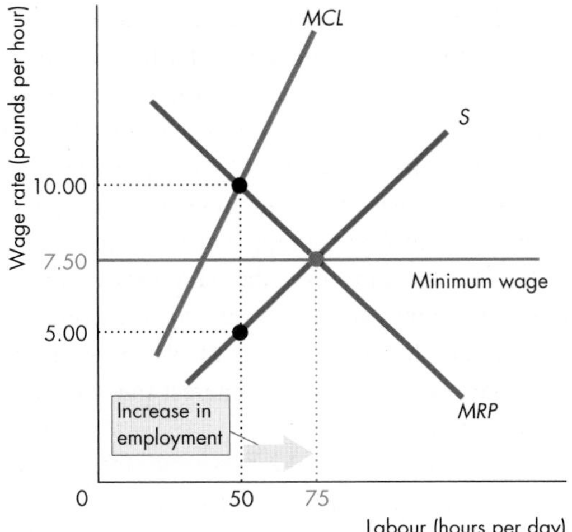

In a monopsony labour market, the wage rate is £5 an hour and 50 hours are employed. If a minimum wage law increases the wage rate to £7.50 an hour, employment increases to 75 hours.

the wage rate up to 75 hours. The law has not affected the supply of labour curve or the marginal cost of labour at employment levels above 75 hours. The minimum wage law has succeeded in raising the wage rate by £2.50 an hour and increasing the amount of labour employed by 25 hours.

Efficiency Wages

An **efficiency wage** is a wage rate that a firm pays above the competitive equilibrium wage rate with the aim of attracting the most productive workers.

In a perfectly competitive labour market, firms and workers are well informed. Workers know exactly what they are being hired to do and firms can observe the marginal productive of each worker. In this state of complete knowledge of all the relevant factors, a firm would never pay more than the going competitive market wage rate.

In some labour markets, the employer is not able to observe a worker's marginal product. It is costly to monitor all the actions of every worker. For example, if McDonald's employed enough managers to keep a close watch on the activities of all the servers, its costs would be very high. And who would monitor all those managers? Because it is costly to monitor everything that a worker does, workers have some power. They might work hard or shirk.

If every firm pays its workers the going competitive wage rate, some workers will choose to work hard and some will choose to shirk. And threatening to fire a shirker won't help much because the shirker knows another job can be found at the going wage and the firm doesn't know if it will replace one shirker with a hard worker or another shirker.

If a firm pays a wage rate above the competitive level – an efficiency wage – the threat of being fired for shirking has some force. A fired worker can expect to find another job but only at the lower market equilibrium wage rate. So the worker now has an incentive not to shirk. Also, hard workers will be more likely to want to work for the firm, so if a shirking worker is fired, most likely the firm will attract a hard worker as the replacement.

So a firm that pays an efficiency wage attracts more productive workers but at the cost of a higher wage bill. So the firm must decide just how much more than the competitive wage to pay. It makes this decision by making the marginal improvement in productivity equal the marginal cost of the higher wage rate. If most firms pay an efficiency wage, the quantity of labour supplied will exceed the quantity demanded and unemployment will arise that strengthens the incentive that workers face and further discourage shirking.

Review Quiz

Study Plan 17.3

1. What are the methods that trades unions use to increase the wage rates of their members above the levels of non-union wage rates?
2. What is a monopsony and why is a monopsony able to pay a lower wage rate than a firm in a competitive labour market?
3. How is the wage rate determined when a union faces a monopsony?
4. What is the effect of a minimum wage law on the level of employment in a monopsony labour market?
5. What is an efficiency wage and how does it work?

You've now seen how wage rates and employment levels are determined in labour markets. And you've seen that where market power is present in the labour market, the outcome is very different from that in competitive labour markets. Your next task is to study capital markets.

Capital Markets

Capital markets are the channels through which firms obtain *financial* resources to buy *physical* capital – the tools, instruments, machines, buildings and other constructions that firms use to produce goods and services. These capital resources are called *physical capital* to emphasize that they are real physical objects. The markets in which each item of physical capital is traded are not the capital markets. They are goods markets just like the ones that you've studied in Chapters 11, 12 and 13. For example, the prices and quantities of tower cranes are determined in the markets for tower cranes.

A firm buys many different items of capital during a given time period. The money value of those capital goods is called the firm's *investment*. But it is the objects themselves that are the capital, not the money value they represent.

The financial resources used to buy physical capital are called *financial capital*. These financial resources come from saving. The "price of capital", which adjusts to make the quantity of capital supplied equal to the quantity demanded, is the interest rate.

For most of us, capital markets are where we make our biggest-ticket transactions. We borrow in a capital market to buy a home. And we lend in capital markets to build up a fund on which to live when we retire.

Because we make our biggest transactions in capital markets, we are very concerned about the interest rate. When we save, we want to receive the highest possible interest rate. And when we borrow, we want to pay the lowest possible rate.

The ideas you've already met in your study of the labour market apply to the capital market as well. But capital has some special features. Its main special feature is that people must compare *present* costs with *future* returns. We'll discover how these comparisons are made by studying the demand for capital.

The Demand for Capital

A firm's demand for financial capital stems from its demand for physical capital, and the amount that a firm plans to borrow in a given time period is determined by its planned investment – its planned purchases of new capital. This decision is driven by the firm's attempt to maximize profit. The factors that determine investment and borrowing plans are the marginal revenue product of capital and the interest rate. Let's see how these factors influence Tina's investment decisions.

Box 17.2
The *Real* Interest Rate

The real interest rate is the interest rate measured after removing the effects of inflation. Interest is paid in money, and if money is losing value because prices are rising, the true, or real interest rate is less than the advertised market interest rate. Suppose, for example, that prices are rising by 5 per cent a year. If you lend a pound and get repaid after a year, or if you borrow a pound and repay the loan after a year, the value of the money that repays the loan is worth 5 per cent less than the original amount. We must subtract this amount from the market interest rate to find the real interest rate.

Figure 1 shows the real interest rate from 1986 to 2006. You can see that the real interest rate has fluctuated around a falling trend from about 7 per cent a year to about 1 per cent a year. On the average, the real interest rate has been 3.7 per cent per year. Capital markets are global and funds move from one country to another in search of the highest return and the lowest borrowing cost. These movements keep interest rates similar, though not identical, around the world.

Figure 1

The Real Interest Rate: 1986–2006

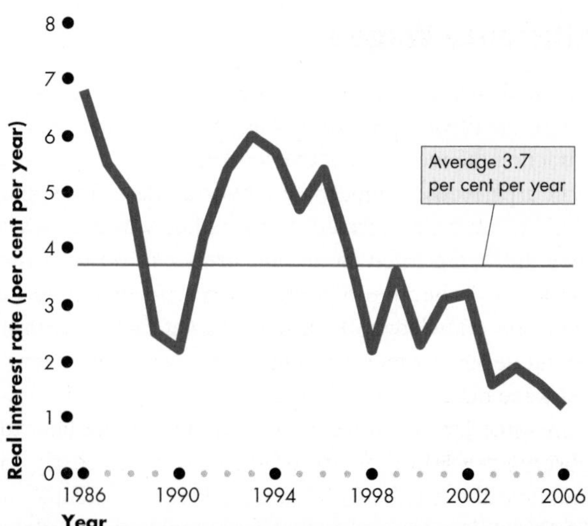

Source of data: Bank of England and Office for National Statistics.

Marginal Revenue Product of Capital

The *marginal revenue product of capital* is the change in total revenue that results from employing one more unit of capital. Suppose that Tina, an accountant who operates Taxfile plc, buys a new computer and software, which increases Taxfile's revenue by £1,150 a year for the next two years. Then the marginal revenue product of this computer is £1,150 a year.

The marginal revenue product of capital diminishes as the quantity of capital increases. Capital is just like labour in this respect. If Tina buys a second computer, Taxfile's total revenue will increase by less than the £1,150 generated by the first computer.

Interest Rate

The interest rate is the opportunity cost of the funds borrowed to finance investment. The interest rate is also the opportunity cost of a firm using its own funds because it could lend those funds to another firm and earn the going interest rate on the loan. The higher the interest rate, the smaller is the quantity of planned investment and borrowing in the capital market.

Firms demand the quantity of capital that makes the marginal revenue product of capital equal to the expenditure on capital. But the expenditure on capital is a present outlay and the marginal revenue product is a future return. The higher the interest rate, the smaller is the present value of future returns, and so the smaller is the quantity of planned investment. (An Appendix on pp. 405–408 explains the technical details on comparing present and future values.)

Demand Curve for Capital

A firm's demand curve for capital shows the relationship between the quantity of financial capital demanded by the firm and the interest rate, other things remaining the same. Figure 17.7(a) shows Tina's demand curve for capital. The lower the interest rate, the greater is the number of computers that Tina buys.

Figure 17.7(b) shows the market demand curve for capital, *KD*, which is the horizontal sum of the demand curves of each firm. In the figure, the quantity of capital demanded in the entire capital market is £150 billion when the interest rate is 6 per cent a year.

You've seen how the demand for capital is determined. Let's now look at the supply side of the capital market.

Figure 17.7

A Firm's Demand and the Market Demand for Capital

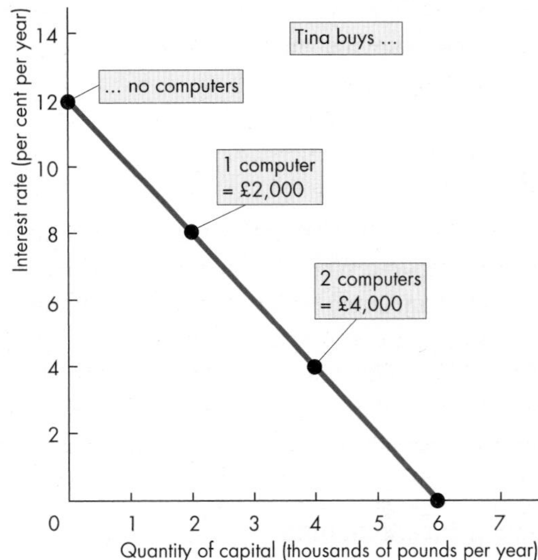

(a) Tina's demand curve for capital

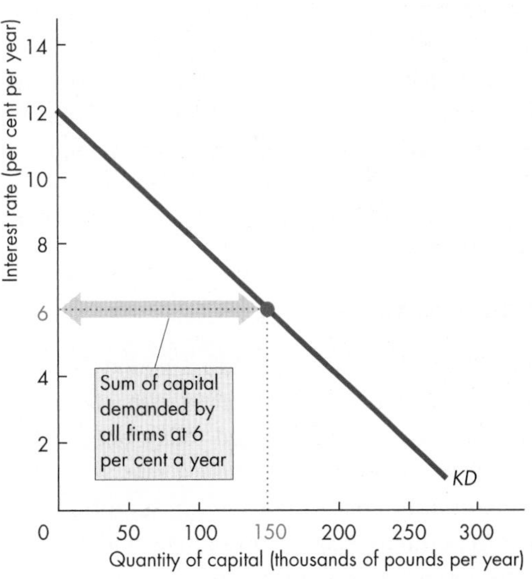

(b) Market demand curve for capital

Part (a) shows Tina's demand for capital. As the interest rate falls, the quantity of capital Tina demands increases. That is, for each firm, the lower the interest rate, the greater is the quantity of capital demanded.

Part (b) illustrates the market demand for capital. The market demand for capital curve is the horizontal sum of the firms' demand curves.

The Supply of Capital

The quantity of capital supplied results from people's saving decisions. The main factors that determine household saving are:

- Current income
- Expected future income
- The interest rate

Current Income

Saving is the act of converting *current* income into *future* consumption. When Aaron's income increases, he plans to consume more both now and in the future. But to increase *future* consumption, Aaron must save today. So, other things remaining the same, the higher Aaron's current income, the more he saves. The relationship between saving and current income is remarkably stable.

Expected Future Income

If Aaron's current income is high and his expected future income is low, he will have a high level of saving. But if Aaron's current income is low and his expected future income is high, he will have a low (perhaps even negative) level of saving.

Students have low current incomes compared with expected future incomes, so they tend to consume more than they earn. In middle age, most people are earning more than they expect to earn when they retire, so they save for their retirement years.

The Interest Rate

A pound saved today grows into a pound plus interest tomorrow. The higher the interest rate, the greater is the amount that a pound saved today becomes in the future. Thus the higher the interest rate, the greater is the opportunity cost of current consumption. With a higher opportunity cost of current consumption, Aaron cuts his current consumption and increases his saving.

Supply Curve of Capital

The supply curve of capital shows the relationship between the quantity of capital supplied and the interest rate, other things remaining the same. The curve KS_0 in Figure 17.8 is a supply curve of capital. Let's now use what we've learned about the demand for and supply of capital and see how the interest rate is determined.

The Interest Rate

The interest rate coordinates people's saving and investment plans through capital markets. If saving exceeds investment, the interest falls and if saving is less than investment, the interest rate rises. By adjusting in response to a surplus or shortage of funds, the interest rate makes saving and investment plans compatible.

Figure 17.8 illustrates these adjustments in the capital market. The demand for capital is KD_0 and the supply of capital is KS_0. The equilibrium real interest rate is 6 per cent a year, and the quantity of capital – amount of investment by firms and saving by households – is £150 billion.

If the interest rate exceeded 6 per cent a year, the quantity of capital supplied would exceed the quantity demanded and the interest rate would fall. The interest rate would keep falling until the capital surplus was eliminated.

If the interest rate were less than 6 per cent a year, the quantity of capital demanded would exceed the quantity supplied and the interest rate would rise. The interest rate would keep rising until the capital shortage was eliminated.

Figure 17.8

myeconlab

Capital Market Equilibrium

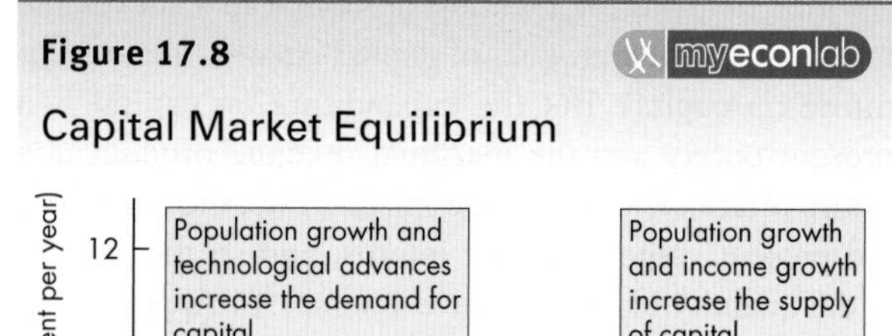

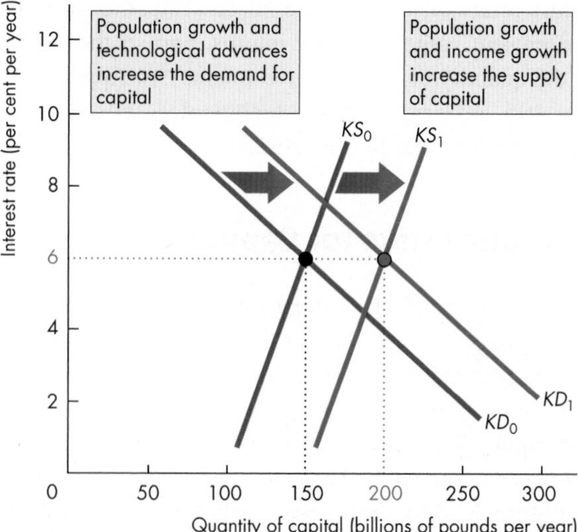

Initially, the demand for capital is KD_0 and the supply of capital is KS_0. The equilibrium interest rate is 6 per cent a year and the capital stock is £150 billion.

Over time, both the demand and supply of capital increase, to KD_1 and KS_1. The quantity of capital increases, but the interest rate is constant.

Changes in Demand and Supply in the Capital Market

Over time, both the demand for capital and the supply of capital increase. In Figure 17.8, the demand curve shifts rightward to KD_1 and the supply curve shifts to KS_1. Both curves shift because the same or related forces influence them. Population growth increases both demand and supply. Technological advances increase demand and bring higher incomes, which in turn increase supply. Because both demand and supply increase over time, the quantity of capital increases but the real interest rate remains constant.

In reality, the real interest rate fluctuates, as you can see in Box 17.2 Figure 1 on p. 392. The reason is that the demand for capital and the supply of capital do not change in step. Sometimes rapid technological change brings an increase in the demand for capital *before* it brings the higher incomes that increase the supply of capital. When this sequence of events occurs, the real interest rate rises. The 1990s was such a time.

At other times, the demand for capital grows slowly or even decreases temporarily. In this situation, supply outgrows demand and the real interest rate falls and may even become negative. The mid-1970s was such a period.

Review Quiz

Study Plan 17.4

1 What is the distinction between *physical* capital and *financial* capital and what is the capital market?
2 What is special about the comparison of the marginal product of capital with the expenditure on capital?
3 What are the main influences on a firm's demand for capital?
4 Why does the quantity of capital demanded depend on the interest rate?
5 What are the main influences on the supply of capital?
6 What have been the main changes in the interest rate and how can we use the demand and supply of capital to explain those changes?

The lessons we've just learned about capital markets can be used to understand the prices of non-renewable natural resources. Let's see how.

Natural Resource Markets

Natural resources, or what economists call *land*, fall into two categories:

1 Renewable
2 Non-renewable

Renewable natural resources are natural resources that are repeatedly replenished by nature. Examples are land (in its everyday sense), rivers, lakes, rain, forests and sunshine.

Non-renewable natural resources are natural resources that nature does not replenish. Once used, they are no longer available. Examples are coal, natural gas and oil – the so-called hydrocarbon fuels.

The demand for natural resources as inputs into production is based on the same principle of marginal revenue product as the demand for labour (and the demand for capital). But the supply of natural resources is special. Let's look first at the supply of renewable natural resources.

The Supply of a Renewable Natural Resource

The quantity of land and other renewable natural resources is fixed. The quantity supplied cannot be changed by individual decisions. People can vary the amount of land they own. But when one person buys some land, another person sells it. The aggregate quantity of land supplied of any particular type and in any particular location is fixed, regardless of the decisions of any individual. This fact means that the supply of each particular piece of land is perfectly inelastic.

Figure 17.9 illustrates such a supply. Regardless of the rent available, the quantity of land supplied in Oxford Street, London is a fixed number of square metres.

Because the supply of land is fixed regardless of its price, price is determined by demand. The greater the demand for a specific piece of land, the higher is its price.

Expensive land can be, and is, used more intensively than inexpensive land. For example, high-rise buildings enable land to be used more intensively. However, to use land more intensively, it has to be combined with another factor of production: capital. An increase in the amount of capital per block of land does not change the supply of land itself.

Figure 17.9

The Supply of Land

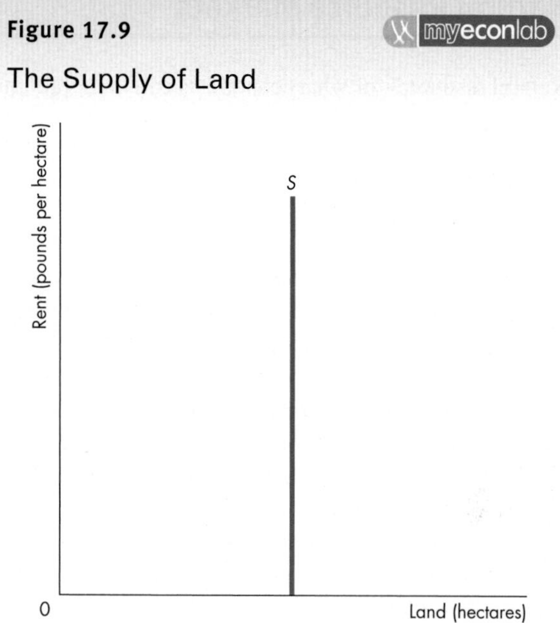

The supply of a given piece of land is perfectly inelastic. No matter what the rent, no more land than exists can be supplied.

Although the supply of each type of land is fixed and its supply is perfectly inelastic, each individual firm, operating in competitive land markets, faces an elastic supply of land. For example, Oxford Street, London has a fixed amount of land, but McDonald's could rent space from Selfridges, the department store, if they want to open a new outlet. Each firm can rent the quantity of land that it demands at the going rent, as determines in the marketplace. So provided land markets are highly competitive, firms are price takers in these markets, just as they are in the markets for other factors of production.

The Supply of Non-renewable Natural Resource

The *stock* of a natural resource is the quantity in existence at a given time. This quantity is fixed and is independent of the price of the resource. The *known* stock of a natural resource is the quantity that has been discovered. This quantity increases over time because advances in technology enable ever less accessible sources to be discovered. Both of these *stock* concepts influence the price of a non-renewable natural resource. But the influence is indirect. The direct influence on price is the rate at which the resource is supplied for use in production – called the flow supply.

The flow supply of a non-renewable natural resource is *perfectly elastic* at a price that equals the present value of the expected price next period.

To see why, think about the economic choices of Saudi Arabia, a country that possesses a large inventory of oil. Saudi Arabia can sell an additional billion barrels of oil right now and use the income it receives to buy US or EU bonds. Or it can keep the billion barrels in the ground and sell them next year. If it sells the oil and buys bonds, it earns the interest rate on the bonds. If it keeps the oil and sells it next year, it earns the amount of the price increase or loses the amount of the price decrease between now and next year.

If Saudi Arabia expects the price of oil to rise next year by a percentage that equals the current interest rate, the price that it expects next year equals $(1 + r)$ multiplied by this year's price. For example, if this year's price is £30 a barrel and the interest rate is 5 per cent $(r = 0.5)$, then next year's expected price is $1.05 \times$ £30, which equals £31.50 a barrel.

With the price expected to rise to £31.50 next year, Saudi Arabia is indifferent between selling now for £30 and not selling now but waiting until next year and selling for £31.50. Saudi Arabia expects to make the same return either way. So at £30 a barrel, Saudi Arabia will sell whatever quantity is demanded.

But if Saudi Arabia expects the price to rise next year by a percentage that exceeds the current interest rate, then Saudi Arabia expects to make a bigger return by hanging onto the oil than by selling the oil and buying bonds. So it keeps the oil and sells none.

And if Saudi Arabia expects the price to rise next year by a percentage that is less than the current interest rate, the bond gives a bigger return than the oil, so Saudi Arabia sells as much oil as it can.

Recall the idea of discounting and present value. The minimum price at which Saudi Arabia is willing to sell oil is the present value of the expected future price. At this price, it will sell as much oil as buyers demand. So its supply is perfectly elastic.

Price and the Hotelling Principle

Figure 17.10 shows the equilibrium in a natural resource market. Because supply is perfectly elastic at the present value of next period's expected price, the actual price of the natural resource equals the present value of next period's expected price. Also, because the current price is the present value of the expected future price, the price of the resource is expected to rise at a rate equal to the interest rate.

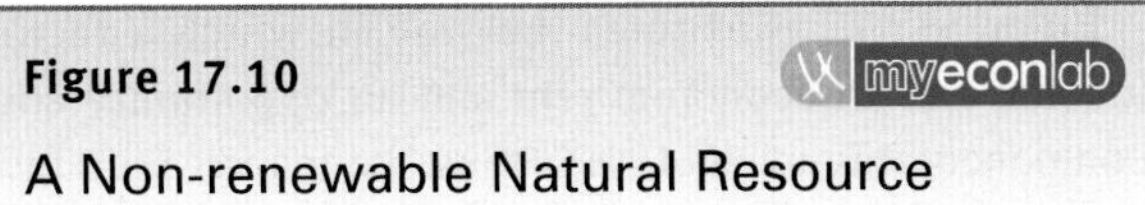

Figure 17.10

A Non-renewable Natural Resource

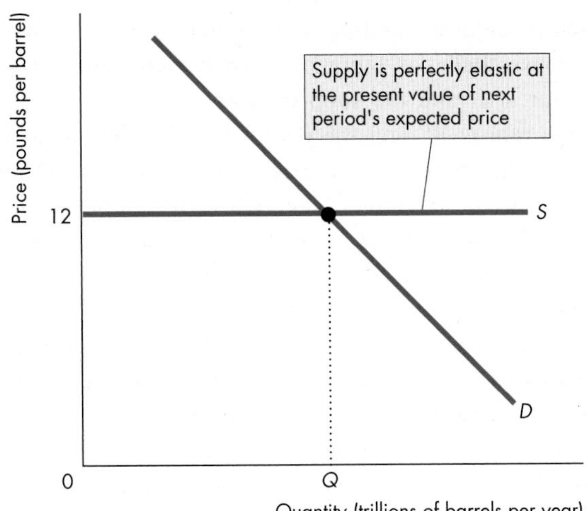

The supply of a non-renewable natural resource is perfectly elastic at the *present value* of next period's expected price. The demand for a non-renewable natural resource is determined by its marginal revenue product. The price is determined by supply and equals the *present value* of next period's expected price.

Figure 17.11

Falling and Rising Resource Prices

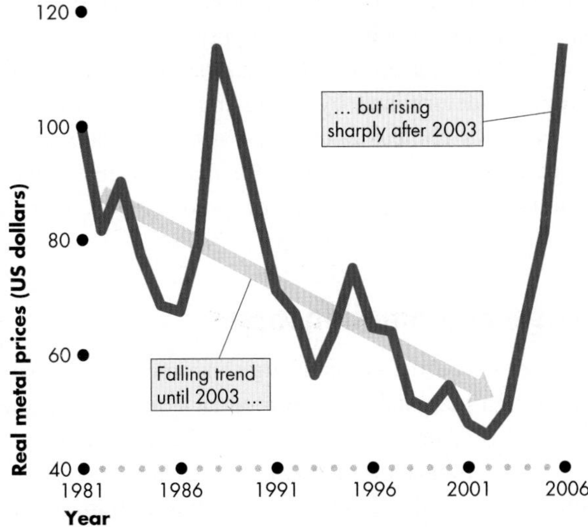

The prices of metals (here an average of the prices of aluminium, copper, iron ore, lead, manganese, nickel, silver, tin and zinc) tended between 1981 and 2003, not rise as predicted by the Hotelling Principle. The reason is that unanticipated advances in technology decreased the cost of extracting metals and greatly increased the exploitable known reserves. But prices rocketed after 2003.

Source of data: International Monetary Fund, World Economic Outlook Database.

The proposition that the price of a resource is expected to rise at a rate equal to the interest rate is called the **Hotelling Principle**. It was first realized by Harold Hotelling, a mathematician and economist at Columbia University. But as Figure 17.11 shows, *actual* prices do not follow the path *predicted* by the Hotelling Principle. Why do the prices of non-renewable natural resources sometimes fall rather than follow their expected path and increase over time?

The key reason is that the future is unpredictable. Expected technological change is reflected in the price of a natural resource. But a previously unexpected new technology that leads to the discovery or the more efficient use of a non-renewable natural resource causes its price to fall. Over the years, as technology has advanced, we have become more efficient in our use of non-renewable natural resources. And we haven't just become more efficient. We've become more efficient than we expected to. We have repeatedly been surprised by our good fortune in discovering more fuel-efficient technologies and in discovering previously unexpected sources of fuels.

When this period of pleasant surprises comes to an end, prices will begin to rise as predicted by the Hotelling Principle.

Review Quiz

Study Plan 17.5

1. Define a renewable natural resource and a non-renewable natural resource and provide some examples of each.
2. Why is the supply of a renewable natural resource such as land perfectly inelastic?
3. At what price is the flow supply of a non-renewable natural resource perfectly elastic and why?
4. Why is the price of a non-renewable natural resource expected to rise at a rate equal to the interest rate?
5. Why do the prices of non-renewable natural resources not follow the path predicted by the Hotelling Principle?

People supply resources to earn income. But some peoples earn enormous incomes. Are such incomes necessary to induce people to work and supply other resources? Let's now answer this question.

Income, Economic Rent and Opportunity Cost

You've now seen how factor prices are determined by the interaction of demand and supply. You've also seen that demand is determined by marginal productivity and supply is determined by the resources available and by people's choices about their use. The interaction of demand and supply in factor markets determines who receives a large income and who receives a small income.

Large and Small Incomes

A chief executive earns a large income because she has a high marginal revenue product – reflected in the demand for her services – and the supply of people with the combination of talents needed for this kind of job is small – reflected in the supply. Equilibrium occurs at a high wage rate and a small quantity employed.

People who work at fast-food restaurants earn a low wage rate because they have a low marginal revenue product – reflected in the demand for their services – and many people are able and willing to supply their labour for these jobs. Equilibrium occurs at a low wage rate and a large number of fast-food workers employed.

If the demand for chief executives increases, their incomes increase by a large amount and the number of chief executives barely changes. If the demand for fast-food workers increases, the number of people doing these jobs increases by a large amount and the wage rate barely changes.

Another difference between a chief executive and a fast-food worker is that if the chief executive were hit with a pay cut, she would probably still supply her services, but if a fast-food worker were hit with a pay cut, he would probably quit. This difference arises from the interesting distinction between economic rent and opportunity cost.

Economic Rent and Opportunity Cost

The total income of a factor of production is made up of its economic rent and its opportunity cost. **Economic rent** is an income received by the owner of a factor over and above the amount required to induce that owner to offer the factor for use. Any factor of production can receive an economic rent. The income required to induce the supply of a factor of production is the opportunity cost of using a factor of production – the value of the factor in its next best use.

Figure 17.12 illustrates the way in which a factor income has an economic rent and an opportunity cost component. Figure 17.12(a) shows the market for a factor of production. It could be *any* factor of production – labour, capital, land or entrepreneurship – but we'll suppose that it is labour. The demand curve for the labour is D and the supply curve of labour is S. The wage rate is W, and the quantity of labour employed is C. The income earned is the sum of the red and green areas. The red area below the supply curve measures opportunity cost. The green area above the supply curve but below the factor price measures economic rent.

To see why the area below the supply curve measures opportunity cost, recall that a supply curve can be interpreted in two different ways. It shows the quantity supplied at a given price and it shows the minimum price at which a given quantity is willingly supplied. If suppliers receive only the minimum amount required to induce them to supply each unit of the factor, they will be paid a different price for each unit. The prices will trace the supply curve and the income received will be entirely opportunity cost – the red area in Figure 17.12(a).

The concept of economic rent is similar to the concept of producer surplus that you met in Chapter 5. The economic rent is the price a person receives for the use of a factor minus the minimum price at which a given quantity of the factor is willingly supplied.

Economic rent is *not* the same thing as the "rent" that a farmer pays for the use of some land or the "rent" that you pay on your flat. Everyday "rent" is a price paid for the services of land or a building. *Economic rent* is a component of the income received by any factor of production.

The portion of factor income that consists of economic rent depends on the elasticity of the supply of the factor. When the supply of a factor is perfectly inelastic, its entire income is economic rent. A large part of the income received by a chief executive is economic rent. When the supply of a factor of production is perfectly elastic, none of its income is economic rent. Most of the income earned by low-skilled workers is opportunity cost. In general, when the supply curve is neither perfectly elastic nor perfectly inelastic, some part of the factor income is economic rent and the other part opportunity cost – as Figure 17.12(a) illustrates.

Figures 17.12(b) and 17.12(c) show the other two possibilities. Part (b) shows the market for a particular block of land in London. The quantity of land is fixed in size at L hectares. So the supply curve of land is

Figure 17.12

Economic Rent and Opportunity Cost

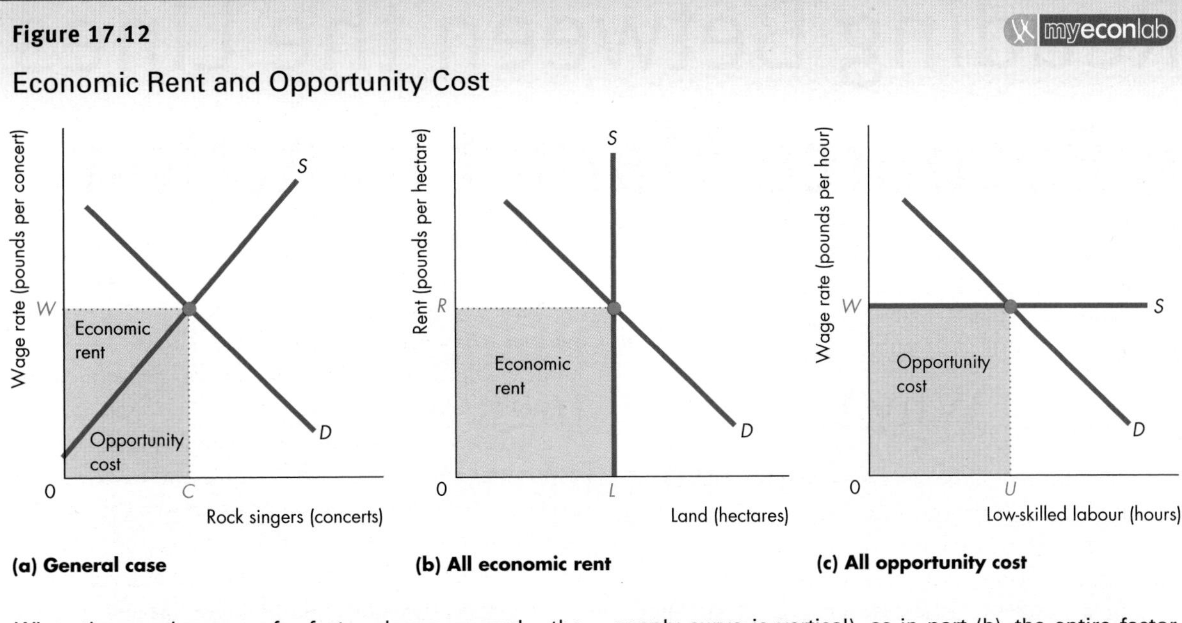

When the supply curve of a factor slopes upward – the general case – as in part (a), part of the factor income is economic rent (the green area) and part is opportunity cost (the red area).

When the supply of a factor is perfectly inelastic (the supply curve is vertical), as in part (b), the entire factor income is economic rent.

When the supply of a factor is perfectly elastic (the supply curve is horizontal), as in part (c), the entire factor income is opportunity cost.

vertical – perfectly inelastic. No matter what the rent on the land is, there is no way of increasing the quantity supplied.

The demand for that block of land is determined by its marginal revenue product, which depends on the uses to which the land can be put. In central London, the marginal revenue product is high because there is a great deal of capital and business there. The marginal revenue product of this land is shown by the demand curve in Figure 17.12(b). The entire income accruing to the owner of the land is the green area in the figure. This income is economic rent. The rent charged for this piece of land depends entirely on its marginal revenue product – on the demand curve. If the demand curve shifts rightward, the rent rises. If the demand curve shifts leftward, the rent falls. The quantity of land supplied remains constant at *L*.

Figure 17.12(c) shows the market for a factor of production that is in perfectly elastic supply. An example of such a market might be unskilled labour in India or China. In these countries, lots of people flock to the cities and are available for work at the going wage rate (in this case, *W*). In these labour markets, the supply of labour is almost perfectly elastic. The entire income earned by these unskilled workers is opportunity cost. They receive no economic rent at all.

Review Quiz

Study Plan 17.6

1. Why do premier league football players earn larger incomes than bus drivers?
2. What is the distinction between an economic rent and an opportunity cost?
3. Is the income that Manchester United pays Wayne Rooney an economic rent, compensation for his opportunity cost, or a combination of economic rent and opportunity cost? Explain.
4. Is coffee more expensive in London than in Lincoln because rents are higher in London or are rents higher in London because people in London are willing to pay more for a coffee?

The next chapter looks at how the market economy distributes income and how governments redistribute income and modify the market outcome. But first, take a look at the global market for oil in *Reading Between the Lines* on pp. 400–401.

Reading Between the Lines
A Resource Market in Action

The Sunday Times, 11 September 2005

Why the dog of high oil prices is not barking

David Smith

. . . America summoned . . . big oil-consuming nations to an emergency conference in Washington in February 1974, the main outcome of which was the creation of the International Energy Agency (IEA). The main purpose of the IEA . . . was to ensure members carried enough oil stocks to avoid being held to ransom by OPEC.

. . . A few days ago . . . the IEA's members agreed to release some of their stocks to tide America over the wake of the Hurricane Katrina. . . . It worked . . . to the extent of bringing crude prices down into the mid-$60s.

. . . During the oil shocks of the 1970s, finance ministers would gather at the OECD in Paris and survey the wreckage. Last week the OECD, the advanced countries' club, gave us its current view on the impact of high oil prices today. And pretty relaxed it was. . . . The dog of high oil prices isn't barking.

Why is this? . . . In advanced countries, . . . the switch from heavy industry to services, and to more fuel-efficient transport, has reduced the so-called 'oil intensity' of economic growth. Each 1% of growth in Britain requires 0.4% extra oil. In the past, 1% growth required 1% or more oil . . .

The Essence of the Story

- Hurricane Katrina cut US oil production in summer 2005.
- The IEA releases some of its oil stocks in response.
- The price of crude fell to the mid-$60s a barrel.
- The OECD are not overly concerned about the rising oil prices, stating that advanced countries need less oil for growth now than in the past.

Economic Analysis

- The global market for crude oil is an interesting example of a non-renewable natural resource market.
- The market is hit by many surprises, one of which was Hurricane Katrina (29 August 2005), which destroyed New Orleans and cut US crude oil production.
- Figure 1 shows the daily price of crude oil from 1 August to 21 September 2005. One week before Katrina, the price was $65 a barrel. At its peak after Katrina, the price was $69 a barrel. Why didn't the price rise by more?
- Part of the answer is that US production is a small part of global production. Another part of the answer is that the International Energy Agency (the IEA) releases oil from stocks to avoid a serious shortage.
- The world oil price reacted to Katrina as predicted by the theory of resource price determination that you've studied in this chapter.
- Figure 2 shows what happened to supply and the price.
- The decrease in US production of nearly 1 million barrels a day meant that the oil market had to allocate the smaller quantity among competing uses.
- Rational traders (including the IEA) anticipated the new equilibrium price of $69 a barrel. They were ready to buy into stocks or sell from stocks, so the market supply is perfectly elastic at this price. The supply curve shifts from S_0 before Katrina to S_1 after Katrina and the price increased.
- Figure 3 shows the long-term trend in the real price of crude oil. The price is on a slightly upward trend as predicted by the Hotelling Principle. But more efficient technologies for extracting and using oil have prevented the price from rising as fast as Hotelling predicts.

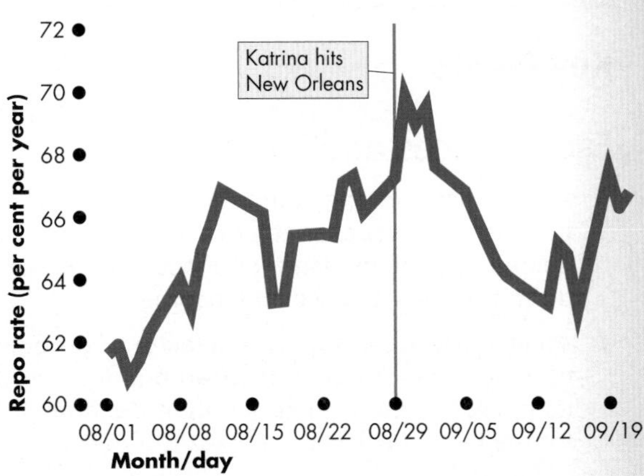

Figure 1 The daily price of crude oil in summer 2005

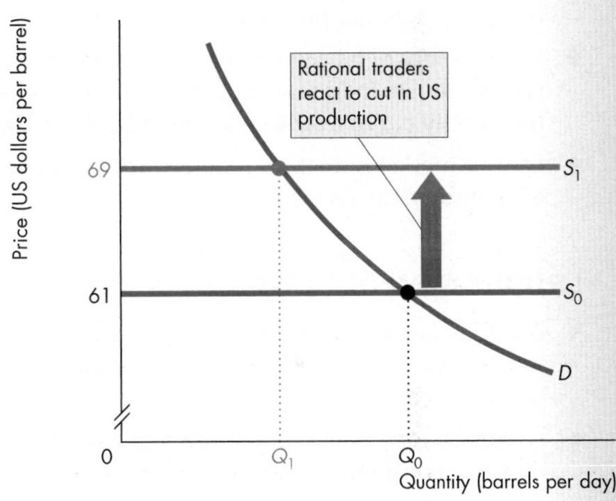

Figure 2 The market for oil in summer 2005

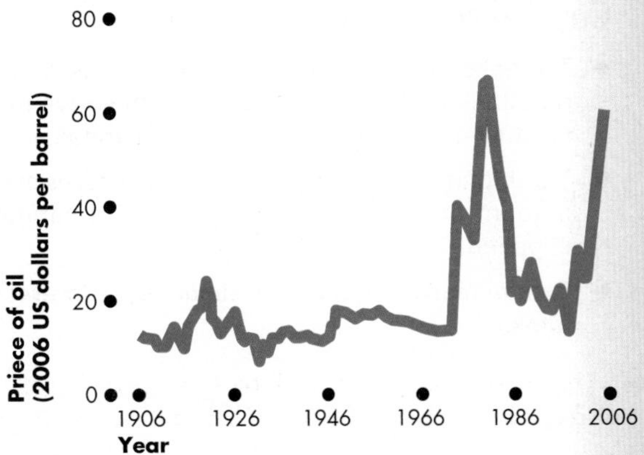

Figure 3 A hundred years of the real price of oil

Summary

Key Points

Factor Prices and Incomes (p. 378)

- An increase in the demand for a factor of production increases it price and income; a decrease in the demand for a factor of production decreases its price and income.
- An increase in the supply of a factor of production increases the quantity used but decreases its price. Income increases only if the demand for the factor is elastic.

Labour Markets (pp. 379–386)

- The demand for labour is determined by the marginal revenue product.
- The quantity of labour supplied increases as the real wage rate increases, but at high wage rates, the supply curve eventually bends backwards.
- Labour market equilibrium determines the level of employment and the wage rate.

Labour Market Power (pp. 387–391)

- A trades union can raise the wage rate restricting the supply or increasing the demand for labour.
- A monopsony can lower the wage rate below that in a competitive labour market.
- In monopsony, a minimum wage law can raise the wage rate and increase employment.

Capital Markets (pp. 392–395)

- To make an investment decision, firms compare the *present value* of the marginal revenue product of capital with the price of capital.
- The higher the interest rate, the greater is the amount of saving and the quantity of capital supplied.
- Capital market equilibrium determines interest rates.

Natural Resource Markets (pp. 395–397)

- The demand for a natural resource is determined by marginal revenue product.
- The supply of land is inelastic.
- The supply of non-renewable natural resources is perfectly elastic at a price equal to the present value of the expected future price.
- The price of non-renewable natural resources is expected to rise at a rate equal to the interest rate but fluctuates and might fall.

Income, Economic Rent and Opportunity Cost (pp. 398–399)

- Economic rent is the income received by a factor over and above the amount needed to induce the factor owner to supply the resource for use.
- The rest of a factor's income is opportunity cost.
- When the supply of a factor is perfectly inelastic, its entire income is made up of economic rent. When the supply of a factor is perfectly elastic, its entire income is made up of opportunity cost.

Key Figures and Tables

Key Terms

Problems

Tests, Study Plan and Solutions* 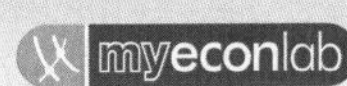

1 The figure illustrates a European market for strawberry pickers:

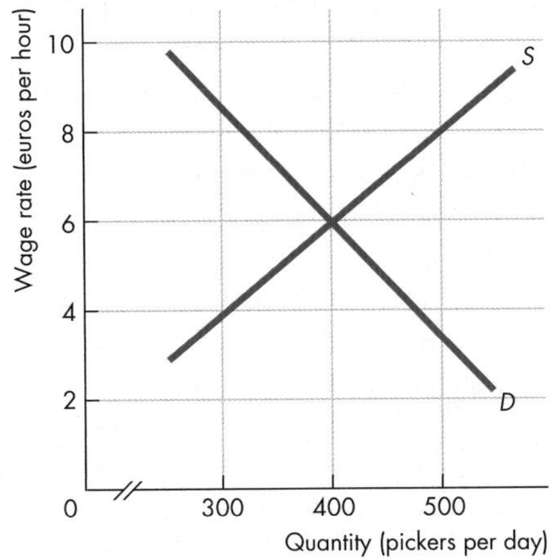

a What is the wage rate paid to strawberry pickers?

b How many strawberry pickers get employed?

c What is the income received by strawberry pickers?

If the demand for strawberry pickers increases by 100 a day,

d What is the new wage rate paid to the pickers?

e How many additional pickers get employed?

f What is the total income paid to pickers?

2 The European fish packing industry is competitive and Wanda owns a fish shop. She employs students to sort and pack the fish. Students can pack the following amounts of fish in an hour:

Number of students	Quantity of fish (kilograms)
1	20
2	50
3	90
4	120
5	145
6	165
7	180
8	190

The market price of fish is 50 cents a kilogram and the wage rate of packers is €7.50 an hour.

a Calculate the marginal product of the students and draw the marginal product curve.

b Calculate the marginal revenue product of the students and draw the marginal revenue product curve.

c Find Wanda's demand for labour curve.

d How many students does Wanda employ?

3 Back at Wanda's fish shop described in problem 2, the market price of fish falls to €33.33 a kilogram. If fish packers' wages remain at €7.50 an hour, what happens to:

a Wanda's marginal product?

b Wanda's marginal revenue product?

c Wanda's demand for labour curve?

d Number of students Wanda employs?

4 At Wanda's fish shop described in problem 2, the wage rate paid to packers increases to €10 an hour. If the market price of fish remains at 50 cents a kilogram:

a What happens to marginal revenue product?

b What happens to Wanda's demand for labour curve?

c How many students does Wanda employ?

5 Use the information in problem 2 to calculate Wanda's marginal revenue, marginal cost and marginal revenue product. Show that when Wanda is making maximum profit, marginal cost equals marginal revenue and marginal revenue product equals the wage rate.

6 **Biggest trade union set to be approved**

The creation of the largest trade union, with about 2m members, is expected to be approved tomorrow when the results of ballots of Amicus and T&G members are revealed. The merger plan has raised concerns about the combined union's potential influence over the Labour party and the rest of the trade union movement.

Financial Times, 7 March 2007

a Why do you think Amicus and T&G members voted to merge?

b Who wins from this new union? Who loses?

c How can this union try to change the demand for labour?

d What do you think "union's potential influence over the rest of the trade union movement" means for how the UK labour market works?

7 Keshia operates a bookkeeping service. She is considering buying four new computers, which will each

* Solutions to odd-numbered problems are provided.

have a life of three years and after that will be worthless. The price of each computer is £1,600. The marginal revenue product of the first computer in each year is £700. The marginal revenue product of the second computer in each year is £625. The marginal revenue product of the third computer in each year is £575. And the marginal revenue product of the fourth computer in each year is £500. How many computers will Keshia buy if the interest rate is

a 2 per cent a year

b 4 per cent a year

c 6 per cent a year

8 **Baronet rides to the rescue of parkland under threat**

A group of residents in Salford who are campaigning to block a proposed housing development . . . discovered that the plot was once a farm owned by the ancestors of Sir Peter Heywood, the 6th Baronet of Claremont, and that they had sold it to the council in 1902 on the condition that it be used only for recreation. . . . Council officials had claimed that there was little chance of tracking down descendants . . . [but now] may be forced to rethink its plan to sell the land for £1.5 million.

The Times, 4 April 2007

a Why would the plot of land in Salford be worth £1.5 million? Include in your answer a discussion of the demand for land and the supply of land.

b If the land were sold, would the council earn economic rent or opportunity cost?

c Is the supply of land in Salford perfectly inelastic?

Critical Thinking

1 Study the *Reading Between the Lines* on pp. 400–401 and then answer the following questions:

a What determines the price of a natural resource such as crude oil?

b How did Hurricane Katrina affect the price of oil in summer 2005?

c How has the price of oil moved over the past 100 years? Explain the price movements in terms of the Hotelling Principle.

d Do you expect the price of oil to keep rising? Explain why or why not.

e Will the oil age end because the world runs out of oil? Explain why or why not.

2 Think about the high salaries awarded to the Chief Executives of modern companies and then answer the following questions:

a What determines the demand for chief executives?

b What determines the supply of chief executives?

c What do you think chief executives would do if they didn't work in industry?

d What does your answer to part (c) tell you about the opportunity cost of these chief executives?

e What does your answer to part (c) tell you about the economic rent received by these chief executives?

f Why don't top executives have contracts that give them their entire marginal revenue product?

g Why is the economic rent of most executives less than the top chief executives?

h Would an inexperienced executive gain as much economic rent as executives with good track records? Explain your answer?

3 "We are running out of natural resources and must take urgent action to conserve our precious reserves." "There is no shortage of resources that the market cannot cope with." Identify the pros and cons for each view, and discuss each in turn. What is your view and why?

4 Why do we keep finding new reserves of oil? Why don't we do a big once-and-for-all survey to catalogue the earth's entire inventory of natural resources?

Web Activities

Links to Websites

1 Find data on the earnings of leading golfers, tennis players and footballers. Then answer the following questions:

a What determines the demand for a top-performing professional sports person?

b What determines the supply of a top-performing professional sports person?

c What do you think Luke Donald, Andy Murray and Wayne Rooney would do if they didn't play their sports?

d What does your answer to part (c) tell you about the opportunity cost of these players?

e What does your answer to part (c) tell you about the economic rent received by these players?

f What would be the effects of a super income tax on the mega incomes of sports stars?

Chapter 17 Appendix

Present Value and Discounting

After studying this appendix you will be able to:

- Explain how to calculate the present value of a future amount of money
- Explain how a firm uses a present value calculation to make an investment decision
- Explain the relationship between present value and the interest rate

Comparing Current and Future Values of Money

To decide how much capital to buy, a firm must compare the present expenditure on capital with the future marginal revenue product of capital. To make such a comparison, we convert the future return into a "present value".

The **present value** of a future amount of money is the amount that, if invested today, will grow to be as large as that future amount when the interest it will earn is taken into account.

So the present value of a future amount of money is smaller than the future amount. The calculation that we use to convert the future amount of money to a present value is called **discounting**.

The easiest way to understand discounting and present value is to consider how a present value grows to a future amount of money because of *compound interest*.

Compound Interest

Compound interest is the interest on an initial investment plus the interest on the interest that the investment has previously earned. Because of compound interest, a present amount of money (a present value) grows into a larger future amount. The future amount is equal to the present amount (present value) plus the interest it will earn in the future.

That is:

$$\text{Future amount} = \text{Present value} + \text{Interest income}$$

The interest income is equal to the present value multiplied by the interest rate, r, so:

$$\text{Future amount} = \text{Present value} + (r \times \text{Present value})$$

or:

$$\text{Future amount} = \text{Present value} \times (1 + r)$$

If you have £100 today and the interest rate is 10 per cent a year ($r = 0.1$), one year from today you will have £110 – the original £100 plus £10 interest. Check that the above formula delivers that answer:

$$£100 \times 1.1 = £110$$

If you leave this £110 invested to earn 10 per cent during a second year, at the end of that year, you will have

$$\text{Amount after 2 years} = \text{Present value} \times (1 + r)^2$$

With the numbers of the previous example, you invest £100 today at an interest rate of 10 per cent a year, which means that $r = 0.1$. After one year you have £110 – the original £100 plus £10 interest. And after the second year, you have £121. In the second year, you earned £10 on your initial £100 plus £1 on the £10 interest that you earned in the first year.

Check that the above formula delivers that answer:

$$£100 \times (1.1)^2 = £100 \times 1.21 = £121$$

If you leave your £100 invested for n years, it will grow to:

$$\text{Amount after } n \text{ years} = \text{Present value} \times (1 + r)^n$$

With an interest rate of 10 per cent a year, your £100 will be £195 after 7 years ($n = 7$) – almost double the present value of £100.

Discounting a Future Amount

We have just calculated the future value of a present amount of money. You've seen how £100 today grows to £110 after one year, £121 after 2 years, and £195 after 7 years if the interest rate is 10 per cent a year. To calculate the present value of these future amounts, one year, two years, and n years in the future, we just work backward.

To find the present value of an amount one year in the future, we divide the future amount by $(1 + r)$.

That is:

$$\text{Present value} = \frac{\text{Amount of money one year in the future}}{(1 + r)}$$

Let's check that we can use the present value formula by calculating the present value of £110 one year from now when the interest rate is 10 per cent a year. You'll be able to guess that the answer is £100 because we just calculated that £100 invested today at 10 per cent a year becomes £110 in one year. Thus it follows immediately that the present value of £110 in one year's time is £100. But let's use the formula. Putting the numbers into the above formula, we have:

$$\text{Present value} = \frac{£110}{(1 + 0.1)} = \frac{£110}{1.1} = £100$$

To calculate the present value of an amount of money two years in the future, we use the formula:

$$\text{Present value} = \frac{\text{Amount of money two years in future}}{(1 + r)^2}$$

Use this formula to calculate the present value of £121 two years from now at an interest rate of 10 per cent a year. With these numbers the formula gives:

$$\text{Present value} = \frac{£121}{(1 + 0.1)^2} = \frac{£121}{(1.1)^2} = \frac{£121}{1.21} = £100$$

We can calculate the present value of an amount of money any number of years in the future by using a formula based on the two that we've already used. The general formula is:

$$\text{Present value} = \frac{\text{Amount of money } n \text{ years in future}}{(1 + r)^n}$$

For example, if the interest rate is 10 per cent a year, £100 to be received 10 years from now has a present value of £38.55. That is, if £38.55 is invested today at an interest rate of 10 per cent a year, it will accumulate to £100 in 10 years. (You might check that calculation on your pocket calculator.)

Present Value of a Sequence of Future Amounts

You've seen how to calculate the present value of an amount of money one year in the future, two years in the future, and *n* years in the future. Most practical applications of present value calculate the present value of a sequence of future amounts of money that spread over several years. To calculate the present value of a sequence of amounts over several years, we use the formula you have learned and apply it to each year. We then sum the present values for each year to find the present value of the sequence of amounts.

For example, suppose that a firm expects to receive £100 a year for each of the next five years. And suppose that the interest rate is 10 per cent per year (0.1 per year). The present value of these five payments of £100 each is calculated by using the following formula:

$$PV = \frac{£100}{1.1} + \frac{£100}{1.1^2} + \frac{£100}{1.1^3} + \frac{£100}{1.1^4} + \frac{£100}{1.1^5}$$

which equals:

$$PV = £90.91 + £82.64 + £75.13 + £68.30 + £62.09 = £379.07$$

You can see that the firm receives £500 over five years. But because the money arrives in the future, it is not worth £500 today. Its present value is only £379.07. And the further in the future it arrives, the smaller is its present value. The £100 received one year in the future is worth £90.91 today. And the £100 received five years in the future is worth only £62.09 today.

Many personal and business decisions turn on calculations like the one we've just made. Should you rent or or buy a flat? Should you pay off your student loan? How much do you need to save each month to be able to retire and tour the world when you're 40? To find the answers, you must do some present value calculations. And if you run a business, how much should you invest in new capital. This everyday business decision is made by calculating the present value of the expected future revenues that a new item of capital will earn. Let's now see how an investment decision is made.

Present Value and Investment Decision

Tina runs Taxfile plc, a firm that sells advice to UK taxpayers. Tina is considering buying a new computer that costs £2,000. The computer has a life of two years, after which it will be worthless. If Tina buys the computer, she will pay out £2,000 now and she expects to generate business that will bring in an additional £1,150 at the end of each of the next two years.

To calculate the present value, *PV*, of the marginal revenue product of a new computer, Tina uses the formula:

$$PV = \frac{MRP_1}{(1+r)} + \frac{MRP_2}{(1+r)^2}$$

Here, MRP_1 is the marginal revenue product received by Tina at the end of the first year. It is converted to a present value by dividing it by $(1 + r)$. The term MRP_2 is the marginal revenue product received at the end of the second year. It is converted to a present value by dividing it by $(1 + r)^2$.

If Tina can borrow or lend at an interest rate of 4 per cent a year, the present value (*PV*) of her marginal revenue product is given by:

$$PV = \frac{£1{,}150}{(1+0.04)} + \frac{£1{,}150}{(1+0.04)^2}$$

$$PV = £1{,}106 + £1{,}063$$

$$PV = £2{,}169$$

The present value (*PV*) of £1,150 one year in the future is £1,150 divided by 1.04 (4 per cent as a proportion is 0.04). The present value of £1,150 two years in the future is £1,063 divided by $(1.04)^2$. Working out these two present values and then adding them gives Tina the present value of the future stream of marginal revenue products, which is £2,169.

Part (a) of Table A17.1 summarizes the data and part (b) puts Tina's numbers into the present value formula and calculates the present value of the marginal revenue product of a computer. Review these calculations and be sure that you understand them.

Table A17.1

Net Present Value of an Investment – Taxfile plc

(a) Data

Price of computer	2,000
Life of computer	2 years
Marginal revenue product	£1,150 at end of each year
Interest rate	4% a year

(b) Present value of the flow of marginal revenue product:

$$PV = \frac{MRP_1}{(1+r)} + \frac{MRP_2}{(1+r)^2}$$
$$= \frac{£1{,}150}{1.04} + \frac{£1{,}150}{(1.04)^2}$$
$$= £1{,}106 + £1.063$$
$$= £2{,}169$$

(c) Net present value of investment:

$NPV = PV$ of marginal revenue product – Price of computer
$= £2{,}169 - £2{,}000$
$= £169$

Tina's Decision to Buy

Tina decides whether to buy the computer by comparing the present value of its flow of marginal revenue product with its purchase price. She makes this comparison by calculating the net present value or *NPV* of the computer. **Net present value** is the present value of the future return – the future flow of marginal revenue product generated by the capital minus the price of the capital. If net present value is positive, the firm buys additional capital. If net present value is negative, the firm does not buy additional capital.

Table A17.1(c) shows the calculation of Tina's net present value of a computer. The net present value (*NPV*) is £169. Because the net present value is greater than zero, if Tina buys this computer, she will be £169 better off than if she doesn't buy it. So Tina buys the computer.

Tina can buy any number of computers that cost £2,000 and have a life of two years. But like all other factors of production, capital is subject to diminishing marginal returns. The greater the amount of capital employed, the smaller is its marginal revenue product. So if Tina buys a second computer or a third one, she gets successively smaller marginal revenue products from the additional computers.

Table A17.2(a) sets out Tina's marginal revenue products for one, two and three computers. The marginal

Table A17.2

Taxfile's Investment Decision

(a) Data

Price of computer	£2,000
Life of computer	2 years
Marginal revenue product:	
Using 1 computer	£1,150 a year
Using 2 computers	£1,100 a year
Using 3 computers	£1,050 a year

(b) Present value of the flow of marginal revenue product

If $r = 0.04$ (4% a year):

Using 1 computer: $PV = \frac{£1,150}{1.04} + \frac{£1,150}{(1.04)^2} = £2,169$

Using 2 computers: $PV = \frac{£1,100}{1.04} + \frac{£1,100}{(1.04)^2} = £2,075$

Using 3 computers: $PV = \frac{£1,050}{1.04} + \frac{£1,050}{(1.04)^2} = £1,980$

If $r = 0.08$ (8% a year):

Using 1 computer: $PV = \frac{£1,150}{1.08} + \frac{£1,150}{(1.08)^2} = £2,051$

Using 2 computers: $PV = \frac{£1,100}{1.08} + \frac{£1,100}{(1.08)^2} = £1,962$

If $r = 0.12$ (12% a year):

Using 1 computer: $PV = \frac{£1,150}{1.12} + \frac{£1,150}{(1.12)^2} = £1,944$

revenue product of one computer (the case just reviewed) is £1,150 a year. The marginal revenue product of a second computer is £1,100 a year and the marginal revenue product of a third computer is £1,050 a year. Table A17.2(b) shows the calculations of the present values of the marginal revenue products of the first, second and third computers.

You've seen that with an interest rate of 4 per cent a year, the net present value of one computer is positive. At an interest rate of 4 per cent a year, the present value of the marginal revenue product of a second computer is £2,075, which exceeds its price by £75. So Tina buys a second computer. But at an interest rate of 4 per cent a year, the present value of the marginal revenue product of a third computer is £1,980, which is £20 less than the price of a computer. So Tina does not buy a third computer.

Present Value and the Interest Rate

The higher the interest rate, the smaller is the present value of a given future amount of money. The numbers in Table A17.2(b) illustrate this fact. When the interest rate rises to 8 per cent, the present value of the first computer falls to £2,051 and when the interest rate rises to 12 per cent a year, the present value of the first computer falls to £1,944.

Because a firm invests only if the net present value is positive, other things remaining the same, as the interest rate rises, the quantity of capital demanded decreases.

The calculations in Table A17.2 generate Taxfile's demand curve for capital in Figure A17.1, which shows the value of the computers demanded at each interest rate.

The higher the interest rate, the smaller is the quantity of *physical* capital demanded. But to finance the purchase of physical capital, firms demand *financial* capital. So the higher the interest rate, the smaller is the quantity of *financial* capital demanded.

Figure A17.1

Taxfile plc's Demand for Capital

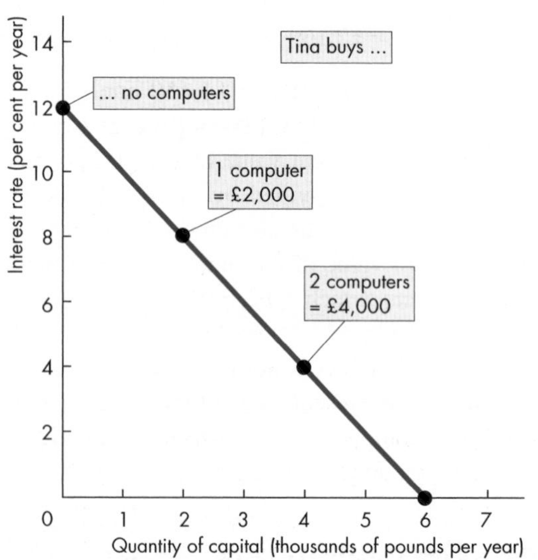

The higher the interest rate, the smaller is the present value of a future amount of money and the smaller is the quantity of capital demanded.

CHAPTER

18

Economic Inequality and Redistribution

After studying this chapter you will be able to:

- Describe the inequality in income and wealth in the United Kingdom and Europe and the trends in inequality
- Explain the features of the labour market that contribute to economic inequality
- Describe the scale of income redistribution by governments

Rags to Riches

J. K. Rowling earns more than £20 million a year and is Britain's highest-earning woman. But before she had the inspiration to write the Harry Potter stories, she was a typical single mother. Many single mothers earn almost nothing and rely on government benefits for their survival. Why are some people incredibly rich while others are abjectly poor? What contribution do government redistribution policies make to economic inequality and poverty? Find some answers in this chapter. And in *Reading Between the Lines* at the end of this chapter, take a close look at the difference to inequality the UK government's taxes and welfare and other benefits make.

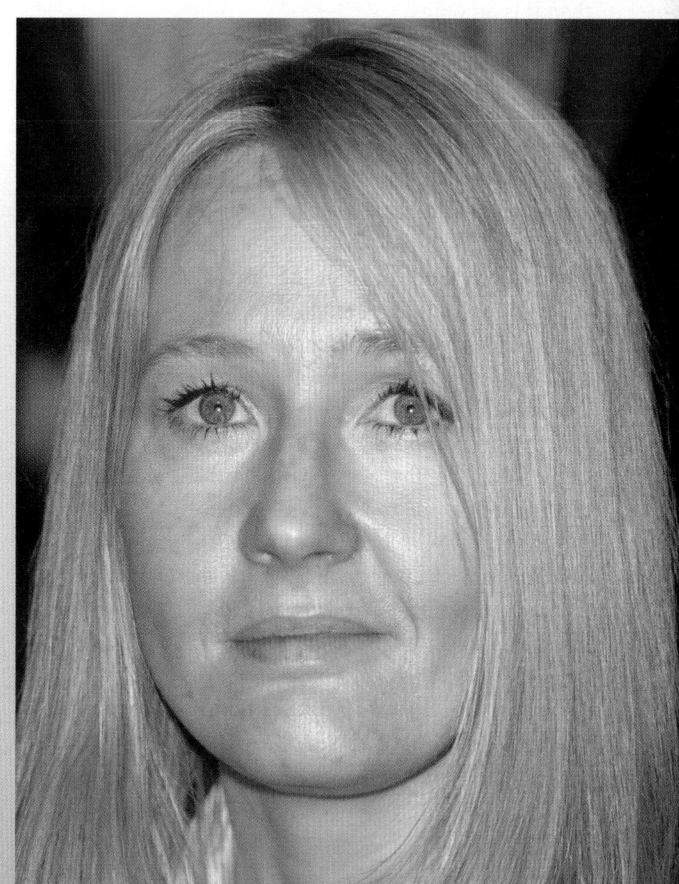

Measuring Economic Inequality

The most commonly used measure of economic inequality is the distribution of annual income. The Office for National Statistics defines as **original income** the income that households receive from market activity before government intervention. Original income equals wages, interest, rent and profit earned in factor markets and before paying income taxes.

The Distribution of Original Income

Figure 18.1 shows the distribution of original income across the 24.5 million households in the United Kingdom in 2004–2005. Note that the *x*-axis measures household income and the *y*-axis is percentage of households. The income numbers are expressed as average weekly incomes (annual income divided by 52).

The most common household original income, called the *mode* income, was received by the 11 per cent of the households whose incomes fell between £107 and £174 a week. The value of £140 marked on Figure 18.1 is the middle of that range.

The income that separates households into two equal groups, called the *median* income, was about £400 a week. One half of UK households had incomes greater than this amount, and the other half had incomes less than this amount.

The average household original income in 2004–2005, called the *mean* income, was £530 a week.

You can see in Figure 18.1 that the mode income is less than the median income and the median income is less than the mean income. This feature of the distribution of income tells us that there are more households with low incomes than with high incomes. And some of the high incomes are very high – well off the scale shown in the figure.

The income distribution in Figure 18.1 is called a *positively skewed* distribution, which means that it has a long tail of high values. This distribution shape contrasts with a *bell-shaped* distribution such as the distribution of people's heights. In a bell-shaped distribution, the mean, median and mode are all equal.

Another way of looking at the distribution of income is to measure the percentage of total income received by each given percentage of households. Data are reported for five groups – called *quintiles* or fifth shares – each consisting of 20 per cent of households.

Figure 18.2 shows the distribution based on these shares in 2004–2005. The poorest 20 per cent of households received 3 per cent of total income; the second poorest 20 per cent received 8 per cent of total income; the middle 20 per cent received 15 per cent of total income; the next highest 20 per cent received 24 per cent of total income; and the highest 20 per cent received 50 per cent of total income.

The distribution of income in Figure 18.1 and the quintile shares in Figure 18.2 tell us that income is distributed unequally. But we need a way of comparing the distribution of income in different periods and using different measures. A neat graphical tool called the *Lorenz curve* enables us to make such comparisons.

Figure 18.1

The Distribution of Original Income in the United Kingdom in 2004–2005

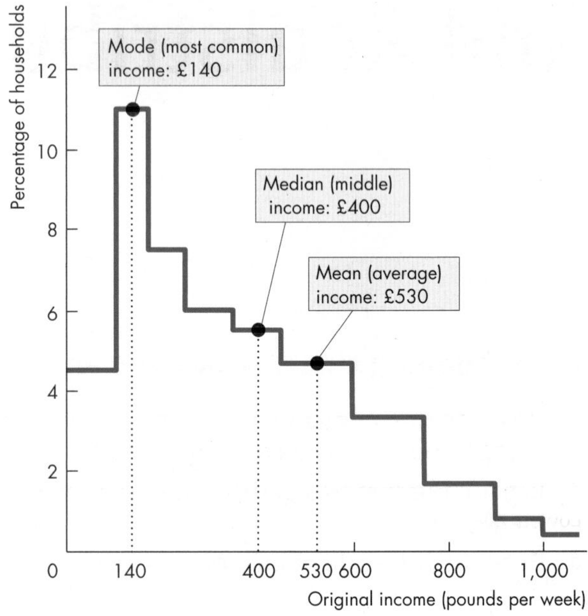

The distribution of original income – income from market activity and before government intervention – is positively skewed. The mode (most common) income is less than the median (middle) income, which in turn is less than the mean (average) income. The percentage of households with an income above £1,000 a week (not shown) falls off slowly and the highest incomes are more than £100,000 a week.

Source of data: Office for National Statistics, "The effects of taxes and benefits on household income, 2004–2005" by Francis Jones.

Figure 18.2 myeconlab

UK Quintile Shares in 2004–2005

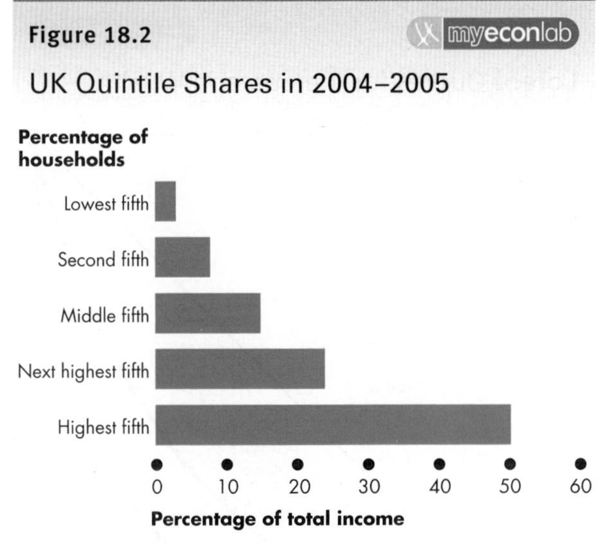

Households (percentage)	Income (percentage of total income)
Lowest 20	3
Second 20	8
Middle 20	15
Next highest 20	24
Highest 20	50

In 2004–2005, the poorest 20 per cent of households received 3 per cent of total income; the second poorest 20 per cent received 8 per cent; the middle 20 per cent received 15 per cent; the next highest 20 per cent received 24 per cent; and the highest 20 per cent received 50 per cent.

Source of data: Office for National Statistics.

Figure 18.3 myeconlab

The Income Lorenz Curve in 2004–2005

	Households		Income	
	Percentage	Cumulative percentage	Percentage	Cumulative percentage
A	Lowest 20	20	3	3
B	Second 20	40	8	11
C	Middle 20	60	15	26
D	Next highest 20	80	24	50
E	Highest 20	100	50	100

The cumulative percentage of income is graphed against the cumulative percentage of households. Points *A* to *E* on the Lorenz curve correspond to the rows of the table.

If incomes were distributed equally, each 20 per cent of households would receive 20 per cent of total income and the Lorenz curve would fall along the line of equality. The Lorenz curve shows that income is unequally distributed.

Source of data: Office for National Statistics.

The Income Lorenz Curve

The income **Lorenz curve** graphs the cumulative percentage of income against the cumulative percentage of households. Figure 18.3 shows the income Lorenz curve using the quintile shares from Figure 18.2. The table shows the percentage of income of each quintile group. For example, row *A* tells us that the lowest quintile of households receives 3 per cent of total income. The table also shows the *cumulative* percentages of households and income. For example, row *B* tells us that the lowest two quintiles (lowest 40 per cent) of households receive 11 per cent of total original income – 3 per cent for the lowest quintile and 8 per cent for the next lowest.

If income were distributed equally across all the households, each quintile would receive 20 per cent of total income and the cumulative percentages of income received by the cumulative percentages of households would fall along the straight line labelled "Line of equality". The actual distribution of income is shown by the curve labelled "Income Lorenz curve". The closer the Lorenz curve is to the line of equality, the more equal is the distribution.

The Distribution of Wealth

The distribution of wealth provides another way of measuring economic inequality. A household's wealth is the value of the things that it owns. Wealth includes the value of money in the bank, shares and bonds, houses, land and any other assets of value such as works of art and cars.

Wealth is measured at a *point in time*. For example, we might value a household's wealth on the last day of the year. The point-in-time measurement of wealth contrasts with the measurement of income, which is the amount that the household receives *over a given period of time*. For example, we measure a household's income over a week, a month or a year.

Figure 18.4 shows the Lorenz curve for wealth in the United Kingdom in 2004–2005. Average household wealth is probably in the region of £150,000. But the variation around this value is enormous.

Because wealth is distributed extremely unequally, the quintile shares data on the distribution of wealth are not very revealing. The lowest quintile owns nothing, and the next lowest quintile owns almost nothing. It is more revealing to look at the distribution of wealth by placing households in *unequal* groups. That is what we do in Figure 18.4. The poorest 50 per cent of households own only 7 per cent of total wealth (row *A*' in the table in Figure 18.4). The next 25 per cent of households own 21 per cent of total wealth (row *B*' in the table). So the poorest 75 per cent of households own only 28 per cent of total wealth and the richest 25 per cent of households own 72 per cent of total wealth. Because this group owns such a large percentage of total wealth, we break it into smaller bits in rows *C*' to *E*'. The richest 1 per cent of households own 21 per cent of total wealth (row *E*').

Figure 18.4 shows the income Lorenz curve (from Figure 18.3) alongside the wealth Lorenz curve. You can see that the Lorenz curve for wealth is much farther away from the line of equality than is the Lorenz curve for income, which means that the distribution of wealth is much more unequal than the distribution of income.

Figure 18.4 myeconlab

Lorenz Curves for Income and Wealth

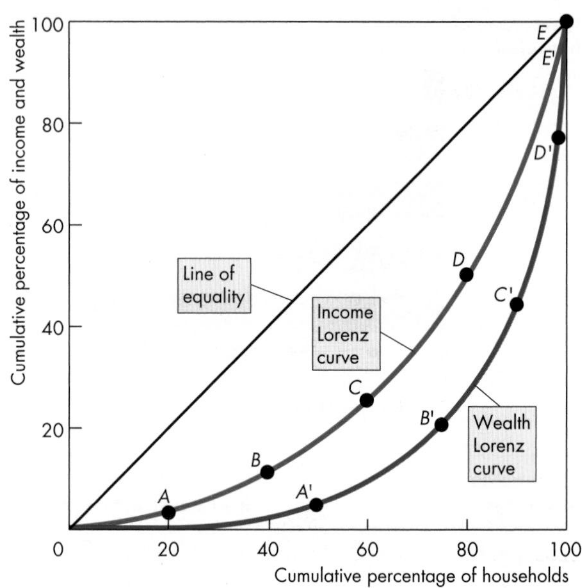

	Households		Wealth	
	Percentage	Cumulative percentage	Percentage	Cumulative percentage
A'	Lowest 50	50	7	7
B'	Next 25	75	21	28
C'	Next 15	90	19	47
D'	Next 9	99	32	79
E'	Highest 1	100	21	100

The cumulative percentage of wealth is graphed against the cumulative percentage of households. Points *A*' to *E*' on the Lorenz curve for wealth correspond to the rows of the table. By comparing the Lorenz curves for income and wealth, we can see that wealth is distributed much more unequally than income.

Source of data: Office for National Statistics, *Social Trends*, 2006.

Wealth versus Income

We've seen that wealth is much more unequally distributed than income. Which distribution provides the better description of the degree of inequality? To answer this question, we need to think about the connection between wealth and income.

Wealth is a stock of assets and income is the flow of earnings that results from the stock of wealth. Suppose that a person owns assets worth £1 million – has a wealth of £1 million. If the rate of return on assets is 5 per cent a year, then this person receives an income of £50,000 a year from those assets. We can describe this person's economic condition by using either the wealth of £1 million or the income of £50,000. When the rate of return is 5 per cent a year, £1 million of wealth equals

£50,000 of income in perpetuity. Wealth and income are just different ways of looking at the same thing.

But in Figure 18.4, the distribution of wealth is more unequal than the distribution of income. Why? It is because the wealth data do not include the value of human capital, while the income data measure income from all wealth, including human capital.

Table 18.1 illustrates the consequence of omitting human capital from the wealth data. Lee has twice the wealth and twice the income of Peter. But Lee's human capital is less than Peter's – £200,000 compared with £499,000. And Lee's income from human capital of £10,000 is less than Peter's income from human capital of £24,950. Lee's other capital is larger than Peter's – £800,000 compared with £1,000. And Lee's income from other capital of £40,000 is larger than Peter's income from other capital of £50.

When Lee and Peter are surveyed by the Office for National Statistics in a national wealth and income survey, their incomes are recorded as £50,000 and £25,000, respectively, which implies that Lee is twice as well off as Peter. And their tangible assets are recorded as £800,000 and £1,000, respectively, which implies that Lee is 800 times as wealthy as Peter.

Because the national survey of wealth excludes human capital, the income distribution is a more accurate measure of economic inequality than the wealth distribution.

Table 18.1

Capital, Wealth and Income

	Lee		Peter	
	Wealth	**Income**	**Wealth**	**Income**
Human capital	200,000	10,000	499,000	24,950
Other capital	800,000	40,000	1,000	50
Total	£1,000,000	£50,000	£500,000	£25,000

When wealth is measured to include the value of human capital as well as other forms of capital, the distribution of income and the distribution of wealth display the same degree of inequality.

Annual or Lifetime Income and Wealth?

A household's income changes over time. It starts out low, grows to a peak when the household's workers reach retirement age and then falls after retirement.

Also, a typical household's wealth changes over time. Like income, wealth starts out low, grows to a peak at the point of retirement and then falls.

Suppose we look at three households that have identical lifetime incomes. One household is young, one is middle-aged and one is retired. The middle-aged household has the highest income and wealth, the retired household has the lowest and the young household falls in the middle.

The distributions of annual income and wealth in a given year are unequal, but the distributions of lifetime income and wealth are (by assumption) equal.

Although some of the inequality in annual income arises because different households are at different stages in the life cycle, after allowing for this factor, a substantial amount of inequality remains.

So far, we have examined the extent of inequality in income and wealth in a few recent years. What are the trends in inequality? Is the distribution of income becoming less equal or more equal? We can see trends in the income distribution by looking at a number of years.

Trends in Inequality

To see trends in the income distribution, we need a measure that enables us to rank distributions on the scale of more equal and less equal. No perfect scale exists, but one that is much used is called the Gini coefficient.

The **Gini coefficient** is based on the Lorenz curve and equals the area between the line of equality and the Lorenz curve as a percentage of the entire area beneath the line of equality. If income is distributed equally, the Lorenz curve is the same as the line of equality, so the Gini coefficient is zero. If one person has all the income and everyone else has none, the Gini coefficient is 100. Gini coefficients based on the distribution of original (or market) income are typically between 40 and 50 in most rich industrial countries today.

Figure 18.5 shows the UK Gini coefficient from 1980 to 2005. The Gini coefficient has clearly increased, which means that on this measure, incomes have become more unequal.

The major increase in inequality occurred during the 1980s, but inequality continued to increase into the early 1990s. From 1994 to 2005, inequality decreased.

No one knows for sure why these changes in inequality have occurred, but a possibility that we'll explore in the next section is that they are the result of technological change in the information-age economy.

Figure 18.5

The UK Gini Coefficient: 1980–2005

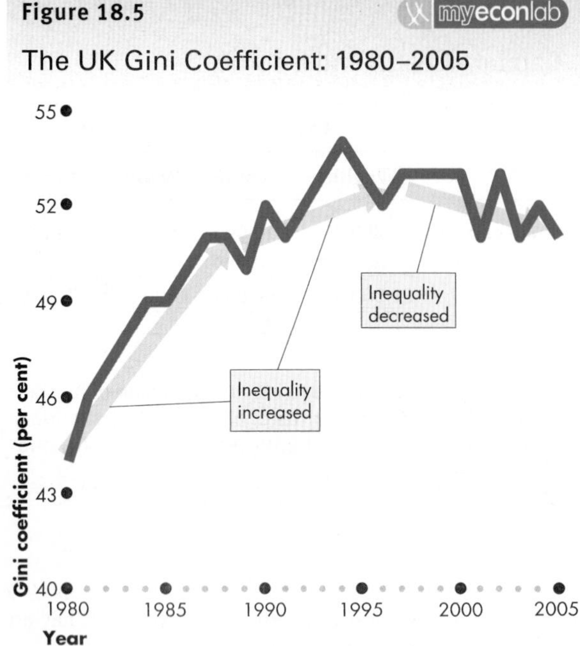

Measured by the Gini coefficient, the distribution of income in the United Kingdom became more unequal between 1980 and 1994. Between 1994 and 2005, the distribution of income became less unequal.

Source of data: Office for National Statistics.

Who Are the Rich and the Poor?

The lowest-income household in the United Kingdom today is likely to be a retired person over 75 years of age, living alone in housing association accommodation, somewhere in Wales. Another very low income household is that of an unemployed unskilled person living alone in a council house somewhere in Northern Ireland or Wales. The highest-income household is likely to be one with two professionals living together in a house that they own, aged between 30 and 50, both graduates living somewhere in the south east of England.

These snapshot profiles are the extremes of the characteristics shown in Figure 18.6. The figure illustrates the role of job type, economic status, household size and type, age of the householder, whether living in rented or owned housing and major region of residence.

All of these factors influence the likelihood that a household is poor and living on an income well below average or well off and living on an income well above the average. Job type, economic status and age are the three biggest contributors to economic wellbeing.

Box 18.1

Poverty in the European Union

Defining the *poverty line* as 60 per cent of median EU income, poverty rates vary throughout the European Union. The *poverty rate* is the percentage of people who fall below the *poverty line*.

Figure 1 shows that 6 of the established members have poverty rates that exceed the EU average. The accession of the new member states such as Romania in 2006 lowered EU median income and increased the number of member states with relatively high poverty rates.

Defining the poverty line as 60 per cent of median EU income, 19 per cent of UK households lived in poverty in 2004. But defining the poverty line as 60 per cent of median UK income, 17 per cent of UK households lived in poverty in 2004. Using this UK-based measure, poverty rates were at their highest in 1991, when 21 per cent of households lived in poverty and at their lowest in 1977, when just 10 per cent of UK households lived in poverty.

Figure 1

Poverty in the European Union

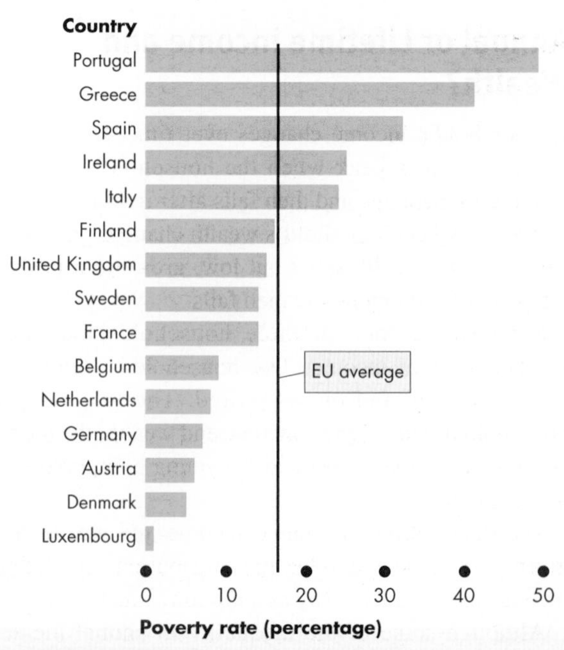

Sources of data: Office for National Statistics, *Social Trends*, 2006 and Eurostat.

Figure 18.6

The Distribution of Income by Selected Household Characteristics in 2004–2005

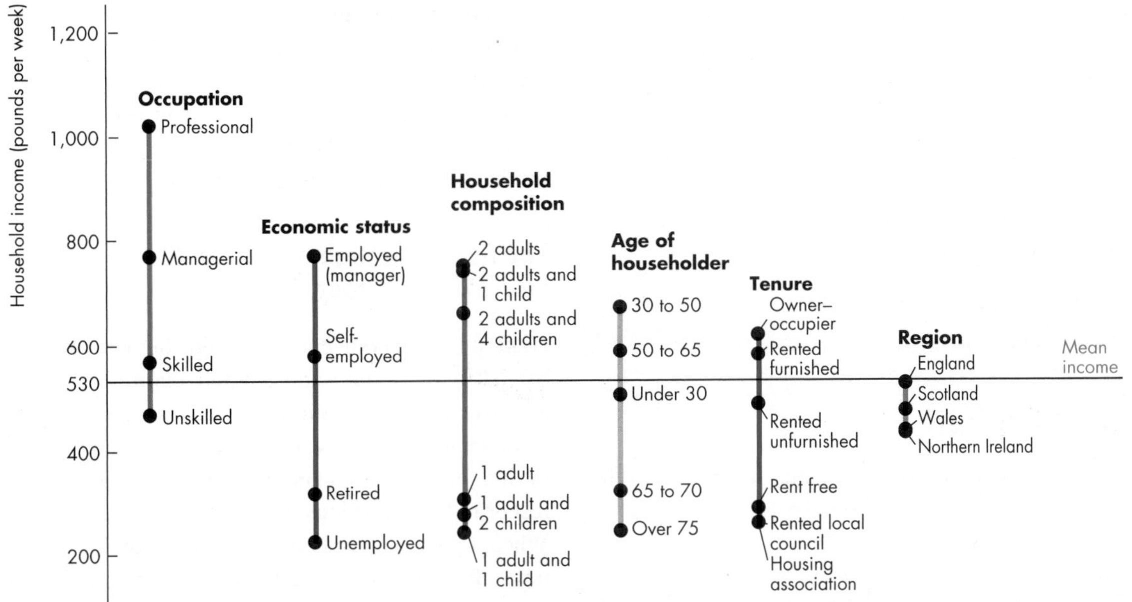

Single adults, single parents, those who are unemployed and those aged over 75 are likely to be among the poorest households in the United Kingdom. Other poor households are those in which the main earner is employed as a manual worker and those that live in local council accommodation. Households in Northern Ireland and Wales are on average poorer than those in England and Scotland.

Source of data: Office for National Statistics, *Family Spending: A Report on the 2002/2005 Family Expenditure Survey*, 2006.

Poverty

The poorest households are considered to be living in **poverty**, a state in which a household's income is too low for it to be able to buy the quantities of food, shelter and clothing that are deemed necessary. Poverty is a relative concept, not an absolute one. The *poverty line* is a benchmark defines as 60 per cent of the median income. A person with an income below this line is defined to be living in poverty. The *poverty rate* is the percentage of people who are living below the poverty line.

Box 18.1 gives some numbers on poverty rates in the European Union and the United Kingdom. You can see that this definition of poverty crucially depends on the population being considered. In Box 18.1, the reference population is the EU and the poverty rate is more a measure of average income per person than of true poverty.

Because measures of poverty are relative, they don't provide information about the absolute level of poverty and how it is changing. People who are living in poverty in the United Kingdom would be considered well off in black townships of South Africa. And people living in poverty in Ireland today would have been considered reasonably well off compared to the people of rural Ireland 40 years ago.

Review Quiz

Study Plan 18.1

1. Which is distributed more unequally: income or wealth? Why? Which is the better measure of inequality?
2. What does a Lorenz curve show and how do we use it to gauge the degree of inequality?
3. What is the Gini coefficient and how is it used to measure inequality?
4. Has the distribution of income in the United Kingdom become more unequal or less unequal? When did the largest changes occur?
5. What are the main characteristics of low-income households?
6. Describe a measure of the poverty line and explain how it is used.

The Sources of Economic Inequality

We've described economic inequality in the United Kingdom. Our task now is to explain it. We began this task in Chapter 17 by learning about the forces that influence demand and supply in the markets for labour, capital and land. We're now going to deepen our understanding of these forces.

Economic inequality arises from unequal labour market outcomes and from unequal ownership of capital. We'll begin by looking at labour markets and two features of them that contribute to differences in income:

- Human capital
- Discrimination

Human Capital

A clerk in a barrister's office earns less than a tenth of the amount earned by the barrister he assists. An operating room assistant earns less than a tenth of the amount earned by the surgeon she works with. A bank clerk earns less than a tenth of the amount earned by the bank's managing director. These differences in earnings arise from differences in human capital. We can explain these differences by using a model of competitive labour markets.

We'll study a model economy with two levels of human capital, which we'll call high-skilled labour and low-skilled labour. The low-skilled labour might represent the barrister's clerk, the operating room assistant or the bank clerk, and the high-skilled labour might represent the barrister, the surgeon or the bank's managing director.

We'll first look at the demand side of the markets for these two types of labour.

The Demand for High-skilled and Low-skilled Labour

High-skilled workers can perform tasks that low-skilled labour would perform badly or perhaps cannot perform at all. Imagine an untrained person doing open-heart surgery. High-skilled labour has a higher marginal revenue product than low-skilled labour. As we learned in Chapter 17, a firm's demand for labour curve is the same as the marginal revenue product of labour curve.

Figure 18.7(a) shows the demand curves for high-skilled and low-skilled labour. The demand curve for high-skilled labour is D_H, and that for low-skilled labour is D_L. At any given level of employment, firms are willing to pay a higher wage rate to a high-skilled worker than to a low-skilled worker.

The vertical distance between the two wage rates measures the marginal revenue product of skill. For example, at an employment level of 2,000 hours, firms are willing to pay £12.50 an hour for a high-skilled worker but only £5 an hour for a low-skilled worker. The difference is £7.50 an hour, so the marginal revenue product of skill is £7.50 an hour.

The Supply of High-skilled and Low-skilled Labour

High-skilled labour contains more human capital than low-skilled labour, and human capital is costly to acquire. The opportunity cost of acquiring human capital includes actual expenditures on such things as tuition fees and room and board and costs in the form of lost or reduced earnings while the skill is being acquired. When a person goes to school, college or university full time, that cost is the total earnings forgone. But some people acquire skills on the job – on-the-job training.

Usually, a worker undergoing on-the-job training is paid a lower wage than someone who is doing a comparable job but not undergoing training. In such a case, the cost of acquiring the skill is the wage paid to a person not being trained minus the wage paid to a person being trained.

The position of the supply curve of high-skilled labour reflects the cost of acquiring human capital. Figure 18.7(b) shows two supply curves: one for high-skilled labour and the other for low-skilled labour. The supply curve for high-skilled labour is S_H, and that for low-skilled labour is S_L.

The high-skilled labour supply curve lies above the low-skilled labour supply curve. The vertical distance between the two supply curves measures the compensation that high-skilled labour requires for the cost of acquiring the skill. For example, suppose that the quantity of low-skilled labour supplied is 2,000 hours at a wage rate of £5 an hour. This wage rate compensates the low-skilled workers mainly for their time on the job.

To induce high-skilled workers to supply 2,000 hours of labour, firms must pay a wage rate of £8.50 an hour. This wage rate for high-skilled labour is higher than the wage rate for low-skilled labour because high-skilled workers must be compensated not only for the time on the job but also for the time and other costs of acquiring the skill. The difference is £3.50 an hour, so the cost of acquiring the skill is £3.50 an hour.

Figure 18.7

Skill Differentials

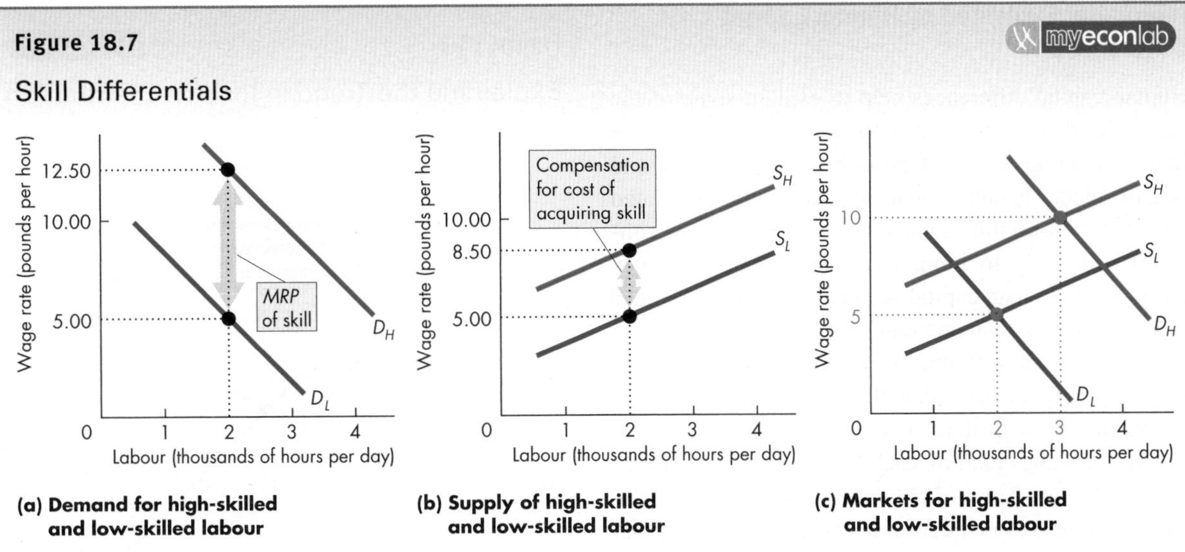

Part (a) illustrates the marginal revenue product of skill. Low-skilled workers have a marginal revenue product that gives rise to the demand curve marked D_L. High-skilled workers have a higher marginal revenue product than low-skilled labour. So the demand curve for high-skilled labour, D_H, lies to the right of D_L. The vertical distance between these two curves is the marginal revenue product of the skill.

Part (b) shows the effects of the cost of acquiring skills on the supply curves of labour. The supply curve for low-skilled labour is S_L. The supply curve for high-skilled labour is S_H. The vertical distance between these two curves is the required compensation for the cost of acquiring a skill.

Part (c) shows the equilibrium employment and the wage differential. Low-skilled workers earn £5 an hour and 2,000 hours of low-skilled labour are employed. High-skilled workers earn £10 an hour and 3,000 hours of high-skilled labour are employed. The wage rate for high-skilled labour always exceeds that for low-skilled labour.

Wage Rates of High-skilled and Low-skilled Labour

To work out the wage rates of high-skilled and low-skilled labour, we have to bring together the effects of skill on the demand for and supply of labour.

Figure 18.7(c) shows the demand curves and the supply curves for high-skilled and low-skilled labour. These curves are exactly the same as those plotted in parts (a) and (b). Equilibrium occurs in the market for low-skilled labour where the supply and demand curves for low-skilled labour intersect. The equilibrium wage rate is £5 an hour and the quantity of low-skilled labour employed is 2,000 hours. Equilibrium in the market for high-skilled labour occurs where the supply and demand curves for high-skilled labour intersect. The equilibrium wage rate is £10 an hour and the quantity of high-skilled labour employed is 3,000 hours.

As you can see in part (c), the equilibrium wage rate of high-skilled labour is higher than that of low-skilled labour. There are two reasons why this occurs. First, high-skilled labour has a higher marginal revenue product than low-skilled labour, so at a given wage rate, the quantity of high-skilled labour demanded exceeds that of low-skilled labour. Second, skills are costly to acquire, so at a given wage rate, the quantity of high-skilled labour supplied is less than that of low-skilled labour. The wage differential (in this case, £5 an hour) depends on both the marginal revenue product of the skill and the cost of acquiring it. The higher the marginal revenue product of the skill, the larger is the vertical distance between the demand curves. The more costly it is to acquire a skill, the larger is the vertical distance between the supply curves. The higher the marginal revenue product of the skill and the more costly it is to acquire, the larger is the wage differential between high-skilled and low-skilled labour.

Do Education and Training Pay?

Rates of return on a university education have been estimated to be as high as 35 per cent for women and 17.5 per cent for men. A solid secondary education ending with 5 or more GCEs generates returns that exceed 20 per cent. These returns suggest that a degree is a better investment than almost any other that a person can undertake!

Inequality Explained by Human Capital Differences

Human capital differences help to explain some of the inequality that we observe. You saw in Figure 18.6 that high-income households tend to be better educated and middle-aged. Human capital differences are correlated with these household characteristics. Education contributes directly to human capital. Age contributes indirectly to human capital because older workers have more experience than do younger workers.

Human capital differences can also explain some of the inequality associated with sex and race. A larger proportion of men than of women and a larger proportion of whites than of visible minorities have a university degree. These differences in education levels among the sexes and the races are becoming smaller, but they have not yet been eliminated.

Interruptions to a career reduce the effectiveness of job experience in contributing to human capital. Historically, job interruptions have been more common for women than for men because women's careers have been interrupted for bearing and rearing children. This factor is a possible source of lower wages, on average, for women. Although maternity leave and day-care facilities are making career interruptions for women less common, this factor remains a problem for many women.

Trends in Inequality Explained by Human Capital Trends

You've seen that income inequality increased during the 1980s and 1990s. Human capital differences are a possible explanation for this trend, and Figure 18.8 illustrates how. The supply of low-skilled labour (part a) and that of high-skilled labour (part b) are S, and initially, the demand in each market is D_0. The low-skilled wage rate is £5 an hour, and the high-skilled wage rate is £10 an hour.

Information technologies such as computers and laser scanners are *substitutes* for low-skilled labour: they perform tasks that previously were performed by low-skilled labour. The introduction of these technologies has decreased the demand for low-skilled labour (part a), decreased the number of low-skilled jobs and lowered the wage rate of low-skilled workers.

These same technologies require high-skilled labour to design, programme and run them. Information technologies and high-skilled labour are *complements*, so the introduction of these technologies has increased the demand for high-skilled labour (part b), increased the number of high-skilled jobs and raised the wage rate of high-skilled workers.

Figure 18.8

Explaining the Trend in Income Distribution

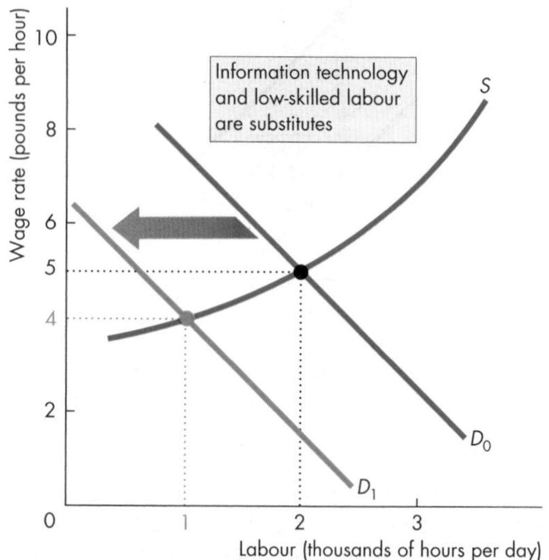

(a) A decrease in demand for low-skilled labour

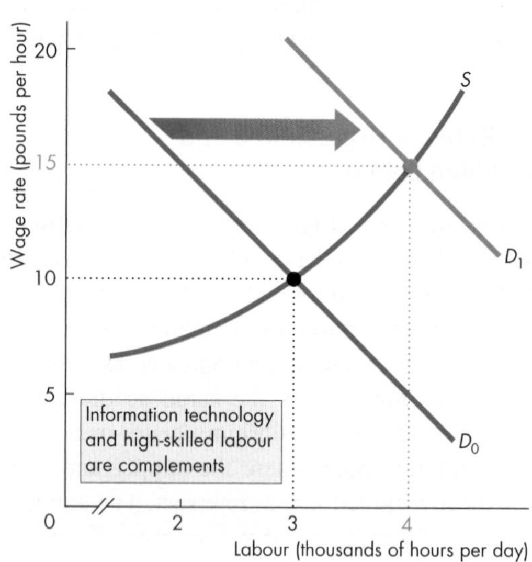

(b) An increase in demand for high-skilled labour

Low-skilled labour in part (a) and information technologies are substitutes. When these technologies were introduced, the demand for low-skilled labour decreased and the quantity of this type of labour employed and its wage rate decreased. High-skilled labour in part (b) and information technologies are complements. When these technologies were introduced, the demand for high-skilled labour increased and the quantity of this type of labour employed and its wage rate increased.

Discrimination

Human capital differences can explain some of the economic inequality that we observe. But it can't explain all of it. Discrimination is another possible source of inequality.

An Example of Discrimination

Suppose that women and men have identical abilities as investment advisers. Figure 18.9 shows the supply curves of women, S_W (in part a), and of men, S_M (in part b). The marginal revenue product of investment advisers shown by the two curves labelled *MRP* is the same for both groups.

If everyone is free of sex prejudice, the market determines a wage rate of £40,000 a year for investment advisers. But if the customers are prejudiced against women, this prejudice is reflected in the wage rate and employment. Suppose that the perceived marginal revenue product of the women, when discriminated against, is MRP_{DA}. Suppose that the perceived marginal revenue product for men, the group discriminated in favour of, is MRP_{DF}. With these *MRP* curves, women earn £20,000 a year and only 1,000 women work as investment advisers. Men earn £60,000 a year, and 3,000 of them work as investment advisers.

Counteracting Forces

Economists disagree about whether prejudice actually causes wage differentials and one line of reasoning implies that it does not. In the example you've just studied, customers who buy from men pay a higher service charge for investment advice than do the customers who buy from women. This price difference acts as an incentive to encourage people who are prejudiced to buy from the people against whom they are prejudiced.

This force could be strong enough to eliminate the effects of discrimination altogether. Suppose, as is true in manufacturing, that a firm's customers never meet its workers. If such a firm discriminates against women, it can't compete with firms that hire women because its costs are higher than those of the non-prejudiced firms. Only firms that do not discriminate survive in a competitive industry.

Whether because of discrimination or from some other source, women do earn lower incomes than men. Another possible source of lower wage rates of women arises from differences in the relative degree of specialization of women and men.

Figure 18.9 myeconlab

Discrimination

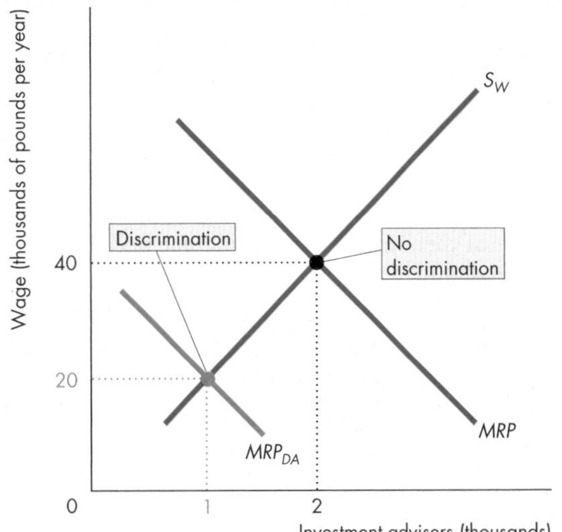

(a) Females

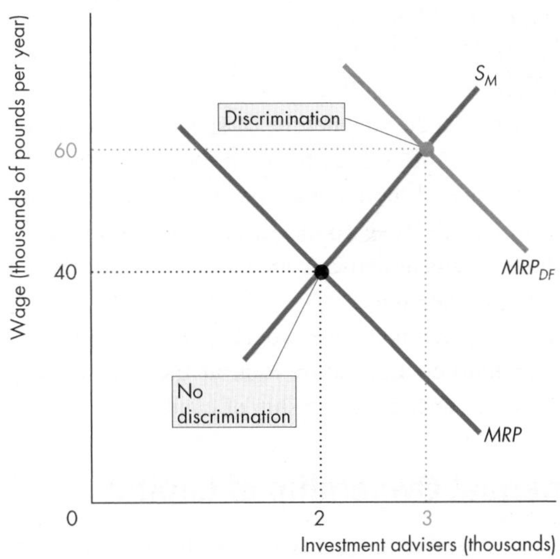

(b) Males

With no discrimination, the wage rate is £40,000 a year and 2,000 of each group are employed. With discrimination against women, the marginal revenue product curve in part (a) is MRP_{DA}.

With discrimination in favour of men, the marginal revenue product curve in part (b) is MRP_{DF}. The wage rate for women falls to £20,000 a year, and only 1,000 are employed. The wage rate for men rises to £60,000 a year, and 3,000 are employed.

Differences in the Degree of Specialization

Couples must choose how to allocate their time between working for a wage and doing jobs in the home, such as cooking, cleaning, shopping, organizing vacations and, most important, bearing and rearing children. Let's look at the choices of Bob and Sue.

Bob might specialize in earning an income and Sue in taking care of the home. Or Sue might specialize in earning an income and Bob in taking care of the home. Or both of them might earn an income and share home production jobs.

The allocation they choose depends on their preferences and on the earning potential of each of them. The choice of an increasing number of households is for each person to diversify between earning an income and doing some home chores. But in most households, Bob will specialize in earning an income and Sue will both earn an income and bear a larger share of the task of running the home. With this allocation, Bob will probably earn more than Sue. If Sue devotes time and effort to ensuring Bob's mental and physical well-being, the quality of Bob's market labour will be higher than it would be if he were diversified. If the roles were reversed, Sue would be able to supply market labour that earns more than Bob.

To test whether the degree of specialization accounts for earnings differences between the sexes, economists have compared the incomes of never-married men and women. They have found that, on the average, with equal amounts of human capital, the wages of these two groups are the same.

We've examined some sources of inequality in the labour market. Let's now look at the way inequality arises from unequal ownership of capital.

Unequal Ownership of Capital

You've seen that inequality in wealth (excluding human capital) is much greater than inequality in income. This inequality arises from saving and transfers of wealth from one generation to the next.

The higher a household's income, the more that household tends to save and pass on to the next generation. Saving is not always a source of increased inequality. If a household's saving redistributes an uneven income over the household's life, consumption will fluctuate less than its income and saving decreases inequality. If a lucky generation that has a high income saves a large part of that income and leaves capital to a succeeding generation that is unlucky, this act of saving also decreases the degree of inequality. But two features of intergenerational transfers of wealth lead to increased inequality: people can't inherit debts, and marriage tends to concentrate wealth.

Can't Inherit Debt

Although a person may die in debt – with negative wealth – a debt can't be forced onto the next generation of a family. So inheritance only adds to a future generation's wealth; it cannot decrease it.

Most people inherit nothing or a very small amount. A few people inherit an enormous fortune. As a result, intergenerational transfers make the distribution of income persistently more unequal than the distribution of ability and job skills. A household that is poor in one generation is more likely to be poor in the next. A household that is wealthy in one generation is more likely to be wealthy in the next. And marriage reinforces this tendency.

Marriage and Wealth Concentration

People tend to marry within their own socioeconomic class – a phenomenon called *assortative mating*. In everyday language, "like attracts like". Although there is a good deal of folklore that "opposites attract", perhaps such Cinderella tales appeal to us because they are so rare in reality. Wealthy people seek wealthy partners.

Because of assortative mating, wealth becomes more concentrated in a small number of families and the distribution of wealth becomes more unequal.

Review Quiz

Study Plan 18.2

1. What role does human capital play in accounting for income inequality?
2. What role might discrimination play in accounting for income inequality?
3. What are the possible reasons for income inequality by sex and age group?
4. Does inherited wealth make the distribution of income less equal or more equal?
5. Why does wealth inequality persist across generations?

Next we're going to see how taxes and government policies redistribute income and wealth and decrease the degree of economic inequality.

Income Redistribution

Governments use three main types of policies to redistribute income. They are:

- Income taxes
- Benefit payments
- Subsidized welfare services

Income Taxes

Income taxes may be progressive, regressive or proportional. A **progressive income tax** is one that taxes income at an average rate that increases with income. A **regressive income tax** is one that taxes income at an average rate that decreases with income. A **proportional income tax** (also called a *flat-rate income tax*) is one that taxes income at a constant average rate regardless of the level of income.

Income taxes are progressive in all EU member states. For example, in 2007/08 in the United Kingdom, people who earned £5,225 or less paid no income tax. A tax of 10 per cent was paid on the first £2,230 earned over £5,225 and a tax of 22 per cent was paid on the next £34,600 earned. Any income above this amount is taxed at 40 per cent.

Benefit Payments

Benefit payments redistribute income by making direct payments to people with low incomes. In 2007/08, the UK government paid out £184 billion in benefits, 31 per cent of total government expenditure. The main types of benefit payments are:

- Income support payments
- Tax credits
- State pensions

Income Support Payments

Governments use a wide range of income support payments to raise household incomes and reduce poverty. These include income support, unemployment benefits, disability payments and child support payments. For example, in the United Kingdom, the Job Seekers' Allowance is paid for a limited period to individuals who have lost their jobs involuntarily and have no other main source of income. This allowance was £87 a week for people over 24 years of age in 2007/08.

Tax Credits

Tax credits are a method of helping low-income employed individuals and families. A tax credit increases a household's disposable income. In 2007/08, the working tax credit for a single person caring for one child was a maximum of £175 a week. An additional child tax credit is also available to couples who have joint incomes of up to £58,175.

State Pensions

State pensions for the elderly are the main component of government benefit payments in all EU member states. These pensions are paid for out of current taxes, so they result in redistribution from people currently working to those retired. In the United Kingdom in 2007, more than 7 million people received a state pension of up to £87.30 a week for a single person (more for a couple).

Subsidized Welfare Services

A great deal of redistribution takes place in most European countries through the subsidized provision of welfare goods and services. These are the goods and services provided by the government at prices below marginal cost. Taxpayers who consume these goods and services receive a transfer in kind from taxpayers who do not consume them. The two most important areas in which this form of redistribution takes place are education – from nursery care through to university – and healthcare.

In the United Kingdom, 50 per cent of government expenditure is on benefits in kind: 24 per cent on the National Health Service, 21 per cent on education and the remainder on other services. The National Health Service provides almost all healthcare services free at the point of demand. Primary and secondary education is provided free for all children in the United Kingdom.

In the European Union, the extent and method of subsidizing education and healthcare services varies greatly across member states. For example, in some countries healthcare is free at the point of demand, and in other countries healthcare is privately provided and the government reimburses patients' costs. In some countries, people are required to pay into compulsory health insurance systems.

Whatever the method, subsidized provision of services improves access to good-quality healthcare and education and reduces inequality in health status and basic human capital.

Box 18.2
Redistribution in the European Union

EU governments use both progressive income taxes and benefit payments to redistribute income.

The role of income tax varies a great deal. Income taxes constitute just 14 per cent of all tax revenue in the United Kingdom and Ireland, 19 per cent in Spain and Portugal, 25 per cent in Finland and the Netherlands and more than 30 per cent in Sweden and Denmark.

Benefit payments also vary. Figure 1 compares government spending per person on cash benefit payments (as a percentage of total income).

Benefit spending as a percentage of income is much higher in Germany, France and the rich northern countries than in the poorer southern countries of the European Union. Benefit spending increases with country wealth and is associated with lower poverty rates.

Figure 2 shows the impact of taxes and benefits in the United Kingdom for the five quintile income groups, from poorest fifth to richest fifth.

On the average, the poorest fifth received £6,410 in cash benefits each year, whereas the richest fifth received only £3,780. (The richest group receives benefits because some benefits, such as pensions, are universally available.) The effect of cash benefits and tax credits is limited by low take-up rates.

Benefits in kind – mainly health benefits provided by the National Health Service and free or heavily subsidized education – are strongly progressive and represent 50 per cent of post-tax income for the poorest fifth but only 6 per cent for the richest fifth.

Income taxes have a strong effect on the distribution of income. The richest fifth pay £15,200 in income taxes each year and the poorest fifth pay £1,040 each year.

Expenditure taxes such as VAT have a smaller effect because the poorest groups spend proportionately more of their income on goods and services.

Overall, the net impact of UK taxes and benefits is a redistribution of income from the 40 per cent of households with highest incomes to the 40 per cent with lowest incomes, with a small net loss to the middle 20 per cent of households.

Figure 1

Benefits in the European Union

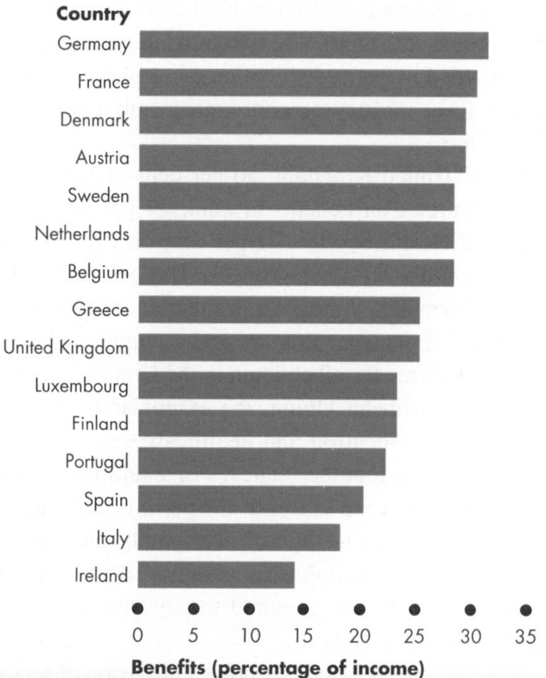

Source of data: European Commission, *Europe in Figures, Eurostat Yearbook, 2006–07.*

Figure 2

The Effect of Taxes and Benefits on the Distribution of Income

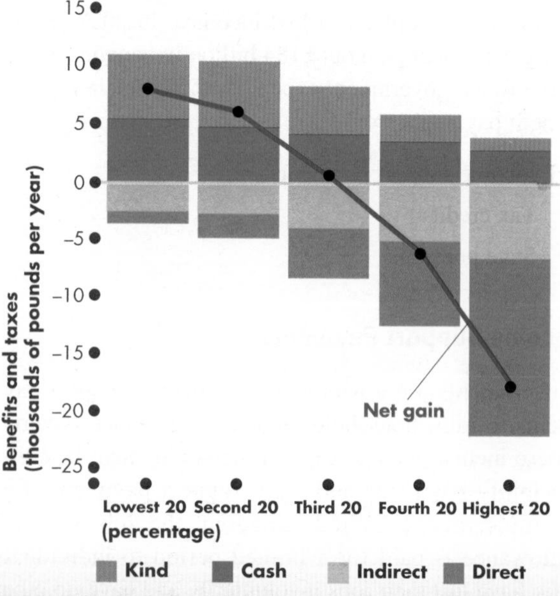

Source of data: Office for National Statistics, *Social Trends,* 2006.

The Big Trade-off

All income redistribution runs up against the *big trade-off* between equity and efficiency – see Chapter 5, p. 109. To achieve greater equity, we want to redistribute from the richest to the poorest. But to do so, we must impose taxes on the rich and pay benefits to the poor. And the more we redistribute, the higher must be the tax rates and the more generous the benefit rates. Both taxes and benefits bring inefficiency, which is the cost that must be borne to achieve greater equity.

Inefficient Taxes

Taxes are inefficient because they drive a wedge between marginal cost and marginal benefit and create deadweight loss. (Pigovian taxes that correct an externality are an exception – see Chapter 15, p. 348.) When a 40 per cent income tax is imposed on a high-income person, the marginal product of that person is 40 per cent greater that the marginal cost to that person of working. A potentially large deadweight loss arises. The taxes on the rich reduce their incentive to work and save. And the weaker incentive to save spills over to the poor because it means less capital is accumulated and fewer jobs are created.

Inefficient Benefits

Benefits for the poor are also inefficient. They lower the incentive of low-skilled people to work. More seriously, benefits lower the incentive to acquire human capital and move into a higher income group.

The inefficiencies arising from taxes and benefits result is less output and consumption for everybody – rich and poor. The disincentive effect of the benefits system is so severe that it gives rise to what is called a benefit trap.

The Benefit Trap

The benefits system can catch people in a *benefit trap* that arises because, in some cases, if a person takes a job or works longer hours, the loss of benefits exceeds the income earned. If a person loses £1 of benefit for every extra £1 earned – a *withdrawal rate* of 100 per cent – there is no gain from working. The person in effect faces a tax rate of 100 per cent, much higher than all other taxpayers!

There are two main types of benefit trap – the unemployment trap and the poverty trap. In the unemployment trap, people make decisions based on the expected wage they might earn compared to the benefits they will lose if they take a job. If the expected wage is only slightly higher than the level of unemployment benefit, the rational choice is to remain unemployed.

In the poverty trap, people are in low-paid work but are receiving benefits. They may want to work longer hours to earn an extra £10, but they will pay tax on the extra £10 and lose up to £10 of benefit. Again, the rational choice is often not to work more hours.

The 1986 Social Security Act removed tax rates that exceeded 100 per cent by allowing benefits to be calculated on post-tax income rather than on before-tax income. The change eased the severity of the poverty trap, but it left many more people facing extremely high marginal tax rates of between 60 and 90 per cent.

In 1998, the UK government raised benefit levels, cut the rate at which benefits are withdrawn as extra income is earned and introduced a system of paying benefits as tax credits. The lower withdrawal rate and higher levels of benefits reduced the poverty trap further. But the problem remains and would be removed only by moving to a system that treats benefits like any other source of income for the purpose of calculating taxes.

Review Quiz

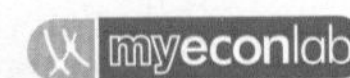

Study Plan 18.3

1. What are the methods that governments use to redistribute income?
2. To what extent does government policy succeed in redistributing income in the United Kingdom?
3. Why has the UK government introduced a system of tax credits to replace many cash benefits?
4. Can you explain what is meant by a benefit trap? Can you give an example?
5. Why is the UK government unlikely to introduce a negative income tax?

We've examined economic inequality in the United Kingdom, and we've seen how inequality arises. We've also seen that inequality has been increasing. *Reading Between the Lines* on pp. 424–425 looks at the increasing burden of income tax in the United Kingdom.

The next chapter studies some problems for the market economy that arise from uncertainty and incomplete information. But unlike the cases we studied in Chapters 15 and 16, the market does a good job of coping with the problems, as you're about to discover.

Reading Between the Lines

Taxation: The Rising Tax Burden

The Sunday Times, 1 October 2006

The tax for an average lifetime: £600,000 and rising

David Smith

The average British household pays more than £600,000 in taxes over a lifetime and even the poorest hand over nearly £250,000 to the Treasury, according to new calculations based on official figures.

The figures, in today's prices, have been calculated by the Taxpayers Alliance. "These figures are quite shocking", said Corin Taylor, head of research at the Alliance. . . .

In the case of other taxes, differences are less pronounced. The poorest households can expect to pay £30,000 in council tax over a lifetime compared with £62,000 for the richest. VAT costs the poorest fifth of the population an average of £67,000, compared with £165,000 for the richest.

The richest fifth of households pay nearly £1.2m in lifetime taxes, though this average disguises a wide range. Some of Britain's richest people pay well over £1m a year in tax. . . .

The tax burden has risen to near-record levels . . . and is set to climb further as a result of "fiscal drag" – people being moved into higher tax brackets.

The Centre for Policy Studies's . . . calls for the abolition of inheritance tax and capital gains tax, together with an increase in income tax allowances to take the lower-paid out of income tax altogether.

The Essence of the Story

- The average tax paid over a lifetime is £600,000 in the United Kingdom.
- The richest pay more than the poorest in tax, but even the poorest households pay £250,000 in tax over a lifetime.
- The lifetime tax burden is rising as more people are moved into higher tax brackets by the effects of inflation.
- Some groups argue the tax system would be better if the poorest households did not pay income tax at all.

Economic Analysis

- In this chapter we described how government redistributes income through benefit payments paid for by taxation.
- The news article makes it clear that the poorest 20 per cent do not escape tax payments and we can now look at how this affects redistribution in more detail.
- Figure 1 shows the estimated tax burden over a lifetime for the quintile groups from the poorest to the richest 20 per cent of UK households.
- The lifetime tax burden for poorest quintile group is 20 per cent of the lifetime tax burden of the richest quintile group.
- But the high tax burden for the poorest is counterbalanced by the provision of benefit payments. The overall impact on UK household income is shown in Figure 2.
- Figure 2 shows the scale of UK household income redistribution as a Lorenz curve. The blue line is original income and the red line is final income (after all taxes and benefits).
- The income distribution after taxes and benefits is less unequal. The richest quintile group have 16 times the income of the poorest group before taxes and benefits but just 4 times the income after taxes and benefits.
- The proposed reform is that the poorest households should not pay income tax at all. This proposal could increase income redistribution still more but is unlikely to come about.
- To maintain tax revenue, the tax burden would need to rise on all other groups including the median voter group, who already suffer a net loss from the UK tax and benefit system.
- In addition, if the rise in the average tax rate for the median voter involved a rise in the marginal rate of income tax, labour market inefficiency might rise.

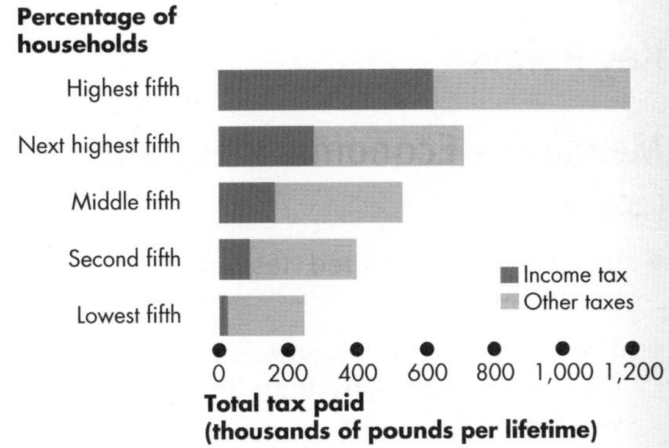

Figure 1 The distribution of lifetime tax payments

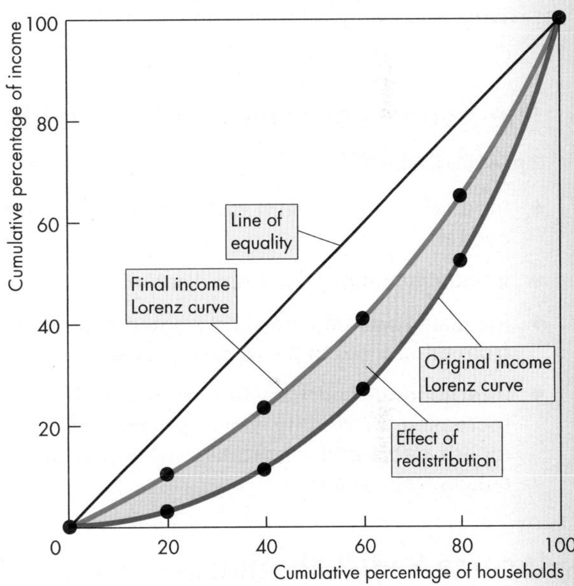

Figure 2 The effect of tax and benefits on income redistribution

- Allowing people to get dragged into a higher tax bracket by not adjusting taxes to inflation is one way that governments can maintain tax revenue without announcing unpopular tax changes.
- Whether the poorest pay too much tax over a lifetime is a difficult question and one that will remain on the political agenda.

Summary

Key Points

Measuring Economic Inequality
(pp. 410–415)

- Income is distributed less unequally than wealth.
- The distribution of income is a more accurate measure of inequality than the distribution of wealth.
- Income inequality increased between 1980 and 1994 but decreased between 1994 and 2005.
- The poorest people tend to be older, out of work and living in low-income areas.

The Sources of Economic Inequality
(pp. 416–420)

- Inequality arises from differences in human capital.
- Inequality might arise from discrimination.
- Inequality between men and women might arise from differences in the degree of specialization.
- Intergenerational transfers of wealth lead to increased inequality because people can't inherit debts and assortative mating tends to concentrate wealth.

Income Redistribution (pp. 421–423)

- Governments redistribute income through progressive income taxes and the payment of cash benefits and benefits in kind.
- Redistribution in the United Kingdom transfers income from the richest 40 per cent of households to the poorest 40 per cent and has little effect on the middle 20 per cent.
- Redistribution suffers from the big trade-off between equity and efficiency because the process uses resources and weakens incentives to work and save.
- Reforms to the benefits system try to lessen the severity of the benefit trap.

Key Figures

Key Terms

Problems

Tests, Study Plan and Solutions* 

1 The table shows shares of original (or market) income in the United States in 2005.

Households (percentage)	Income (per cent of total)
Lowest 20	3.4
Second 20	8.6
Third 20	14.6
Fourth 20	23.0
Highest 20	50.4

a Draw a Lorenz curve for the United States and compare it with the Lorenz curve for the United Kingdom shown in Figure 18.3.

b Which country has the higher Gini coefficient?

c Was US income distributed more equally or less equally than UK income?

d Can you think of some reasons for the differences in the distribution of income in the United States and United Kingdom?

2 The following figure shows the demand for and supply of low-skilled labour.

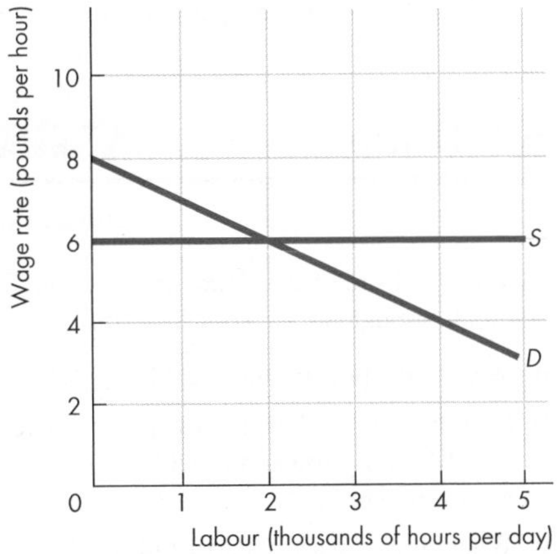

The marginal revenue product of a high-skilled worker is £8 an hour greater than that of a low-skilled worker. (The marginal revenue product at each employment level is £8 greater than that of a low-skilled worker.) The cost of acquiring the skill adds £6 an hour to the wage that must be offered to attract high-skilled labour.

a What is the wage rate of low-skilled labour?

b How many hours of low-skilled labour are employed?

c What is the wage rate of high-skilled labour?

d How many hours of high-skilled labour are employed?

e Why does the wage rate of a high-skilled worker exceed that of a low-skilled worker by exactly the cost of acquiring the skill?

3 The following figure shows the demand for and supply of workers who are discriminated against. Suppose that there is a group of workers in the same industry who are not discriminated against, and their marginal revenue product is perceived to be twice the marginal revenue product of the workers who are discriminated against. Suppose also that the supply of workers who do not face discrimination is 2,000 hours per day less at each wage rate.

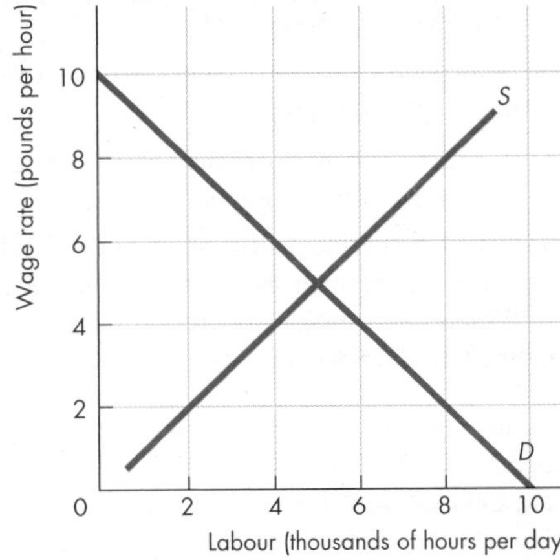

a What is the wage rate of a worker who is discriminated against?

b What is the wage rate of a worker who does not face discrimination?

c What is the quantity of workers employed who are discriminated against?

d What is the quantity of workers employed who do not face discrimination?

4 The table shows three tax payments schemes.

Before-tax income (euros)	Plan A tax (euros)	Plan B tax (euros)	Plan C tax (euros)
10,000	1,000	1,000	2,000
20,000	2,000	4,000	2,000
30,000	3,000	9,000	2,000

Which tax payment plan:

a Is proportional?

b Is regressive?

c Is progressive?

d Increases inequality?

* Solutions to odd-numbered problems are provided.

e Lessens inequality?

f Has no effect on inequality?

5 The table shows the total income shares[1] in South Africa in 2000.

Households (percentage)	Income of Blacks	Income of Whites
	(per cent of total)	
Lowest 20	2.6	3.7
Second 20	5.5	8.0
Third 20	9.2	12.8
Fourth 20	16.7	20.4
Highest 20	66.0	55.1

a Draw the Lorenz curve for the income of Blacks in South Africa in 2000.

b Draw the Lorenz curve for the income of Whites in South Africa in 2000.

c Compare the Gini Coefficient for income of Blacks with that of Whites? Explain your answer.

d Compare the inequality of income of Whites in South Africa with that in the United Kingdom? Which distribution of total income is more unequal? Explain your answer.

6 Incomes in China and India are a small fraction of incomes in the United States. But incomes in China and India are growing at more than twice the rate of those in the United States. Given this information, what can you say about:

a Changes in inequality between people in China and India and people in the United States?

b The world Lorenz curve and Gini ratio?

Critical Thinking

1 Read the *Reading Between the Lines* on pp. 424–425 and then answer the following questions:

a Describe the differences in lifetime tax payments by different income groups.

b Why might it be argued that the poor pay too much tax?

c Why might it be argued that the poor are better off as a result of the tax system?

d What is the proposed reform of the tax system in the article?

e How do you think the tax system should be changed to influence UK income distribution?

2 Many professional footballers earn huge salaries, but most earn modest salaries.

a Which do you predict is the more unequal distribution: that for the United Kingdom as a whole or that for professional footballers?

b Which distribution do you predict has the higher average: that for the United Kingdom as a whole or that for professional footballers?

3 **Only work ends poverty, says minister**
Work is the only route out of poverty, and the welfare state will never pay enough in benefits to lift people out of it, according to Jim Murphy, the employment and welfare minister. . . . His comments . . . were greeted with consternation by anti-poverty campaigners. . . . "The more successful they are in getting people off benefit and into work, the more important it is that those who are left behind, and who cannot work, still have a decent standard of living."

FT.com, 26 March 2007

a What does the minister mean when he says "the welfare state will never pay enough in benefits to lift people out of [poverty]"?

b Why are the anti-poverty campaigners aghast? Explain your answer.

c How will the minister's suggestion help those who cannot work have a decent standard of living?

Web Activities

Links to Websites

1 Visit the website of the Office for National Statistics, and look through *Social Trends*, 2006.

a What is the poverty line used in *Social Trends*?

b How has the distribution of income changed over time? Which groups are getting richer and which groups poorer?

c What other ways are there of measuring poverty?

d Do the poorest have access to the same level of goods and services as the richest? Does it matter?

2 Download the World Bank's Deininger and Squire Data Set on income distribution in a large number of countries.

a Which country in the data set has the most unequal distribution?

b Which country has the least unequal distribution?

c Can you think of reasons for the differences in income distribution in the two countries you've identified?

[1] Source of data:
http://www.econ.kuleuven.be/ces/seminars/paper%20vdberg.pdf

CHAPTER

19

Uncertainty and Information

After studying this chapter you will be able to:

- Explain how people make decisions when they are uncertain about the consequences
- Explain why people buy insurance and how insurance companies make a profit
- Explain why buyers search
- Explain how markets cope with private information
- Explain how people use financial markets to lower risk
- Explain how the presence of uncertainty and incomplete information influence the ability of markets to achieve an efficient outcome

Lotteries and Lemons

Life is like a lottery. You work hard at university but what will the payoff be? Will you get a good job or a miserable one?

You drive through a green light and notice a car moving on your left. You hope the driver stops, but if he doesn't you'll make an insurance claim.

Buying a used car can be fun but it can also be scary. You might get a lemon!

"Don't put all your eggs in one basket" is well-known advice. How does it apply to investing in shares?

Find some answers in this chapter. And in *Reading Between the Lines* at the end of the chapter, find out why you don't want to be in a course where everyone gets an A!

Uncertainty and Risk

A former US Secretary of Defense, Donald Rumsfeld, became famous for his descriptions of uncertainty. "I would not say that the future is necessarily less predictable than the past. I think the past was not predictable when it started," he once remarked. The future is unpredictable – uncertain – and it always has been and always will be.

What exactly is uncertainty? And what is risk? Is uncertainty the same as risk? Let's define uncertainty and risk and distinguish between them.

Assessing Uncertainty and Risk

Uncertainty is a situation in which more than one event may occur but we don't know which one. For example, when farmers plant their crops, they are uncertain about the weather during the growing season.

In ordinary speech, risk is the probability of incurring a loss (or some other misfortune). In economics, **risk** is a situation in which more than one outcome may occur and the *probability* of each possible outcome can be estimated. A *probability* is a number between 0 and 1 that measures the chance of some possible event occurring. A zero probability means that the event will not happen. A probability of 1 means that the event will occur for sure – with certainty. A probability of 0.5 means that the event is just as likely to occur as not. An example is the probability of a tossed coin falling heads. In a large number of tosses, about half of them will be heads and the other half tails.

Sometimes, probabilities can be measured exactly. For example, the probability that a tossed coin will come down heads is based on the fact that in a large number of tosses, half are heads and half are tails; the probability that a car in London in 2007 will be involved in an accident can be estimated by using police and insurance records of previous accidents; the probability that you will win a lottery can be estimated by dividing the number of tickets you have bought by the total number of tickets bought.

Some situations cannot be described by using probabilities based on past observed events. These situations may be unique events, such as the introduction of a new product. what quantity of the new product will sell and at what price? Because the product is new, there is no previous experience on which to base a probability. But the questions can be answered by looking at past experience with *similar* new products, supported by some judgements. Such judgements are called *subjective probabilities*.

Regardless of whether the probability of some event occurring is based on actual data or judgements – or even guesses – we can use probability to study the way in which people make decisions in the face of uncertainty. The first step in doing this is to describe how people assess the cost of risk.

The Cost of Risk

Some people are more willing to bear risk than others, but almost everyone prefers less risk to more, other things remaining the same. We measure people's attitudes towards risk by using their utility of wealth schedules and curves. The **utility of wealth** is the amount of utility a person attaches to a given amount of wealth. The greater a person's wealth, other things remaining the same, the higher is the person's total utility. Greater wealth brings higher total utility, but as wealth increases, each additional unit of wealth increases total utility by a smaller amount. That is, the *marginal utility of wealth* diminishes.

Figure 19.1 sets out Tania's utility of wealth schedule and curve. Each point *A* to *E* on Tania's utility of wealth curve corresponds to the row of the table identified by the same letter. You can see that as her wealth increases, so does her total utility of wealth. You can also see that her marginal utility of wealth diminishes. When wealth increases from £3,000 to £6,000, total utility increases by 20 units, but when wealth increases by a further £3,000 to £9,000, total utility increases by only 10 units.

We can use Tania's utility of wealth curve to measure her cost of risk. Let's see how Tania evaluates two summer jobs that involve different amounts of risk.

One job, working as a painter, pays enough for her to save £5,000 by the end of the summer. There is no uncertainty about the income from this job and hence no risk. If Tania takes this job, by the end of the summer her wealth will be £5,000.

The other job, working as a telemarketer selling subscriptions to a magazine, is risky. If she takes this job, her wealth at the end of the summer depends entirely on her success at selling. She might be a good sales person or a poor one. A good sales person makes £9,000 in a summer, and a poor one makes £3,000. Tania has never tried telemarketing, so she doesn't know how successful she'll be. She assumes that she has an equal chance – a probability of 0.5 – of making either £3,000 or £9,000.

Which outcome does Tania prefer: £5,000 for sure from the painting job or a 50 per cent chance of either £3,000 or £9,000 from the telemarketing job?

Figure 19.1

The Utility of Wealth

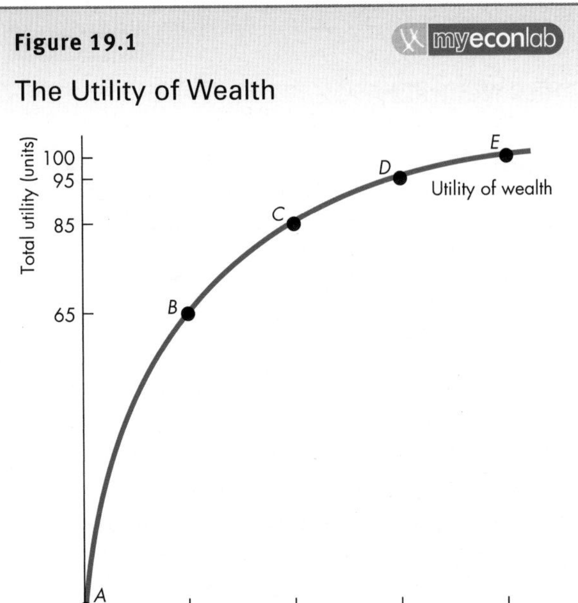

	Wealth (thousands of pounds)	Total utility (units)	Marginal utility (units)
A	0	0	
			65
B	3	65	
			20
C	6	85	
			10
D	9	95	
			5
E	12	100	

The table shows Tania's utility of wealth schedule, and the figure shows her utility of wealth curve. Utility increases as wealth increases, but the marginal utility of wealth diminishes.

Figure 19.2

Choice Under Uncertainty

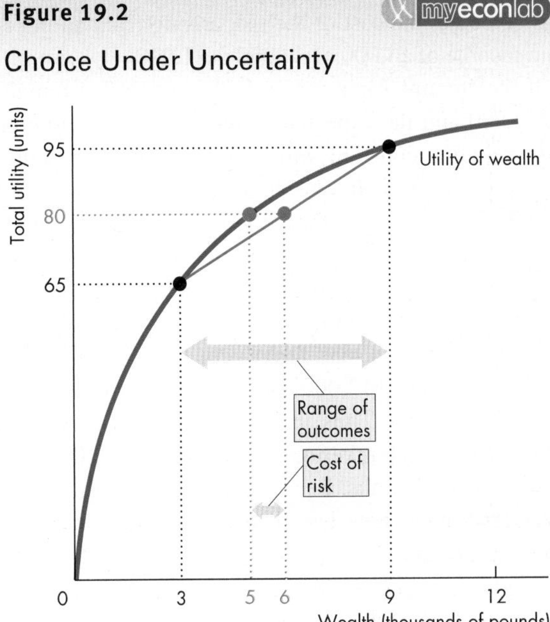

If Tania's wealth is £5,000 and she faces no risk, her utility is 80 units. If she faces an equal probability of having £9,000 with a utility of 95 or £3,000 with a utility of 65, her expected wealth is £6,000. But her expected utility is 80 units – the same as with £5,000 and no uncertainty. Tania is indifferent between these two alternatives. Tania's extra £1,000 of expected wealth is just enough to offset her extra risk.

When there is uncertainty, people do not know the *actual* utility they will get from taking a particular action. But it is possible to calculate the utility they *expect* to get. **Expected utility** is the average utility arising from all possible outcomes. So, to choose her summer job, Tania calculates the expected utility from each job. Figure 19.2 shows how she does this.

If Tania takes the painting job, she has £5,000 of wealth and 80 units of utility. There is no uncertainty, so her expected utility equals her actual utility: 80 units. But suppose she takes the telemarketing job. If she makes £9,000, her utility is 95 units, and if she makes £3,000, her utility is 65 units. Tania's *expected income* is the average of these two outcomes and is (£9,000 × 0.5) + (£3,000 × 0.5), which equals £6,000. This average is called a *weighted average*, the weights being the probabilities of each outcome (both 0.5 in this case). Tania's *expected utility* is the average of these two possible total utilities and is (95 × 0.5) + (65 × 0.5), which equals 80 units.

Tania chooses the job that maximizes her expected utility. In this case, the two alternatives give the same expected utility – 80 units – so she is indifferent between them. She is equally likely to take either job. The difference between Tania's expected wealth of £6,000 from the risky job and £5,000 from the no-risk job – £1,000 – is just large enough to offset the additional risk that Tania faces.

The calculations that we've just done enable us to measure Tania's cost of risk. The cost of risk is the amount by which expected wealth must be increased to give the same expected utility as a no-risk situation. In Tania's case, the cost of the risk arising from an uncertain income of £3,000 or £9,000 is £1,000.

If the amount Tania can make from painting remains at £5,000 and the expected income from telemarketing also remains constant while its range of uncertainty increases, Tania will take the painting job. To see this conclusion, suppose that good telemarketers make £12,000 and poor ones make nothing. The average income from telemarketing is unchanged at £6,000, but the range of uncertainty has increased. The table in Figure 19.1 shows that Tania gets 100 units of utility from a wealth of £12,000 and zero units of utility from a wealth of zero. Thus in this case, Tania's expected utility from telemarketing is $(100 \times 0.5) + (0 \times 0.5)$, which equals 50 units. Because the expected utility from telemarketing is now less than that from painting, she chooses painting.

Risk Aversion and Risk Neutrality

The cost of risk to a person depends on individual preferences. And there is a distribution of attitudes towards risk. At one extreme are people who dislike risk so intensely that they would pay a very high price to avoid it. At the other extreme are people for whom the cost of risk bearing is small. We call the attitude towards risk **risk aversion**.

Tania is *risk averse*. The shape of the utility of wealth curve tells us about the attitude towards risk – about the person's *degree of risk aversion*. The more rapidly a person's marginal utility of wealth diminishes, the more risk averse that person is. You can see this fact best by considering the case of *risk neutrality*. A risk-neutral person cares only about *expected wealth* and doesn't mind how much uncertainty there is.

Cricket provides lots of examples of varying attitudes towards risk. When Kevin Pietersen swings at a tight ball from Makhaya Ntini in the hope of hitting a six, he displays a low degree of risk aversion. And when Herschelle Gibbs plays a perfect defensive stroke against a Yorker from Andrew 'Freddie' Flintoff, he is displaying a high degree of risk aversion.

Figure 19.3 shows the utility of wealth curve of a risk-neutral person. It is a straight line, and the marginal utility of wealth is constant. If this person has an expected wealth of £6,000, expected utility is 50 units regardless of the range of uncertainty around that average. An equal probability of having £3,000 or £9,000 gives the same expected utility as a certain £6,000. When Tania's risk increased to this range, she needed an extra £1,000.

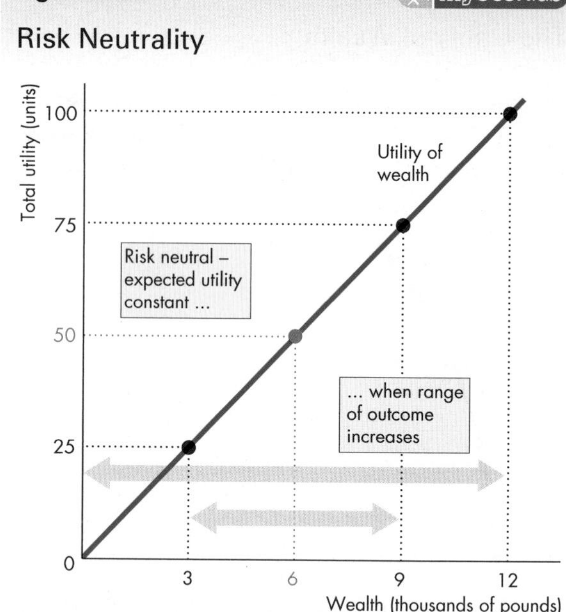

People's dislike of risk implies a diminishing marginal utility of wealth. A (hypothetical) risk-neutral person has a linear utility of wealth curve and a constant marginal utility of wealth. For a risk-neutral person, expected utility does not depend on the range of uncertainty. The cost of risk is zero.

This person does not. Even if the range of risk becomes £0 to £12,000, the risk-neutral person still gets the same expected utility as a certain £6,000 gives.

Most people are risk averse, and their utility of wealth curves look like Tania's. But the case of risk neutrality shows why the shape of the utility of wealth curve indicates a person's degree of risk aversion.

Review Quiz

Study Plan 19.1

1. How do people make decisions when they are faced with uncertain outcomes? What do they try to achieve?
2. How can we measure the cost of risk?
3. What determines the amount that someone would be willing to pay to avoid risk? Is the cost of risk the same for everyone?
4. What is a risk-neutral person and how much would such a person pay to avoid risk?

Because most people are risk averse, they buy insurance. Let's see how people gain from insurance.

Insurance

One way of reducing the risk we face is to buy insurance. How does insurance reduce risk? Why do people buy insurance? And what determines the amount we spend on insurance? Before we answer these questions, let's look at the insurance industry in the United Kingdom today.

Insurance Industry in the United Kingdom

We spend close to 15 per cent of our income, on the average, on private insurance. That's as much as we spend on housing and more than we spend on cars and food. In addition, we buy insurance through our taxes in the form of National Insurance and unemployment insurance. When we buy private insurance, we enter into an agreement with an insurance company to pay an agreed price – called a premium – in exchange for benefits to be paid to us if some specified event occurs.

The main types of insurance we buy are:

- Life insurance
- Property and casualty insurance

Life Insurance

Life insurance reduces the risk of financial loss in the event of death and provides a convenient way of spreading consumption over a person's life cycle. Almost 50 per cent of households in the United Kingdom have life insurance and the total amount paid in premiums is running close to £80 billion a year.

Property and Casualty Insurance

Property and casualty insurance reduces the risk of financial loss in the event of an accident involving damage to persons or property. It includes car insurance – its biggest component – and the insurance of homes and their contents.

How Insurance Works

Insurance works by pooling risks. It is possible and profitable because people are risk averse. The probability of any one person having a serious car accident is small, but the cost of an accident to the person involved is enormous. For a large population, the probability of one person having an accident is the proportion of the population that does have an accident. Because this probability can be estimated, the total cost of accidents can be predicted. An insurance company can pool the risks of a large population and share the costs. It does so by collecting premiums from everyone and paying out benefits to those who suffer a loss. If the insurance company does its calculations correctly, it collects at least as much in premiums as it pays out in benefits and operating costs.

To see why people buy insurance and why it is profitable, let's consider an example. Dan has the utility of wealth curve shown in Figure 19.4. He owns a car worth £10,000, and that is his only wealth. If there is no risk of his having an accident, his utility will be 100 units. But there is a 10 per cent chance (a probability of 0.1) that he will have an accident within a year. Suppose Dan does not buy insurance. If he does have an accident, his car is worthless, and with no insurance, he has no wealth and no utility. Because the probability of an accident is 0.1, the probability of not having an accident is 0.9. Dan's expected wealth, therefore, is £9,000

Figure 19.4

The Gains from Insurance

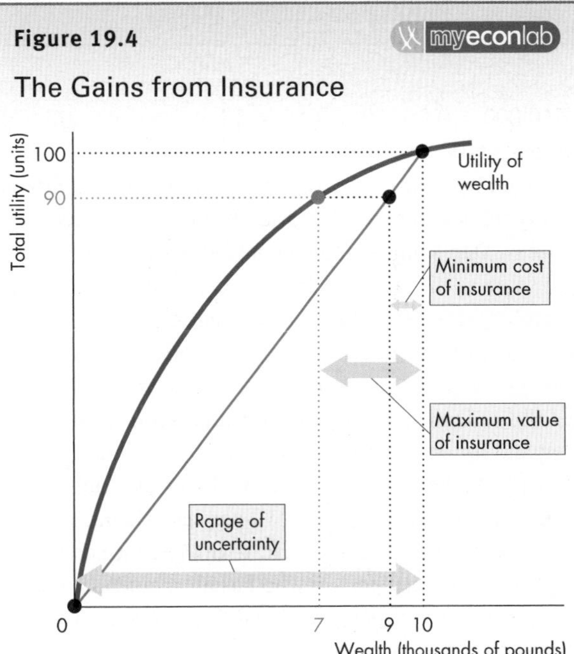

Dan has a car valued at £10,000 that gives him a utility of 100 units, but there is a 0.1 probability that he will have an accident, making his car worthless (wealth and utility equal to zero). With no insurance, his expected wealth is £9,000 and his expected utility is 90 units. His guaranteed wealth is £7,000. Dan will pay up to £3,000 for insurance. If an insurance company can offer Dan insurance for £1,000, there is a potential gain from insurance for both Dan and the insurance company.

Table 19.1

Risk Taking versus Insurance

(a) Possible Outcomes

Probability	**No accident 0.9**		**Accident 0.1**	
	Wealth	**Utility**	**Wealth**	**Utility**
No insurance	£5,000	100	£0	0
Insurance	£4,000	95	£4,000	95

(b) Expected Outcomes

	Expected Wealth	**Expected utility**
No insurance	(£5,000 × 0.9) + (£0 × 0.1) = £4,500	(100 × 0.9) + (0 × 0.1) = 90
Insurance	(£4,000 × 0.9) + (£4,000 × 0.1) = £4,000	(95 × 0.9) + (95 × 0.1) = 95

Part (a) sets out the possible outcomes. The probablity of having an accident is 0.9. If an accident occurs and Dan has no insurance, his wealth falls from £5,00 to £0. Whereas with insurance that costs £1,000, his wealth remains at £4,000 and his utility is 95 units.

Part (b) shows Dan's expected outcomes. With no insurance, his expected wealth is £4,500 and his expected utility is 90 units. By buying insurance for £1,000, Dan's expected wealth falls to £4,000, but he has no uncertainty and his expected utility rises to 95 units.

(£10,000 × 0.9 + £0 × 0.1), and his expected utility is 90 units (100 × 0.9 + 0 × 0.1).

Given his utility of wealth curve, Dan has 90 units of utility if his wealth is £7,000 and he faces no uncertainty. That is, Dan's utility of a guaranteed wealth of £7,000 is the same as his utility of a 90 per cent chance of having wealth of £10,000 and a 10 per cent chance of having nothing. If the cost of an insurance policy that pays out in the event of an accident is less than £3,000 (£10,000 – £7,000), Dan will buy the policy. Thus Dan has a demand for car insurance at premiums less than £3,000.

Suppose there are lots of people like Dan, each with a £10,000 car and each with a 10 per cent chance of having an accident within the year. If an insurance company agrees to pay each person who has an accident £10,000, the company will pay out £10,000 to one tenth of the population, or an average of £1,000 per person. This amount is the insurance company's minimum premium for such insurance. It is less than the value of insurance to Dan because Dan is risk averse. He is willing to pay something to reduce the risk he faces.

Now suppose that the insurance company's operating expenses are a further £1,000 and that it offers insurance for £2,000. The company now covers all its costs – the amounts paid out to policy holders for their losses plus the company's operating expenses. Dan – and all the other people like him – will maximize his utility by buying this insurance.

Review Quiz

Study Plan 19.2

1. What types of insurance do we buy and how large a percentage of our incomes do we spend on insurance (on the average)?
2. How does insurance work? How can people avoid unwanted outcomes by insuring against them?
3. How can an insurance company offer people a deal worth taking? Why don't the amounts paid in by insurers only just cover the amounts paid out by insurance companies to claimants?

Much of the uncertainty that we face arises from ignorance. We just don't know all the things we could benefit from knowing. But knowledge or information is not free. And government intervention is of little use in dealing with this problem. Governments usually are even less well informed than buyers and sellers. Faced with incomplete information, we must make decisions about how much information to acquire. Let's now study the choices we make about obtaining information and how markets cope with incomplete information.

Information

We spend a huge quantity of our scarce resources on economic information. **Economic information** includes data on the prices, quantities and qualities of goods and services and resources.

In the models of perfect competition, monopoly and monopolistic competition, information is free. Everyone has all the information he or she needs. Households are completely informed about the prices of the goods and services they buy and the factors of production they sell. Similarly, firms are completely informed about consumers' preferences and about the prices and products of other firms.

In contrast, information is scarce in the real world. If it were not, we wouldn't need the *Financial Times* and the BBC. And we wouldn't need to shop around for bargains or spend time looking for a job. The opportunity cost of economic information – the cost of acquiring information on the prices, quantities and qualities of goods and services and resources – is called **information cost**.

The fact that many economic models ignore information costs does not make these models useless. They give us insights into the forces generating trends in prices and quantities over periods long enough for information limits not to be important. But to understand how markets work hour by hour and day by day, we must take information problems into account. Let's look at some of the consequences of information cost.

Searching for Price Information

When many firms sell the same good or service, there is a range of prices and buyers want to find the lowest price. But searching takes time and is costly. So buyers must balance the expected gain from further search against the cost of further search. To perform this balancing act, buyers use a decision rule called the *optimal-search rule* – or *optimal-stopping rule*. The optimal-search rule is:

- Search for a lower price until the expected marginal benefit of additional search equals the marginal cost of search.
- When the expected marginal benefit from additional search is less than or equal to the marginal cost, stop searching and buy.

To implement the optimal-search rule, each buyer chooses her or his own reservation price. The buyer's **reservation price** is the highest price that the buyer is willing to pay for a good. The buyer will continue to search for a lower price if the lowest price so far found exceeds the reservation price but will stop searching and buy if the lowest price found is less than or equal to the reservation price. At the buyer's reservation price, the expected marginal benefit of search equals the marginal cost of search.

Figure 19.5 illustrates the optimal-search rule. Suppose you've decided to buy a used Ford Focus. Your marginal cost of search is £*C* per dealer visited and is shown by the horizontal red line in the figure. This cost includes the value of your time, which is the amount that you could have earned by working instead of driving around used car lots, and the amount spent on transportation and advice. Your expected marginal benefit of visiting one more dealer depends on the lowest price that you've found. The lower the price you've already found, the lower is your expected marginal benefit of visiting one more dealer, as shown by the blue curve in the figure.

Figure 19.5 myeconlab

Optimal-search Rule

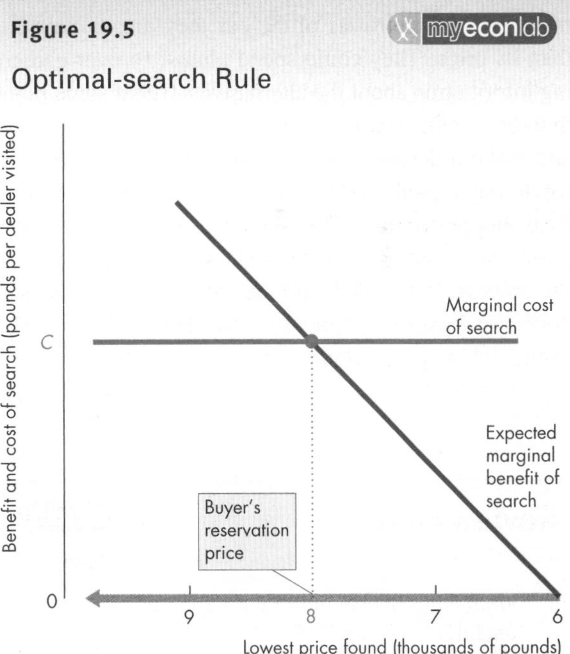

The marginal cost of search is constant at £*C*. As the lowest price found (measured from right to left on the *x*-axis) declines, the expected marginal benefit of further search diminishes. The lowest price found at which the marginal cost equals the expected marginal benefit is the reservation price. The optimal-search rule is to search until the reservation price is found and then buy at that lowest found price.

The price at which expected marginal benefit equals marginal cost is your reservation price – £8,000 in the figure. If you find a price equal to or below your reservation price, you stop searching and buy. If you find a price that exceeds your reservation price, you continue to search for a lower price. Individual shoppers differ in their marginal cost of search and so have different reservation prices. As a result, identical items can be found selling for a range of prices.

Buyers who have a high value on their time, stop searching after a short time and pay the highest prices. Buyers who have the lowest value on their time search the longest and pay the lowest prices.

Demand and supply determine the average and the range of prices. A dealer whose prices are too high will get few buyers and will eventually cut the price. And a dealer whose price is too low will run out of stock and eventually raise the price.

A Real Car Shopping Trip

Real car shoppers are confronted with a much bigger problem than the one we've just studied. There are many more dimensions of the car they are looking for than its price. They could spend almost forever gathering information about the alternatives. But at some point in their search, they decide they've done enough looking and make a decision to buy. Your imaginary shopping trip to buy a used Ford Focus rationalizes their decision. Real shoppers think, "The benefits I expect from further search are insufficient to make it worth going on with the process." They don't do the calculations we've just done – at least, not explicitly – but their actions can be explained by those calculations.

Review Quiz

Study Plan 19.3

1 What types of economic information do people find useful?
2 Why is economic information scarce and how do people economize on its use?
3 What is the buyer's reservation price?
4 What determines the opportunity cost of economic information?
5 How do you decide to keep searching for an item, rather than stop searching?
6 How do you decide when to stop searching for a lower-priced item to buy?

Private Information

So far we have looked at situations in which information is available to everyone and can be obtained with an expenditure of resources. But not all situations are like this. For example, someone might have private information. **Private information** is information that is available to one person but is too costly for anyone else to obtain.

Private information affects many economic transactions. One is your knowledge about your driving. You know much more than your car insurance company does about how carefully and defensively you drive. Another is your knowledge about your work effort. You know far more than your employer about how hard you work. Yet another is your knowledge about the quality of your car. You know whether it's a lemon. But the person to whom you are about to sell it does not and can't find out until after he or she has purchased the car from you.

Private information creates two problems:

1 Moral hazard
2 Adverse selection

Moral hazard exists when one of the parties to an agreement has an incentive after the agreement is made to act in a manner that brings additional benefits to himself or herself at the expense of the other party. Moral hazard arises because it is too costly for the injured party to monitor the actions of the advantaged party. For example, Jackie hires Mitch as a sales person and pays him a fixed wage regardless of his sales. Mitch faces a moral hazard. He has an incentive to put in the least possible effort, benefiting himself and lowering Jackie's profits. For this reason, sales people are usually paid by a formula that makes their income higher the greater is the volume (or value) of their sales.

Adverse selection is the tendency for people to enter into agreements in which they can use their private information to their own advantage and to the disadvantage of the less informed party. For example, if Jackie offers sales people a fixed wage, she will attract lazy sales people. Hardworking sales people will prefer not to work for Jackie because they can earn more by working for someone who pays by results. The fixed-wage contract adversely selects those with private information (knowledge about their work habits) who can use that knowledge to their own advantage and to the disadvantage of the other party.

A variety of devices have evolved that enable markets to function in the face of moral hazard and adverse selection. We've just seen one, the use of incentive payments for sales people. Let's look at some more and also see how moral hazard and adverse selection influence three real-world markets:

- The market for used cars
- The market for loans
- The market for insurance

The Market for Used Cars

When a person buys a car, it might turn out to be a lemon. If the car is a lemon, it is worth less to the buyer and to everyone else than if it has no defects. Does the used car market have two prices reflecting these two values – a low price for lemons and a higher price for cars without defects? It does not. To see why, let's look at a used car market, first with no dealer warranties and second with warranties.

Used Cars Without Warranties

To make the points as clearly as possible, we'll make some extreme assumptions. There are just two kinds of cars: lemons and those without defects. A lemon is worth £1,000 to both its current owner and anyone who buys it. A car without defects is worth £5,000 to both its current owner and potential future owners. Whether a car is a lemon is private information that is available only to the current owner. Buyers of used cars can't tell whether they are buying a lemon until after they have bought the car and learned as much about it as its current owner knows. There are no dealer warranties.

Because buyers can't tell the difference between a lemon and a good car, they are willing to pay only one price for a used car. What is that price? Are they willing to pay £5,000, the value of a good car? They are not, because there is at least some probability that they are buying a lemon worth only £1,000. If buyers are not willing to pay £5,000 for a used car, are the owners of good cars willing to sell? They are not, because a good car is worth £5,000 to them, so they hang onto their cars. Only the owners of lemons are willing to sell – as long as the price is £1,000 or higher. But, reason the buyers, if only the owners of lemons are selling, all the used cars available are lemons, so the maximum price worth paying is £1,000. Thus the market for used cars is a market for lemons, and the price is £1,000.

Moral hazard exists in the car market because sellers have an incentive to claim that lemons are good cars. But, given the assumptions in the above description of the car market, no one believes such claims. Adverse selection exists, resulting in only lemons actually being traded. The market for used cars is not working well. Good used cars just don't get bought and sold, but people want to be able to buy and sell good used cars. How can they do so? The answer is by introducing warranties into the market.

Used Cars with Warranties

Buyers of used cars can't tell a lemon from a good car, but car dealers sometimes can. For example, they might have regularly serviced the car. So they know whether they are buying a lemon or a good car and can offer £1,000 for lemons and £5,000 for good cars.[1] But how can they convince buyers that it is worth paying £5,000 for what might be a lemon? The answer is by giving a guarantee in the form of a warranty. The dealer signals which cars are good and which are lemons. A **signal** is an action taken outside a market that conveys information that can be used by that market. There are many examples of signals, one of which is students' grades. Your grade acts as a signal to potential employers.

In the case of the used cars, dealers take actions in the market for car repairs that can be used by the market for cars. For each good car sold, the dealer gives a warranty. The dealer agrees to pay the costs of repairing the car if it turns out to have a defect. Cars with a warranty are good; cars without a warranty are lemons.

Why do buyers believe the signal? It is because the cost of sending a false signal is high. A dealer who gives a warranty on a lemon ends up paying the high cost of repairs – and risks gaining a bad reputation. A dealer who gives a warranty only on good cars has no repair costs and a reputation that gets better and better. It pays to send an accurate signal. It is rational, therefore, for buyers to believe the signal. Warranties break the lemon problem and enable the used car market to function with two prices, one for lemons and one for good cars.

The Market for Loans

The market for bank loans is one in which private information plays a crucial role. Let's see how.

The quantity of loans demanded by borrowers depends on the interest rate. The lower the interest rate, the greater is the quantity of loans demanded – the

[1] Here, to keep the numbers simple, we'll ignore dealer profits margins and costs of doing businee.The principles remain the same.

demand curve for loans is downward-sloping. The supply of loans by banks and other lenders depends on the cost of lending. This cost has two parts. One is interest, and this interest cost is determined in the market for bank deposits – the market in which the banks borrow the funds that they lend. The other part of the cost of lending is the cost of bad loans – loans that are not repaid – called the default cost. The interest cost of a loan is the same for all borrowers. The default cost of a loan depends on the quality of the borrower.

Borrowers of Unknown Risk

Suppose that borrowers fall into two classes: low-risk and high-risk. Low-risk borrowers seldom default on their debts and then only for reasons beyond their control. For example, a firm might borrow to finance a project that fails and be unable to repay the bank. High-risk borrowers take high risks with the money they borrow and frequently default on their loans. For example, a firm might borrow to speculate in high-risk mineral prospecting that has a very small chance of paying off.

If banks can separate borrowers into risk categories, they supply loans to low-risk borrowers at one interest rate and to high-risk borrowers at another, higher interest rate. Real banks do this as much as possible. But they cannot always separate their borrowers. They have no sure way of knowing whether they are lending to a low-risk or a high-risk borrower.

So the banks charge the same interest rate to both low-risk and high-risk borrowers. If they offered loans to everyone at the low-risk interest rate, borrowers would face moral hazard and the banks would attract a lot of high-risk borrowers – adverse selection. Most borrowers would default, and the banks would incur economic losses. If the banks offered loans to everyone at the high-risk interest rate, most low-risk borrowers, with whom the banks would like to do profitable business, would be unwilling to borrow.

Signalling and Loan Rationing

Faced with moral hazard and adverse selection, banks use signals to discriminate between borrowers, and they ration or limit loans to amounts below the amounts demanded. To restrict the amounts they are willing to lend to borrowers, banks use signals such as length of time in a job, ownership of a home, marital status, age, and business record.

Figure 19.6 shows how the market for loans works in the face of moral hazard and adverse selection. The demand for loans is D, and the supply is S. The supply curve is horizontal – perfectly elastic supply – because it is assumed that banks have access to a large quantity of funds that have a constant marginal cost of r. With no loan limits, the interest rate is r and the quantity of loans is Q. Because of moral hazard and adverse selection, the banks set loan limits based on signals and restrict the total loans to L. At the interest rate r, there is an excess demand for loans. A bank cannot increase its profit by making more loans because it can't identify the type of borrower taking the loans. Because the signals used mean that more high-risk borrowers are unsatisfied than low-risk borrowers, it is likely that additional loans will be biased towards high-risk (and high-cost) borrowers.

The Market for Insurance

People who buy insurance face moral hazard, and insurance companies face adverse selection. Moral hazard arises because a person with insurance against a loss has less incentive than an uninsured person to avoid the

Figure 19.6 myeconlab

The Market for Loans

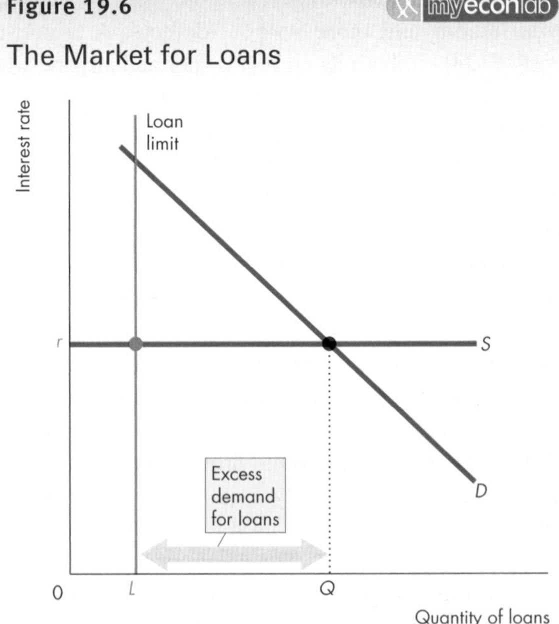

If a bank supplied loans on demand at the going interest rate r, the quantity of loans would be Q, but most of the loans would be taken by high-risk borrowers. Banks use signals to distinguish between low-risk and high-risk borrowers, and they limit the total loans to L and ration them. Banks have no incentive to increase interest rates and increase the quantity of loans because the additional loans would be to high-risk borrowers.

loss. For example, a business with fire insurance has less incentive to install a fire alarm or sprinkler system than a business with no fire insurance does. Adverse selection arises because people who create greater risks are more likely to buy insurance. For example, a person with a family history of serious illness is more likely to buy health insurance than is a person with a family history of good health.

Insurance companies have an incentive to find ways around the moral hazard and adverse selection problems. By doing so, they can lower premiums for low-risk people and raise premiums for high-risk people. Let's see how car insurance companies use signalling to get around these private information problems.

"No-Claim" Bonus as a Signal

One device that car insurance companies use is the "no-claim" bonus. A driver accumulates a no-claim bonus by driving safely and avoiding accidents and claims. The greater the bonus, the greater is the incentive to drive carefully. The safest drivers get the biggest bonus so pay the least for their car insurance.

Deductible as a Signal

Car insurance companies also use a deductible as a signal. A deductible is the amount of a loss that the insured person agrees to bear. The premium is smaller the greater is the deductible, and the decrease in the premium is more than proportionate to the increase in the deductible. By offering insurance with full coverage – no deductible – on terms that are attractive only to the highest-risk people and by offering coverage with a deductible on more favourable terms that are attractive to other people, insurance companies can do profitable business with everyone. High-risk people choose policies with low deductibles and high premiums; low-risk people choose policies with high deductibles and low premiums.

Review Quiz

Study Plan 19.4

1 How does private information create moral hazard and adverse selection?
2 How do markets for cars use warranties to cope with private information?
3 How do markets for insurance use no-claim bonuses to cope with private information?

Managing Risk in Financial Markets

Risk is a dominant feature of markets for stocks and bonds – indeed for any asset whose price fluctuates. One thing people do to cope with risky asset prices is diversify their asset holdings.

Diversification to Lower Risk

The idea that diversification lowers risk is very natural. It is just an application of not putting all one's eggs into the same basket. How exactly does diversification reduce risk? Let's consider an example.

Suppose there are two risky projects that you can undertake. Each involves investing £100,000. The two projects are independent of each other, but they both promise the same degree of risk and return.

On each project, you will either make £50,000 or lose £25,000, and the chance that either of these will happen is 50 per cent. The expected return on each project is (£50,000 × 0.5) + (–£25,000 × 0.5), which is £12,500. But because the two projects are completely independent, the outcome of one project in no way influences the outcome of the other.

Undiversified

Suppose you risk everything, investing the £100,000 in either Project 1 or Project 2. You will either make £50,000 or lose £25,000. Because the probability of each of these outcomes is 50 per cent, your expected return is the average of these two outcomes – an expected return of £12,500. But in this case in which only one project is chosen, there is no chance that you will actually make a return of £12,500.

Diversified

Now suppose that you put 50 per cent of your money into Project 1 and 50 per cent into Project 2. (Someone else puts up the other money in these two projects.) Because the two projects are independent, you now have four possible returns:

1 Lose £12,500 on each project, and your return is –£25,000.
2 Make £25,000 on Project 1 and lose £12,500 on Project 2, and your return is £12,500.

3 Lose £12,500 on Project 1 and make £25,000 on Project 2, and your return is £12,500.

4 Make £25,000 on each project, and your return is £50,000.

Each of these four possible outcomes is equally probable – each has a 25 per cent chance of occurring. You have lowered the chance that you will earn £50,000, but you have also lowered the chance that you will lose £25,000. And you have increased the chance that you will actually make your expected return of £12,500. By diversifying your portfolio of assets, you have reduced its riskiness while maintaining an expected return of £12,500.

If you are risk averse – if your utility of wealth curve looks like Tania's, which you studied earlier in this chapter – you'll prefer the diversified portfolio to the one that is not diversified. That is, your expected utility with a diversified set of assets is greater.

A common way to diversify is to buy shares of the stock in different corporations. Let's look at the market in which these stocks are traded.

The Stock Market

The price of a share of a company's stock is determined by demand and supply. But demand and supply in the stock market is dominated by one thing: the expected future price. If the price of a share of stock today is higher than the expected price tomorrow, people will sell the share today. If the price of a share today is less than its expected price tomorrow, people will buy the share today. As a result of such trading, today's price equals tomorrow's expected price, and so today's price embodies all the relevant information that is available about the stock. A market in which the actual price embodies all currently available relevant information is called an **efficient market**.

In an efficient market, it is impossible to forecast changes in price. Why? If your forecast is that the price is going to rise tomorrow, you will buy now. Your action of buying today is an increase in demand today and increases today's price. It's true that your action – the action of a single trader – is not going to make much difference to a huge market like the London Stock Exchange. But if traders in general expect a higher price tomorrow and they all act today on the basis of that expectation, then today's price will rise. It will keep on rising until it reaches the expected future price, because only at that price do traders see no profit in buying more stock today.

There is an apparent paradox about efficient markets. Markets are efficient because people try to make a profit. They seek a profit by buying at a low price and selling at a high price. But the very act of buying and selling to make a profit means that the market price moves to equal its expected future value. When it has done that, no one, not even those who are seeking to profit, can predictably make a profit. Every profit opportunity seen by traders leads to an action that produces a price change that removes the profit opportunity for others. The stockbroker in the cartoon is being refreshingly honest with his client in the advice he's offering.

"We're expecting stocks to rally but we don't know which ones and when."

So an efficient market has two features:

1 Its price equals the expected future price and embodies all the available information.

2 No *forecastable* profit opportunities are available.

The key thing to understand about an efficient market such as the stock market is that if something can be anticipated, it will be, and the anticipation of a future event will affect the current price of a stock.

Review Quiz

Study Plan 19.5

1 How does diversification lower risk and how does it affect the expected rate of return?

2 What does it mean to say that the stock market is efficient? Is the term "efficient" being used in the normal way?

Uncertainty, Information and the Invisible Hand

A recurring theme throughout microeconomics is the big question: When do choices made in the pursuit of self-interest also promote the social interest? When does the invisible hand work well and when does it fail us? You've learned about the concept of efficiency, a major component of what we mean by the social interest. And you've seen that while competitive markets generally do a good job in helping to achieve efficiency, impediments such as monopoly and the absence of well-defined property rights can prevent the attainment of an efficient use of resources.

How do uncertainty and incomplete information affect the ability of self-interested choices to lead to a social interest outcome? Are these features of economic life another reason why markets fail and why some type of government intervention is required to achieve efficiency?

These are hard questions, and there are no definitive answers. But there are some useful things that we can say about the effects of uncertainty and a lack of complete information on the efficiency of resource use. We'll begin our brief review of this issue by thinking about information as just another good.

Information as a Good

More information is generally useful. And less uncertainty about the future is generally useful. Think about information as one of the goods that we want more of.

The most basic lesson about efficiency that you learned in Chapter 2 can be applied to information. Along our production possibilities frontier, we face a trade-off between information and all other goods and services. Information, like everything else, can be produced at an increasing opportunity cost – an increasing marginal cost. For example, we could get more accurate weather forecasts, but only at increasing marginal cost, as we increased the amount of information that we gather from the atmosphere and the amount of money that we spend on super-computers to process the data.

The principle of decreasing marginal benefit also applies to information. More information is valuable, but the more you know, the less you value another increment in information. For example, knowing that it will rain tomorrow is valuable information. Knowing the amount of rain to within an inch is even more useful. But knowing the amount of rain to within a millimetre probably isn't worth much more.

Because the marginal cost of information is increasing and the marginal benefit is decreasing, there is an efficient amount of information. It would be inefficient to be overinformed.

In principle, competitive markets in information might deliver this efficient quantity. Whether they actually do so is hard to determine.

Monopoly in Markets That Cope with Uncertainty

There are probably large economies of scale in providing services that cope with uncertainty and incomplete information. The banking and insurance industries, for example, are highly concentrated. Where monopoly elements exist, exactly the same inefficiency issues arise as they do in markets where uncertainty and incomplete information are not big issues. So it is likely that in some information markets, including markets for loans and insurance markets, there is underproduction arising from the attempt to maximize monopoly profit.

But in other markets, such as that for used cars, there is intense competition and most likely these markets, helped with signals, achieve efficient outcomes.

Review Quiz

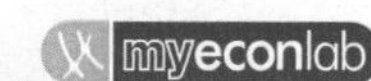

Study Plan 19.6

1. Thinking about information as a good, what information would you be willing to pay for?
2. Of the information you are willing to pay for, what can you buy in an information market and what can't you buy?
3. Why are some of the markets that provide information likely to be dominated by monopoly?

We've seen how people cope with uncertainty and how markets work when there are information problems. *Reading Between the Lines* on pages 442–443 looks at the way university marks work as signals in the labour market and sort students by ability so that employers can hire the type of labour they seek. You'll discover that grade inflation is inefficient.

The next part of this book studies macroeconomics. It builds on what you learned in Chapter 2 about production possibilities and shows how economic growth expands these possibilities. It also studies fluctuations in production, employment and prices.

Reading Between the Lines
Grades as Signals

The Economist, 18 March 2004

Grade expectations

FIRST-CLASS degrees used to be awarded very sparingly. According to one Cambridge joke, examiners in philosophy used to shun awarding firsts, because that would imply that the candidate was as clever as the examiner, which would be logically absurd.

That's changed. New statistics this week showed that the number of firsts awarded by Britain's 19 top universities had risen by half in the past five years. In 1998 they gave 6,314; last year it was 9,475. This caused much harrumphing about dumbing down. It follows similar howls about mushrooming top grades in schools.

There are some innocent explanations. Numbers have risen (although not nearly enough to account for the improvement). Students may be better: perhaps working a bit harder, or with teaching more focused on the all-important exam, rather than on woolly stuff like thinking and ideas.

More likely, though, the drift towards firsts reflects more worrying problems. Marking finals at top universities used to be prestigious, well paid and solidly protected from outside pressure. That ensured hard, careful work by senior dons. Now examining is seen as drudgery, best farmed out to junior staff.

Dons also complain that increasing government scrutiny means they are under pressure not to fail students or give poor grades. That would suggest that they had failed to select and teach students properly. It is wiser to be kind. . . .

The Essence of the Story

- Britain's 19 top universities gave 6,314 first class honours degrees in 1968 and 9,475 in 2003.
- The total number of students has increased but not by enough to account for the large increase in the number of firsts.
- Students may be better, working harder, or taught with greater focus on exams.
- But more likely softer grading is the explanation.
- University teachers complain that they are under pressure not to fail students.
- Avoiding failures brings softer courses and higher grades.

Economic Analysis

- Accurate grades provide valuable information to students and potential employers about a student's ability.
- Universities try to provide accurate grades but face pressures to grade more softly.
- Figure 1 shows a labour market for university graduates when there is grade inflation.
- Students with high ability are not distinguished from other students, and the supply curve represents the supply of students of all ability levels.
- The demand curve shows the employers' willingness to hire new workers without knowledge of their ability.
- All graduates get jobs at the same low wage rate.
- Figures 2 and 3 show the outcome with accurate grading. In Figure 2, students with high grades get high-wage jobs and in Figure 3, students with low grades get low-wage jobs.
- Even with grade inflation, employers discover ability from on-the-job performance and eventually, even with grade inflation, earnings reflect ability.
- But accurate grades are valuable because they enable employers and graduates to avoid the costly process of discovering and revealing true ability on the job and get people into the right jobs at the time of graduation.

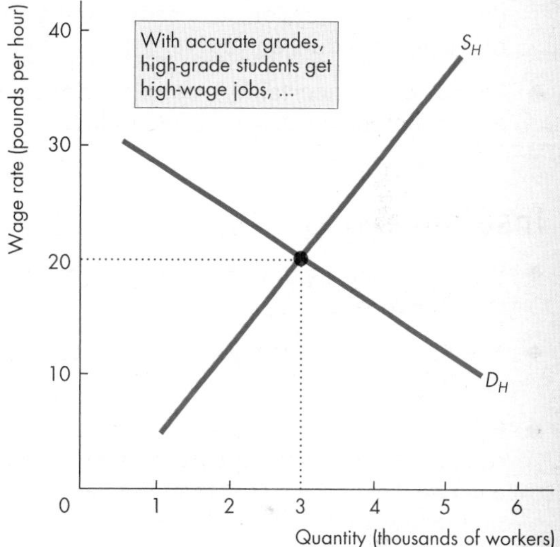

Figure 2 The market for A students

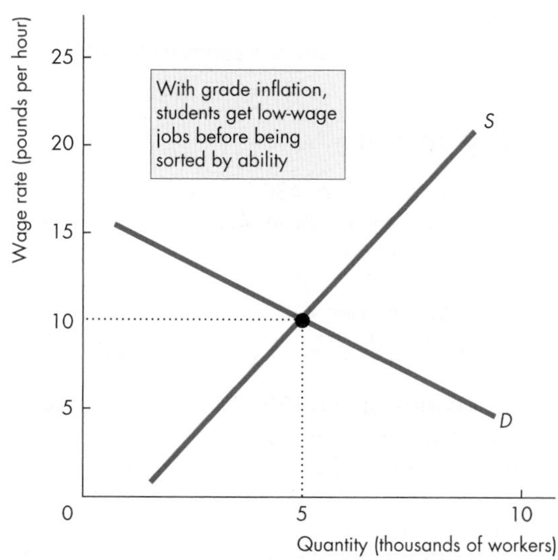

Figure 1 Market with grade inflation

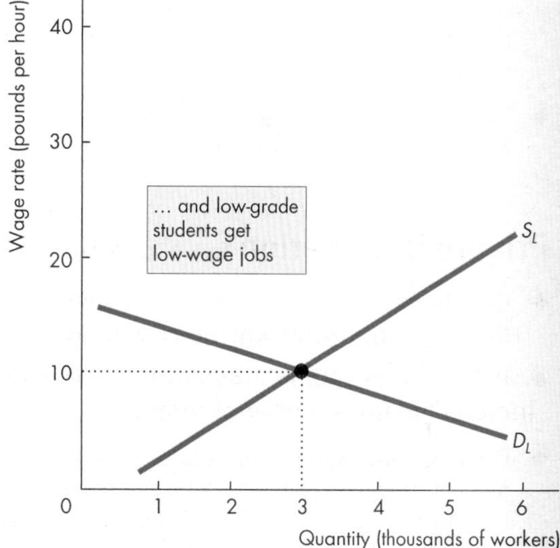

Figure 3 The market for D students

Summary

Key Points

Uncertainty and Risk (pp. 430–432)

- Uncertainty is a situation in which more than one event may occur but we don't know which one.
- Risk is uncertainty with probabilities attached to outcomes.
- A person's attitude toward risk, called the degree of risk aversion, is described by a utility of wealth schedule and curve.
- Faced with uncertainty, people choose the action that maximizes expected utility.

Insurance (pp. 433–434)

- We spend our income on insurance to reduce the risk we face.
- The main types of insurance are life and property and casualty.
- By pooling risks, insurance companies can reduce the risks people face (from insured activities) at a lower cost than the value placed on the lower risk.

Information (pp. 435–436)

- Buyers search for the least-cost source of supply and stop when the expected marginal benefit of search equals the marginal cost of search.
- The price at which the search stops is less than or equal to the buyer's reservation price.

Private Information (pp. 436–439)

- Private information is one person's knowledge that is too costly for anyone else to discover.
- Private information creates the problems of moral hazard and adverse selection.
- Devices that enable markets to function in the face of moral hazard and adverse selection are incentive payments, guarantees such as warranties, rationing and signals.

Managing Risk in Financial Markets (pp. 439–440)

- Risk can be reduced by diversifying asset holdings, which combines the returns on projects that are independent of each other.
- Share prices are determined by the expected future price of the stock.
- Expectations about future share prices are based on all the information that is available and regarded as relevant.
- A market in which the price equals the expected price is an efficient market.

Uncertainty, Information and the Invisible Hand (p. 441)

- Less uncertainty and more information can be viewed as a good that has increasing marginal cost and decreasing marginal benefit.
- Competitive information markets might be efficient, but economies of scale might bring inefficient underproduction of information and insurance.

Key Figures

Key Terms

Problems

Tests, Study Plan and Solutions* 

1 The figure shows Sophie's utility of wealth curve.

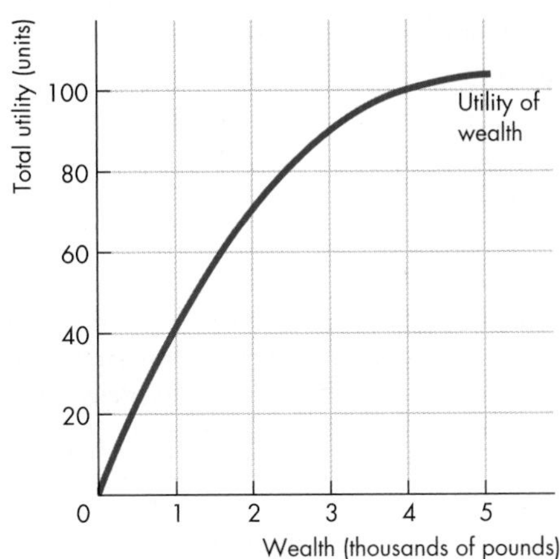

Sophie is offered a job as a sales person in which there is a 50 per cent chance that she will make £4,000 a month and a 50 per cent chance that she will make nothing.

a What is Sophie's expected income from taking this job?

b What is Sophie's expected utility from taking this job?

c How much would another firm have to offer Sophie with certainty to persuade her not to take the risky sales job?

d What is Sophie's cost of risk?

2 The table sets out Jimmy's and Zenda's utility of wealth schedules:

Wealth	Jimmy's utility	Zenda's utility
0	0	0
100	200	512
200	300	640
300	350	672
400	375	678
500	387	681
600	393	683
700	396	684

a What are Jimmy's and Zenda's expected utilities from a bet that gives them a 50 per cent chance of having a wealth of £600 and a 50 per cent chance of having nothing?

b Calculate Jimmy's and Zenda's marginal utility of wealth schedules.

c Who is more risk averse, Jimmy or Zenda? How do you know?

d Who is more likely to buy insurance, Jimmy or Zenda?

3 Suppose that Jimmy and Zenda in problem 2 have £400 each and that each sees a business project that involves committing the entire £400 to the project. They reckon that the project could return £600 (a profit of £200) with a probability of 0.85 or £200 (a loss of £200) with a probability of 0.15. Who goes for the project and who hangs onto the initial £400?

4 Sophie in problem 1 has built a small weekend shack on a steep, unstable hillside. She spent all her wealth, which is £5,000, on this project. There is a 75 per cent chance that the house will be washed down the hill and be worthless. How much is Sophie willing to pay for an insurance policy that pays her £5,000 if the house is washed away?

5 Sophie in problem 1 is shopping for a new car. She plans to borrow the money to pay for the car from the bank. Describe in detail the search problems that Sophie faces. What information does she find useful? How does she obtain it? How does she make her decisions?

6 Zaneb is a high-school teacher and is well known in her community for her honesty and integrity. She is shopping for a new car and plans to borrow the money to pay for it from her local bank.

a Does Zaneb create any moral hazard or adverse selection problems either for the bank or the car dealer? Explain your answer.

b Do the bank or the car dealer create any moral hazard or adverse selection problems for Zaneb? Explain your answer.

c What arrangements is Zaneb likely to encounter that are designed to help cope with the moral hazard and adverse selection problems she encounters in her car buying and bank loan transactions?

7 Suppose that there are three national football leagues: the Time League, the Goal Difference League, and the Bonus for Win League. The leagues are of equal quality, but the players in each league are paid differently. In the Time League, they are paid by the hour for time spent practising and time spent playing. In the Goal Difference league, they are paid an amount that depends on the number of points that the team scores minus the number of points scored against it. In the

* Solutions to odd-numbered problems are provided.

Bonus for Win League, the players are paid one wage for a loss, a higher wage for a tie, and the highest wage of all for a win.

- **a** Briefly describe the predicted differences in the quality of the games played by each of these leagues.
- **b** Which league will be the most attractive to players?
- **c** Which league will generate the largest profits?

8 Wayne Rooney has a contract with Manchester United that makes him the highest-ever earning British footballer. The 21-year-old has signed up for another six years at United, which, when added together with his commercial work, will net him up to £100 million. His salary alone over that period will be £35 million.

Entertainment Wise, 26 November 2006

- **a** Provide some example of private information that Wayne Rooney possesses.
- **b** Does a football player present a moral hazard to his team?
- **c** Does a football player present adverse selection problems to his team?
- **d** How does Manchester United get the best possible performance out of Wayne Rooney?

9 At 11:10 a.m. on 21 November 2006, one share of Google traded for $504.07. Viewed from that time and date, if the market for Google shares is efficient

- **a** What would you expect the price of one share of Google to be on 22 November 2006?
- **b** What profit would you expect to earn by selling one share of Google today or by holding that share for another week and then selling it?

10 Explain why you would increase your expected utility by spreading your wealth across the stocks of Google, BP, eBay and Microsoft instead of putting all your wealth into the stocks of just one of these companies. Would you also increase your expected wealth? Explain why or why not.

Critical Thinking

1 After you have studied *Reading Between the Lines* on pp. 442–443, answer the following questions:

- **a** What information do accurate grades provide that grade inflation hides?
- **b** If grade inflation became widespread in secondary schools and universities, what new arrangements do you predict would emerge to provide better information about student ability?
- **c** Do you think grade inflation is in anyone's self-interest? Explain who benefits and how the benefit from grade inflation.
- **d** How do you think grade inflation might be controlled?

2 Why do you think it is not possible to buy insurance against having to put up with a low-paying, miserable job? Explain why a market in insurance of this type would not work.

3 Although you can't buy insurance against the risk of being sold a lemon, the market does give you some protection. How? What are the main ways in which markets overcome the lemon problem?

4 GlaxoSmithKline discovers a new drug that is expected to bring big profits. What happens to the price of GlaxoSmithKline's stock? Why wouldn't people put all their wealth into GlaxoSmithKline's stock?

Web Activities

Links to Websites

1 Obtain information on the prices of three company stocks that interest you.

- **a** Describe the change in the prices of the shares of these stocks over the past month.
- **b** If you had bought £1,000 of each of these stocks (a total of £3,000) one month ago, how much would your stock be worth today?
- **c** If you had £3,000, would you use some of it to buy these stocks? How much would you put in each stock? How much would you keep in cash?
- **d** Form a group with other students and compare your answers to part (c). Which of you is the most risk averse? Which of you is the least risk averse? Explain your answer.

PART

5

Macroeconomic Overview

Talking with David Smith

David Smith is Economics Editor of The Sunday Times *and a regular contributor to several magazines including* Management Today, Financial World, The Manufacturer, Business Voice and Professional Investor. *He also edits the Economic Science Research Council journal* The Edge.

He studied economics at the Universities of Wales, Oxford and London and before joining The Sunday Times, *worked at* The Times, Financial Weekly, Now! Magazine, *the Henley Centre for Forecasting and Lloyds Bank.*

David Smith is the author of eight books, including The Rise and Fall of Monetarism, Mrs Thatcher's Economics, North and South, From Boom to Bust, UK Current Economic Policy, Eurofutures *and, most recently,* The Dragon & the Elephant, *a book about China and India.*

Kent Matthews talked with David Smith about the challenges facing the global and UK economies today.

What are the big issues facing the world economy?

I think there are three, all connected with globalization. The first is the successful integration of China and India into the global economy. Their rapid growth brings the biggest shock to the world economy, probably for all time. I believe this is overwhelmingly a positive shock that if properly handled, will bring several decades of global economic growth. The risk, which has to be avoided, is of a protectionist response to these low-cost, competitive economies.

The second challenge arises because there are losers as well as winners from globalization. I believe the winners easily outnumber the losers. But the losers, the displaced workers in advanced economies and the many people in developing countries who miss out on rising prosperity, must be given access to the gains.

Third, the world economy remains unbalanced. There is something of a Faustian pact between the Asian economies, particularly Japan and China, and the United States: they run large trade surpluses and support the US trade deficit by buying US financial assets. It has worked so far but may not be sustainable in the long term. At some stage the imbalances will bite back.

What do you mean by the imbalances biting back and what damage can they do to the global economy?

What I mean is that in the absence of large-scale capital inflows, the dollar would fall sharply. A "disorderly" fall in the dollar, say of 40 or 50 per cent, would seriously destabilise the global economy. The hope is that this can be avoided by a gradual reduction in the US deficit.

Do you think the growth in China and India can be sustained over the long term?

I am optimistic about both economies but there are big challenges ahead. In the case of China, it is the challenge of reconciling economic freedom with greater political freedom. For India, it means ensuring the very poorest start benefiting from an economic miracle that has so far been confined to a few limited groups. There is also an urgent need to modernize the infrastructure. Both countries also need to tackle corruption. These economies will face setbacks and, in the case of China, growth will slow to something more sustainable, say 5 per cent a year, relatively soon. How the governments handle the setbacks, and manage rising expectations, will determine how successful they are in the long run.

What are the big issues facing the UK economy?

The UK's macroeconomic performance has been transformed over the last decade and a half. Growth has been steady and continuous and inflation has been both remarkably low and stable. The inflation targeting regime adopted in the early 1990s, reinforced by Bank of England independence in 1997, appears to have resulted in an improved unemployment–inflation trade-off by anchoring inflation expectations. One challenge for the authorities, therefore, is not to let that achievement slip away. That means communicating policy properly to economic actors and, perhaps, even greater policy transparency than we have had so far. Members of the Bank's monetary policy committee (MPC) are not sufficiently engaged in the public debate.

The bigger challenges, however, are microeconomic. Britain made great strides during the 1980s, particularly in respect of labour market reform. The UK economy, under both Conservative and Labour governments, has retained its openness. But there remain some fundamental supply-side challenges. They concern the relative low level of skills – particularly intermediate skills – and mixed educational performance. I am also troubled by the re-regulation of the economy and the shift, under the Labour government, to higher taxes accompanied by much greater tax complexity. When Britain is no longer competitive on tax, this exposes the economy's shortcomings in terms of skills, a relatively poor investment record, a weak transport infrastructure and, in sum, low productivity. These are the big economic issues facing the United Kingdom. Other challenges, such as the environment and an ageing population, become much easier to tackle if the economy is efficient and competitive.

Do you think the MPC has had good luck? Do you think money should play a bigger role in the MPC's thinking?

When the Bank of England was made independent there was a lot of nervousness about whether the country was ready for it. Did the United Kingdom have a low inflation mentality? In fact, events conspired to make the Bank's task rather easier than it could have expected. In particular, the strength of sterling (unusual for the United Kingdom) helped hold down import prices, and falling goods prices, particularly from China, were also very helpful. The monetary policy record has gone from being one of the worst to being among the best. Luck played a part in that but so did robust and responsive decision making.

Different MPC members have different takes on how they approach the rate-setting task, and on the importance of money. If there is an overriding approach, however, it is based on the output gap. The closer the economy is to capacity, and the more rapid that growth is in relation to trend, the greater inflationary pressures are likely to be, and vice versa. Assessing the output gap is, of course, always problematical, while the statistical signals about the current strength of the economy are often mixed and subject to revision. Money is one of the indicators the MPC uses to determine the economy's strength. Other things being equal, the faster the growth in M4, broad money, the stronger the economy is likely to be and the greater the inflationary pressures. I think using M4 in that way is about right, given that it too is subject to distortions. I certainly would not advocate a return to the monetary targeting of the past.

Who are the economists that have inspired you?

Adam Smith was plainly an inspiration, as he should be an inspiration to all economists. But also Alfred Marshall, who contributed so much and who said economics was about the "ordinary business of life". When I was studying economics you could admire Keynes or you could admire Friedman, but you couldn't admire both. Thank goodness that has changed. Both were the giants of 20th century economics and importantly, both engaged in the political debate and were practitioners as well as theorists. I admire economists who have done this, such as Alan Greenspan and Mervyn King, the Bank of England governor. I also admire the game theorists and behavioural economists who have taken the subject into new areas in recent years. In this context I must mention Ken Binmore and his team at University College, London. Their game theory design of the 3G mobile phone auction in 2000 succeeded in raising £22.5 billion for the UK government.

What advice would you give to a student of economics?

Work hard and read as much as you can. You will look back nostalgically on the days when you had time to read everything. Explore areas that aren't necessarily on your course curriculum. In choosing economics, you have made a very wise choice of subject. Some students will go on to greatness in the subject. Many others will use it as a base for different careers. Economics, I think, sets you up better than most disciplines. It encourages a logical way of thinking that is invaluable in tackling a wide range of practical problems. Economists are good at spotting flaws in others' arguments and in constructing new ones. I have certainly found it useful in the sometimes illogical world of journalism.

A First Look at Macroeconomics

CHAPTER 20

After studying this chapter you will be able to:

- Describe the origins and issues of macroeconomics
- Describe the trends and fluctuations in economic growth and explain its benefits and costs
- Describe the trends and fluctuations in unemployment and explain why it is a problem
- Describe the trends and fluctuations in inflation and explain why it is a problem
- Describe the trends and fluctuations in government and international deficits and why they matter
- Identify the macroeconomic policy challenges and the tools available for meeting them

Boom or Bust

Are we better off today than our parents were in the swinging 60s and our Victorian great grandparents were 100 years ago? Are the booms and busts of economic life getting better or worse? Is mass unemployment a horror of the past that we need no longer fear? Have we conquered inflation – rising prices that wipe out people's savings? Can the government manage the economy to make it perform better? Are government and international deficits becoming a problem? This chapter takes a first look at these questions and sets the scene for your study of macroeconomics. And *Reading Between the Lines* at the end of the chapter (pp. 464–465) looks at the global imbalances and the dangers for the world economy.

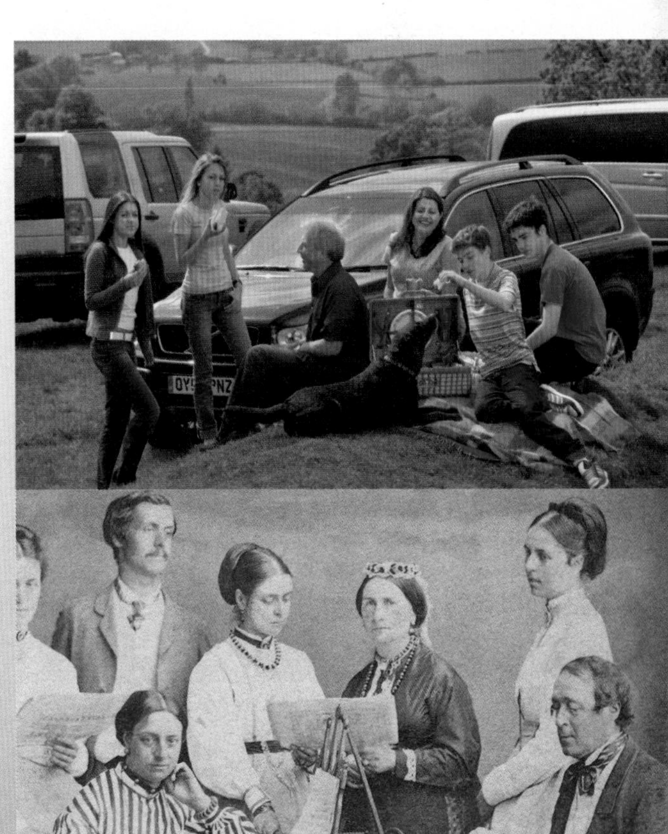

Origins and Issues of Macroeconomics

Economists began to study economic growth, inflation and international payments as long ago as the 1750s, and this work was the forerunner of macroeconomics. But macroeconomics did not emerge until the **Great Depression**, a decade (1929–1939) of high unemployment and stagnant production throughout the world economy. In the depression's worst year, 1931, total UK production fell by more than 5 per cent and in the following year unemployment reached a record 15 per cent of the workforce. The entire period between the two world wars of the last century (1919–1939) were years of human misery on a scale that is hard to imagine today. A state of pessimism about the ability of the market economy to work properly led many people to the view that private enterprise, free markets and democratic political institutions could not survive.

The science of economics had no solutions to the Great Depression. An alternative economic system of central planning and the political system of socialism seemed increasingly attractive to many people. It was in this climate of economic depression and political and intellectual turmoil that macroeconomics was born. Its origin was the publication in 1936 of John Maynard Keynes' *The General Theory of Employment, Interest and Money*.

Short-term versus Long-term Goals

Keynes' theory was that depression and high unemployment result from insufficient spending and that to cure these problems, the government must increase its own spending or try to stimulate private spending. Keynes' focus was on the *short term*. He wanted to cure an immediate and serious problem almost regardless of what the *long-term* consequences of the cure might be. 'In the long run,' said Keynes, 'we're all dead.'

But Keynes believed that after his cure for depression had restored the economy to a normal condition, the long-term problems of inflation and economic growth would become the central ones. He even suspected that his cure for depression, increased government spending, might trigger inflation and also might lower the long-term growth rate of production. With a lower long-term growth rate, the economy would create fewer jobs. If this outcome did occur, a policy aimed at lowering unemployment in the short term might end up increasing it in the long term.

By the late 1960s and through the 1970s, Keynes' predictions became a reality. Full employment was achieved but inflation increased and economic growth slowed. Later, unemployment became stubbornly high in many countries. The causes of these developments are complex, but they point to an inescapable conclusion: the long-term problems of inflation, slow growth and persistent unemployment and the short-term problems of depression and economic fluctuations intertwine and are most usefully studied together. So although macroeconomics was born during the Great Depression, its emphasis today is broader than depression economics. The macroeconomics that you will learn is a subject that tries to understand long-term economic growth and inflation as well as short-term economic fluctuations and unemployment.

The Road Ahead

There is no unique way to study macroeconomics. Because its birth was a product of economic depression, the common practice for many years was to pay most attention to short-term output fluctuations and unemployment, but never to lose sight of the long-term issues completely.

When a rapid inflation emerged during the late 1960s and 1970s, inflation returned to prominence. During the 1980s, when long-term economic growth slowed in the United Kingdom and other rich industrial countries, economists redirected their energy towards economic growth. During the 1990s, when information technologies further shrank the globe, the international dimension of macroeconomics became more prominent.

The result of all these events is that modern macroeconomics is a broad subject that pays attention to all the issues we've just identified: economic growth and fluctuations, unemployment and inflation. It also studies government and international deficits.

Over the past 40 years, economists have developed a clearer understanding of the forces that determine macroeconomic performance and they have devised policies that they hope will improve this performance.

Your main goal is to become familiar with the theories of macroeconomics and the policies they make possible. To set you on your path towards this goal, we're going to take a first look at the issues of economic growth, unemployment, inflation and government and international surpluses and deficits and learn why these phenomena merit our attention.

Study Plan 20.1

Economic Growth

Your parents are richer than your grandparents were when they were young. But are you going to be richer than your parents are? Are your children going to be richer than you? The answers depend on the rate of economic growth. **Economic growth** is the expansion of the economy's production possibilities. It can be pictured as an outward shift of the production possibilities frontier (*PPF*) – see Chapter 2, p. 42.

We measure economic growth as the increase in real gross domestic product. We define *real gross domestic product* (also called *real GDP*) and how it is measured in Chapter 21 (see pp. 470–474) but for now, you can think of it as the value of the economy's total production measured in the prices of a single year. Real GDP in the United Kingdom is currently measured in prices that prevailed in 2005 (called 2005 pounds). We use the pound prices of a single year so that we can eliminate the influence of *inflation* – the increase in the average level of prices – and determine how much production has grown from one year to another.

Real GDP is not a perfect measure of total production because it does not include everything that is produced. It excludes the things we produce for ourselves at home (preparing meals, doing laundry, cleaning and doing odd jobs). It also excludes production that people hide to avoid taxes or because the activity is illegal – the underground economy. But despite its shortcomings, real GDP is the best measure of total production available. Let's see what it tells us about economic growth.

UK Economic Growth

Figure 20.1 shows real GDP in the United Kingdom from 1960 to 2006 and it highlights two features of economic growth:

- The growth of potential GDP
- Fluctuations of real GDP around potential GDP

The Growth of Potential GDP

When all the economy's labour, capital, land and entrepreneurial ability are fully employed, the value of production is called **potential GDP**. Real GDP fluctuates around potential GDP and the long-term economic growth rate is measured by the growth rate of potential GDP. It is shown by the steepness of the potential GDP line – the black line in Figure 20.1.

You can see that the potential GDP line is steeper in the 1960s than in the 1970s and becomes steeper in the early 1980s and again in the late 1990s and 2000s.

From 1960 to 1973, potential GDP grew at 2.8 per cent a year. The growth rate slowed from 1973 to 1979 to 1.9 per cent a year in a phenomenon called the **productivity growth slowdown**. The growth rate of potential GDP increased briefly to 2.2 per cent a year during the 1980s and then increased to 2.6 per cent a year during the 1990s and 2000s.

Why did the productivity growth slowdown occur? This question is controversial. We explore the causes of the productivity growth slowdown in Chapter 31. Whatever its cause, the productivity growth slowdown means that we all have smaller incomes today than we would have had if the economy had kept growing at its 1960s rate.

Let's now look at real GDP fluctuations around potential GDP.

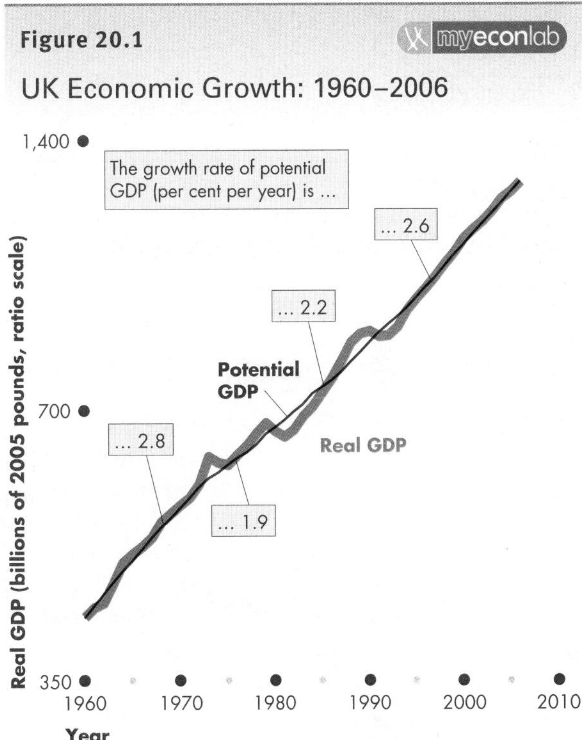

Figure 20.1
UK Economic Growth: 1960–2006

The economic growth rate, measured by the growth of potential GDP, was 2.8 per cent a year from 1960 to 1973 but slowed to 1.9 per cent a year from 1973 to 1979, increased to 2.2 in the 1980s and to 2.6 per cent in the 1990s and the 2000s. Real GDP fluctuates around potential GDP.

Sources of data: Office for National Statistics; International Monetary Fund, *World Economic Outlook*.

Fluctuations Around Potential GDP

Real GDP fluctuates around potential GDP in a business cycle. A **business cycle** is the periodic but irregular up-and-down movement in economic activity.

The business cycle is measured by fluctuations in real GDP around potential GDP. When real GDP is less than potential GDP, some resources are underused. For example, some labour is unemployed and capital is underutilized. When real GDP is greater than potential GDP, resources are overused. Many people work longer hours than they are willing to put up with in the long run, capital is worked so intensively that it is not maintained in prime working order, delivery times lengthen, bottlenecks occur and unfilled orders increase.

A business cycle is not a regular, predictable or repeating cycle like the phases of the moon. The timing of a business cycle changes unpredictably. But business cycles do have some things in common.

Every business cycle has two phases:

1 Recession
2 Expansion

and two turning points:

1 A peak
2 A trough

Figure 20.2 shows these features of the most recent business cycle in the United Kingdom. A **recession** is a period during which real GDP decreases – the growth rate of real GDP is negative – for at least two successive quarters. The most recent recession, which is highlighted in the figure, began in the second quarter of 1990 and ended in the first quarter of 1992. This recession was unusually long and, during the two-year period, real GDP decreased by 2.5 per cent.

An **expansion** is a period during which real GDP increases. The most recent expansion began in the second quarter of 1992. It was an unusually long one. By the end of 2006, it had run for almost 14 years and real GDP had expanded by almost 50 per cent.

When an expansion ends and a recession begins, the turning point is called a *peak*. A peak occurred in the second quarter of 1990. When a recession ends and an expansion begins, the turning point is called a *trough*. A trough occurred in the first quarter of 1992.

Figure 20.2

The Most Recent UK Business Cycle

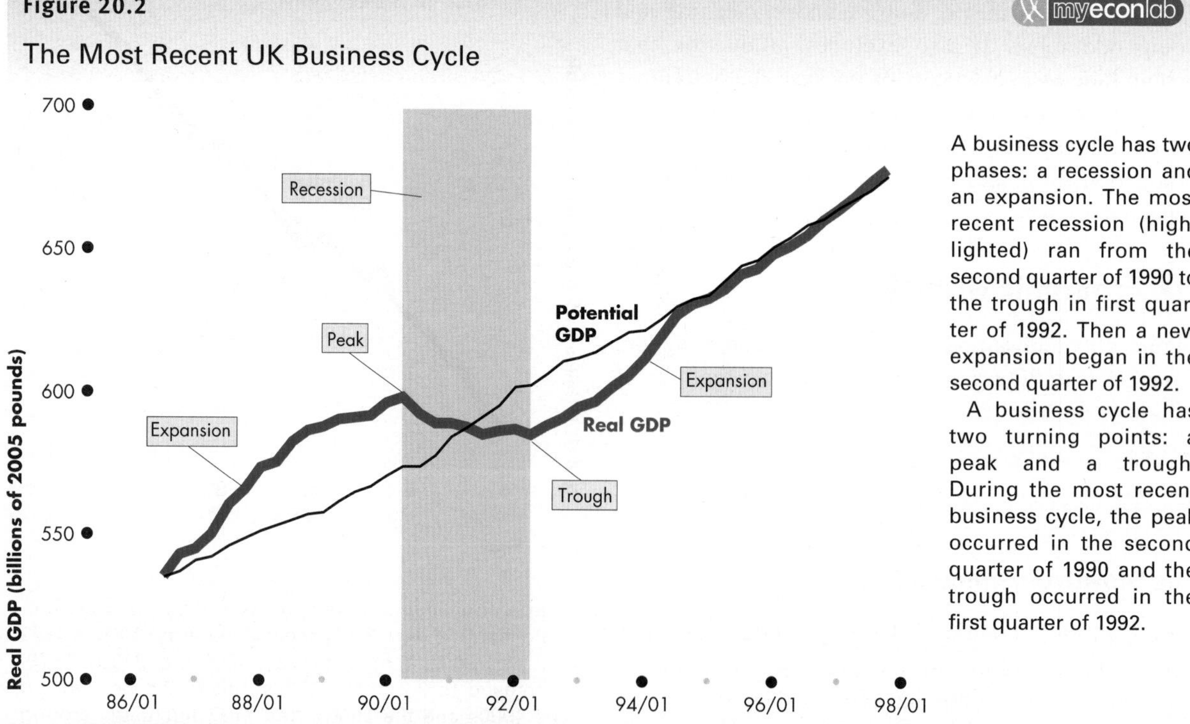

A business cycle has two phases: a recession and an expansion. The most recent recession (highlighted) ran from the second quarter of 1990 to the trough in first quarter of 1992. Then a new expansion began in the second quarter of 1992.

A business cycle has two turning points: a peak and a trough. During the most recent business cycle, the peak occurred in the second quarter of 1990 and the trough occurred in the first quarter of 1992.

Sources of data: Office for National Statistics; International Monetary Fund, *World Economic Outlook*; and authors' assumptions.

The Most Recent Recession in Historical Perspective

The recession of 1990–1992 seemed pretty severe while we were passing through it, but compared with some earlier recessions it was mild. You can see how mild it was by looking at Figure 20.3, which shows a longer history of economic growth. The biggest decreases in real GDP occurred immediately after the First World War, ten years later during the Great Depression and in the period immediately following the Second World War. In more recent times, milder decreases in real GDP occurred during the mid-1970s – the time of oil price hikes by OPEC – and during the early 1980s and early 1990s.

You can see that the economic downturns that occurred before the Second World War were more severe and prolonged than the recessions that came in the post-war years.

The last truly great depression occurred before governments started taking policy actions to stabilize the economy. It also occurred before the birth of modern macroeconomics. Is the absence of another great depression a sign that macroeconomics has contributed to economic stability? Some people believe it is. Others doubt it. We'll evaluate these opinions on a number of occasions in this book.

We've looked at how UK real GDP has increased over the long term and we've seen that economic growth slowed during the 1970s. We've also seen that recessions have interrupted the broad upward sweep of real GDP. Is the UK experience typical? Do other countries share this experience? Let's see if they do.

Figure 20.3

myeconlab

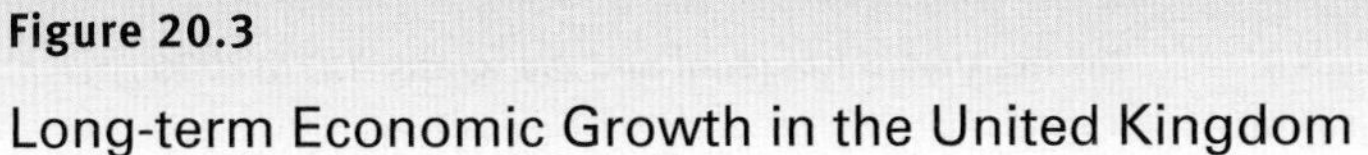

Long-term Economic Growth in the United Kingdom

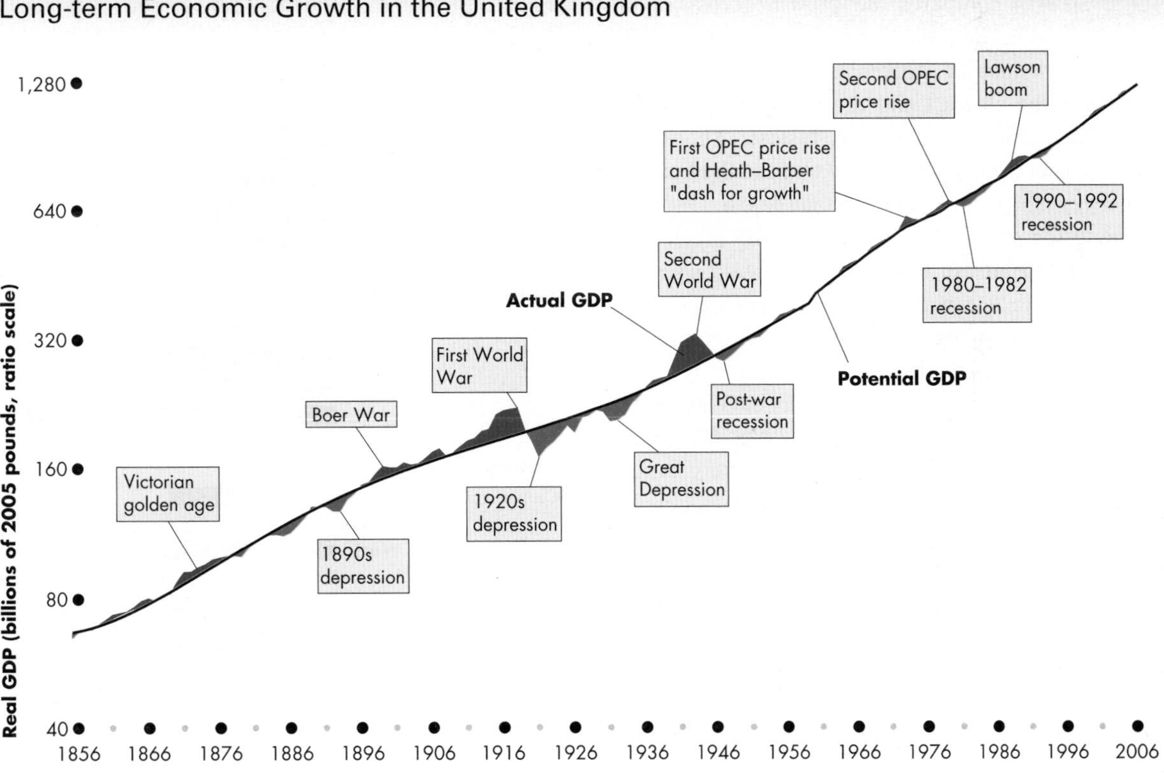

The thin black line shows potential GDP. Along that line, real GDP grew at an average rate of 2 per cent a year between 1856 and 2006. The blue areas show when real GDP was above potential GDP and the red areas show when it was below potential GDP. The labels indicate the events associated with some of the major deviations from potential GDP.

Sources of data: Real GDP 1856–1947: C. H. Feinstein, *National Income Expenditure and Output of the United Kingdom, 1855–1965*, Cambridge, Cambridge University Press, 1972; Real GDP 1948–2006: Office for National Statistics; Potential GDP: International Monetary Fund, *World Economic Outlook* and authors' assumptions.

Economic Growth Around the World

First, we'll compare UK economic growth over time with that in other countries. Then we'll look at longer-term differences in growth rates among countries and groups of countries.

Growth Rates Over Time

Figure 20.4(a) shows the UK and world growth rates from 1976 to 2006. You can see a striking fact: the UK real GDP growth rate fluctuates much more than the real GDP growth rate in the rest of the world. In several years, UK real GDP actually fell – a negative growth rate – but economic growth in the rest of the world was never negative during the 30 years shown in the figure.

Persistent Growth Rate Differences

Figure 20.4(b) compares the growth across several countries and regions on average from 1996 to 2006. Among the industrial economies (the red bars), Japan has grown the slowest and the newly industrialized Asian economies have grown fastest. The United Kingdom is in the middle of these two and the Euro area lies between the United Kingdom and Japan.

Among the developing economies (the green bars), the most rapid growth has occurred in Asia where the average growth rate was more than 7 per cent a year. The slowest growing developing countries are in Central and South America.

The transition economies (purple bar) grew at a moderate rate during the ten years to 2006. These countries in Central and Eastern Europe are making a transition from a command economy to a market economy.

World average growth (the blue bar) has been a bit more than 4 per cent a year, substantially greater than the UK and Euro area growth rates.

Consequences of Persistent Differences

The persistent differences in growth rates have brought dramatic change to nations' shares of world real GDP. The slow-growing UK share fell from 3.7 per cent in 1980 to 2.9 per cent in 2006 and the Euro area's share fell from 18.6 per cent in 1991 to 14.4 per cent in 2006. The fast-growing nations of Asia have become a significantly bigger part of the global economy. China's share increased from 3.4 per cent in 1980 to 16.1 per cent in 2006 and India's share increased from 3.3 per cent in 1980 to 6.0 per cent in 2006.

Figure 20.4 myeconlab

Economic Growth Around the World

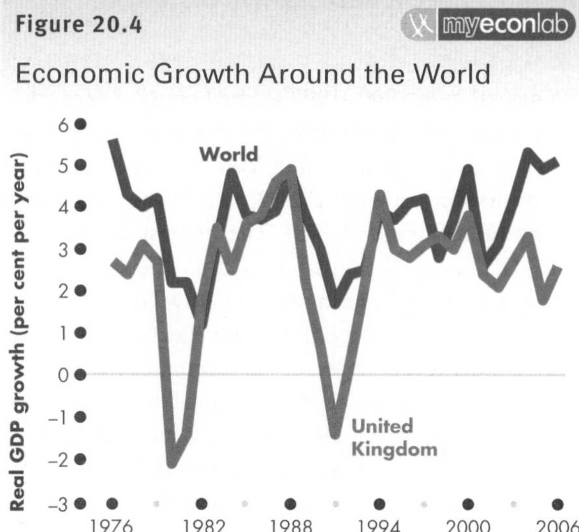

(a) The United Kingdom and the world: 1976–2006

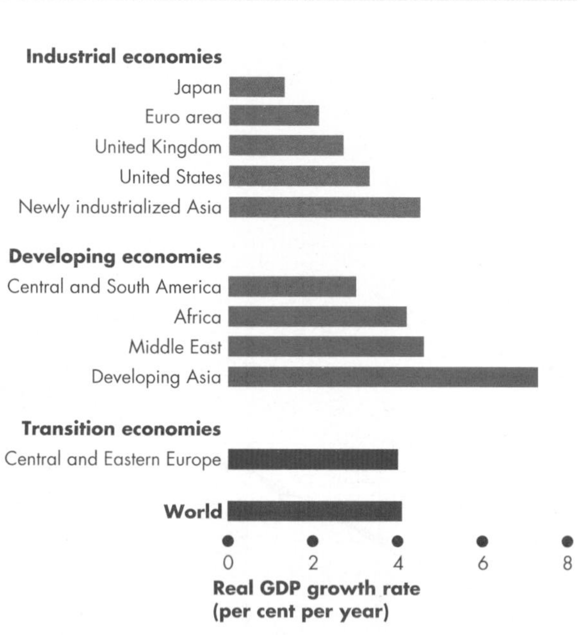

(b) Countries and regions compared: 1992–2006 average

In part (a), economic growth fluctuates much more in the United Kingdom than in the world economy, but the fluctuations across countries are correlated.

In part (b), growth rate differences persist. Between 1992 and 2006, developing Asian economies (China and India) grew fastest and Asia's richest economy, Japan, grew slowest. The UK growth rate was below the world average growth rate.

Source of data: International Monetary Fund, *World Economic Outlook*.

The Lucas Wedge and the Okun Gap

You've seen that productivity growth slowed during the 1970s. And you've seen that real GDP growth fluctuates, so real GDP falls below potential GDP from time to time. How costly are the growth slowdown and lost output over the business cycle?

Two measures provide the answers:

- The Lucas wedge
- The Okun gap

The Lucas Wedge

The *Lucas wedge* is the accumulated loss of output that results from a slowdown in the growth rate of real GDP. It is given this name because Robert E. Lucas Jr., a leading macroeconomist and Nobel Laureate, drew attention to it and remarked that once you begin to think about the benefits of faster economic growth, it is hard to think about anything else!

Figure 20.5(a) shows the Lucas wedge that arises from the productivity growth slowdown of the 1970s. The black line in the figure tracks the path that potential GDP would have followed if its 1960s growth rate had been maintained through the 36 years to 2006.

The Lucas wedge is a staggering £5.7 trillion – four and a half times real GDP in 2006. This number is a measure of the cost of slower productivity growth.

The Okun Gap

Real GDP minus potential GDP is the **output gap**. When the output gap is negative it is called an *Okun gap*. It is given this name because Arthur M. Okun, a policy economist who was chairman of President Lyndon Johnson's Council of Economic Advisors during the 1960s, drew attention to it as a source of loss from economic fluctuations.

Figure 20.5(b) shows the Okun gap from the recessions that occurred during the same years for which we've just calculated the Lucas wedge.

The Okun gaps in the four recessions since 1970 sum to £164 billion – about one-eighth of real GDP in 2006. This number is a measure of the cost of business cycle fluctuations.

You can see that the Lucas wedge is a much bigger deal than the Okun gap – about 35 times as big a deal! Smoothing the business cycle saves spells of high unemployment and lost output. But maintaining a high productivity growth rate makes a dramatic and persistent difference to the standard of living.

Figure 20.5 myeconlab

The Lucas Wedge and the Okun Gap

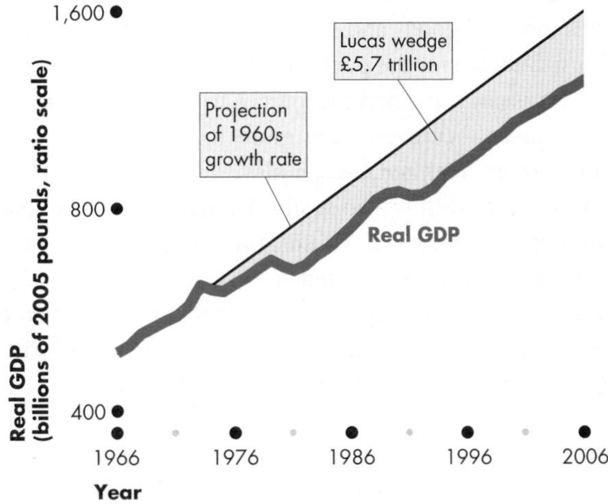

(a) The Lucas wedge

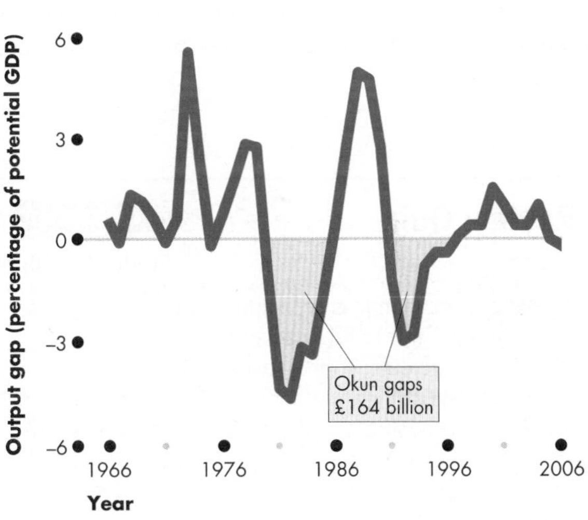

(b) The Okun gap

In part (a), the Lucas wedge that arises from the productivity growth slowdown of the 1970s is a staggering £5.7 trillion or about 4.5 times the real GDP of 2006.

In part (b), the Okun gap that arises from the lost production in the recessions since the early 1970s amounts to £164 billion or about one-eighth of real GDP in 2006.

Over this 36-year period, the Lucas wedge is about 35 times as large as the Okun gap.

Sources of data: Office for National Statistics; International Monetary Fund, *World Economic Outlook;* and authors' assumptions.

Benefits and Costs of Economic Growth

The Lucas wedge is a measure of the pound value of lost real GDP if the growth rate slows. But this cost translates into real goods and services. It is a cost in terms of less healthcare for the poor and elderly, more cancer and AIDS research and more resources to improve our roads and houses. We even have more to spend on cleaner rivers, more trees and cleaner air.

But fast growth is also costly. Its main cost is forgone *current* consumption. To sustain a high growth rate, resources must be devoted to advancing technology and accumulating capital rather than to *current* consumption. This cost cannot be avoided. But it brings the benefit of greater consumption in the future – see Chapter 2, p. 42.

Two other possible costs of faster growth are a more rapid depletion of non-renewable natural resources, such as oil and natural gas, and increased pollution of the air, rivers and oceans. But neither of these two costs is inevitable. The technological advances that bring economic growth help us to economize on our use of natural resources and to clean up the environment. For example, more efficient car engines cut petrol use and carbon emissions.

Review Quiz

Study Plan 20.2

1. What is economic growth and how is the long-term economic growth rate measured?
2. What is the distinction between real GDP and potential GDP?
3. What is a business cycle and what are its phases?
4. What is a recession?
5. In what phase of the business cycle was the UK economy during 2006?
6. What happened to economic growth in the United Kingdom and other countries during the 1970s?
7. What is the Lucas wedge and what is the Okun gap? How big are they?
8. What are the benefits and the costs of long-term economic growth?

We've seen that real GDP grows and that it fluctuates over the business cycle. The business cycle brings fluctuations in jobs available and unemployment. Let's now examine these core macroeconomic problems.

Jobs and Unemployment

What kind of labour market will you enter when you graduate? Will there be plenty of good jobs to choose from, or will there be so much unemployment that you will be forced to take a low-paying job that doesn't use your education? The answer depends, to a large degree, on the total number of jobs available and on the unemployment rate.

Jobs

Between 1979 and 2005, 13 million jobs were created in the European Union. This number may appear to be impressive but let's put it in an international perspective. In the United States – a comparably sized economy – 46.6 million jobs were created over the same period. In the United Kingdom, the number of jobs created was 3.0 million. But these figures hide the details – a general switch from manufacturing jobs to service jobs, from male to female workers and from full-time to part-time jobs.

New jobs are created every month, but many jobs are destroyed. The pace of job creation and destruction fluctuates over the business cycle. More jobs are destroyed than created during a recession, so the number of jobs decreases. But more jobs are created than destroyed during a recovery and expansion, so the number of jobs increases. For example, in the United Kingdom 1.7 million jobs were lost between 1979 and 1983. In the long recovery to 1989, 3.2 million jobs were created, in the recession of 1990–1992 the number of jobs fell by nearly 1.9 million and in the recovery from 1993 to 2005, 3.1 million jobs were created.

Unemployment

Not everyone who wants a job can find one. On one day in any recent year, around 900,000 men and 600,000 women in the United Kingdom are unemployed. During a recession, unemployment rises above this level and during an expansion, it falls below this level. For example, in the 1990–1992 recession, almost 3 million people were looking for jobs. In the economic expansion of 2001, the number of job seekers fell to 1.4 million.

These unemployment numbers are large. The number of people unemployed during this recession is equivalent to the combined populations of Birmingham, Leeds, Sheffield, Liverpool and Manchester.

To place the number of unemployed people in perspective, we use a measure called the unemployment rate. The **unemployment rate** is the number of unemployed people expressed as a percentage of all the people who have jobs or are looking for one. (The concepts of the unemployment rate, along with other measures of the labour market, is explained more fully in Chapter 22, pp. 490–492.)

The unemployment rate is not a perfect measure of the underutilization of labour for two reasons. First, it excludes people who are so discouraged that they have given up the effort to find work. Many people switch between the unemployment and discouraged worker categories in both directions every month. Second, the unemployment rate measures unemployed persons rather than unemployed labour hours. So the unemployment rate does not tell us about the number of people who have a part-time job but want a full-time job.

Despite these two limitations, the unemployment rate is the best available measure of underused labour resources. Let's look at some facts about unemployment.

Unemployment in the United Kingdom

Figure 20.6 shows the unemployment rate in the United Kingdom from 1906 to 2006. Three features stand out.

First, the United Kingdom has had some spells of very high unemployment. During the period between the two world wars (1919–1939), the unemployment rate was persistently high. It reached a peak of 16 per cent in 1932, the worst year of the Great Depression. The unemployment rate was also high during the recessions of the 1970s, 1980–1982 and 1990–1992.

Second, the unemployment rate has fluctuated a great deal. After a period of mild fluctuations during the 1960s and early 1970s, the swings in unemployment became large during the 1980–1982 and 1990–1992 recessions and the expansions that followed them.

Third, unemployment has never fallen to zero. Since the Second World War, the average unemployment rate has been close to 5 per cent.

How does UK unemployment compare with unemployment in other countries?

Figure 20.6

myeconlab

One Hundred Years of Unemployment in the United Kingdom: 1906–2006

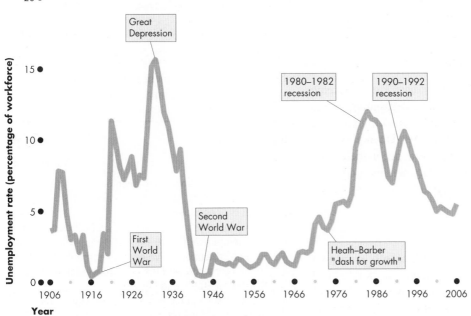

Unemployment is a persistent feature of economic life, but its rate varies. At its worst – during the Great Depression – nearly 16 per cent of the workforce was unemployed. Even in recent recessions, the unemployment rate climbed to 11 per cent. Between 1945 and the late 1960s, the unemployment rate remained steady. During the 1970s, the unemployment rate increased and during the late 1990s and 2000s, it tended to decrease.

Sources of data: C. H. Feinstein, *National Income Expenditure and Output of the United Kingdom, 1855–1965*, Cambridge, Cambridge University Press, 1972; and Office for National Statistics.

Unemployment Around the World

Figure 20.7 shows the unemployment rate in the United States, the European Union and Japan. Over the period shown in this figure, US unemployment averaged 6.1 per cent, much higher than Japanese unemployment, which averaged 3.3 per cent, but lower than unemployment in the European Union, which averaged 8.8 per cent.

The figure shows that unemployment fluctuates over the business cycle. Like EU unemployment, US and Japanese unemployment increases during a recession and decreases during an expansion. The cycle in US unemployment is out of phase with the cycle in EU unemployment. Japanese unemployment remained low and relatively stable until the mid-1990s but since then has drifted upward and by 2006 was only just below that in the United States.

We've looked at some facts about unemployment in the United Kingdom and in other countries. Let's now look at some of the consequences of unemployment that make it a serious problem.

Figure 20.7

Unemployment in the Industrial Economies

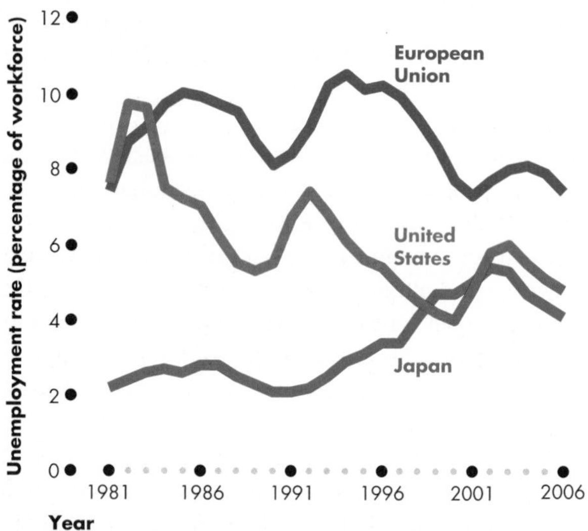

The EU and US unemployment rates were similar in the early 1980s, but the US unemployment rate fell during the 1990s whereas the EU rate remained high. Both the EU and US unemployment rates cycle but the peaks and troughs occur at different times. Japan's unemployment rate barely changed during the 1980s but increased towards the US rate during the 1990s.

Source of data: International Monetary Fund, *World Economic Outlook*.

Why Unemployment Is a Problem

Unemployment is a serious economic, social and personal problem for two main reasons:

- Lost production and incomes
- Lost human capital

Lost Production and Incomes

The loss of a job brings an immediate loss of income and production. These losses can be devastating for the people who bear them and make unemployment a frightening prospect for everyone. Unemployment benefits such as the jobseeker's allowance in the United Kingdom creates a short-term safety net, but it does not provide the same living standard as having a job does.

Lost Human Capital

Prolonged unemployment can permanently damage a person's job prospects. For example, a middle-aged manager loses his job when his firm downsizes. Short of income, he takes a job as a taxi driver. After a year he discovers that he cannot compete with young MBA graduates. He eventually finds a job as a shop manager and at a lower wage than his previous managerial job. He has lost some of his human capital.

The costs of unemployment are spread unequally, which makes unemployment a highly charged political problem as well as a serious economic problem.

Review Quiz

Study Plan 20.3

1. How many new jobs have been created in the United Kingdom between 1979 and 2005?
2. What is unemployment?
3. What have been the main trends and cycles in the UK unemployment rate since 1932?
4. How has the unemployment rate in the European Union compared with the unemployment rates in the United States and Japan?
5. What are the main costs of unemployment that make it a serious problem?

Let's now turn to the third major macroeconomic issue: inflation.

Inflation

What will it *really* cost you to pay off your student loan? What will your parent's life savings buy when they retire? The answers depend on what happens to prices.

We measure the *level* of prices – the **price level** – as the average of the prices that people pay for all the goods and services that they buy. A common measure of the price level is the *Retail Prices Index* (RPI), which is explained in Chapter 23.

We measure the **inflation rate** as the annual percentage change in price level. For example, if the RPI (the price *level*) rises from 200 to 204 in a year, the inflation rate is 2 per cent a year.

Inflation occurs when the price level is rising persistently. A one-time jump in the price of petrol isn't inflation. Inflation is a *persistent* rise in the *average* of all prices.

If the inflation rate is negative, the price level is falling over time and we have **deflation**.

Inflation in the United Kingdom

Figure 20.8 shows the UK inflation rate from 1962 to 2006. You can see from the figure that the inflation rate rises and falls over the years, but is always positive – we have not experienced *deflation*. (The last time deflation occurred in the United Kingdom was during the 1930s.)

You can see that during the early 1960s the inflation rate was between 2 and 3 per cent a year. Inflation began to increase in the late 1960s, but the largest increases occurred in 1975 and 1980. These were years in which the actions of the Organization of the Petroleum Exporting Countries (OPEC) resulted in exceptionally large increases in the price of oil, but domestic UK policies also contributed to the inflation process.

Inflation was brought under control in the early 1980s when the Thatcher government instructed the Bank of England to push interest rates up and people cut back on their spending. During the Lawson boom of the late 1980s, inflation increased again. But since the early 1990s, the UK inflation rate has remained low.

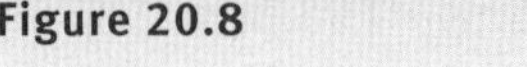

Figure 20.8

myeconlab

Inflation in the United Kingdom: 1962–2006

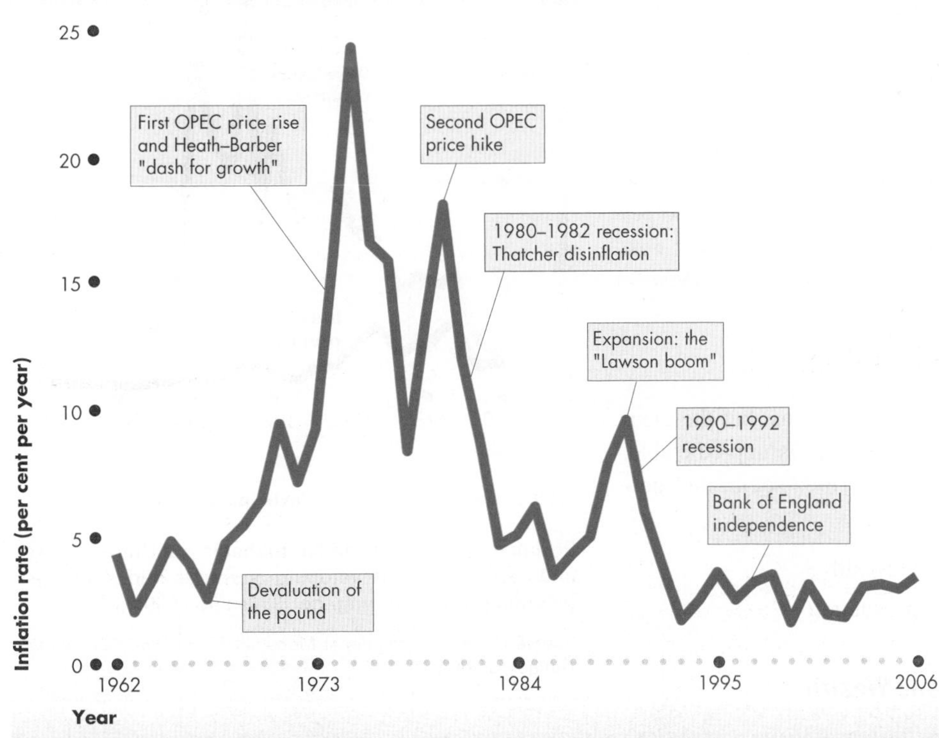

Inflation is a persistent feature of economic life in the United Kingdom. The inflation rate was low in the first half of the 1960s, but it increased during the second half with the rise in the world inflation rate. The inflation rate increased further with the OPEC oil price hikes in the 1970s but declined during the Thatcher years of the 1980s. The inflation rate has remained low since the early 1990s.

Source of data: Office for National Statistics.

Inflation Around the World

Figure 20.9(a) shows inflation in the major industrial economies from 1970 to 2006. You can see that the inflation rates in the United States, the European Union and Japan have had a similar pattern. You can see that they all shared the burst of double-digit inflation during the 1970s, the fall in inflation during the 1980s and low inflation in the 1990s.

You can see in Figure 20.9(b) that the average inflation rate of the developing countries exceeds that of the industrial countries. The gap was widest during the 1980s and 1990s and it narrowed during the 2000s as the developing countries lowered their inflation rates. But inflation remains a problem for some developing countries. Zimbabwe, for example, had an inflation rate of 17 per cent a month, or 1,200 per cent a year in 2006.

Figure 20.9

myeconlab

Inflation Around the World

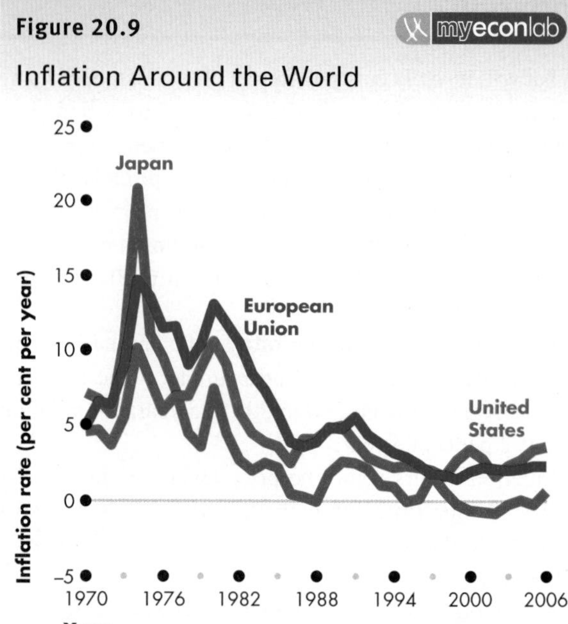

(a) Inflation in industrial economies

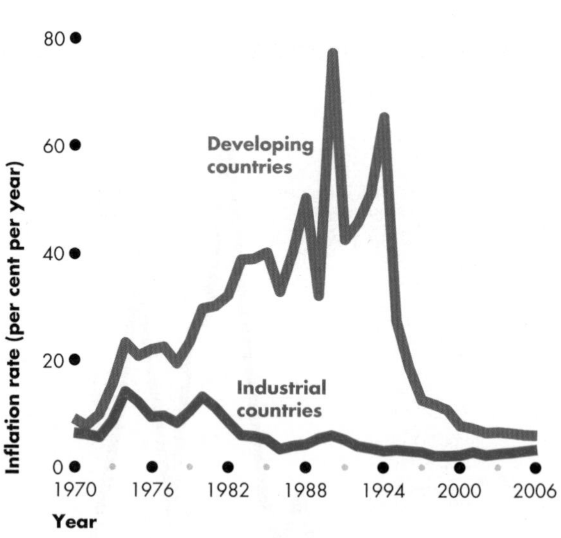

(b) Industrial countries and developing countries

EU inflation has been similar to that in the United States and Japan. Some developing countries had a serious inflation problem during the 1980s and 1990s.

Source of data: International Monetary Fund, *World Economic Outlook*; and OECD.

Hyperinflation

Inflation in Zimbabwe today is serious. But even that inflation rate doesn't match the worst that has occurred. The most serious type of inflation is called **hyperinflation** – an inflation rate that exceeds 50 per cent a month. At the height of a hyperinflation, workers are often paid twice a day because money loses its value so quickly. As soon as workers are paid, they rush out to spend their wages before the money loses too much value.

Hyperinflation is rare, but several European countries experienced it during the 1920s after the First World War and again during the 1940s after the Second World War. In 1994, the African nation of Zaire had a hyperinflation that peaked at 76 per cent *a month*, which is 88,000 per cent a year! And in Brazil, a cup of coffee that cost 15 cruzeiros in 1980 cost 22 *billion* cruzeiros in 1994.

Why Inflation Is a Problem

Inflation is a problem for several reasons, but the main one is that once it takes hold, its rate is unpredictable. Unpredictable inflation brings serious social and personal problems because it:

- Redistributes income and wealth
- Diverts resources from production

Redistributes Income and Wealth

Inflation makes the economy behave like a casino in which some people gain and some lose and no one can predict where the gains and losses will fall. Gains and losses occur because of unpredictable changes in the value of money. Money is used as a measuring rod of value in the transactions that we undertake. Borrowers and lenders, workers and employers, all make contracts in terms of money. If the value of money varies unpredictably over time, then the amounts *really* paid and received – the quantities of goods that the money will buy – also fluctuate unpredictably. Measuring value with a measuring rod whose units vary is a bit like trying to measure a piece of cloth with an elastic ruler. The size of the cloth depends on how tightly the ruler is stretched.

Diverts Resources from Production

In a period of rapid, unpredictable inflation, resources get diverted from productive activities to forecasting inflation. It becomes more profitable to forecast the inflation rate correctly than to invent a new product. Doctors, lawyers, accountants, farmers – just about everyone – can make themselves better off, not by specializing in the profession for which they have been trained but by spending more of their time dabbling as amateur economists and inflation forecasters and managing their investment portfolios.

From a social perspective, this diversion of talent resulting from inflation is like throwing scarce resources onto the garbage heap. This waste of resources is a cost of inflation. You will learn more about inflation and the costs of reducing it in Chapter 30.

Review Quiz

Study Plan 20.4

1 What is inflation and how does it influence the value of money?
2 How is inflation measured?
3 What has been the UK inflation record since 1962?
4 How does inflation in the United Kingdom compare with inflation in other industrial countries and in developing countries?
5 Why is inflation a serious problem?

We've now looked at economic growth and fluctuations, unemployment and inflation. Let's turn to the fourth macroeconomic issue: surpluses and deficits. What happens when a government spends more than it collects in taxes? And what happens when a nation buys more from other countries than it sells to them? Do governments and nations face the problem that you and we would face if we spent more than we earned? Do they run out of funds? Let's look at these questions.

Surpluses and Deficits

In only eight of the past 30 years has the UK government had a budget surplus. And for the past 20 years, the United Kingdom has had a persistent international deficit. What exactly are a government budget deficit and a nation's international deficit?

Government Budget Balance

If a government collects more in taxes than it spends, it has a surplus – a **government budget surplus**. If a government spends more than it collects in taxes, it has a deficit – a **government budget deficit**. The UK government had a surplus from 1987 to 1990 and again from 1998 to 2000. Aside from these two brief spells of surplus, the government has generally had a budget deficit.

Figure 20.10(a) shows the UK government budget surplus and deficit from 1976 to 2006. We measure the budget surplus or deficit as a percentage of GDP so that we can compare the surplus or deficit in one year with that in another year. You can think of this measure as the number of pence of surplus or deficit per pound of income earned by an average person.

When the UK government has had a budget surplus, it has generally been modest. The budget surplus peaked at about 4 per cent of GDP in 2000. But when the UK government has had a budget deficit, it was on occasion extremely large. For example, in 1976, the budget deficit was 7 per cent of GDP and it returned to a similarly large percentage of GDP during the 1990–1992 recession. A government budget deficit generally swells during a recession and shrinks during an expansion.

International Deficit

When we import goods and services from the rest of the world, we make payments to the rest of the world. When we export goods and services to the rest of the world, we receive payments from the rest of the world. If our imports exceed our exports, we have an international deficit.

Figure 20.10(b) shows the UK international balance from 1976 to 2006. The figure shows the balance on the **current account**, which includes UK exports minus UK imports but also takes into account interest payments paid to and received from the rest of the world. (Again to compare one year with another, the figure shows the current account as a percentage of GDP.)

Figure 20.10

myeconlab

The UK Government Budget and International Surpluses and Deficits: 1976–2006

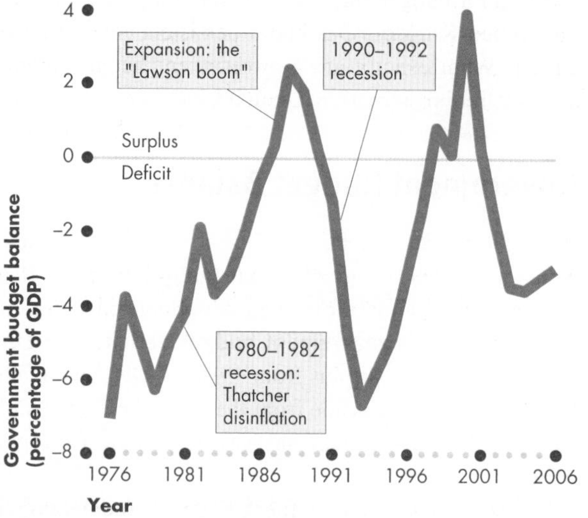

(a) Government budget balance

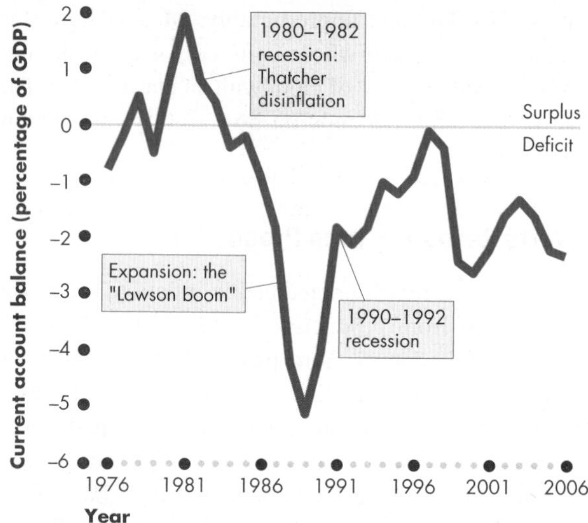

(b) Current account balance

In part (a), the UK government had a persistent budget deficit during the 1970s and most of the 1980s. The budget deficit became large during the 1990–1992 recession. A budget surplus emerged in 1998, but since 2001 the government budget has again been in deficit.

In part (b), the UK current account shows the balance of UK exports minus UK imports. The current account balance fluctuates. In 1980, a current account surplus emerged. But by the mid-1980s, a current account deficit had returned and has remained a deficit.

Source of data: Office for National Statistics.

From 1980 to 1984, the United Kingdom had a current account surplus. But since then the United Kingdom has had a persistent current account deficit.

Do Surpluses and Deficits Matter?

What happens when a government cannot cover its spending with taxes, or when a country buys more from other countries than it sells to them?

If you spend more than you earn, you have a deficit. And to cover your deficit, you go into debt. But when you borrow, you must pay interest on your debt. Just like you, if a government or a nation has a deficit, it must borrow. And like you, the government and the nation must pay interest on their debts.

Whether borrowing and paying out huge amounts of interest is a good idea depends on what the borrowed funds are used for. If you borrow to finance a holiday, you must eventually tighten your belt, cut spending and repay your debt, as well as pay the interest on the debt. But if you borrow to invest in a business that earns a large profit, you might be able to repay your debt and pay the interest on it while increasing your spending. It is the same with a government and a nation.

A government or a nation that borrows to increase its consumption might be heading for trouble later. But a government or a nation that borrows to buy assets that earn a profit might be making a sound investment.

You will learn more about the government budget in Chapter 26 and about the current account deficit in Chapter 33.

Review Quiz

Study Plan 20.5

1. What determines a government's budget deficit or budget surplus?
2. How has the budget of the UK government evolved since 1976?
3. What is a country's current account deficit?
4. How has the UK current account changed since 1976?

Macroeconomic Policy Challenges and Tools

Now that you have reviewed the performance of the economy, you've seen that economic growth has slowed, we always have some unemployment and in a recession its rate is high, inflation persistently erodes the value of our money and government and international deficits persistently swell our debts. You are perhaps wondering whether something can be done to improve our macroeconomic performance.

Economists think that much can be done, but they don't agree on the most effective approach. Their views fall into two broad schools: classical and Keynesian.

The Classical and Keynesian Views

The *classical* view, first stated in Adam Smith's *Wealth of Nations* published in 1776, is that the only economic role for government is to enforce property rights. The economy behaves best, in the classical view, if the government leaves people free to pursue their own self-interest. Attempts by government to improve macroeconomic performance will not succeed.

The *Keynesian* view, which originated in Keynes' *General Theory of Employment, Interest and Money* published in 1936 and was inspired by the Great Depression, is that the economy behaves badly if left alone and that government action is needed to achieve and maintain full employment.

We'll explore these views in greater detail at a number of points in the chapters that follow.

Policy Challenges and Tools

Today five widely agreed challenges for macroeconomic policy in most developed countries are to:

1 Boost economic growth
2 Keep inflation low
3 Stabilize the business cycle
4 Lower unemployment
5 Reduce government and international deficits

How can we do all these things? What are the tools available to pursue the macroeconomic policy challenges? Macroeconomic policy tools are divided into:

- Fiscal policy
- Monetary policy

Fiscal Policy

Making changes in taxes and in government spending is called **fiscal policy**. This range of actions is under the control of the government. Fiscal policy can be used to try to boost long-term growth by creating incentives that encourage saving, investment and technological change. Fiscal policy can also be used to try to smooth out the business cycle. When the economy is in a recession, the government might cut taxes or increase its spending. Conversely, when the economy is in a rapid expansion, the government might increase taxes or cut its spending in an attempt to slow real GDP growth and prevent inflation from increasing. Fiscal policy is discussed in Chapter 26.

Monetary Policy

Changing interest rates and changing the quantity of money in the economy is called **monetary policy**. These actions are under the control of the Bank of England in the United Kingdom and the European Central Bank (ECB) in the Eurozone economies (the EU countries that use the euro). The principal aim of monetary policy is to keep inflation in check. To achieve this objective, the Bank of England and the ECB prevent the quantity of money from expanding too rapidly. Monetary policy can also be used to smooth the business cycle. When the economy is in recession, the Bank of England and the ECB might lower interest rates, and when the economy is in a rapid expansion, they might raise interest rates in an attempt to slow real GDP growth and prevent inflation from increasing. We study the monetary system in Chapter 27 and monetary policy in Chapter 28.

Review Quiz

Study Plan 20.6

1 What are the macroeconomic policy challenges?
2 What are the main tools of macroeconomic policy?
3 Distinguish between fiscal policy and monetary policy.

In the following chapters, you will learn about the causes of economic growth, business cycles, unemployment, inflation and deficits as well as the macroeconomic policy choices and challenges. But first, *Reading Between the Lines* on pp. 464–465 analyzes the international imbalances in the world economy.

Reading Between the Lines

International Imbalances and the World Economy

The Financial Times, 12 June 2006

FT

World Economy

Lex Column

World Economy Life is like riding a bicycle, Albert Einstein observed. To keep your balance you must keep moving. Fortunately, for the world's policy makers, their economies have progressed nicely so far this year. Unfortunately, the world economy's hazardous imbalances have also continued to widen, as finance ministers from the Group of Eight industrial nations noted at their weekend summit.

The warning signs are familiar, starting with massive US current account deficit. April's trade figures were better than expected, partly because the US paid less than thought for oil. But the real trade deficit still hit a record, after stripping out petroleum. Given how US exports are dwarfed by imports, the former would need to grow more than 1.5 times faster than the latter, merely to keep the gap steady.

What remains less appreciated is how difficult tackling the deficit could prove. A weaker dollar is the obvious remedy. But that would probably hobble the new-found economic strength of Japan and especially, Europe. It would also take time to boost exports – partly because of the familiar lag for changes in relative prices to actually shift the buying patterns of companies and consumers.

More seriously, it is not clear that US producers of tradeable goods have the capacity to benefit swiftly from their improved competitiveness. Doing so will require a massive shift of resources across different sectors, as aggregate manufacturing capacity utilisation has already risen above its long-run average. It might also allow foreign producers to pass on more pain to US consumers from a weaker dollar than has lately been the case.

Already, there are signs of rising price pressures on imports from Europe, Mexico and Canada, and there is a risk China might eventually follow suit.

That would make the Federal Reserve's task of containing inflation even trickier. It also suggests the eventual rebalancing could prove painful, not least for US consumers.

The Essence of the Story

- At a Group of Eight meeting in summer 2006, finance ministers discussed the imbalance in the world economy.
- A large US current account deficit is the main feature of the imbalance.
- Reducing the US current account deficit is a difficult task.
- A depreciation of the dollar is the obvious solution but that poses other dangers.
- It would take time to boost exports.
- It would also bring higher import prices and make it harder for the Federal Reserve to contain inflation.

Economic Analysis

- The US current account deficit reached nearly \$900 billion in 2006. Figure 1 shows how the current account deficit has increased.
- Matching the US current account deficit are current account surpluses in the rest of the world.
- China and Japan have large surpluses – China \$180 billion and Japan \$170 billion in 2006.
- But the rest of the world, which includes other Asian economies and the oil exporting countries of the Middle East, had a surplus of \$520 billion in 2006.
- To lower its deficit, the United States must increase its exports and decrease its imports.
- Figure 2 shows that the United States had no spare capacity in 2006 to increase is exports because its output gap – real GDP minus potential GDP – was zero. Real GDP was the same as potential GDP.
- A depreciation of the US dollar would make imports from Japan and China more expensive in the United States and might encourage Americans to cut their imports. But it would also bring higher US inflation, raising US consumer prices and US wage rates.
- Figure 3 shows that US inflation has already started to rise. To check the rise in inflation the US central bank, the Federal Reserve, might raise the US interest rate and slow down the US economy.
- A slowdown in the US economy would lower US imports from China and Japan and other countries.
- But lower US imports mean lower exports for other countries, which would slow down the world economy and lower US exports to China and Japan and other countries.
- There are no easy answers to the imbalance in the global economy.

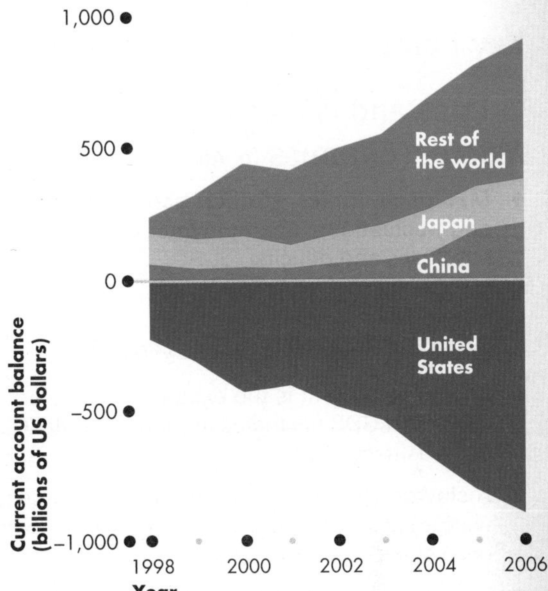

Figure 1 Current account balances

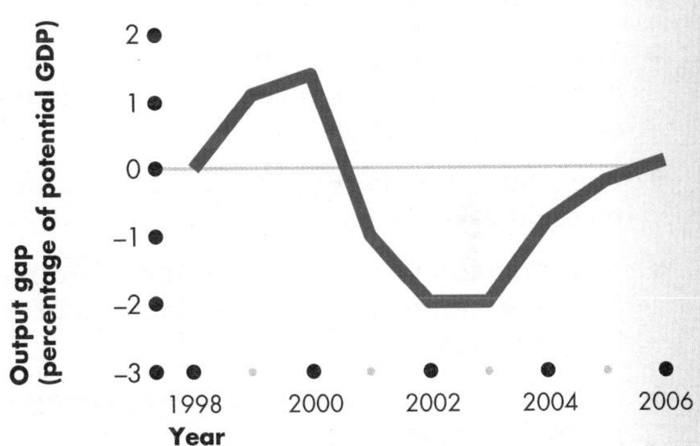

Figure 2 Output gaps in the United States

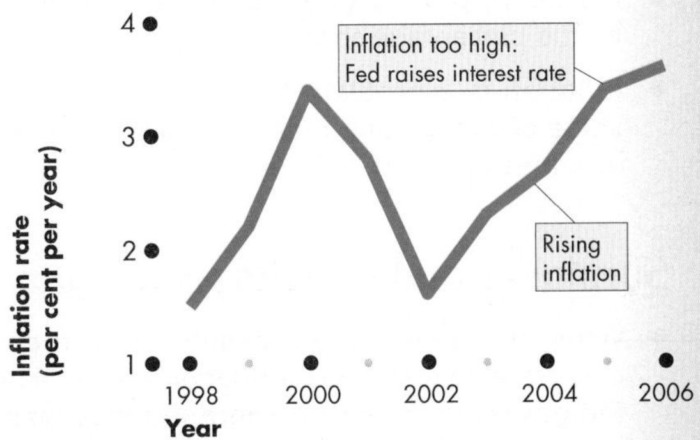

Figure 3 US inflation

Summary

Key Points

Origins and Issues of Macroeconomics (p. 450)

- Macroeconomics studies economic growth and fluctuations, unemployment, inflation and surpluses and deficits.

Economic Growth (pp. 451–456)

- Economic growth is the expansion of potential GDP. Real GDP fluctuates around potential GDP in a business cycle.
- A slowdown in productivity growth (the Lucas wedge) is more costly than business cycle recessions (the Okun gap).
- Economic growth increases future consumption but lowers current consumption.

Jobs and Unemployment (pp. 456–458)

- The economy creates more jobs than it loses in an expansion and loses more jobs than it creates in a recession.
- The unemployment rate increases during a recession and decreases during an expansion.
- The unemployment rate in the European Union is higher than that in Japan and the United States.
- Unemployment can permanently damage a person's job prospects.

Inflation (pp. 459–461)

- Inflation, a process of rising prices, is measured by the percentage change in the RPI.
- Inflation is a problem because it lowers the value of money and makes money less useful as a measuring rod of value.

Surpluses and Deficits (pp. 461–462)

- When the government spends more than it collects in taxes, it has a budget deficit. When the government collects more in taxes than it spends, it has a budget surplus.
- When imports exceed exports, a nation has a current account deficit.

Macroeconomic Policy Challenges and Tools (p. 463)

- The macroeconomic policy challenge is to use fiscal policy and monetary policy to boost long-term growth, keep inflation low, stabilize the business cycle, lower unemployment and reduce government and international deficits.

Key Figures

Key Terms

Problems

Data Grapher, Tests, Study Plan and Solutions*

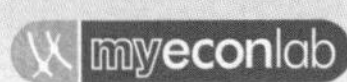

1 Use the Data Grapher to answer the following questions. In which country in 2006 was:

a The growth rate of real GDP highest: Canada, France, Japan or the United States?

b The unemployment rate highest: Canada, Japan, the United Kingdom or the United States?

2 Use the Data Grapher to answer the following questions. In which country in 2006 was:

a The inflation rate lowest: Canada, the United Kingdom, Japan or the United States?

b The government budget surplus (as a percentage of GDP) largest: Canada, the United Kingdom or the United States?

3 The graph shows real GDP growth rate in Greece and Turkey from 1998 to 2002.

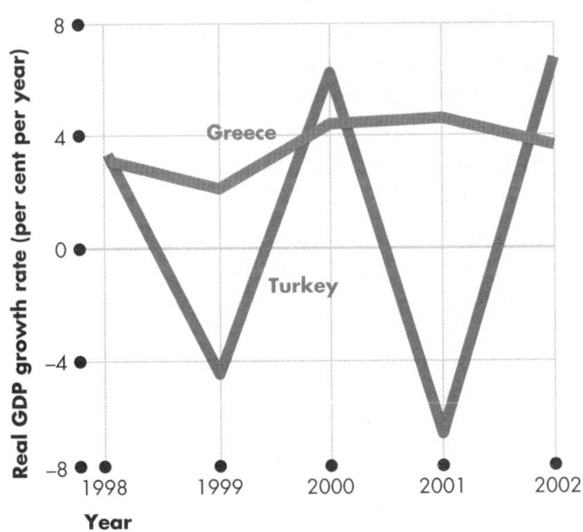

a In which years did economic growth in Greece increase? And in which year was growth the fastest?

b In which years did economic growth in Turkey decrease? And in which year was growth the slowest?

c Compare the paths of economic growth in Greece and Turkey during this period.

d Which economy, that of Greece or Turkey, had the fastest *average* growth rate during this period?

4 The figure at the top of the next column shows real GDP per person in Australia and Japan from 1992 to 2002.

a In which years did economic growth in Australia increase? And in which year was growth the fastest?

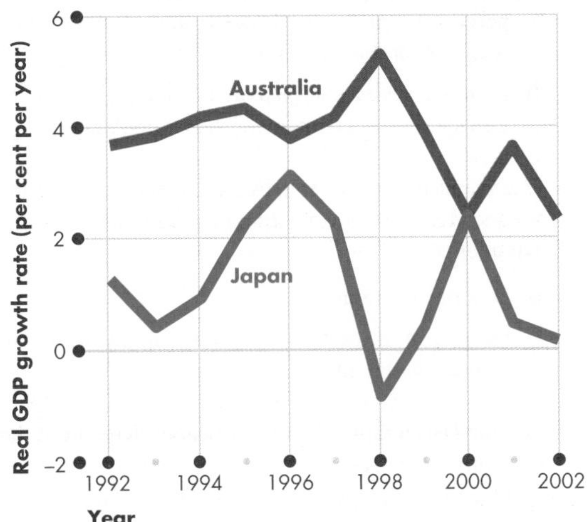

b In which years did economic growth in Japan decrease? And in which year was growth the slowest?

c Compare the paths of economic growth in Australia and Japan during this period.

5 The graph shows real GDP in Germany from 1989 to 2003.

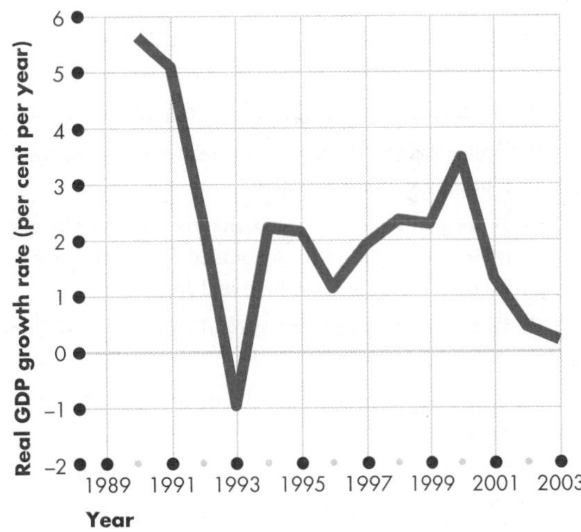

a How many recessions did Germany experience during this period?

b In which years, if any, did Germany experience a business cycle peak and a business cycle trough?

c In which years, if any, did Germany experience an expansion?

d In which years do you think Germany most likely had a negative output gap (an Okun gap)?

* Solutions to odd-numbered problems are provided.

6 Use the Data Grapher to answer the following questions. Which country, in 2002, had:

a The largest government budget deficit (as a percentage of GDP): Canada, Japan, the United Kingdom or the United States?

b A current account surplus (as a percentage of GDP): Canada, Japan, Germany or the United States?

7 Use the Data Grapher to make a scatter diagram of the inflation rate and the unemployment rate in the United Kingdom.

a Describe the relationship.

b Do you think that low unemployment brings an increase in the inflation rate?

8 Use the Data Grapher to make a scatter diagram of the government budget deficit as a percentage of GDP and the unemployment rate in the United Kingdom.

a Describe the relationship.

b Do you think that low unemployment brings a decrease in the budget deficit?

Critical Thinking

1 Study *Reading Between the Lines* on pp. 464–465 and then answer the following questions:

a What is the trend in the US current account deficit?

b What are the trends in the current account surpluses of China and Japan?

c What percentage (approximately) of the US current account deficit is accounted for by the current account surpluses of China and Japan?

d Why do you think the global imbalance is considered a problem?

e Why will lowering the US deficit be difficult to achieve?

f Why might the response of the Federal Reserve to the adjustment cause a problem for the global economy?

2 **Suddenly Rich, Poor Old Ireland Seems Bewildered**

It was not so long ago . . . that Ireland was a threadbare nation, barely relevant in European affairs. . . . In a little more than a decade, the so-called Celtic Tiger was transformed from one of the poorest countries in Western Europe to one of the richest in the world. Its gross domestic product per person, not quite 70 per cent of the EU average in 1987, sprang to 136 per cent of the Union's average by 2003, while the unemployment rate sank to 4 per cent from 17 per cent.

The New York Times, 2 February 2005

a Describe Ireland's economic trends since 1987.

b In what phase of the business cycle was Ireland in 2005?

c Is there a relationship between the phase of the business cycle and unemployment?

d Compare the change in unemployment in Ireland with that in the United States over the past decade. Give some reasons for the differences in unemployment rates between the two countries.

Web Activities

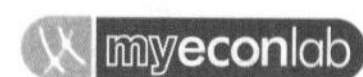

Links to Websites

1 Obtain the latest data on real GDP, unemployment and inflation in the Eurozone countries (countries that use the euro).

a Draw a graph of the real GDP growth rate, the inflation rate and the unemployment rate since 2001.

b What dangers does the Eurozone economy face today?

c What actions, if any, do you think might be needed by the European Central Bank to keep the economy strong?

2 Obtain data on the unemployment rate for your region of the country.

a Compare the unemployment rate in your region with that in the United Kingdom as a whole.

b Compare the unemployment rate in your region with that in the neighbouring regions.

3 Obtain data on the following variables for the United Kingdom for the most recent period available. Describe how the following variables have changed over the last year:

a The unemployment rate

b The inflation rate

c The government budget surplus or deficit

d The current account deficit

4 Obtain data on the the growth rate of real GDP for the United Kingdom and for the world economy for the most recent period available. What do these growth rates imply about the United Kingdom's share of the global economy?

Measuring GDP and Economic Growth

CHAPTER

21

After studying this chapter you will be able to:

- Define GDP and use the circular flow model to explain why GDP equals aggregate expenditure and aggregate income
- Explain the two methods used by the Office for National Statistics to measure UK GDP
- Explain how the Office for National Statistics measures *real* GDP and the GDP deflator to separate economic growth and inflation
- Explain the uses and the limitations of real GDP

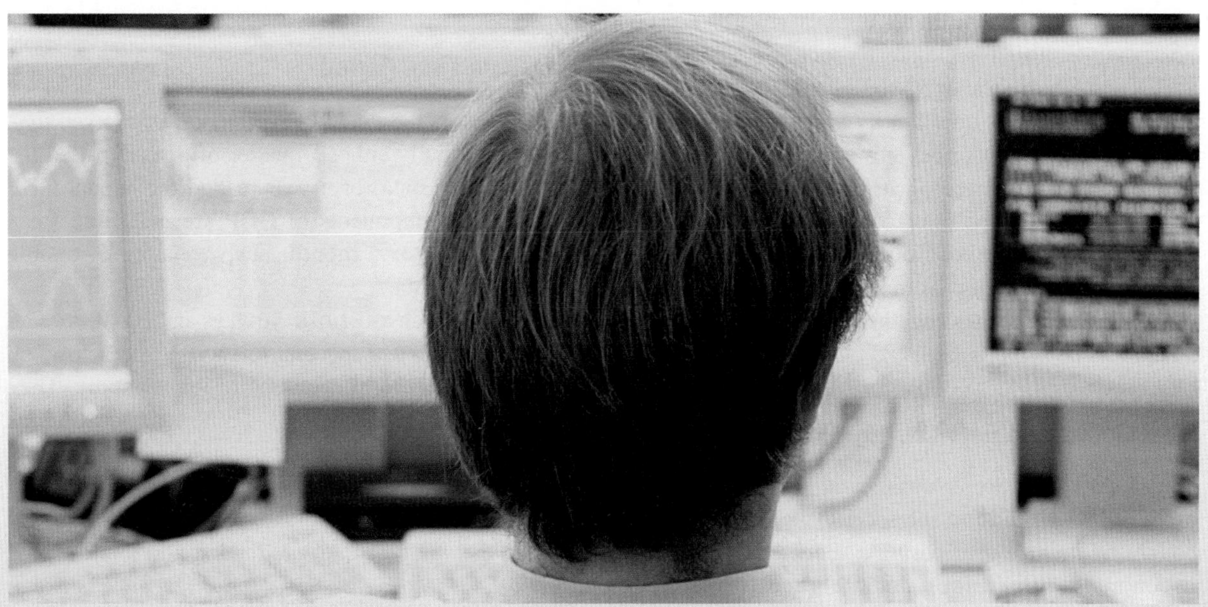

Economic Barometer

Every three months, you see a news report about gross domestic product or GDP. How do economic statisticians add up all the economic activity in a country to arrive at the GDP number. And how do we use GDP numbers to compare economic well-being over time and among rich and poor countries? Find the answers in this chapter and apply what you learn by looking at China's GDP in *Reading Between the Lines*.

Gross Domestic Product

What exactly is GDP, how is it calculated, what does it mean and why do we care about it? You are going to discover the answers to these questions in this chapter. First, what is GDP?

GDP Defined

GDP or **gross domestic product** is the market value of all the final goods and services produced within a country in a given time period – usually a year. This definition has four parts:

- Market value
- Final goods and services
- Produced within a country
- In a given time period

We examine each in turn.

Market Value

To measure total production, we must add together the production of apples and oranges, computers and popcorn. Just counting the items doesn't get us very far. For example, which is the greater total production: 100 apples and 50 oranges, or 50 apples and 100 oranges?

GDP answers this question by valuing items at their *market values* – at the prices at which each item is traded in markets. If the price of an apple is 10 pence, the market value of 50 apples is £5. If the price of an orange is 20 pence, the market value of 100 oranges is £20. By valuing production at market prices, we can add the apples and oranges together. The market value of 50 apples and 100 oranges is £5 plus £20, or £25.

Final Goods and Services

To calculate GDP, we value the *final goods and services* produced. A **final good** (or service) is an item that is bought by its final user during a specified time period. It contrasts with an **intermediate good** (or service), which is an item that is produced by one firm, bought by another firm and used as a component of a final good or service.

For example, a Ford Focus is a final good, but a tyre on the Ford Focus is an intermediate good. A Dell computer is a final good, but an Intel Pentium chip inside it is an intermediate good. If we were to add the value of intermediate goods and services produced to the value of final goods and services, we would count the same thing many times – a problem called *double counting*. The value of a Ford Focus already includes the value of the tyres, and the value of a Dell PC already includes the value of the Pentium chip inside it.

Some goods can be an intermediate good in some situations and a final good in other situations. For example, the ice cream that you buy on a hot summer day is a final good, but the ice cream that a café buys and uses to make sundaes is an intermediate good. The sundae is the final good. So whether a good is an intermediate good or a final good depends on what it is used for, not on what it is.

Produced Within a Country

Only goods and services that are produced *within a country* count as part of that country's GDP. When James Dyson, a British entrepreneur who makes vacuum cleaners, produces them in Malaysia, the market value of those cleaners is part of Malaysia's GDP, not part of GDP in the United Kingdom. Toyota, a Japanese firm, produces cars in Deeside, Wales, and the value of this production is part of UK GDP, not part of Japan's GDP.

In a Given Time Period

GDP measures the value of production *in a given time period* – normally either a quarter of a year (called the quarterly GDP data) or a year (called the annual GDP data). Some components of GDP are measured for a period as short as a month, but we have no reliable monthly GDP data.

Businesses such as British Airways and HSBC as well as governments use the quarterly GDP data to keep track of the short-term evolution of the economy. They use the annual GDP data to examine long-term trends and changes in production and the standard of living.

GDP measures not only the value of total production but also total income and total expenditure. The equality between the value of total production and total income is important because it shows the direct link between productivity and living standards. Our standard of living rises when our incomes rise and we can afford to buy more goods and services. But we must produce more goods and services if we are to be able to buy more goods and services.

Rising incomes and a rising value of production go together. To see why, we study the circular flow of expenditure and income.

GDP and the Circular Flow of Expenditure and Income

Figure 21.1 illustrates the circular flow of expenditure and income. The economy consists of households, firms, governments and the rest of the world (the purple diamonds), which trade in factor markets, goods (and services) markets and financial markets. Let's focus first on households and firms.

Households and Firms

Households sell and firms buy the services of labour, capital and land in factor markets. For these factor services, firms pay income to households: wages for labour services, interest for the use of capital and rent for the use of land. A fourth factor of production, entrepreneurship, receives profit.

Firms' retained earnings – profits that are not distributed to households – are also part of the household sector's income. You can think of retained earnings as being income that households save and lend back to firms. Figure 21.1 shows the *aggregate income* received by all households in payment for factor services by the blue dots labelled *Y*.

Households buy and firms sell consumption goods and services – such as beer, pizzas and dry cleaning services – in goods markets. Total payment for these goods and services is **consumption expenditure**, shown by the red dots labelled *C*.

Firms buy and sell new capital equipment – such as computer systems, aeroplanes, trucks, trains and assembly line equipment – in goods markets.

Some of what firms produce is not sold but is added to their stocks (or inventories). For example, if Ford produces 1,000 cars and sells 950 of them, the other 50 cars remain unsold and the firm's stock of cars increases by 50. When a firm adds unsold output to its stocks, we can think of the firm as buying goods from itself. The purchase of new plant, equipment and buildings, and the additions to stocks, are **investment**, shown by the red dots labelled *I*.

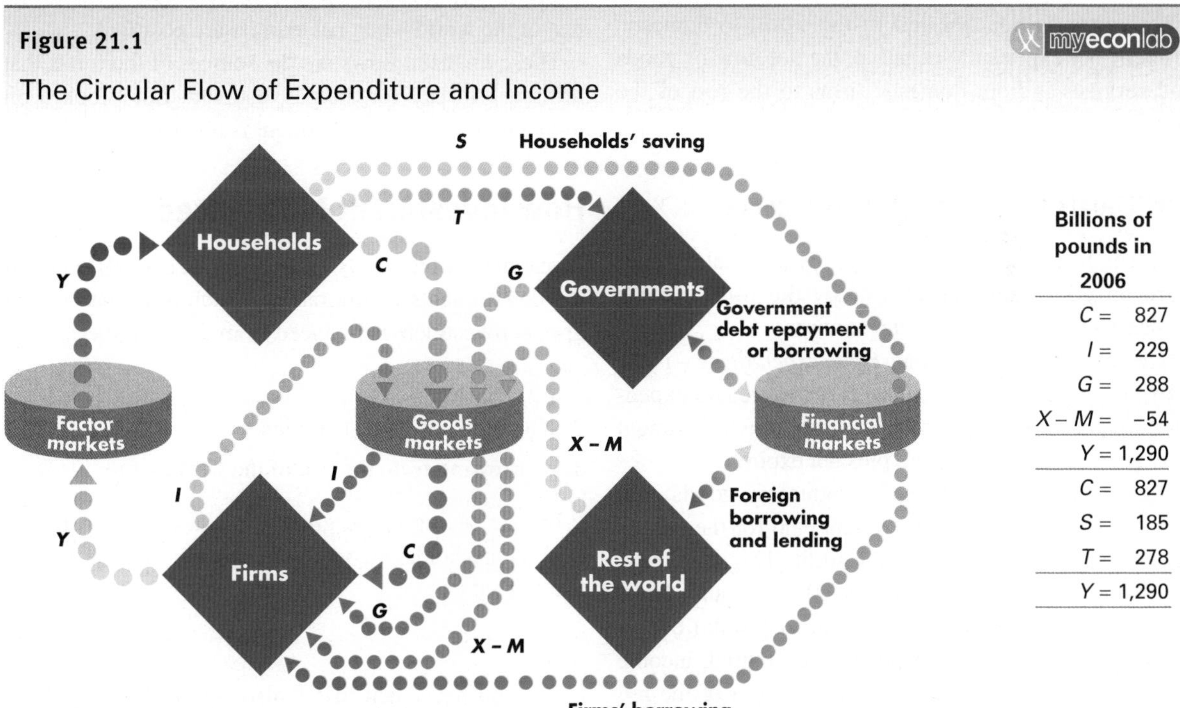

Figure 21.1

The Circular Flow of Expenditure and Income

In the circular flow of expenditure and income, households make consumption expenditures (*C*); firms make investment expenditures (*I*); governments purchase goods and services (*G*); the rest of the world purchases net exports (*X* – *M*) (red flows). Households receive incomes (*Y*) from firms (blue flow).

Aggregate income (blue flow) equals aggregate expenditure (red flows). Households use their income to consume (*C*), save (*S*) and pay net taxes (*T*). Firms borrow to finance their investment expenditures and governments and the rest of the world borrow to finance their deficits or lend their surpluses (green flows).

Governments

Governments buy goods and services from firms. The government expenditure on goods and services is called **government expenditure**, In Figure 21.1, government expenditure on goods and services is shown as the red flow G. Governments use taxes to pay for their expenditure. The green dots labelled T show taxes as net taxes. **Net taxes** are taxes paid to governments minus transfer payments received from governments. *Transfer payments* are cash transfers from governments to households and firms such as social security benefits, unemployment benefits, subsidies and interest on the government's debt.

Rest of World

Firms sell goods and services to the rest of the world, **exports**, and buy goods and services from the rest of the world, **imports**. The value of exports (X) minus the value of imports (M) is called **net exports**. Figure 21.1 shows net exports by the red flow $X - M$.

If net exports are positive, the net flow of goods and services is from the rest of the world to domestic firms. If net exports are negative, the net flow of goods and services is from domestic firms to the rest of the world.

GDP Equals Expenditure Equals Income

GDP can be measured in two ways: by the total expenditure on goods and services or by the total income earned by producing goods and services.

The total expenditure – *aggregate expenditure* – is the sum of the red flows in Figure 21.1. Aggregate expenditure equals consumption expenditure plus investment plus government expenditure plus net exports.

Aggregate income earned producing goods and services is equal to the total amount paid for the factors used – wages, interest, rent and profit. This amount is shown by the blue flow in Figure 21.1. Because firms pay out as incomes (including retained profits) everything they receive from the sale of their output, income (the blue flow) equals expenditure (the sum of the red flows). That is:

$$Y = C + I + G + X - M$$

The table in Figure 21.1 shows the UK numbers for 2006. You can see that the sum of the expenditures is £1,290 billion, which also equals aggregate income.

Because aggregate expenditure equals aggregate income, these two methods of valuing GDP give the same answer. So:

GDP equals aggregate expenditure and equals aggregate income.

The circular flow model is the foundation on which the national economic accounts are built.

Financial Flows

The circular flow model enables us to see the link between the expenditure and income flows and the flows through the financial markets that finance deficits and pay for investment. These flows are shown in green in Figure 21.1.

Households' **saving** (S) is the amount that households have left after they have paid their net taxes and bought their consumption goods and services. Government borrowing finances a government budget deficit. (Government lending occurs if the government has a budget surplus.) A country borrows from the rest of the world to pay for negative net exports (and lends to the rest of the world when net exports are positive).

These financial flows are the sources of the funds that firms use to pay for their investment. Let's look a bit more closely at how investment is financed.

How Investment Is Financed

Investment, which adds to the stock of capital, is one of the determinants of the rate at which aggregate output grows. Investment is financed from three sources:

1 Private saving
2 Government budget surplus
3 Borrowing from the rest of the world

Private saving is the green flow labelled S in Figure 21.1. Households' income is consumed, saved or paid in taxes. That is:

$$Y = C + S + T$$

But you have seen that Y also equals the sum of the components of aggregate expenditure. That is:

$$Y = C + I + G + X - M$$

Use these two equations to obtain:

$$I + G + X - M = S + T$$

Now subtract G and X from both sides of the last

equation and add M to both sides to obtain:

$$I = S + (T - G) + (M - X)$$

In this equation, $(T - G)$ is the government budget surplus and $(M - X)$ is borrowing from the rest of the world. If net taxes (T) exceed government expenditure (G), the government budget surplus equals $(T - G)$ and the surplus contributes towards paying for investment. If net taxes are less than government expenditure the government has a budget deficit equal to $(T - G)$, which is negative. This deficit subtracts from the sources that finance investment.

If UK imports (M) exceed UK exports (X), the United Kingdom borrows an amount equal to $(M - X)$ from the rest of the world. So part of the rest of the world's saving finances investment in the United Kingdom. If UK exports exceed UK imports, the United Kingdom lends an amount equal to $(X - M)$ to the rest of the world. So part of saving in the United Kingdom finances investment in other countries.

The sum of private saving (S) and government saving $(T - G)$ is called **national saving**. So national saving and foreign borrowing finance investment.

In 2006, investment in the United Kingdom was £229 billion. This investment was financed by national saving of £175 billion and foreign borrowing of £54 billion.

Gross and Net Domestic Product

What does the "gross" in GDP mean? *Gross* means before deducting the depreciation of capital. The opposite of gross is net, which means after deducting the depreciation of capital. To understand what the depreciation of capital is and how it affects aggregate expenditure and income, we need to expand the accounting framework that we use and distinguish between flows and stocks.

Flows and Stocks in Macroeconomics

A **flow** is a quantity per unit of time. The water running from an open tap into a bath is a flow. So is the number of CDs you buy in a month and the amount of income you earn in a month. GDP is a flow – the value of goods and services produced in a country *during a given time period*. Saving and investment are flows.

A **stock** is a quantity that exists at a point in time. The water in a bath is a stock. So is the number of CDs that you own and the amount of money in your bank account today. The two key stocks in macroeconomics are wealth and capital. The flows of saving and investment change these stocks.

Wealth and Saving

The value of all the things that people own is called **wealth**. What people own (a stock) is related to what they earn (a flow). People earn an income, which is the amount they receive during a given time period from supplying the services of factors of production. Income that is left after paying net taxes is either consumed or saved. *Consumption expenditure* is the amount spent on consumption goods and services. *Saving* is the amount of income remaining after making consumption expenditures. So saving adds to wealth.

For example, at the end of the year, you have £50 in your bank account and computer equipment worth £1,000. That's all you own. Your wealth is £1,050. Suppose that over the summer you earn an income of £3,000. You are extremely careful and spend only £500 on consumption goods and services. When university starts again, you have £2,550 in your bank account. Your wealth is now £3,550. Your wealth has increased by £2,500, which equals your saving of £2,500. And your saving of £2,500 equals your income during the summer of £3,000 minus your consumption expenditure of £500.

National wealth and national saving work just like this personal example. The wealth of a nation at the start of a year equals its wealth at the start of the previous year plus its saving during the year. So a nation's saving equals its income minus its consumption expenditure.

Capital and Investment

Capital is the plant, equipment, buildings and stocks or inventories of raw materials and semifinished goods that are used to produce other goods and services. The stock of capital in the economy exerts a big influence on GDP.

Two flows change the stock of capital: investment and depreciation. *Investment*, the purchase of new capital, increases the stock of capital. (Investment includes additions to inventories.) **Depreciation** is the decrease in the stock of capital that results from wear and tear and obsolescence. The total amount spent on purchases of new capital and on replacing depreciated capital is called **gross investment**. The amount by which the stock of capital increases is called **net investment**.

$$\text{Net investment} = \text{Gross investment} - \text{Depreciation}$$

Figure 21.2 illustrates these concepts. On 1 January 2007, Wayne's DVDs Inc. had 3 machines. This quantity was its initial capital. During 2007, Wayne's scrapped 1 machine. This quantity is its depreciation. After depreciation, Wayne's stock of capital was down to 2 machines. But also during 2007, Wayne's bought 2 new machines. This amount is its gross investment. By 31 December 2007, Wayne's DVDs had 4 machines so its capital had increased by 1 machine. This amount is Wayne's net investment. Wayne's net investment equals its gross investment (the purchase of 2 new machines) minus its depreciation (1 machine scrapped).

The example of Wayne's DVDs can be applied to the economy as a whole. The nation's capital stock decreases because capital depreciates and increases because of gross investment. The change in the nation's capital stock from one year to the next equals its net investment.

Back to the Gross in GDP

We can now see the distinction between gross domestic product and net domestic product. On the income side of the flows that measure GDP, a firm's *gross* profit is its profit *before* subtracting *depreciation*. A firm's gross profit is part of aggregate income, so depreciation is counted as part of gross income and GDP. Similarly, on the expenditure side of the flows that measure GDP. A firm's *gross investment* includes depreciation, so depreciation is counted as part of aggregate expenditure and total expenditure is a gross measure.

Net domestic product excludes depreciation. Like GDP, net domestic product can be viewed as the sum of incomes or expenditures. Net income includes firms' *net* profit – profits *after* subtracting depreciation. Net expenditure includes *net* investment, which also excludes depreciation.

Figure 21.2 myeconlab

Capital and Investment

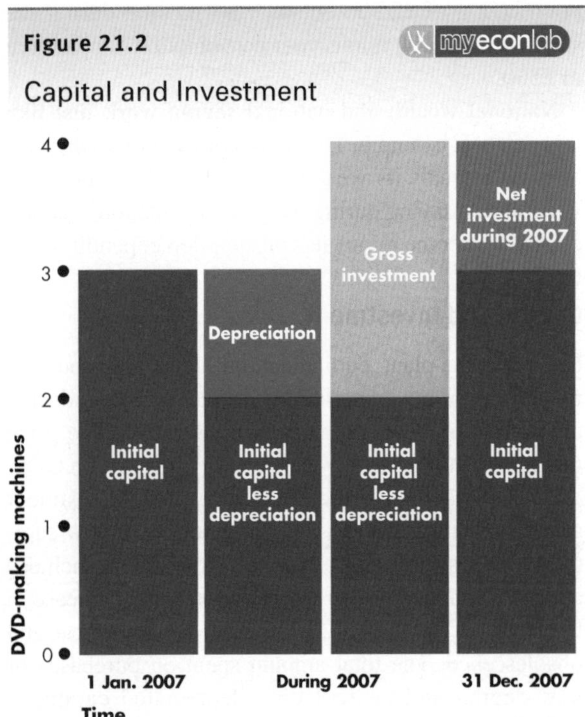

Wayne's DVDs has a capital stock at the end of 2007 that equals its capital stock at the beginning of 2007 plus its net investment during 2007.

Net investment is equal to gross investment less depreciation. Wayne's gross investment was the 2 new machines bought during the year, and its depreciation was the 1 machine that Wayne's scrapped during the year. Wayne's net investment was 1 machine.

The Short Term Meets the Long Term

The flows and stocks that you have just studied influence GDP growth and fluctuations. One of the reasons why GDP grows is that the capital stock grows. Investment adds to capital, so GDP grows because of investment. But investment fluctuates, which brings fluctuations to GDP. So capital and investment, along with wealth and saving, are part of the key to understanding both the growth and fluctuations of GDP.

Investment and saving interact with income and consumption expenditure in a circular flow of expenditure and income. In this circular flow, income equals expenditure, which also equals the value of production. This equality is the foundation on which a nation's economic accounts are built and from which its GDP is measured.

Review Quiz

Study Plan 21.1

1. Define GDP and distinguish between a final good and an intermediate good. Provide examples.
2. Why does GDP equal aggregate income and also equal aggregate expenditure?
3. How can investment be financed? What determines national saving?
4. What is the distinction between gross and net?
5. Define capital and explain how the flows of investment and depreciation change the stock of capital.

Let's now see how the ideas that you have just studied can be used in practice. We'll see how GDP and its components are measured in the United Kingdom today.

Measuring UK GDP

The Office for National Statistics uses the concepts that you met in the circular flow model to measure GDP and its components, which it publishes in the *United Kingdom National Accounts – The Blue Book.*

Because the value of aggregate output equals aggregate expenditure and aggregate income, there are two approaches available for measuring GDP, and both are used. They are:

- The expenditure approach
- The income approach

The Expenditure Approach

The *expenditure approach* measures GDP as the sum of consumption expenditure (C), investment (I), government expenditure on goods and services (G) and net exports of goods and services ($X - M$), corresponding to the red flows in the circular flow model in Figure 21.1. Table 21.1 shows the results of this approach for 2005. The table also shows the terms used in the *United Kingdom National Accounts – The Blue Book.*

Consumption expenditure is the expenditure by households on goods and services produced in the United Kingdom and the rest of the world. It includes goods such as beer, CDs, books and magazines; and services such as insurance, banking and legal advice. It does *not* include the purchase of new houses, which is counted as part of investment.

Investment is expenditure on capital equipment and buildings by firms and expenditure on new residential houses by households. It also includes the change in firms' stocks or inventories.

Government expenditure is the expenditure on goods and services by all levels of government – from Westminster to the local town hall. This item includes expenditure on national defence, law and order, street lighting and refuse collection. It does *not* include *transfer payments* because they are not purchases of goods and services.

Net exports are the value of UK exports minus the value of UK imports. When a UK company sells a car to a buyer in the United States, the value of that car is part of UK exports. When your local Skoda dealer stocks up on the latest model, its expenditure is part of UK imports.

Table 21.1 shows the relative magnitudes of the four items of aggregate expenditure.

Table 21.1

GDP: The Expenditure Approach

Item	Symbol	Amount in 2006 (billions) of pounds)	Percentage of GDP
Consumption expenditure (Final consumption expenditure: personal)	C	827	64.1
Investment (Gross capital formation)	I	229	17.8
Government expenditure (Final consumption expenditure: governments)	G	288	22.3
Net exports (External balance of goods and services)	$X - M$	−54	−4.2
Gross domestic product	Y	1,290	100.0

The expenditure approach measures GDP as the sum of consumption expenditure (C), investment (I) government expenditure (G) and net exports ($X - M$). In 2006, GDP as measured by the expenditure approach was £1,290. Almost two-thirds of aggregate expenditure is consumption expenditure.

Source of data: Office for National Statistics, *United Kingdom National Accounts.*

The Income Approach

The *income approach* measures GDP by summing all the incomes paid by firms to households for the services of the factors of production they hire – wages for labour, interest for capital, rent for land and profit for entrepreneurship. Let's see how the income approach works.

In the *United Kingdom National Accounts – The Blue Book*, incomes are divided into three categories:

1 Compensation of employees
2 Gross operating surplus
3 Mixed incomes

Compensation of employees is the total payments by firms for labour services. This item includes the net wages and salaries (called take-home pay) plus taxes withheld plus fringe benefits such as social security and pension fund contributions.

Gross operating surplus is the total profit made by companies and the surpluses generated by publicly owned enterprises. Some of these profits are paid to households in the form of dividends, and some are retained by companies as undistributed profits. The surpluses from public enterprises are either retained by the enterprises or paid to the government as part of its general revenue. They are all income.

Mixed income is a combination of rental income and income from self-employment. *Rental income* is the payment for the use of land and other rented inputs. It includes payments for rented housing and imputed rent for owner-occupied housing. (Imputed rent is an estimate of what homeowners would pay to rent the housing they own and use themselves. By including this item in the national accounts, we measure the total value of housing services, whether they are owned or rented.)

Income from self-employment is a mixture of the elements that we have just reviewed. The proprietor of an owner-operated business supplies labour, capital and perhaps land and buildings to the business.

Table 21.2 shows these three components of aggregate income and their relative magnitudes.

The sum of the incomes is called *gross domestic income at factor cost*. The term *factor cost* is used because it is the cost of the *factors of production* used to produce final goods and services. When we sum all the expenditures on final goods and services, we arrive at a total called *domestic product at market prices*. Market prices and factor cost would be the same except for indirect taxes and subsidies.

An *indirect tax* is a tax paid by consumers when they buy goods and services. (In contrast, a *direct tax* is a tax on income.) Sales taxes, VAT and taxes on alcohol, petrol and tobacco products are indirect taxes. Because of indirect taxes, consumers pay more for some goods and services than producers receive. Market price exceeds factor cost. For example, with VAT at 17.5 per cent, when you pay £11.75 for a CD (market price), the producer receives £10 (the factor cost). The VAT you pay is £1.75.

A *subsidy* is a payment by the government to a producer. Payments made to farmers under the EU Common Agricultural Policy are subsidies. Because of subsidies, consumers pay less for some goods and services than producers receive. Factor cost exceeds market price.

To get from factor cost to market price, we add indirect taxes and subtract subsidies. Making this adjustment brings us to GDP – the value of production in market prices.

Table 21.2

GDP: The Income Approach

Item	Amount in 2006 (billions of pounds)	Percentage of GDP
Compensation of employees	717	55.6
Gross operating surplus	330	25.6
Mixed income	79	6.1
Gross domestic income at factor cost	1,126	
Indirect taxes *less* Subsidies	164	12.7
Gross domestic product	1,290	100.0

The sum of all factor incomes equals gross domestic income at factor cost. GDP equals net domestic income at factor cost plus indirect taxes less subsidies. In 2006, GDP measured by the factor incomes approach was £1,290 billion. Compensation of employees was by far the largest part of total factor income.

Source of data: Office for National Statistics, *United Kingdom National Accounts*.

Review Quiz

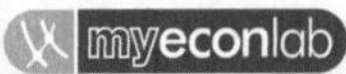

Study Plan 21.2

1 Why does GDP measured by the expenditure approach equal GDP measured by the income approach?
2 What is the distinction between expenditure on final goods and expenditure on intermediate goods?

You now know how GDP is defined and measured. Because GDP is measured in pounds it can change for two reasons: prices can change or the quantities of goods and services produced can change. It is the quantities of goods and services produced rather than just their money value that determines the standard of living. Your next task is to learn how we unscramble two sources of change in GDP – inflation and economic growth – to reveal changes in the quantity of goods and services produced, changes in what we call *real* GDP.

Measuring Economic Growth

You've seen that GDP measures total expenditure on final goods and services in a given period. In 2006, GDP was £1,290 billion. A year before, in 2005, GDP was £1,226 billion. Because GDP was greater in 2006 than in 2005, we know that one or two things must have happened during 2006:

1 We produced more goods and services in 2006 than we produced in 2005.
2 We paid higher prices for our goods and services in 2006 than we paid in 2005.

Producing more goods and services contributes to an improvement in our standard of living. Paying higher prices means that our cost of living has increased. So it matters a great deal why GDP has increased.

You're now going to learn how economists at the Office for National Statistics separate the change in GDP into two parts. One part tells us the change in quantity of goods and services produced and the other part tells us the change in the prices paid for goods and services. The method that the Office for National Statistics uses has changed in recent years and you will learn both the old and the new methods.

We measure the change in production by using a number that we call real gross domestic product. **Real gross domestic product (real GDP)** is the value of final goods and services produced in a given year when valued at constant prices. By comparing the value of the goods and services produced at constant prices, we can measure the change in the quantity of production.

Calculating Real GDP

Table 21.3 shows the quantities produced and the prices in 2005 for an economy that produces only two goods: balls and bats. The first step towards calculating real GDP is to calculate nominal GDP. **Nominal GDP** is the value of the final goods and services produced in a given year valued at the prices that prevailed in that same year. Nominal GDP is just a more precise name for GDP that we use when we want to be emphatic that we are not talking about real GDP.

Nominal GDP Calculation

To calculate nominal GDP in 2005, we sum the expenditures on balls and bats in that year as follows:

Expenditure on balls = 100 balls × £1 = £100

Expenditure on bats = 20 bats × £5 = £100

Nominal GDP in 2005 = £100 + £100 = £200

Table 21.4 shows the quantities produced and the prices in 2006. The quantity of balls produced increased to 160, and the quantity of bats produced increased to 22. The price of a ball fell to 50 pence, and the price of a bat increased to £22.50. To find nominal GDP in 2006, we sum the expenditures on balls and bats in that year as follows:

Expenditure on balls = 160 balls × £0.50 = £80

Expenditure on bats = 22 bats × £22.50 = £495

Nominal GDP in 2006 = £80 + £495 = £575

To calculate real GDP, we choose one year, called the *base year*, against which to compare the other years. In the United Kingdom today, the base year is 2003. The choice of the base year is not important. It is just a common reference point. We'll use 2005 as the base year. By definition, in the base year, real GDP equals nominal GDP. So real GDP in 2005 is £200.

Base-year Prices Value of Real GDP

The base-year prices method of calculating real GDP, which is the old method, values the quantities produced in a year at the prices of the base year. Table 21.5 on the next page shows the prices for 2005 and the quantities produced in 2006 (based on the information in Tables 21.3 and 21.4).

Table 21.3

GDP Data for 2005

Item	Quantity	Price
Balls	100	£1.00 each
Bats	20	£5.00 each

Table 21.4

GDP Data for 2006

Item	Quantity	Price
Balls	160	£0.50 each
Bats	22	£22.50 each

Table 21.5

2006 Quantities and 2005 Prices

Item	Quantity	Price
Balls	160	£1.00 each
Bats	22	£5.00 each

The value of the 2006 quantities at the 2005 prices is calculated as follows:

Expenditure on balls = 160 balls × £1.00 = £160

Expenditure on bats = 22 bats × £5.00 = £110

Value of the 2006 quantities at 2005 prices = £270

If we use the old base-year prices method, £270 would be recorded as real GDP in 2006.

Chained Volume Measure Calculation

The **chained volume measure** method, which is the new method of calculating real GDP, uses the prices of two adjacent years to calculate the real GDP growth rate. So to find the real GDP growth rate in 2006, we compare the quantities produced in 2005 and 2006 by using both the 2005 prices and the 2006 prices. We then average the two sets of numbers in a way that we'll now describe.

To compare the quantities produced in 2005 and 2006 at 2006 prices, we need to calculate the value of 2005 quantities at 2006 prices. Table 21.6 summarizes these quantities and prices. The value of the 2005 quantities at the 2006 prices is calculated as follows:

Expenditure on balls = 100 balls × £0.50 = £50

Expenditure on bats = 20 bats × £22.50 = £450

Value of the 2005 quantities at 2006 prices = £500

We now have two comparisons between 2005 and 2006. At the 2005 prices, the value of production increased from £200 in 2005 to £270 in 2006. The increase in value is £70, and the percentage increase is (£70 ÷ £200) × 100, which is 35 per cent. At the 2006 prices, the value of production increased from £500 in 2005 to £575 in 2006. The increase in value is £75, and the percentage increase is (£75 ÷ £500) × 100, which is 15 per cent.

The new method of calculating real GDP uses the average of these two percentage increases. The average of 35 per cent and 15 per cent is (35 + 15) ÷ 2, which equals 25 per cent. Real GDP in 2006 is 25 per cent greater than it was in 2005. Real GDP in 2005 is £200, so real GDP in 2006 is £250.

Table 21.6

2005 Quantities and 2006 Prices

Item	Quantity	Price
Balls	100	£0.50 each
Bats	20	£22.50 each

Chain Linking

The calculation that we've just described is repeated each year. Each year is compared with its preceding year. So in 2007, the calculations are repeated but using the prices and quantities of 2006 and 2007.

Real GDP in 2007 equals real GDP in 2006 increased by the calculated percentage change in real GDP for 2007. For example, suppose that real GDP for 2007 is calculated to be 20 per cent greater than that in 2006. You know that real GDP in 2006 is £250. So real GDP in 2007 is 20 per cent greater than this value and is £300. In every year, real GDP is valued in base-year (2005) pounds.

By applying the calculated percentage change in real GDP in each year to the real GDP of the preceding year, real GDP in each year is linked back to the pounds of the base year like the links in a chain.

Calculating the Price Level

You've seen how real GDP reveals the change in the quantity of goods and services produced. We're now going to see how we can find the change in prices that increases our cost of living.

The average level of prices is called the **price level**. One measure of the price level is the **GDP deflator**, which is an average of current-year prices expressed as a percentage of base-year prices. We calculate the GDP deflator by using nominal GDP and real GDP in the formula:

GDP deflator = (Nominal GDP ÷ Real GDP) × 100

You can see why the GDP deflator is a measure of the price level. If nominal GDP rises but real GDP remains unchanged, the price level must have risen. The larger the nominal GDP for a given real GDP, the higher is the price level and the larger is the GDP deflator.

Table 21.7

Calculating the GDP Deflator

Year	Nominal GDP	Real GDP	GDP Deflator
2005	£200	£200	100
2006	£575	£250	230

Table 21.7 shows how the GDP deflator is calculated. In 2005, the base year, real GDP equals nominal GDP, so the GDP deflator is 100. In 2006, the GDP deflator is 230, which equals nominal GDP of £575 divided by real GDP of £250 and then multiplied by 100.

Deflating the GDP Balloon

You can think of GDP as a balloon that is blown up by growing production and rising prices. In Figure 21.3, the GDP deflator lets the inflation air – the contribution of rising prices – out of the nominal GDP balloon so that we can see what has happened to *real* GDP. In Figure 21.3, the base year is 1986 and the red balloon for 1986 shows real GDP in that year. The green balloon shows *nominal* GDP in 2006. The red balloon for 2006 shows real GDP for that year. To see real GDP in 2006, we *deflate* nominal GDP using the GDP deflator.

Review Quiz

Study Plan 21.3

1. What is the distinction between nominal GDP and real GDP?
2. What is the old method of calculating real GDP?
3. What is the chained volume measure of real GDP?
4. How is the chained volume measure of real GDP calculated?
5. How is the GDP deflator calculated?

You now know how to calculate real GDP and the GDP deflator. Your next task is to learn how to use real GDP to make economic welfare comparisons and to see some of its limitations.

Figure 21.3

The UK GDP Balloon

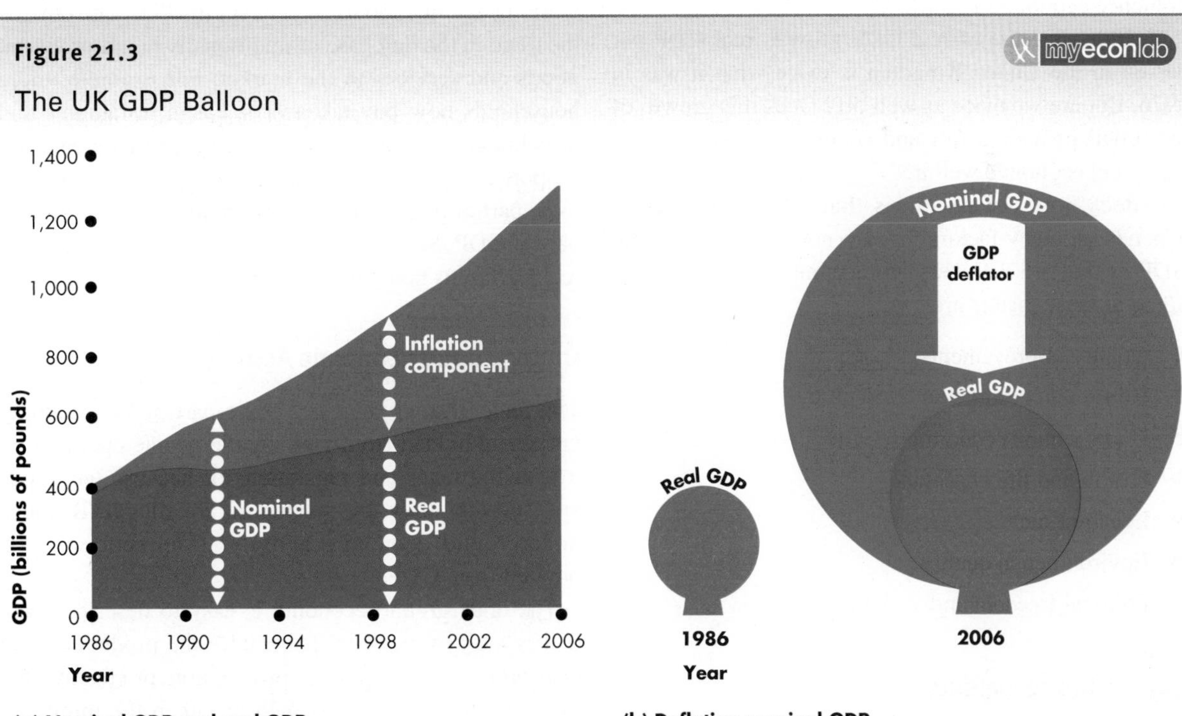

Part of the rise in GDP comes from inflation and part from increased production – an increase in real GDP. The GDP deflator lets inflation air out of the GDP balloon so that we can see the extent to which production has increased.

Source of data: Office for National Statistics.

The Uses and Limitations of Real GDP

We use estimates of real GDP for three main purposes. They are to make:

- Economic welfare comparisons over time
- Economic welfare comparisons across countries
- Business cycle forecasts

Although real GDP is used for these three purposes, it is not a perfect measure for any of them. But neither is it a seriously misleading measure. We'll describe the uses and evaluate the limitations of real GDP in each of the three cases.

Economic Welfare Comparisons Over Time

Economic welfare is a comprehensive measure of the general state of well-being. Economic welfare improves when the production per person of all the goods and services grows. The goods and services that make up real GDP growth are only a part of all the items that influence economic welfare.

In 2006, because of real GDP growth, real GDP per person in the United Kingdom is twice what it was in 1976. But are we twice as well off? Does this growth of real GDP provide a full and accurate measure of the change in economic welfare?

It does not. The reason is that economic welfare depends on many factors that are not measured by real GDP or that are not measured accurately by real GDP. Some of these factors are:

- Quality improvements
- Household production
- Underground economic activity
- Health and life expectancy
- Leisure time
- Environmental quality
- Political freedom and social justice

Quality Improvements

The price indices that are used to measure inflation give an upward-biased estimate of true inflation. (You will learn about the sources of this bias on p. 503.) If we overestimate the rise in prices, we underestimate the growth of real GDP. When car prices rise because cars have become better (safer, more fuel efficient, more comfortable), the GDP deflator counts the price increase as inflation. So what is really an increase in production is counted as an increase in price rather than an increase in real GDP. It is deflated away by the wrongly measured higher price level. The magnitude of this bias is probably less than 1 percentage point a year, but its exact magnitude is not known.

Household Production

An enormous amount of production takes place every day in our homes. Changing a light bulb, cutting the grass, washing the car and growing vegetables are all examples of productive activities that do not involve market transactions and are not counted as part of GDP.

If these activities grew at the same rate as real GDP, then not measuring them would not be a problem. But it is likely that market production, which is part of GDP, is increasingly replacing household production, which is not part of GDP. Two trends point in this direction. One is the trend in female employment, which has increased from 44 per cent of the female population of working age in 1966 to 54 per cent in 2006. The other is the trend in the purchase of traditionally home-produced goods and services in the market. For example, more households now buy takeaways, eat in restaurants and use childcare services. This trend means that increasing proportions of food preparation and childcare that used to be part of household production are now measured as part of GDP. So real GDP grows more rapidly than does real GDP plus home production.

Underground Economic Activity

The *underground economy* is the part of the economy purposely hidden from view by the people operating in it to avoid taxes and regulations or because the goods and services they are producing are illegal. Because underground economic activity is unreported, it is omitted from GDP.

The underground economy is easy to describe, even if it is hard to measure. It includes the production and distribution of illegal drugs, prostitution, production that uses illegal labour that is paid less than the minimum wage, and jobs done for cash to avoid paying income taxes. This last category might be quite large and includes tips earned by taxi drivers, hairdressers and hotel and restaurant workers.

Estimates of the scale of the underground economy range between 3.5 and 13.5 per cent of GDP (£45 billion to £174 billion) in the United Kingdom and much more in some countries, particularly in Eastern European countries that are making the transition from centrally planned economies to market economies.

If the underground economy is a constant proportion of the total economy, the growth rate of real GDP provides a useful estimate of *changes* in economic welfare. But production can shift from the underground economy to the rest of the economy, and it can shift the other way. The underground economy expands relative to the rest of the economy if taxes rise sharply or if regulations become especially restrictive. And the underground economy shrinks relative to the rest of the economy if the burdens of taxes and regulations ease.

During the 1980s, when tax rates were cut, there was an increase in tax revenues. Some of this increase may have been due to the existing workforce, particularly high-paid labour, working harder, taking greater risks and being more productive, but some of it could have been due to a switch from what was previously underground activity to recorded activity. So some part (but probably a small part) of the expansion of real GDP during the 1980s represented a shift of economic activity from the underground economy rather than an increase in production.

Health and Life Expectancy

Good health and a long life – the hopes of everyone – do not show up in real GDP, at least not directly. A higher real GDP does enable us to spend more on medical research, healthcare, healthy food and exercise equipment. And as real GDP has increased, our life expectancy has lengthened – from 70 years at the end of the Second World War to approaching 80 years today. Infant deaths and death in childbirth, two fearful scourges of the nineteenth century, have been greatly reduced.

But we face new health and life expectancy problems every year. AIDS, drug abuse, suicide and murder are taking young lives at a rate that causes serious concern. When we take these negative influences into account, we see that real GDP growth overstates the improvements in economic welfare.

Leisure Time

Leisure time is an economic good that adds to our economic welfare. Other things remaining the same, the more leisure we have, the better off we are. Our time spent working is valued as part of GDP, but our leisure time is not. Yet from the point of view of economic welfare, that leisure time must be at least as valuable to us as the wage that we earn for the last hour worked. If it were not, we would work instead of taking the leisure. Over the years, leisure time has steadily increased. The working week has become shorter and the number and length of holidays have increased. These improvements in economic well-being are not reflected in GDP.

Environmental Quality

Economic activity directly influences the quality of the environment. The burning of hydrocarbon fuels is the most visible activity that damages our environment. But it is not the only example. The depletion of non-renewable resources, the mass clearing of forests, and the pollution of lakes and rivers are other major environmental consequences of industrial production.

Resources used to protect the environment are valued as part of GDP. For example, the value of catalytic converters that help to protect the atmosphere from carbon emissions are part of GDP. But if we did not use such pieces of equipment and instead polluted the atmosphere, we would not count the deteriorating air that we were breathing as a negative part of GDP.

An industrial society possibly produces more atmospheric pollution than does an agricultural society. But pollution does not always increase as we become wealthier. Wealthy people value a clean environment and are willing to pay for one. Compare the pollution that was revealed in East Germany in the late 1980s with pollution in the United Kingdom. East Germany, a poor country, polluted its rivers, lakes and atmosphere in a way that is unimaginable in the United Kingdom or in wealthy West Germany.

Political Freedom and Social Justice

Most people value political freedoms such as those provided by the western democracies. They also value social justice or fairness – equality of opportunity and of access to social security safety nets that protect people from the extremes of misfortune.

A country might have a very large real GDP per person but have limited political freedom and equity. For example, a small elite might enjoy political liberty and extreme wealth, while the vast majority are effectively enslaved and live in abject poverty. Such an economy would generally be regarded as having less economic welfare than one that had the same amount of real GDP but in which political freedoms were enjoyed by everyone. Today, China is the world's fastest-growing economy but the Chinese people have limited political freedoms. India's economy is growing less quickly than China's but the people of India enjoy a democratic political system. Economists have no easy way to determine which of these two countries is better off.

Box 21.1

How Much Poorer Is China Than the United States?

In 2006, real GDP per person in the United States was almost $44,000. The official Chinese statistics say that real GDP per person in China in 2006 was 15,500 yuan (the yuan is the currency of China). On the average during 2006, $1 was worth 9.9 yuan. If we use this exchange rate to convert Chinese yuan into US dollars, we get a value of $1,566. This comparison of China and the United States makes China look extremely poor. In 2006, GDP per person in the United States was 28 times that in China.

The green line in Figure 1 shows the story of real GDP in China from 1981 to 2006 based on converting the yuan to the US dollar at the market exchange rate.

Figure 1

Two Views of Real GDP in China

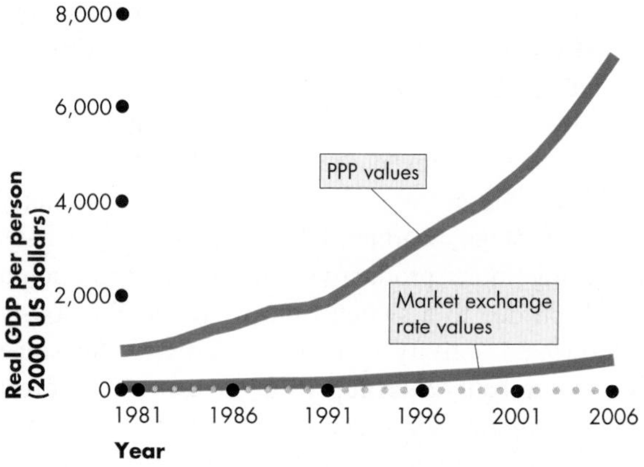

Sources of data: International Monetary Fund, *World Economic Outlook* database, April 2006; Alan Heston, Robert Summers and Bettina Aten, Penn World Table Version 6.1 Center for International Comparisons at the University of Pennsylvania (CICUP), October 2002.

Purchasing Power Parity Comparison

The red line in Figure 1 shows another story based on an estimate of China's real GDP per person that is much larger than the measure we've just calculated. Let's see how this alternative measurement is made.

GDP in the United States is measured by using prices that prevail in the United States. China's GDP is measured by using prices that prevail in China. But the *relative* prices in the two countries are very different. Some goods that are expensive in the United States cost very little in China, so these items get a smaller weight in China's real GDP than they get in US real GDP. If, instead of using China's prices, all the goods and services produced in China are valued at the prices prevailing in the United States, then a more valid comparison can be made of GDP in the two countries. Such a comparison uses prices called purchasing power parity prices, or PPP prices.

Alan Heston, Robert Summers and Bettina Aten, economists in the Center for International Comparisons at the University of Pennsylvania, have used PPP prices to construct real GDP data for more than 100 countries. And the IMF now uses a method similar to that of Heston, Summers and Aten to calculate PPP estimates of GDP in all countries. The PPP comparisons tell a remarkable story about China.

According to the PPP comparisons, US GDP per person in 2006 was 5 times that of China's, not the 28 times shown at the market exchange rate. Figure 1 shows the PPP view of China's real GDP and compares it with the market exchange rate view.

Uncertainty and Measurement Errors

A prominent China scholar, Thomas Rawski of the University of Pittsburgh, doubts both sets of data shown in Figure 1. He believes that the growth rate of China's real GDP has been exaggerated for some years and that even the market exchange rate data overstate real GDP in China.

US real GDP is measured reliably. But China's is not. The alternative measures of China's real GDP are unreliable, and the truth about GDP in China is not known. But China's real GDP is growing, and many businesses are paying close attention to the prospects of expanding their activities in China and other fast-growing Asian economies.

The Bottom Line

Do we get the wrong message about the growth in economic welfare by looking at the growth of real GDP? The influences that are omitted from real GDP are probably important and could be large.

Developing countries have a larger underground economy and a larger amount of household production than do developed countries. So as an economy develops and grows, part of the apparent growth might reflect a switch from underground to regular production and from home production to market production. This measurement error overstates the economic growth rate and the improvement in economic welfare.

Other influences on living standards include the amount of leisure time available, the quality of the environment, the security of jobs and homes, the safety of city streets, and so on. It is possible to construct broader measures that combine the many influences that contribute to human happiness. Real GDP will be one element in these broader measures, but it will by no means be the whole of them.

Economic Welfare Comparisons Across Countries

All the problems we've just reviewed affect the economic welfare of every country. So to make international comparisons of economic welfare, factors additional to real GDP must be used. But real GDP comparisons are a major component of international welfare comparisons and two special problems arise in making international comparisons.

First, the real GDP of one country must be converted into the same currency units as the real GDP of the other country. Second, the same prices must be used to value the goods and services in the countries being compared. Box 21.1 looks at these two problems by using a striking comparison between the United States and China, and *Reading Between the Lines* on pp. 484–485 takes a further look at the measurement of China's GDP.

Business Cycle Forecasts

If policy makers plan to raise interest rates to slow an expansion that they believe is too strong, they look at the latest estimates of real GDP. But suppose that for the reasons that we've just discussed, real GDP is mis-measured. Does this mis-measurement hamper our ability to identify the phases of the business cycle? It does not. The reason is that although the omissions from real GDP do change over time, they probably do not change in a systematic way with the business cycle. So inaccurate measurement of real GDP does not necessarily cause a wrong assessment of the phase of the business cycle.

The fluctuations in economic activity measured by real GDP tell a reasonably accurate story about the phase of the business cycle that the economy is in. When real GDP grows, the economy is in a business cycle expansion; when real GDP shrinks (for two quarters), the economy is in a recession. Also, as real GDP fluctuates, so do production and jobs.

But real GDP fluctuations probably exaggerate or overstate the fluctuations in total production and economic welfare. The reason is that when business activity slows in a recession, household production increases and so does leisure time. When business activity speeds up in an expansion, household production and leisure time decrease. Because household production and leisure time increase in a recession and decrease in an expansion, real GDP fluctuations tend to overstate the fluctuations in both total production and economic welfare. But the directions of change of real GDP, total production and economic welfare are probably the same.

Review Quiz

Study Plan 21.4

1. Does real GDP measure economic welfare? If not, why not?
2. Does real GDP measure total production of goods and services? If not, what are the main omissions?
3. How can we make valid comparisons of real GDP over time?
4. Does the growth rate of real GDP measure the economic growth rate accurately? If not, why not?
5. How can we make international comparisons of real GDP?
6. Do the fluctuations in real GDP measure the business cycle accurately? If not, why not?

You've now studied the methods used to measure GDP, real GDP and economic growth, and you've learned about some of the limitations of these measures. In *Reading Between the Lines* on pp. 484–486, you can see that measurement has been a serious problem for China. Your task in the next chapter is to learn how we monitor employment and unemployment and retail prices.

Reading Between the Lines
Measuring Real GDP in China

The Financial Times, 20 December 2005

FT

China revises size of economy up by 17%

Mure Dickie

China's economy was the sixth biggest in the world last year, Beijing announced on Tuesday, unveiling a 16.8 per cent upward revision to official gross domestic product that pushed Italy into seventh place.

The revision, based on a nationwide census that recorded previously ignored activity in the fast-growing service sector, put China's GDP in 2004 at Rmb 15,988bn ($1,983bn, €1,652bn, £1,119bn).

The change implies that China's growth in recent years has been faster than GDP data showed and offers comfort to those concerned about the economy's relative reliance on investment and manufacturing.

The census put the output of China's services sector at Rmb 6,502bn, raising its share of GDP from 32 per cent to 41 per cent, said Li Deshui, commissioner of the National Bureau of Statistics. . . .

The new rosy picture of economic strength could fuel calls from the US for China to revalue significantly its currency, which critics say is being held at a level that grants an unfair trade advantage. . . .

However, Mr. Li took pains to stress that China's newly revised 2004 per capita GDP still ranked lower than 100th in the world, and that more than 100m Chinese still lived in poverty. . . .

The scale of the revision is a reminder of the sketchy nature of much of Chinese economic data. Some economists say the official data still understates economic activity. Dong Tao of Credit Suisse First Boston estimated that China's service sector accounted for more than 50 per cent of the economy rather than the revised 41 per cent.

The Essence of the Story

- The Chinese government revised its measure of GDP up by nearly 17 per cent in 2004.
- The census of production showed that government statisticians had underestimated the value of a fast-growing service sector.
- This revised estimate of GDP makes China the sixth largest economy in the world.
- Economists say that the scale of the revision will not be reflected in a change in the estimates of investment spending.
- GDP per person in China remains very low and is lower than 100th in the world.
- The size of the revision indicates the unreliabilty of Chinese economic data.

Economic Analysis

- China has not yet established a reliable and independent system of national accounts and estimates of GDP are based on small samples of data.
- Consequently, China's GDP measure is subject to large errors and revisions.
- Figure 1 shows estimates of China's GDP before and after revisions that were made in 2005.
- Initially, China's service sector was thought to account for 32 per cent of GDP but now it is believed to account for 41 per cent of GDP.
- The scale of the GDP revision raises doubts about the accuracy of China's data. It also poses questions about how to compare China with other countries.
- Figure 2 shows two measures of GDP in 2005 in 11 countries. The blue bars show GDP valued at the market exchange rate and the red bars show GDP using PPP values (see p. 482).
- With the revised estimate of China's GDP, and using the market exchange rate, China becomes the fourth largest economy in the world just ahead of the United Kingdom.
- Using PPP to value GDP, China becomes the second largest economy and not far behind the United States.
- China may be the fourth (or second) largest economy but it has a huge population of nearly 1.4 billion people.
- Figure 3 shows that China's GDP per person has only recently exceeded that threshold used by the World Bank to classify a country as a low-income developing economy.
- At a GDP per person of $US1,740 (at the market exchange rate), China remains a poor country.

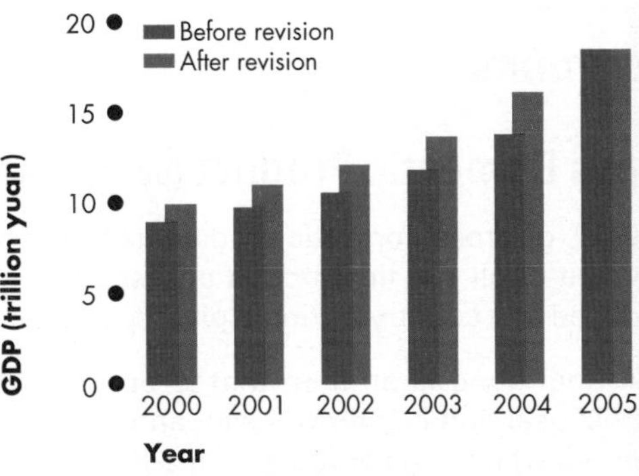

Figure 1 China's GDP before and after revision

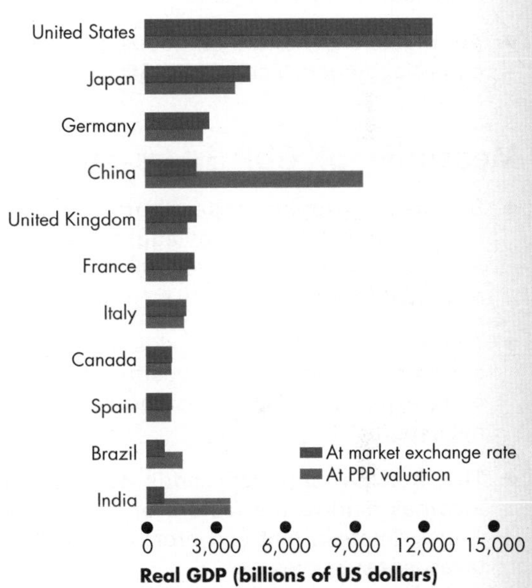

Figure 2 The size of national economies in 2005

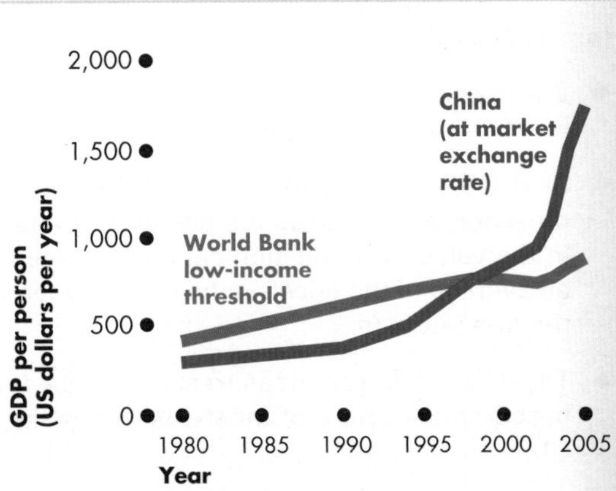

Figure 3 Income per person in China

Summary

Key Points

Gross Domestic Product (pp. 470–474)

- GDP, or gross domestic product, is the market value of all the final goods and services produced in a country during a given period.
- A final good is an item that is bought by its final user and it contrasts with an intermediate good, which is a component of a final good.
- GDP is calculated by using the expenditure and income totals in the circular flow model of expenditure and income.
- Aggregate expenditure on goods and services equals aggregate income and GDP.

Measuring UK GDP (pp. 475–476)

- Because aggregate expenditure, aggregate income and the value of aggregate output are equal, we can measure GDP by either the expenditure approach or the income approach.
- The expenditure approach adds together consumption expenditure, investment, government expenditure on goods and services and net exports.
- The income approach adds together the incomes paid to the factors of production – wages, interest, rent and profit – and indirect taxes less subsidies.

Measuring Economic Growth (pp. 477–479)

- We measure economic growth by comparing real GDP across a number of years.
- Real GDP is measured by a chained volume measure, which shows the percentage change in the value of production each year based on an average of the prices in the current year and the previous year.
- The GDP deflator measures the price level based on the prices of the items that make up GDP.

The Uses and Limitations of Real GDP (pp. 480–483)

- Real GDP is used to compare economic welfare over time and across countries and to access the phase of the business cycle.
- Real GDP is not a perfect measure of economic welfare. It excludes household and underground production, environmental damage and the value of health, life expectancy, leisure time, and political freedom and social justice.
- Fluctuations of real GDP provide a good indication of the phases of the business cycle.

Key Figure and Tables

Key Terms

Problems

Tests, Study Plan and Solutions* 

1 The figure below shows the flows of expenditure and income on Lotus Island. During 2005: *A* was £10 million; *B* was £30 million; *C* was £12 million; *D* was £15 million; and *E* was £3 million. Calculate:

a Aggregate expenditure.

b Aggregate income.

c GDP.

d Government budget deficit.

e Household saving.

f Government saving.

g Foreign borrowing.

h National saving.

2 In problem 1, during 2006: *A* was £10 million; *B* was £50 million; *C* was £15 million; *D* was £15 million; and *E* was –£5 million. Calculate the quantities in problem 1 during 2006.

3 Martha owns a copy shop that has 10 copiers. One copier wears out each year and is replaced. In addition, this year Martha will expand her business to 14 copiers. Calculate Martha's initial capital stock, depreciation, gross investment, net investment and final capital stock.

4 Martha in problem 3 buys paper from XYZ Paper Mills. Is Martha's expenditure on paper part of GDP? If not, how does the value of paper Martha buys get counted in GDP?

5 In the United Kingdom in 2005:

Item	Billions of pounds
Wages paid to labour	685
Consumption expenditure	791
Taxes	394
Transfer payments	267
Profits	273
Investment	209
Government expenditure	267
Exports	322
Saving	38
Imports	366

a Calculate GDP in the United Kingdom and explain whether you used the expenditure approach or the income approach.

b How was investment financed in 2005?

6 Tropical Republic produces only bananas and coconuts. The base year is 2006. The table gives the quantities produced and the prices.

	2005	2006
Quantities		
Bananas	1,000	1,100
Coconuts	500	525
Prices		
Bananas	£0.20 each	£0.30 each
Coconuts	£1.00 each	£0.80 each

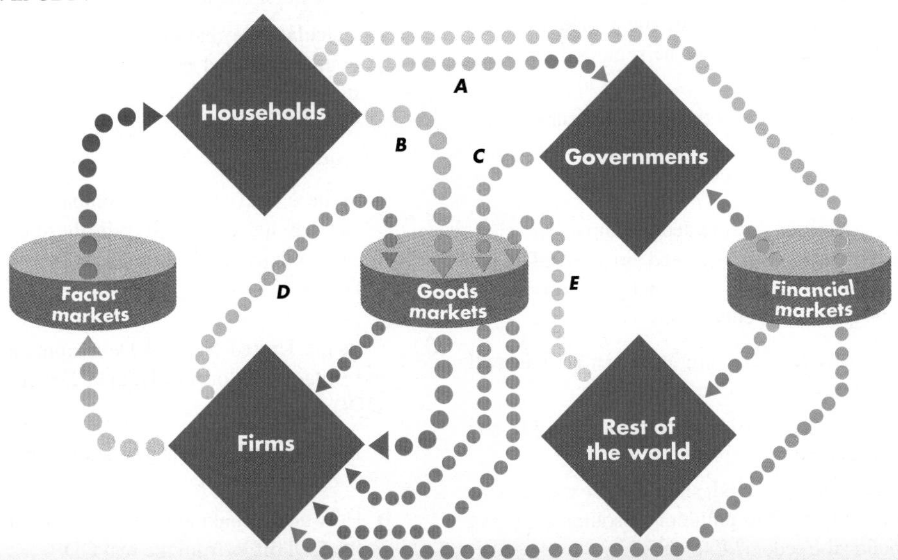

* Solutions to odd-numbered problems are provided.

a Calculate nominal GDP in 2005 and 2006.

b Calculate real GDP in 2006 using the base-year prices method.

c What is the GDP deflator in 2006?

7 Tropical Republic (in problem 6) decides to use the chained volume measure method to calculate real GDP. Using this method:

a Calculate the growth rate of real GDP in 2006.

b The GDP deflator in 2006.

c Compare and comment on the differences in real GDP calculated using the base-year prices and the chain volume measure methods.

Critical Thinking

1 Study *Reading Between the Lines* on pp. 484–485 and then answer the following questions:

a How much has China's GDP been revised upwards in 2005?

b What is the reason for the upward revision?

c What position has the revised measure of GDP put China into in the world economic ranking using market exchange rates as the valuation method?

d What position has the revised measure of GDP put China into in the world economic ranking using PPP as the valuation method?

e Which method of valuation do you think provides the more accurate account of China's real GDP and the real GDP of other countries?

f Why, despite being one of the world's largest economies, can China not be regarded as a rich economy?

g What problems do you think the inaccurate measurement of GDP poses for the government of China in formulating economic policy?

2 The United Nations has created a Human Development Index (HDI) that is based on real GDP per person, life expectancy at birth and indicators of the quality and quantity of education.

a Explain why the HDI might be better than real GDP as a measure of economic welfare.

b Which items in the HDI are part of real GDP and which items are not in real GDP?

c Do you think the HDI should be expanded to include items such as pollution, resource depletion and political freedom? Explain why.

d Are there any other factors that influence economic welfare that you think should be included in a comprehensive measure?

Web Activities

Links to Websites

1 Visit the Office for National Statistics and obtain data on GDP and the components of aggregate expenditure and aggregate income for the United Kingdom. The data are in constant prices (real GDP) and in current market prices (nominal GDP).

a What is the value of nominal GDP in the most recent quarter?

b What is the value of real GDP in the most recent quarter using the chain volume measure?

c What is the GDP deflator in the most recent quarter?

d What is the value of real GDP in the same quarter the previous year?

e By how much has real GDP changed over this last year? (Express your answer as a percentage.)

f Did real GDP increase or decrease and what does the change tell you about the state of the economy over this last year?

2 Visit the International Monetary Fund's World Economic Outlook Database. There, you can obtain economic data for 181 countries going back to 1980.

a Obtain the data series called "Gross domestic product per capita, constant prices, national currency" and "Gross domestic product based on purchasing-power-parity (PPP) per capita GDP, current international dollar" for the United Kingdom and any three other countries.

b Calculate the real GDP growth rates for the four countries based on the two different real GDP measures.

c Make a time-series graph of the eight real GDP growth rates.

d Write a brief report that compares the growth and fluctuations in real GDP in these economies and the similarities and differences that arise when PPP is used.

3 Visit the United Nations Development Programme and obtain data on the Human Development Index (HDI).

a For the countries that you studied in Web Activity 2, obtain the HDI.

b How do the rankings of the four countries based on the HDI differ from the real GDP?

c Write a brief report that assesses whether the HDI provides a better assessment of a country's economic welfare than does GDP.

CHAPTER 22

Monitoring Jobs and the Price Level

After studying this chapter you will be able to:

- ◆ Define the unemployment rate, the economic activity rate, the employment rate, aggregate hours and the real wage rate
- ◆ Describe the sources of unemployment, its duration, the groups most affected by it and how it fluctuates over the business cycle
- ◆ Explain how we measure the price level and the inflation rate

Vital Signs

Each month, we track the the course of employment and unemployment as measures of economic health. How do we measure employment and unemployment? What does the unemployment rate tell us? Is it a reliable vital sign for the economy?

Having a good job that pays a decent wage is only one half of the equation that translates into a good standard of living. The other half is the cost of living. We track the cost of the items we buy with two other numbers that are published every month: the CPI and RPI. How are these numbers calculated, and do they provide a good guide to the changes in our cost of living?

These are the questions we study in this chapter. And at the end of the chapter in *Reading Between the Lines*, we put the spotlight on the CPI and RPI.

Jobs and Wages

The state of the labour market has a large impact on our incomes and our lives. We become concerned when jobs are hard to find and more relaxed when they are plentiful. But we want a good job, which means that we want a well-paid and interesting job. You are now going to learn how economists monitor the health of the labour market.

Labour Force Survey

Every working day, interviewers employed by the Social and Vital Statistics Division of the Office for National Statistics contact close to 1,000 households (60,000 in a three-month period) and ask them questions about the age and labour market status of the household's members. This survey is called the Labour Force Survey. The Office for National Statistics (ONS) uses the information obtained from the Labour Force Survey (LFS) to describe the changing anatomy of the labour market.

Figure 22.1 shows the population categories used by the ONS and the relationships among them. The population divides into two groups: the working-age population and others. The **working-age population** is the total number of men aged 16 to 64 and women aged 16 to 59 who are not in prison, hospital or some other form of institutional care.

Members of the working-age population are either economically active or economically inactive. The **economically active** – also called the **workforce** – are people who have a job or are willing and able to take a job. The **economically inactive** are people who don't want a job. Most of the economically inactive are in full-time education or have retired.

The economically active (people in the workforce) are either employed or unemployed. To be counted as employed in the LFS, a person must have either a full-time job or a part-time job. A student who does part-time work while at college is counted as employed. To be counted as *un*employed in the LFS, people must be available for work within the two weeks following their interview and must be in one of three categories:

1 Without work, but having made specific efforts to find a job within the previous four weeks.

2 Waiting to be called back to a job from which they have been laid off.

3 Waiting to start a new job within 30 days.

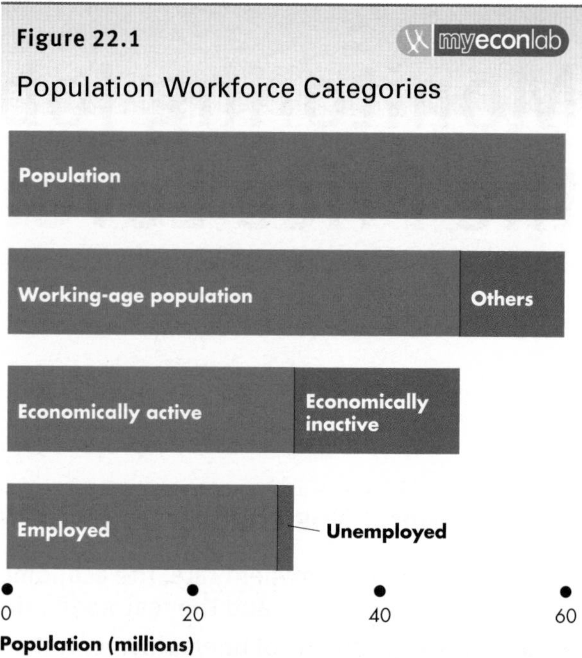

The population is divided into the working-age population and the young and institutionalized. The working-age population is divided into those who are economically active (in the workforce) and those who are economically inactive. The economically active are either employed or unemployed.

Source of data: Office for National Statistics.

People in the working-age population who are neither employed nor unemployed are classified as economically inactive.

In 2006, the population of the United Kingdom was 59.4 million. There were 11.2 million below or above working age or living in institutions. So the working-age population in 2006 was 48.2 million. Of this number, 17.5 million were economically inactive (not in the workforce). The remaining 30.7 million were economically active. Of the economically active, 29 million were employed and 1.7 million were unemployed.

Three Labour Market Indicators

The Office of National Statistics calculates three indicators of the state of the labour market which are shown in Figure 22.2. They are:

- The unemployment rate
- The economic activity rate
- The employment rate

The Unemployment Rate

The amount of unemployment is an indicator of the extent to which people who want jobs can't find them. The **unemployment rate** is the percentage of economically active people who are unemployed.

$$\text{Unemployment rate} = \frac{\text{Number of people unemployed}}{\text{Workforce}} \times 100$$

and

$$\text{Workforce} = \text{Number employed} + \text{Number unemployed}$$

In the United Kingdom in 2006, the number of people employed was 29 million and the number unemployed was 1.7 million. By using the above equations, the workforce was 30.7 million (29 million plus 1.7 million) and the unemployment rate was 5.5 per cent (1.7 million divided by 30.7 million, multiplied by 100).

Figure 22.2 shows the unemployment rate (orange line and plotted against the right scale) between 1966 and 2006. The average unemployment rate was 2.3 per cent during the 1960s and 1970s but 8.9 per cent during the 1980s and 1990s. The unemployment rate fluctuates and reached peak values at the end of recessions in 1980–1982 and 1990–1992.

The Economic Activity Rate

The number of people in the workforce is an indicator of the willingness of the people of working age to take jobs. The **economic activity rate** is the percentage of the working-age population who are economically active. They are the members of the workforce.

$$\text{Economic activity rate} = \frac{\text{Workforce}}{\text{Working-age population}} \times 100$$

In 2006, the workforce was 30.7 million and the working-age population was 48.2 million. By using the above equation, you can calculate the economic activity rate. It was 63.7 per cent (30.7 million divided by 48.2 million, multiplied by 100).

Figure 22.2 shows the economic activity rate (graphed in red and plotted against the left scale). It rose slightly from 61 per cent in 1966 to 63.5 per cent in 2006. It also had some mild fluctuations, which result from unsuccessful job seekers becoming discouraged workers.

Discouraged workers are people who are available and willing to work but who have stopped actively looking for jobs in the past four weeks. These workers often temporarily leave the workforce during a recession and re-enter during an expansion. Fluctuations in the economic activity rate give an estimate of the number of discouraged workers.

Figure 22.2

myeconlab

Employment, Unemployment and Economic Activity Rates: 1966–2006

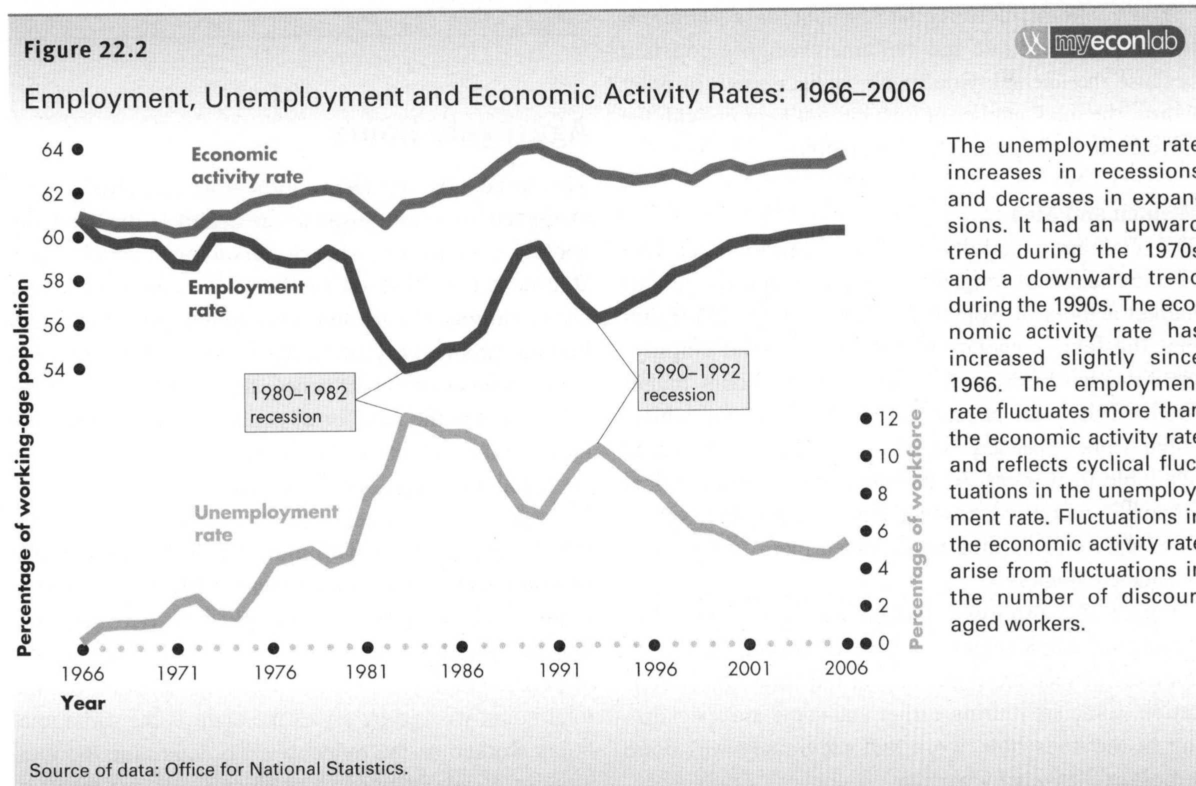

The unemployment rate increases in recessions and decreases in expansions. It had an upward trend during the 1970s and a downward trend during the 1990s. The economic activity rate has increased slightly since 1966. The employment rate fluctuates more than the economic activity rate and reflects cyclical fluctuations in the unemployment rate. Fluctuations in the economic activity rate arise from fluctuations in the number of discouraged workers.

Source of data: Office for National Statistics.

The Employment Rate

The number of people of working age who have jobs is an indicator of the availability of jobs and the degree of match between people's skills and jobs. The **employment rate** is the percentage of the people of working age who have jobs. That is:

$$\text{Employment rate} = \frac{\text{Number of people employed}}{\text{Working-age population}} \times 100$$

In 2006, the number of people employed in the United Kingdom was 29 million and the working-age population was 48.2 million. By using the above equation, you can calculate the employment rate. It was 60.2 per cent (29 million divided by 48.2 million, multiplied by 100).

Figure 22.2 shows the UK employment rate (graphed in blue and plotted against the left scale). It fell slightly from 60.9 per cent in 1966 to 60.1 per cent in 2006, but it has fluctuated and reached a trough of 54.4 per cent in 1983. The increase in the employment rate since 1983 means that the economy has created jobs at a faster rate than the working-age population has grown. This labour market indicator also fluctuates, and its fluctuations coincide with but are opposite to those in the unemployment rate. The employment rate falls during a recession and increases during an expansion.

The economic activity rate has increased whereas the employment rate has remained roughly constant because the unemployment rate has increased. In other words, the total number of jobs has not kept up with the increase in the working-age population.

Women and Men

The economic activity rate and employment rate obscure an interesting difference between the labour market activity of women and men. Figure 22.3 shows that the female economic activity rate and employment rate have increased. Shorter working hours, higher productivity and an increased emphasis on white-collar work expanded the job opportunities and wages available to women. At the same time, technological advances increased productivity in the home, which freed up women's time and enabled them to take jobs outside the home.

Figure 22.3 also shows that the male economic activity rate and employment rate have *decreased*. Increasing numbers of men are remaining in full-time higher education, some are retiring earlier and some are specializing in the household work that previously was done almost exclusively by women.

Figure 22.3 myeconlab

The Changing Face of the UK Labour Market

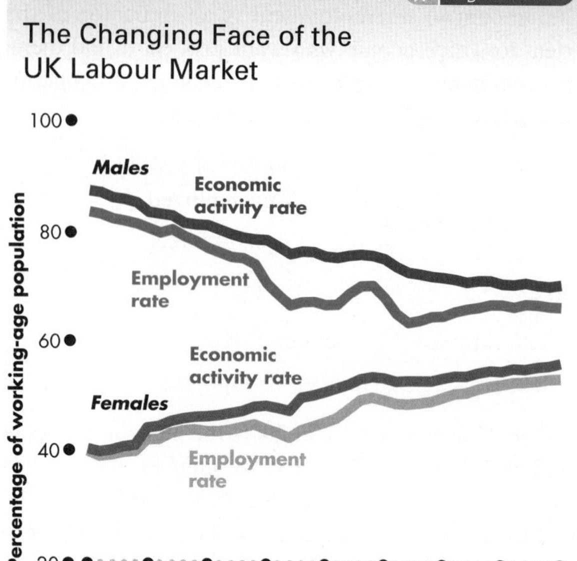

The female economic activity rate and employment rate have increased as more women have taken new white-collar jobs and part-time jobs. The male economic activity rate and employment rate have decreased as more men have remained in higher education, retired earlier and specialized in household work.

Source of data: Office for National Statistics, *Labour Market Trends*, June 2007.

Aggregate Hours

The three labour market indicators that we've just examined are useful signs of the health of the economy and directly measure what matters to most people: jobs. But these indictors don't tell us the quantity of labour used to produce GDP, and we cannot use them to calculate the productivity of labour. Labour productivity is significant because it influences the wages people earn.

The reason the number of people employed does not measure the quantity of labour employed is that all jobs are not all the same. Some jobs are part time and involve just a few hours a week. Others are full time, and some jobs involve regular overtime work. For example, one shop might hire six students who each work for three hours a day. Another shop might hire two full-time workers who each work nine hours a day. The number of people employed in these two shops is eight, but the total hours worked by six of the eight is the same total hours worked as the other two. To determine the total amount of labour used to produce GDP, we measure labour in hours rather than in jobs. **Aggregate hours** are the total number of hours worked by all the people employed, both full time and part time, during a year.

Figure 22.4(a) shows aggregate hours in the UK economy from 1976 to 2006. You can see in the figure that aggregate hours fluctuate a great deal. You can also see a moderate upward trend in aggregate hours: in 2006 they were 7.5 per cent higher than they had been 30 years earlier in 1976.

Aggregate hours have increased but by less than the increase in employment. Between 1976 and 2006, employment increased by 4 million – an increase of 16 per cent. With the employment rate almost constant at about 60 per cent of the working-age population, this increase in employment came from an increase in the working-age population.

Why, when the number of people employed has increased by 4 million or 16 per cent, have aggregate hours increased by only 7.5 per cent? The answer is that average weekly hours per worker have fallen.

Figure 22.4(b) shows average weekly hours per worker. Average hours per worker decreased from around 35.5 hours a week in 1976 to 32 hours a week in 2006. A large decrease occurred during the 1980–1982 recession and an even larger decrease of 2 hours per week occurred during the 1990–1992 recession.

The average working week shortened partly because of a slight decrease the average hours worked by full-time workers, but also because the number of part-time jobs increased faster than the number of full-time jobs.

Fluctuations in aggregate hours and average hours per worker line up with the business cycle. Figure 22.4 highlights the past three recessions during which aggregate hours decreased and average hours per worker decreased more quickly than the trend.

The Real Wage Rate

The **real wage rate** is the quantity of goods and services that an hour's work can buy. It is equal to the money wage rate (pounds per hour) divided by the price level. If we use the GDP deflator to measure the price level, the real wage rate is expressed in 2005 pounds because the GDP deflator is 100 in 2005. The real wage rate is a significant economic variable because it measures the cost of and reward for labour.

Changes in the real wage rate reflect changes in what an hour of work will buy and any effects of inflation have been removed.

What has happened to the real wage rate in the United Kingdom? The answer is not simple because there are

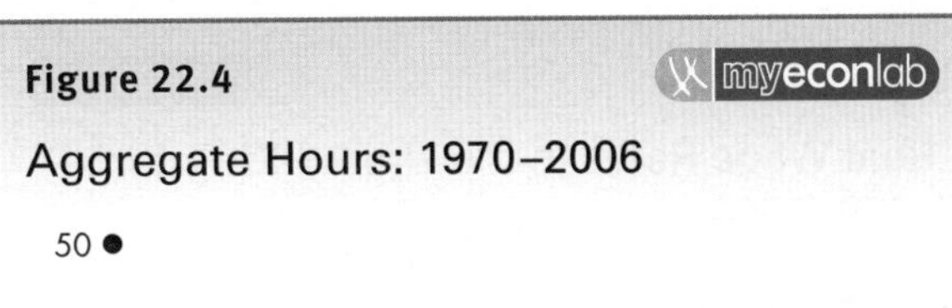

Figure 22.4

Aggregate Hours: 1970–2006

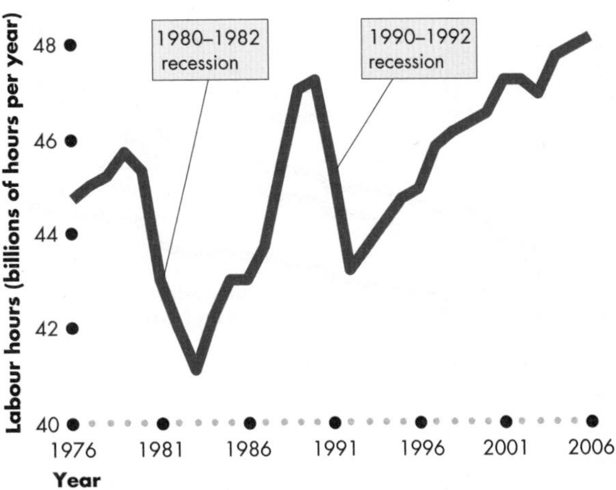

(a) Aggregate hours

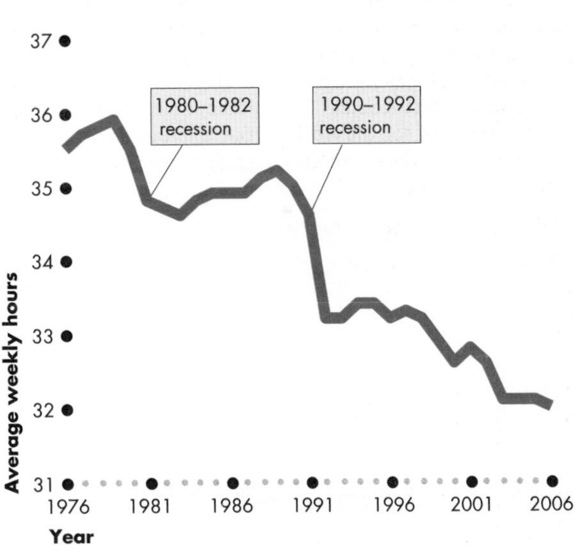

(b) Average weekly hours per person

Aggregate hours, part (a), measure the total labour used to produce real GDP more accurately than does the number of people employed because an increasing proportion of jobs are part time. Between 1976 and 2006, aggregate hours increased by 7.5 per cent. Fluctuations in aggregate hours coincide with the business cycle. Aggregate hours have increased by less than the increase in employment because the average working week in part (b) has shortened.

Sources of data: Office for National Statistics, *Labour Market Trends*, June 2007; and authors' assumptions.

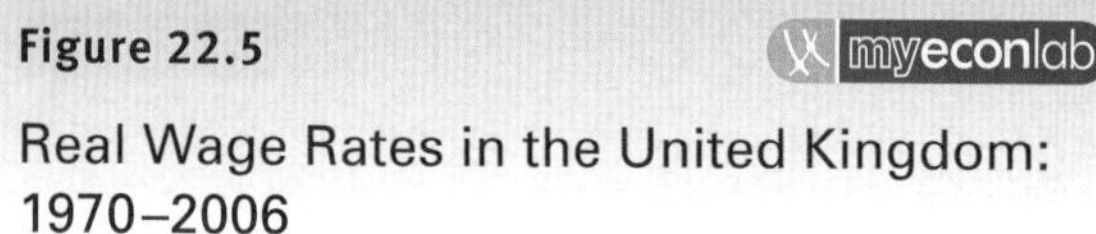

Figure 22.5

Real Wage Rates in the United Kingdom: 1970–2006

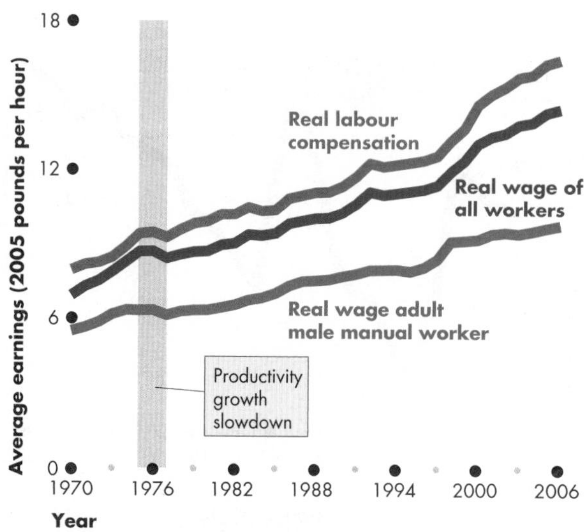

Three measures of the average hourly real wage rate show an upward trend. All three measures also show the productivity growth slowdown of the mid-1970s and the acceleration of earnings growth during the 1990s. The highest measure (red line) includes all benefits and is the broadest measure. The middle measure (blue line) is an average for all workers but excludes non-wage benefits. The lowest measure (green line) covers only manual workers.

Sources of data: Office for National Statistics; and authors' assumptions.

several alternative ways of estimating the real wage rate. We will look at the three alternative measures.

Average Hourly Earnings of Adult Manual Workers

The Office for National Statistics conducts a periodic survey of the *average hourly earnings of adult manual workers*. This measure of the real wage rate is useful because it is readily available and frequently updated. But it does not cover the entire workforce, so it is not as useful as broader measures.

In 2005 pounds, this measure of the hourly real wage was £5.49 in 1970 and £9.76 in 2006 – an increase of 77.8 per cent over the 36 years or an average increase of 1.5 per cent per year. The green line in Figure 22.5 shows the history of this wage rate.

Total Wages and Salaries per Hour

A second measure of the hourly real wage rate is based on the national income accounts. It is calculated by dividing total wages and salaries by aggregate hours. This measure of the hourly wage rate is broader than the first and includes the incomes of all types of labour, whether their rate of pay is calculated by the hour or not. It includes managers and supervisors as well as manual workers. The blue line in Figure 22.5 shows this measure in a sustained upward trend over the 36-year period.

Total Labour Compensation per Hour

An increasing proportion of the total labour cost takes the form of employer's add-on costs, such as employer's National Insurance contributions and graduated pension contributions. To take this trend into account, we use a third measure of the hourly real wage rate, which equals *real labour compensation* – wages, salaries and supplements – divided by aggregate hours. This measure is the most comprehensive one available, and it shows that the average hourly wage rate has increased.

All three measures of the real wage rate show that there was a common slowdown coinciding with the productivity growth slowdown of the mid-1970s. And all three show a surge during the 1990s.

Review Quiz

Study Plan 22.1

1. What are the trends in the unemployment rate, the economic activity rate and the employment rate?
2. How do the unemployment rate, economic activity rate and the employment rate fluctuate over the business cycle?
3. Has the female economic activity rate been similar to or different from the male economic activity rate? If they differ, describe how.
4. Why have aggregate hours changed since 1970?
5. How have average hourly real wage rates changed during the 1990s and 2000s?

You've now seen how we measure employment, unemployment, aggregate hours and the real wage rate. Your next task is to study the anatomy of the labour market a bit more deeply and see why unemployment is ever present, even at full employment.

Unemployment and Full Employment

How do people become unemployed, how long do they remain unemployed and who is at greatest risk of becoming unemployed? Let's answer these questions by looking at the anatomy of unemployment.

The Anatomy of Unemployment

People become unemployed if they:

1 Lose their jobs
2 Leave their jobs
3 Enter or re-enter the workforce

People end a spell of unemployment if they:

1 Are hired or recalled
2 Withdraw from the workforce

People who are laid off, either permanently or temporarily, from their jobs are called *job losers*. Some job losers become unemployed but some immediately withdraw from the workforce. People who voluntarily leave their jobs are called *job leavers*. Like job losers, some job leavers become unemployed and search for a better job, whereas others withdraw from the workforce temporarily or permanently retire from work.

People who enter or re-enter the workforce are called *entrants* and *re-entrants*. Entrants are mainly people who have just left school. Some entrants get a job straight away and are never unemployed, but many spend time searching for their first job and during this period they are unemployed.

Re-entrants are people who have previously withdrawn from the workforce. Most of these people are formerly discouraged workers or women returning to the labour market after an extended absence while raising a family. Figure 22.6 shows these labour market categories.

Let's see how much unemployment arises from the three different ways in which people can become unemployed.

The Sources of Unemployment

Figure 22.7 (overleaf) shows the proportion of unemployment by reason for becoming unemployed. During the 1990s when when the average unemployment rate was 8.2 per cent, 58 per cent of the unemployed were job losers and 28 per cent were entrants and re-entrants. In 2000, when the unemployment rate was 5.6 per cent, job losers were 37 per cent of the unemployed and 49 per cent were entrance and re-entrants.

Job leavers are the smallest and most stable source of unemployment. On any given day in 2000, 14 per cent of people unemployed were job leavers. The willingness to leave a job and look for a new one varies only very slightly with the unemployment rate. In the 1990s, when the unemployment rate averaged 8.2 per cent, the percentage of people who were unemployed because they had left their jobs was the same as it was in 2000 when the unemployment rate was only 5 per cent.

Figure 22.6 myeconlab

Labour Market Flows

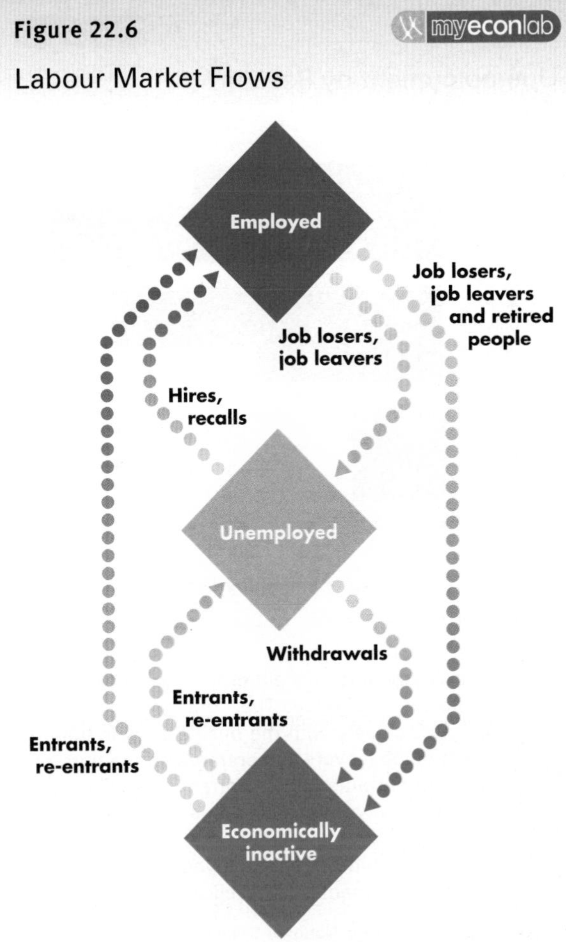

Unemployment results from employed people losing or leaving their jobs (job losers and job leavers) and from people entering the workforce (entrants and re-entrants). Unemployment ends because people get hired or recalled or because they withdraw from the workforce.

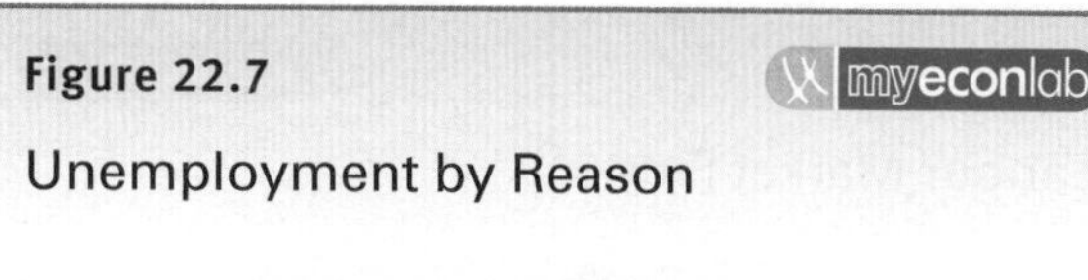

Figure 22.7

Unemployment by Reason

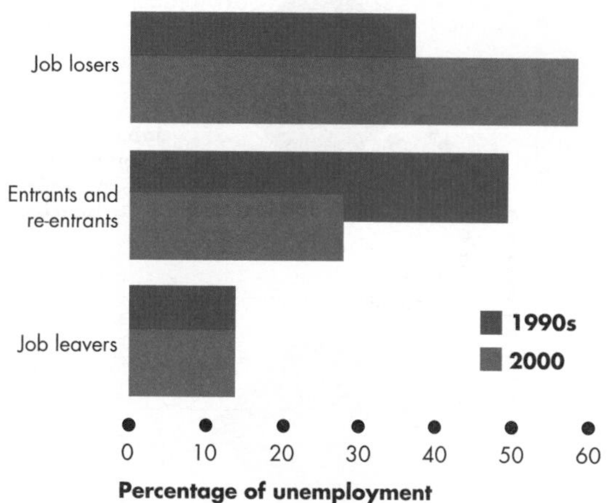

Most unemployment results either from job loss or from re-entry into the workforce. The number of job losers fluctuates more closely with the business cycle than do the numbers of job leavers and entrants and re-entrants. The number of entrants and re-entrants also fluctuates with the business cycle because some workers become discouraged and leave the workforce. Job leavers are the least common type of unemployed people and this source of unemployment is not cyclical.

Source of data: Office for National Statistics, *The Labour Force Survey*.

Figure 22.8

Unemployment by Duration

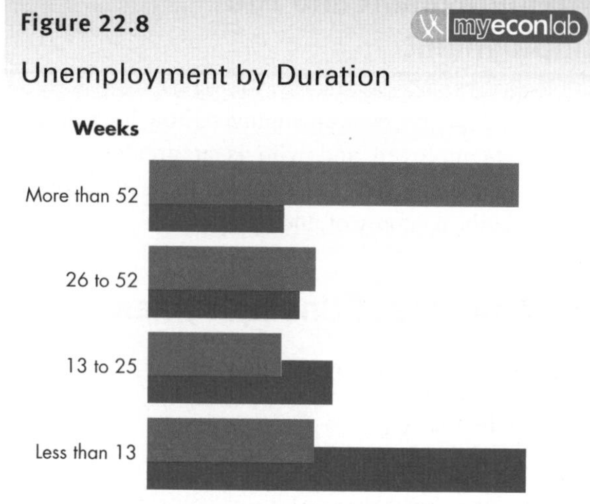

At a business cycle peak (low unemployment), 45 per cent of unemployment lasts for under 13 weeks, 22 per cent lasts for 13–25 weeks, 18 per cent lasts for 26–52 weeks and 16 per cent lasts for one year or more. At a business cycle trough (high unemployment), only 20 per cent of unemployment lasts for under 13 weeks, 16 per cent lasts for 13–25 weeks, 20 per cent lasts for 26–52 weeks and 44 per cent lasts for one year or more.

Sources of data: Office for National Statistics, *The Labour Force Survey*; and Quantime Ltd.

The Duration of Unemployment

Some people are unemployed for a week or two, and others are unemployed for periods of a year or more. Figure 22.8 examines the duration of unemployment at the peak and the trough of the business cycle. We can see that the proportion of the unemployed who were jobless for under 13 weeks is higher in the peak than in the trough and the proportion who were jobless for more than 13 weeks is lower in the peak than in the trough.

People who have been unemployed for over one year experience *long-term unemployment*. In the peak of 1989, 16 per cent of the jobless population were classified as long-term unemployed; in the trough of 1992, that proportion increased to 44 per cent. The proportion of the long-term unemployed has remained stubbornly in excess of 16 per cent over the business cycle. The high proportion of people who experience long-term unemployment presents a serious social problem both in the United Kingdom and in the European Union.

The Demographics of Unemployment

Figure 22.9 shows unemployment for different demographic and ethnic groups. Figure 22.9(a) shows that the high unemployment rates occur among young workers, especially teenagers and ethnic minority groups, especially blacks. In the third quarter of 2006, the unemployment rate of all ethnic minorities was 12 per cent but for blacks it was 15 per cent compared with whites for whom it was only 5.1 per cent. Teenagers also have a higher than average unemployment rate. In 2006, the unemployment rate of all 16–17 year-olds was 25.4 per cent, whereas that of 18–24 year-olds was 12.7 per cent.

Figure 22.9(b) shows that the gap between white and non-white unemployment rates increases in the trough and decreases in the peak .

Why are teenage unemployment rates so high? There are three reasons. First, young people are still in the process of discovering what they are good at and trying different lines of work. So they leave their jobs more

Figure 22.9 myeconlab

Unemployment by Demographic Group

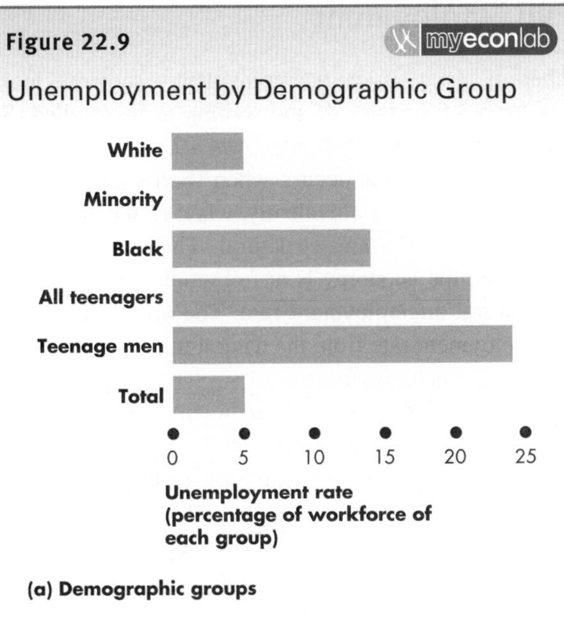

(a) Demographic groups

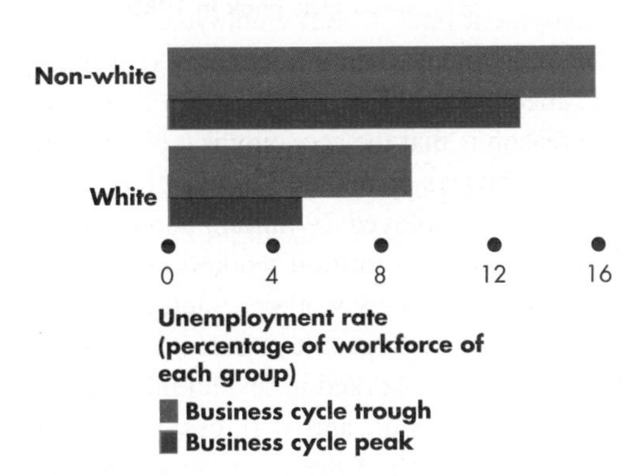

(b) Ethnic groups

Teenagers experience unemployment rates nearly five times higher than the average, and unemployment among blacks is nearly three times the average. Even at a business cycle trough, when unemployment is at its highest rate, the ratio of non-white to white unemployment is 1.7.

Source of data: Office for National Statistics, *Labour Market Trends*, December 2003.

frequently than older workers. Second, firms sometimes hire teenagers on a short-term trial basis. So the rate of job loss is higher for teenagers than for other people. Third, most teenagers are not in the workforce but are at school. If we count being in full-time education as having a job, the true teenage unemployment rate is much lower than the reported teenage unemployment rate.

Ethnic minorities' unemployment rates are higher than white unemployment rates. One reason is that ethnic minorities face unequal opportunities and possible discrimination in the labour market. In the peak of the business cycle, unemployment among non-whites is 2.6 times higher than unemployment among whites. Even in the trough of the business cycle, when unemployment is higher all round, the ratio of non-white to white unemployment falls to only 1.7.

Types of Unemployment

Unemployment is classified into three types that are based on its sources. They are:

- Frictional unemployment
- Structural unemployment
- Cyclical unemployment

Frictional Unemployment

The unemployment that arises from normal labour turnover – from people entering and leaving the workforce and from the ongoing creation and destruction of jobs – is called **frictional unemployment**. Frictional unemployment is a permanent and healthy phenomenon in a dynamic growing economy.

The unending flow of people into and out of the workforce and the processes of job creation and job destruction create the need for people to search for jobs and for businesses to search for workers. Businesses always have unfilled jobs and people are always seeking jobs. Look in your local newspaper and you will see that there are always some jobs being advertised. Businesses don't usually hire the first person who applies for a job, and unemployed people don't usually take the first job that comes their way. Instead, both firms and workers spend time searching out what they believe will be the best match available. By this process of search, people can match their own skills and interests with the available jobs and find a satisfying job and income. While these unemployed people are searching, they are frictionally unemployed.

The amount of frictional unemployment depends on the rate at which people enter and re-enter the workforce and on the rate at which jobs are created and destroyed. During the 1970s, the amount of frictional unemployment increased as a consequence of the post-war baby boom that began during the 1940s. By the late 1970s, the baby boom had created a bulge in the number of people leaving school. As these people entered the workforce, the amount of frictional unemployment increased.

The amount of frictional unemployment is also influenced by the level of unemployment benefits. The greater the number of people covered by unemployment benefits and the more generous the benefits, the longer is the average time taken in job search and the greater is the amount of frictional unemployment. Studies of variations in unemployment rates and benefits across the member states of the European Union show this factor to be important.

Structural Unemployment

The unemployment that arises when changes in technology or international competition change the skills needed to perform jobs or change the location of jobs is called **structural unemployment**. Structural unemployment usually lasts longer than frictional unemployment because workers must usually retrain and possibly relocate to find a job. For example, on the day the shipyards in the Upper Clyde announced the loss of 600 jobs, a computer chip company in Gwent announced the creation of 750 new jobs. The unemployed former shipyard workers remained unemployed for several months until they moved home, retrained and got one of the new jobs created in other parts of the country.

Structural unemployment is painful, especially for older workers for whom the best available option might be to retire early or to take a lower-skilled, lower-paid job. For example, a Humberside shipyard worker who is made redundant may reluctantly remain unemployed rather than retrain, take a lower wage for another type of job, or move south to where new jobs are being created.

At some times the amount of structural unemployment is modest. At other times it is large and at such times, structural unemployment can become a serious long-term problem. It was especially large during the late 1970s and early 1980s. During those years, oil price hikes and an increasingly competitive international environment destroyed jobs in traditional industries. Structural unemployment was also present during the early 1990s as many businesses "downsized".

Cyclical Unemployment

The fluctuating unemployment over the business cycle is **cyclical unemployment**. Cyclical unemployment increases during a recession and decreases during an expansion. A worker in a car component factory who is laid off because the economy is in a recession and who gets rehired some months later when the expansion begins has experienced cyclical unemployment.

Full Employment

There is always *some* unemployment – someone looking for a job or laid off and waiting to be recalled. So what do we mean by *full employment*?

Full employment occurs when there is no cyclical unemployment or, equivalently, when all the unemployment is frictional and structural. The unemployment rate when the economy is at full employment is called the **natural unemployment rate**. The divergence of the unemployment rate from the natural unemployment rate is cyclical unemployment.

There can be quite a lot of unemployment at full employment, and the terms "full employment" and "natural unemployment rate" are examples of technical economic terms that do not correspond with everyday language. For most people – and especially for unemployed workers – there is nothing *natural* about unemployment.

So why do economists call a situation with a lot of unemployment one of "full employment"? And why is the unemployment when the economy is at full employment called "natural"?

The reason is that the economy is a complex mechanism that is always changing. For example, in 2006, the UK economy employed 29 million people. During that year, about a half a million workers retired and more than half a million new workers entered the workforce. Another million or so people re-entered the workforce.

All these people worked in several million businesses that produced goods and services valued at about £1,250 billion. Some of these businesses shrank as they faced increasing competition. Some of them failed, and others expanded. This process of business contraction, failure and expansion created a million or so job losers. All of this change creates frictions and dislocations that are unavoidable – natural. And the unemployment that the process creates is unavoidable.

There is not much controversy about the existence of a natural unemployment rate. Nor is there much disagreement that it changes. The natural unemployment rate arises from the existence of frictional and structural unemployment, and it fluctuates because the frictions and the amount of structural change fluctuate.

But economists don't agree about the size of the natural unemployment rate and the extent to which it fluctuates. Some economists believe that the natural unemployment rate fluctuates frequently and that at times of rapid demographic and technological change the natural unemployment rate can be high. Others think that the natural unemployment rate changes slowly.

Figure 22.10 myeconlab

UK Real GDP and Unemployment: 1986–2006

Real GDP (billions of 2005 pounds, ratio scale)

1,350

950

750

Potential GDP

Real GDP

1986 1991 1996 2001 2006

Year

(a) Real GDP and potential GDP

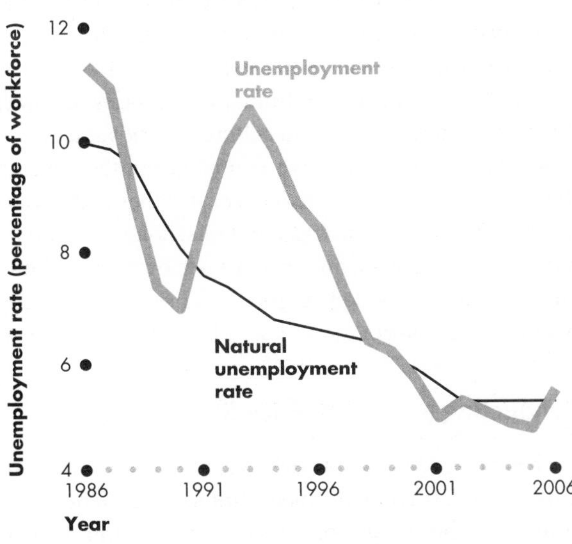

(b) Unemployment and the natural unemployment rate

As real GDP fluctuates around potential GDP in part (a), the unemployment rate fluctuates around the natural unemployment rate in part (b). In the recession of 1990–1992, the unemployment rate peaked at 10 per cent. The labour market reforms of the 1980s helped to reduce the natural unemployment rate. The graph shows one estimate of how far it fell.

Sources of data: Office for National Statistics; and authors' assumptions and calculations.

Real GDP and Unemployment Over the Business Cycle

The quantity of real GDP at full employment is called **potential GDP**. You will study the forces that determine potential GDP in Chapter 24 (pp. 539–540). Over the business cycle, real GDP fluctuates around potential GDP and the unemployment rate fluctuates around the natural unemployment rate. Figure 22.10 illustrates these fluctuations in the United Kingdom between 1986 and 2006 – real GDP in part (a) and the unemployment rate in part (b).

When the economy is at full employment, the unemployment rate equals the natural unemployment rate and real GDP equals potential GDP. When the unemployment rate is less than the natural unemployment rate, real GDP is greater than potential GDP. And when the unemployment rate is greater than the natural unemployment rate, real GDP is less than potential GDP.

Figure 22.10(b) shows an estimate of the natural unemployment rate that is consistent with the estimate of potential GDP in part (a).

Keep in mind that economists do not know the magnitude of either potential GDP or the natural unemployment rate. The picture presented in the figure is only one estimate. In the figure, the natural unemployment rate is 10 per cent in 1986 and it falls steadily through the 1980s and 1990s to 5.2 per cent by 2006. This estimate of the natural unemployment rate in the United Kingdom is one that many, but not all, economists would accept.

Review Quiz

Study Plan 22.2

1. What are the categories of people who become unemployed?
2. Define frictional, structural and cyclical unemployment and provide an example of each type of unemployment.
3. What is the natural unemployment rate?
4. What factors might make the natural unemployment rate change?
5. How does the unemployment rate fluctuate over the business cycle?

Your final task in this chapter is to learn about another vital sign that gets monitored every month, the Retail Prices Index (RPI). What is the RPI, how do we measure it and what does it mean?

Price Level and Inflation

The Office for National Statistics calculates two price indexes every month. They are the **Retail Prices Index (RPI)** and the **Consumer Prices Index (CPI)** and both measure an average of the prices paid by consumers for a fixed "basket" of goods and services.[1] What you learn in this section will help you to make sense of the RPI and the CPI and relate them to your own economic life. The price indexes tell you what has happened to the value of the money in your pocket.

Reading the RPI and CPI

The RPI is defined to equal 100 for a period called the **reference base period**. Currently, the reference base period is January 1987. That is, for January 1987, the RPI equals 100. In January 2006, the RPI was 193.4. This number tells us that the average of the prices paid by households for a particular basket of consumer goods and services was 93.4 per cent higher in January 2006 than it was in January 1987.

In January 2006, the RPI was 193.4 and in January 2005, it was 188.9. These numbers tells us that the average of the prices paid by households for a particular basket of consumer goods and services increased during the year by 4.5 points, or by 2.4 per cent.

The reference base period for the CPI is 2005 and in January 2006, the CPI was 100.5. We read the CPI and calculate percentage changes in it in the same way as you've just seen for the RPI. In January 2005, the CPI was 98.6. The increase in the 12 months was 1.9 index points or a 1.9 per cent increase.

Constructing the RPI and CPI

Constructing the RPI and the CPI is a huge operation that costs millions of pounds and involves three stages:

- Selecting the basket
- Conducting a monthly price survey
- Calculating the price index

Selecting the Basket

The first stage in constructing a price index is to select the "basket" of goods and services that the index will cover. The RPI basket contains the goods and services bought by an average household in the United Kingdom. The idea is to make the relative importance of the items in the RPI basket the same as that in the budget of an average household. For example, because people spend more on housing than on bus rides, the RPI places more weight on the price of housing than on the price of a bus ride.

To be representative of typical households, the RPI basket does not take account of the spending patterns of the 4 per cent of households with the highest incomes or of pensioner households.

The CPI basket is a bit different from the RPI basket and covers *all* expenditure on consumer goods and services made in the United Kingdom by private households, residents of institutions and tourists.

To determine the spending patterns of households and to select the RPI and CPI baskets, the ONS conducts periodic expenditure surveys. These surveys are costly and so are undertaken infrequently. Figure 22.11 shows the RPI and CPI baskets in 2006.

For the RPI, there are five major categories of which by far the largest is housing and household expenditure. Travel and leisure comes next and is larger than food, alcoholic drinks and tobacco combined.

The ONS breaks down each of these categories into ever smaller ones, right down to distinguishing between packaged and loose new potatoes!

The CPI basket contains 12 major categories of which transport, and recreation and culture, are the largest.

As you look at the relative importance of the items in the RPI and CPI baskets, remember that they apply to an *average* household. *Individual* households are spread around the average. Think about your own expenditure and compare the basket of goods and services you buy with the RPI basket.

Conducting a Monthly Price Survey

Each month, ONS employees check 110,000 prices of more than 550 types of goods and services. They visit shops in about 150 places throughout the United Kingdom to see the goods and the prices to ensure accuracy. Because the RPI aims to measure price *changes*, it is important that the prices recorded each month refer to exactly the same item. For example, suppose the price of a packet of biscuits has decreased but a packet now contains fewer biscuits. Has the price of biscuits decreased, remained the same or increased? The ONS price checker must record the details of changes in quality or packaging so that price changes can be isolated from other changes.

[1] A third price index, the Retail Prices Index Excluding Mortgage Interest (RPIX), is also published.

Calculating the Price Index

The RPI and CPI calculations have three steps:

1 Find the cost of the basket at base-period prices.
2 Find the cost of the basket at current-period prices.
3 Calculate the index for the base period and the current period.

Figure 22.11

The RPI and CPI Baskets

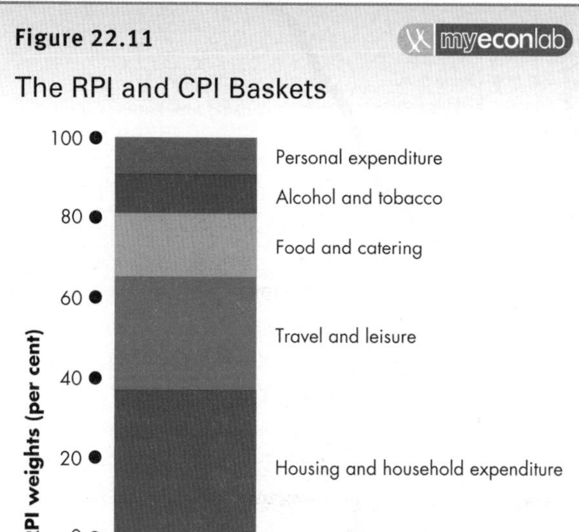

(a) The RPI basket

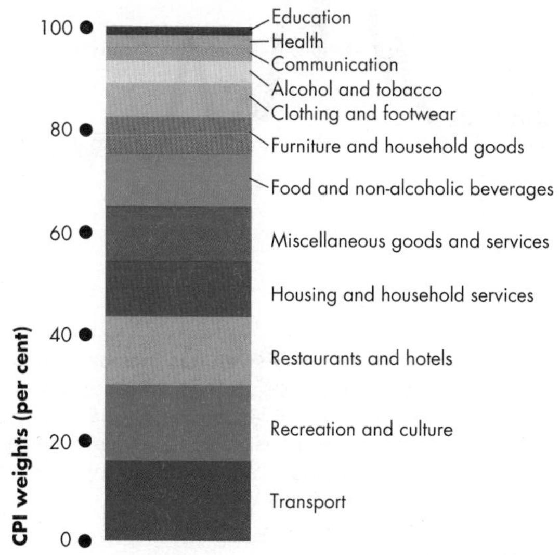

(b) The CPI basket

The RPI basket contains items that a typical household buys. The CPI basket is broader and contains all the consumer items bought in the United Kingdom.

Source of data: Office for National Statistics.

We'll work through these three steps for a simple example of an RPI calculation. Suppose the RPI basket contains only two goods and services: oranges and haircuts. We'll construct an annual price index rather than a monthly index with the reference base period 2006 and the current period 2007.

Table 22.1 shows the quantities in the RPI basket and the prices in the base period and current period. Part (a) contains the data for the base period. In that period, consumers bought 10 oranges at £1 each and 5 haircuts at £8 each. To find the cost of the RPI basket in the base-period prices, multiply the quantities in the basket by the base-period prices. The cost of oranges is £10 (10 at £1 each), and the cost of haircuts is £40 (5 at £8 each). So total cost of the RPI basket in the base period is £50 (£10 + £40).

Part (b) contains the price data for the current period. The price of an orange increased from £1 to £2, which is a 100 per cent increase (£1 ÷ £1 × 100 = 100). The price of a haircut increased from £8 to £10, which is a 25 per cent increase (£2 ÷ £8 × 100 = 25).

A price index provides a way of averaging these price increases by comparing the cost of the basket rather than the price of each item. To find the cost of the RPI basket in the current period, 2007, multiply the quantities in the basket by their 2007 prices. The cost of oranges is £20 (10 at £2 each), and the cost of haircuts is £50 (5 at £10 each). So total cost of the basket at current-period prices is £70 (£20 + £50).

Table 22.1

The RPI: A Simplified Calculation

(a) The cost of the RPI basket at base-period prices: 2006

RPI basket			
Item	**Quantity**	**Price**	**Cost of basket**
Oranges	10	£1	£10
Haircuts	5	£8	£40
Cost of the RPI basket at base-period prices			£50

(b) The cost of the RPI basket at current-period prices: 2007

RPI basket			
Item	**Quantity**	**Price**	**Cost of basket**
Oranges	10	£2	£20
Haircuts	5	£10	£50
Cost of the RPI basket at current-period prices			£70

You've now taken the first two steps towards calculating a RPI: calculating the cost of the RPI basket in the base period and the current period. The third step uses the numbers you've just calculated to find the value of the RPI in 2006 and 2007.

To calculate the RPI, we use the formula:

$$\text{RPI} = \frac{\text{Cost of basket at current-period prices}}{\text{Cost of basket at base-period prices}} \times 100$$

In Table 22.1 you have established that in 2006 the cost of the RPI basket was £50 and in 2007 it was £70. You also know that the base period is 2006. So the cost of the RPI basket at base-period prices is £50. If we use these numbers in the formula above, we can find the RPI for 2006 and 2007. For 2006:

$$\text{RPI in 2006} = \frac{£50}{£50} \times 100 = 100$$

For 2007:

$$\text{RPI in 2007} = \frac{£70}{£50} \times 100 = 140$$

The principles that you've applied in this simplified RPI calculation apply to the more complex calculations performed every month by the ONS.

Measuring Inflation

A major purpose of the RPI is to measure *changes* in the cost of living and in the value of money. To measure these changes, we calculate the **inflation rate**, which is the percentage change in the price level from one year to the next. To calculate the inflation rate, we use the formula:

$$\text{Inflation rate} = \frac{(\text{RPI this year} - \text{RPI last year})}{\text{RPI last year}} \times 100$$

We can use this formula to calculate the inflation rate in 2006. The RPI in December 2005 was 194.1, and the RPI in December 2006 was 202.7. So the inflation rate during 2006 was:

$$\text{Inflation rate} = \frac{(202.7 - 194.1)}{191.4} \times 100$$

$$= 4.4 \text{ per cent}$$

Figure 22.12 myeconlab

The RPI and the Inflation Rate

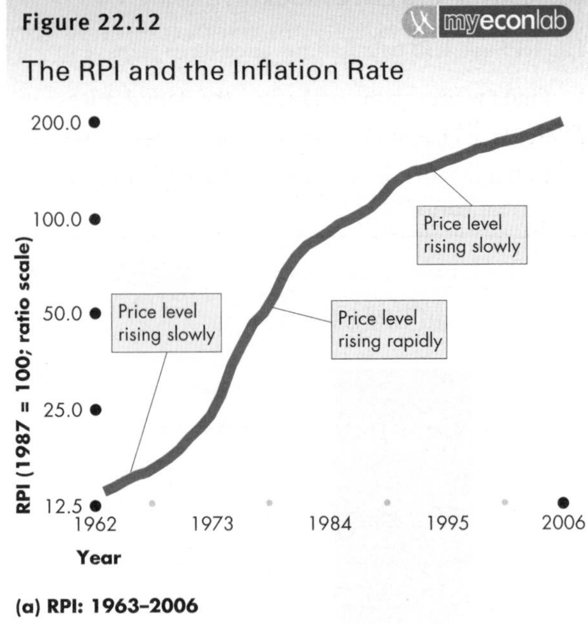

(a) RPI: 1963–2006

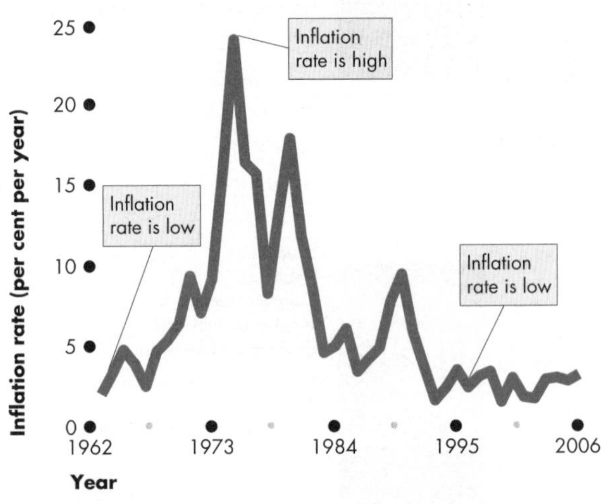

(b) Inflation rate: 1963–2006

In part (a), the RPI (the price level) has increased every year. In part (b), the inflation rate has averaged 5.5 per cent a year. During the 1970s and early 1980s, the inflation rate was high and peaked at 25 per cent a year. But after 1983, the inflation rate fell to an average of 3 per cent a year.

Source of data: Office for National Statistics.

Figure 22.12 shows the RPI and the inflation rate in the United Kingdom during the 44 years between 1962 and 2006. The two parts of the figure are related. The figure shows that when the price *level* in part (a) rises rapidly, the inflation rate in part (b) is high, and when the price level in part (a) rises slowly, the inflation rate in part (b) is low. Notice in part (a) that the RPI increased every year during this period. During the late 1970s and 1980s, the RPI was increasing rapidly, but its rate of increase slowed during the late 1980s and 1990s.

The RPI is not a perfect measure of the price level, and changes in the RPI can overstate the inflation rate. Let's look at the sources of bias in price indexes such as the RPI and CPI against which the ONS must guard.

Biased Price Indexes

The main sources of bias in a price index are:

- New goods bias
- Quality change bias
- Substitution bias

New Goods Bias

New goods keep replacing old goods. For example, CDs have replaced LP records and PCs have replaced typewriters. If you want to compare the price level in 2005 with that in 1975, you somehow have to compare the price of a CD and a computer today with that of an LP and typewriter in 1975. Because CDs and PCs are more expensive today than LPs and typewriters, the arrival of these new goods puts an upward bias into the estimate of the price level.

Quality Change Bias

Most goods undergo constant quality improvement. Cars, computers, CD players and even textbooks get better year after year. Quality improvements often increase the price, but such price increases are not inflation. For example, suppose that a 1999 car is 5 per cent better and costs 5 per cent more than a 1995 car. Adjusted for the quality change, the price of the car has not changed. But in calculating the RPI, the price of the car will have increased by 5 per cent.

Estimates have been made of the quality change bias, especially for obvious changes such as those in cars and computers. Allowing for quality improvements changes the inflation picture by 1 percentage point a year, on average, according to some economists.[2] That is, correctly measured, the inflation rate might be as much as 1 percentage point a year less than the published numbers.

Substitution Bias

A change in the price index measures the percentage change in the price of a *fixed* basket of goods and services. But changes in relative prices lead consumers to seek less costly items. For example, by shopping more frequently at discount shops and less frequently at corner shops, consumers can cut the prices they pay. By using discount fares on airlines, they can cut the cost of travel. This kind of substitution of cheaper items for more costly items is not picked up by the price index. Because consumers make such substitutions, a price index based on a fixed basket overstates the effects of a given price change on the inflation rate.

Some Consequences of Bias in the RPI and CPI

The RPI is also used to calculate increases in pensions and other government outlays. So a bias in the RPI could end up swelling government expenditure (and taxes). The CPI is used by the Bank of England to determine whether the interest rate needs to be raised or lowered. So a bias in the CPI could lead to an inappropriate policy decision.

Mindful of these potentially harmful effects, our price indexes are constructed with the greatest possible care to minimize the biases we've just examined.

Review Quiz

Study Plan 22.3

1. What are the RPI and CPI and how are they calculated?
2. What is the relationship between the RPI and the inflation rate?
3. How might a price index be biased?
4. What problems arise from biased RPI and CPI?

You've now completed your study of the measurement of macroeconomic performance. Your task in the following chapters is to learn what determines that performance and how policy actions might improve it. But first, take a close-up look at the acceleration in inflation in 2006 in *Reading Between the Lines* on pp. 504–506.

[2] S. Checchetti and M. Wynne, "Inflation measurement and the ECB's pursuit of price stability: a first assessment", *Economic Policy*, 37, 2003.

Reading Between the Lines

The Monthly Inflation Rate

The Financial Times, 12 December 2006

FT

UK inflation accelerates as transport costs rise

Jamie Chisholm

The Bank of England's target measure of inflation jumped to a record high last month, as the decline in transport costs slowed and housing costs rose. . . .

The Office for National Statistics said that the consumer price index rose by 0.3 per cent between October and November.

This meant that in the year to November, the CPI climbed by 2.7 per cent, up from 2.4 per cent the previous month and the fastest pace of increase since the series began in January 1997.

This is the seventh successive month that the CPI has been above the Bank's target of 2 per cent, . . . although the measure was projected to spike higher towards the end of the year. . . .

The ONS said that the main cause of the acceleration in inflation was the cost of transport, particularly petrol, which saw prices fall more slowly than they had done for the comparable period last year.

Further upward momentum was provided by increases in utility bills and slower falls in the prices of electronic equipment. . . .

However, Howard Archer [of Global Insight] saw evidence that shop-owners were adding to inflationary pressures by attempting to widen their profit margins.

"While consumer price inflation was pushed up by higher utility prices and unfavourable base effects, the rise in core inflation to 1.6 per cent from 1.4 per cent in October and a low of 0.9 per cent in July will heighten the Bank's concern that retailers are seeking to push through more price rises," he said. . . .

The measure of inflation most used for wage settlements is the Retail Price Index. The RPI, which includes interest payments on mortgages, climbed in the 12 months to November by 3.9 per cent, up from 3.7 per cent in October and the highest reading since May 1998.

The Essence of the Story

- The CPI rose by 0.3 per cent in November and by 2.7 per cent in the year to November.
- The inflation rate has been higher than the target of 2 per cent for seven successive months.
- The ONS says the rise in inflation was caused by transport costs, particularly higher petrol prices.
- Higher utility bills and a slower fall in the prices of electronic goods also contributed.
- The Retail Prices Index (RPI) rose to 3.9 per cent in the 12 months to November 2006 which was the highest level since May 1998.

Economic Analysis

- The CPI and the RPI are index numbers that measure the UK price level.
- Both index numbers are obtained by comparing the price of a basket of goods and services purchased in the United Kingdom in different time periods.
- Figure 1 shows the CPI for each month from January 2003 to November 2006. In January 2003 the CPI was 95.7 and in November 2006 it was 103.4 – an increase of 8 per cent.
- Figure 2 shows the inflation rate measured by both the CPI and the RPI. Both measures show a rise in the inflation rate throughout most of 2006.
- The official target for inflation is 2 per cent a year based on the CPI. But based on the RPI, the inflation rate reached 3.9 per cent a year.
- Wage bargaining for the cost of living is based on the RPI.
- The newspaper article says the main reason for the rise in the CPI is the increase in the cost of transport.
- Figure 3 shows the percentage changes in each component of the CPI basket between October and November 2006 expressed as annualized percentage changes.
- These price changes tell us about the changes in *relative prices*. They do not tell us anything about inflation. Nor do they tell us why the inflation rate increased.
- It is a common mistake in the media to say that the inflation rate increased (or decreased) because a particular price increased (or decreased).
- An increase in the price of petrol has increased the cost of transportation, which increases the relative price of transportation. But as Figure 3 shows, many relative prices have changed.

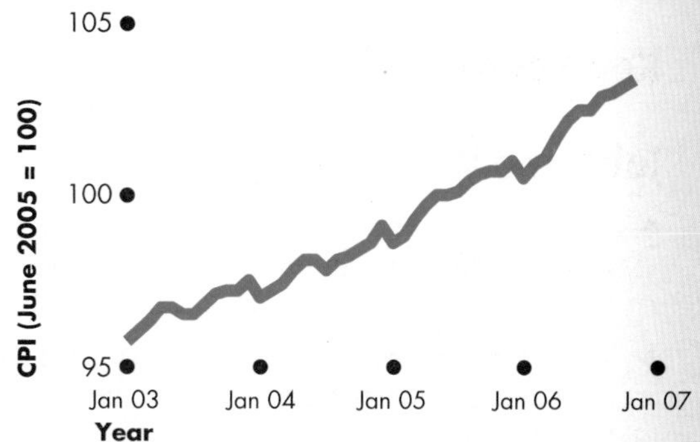

Figure 1 The Consumer Prices Index

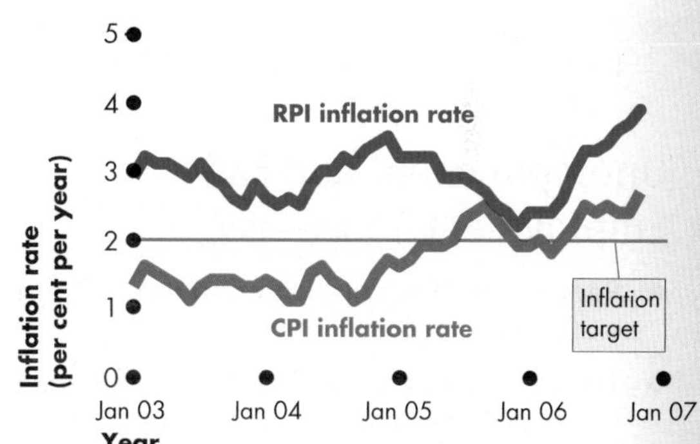

Figure 2 Two measures of the inflation rate

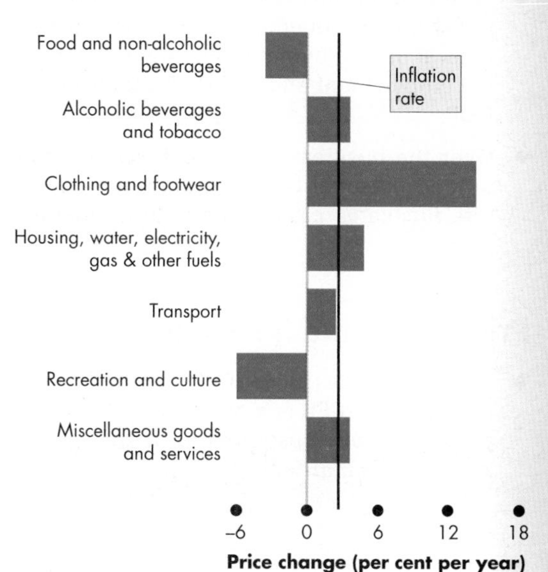

Figure 3 Relative price changes between October and November 2006

Summary

Key Points

Jobs and Wages (pp. 490–494)

- The unemployment rate, the economic activity rate and the employment rate fluctuate with the business cycle.
- The female economic activity rate has increased, but the male economic activity rate has decreased.
- Aggregate hours fluctuate with the business cycle. Average weekly hours per worker have decreased.
- Real hourly wage rates have increased but at a pace that slowed during the 1970s.

Unemployment and Full Employment (pp. 495–499)

- People are constantly entering and leaving the state of unemployment.
- The duration of unemployment fluctuates over the business cycle. But demographic patterns in unemployment are constant.
- Three types of unemployment are frictional, structural and cyclical.
- When all the unemployment is frictional and structural, the unemployment rate equals the natural unemployment rate, the economy is at full employment and real GDP equals potential GDP.
- Over the business cycle, real GDP fluctuates around potential GDP and the unemployment rate fluctuates around the natural unemployment rate.

Price Level and Inflation (pp. 500–503)

- The Retail Prices Index (RPI) and the Consumer Prices Index (CPI) is a measure of the average prices paid by consumers for a specified basket of goods and services.
- The RPI and the CPI are defined to equal 100 in the reference base period.
- The inflation rate is the percentage change in the RPI (or CPI) from one year to the next.
- The RPI and CPI probably overstate the inflation rate because of the bias that arises from new goods, quantity changes, commodity substitution, and outlet substitution.
- The RPI bias increases government outlays and the CPI bias might lead to inappropriate policy.

Key Figures

Key Terms

Problems

Tests, Study Plan and Solutions* 

1 In 2004, the Labour Force Survey measured the UK workforce at 29,839,000, employment at 28,410,000, and the working-age population at 47,324,000. Calculate for 2004:

a The unemployment rate.

b The economic activity rate.

c The employment rate.

2 During 2005, the working-age population increased by 277,000, employment increased by 156,000 and the number of economically active people increased by 41,000. Use the data in problem 1 to calculate the change in unemployment and the change in the number of discouraged workers during 2005.

3 In January 2003, the unemployment rate was 5.1 per cent. In January 2004, the unemployment rate was 4.7 per cent. What do you predict happened between January 2003 and January 2004 to the numbers of:

a Job losers and job leavers?

b Entrants and re-entrants into the workforce?

4 In Botswana, the 2006 Labour Force Survey estimated the working-age population at 798,460 males and 904,369 females. The total employed population was 287,303 males and 261,290 females. The total number of the unemployed was 50,876 males and 63,546 females. Calculate for 2006:

a The number of economically active people.

b The unemployment rate.

c The economic activity rate.

d The employment rate.

e The male economic activity rate, employment rate and unemployment rate.

f The female economic activity rate, employment rate and unemployment rate.

g Compare the values of the male and female labour market indicators.

5 The IMF *World Economic Outlook* reports the following unemployment rates:

Region	May 2005	May 2006
Euro area	8.7	7.9
United States	5.2	4.6
Japan	4.4	4.0

a What do these numbers tell you about the phase of the business cycle in the United States, the Euro area and Japan in May 2006?

b What do you think these numbers tell us about the relative size of the natural unemployment rates in the United States, the Euro area and Japan?

c Do these numbers tell us anything about the relative size of the economically active rates and employment rate in the three regions?

d Why might these unemployment numbers understate or overstate the true amount of unemployment?

6 Statistics South Africa reports the following CPI data:

June 2004 129.2

June 2005 133.8

June 2006 138.6

a What do these numbers tell you about the price level in these three years?

b Calculate the inflation rates for the years ended June 2005 and June 2006.

c How did the inflation rate change in 2006?

d Why might these CPI numbers be biased?

e What might Statistics South Africa do to minimize the bias in the CPI numbers?

7 A typical family on Sandy Island consumes only juice and cloth. Last year, which was the reference base period, the family spent £40 on juice and £25 on cloth. Last year, juice was £4 a bottle and cloth was £5 a length. This year, juice is £4 a bottle and cloth is £6 a length. Calculate

a The RPI basket.

b The RPI in the current year.

c The inflation rate in the current year.

8 The IMF *World Economic Outlook* reports the following price level data (2000 = 100):

Region	2003	2004	2005
Euro area	106.7	109.0	111.4
United States	106.8	109.7	113.4
Japan	98.1	98.1	97.8
Zimbabwe	1,880.5	8,462.1	28,586.6

a Comparing just the Euro area and United States, which had the higher inflation rate before 2004 and which has the higher inflation rate after 2004?

b Describe the path of the price level in Japan.

c Describe the path of the price level in Zimbabwe. Did the inflation rate increase or decrease in 2005?

* Solutions to odd-numbered problems are provided.

Critical Thinking

1 Study *Reading Between the Lines* on pp. 504–505 and then answer the following questions:

a Describe the changes in the CPI that occurred during 2006.

b What has happened to inflation as measured by the CPI and the RPI in 2006?

c Explain the difference between a change in relative price and inflation. Which relative price changed the most in November 2006?

d If you were the reporter writing an article on the inflation figures in November 2006 how would you do it better?

2 The data below show the unemployment rate, *U*, and the OECD estimate of the natural unemployment rate, *U**, for five large economies in 2001 and 2003.

Country	*U* 2001	*U** 2001	*U* 2003	*U** 2003
United States	4.7	5.1	6.0	5.1
United Kingdom	5.0	5.5	4.9	5.2
Germany	7.8	7.2	9.3	7.2
France	8.5	9.2	9.4	9.0
Italy	9.4	9.0	8.6	8.8

a In which countries did the unemployment rate decrease between 2001 and 2003?

b In which countries is the unemployment rate above the natural unemployment rate and in which countries is it below the natural unemployment rate?

c In which countries is real GDP above potential GDP? And in which countries is it below potential GDP?

d If the unemployment rate is below the natural rate, what do you think will happen to the economy if the government does nothing?

e Why do you think the natural unemployment rates are higher in France and Italy than in the United Kingdom?

f If the unemployment rate is above the natural rate, what do you think the government of that country should do about it?

3 You've seen that the average weekly hours have fallen over the years. Do you think that a shorter workweek is a problem or a benefit? Do you expect the average workweek to keep getting shorter? Why or why not?

4 An increasing number of jobs are part-time jobs. Can you think of some reasons for this trend? Who benefits from part-time jobs: the employer, the worker, or both? Explain with examples.

Web Activities

Links to Websites

1 Obtain data on unemployment in your economic region of the United Kingdom.

a What have been the changes in the employment rate, unemployment rate and the economic activity rate in your own region during the past two years?

b On the basis of what you know about your own region, how would you set about explaining these trends?

c Compare unemployment in your region with that in the United Kingdom as a whole.

d Why do you think your region might have a higher or a lower unemployment rate than the UK average?

e Try to identify those industries that have expanded most and those that have shrunk in your region.

f What are the problems in your region's labour market that you think local government and development agencies can solve?

2 Obtain data on the RPI for the United Kingdom and the CPI for the United Kingdom and the other EU countries.

a Describe the changes in the inflation rates of the EU countries during the past two years.

b Which EU countries have had the lowest inflation rates and which have had the highest?

c Why might the price index for one country differ from that of another?

d Compare the inflation rates as measured by the RPI and the CPI for the United Kingdom?

e Why do you think the inflation rates as measured by the RPI and the CPI are different? Is either measure of inflation "correct"? Explain why or why not.

f Suppose that someone proposed replacing the RPI with the CPI for the purpose of linking wage rates and pensions. Who would be in favour of this proposal and who would oppose it. Why?

3 Obtain the most recent data available on the price level in Zimbabwe.

a Describe the changes in the price level during the past two years.

b Describe the changes in the inflation rate during the past two years.

c If the inflation rate in the economy in which you live was as high as it is today in Zimbabwe, what would you do differently to cope with the rapid inflation?

CHAPTER

23

Aggregate Supply and Aggregate Demand

After studying this chapter you will be able to:

- Define and explain what determines aggregate supply
- Define and explain what determines aggregate demand
- Explain macroeconomic equilibrium and the effects of fluctuations in aggregate supply and aggregate demand
- Explain UK economic growth, inflation and the business cycle by using the *AS–AD* model
- Explain the main schools of thought in macroeconomics today

Catching the Wave

If you want a good economic ride, you must catch the wave like a champion surfer. But economic waves are hard to read. What makes the economy ebb and flow in waves around its long-term growth trend? Why do the waves sometimes rise high and then crash, and sometimes rise and roll on a long high? This chapter explains a *model* of real GDP and the price level that summarizes the consensus view of macroeconomists on the sources of economic growth, inflation and the business cycle. *Reading Between the Lines* at the end of the chapter applies this model to the UK economy in 2006.

Aggregate Supply

The aggregate supply–aggregate demand model enables us to understand three features of macroeconomic performance:

1 Growth of potential GDP
2 Inflation
3 Business cycle fluctuations

The model uses the concepts of *aggregate* supply and *aggregate* demand to determine *real GDP* and the *price level* (GDP deflator). We begin by looking at the limits to production that influence aggregate supply.

Aggregate Supply Fundamentals

The *quantity of real GDP supplied* (Y) depends on three factors:

1 The quantity of labour (L)
2 The quantity of capital (K)
3 The state of technology (T)

The influence of these three factors on the quantity of real GDP supplied is described by the **aggregate production function**, which is written as the equation:

$$Y = F(L, K, T)$$

In words, the quantity of real GDP supplied is determined by (is a function F of) the quantities of labour and capital and the state of technology. The larger any L, K or T, the greater is Y.

At any given time, capital and the state of technology are fixed. They depend on decisions made in the past. The population is also fixed. But the quantity of labour is not fixed. It will depend on the decisions made by people and firms about the supply of and demand for labour.

The labour market can be in any one of three states: at full employment, above full employment or below full employment.

Even at full employment, there are always some people looking for jobs and some firms looking for people to hire. The reason is that there is a constant churning of the labour market. Every day, some jobs are destroyed as businesses reorganize or fail. Some jobs are created as new businesses start up or existing ones expand. Some workers decide, for any of a thousand personal reasons, to leave their jobs. And other people decide to start looking for a job. This constant churning in the labour market prevents unemployment from ever disappearing. The unemployment rate at full employment is the *natural unemployment rate*.

Another way to think about full employment is as a state of the labour market in which the quantity of labour demanded equals the quantity supplied. Firms demand labour only if it is profitable to do so. And the lower the wage rate, which is the cost of labour, the greater is the quantity of labour demanded. People supply labour only if doing so is the most valuable use of their time. And the higher the wage rate, which is the return to labour, the greater is the quantity of labour supplied. The wage rate that makes the quantity of labour demanded equal to the quantity of labour supplied is the equilibrium wage rate. At this wage rate, there is full employment.

The quantity of real GDP supplied at full employment is *potential GDP*. Potential GDP depends on the full employment quantity of labour, the quantity of capital and the state of technology.

Over the business cycle, employment fluctuates around full employment and real GDP fluctuates around potential GDP. Real GDP goes below potential GDP in a recession and above potential GDP in an expansion.

To study aggregate supply in different states of the labour market, we distinguish two time frames:

- Long-run aggregate supply
- Short-run aggregate supply

Long-run Aggregate Supply

The economy is constantly bombarded by events that move real GDP away from potential GDP and, equivalently, the unemployment rate away from the natural rate. Following such an event, forces operate to push real GDP back towards potential GDP and restore full employment. The **macroeconomic long run** is a time-frame that is sufficiently long for these forces to succeed so that real GDP equals potential GDP and full employment prevails.

Long-run aggregate supply is the relationship between the quantity of real GDP supplied and the price level when real GDP equals potential GDP. Figure 23.1 illustrates this relationship as the vertical long-run aggregate supply curve, *LAS*. Along this curve, as the price level changes, real GDP remains at potential GDP, which in Figure 23.1 is £1,300 billion. The long-run aggregate supply curve is always vertical and located at potential GDP.

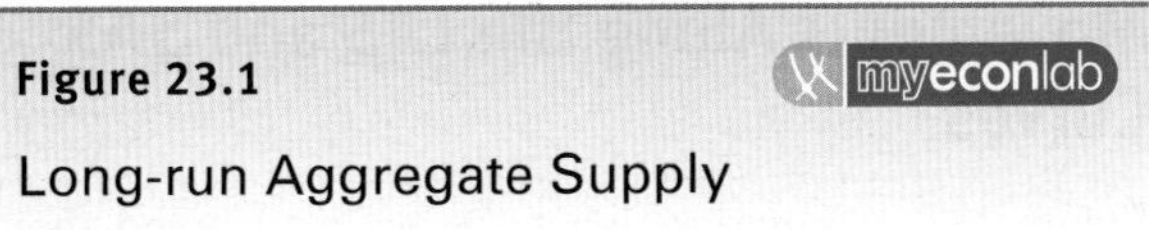

Figure 23.1

Long-run Aggregate Supply

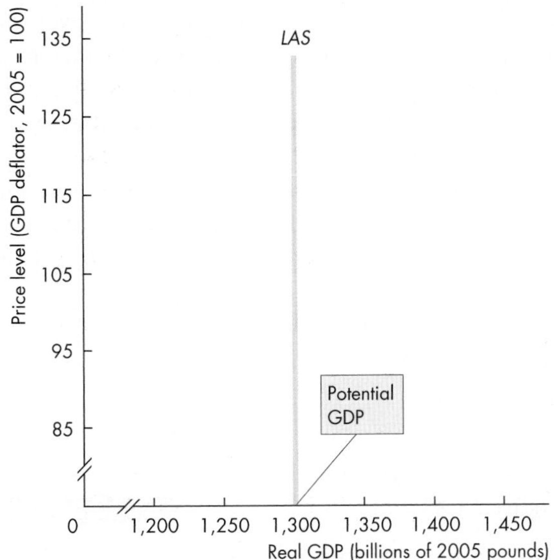

The long-run aggregate supply curve (*LAS*) shows the relationship between potential GDP and the price level. Potential GDP is independent of the price level, so the *LAS* curve is vertical at potential GDP.

The long-run aggregate supply curve is vertical because potential GDP is independent of the price level. The reason for this independence is that a movement along the long-run aggregate supply curve is accompanied by changes in *two* sets of prices: the prices of goods and services (the price level) and the prices of factors of production. Along the long-run aggregate supply curve, a 10 per cent increase in the prices of goods and services is matched by a 10 per cent increase in the money wage rate and the prices of other factors of production. That is, the price level, wage rate and other factor prices all change by the same percentage and so *relative prices* and the *real wage rate* are unchanged. When the price level changes but relative prices and the real wage rate remain constant, real GDP also remains constant.

Production at Liz's Meat Pies

You can see why real GDP remains constant when all prices change by the same percentage if you think about production decisions at Liz's meat pie plant. The plant is producing the quantity of pies that maximizes profit. The plant can increase production but only by incurring a higher *marginal cost* (see Chapter 2, p. 39). So the firm has no incentive to change production.

Short-run Aggregate Supply

The **macroeconomic short run** is a period during which some money prices are sticky so that real GDP might be below, above, or at potential GDP and the unemployment rate might be above, below, or at the natural unemployment rate.

Short-run aggregate supply is the relationship between the quantity of real GDP supplied and the price level in the short run, when the money wage rate, the prices of other factors of production, and potential GDP remain constant. Short-run aggregate supply is described by a short-run aggregate supply schedule and curve.

Figure 23.2 (on the next page) shows a short-run aggregate supply curve (*SAS*) and short-run aggregate supply schedule. Each point of the *SAS* curve corresponds to a row of the schedule. For example, point *A* on the short-run aggregate supply curve and row *A* of the schedule tell us that if the price level is 95, the quantity of real GDP supplied is £1,200 billion.

At point *C*, the price level is 105 and the quantity of real GDP supplied is £1,300 billion, which equals potential GDP. If the price level is higher than 105, real GDP exceeds potential GDP; if the price level is below 105, real GDP is less than potential GDP.

Back at Liz's Meat Pies

You can see why the short-run aggregate supply curve slopes upward by returning to Liz's meat pie plant. The plant produces the quantity of pies that maximizes profit. If the price of a pie rises and the money wage rate and Liz's other costs don't change, the *relative price* of a pie rises and Liz has an incentive to increase her production. The higher relative price of a pie covers the higher *marginal cost* of producing more pies, so Liz increases production.

Similarly when the price of a pie falls and the money wage rate and Liz's other costs don't change, the lower relative price of a pie is not sufficient to cover the marginal cost of a pie, so Liz decreases production.

Again, what's true for meat pie producers is true for the producers of all goods and services. So when the price level rises and the money wage rate and prices of other factors of production remain constant, the quantity of real GDP supplied increases.

Figure 23.2 myeconlab

Short-run Aggregate Supply

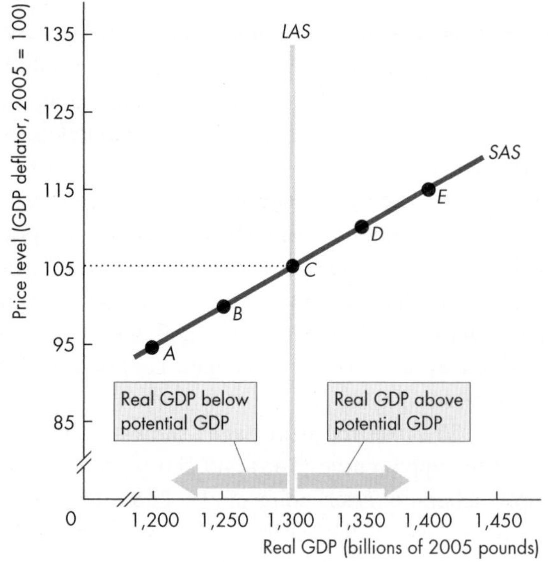

	Price level (GDP deflator)	Real GDP (billions of 2005 pounds)
A	95	1,200
B	100	1,250
C	105	1,300
D	110	1,350
E	115	1,400

The short-run aggregate supply curve shows the relationship between the quantity of real GDP supplied and the price level when the money wage rate, other resource prices and potential GDP remain the same. The short-run aggregate supply curve, *SAS*, is based on the schedule in the table.

The *SAS* curve is upward-sloping because firms' marginal costs increase as output increases, so a higher price is needed, relative to the prices of productive resources, to bring forth an increase in the quantity produced.

On the *SAS* curve, when the price level is 105, real GDP equals potential GDP (£1,300 billion). If the price level is greater than 105, real GDP exceeds potential GDP; if the price level is below 105, real GDP is less than potential GDP.

Movements Along the *LAS* and *SAS* Curves

Figure 23.3 summarizes what you've just learned about the *LAS* and *SAS* curves. When the price level, the money wage rate, and the prices of other factors of production rise by the same percentage, relative price remains constant and real GDP remains at potential GDP. There is a *movement along* the *LAS* curve.

When the price level rises but the money wage rate and the prices of other factors of production remain the same, the quantity of real GDP supplied increases and there is a *movement along* the *SAS* curve.

Let's next study the influences that bring changes in aggregate supply.

Figure 23.3 myeconlab

Movements Along the Aggregate Supply Curves

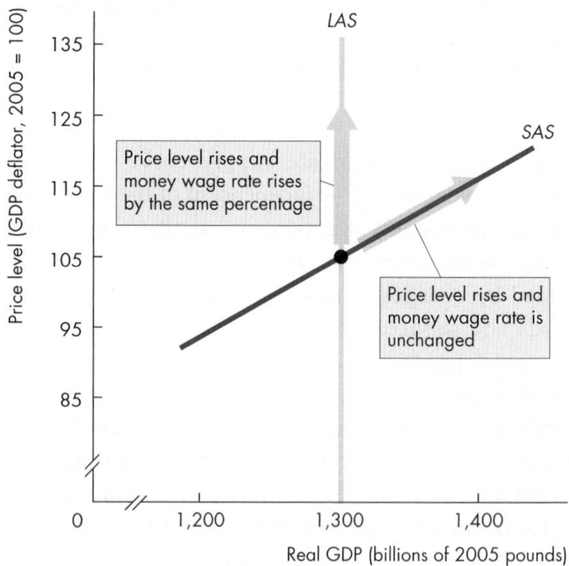

A rise in the price level with no change in the money wage rate and other resource prices brings an increase in the quantity of real GDP supplied and a movement along the short-run aggregate supply curve, *SAS*.

A rise in the price level with equal percentage increases in the money wage rate and other resource prices keeps the quantity of real GDP supplied constant at potential GDP and brings a movement along the long-run aggregate supply curve, *LAS*.

Changes in Aggregate Supply

You've just seen that a change in the price level brings a movement along the aggregate supply curves but does not change aggregate supply. Aggregate supply changes when any influence on production plans other than the price level changes. Let's begin by looking at factors that change potential GDP.

Changes in Potential GDP

When potential GDP changes, both long-run aggregate supply and short-run aggregate supply change. Potential GDP changes for three reasons:

- A change in the full-employment quantity of labour
- A change in the quantity of capital
- An advance in technology

An increase in the full-employment quantity of labour, an increase in the quantity of capital or an advance in technology increases potential GDP. And an increase in potential GDP changes both the long-run aggregate supply and short-run aggregate supply.

Figure 23.4 shows these effects of a change in potential GDP. Initially, potential GDP is £1,300 billion, the long-run aggregate supply curve is LAS_0, and the short-run aggregate supply curve is SAS_0. If an increase in the quantity of capital or a technological advance increases potential GDP to £1,400 billion, long-run aggregate supply increases and the long-run aggregate supply curve shifts rightward to LAS_1. Short-run aggregate supply also increases, and the short-run aggregate supply curve shifts rightward to SAS_1.

Let's look more closely at the influences on potential GDP and the aggregate supply curves.

A Change in the Full-employment Quantity of Labour

A meat pie production plant that employs 100 workers produces more pies than an otherwise identical plant that employs 10 workers. The same is true for the economy as a whole. The larger the quantity of labour employed, the greater is GDP.

Over time, potential GDP increases because the labour force increases. But (with constant capital and technology) *potential* GDP increases only if the full-employment quantity of labour increases. Fluctuations in employment over the business cycle bring fluctuations in real GDP. But these changes in real GDP are fluctuations around potential GDP and long-run aggregate supply.

Figure 23.4

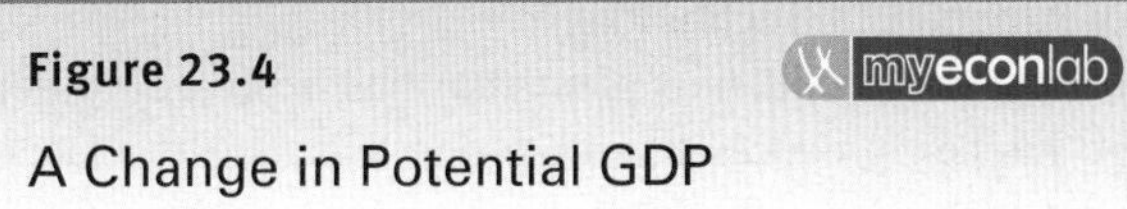

A Change in Potential GDP

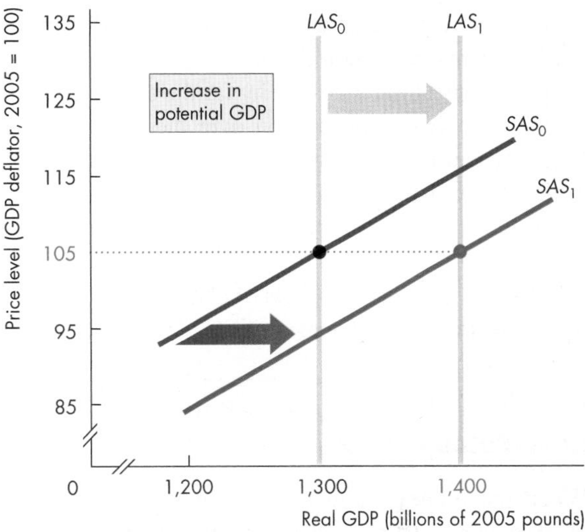

An increase in potential GDP increases both long-run aggregate supply and short-run aggregate supply and shifts both aggregate supply curves rightward from LAS_0 to LAS_1 and from SAS_0 to SAS_1.

Change in the Quantity of Capital

A meat pie plant that has two production lines has more capital and produces more output than an otherwise identical plant that has one production line. For the economy, the larger the quantity of capital, the more productive is the workforce, the greater is its potential GDP. Potential GDP per person in capital-rich EU economies is vastly greater than that in capital-poor China and Russia.

Capital includes *human capital*. One pie production plant is managed by an economics graduate with an MBA and has a workforce with an average of 10 years of experience. This plant produces a much larger output than an otherwise identical plant that is managed by someone with no business training or experience and that has a young workforce that is new to bottling. The first plant has a greater amount of human capital than the second. For the economy as a whole, the larger the quantity of *human capital* – the skills that people have acquired in school and through on-the-job-training – the greater is potential GDP.

An Advance in Technology

A meat pie production plant that has a pre-computer age kitchen produces less than one that uses the latest robot technology. Technological change enables firms to produce more from any given amount of inputs. So even with fixed quantities of labour and capital, improvements in technology increase potential GDP.

Technological advances are by far the most important source of increased production over the past two centuries. Because of technological advances, one farmer in the United Kingdom today can feed 100 people and one auto worker can produce almost 14 cars and trucks in a year.

Let's now look at the effects of changes in the money wage rate and other resource prices.

Changes in the Money Wage Rate and Other Resource Prices

When the money wage rate or the money prices of other resources (such as the price of oil) change, short-run aggregate supply changes but long-run aggregate supply does not change.

Figure 23.5 shows the effect on aggregate supply of an increase in the money wage rate. Initially, the short-run aggregate supply curve is SAS_0. A rise in the money wage rate *decreases* short-run aggregate supply and shifts the short-run aggregate supply curve leftward to SAS_2.

The money wage rate (and other resource prices) affect short-run aggregate supply because they influence firms' costs. The higher the money wage rate, the higher are firms' costs and the smaller is the quantity that firms are willing to supply at each price level. So an increase in the money wage rate decreases short-run aggregate supply.

A change in the money wage rate does not change long-run aggregate supply because on the *LAS* curve, a change in the money wage rate is accompanied by an equal percentage change in the price level. With no change in *relative* prices, firms have no incentive to change production and real GDP remains constant at potential GDP. With no change in potential GDP, the long-run aggregate supply curve remains at *LAS*.

What Makes the Money Wage Rate Change?

The money wage rate can change for two reasons: departures from full employment and expectations about inflation. Unemployment above the natural rate puts downward pressure on the money wage rate, and unemployment below the natural rate puts upward pressure on the money wage rate. An expected increase in the inflation rate makes the money wage rate rise faster, and an expected decrease in the inflation rate slows the rate at which the money wage rate rises.

Figure 23.5 myeconlab

A Change in the Money Wage Rate

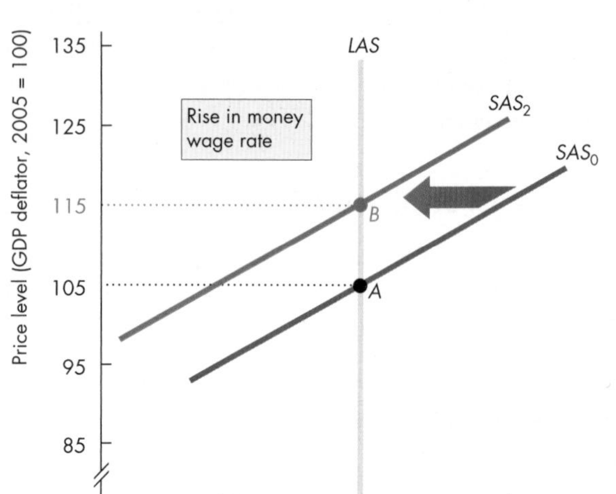

A rise in the money wage rate decreases short-run aggregate supply and shifts the short-run aggregate supply curve leftward from SAS_0 to SAS_2. A rise in the money wage rate does not change potential GDP, so the long-run aggregate supply curve does not shift.

Review Quiz

Study Plan 23.1

1. If the price level rises and if the money wage rate also rises by the same percentage, what happens to the quantity of real GDP supplied? Along which aggregate supply curve does the economy move?
2. If the price level rises and the money wage rate remains constant, what happens to the quantity of real GDP supplied? Along which aggregate supply curve does the economy move?
3. If potential GDP increases, what happens to aggregate supply? Is there a shift of or a movement along the *LAS* curve and the *SAS* curve?
4. If the money wage rate rises and potential GDP remains the same, what happens to aggregate supply? Is there a shift of or a movement along the *LAS* curve and the *SAS* curve?

Aggregate Demand

The quantity of real GDP demanded is the sum of the real consumption expenditure (C), investment (I), government expenditure (G), and exports (X) minus imports (M). That is:

$$Y = C + I + G + X - M$$

The *quantity of real GDP demanded* is the total amount of final goods and services produced in the United Kingdom that people, businesses, governments and foreigners plan to buy.

These buying plans depend on many factors. The four main ones are:

1 The price level
2 Expectations
3 Fiscal policy and monetary policy
4 The world economy

We first focus on the relationship between the quantity of real GDP demanded and the price level. To study this relationship, we keep all other influences on buying plans the same and ask: How does the quantity of real GDP demanded vary as the price level varies?

The Aggregate Demand Curve

Other things remaining the same, the higher the price level, the smaller is the quantity of real GDP demanded. This relationship between the quantity of real GDP demanded and the price level is called **aggregate demand**. Aggregate demand is described by an aggregate demand schedule and an aggregate demand curve.

Figure 23.6 shows an aggregate demand curve (*AD*) and an aggregate demand schedule. Each point on the *AD* curve corresponds to a row of the schedule. For example, point *C'* on the *AD* curve and row *C'* of the schedule tell us that if the price level is 105, the quantity of real GDP demanded is £1,300 billion.

The aggregate demand curve slopes downward for two reasons:

◆ Wealth effect
◆ Substitution effects

Wealth Effect

When the price level rises but other things remain the same, *real* wealth decreases. Real wealth is the amount of money in the bank, bonds, shares and other assets that people own, measured not in dollars but in terms of the goods and services that this money, bonds and shares will buy.

People save and hold money, bonds, shares and other assets for many reasons. One reason is to build up funds

Figure 23.6

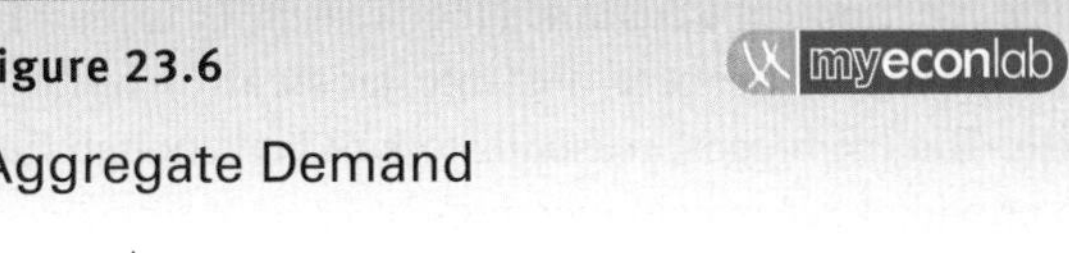

Aggregate Demand

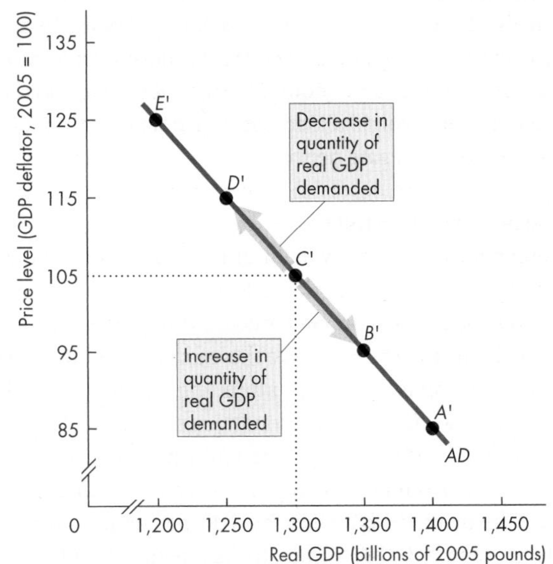

	Price level (GDP deflator)	Real GDP (billions of 2005 pounds)
A'	85	1,400
B'	95	1,350
C'	105	1,300
D'	115	1,250
E'	125	1,200

The aggregate demand curve (*AD*) shows the relationship between the quantity of real GDP demanded and the price level. The aggregate demand curve is based on the aggregate demand schedule in the table. Each point *A'* to *E'* on the curve corresponds to the row in the table identified by the same letter. For example, when the price level is 105, the quantity of real GDP demanded is £1,300 billion, shown by point *C'* in the figure.

A change in the price level with all other influences on aggregate buying plans remaining the same brings a change in the quantity of real GDP demanded and a movement along the *AD* curve.

for education expenses. Another reason is to build up enough funds to meet possible medical or other big bills. But the biggest reason is to build up enough funds to provide a retirement income.

If the price level rises, real wealth decreases. People then try to restore their wealth. To do so, they must increase saving and, equivalently, decrease current consumption. Such a decrease in consumption is a decrease in aggregate demand.

Maria's Wealth Effect

You can see how the wealth effect works by thinking about Maria's buying plans. Maria lives in Moscow, Russia. She has worked hard all summer and saved 20,000 rubles (the ruble is the currency of Russia), which she plans to spend attending graduate school when she has finished her economics degree. So Maria's wealth is 20,000 rubles. Maria has a part-time job, and her income from this job pays her current expenses. The price level in Russia rises by 100 per cent, and now Maria needs 40,000 rubles to buy what 20,000 once bought. To try to make up some of the fall in value of her savings, Maria saves even more and cuts her current spending to the bare minimum.

Substitution Effects

When the price level rises and other things remain the same, interest rates rise. The reason is related to the wealth effect that you've just studied. A rise in the price level decreases the real value of the money in people's pockets and bank accounts. With a smaller amount of real money around, banks can get a higher interest rate on loans. But faced with higher interest rates, people and businesses delay plans to buy new capital and consumer durable goods and cut back on spending.

This substitution effect involves substituting goods in the future for goods in the present and is called an *intertemporal* substitution effect – a substitution across time. Saving increases to increase future consumption.

To see this intertemporal substitution effect more clearly, think about your own plan to buy a new computer. At an interest rate of 5 per cent a year, you might borrow £1,000 and buy the new machine you've been researching. But at an interest rate of 10 per cent a year, you might decide that the payments would be too high. You don't abandon your plan to buy the computer, but you decide to delay your purchase.

A second substitution effect works through international prices. When the UK price level rises and other things remain the same, UK-made goods and services become more expensive relative to foreign-made goods and services. This change in *relative prices* encourages people to spend less on UK-made items and more on foreign-made items. For example, if the UK price level rises relative to the Swedish price level, Swedes buy fewer UK-made cars (UK exports decrease) and Britons buy more Swedish-made cars (UK imports increase). GDP in the United Kingdom decreases.

Maria's Substitution Effects

In Moscow, Russia, Maria makes some substitutions. She was planning to trade in her old motor scooter and get a new one. But with a higher price level and faced with higher interest rates, she decides to make her old scooter last one more year. Also, with the prices of Russian goods sharply increasing, Maria substitutes a low-cost dress made in Malaysia for the Russian-made dress she had originally planned to buy.

Changes in the Quantity of Real GDP Demanded

When the price level rises and other things remain the same, the quantity of real GDP demanded decreases – a movement up the *AD* curve as shown by the arrow in Figure 23.6. When the price level falls and other things remain the same, the quantity of real GDP demanded increases – a movement down the *AD* curve.

We've now seen how the quantity of real GDP demanded changes when the price level changes. How do other influences on buying plans affect aggregate demand?

Changes in Aggregate Demand

A change in any factor that influences buying plans other than the price level brings a change in aggregate demand. The main factors are:

- Expectations
- Fiscal policy and monetary policy
- The world economy

Expectations

Expectations about future disposable income, inflation and profit influence people's decisions about spending today. An increase in expected future disposable income, other things remaining the same, increases the amount of consumption goods (especially items such as cars) that people plan to buy today and increases aggregate demand today.

An increase in the expected future inflation rate increases aggregate demand today because people decide to buy more goods and services at today's relatively lower prices. An increase in expected future profit increases the investment that firms plan to undertake today and increases aggregate demand today.

Figure 23.7 myeconlab

Changes in Aggregate Demand

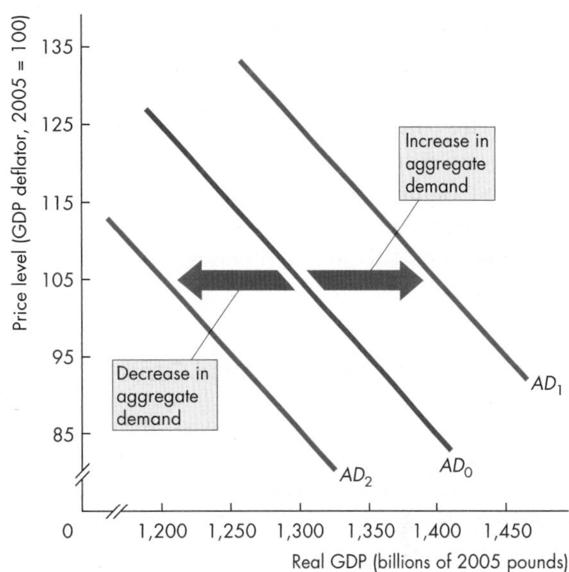

Aggregate demand

Decreases if:	*Increases if:*
◆ Expected future disposable income, inflation or profit decreases	◆ Expected future disposable income, inflation or profit increases
◆ Fiscal policy decreases government expenditure on goods and services, increases taxes or decreases transfer payments	◆ Fiscal policy increases government expenditure on goods and services, decreases taxes or increases transfer payments
◆ Monetary policy increases interest rates and decreases the quantity of money	◆ Monetary policy decreases interest rates and increases the quantity of money
◆ The foreign exchange rate increases or foreign income decreases	◆ The foreign exchange rate decreases or foreign income increases

Fiscal Policy and Monetary Policy

The government's attempt to influence the economy by setting and changing taxes, making transfer payments, and purchasing goods and services is called **fiscal policy**. A tax cut or an increase in transfer payments – for example, unemployment benefits or welfare payments – increases aggregate demand. Both of these influences operate by increasing households' disposable income. **Disposable income** is aggregate income minus taxes plus transfer payments. The greater the disposable income, the greater is the quantity of consumption goods and services that households plan to buy and the greater is aggregate demand.

Government expenditures on goods and services are one component of aggregate demand. So if the government spends more on hospitals, schools and motorways, aggregate demand increases.

Monetary policy consists of changes in interest rates and in the quantity of money in the economy. The quantity of money in the United Kingdom is determined by the Bank of England and the banks (in a process described in Chapters 27 and 28). An increase in the quantity of money increases aggregate demand.

To see why money affects aggregate demand, imagine that the Bank of England borrows the army's helicopters, loads them with millions of new £5 notes and sprinkles these notes like confetti across the nation.

People gather the newly available money and plan to spend some of it. So the quantity of goods and services demanded increases. But people don't plan to spend all the new money. They save some of it and lend it to others through the banks. Interest rates fall, and with lower interest rates, people plan to buy more consumer durables and firms plan to increase their investment.

The World Economy

Two main influences that the world economy has on aggregate demand are the foreign exchange rate and foreign income. The *foreign exchange rate* is the amount of a foreign currency that you can buy with a pound. Other things remaining the same, a rise in the foreign exchange rate decreases aggregate demand. To see how the foreign exchange rate influences aggregate demand, suppose that £1 is worth 2,000 South Korean won. You can buy a Samsung TV (made in South Korea) that costs 400,000 won for £200. If the price of a Ferguson TV (made in the United Kingdom) is the same, you may be willing to buy the Ferguson TV.

Now suppose the foreign exchange rate rises to 2,200 won per pound. At 2,200 won per pound, the Samsung

TV now costs only £18.82 and is now cheaper than the Ferguson TV. People around the world will switch from the UK-made TV to the South Korean-made TV. UK exports will decrease and UK imports will increase. UK aggregate demand will decrease.

An increase in foreign income increases UK exports and increases the UK aggregate demand – the aggregate demand for UK-produced goods and services. For example, an increase in income in the United States, Japan and Germany increases the American, Japanese and German consumers' and producers' planned expenditures on UK-produced consumption goods and capital goods.

Shifts of the Aggregate Demand Curve

When aggregate demand changes, the aggregate demand curve shifts. Figure 23.7 shows two changes in aggregate demand and summarizes the factors that bring about such changes.

Aggregate demand increases and the aggregate demand curve shifts rightward from AD_0 to AD_1 when expected future disposable income, inflation or profit increases; government expenditures increase; taxes are cut; transfer payments increase; the quantity of money increases and interest rates fall; the foreign exchange rate falls; or foreign income increases.

Aggregate demand decreases and the aggregate demand curve shifts leftward from AD_0 to AD_2 when expected future disposable income, inflation or profit decreases; government expenditures decrease; taxes increase; transfer payments decrease; the quantity of money decreases and interest rates rise; the foreign exchange rate rises; or foreign income decreases.

Review Quiz

Study Plan 23.2

1 What does the aggregate demand curve show?
2 What factors change and what factors remain the same when there is a movement along the aggregate demand curve?
3 Why does the aggregate demand curve slope downward?
4 How do changes in expectations, fiscal policy and monetary policy change aggregate demand and shift the aggregate demand curve?
5 How do changes in and the world economy change aggregate demand and shift the aggregate demand curve?

Macroeconomic Equilibrium

The purpose of the aggregate supply–aggregate demand model is to explain changes in real GDP and the price level. To achieve this purpose, we combine aggregate supply and aggregate demand and determine macroeconomic equilibrium. There is a macroeconomic equilibrium for each of the time frames for aggregate supply: a long-run equilibrium and a short-run equilibrium. Long-run equilibrium is the state towards which the economy is heading. Short-run equilibrium is the normal state of the economy as it fluctuates around potential GDP.

We'll begin our study of macroeconomic equilibrium by looking at the short run.

Short-run Macroeconomic Equilibrium

The aggregate demand curve tells us the quantity of real GDP demanded at each price level, and the short-run aggregate supply curve tells us the quantity of real GDP supplied at each price level. **Short-run macroeconomic equilibrium** occurs when the quantity of real GDP demanded equals the short-run quantity of real GDP supplied at the point of intersection of the *AD* curve and the *SAS* curve. Figure 23.8 illustrates such an equilibrium at a price level of 105 and real GDP of £1,300 billion (point *C* and *C'*).

To see why this position is the equilibrium, think about what happens if the price level is something other than 105. Suppose, for example, that the price level is 115 and that real GDP is £1,400 billion (at point *E* on the *SAS* curve). The quantity of real GDP demanded is less than £1,400 billion, so firms are unable to sell all their output. Unwanted inventories (stocks) pile up, and firms cut both production and prices. Production and prices are cut until firms can sell all their output. This situation occurs only when real GDP is £1,300 billion and the price level is 105.

Now suppose that the price level is 95 and real GDP is £1,200 billion (at point *A* on the *SAS* curve). The quantity of real GDP demanded exceeds £1,200 billion, so firms are unable to meet demand for their output. Inventories (stock) decrease and customers clamour for goods and services. So firms increase production and raise prices. Production and prices increase until firms can meet demand. This situation occurs only when real GDP is £1,300 billion and the price level is 105.

Figure 23.8

Short-run Macroeconomic Equilibrium

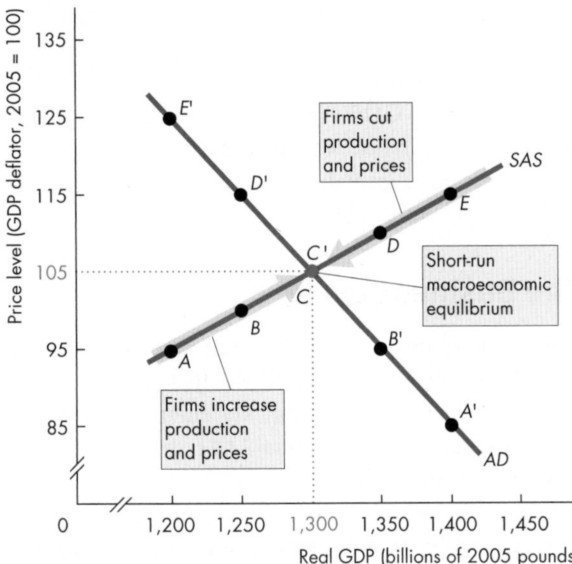

Short-run macroeconomic equilibrium occurs when real GDP demanded equals real GDP supplied – at the intersection of the aggregate demand curve (*AD*) and the short-run aggregate supply curve (*SAS*). Here, such an equilibrium occurs at points *C* and *C'* where the price level is 105 and real GDP is £1,300 billion.

If the price level was 115 and real GDP was £1,400 billion (point *E*), firms would not be able to sell all their output. They would decrease production and cut prices.

If the price level was 95 and real GDP was £1,200 billion (point *A*), people would not be able to buy all the goods and services they demanded. Firms would increase production and raise their prices.

Only when the price level is 105 and real GDP is £1,300 billion can firms sell all they produce and people buy all they demand. The economy is in short-run macroeconomic equilibrium.

In short-run macroeconomic equilibrium, the money wage rate is fixed. It does not adjust to bring full employment. So in the short run, real GDP can be greater than or less than potential GDP. But in the long run, the money wage rate does adjust and real GDP moves towards potential GDP. We are going to study this adjustment process. But first, let's look at the economy in long-run equilibrium.

Long-run Macroeconomic Equilibrium

Long-run macroeconomic equilibrium occurs when real GDP equals potential GDP – equivalently, when the economy is on its *long-run* aggregate supply curve. Figure 23.9 shows *long-run* equilibrium, which occurs at the intersection of the aggregate demand curve and the long-run aggregate supply curve (the blue curves). Long-run equilibrium comes about because the money wage rate adjusts. Potential GDP and aggregate demand determine the price level, and the price level influences the money wage rate. In long-run equilibrium, the money wage rate has adjusted to put the (green) short-run aggregate supply curve through the long-run equilibrium point.

We'll look at this money wage adjustment process later in this chapter. But first, let's see how the *AS–AD* model helps us to understand economic growth and inflation.

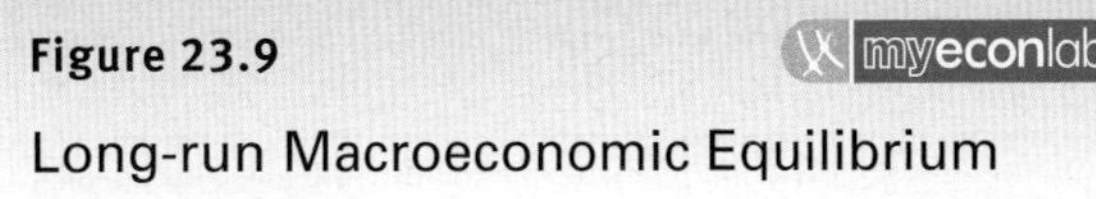

Figure 23.9

Long-run Macroeconomic Equilibrium

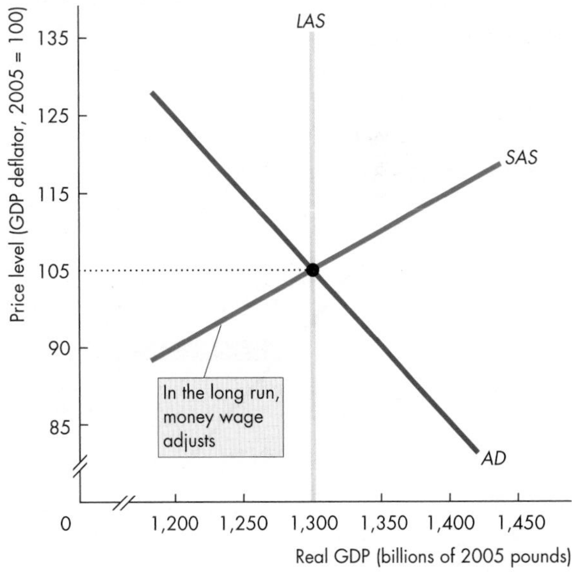

In long-run macroeconomic equilibrium, real GDP equals potential GDP. So long-run equilibrium occurs where the aggregate demand curve *AD* intersects the long-run aggregate supply curve *LAS*. In the long run, aggregate demand determines the price level and has no effect on real GDP. The money wage rate adjusts in the long run, so the *SAS* curve intersects the *LAS* curve at the long-run equilibrium price level.

Economic Growth and Inflation

Economic growth occurs because over time, the quantity of labour grows, capital is accumulated and technology advances. These changes increase potential GDP and shift the long-run aggregate supply curve rightward. Figure 23.10 shows such a shift. The growth rate of potential GDP is determined by the pace at which labour grows, capital is accumulated and technology advances.

Inflation occurs when, over time, aggregate demand increases by more than long-run aggregate supply. That is, inflation occurs if the aggregate demand curve shifts rightward by more than the rightward shift in the long-run aggregate supply curve. Figure 23.10 shows such shifts.

If aggregate demand increased at the same pace as long-run aggregate supply, we would experience real GDP growth with no inflation.

In the long run, the main influence on aggregate demand is the growth rate of the quantity of money.

Figure 23.10

Economic Growth and Inflation

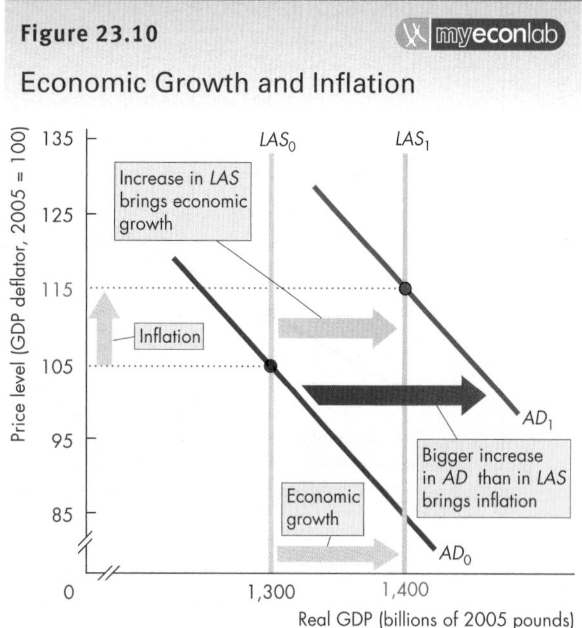

Economic growth is the persistent increase in potential GDP. Economic growth is shown as an ongoing rightward movement in the *LAS* curve. Inflation is the persistent rise in the price level. Inflation occurs when aggregate demand increases by more than the increase in long-run aggregate supply.

At times when the quantity of money increases rapidly, aggregate demand increases quickly and the inflation rate is high. When the growth rate of the quantity of money slows, other things remaining the same, the inflation rate eventually decreases.

Our economy experiences growth and inflation, like that shown in Figure 23.10. But it does not experience *steady* growth and *steady* inflation. Real GDP fluctuates around potential GDP in a business cycle, and inflation also fluctuates. When we study the business cycle, we ignore economic growth. By doing so, we can see the business cycle more clearly.

The Business Cycle

The business cycle occurs because aggregate demand and short-run aggregate supply fluctuate but the money wage rate does not adjust quickly enough to keep real GDP at potential GDP. Figure 23.11 shows three types of short-run equilibrium.

In part (a) there is a below full-employment equilibrium. A **below full-employment equilibrium** is a macroeconomic equilibrium in which potential GDP exceeds real GDP. When potential GDP exceeds real GDP, the *output gap* (which you saw in Chapter 20, p. 455) is negative. A negative gap is called a **recessionary gap**. The name that reminds us that the gap has opened between real GDP and potential GDP either because the economy has experienced a recession or because real GDP, while growing, has grown more slowly than potential GDP.

The below full-employment equilibrium illustrated in Figure 23.11(a) occurs where aggregate demand curve AD_0 intersects short-run aggregate supply curve SAS_0 at a real GDP of £1,280 billion and a price level of 105. The recessionary gap is £20 billion. The UK economy was in a situation similar to that shown in Figure 23.11(a) in 1980–1981 and again in 1990–1992. In those years, real GDP was less than potential GDP and the UK economy was in a recession.

Figure 23.11(b) is an example of the economy at full employment. **Full-employment equilibrium** is a macroeconomic equilibrium in which real GDP equals potential GDP. In this example, the equilibrium occurs where the aggregate demand curve AD_1 intersects the short-run aggregate supply curve SAS_1 at an actual and potential GDP of £1,300 billion. The economy was in a situation such as that shown in Figure 23.11(b) in 2005.

Figure 23.11(c) illustrates an above full-employment equilibrium. An **above full-employment equilibrium** is a macroeconomic equilibrium in which real GDP exceeds potential GDP. When real GDP exceeds potential GDP, the *output gap* is positive and is called an **inflationary gap**. This name reminds us that a gap has opened up between real GDP and potential GDP and that this gap creates inflationary pressure – a tendency for the price level to rise more quickly.

The above full-employment equilibrium shown in Figure 23.11(c) occurs where the aggregate demand curve AD_2 intersects the short-run aggregate supply curve SAS_2 at a real GDP of £1,320 billion and a price level of 105. There is an inflationary gap of £20 billion. The UK economy was in a situation similar to that depicted in Figure 23.11(c) in 2006.

The economy moves from one type of equilibrium to another as a result of fluctuations in aggregate demand and in short-run aggregate supply. These fluctuations produce fluctuations in real GDP and the price level. Figure 23.11(d) shows how real GDP fluctuates around potential GDP.

Let's now look at some of the sources of these fluctuations around potential GDP.

Figure 23.11

The Business Cycle

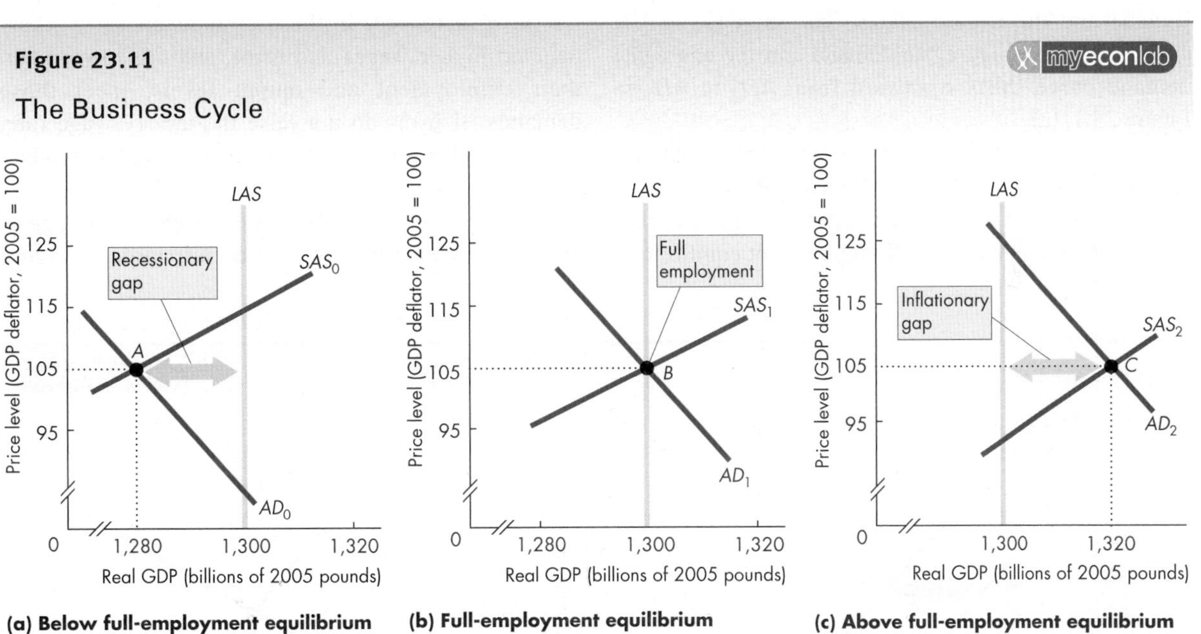

(a) Below full-employment equilibrium **(b) Full-employment equilibrium** **(c) Above full-employment equilibrium**

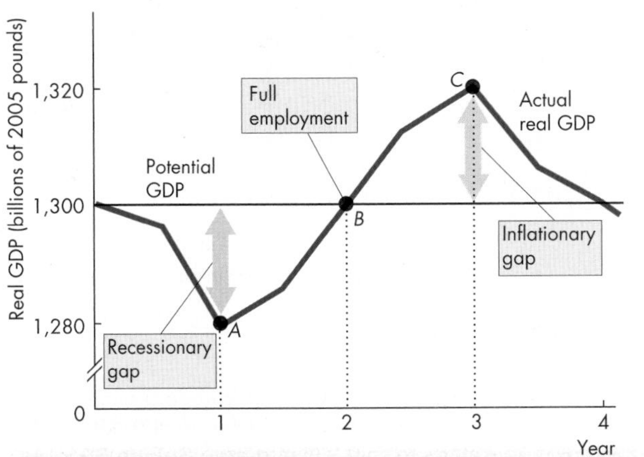

(d) Fluctuations in real GDP

Part (a) shows a below full-employment equilibrium in year 1, part (b) shows long-run equilibrium in year 2, and part (c) shows an above full-employment equilibrium in year 3. Part (d) shows how real GDP fluctuates around potential GDP in a business cycle.

In year 1, a recessionary gap exists and the economy is at point *A*, in parts (a) and (d). In year 2, the economy is in long-run equilibrium and the economy is at point *B* in parts (b) and (d). In year 3, an inflationary gap exists and the economy is at point *C* in parts (c) and (d).

Fluctuations in Aggregate Demand

One reason real GDP fluctuates around potential GDP is that aggregate demand fluctuates. Let's see what happens when aggregate demand increases.

Figure 23.12(a) shows an economy at full employment. The aggregate demand curve is AD_0, the short-run aggregate supply curve is SAS_0, and the long-run aggregate supply curve is *LAS*. Real GDP equals potential GDP at £1,300 billion, and the price level is 105.

Now suppose that the world economy expands and that the demand for UK-made goods increases in Japan, Canada and the United States. The increase in UK exports increases aggregate demand and the aggregate demand curve shifts rightward from AD_0 to AD_1 in Figure 23.12(a).

Faced with an increase in demand, firms increase production and raise prices. Real GDP increases to £1,350 billion and the price level rises to 110. The economy is now in an above full-employment equilibrium. Real GDP exceeds potential GDP, and there is an inflationary gap.

The increase in aggregate demand has increased the prices of all goods and services. Faced with higher prices, firms have increased their output rates. At this stage, prices of goods and services have increased but the money wage rate has not changed. (Recall that as we move along a short-run aggregate supply curve, the money wage rate is constant.)

Because the price level has increased and the money wage rate is unchanged, workers have experienced a fall in the buying power of their wages and firms' profits have increased. In these circumstances, workers demand higher wages and firms, anxious to maintain their employment and output levels, meet those demands. If firms do not raise the money wage rate, they will either lose workers or have to hire less productive ones.

As the money wage rate rises, the short-run aggregate supply curve begins to shift leftward. In Figure

Figure 23.12

myeconlab

An Increase in Aggregate Demand

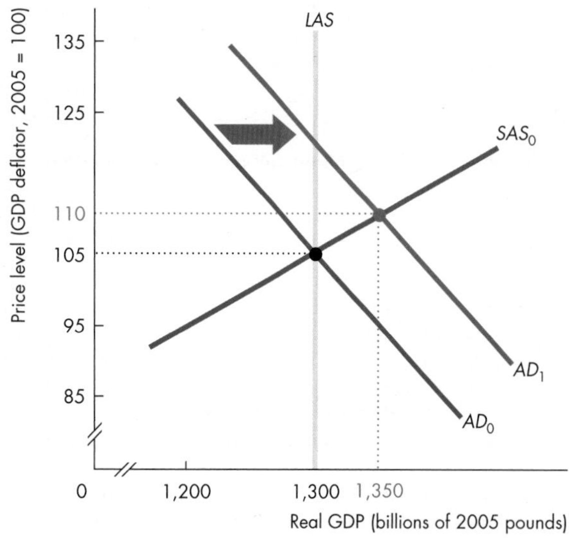

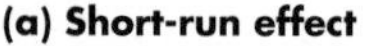

(a) Short-run effect

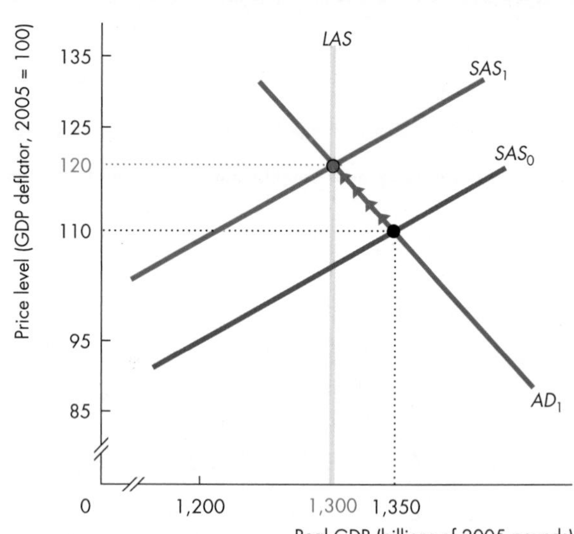

(b) Long-run effect

An increase in aggregate demand shifts the aggregate demand curve from AD_0 to AD_1. In the short run (part a), real GDP increases from £1,300 billion to £1,350 billion and the price level rises from 105 to 110. The economy has moved up along the *SAS* curve. In this situation, an inflationary gap exists.

In the long run (part b), with an inflationary gap, the money wage rate starts to rise. The short-run aggregate supply curve starts to shift leftward from SAS_0 to SAS_1. As the *SAS* curve shifts leftward, it intersects the aggregate demand curve AD_1 at higher price levels and real GDP decreases. Eventually, the price level rises to 120 and real GDP decreases to £1,300 billion – potential GDP.

23.12(b), the short-run aggregate supply curve shifts from SAS_0 towards SAS_1. The rise in the money wage rate and the shift in the *SAS* curve produce a sequence of new equilibrium positions. Along the adjustment path, real GDP decreases and the price level rises. The economy moves up along its aggregate demand curve as the arrowheads show.

Eventually, the money wage rate rises by the same percentage as the price level. At this time, the aggregate demand curve AD_1 intersects SAS_1 at a new long-run equilibrium. The price level has risen to 120, and real GDP is back where it started, at potential GDP.

A decrease in aggregate demand has similar but opposite effects to those of an increase in aggregate demand. That is, a decrease in aggregate demand shifts the aggregate demand curve leftward. Real GDP decreases to less than potential GDP and a recessionary gap emerges. Firms cut prices. The lower price level increases the purchasing power of wages and increases firms' costs relative to their output prices because the money wage rate remains unchanged. Eventually, the money wage rate falls and the short-run aggregate supply curve shifts rightward. But the money wage rate changes slowly, so real GDP slowly returns to potential GDP and the price level falls slowly.

Let's now work out how real GDP and the price level change when aggregate supply changes.

Fluctuations in Aggregate Supply

Fluctuations in short-run aggregate supply can bring fluctuations in real GDP around potential GDP. Suppose that initially, real GDP equals potential GDP. Then there is a large but temporary rise in the price of oil. What happens to real GDP and the price level?

Figure 23.13 answers this question. The aggregate demand curve is AD_0, the short-run aggregate supply curve is SAS_0 and the long-run aggregate supply curve is *LAS*. Equilibrium real GDP is £1,300 billion, which equals potential GDP, and the price level is 105. Then the price of oil rises. Faced with higher energy and transportation costs, firms decrease production. Short-run aggregate supply decreases and the short-run aggregate supply curve shifts leftward to SAS_1. The price level rises to 115 and real GDP decreases to £1,250 billion.

Because real GDP decreases, the economy experiences recession. Because the price level increases, the economy experiences inflation. A combination of recession and inflation, called *stagflation*, actually occurred in the United Kingdom in the mid-1970s.

Figure 23.13

A Decrease in Aggregate Supply

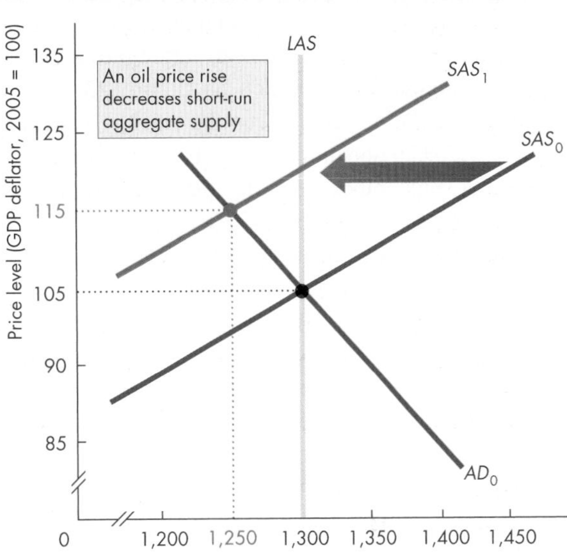

An increase in the price of oil decreases short-run aggregate supply and shifts the short-run aggregate supply curve leftward from SAS_0 to SAS_1. Real GDP decreases from £1,300 billion to £1,250 billion, and the price level increases from 105 to 115. The economy experiences both recession and inflation – a situation known as stagflation.

Review Quiz

Study Plan 23.3

1. Does economic growth result from increases in aggregate demand, short-run aggregate supply or long-run aggregate supply?
2. Does inflation result from increases in aggregate demand, short-run aggregate supply or long-run aggregate supply?
3. Describe the three types of short-run macroeconomic equilibrium.
4. How do fluctuations in aggregate demand and short-run aggregate supply bring fluctuations in real GDP around potential GDP?

Let's put our new knowledge of aggregate supply and aggregate demand to work and see how we can explain recent macroeconomic performance in the United Kingdom.

Economic Growth, Inflation and Cycles in the UK Economy

The economy is continually changing. If you imagine the economy as a video, then an aggregate supply–aggregate demand figure such as Figure 23.13 is a freeze-frame. We're going to run the video – an instant replay – but keep our finger on the freeze-frame button and look at some important parts of the previous action. Let's run the video from 1960 to 2006.

Figure 23.14 shows the state of the economy in 1960 at the point where the aggregate demand curve AD_{60} and the short-run aggregate supply curve SAS_{60} intersect. Real GDP was £414 billion and the price level was 6 (with 2005 as the base year). By 2006, the economy had reached the intersection of aggregate demand curve AD_{06} and short-run aggregate supply curve SAS_{06}. Real GDP was £1,257 billion and the price level was 102.

The path traced by the blue and red dots between 1960 and 2006 in Figure 23.14 shows three key features:

- Economic growth
- Inflation
- Business cycles

Economic Growth

The rightward movement of the points in Figure 23.14 shows economic growth. The faster the growth rate, the larger is the horizontal distance between successive dots. The force generating economic growth is an increase in long-run aggregate supply, which occurs because the quantity of labour grows, we accumulate physical capital and human capital and our technologies advance.

Figure 23.14

Aggregate Supply and Aggregate Demand: 1960–2006

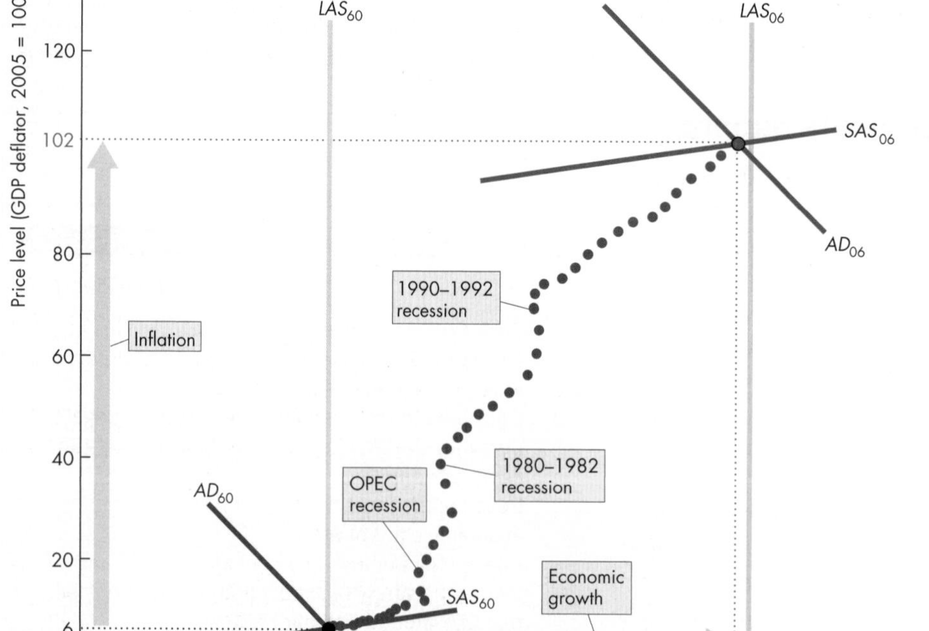

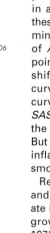

Each point shows the price level and real GDP in a given year. In 1960, these variables were determined by the intersection of AD_{60} and SAS_{60}. Each point is generated by the shifting AD and SAS curves. By 2006, these curves were AD_{06} and SAS_{06}. Real GDP grew and the price level increased. But economic growth and inflation did not proceed smoothly.

Real GDP grew quickly and inflation was moderate in the 1960s; real GDP growth sagged in 1974–1975 and again in 1980–1982 and in 1990–1992. But growth speeded up during the recoveries from the 1980–1982 and 1990–1992 recessions.

Inflation was rapid during the 1970s but slowed during the 1980s.

Source of data: Office for National Statistics.

Inflation

The price level rises over the years – shown in Figure 23.14 by the upward movement of the points. The more rapid the inflation rate, the larger is the vertical distance between successive dots in the figure. The main force generating the persistent increase in the price level is a tendency for aggregate demand to increase at a faster pace than the increase in long-run aggregate supply. All of the factors that increase aggregate demand and shift the aggregate demand curve influence the pace of inflation. But one factor – the growth of the quantity of money – is the main source of *persistent* increases in aggregate demand and persistent inflation.

Business Cycles

Over the years, the economy grows and shrinks in cycles – shown in Figure 23.14 by the wavelike pattern made by the points, with recessions highlighted in red. The cycles arise because both the expansion of short-run aggregate supply and the growth of aggregate demand do not proceed at a fixed, steady pace. Although the economy has cycles, recessions do not usually follow quickly on the heels of their predecessors; "double-dip" recessions like the one in the cartoon are rare.

"Please stand by for a series of tones. The first indicates the official end of the recession, the second indicates prosperity, and the third the return of the recession."

The Evolving Economy: 1960–2006

During the 1960s, real GDP growth was rapid and inflation was low. This was a period of rapid increases in aggregate supply and of moderate increases in aggregate demand.

The 1970s were years of rapid inflation and slow growth. The major sources of these developments were a series of massive oil price increases that slowed the rightward shift of the long-run aggregate supply curve and rapid increases in the quantity of money that shifted the aggregate demand curve rightward. The short-run aggregate supply curve shifted leftward at a faster pace than the aggregate demand shifted rightward.

The rest of the 1970s saw high inflation – the price level increased quickly – and only moderate growth in real GDP. By 1979, inflation was a major problem and the government decided to take strong action against inflation. The Bank of England raised interest rates to previously unknown levels. Consequently, aggregate demand decreased. The decrease in aggregate demand put the UK economy in a deep recession.

The economy began to expand after 1982, with improved aggregate supply policies, which increased potential GDP. Steady growth moved the UK economy to above full-employment in 1987 to 1990. Inflation increased during this period and the UK economy was in this condition when a decrease in aggregate demand led to the 1990–1992 recession. The economy again embarked on a path of expansion over the rest of the 1990s until 2006, where the economy was at or perhaps a bit above full employment.

Review Quiz

Study Plan 23.4

1. How does the *AS–AD* model explain the economic growth and inflation of the past 40 years?
2. How does the *AS–AD* model explain the business cycles of the 1970s, 1980s and 1990s?

The *AS–AD* model explains economic growth, inflation, and the business cycle. The model is a useful one because it enables us to keep our eye on the big picture. But it lacks detail. It does not tell us as much as we need to know about the deeper forces that lie behind aggregate supply and aggregate demand. But we can use the *AS–AD* model to explain and illustrate the views of the alternative schools of thought in macroeconomics.

Macroeconomic Schools of Thought

Macroeconomics is an active field of research and much remains to be learned about the forces that make our economy grow, bring inflation, and generate business cycles. There is a greater degree of consensus and certainty about economic growth and inflation trends – the longer term changes in real GDP and the price level – than there is about the business cycle – the short-term fluctuations in these variables. Here, we'll look only at differences of view about short-term fluctuations.

The *AS–AD* model that you've studied in this chapter provides a good foundation for understanding the range of views that macroeconomists hold about this topic. But what you will learn here is just a first glimpse at the scientific controversy and debate. We'll return to these issues at various later points in the text and deepen your appreciation of the alternative views.

Classification usually requires simplification. And classifying macroeconomists is no exception to this general rule. The classification that we'll use here is simple, but it is not misleading. We identify three macroeconomic schools of thought and examine the views of each group in turn. We examine:

- The Classical view
- The Keynesian view
- The Monetarist view

The Classical View

A **classical** macroeconomist believes that the economy is self-regulating and that it is always at full employment. The term "classical" derives from the name of the founding school of economics that includes Adam Smith, David Ricardo and John Stuart Mill.

A **new classical** view is that business cycle fluctuations are the efficient responses of a well-functioning market economy that is bombarded by shocks that arise from the uneven pace of technological change.

The classical view can be understood in terms of beliefs about aggregate demand and aggregate supply.

Aggregate Demand Fluctuations

In the classical view, technological change is the most significant influence on both aggregate demand and aggregate supply. For this reason, classical macroeconomists don't use the *AS–AD* framework. But their views can be interpreted in this framework. A technological change that increases the productivity of capital brings an increase in aggregate demand because firms increase their expenditure on new plant and equipment. A technological change that lengthens the useful life of existing capital decreases the demand for new capital, which decreases aggregate demand.

Aggregate Supply Response

In the classical view, the money wage rate that lies behind the short-run aggregate supply curve is instantly and completely flexible. The money wage rate adjusts so quickly to maintain equilibrium in the labour market that real GDP always adjusts to equal potential GDP.

Potential GDP itself fluctuates for the same reasons that aggregate demand fluctuates: technological change. When the pace of technological change is rapid, potential GDP increases quickly and so does real GDP. When the pace of technological change slows, so does the growth rate of potential GDP.

Classical Policy

The classical view of policy emphasizes the potential for taxes to stunt incentives and create inefficiency. By minimizing the disincentive effects that taxes have, employment, investment and technological advance are at their efficient levels and the economy expands at an appropriate and rapid pace.

The Keynesian View

A **Keynesian** macroeconomist believes that left alone, the economy would rarely operate at full employment and that to achieve and maintain full employment, active help from fiscal policy and monetary policy is required. The term "Keynesian" derives from the name of one of the twentieth century's most famous economists, John Maynard Keynes.

The Keynesian view is based on beliefs about the forces that determine aggregate demand and short-run aggregate supply.

Aggregate Demand Fluctuations

In the Keynesian view, *expectations* are the most significant influence on aggregate demand. And expectations are based on herd instinct or, what Keynes himself called "animal spirits". A wave of pessimism about future profit prospects can lead to a fall in aggregate demand and plunge the economy into recession.

Aggregate Supply Response

In the Keynesian view, the money wage rate that lies behind the short-run aggregate supply curve is extremely sticky downward. Basically, the money wage rate doesn't fall. So if there is a recessionary gap, there is no automatic mechanism for getting rid of it. If it were to happen, a fall in the money wage rate would increase short-run aggregate supply and restore full employment. But the money wage rate doesn't fall, so the economy remains stuck in recession.

A modern version of the Keynesian view known as the **new Keynesian** view holds that not only is the money wage rate sticky but that prices of goods and services are also sticky. With a sticky price level, the short-run aggregate supply curve is horizontal at a fixed price level.

Policy Response Needed

The Keynesian view calls for fiscal policy and monetary policy to actively offset the changes in aggregate demand that bring recession. By stimulating aggregate demand in a recession, full employment can be restored.

The Monetarist View

A **monetarist** is a macroeconomist who believes that the economy is self-regulating and that it will normally operate at full employment, provided that monetary policy is not erratic and that the pace of money growth is kept steady. The term "monetarist" was coined by an outstanding twentieth century economist, Karl Brunner, to describe his own and Milton Friedman's views.

The monetarist view can be interpreted in terms of beliefs about the forces that determine aggregate demand and short-run aggregate supply.

Aggregate Demand Fluctuations

In the monetarist view, the quantity of money is the most significant influence on aggregate demand. And the quantity of money is determined by the Bank of England. If the Bank of England keeps money growing at a steady pace, aggregate demand fluctuations will be minimized and the economy will operate close to full employment. But if the Bank of England decreases the quantity of money or even just slows its growth rate too abruptly, the economy will go into recession. In the monetarist view, all recessions result from inappropriate monetary policy.

Aggregate Supply Response

The monetarist view of short-run aggregate supply is the same as the Keynesian view – the money wage rate is sticky. If the economy is in recession, it will take an unnecessarily long time for it to return unaided to full employment.

Monetarist Policy

The monetarist view of policy is the same as the classical view on fiscal policy. Taxes should be kept low to avoid disincentive effects that decrease potential GDP. Provided that the quantity of money is kept on a steady growth path, no active stabilization is needed to offset changes in aggregate demand.

The Way Ahead

You will encounter classical, Keynesian, and monetarist views in the chapters that follow. In the next chapter, we study the classical model. Then we study the Keynesian model. From there, we study money and inflation and lay the foundation for a deeper look at the sources of macroeconomic fluctuations and economic growth. We finish with a close look at the fiscal policies and monetary policies that try to achieve faster growth, stable prices and a smoother cycle.

Review Quiz

Study Plan 23.5

1 What are the defining features of classical macroeconomics and what policies do classical macroeconomists recommend?
2 What are the defining features of Keynesian macroeconomics and what policies do Keynesian macroeconomists recommend?
3 What are the defining features of monetarist macroeconomics and what policies do monetarist macroeconomists recommend?

To complete your study of the *AS–AD* model, take a look at the UK economy in 2005 and 2006 through the eyes of this model in *Reading Between the Lines* on pp. 528–529.

Reading Between the Lines

Aggregate Supply and Aggregate Demand in Action

The Financial Times, 24 November 2006

Business investment drives UK economy forward

Jamie Chisholm

A surge in business investment helped the UK economy grow above its long-term trend in the third quarter, figures released on Friday confirmed. . . .

The Office for National Statistics confirmed its earlier assessment that GDP grew 0.7 per cent between July and September, compared with the previous three months. Against the same period a year ago, GDP was up by 2.7 per cent, rounded down from 2.8 per cent. . . .

Gross fixed capital formation, or public and private sector investment, climbed by 2.3 per cent in the third quarter against the previous three months, up sharply from the 0.6 increase recorded for the second quarter of 2006. Of this, investment by business was up by 3.1 per cent.

Purchases of services and semi-durable goods helped household spending to rise by 0.4 per cent quarter-on-quarter, but this was a slower pace of growth than the 0.9 per cent seen in the second quarter.

The services sector remained buoyant, expanding by 0.8 per cent between the second and third quarter, while manufacturing continued to rebound, up 0.6 per cent over the same period. . . .

Howard Archer at Global Insight said: "GDP growth now seems set to come in around 2.6 per cent for the whole of 2006. The Bank of England expects growth to accelerate to 3.0 per cent in 2007, but we suspect that it is more likely to be around 2.5 per cent as the upside is limited by slower global growth and the significant headwinds facing the consumer."

These headwinds, said Mr Archer, included higher interest rates and utility bills, moderate earnings growth, an increasing tax burden and rising debt levels.

The Essence of the Story

- Real GDP in the third quarter of 2006 was 2.7 per cent higher than the same quarter in 2005.
- The stronger growth resulted from stronger growth in investment expenditure in the third quarter.
- The rapid growth of GDP has pushed the economy above potential GDP.

Economic Analysis

- Figure 1 shows the real GDP growth and growth of investment from the first quarter of 2005 to the third quarter of 2006. You can see that the growth rate increased during the first three quarters of 2006 and growth in investment has been particularly high.
- Figure 2 shows the economy in the third quarter of 2005. The long-run aggregate supply curve was LAS_{05} with potential GDP at £308 billion (quarterly rate).
- The short-run aggregate supply curve was SAS_{05}, the aggregate demand curve was AD_{05} and equilibrium real GDP was £307 billion.
- There was a recessionary gap in the first quarter of 2005 of £1 billion or about 0.3 per cent of potential GDP.
- Figure 3 shows the changes in the economy during the year to the third quarter of 2006. The long-run aggregate supply curve shifted rightward to LAS_{06} with potential GDP at £315 billion. This increase in potential GDP represents an economic growth rate of 2.3 per cent a year.
- The short-run aggregate supply curve shifted to SAS_{06}, the aggregate demand curve shifted to AD_{06} and equilibrium real GDP increased to equal potential GDP at 315 billion.
- In the year to the third quarter of 2006, real GDP grew faster than potential GDP – a situation described in the news article as GDP growing "above its long term trend".
- If aggregate demand grows faster than potential GDP during 2007, an inflationary gap will arise.
- The increase in investment will eventually speed potential GDP growth. But this effect comes over a longer period and does not increased aggregate supply immediately.

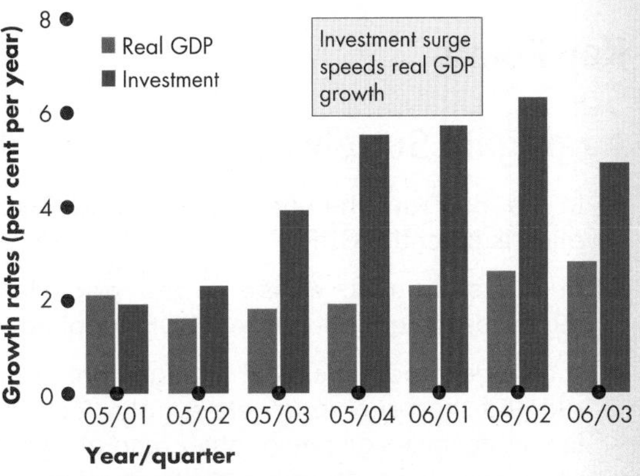

Figure 1 Real GDP and investment growth

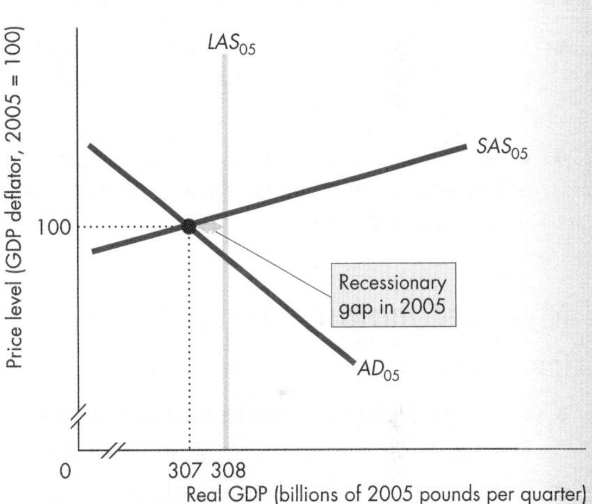

Figure 2 The economy in 2005 third quarter

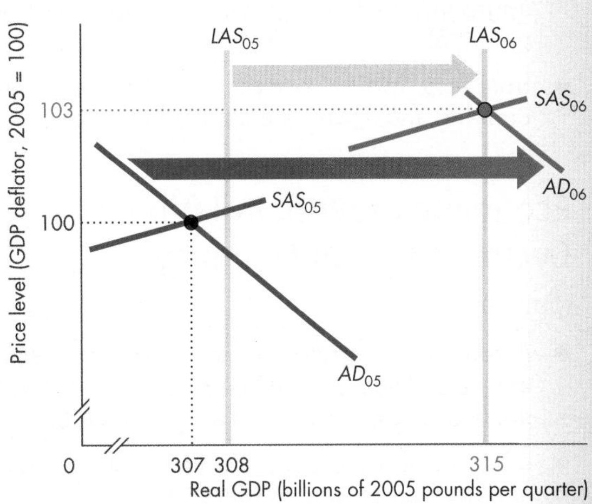

Figure 3 The changes in the year to 2006 third quarter

Summary

Key Points

Aggregate Supply (pp. 510–514)

- In the long run, the quantity of real GDP supplied is potential GDP.
- In the short run, a rise in the price level increases the quantity of real GDP supplied.
- A change in potential GDP changes both long-run and short-run aggregate supply. A change in the money wage rate or other resource prices changes only short-run aggregate supply.

Aggregate Demand (pp. 515–518)

- A rise in the price level decreases the quantity of real GDP demanded because of wealth and substitution effects.
- Changes in expectations, fiscal policy, monetary policy and the world economy change aggregate demand.

Macroeconomic Equilibrium (pp. 518–523)

- Aggregate demand and short-run aggregate supply determine real GDP and the price level.
- In the long run, real GDP equals potential GDP and aggregate demand determines the price.
- Economic growth occurs because potential GDP increases and inflation occurs because aggregate demand grows more quickly than potential GDP.
- Business cycles occur because aggregate demand and aggregate supply fluctuate.

Economic Growth, Inflation and Cycles in the UK Economy (pp. 524–525)

- Potential GDP grew fastest during the 1960s, and late 1990s and 2000s, and slowest during the late 1970s, early 1980s and early 1990s.
- Inflation persists because aggregate demand grows faster than potential GDP.
- Cycles occur because aggregate supply and aggregate demand change at an uneven pace.

Macroeconomic Schools of Thought (pp. 526–527)

- Classical economists believe that the economy is self-regulating and always at full employment.
- Keynesian economists believe that full employment can be achieved only with active policy.
- Monetarist economists believe that recessions result from inappropriate monetary policy.

Key Figures

Key Terms

Problems

Tests, Study Plan and Solutions* 

1 The following events have occurred at times in the history of the United Kingdom:

(i) A deep recession hits the world economy.

(ii) Oil prices rise sharply.

(iii) Businesses expect huge losses in the near future.

a Explain for each event whether it changes short-run aggregate supply, long-run aggregate supply, aggregate demand or some combination of them.

b Explain the separate effects of each event on UK real GDP and the price level, starting from a position of long-run equilibrium.

c Explain the combined effects of these events on UK real GDP and the price level, starting from a position of long-run equilibrium.

d Describe what a classical macroeconomist, a Keynesian and a monetarist would want to do in response to each of the above events.

2 The following events have occurred at times in the history of Spain:

(i) A strong expansion in the world economy.

(ii) Businesses expect huge profits in the near future.

(iii) The government of Spain increases its expenditure on goods and services.

a Explain for each event whether it changes short-run aggregate supply, long-run aggregate supply, aggregate demand or some combination of them.

b Explain the separate effects of each event on real GDP and the price level in Spain, starting from a position of long-run equilibrium.

c Explain the combined effects of these events on real GDP and the price level in Spain, starting from a position of long-run equilibrium.

3 The economy of Mainland has the following aggregate demand and short-run aggregate supply schedules:

Price level	Real GDP demanded	Real GDP supplied in the short run
	(billions of 2005 euros)	
90	450	350
100	400	400
110	350	450
120	300	500
130	250	550
140	200	600

a What is the short-run macroeconomic equilibrium in Mainland?

b Mainland's potential GDP is €500 billion. Does Mainland have an inflationary gap or a recessionary gap and what is its magnitude?

4 In Mainland, described in problem 3, what is the magnitude and direction of the change in real GDP and the price level when each of the following events occur:

a Aggregate demand increases by €100 billion.

b The money wage rises and short-run aggregate supply changes by €100 billion.

c Potential GDP increases by €150 billion.

5 In Japan, potential GDP is 600 trillion yen and the table shows aggregate demand and short-run aggregate supply schedules.

Price level	Real GDP demanded	Real GDP supplied in the short run
	(billions of 2000 yen)	
75	600	400
85	550	450
95	500	500
105	450	550
115	400	600
125	350	650
135	300	700

a Draw a graph of the aggregate demand curve and short-run aggregate supply curve.

b What is the short-run equilibrium real GDP and price level?

c Does Japan have an inflationary gap or a recessionary gap and what is its magnitude?

6 US real GDP during the second quarter of 2006 was \$11,388 billion compared to \$11,002 billion in the same quarter of 2005. The GDP deflator was 115.9, up from 112.2 in the second quarter of 2005. Potential GDP was estimated to be \$11,491 billion in the second quarter of 2006 and \$11,146 billion a year earlier.

a Draw a graph of the aggregate demand curve, the short-run aggregate supply curve, and the long-run aggregate supply curve in 2005 that is consistent with these numbers.

b On the graph, show how the aggregate demand curve, the short-run aggregate supply curve, and the long-run aggregate supply curve shifted during the year to the second quarter of 2006.

* Solutions to odd-numbered problems are provided.

7 In the economy shown in the graph, initially the short-run aggregate supply is SAS_0 and aggregate demand is AD_0. Then some events change aggregate demand and the aggregate demand curve shifts rightward to AD_1. Later, some other events change aggregate supply and shift the short-run aggregate supply curve leftward to SAS_1.

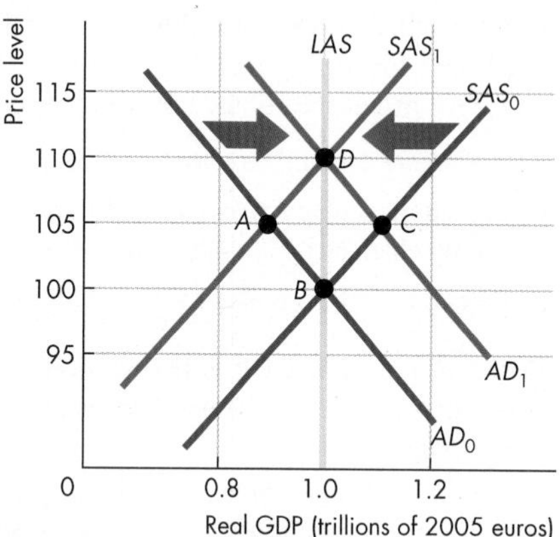

a What is the equilibrium point after the change in aggregate demand?

b What is the equilibrium point after the change in aggregate supply?

c What events could have changed aggregate demand from AD_0 to AD_1?

d What events could have changed aggregate supply from SAS_0 to SAS_1?

Critical Thinking

1 After you have studied *Reading Between the Lines* on pp. 528–529, answer the following questions.

a Describe the growth of the UK economy during the period between 2000 and the third quarter of 2006.

b Did the United Kingdom have a recessionary gap, an inflationary gap or full employment in the third quarter of 2006?

c Use the *AS–AD* model to illustrate the UK economy during 2006.

d Suppose that aggregate demand continues to expand rapidly through the rest of 2006 and that the Bank of England does not act strongly enough to dampen the expansion. Use the *AS–AD* model to illustrate the state of the economy at the beginning of 2007. Indicate whether there is full employment, a recessionary gap or an inflationary gap.

e Suppose that aggregate demand continues to expand rapidly through the rest of 2006 but that the Bank of England does act strongly enough to dampen the expansion. Use the *AS–AD* model to illustrate the state of the economy at the beginning of 2007. Indicate whether there is full employment, a recessionary gap or an inflationary gap.

2 The International Monetary Fund's World Economic Outlook database provides the following data for India in 2004, 2005 and 2006.

	2004	2005	2006
Real GDP growth rate	8.1	8.3	7.3
Inflation rate	4.2	4.7	4.6

a What changes in long-run and short-run aggregate supply and aggregate demand are consistent with these numbers?

b Draw a graph to illustrate your answer to part (a).

c List the main factors that might have produced the changes in aggregate supply and aggregate demand that you have described in your answer to part (a).

d From the above data, do you think India has an inflationary gap, a recessionary gap or is at full employment?

Web Activities

Links to Websites

1 Visit the Office for National Statistics to obtain the data on real GDP and the price level for the United Kingdom.

a Use the data to update Figure 23.14.

b What has happened to real GDP and the price level?

c What has happened to aggregate demand and short-run aggregate supply since 2006?

d Use this information to assess whether real GDP in 2007 was above, below or at potential GDP.

2 Find data on recent change in and forecasts of real GDP and the price level in the European Union.

a What is your forecast of EU real GDP for the coming year?

b What is your forecast of the EU price level for the coming year?

c What is your forecast of the growth rate of real GDP?

d What is your forecast of the EU inflation rate?

In the Long Run: The Classical Model

CHAPTER 24

After studying this chapter you will be able to:

- Explain the purpose of the classical model
- Describe the relationship between the quantity of labour employed and real GDP
- Explain what determines full employment, the real wage rate and potential GDP
- Explain what determines unemployment at full employment
- Explain how borrowing and lending interact to determine saving, investment and the real interest rate
- Use the classical model to explain changes in potential GDP and the standard of living
- Explain the links between the labour market and aggregate supply

Our Economy's Compass

Economic growth is like a voyage of discovery through an unknown ocean. Battered by waves and winds, the explorer's ship keeps getting knocked off course. But with the help of a compass, it always returns to the main path forward. The economy is battered by forces that bring a recessionary or inflationary gap. But the economy also has compass. Powerful market forces keep returning the economy to full employment.

In this chapter you learn about the economy's compass. And in *Reading Between the Lines*, you will apply what you learn to help you better understand productivity growth in the UK economy in recent years.

The Classical Model: A Preview

Economists have made progress in understanding how the economy works by dividing the variables that describe macroeconomic performance into real variables and nominal variables.

Real variables, which include real GDP, employment and unemployment, the real wage rate, consumption, saving, investment and the real interest rate, measure quantities that tell us what is *really* happening to economic well-being.

Nominal variables, which include the price level (RPI, CPI and GDP deflator), the inflation rate, nominal GDP, the nominal wage rate and the nominal interest rate, measure objects that tell us how *pound values* and the cost of living are changing.

The Classical Model

This separation of macroeconomic performance into a real part and a nominal (or money) part is based on a huge insight called the **classical dichotomy**, which states:

> **At full employment, the forces that determine real variables are independent of those that determine nominal variables.**

In practical terms, the classical dichotomy means that we can explain why real GDP per person in the United Kingdom is 30 times that in Burundi by looking only at the real parts of the two economies and ignoring differences in their price levels and inflation rates. Similarly, we can explain why real GDP per person in the United Kingdom in 2006 was more than twice that in 1966 without considering what has happened to the value of the pound between those two years.

The **classical model** – a model of the economy that determines the *real* variables – real GDP, employment and unemployment, the real wage rate, consumption, saving, investment and the real interest rate – at full employment.

Most economists believe that the economy is rarely at full employment and that the business cycle is a fluctuation around full employment, so the classical model explains only one aspect of macroeconomic performance. Some classical economists think that the economy is always at full employment and that the business cycle is a fluctuation of the full-employment economy. Regardless of which view of the cycle an economist takes, all agree that the classical model that you're now going to study provides powerful insights into macroeconomic performance.

Study Plan 24.1

Real GDP and Employment

To produce more output, we must use more labour or more capital or develop technologies that are more productive. It takes time to change the quantity of capital and the state of technology. But the quantity of labour employed can change quickly. So we can change real GDP quickly by changing the quantity of labour employed.

Aggregate Production Possibilities

When you studied the limits to production in Chapter 2 (see p. 36) you learned about the *production possibilities frontier*, which is the boundary between those combinations of goods and services that can be produced and those that cannot. An *aggregate* production possibilities frontier describes the limits to real GDP. The aggregate production possibilities frontier shows the limits to what is attainable for two special "goods" – real GDP and the quantity of leisure time.

Aggregate Production Possibilities Frontier

Real GDP is a measure of all the final goods and services produced in the economy in a given time period (see Chapter 21, p. 479). We measure real GDP as a number of 2005 pounds, but the measure is a *real* one. Real GDP is not a quantity of pounds. It is a quantity of goods and services. Think of it as a number of big shopping carts filled with goods and services. Each cart contains some of each of the different goods and services produced and one cartload of items costs £1 billion. To say that real GDP is £1,300 billion means that real GDP is 1,300 big shopping carts of goods and services.

The quantity of leisure time is the number of hours we spend not working. It is the time we spend playing or watching sports, seeing movies, going to concerts and hanging out with friends. It also includes the time we spend searching for a job if we don't have one.

Each hour that we spent pursuing fun could have been an hour spent working. So when the quantity of leisure time increases by one hour, the quantity of labour employed decreases by one hour. If we spent all our time having fun rather than working we would not produce anything. Real GDP would be zero. The more leisure we forgo, the greater is the quantity of labour employed and the greater is real GDP.

The relationship between leisure time and real GDP is a *production possibilities frontier* (*PPF*). Figure 24.1(a)

Figure 24.1 myeconlab

Production Possibilities and the Production Function

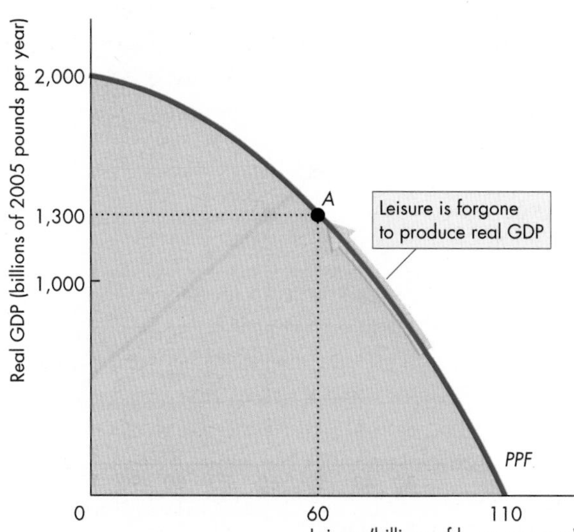

(a) Production possibilities frontier

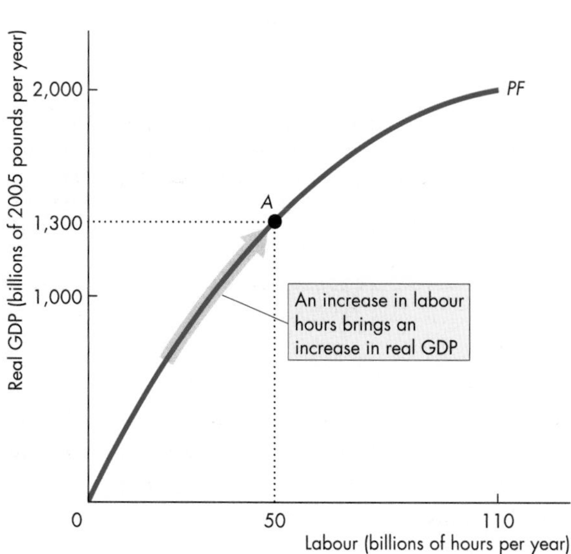

(b) Production function

On the *PPF* in part (a), if we enjoy 110 billion hours of leisure, we produce no real GDP. If we take only 60 billion hours of leisure and work for 50 billion hours, we produce a real GDP of £1,300 billion, at point *A*.

At point *A* on the production function *PF* in part (b), we work for 50 billion hours and produce £1,300 billion of real GDP.

shows an example of this frontier. Here, an economy has 110 billion hours of time available. If people use all these hours to pursue leisure, no labour is employed and real GDP is zero. As people forgo leisure and work more, real GDP increases. If people took 60 billion hours in leisure and spent 50 billion hours working, real GDP would be £1,300 billion at point *A*. If people spent all the available hours working, real GDP would be £2,000 billion.

The downward slope of the *PPF* describes the trade-off between leisure and real GDP. The outward bow of the *PPF* displays increasing opportunity cost. In this case, the opportunity cost of a given amount of real GDP is the amount of leisure forgone to produce the real GDP. The additional hours of leisure forgone to produce a given additional amount of real GDP increases as real GDP increases. The reason is that we use the most productive labour first and, as we use more labour, we use increasingly less productive labour.

Production Function

The **production function** is the relationship between real GDP and the quantity of labour employed when all other influences on production remain the same. The production function (*PF*) is like a mirror image of the *PPF* of leisure and real GDP. Figure 24.1(b) shows the production function for the economy whose *PPF* is shown in Figure 24.1(a). When the quantity of labour employed is zero, real GDP is also zero. And as the quantity of labour employed increases, so does real GDP. When 50 billion labour hours are employed, real GDP is £1,300 billion (at point *A*).

A decrease in leisure hours and the corresponding increases in the quantity of labour employed bring movements along the production possibilities frontier and along the production function and increases real GDP. The arrows along the *PPF* and the *PF* curves in Figure 24.1 show these movements. An example of such movements occurred during the first four years of the Second World War when employment and real GDP surged.

Review Quiz

Study Plan 24.2

1. What is the relationship between the leisure time–real GDP *PPF* and the production function?
2. What does the outward-bowed shape of the leisure time–real GDP *PPF* imply about the opportunity cost of real GDP and why is the *PPF* bowed outward?

The Labour Market and Potential GDP

You've seen that in a given year, with a given amount of physical and human capital and given technology, real GDP depends on the quantity of labour hours employed. To produce more real GDP, we must employ more labour hours. The labour market determines the quantity of labour hours employed and the quantity of real GDP supplied. We'll learn how by studying:

- The demand for labour
- The supply of labour
- Labour market equilibrium and potential GDP

The Demand for Labour

The *quantity of labour demanded* is the labour hours hired by all the firms in the economy. The **demand for labour** is the relationship between the quantity of labour demanded and the real wage rate when all other influences on firms' hiring plans remain the same. The **real wage rate** is the quantity of goods and services that an hour of labour earns. In contrast, the **money wage rate** is the number of pounds that an hour of labour earns. A real wage rate is equal to a money wage rate divided by the price of a good. For the economy as a whole, the average real wage rate equals the average money wage rate divided by the price level multiplied by 100. So we express the real wage rate in constant pounds. (Today, we express this real wage rate in 2005 pounds.)

Other things remaining the same, the lower the real wage rate, the greater is the quantity of labour demanded. The *real* wage rate influences the quantity of labour demanded because what matters to firms is how much output they must sell to earn the number of pounds they pay (the money wage rate).

We can represent the demand for labour as either a demand schedule or a demand curve. The table in Figure 24.2 shows part of a demand for labour schedule and the graph shows the corresponding demand for labour curve. For example, if the real wage rate is £20.00 an hour, the quantity of labour demanded is 40 billion hours a year (row *A* and point *A*) and if the real wage rate is £17.50 an hour, the quantity of labour demanded is 50 billion hours a year (row *B* and point *B*). The demand for labour curve is the downward sloping curve *LD*.

Why does the quantity of labour demanded *increase* as the real wage rate *decreases*? That is, why does the demand for labour curve slope downward?

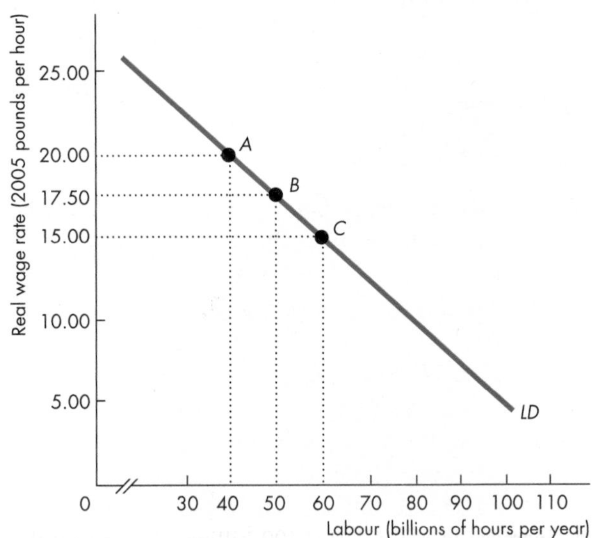

	Real wage rate (2005 pounds per hour)	Quantity of labour demanded (billions of hours per year)
A	20.00	40
B	17.50	50
C	15.00	60

The table shows part of a demand for labour schedule. Points *A*, *B* and *C* on the demand for labour curve correspond to the rows of the table. The lower the real wage rate, the greater is the quantity of labour demanded. The demand for labour curve slopes downward.

The basic answer is that productivity of each additional hour of labour is less than the productivity of the previously employed hour – the marginal product of labour diminishes.

The Diminishing Marginal Product of Labour

The **marginal product of labour** is the additional real GDP produced by an additional hour of labour when all other influences on production remain the same. The marginal product of labour is governed by the **law of diminishing returns**, which states that as the quantity of labour increases, other things remaining the same, the marginal product of labour decreases.

The Law of Diminishing Returns

Diminishing returns arise because the amount of capital is fixed. Two people operating one machine are not twice as productive as one person operating one machine. Eventually, as more labour is hired, workers get in each other's way and output barely increases.

Marginal Product Calculation

We calculate the marginal product of labour as the change in real GDP divided by the change in the quantity of labour employed. Figure 24.3(a) shows some marginal product calculations and Figure 24.3(b) shows the marginal product curve.

In Figure 24.3(a), when the quantity of labour employed increases from 30 billion hours to 50 billion hours, an increase of 20 billion hours, real GDP increases from £900 billion to £1,300 billion, an increase of £400 billion. The marginal product of labour equals the increase in real GDP (£400 billion) divided by the increase in the quantity of labour employed (20 billion hours), which is £20 an hour.

When the quantity of labour employed increases from 50 billion hours to 70 billion hours, an increase of 20 billion hours, real GDP increases from £1,300 billion to £1,600 billion, an increase of £300 billion. The marginal product of labour equals £300 billion divided 20 billion hours, which is £15 an hour.

In Figure 24.3(b), as the quantity of labour employed increases, the marginal product of labour diminishes. Between 30 billion and 50 billion hours (at 40 billion hours), marginal product is £20 an hour – at point *A*. And between 50 billion and 70 billion hours (at 60 billion hours), marginal product is £15 an hour – at point *C*.

The diminishing marginal product of labour limits the demand for labour.

Diminishing Marginal Product and the Demand for Labour

Firms are in business to maximize profits. Each hour of labour that a firm hires increases output but adds to costs. Initially, an extra hour of labour produces more output than the real wage that the labour costs. Marginal product exceeds the real wage rate. But each additional hour of labour produces less additional output – the marginal product of labour diminishes.

As a firm hires more labour, eventually the extra output from an extra hour of labour is exactly what that hour of labour costs. At this point, marginal product equals the real wage rate. Hire one less hour and

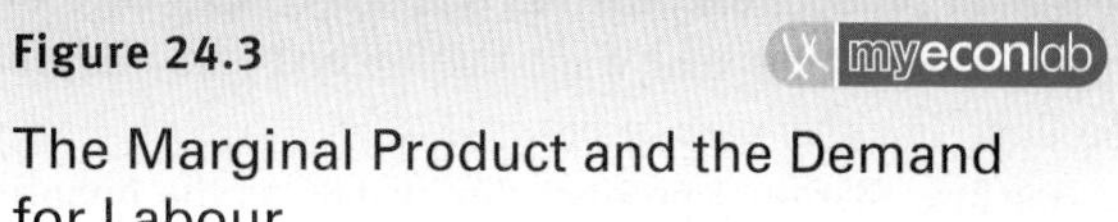

Figure 24.3 myeconlab

The Marginal Product and the Demand for Labour

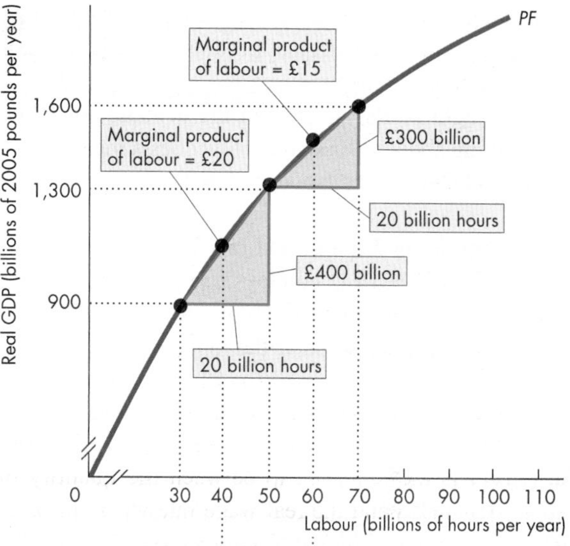

(a) Calculating marginal product

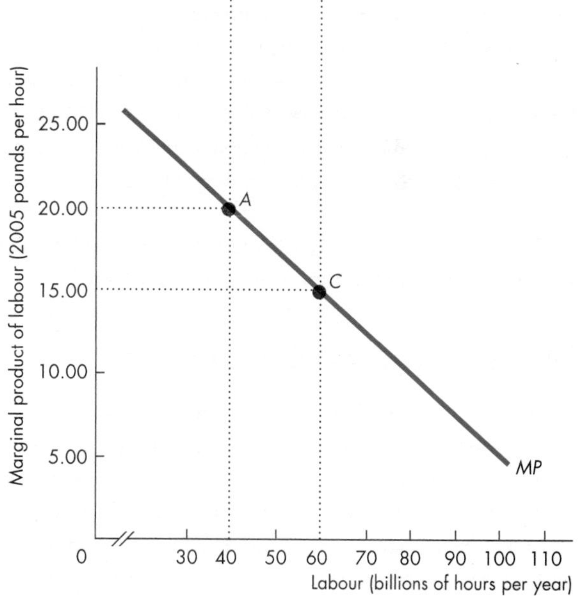

(b) The marginal product curve

In part (a), between 30 billion and 50 billion hours, the marginal product of labour is £20 an hour. Between 50 billion and 70 billion hours, the marginal product of labour is £15 an hour. In part (b), at 40 billion hours (between 30 billion and 50 billion), the marginal product of labour is £20 an hour at point *A* on the *MP* curve. The *MP* curve is the demand for labour curve.

marginal product exceeds the real wage rate. Hire one more hour and the real wage rate exceeds the marginal product. In either case, profit is less.

Because marginal product diminishes as the quantity of labour employed increases, the lower the real wage rate, the greater is the quantity of labour that a firm can profitably hire. The marginal product curve is the same as the demand for labour curve.

You might better understand the demand for labour by thinking about an example. How does a meat pie factory decide how much labour to hire?

The Demand for Labour at Liz's Meat Pie Plant

Suppose that when Liz employs one additional hour of labour, output increases by 3 pies an hour. Marginal product is 3 pies an hour. If the money wage rate is £6 an hour and if meat pies sell for £2 each, the real wage rate is 3 pies an hour. (We calculate the real wage rate as the money wage rate of £6 an hour divided by a price of a pie, £2, which equals a real wage rate of 3 pies an hour.) Because marginal product diminishes, we know that if Liz did not hire this hour of labour, marginal product would exceed 3 pies. Because Liz can hire the hour of labour for a real wage rate of 3 pies, it pays Liz to do so.

If the price of a meat pie remains at £2 and the money wage rate falls to £4 an hour, the real wage rate falls to 2 pies an hour and Liz increases the quantity of labour demanded. Similarly, if the money wage rate remains at £6 an hour and the price of a meat pie rises to £3, the real wage rate falls to 2 pies an hour and Liz increases the quantity of labour demanded.

When the firm pays a real wage rate equal to the marginal product of labour, it is maximizing profit.

Changes in the Demand for Labour

A change in the real wage rate brings a change in the quantity of labour demanded, which is shown by a movement along the demand curve. A change in any other influence on a firm's decision to hire labour brings a change in the demand for labour, which is shown by a shift of the demand curve. These other influences are the quantities of physical and human capital and technology. An increase in capital or an advance in technology shifts the production function upward. These same forces increase the marginal product of labour and shift the demand for labour curve rightward. Labour-saving technological change decreases the demand for some types of labour, but overall advances in technology increase the demand for labour.

The Supply of Labour

The *quantity of labour supplied* is the number of labour hours that all the households in the economy plan to work. The **supply of labour** is the relationship between the quantity of labour supplied and the real wage rate when all other influences on work plans remain the same.

We can represent the supply of labour as either a supply schedule or a supply curve. The table in Figure 24.4 shows a supply of labour schedule. It tells us the quantity of labour supplied at three different real wage rates. For example, if the real wage rate rises from £7.50 an hour (row *A*) to £17.50 an hour (row *B*), the quantity of labour supplied increases from 40 billion hours to 50 billion hours a year.

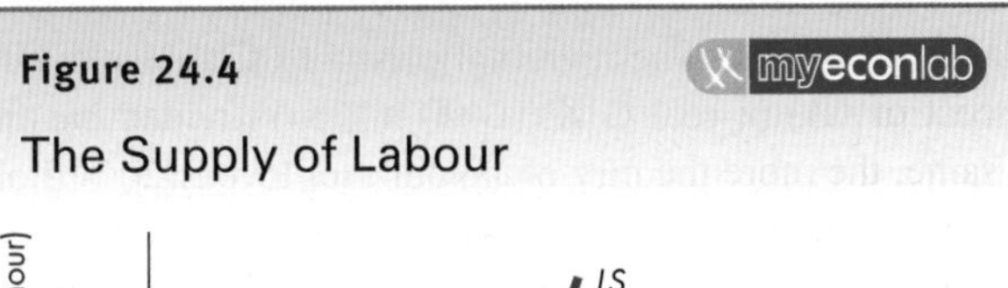

Figure 24.4

The Supply of Labour

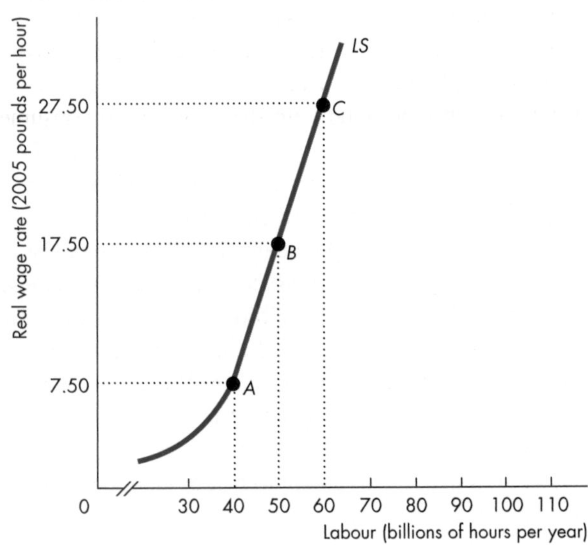

	Real wage rate (2005 pounds per hour)	Quantity of labour supplied (billions of hours per year)
A	7.50	40
B	17.50	50
C	27.50	60

The table shows part of a supply of labour schedule. Points *A*, *B* and *C* on the supply of labour curve correspond to the rows of the table. The higher the real wage rate, the greater is the quantity of labour supplied.

The curve *LS* is a supply of labour curve. Points *A*, *B* and *C* on the curve correspond to rows *A*, *B* and *C* of the supply schedule.

The *real* wage rate influences the quantity of labour supplied because what matters to people is not the number of pounds they earn (the money wage rate) but what those pounds will buy.

The quantity of labour supplied increases as the real wage rate increases for two reasons:

- Hours per person increase
- Economic activity rate increases

Hours per Person Increase

In choosing how many hours to work, a household considers the opportunity cost of not working. This opportunity cost is the real wage rate. The higher the real wage rate, the greater is the opportunity cost of taking leisure and not working. And as the opportunity cost of taking leisure rises, other things remaining the same, the more the household chooses to work.

But other things don't remain the same. The higher the real wage rate, the greater is the household's income. And the higher the household's income, the more it wants to consume. One item that it wants to consume more of is leisure.

So a rise in the real wage rate has two opposing effects. By increasing the opportunity cost of leisure, it makes the household want to consume less leisure and to work more. And by increasing the household's income, it makes the household want to consume more leisure and to work fewer hours. For most households, the opportunity cost effect is stronger than the income effect. So the higher the real wage rate, the greater is the amount of work that the household chooses to do.

Economic Activity Rate Increases

Almost everyone has productive opportunities outside the labour force. If the value of one of these other productive activities exceeds the real wage rate, a person will not join the labour force. For example, a parent might work full time caring for her or his child. The alternative is to pay for the child to attend a childcare centre. The parent will choose to work only if he or she can earn a high enough wage rate per hour to pay the cost of childcare, pay the transport costs and taxes involved and have income enough left over to make the work effort worthwhile.

The higher the real wage rate, the more likely it is that a person will choose to work and so the greater is the economic activity rate.

Labour Supply Response

The quantity of labour supplied increases as the real wage rate rises. But the quantity of labour supplied is not highly responsive to the real wage rate. A large percentage change in the real wage rate brings only a small percentage change in the quantity of labour supplied.

Changes in the Supply of Labour

A change in the real wage rate brings a change in the quantity of labour supplied, which is shown by a movement along the supply curve. A change in any other influence on a household's decision to work brings a change in the supply of labour, which is shown by a shift of the supply curve.

The other major influence on the supply of labour is the working-age population. Over time, as the working-age population increases – either because the number of births exceeds the number of deaths, or from immigration – the supply of labour increases.

Other factors that include technology in the home and social attitudes also influence the supply of labour and especially the supply of female labour. Advances in technology in the home along with greater opportunities for women have shifted the supply of labour curve rightward.

Let's now see how the labour market determines employment, the real wage rate and potential GDP.

Labour Market Equilibrium and Potential GDP

The forces of supply and demand operate in labour markets just as they do in the markets for goods and services. The price of labour is the real wage rate. A rise in the real wage rate eliminates a shortage of labour by decreasing the quantity demanded and increasing the quantity supplied. A fall in the real wage rate eliminates a surplus of labour by increasing the quantity demanded and decreasing the quantity supplied. If there is neither a shortage nor a surplus, the labour market is in equilibrium.

In macroeconomics, we study the economy-wide labour market to determine the total quantity of labour employed and the average real wage rate.

Labour Market Equilibrium

Figure 24.5(a) shows a labour market in equilibrium. The demand for labour curve *LD* and the supply of labour curve *LS* are the same as those in Figure 24.2 and Figure 24.4, respectively.

Figure 24.5

The Labour Market and Potential GDP

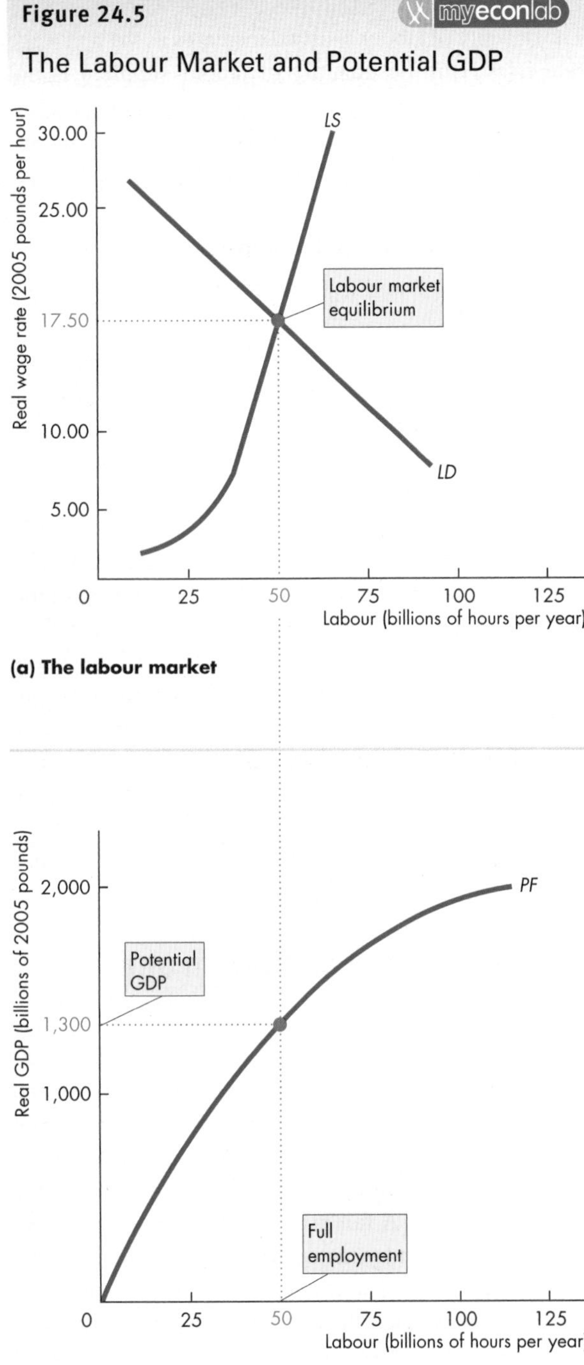

The economy is at full employment in part (a) when the quantity of labour demanded equals the quantity of labour supplied. The equilibrium real wage rate is £17.50 an hour and equilibrium employment is 50 billion hours a year.

Part (b) shows potential GDP. It is the quantity of real GDP determined by the production function and the full-employment quantity of labour.

If the real wage rate exceeds £17.50 an hour, the quantity of labour supplied exceeds the quantity demanded. There is a surplus of labour and the real wage rate falls. If the real wage rate is less than £17.50 an hour, the quantity of labour demanded exceeds the quantity supplied. There is a shortage of labour and the real wage rate rises.

If the real wage rate is £17.50 an hour, the quantity of labour demanded equals the quantity supplied. There is neither a shortage nor a surplus of labour and the labour market is in equilibrium. The real wage rate remains constant.

Equilibrium employment is 50 billion hours a year. The labour market equilibrium is a *full-employment* equilibrium.

Potential GDP

You've seen that the quantity of real GDP depends on the quantity of labour employed. The production function tells us how much real GDP a given amount of employment can produce. At the labour market equilibrium, employment is at its full-employment level. And the quantity of real GDP produced by the full-employment quantity of labour is *potential GDP*. So the equilibrium level of employment produces potential GDP.

Figure 24.5(b) shows potential GDP. The equilibrium level of employment in Figure 24.5(a) is 50 billion hours. The production function in Figure 24.5(b) tells us that 50 billion hours of labour can produce a real GDP of £1,300 billion. This amount is potential GDP.

Review Quiz

Study Plan 24.3

1 What is the classical model and what is the classical dichotomy?
2 What is the relationship between the leisure time–real GDP *PPF* and the production function.
3 What does the outward-bowed shape of the leisure time–real GDP *PPF* imply about the opportunity cost of real GDP and why is the *PPF* bowed outward?
4 Why does a rise in the real wage rate bring a decrease in the quantity of labour demanded, other things remaining the same?
5 Why does a rise in the real wage rate bring an increase in the quantity of labour supplied, other things remaining the same?
6 How is potential GDP determined?

Unemployment at Full Employment

So far, we've focused on the forces that determine the real wage rate, the quantity of labour employed and potential GDP. We're now going to bring unemployment into the picture and study the real factors that influence the natural unemployment rate.

In Chapter 22, we learned how unemployment is measured. We described how people become unemployed (they lose jobs, leave jobs and enter or re-enter the workforce) and we classified unemployment (it can be frictional, structural and cyclical). We also learned that we call the unemployment rate at full employment the *natural unemployment rate*.

But measuring, describing and classifying unemployment do not *explain* it. *Why* is there always some unemployment? Why does the unemployment rate vary over time? Why was the unemployment rate lower during the 1960s and the late 1990s than during the 1980s and early 1990s?

Part of the answer is that fluctuations in aggregate demand bring fluctuations in the unemployment rate around the natural rate. But the churning economy also brings fluctuations in the natural rate. Here we look at the forces that determine the natural unemployment rate.

Unemployment is always present for three broad reasons:

- Job search
- Job rationing
- Hysteresis

Job Search

Job search is the activity of looking for an acceptable vacant job. There are always some people who have not yet found a suitable job and who are actively searching for one. The reason is that the labour market is in a constant state of change.

The failure of existing businesses destroys jobs. The expansion of existing businesses and the start up of new businesses that use new technologies and develop new markets create jobs. As people pass through different stages of life, some enter or re-enter the labour market. Others leave their jobs to look for better ones and still others retire.

This constant churning in the labour market means that there are always some unemployed people looking for jobs.

The amount of job search depends on a number of factors, one of which is the real wage rate. In Figure 24.6, when the real wage rate is £17.50 an hour, the economy is at the full-employment equilibrium. The amount of job search that takes place at this real wage rate generates unemployment at the natural rate.

If the real wage rate is above the full-employment equilibrium – for example, at £22.50 an hour – there is a surplus of labour. At this higher real wage rate, more job search takes place and the unemployment rate exceeds the natural rate.

If the real wage rate is below the full-employment equilibrium – for example, at £12.50 an hour – there is a shortage of labour. At this real wage rate, less job search takes place and the unemployment rate falls below the natural rate.

The market forces of supply and demand move the real wage rate towards the full-employment equilibrium. And these same forces move the amount of job search

Figure 24.6

myeconlab

Job Search Unemployment

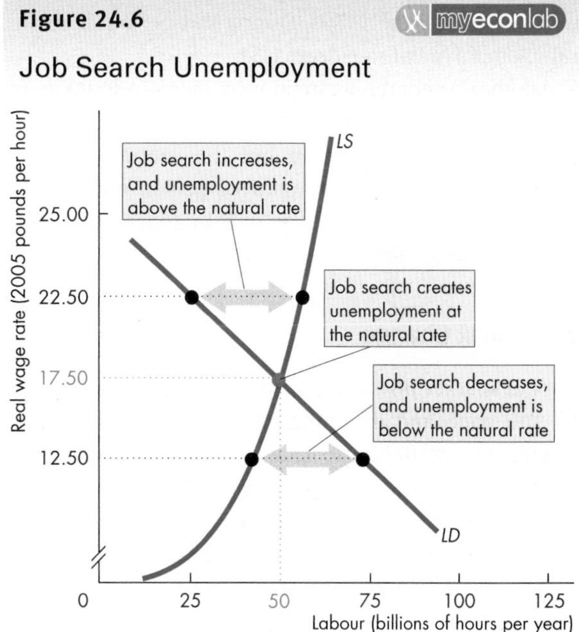

When the real wage rate is at the full-employment equilibrium – £17.50 an hour in this example – job search puts unemployment at the natural rate. If the real wage rate is above the full-employment equilibrium, there is a surplus of labour. Job search increases and unemployment rises above the natural rate. If the real wage rate is below the full-employment equilibrium, there is a shortage of labour. Job search decreases and unemployment falls below the natural rate.

towards the level that creates unemployment at the natural rate.

But other influences on the amount of job search bring changes, over time, in the natural unemployment rate. The main sources of these changes are:

- Demographic change
- Structural change
- Unemployment benefits

Demographic Change

An increase in the proportion of the working-age population brings an increase in the entry rate into the workforce and an increase in the unemployment rate. The "baby boom" – a bulge in the birth rate that occurred in from late 1940s to the late 1950s – increased the proportion of new entrants into the workforce during the 1970s and increased the natural unemployment rate.

As the birth rate declined, the bulge moved into higher age groups, and the proportion of new entrants declined during the 1980s. During this period, the natural unemployment rate decreased.

Another demographic trend is an increase in the number of households with two working adults. If unemployment hits one person but the second person's income continues, the unemployed person might spend more time in job search, which increases frictional unemployment.

Structural Change

Labour market flows and unemployment are influenced by the pace and direction of technological change. Sometimes technological change brings a *structural slump*, a condition in which some industries die and regions suffer and other industries are born and regions flourish. When these events occur, labour turnover is high – the flows between employment and unemployment and the pool of unemployed people increases. The decline of traditional heavy industries such as shipbuilding, steel and coal and the rapid expansion of industries that produce electronics and car components are examples of the effects of technological change and were the source of the increase in the natural unemployment rate during the 1970s and early 1980s.

Supply-side policies that increased job market flexibility during the 1980s resulted in the labour market being able to adjust more rapidly to technological shocks.

Unemployment Benefits

The length of time that an unemployed person spends searching for a job depends, in part, on the opportunity cost of job search. An unemployed person who received no income benefits faces an opportunity cost of job search equal to the wage rate available without further search. Unemployment benefits lower this opportunity cost.

The opportunity cost of job search has fallen over the years as unemployment benefits have increased. In 1966, unemployment benefits included a flat-rate component and an earnings-related component. As a result of these changes, the natural unemployment rate was on an upward trend during the 1970s.

But not all of the changes in unemployment benefits have been increases. Concern over the incentive effects of high benefits has brought some decreases. For example, in 1982, earnings-related benefit was abolished in the United Kingdom and during the 1990s the conditions for the receipt of benefit were tightened. These changes contributed to a decrease in the natural rate during the 1980s and 1990s.

Job-search unemployment is present even when the quantity of labour demanded equals the quantity supplied. The other possible explanations of unemployment are based on the view that the quantity of labour demanded does not always equal the quantity supplied.

Job Rationing

Markets *allocate* scarce resources by adjusting the market price to make buying plans and selling plans agree. Another word that has a meaning similar to "allocate" is "ration". Markets *ration* scarce resources by adjusting prices. In the labour market, the real wage rate rations employment and therefore rations jobs. Changes in the real wage rate keep the number of people seeking work and the number of jobs available in balance.

But the real wage rate is not the only instrument for rationing jobs. In some industries, the real wage rate is set above the market equilibrium. **Job rationing** is the practice of paying a real wage rate above the equilibrium level and then rationing jobs by some method.

Three reasons why the real wage rate might be set above the equilibrium level are:

- Efficiency wage
- Insider interest
- Minimum wage

Efficiency Wage

An **efficiency wage** is a real wage rate set above the equilibrium real wage rate that balances the costs and benefits of this higher wage rate to maximize the firm's profit.

The cost of paying a higher wage is direct. It is the addition to the firm's wage bill. The benefits of paying a higher wage rate are indirect.

First, a firm that pays a high wage rate can attract the most productive workers. Second, the firm can get greater productivity from its workforce if it threatens to fire those who do not perform at the desired standard. The threat of losing a well-paid job stimulates greater work effort. Third, workers are less likely to quit their jobs, so the firm faces a lower rate of labour turnover and lower training costs. Fourth, the firm's recruiting costs are lower. The firm always faces a steady stream of available new workers.

Faced with benefits and costs, a firm offers a wage rate that balances productivity gains from the higher wage rate against its additional cost. This wage rate maximizes the firm's profit and is the efficiency wage.

The payment of efficiency wages is another reason the natural unemployment rate is not zero.

Insider Interest

Why don't firms cut their wage costs by offering jobs to unemployed workers at a wage rate below that paid to existing workers? One explanation, called **insider–outsider theory**, is that to be productive, new workers – outsiders – must receive on-the-job training from existing workers – insiders. If insiders provide such training to outsiders who are paid a lower wage rate, the insiders' bargaining position is weakened. So insiders will not train outsiders unless outsiders and insiders receive the same wage rate.

When bargaining for a wage deal, unions represent only the interests of insiders, so the real wage rate agreed exceeds the equilibrium wage rate and there are always outsiders unable to find work. So the pursuit of rational self-interest by insiders is another reason the natural unemployment rate is not zero.

Minimum Wage

A **minimum wage** is the lowest wage rate at which a firm may legally hire labour. If the minimum wage is set *below* the equilibrium wage, the minimum wage has no effect. The minimum wage and market forces are not in conflict. But if a minimum wage is set *above* the equilibrium wage, the minimum wage is in conflict with the market forces and does have some effects on the labour market.

The UK minimum wage in October 2007 (£5.52 an hour for workers aged 22 and over, £4.60 an hour for workers aged 18 to 21 and £3.40 an hour for workers aged 16 and 17) is most likely above the market equilibrium wage rate.

Hysteresis

The unemployment rate fluctuates around the natural unemployment rate. But the natural unemployment rate itself might depend on the past actual unemployment rate – a dependence called **hysteresis**.

When hysteresis is present, a high unemployment rate increases the natural unemployment rate and keeps unemployment high; a low unemployment rate lowers the natural unemployment rate and keeps unemployment low.

Hysteresis might arise from the connection between human capital and unemployment. Work experience increases human capital and unemployment depreciates human capital. People who experience long bouts of unemployment find it hard to get new jobs as good as the ones they have lost because their human capital has depreciated.

An increase in the number of long-term unemployed workers means an increase in the amount of human capital lost and possibly a permanent increase in the natural unemployment rate.

Review Quiz

Study Plan 24.4

1. What brings unemployment at full employment?
2. Why does the natural unemployment rate fluctuate?
3. What is job search and why does it occur?
4. What is job rationing and why does it occur?
5. Explain how three sources of job rationing bring unemployment.
6. How does hysteresis influence unemployment?

You've now seen how the classical model enables us to see the forces that determine the real wage rate, employment, potential GDP and the natural unemployment rate.

The classical model also shows how the interest rate and the allocation of real GDP between consumption and investment in new capital are determined in the market for loanable funds, which we study next.

Capital and Interest

Potential GDP depends on the quantities of factors of production, one of which is capital. The **capital stock** is the total quantity of plant, equipment, buildings and inventories. The capital stock includes business capital such as communication satellites and computers as well as the inventories that businesses carry. It also includes houses and apartments. And it includes government-owned *social infrastructure capital* such as roads, dams and railways, schools, universities, national defence systems and the justice system that establishes and enforces property rights.

The capital stock is determined by investment decisions (see Chapter 21, pp. 473–474). The funds that finance investment are obtained in the market for loanable funds.

The Market for Loanable Funds

The **market for loanable funds** is the market in which households, firms, governments, banks and other financial institutions borrow and lend.

In the UK economy, there are many interrelated loans markets. There are markets in which the stocks of corporations are traded. Stocks are securities issued by corporations, and stock markets determine the prices and rates of return earned on stocks. The London Stock Exchange is an example of this type of market. There are markets in which bonds are traded. Bonds are securities issued by corporations and governments. There are markets in all types of loans, such as credit card loans and student loans.

In macroeconomics, we lump all these individual markets for loans into the one big loanable funds market. Think of this market as the aggregate (or sum) of all the different markets in which households, firms, governments, banks and other financial institutions borrow and lend.

Flows in the Market for Loanable Funds

The *circular flow model* (see Chapter 21, pp. 471–472) provides the accounting framework that explains the flows in the loanable funds market. Loanable funds are used for three purposes:

1 Business investment
2 Government budget deficit
3 International investment or lending

And loanable funds come from three sources:

1 Private saving
2 Government budget surplus
3 International borrowing

Firms often use retained earnings to finance business investment. These earnings belong to the firm's stockholders and are borrowed from the stockholders, rather than being paid to them as dividends. To keep the accounts in the clearest possible way, we think of these retained earnings as being both demanded and supplied in the loanable funds market. They are included as business investment on the demand side and as private saving on the supply side.

We measure all the flows of loanable funds in real terms – in constant 2005 pounds.

You're now going to see how these real flows and their opportunity cost or price are determined by studying:

- The demand for loanable funds
- The supply of loanable funds
- Equilibrium in the market for loanable funds

The Demand for Loanable Funds

The *quantity of loanable funds demanded* is the total quantity of funds demanded to finance investment, the government budget deficit and international investment or lending during a given period. This quantity depends on:

1 The real interest rate
2 The expected profit rate
3 Government and international factors

To focus on the demand for loanable funds, we ask: how does the quantity of loanable funds demanded vary as the real interest rate varies, with all other influences on borrowing plans remaining the same?

The Demand for Loanable Funds Curve

The **demand for loanable funds** is the relationship between the quantity of loanable funds demanded and the real interest rate when all other influences on borrowing plans remain the same.

Business investment is the main item that makes up the demand for loanable funds, and the other two items – the government budget deficit and international investment and lending – can be thought of as amounts to be added to investment. Other things remaining the same, investment decreases if the real interest rate rises and increases if the real interest rate falls. Equivalently, the quantity of loanable funds demanded decreases if the real interest rate rises and increases if the real interest rate falls.

Figure 24.7 illustrates the demand for loanable funds when investment is the only source of demand (there is no government deficit or international investment or lending). The table shows investment at three real interest rates. Each point (*A* through *C*) on the demand for loanable funds curve corresponds to a row in the table.

Figure 24.7

myeconlab

The Demand for Loanable Funds

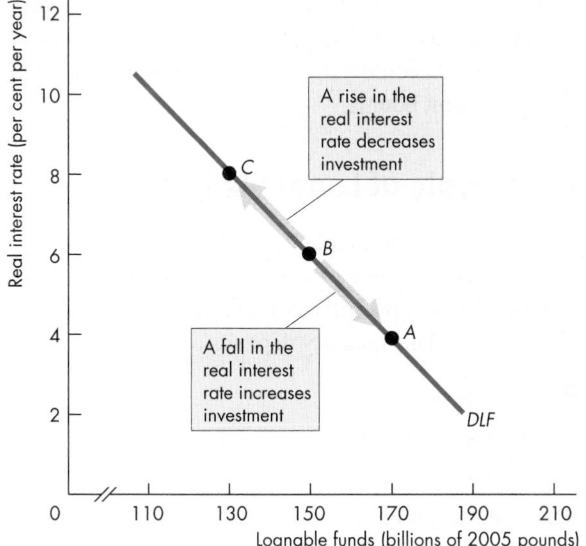

	Real interest rate (per cent per year)	Investment (billions of 2005 pounds)
A	8	130
B	6	150
C	4	170

The demand for loanable funds curve shows the effects of a change in the real interest rate on investment and the quantity of loanable funds demanded, other things remaining the same. A change in the real interest rate brings a change in investment and a movement along the demand for loanable funds curve.

If the real interest rate is 6 per cent a year, investment is £150 billion and the quantity of funds demanded is £150 billion. A change in the real interest rate brings a movement along the demand for loanable funds curve. A rise in the real interest rate decreases investment and brings a movement up the demand curve. A fall in the real interest rate increases investment and brings a movement down the demand curve.

Why does the quantity of loanable funds demanded depend on the real interest rate? And what exactly is the *real* interest rate?

The Real Interest Rate and the Opportunity Cost of Loanable Funds

The **real interest rate** is the quantity of goods and services that a unit of capital earns. In contrast, the **nominal interest rate** is the number of pounds that a unit of capital earns.

To measure the real interest rate, we begin with the nominal interest rate expressed as a percentage per year of the number of pounds loaned or borrowed. If your bank pays you £3 interest a year on a £100 savings deposit, you've earned a nominal interest rate of 3 per cent per year.

The next step is to adjust the nominal interest rate for inflation. The real interest rate is approximately equal to the nominal interest rate minus the inflation rate.

You can see why if you think about what you can buy with the interest on a £100 savings deposit in one year. If the nominal interest rate is 3 per cent a year, you will have £103 in your savings account after one year. Suppose that during the year, all prices increased by 2 per cent – a 2 per cent inflation rate. You need £102 to buy what a year earlier cost £100. So you can buy £1 worth more of goods and services than you could have bought a year earlier. You've earned goods and services worth £1, which is a real interest rate of 1 per cent a year. And the bank has paid a real interest rate of 1 per cent a year. So the real interest rate is the 3 per cent nominal interest rate minus the 2 per cent inflation rate.[1]

The real interest rate is the opportunity cost of loanable funds, and it is the opportunity cost of funds regardless of their source. The real interest paid on borrowed

[1] The exact real interest rate formula, which allows for the change in the purchasing power of both the interest and the loan is: Real interest rate = (Nominal interest rate – Inflation rate) ÷ (1 + Inflation rate/100). If the nominal interest rate is 4 per cent a year and the inflation rate is 3 per cent a year, the real interest rate is (4 – 3) ÷ (1 + 0.03) = 0.97 per cent a year.

funds is an obvious cost. But the real interest rate is also the opportunity cost of using retained earnings. These funds could be loaned to another firm, so the real interest rate forgone is the opportunity cost of using retained earnings.

Now that you know what the real interest rate is, we can study its influence on the quantity of loanable funds demanded. To do so, we look at a firm's investment decision.

The Investment Decision

How does Google decide how much to invest in servers and software to create a new Internet search system? Google's decision is influenced by the interplay of two factors:

1 The real interest rate

2 The expected profit rate

To decide whether to invest in a new Internet search system, Google compares the expected profit rate with the real interest rate. The expected profit rate is the benefit of the investment, and the real interest rate is the opportunity cost of the investment. Only if the benefit exceeds the cost, is it profitable to invest.

Imagine that Google is deciding how much to invest in a new Internet search system that will operate for one year and then be scrapped and replaced by an even better system. The firm believes that if it invests £50 million in a system to serve the US market, it will earn a profit of £10 million, or 20 per cent a year. Google also believes that if it invests another £50 million in a system to serve the European market, it will earn a profit of £5 million or 10 per cent a year. And Google believes that if it invests yet another £50 million in a system to serve the Asian market, it will earn a profit of £2.5 million or 5 per cent a year.

Suppose that Google can borrow in the loanable funds market at an interest rate of 9 per cent a year. How much will it borrow and invest in the new search systems? The answer is that Google will borrow £100 million and build the US and European systems but not the Asian system. If the interest rate rises to 15 per cent a year, Google will drop the European plans and invest only £50 million in the US system. And if the interest rate falls to 4 per cent a year. Google will go for all three projects and invest £3,150 million.

The higher the real interest rate, the smaller is the number of projects that are worth undertaking and the smaller is the amount of investment.

Changes in the Demand for Loanable Funds

A change in the real interest rate brings a change in investment and a change in the quantity of loanable funds demanded, which is shown by a movement along the demand curve.

A change in any other influence on a firm's decision to invest and borrow funds is shown by a shift of the demand curve. These other influences are all the factors that affect a firm's expected profit. Other things remaining the same, the greater the expected profit rate from new capital, the greater is the amount of investment and the greater is the demand for loanable funds.

Technology is a major influence of expected profit. Some firms strive to be first to market with a new technology. And some firms wait to see how a new technology performs before adopting it. But the profits of all firms are influenced by advances in technology, and investment plans must be constantly reassessed.

In a period of rapid and far-reaching technological change, such as that of the information revolution of the 1990s, firms become extremely optimistic about profits and investment booms.

The Supply of Loanable Funds

The quantity of loanable funds supplied is the total funds available from private saving, the government budget surplus and international borrowing during a given period. This quantity depends on:

- The real interest rate
- Disposable income
- Wealth
- Expected future income
- Government and international factors

To focus on the relationship between the quantity of loanable funds supplied and the real interest rate, we hold all other influences on lending plans constant and ask: how does the quantity of loanable funds supplied vary as the real interest rate varies?

The Supply of Loanable Funds Curve

The **supply of loanable funds** is the relationship between the quantity of loanable funds supplied and the real interest rate when all other influences on lending plans remain the same. Saving is the main item that makes up the supply of loanable funds, and the government budget surplus and international borrowing (when they are not zero) can be thought of as amounts to be added to saving. Other things remaining the same, saving increases if the real interest rate rises and decreases if the real interest rate falls. Equivalently, the quantity of loanable funds supplied increases if the real interest rate rises and decreases if the real interest rate falls.

Figure 24.8 illustrates this relationship when saving is the only source of supply of funds (when there is no government budget surplus or international borrowing). The table shows saving at three real interest rates. Saving provides loanable funds, and the relationship between the quantity of loanable funds supplied and the real interest rate, other things remaining the same, is the supply of loanable funds.

Figure 24.8

myeconlab

The Supply of Loanable Funds

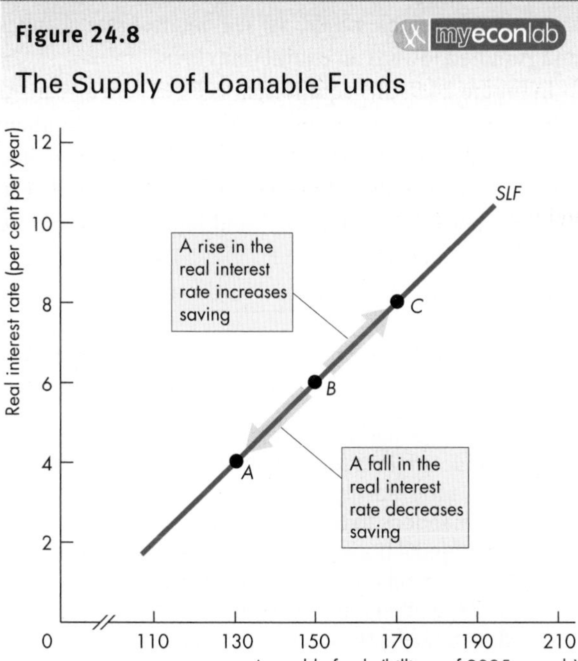

	Real interest rate (per cent per year)	Saving (billions of 2005 pounds)
A	4	130
B	6	150
C	8	170

The supply of loanable funds curve shows the effects of a change in the real interest rate on the quantity of loanable funds supplied, other things remaining the same. A change in the real interest rate brings a change in saving and a movement along the supply of loanable funds curve.

Each point (*A* through *C*) on the supply of loanable funds curve corresponds to a row in the table. If the real interest rate is 6 per cent a year, saving is £150 billion and the quantity of funds supplied is £150 billion. A change in the real interest rate brings a movement along the supply of loanable funds curve. If the real interest rate rises, saving increases and there is a movement up the supply of loanable funds curve. If the real interest rate falls, saving decreases and there is a movement down the supply of loanable funds curve.

Saving increases when the real interest rate increases because the real interest rate is the opportunity cost of consumption. A pound consumed is a pound not saved, so the interest that could have been earned on that saving is forgone. This opportunity cost arises regardless of whether a person is a lender or a borrower. For a lender, saving less this year means receiving less interest next year. For a borrower, saving less this year means paying less off a loan this year and paying more interest next year.

You can see why the real interest rate influences saving by thinking about student loans. If the real interest rate on student loans jumps to 20 per cent a year, students will save more (will buy cheaper food and find lower-rent accommodations) to pay off their loans as quickly as possible. If the real interest rate on student loans falls to 1 per cent a year, students will save less and take out larger loans.

Changes in the Supply of Loanable Funds

A change in the real interest rate brings a change in saving and a change in the quantity of loanable funds supplied, which is shown by a movement along the supply curve. A change in any other influence on saving and lending plans is shown by a shift of the supply curve. These other influences are disposable income, wealth and expected future income.

The greater a household's disposable income, other things remaining the same, the greater is its saving.

A household's *wealth* is its assets (what it owns) minus its debts (what it owes). The purchasing power of a household's wealth is the *real* value of its wealth. It is the quantity of goods and services that the household's wealth can buy. The greater a household's real wealth, other things remaining the same, the less is its saving.

The higher a household's expected future income, other things remaining the same, the lower is its saving.

So an increase in income, decrease in wealth, or decrease in expected future income increases the supply of loanable funds and shifts the supply curve rightward.

Equilibrium in the Loanable Funds Market

You've seen that other things remaining the same, the quantities of loanable funds demanded and supplied depend on the real interest rate. The higher the real interest rate, the greater is the amount of saving and the larger is the quantity of loanable funds supplied and the smaller is the amount of investment and the smaller is the quantity of loanable funds demanded. There is one interest rate at which the quantities of loanable funds demanded and supplied are equal, and that is the equilibrium real interest rate.

Figure 24.9 shows how the demand for and supply of loanable funds determine the real interest rate. The *DLF* curve is the demand curve and the *SLF* curve is the supply curve. When the real interest rate exceeds 6 per cent a year, saving exceeds investment. Borrowers have an easy time finding the funds they want, but lenders are unable to lend all the funds they have available. The real interest rate falls and continues to fall until the quantity of funds supplied equals the quantity of funds demanded. At this real interest rate, saving equals investment.

Alternatively, when the interest rate is less than 6 per cent a year, saving is less than investment. Borrowers can't find the loans they want, but lenders are able to lend all the funds they have available. So the real interest rate rises and continues to rise until the supply of funds equals the demand for funds and saving equals investment. Regardless of whether there is a surplus or a shortage of loanable funds, the real interest rate changes and is pulled toward an equilibrium level.

In Figure 24.9, this equilibrium is 6 per cent a year. At this interest rate, there is neither a surplus nor a shortage of funds. Borrowers can get the funds they demand, and lenders can lend all the funds they have available. The plans of borrowers (investors) and lenders (savers) are consistent with each other.

Figure 24.9 myeconlab

Equilibrium in the Loanable Funds Market

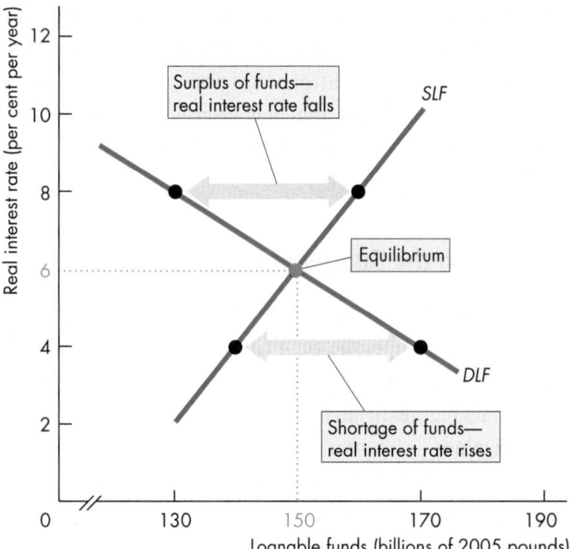

In the loanable funds market, the demand is *DLF*, and the supply is *SLF*. If the real interest rate were 4 per cent a year, the quantity of loanable funds demanded would exceed the quantity supplied and the real interest rate would rise. If the real interest rate were 8 per cent a year, the quantity of loanable funds supplied would exceed the quantity demanded and the real interest rate would fall.

When the real interest rate is 6 per cent a year, the quantity of loanable funds demanded equals the quantity supplied, the real interest rate is at its equilibrium. Saving equals investment.

Review Quiz

Study Plan 24.5

1. What is the market for loanable funds?
2. What determines the demand for loanable funds?
3. What is the real interest rate?
4. What happens to the quantity of loanable funds demanded if the real interest rate falls and other things remain the same; and if the real interest rate rises and other things remain the same?
5. What happens to quantity of loanable funds demanded if the expected profit rate increases and other things remain the same; and if the expected profit rate decreases and other things remain the same?
6. What determines the supply of loanable funds?
7. How does the real interest rate influence the quantity of loanable funds supplied?
8. How do disposable income, wealth and expected future income influence the supply of loanable funds?
9. How is the real interest rate determined?

You now know the components of the classical model and what the model determines. To complete your study of the classical model, let's see what it tells us about the UK economy today.

The Dynamic Classical Model

You've now seen how the classical model determines potential GDP, employment and the real wage rate, the natural rate of unemployment, investment, saving and the real interest rate. You're now going to see that the classical model is a dynamic model that has rich implications for how the economy changes over time and deepens our understanding of the forces that change real GDP.

Real GDP increases if:

1 The economy recovers from recession.

2 Potential GDP increases.

Recovery from recession means the economy moves along the production function (or along the leisure time-real GDP *PPF*), from a point at which real GDP and employment are too low and unemployment is too high, to the full-employment equilibrium point. Equivalently, the economy moves along its short-run aggregate supply curve. Economists have a lot to say about such a move. And you learned about this type of short-term change in Chapter 23.

Increasing potential GDP means expanding production possibilities and moving to a new full-employment equilibrium. It is this source of change in real GDP – a change in potential GDP – that we are going to study in the rest of this chapter.

We can place all the influences on potential GDP in two groups, those that bring:

- Increases in productivity
- Increases in the supply of labour

Increases in Productivity

When we talk about *productivity*, we usually mean labour productivity. **Labour productivity** is real GDP per hour of labour. Three factors influence labour productivity:

- Physical capital
- Human capital
- Technology

Saving and investment increase physical capital. Education and on-the-job training and experience increase human capital. And research and development bring technological advances. We study the way these forces interact to determine the growth rate of potential GDP in Chapter 31.

Here, we study the effects on the labour market and potential GDP of a one-time increase in physical capital, or human capital, or advance in technology.

We will see how the real wage rate, employment and potential GDP change when any of these three influences on labour productivity change.

Physical Capital

A computer and high-speed Internet connection saves a student many hours of walking through library stacks and writing and rewriting to complete a term paper. A student with a computer is more productive than a student with a pencil and note pad.

A farm worker equipped with only a stick and primitive tools can cultivate almost no land and grow barely enough food to feed a single family. A farmer equipped with a steel plough pulled by an animal can cultivate more land and produce enough food to feed a small village. A farmer equipped with a modern tractor, plough and harvester can cultivate thousands of hectares and produce enough food to feed hundreds of people.

By increasing the amount of physical capital on our farms and in our factories, shops and offices and even in our universities, labour productivity increases enormously.

Human Capital

An economy's *human capital* is the knowledge and skill that people have obtained from education and on-the-job training. The average university graduate has a greater amount of human capital than the average school leaver. Consequently, the university graduate is able to perform some tasks that are beyond the ability of the school leaver. The university graduate is more productive. For the nation as a whole, the greater the amount of education its citizens complete, the greater is its real GDP, other things remaining the same.

Regardless of how much education a person has completed, not much production is accomplished on the first day at work. Learning about the new work environment consumes the newly hired worker. But as time passes and experience accumulates, the worker becomes more productive. We call this on-the-job training activity *learning-by-doing*.

Learning-by-doing can bring incredible increases in labour productivity. The more experienced the workforce, the greater is its labour productivity and other things remaining the same, the greater is real GDP.

Technology

A student equipped with a pen can complete a readable page of writing in perhaps 10 minutes. This same task takes 5 minutes with a typewriter and 2 minutes with a computer. This example shows the enormous impact of technology on labour productivity.

Productivity and the Production Function

Any influence on production that increases labour productivity shifts the production function upward. Real GDP increases for each hour of labour. In Figure 24.10, the production function is initially PF_0. Then an increase in physical capital or human capital or an advance in technology occurs. The production function shifts upward to PF_1.

Labour productivity in the United Kingdom increases on the average 2.1 per cent per year, so the UK production function shifts upward by that amount each year, on the average. In the United States, it shifts upward a bit faster than in the United Kingdom. And in most other EU countries, it shifts upward a bit slower than in the United Kingdom.

Figure 24.10 myeconlab

An Increase in Labour Productivity

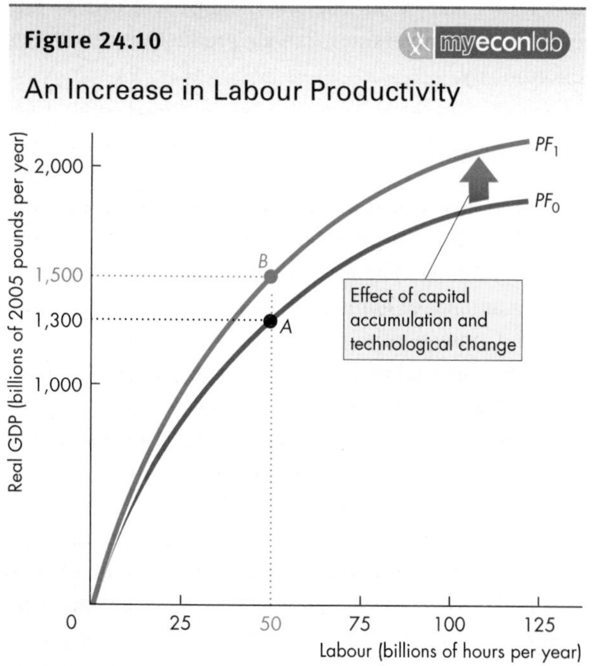

On PF_0, 50 billion labour hours can produce a real GDP of £1,300 billion (point *A*). An increase in physical or capital or an advance in technology increases labour productivity and shifts the production function upward to PF_1. Now, 50 billion labour hours can produce a real GDP of £1,500 billion (point *B*).

Productivity and Potential GDP

You've seen how an increase in labour productivity increases production possibilities. How does it change the real wage rate, employment and potential GDP? Let's find out.

An increase in any of the three factors (physical capital, human capital and technology) that increases productivity and shifts the production function upward increases the real GDP that each quantity of labour can produce. It also increases the marginal product of labour and so increases the demand for labour. Some physical capital replaces some types of labour. So the demand for those types of labour decreases when capital increases. But an increase in physical capital creates a demand for the types of labour that build, sell and maintain the additional capital. The increases in demand for labour are always larger than the decreases in demand, and the economy-wide demand for labour increases.

With an increase in the economy-wide demand for labour, the real wage rate rises and the quantity of labour supplied increases. Equilibrium employment increases.

Potential GDP increases for two reasons. First, a given level of employment produces more real GDP. Second, equilibrium employment increases.

Illustrating the Effects of an Increase in Labour Productivity on Potential GDP

Figure 24.11 shows the effects of an increase in labour productivity that result from an increase in capital or an advance in technology. In part (a), the demand for labour initially is LD_0 and the supply of labour is *LS*. The real wage rate is £17.50 an hour and full employment is 50 billion hours a year. In part (b), the production function initially is PF_0. With 50 billion hours of labour employed, potential GDP is £1,300 billion.

Now an increase in capital or an advance in technology increases the labour productivity. In Figure 24.11(a), the demand for labour increases and the demand curve shifts rightward to LD_1. In Figure 24.12(b), the increase in labour productivity shifts the production function upward to PF_1.

In Figure 24.11(a), at the original real wage rate of £17.50 an hour, there is now a shortage of labour. So the real wage rate rises. In this example, it keeps rising until it reaches £22.50 an hour. At £22.50 an hour, the quantity of labour demanded equals the quantity of labour supplied and full employment increases to 56 billion hours a year.

Figure 24.11 myeconlab

The Effects of an Increase in Labour Productivity

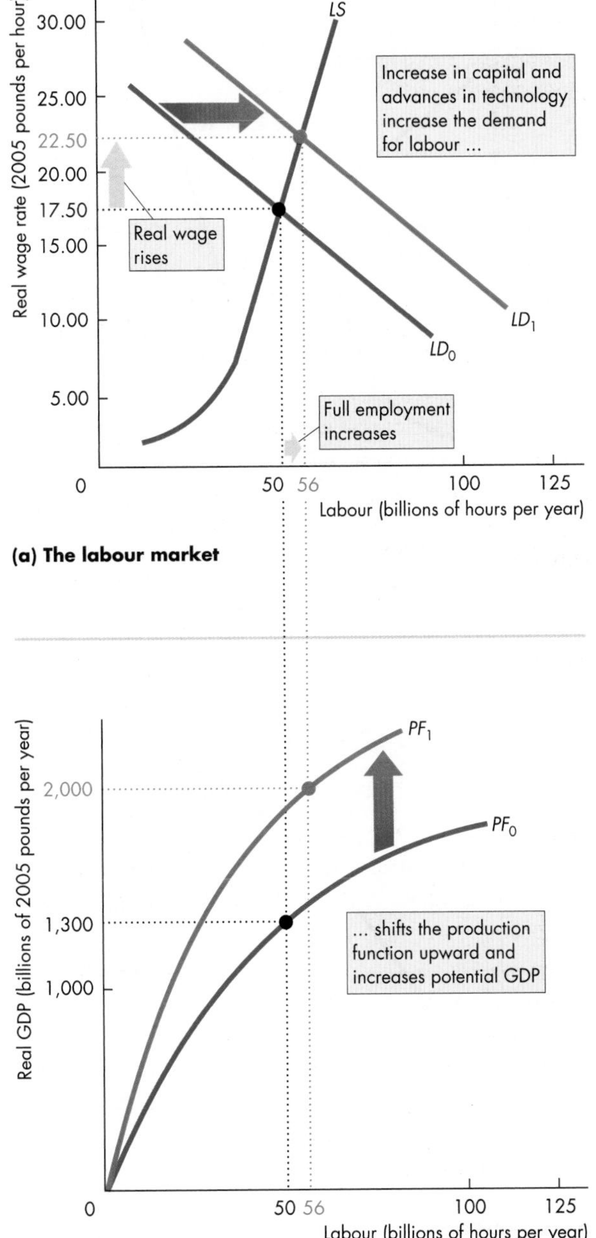

An increase in labour productivity shifts the demand for labour curve rightward from LD_0 to LD_1 in part (a) and the production function upward from PF_0 to PF_1 in part (b). The real wage rate rises from £17.50 to £22.50 an hour, full employment increases from 50 billion to 56 billion hours. Potential GDP increases from £1,300 billion to £2,000 billion.

Figure 24.12(b) shows the effects on potential GDP of an increase in full employment combined with the new production function. As full employment increases from 50 billion hours to 56 billion hours, potential GDP increases from £1,300 billion to £2,000 billion.

Potential GDP per hour of labour also increases. Initially, with potential GDP at £1,300 billion and labour hours at 50 billion, potential GDP per hour of labour was £26. With the increase in labour productivity, potential GDP is £2,000 billion and labour hours are 56 billion, so potential GDP per hour of labour is £35.71.

Increases in the Supply of Labour

The supply of labour can increase for two reasons:

1 An increase in the working-age population

2 An increase in the economic activity rate (see Chapter 22, p. 491).

The working-age population can increase because the rate at which people reach working age exceeds the rate at which people reach the retirement age, or because of immigration. The main sources of increases in the economic activity rate are changes in technology and changes in attitudes that have increased the female economic activity rate.

An increase in the supply of labour has a direct impact on production possibilities. With more labour available and with capital and technology remaining the same, production possibilities expand and the *PPF* shifts outward.

But does an increase in the supply of labour increase potential GDP and potential GDP *per person*?

The answers to these questions have intrigued economists for many years. And they cause heated political debate today. In China, for example, families are under enormous pressure to limit the number of children they have. In other countries, for example France, the government encourages large families. With a time lag of about 16 years, these policies limit (in China) or expand (in France) the size of the working-age population.

Immigration is also a hot political issue. Do immigrants from Poland end up lowering UK potential GDP and potential GDP per person?

We can study the effects of an increase in population or increase in the economic activity rate and the resulting increase in the supply of labour by using the classical model.

In Figure 24.12(a), the demand for labour is *LD* and initially the supply of labour is LS_0. At full employment, the real wage rate is £17.50 an hour and employment is 50 billion hours a year. In Figure 24.12(b), the production function (*PF*) shows that with 50 billion hours of labour employed, potential GDP is £1,300 billion.

Now the population increases and the supply of labour increases. The labour supply curve shifts rightward to LS_1. At a real wage rate of £17.50 an hour, there is now a surplus of labour. So the real wage rate falls. In this example, it falls until it reaches £12.50 an hour. At £12.50 an hour, the quantity of labour demanded equals the quantity of labour supplied. Full employment increases to 70 billion hours a year.

Figure 24.12(b) shows the effect of the increase in full employment on real GDP. As the full-employment quantity of labour increases from 50 billion hours to 70 billion hours, potential GDP increases from £1,300 billion to £1,700 billion.

So an increase in population increases employment, increases potential GDP and lowers the real wage rate.

An increase in population also decreases potential GDP per hour of labour. You can see this decrease by dividing potential GDP by total labour hours. Initially, with potential GDP at £1,300 billion and labour hours at 50 billion, potential GDP per hour of labour was £26. With the increase in population, potential GDP is £1,700 billion and labour hours are 70 billion. Potential GDP per hour of labour is £24.29. Diminishing returns is the source of the decrease in potential GDP per hour of labour.

You've seen that an increase in population increases potential GDP and decreases potential GDP per hour of labour. Some people challenge this conclusion and argue that people are the ultimate economic resource. They claim that a larger population brings forth a greater amount of scientific discovery and technological advance. Consequently, these people argue that an increase in population never takes place in isolation. It is always accompanied by an increase in labour productivity. Let's now look at the effects of this influence on potential GDP.

We've studied the effects of an increase in population and an increase in labour productivity separately. In reality, these changes occur together. Real GDP and employment both increase. The real wage rate typically increases because the effects of a labour productivity increase are greater than those of a population increase. Box 24.1 examines these combined effects in the UK economy.

Figure 24.12

The Effects of an Increase in the Supply of Labour

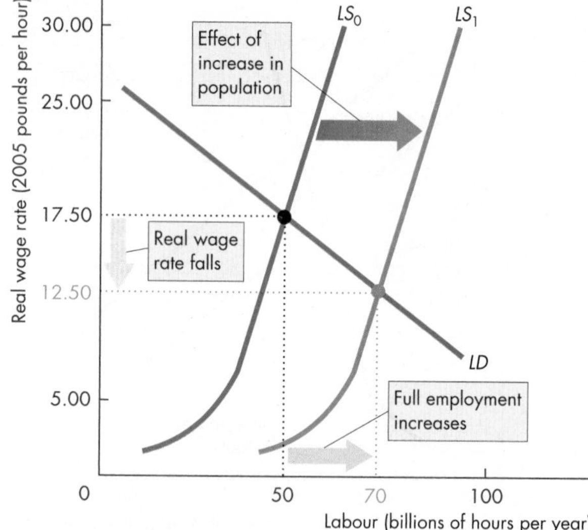

(a) The labour market

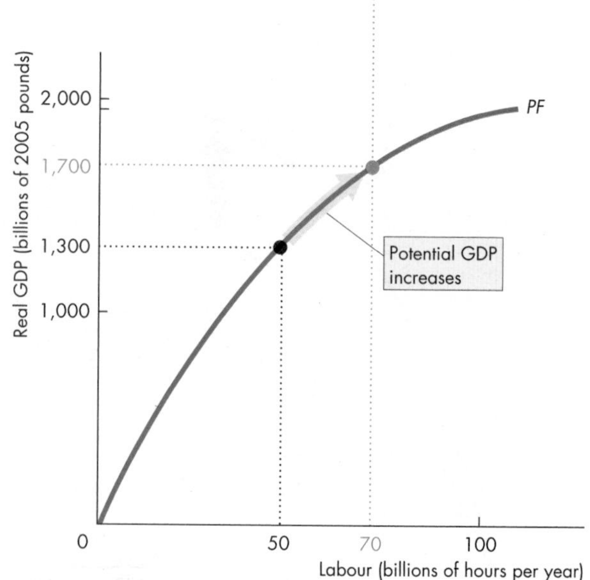

(b) Potential GDP

An increase in population increases the supply of labour. In part (a), the supply of labour curve shifts rightward from LS_0 to LS_1. The real wage rate falls and the quantity of labour employed at full employment increases. In part (b), the increase in full employment increases potential GDP. Because the marginal product of labour diminishes, the increased population increases potential GDP but potential GDP per hour of labour decreases.

Box 24.1

Population and Productivity in the United Kingdom

The UK economy was close to full employment in 2005. It was also close to full employment in 1975. In 1975, employment was 45 billion hours, the real wage rate was £9.41 an hour and real GDP was £606 billion. (we are using 2005 pounds.) By 2005, labour hours had increased to 48 billion hours, the real wage rate was £16.26 an hour and real GDP had increased to £1,225 billion (we are using 2005 pounds).

The classical model points us to the things that changed to increase employment, the real wage rate and potential GDP.

First, advances in technology and investment that brought us the Internet, the mobile phone, MP3 audio as well as robots in factories and warehouses, increased productivity. These advances in technology and investment increased the marginal product of labour and increased the demand for labour. Second, the population expanded, increased the working-age population and increased the supply of labour.

Figure 1 illustrates the combined effects of these changes. In 1975, the demand for labour curve was LD_{75}, the supply of labour was LS_{75} and the production function was PF_{75}. Employment was 45 billion hours, the real wage rate was £9.41 an hour and real GDP was £606 billion.

By 2005, the demand for labour curve had shifted to LD_{05}, the production function had shifted to PF_{05}. The real wage rate increased to £16.26 an hour, employment had increased to 48 billion hours and real GDP had increased to £1,225 billion.

Figure 1

The UK Economy: 1975–2005

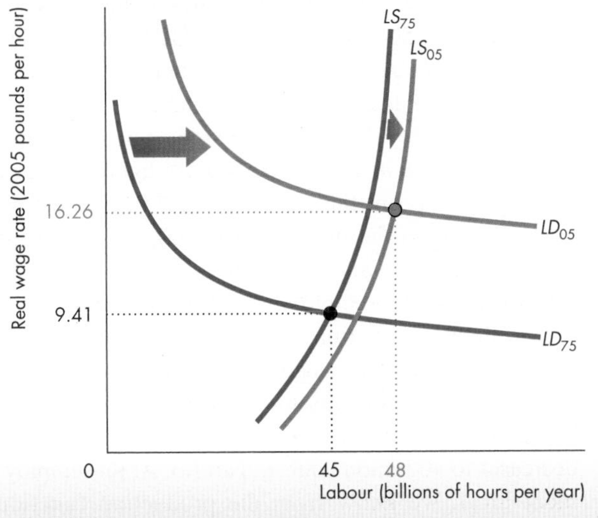

(a) The labour market

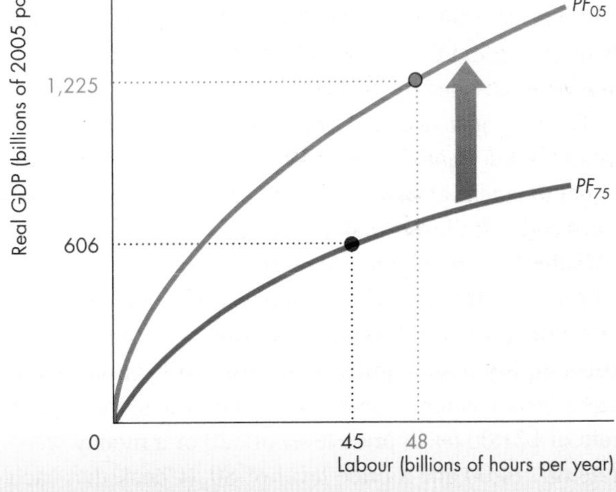

(b) The production function

Review Quiz

Study Plan 24.6

1 How does an increase in population change potential GDP, employment and the real wage rate?
2 How does an increase in capital change potential GDP, employment and the real wage rate?
3 How does an advance in technology change potential GDP, employment and the real wage rate?

You've now seen how the economy operates at full employment and how the classical model explains the determination of potential GDP and changes in potential GDP, employment and the real wage rate as the economy moves from one full-employment equilibrium to the next. Your final task in this chapter is to use the classical model to derive the long-run and short-run aggregate supply curves.

The Labour Market and Aggregate Supply

You can use what you've learned about the labour market and potential GDP to gain a deeper understanding of long-run aggregate supply and short-run aggregate supply that you met in Chapter 23 (pp. 510–514).

Long-run Aggregate Supply

In Chapter 23, we defined *long-run aggregate supply* as the relationship between the quantity of real GDP supplied and the price level when real GDP equals potential GDP. And we said that the long-run aggregate supply curve is vertical because potential GDP is independent of the price level.

You can now see that this statement is correct and is implied by the classical model. Potential GDP is the quantity of real GDP produced by a fully employed labour force. And the quantity of labour employed at full employment is the equilibrium quantity – the quantity that balances the labour supply decisions of households and the labour demand decisions of firms. The "price" that achieves this equilibrium is the real wage rate. And the real wage rate is equal to the money wage rate divided by the price level.

There is just one real wage rate that achieves full-employment equilibrium and results in real GDP being equal to potential GDP. But there are many money wage rates and price levels that achieve this outcome.

If the full-employment equilibrium real wage rate is £17.50 (in 2005 pounds), a money wage rate of £17.50 and a price level of 100 is one possible way of achieving full-employment equilibrium. But full-employment equilibrium would also be achieved at a money wage rate of £21.00 and a price level of 120 or a money wage rate of £14.00 and a price level of 80. (Check that each of these situations has a real wage rate of £17.50 – £21.00 × 100 ÷ 120 = £17.50 and £14.00 × 100 ÷ 80 = £17.50.)

Because the quantity of real GDP supplied is potential GDP at price levels of 80, 100 and 120 (and every other price level and money wage rate that equals a real wage rate of £17.50), the long-run aggregate supply curve is vertical at potential GDP.

Movements along this long-run aggregate supply curve involve a change in the price level and a change in the money wage rate by the same percentage so the *real wage rate* (a *relative price*) remains constant and real GDP also remains constant.

Short-run Aggregate Supply

In the short run, the money wage rate is fixed and along the short-run aggregate supply curve, as the price level changes the real wage rate changes. A change in the real wage changes the quantity of labour demanded and the quantity of real GDP supplied.

Figure 24.13 illustrates the short-run aggregate supply curve are derived from the labour market and production function.

Figure 24.13(a) shows the three short-run equilibrium levels of the real wage rate and employment. The money wage rate is fixed at £17.50 an hour. If the price level is 100, the real wage rate is £17.50 an hour and 50 billion hours of labour are employed – point *B*. If the price level is 83.3, the real wage rate is £21 an hour and employment is 40 billion hours – point *A*. If the price level is 125, the real wage rate is £14 an hour and employment is 60 billion hours – point *C*.

Figure 24.13(b) shows the production function and the quantities of real GDP produced at each employment level. For example, when employment is 40 billion hours, real GDP is £1,120 billion – point *A*. When employment is 50 billion hours, real GDP is £1,300 billion – point *B*. And when employment is 60 billion hours, real GDP is £1,470 billion – point *C*.

Figure 24.13(c) shows the short-run aggregate supply curve. At point *B* in all three parts of the figure, the price level is 100. From the labour market in part (a) we know that when the price level is 100, the real wage is £17.50 an hour and 50 billion hours of labour are employed. At this employment level, we know from the production function in part (b) that real GDP is £1,300 billion and the economy is at full employment.

If the price level falls to 83.3, the real wage rises to £21 an hour and the quantity of labour demanded decreases to 40 billion hours in part (a). At this employment level, we know from the production function in part (b) that real GDP decreases to £1.120 billion. The economy moves to point *A* on the *SAS* curve in part (c).

If the price level rises to 125, the real wage falls to £14 an hour and the quantity of labour demanded increases to 60 billion hours in part (a). At this employment level, we know from the production function in part (b) that real GDP increases to £1,470 billion. The economy moves to point *C* on the *SAS* curve in part (c).

Along the long-run aggregate supply curve in part (c), as the price level changes, the money wage rate changes to keep the real wage rate at the full-employment equilibrium level. Real GDP remains at £1,300 billion.

Figure 24.13

myeconlab

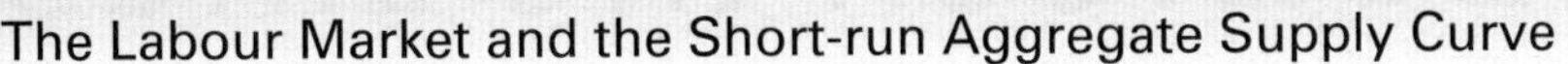

The Labour Market and the Short-run Aggregate Supply Curve

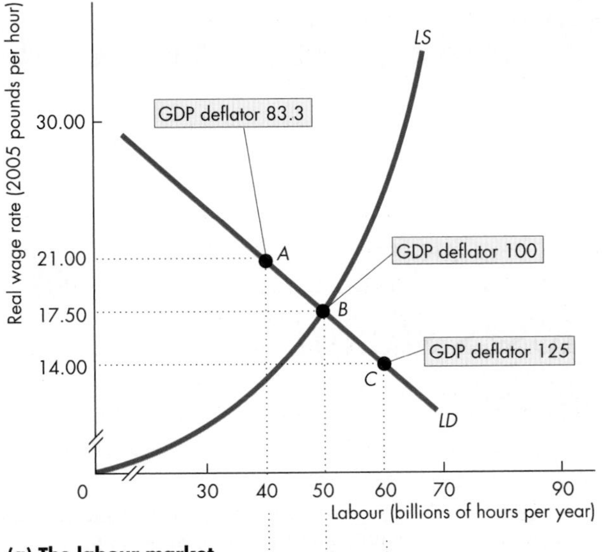

(a) The labour market

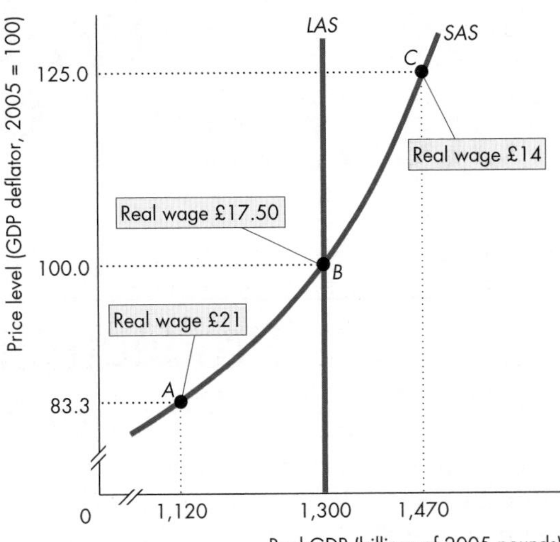

(c) Aggregate supply curves

Real GDP (billions of 2005 pounds)

1,470
1,300
1,120
900
700
500
0

PF

A
B
C

30 40 50 60 70 90

Labour (billions of hours per year)

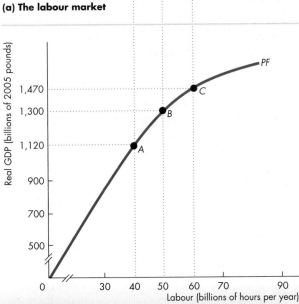

(b) Potential GDP

The money wage rate is fixed at £17.50 an hour. In part (a), the demand for labour curve, *LD*, intersects the supply of labour curve, *LS*, at a real wage rate of £17.50 an hour and 50 billion hours of employment. If the GDP deflator is 100, the economy operates at point *B*. In part (b), the production function, *PF*, determines real GDP of £1,300 billion at point *B*. In part (c), the economy is at point *B* on its short-run aggregate supply curve, *SAS*, and long-run aggregate supply curve, *LAS*.

If the GDP deflator is 83.3, the real wage rate is £21 an hour and the economy is at point *A*. Employment is 40 billion hours in part (a) and real GDP is £1,120 billion in part (b). The economy is at point *A* on its short-run aggregate supply curve, *SAS*, in part (c) and below its long-run aggregate supply curve.

If the GDP deflator is 125, the real wage rate is £14 an hour and the economy is at point *C*. Employment is 60 billion hours in part (a) and real GDP is £1,480 billion in part (b). The economy is at point *C* on its short-run aggregate supply curve in part (c) and above its long-run aggregate supply curve.

Review Quiz

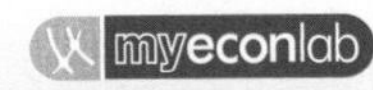

Study Plan 24.7

1 Why does real GDP remain at potential GDP as the price level changes on the long-run aggregate supply curve?
2 Why does real GDP change as the price level changes on the short-run aggregate supply curve?

You've now completed your study of the classical model. You can apply some of the things you've learned in *Reading Between the Lines* on pp. 556–557, where we examine recent trends in labour productivity growth in the United Kingdom. In the next chapter, we focus on the short run and study the forces that make real GDP fluctuate around potential GDP.

Reading Between the Lines

Productivity, Employment and Potential GDP

The Financial Times, 23 January 2007

FT

Productivity loses steam under Labour

Chris Giles

Productivity growth in the UK has slowed under Labour, raising doubts over the long-term outlook for prosperity and the ability of the economy to sustain fast growth without sparking inflation.

In its annual assessment of labour productivity across the world, the Conference Board, the international business organisation, estimates that UK output per hour worked rose by 1.7 per cent in 2006, below the UK's long-run average of 2.1 per cent.

Even though the economy grew faster at 2.7 per cent, rapid growth in employment limited the contribution of productivity, which governs the long-term health of the economy.

More worryingly for Gordon Brown, the Chancellor, the assessment of the UK shows that productivity growth between 2000 and 2006 slowed to an annual average of 1.9 per cent, compared with an average of 2.1 per cent between 1987 and 2000 when the Conservatives were in office and an even higher rate when Labour was first in power. . . .

Lower productivity growth makes the Bank of England's life more difficult, since it cannot let the economy grow so fast without taking big risks with inflation. . . .

The UK's productivity record is not spectacular compared either with its own past performance or with the US, but it has been more distinguished than most other big European Union economies.

While the UK achieved 2.1 per cent annual average labour productivity growth between 1995 and 2006, the conference board estimates that Germany's rate was 1.7 per cent, France's 1.9 per cent, Italy's 0.4 per cent and Spain's −0.2 per cent. . . .

The UK productivity growth has occurred alongside reasonable growth in number of hours worked. In France and Germany, it has not been accompanied to the same extent by rising employment, limiting the effect on living standards.

The Essence of the Story

- UK real GDP grew by 2.7 per cent in 2006 but labour productivity grew by only 1.7 per cent.
- The UK labour productivity growth rate averaged 2.1 per cent between 1987 and 2006 and 1.9 per cent a year between 2000 and 2006.
- Labour productivity growth in the United Kingdom is below that in the United States but above that in some other EU economies.

Economic Analysis

- Figure 1 shows the UK productivity growth rate – the growth rate of real GDP per hour of labour – from 1987 to 2006.
- Before 1997 (with a Conservative government) and after 1997 (with a Labour government), the average productivity growth rate was 2.1 per cent per year. But after 2000, the productivity growth rate decreased.
- Did Labour government policies slow the productivity growth rate? Most likely not. Year-to-year fluctuations in productivity growth are large and the path since 2000 will most likely turn out to be a temporary departure from the long-term trend of 2.1 per cent.
- A more striking feature of productivity growth is its relative stability after 1997 compared to the late 1980s and early 1990s.
- Labour productivity growth results from capital accumulation and technological change that shift the production function upward.
- Figure 2 shows the UK production function in 1987, 2000 and 2006. In 1987, the economy was at point *A*; by 2000, it was at point *B;* and by 2006, it was at point *C*. Real GDP increased because both employment and labour productivity increased.
- An upward shift in the production function increases the marginal product of labour, which increases the demand for labour.
- Figure 3 shows the UK labour market. In 1987, the demand for labour was LD_{87}, the supply of labour was LS_{87} and the labour market was in equilibrium at point *A*'.
- By 2000, the demand for labour had increased to LD_{00}, and by 2006, it had increased to LD_{06}.
- Immigration from new EU countries such as Poland and Slovakia and the UK's natural population growth increased the supply of labour to LS_{00} by 2000 and to LS_{06} by 2006. The labour market was in equilibrium at point *B*' in 2000 and at point C' in 2006.

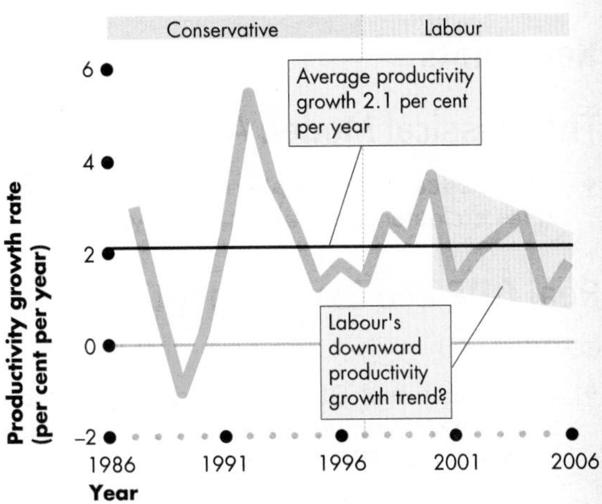

Figure 1 Politics and productivity growth

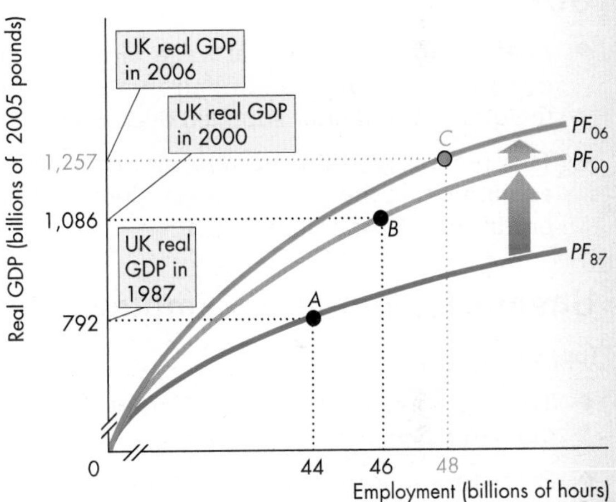

Figure 2 The UK production function

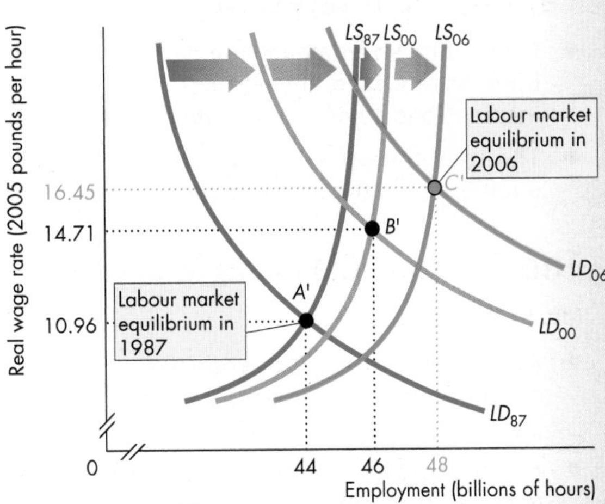

Figure 3 The UK labour market

Summary

Key Points

The Classical Model: A Preview (p. 534)

- The classical model explains how the real variables are determined at full employment.

Real GDP and Employment (pp. 534– 535)

- To produce real GDP, we must forgo leisure and work more. As the quantity of labour increases real GDP increases.

The Labour Market and Potential GDP (pp. 536–540)

- *Ceteris paribus*, as the real wage rate falls, the quantity of labour demanded increases and the quantity of labour supplied decreases.
- The real wage rate adjusts to bring about equilibrium in the labour market. The real GDP produced equals potential GDP.

Unemployment at Full Employment (pp. 541–543)

- The unemployment rate at full employment is the natural unemployment rate.
- Persistent unemployment arises from job search, job rationing and hysteresis.

Capital and Interest (pp. 544–548)

- Other things remaining the same, as the real interest rate falls, investment and borrowing increase and saving and lending decrease.
- The real interest rate adjusts to bring about equilibrium in the loanable funds market.

The Dynamic Classical Model (pp. 549–553)

- An increase in labour productivity increases equilibrium employment, potential GDP and potential GDP per hour of labour.
- An increase in population or the economic activity rate increases employment, increases potential GDP, but *decreases* potential GDP per hour of labour.

The Labour Market and Aggregate Supply (pp. 554–555)

- In the long-run, when the price level changes, the real wage rate, employment and real GDP remain constant.
- In the short-run, the money wage rate is constant so a change in the price level changes the real wage rate, employment and real GDP.

Key Figures

Key Terms

Problems

Tests, Study Plan and Solutions* myeconlab

1 Robinson Crusoe lives on a desert island on the equator. He has 12 hours of daylight every day to allocate between leisure and work. The table shows seven alternative combinations of leisure and real GDP in the economy of Crusoe:

Possibility	Leisure (hours per day)	Real GDP (euros per day)
A	12	0
B	10	10
C	8	18
D	6	24
E	4	28
F	2	30
G	0	30

a Make a table and a graph of Crusoe's production function.

b Find Crusoe's marginal product of labour at different quantities of labour.

2 Use the information about Robinson Crusoe's economy in problem 1 and the fact that at a real wage of €4.50 an hour, Crusoe is willing to work any number of hours between 0 and 12.

a Make a table that shows Crusoe's demand for labour schedule and draw Crusoe's demand for labour curve.

b Make a table that shows Crusoe's supply of labour schedule and draw Crusoe's supply of labour curve.

c What is the equilibrium real wage rate and quantity of labour in Crusoe's economy?

d Find Crusoe's potential GDP.

3 The figure (in the next column) describes the labour market in Cocoa Island. In addition (not shown in the figure) a survey tells us that when Cocoa Island is at full employment, people spend 1,000 hours a day in job search.

a Find the full-employment equilibrium real wage rate and quantity of labour employed.

b Calculate the natural unemployment rate.

c If the government introduces a minimum wage of €4 an hour, how much unemployment is created?

4 A mobile phone assembly plant costs €10 million and has a life of one year. The firm will have to hire labour at a cost of €3 million and buy parts and fuel at a cost of a further €3 million. If the firm builds the plant, it will be able to produce mobile phones that will sell for

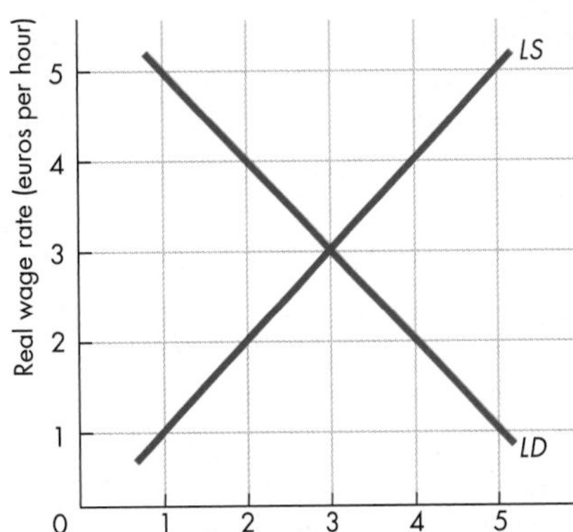

a total of €17 million. Does it pay the firm to invest in this new plant at the following real interest rates:

a 5 per cent a year?

b 10 per cent a year?

c 15 per cent a year?

5 In 2004, the Batman family (Batman and Robin) had a disposable income of €50,000, wealth of €100,000 and an expected future income of €50,000 a year. At an interest rate of 4 per cent a year, the Batmans would save €10,000; at 6 per cent a year, they would save €12,500; and at 8 per cent a year, they would save €15,000.

a Draw a graph of the Batman family's supply of loanable funds curve for 2004.

b In 2005, everything remained the same as the year before except that the Batmans expected their future income to rise to €60,000 a year. Show the influence of this change on the Batmans' supply of loanable funds.

6 If the European Union cracked down on illegal immigrants and returned millions of workers to their countries of origin, what would happen in the European Union to:

a Potential GDP?

b Employment?

c The real wage rate?

7 If a large increase in investment increased the marginal product of labour, what would happen to:

a Potential GDP?

b Employment?

c The real wage rate?

* Solutions to odd-numbered problems are provided.

8 The United States was at full employment in 1986 and again in 2005. In 1986, 198 billion hours of labour produced real GDP of $6 trillion (2000 dollars), and the real wage rate was $18 an hour. Between 1986 and 2005, capital per worker increased and technology advanced. At the same time, the population and the supply of labour increased. In 2005, the full employment quantity of labour was 254 billion hours and the real wage rate was $26 an hour and real GDP was $11.8 trillion (2000 dollars).

a Draw a graph of the US labour market that shows the demand for labour, the supply of labour and the real wage rate in 1986 and 2005.

b Draw a graph of the US production function in 1986 and 2005. Make sure your graph shows potential GDP in both years.

Critical Thinking

1 Study *Reading Between the Lines* on pp. 556–557 and then answer the following questions:

a By how much did real GDP grow between:

(i) 1987 and 2000 and (ii) 2000 and 2006?

b By how much did labour hours worked grow between:

(i) 1987 and 2000 and (ii) 2000 and 2006?

c By how much did labour productivity grow between:

(i) 1987 and 2000 and (ii) 2000 and 2006?

d What happened to the share of GDP received by labour between:

(i) 1987 and 2000 and (ii) 2000 and 2006?

[*Hint: You can answer from the information in Figures 2 and 3 on p. 557*]

e Do you think that there is strong evidence of a decrease in labour productivity growth between 2000 and 2006?

f Can you think of any reasons why productivity growth fluctuated much less during the late 1990s and 2000s than it did during the 1980s and early 1990s?

2 You are working as an Economic Assistant in the Treasury and must write a memo for the Chancellor that provides a checklist of policy initiatives that will increase potential GDP. Be as imaginative as possible but justify each of your suggestions with reference to the concepts and tools that you have learned about in this chapter.

3 **Tsunami social cost yet to come**

Relief experts estimate it could take up to a decade for some places to fully recover, and reconstruction will cost about $9 billion. . . . An assessment by the Indonesian government estimated total damage from the tsunami at $4.5 billion to $5 billion. . . . Housing, commerce, agriculture, fisheries and transport vehicles and services suffered losses of $2.8 billion, or 63 per cent of the total. . . .

CNN, 19 December 2005

a What happened to Indonesia's full-employment quantity of labour as a result of the December 2004 tsunami?

b Did Indonesia move along its production function or did its production function shift?

c What was the effect of the tsunami on Indonesia's potential GDP?

d According to the CNN news article, "people hardest hit by the tsunami were those who fell outside the 'formal' economy – mainly fishermen, farmers, women and people running small businesses". Does this information change your answers to parts (a), (b) and (c)? Explain why.

Web Activities

Links to Websites

1 Obtain information about the economy of Russia during the 1990s and 2000s.

a What happened to the the production function, the demand for labour and the supply of labour in Russia during the 1990s?

b Tell a story about the Russian economy during these years using only the concepts and tools that you have learned about in this chapter.

c Compare and contrast Russia's economy of the 1990s with that of the 2000s. What do you think made the difference?

2 Obtain information about the economy of China during the 1990s.

a What happened to the the production function, the demand for labour and the supply of labour in China during the 1990s?

b Tell a story about the Chinese economy during these years using only the concepts and tools that you have learned about in this chapter.

CHAPTER 25

In the Short Run: The Keynesian Model

After studying this chapter you will be able to:

- ◆ Explain how expenditure plans are determined when the price level is fixed
- ◆ Explain how equilibrium real GDP is determined when the price level is fixed
- ◆ Explain the expenditure multiplier when the price level is fixed
- ◆ Explain the relationship between aggregate expenditure and aggregate demand and explain the multiplier when the price level changes

Economic Amplifier or Shock Absorber?

Investment and exports fluctuate like the volume of Christina Aguilera's voice and the uneven surface of a country road. How does the economy react to these fluctuations? Does it react like a BMW to absorb the shocks and provide a smooth ride for its passengers? Or does it react like the amplifier that carries Christina Aguilera's voice around an open air stadium and enlarge and spread the shocks to affect the millions of participants in an economic concert? You will explore these questions in this chapter and at the end, in *Reading Between the Lines*, we will apply what you learn to examine the effects on consumption expenditure of interest rate changes.

Fixed Prices and Expenditure Plans

Economists have made progress in understanding the business cycle by studying a model economy in which the price level is fixed. In this model economy, all the firms are like your local supermarket. They set their prices, advertise their products and services, and sell the quantities their customers are willing to buy. If firms persistently sell a greater quantity than they plan to and are constantly running out of inventory, they eventually raise their prices. And if firms persistently sell a smaller quantity than they plan to and have inventories piling up, they eventually cut their prices. But in the very short term, their prices are fixed. Firms hold the prices they have set, and the quantities they sell depend on demand, not supply.

Fixed prices have two implications for the economy as a whole:

1 Because each firm's price is fixed, the *price level* is fixed.

2 Because demand determines the quantities that each firm sells, *aggregate demand* determines the aggregate quantity of goods and services sold, which equals *real GDP*.

The Keynesian Model

The idea that aggregate demand determines real GDP is the basis of the **Keynesian model** – a model of the economy that determines real GDP in the very short run. We begin our study of the Keynesian model by identifying the forces that determine expenditure plans.

Expenditure Plans

Aggregate expenditure has four components:

1 Consumption expenditure

2 Investment

3 Government expenditure on goods and services

4 Net exports (exports minus imports)

These four components of aggregate expenditure sum to real GDP (see Chapter 21, p. 472).

Aggregate planned expenditure is equal to *planned* consumption expenditure plus *planned* investment plus *planned* government expenditure on goods and services plus *planned* exports minus *planned* imports. Planned investment, government expenditure, and exports don't depend on the current level of real GDP. But planned consumption expenditure does depend on real GDP because it depends on income. Also, because some consumer goods are imported, planned imports depend on real GDP.

A Two-way Link Between Aggregate Expenditure and Real GDP

Because real GDP influences consumption expenditure and imports, and because consumption expenditure and imports are components of aggregate expenditure, there is a two-way link between aggregate expenditure and real GDP. Other things remaining the same:

- An increase in real GDP increases aggregate expenditure, and
- An increase in aggregate expenditure increases real GDP.

You are going to learn how this two-way link between aggregate expenditure and real GDP determines real GDP when the price level is fixed. The starting point is to consider the first piece of the two-way link: the influence of real GDP on planned consumption expenditure and saving.

Consumption Function and Saving Function

Several factors influence consumption expenditure and saving. Among the more important of them are:

1 Disposable income

2 The real interest rate

3 Wealth

4 Expected future income

Disposable income equals aggregate income minus taxes plus transfer payments. Aggregate income equals real GDP. So to explore the two-way link between real GDP and planned consumption expenditure, we focus on the relationship between consumption expenditure and disposable income when the other three factors are constant.

Real GDP is Y, taxes minus transfer payments are net taxes (T), so the equation for disposable income (YD) is:

$$YD = Y - T$$

Disposable income is either spent on consumption goods and services – consumption expenditure (C) – or saved (S). So planned consumption expenditure plus planned saving equals disposable income. That is:

$$YD = C + S$$

The table in Figure 25.1 shows some examples of planned consumption expenditure and planned saving at different levels of disposable income. The greater is disposable income, the greater is consumption expenditure and the greater is saving. Also, at each amount of disposable income, consumption expenditure plus saving equals disposable income.

The relationship between consumption expenditure and disposable income, with other things remaining the same, is the **consumption function**.

The relationship between saving and disposable income, with other things remaining the same, is the **saving function**.

Figure 25.1

Consumption Function and Saving Function

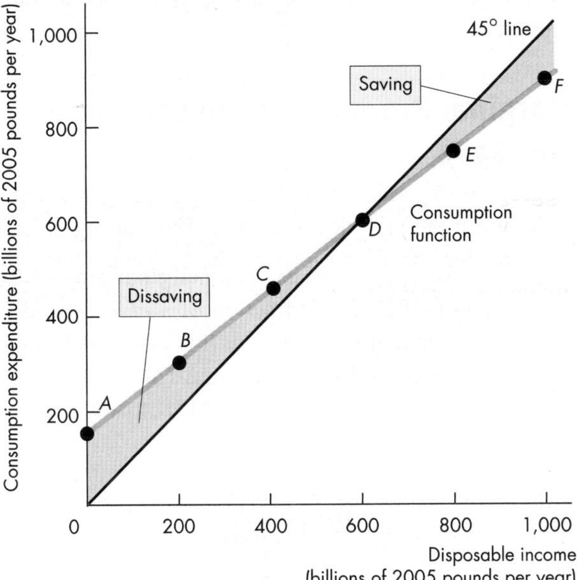

(a) Consumption function

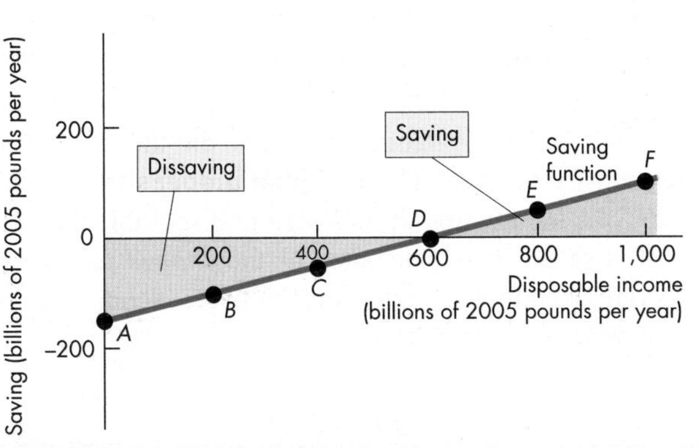

(b) Saving function

	Disposable income	Planned consumption expenditure	Planned saving
	(billions of 2005 pounds per year)		
A	0	150	−150
B	200	300	−100
C	400	450	−50
D	600	600	0
E	800	750	50
F	1,000	900	100

The table shows consumption expenditure and saving plans at various levels of disposable income. When disposable income is £800 (row *E*) planned consumption expenditure is £750 and planned saving is £50.

Part (a) of the figure shows the consumption function (the relationship between consumption expenditure and disposable income). The height of the consumption function measures consumption expenditure at each level of disposable income.

Part (b) shows the saving function (the relationship between saving and disposable income). The height of the saving function measures saving at each level of disposable income. Points *A* to *F* on the consumption and saving functions correspond to the rows in the table.

The height of the 45° line in part (a) measures disposable income. So along the 45° line, consumption expenditure equals disposable income. Consumption expenditure plus saving equals disposable income.

When the consumption function is above the 45° line, saving is negative (dissaving occurs). When the consumption function is below the 45° line, saving is positive. At the point where the consumption function intersects the 45° line, all disposable income is consumed and saving is zero.

Consumption Function

Figure 25.1(a) shows a consumption function. The y-axis measures consumption expenditure and the x-axis measures disposable income. Along the consumption function, the points labelled A through F correspond to the rows of the table. For example, point E shows that when disposable income is £800 billion, consumption expenditure is £750 billion. Along the consumption function, as disposable income increases, consumption expenditure also increases.

At point A on the consumption function, consumption expenditure is £150 billion even though disposable income is zero. This consumption expenditure is called *autonomous consumption* and is the amount of consumption expenditure that would take place in the short run even if people had no current income. You can think of this amount as the expenditure on the vital necessities of life. When consumption expenditure exceeds disposable income, past savings are used to pay for current consumption. Such a situation cannot last forever, but it can occur temporarily.

Consumption expenditure in excess of autonomous consumption is called *induced consumption* – expenditure that is induced by an increase in disposable income.

45° Line

Figure 25.1(a) also contains a 45° line, the height of which measures disposable income. At each point on this line, consumption expenditure equals disposable income. In the range over which the consumption function lies above the 45° line – between points A and D – consumption expenditure exceeds disposable income. In the range over which the consumption function lies below the 45° line – between points D and F – consumption expenditure is less than disposable income. And at the point at which the consumption function intersects the 45° line – at point D – consumption expenditure equals disposable income.

Saving Function

Figure 25.1(b) shows a saving function. The x-axis is exactly the same as that in part (a). The y-axis measures saving. Again, the points marked A through F correspond to the rows of the table. For example, point E shows that when disposable income is £800 billion, saving is £50 billion. Along the saving function, as disposable income increases, saving also increases. At disposable incomes below £600 billion (point D), saving is negative. Negative saving is called *dissaving*. At disposable incomes above £600 billion, saving is positive, and at £600 billion, saving is zero.

Notice the connection between the two parts of Figure 25.1. When consumption expenditure exceeds disposable income in part (a), saving is negative in part (b). When consumption expenditure is less than disposable income in part (a), saving is positive in part (b). And when consumption expenditure equals disposable income in part (a), saving is zero in part (b).

When saving is negative (when consumption expenditure exceeds disposable income), past savings are used to pay for current consumption. Such a situation cannot last forever, but it can occur if disposable income falls temporarily.

Marginal Propensities to Consume and Save

The extent to which consumption expenditure changes when disposable income changes depends on the marginal propensity to consume. The **marginal propensity to consume** (*MPC*) is the fraction of a *change* in disposable income that is consumed. It is calculated as the *change* in consumption expenditure (ΔC) divided by the *change* in disposable income (ΔYD) that brought it about. That is:

$$MPC = \frac{\Delta C}{\Delta YD}$$

In Figure 25.1, the *MPC* equals 0.75. To calculate this number, notice that when disposable income increases from £600 billion to £800 billion, consumption expenditure increases from £600 billion to £750 billion. The £200 billion increase in disposable income increases consumption expenditure of £150 billion. The *MPC* is £150 billion divided by £200 billion, which equals 0.75.

The amount by which saving changes when disposable income changes depends on the marginal propensity to save. The **marginal propensity to save** (*MPS*) is the fraction of a *change* in disposable income that is saved. It is calculated as the *change* in saving (ΔS) divided by the *change* in disposable income (ΔYD) that brought it about. That is:

$$MPS = \frac{\Delta S}{\Delta YD}$$

In Figure 25.1, the *MPS* equals 0.25. To calculate this number, notice that an increase in disposable income from £600 billion to £800 billion increases saving from zero to £50 billion. The £200 billion increase in disposable income increases saving by £50 billion. The *MPS* is £50 billion divided by £200 billion, which equals 0.25.

The marginal propensity to consume plus the marginal propensity to save always equals 1. They sum to 1 because consumption expenditure and saving exhaust disposable income. Part of each pound increase in disposable income is consumed, and the remaining part is saved. You can see that these two marginal propensities sum to 1 by using the equation:

$$\Delta C + \Delta S = \Delta YD$$

Divide both sides of the equation by the change in disposable income to obtain:

$$\frac{\Delta C}{\Delta YD} + \frac{\Delta S}{\Delta YD} = 1$$

$\Delta C/\Delta YD$ is the *marginal propensity to consume* (*MPC*) and $\Delta S/\Delta YD$ is the *marginal propensity to save* (*MPS*), so:

$$MPC + MPS = 1$$

Figure 25.2 shows that when the *MPC* is 0.75, the *MPS* is 0.25. The sum of *MPC* and *MPS* equals 1.

Slopes and Marginal Propensities to Consume and Save

The slope of the consumption function is the marginal propensity to consume and the slope of the saving function is the marginal propensity to save.

Figure 25.2(a) shows the *MPC* as the slope of the consumption function. A £200 billion increase in disposable income from £600 billion to £800 billion is the base of the red triangle. The increase in consumption expenditure that results from this increase in disposable income is £150 billion and is the height of the triangle. The slope of the consumption function is given by the formula "slope equals rise over run" and is £150 billion divided by £200 billion, which equals 0.75 – the *MPC* is 0.75.

Figure 25.2(b) shows the *MPS* as the slope of the saving function. A £200 billion increase in disposable income from £600 billion to £800 billion (the base of the red triangle) increases saving by £50 billion (the height of the triangle). The slope of the saving function is £50 billion divided by £200 billion, which equals 0.25 – the *MPS* is 0.25.

Figure 25.2

Marginal Propensities to Consume and Save

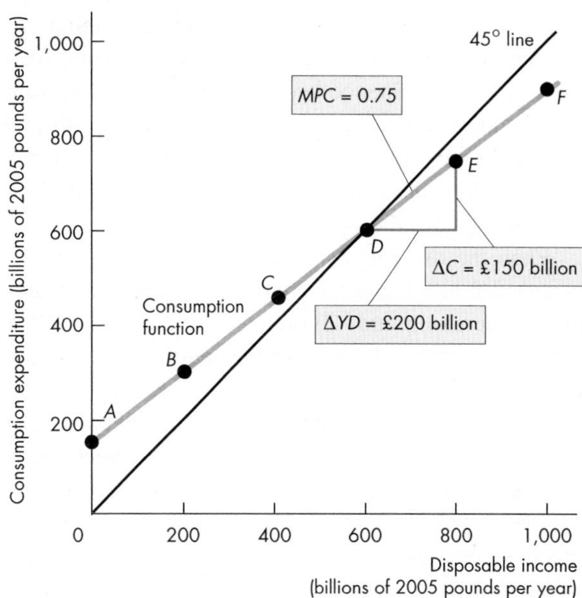

(a) Consumption function

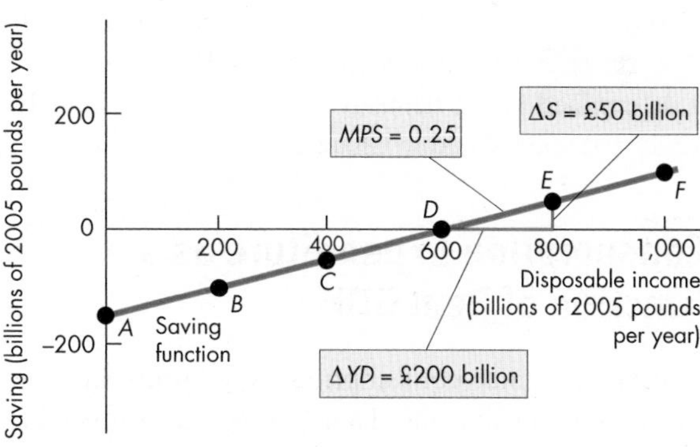

(b) Saving function

The marginal propensity to consume, *MPC*, is equal to the change in consumption expenditure divided by the change in disposable income, other things remaining the same. It is measured by the slope of the consumption function. In part (a), the *MPC* is 0.75.

The marginal propensity to save, *MPS*, is equal to the change in saving divided by the change in disposable income, other things remaining the same. It is measured by the slope of the saving function. In part (b), the *MPS* is 0.25.

Other Influences on Consumption Expenditure and Saving

A change in disposable income leads to changes in consumption expenditure and saving and brings movements along the consumption function and saving function.

Along the consumption function and the saving function, all other influences on consumption expenditure and saving (such as the real interest rate, wealth and expected future disposable income) are fixed. A change in any of these other influences shifts both the consumption function and the saving function.

When the real interest rate falls or when wealth or expected future income increases, consumption expenditure increases and saving decreases. Figure 25.3 shows the effects of these changes on the consumption function and the saving function. The consumption function shifts upward from CF_0 to CF_1, and the saving function shifts downward from SF_0 to SF_1. Such shifts commonly occur during the expansion phase of the business cycle because, at that time, expected future income increases.

When the real interest rate rises or when wealth or expected future income decreases, consumption expenditure decreases and saving increases. The consumption function shifts downward, and the saving function shifts upward. Such shifts often occur when a recession begins because, at that time, expected future income decreases.

Although the real interest rate is taken as given in the short run of the Keynesian model, you have seen how it is determined by the demand for and supply of loanable funds that you studied in Chapter 24 (see p. 548).

Figure 25.3 

Shifts in the Consumption and Saving Functions

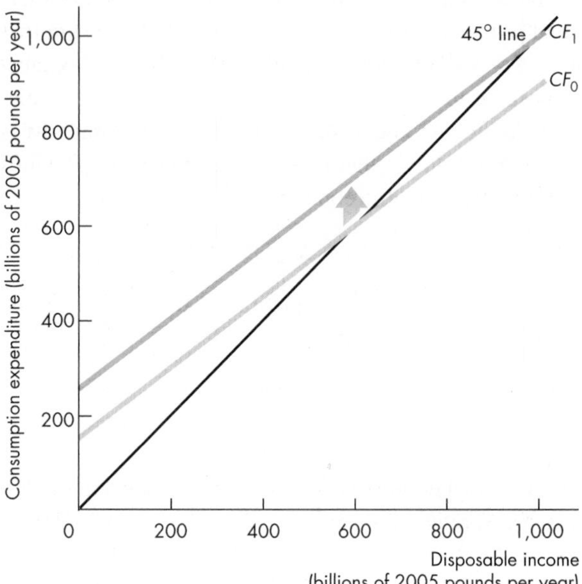

(a) Consumption function

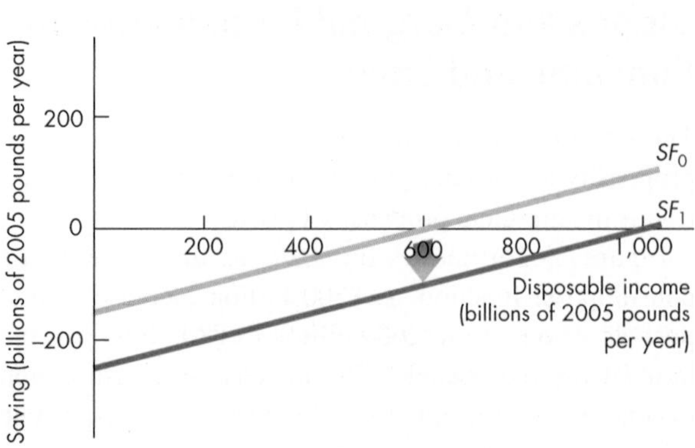

(b) Saving function

A fall in the real interest rate, an increase in wealth or an increase in expected future disposable income increases consumption expenditure, shifts the consumption function upward from CF_0 to CF_1 and shifts the saving function downward from SF_0 to SF_1.

Similarly, a rise in the real interest rate, a decrease in wealth, or a decrease in expected future disposable income shifts the consumption function downward from and shifts the saving function upward.

Consumption Expenditure as a Function of Real GDP

You've seen that consumption expenditure changes when disposable income changes. You've also seen that disposable income is equal to real GDP minus net taxes. So consumption expenditure is a function of real GDP. An increase in real GDP increases disposable income, which increases consumption expenditure. But an increase in real GDP also increases net taxes. So when real GDP increases, consumption expenditure increases but by less than it would if net taxes were unchanged. We use this link between consumption expenditure and real GDP to determine equilibrium expenditure. But before we do so, we need to look at one other component of aggregate expenditure: imports. Like consumption expenditure, imports are influenced by real GDP.

Box 25.1
The UK Consumption Function

Figure 1 shows the UK consumption function. Each blue dot represents consumption expenditure and disposable income for a particular year. (The dots are for the years 1970 to 2005 and the dots of four of the years are identified.)

The line CF_{70} is an estimate of the UK consumption function in 1970, and the line CF_{05} is an estimate of the UK consumption function in 2005.

The slope of the consumption function in the figure is 0.8, which means that a £100 billion increase in disposable income brings a £80 billion increase in consumption expenditure. This slope, which is an estimate of the marginal propensity to consume, is the average over the period 1970–2005 and it is the middle of the range of values that economists have estimated for the marginal propensity to consume.

The consumption function shifts upward over time as other influences on consumption expenditure change. Of these other influences, the real interest rate and wealth fluctuate and so bring upward *and* downward shifts in the consumption function. But rising expected future disposable income brings a steady upward shift in the consumption function. As the consumption function shifts upward, autonomous consumption expenditure increases.

Figure 1

The UK Consumption Function

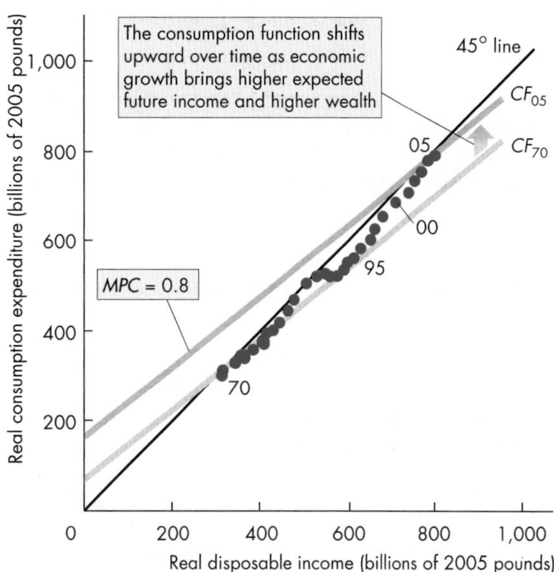

Source of data: Office for National Statistics.

Import Function

UK imports are determined by a number of factors, but in the short run with fixed prices, one factor dominates: real GDP in the United Kingdom. Other things remaining the same, the greater the UK real GDP, the larger is the quantity of UK imports. So an increase in UK real GDP brings an increase in UK imports.

The relationship between imports and real GDP is determined by the marginal propensity to import. The **marginal propensity to import** is the fraction of an increase in real GDP that is spent on imports. It is calculated as the change in imports divided by the change in real GDP that brought it about, other things remaining the same. For example, if a £100 billion increase in real GDP increases imports by £20 billion, the marginal propensity to import is 0.2.

Review Quiz

Study Plan 25.1

1. Which components of aggregate planned expenditure are influenced by real GDP?
2. Define the marginal propensity to consume.
3. What is your estimate of your own marginal propensity to consume? After you graduate and begin work, will your marginal propensity to consume change? Why or why not?
4. How do we calculate the effects of real GDP on consumption expenditure and imports?

Your next task is to study the second piece of the two-way link between aggregate expenditure and real GDP and see how all the components of aggregate planned expenditure interact to determine real GDP.

Real GDP with a Fixed Price Level

You are now going to learn how expenditure plans determine real GDP when the price level is fixed. We begin by studying the relationship between aggregate planned expenditure and real GDP. We describe this relationship either by an aggregate expenditure schedule or by an aggregate expenditure curve. The *aggregate expenditure schedule* lists aggregate planned expenditure generated at each level of real GDP. The *aggregate expenditure curve* is a graph of the aggregate expenditure schedule.

Then we'll learn about the key distinction between *planned* expenditure and *actual* expenditure. And finally, we'll define and learn what determines equilibrium expenditure and real GDP.

Figure 25.4

Aggregate Expenditure

myeconlab

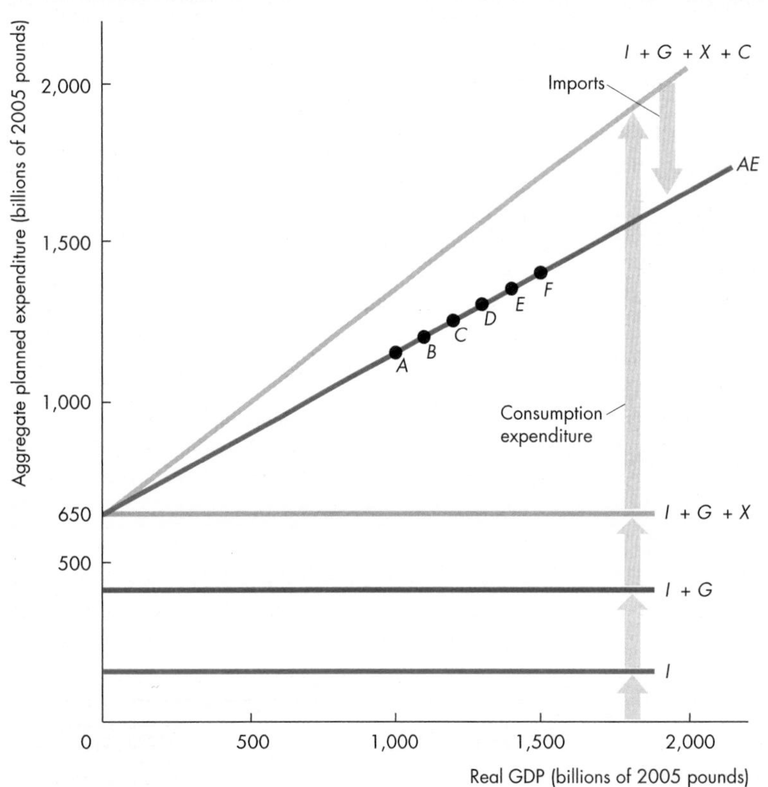

Aggregate planned expenditure is the sum of planned consumption expenditure, investment, government expenditure and exports minus imports. When real GDP is zero, aggregate planned expenditure is £650 billion. When real GDP is £1,000 billion, (row *A* of the table) planned consumption expenditure is £700 billion, planned investment is £150 billion, planned government expenditure is £260 billion, planned exports are £240 billion, and planned imports are £200 billion, so aggregate planned expenditure is £1,150 billion.

The graph shows the relationship between the components of aggregate expenditure and real GDP. The green, blue and orange arrows show investment, government expenditure and exports – the expenditures that do not vary with real GDP. The red and purple arrows show consumption expenditure and imports – the expenditures that vary with real GDP. The red curve *AE* is the aggregate planned expenditure curve.

	Real GDP (*Y*)	Consumption expenditure (*C*)	Investment (*I*)	Government expenditure (*G*)	Exports (*X*)	Imports (*M*)	Aggregate planned expenditure (*AE* = *C* + *I* + *G* + *X* − *M*)
		Planned expenditure (billions of 2005 pounds)					
	0	0	150	260	240	0	650
A	1,000	700	150	260	240	200	1,150
B	1,100	770	150	260	240	220	1,200
C	1,200	840	150	260	240	240	1,250
D	1,300	910	150	260	240	260	1,300
E	1,400	980	150	260	240	280	1,350
F	1,500	1,050	150	260	240	300	1,400

Aggregate Planned Expenditure and Real GDP

The table in Figure 25.4 sets out an aggregate expenditure schedule together with the components of aggregate planned expenditure. To calculate aggregate planned expenditure at a given real GDP, we add the various components together. The first column of the table shows real GDP and the second column shows the consumption expenditure generated by each level of real GDP. A £1,000 billion increase in real GDP generates a £700 billion increase in consumption expenditure – the *MPC* is 0.7.

The next two columns show investment and government expenditure on goods and services. Investment depends on factors such as the real interest rate and the expected future profit. But at a given point in time, these factors generate a particular level of investment. Suppose this level of investment is £150 billion. Also, suppose that government expenditure on goods and services are £260 billion.

The next two columns show exports and imports. Exports are influenced by income in the rest of the world, prices of foreign-produced goods and services relative to the prices of similar UK-produced goods and services, and foreign exchange rates. But exports are not directly affected by UK real GDP. In the table, exports appear as a constant £240 billion. In contrast, imports increase as real GDP increases. A £100 billion increase in real GDP generates a £20 billion increase in imports – the marginal propensity to import is 0.2.

The final column of the table shows aggregate planned expenditure – the sum of planned consumption expenditure, investment, government expenditure and exports minus imports.

Figure 25.4 plots an aggregate expenditure curve. Real GDP is shown on the x-axis and aggregate planned expenditure on the y-axis. The aggregate expenditure curve is the red line *AE*. Points *A* to *F* on this curve correspond to the rows of the table. The *AE* curve is a graph of aggregate planned expenditure (the last column) plotted against real GDP (the first column).

Figure 25.4 also shows the components of aggregate expenditure. The constant components – investment (I), government expenditure (G), and exports (X) – are shown by the vertical gaps between the horizontal lines. Consumption expenditure (C) is the vertical gap between the lines labelled $I + G + X + C$ and $I + G + X$.

To construct the *AE* curve, subtract imports (M) from the $I + G + X + C$ line. Aggregate expenditure is expenditure on UK-produced goods and services. But the components of aggregate expenditure, C, I and G include expenditure on imported goods and services. For example, if you buy a new mobile phone, your expenditure is part of consumption expenditure. But if the mobile phone is a Nokia made in Finland, your expenditure on it must be subtracted from consumption expenditure to find out how much is spent on goods and services produced in the United Kingdom – on UK real GDP. Money paid to Nokia for mobile phone imports from Finland does not add to aggregate expenditure in the United Kingdom.

Because imports are only a part of aggregate expenditure, when we subtract imports from the other components of aggregate expenditure, aggregate planned expenditure still increases as real GDP increases, as you can see in Figure 25.4.

Consumption expenditure minus imports, which varies with real GDP, is called **induced expenditure**. The sum of investment, government expenditure and exports, which does not vary with real GDP, is called **autonomous expenditure**. Consumption expenditure and imports can also have an autonomous component – a component that does not vary with real GDP. Another way of thinking about autonomous expenditure is that it would be the level of aggregate planned expenditure if real GDP were zero.

In Figure 25.4, autonomous expenditure is £650 billion – aggregate planned expenditure when real GDP is zero. For each £100 billion increase in real GDP, induced expenditure increases by £50 billion.

The aggregate expenditure curve summarizes the relationship between aggregate planned expenditure and real GDP. But what determines the point on the aggregate expenditure curve at which the economy operates? What determines *actual* aggregate expenditure?

Actual Expenditure, Planned Expenditure and Real GDP

Actual aggregate expenditure is always equal to real GDP, as we saw in Chapter 21 (p. 472). But aggregate *planned* expenditure does not necessarily equal actual aggregate expenditure and real GDP. How can actual expenditure and planned expenditure differ from each other? Why don't expenditure plans get implemented? The main reason is that firms might end up with greater inventories or stocks or with smaller inventories or stocks than planned. People carry out their consumption expenditure plans, the government implements its planned expenditure on goods and services, and net exports are as planned. Firms carry out their plans to purchase new buildings, plant and equipment. But one component of investment is the increase in firms' inventories or stocks of goods. If aggregate planned expenditure is less than real GDP, firms don't sell all the goods and services they produce and they end up with more inventories than they has planned. They have unplanned inventories or stocks. If aggregate planned expenditure is greater than real GDP, firms sell more goods and services than they produce and inventories or stocks fall to below the level that firms had planned.

Equilibrium Expenditure

Equilibrium expenditure is the level of aggregate expenditure that occurs when aggregate *planned* expenditure equals real GDP. Equilibrium expenditure is a level of aggregate expenditure and real GDP at which everyone's spending plans are fulfilled. When the price level is fixed, equilibrium expenditure determines real GDP. When aggregate planned expenditure and actual aggregate expenditure are unequal, a process of convergence

Figure 25.5

myeconlab

Equilibrium Expenditure

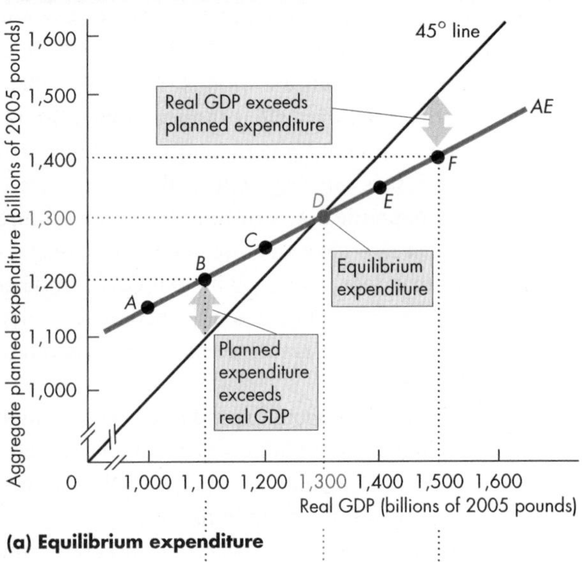

(a) Equilibrium expenditure

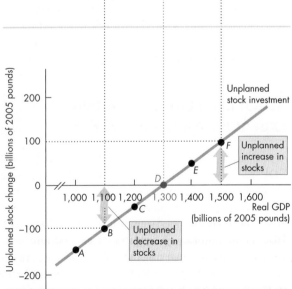

(b) Unplanned stock changes

	Real GDP (*Y*)	Aggregate planned expenditure (*AE*)	Unplanned stock change (*Y* – *AE*)
		(billions of 2005 pounds)	
A	1,000	1,150	–150
B	1,100	1,200	–100
C	1,200	1,250	–50
D	**1,300**	**1,300**	**0**
E	1,400	1,350	50
F	1,500	1,400	100

The table shows expenditure plans at different levels of real GDP. When real GDP is £1,300 billion, aggregate planned expenditure equals real GDP.

Part (a) of the figure illustrates equilibrium expenditure, which occurs when aggregate planned expenditure equals real GDP at the intersection of the 45° line and the *AE* curve. Part (b) of the figure shows the forces that bring about equilibrium expenditure.

When aggregate planned expenditure exceeds real GDP, firms' inventories or stocks decrease – for example, point *B* in both parts of the figure. Firms have an unplanned decrease in inventories, so they increase production. Real GDP increases.

When aggregate planned expenditure is less than real GDP, firms' inventories or stocks increase – for example, point *F* in both parts of the figure. Firms have an unplanned increase in inventories, so they decrease production. Real GDP decreases.

When aggregate planned expenditure equals real GDP, there are no unplanned inventory or stock changes and real GDP remains constant at equilibrium expenditure.

towards equilibrium expenditure occurs. And throughout this convergence process real GDP adjusts. Let's examine equilibrium expenditure and the process that brings it about.

Figure 25.5(a) illustrates equilibrium expenditure. The table sets out aggregate planned expenditure at various levels of real GDP. These values are plotted as points *A* through *F* along the *AE* curve. The 45° line shows all the points at which aggregate planned expenditure equals real GDP. So where the *AE* curve lies above the 45° line, aggregate planned expenditure exceeds real GDP; where the *AE* curve lies below the 45° line, aggregate planned expenditure is less than real GDP; and where the *AE* curve intersects the 45° line, aggregate planned expenditure equals real GDP. Point *D* illustrates equilibrium expenditure. At this point, real GDP is £1,300 billion.

Convergence to Equilibrium

What are the forces that move aggregate expenditure towards its equilibrium level? To answer this question, we must look at a situation in which aggregate expenditure is away from its equilibrium level. Suppose that in Figure 25.5, actual aggregate expenditure is £1,100 billion. But aggregate *planned* expenditure is £1,200 billion, point *B* in Figure 25.5(a). Aggregate planned expenditure exceeds *actual* expenditure. When people spend £1,200 billion, and firms produce goods and services worth £1,100 billion, firms' inventories (stocks) fall by £100 billion, point *B* in Figure 25.5(b). Because the change in stocks is part of investment, *actual* investment is £100 billion less than *planned* investment.

Real GDP doesn't remain at £1,100 billion for very long. Firms have inventory (stock) targets based on their sales. When stocks fall below target, firms increase production to restore stocks to their target levels. To increase stocks, firms hire additional labour and increase production.

Suppose that firms increase production in the next period by £100 billion. Real GDP increases by £100 billion to £1,200 billion. But again, aggregate planned expenditure exceeds real GDP. When real GDP is £1,200 billion, aggregate planned expenditure is £1,250 billion, point *C* in Figure 25.5(a). Again, stocks decrease, but this time by less than before. With real GDP of £1,200 billion and aggregate planned expenditure of £1,250 billion, stocks decrease by £50 billion, point *C* in Figure 25.5(b). Again, to restore stocks, firms hire additional labour and production increases; real GDP increases yet further.

The process that we have just described – planned expenditure exceeds real GDP, inventories (stocks) decrease and production increases to restore the stocks back to their target levels – ends when real GDP has reached £1,300 billion. At this real GDP, there is equilibrium expenditure. Unplanned inventory (stock) changes are zero. Firms do not change their production.

You can do a similar experiment to the one we've just done, but starting with a level of real GDP greater than equilibrium expenditure. In this case, planned expenditure is less than actual expenditure, stocks pile up and firms cut production. As before, real GDP keeps on changing (decreasing this time) until it reaches its equilibrium level of £1,300 billion.

This process of convergence to equilibrium is driven by changes in production and real GDP, not by changes in prices. Throughout the entire process the price level (and the price of every firm's output) remains fixed.

Review Quiz

Study Plan 25.2

1. Explain the relationship between aggregate planned expenditure and real GDP.
2. Distinguish between autonomous expenditure and induced expenditure.
3. What is the relationship between aggregate planned expenditure and real GDP at equilibrium expenditure?
4. What adjusts to achieve equilibrium expenditure?
5. If real GDP and aggregate expenditure are less than equilibrium expenditure, what happens to firms' inventories or stocks? How do firms change their production? What happens to real GDP?
6. If real GDP and aggregate expenditure are greater than their equilibrium expenditure, what happens to firms' inventories or stocks? How do firms change their production? What happens to real GDP?

We've learned that when the price level is fixed, real GDP is determined by equilibrium expenditure. And we have seen how unplanned changes in inventories or stocks and the production response they generate bring a convergence towards equilibrium expenditure. We're now going to study *changes* in equilibrium expenditure and discover an economic amplifier called the *multiplier*.

The Multiplier

Investment and exports can change for many reasons. A fall in the real interest rate might induce firms to increase their planned investment. A wave of innovation, such as occurred with the spread of multimedia computers in the 1990s, might increase expected future profits and lead firms to increase their planned investment. An economic boom in the United States and Canada might lead to a large increase in their expenditure on UK-produced goods and services – UK exports. These are all examples of increases in autonomous expenditure in the United Kingdom.

When autonomous expenditure increases, aggregate expenditure increases, and so do equilibrium expenditure and real GDP. But the increase in equilibrium expenditure and real GDP is *larger* than the change in autonomous expenditure. The **multiplier** is the amount by which a change in autonomous expenditure is magnified or multiplied to determine the change in equilibrium expenditure and real GDP.

To understand the basic idea of the multiplier, we'll work with an example economy in which there are no income taxes and no imports. So we'll first assume that these factors are absent. Then, when you understand the basic idea, we'll bring these factors back into play and see what difference they make to the multiplier.

The Basic Idea of the Multiplier

Suppose that investment increases. The additional expenditure by businesses means that aggregate expenditure and real GDP increases. The increase in real GDP increases disposable income, and with no income taxes, real GDP and disposable income increase by the same amount. The increase in disposable income brings an increase in consumption expenditure. And the increased consumption expenditure adds even more to aggregate expenditure. Real GDP and disposable income increase further, and so does consumption expenditure. The initial increase in investment brings an even bigger increase in aggregate expenditure because it induces an increase in consumption expenditure. The magnitude of the increase in aggregate expenditure that results from an increase in autonomous expenditure is determined by the *multiplier*.

The table in Figure 25.6 sets out aggregate planned expenditure. When real GDP is £1,200 billion, aggregate planned expenditure is £1,225 billion. For each £100 billion increase in real GDP, aggregate planned expenditure increases by £75 billion. This aggregate expenditure schedule is shown in the graph as the aggregate expenditure curve AE_0.

Initially, equilibrium expenditure is £1,300 billion. You can see this equilibrium in row *B* of the table, and in the graph where the curve AE_0 intersects the 45° line at the point marked *B*.

Now suppose that autonomous expenditure increases by £50 billion. What happens to equilibrium expenditure? You can see the answer in Figure 25.6. When this increase in autonomous expenditure is added to the original aggregate planned expenditure, aggregate planned expenditure increases by £50 billion at each level of real GDP. The new aggregate expenditure curve is AE_1. The new equilibrium expenditure, highlighted in the table (row *D'*), occurs where AE_1 intersects the 45° line and is £1,500 billion (point *D'*). At this point, aggregate planned expenditure equals real GDP. Equilibrium expenditure is £1,500 billion.

The Multiplier Effect

In Figure 25.6, the increase in autonomous expenditure of £50 billion increases equilibrium expenditure from £1,300 billion to £1,500 billion – an increase of £200 billion. That is, the change in autonomous expenditure leads, like Christina Aguilera's voice, to an amplified change in equilibrium expenditure. This amplified change is the multiplier effect – equilibrium expenditure increases by more than the increase in autonomous expenditure. The multiplier is greater than 1.

Initially, when autonomous expenditure increases, aggregate planned expenditure exceeds real GDP. As a result, firm's inventories (stocks) decrease. Firms respond by increasing production so as to restore their inventories to their target levels. As production increases, so does real GDP. With a higher level of real GDP, *induced expenditure* increases. So equilibrium expenditure increases by the sum of the initial increase in autonomous expenditure and the increase in induced expenditure. In this example, the initial increase in autonomous expenditure is £50 billion and induced expenditure increases by £150 billion, so equilibrium expenditure increases by £200 billion.

Although we have just analysed the effects of an *increase* in autonomous expenditure, the same analysis applies to a decrease in autonomous expenditure. If initially the aggregate expenditure curve is AE_1, equilibrium expenditure and real GDP are £1,500 billion. A decrease in autonomous expenditure of £50 billion shifts the aggregate expenditure curve downward by

Figure 25.6

The Multiplier

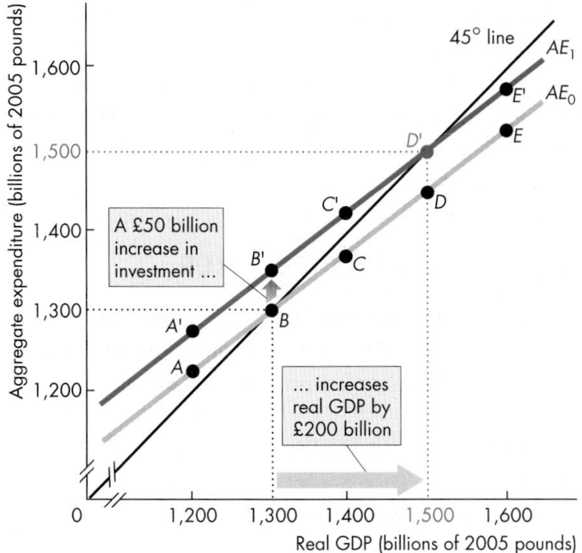

Real GDP (Y)	Aggregate planned expenditure			
	Original (AE_0)		New (AE_1)	
	(billions of 2005 pounds)			
1,200	*A*	1,225	*A'*	1,275
1,300	***B***	**1,300**	*B'*	1,350
1,400	*C*	1,375	*C'*	1,425
1,500	*D*	1,450	***D'***	**1,500**
1,600	*E*	1,525	*E'*	1,575

A £50 billion increase in autonomous expenditure shifts the *AE* curve upward by £50 billion from AE_0 to AE_1. Equilibrium expenditure increases by £200 billion from £1,300 billion to £1,500 billion. The increase in equilibrium expenditure is 4 times the increase in autonomous expenditure, so the multiplier is 4.

£50 billion to AE_0. Equilibrium expenditure decreases from £1,500 billion to £1,300 billion. The decrease in equilibrium expenditure (£200 billion) is larger than the decrease in autonomous expenditure that brought it about (£50 billion).

Why Is the Multiplier Greater Than 1?

We've seen that equilibrium expenditure increases by more than the increase in autonomous expenditure. This makes the multiplier greater than 1. How come? Why does equilibrium expenditure increase by more than the increase in autonomous expenditure?

The multiplier is greater than 1 because of induced expenditure – an increase in autonomous expenditure *induces* further increases in expenditure. If Vodafone spends £10 million on a new telephone-video system, aggregate expenditure and real GDP immediately increase by £10 million. But that is not the end of the story. Electrical engineers and video-system designers now have more income, and they spend part of the extra income on consumption goods and services.

Real GDP now increases by the initial £10 million plus the extra consumption expenditure induced by the £10 million increase in income. The producers of consumption goods and services now have increased incomes, and they, in turn, spend part of the increase in their incomes on consumption goods and services. Additional income induces additional expenditure, which creates additional income.

The Size of the Multiplier

The economy is in a recession and now profit prospects start to look better. Firms are making plans for large increases in investment. The world economy is also heading towards expansion, and exports are increasing. The question on everyone's lips is: how strong will the expansion be? This is a hard question to answer. But an important ingredient in the answer is working out the size of the multiplier.

The *multiplier* is the amount by which a change in autonomous expenditure is multiplied to determine the change in equilibrium expenditure that it generates. To calculate the multiplier, we divide the change in equilibrium expenditure by the change in autonomous expenditure. Let's calculate the multiplier for the example in Figure 25.6. Initially, equilibrium expenditure is £1,300 billion. Then autonomous expenditure increases by £50 billion, and equilibrium expenditure increases by £200 billion to £1,500 billion. So:

$$\text{Multiplier} = \frac{\text{Change in equilibrium expenditure}}{\text{Change in autonomous expenditure}}$$

$$= \frac{£200 \text{ billion}}{£50 \text{ billion}} = 4$$

The Multiplier and the Slope of the *AE* Curve

What determines the magnitude of the multiplier? The answer is the slope of the *AE* curve. The steeper the slope of the *AE* curve, the larger is the multiplier. To see why, think about what the slope of the *AE* curve tells you. It tells you by how much induced expenditure increases when real GDP increases. The steeper the *AE* curve, the greater is the increase in induced expenditure that results from a given increase in real GDP. Let's do a calculation to show the relationship between the slope of the *AE* curve and the multiplier.

The change in real GDP (ΔY) equals the change in induced expenditure (ΔN) plus the change in autonomous expenditure (ΔA). That is:

$$\Delta Y = \Delta N + \Delta A$$

But the change in induced expenditure is determined by the change in real GDP and the slope of the *AE* curve. To see why, begin with the fact that the slope of the *AE* curve equals the "rise", ΔN, divided by the "run", ΔY. That is:

$$\text{Slope of } AE \text{ curve} = \Delta N \div \Delta Y$$

So:

$$\Delta N = \text{Slope of } AE \text{ curve} \times \Delta Y$$

Now use this equation to replace ΔN in the first equation above to give:

$$\Delta Y = (\text{Slope of } AE \text{ curve} \times \Delta Y) + \Delta A$$

Now, solve for ΔY as:

$$(1 - \text{Slope of } AE \text{ curve}) \times \Delta Y = \Delta A$$

and rearrange to give:

$$\Delta Y = \frac{\Delta A}{1 - \text{Slope of the } AE \text{ curve}}$$

Finally, divide both sides of this equation by ΔA:

$$\text{Multiplier} = \frac{\Delta Y}{\Delta A} = \frac{1}{1 - \text{Slope of the } AE \text{ curve}}$$

Using the numbers for Figure 25.6, the slope of the *AE* curve 0.75, so the multiplier is:

$$\text{Multiplier} = \frac{1}{1 - 0.75} = \frac{1}{0.25} = 4$$

When there are no income taxes and no imports, the slope of the *AE* curve equals the marginal propensity to consume (*MPC*). So the multiplier is:

$$\text{Multiplier} = \frac{1}{(1 - MPC)}$$

But (1 – *MPC*) equals *MPS*. So another formula for the multiplier is:

$$\text{Multiplier} = \frac{1}{MPS}$$

Because the marginal propensity to save (*MPS*) is a fraction – a number between 0 and 1 – the multiplier is greater than 1.

Imports and Income Taxes

The multiplier is determined, in general, not only by the marginal propensity to consume but also by the marginal propensity to import and by the marginal tax rate.

Imports make the multiplier smaller than it otherwise would be. To see why, think about what happens following an increase in UK investment. An increase in investment increases real GDP, which in turn increases consumption expenditure in the United Kingdom. But part of this increase in consumption expenditure is expenditure on imported goods and services, not expenditure on UK-produced good and services. Only expenditure on goods and services produced in the United Kingdom increases real GDP in the United Kingdom. The larger the marginal propensity to import, the smaller is the change in UK real GDP.

Income taxes also make the multiplier smaller than it otherwise would be. Again, think about what happens following an increase in investment. An increase in investment increases real GDP. But because income taxes increase, disposable income increases by less than the increase in real GDP. Consequently, consumption expenditure increases by less than it would if taxes had not changed. The larger the income tax rate, the smaller is the change in disposable income and real GDP.

The marginal propensity to import and the marginal tax rate together with the marginal propensity to consume determine the multiplier. And their combined influence determines the slope of the *AE* curve.

Figure 25.7 compares two situations. In Figure 25.7(a) there are no imports and no taxes. The slope of the *AE* curve equals the marginal propensity to consume, which is 0.75. The multiplier is 4. In Figure 25.7(b), imports and income taxes decrease the slope of the *AE* curve to 0.5. The multiplier is 2.

Figure 25.7

The Multiplier and the Slope of the *AE* Curve

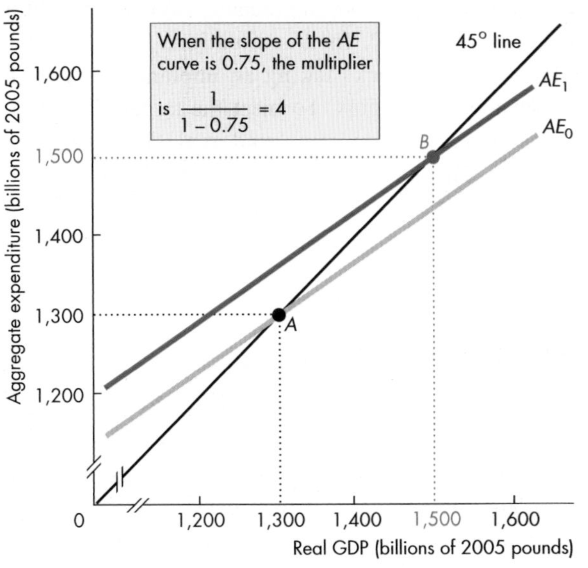

(a) Multiplier is 4

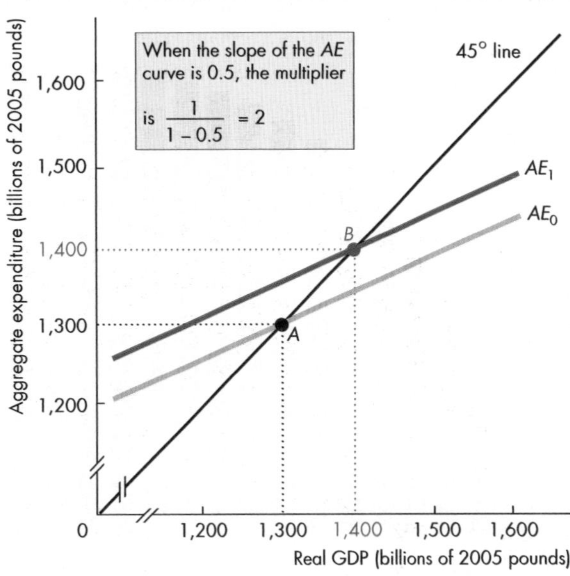

(b) Multiplier is 2

Imports and income taxes make the *AE* curve less steep and reduce the value of the multiplier. In part (a), with no imports and income taxes, the slope of the *AE* curve is 0.75 (the marginal propensity to consume) and the multiplier is 4.

But with imports and income taxes, the slope of the *AE* curve is less than the marginal propensity to consume. In part (b), the slope of the *AE* curve is 0.5. In this case, the multiplier is 2.

Over time, changes in the marginal propensity to consume, the marginal propensity to import and tax rates change the value of the multiplier. These changes make the multiplier hard to predict. But they do not alter the fundamental fact that an initial change in autonomous expenditure leads to a magnified change in aggregate expenditure and real GDP.

The Mathematical Note on pp. 584–585 shows the effects of taxes, imports, and the *MPC* on the multiplier.

The Multiplier Process

The multiplier effect isn't a one-shot, overnight event. It is a process that plays out over a few months. Figure 25.8 (on the next page) illustrates the multiplier process. In round 1, autonomous expenditure increases by £50 billion. At this time, real GDP increase by £50 billion (the green bar in round 1). This increase in real GDP increases induced expenditure in round 2. With the slope of the *AE* curve equal to 0.75, induced expenditure increases by 0.75 times the increase in real GDP, so the increase in real GDP of £50 billion induces a further increase in expenditure of £37.5 billion. This change in induced expenditure (the green bar in round 2), when added to the previous increase in expenditure (the blue bar in round 2), increases aggregate expenditure and real GDP by £87.5 billion. The round 2 increase in real GDP induces a round 3 increase in expenditure. The process repeats through successive rounds. Each increase in real GDP is 0.75 times the previous increase. The cumulative increase in real GDP gradually approaches £200 billion.

Now that you've studied the multiplier, we can use it to gain some insights into what happens at business cycle turning points.

Business Cycle Turning Points

At business cycle turning points, the economy moves from expansion to recession or from recession to expansion. Economists understand these business cycle turning points like seismologists understand

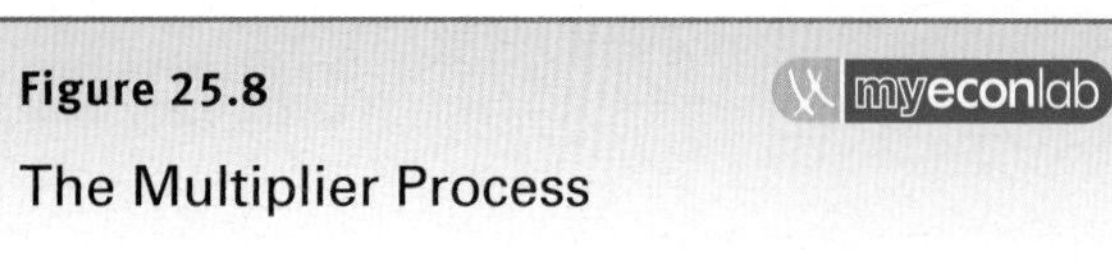

Figure 25.8

The Multiplier Process

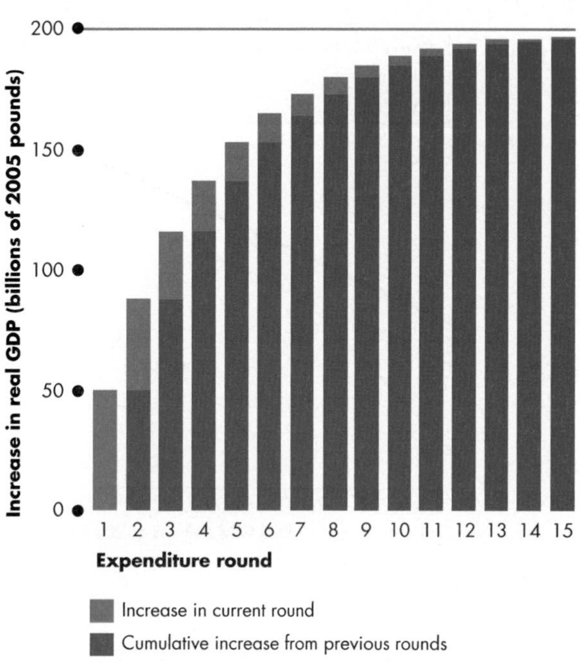

Autonomous expenditure increases by £50 billion. In round 1, real GDP increases by the same amount. With the slope of the *AE* curve equal to 0.75, each additional pound of real GDP induces an additional 0.75 of a pound of induced expenditure.

The round 1 increase in real GDP brings an increase in induced expenditure of £37.5 billion in round 2. At the end of round 2, real GDP has increased by £87.5 billion.

The extra £37.5 billion of real GDP in round 2 brings a further increase in induced expenditure of £28.1 billion in round 3. Real GDP increases yet further to £115.6 billion.

This process continues with real GDP increasing by ever smaller amounts. When the process comes to an end, real GDP has increased by a total of £200 billion.

earthquakes. They know quite a lot about the forces and mechanisms that produce them, but they can't predict them. The forces that bring business cycle turning points are the swings in investment and exports. The mechanism that gives momentum to the economy's new direction is the multiplier. Let's use what we've now learned to examine these turning points.

An Expansion Begins

An expansion is triggered by an increase in autonomous expenditure. At the moment the economy turns the corner into an expansion, aggregate planned expenditure exceeds real GDP. In this situation, firms see their inventories or stocks taking an unplanned dive. The expansion now begins. To meet the targets for stocks, firms increase production and real GDP begins to increase. This initial increase in real GDP brings higher incomes that stimulate consumption expenditure. The multiplier process kicks in and the expansion picks up speed.

A Recession Begins

The process we've just described works in reverse at a business cycle peak. A recession is triggered by a decrease in autonomous expenditure. At the moment the economy turns the corner into recession, real GDP exceeds aggregate planned expenditure. In this situation, firms see unplanned inventories or stocks piling up. The recession now begins. To decrease their stocks, firms cut production and real GDP begins to decrease. This initial decrease in real GDP brings lower incomes that cut consumption expenditure. The multiplier process reinforces the initial cut in autonomous expenditure and the recession takes hold.

The Next Recession

The last recession in the United Kingdom was in the years 1990–1992. The economy slowed down during 2005 and was the fall in house prices (the largest component of consumers' wealth) a signal of an even sharper contraction in 2006? The fall in house prices halted in the third quarter of 2005 and rose during 2006.

Review Quiz

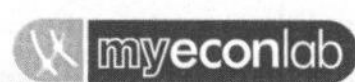

Study Plan 25.3

1. What is the multiplier? What does it determine?
2. Why does the multiplier matter?
3. How do the marginal propensity to consume, the marginal propensity to import and the income tax rate influence the multiplier?
4. How do fluctuations in autonomous expenditure influence real GDP? If autonomous expenditure decreases, which phase of the business cycle does the economy enter?

The Multiplier and the Price Level

We have just considered adjustments in spending that occur in the very short run when the price level is fixed. In this time frame, the economy's potholes, which are changes in investment and exports, are not smoothed by shock absorbers like those on the car travelling along a country road. Instead, they are amplified like Christina Aguilera's voice. But these outcomes occur only when the price level is fixed. We now investigate what happens after a long enough time lapse for the price level to change.

Adjusting Quantities and Prices

When firms can't keep up with sales and their inventories or stocks fall below target, they increase production, but at some point they raise their prices. Similarly, when firms find unwanted stocks piling up, they decrease production, but eventually they cut their prices.

So far, we've studied the macroeconomic consequences of firms changing their production levels when their sales change, but we've not looked at the effects of price changes. When individual firms change their prices, the economy's price level changes.

To study the simultaneous determination of real GDP and the price level, we use the *aggregate supply–aggregate demand model*, which is explained in Chapter 23. But to understand how aggregate demand adjusts, we need to work out the connection between the aggregate supply–aggregate demand model and the equilibrium expenditure model that we've used in this chapter. The key to understanding the relationship between these two models is the distinction between the aggregate *expenditure* and aggregate *demand* and the related distinction between the *aggregate expenditure curve* and the *aggregate demand curve*.

Aggregate Expenditure and Aggregate Demand

The aggregate expenditure curve is the relationship between the aggregate planned expenditure and real GDP, when all other influences on aggregate planned expenditure remain the same. The aggregate demand curve is the relationship between the aggregate quantity of goods and services demanded and the price level, when all other influences on aggregate demand remain the same. Let's explore the links between these two relationships.

Deriving the Aggregate Demand Curve

When the price level changes, aggregate planned expenditure changes and the quantity of real GDP demanded changes. The aggregate demand curve slopes downward. Why?

There are two main reasons:

- Wealth effect
- Substitution effects

Wealth Effect

Other things remaining the same, the higher the price level, the smaller is the purchasing power of people's real wealth. For example, suppose you have £100 in the bank and the price level is 105. If the price level rises to 125, your £100 will buy fewer goods and services. You are less wealthy. With less wealth, you will probably want to spend a bit less and save a bit more. The higher the price level, other things remaining the same, the higher is saving and the lower is consumption expenditure and aggregate planned expenditure.

Substitution Effects

For a given expected future price level, a rise in the price level today makes current goods and services more expensive relative to future goods and services and results in a delay in purchases – an *intertemporal substitution*. A rise in the UK price level, other things remaining the same, makes UK-produced goods and services more expensive relative to foreign-produced goods and services. As a result, UK imports increase and UK exports decrease – an *international substitution*.

When the price level rises, each of these effects reduces aggregate planned expenditure at each level of real GDP. As a result, when the price level *rises*, the aggregate expenditure curve shifts *downward*. A fall in the price level has the opposite effect. When the price level *falls*, the aggregate expenditure curve shifts *upward*.

Figure 25.9(a) shows the shifts of the *AE* curve. When the price level is 105, the aggregate expenditure curve is AE_0, which intersects the 45° line at point *B*. Equilibrium expenditure is £1,300 billion. If the price level increases to 125, the aggregate expenditure curve shifts downward to AE_1, which intersects the 45° line at point *A*. Equilibrium expenditure decreases to £1,200 billion. If the price level decreases to 85, the aggregate

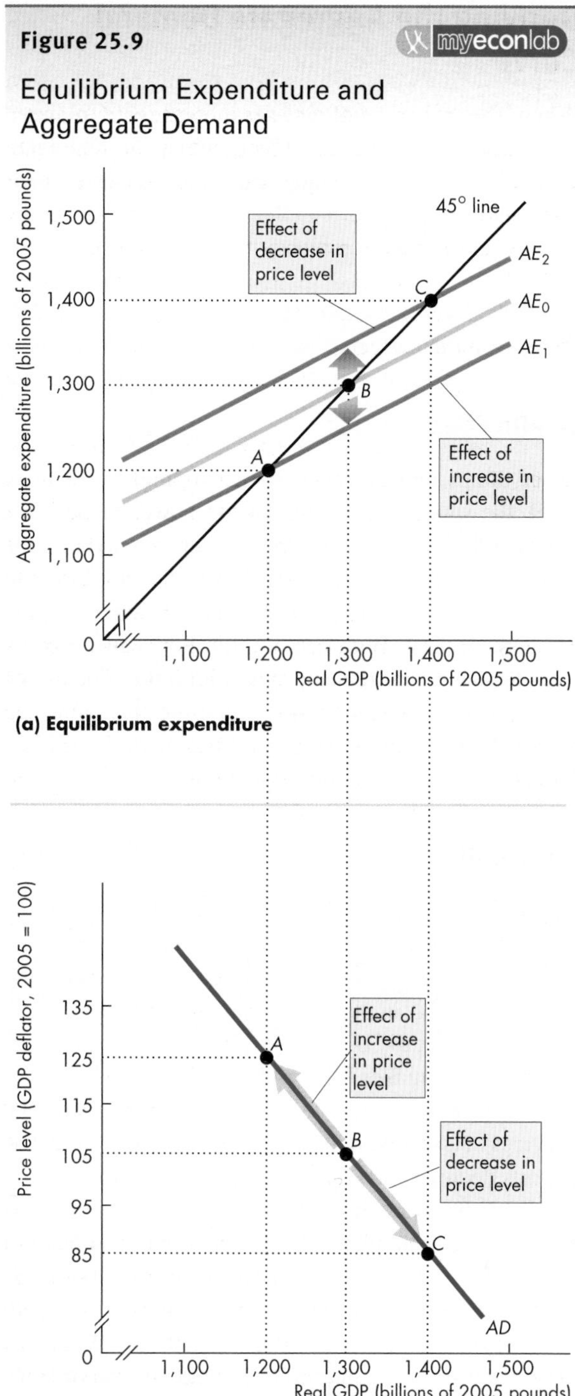

Figure 25.9 Equilibrium Expenditure and Aggregate Demand

When the price level is 105, the *AE* curve is AE_0 and equilibrium expenditure is £1,300 billion at point *B*. When the price level rises to 125, the *AE* curve is AE_1 and equilibrium expenditure is £1,400 billion at point *A*. When the price level falls to 85, the *AE* curve is AE_2 and equilibrium expenditure is £1,200 billion at point *C*. Points *A*, *B* and *C* on the *AD* curve correspond to the equilibrium expenditure points *A*, *B* and *C*.

expenditure curve shifts upward to AE_2, which intersects the 45° line at point *C*. Equilibrium expenditure increases to £1,400 billion.

We've just seen that when the price level changes, other things remaining the same, the aggregate expenditure curve shifts and the equilibrium expenditure changes. But when the price level changes, other things remaining the same, there is a movement along the aggregate demand curve.

Figure 25.9(b) shows the movements along the aggregate demand curve. At a price level of 105, the aggregate quantity of goods and services demanded is £1,300 billion – point *B* on the *AD* curve. If the price level rises to 125, the aggregate quantity of goods and services demanded decreases to £1,200 billion. There is a movement up along the aggregate demand curve to point *A*. If the price level falls to 85, the aggregate quantity of goods and services demanded increases to £1,400 billion. There is a movement down along the aggregate demand curve to point *C*.

Each point on the aggregate demand curve corresponds to a point of equilibrium expenditure. The equilibrium expenditure points *A*, *B* and *C* in Figure 25.9(a) correspond to the points *A*, *B* and *C* on the aggregate demand curve in Figure 25.9(b).

Changes in Aggregate Expenditure and Aggregate Demand

When any influence on aggregate planned expenditure other than the price level changes, both the aggregate expenditure curve and the aggregate demand curve shift. For example, an increase in investment or exports increases both aggregate planned expenditure and aggregate demand and shifts both the *AE* curve and the *AD* curve. Figure 25.10 illustrates the effect of such an increase.

Initially, the aggregate expenditure curve is AE_0 in part (a) and the aggregate demand curve is AD_0 in part (b). The price level is 105, real GDP is £1,300 billion, and the economy is at point *A* in both parts of Figure 25.10.

Now suppose that investment increases by £100 billion. At a constant price level of 105, the aggregate expenditure curve shifts upward to AE_1. This curve intersects the 45° line at an equilibrium expenditure of £1,500 billion (point *B*). This equilibrium expenditure of £1,500 billion is the aggregate quantity of goods and services demanded at a price level of 105, as shown by point *B* in part (b). Point *B* lies on a new aggregate

Figure 25.10

A Change in Aggregate Demand

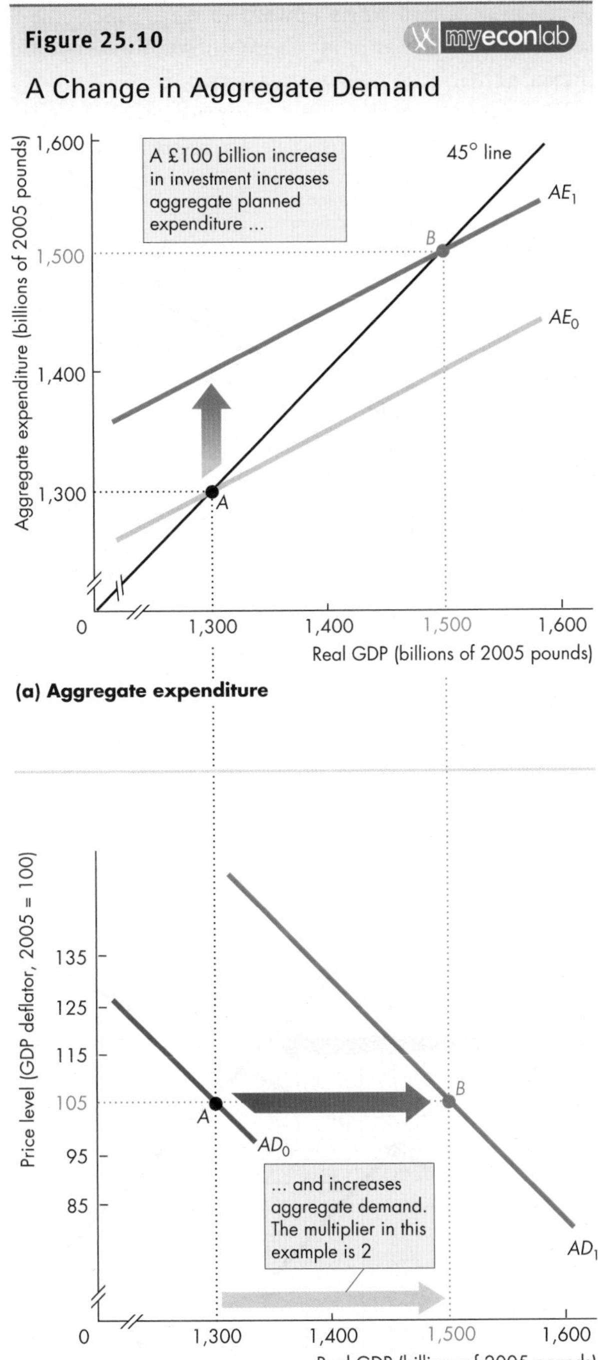

The price level is 105. When the aggregate expenditure curve is AE_0 in part (a), the aggregate demand curve is AD_0 in part (b). An increase in autonomous expenditure shifts the *AE* curve upward to AE_1. In the new equilibrium, real GDP is £1,500 billion (at point *B*). Because the quantity of real GDP demanded at a price level of 105 increases to £1,500 billion, the *AD* curve shifts rightward to AD_1.

demand curve. The aggregate demand curve has shifted rightward to AD_1.

But how do we know by how much the *AD* curve shifts? The multiplier determines the answer. The larger the multiplier, the larger is the shift in the aggregate demand curve that results from a given change in autonomous expenditure. In this example, the multiplier is 2. A £100 billion increase in investment produces a £200 billion increase in the aggregate quantity of goods and services demanded at each price level. That is, a £100 billion increase in autonomous expenditure shifts the aggregate demand curve rightward by £200 billion.

A decrease in autonomous expenditure shifts the aggregate expenditure curve downward and shifts the aggregate demand curve leftward. You can see these effects by reversing the change that we've just described. If the economy is initially at point *B* on the aggregate expenditure curve AE_1 and on the aggregate demand curve is AD_1, a decrease in autonomous expenditure shifts the aggregate expenditure curve downward to AE_0. The aggregate quantity of goods and services demanded decreases from £1,500 billion to £1,300 billion, and the aggregate demand curve shifts leftward to AD_0.

Let's summarize what we have just discovered:

If some factor other than a change in the price level increases autonomous expenditure, the *AE* curve shifts upward and the *AD* curve shifts rightward. The size of the *AD* curve shift equals the change in autonomous expenditure multiplied by the multiplier.

Equilibrium Real GDP and the Price Level

In Chapter 23, we learned that aggregate demand and short-run aggregate supply determine equilibrium real GDP and the price level. We've now put aggregate demand under a more powerful microscope and have discovered that a change in investment (or in any component of autonomous expenditure) changes aggregate demand and shifts the aggregate demand curve. The magnitude of the shift depends on the multiplier.

But whether a change in autonomous expenditure results ultimately in a change in real GDP, a change in the price level, or a combination of the two depends on aggregate supply. There are two time frames to consider: the short run and the long run. First we'll see what happens in the short run.

An Increase in Aggregate Demand in the Short Run

Figure 25.11 describes the economy. In part (a), the aggregate expenditure curve is AE_0, and equilibrium expenditure is £1,300 billion – point *A*. In part (b), aggregate demand is AD_0 and the short-run aggregate supply curve is *SAS*. (Chapter 23, pp. 511–514 explains the *SAS* curve.) Equilibrium is at point *A*, where the aggregate demand and short-run aggregate supply curves intersect. The price level is 105 and real GDP is £1,300 billion.

Now suppose that investment increases by £100 billion. With the price level fixed at 105, the aggregate expenditure curve shifts upward to AE_1. Equilibrium expenditure increases to £1,500 billion – point *B* in part (a). In part (b), the aggregate demand curve shifts rightward by £200 billion, from AD_0 to AD_1. How far the *AD* curve shifts is determined by the multiplier when the price level is fixed.

But with this new *AD* curve, the price level does not remain fixed. The price level rises and as it does so, the *AE* curve shifts downward. The short-run equilibrium occurs when the aggregate expenditure curve has shifted downward to AE_2 and the new aggregate demand curve, AD_1, intersects the short-run aggregate supply curve at point *C*. Real GDP is £1,430 billion and the price level is 118.

When the price level effects are taken into account, the increase in investment still has a multiplier effect on real GDP, but the multiplier effect is smaller than it would be if the price level were fixed. The steeper the slope of the *SAS* curve, the larger is the increase in the price level and the smaller is the multiplier effect on real GDP.

An Increase in Aggregate Demand in the Long Run

Figure 25.12 illustrates the effect of an increase in aggregate demand starting at full employment. Real GDP equals potential GDP, which is £1,300 billion. The long-run aggregate supply curve is *LAS*. Initially, the economy is at point *A* in part (a) and part (b).

Investment increases by £100 billion. The aggregate expenditure curve shifts upward to AE_1 and the aggregate demand curve shifts rightward to AD_1. With no change in the price level, the economy would move to point *B* and real GDP would increase to £1,500 billion. But in the short run, the price level rises to 118 and real GDP increases to £1,430 billion. With the higher price

Figure 25.11 myeconlab

The Multiplier in the Short Run

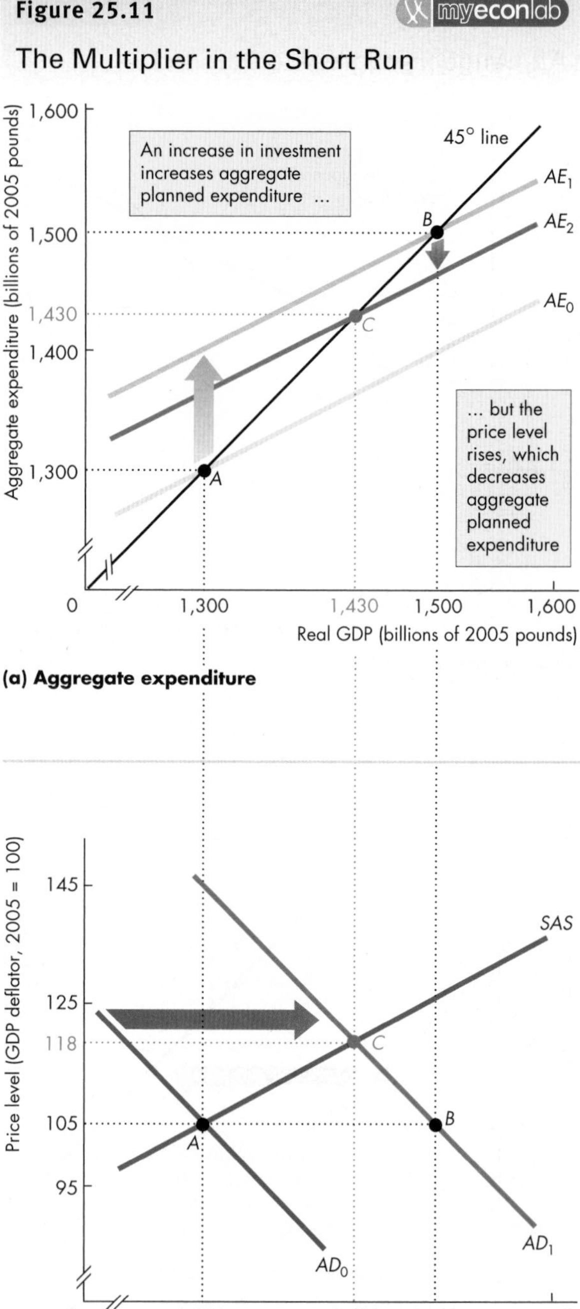

An increase in investment shifts the *AE* curve from AE_0 to AE_1 in part (a) and shifts the *AD* curve from AD_0 to AD_1 in part (b). The price level does not remain at 105 but rises, and the higher price level shifts the *AE* curve downward from AE_1 to AE_2. The economy moves to point *C*. In the short run, when prices are flexible, the multiplier is smaller than when the price level is fixed.

Figure 25.12

myeconlab

The Multiplier in the Long Run

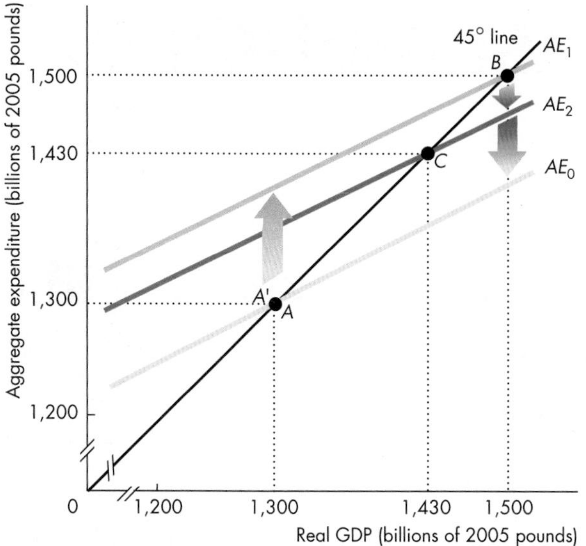

(a) Aggregate expenditure

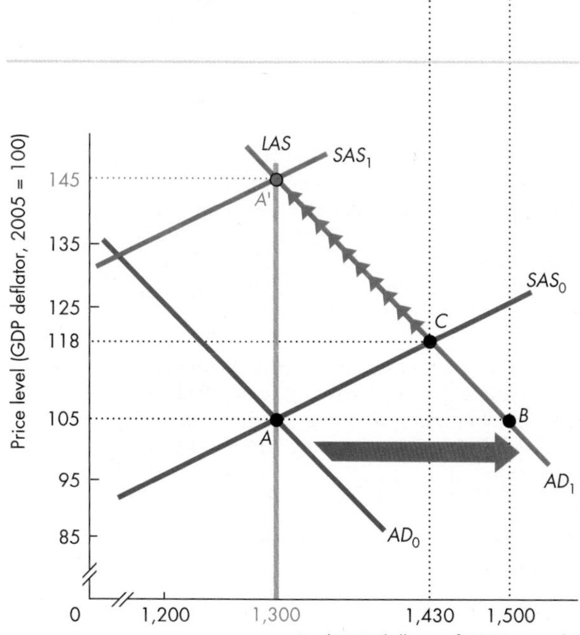

(b) Aggregate demand

Starting from point A, an increase in investment shifts the AE curve to AE_1 and shifts the AD curve to AD_1. In the short run, the economy moves to point C. In the long run, the money wage rate rises, the SAS curve shifts to SAS_1, the price level rises, the AE curve shifts back to AE_0 and real GDP decreases. The economy moves to point A' and in the long run, the multiplier is zero.

level, the aggregate expenditure curve shifts from AE_1 to AE_2. The economy is now in a short-run equilibrium at point C.

But real GDP now exceeds potential GDP. The workforce is more than fully employed, and in the long run shortages of labour increase the money wage rate. The higher money wage rate increases costs, which decreases short-run aggregate supply. The SAS curve begins to shift leftward towards SAS_1. The price level rises further and real GDP decreases. There is a movement along AD_1, and the AE curve shifts downward from AE_2 towards AE_0. When the money wage rate and the price level have increased by the same percentage, real GDP again equals potential GDP and the economy is at point A'. In the long run, the multiplier is zero.

Review Quiz

Study Plan 25.4

1. How does a change in the price level influence the AE curve and the AD curve?
2. If autonomous expenditure increases with no change in the price level, what happens to the AE curve and the AD curve?
3. How does an increase in autonomous expenditure change real GDP in the short run? Does real GDP change by the same amount as the change in aggregate demand? Why or why not?
4. How does real GDP change in the long run when autonomous expenditure increases? Does real GDP change by the same amount as the change in aggregate demand? Why or why not?

We've seen that when the price level is fixed, changes in autonomous expenditure are amplified. But we've also seen that when the price level changes, the amplification effect is smaller in the short run when the money wage rate is fixed and zero in the long run when the money wage rate is flexible.

You are now ready to build on what you've learned about aggregate expenditure and aggregate demand and study the roles of fiscal policy and monetary policy in smoothing the business cycle. In Chapter 26, we study fiscal policy and in Chapters 27 and 28, we study monetary policy – interest rates and the quantity of money. But before you leave the current topic, look at *Reading Between the Lines* on pp. 582–583, which looks at some influences on the UK consumption function in the past few years.

Reading Between the Lines

Shifts in the Consumption Function

The Financial Times, 3 February 2007

FT

Bank see low risk as value of homes rise

Scheherazade Daneshkhu

Mervyn King, Bank of England governor, warned last November that: 'All lenders and all borrowers should think very carefully before they either lend or borrow'.

Yet in spite of his strictures, the Bank does not currently see a risk to the economy from the sharp rise in household debt and insolvencies.

So why the insouciance? First, while recognising that each bankruptcy represents personal hardship, the numbers are not big enough to pose a danger to the economy. The 107,288 personal insolvencies last year represent 0.25 per cent of the adult population in England and Wales. In the recession of the 1990s, 0.1 per cent of the population was insolvent.

Second, the Bank's regular survey of household indebtedness has consistently found that those most prone to default are people on low incomes with high credit card and other unsecured debts. They are likely to be renting and unable to tap into the rising value of their homes. Put bluntly, the direct economic effect of these people spending less in the future is small.

Third, although household debt has doubled since 1999, that has been more than outpaced by the rising value of homes, shares and other assets, Robert Lind of ABN AMRO bank, said: "Contrary to popular mythology, high income households are the predominant holders of debt in the UK. These households are better able to manage their debt, which makes them less vulnerable to higher interest rates".

. . .

This does not mean that high debt levels are insignificant – the growing cost of servicing debt because of rising interest rates means people have less money to spend on other things.

. . .

The Essence of the Story

- Higher interest rates mean people have less money to spend on other things.
- Low-income people who have high credit card debt, reduce their consumption expenditure when the interest rate rises. But their effect on the economy is small.
- The values of homes, shares and other assets have risen faster than debts, so high-income people are not much influenced by a higher interest rate.

Economic Analysis

- The *real* interest rate – the nominal interest rate minus the inflation rate – is the opportunity cost of consumption. If you spend £1 today, then one year from today you forgo consumption of £1 plus the real interest the £1 would earn.
- A low *real* interest rate provides an incentive to increase consumption expenditure, decrease saving and increase debt. It shifts the consumption function upward.
- A high *real* interest rate provides the opposite incentive to decrease consumption expenditure, increase saving and pay off debt. It shifts the consumption function downward.
- Figure 1 shows that the growth in consumption expenditure was low during most of 2005 but increased in 2006.
- Figure 2 shows the average monthly real interest rate paid by mortgage holders during 2005 and 2006. Even though the nominal mortgage rate rose, the real interest rate fell during most of 2006.
- Figure 2 also shows that house prices increased at a rapid rate at the beginning of 2005 and during 2006.
- When house prices increase rapidly, household wealth increases because house values outpace the rate at which new debt is incurred.
- Figure 3 shows that the fall in the real interest rate and the rise in household wealth during 2006 shifted the consumption function up from CF_0 up to CF_1.
- Figure 3 also shows that the consumption function was also CF_1 at the beginning of 2005 when house prices were rising rapidly and making people feel more wealthy.

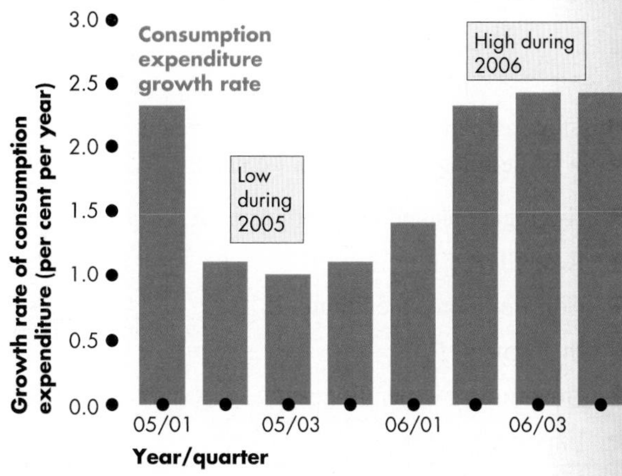

Figure 1 Consumption expenditure growth

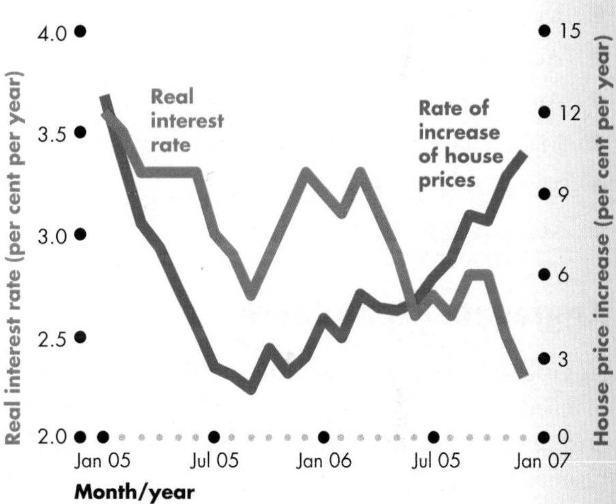

Figure 2 House prices and the real interest rate

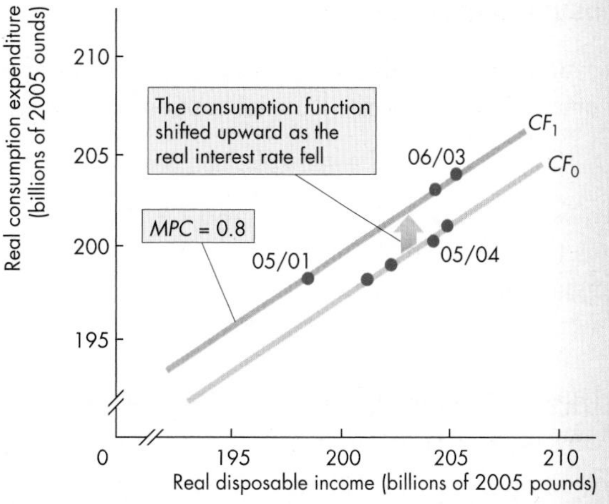

Figure 3 The consumption function in 2005 and 2006

Mathematical Note

The Algebra of the Multiplier

This note explains the multiplier in greater detail. We begin by defining the symbols we need:

- Aggregate planned expenditure, AE
- Real GDP, Y
- Consumption expenditure, C
- Investment, I
- Government expenditures, G
- Exports, X
- Imports, M
- Net taxes, T
- Disposable income, YD
- Autonomous expenditure, A
- Autonomous consumption expenditure, a
- Marginal propensity to consume, b
- Marginal propensity to import, m
- Marginal tax rate, t

Aggregate Expenditure

Aggregate planned expenditure (AE) is the sum of planned consumption expenditure (C), investment (I), government expenditure (G), and exports (X) minus the planned amount of imports (M). That is:

$$AE = C + I + G + X - M$$

Consumption Function

Consumption expenditure (C) depends on disposable income (YD) and we write the consumption function as:

$$C = a + bYD$$

Disposable income (YD) equals real GDP minus net taxes ($Y - T$). So replacing YD with ($Y - T$), the consumption function becomes:

$$C = a + b(Y - T)$$

Net taxes equal real GDP (Y) multiplied by the marginal tax rate (t). That is:

$$T = tY$$

Use this equation in the previous one to obtain:

$$C = a + b(1 - t)Y$$

This equation describes consumption expenditure as a function of real GDP.

Import Function

Imports depend on real GDP and the import function is:

$$M = mY$$

Aggregate Expenditure Curve

Use the consumption function and the import function to replace C and M in the aggregate planned expenditure equation. That is:

$$AE = a + b(1 - t)Y + I + G + X - mY$$

Collect the terms on the right-side of the equation that involve Y to obtain:

$$AE = [a + I + G + X] + [b(1 - t) - m]Y$$

Autonomous expenditure (A) is $[a + I + G + X]$, and the slope of the AE curve is $[b(1 - t) - m]$. So the equation for the AE curve, which is shown in Figure 1, is:

$$AE = A + [b(1 - t) - m]Y$$

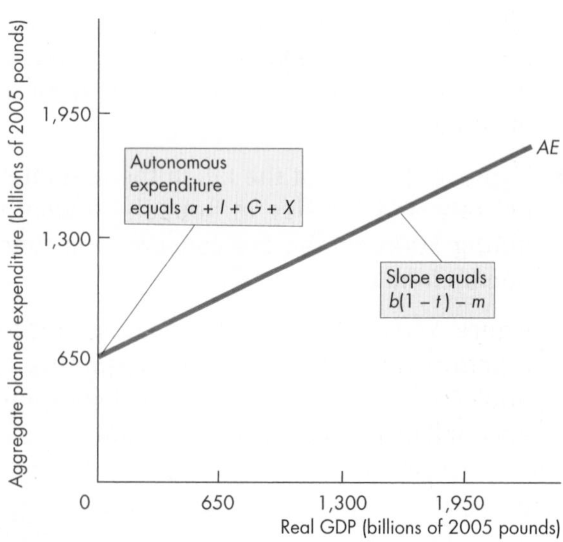

Figure 1 The *AE* curve

Equilibrium Expenditure

Equilibrium expenditure occurs when aggregate planned expenditure (AE) equals real GDP (Y). That is:

$$AE = Y$$

In Figure 2, the scales of the x-axis (real GDP) and the y-axis (aggregate planned expenditure) are identical, so the 45° line shows the points at which aggregate planned expenditure equals real GDP. That is, along the 45° line, AE equals Y.

Figure 2 shows the point of equilibrium expenditure at the intersection of the AE curve and the 45° line.

To calculate equilibrium expenditure and real GDP, we solve the equations for the AE curve and the 45° line for the two unknown quantities AE and Y. So, starting with:

$$AE = A + [b(1 - t) - m]Y$$

$$AE = Y$$

replace AE with Y in the AE equation to obtain:

$$Y = A + [b(1 - t) - m]Y$$

The solution for Y is:

$$Y = \frac{1}{1 - [b(1 - t) - m]} A$$

The Multiplier

The multiplier equals the change in equilibrium expenditure and real GDP (Y) that results from a change in autonomous expenditure (A) divided by the change in autonomous expenditure. A change in autonomous expenditure (ΔA) changes equilibrium expenditure and real GDP (ΔY) by:

$$\Delta Y = \frac{1}{1 - [b(1 - t) - m]} \Delta A$$

$$\text{Multiplier} = \frac{1}{1 - [b(1 - t) - m]}$$

The size of the multiplier depends on the slope of the AE curve and the larger the slope, the larger is the multiplier. So the multiplier is larger:

1 The greater the marginal propensity to consume (b)

2 The smaller the marginal tax rate (t)

3 The smaller the marginal propensity to import (m)

An economy with no imports and no marginal taxes has $m = 0$ and $t = 0$. In this special case, the multiplier equals $1/(1 - b)$. If b is 0.75, the multiplier is 4 as shown in Figure 3. In an economy with $b = 0.75$, $t = 0.2$, and $m = 0.1$, the multiplier is $1 \div [1 - 0.75(1 - 0.2) - 0.1]$, which equals 2. Make up some more examples to show the effects of different values of b, t and m on the multiplier.

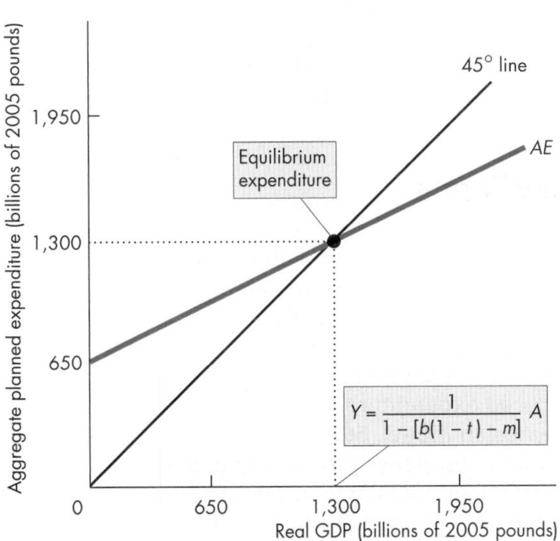

Figure 2 Equilibrium expenditure

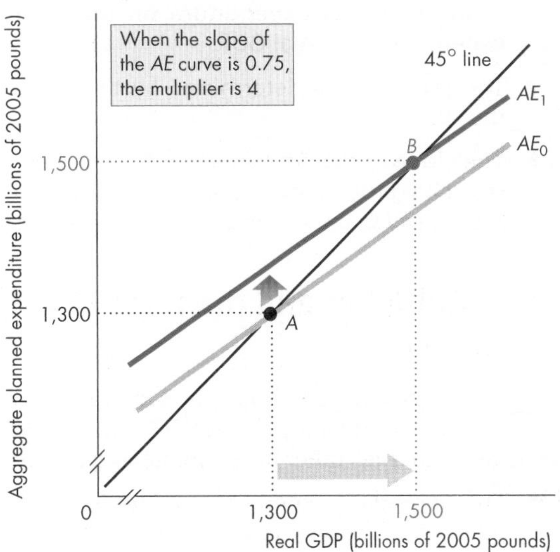

Figure 3 The multiplier

Summary

Key Points

Fixed Prices and Expenditure Plans

(pp. 562–567)

- When the price level is fixed, expenditure plans determine real GDP.
- Consumption expenditure is determined by disposable income, and the marginal propensity to consume (*MPC*) determines the change in consumption expenditure brought about by a change in disposable income. Real GDP is the main influence on disposable income.
- Imports are determined by real GDP, and the marginal propensity to import determines the change in imports brought about by a change in real GDP.

Real GDP with a Fixed Price Level

(pp. 568–571)

- Aggregate *planned* expenditure depends on real GDP.
- Equilibrium expenditure occurs when aggregate planned expenditure equals actual expenditure and real GDP.

The Multiplier (pp. 572–576)

- The multiplier is the magnified effect of a change in autonomous expenditure on equilibrium expenditure and real GDP.
- The multiplier is determined by the slope of the *AE* curve.
- The slope of the *AE* curve is influenced by the marginal propensity to consume, the marginal propensity to import and the income tax rate.

The Multiplier and the Price Level

(pp. 577–581)

- The aggregate demand curve is the relationship between the quantity of real GDP demanded and the price level, other things remaining the same.
- The aggregate expenditure curve is the relationship between aggregate planned expenditure and real GDP, other things remaining the same.
- At a given price level, there is a given aggregate expenditure curve. A change in the price level changes aggregate planned expenditure and shifts the aggregate expenditure curve. A change in the price level also creates a movement along the aggregate demand curve.
- A change in autonomous expenditure that is not caused by a change in the price level shifts the aggregate expenditure curve and shifts the aggregate demand curve. The magnitude of the shift of the aggregate demand curve depends on the multiplier and the change in autonomous expenditure.
- The multiplier decreases as the price level changes. The multiplier in the long run is zero.

Key Figures

Key Terms

Problems

Tests, Study Plan and Solutions* 

1 The table sets out data about Heron Island.

Disposable income	Consumption expenditure
(millions of euros per year)	
300	340
400	420
500	500
600	580
700	660

a Calculate the marginal propensity to consume.

b Calculate saving at each disposable income.

c Calculate the marginal propensity to save.

2 The table sets out some data on Cocoa Isle.

Disposable income	Saving
(millions of dollars per year)	
0	-5
100	20
200	45
300	70
400	95

a Calculate the marginal propensity to save.

b Calculate consumption expenditure at each level of disposable income.

c Calculate the marginal propensity to consume.

3 The figure illustrates the components of aggregate planned expenditure on Turtle Island. Turtle Island has no imports or exports, the people of Turtle Island pay no income taxes, and the price level is fixed.

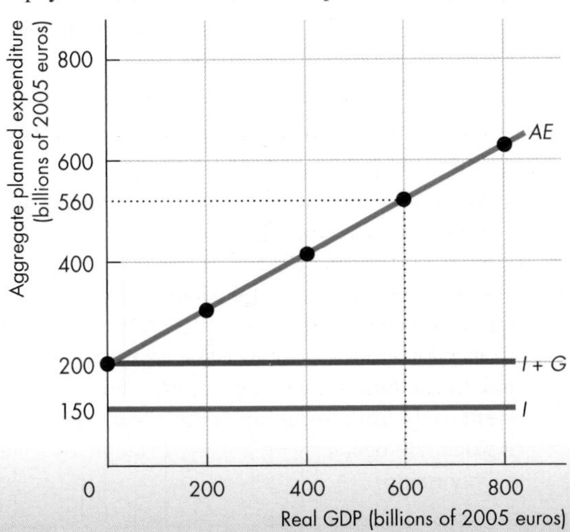

a Calculate autonomous expenditure.

b Calculate the marginal propensity to consume.

c What is aggregate planned expenditure when real GDP is €600 billion?

d If real GDP is €400 billion, what is happening to inventories or stocks?

e If real GDP is €600 billion, what is happening to inventories or stocks?

f Calculate the multiplier.

4 The spreadsheet figure lists the components of aggregate planned expenditure in Spice Bay. The numbers are in billions of cloves, the currency of the Bay.

	A	B	C	D	E	F
1	*Y*	*C*	*I*	*G*	*X*	*M*
2	100	110	50	60	60	15
3	200	170	50	60	60	30
4	300	230	50	60	60	45
5	400	290	50	60	60	60
6	500	350	50	60	60	75
7	600	410	50	60	60	90

a Calculate autonomous expenditure.

b Calculate the marginal propensity to consume.

c What is aggregate planned expenditure when real GDP is 200 billion cloves?

d If real GDP is 200 billion cloves, what is happening to inventories or stocks?

e If real GDP is 500 billion cloves, what is happening to inventories or stocks?

f Calculate the multiplier.

5 You are given the following information about the Canadian economy. Autonomous consumption expenditure is \$50 billion and the marginal propensity to consume is 0.7. Investment is \$200 billion, and government expenditure on goods and services is \$250 billion. Net taxes are \$250 billion – net taxes are assumed to be constant and not vary with income. Exports are \$500 billion and imports are \$450 billion.

a What is the consumption function?

b What is the equation of the *AE* curve?

c Calculate equilibrium expenditure.

d If investment decreases to \$150 billion, what is the change in equilibrium expenditure?

* Solutions to odd-numbered problems are provided.

6 Suppose that the economy is at full employment, the price level is 100, and the investment multiplier is 2. Investment increases by $100 billion.

a What is the change in equilibrium expenditure?

b What is the immediate change in the quantity of real GDP demanded?

c In the short run, does real GDP increase by more than, less than, or the same amount as the increase in the quantity of real GDP demanded in part (b)?

d In the short run, does the price level remain at 100? Explain why or why not.

e In the long run, does real GDP increase by more than, less than, or the same amount as the increase in the quantity of real GDP demanded in part (b)?

f Explain how the price level changes in the long run.

g Compare the multipliers in the short run and the long run.

Critical Thinking

1 Study *Reading Between the Lines* on pp. 582–583 and then answer the following questions.

a What has happened to the real interest rate in the UK economy during 2005 and 2006?

b Why might a rise in the mortgage rate not be associated with a fall in consumption if other things were also changing in the economy?

c What were the 'other things' that were going on in the UK economy during 2006 that might have influenced consumer spending?

d What happened to consumer spending in the United Kingdom in 2006?

e What is your prediction for the real interest rate and consumption expenditure in the United Kingdom in 2007?

f Use the links on MyEconLab to obtain data on the growth of real consumption expenditure in the United Kingdom in 2007 and check your prediction.

2 **UK business investment 'buoyant'**

Business investment rose sharply in the UK towards the end of 2006, official figures show, suggesting boardroom confidence about economic prospects . . .

BBC, 22 February 2007

a Does the increase in UK investment create a movement along the *AE* curve or does it shift the *AE* curve?

b Suppose that UK investment increases by £120 billion in 2007 and the multiplier is 1.5. If other things remain the same, what is the increase in real GDP?

c Suppose that the UK economy is at full employment in 2007 when investment increases by £120 billion. Will there still be a multiplier effect?

d Suppose that the UK economy is above full employment in 2007 when investment increases by £120 billion in 2007. What in this case will happen to aggregate expenditure, aggregate demand, real GDP and the price level?

3 **US Economy Is Still Growing at Rapid Pace**

. . . strong global growth is lifting American exports, economists say. Last week the International Monetary Fund predicted that the world economy would grow at 4.9 percent this year, up from 4.8 percent in 2005.

The New York Times, 28 April 2006

a Suppose that US exports increase by $10 billion in 2006 and the multiplier is 2. If other things remain the same, what is the increase in real GDP?

b Suppose that US exports increase by $100 billion in 2006 and US imports increase by the same amount. Will there still be a multiplier effect in the US economy?

Web Activities

Links to Websites

1 Visit the Penn World Table and obtain data on real GDP per person and consumption as a percentage of real GDP for the United States, China, South Africa and Mexico since 1980.

a In a spreadsheet, multiply your real GDP data by the consumption percentage and divide by 100 to obtain data on real consumption expenditure per person.

b Make graphs like the figure in Box 25.1 on p. 567 to show the relationship between consumption and real GDP for these four countries.

c Based on the numbers you've obtained, in which country do you expect the multiplier to be largest (other things remaining the same)?

d What other data do you need to calculate the multipliers for these countries?

2 You are an economic assistant working for the Treasury. You've been asked to draft a note to the Chancellor of the Exchequer that explains the power and limitations of the multiplier. The Chancellor wants only 250 words of crisp, clear, jargon-free explanation together with a lively example by tomorrow morning.

Macroeconomic Policy

PART 6

Improving Economic Health

To cure a disease, doctors must first understand how it responds to different treatments. It helps to understand the mechanisms that operate to cause the disease, but sometimes a workable cure can be found even before the full story of the cause has been told.

Curing economic ills is similar to curing our medical ills. We need to understand how the economy responds to the treatments we might prescribe for it. And sometimes, we want to try a cure even though we don't fully understand the reasons for the problem we're trying to control.

You've seen how labour market equilibrium determines potential GDP and how changes in aggregate demand and aggregate supply with sticky wages bring fluctuations around potential GDP. And you've learned about the key sources of fluctuations in aggregate demand and aggregate supply.

The chapters in this part build on everything you've studied in macroeconomics. The central tools they use are the demand and supply model of Chapter 3, the *AS–AD* model of Chapter 23, and the classical and Keynesian models of Chapters 24 and 25. We now use these models to explain how macroeconomic policy influences the economy.

Chapter 26 explains the effects of fiscal policy. Here you will learn how government budgets can be used both to stabilize the cycle and to increase potential GDP and speed the growth rate. Chapter 27 describes the monetary system and Chapter 28 explains how monetary policy decisions are made and how they ripple through the economy to influence real GDP and ultimately, the inflation rate. A more advanced and optional Chapter 29 brings fiscal policy and monetary policy together and examines their interactions.

Chapters 30 to 34 provide a deeper look at four major policy issues: inflation, economic growth, business cycles and international finance. In these more advanced chapters you will learn what is known about the causes of inflation and the way to prevent it; the sources of faster real GDP growth and the policies that can foster it; business cycles and how they might be tamed; and currency fluctuations and international deficits and debts and the challenges they pose for the stability of the global economy.

CHAPTER 26

Fiscal Policy

After studying this chapter you will be able to:

- Describe the recent history of UK government revenues, outlays and the budget deficits
- Define and explain the fiscal policy multipliers
- Explain the demand-side effects of fiscal policy in the short run and the long run
- Explain the supply-side effects of fiscal policy

Balancing Acts in Westminster

Every spring, the Chancellor of the Exchequer (the UK minister of finance) presents his budget – his plans for government spending and taxes – to Parliament. What are the effects of government spending on the economy? Does it create jobs or does it destroy them? Does a pound spent by the government have the same effects as a pound spent by someone else? What happens if governments spend more than they receive in revenue and run into debt? Does government debt damage economic growth and the well-being of future generations? You will find some of the answers in this chapter. And in *Reading Between the Lines* at the end of the chapter, you can see how low taxes and small government can stimulate production and jobs.

Government Budgets

A government's **budget** is an annual statement of projected outlays and revenues during the next year together with the laws and regulations that will support those outlays and revenues. The finance minister – the Chancellor of the Exchequer in the United Kingdom – presents the budget to Parliament in what is often a piece of political theatre and always a major media event.

A government's budget has three major purposes:

1 To state the scale and allocation of the government's outlays and its plans to finance its activities

2 To stabilize the economy

3 To encourage the economy's long-term growth and balanced regional development

Before the Second World War, the budget had only the first of these goals – to plan and finance the business of government.

But during the late 1940s and early 1950s, the budget began to assume its second purpose – stabilization of the economy.

In more recent years, the budget has assumed its third goal of helping to secure faster sustained economic growth and to seek balance across regions.

Today, the budget is the tool used by a government in pursuit of its fiscal policy. *Fiscal policy* is a government's use of its budget to achieve macroeconomic objectives such as full employment, sustained economic growth and price-level stability. It is the fiscal policy aspects of the budget that we focus on in this chapter.

Government budgets differ in size and detail, but they all have the same components. Here, we'll illustrate a government budget by looking at the United Kingdom.

Table 26.1

The Government Budget in 2007/08

Item		Projections (billions of pounds)	
Revenues			**553**
Taxes on income and wealth		207	
Taxes on expenditure		121	
National Insurance contributions		95	
Other receipts and royalties		130	
Outlays			**587**
Expenditure on goods and services		373	
Health	104		
Education	77		
Law and order	33		
Defence	32		
Other	127		
Transfer payments		184	
Debt interest		30	
Budget balance (surplus +/deficit –)			**–34**

Source of data: HM Treasury, *Budget 2007*.

Highlights of the UK Budget in 2007

Table 26.1 shows the main items in the UK government's budget. The numbers are projections for the fiscal year beginning in April 2007. The three main items in the budget are:

- Revenues
- Outlays
- Budget balance

Revenues

Revenues come from four sources:

1 Taxes on income and wealth

2 Taxes on expenditure

3 National Insurance contributions

4 Other receipts and royalties

The largest source of revenue is *taxes on income and wealth*, which were projected to be £207 billion in 2007/08. These are the taxes paid by individuals on their incomes and wealth and the taxes paid by businesses on their profits.

The second largest source of revenue is *other receipts and royalties*. This item includes oil royalties, stamp duties, car taxes, miscellaneous rents, dividends from abroad and profits from nationalized industries.

Third in size are *taxes on expenditure*, which in 2007/08 were projected at £121 billion. These taxes include VAT and special duties and taxes on gambling, alcoholic drinks, petrol, luxury items and imported goods.

Fourth in size are *National Insurance contributions*, projected to be £95 billion in 2007/08. This revenue comes from contributions paid by workers and employers to fund the welfare and healthcare programmes.

Outlays

Outlays are classified in three broad categories:

1 Expenditures on goods and services
2 Transfer payments
3 Debt interest

Expenditures on goods and services are by far the largest item at £373 billion in 2007/08.

The table lists some of the larger components of these expenditures. Health (expenditure on the National Health Service) took £104 billion and education took another £77 billion. The provision of law and order and defence, the two traditional roles of government, took only £65 billion between them.

Transfer payments – £184 billion in 2007/08 – are payments to individuals, businesses, other levels of government and the rest of the world. These payments include National Insurance benefits, healthcare benefits, unemployment benefits, welfare supplements, grants to local authorities and aid to developing countries.

Debt interest, which in 2007/08 is projected to be £30 billion, is the interest on the government debt minus interest received by the government on its own investments.

The bottom line of the government budget is the balance – the surplus or deficit.

Budget Balance

The government's budget balance is equal to its revenues minus its outlays. That is:

Budget balance = Revenues – Outlays

If revenues exceed outlays, the government has a **budget surplus**. If outlays exceed revenues, the government has a **budget deficit**. If revenues equal outlays, the government has a **balanced budget**. In fiscal year 2007/08, with projected outlays of £587 billion and revenue of £553 billion, the projected government deficit is £34 billion.

How typical is the budget of 2007/08? Let's look at its recent history.

The Budget in Historical Perspective

Figure 26.1 shows the government's revenues, outlays and budget balance since fiscal year 1965/66. The figure expresses the revenues, outlays and the budget balance as percentages of GDP. Expressing them in this way lets us see how large government is relative to the size of the

Figure 26.1 myeconlab

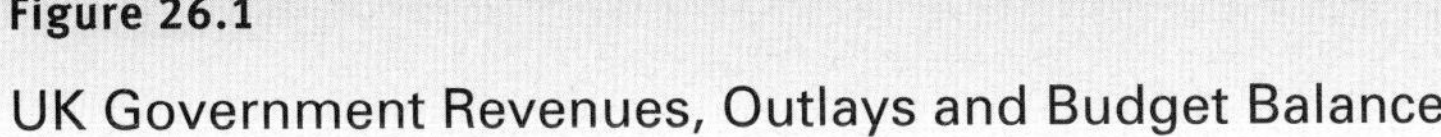

UK Government Revenues, Outlays and Budget Balance

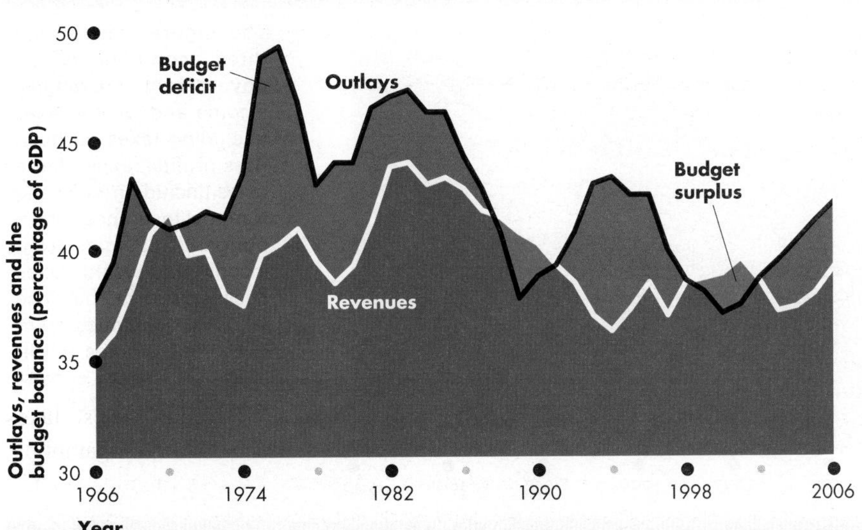

The figure records the UK government's revenues, outlays and budget deficit as percentages of GDP. During the 1970s, the budget deficit became large and persisted well into the 1980s. A budget surplus appeared in the late 1980s, but income tax cuts and an increase in outlays turned the budget into a deficit again in the early 1990s. The budget was in balance in 1997/98, in surplus from 1998/99 to 2000/01, in balance in 2001/02 but once again returned to a deficit in 2002/03.

Source of data: HM Treasury, *Budget 2007*.

economy, and it helps us to study *changes* in the scale of government over time. You may think of these percentages of GDP as telling you how many pence of each pound that we earn get paid to and spent by the government.

Throughout most of this period there was a budget deficit. The deficit increases in recessions and decreases in expansions. The deficit rose to a peak following the recession of the 1970s. Government revenues were actually higher than outlays in the fiscal years 1987/89. But the budget deficit increased again during the 1990s but has fallen sharply and turned into a budget surplus in recent years.

Why did the government deficit grow so sharply in the 1990s? The immediate answer is that outlays increased and revenues decreased. But which components of outlays increased and which sources of revenues decreased? Let's look at revenues and outlays in a bit more detail.

Revenues

Figure 26.2 shows the components of revenues received by the government as a percentage of GDP, from 1989 to 2005. Government revenues as a percentage of GDP increased from 1989 to 1991 and then decreased in the following three years. This decrease occurred because the 1990–1992 recession decreased tax revenues. Firms' profits fell, which lowered the taxes on business profits, and as the unemployment rate increased, the revenue from personal income taxes decreased. Tax revenues increased from 1994 to 2000 as the economy settled into a long boom. They then settled to a plateau as the economy grew at a steady rate.

Outlays

Figure 26.3 shows the components of government outlays as percentages of GDP, between 1989 and 2005. Total outlays increased as a proportion of GDP during the first half of the 1990s. The main source of the increased outlays was a large increase in transfer payments that resulted from the recession. A sharp rise in unemployment and in early retirements increased benefit and welfare payments.

A small part of UK government outlays is the interest payment on government debt. The amount of interest paid depends on the debt. A large debt means a high interest payment. A small debt means a low interest payment. Compared with many other EU countries, the United Kingdom has a relatively low ratio of debt to GDP, so its interest payments are modest. But for some countries, high interest payments on debt make controlling the deficit a challenge.

Figure 26.2

myeconlab

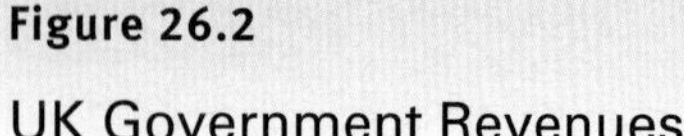

UK Government Revenues

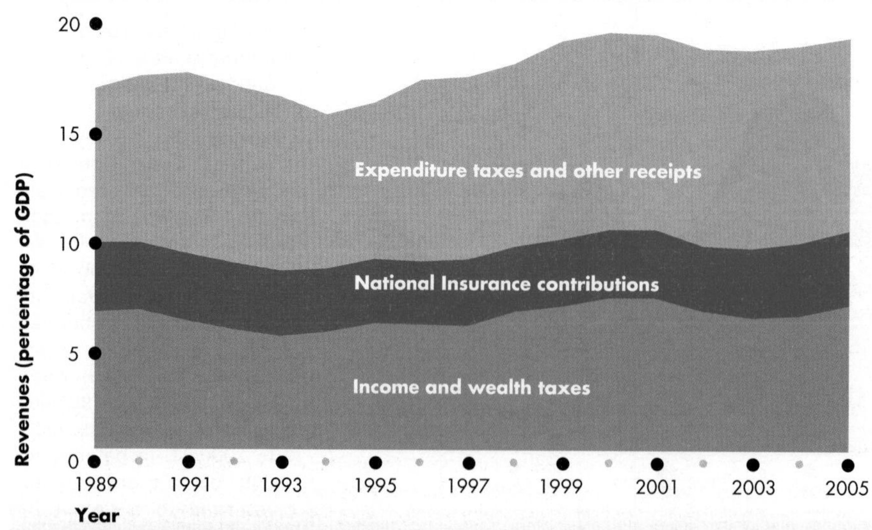

The figure shows the three components of government revenues: income and wealth taxes (including taxes on business profits), expenditure taxes (including VAT) and National Insurance contributions. Revenues from income and wealth taxes declined in 1993 but rose in 1994. Revenues from expenditure taxes fell in 1994 but rose consistently through to 2001.

Source of data: HM Treasury, *Budget 2007*.

Figure 26.3

myeconlab

UK Government Outlays

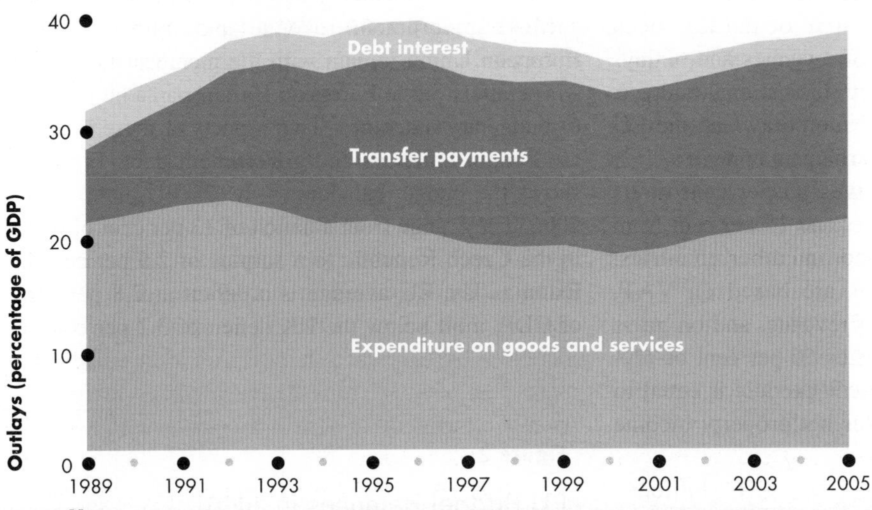

The figure shows three components of government outlays: expenditures on goods and services, transfer payments and debt interest. Expenditures on goods and services fell steadily from 1992 until 2000, when they began to rise again. Transfer payments increased during the 1990–1991 recession and have remained steady. Debt interest has fallen since 1996.

Source of data: HM Treasury, *Budget 2007*.

Deficit, Debt and Capital

Government debt is the total amount of borrowing by the government. It is the past deficits minus the past surpluses minus the receipts from the sale of assets.

When the government has a budget deficit, its debt increases, and when it has a budget surplus, its debt decreases. If a government sells state-owned assets, it can reduce its debt even though its tax revenues are less than its outlays.

Figure 26.4 shows the history of government debt in the United Kingdom from 1976 to 2006. The United Kingdom started the period as a high debt country. It steadily reduced its debt in the 1970s and accelerated the reduction in the 1980s through an aggressive programme of sales of state assets.

Like individuals and businesses, governments borrow to buy assets. Governments own public assets such as roads, bridges, schools and universities, public libraries and defence equipment. The value of UK government assets exceeded £500 billion in 2005, whereas its debt was £835 billion.

So although the UK government has some debt, that debt is not a problem and is not out of line with the assets it owns.

But how do the UK deficit and debt compare with deficits and debts in other major economies and the European Union?

Figure 26.4

myeconlab

UK Government Debt

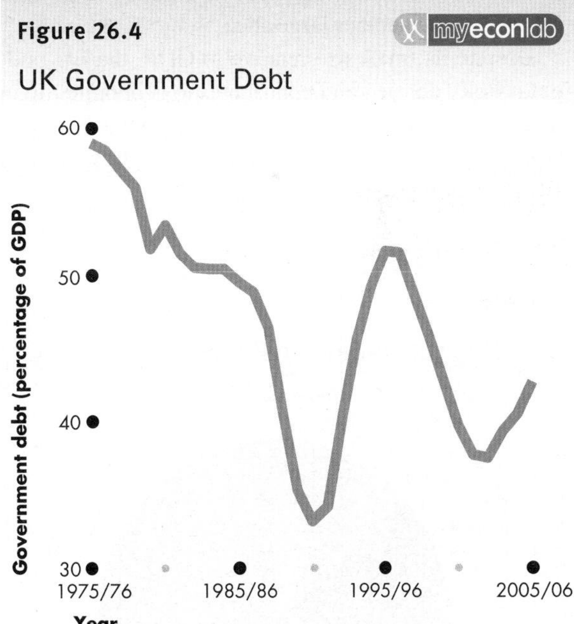

In 1976, UK government debt was 59 per cent of GDP. During the 1970s and 1980s the government reduced its debt. An aggressive programme of privatization of state assets hastened the reduction in debt during the 1980s. The United Kingdom saw a sharp rise in debt after the 1990–1992 recession, a fall from 1997 to 2002, but as a percentage of GDP, UK debt has risen since 2003.

Source of data: HM Treasury.

Box 26.1

EU Government Budget Balances and Debts

The budget of each member state of the European Union has similar categories of revenues and outlays to the UK budget. In addition to the national budgets, the Council of the European Union draws up the EU budget, which the European Parliament approves.

The European Union receives 85 per cent of its revenue from the member states and 15 per cent from EU tariffs on imports from non-member countries. Member states' contributions are based on VAT, which provides 35 per cent of revenue, and on gross national product, which produces 50 per cent of revenue. (A country's gross *national* product is equal to its gross *domestic* product plus net property income from the rest of the world.)

The total EU budget in 2006 was €102 billion – equivalent to less than 1 per cent of EU GDP.

Figure 1 shows how the European Union spends its resources. Agriculture – the Common Agricultural Policy – takes the biggest slice of the budget pie. Structural measures – grants to weaker economic regions – take another large slice.

Despite its small size relative to GDP, the EU budget is hotly debated and contributes to economic life in many EU countries. For example, Ireland has benefited from both the Common Agricultural Policy and the EU structural programmes.

Figure 1

EU Budget Outlays in 2006

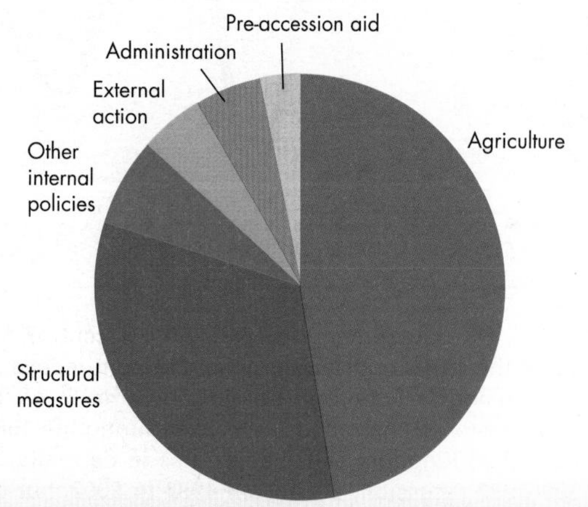

Most government revenue and outlays in the European Union remain with the member states. The 27 members of the European Union span a huge range of budgetary outcomes. Two aspects of these budgets are budget balances and government debt. Figure 2 shows the budget balances of the 25 EU members in 2006. They range from a deficit of 13 per cent of GDP in the Czech Republic to a surplus of 2.6 per cent in Estonia. The EU average is a deficit at 2.8 per cent of GDP, a bit below the UK deficit of 3.2 per cent of

Figure 2

EU Budget Balances in 2006

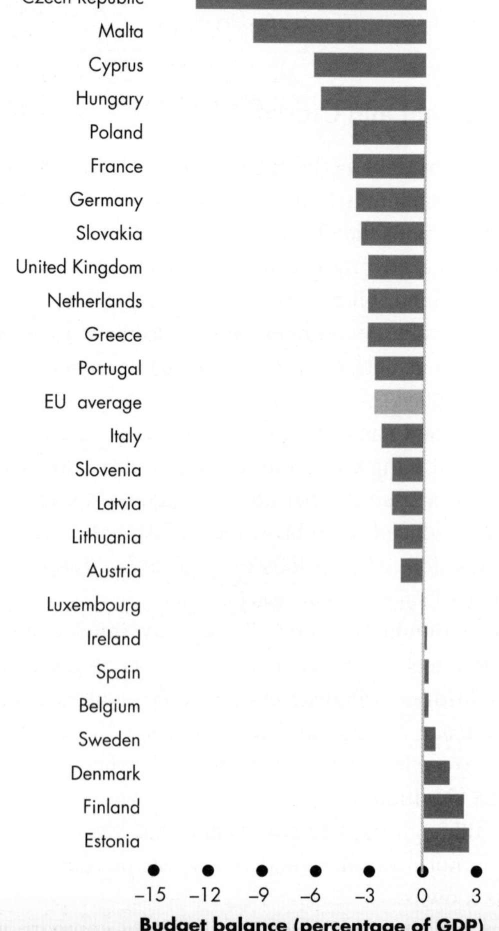

Source of data for Figures 1, 2 and 3: Eurostat.

◀

GDP. Two other large EU members, France and Germany, have deficits that are greater than the UK deficit.

Figure 3 shows the EU government debt in 2006. It ranges from a high of 106 per cent of GDP in Italy to a low of 5 per cent in Luxembourg. The EU average debt is 63 per cent of GDP, which is substantially above the UK debt of 40 per cent of GDP. Three other large EU members, France, Germany and Italy, each have debt that exceeds the UK debt.

There is no correlation between debt and the budget balance. Some EU countries with large debt are running low deficits to bring the debt down.

Figure 3

EU Government Debt in 2006

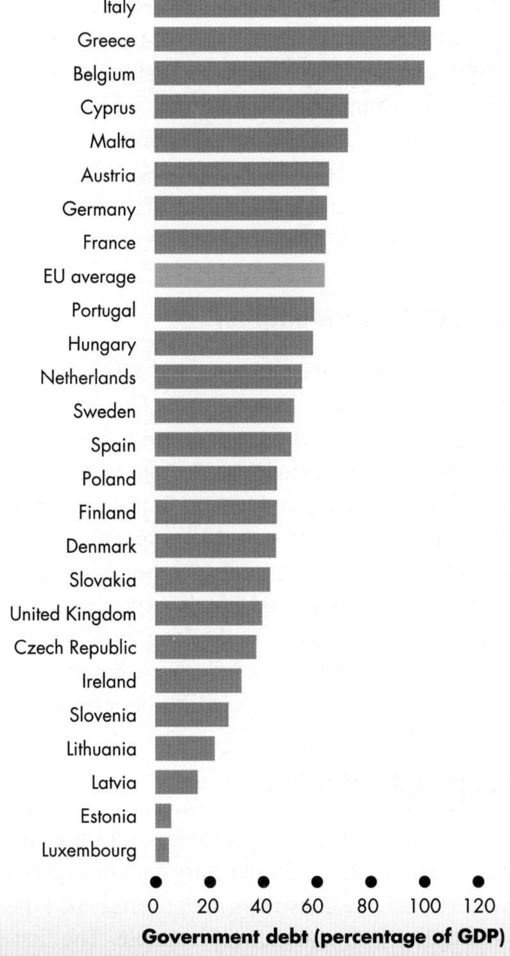

UK and EU Budget Balances and Debt in a Global Perspective

You've seen that the United Kingdom had a budget surplus in 2006 of £35 billion (2.8 per cent of GDP) and that the EU average budget deficit is 2.8 per cent of EU GDP. How do these balances stack up against the rest of the world?

The answer is that the UK and other EU member's budget balances are among the smallest. Japan has been running a budget deficit of more than 6 per cent of GDP for some years. The developing countries of Africa and Asia have deficits of about 4 per cent of their GDPs. The United States has a larger deficit than the EU average.

Among the few countries that have smaller balances than the European average are the newly industrialized Asian economies (Hong Kong, Singapore, South Korea and Taiwan), Australia and Canada, all of which have surpluses.

There is nothing inherently wrong with a government running a deficit, provided the resources are being used to add to the stock of social capital. There is also a case for a government running a deficit if it wants to try to lift its economy from recession.

Review Quiz

Study Plan 26.1

1. What are the functions of a government's budget?
2. What are the goals of fiscal policy?
3. Describe the main sources of revenues and outlays in the budget of the UK government?
4. Under what circumstances does a government have a budget surplus?
5. Which members of the European Union ran a budget deficit in 2006?
6. Which members of the European Union had the largest debt levels in 2006?
7. Explain the connection between a government's budget deficit and its debt.

We have now described the government budget. Your next task is to study the effects of fiscal policy on the economy. We'll begin by learning about its effects on expenditure plans when the price level is fixed. You will see that fiscal policy has multiplier effects like the multiplier explained in Chapter 25. Then we'll study the influences of fiscal policy on aggregate demand and aggregate supply and look at its short-run and long-run effects on real GDP and the price level.

Fiscal Policy Multipliers

Fiscal policy actions can be either automatic or discretionary. **Automatic fiscal policy** is a change in fiscal policy that is triggered by the state of the economy. For example, an increase in unemployment triggers an *automatic* increase in payments to unemployed workers. A fall in incomes triggers an *automatic* decrease in tax revenues. That is, fiscal policy adjusts automatically. **Discretionary fiscal policy** is a policy action that is initiated by the Chancellor of the Exchequer. It requires a change in tax laws or in some spending programme. For example, a cut in tax rates and an increase in defence spending are discretionary fiscal policy actions. That is, discretionary fiscal policy is a deliberate policy action.

We begin by studying the effects of *discretionary* changes in government spending and taxes. To focus on the essentials, we'll initially study a model economy that is simpler than the one in which we live. In our model economy, there is no international trade and the taxes are autonomous. **Autonomous taxes** are taxes that do not vary with real GDP. They are fixed by the government and they change only when the government changes them.

Autonomous taxes are rare in reality and they are generally considered to be unfair because rich people and poor people pay the same amount of tax. (It is said that the former Prime Minister, Margaret Thatcher, lost her job because of the unpopularity of an autonomous tax called the 'poll tax', which was a fixed tax per person to pay for local government services.)

We use autonomous taxes in our model economy because they make the principles we are studying easier to understand. Once we've grasped the principles, we'll explore our real economy with its international trade and income taxes – taxes that *do* vary with real GDP.

Like our real economy, the model economy we study is constantly bombarded by spending fluctuations. Business investment in new buildings, plant and equipment and inventories fluctuate because of swings in profit expectations and interest rates. These fluctuations set up multiplier effects that begin a recession or an expansion. If a recession takes hold, unemployment increases and incomes fall. If an expansion becomes too strong, inflationary pressures build up. To minimize the effects of these swings in spending, the government might change either its expenditures on goods and services or taxes. By changing either of these items, the government can influence aggregate expenditure and real GDP, but the government's budget deficit or surplus also changes. An alternative fiscal policy action is to change both expenditures and taxes together so that the budget balance does not change. We are going to study the initial effects of these discretionary fiscal policy actions in the very short run when the price level is fixed. Each of these actions creates a multiplier effect on real GDP. These multipliers are the:

- Government expenditure multiplier
- Autonomous tax multiplier
- Balanced budget multiplier

Government Expenditure Multiplier

The **government expenditure multiplier** is the amount by which a change in government expenditure on goods and services is multiplied to determine the change in equilibrium expenditure and real GDP that it generates.

Government expenditure is a component of aggregate expenditure. So when government expenditure on goods and services changes, aggregate expenditure and real GDP change. The change in real GDP induces a change in consumption expenditure, which brings an additional change in aggregate expenditure. A multiplier process ensues. This multiplier process is like the one described in Chapter 25, pp. 572–575. Let's look at an example.

A Peace Dividend Multiplier

After the end of the Cold War, the UK government decreased its defence expenditure. One cut was the downgrading of a naval base at Rosyth, Scotland. The cut in government expenditure decreased the region's GDP and increased unemployment in the area. Because military personnel and other workers spent most of their incomes locally, consumption expenditure in the region decreased. Retail shops and hotels experienced falling trade and laid off workers. In the long term, the Rosyth area will develop alternative industries, but in the short term, it experienced a negative multiplier effect.

The Size of the Multiplier

Our task is to find equilibrium expenditure and the change in real GDP when the government expenditure changes. Table 26.2 illustrates the government expenditure multiplier with a numerical example. The first column lists various possible levels of real GDP. The second column shows *induced expenditures* – induced

Table 26.2

The Government Expenditure Multiplier

	Real GDP (*Y*)	Induced expenditure (*N*)	Initial autonomous expenditure (*A*)	Initial aggregate planned expenditure ($AE = N + A$)	New autonomous expenditure (*A'*)	New aggregate planned expenditure ($AE' = N + A'$)
				(billions of pounds)		
A	1,200	900	325	1,225	375	1,275
B	**1,300**	**975**	**325**	**1,300**	375	1,350
C	1,400	1,050	325	1,375	375	1,425
D	**1,500**	**1,125**	325	1,450	**375**	**1,500**
E	1,600	1,200	325	1,525	375	1,575
F	1,700	1,275	325	1,600	375	1,650

consumption expenditure minus imports. In this example, a £100 billion increase in real GDP induces a £75 billion increase in aggregate planned expenditure. For example when real GDP increases from £1,200 billion (row *A*) to £1,300 billion (row *B*), induced expenditure increases from £900 billion to £975 billion. This relationship between real GDP and induced expenditure means that the *slope of the aggregate expenditure* (*AE*) *curve* is 0.75.

The third column shows the initial level of autonomous expenditure – the sum of investment, government expenditure, exports and the autonomous component of consumption expenditure. Autonomous expenditure is initially equal to £325 billion.

The next column shows the initial level of aggregate planned expenditure. It is the sum of induced expenditure and the initial level of autonomous expenditure.

Equilibrium expenditure and real GDP occur when aggregate planned expenditure equals actual expenditure. In this example, equilibrium expenditure is £1,300 billion (highlighted in row *B* of the table).

The final two columns of the table show what happens when government expenditure increases by £50 billion. The new level of autonomous expenditure is £375 billion. And at each level of real GDP the new level of aggregate planned expenditure is £50 billion higher than the initial level. For example, at the initial real GDP of £1,300 billion (row *B*), aggregate planned expenditure increases to £1,350 billion.

Because at the initial equilibrium real GDP, aggregate planned expenditure exceeds real GDP, inventories decrease. So firms increase production. Output, incomes and expenditure increase. Increased incomes bring a further increase in induced expenditure, which is less than the increase in income. Aggregate planned expenditure increases and eventually a new equilibrium is reached. The new equilibrium is at a real GDP of £1,500 billion (highlighted in row *D*).

A £50 billion increase in government expenditure has increased equilibrium expenditure and real GDP by £200 billion. So the government expenditure multiplier is 4. Just as in the case of the investment multiplier, the size of the multiplier depends on the slope of the *AE* curve and is:

$$\text{Government multiplier} = \frac{1}{(1 - \text{Slope of } AE \text{ curve})}$$

Let's use this formula with the numbers in the above example. You've seen that the slope of the *AE* curve is 0.75 so the multiplier is:

$$\text{Government exp multiplier} = \frac{1}{1 - 0.75} = \frac{1}{0.25} = 4$$

Figure 26.5 (overleaf) illustrates the government expenditure multiplier. Initially, aggregate planned expenditure is shown by the curve labelled AE_0. The points on this curve, labelled *A* to *F*, correspond with the rows of Table 26.2. This aggregate expenditure curve intersects the 45° line at the equilibrium level of real GDP, which is £1,300 billion.

Figure 26.5 myeconlab

The Government Expenditure Multiplier

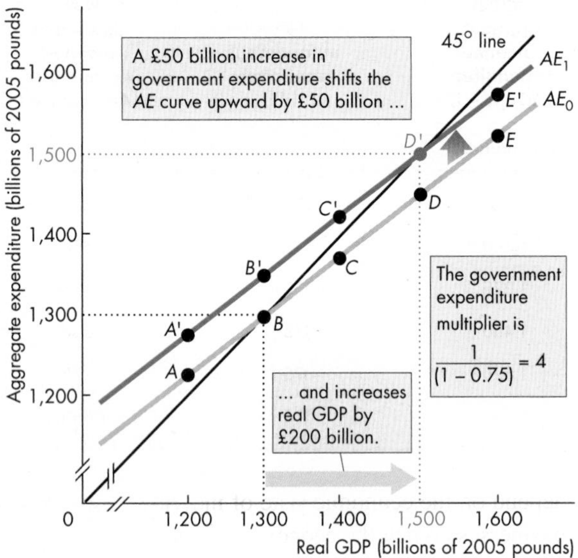

Initially, the aggregate expenditure curve is AE_0 and real GDP is £1,300 billion (at point *B*). An increase in government expenditure of £50 billion increases aggregate planned expenditure at each level of real GDP by £50 billion. The aggregate expenditure curve shifts upward from AE_0 to AE_1 – a parallel shift.

At the initial real GDP of £1,300 billion, aggregate planned expenditure is now £1,350 billion. Because aggregate planned expenditure is greater than real GDP, real GDP increases. The new equilibrium is reached when real GDP is £1,500 billion – the point at which the AE_1 curve intersects the 45° line (at *D'*). In this example, the government expenditure multiplier is 4.

When government expenditure increases by £50 billion, the aggregate expenditure curve shifts upward by that amount to AE_1. With this new aggregate expenditure curve, equilibrium real GDP increases to £1,500 billion. The increase in real GDP is 4 times the increase in government expenditure. The government expenditure multiplier is 4.

You've seen that in the very short term, when the price level is fixed, an increase in government expenditure increases real GDP. But to produce more output, more people must be employed, so in the short term, an increase in government expenditure can create jobs.

Increasing its expenditures on goods and services is one way in which the government can try to stimulate the economy. A second way in which the government might act to increase real GDP in the very short run is by cutting taxes or increasing transfer payments. And the government might change autonomous taxes (or transfer payments) or induced taxes (or transfer payments.) Let's see how these actions work.

Autonomous Tax Multiplier

The **autonomous tax multiplier** is the magnification effect of a change in autonomous taxes on equilibrium expenditure and real GDP. An *increase* in taxes *decreases* disposable income, which decreases consumption expenditure. The amount by which consumption expenditure initially changes is determined by the marginal propensity to consume. In Chapter 25 (Box 25.1), the UK marginal propensity to consume is 0.8, so a £1 tax cut increases disposable income by £1 and increases aggregate expenditure initially by 80 pence.

This initial change in aggregate expenditure has a multiplier just like the government expenditure multiplier. We've seen that the government expenditure multiplier is 1/(1 – Slope of the *AE* curve). Because a tax *increase* leads to a *decrease* in expenditure, the autonomous tax multiplier is *negative*. And because a change in autonomous taxes changes aggregate expenditure initially by only the *MPC* multiplied by the tax change, the autonomous tax multiplier is equal to:

$$\text{Autonomous tax multiplier} = \frac{-MPC}{(1 - \text{Slope of } AE \text{ curve})}$$

Figure 26.6 illustrates the autonomous tax multiplier. Initially, the aggregate expenditure curve is AE_0 and equilibrium expenditure is £1,300 billion. Taxes increase by £100 billion and disposable income falls by that amount. With a marginal propensity to consume of 0.8, aggregate expenditure decreases initially by £80 billion and the aggregate expenditure curve shifts downward by that amount to AE_1. Equilibrium expenditure and real GDP fall by £320 billion to £980 billion. The autonomous tax multiplier is –3.2.

$$\text{Autonomous tax multiplier} = \frac{-0.8}{(1 - 0.75)} = -3.2$$

The autonomous tax multiplier also tells us the effects of a change in autonomous transfer payments – negative taxes. An *increase* in transfer payments has the same effect as a *decrease* in taxes. So the autonomous transfer

Figure 26.6

The Autonomous Tax Multiplier

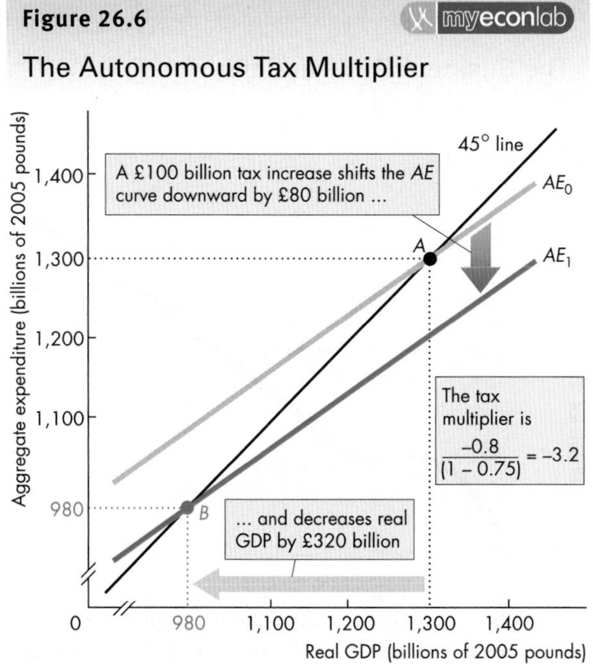

Initially, the aggregate expenditure curve is AE_0, and equilibrium expenditure is £1,300 billion. The marginal propensity to consume is 0.8. Autonomous taxes increase by £100 billion, so disposable income decreases by £100 billion.

The decrease in aggregate expenditure is found by multiplying this change in disposable income (£100 billion) by the marginal propensity to consume (0.8). The decrease in aggregate expenditure is £80 billion and the aggregate expenditure curve shifts *downward* by this amount to AE_1.

Equilibrium expenditure decreases by £320 billion, and the autonomous tax multiplier is –3.2.

payments multiplier equals the negative of the autonomous tax multiplier.

Balanced Budget Multiplier

The **balanced budget multiplier** is the multiplier that arises from a fiscal policy action that changes *both* government expenditure and taxes by the *same* amount so that the government's budget balance remains *unchanged.*

Because the tax multiplier is smaller than the government expenditure multiplier, the balanced budget multiplier is greater than zero. With no imports and no income taxes, the balanced budget multiplier is one. But this special case does not apply when there are imports and income taxes. Nonetheless, the balanced budget multiplier is always greater than zero.

Induced Taxes and Transfer Payments

In the examples we've studied so far, taxes are autonomous. But in reality, net taxes (taxes minus transfer payments) vary with the state of the economy.

On the revenue side of the budget, tax laws define the tax *rates* to be paid, not the tax *pounds* to be paid. Tax *pounds* paid depend on tax *rates* and incomes. But incomes vary with real GDP, so tax revenues depend on real GDP. When the economy expands, induced taxes increase because real GDP increases. When the economy is in a recession, induced taxes decrease because real GDP decreases.

On the outlays side of the budget, the government creates programmes that entitle suitably qualified people and businesses to receive benefits. For example, the government pays unemployed workers a job-seeker's allowance. The spending on such programmes is not fixed in pounds and it results in transfer payments that depend on the economic state of individual citizens and businesses. When the economy is in a recession, unemployment is high, the number of people experiencing economic hardship increases and a larger number of firms and farms experience hard times. Transfer payments increase. When the economy expands, transfer payments decrease.

Net taxes (taxes minus transfer payment) that vary with real GDP are called **induced taxes**. And the change in induced taxes equals the change in real GDP multiplied by the marginal tax rate. The *marginal tax rate* is the proportion of an additional pound of real GDP that flows to the government in net taxes. The higher the marginal tax rate, the larger is the proportion of an additional pound of real GDP that is paid to the government and the smaller is the induced change in aggregate expenditure.

An increase in the marginal tax rate decreases disposable income, decreases consumption expenditure and has a multiplier effect on real GDP. But an increase in the marginal tax rate also decreases the magnitude of the autonomous expenditure multipliers (the investment, government expenditure, autonomous tax and autonomous transfer payments multipliers). It does so by decreasing the slope of the *AE* curve. With a high marginal tax rate, when real GDP increases, induced taxes increase by more and disposable income and consumption expenditure by less than they do with a low marginal tax rate. So aggregate expenditure increases by less than it otherwise would have. The *AE* curve is flatter, its slope is smaller, and the autonomous expenditure multipliers are smaller.

International Trade and Fiscal Policy Multipliers

Not all expenditure on final goods and services in the United Kingdom is expenditure on UK-produced goods and services. Some of it is on imports – foreign-produced goods and services. Imports affect the fiscal policy multipliers in the same way as they influence the investment multiplier, as explained in Chapter 25 (see pp. 572–576). The extent to which an additional pound of real GDP is spent on imports is determined by the *marginal propensity to import.* Expenditure on imports does not generate UK real GDP and so does not lead to an increase in UK consumption expenditure. The larger the marginal propensity to import, the smaller is the increase in consumption expenditure induced by an increase in real GDP and the smaller are the government expenditure and autonomous tax multipliers. (The mathematical note on pp. 612–613 explains the details of the effects of induced taxes and transfer payments and imports on the fiscal policy multipliers.)

So far, we've studied *discretionary* fiscal policy. Let's look at *automatic* stabilizers.

Automatic Stabilizers

Automatic stabilizers are mechanisms that operate to stabilize real GDP without the need for explicit action by the government. Their name is borrowed from engineering and conjures up images of shock absorbers, thermostats and sophisticated devices that keep aircraft and ships steady in turbulent air and seas. But automatic fiscal stabilizers do not actual stabilize. They just make fluctuations less severe. These stabilizers operate because income taxes and transfer payments fluctuate with real GDP. As real GDP falls, tax revenues fall, transfer payments rise and the budget balance changes. Let's look at the budget balance over the business cycle.

Budget Balance Over the Business Cycle

Figure 26.7 shows the business cycle and fluctuations in the budget balance between 1986 and 2006. Part (a) shows the fluctuations of real GDP around potential GDP. Part (b) shows the government budget balance. Both parts highlight the most recent recession by shading this period. By comparing the two parts of the figure, you can see the relationship between the business cycle and the budget deficit. As a rule, when the economy is in the expansion phase of a business cycle, the budget balance increases.

Figure 26.7

The Business Cycle and the Budget Balance

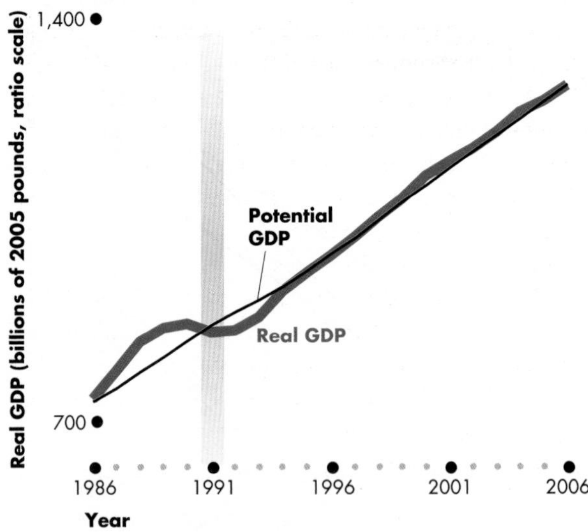

(a) Real GDP and potential GDP

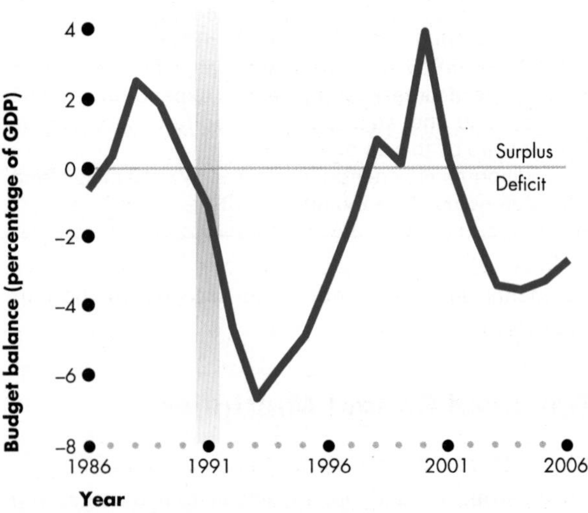

(b) The UK government budget balance

As real GDP fluctuates around potential GDP in part (a), the budget deficit fluctuates in part (b). During a recession (shaded areas), the budget balance decreases. The budget balance also decreases *before* a recession as real GDP growth slows and *after* a recession before real GDP growth speeds up. When the growth rate of real GDP is high during an expansion, the budget balance increases.

Source of data: Office for National Statistics.

As the expansion slows and before the recession begins, the budget balance decreases. It continues to decrease during the recession and for a further period after the recession is over. Then, when the expansion is well under way, the budget balance increases again.

The budget balance fluctuates with the business cycle because both revenues and outlays fluctuate with real GDP. As real GDP increases during an expansion, tax revenues increase and transfer payments decrease, so the budget balance automatically increases. As real GDP decreases during a recession, tax revenues decrease and transfer payments increase, so the budget balance automatically decreases.

Fluctuations in investment or exports have a multiplier effect on real GDP. But automatic fluctuations in tax revenues (and the budget balance) act as an automatic stabilizer. They decrease the swings in disposable income and make the multiplier smaller. They dampen both the expansions and recessions.

Cyclical and Structural Balances

Because the government budget balance fluctuates with the business cycle, we need a method of measuring the balance so that we know whether it is a temporary cyclical phenomenon or a persistent structural phenomenon. A temporary cyclical surplus or deficit vanishes when full employment returns. A persistent structural surplus or deficit requires government action to remove it.

To determine whether the budget balance is persistent and structural, or temporary and cyclical, economists have developed the concepts of the structural budget balance and the cyclical budget balance. The **structural surplus or deficit** is the budget balance that would occur if the economy were at full employment and real GDP were equal to potential GDP. The **cyclical surplus or deficit** is the actual surplus or deficit minus the structural surplus or deficit. That is, the cyclical surplus or deficit is the part of the budget balance that arises purely because real GDP does not equal potential GDP.

For example, suppose that the budget deficit is £10 billion and the structural deficit is £2.5 billion. Then the cyclical deficit is £7.5 billion.

Figure 26.8 illustrates the concepts of cyclical surplus or deficit and structural surplus or deficit. The blue curve shows government outlays. The outlays curve slopes downward because transfer payments, a component of government outlays, decrease as real GDP increases. The green curve shows revenues. The revenues curve slopes upward because most tax revenues increase as income and real GDP increases.

Figure 26.8 myeconlab

Cyclical and Structural Deficits and Surpluses

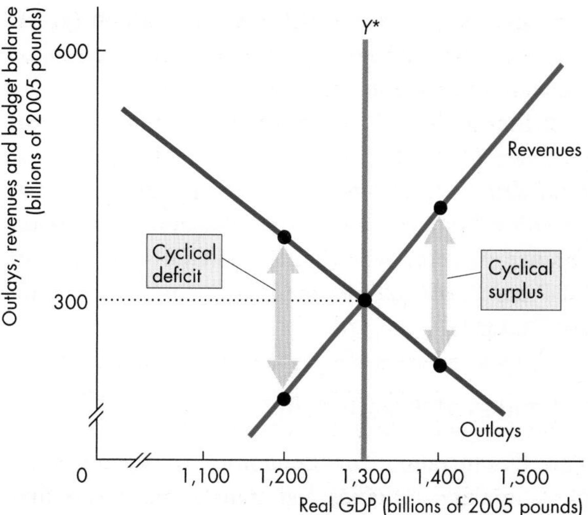

(a) Cyclical deficit and cyclical surplus

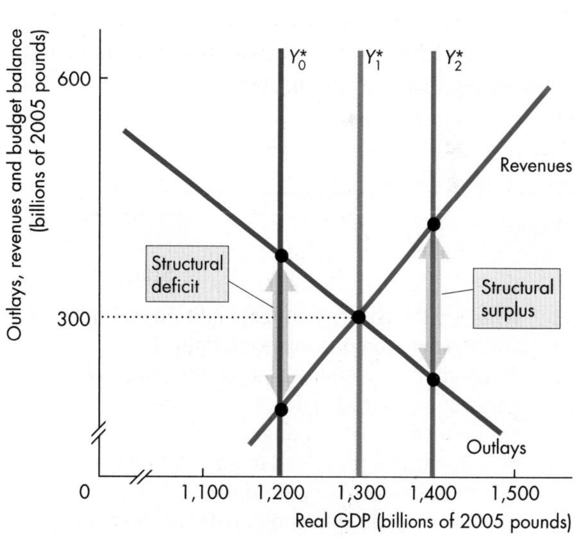

(b) Structural deficit and structural surplus

In part (a), potential GDP is £1,300 billion. When real GDP is less than potential GDP, the budget is in a *cyclical deficit*. When real GDP exceeds potential GDP, the budget is in a *cyclical surplus*. The government has a *balanced budget* when real GDP equals potential GDP.

In part (b), when potential GDP is £1,200 billion, the budget deficit is a *structural deficit*. But when potential GDP is £1,400 billion, the budget surplus is a *structural surplus*.

In Figure 26.8(a), potential GDP is £1,300 billion. If real GDP equals potential GDP, the government has a *balanced budget*. Outlays and revenues each equal £300 billion. If real GDP is £1,200 billion (less than potential GDP), outlays exceed revenues and there is a *cyclical deficit*. If real GDP is £1,400 billion (greater than potential GDP), outlays are less than revenues and there is a *cyclical surplus*.

In Figure 26.8(b), if both real GDP and potential GDP are £1,200 billion, the budget deficit is a *structural deficit*. If both real GDP and potential GDP are £1,300 billion, the budget is balanced – a structural balance of zero. When both real GDP and potential GDP are £1,400 billion, the budget surplus is a *structural surplus*.

Estimates of Structural Balances

The Organization for Economic Cooperation and Development (OECD) estimates that the United Kingdom had a structural deficit of 2.7 per cent of potential GDP in 2006. Other EU members that have a larger structural deficit than the United Kingdom include the Czech Republic, Greece, Hungary and Italy. A country with a structural deficit needs to take steps either to bring outlays under control or to increase revenues. Countries with a structural surplus have room for spending increases or tax cuts.

Review Quiz

Study Plan 26.2

1 What are the government expenditure multiplier and the autonomous taxes multiplier?
2 Which multiplier effect is larger: the multiplier effect of a change in government expenditure or the multiplier effect of a change in autonomous taxes?
3 How do income taxes and imports influence the size of the fiscal policy multipliers?
4 How do income taxes and transfer payments work as automatic stabilizers to dampen the business cycle?
5 How do we tell whether a budget deficit needs government action to remove it?

Your next task is to see how, with the passage of more time and with price level adjustments, these multiplier effects change.

Fiscal Policy Multipliers and the Price Level

We've seen how real GDP responds to changes in fiscal policy when the price level is fixed and all the adjustments that take place are in spending, income and production. Once production starts to change, regardless of whether it increases or decreases, prices also start to change. The price level and real GDP change together, and the economy moves to a new short-run equilibrium.

To study the simultaneous changes in real GDP and the price level that result from fiscal policy, we use the *AS–AD* model of Chapter 23. In the long run, both the price level and the money wage rate respond to fiscal policy. As these further changes take place, the economy gradually moves towards a new long-run equilibrium. We also use the *AS–AD* model to study these adjustments.

We begin by looking at the effects of fiscal policy on aggregate demand and the aggregate demand curve.

Fiscal Policy and Aggregate Demand

You learned about the relationship between aggregate demand, aggregate expenditure, and equilibrium expenditure in Chapter 25, pp. 577–579. You are now going to use what you learned to work out what happens to aggregate demand, the price level and real GDP when fiscal policy changes. We'll start by looking at the effects of a change in fiscal policy on aggregate demand.

Figure 26.9 shows the effects of an increase in government expenditure on aggregate demand. Initially, the aggregate expenditure curve is AE_0 in part (a) and the aggregate demand curve is AD_0 in part (b). The price level is 105, real GDP is £1,300 billion and the economy is at point *A* in both parts of the figure.

Now suppose that government expenditure increases by £50 billion. At a constant price level of 105, the aggregate expenditure curve shifts upward from AE_0 to AE_1. This curve intersects the 45° line at an equilibrium expenditure of £1,500 billion at point *B*. This amount is the aggregate quantity of goods and services demanded at a price level of 105, as shown by point *B* in part (b). Point *B* lies on a new aggregate demand curve. The aggregate demand curve has shifted rightward to AD_1.

The government expenditure multiplier determines the distance by which the aggregate demand curve shifts

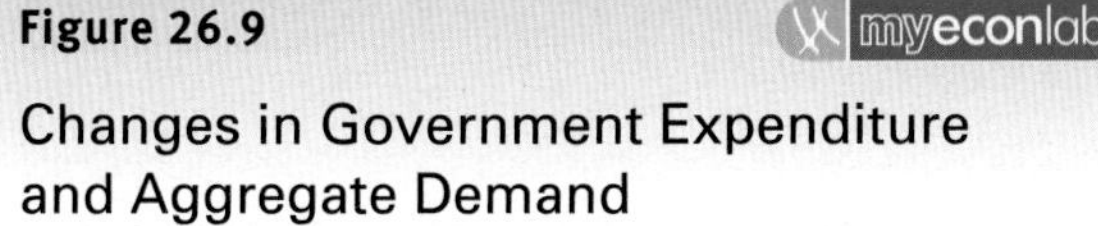

Figure 26.9

Changes in Government Expenditure and Aggregate Demand

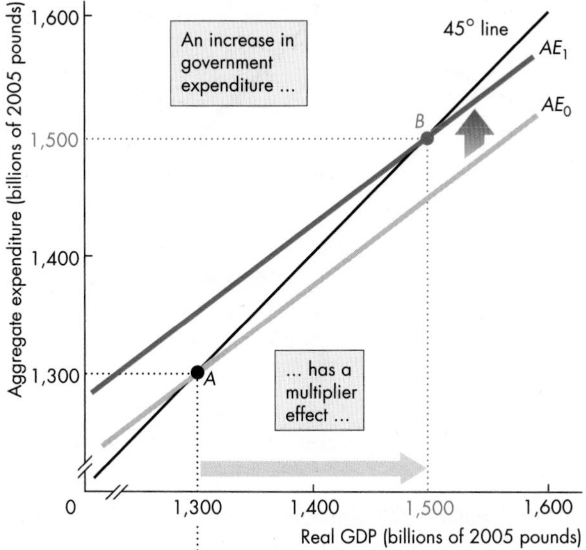

(a) Aggregate expenditure

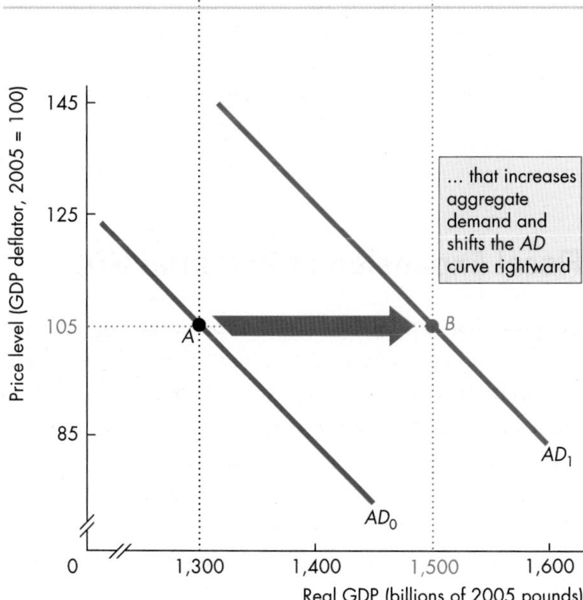

(b) Aggregate demand

The price level is 105. When the aggregate expenditure curve is AE_0 in part (a), the aggregate demand curve is AD_0 in part (b). An increase in government expenditure shifts the AE curve to AE_1 and real GDP increases to £1,500 billion. The aggregate demand curve shifts rightward to AD_1.

rightward. The larger the multiplier, the larger is the shift of the aggregate demand curve that results from a given change in government expenditure. In this example, a £50 billion increase in government expenditure produces a £200 billion increase in the aggregate quantity of goods and services demanded at each price level. The multiplier is 4. So the £50 billion increase in government expenditure shifts the aggregate demand curve rightward by £200 billion.

Figure 26.9 shows the effects of an increase in government expenditure. But a similar effect occurs for *any* expansionary fiscal policy. An **expansionary fiscal policy** is an increase in government expenditure on goods and services or a decrease in net taxes. But the distance that the aggregate demand curve shifts is smaller for a decrease in taxes than for an increase in government expenditure of the same size.

Figure 26.9 can also be used to illustrate the effects of a **contractionary fiscal policy** – a decrease in government expenditure on goods and services or an increase in net taxes. In this case, start at point B in each part of the figure and decrease government expenditure or increase taxes. Aggregate demand decreases and the aggregate demand curve shifts leftward from AD_1 to AD_0.

Equilibrium GDP and the Price Level in the Short Run

We've seen how an increase in government expenditure increases aggregate demand. Let's now see how it changes real GDP and the price level. Figure 26.10(a) – overleaf – describes the economy. Aggregate demand is AD_0 and the short-run aggregate supply curve is SAS. (Check back to Chapter 23, pp. 511–513 if you need to refresh your understanding of the short-run aggregate supply curve.) Equilibrium is at point A, where the aggregate demand and short-run aggregate supply curves intersect. The price level is 105, and real GDP is £1,300 billion.

An increase in government expenditure of £50 billion shifts the aggregate demand curve rightward from AD_0 to AD_1. While the price level is fixed at 105, the economy moves towards point B and real GDP increases towards £1,500 billion. But during the adjustment process, the price level does not remain constant. It gradually rises and the economy moves along the short-run aggregate supply curve to the point of intersection of the short-run aggregate supply curve and the new aggregate demand curve – point C. The price level rises to 118 and real GDP increases to £1,430 billion.

Figure 26.10

myeconlab

Fiscal Policy, Real GDP and the Price Level

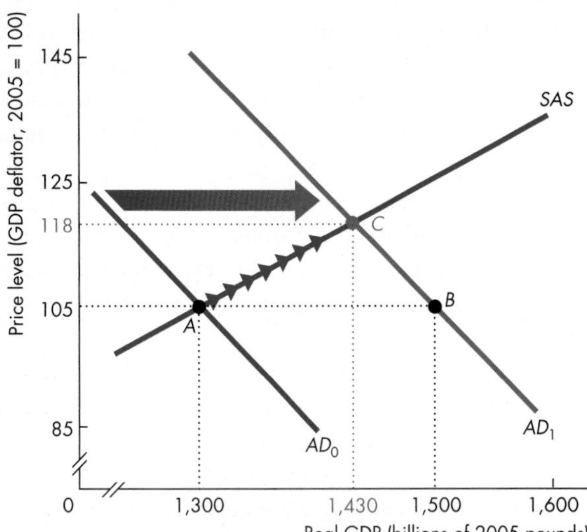

(a) Fiscal policy with unemployment

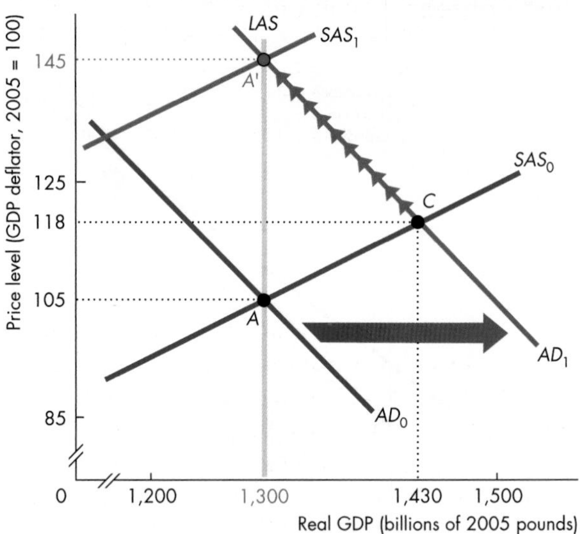

(b) Fiscal policy at full employment

An increase in government expenditure shifts the *AD* curve from AD_0 to AD_1 in part (a). With a fixed price level, the economy would have moved to point *B*. But the price level rises and in the short run the economy moves along the *SAS* curve to point *C*. The price level increases to 118, and real GDP increases to £1,430 billion.

At point *C*, real GDP exceeds potential GDP and unemployment is below the natural rate in part (b). The money wage rate starts to rise, and short-run aggregate supply decreases. The *SAS* curve shifts towards SAS_1. In the long run, the economy moves to point *A'*. The price level rises to 145 and real GDP returns to £1,300 billion.

When we take account of the change in the price level, the increase in government expenditure still has a multiplier effect on real GDP, but the effect is smaller than it would be if the price level had remained constant. The steeper the short-run aggregate supply curve, the larger is the increase in the price level and the smaller is the increase in real GDP. So the steeper the short-run aggregate supply curve, the smaller is the government expenditure multiplier. But it is not zero.

In the long run, real GDP equals potential GDP – the economy is at full employment. When real GDP equals potential GDP, an increase in aggregate demand has the same short-run effect as we have just worked out, but the long-run effect is different. The increase in aggregate demand raises the price level but in the long-run, real GDP remains at potential GDP.

To study this case, let's see what happens if the government embarks on an expansionary fiscal policy when real GDP equals potential GDP.

Fiscal Expansion at Potential GDP

Suppose that real GDP is equal to potential GDP, which means that unemployment is equal to the natural unemployment rate. But suppose also that both the unemployment rate and the natural unemployment rate are high and that most people, including the government, mistakenly think that the unemployment rate must be above the natural rate. In this situation, the government tries to lower the unemployment rate by using an expansionary fiscal policy.

Figure 26.10(b) shows the effect of an expansionary fiscal policy when real GDP equals potential GDP. In this example, potential GDP is £1,300 billion. Aggregate demand increases and the aggregate demand curve shifts rightward from AD_0 to AD_1. The short-run equilibrium, point *C*, is an above full-employment equilibrium. Now the money wage rate begins to increase. The higher wage rate increases firms' costs, and short-run aggregate supply decreases. The *SAS* curve begins to shift leftward from SAS_0 to SAS_1. The economy moves up the aggregate demand curve AD_1 towards point *A'*.

When all adjustments to the money wage rate and the price level have been made, the price level is 145 and real GDP is again at potential GDP of £1,300 billion. The multiplier in the long run is zero. There has been only a temporary decrease in unemployment and increase in real GDP, but a permanent rise in the price level.

Limitations of Fiscal Policy

Because the short-run fiscal policy multipliers are not zero, expansionary fiscal policy can be used to increase real GDP and decrease the unemployment rate in a recession. Contractionary fiscal policy can also be used, if the economy is overheating, to decrease real GDP and help to keep inflation in check. But two factors limit the use of fiscal policy.

First, the legislative process is slow, which means that it is difficult to take fiscal policy actions in a timely way. The economy might be able to benefit from fiscal stimulation right now, but it will take Parliament many months, perhaps more than a year, to act. By the time the action is taken, the economy might need an entirely different fiscal medicine.

Second, it is not always easy to tell whether real GDP is below (or above) potential GDP. A change in aggregate demand can move real GDP away from potential GDP, or a change in aggregate supply can change real GDP and change potential GDP. This difficulty is a serious one because, as you've seen, fiscal stimulation might occur too close to full employment, in which case it will increase the price level and have no long-run effect on real GDP.

Review Quiz

Study Plan 26.3

1. How do changes in the price level influence the multiplier effects of fiscal policy on real GDP?
2. What is the long-run fiscal multiplier effect on real GDP and the price level?

So far, we've ignored any potential effects of fiscal policy on aggregate supply. Yet many economists believe that the supply-side effects of fiscal policy are the biggest. Let's now look at these effects.

Supply-side Effects of Fiscal Policy

Tax cuts increase disposable income and increase aggregate demand. But tax cuts also strengthen incentives and increase aggregate supply. The strength of the supply-side effects of tax cuts is not known with certainty. Some economists believe that the supply-side effects are large and exceed the demand-side effects. Other economists, while agreeing that supply-side effects are present, believe that they are relatively small.

The controversy over the magnitude of the effects of taxes on aggregate supply is a political controversy. Generally speaking, people on the conservative or right wing of the political spectrum believe that supply-side effects are powerful, and people on the liberal or left wing of the political spectrum view supply-side effects as being small.

Regardless of which view is correct, we can study the supply-side effects of tax cuts by using the *AS–AD* model. Let's study the effects of taxes on potential GDP and then see how the supply-side effects and demand-side effects together influence real GDP and the price level.

Fiscal Policy and Potential GDP

Potential GDP depends on the full-employment quantity of labour, the quantity of capital and the state of technology. Taxes can influence all three of these factors. The main tax to consider is the income tax. By taxing the incomes people earn when they work or save, the government weakens the incentives to work and save. The result is a smaller quantity of labour and capital and a smaller potential GDP. Also, the income tax weakens the incentive to develop new technologies that increase income. So the pace of technological change might be slowed, which slows the growth rate of potential GDP. Let's look at the effect of the income tax on both the quantity of labour and the quantity of capital.

Labour Market Taxes

The quantity of labour is determined by demand and supply in the labour market. Figure 26.11(a) – overleaf – shows the demand for labour is *LD* and the supply is *LS*. The equilibrium real wage rate is £15 an hour and 60 billion hours of labour per year are employed.

Now suppose that two taxes are introduced: an income tax and a payroll tax. The income tax weakens

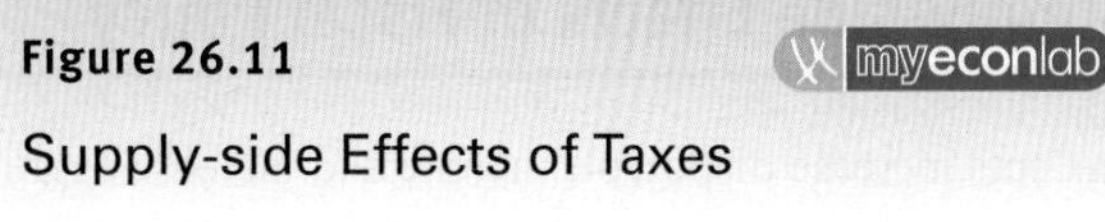

Figure 26.11

Supply-side Effects of Taxes

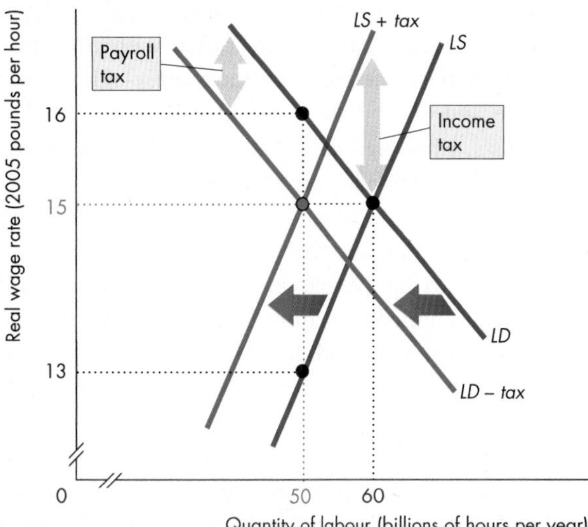

(a) The labour market

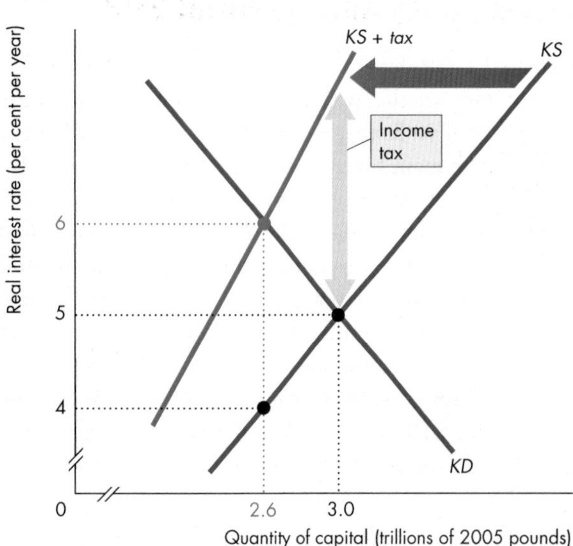

(b) The capital market

In part (a), an income tax decreases the supply of labour from *LS* to *LS* + *tax* and a payroll tax decreases the demand for labour from *LD* to *LD* – *tax*. The quantity of labour decreases. In part (b), the income tax decreases the supply of capital from *KS* to *KS* + *tax*. The quantity of capital decreases. With less labour and less capital, potential GDP decreases.

the incentive to work and decreases the supply of labour. The supply curve shifts leftward to *LS* + *tax*. A payroll tax makes it more costly to employ labour and decreases the demand for labour. The demand curve shifts leftward to *LD* – *tax*. With the new decreased supply and demand, the quantity of labour employed decreases to 50 billion hours a year. The *before-tax* real wage rate remains at £15 an hour (but it might rise or fall depending on whether demand or supply decreases more). The *after-tax* real wage rate falls to £13 an hour, and the cost of hiring labour rises to £16 an hour.

Capital and the Income Tax

The quantity of capital is determined by demand and supply in the capital market. Figure 26.11(b) shows the capital market. The demand for capital is *KD* and the supply is *KS*. The equilibrium real interest rate is 5 per cent a year and the quantity of capital is £3 trillion.

A tax on the income from capital weakens the incentive to save and decreases the supply of capital. The supply curve shifts leftward to *KS* + *tax*. With the new decreased supply, the quantity of capital decreases to £2.6 trillion. The *before-tax* interest rate rises to 6 per cent a year, and the *after-tax* interest rate falls to 4 per cent a year.

Potential GDP and the *LAS* Curve

Because the taxes decrease the equilibrium quantities of labour and capital, they also decrease potential GDP. But potential GDP determines long-run aggregate supply. So the taxes decrease long-run aggregate supply and shift the *LAS* curve leftward.

Supply Effects and Demand Effects

Let's now bring the supply-side effects and demand-side effects of fiscal policy together. Figure 26.12(a) shows the most likely effects of a tax cut. The tax cut increases aggregate demand and shifts the *AD* curve rightward, just as before. But a tax cut that increases the incentive to work and save also increases aggregate supply. It shifts the long-run and short-run aggregate supply curves rightward. Here we focus on the short run and show the effect on the *SAS* curve, which shifts rightward to SAS_1. In this example, the tax cut has a large effect on aggregate demand and a small effect on aggregate supply. The *AD* curve shifts rightward by a larger amount than the rightward shift in the *SAS* curve. The

Figure 26.12

Two Views of the Supply-side Effects of Fiscal Policy

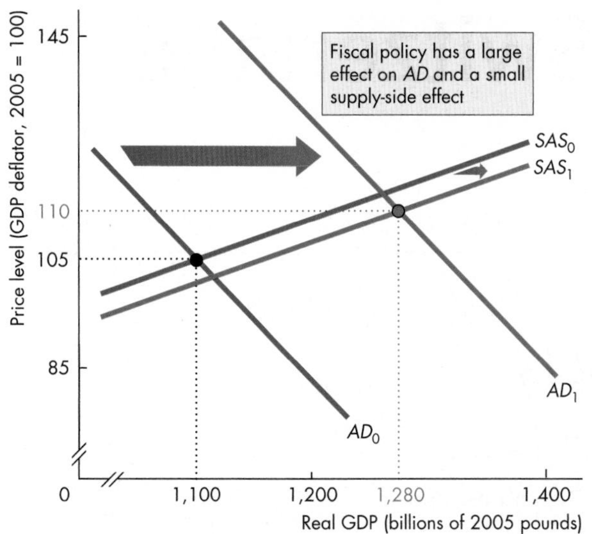

(a) The traditional view

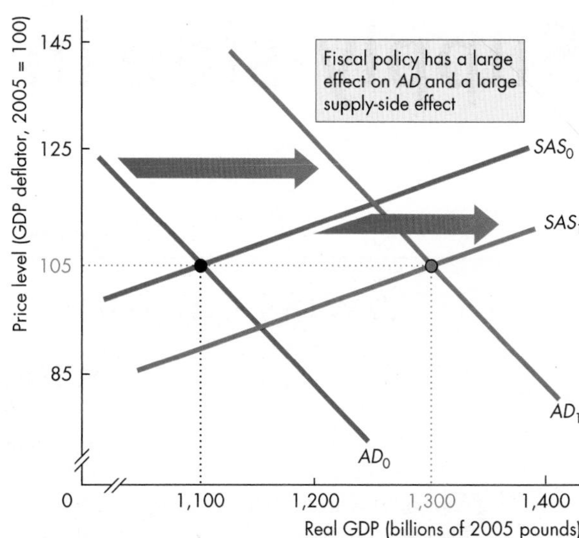

(b) The supply-side view

An expansionary fiscal policy such as a tax cut increases aggregate demand and shifts the *AD* curve rightward from AD_0 to AD_1 (both parts). Such a policy change also has a supply-side effect. If the supply-side effect is small, the *SAS* curve shifts rightward from SAS_0 to SAS_1 in part (a). The demand-side effect dominates the supply-side effect, real GDP increases and the price level rises.

If the supply-side effect of a tax cut is large, the *SAS* curve shifts rightward from SAS_0 to SAS_1 in part (b). In this case, the supply-side effect is the same as the demand-side effect – £200 billion. Real GDP increases and the price level remains constant. But if the supply-side effect were larger than the demand-side effect, the price level would actually fall.

outcome is a rise in the price level and an increase in real GDP. But notice that the price level rises by *less* and real GDP increases by *more* than would occur if there were no supply-side effects.

Figure 26.12(b) shows the effects that supply-siders believe occur. A tax cut has a large effect on aggregate demand, but it has a similarly large effect on aggregate supply. The *AD* curve and the *SAS* curve shift rightward by similar amounts. In this particular case, the price level remains constant and real GDP increases. A slightly larger increase in aggregate supply would have brought a fall in the price level, a possibility that some supply-siders believe could occur.

The general point with which everyone agrees is that a tax cut that strengthens the incentives to work and save increases real GDP by more and is less inflationary than an equal-size expansionary fiscal policy that does not change incentives or that weakens them.

Review Quiz

Study Plan 26.4

1. How do income taxes and payroll taxes influence the labour market, and how would a cut in these taxes influence real GDP?
2. How would an income tax cut influence aggregate supply and aggregate demand?
3. How would an income tax cut influence real GDP and the price level?

You've seen how fiscal policy influences real GDP and potential GDP. *Reading Between the Lines* on pp. 610–611 looks at how tax competition from Switzerland drives jobs and capital to relocate from the European Union to Switzerland.

Your next task is to study the other main arm of macroeconomic policy: monetary policy.

Reading Between the Lines

Supply-side in Switzerland

The Financial Times, 16 February 2007

FT

Swiss canton's tax regime irks Brussels

Haig Simonian

Stroll down the Banhoffstrasse, and the most immediate impression of Zug, a town of 26,000 people, is of a developing country boomtown rather than Swiss backwater.

Large anonymous office blocks line the boulevard from the bustling station. Expensive shops, luxury car dealerships and marble clad banks break up the monotony. Money is in the air.

But Zug's wealth has not been made from diamonds or oil – although both happen to be extensively traded there – but tax.

This week, the European Commission identified the capital of the eponymous canton, and neighbouring Schwyz, as examples of "unfair" fiscal competition practised by Switzerland to the detriment of European Union members.

The complaint, brewing since autumn 2005, was based on a 1972 free trade agreement between Bern and Brussels, and stoked by Switzerland's recent successes in attracting high profile companies – often away from EU countries. Last month, Kraft Foods of the US joined groups such as Procter and Gamble and Honeywell Bull in upping sticks.

"We don't understand why the Commission has made these accusations now," says Peter Hegglin, the cantonal finance minister. "I'm convinced our position is fully in line with the free trade agreement."

Like most Swiss, Mr Hegglin emphasises the role of tax competition as a cornerstone of Switzerland's extreme form of devolution, where individual cantons and communities set their own levies, and as an instrument to ensure lean, efficient government. . . .

One way was by being more liberal in granting work permits to foreigners than more restrictive Zurich, the country's leading commercial hub.

Business friendly taxation was the other. Zug is now the hub for companies from global commodities traders, such as Glencore, to the regional headquarters of leading pharmaceuticals groups. . . .

The Essence of the Story

- The European Union has high taxes and inflexible labour market policies.
- Some Swiss cantons have low taxes and liberal work-permit policies.
- A few high profile companies have relocated from the European Union to Switzerland to take advantage of the differences in taxes and labour market policies.
- The European Union claims that the lower Swiss taxes have created unfair competition.

Economic Analysis

- Switzerland has lower taxes and more flexible labour market policies than the European Union.
- Some high-profile firms have been induced by the tax and labour market policy differences to move from the European Union to Switzerland.
- The tax and labour market policy differences have increased the quantity of capital, labour productivity and potential GDP in Switzerland.
- These same policy differences have decreased the quantity of capital, labour productivity and potential GDP in the European Union.
- Figure 1 shows that the employment rate in Switzerland is higher than in EU countries.
- Figure 2 shows the effects of Switzerland's policies on its labour market. Lower taxes increase the supply of labour from LS_0 to LS_1. Greater labour productivity increases the demand for labour from LD_0 to LD_1.
- Because both the demand for and supply of labour are higher, employment increases; and because demand increases by more than supply (an assumption but most likely correct), the real wage rate rises.
- Figure 3 shows the effects of Switzerland's tax and labour market policies on its aggregate supply. Potential GDP increases so long-run aggregate supply increases from LAS_0 to LAS_1 and short-run aggregate supply increases from SAS_0 to SAS_1.
- Figure 3 also shows that monetary policy increases aggregate demand from AD_0 to AD_1 to keep the price level steady.

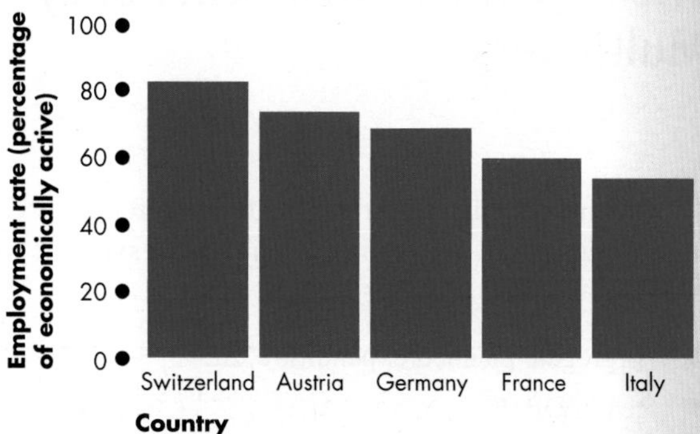

Figure 1 Employment rates

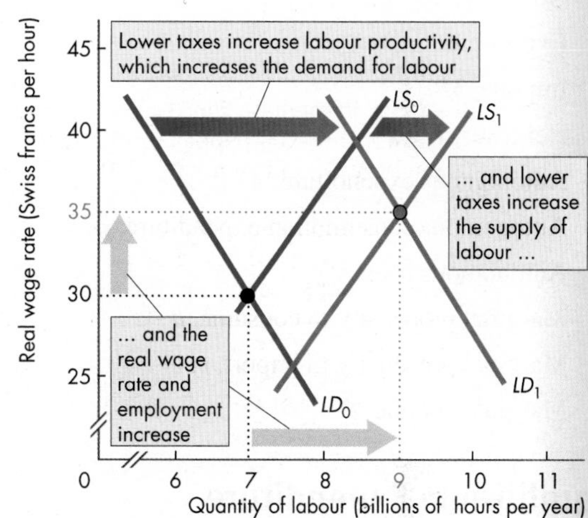

Figure 2 The Swiss labour market

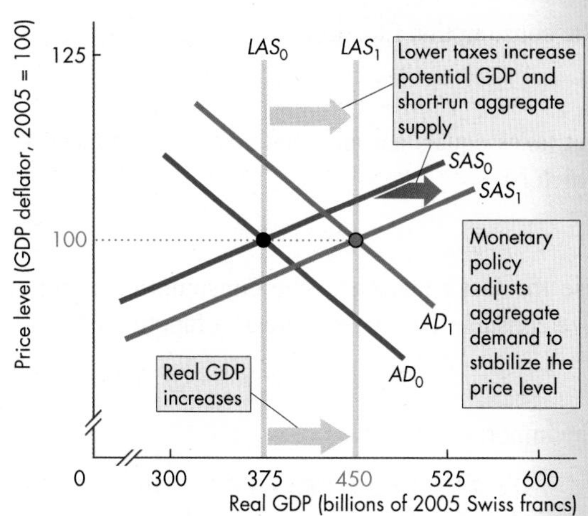

Figure 3 Aggregate demand and aggregate supply in Switzerland

Mathematical Note

The Algebra of the Fiscal Policy Multipliers

This mathematical note derives the formula for the fiscal policy multipliers. We begin by defining the symbols we need:

- Aggregate planned expenditure, AE
- Real GDP, Y
- Consumption expenditure, C
- Investment, I
- Government expenditure, G
- Exports, X
- Imports, M
- Net taxes, T
- Autonomous expenditure, A
- Autonomous consumption expenditure, a
- Autonomous taxes, T_a
- Marginal propensity to consume, b
- Marginal propensity to import, m
- Marginal tax rate, t

Equilibrium Expenditure

Aggregate planned expenditure is:

$$AE = C + I + G + X - M$$

The consumption function is:

$$C = a + b(Y - T)$$

Net taxes equals autonomous taxes plus induced taxes, which is:

$$T = T_a + tY$$

Use the last equation in the consumption function to give consumption expenditure as a function of GDP:

$$C = a - bT_a + b(1 - t)Y$$

The import function is:

$$M = mY$$

Use the consumption function and the import function to replace C and M in the aggregate planned expenditure equation to obtain:

$$AE = a - bT_a + b(1 - t)Y + I + G + X - mY$$

Collect the terms on the right side of the equation that involve Y to obtain:

$$AE = [a - bT_a + I + G + X] + [b(1 - t) - m]Y$$

Autonomous expenditure (A) is given by:

$$A = a - bT_a + I + G + X$$

so:

$$AE = A + [b(1 - t) - m]Y$$

Equilibrium expenditure occurs when aggregate planned expenditure (AE) equals real GDP (Y). That is:

$$AE = Y$$

To calculate equilibrium expenditure we solve the equation:

$$Y = A + [b(1 - t) - m]Y$$

to obtain:

$$Y = \frac{1}{1 - [b(1 - t) - m]}A$$

Government Expenditure Multiplier

The government expenditure multiplier equals the change in equilibrium expenditure (Y) that results from a change in government expenditure (G) divided by the change in government expenditure. Because autonomous expenditure is:

$$A = a - bT_a + I + G + X$$

the change in autonomous expenditure equals the change in government expenditure. That is:

$$\Delta A = \Delta G$$

The government expenditure multiplier is found by working out the change in Y that results from the change in A. You can see from the solution for Y that:

$$\Delta Y = \frac{1}{1 - [b(1 - t) - m]}\Delta G$$

The government expenditure multiplier equals:

$$\frac{1}{1 - [b(1 - t) - m]}$$

In an economy in which $t = 0$ and $m = 0$, the government expenditure multiplier is $1/(1 - b)$. With $b = 0.75$, the government expenditure multiplier equals 4, as part (a) of the figure shows. Make up some examples and use the above formula to show how b, m and t influence the government expenditure multiplier.

Autonomous Tax Multiplier

The autonomous tax multiplier equals the change in equilibrium expenditure (Y) that results from a change in autonomous taxes (T_a) divided by the change in autonomous taxes. Because autonomous expenditure is:

$$A = a - bT_a + I + G + X$$

the change in autonomous expenditure equals *minus b* multiplied by the change in autonomous taxes. That is:

$$\Delta A = -b\Delta T_a$$

You can see from the solution for Y that:

$$\Delta Y = \frac{-b}{1 - [b(1 - t) - m]} \Delta T_a$$

The autonomous tax multiplier equals:

$$\frac{-b}{1 - [b(1 - t) - m]}$$

In an economy in which $t = 0$ and $m = 0$, the autonomous tax multiplier is $-b/(1 - b)$. With $b = 0.75$, the autonomous tax multiplier equals -3, as part (b) of the figure shows. Make up some examples and use the above formula to show how b, m and t influence the autonomous tax multiplier.

Balanced Budget Multiplier

The balanced budget multiplier equals the change in equilibrium expenditure that results from a fiscal policy action that changes *both* government expenditure and taxes by the *same* amount so that the government's budget balance remains *unchanged*.

If government expenditure increase by ΔG and autonomous taxes increase by ΔT_a and $\Delta G = \Delta T_a$, then the budget balance does not change.

The change in government expenditure (ΔG) changes equilibrium expenditure (Y) by:

$$\Delta Y = \frac{1}{1 - [b(1 - t) - m]} \Delta G$$

and the change in autonomous taxes (ΔT_a) changes equilibrium expenditure (Y) by:

$$\Delta Y = \frac{-b}{1 - [b(1 - t) - m]} \Delta T_a$$

So when government expenditure and taxes change together, the change in equilibrium expenditure is:

$$\Delta Y = \frac{1}{1 - [b(1 - t) - m]} \Delta G + \frac{-b}{1 - [b(1 - t) - m]} \Delta T_a$$

But $\Delta G = \Delta T_a$, so:

$$\Delta Y = \frac{1 - b}{1 - [b(1 - t) - m]} \Delta G$$

The balanced budget multiplier is:

$$\frac{1 - b}{1 - [b(1 - t) - m]}$$

In an economy in which $t = 0$ and $m = 0$, the balanced budget multiplier is $(1 - b)/(1 - b)$, which equals 1.

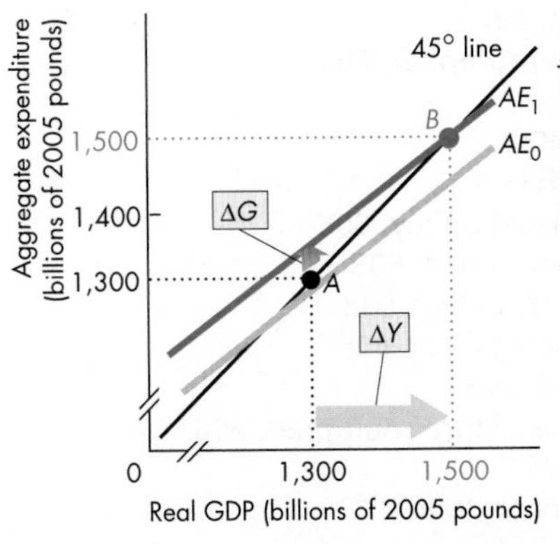

(a) Government expenditure multiplier

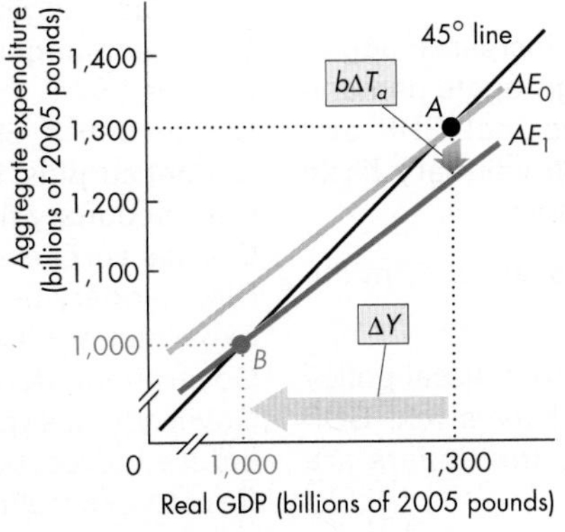

(b) Autonomous tax multiplier

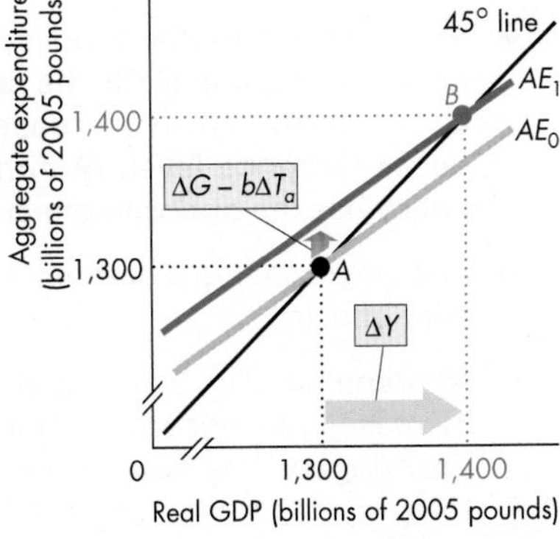

(c) Balanced budget multiplier

Summary

Key Points

Government Budgets (pp. 592–597)

- The government budget finances the activities of the government and is used to conduct fiscal policy.
- Government revenues come from taxes on income and wealth, taxes on expenditure and National Insurance contributions.
- When government outlays exceed revenues, the government has a budget deficit.

Fiscal Policy Multipliers (pp. 598–604)

- Fiscal policy actions are either discretionary or automatic.
- Government expenditure, taxes and transfer payments have multiplier effects on real GDP.
- The government expenditure multiplier equals 1/(1 – Slope of the *AE* curve). The autonomous tax multiplier equals –*MPC*/(1 – Slope of the *AE* curve).
- The autonomous transfer payments multiplier is equal to the magnitude of the tax multiplier but is positive.
- Induced taxes and transfer payments and imports make the fiscal policy multipliers smaller.
- Income taxes and transfer payments act as automatic stabilizers.

Fiscal Policy Multipliers and the Price Level (pp. 604–607)

- An expansionary fiscal policy increases aggregate demand and shifts the aggregate demand curve rightward. It increases real GDP and raises the price level. (A contractionary fiscal policy has the opposite effects.)
- Price level changes dampen fiscal policy multiplier effects.
- At potential GDP, an expansionary fiscal policy increases the price level but leaves real GDP unchanged. The fiscal policy multipliers are zero.

Supply-side Effects of Fiscal Policy (pp. 607–609)

- Fiscal policy has supply-side effects because increases in taxes weaken the incentives to work and save.
- A tax cut increases both aggregate demand and aggregate supply and increases real GDP, but the tax cut has an ambiguous effect on the price level.

Key Figures

Key Terms

Problems

Tests, Study Plan and Solutions* 

1 In the economy of Zap, the marginal propensity to consume is 0.9. Investment is €50 billion, government expenditure on goods and services are €40 billion, and autonomous taxes are €40 billion. Zap has no exports, no imports and no income taxes.

a The government cuts its expenditure on goods and services to €30 billion. What is the change in equilibrium expenditure?

b What is the value of the government expenditure multiplier?

c The government continues to buy €40 billion worth of goods and services and cuts autonomous taxes to €30 billion. What is the change in equilibrium expenditure?

d What is the value of the autonomous tax multiplier?

e The government simultaneously cuts both its expenditure on goods and services and autonomous taxes to €30 billion. What is the change in equilibrium expenditure? Why does equilibrium expenditure decrease?

f If the government wants to increase equilibrium expenditure by €500 billion, but wants to keep its budget balanced, by how much must it increase its expenditures and taxes?

2 Suppose that the price level in the economy of Zap as described in problem 1 is 100. The economy is also at full employment.

a If the government of Zap increases its expenditure on goods and services by €10 billion, what happens to the quantity of real GDP demanded?

b How does Zap's aggregate demand curve change? Draw a two-part graph that is similar to Figure 26.9 to illustrate the change in both the *AE* curve and the *AD* curve.

c In the short run, does equilibrium real GDP increase by more than, less than or the same amount as the increase in the quantity of real GDP demanded?

d In the long run, does equilibrium real GDP increase by more than, less than or the same amount as the increase in the quantity of real GDP demanded?

e In the short run, does the price level in Zap rise, fall or remain unchanged?

f In the long run, does the price level in Zap rise, fall or remain unchanged?

3 The figure shows revenues and outlays of the government of Dreamland. Potential GDP is £40 million.

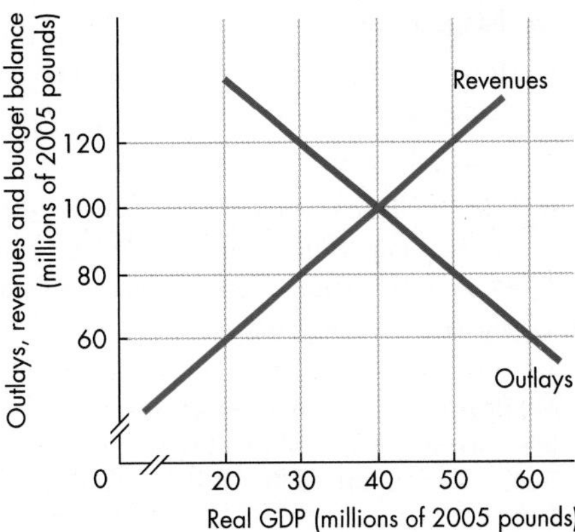

a What is the government's budget balance if real GDP is £40 million?

b Does Dreamland have a structural surplus or deficit if its real GDP is £40 million? What is its size? Explain why.

c What is the government's budget balance if real GDP is £30 million?

d If Dreamland's real GDP is £30 million, does Dreamland have a structural surplus or deficit? What is its size? Explain why.

e If Dreamland's real GDP is £50 million, does Dreamland have a structural surplus or deficit? What is its size? Explain why.

4 The economy is in a recession, and the recessionary gap is large.

a Describe the discretionary and automatic fiscal policy actions that might occur.

b Describe a discretionary fiscal stimulation package that could be used that would not bring a budget deficit.

c Explain the risks of discretionary fiscal policy in this situation.

5 The government is proposing to increase the tax rate on labour income and asks you to report on the supply-side effects of such an action. Answer the following questions using appropriate diagrams. You are being asked about directions of change, not exact magnitudes.

a What will happen to the supply of labour and why?

b What will happen to the demand for labour and why?

---

* Solutions to odd-numbered problems are provided.

c How will the equilibrium level of employment change and why?

d How will the equilibrium before-tax wage rate change and why?

e How will the equilibrium after-tax wage rate change and why?

f What will happen to potential GDP?

g What evidence would you present to the government to support the view that a lower tax on labour income will increase employment, potential GDP and aggregate supply?

6 Suppose that in China in 2008, investment is £400 billion, saving is £400 billion, tax revenues are £500 billion, exports are £300 billion, and imports are £200 billion.

a Calculate government expenditure.

b What is the government budget balance?

c Is the government exerting a positive or negative impact on investment?

7 The economy is in a recession, the recessionary gap is large and there is a budget deficit.

a Do we know whether the budget deficit is structural or cyclical? Explain your answer.

b Do we know whether automatic stabilizers are increasing or decreasing aggregate demand? Explain your answer.

c If a discretionary increase in government expenditure occurs, what happens to the structural deficit or surplus? Explain.

8 The economy is in a boom, the inflationary gap is large and there is a budget deficit.

a Do we know whether the budget deficit is structural or cyclical? Explain your answer.

b Do we know whether automatic stabilizers are increasing or decreasing aggregate demand? Explain your answer.

c If a discretionary decrease in government expenditure occurs, what happens to the structural deficit or surplus? Explain your answer.

Critical Thinking

1 Study *Reading Between the Lines* on pp. 610–611 and then answer the following questions.

a What policy has the local governments of Switzerland conducted to keep local fiscal policy efficient?

b Why have firms in the European Union and elsewhere relocated to Switzerland?

c What is the economic argument for the type of supply-side policy conducted by the local Swiss authorities?

d If the supply-side policy in Switzerland is successful what do you expect to happen to real GDP in Switzerland and the EU countries in the long run?

e In the long run, is the multiplier in Switzerland zero or positive?

Web Activities

Links to Websites

1 Obtain data on the components of government outlays in the main industrial countries. Then use the fiscal policy multiplier to predict which countries have strong automatic stabilizers and which have weak ones. Explain the reasons for your predictions.

2 Visit the HM Treasury Website and obtain the most recent data you can find on the revenues, outlays, and budget surplus or deficit for the United Kingdom.

a Compare the data you obtain with that in Table 26.1.

b Is the most recent budget more or less expansionary than that in Table 26.1? Explain why.

c Predict the effects of the most recent budget on real GDP and the price level.

CHAPTER 27

The Monetary System

After studying this chapter you will be able to:

- Define money and describe its functions
- Explain the economic functions of banks and other financial institutions
- Describe the functions of the central bank
- Explain how the banking system creates money
- Explain what determines the demand for money
- Explain how the quantity of money and interest rate are determined

Money Makes the World Go Round

When you want to buy something, you use coins, notes, write a cheque, or present a debit or credit card. Are all these things money? When you deposit some coins or notes in the bank, is it still money? What happens when the bank lends your money to someone else? How can you still get it back if it's been lent out? Why does the amount of money in the economy matter? How does it affect the interest rate? You can find the answers in this chapter. And in *Reading Between the Lines* at the end of the chapter, you can see how electronic money is changing the way we do business with each other.

What Is Money?

What do cowrie shells, wampum, whales' teeth, tobacco, cattle and pennies have in common? The answer is that all of them are (or have been) forms of money. **Money** is any commodity or token that is generally acceptable as a means of payment. A **means of payment** is a method of settling a debt. When a payment has been made there is no remaining obligation between the parties to a transaction. So what cowrie shells, wampum, whales' teeth, cattle and pennies have in common is that they have served (or still do serve) as the means of payment. But money has three other functions as:

- A medium of exchange
- A unit of account
- A store of value

Medium of Exchange

A *medium of exchange* is an object that is generally accepted in exchange for goods and services. Money acts as such a medium. Without money, it would be necessary to exchange goods and services directly for other goods and services – an exchange called **barter**. Barter requires a *double coincidence of wants*, a situation that rarely occurs. For example, if you want a pizza, you might offer a CD in exchange for it. But you must find someone who is selling pizza and who wants your CD.

A medium of exchange overcomes the need for a double coincidence of wants. And money acts as a medium of exchange because people with something to sell will always accept money in exchange for it. But money isn't the only medium of exchange. You can buy with a credit card. But a credit card isn't money. It doesn't make a final payment and the debt it creates must eventually be settled by using money.

Unit of Account

A *unit of account* is an agreed measure for stating the prices of goods and services. To get the most out of your budget you have to work out, among other things, whether seeing one more film is worth the price you have to pay, not in pounds and pence, but in terms of the number of ice creams, beers or cups of tea that you have to give up. It's easy to do such calculations when all these goods have prices in terms of pounds and pence (see Table 27.1). If a cinema ticket costs £4 and a pint of beer in the Students' Union costs £1, you know straight away that seeing one more film costs you 4 pints of beer. If a cup of tea costs 50 pence, one more cinema ticket costs 8 cups of tea. You need only one calculation to work out the opportunity cost of any pair of goods and services.

But imagine how troublesome it would be if your local cinema posted its price as 4 pints of beer; and if the Students' Union announced that the price of a pint of beer was 2 ice creams; and if the corner shop posted the price of an ice cream as 1 cup of tea; and if the café priced a cup of tea as 5 rolls of mints!

Now how much running around and calculating do you have to do to work out how much that film is going to cost you in terms of the beer, ice cream, tea or mints that you must give up to see it? You get the answer for beer from the sign posted at the cinema, but for all the other goods you're going to have to visit many different shops to establish the prices you need to work out the opportunity costs you face.

Cover up the column labelled "price in money units" in Table 27.1 and see how hard it is to work out the number of local telephone calls it costs to see one film.

It is much simpler for everyone to express their prices in terms of pounds and pence.

Table 27.1

The Unit of Account Function of Money Simplifies Price Comparisons

Good	Price in money units	Price in units of another good
Cinema ticket	£4.00 each	4 pints of beer
Beer	£1.00 per pint	2 ice creams
Ice cream	£0.50 per cone	1 cup of tea
Tea	£0.50 per cup	5 rolls of mints
Mints	£0.10 per roll	1 local phone call

Money as a unit of account. 1 cinema ticket costs £4 and 1 cup of tea costs 50 pence, so a cinema ticket costs 8 cups of tea (£4.00/£0.50 = 8).

No unit of account. You go to a cinema and learn that the price of a ticket is 4 pints of beer. You go to a café and learn that a cup of tea costs 5 rolls of mints. But how many rolls of mints does it cost you to see a film? To answer that question, you go to the Students' Union bar and find that a pint of beer costs 2 ice creams. Now you head for the ice cream shop, where an ice cream costs 1 cup of tea. Now you get out your pocket calculator: 1 cinema ticket costs 4 pints of beer, or 8 ice creams, or 8 cups of tea, or 40 rolls of mints!

Sometimes we use a unit of account that is not money. An example is the European Currency Unit that preceded the euro. Also, the euro existed as a unit of account before it became money – a means of payment – on 1 January 2002.

Store of Value

Money is a *store of value* in the sense that it can be held and exchanged later for goods and services. If money were not a store of value, it could not serve as a means of payment.

Money is not alone in acting as a store of value. A physical object such as a house, a car, a work of art or a computer can act as a store of value. The most reliable and useful stores of value are items that have a stable value. The more stable the value of a commodity or token, the better it can act as a store of value and the more useful it is as money. No store of value has a completely stable value. The value of a house, a car or a work of art fluctuates over time. The value of the commodities and tokens that are used as money also fluctuate over time. And when there is inflation, their values persistently fall.

Because inflation brings a falling value of money, a low inflation rate is needed to make money as useful as possible as a store of value.

Money in the United Kingdom Today

In the United Kingdom today, money consists of:

- Currency
- Deposits at banks and building societies

Currency

The notes and coins that we use in the United Kingdom today are known as **currency**. They are money because the government declares them to be so. The Royal Mint maintains the inventory of coins in circulation and the Bank of England issues notes. (In Scotland and Northern Ireland, private banks also issue notes, but they must hold £1 of Bank of England notes for every £1 they issue.)

Deposits at Banks and Building Societies

Deposits at banks and building societies are also money. This type of money is an accounting entry in an electronic database in the banks' and building societies' computers. They are money because they can be converted instantly into currency and because they are used directly to settle debts. In fact, deposits are the main means of settling debts in modern societies. The owner of a deposit transfers ownership to another person simply by writing a cheque – an instruction to a bank – that tells the bank to change its database, debiting the account of one depositor and crediting the account of another.

The Official UK Measure of Money

The official measure of money in the United Kingdom today is known as M4. **M4** consists of currency held by the public plus bank deposits and building society deposits. M4 does *not* include currency held by banks and building societies and it does *not* include currency or bank deposits owned by the UK government. Figure 27.1 shows the components that make up M4.

Figure 27.1 myeconlab

The Official UK Measure of Money

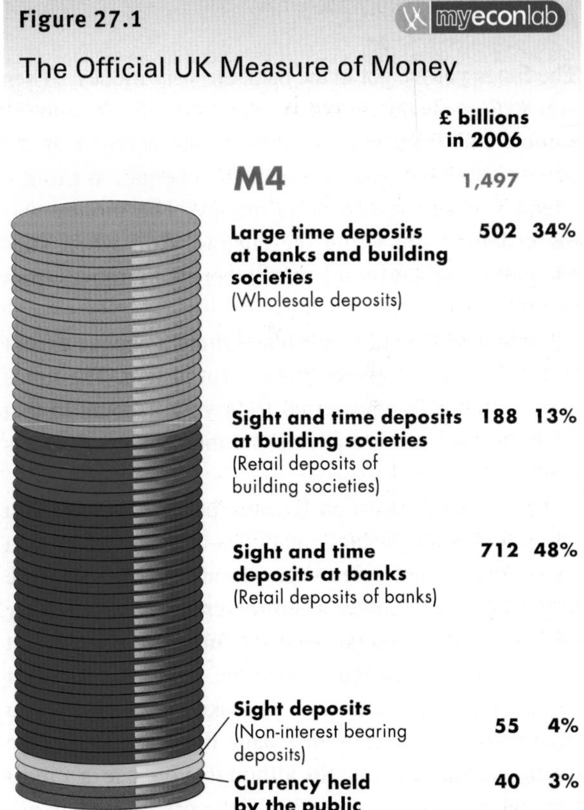

M4 is the official measure of money in the United Kingdom. It is the sum of currency held by the public, bank deposits and building society deposits. Currency represents only 3 per cent of the money in the UK economy.

Source of data: Bank of England.

Are All the Components of M4 Really Money?

Money is the means of payment. So the test of whether something is money is whether it serves as a means of payment. Currency passes the test.

Deposits are divided into two types: sight deposits and time deposits. A *sight deposit* (sometimes called a chequeable deposit) can be transferred from one person to another by writing a cheque or using a debit card. So it is clearly money. A *time deposit* is a deposit that has a fixed term to maturity. Although not usually a chequeable deposit, technological advances in the banking industry have made it easy to switch funds from a time deposit to a sight deposit. Because of the ease with which funds in a time deposit can be switched into a sight deposit, time deposits are included in the definition of money.

Cheques, Debit Cards and Credit Cards Are Not Money

The funds you've got in the bank are your money. When you write a cheque, you are telling your bank to move some funds from your account to the account of the person to whom you've given the cheque. Writing a cheque doesn't create more money. The money was there before you wrote the cheque. And when your cheque is paid, the money is still there but it moves from you to someone else.

Using a debit card is just like writing a cheque except that the transaction takes place in an instant. The funds are electronically transferred from your account to that of the person you are paying the moment your card is read.

A credit card is just an ID card, but one that lets you take a loan at the instant you buy something. When you sign a credit card sales slip, you are saying: "I agree to pay for these goods when the credit card company bills me." Once you get your statement from the credit card company, you must make the minimum payment due (or clear your balance). To make that payment you need money – currency or a bank deposit – to pay the credit card company. So although you use a credit card when you buy something, the credit card is not the *means of payment* and it is not money. The currency or the bank deposit that you use is money.

We've seen that the main component of money is deposits at banks and building societies. These institutions play a crucial role in our economic life and we're now going to examine that role.

Box 27.1
Money in the Eurozone

The official Eurozone measure of money is called M3, but the items included in the Eurozone M3 are very similar to those in M4 in the United Kingdom. Figure 1 shows the numbers. The most interesting feature of euro money is the large amount of currency held by the public, 8 per cent of the total, compared with 3 per cent in the United Kingdom. Think about the reasons for this huge difference!

Figure 1

Official Eurozone Measure of Money

	€ billions in 2006	
M3	7,711	
Marketable instruments	1080	14%
Time deposits	2,930	38%
Sight deposits	3,084	40%
Currency held by the public	617	8%

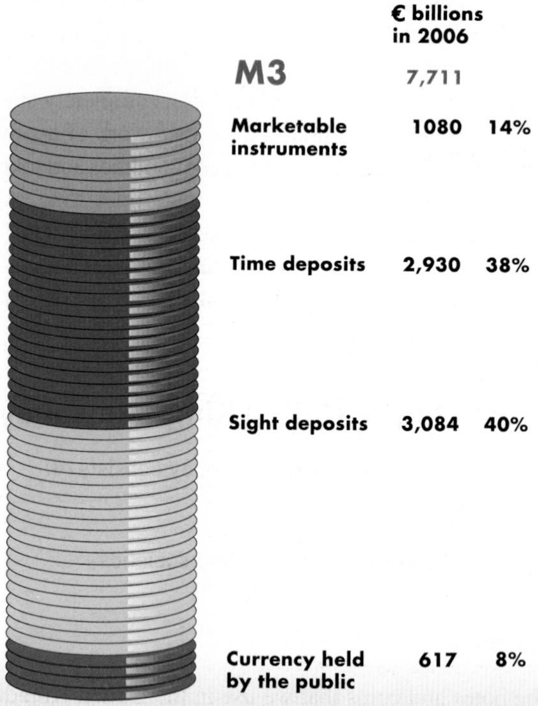

Source of data: European Central Bank.

Review Quiz

Study Plan 27.1

1. What makes something money? What are the functions that money performs? Why do you think Polo mints don't serve as money?
2. What are the largest components of money in the United Kingdom and in the Eurozone today?
3. Are all the components of M4 really money?
4. Why are cheques, debit cards and credit cards not money?

Financial Intermediaries

A firm that takes deposits from households and firms and makes loans to other households and firms is called a **financial intermediary**. There are many types of financial intermediary in different countries whose deposits are components of money. In the United Kingdom, the deposits of two financial intermediaries are money:

- Commercial banks
- Building societies

Commercial Banks

A **commercial bank** is a private firm, licensed by the Bank of England under the Banking Act 1987 to take deposits and make loans. Ten large commercial banks and about 200 others had total deposits of more than £1,200 billion in 2006.

Profit and Prudence: A Balancing Act

The aim of a bank is to maximize its net worth – its value to its shareholders. To achieve this objective, a bank makes loans at interest rates higher than those it pays for deposits. But a bank must perform a delicate balancing act. Lending is risky, and the more the bank ties up its deposits in high-risk, high-interest-rate loans, the bigger is its chance of not being able to repay its depositors. And if depositors perceive a high risk of not being repaid, they withdraw their funds and create a crisis for the bank. So a bank must be prudent in the way it uses its deposits, balancing security for the depositors against profit for its shareholders.

Reserves and Loans

To achieve security for its depositors, a bank divides its funds into two parts: reserves and loans. **Reserves** are cash in a bank's vault plus its deposits at the central bank. (The Bank of England is the central bank in the United Kingdom.) The cash in a bank's vaults is a reserve to meet the demands that its customers place on it – it keeps that ATM replenished every time you and your friends need to use it for a midnight pizza. A commercial bank's deposit at the central bank is similar to your deposit at your own bank. Commercial banks use these deposits in the same way as you use your bank account. A commercial bank deposits cash into or draws cash out of its account at the central bank and writes cheques on that account to settle debts with other banks.

If a bank kept all its assets as cash in its vault or as deposits at the central bank, it wouldn't make any profit. In fact it keeps only a small fraction of its funds in reserves and lends the rest. A bank makes three different types of loans, or, equivalently, holds three different types of assets:

1. *Liquid assets* are government Treasury bills and commercial bills. These assets can be sold and instantly converted into cash with virtually no risk of loss. Because liquid assets are virtually risk free, they earn a low interest rate.
2. *Investment securities* are longer-term government bonds and other bonds. These assets can be sold quickly and converted into cash but at prices that fluctuate. Because their prices fluctuate, these assets are riskier than liquid assets and they have a higher interest rate.
3. *Loans* are lines of credit extended to companies to finance the purchase of capital equipment and stocks and to households – personal loans – to finance consumer durable goods, such as cars or boats. The outstanding balances on credit card accounts are also bank loans. Loans are the riskiest assets of a bank because they cannot be converted into cash until they are due to be repaid. And some borrowers default and never repay. Because they are the riskiest of a bank's assets, they carry the highest interest rate.

Commercial bank deposits are one component of money, building society deposits are another.

Building Societies

A **building society** is a private firm licensed under the Building Societies Act 1986 to accept deposits and make loans. In 2006, 60 building societies had total deposits and mortgage loans of about £200 billion.

The main differences between a building society and a bank are that the former are usually owned by their depositors and borrowers (known as *mutuals*), obtain their funds in the form of savings accounts, make long-term loans for house purchases and keep their reserves not at the Bank England but as deposits in commercial banks.

Since the passage of the 1986 Act, building societies have become more like banks and offer a range of financial products that brings them into direct competition with the banks.

The Economic Functions of Financial Intermediaries

All financial intermediaries make a profit from the spread between the interest rate they pay on deposits and the interest rate at which they lend. Why can financial intermediaries borrow at a low interest rate and lend at a higher one? What services do they perform that make their depositors willing to put up with a low interest rate and their borrowers willing to pay a higher one?

Financial intermediaries provide four main services that people are willing to pay for:

- Creating liquidity
- Minimizing the cost of obtaining funds
- Minimizing the cost of monitoring borrowers
- Pooling risk

Creating Liquidity

Financial intermediaries create liquidity. *Liquid* assets are those that are easily and with certainty convertible into money. Some of the liabilities of financial intermediaries are themselves money; others are highly liquid assets that are easily converted into money.

Financial intermediaries create liquidity by borrowing short and lending long. Borrowing short means taking deposits but standing ready to repay them at short notice (and even at no notice in the case of sight deposits). Lending long means making loan commitments for a prearranged, and often quite long, period of time. For example, when a person makes a deposit with a UK building society, that deposit can be withdrawn at any time. But the building society makes a lending commitment for perhaps up to 25 years to a home buyer.

Minimizing the Cost of Obtaining Funds

Finding someone from whom to borrow can be a costly business. Imagine how troublesome it would be if there were no financial intermediaries. A firm that was looking for £1 million to buy a new production plant would probably have to hunt around for several dozen people from whom to borrow in order to acquire enough funds for its capital project. Financial intermediaries lower such costs. A firm needing £1 million can go to a single financial intermediary to obtain those funds. The financial intermediary has to borrow from a large number of people, but it's not doing that just for this one firm and the £1 million it wants to borrow. The financial intermediary can establish an organization capable of raising funds from a large number of depositors and can spread the cost of this activity over a large number of borrowers.

Minimizing the Cost of Monitoring Borrowers

Lending money is a risky business. There's always a danger that the borrower may not repay. Most of the money lent gets used by firms to invest in projects that they hope will return a profit. But sometimes these hopes are not fulfilled. Checking up on the activities of a borrower and ensuring that the best possible decisions are being made for making a profit and avoiding a loss is a costly and specialized activity. Imagine how costly it would be if each and every household that lent money to a firm had to incur the costs of monitoring that firm directly. By depositing funds with a financial intermediary, households avoid those costs. The financial intermediary performs the monitoring activity by using specialized resources that have a much lower cost than that which each household would incur if it had to undertake the activity individually.

Pooling Risk

As we noted above, lending money is risky. There is always a chance that it will not be repaid – of default. The risk of default can be reduced by lending to a large number of different individuals. In such a situation, if one person defaults on a loan it is a nuisance but not a disaster. In contrast, if only one person borrows and that person defaults on the loan, the entire loan is a write-off. Financial intermediaries enable people to pool risk in an efficient way. Thousands of people lend money to any one financial intermediary and, in turn, the financial intermediary re-lends the money to hundreds, and perhaps thousands, of individual firms. If any one firm defaults on its loan, that default is spread across all the depositors with the intermediary and no individual depositor is left exposed to a high degree of risk.

Review Quiz

Study Plan 27.2

1. What is a financial intermediary?
2. What are the three main types of assets held by banks?
3. What are the main economic functions of a financial intermediary?

Central Banking

A central bank is a public authority that provides banking services to governments and commercial banks, supervises and regulates financial institutions and markets and conducts monetary policy. *Monetary policy* is the attempt to control inflation, moderate the business cycle and provide the foundation for sustained economic growth by influencing the quantity of money, interest rates and the exchange rate. We study monetary policy in Chapter 28. Our aim in this chapter is to learn about the role of a central bank in the process of creating and influencing the quantity of money and the interest rate. We'll briefly describe two central banks:

- The Bank of England
- The European Central Bank

The Bank of England

The **Bank of England** is the central bank of the United Kingdom. It was established by Parliament in 1694 in a deal between a syndicate of wealthy individuals and the government of King William and Queen Mary. The syndicate lent the government £1.2 million in return for the right to issue bank notes. And so the Bank of England notes we use today were born.

The Bank of England was not formally recognized as the central bank until the passage of the Bank of England Act of 1946, which took the Bank into public ownership. For the next 50 years, the government of the day made monetary policy decisions and the Bank of England implemented them. In April 1997, the Bank was given independence to determine monetary policy, subject to objectives determined by the government.

The European Central Bank

The **European Central Bank (ECB)** is the central bank of the Eurozone – the members of the European Union that use the euro as their currency. The ECB was established on 1 June 1998.

National central banks, the largest of which are the Banque de France, Deutsche Bundesbank and Banca d'Italia, provide banking services to their governments and commercial banks and supervise and regulate their national financial institutions and markets. The Executive Board of the ECB together with the Governors of the national central banks of the Eurozone constitute the Governing Council, which is the highest decision-making body in the ECB. Through this membership of the Governing Council, national central banks play a role in setting Eurozone monetary policy.

What are the functions of a central bank?

The Functions of a Central Bank

In describing the functions of a central bank, we will focus on the Bank of England. All central banks have similar functions but in the European Union, as just noted, central banking functions are distributed across the ECB and the former national central banks.

In addition to its monetary policy role that we study in the next chapter, a central bank performs the following functions:

- Government's bank
- Bankers' bank

Government's Bank

The Bank of England provides banking services to the government of the United Kingdom similar to those that HSBC provides to its customers. When you pay your taxes, the funds go into a government deposit account at the Bank of England. When the Department of Health buys a batch of flu shots, it pays by writing a cheque on a Bank of England account.

The Bank offers a service to the government that you'd love your bank to do for you: it manages all the government borrowing. It performs this role by selling government bonds. You will see soon that the Bank of England's actions in the market for government bonds plays a central role in its influence on the quantity of money and the interest rate.

Bankers' Bank

The Bank of England provides banking services to HSBC similar to those that HSBC provides to its customers. A commercial bank keeps some of its reserves as deposits at the central bank. The commercial bank uses these funds to settle debts with other banks. It also withdraws currency when it needs additional funds to top up its cash dispensers.

The Bank of England does *not* provide banking services for businesses and individual citizens.

To appreciate the tools available to the Bank of England to influence the quantity of money, we must first learn about its financial structure, summarized in its balance sheet.

The Bank of England's Balance Sheet

Table 27.1 shows the Bank of England's balance sheet – a statement of the Bank's liabilities and assets. Its largest liability is notes held by the public. These are the £5, £10, £20 and £50 notes that we use in our cash transactions. Some of these notes are part of *currency* – a component of the M4 definition of money (see p. 619). And some of them are in the tills and vaults of the commercial banks – part of the banks' reserves.

The Bank of England's other liability is the reserves of commercial banks.

The liabilities of the Bank of England plus the coins issued by the Royal Mint make up the **monetary base**. Coins are part of the monetary base but do not appear in the Bank of England balance sheet because the Royal Mint, which issues coins, is a branch of the government and not a part of the Bank of England.

The Bank's main assets are government bonds and loans to banks under repurchase agreements. Under a repurchase agreement – known as **repo** – a commercial bank sells a government bond to the Bank of England and simultaneously agrees to repurchase it (buy it back) at a higher price usually two weeks later. This type of agreement is a major source of reserves for the banks.

Let's see how the Bank of England uses the items in its balance as part of its monetary policy tool kit.

The Bank of England's Policy Tools

The Bank of England uses two policy tools to influence the quantity of money and the interest rate. They are:

- Bank Rate
- Open market operations

Table 27.1

Balance Sheet of the Bank of England, 31 January 2007

Assets (billions of pounds)		Liabilities (billions of pounds)	
Government bonds*	13	Notes held by the public	38
Repo loans to banks	45	Bank reserves	20
Total	**58**	**Total**	**58**

*Includes other balancing items. All the data are rounded to the nearest billion pounds.
Source of data: Bank of England.

Bank Rate

Bank Rate is the Bank of England's official interest rate. The Bank pays interest to commercial banks and building societies on their reserve deposits and these institutions pay interest on loans of reserves from the Bank. The interest rates on reserves and loans are linked to Bank Rate.

Bank Rate influences the supply of money. We'll study the details of this influence in the next chapter. Briefly, when the Bank of England raises Bank Rate, other interest rates rise and the quantity of money decreases; and when the Bank lowers Bank Rate, other interest rates fall and the quantity of money increases.

Open Market Operations

An **open market operation** is the purchase or sale of government bonds by the central bank in the open market. The term "open market" refers to commercial banks and the general public but not the government. So when the Bank of England conducts an open market operation, it does a transaction with a bank or some other business but it does not transact with the government.

Open market operations influence the supply of money. We'll study the details of this influence in the next chapter. Briefly, when the central bank sells government bonds it receives payment with bank deposits and bank reserves, which creates tighter monetary and credit conditions. With lower reserves, the banks cut their lending, and the supply of money decreases. When the central bank buys government bonds, it pays for them with bank deposits and bank reserves, which creates looser monetary and credit conditions. With extra reserves, the banks increase their lending and the supply of money increases.

This brief sketch will be expanded in the next section where you will see exactly how the banking system creates money.

Review Quiz

myeconlab

Study Plan 27.3

1. What is a central bank?
2. What are the central banks of the United Kingdom and Eurozone and what functions do they perform?
3. What are the main items in the balance sheet of a central bank?
4. What is the monetary base?
5. What are a central bank's policy tools?

How Banks Create Money

Banks create money.[1] But this doesn't mean that they have smoke-filled back rooms in which counterfeiters are busily working. Remember that most money is deposits, not currency. What banks create is deposits and they do so by making loans.

Creating Deposits by Making Loans

The easiest way to see that banks create deposits is to think about what happens when Helen fills up her car with petrol at a BP service station and pays using her Visa credit card issued by Barclays. When Helen keys in her PIN, she takes a loan from Barclays and obligates herself to repay the loan at a later date. The electronic transfer of funds from Helen's Barclays Visa account to BP's bank is instantaneous. Barclays credits BP's bank account with the value of the sale (less the commission).

You can see that these transactions have created a bank deposit and a loan. Helen has increased the size of her loan (her credit card balance), and BP has increased the size of its bank deposit (minus the bank's commission). And because deposits are money, this transaction has created money.

If Helen and BP use the same bank, no further transactions take place. But the outcome is essentially the same when two banks are involved. If BP's bank is the Royal Bank of Scotland, then Barclays uses its reserves to pay the Royal Bank.

Barclays still has an increase in loans but now it has a decrease in its reserves at the Bank of England; the Royal Bank of Scotland has an increase in its reserves at the Bank of England and an increase in deposits.

The banking system as a whole has an increase in loans and deposits and no change in reserves.

You know that the interest rate that banks pay on deposits is much less than what they receive on loans. So creating deposits by making loans is a profitable business. What keeps this business in check?

Three factors limit the quantity of loans and deposits that the banking system can create:

- The monetary base
- Desired reserves
- Desired currency holdings

[1] In this section, we'll use the term *banks* to refer to commercial banks and building societies – the financial intermediaries whose deposits are money.

The Monetary Base

You've seen that the *monetary base* is the sum of Bank of England notes and banks' deposits at the Bank of England – the Bank of England's liabilities – plus coins issued by the Royal Mint. The size of the monetary base limits the total quantity of money that the banking system can create because banks have a desired level of reserves, households and firms have a desired level of currency holding and both of these desired holdings of the monetary base depend on the quantity of money.

Desired Reserves

A bank's *actual reserves* consist of the currency in its vaults and its deposit at the Bank of England. A bank uses its reserves to meet depositors' demand for currency and to make payments to other banks.

You've seen that banks don't have £100 in notes for every £100 that people have deposited with them. In fact, a typical bank today has about 60 pence in currency and another 26 pence on deposit at the central bank, a total reserve of less than £1, for every £100 deposited in it. But there is no need for panic. These reserve levels are adequate for ordinary business needs.

The fraction of a bank's total deposits that are held in reserves is called the **reserve ratio**. The value of the reserve ratio is influenced by the actions of a bank's depositors. If a depositor withdraws currency from a bank, the reserve ratio decreases. If a depositor puts currency into a bank, the reserve ratio increases.

The **required reserve ratio** is the ratio of reserves to deposits that banks are required, by regulation, to hold. A bank's **desired reserve ratio** is the ratio of reserves to deposits that banks consider to be prudent to hold. A bank's desired reserve ratio exceeds the required reserve ratio. A bank's desired reserves are equal to its deposits multiplied by the desired reserve ratio. Actual *reserves* minus *desired reserves* are **excess reserves**. Whenever banks have excess reserves, they are able to create money. Banks increase their loans and deposits when they have excess reserves and they decrease their loans and deposits when they are short of reserves.

But the greater the desired reserve ratio, the smaller is the quantity of deposits and money that the banking system can create from a given amount of monetary base.

Desired Currency Holdings

People hold money in the form of currency and deposits. The proportion of money held as currency is not a constant but at any point in time people have a definite view as to how much currency they want to hold based on their desired expenditure plans.

In 2006, for every pound of bank deposits 5 pence was held as currency. If building society deposits are included then the amount of currency held for every pound of deposits is only 3 pence.

Because people want to hold some money in the form of currency, when the total quantity of deposits increases, so does the quantity of currency that people want to hold. So currency leaves the banks and building societies when loans are made and deposits increase. We call the leakage of currency from the banking (building societies) system the *currency drain*. We call the ratio of currency to deposits the **currency drain ratio**.

The greater the currency drain ratio, the smaller is the quantity of deposits and the smaller is the quantity of money created by the banks and building societies from a given amount of monetary base.

The Money Creation Process

The money creation process begins when the monetary base increases and the banking system has excess reserves. These excess reserves come from a purchase of securities by the Bank of England from a bank. (Chapter 28, pp. 646–647, explains exactly how the Bank of England conducts such a purchase.)

When the Bank of England buys securities from a bank, the bank's reserves increase but its deposits do not change. So the bank has excess reserves. It lends those excess reserves and a sequence of events then plays out.

The sequence, which Figure 27.2 illustrates, keeps repeating until all the reserves are desired and no excess reserves are being held. The sequence has the following nine steps:

1 Banks have excess reserves.
2 Banks lend excess reserves.
3 Bank deposits increase.
4 The quantity of money increases.
5 New money is used to make payments.
6 Some of the new money remains on deposit.
7 Some of the new money is a currency drain.
8 Desired reserves increase because deposits increase.
9 Excess reserves decrease but remain positive.

Figure 27.2

myeconlab

How the Banking System Creates Money by Making Loans

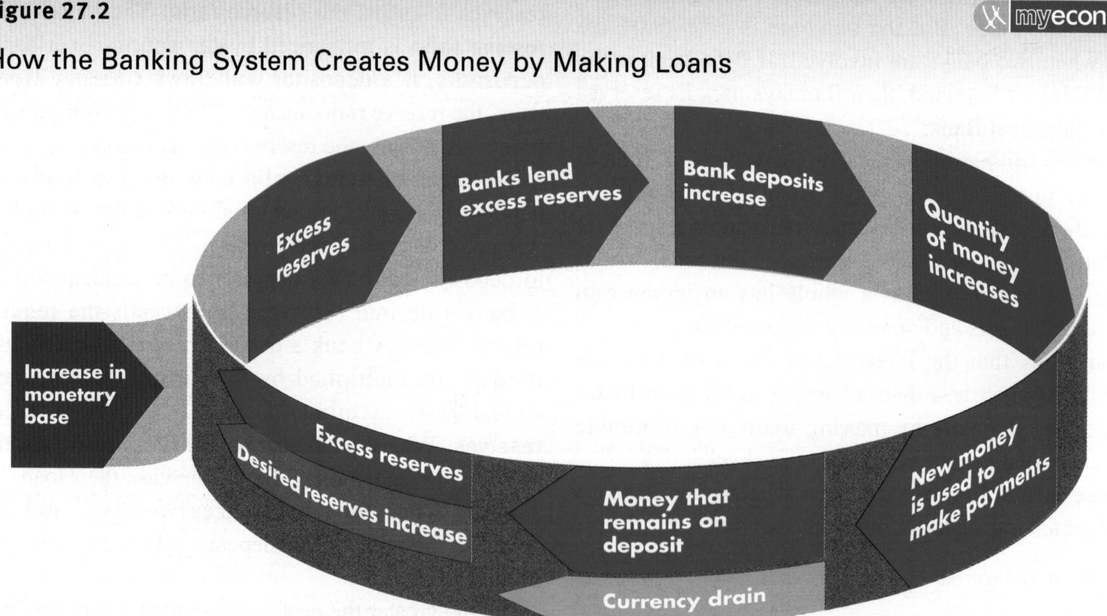

The Bank of England increases the monetary base, which increases bank reserves and creates excess reserves. Banks lend the excess reserves, new bank deposits are created and the quantity of money increases. New money is used to make payments. Some of the new money remains on deposit at banks and some leaves the banks in a currency drain. The increase in bank deposits increases banks' desired reserves. But the banks still have excess reserves, though less than before. The process repeats until excess reserves have been eliminated.

The sequence repeats in a series of rounds, but each round begins with a smaller quantity of excess reserves than did the previous one. The process continues until excess reserves have finally been eliminated.

To make the process of money creation more concrete, let's work through an example for a banking system in which each bank has a desired reserve ratio of 10 per cent (or 0.1) and the currency drain ratio is 50 per cent (or 0.5). Although these ratios are larger than the ones in the UK economy, they make the process end more quickly and enable you to see more clearly the principles at work.

Figure 27.3 keeps track of the numbers. The process begins when all the banks have zero excess reserves except one bank, Suppose it has excess reserves of £100,000. When the bank lends £100,000 of excess reserves, £66,667 remains in the banks as deposits and £33,333 drains off and is held outside the banks as currency. The quantity of money has now increased by £100,000 – the increase in deposits plus the increase in currency.

The increased bank deposits of £66,667 generate an increase in desired reserves of 10 per cent of that amount, which is £6,667. Actual reserves have increased by the same amount as the increase in deposits – £66,667. So the banks now have excess reserves of £60,000. At this stage we have gone around the circle shown in Figure 27.2 once. The process we've just described repeats but begins with excess reserves of £60,000. Figure 27.3 shows the next two rounds. At the end of the process, the quantity of money has increased by £250,000, which is 2.5 times the increase in the monetary base.

The Money Multiplier

The sequence in Figure 27.3 is the first four stages of a process that eventually reaches the totals shown in the final row running tally. To figure out the entire process, look closely at the numbers in the figure. The initial increase in reserves is £100,000 (call it A). At each stage, the loan is 60 per cent (0.6) of the previous loan and the quantity of money increases by 0.6 of the previous increase. Call that proportion L ($L = 0.6$).

Figure 27.3

The Money Creation Process: An Example

Reserves	Deposits	Currency	Money
	£66,667	£33,333	£100,000
£6,667	£106,667	£53,333	£160,000
£10,667	£130,667	£65,333	£196,000
•	•	•	•
£16,667	£166,667	£83,333	£250,000

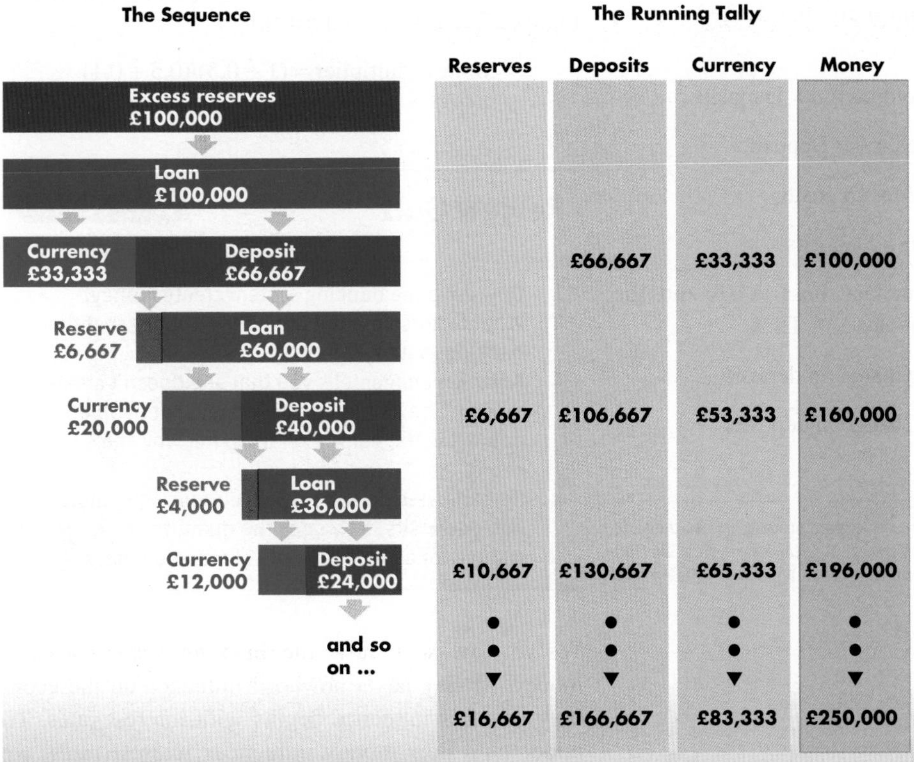

A £100,000 increase in monetary base brings excess reserves. The banks lend those reserves: £33,333 (50 per cent of deposits) leaves the banks in a currency drain and £66,667 remains on deposit. With additional deposits, desired reserves increase by £6,667 (10 per cent) and the banks lend £60,000. The currency drain is £20,000 and £40,000 remains on deposit. The process repeats until the banks have created enough deposits to eliminate their excess reserves. An additional £100,000 of reserves creates £250,000 of money.

We can write down the complete sequence as an equation:

$$A + AL + AL^2 + AL^3 + AL^4 + AL^5 + \ldots$$

Remember, L is a fraction, so at each stage in this sequence the amount of new loans gets smaller. The total number of loans made at the end of the process is the above sum which is[2]:

$$A/(1 - L)$$

If we use the numbers from the example, A = £100,000 and L = 0.6, the total of loans are £100,000/(0.4), which equals £250,000.

The **money multiplier** is the ratio of the change in the quantity of money to the change in monetary base. Here, the monetary base increased by £100,000 and the quantity of money increased by £250,000 so the money multiplier is 2.5.

The magnitude of the money multiplier depends on the desired reserve ratio and the currency drain ratio. Call the monetary base MB and the quantity of money M. When there are no excess reserves,

$$MB = \text{Desired currency holding} + \text{Desired reserves}$$

Also,

$$M = \text{Deposits} + \text{Desired currency holding}$$

Call the currency drain ratio a and the desired reserve ratio b. Then:

$$\text{Desired currency holding} = a \times \text{Deposits}$$

$$\text{Desired reserves} = b \times \text{Deposits}$$

$$MB = (a + b) \times \text{Deposits}$$

$$M = (1 + a) \times \text{Deposits}$$

Call the change in monetary base ΔMB and the change in the quantity of money ΔM. Then:

$$\Delta MB = (a + b) \times \text{Change in deposits}$$

$$\Delta M = (1 + a) \times \text{Change in deposits}$$

[2] Both here and in the expenditure multiplier process in Chapter 25, the sequence of values is called a convergent geometric series. To find the sum of such a series, begin by calling the sum S. Then write out the sum as:

$$S = A + AL + AL^2 + AL^3 + \ldots$$

Multiply by L to give:

$$LS = AL + AL^2 + AL^3 + \ldots$$

and then subtract the second equation from the first to give:

$$S(1 - L) = A \text{ and } S = A/(1 - L)$$

Box 27.2

The UK Money Multiplier

In the United Kingdom in 2007, the monetary base was £60 billion and M4 was £1,500 billion, so M4 was 25 times monetary base. Currency was £40 billion, bank reserves were £20 billion and deposits in M4 were £1,460 billion. So the currency drain ratio, a, was 0.0274 (2.74 per cent) and the bank's reserve ratio, b, was 0.0137 (1.37 per cent). Using these numbers in the formula for the money multiplier gives:

$$\text{Money multiplier} = (1 + 0.0274)/(0.0274 + 0.0137)$$
$$= 25$$

That is, a £1 million change in the monetary base brings approximately a £25 million change in M4. The UK money multiplier is about 25.

Divide the above equation for ΔM by the one for ΔMB, and you see that the money multiplier, which is the ratio of ΔM to ΔMB, is:

$$\text{Money multiplier} = (1 + a)/(a + b)$$

If we use the values of the example summarized in Figure 27.3, $a = 0.5$ and $b = 0.1$:

$$\text{Money multiplier} = (1 + 0.5)/(0.5 + 0.1)$$
$$= 1.5/0.6 = 2.5$$

Review Quiz

Study Plan 27.4

1 How does the banking system create money?
2 What factors limit the quantity of money that the banking system can create?
3 A bank manager tells you that she doesn't create money. She just lends the money that people deposit in the bank. Explain to her why she's wrong.
4 If people decide to hold less currency and more bank deposits, how does the quantity of money change for a given quantity of monetary base?

We've now seen how the banking system creates money. Money has a powerful influence on the economy and this influence begins with interest rates. To understand how money influences interest rates, we must study the demand for money.

The Demand for Money

The amount of money we *receive* each week in payment for our labour is income – a flow. The amount of money that we hold in our wallets or in a sight deposit account at our local bank is an inventory – a stock. There is no limit to how much income – a flow – we would like to receive each week. But there is a limit to how big a stock of money each of us would like to hold, on average.

The Influences on Money Holding

The quantity of money that people choose to hold depends on four main factors. They are:

- The price level
- The interest rate
- Real GDP
- Financial innovation

Let's look at each of them.

The Price Level

The quantity of money measured in current pounds is called the quantity of *nominal money*. The quantity of nominal money demanded is proportional to the price level, other things remaining the same. That is, if the price level (GDP deflator) increases by 10 per cent from 100 to 110, people will want to hold 10 per cent more nominal money than before, other things remaining the same. What matters is not the number of pounds that you hold but their buying power. If you hold £50 to buy your weekly groceries, you will increase your money holding to £55 pounds if the prices of groceries – and your income – increase by 10 per cent.

The quantity of money measured in constant pounds (for example, in 2001 pounds) is called *real money*. Real money is equal to nominal money divided by the price level (multiplied by 100).

The quantity of real money demanded is independent of the price level. In the above example, you held an average of £50 at the original price level. When the price level increased by 10 per cent, you increased your average cash holding by 10 per cent to keep your *real* cash holding constant. Your £55 at the new price level is the same quantity of *real money* as your £50 at the original price level. That is, £50 divided by 1 equals £55 divided by 1.1.

The Interest Rate

A fundamental principle of economics is that as the opportunity cost of something increases, people try to find substitutes for it. Money is no exception. The higher the opportunity cost of holding money, other things remaining the same, the smaller is the quantity of real money demanded.

The interest rate is the opportunity cost of holding money. To see why, recall that the opportunity cost of any activity is the value of the best alternative forgone. The alternative to holding money is holding a savings bond or a Treasury bill that earns interest. By holding money instead, you forgo the interest that you otherwise would have received. This forgone interest is the opportunity cost of holding money.

Money loses value because of inflation. Why isn't the inflation rate part of the cost of holding money? It is. Other things remaining the same, the higher the expected inflation rate, the higher is the interest rate and so the higher is the opportunity cost of holding money.

Real GDP

The quantity of money that households and firms plan to hold depends on the amount they spend, and the quantity of money demanded in the economy as a whole depends on aggregate expenditure – real GDP.

Again, suppose that you hold an average of £50 to finance your weekly purchases of goods. Now imagine that the prices of these goods and of all other goods remain constant, but that your income increases. As a consequence, you now spend more and you also keep a larger amount of money on hand to finance your higher volume of expenditure.

Financial Innovation

Technological change and the arrival of new financial products – called **financial innovation** – change the quantity of money held. The major financial innovations are the widespread use of:

1. Interest-bearing sight deposits
2. Automatic transfers between sight and time deposits
3. Automatic teller machines
4. Credit cards and debit cards

These innovations have occurred because of the development of computing power that has lowered the cost of calculations and record keeping.

The Demand for Money Curve

We summarize the effects of the influences on money holding by using the demand for money curve. The **demand for money** is the relationship between the quantity of real money demanded and the interest rate – the opportunity cost of holding money – all other influences on the amount of money that people wish to hold remaining the same.

Figure 27.4 shows a demand for money curve, *MD*. When the interest rate rises, everything else remaining the same, the opportunity cost of holding money rises and the quantity of money demanded decreases – there is a movement along the demand for money curve. Similarly, when the interest rate falls, the opportunity cost of holding money falls and the quantity of money demanded increases – there is a downward movement along the demand for money curve.

When any influence on the amount of money that people plan to hold changes, there is a change in the demand for money and the demand for money curve shifts. Let's look at these shifts.

Shifts in the Demand for Money Curve

A change in real GDP or a financial innovation changes the demand for money and shifts the demand for money curve. Figure 27.5 illustrates the changes in the demand for money.

A decrease in real GDP decreases the demand for money and shifts the demand curve leftward from MD_0 to MD_1. An increase in real GDP has the opposite effect. It increases the demand for money and shifts the demand curve rightward from MD_0 to MD_2. These changes in the demand for money are similar in magnitude to the changes in real GDP.

The influence of financial innovation on the demand for money curve is more complicated. Financial innovation might increase the demand for some types of deposit and decrease the demand for others and it might decrease the demand for currency.

Box 27.3 looks at the effects of changes in real GDP and financial innovation on the demand for money in the United Kingdom.

Figure 27.4 myeconlab

The Demand for Money

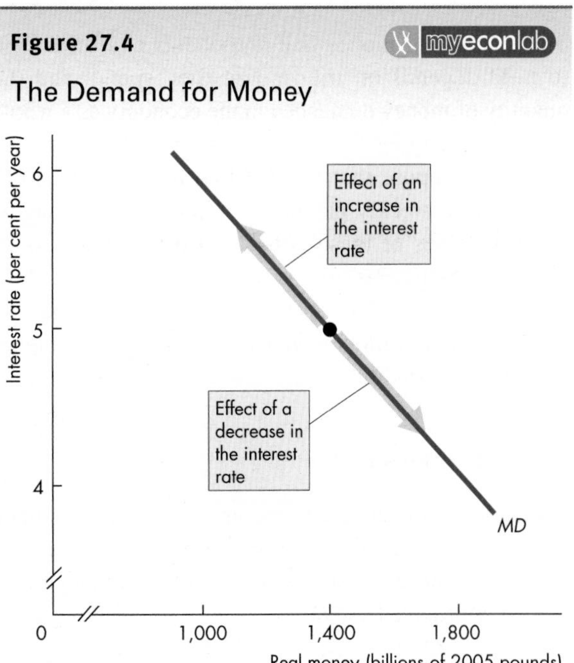

The demand for money curve, *MD*, shows the relationship between the quantity of real money that people plan to hold and the interest rate, other things remaining the same. The interest rate is the opportunity cost of holding money. A change in the interest rate leads to a movement along the demand for money curve.

Figure 27.5 myeconlab

Changes in the Demand for Money

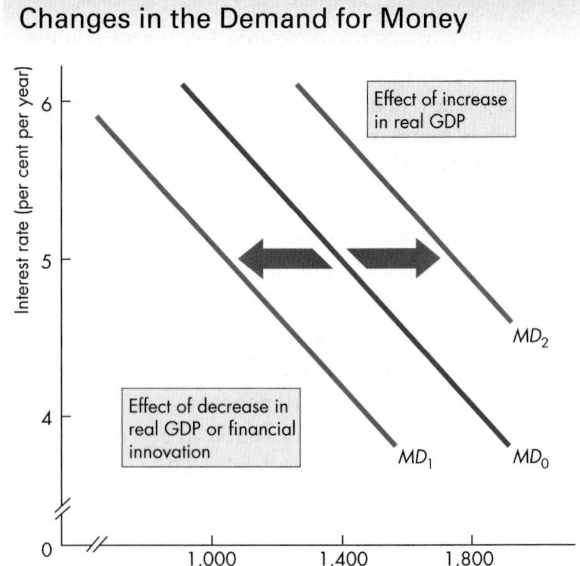

A decrease in real GDP decreases the demand for money and shifts the demand curve leftward from MD_0 to MD_1. An increase in real GDP increases the demand for money and shifts the demand curve rightward from MD_0 to MD_2. Financial innovation can either increase or decrease the demand for money depending on the specific innovation.

Box 27.3
The Demand for Money in the United Kingdom

Figure 1 shows the relationship between the interest rate and the quantity of real M4 money. Each dot shows the interest rate and the amount of real money held in a given year between 1963 and 2003 (with some years identified by two digit numbers).

The figure also shows four demand curves. In 1963, the demand for M4 was MD_{63}. During the rest of the 1960s and the 1970s, the demand for M4 increased and the demand curve shifted rightward to MD_{79}. During the 1980s, the demand for M4 increased further and the demand curve shifted rightward to MD_{89}. The demand for M4 increased yet further during the 1990s and early 2000s when the demand curve shifted rightward to MD_{03}.

These shifts in the demand for M4 money occurred because real GDP increased and because of financial innovation.

On average, with no financial innovation, we would expect the demand for M4 to increase at a rate close to the rate of increase in real GDP.

The magnitude of the increase in the demand for M4 during the 1960s and 1970s was in fact similar to the increase in real GDP.

But during the 1980s, because of financial innovation, the demand for real M4 increased at a pace more than three times that of real GDP as interest-bearing accounts spread. And during the 1990s and early 2000s, the demand for M4 increased at about a half of the increase in real GDP as financial innovations created substitutes for money.

Figure 2 shows the relationship between the interest rate and the demand for real currency. From 1969 to 1979, the demand for currency remained roughly constant at MD_{69}. The positive effects of rising incomes were countered by the negative effects of financial innovation.

Then, during the 1980s and into the 1990s, when the pace of financial innovation increased, the demand for currency decreased and the demand curve shifted leftward to MD_{92}. The financial innovations that increased the demand for M4 decreased the demand for currency.

After 1992, when the pace of financial innovation slowed, rapid income growth increased the demand for currency – the demand curve shifted to MD_{03}.

Figure 1

The Demand for M4 in the United Kingdom

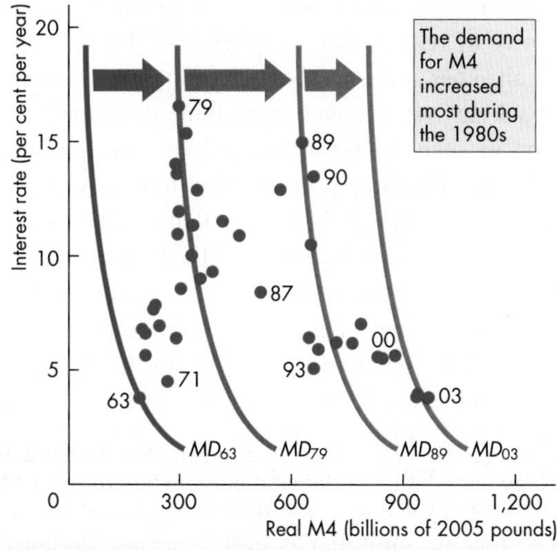

Sources of data: Bank of England and authors' assumptions and calculations.

Figure 2

The Demand for Currency in the United Kingdom

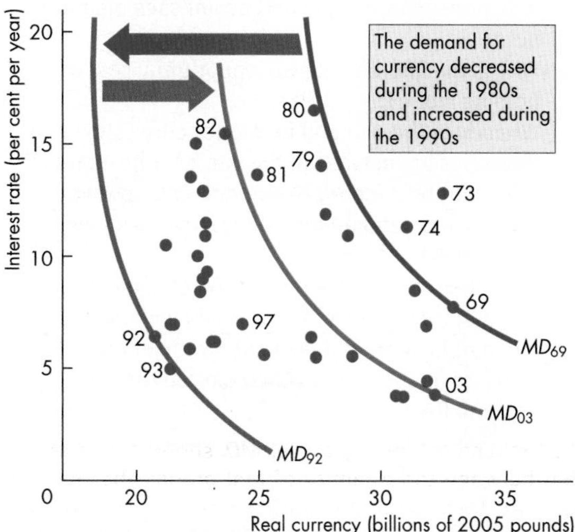

Sources of data: Bank of England and authors' assumptions and calculations.

The Future Demand for Money

How will the demand for money change in the future? The effects of changes in real GDP on the demand for money are predictable. Rising real GDP will, other things remaining the same, bring an increasing demand for money.

But the effects of financial innovation on the future demand for money are difficult to anticipate and predict. Looking back at the 1980s, we see that the introduction of interest-bearing sight deposits and of automatic transfers between sight deposits and time deposits led to a surge in the demand for deposits and so an increase in the demand for M4 – see Box 27.3 (Figure 1) on p. 631.

As people found more convenient means of payment that could earn interest, they also found ways of getting by with less currency in their purses and more plastic to access their bank deposits. The demand for deposits swelled and the demand for currency decreased – see Box 27.3 (Figure 2) on p. 631.

Future advances in information and communication technology are likely to change the demand for money and the demand for its components. New electronic forms of money will replace traditional forms of money in an increasing number of transactions. But there will always be a demand for some form of money.

Review Quiz

Study Plan 27.5

1. What are the main influences on the quantity of real money that people and businesses plan to hold?
2. Why is the interest rate the opportunity cost of holding money?
3. What does the demand for money curve show?
4. How does an increase in the interest rate change the quantity of money demanded and how would you use the demand for money curve to show the effects?
5. How does an increase in real GDP change the demand for money and how would you use the demand for money curve to show the effects?
6. How has financial innovation altered the demand for money?

You now know what determines the demand for money. And you've seen that a key factor is the interest rate – the opportunity cost of holding money. But what determines the interest rate? Let's find out.

Interest Rate Determination

You've seen that the interest rate is the opportunity cost of holding money. You learned in Chapter 3 (p. 58) to think of an opportunity cost as a price. And you also learned how a price is determined in a market. We're now going to see how the interest rate as the opportunity cost (or price) of holding money is determined in the *money market*.

The Money Market

The money market isn't a market in the everyday sense of the word. You don't go to a shop to buy or sell money. But you do demand money – you choose to hold an inventory of currency and bank deposits. The banking system supplies money – the Bank of England supplies currency and the commercial banks and building societies create or supply deposits. So we can think of the demand for money by individuals and firms and the supply of money by banks and other financial institutions as taking place in a market that determines the interest rate.

You've just seen that the quantity of money demanded varies inversely with the interest rate (other things remaining the same) – that the demand for money curve slopes downward. To see how the interest rate is determined, we need to look at the supply of money and equilibrium in the money market.

The Supply of Money

The **supply of money** is the relationship between the quantity of real money supplied and the interest rate with all other influences on the amount of money that the banking system creates remaining the same.

You've seen earlier in this chapter that the banking system creates money by making loans. And you've seen that the amount of money that can be created is limited by the monetary base and the money multiplier.

The greater the monetary base, the greater is the quantity of money that is supplied. The monetary base is determined by decisions of the central bank (the Bank of England in the United Kingdom and the European Central Bank in the Eurozone part of the European Union). You will learn about those decisions in Chapter 28. For now, we'll take the monetary base as given.

The money mulitplier is influenced by the currency drain ratio and the banks' desired reserve ratio. The smaller are either of these ratios, the greater is the money multiplier. What determines these two ratios?

The currency drain ratio is determined mainly by financial technology. It is not very sensitive the interest rate.

The banks' desired reserve ratio is sensitive to the interest rate. The reason is that reserves for a bank play a role similar to that played by money for you. You hold money so that you can make payments. A bank holds reserves so that it can make payments. Banks must pay currency when depositors want to withdraw their funds. And banks must pay other banks when the cheques paid by their customers sum to a greater total than the cheques received by their customers.

A bank's desired reserve (and its desired reserve ratio) is determined in a similar way to your demand for money. The opportunity cost of reserves is the interest rate the bank could earn if it bought a bond or made a loan.

Banks are like all other economic decision makers. They respond to incentives. The higher the interest rate, other things remaining the same, the greater is the percentage of deposits that the banks want to lend and the smaller is the percentage that they want to hold as reserves – the higher the interest rate, the smaller is the desired reserve ratio.

Figure 27.6 myeconlab

The Supply of Money

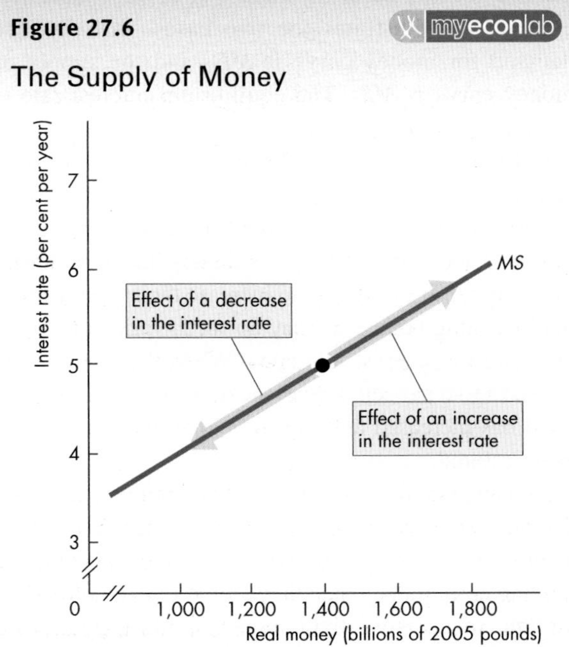

The supply of money curve, *MS*, shows the relationship between the quantity of real money that the banking system supplies and the interest rate, other things remaining the same. A rise in the interest rate – a rise in the opportunity cost of reserves – brings a lower desired reserve ratio and a greater quantity of money supplied.

Because the money multiplier varies inversely with the desired reserve ratio, the higher the interest rate, the greater is the money multiplier and the greater is the quantity of money supplied.

For a given monetary base, the quantity of money supplied increases as the interest rate rises. Figure 27.6 shows that the supply of money curve is upward sloping.

Money Market Equilibrium

Figure 27.7 illustrates money market equilibrium, which determines the interest rate. The demand for money curve is *MD* and the supply of money curve is *MS*.

Equilibrium is achieved by changes in the interest rate. If the interest rate is too high, people demand a smaller quantity of money than the banking system wants to supply. They are holding too much money. In this situation, they try to get rid of money by buying

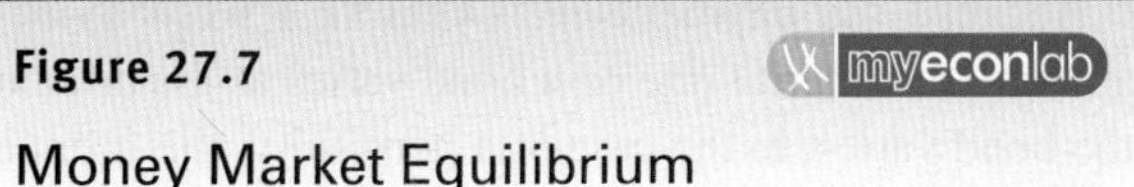

Figure 27.7 myeconlab

Money Market Equilibrium

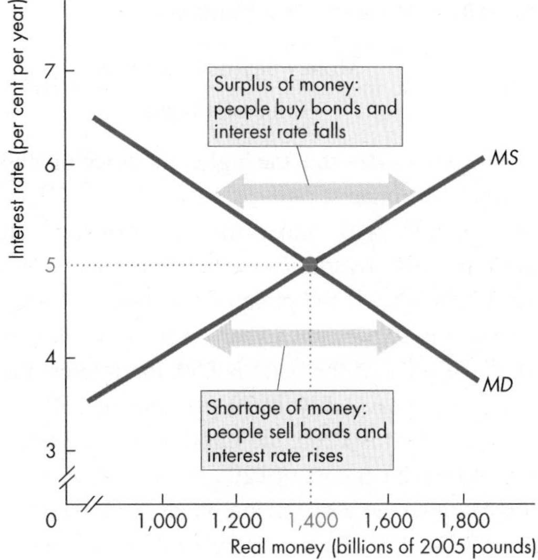

Money market equilibrium occurs when the interest rate has adjusted to make the quantity of money demanded equal to the quantity supplied. Here, equilibrium interest rate is 5 per cent a year. At an interest rate above 5 per cent a year, the quantity of money demanded is less than the quantity supplied, so people buy bonds, and the interest rate falls. At an interest rate below 5 per cent a year, the quantity of real money demanded exceeds the quantity supplied, so people sell bonds and the interest rate rises. Only at 5 per cent a year is the quantity of real money in existence willingly held.

bonds. Conversely, if the interest rate is too low, people demand a larger quantity of money than the quantity that the banking system wants to supply. They are holding too little money. In this situation, they try to get more money by selling bonds.

The Interest Rate and the Price of a Bond

Buying bonds makes the price of a bond rise and selling bonds makes the price of a bond fall. And the interest rate changes in the opposite direction to the price of a bond. Let's see why.

A bond is a promise to make a sequence of future payments. There are many different possible sequences but the simplest one is the case of a bond called a perpetuity – a bond that promises to pay a specified fixed amount of money each year for ever. The issuer of a *perpetuity* will never buy the bond back (redeem it); the bond will remain outstanding for ever and will earn a fixed number of pounds each year.

Because the payment each year is a fixed money amount, the interest rate on a bond varies as the price of the bond varies. In the case of a perpetuity, the formula that links the interest rate to the price of the bond is a particularly simple one. That formula is:

$$\text{Interest rate} = \frac{\text{Money payment per year}}{\text{Price of a bond}} \times 100$$

This formula states that the higher the price of a bond, the lower is the interest rate.

An example will make this relationship clear. Suppose the UK government sells a bond that promises to pay £10 a year. If the price of the bond is £100, the interest rate is 10 per cent a year – £10 is 10 per cent of £100. If the price of the bond is £50, the interest rate is 20 per cent a year – £10 is 20 per cent of £50. If the price of the bond is £200, the interest rate is 5 per cent a year – £10 is 5 per cent of £200.

You can now see why buying bonds, which raises the price of a bond, sends the interest rate down and why selling bonds, which lowers the price of a bond, sends the interest rate up.

Speculative Demand for Money

The *speculative demand for money* arises because some people hold money in anticipation of a fall in the price of bonds. This demand arises from the link between the price of a bond and the interest rate that you've just studied.

The link works two ways. A change in the price of a bond changes the interest rate. But a change in the interest rate changes the price of a bond. If the interest rate is expected to rise in the near future, then the price of a bond must be expected to fall. Similarly, if the interest rate is expected to fall in the near future, then the price of a bond must be expected to rise.

People try to anticipate fluctuations in the interest rate because of its effect on the price of a bond. When the interest rate is expected to rise, holding money is better than holding bonds. Money pays no interest but avoids an expected loss from the fall of the price of bonds. When the interest rate is expected to fall, holding bonds is better than holding money because in this situation bonds not only pay interest but are also expected give a gain from the rise in their price.

Fluctuating Interest Rate

The interest rate fluctuates a great deal. Between 1963 and 2003, the average interest rate on UK Government Treasury bills was close to 9 per cent a year. But the interest rate fluctuated between a low of 4 per cent a year in 2001 and a high of almost 17 per cent a year in 1979.

The interest rate can fluctuate because either the demand for money or the supply of money fluctuates. Figure 27.8 illustrates the two cases. Initially, the demand for money curve is MD_0 and the supply of money curve is MS_0. The equilibrium interest rate is 5 per cent a year.

In Figure 27.8(a), the demand for money increases and the demand curve shifts rightward to MD_1. At an interest rate of 5 per cent a year, there is a shortage of money. People are holding less money than they would like to hold. They attempt to increase their money holding by selling bonds. As they do so, the price of a bond falls and the interest rate rises. When the interest rate has risen to 6 per cent a year, the quantity of money supplied has increased and money market equilibrium has been restored.

A decrease in the demand for money shifts the demand curve leftward to MD_2. At an interest rate of 5 per cent a year, there is a surplus of money. People are holding more money than they would like to hold. They attempt to decrease their money holding by buying bonds. As they do so, the price of a bond rises and the interest rate falls. When the interest rate has fallen to 4 per cent a year, the quantity of money supplied has decreased and money market equilibrium has been restored.

In Figure 27.8(b), the supply of money increases and the supply of money curve shifts rightward to MS_1. At

Figure 27.8

The Fluctuating Interest Rate

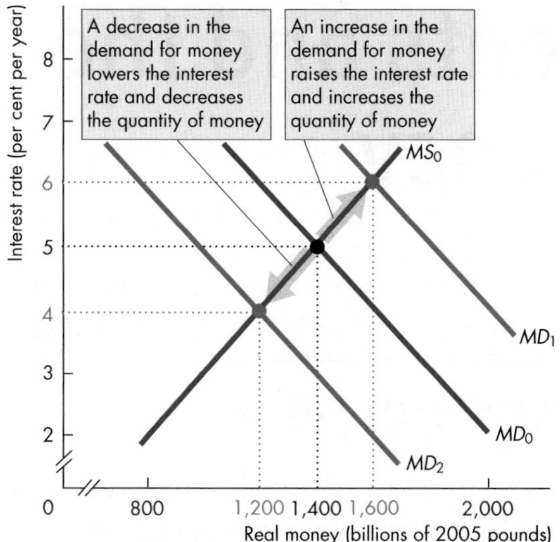

(a) Fluctuations in the demand for money

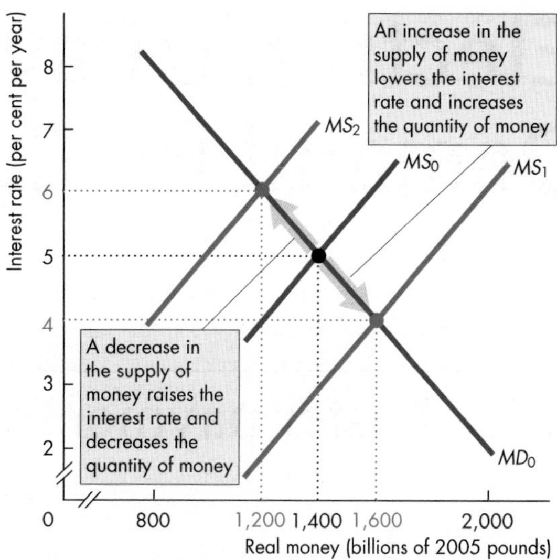

(b) Fluctuations in the supply of money

Fluctuations in the demand for money bring fluctuations in the interest rate and the quantity of money. When the demand for money fluctuates, the interest rate and the quantity of money fluctuate in the same direction.

Fluctuations in the supply of money bring fluctuations in the interest rate and the quantity of money. When the supply of money fluctuates, the interest rate and the quantity of money fluctuate in opposite directions.

an interest rate of 5 per cent a year, there is a surplus of money. People are holding more money than they would like to hold. They attempt to decrease their money holding by buying bonds. As they do so, the price of a bond rises and the interest rate falls. When the interest rate has fallen to 4 per cent a year, the quantity of money demanded has increased and money market equilibrium has been restored.

A decrease in the supply of money shifts the supply curve leftward to MS_2. At an interest rate of 5 per cent a year, there is a shortage of money. People are holding less money than they would like to hold. They attempt to increase their money holding by selling bonds. As they do so, the price of a bond falls and the interest rate rises. When the interest rate has risen to 6 per cent a year, the quantity of money demanded has decreased and money market equilibrium has been restored.

UK Interest Rate Fluctuations

Interest rate fluctuations in the United Kingdom have come from fluctuations in both the demand for money and the supply of money. But most of the fluctuations originate on the supply side of the money market with the actions of the Bank of England. Also, the central bank does not have to stand idly by when the demand for money changes. It can take actions to offset the effect of the change in demand on the interest rate.

Review Quiz

Study Plan 27.6

1. What is a bond and what is the relationship between the price of a bond and the interest rate?
2. How is the interest rate determined?
3. What do people do if they are holding *less* money than they plan to hold and what happens to the interest rate?
4. What do people do if they are holding *more* money than they plan to hold and what happens to the interest rate?
5. What happens to the interest rate if the supply of money increases or decreases?

Your task in the next chapter is to study the actions that the central bank can take. But before moving on, take a look at *Reading Between the Lines* on pp. 636–637 and see how the way we make payments is changing.

Reading Between the Lines

Electronic Payments and the Demand for Currency

The Financial Times, 13 February 2007

FT

Faster payments processing on way

Jane Croft

The government body established to speed up Britain's payment system said yesterday that UK banks were on course to introduce faster processing for internet and telephone banking in November 2007.

The Payment Systems Taskforce, chaired by the Office of Fair Trading, said in its final report yesterday that, from the end of the year, consumers and businesses should be able to make electronic payments within hours, rather than the three days it takes for a transaction to clear at present.

The taskforce said that the BACS Innovation Working Group report had concluded that the value to the UK economy of introducing such a system could be in the range of £498m to £1.10bn over 10 years.

UK customers choosing to make a faster online or phone payment will be making it in near-real-time, meaning the payment will complete end-to-end within a couple of hours.

Although the central system will be ready in November 2007, it will be up to each bank or building society to decide how and when it delivers a full service to all its personal and corporate customers.

The taskforce confirmed that, for the first time, banks would introduce maximum clearing times for cheques, which currently take three days to clear, or four if the cheque is being sent between Scotland or Northern Ireland and the rest of the UK.

The Essence of the Story

- It takes three days to clear a cheque (four days between banks in Scotland or Northern Ireland and the rest of the United Kingdom).
- A central system for processing payments in near real-time (a few hours) will be ready to operate in November 2007.
- Each bank or building society will decide how and when to make the faster service available to its customers.
- The value to the UK economy of the new system is estimated to range from £498 million to £1.10 billion over 10 years.

Economic Analysis

- A new electronic payment system will enable payments to be completed in a few hours instead of the current three to four days it takes to clear a cheque.
- The faster electronic payment system will be attractive to both banks and customers and as more people switch to electronic payments the cost per transaction to the banks and the price to the customer will fall.
- Cheque payments have decreased from 4 billion cheques cleared in the United Kingdom in 1990 to 2.8 billion in 1999 to 1.9 billion in 2006.
- Electronic and phone transmission of payments will also make it less necessary for individuals to hold currency.
- Figure 1 shows that currency has become less and less popular as a means of payment. The ratio of currency to GDP fell steadily during the 1970s and 1980s to around 3.5 per cent of GDP.
- But during the 1990s and 2000s, the currency to GDP ratio has increased slightly.
- Figure 2 interprets the trends in Figure 1. Each dot in the figure shows the quantity of currency as a percentage of GDP and the interest rate for a given year (some of which are identified in the figure).
- You can think of the curves in Figure 2 as demand for currency curves with the effect of GDP on the demand for currency held constant.
- Changes in financial technology decreased the demand for currency and the demand for currency curve (GDP constant) shifted leftward from CD_0 to CD_1 to CD_2 and to CD_3.
- During the 1970s and early 1980s, the interest rate rose and the quantity of currency demanded decreased in a movement up along the demand curve CD_0.
- During the 1990s and 2000s, the interest rate fell and the quantity of currency demanded increased in a movement down along the demand curve CD_3.
- The new electronic payment method will decrease the demand for currency in the future.
- A decrease in the demand for currency decreases the currency drain and increases the money multiplier.
- The demand for currency is unlikely to fall to zero because some people want to make transactions that can't be traced (such as underground economy transactions) and currency is the simplest and most secure way of making untraceable transactions.

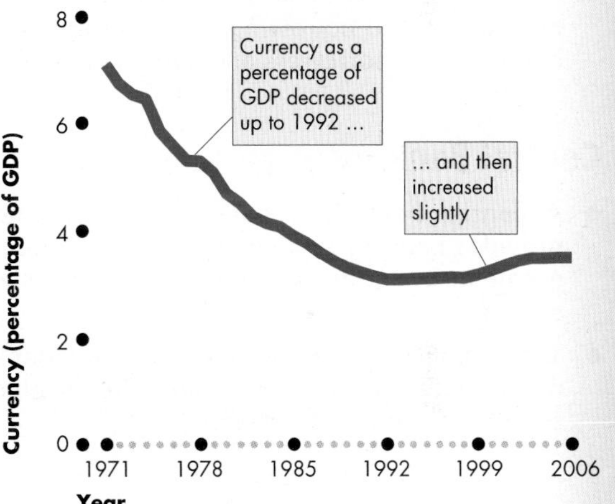

Figure 1 Currency as a percentage of GDP

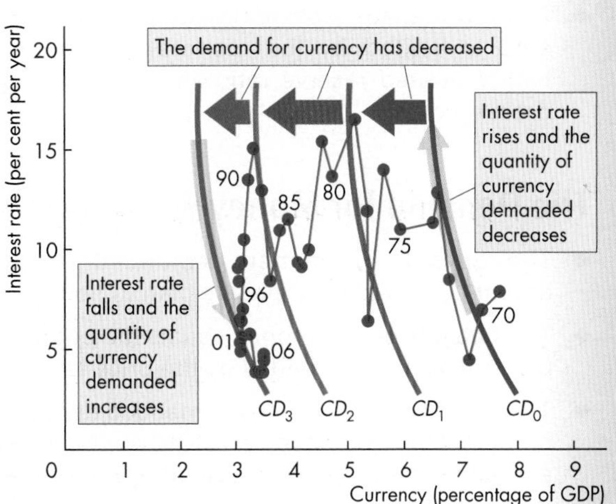

Figure 2 The demand for currency

Summary

Key Points

What is Money? (pp. 618–620)

- Money is the means of payment and it functions as a medium of exchange, unit of account and store of value.
- M4 – currency held by the public and bank and building society deposits – is the main measure of money in the United Kingdom today.

Financial Intermediaries (pp. 621–622)

- Commercial banks and building societies are financial intermediaries whose liabilities are money.
- Financial intermediaries create liquidity, minimize the cost of borrowing, minimize the cost of monitoring borrowers and pool risks.

Central Banking (pp. 623–624)

- A central bank is a public authority that provides banking services to banks and governments and manages the nation's financial system.
- The liabilities of the central bank are bank notes and bank reserves. These items plus coins are the monetary base.

How Banks Create Money (pp. 625–628)

- Banks create money by making loans.
- The total quantity of money that can be created is limited by the monetary base, the banks' desired reserve ratio and the currency drain ratio.

The Demand for Money (pp. 629–632)

- The quantity of money demanded is the amount of money that people plan to hold.
- The quantity of real money equals the quantity of nominal money divided by the price level.
- The quantity of real money demanded depends on the interest rate and real GDP. As the interest rate rises, the quantity of real money demanded decreases.

Interest Rate Determination (pp. 632–635)

- The interest rate adjusts to achieve equilibrium in the money market.
- If the demand for money increases, the prices of bonds fall, the interest rate rises and the quantity of money decreases.
- If the supply of money increases, the prices of bonds rise, the interest rate falls and the quantity of money increases.

Key Figures

Key Terms

Problems

Tests, Study Plan and Solutions* 

1 Which of the following items are money?

a Bank of England notes in the commercial banks' cash machines.

b Your Visa card.

c The coins inside public phones.

d Pound coins in your wallet.

e The cheque you have just written to pay for your rent.

f The student loan you took out in September to pay for your tuition fees.

g British Telecom shares held by individuals.

h The £5 commemorative crown for the Queen's Jubilee.

i UK Government securities.

2 Monica withdraws £1,000 from her savings account at the Leeds Building Society. She keeps £50 in currency and puts the rest into her chequable savings account at HSBC. How do Monica's transactions change M4 and its composition?

3 The banks in Zap have a required reserve ratio of 8 per cent, a desired reserve ratio of 10 per cent and the following items in their balance sheets:

Reserves	£250 million
Loans	£1,000 million
Deposits	£2,000 million

a Calculate the Zap banks' actual reserve ratio.

b Calculate the Zap banks' excess reserves.

c Why do the Zap banks hold reserves?

d How do the Zap banks earn a profit?

e How do the Zap banks create liquidity?

f How do the Zap banks minimize the cost of borrowing and monitoring borrowers?

g How do the Zap banks pool risk?

4 You are given the following information about the economy of Freezone: the people and businesses in Freezone have bank deposits of €500 billion and hold €80 billion in notes issued by the Freezone Central Bank (FCB) and €20 billion in coin issued by the Freezone Mint. The banks hold deposits at the FCB of €50 billion and they keep €5 billion in notes and coin in their vaults and ATM machines. Calculate:

a The liabilities of the FCB.

b The monetary base.

c The quantity of money and its composition – how much is currency and how much is deposits?

d The banks' reserves.

5 In Freezone described in problem 4, the banks' reserves are at their desired level and then the FCB increases the monetary base by €1 billion.

a What happens to the reserves of the banks?

b What do the banks do next?

c What is the currency drain ratio in Freezone?

d If the banks of Freezone make new loans equal to their excess reserves, how much do they loan initially and what is the change in the quantity of loans, deposits, reserves and currency in circulation after one round of bank lending?

e After two rounds of bank lending, what is the change in the quantity of loans, deposits, reserves and currency in circulation?

f When excess reserves are zero, what is the change in the quantity of loans, deposits, reserves and currency in circulation?

g What is the magnitude of the money multiplier in Freezone?

h What is the relationship between the banks' desired reserve ratio, the currency drain ratio and the money multiplier in Freezone?

6 The spreadsheet provides information about the demand for and supply of money in Minland. Column A is the interest rate, *R*. Columns B, C and D show the quantity of money demanded at three different levels of real GDP: Y_0 is £10 billion, Y_1 is £20 billion and Y_2 is £30 billion. Column E shows the quantity of money supplied. Initially, real GDP is £20 billion.

	A	B	C	D	E
1	R	Y_0	Y_1	Y_2	MS
2	6	1	3	5	7
3	5	2	4	6	6
4	4	3	5	7	5
5	3	4	6	8	4
6	2	5	7	9	3
7	1	6	8	10	2

Draw a graph to show the demand for money, supply of money and money market equilibrium in Minland and explain what happens in Minland if the interest rate:

* Solutions to odd-numbered problems are provided.

a Exceeds 4 per cent a year.

b Is less than 4 per cent a year.

c Equals 4 per cent a year.

Suppose that Minland experiences a severe recession. Real GDP falls to £10 billion.

d What happens in Minland if the interest rate is 4 per cent a year?

e What is the equilibrium interest rate?

f Compared with the situation before the recession, does the interest rate in Minland rise or fall? Why?

7 In Minland described in problem 6, a strong business cycle expansion occurs. Real GDP rises to £30 billion. Then a recession hits and real GDP falls to £10 billion. What happens to the interest rate in Minland during the:

a Expansion phase of the cycle?

b Recession phase of the cycle?

8 In Minland described in problem 6, a financial innovation changes the demand for money. People plan to hold £0.5 billion less than the numbers in the spreadsheet.

a What happens to the interest rate?

b What happens to the interest rate if at the same time as the change in the demand for money, the supply of money decreases by £0.5 billion? Explain.

9 In Minland described in problem 6, a new smartcard replaces currency and the demand for money changes. Also, the new smartcard causes business to boom and real GDP increases.

a Draw a demand for money curve and supply of money curve that describe the initial situation and the new situation.

b What would have to happen to the supply of money in Minland if the interest rate was to remain constant through these events?

10 In Minland described in problem 6, a financial crisis occurs. The people begin to distrust the banks and withdraw their deposits. At the same time, they cut up their smartcards and start using currency again. The financial crisis brings a deep recession.

a Draw the demand for money curve and supply of money curve that describe the initial situation and the new situation.

b What would have to happen to the supply of money in Minland if the interest rate was to remain constant through these events?

Critical Thinking

1 Study *Reading Between the Lines* on pp. 636–637 and then answer the following questions:

a What changes in the payments technology are described in the news article?

b What is the implication of the news article for the future amount of currency held?

c What are the trends in currency holding?

d Why do you think currency holdings increased between 2000 and 2006?

e What do you expect the future trends in the use of currency to be and why?

f Based on information that you can find in this chapter, do you predict that credit cards and debit cards are used more widely or less widely in the Eurozone than in the United Kingdom? Explain.

2 Rapid inflation in Brazil caused the cruzeiro, the former currency of Brazil, to lose its ability to function as money. People were unwilling to accept it because it lost value too fast. Which of the following commodities do you think would be most likely to take the place of the cruzeiro and act as money in the Brazilian economy?

a Tractor parts

b Packs of cigarettes

c Loaves of bread

d Impressionist paintings

e Baseball trading cards

Web Activities

Links to Websites

1 Visit Roy Davies's Website, "Money – Past, Present and Future", and study the section on e-money. Then answer the following questions:

a What is e-money and what are the alternative forms that it takes?

b Do you think that the widespread use of e-money will lead to an increase or a decrease in the demand for money? Explain.

c When you buy an item on the Internet and pay for it using PayPal, are you using money? Explain why or why not.

d Why might e-money be superior to cash as a means of payment?

CHAPTER 28

Monetary Policy

After studying this chapter you will be able to:

- Describe the objectives of UK monetary policy and the framework for setting and achieving them
- Explain how the Bank of England makes its interest rate decision and achieves its interest rate target
- Explain the transmission channels through which the Bank of England influences the inflation rate
- Explain and compare alternative monetary policy strategies

The Old Lady and a New Kid

Every month, six eminent economists join the Governor and Deputy Governors of the Bank of England to analyze and deliberate on the state of the UK economy and decide whether to change the interest rate. How does the Bank of England, the Old Lady of Threadneedle Street, make its interest rate decisions? How does it get the interest rate to change? And how do interest rates influence the economy?

A similar meeting takes place every month in Frankfurt, where the European Central Bank, a new kid on the block, makes its decision about the Eurozone interest rate.

This chapter explains monetary policy. And *Reading Between the Lines* at the end of the chapter looks at a recent episode of decision making by the Bank of England.

Monetary Policy Objectives and Framework

A nation's monetary policy objectives and the framework for setting and achieving them stem from the relationship between the central bank and government. Monetary policy-making involves two activities:

1 Setting the policy objectives
2 Achieving the policy objectives

In a few countries, the central bank sets the objectives and decides how to achieve them. And in some countries, the government makes all the monetary policy decisions and tells the central bank what actions to take. But in most countries, including the United Kingdom, the government sets the monetary policy objectives and the central banks decides how to achieve them.

Here, we'll describe the objectives of UK monetary policy and the framework and assignment of responsibility for achieving those objectives.

Monetary Policy Objectives

The objectives of monetary policy are ultimately political and are determined by government. But they are pursued by the actions of the central bank. The Bank of England Act of 1998 sets out the objectives of UK monetary policy.

Bank of England Act 1998

The 1998 Bank of England Act sets out the Bank's monetary policy objectives as being:

(a) to maintain price stability, and
(b) subject to that, to support the economic policy of Her Majesty's Government, including its objectives for growth and employment.[1]

The Act also requires the Chancellor of the Exchequer to specify annually in writing:

(a) what price stability is to be taken to consist of, and
(b) what the economic policy of Her Majesty's Government is to be taken to be.[2]

One of the most important innovations in the 1998 Act is its establishment of the monetary policy committee.

[1] Bank of England Act (1998) section 11.
[2] Bank of England Act (1998) section 12.

Monetary Policy Committee

The Bank of England's **monetary policy committee (MPC)** is the committee in the Bank that has the responsibility for formulating monetary policy. The nine-person committee consists of the Governor and two Deputy Governors of the Bank, two members appointed by the Governor of the Bank after consultation with the Chancellor of the Exchequer, and four members appointed by the Chancellor of the Exchequer. The persons appointed by the Chancellor must have "knowledge or experience which is likely to be relevant to the Committee's functions" – which in practice means that they are academic economists.

Remit for the Monetary Policy Committee

The Chancellor renews and if necessary modifies the remit for the monetary policy committee at roughly annual intervals. This remit is stated in two parts corresponding to the two monetary policy objectives.

Price Stability Objective

The first part of the remit for the monetary policy committee is an operational definition of "price stability". Since the beginning of 2004, this objective has been specified as a target inflation rate of 2 per cent a year as measured by the 12-month increase in the Consumer Prices Index (CPI).

Between May 1997 and 2004, the Chancellor specified that price stability shall be an inflation target of 2.5 per cent a year as measured by the 12-month increase in the Retail Prices Index excluding mortgage interest payments (RPIX). The switch from the RPIX to the CPI was made to bring the UK inflation target into closer alignment with that of the euro area (see Box 28.1 on p. 644).

The change from a 2.5 per cent target to a 2 per cent target does not imply a lower average inflation rate. Mervyn King, the Governor of the Bank of England, has likened the change to measuring the temperature on the centigrade rather than Fahrenheit scale. But the analogy isn't perfect because the difference in the average inflation rates using the RPIX and CPI is a bit more than 0.5 percentage points. So a CPI target of 2 per cent a year is equivalent to a slightly higher inflation rate than the old RPIX 2.5 per cent target. Setting the CPI target at 2 per cent a year means that the definition of price stability has been changed and a slightly higher average inflation rate is now defined to be price stability.

Although the inflation target is renewed annually, the intention is that inflation be locked in at a low and stable rate over the long term. To achieve long-term price stability, deviations from the inflation target in either direction that exceed 1 percentage point require the Governor of the Bank to write an open letter to the Chancellor explaining why the target has been missed and what steps will be taken to bring the inflation rate back to its target. And for every three months that the inflation rate misses its target by more than 1 percentage point, a further explanation must be provided.

Government Economic Policy Objectives

The government's economic policy objectives as they relate to monetary policy are to achieve high and stable levels of economic growth and employment.

Price stability is the key goal and a major contributor to achieving the other goals of government economic policy. Price stability provides the best available environment for households and firms to make the saving and investment decisions that bring economic growth. So price stability encourages the maximum sustainable growth rate of potential GDP.

But in the short run, the Bank of England faces a trade-off between inflation and economic growth and employment. Taking an action that is designed to lower the inflation rate and achieve stable prices might mean slowing the economic growth rate and lowering employment.

In both the primary objective of price stability and the consequential goal of high and stable growth and employment, monetary policy in the United Kingdom is similar to that in the rest of the European Union (see Box 28.1 on p. 644).

Figure 28.1 myeconlab

Inflation Targets and Outcomes

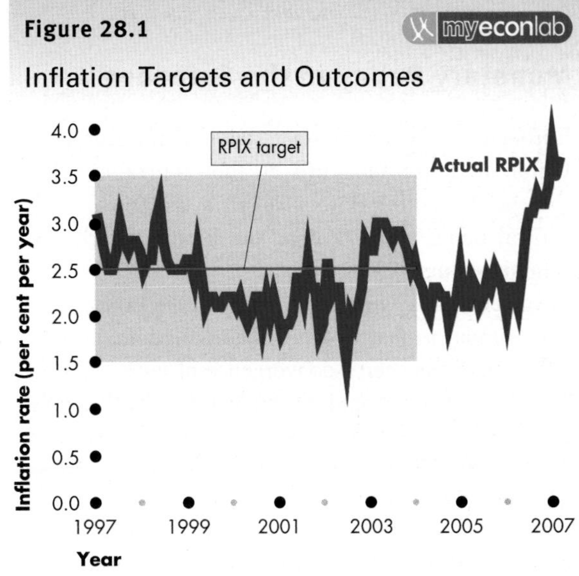

(a) RPIX target: 1997–2003

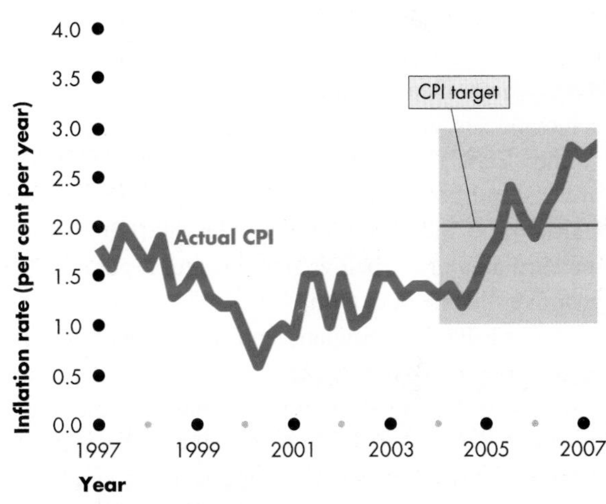

(b) CPI target: 2003–2007

The MPC has achieved its inflation target. During the years in which the target was an inflation rate measured by the RPIX of 2.5 per cent a year, the actual inflation rate was 2.4 per cent a year – in part (a). During the years in which the target was an annual inflation rate measured by the CPI of 2 per cent a year, the actual inflation rate was 1.9 per cent a year – in part (b).

Actual Inflation and the Inflation Target

The performance of UK inflation since May 1997, when the RPIX target of 2.5 per cent a year was set, has been close to target. Figure 28.1 shows just how close.

Figure 28.1(a) compares the RPIX measure and the target of 2.5 per cent a year between May 1997 and December 2003. The average rate of increase in RPIX was 2.4 per cent a year – almost exactly on target. Also the rate never went outside the range of 2.5 per cent plus or minus 1 percentage point (the shaded area).

Figure 28.1(b) compares the CPI measure and target of 2 per cent a year since the beginning of 2004. During this period, the average rate of increase of the CPI was just below target at 1.9 per cent a year.

Although the Bank of England has been close to its inflation target on the average, in March 2007, the CPI increased by 3.1 per cent, and so triggered an open letter from the Governor to the Chancellor.

Box 28.1
Monetary Policy in the Eurozone

Eurozone is the 13 member states of the European Union that use the euro as their currency. The European Central Bank (ECB) is the Eurozone's central bank, a new kid on the block, which was established in 1998.

The conduct of monetary policy in the Eurozone is very similar to that in the United Kingdom. In fact, today there has been a convergence of views on how monetary policy should be conducted and the central banks of most industrial countries pursue monetary policy using similar objectives, tools and decision-making frameworks.

The objectives of monetary policy are laid out in Article 105 of the Treaty Establishing the European Community (the Treaty of Rome), which assigns overriding importance to price stability as the ECB's monetary policy goal. The Treaty also requires the ECB to support broader Community economic policies, which means supporting policies aimed at achieving sustained growth and high employment.

The ECB's Governing Council has defined price stability as "a year-on-year increase in the Harmonised Index of Consumer Prices (HICP) for the euro area of . . . below, but close to, 2 per cent a year over the medium term".

Like the Bank of England and most other central banks, the ECB recognizes "that ensuring price stability is the most important contribution that monetary policy can make to achieve a favourable economic environment and a high level of employment". In other words, price stability is the goal of monetary policy *because it contributes to the achievement of other economic objectives.*

During the months in which the CPI inflation rate was moving upward towards 3 per cent, the RPIX burst through 3.5 per cent and moved towards 4 percent. If the target had not been changed from the RPIX to the CPI, the Governor would have been even busier writing open letters to the Chancellor explaining how the Bank proposed to get back on target.

Rationale for an Inflation Target

Two main benefits flow from adopting an inflation target. The first is that the purpose of the Bank of England's policy actions are more clearly understood by financial market traders. A clearer understanding leads to fewer surprises and mistakes on the part of savers and investors.

The second benefit is that the target provides an anchor for expectations about future inflation. Firmly held expectations of low inflation make the short-run output–inflation (or unemployment–inflation) trade-off as favourable as possible – see Chapter 30, pp. 706–708. Also, firmly held (and correct) inflation expectations help individuals and firms to make better economic decisions, which in turn help to achieve a more efficient allocation of resources and a more stable economic growth rate.

Controversy About Inflation Targeting

Not everyone agrees that the inflation targeting brings benefits. Critics argue that by focusing on inflation, the Bank of England sometimes permits the unemployment rate or real GDP growth rate to suffer.

The fear of these critics is that if the inflation rate begins to edge upward towards and perhaps beyond a full percentage point above target, the Bank of England might reign in aggregate demand and push the economy into recession. At the same time, the Bank might end up permitting the pound to rise on the foreign exchange market and making exports suffer.

One response of supporters of inflation targeting is that by keeping inflation low and stable, monetary policy makes its maximum possible contribution towards achieving full employment and sustained economic growth.

Another response is "look at the record". The last time the United Kingdom was in a recession was at the beginning of the 1990s. Since May 1997 when the Bank of England was made operationally independent and given the goal of price stability, the United Kingdom has not been in a recession.

Review Quiz

Study Plan 28.1

1. What are the objectives of monetary policy?
2. What is the rationale for setting an inflation target?
3. What is the Bank of England's record in achieving the inflation target?

You now know the objective of monetary policy and the Bank of England's record in achieving that objective. Your next task is to learn how the Bank of England conducts monetary policy.

The Conduct of Monetary Policy

In this section, we describe the way in which the Bank of England conducts its monetary policy and we explain the Bank's monetary policy strategy. We evaluate the Bank's strategy in the final section of this chapter, where we describe and compare alternative monetary policy strategies.

Choosing a Policy Instrument

A **monetary policy instrument** is a variable that the Bank can directly control or closely target. As the sole issuer of the monetary base, the Bank is a monopoly. Like all monopolies, it can fix the quantity of its product and leave the market to determine the price; or it can fix the price of its product and leave the market to choose the quantity.

The first decision is whether to fix the price of the pound on the foreign exchange market – the exchange rate. A country that operates a fixed exchange rate cannot pursue an independent monetary policy. The United Kingdom has a flexible exchange rate and pursues an independent monetary policy. (Chapter 33 explains the foreign exchange market and the factors that influence the exchange rate.)

Even with a flexible exchange rate, the Bank still has a choice of policy instrument. It can decide to target the monetary base or a short-term interest rate. While the Bank can set either of these two variables, it cannot set both. The value of one is the consequence of the other. If the Bank decided to decrease the monetary base, the interest rate would rise. If the Bank decided to raise the interest rate, the monetary base would decrease. (You'll see exactly why in the next few pages.) So the Bank must decide which of these two variables to target.

Bank Rate

The Bank's choice of monetary policy instrument is a short-term interest rate. Given this choice, the Bank permits the exchange rate and the quantity of money to find their own equilibrium values and the Bank has no preset views about what those values should be.

The interest rate that the Bank sets is Bank Rate, which is linked to the interest rate that banks earn on reserves and pay on borrowed reserves and to the **repo rate** – the interest rate in the repo market. Banks can borrow and lend reserves in the repo market. A bank that is short of reserves and a bank that has excess reserves can use a repo to move the reserves from one bank to the other. The Bank of England also trades in the repo market as you'll see below.

Figure 28.2 shows the Bank Rate since 1997. You can see that Bank Rate is normally changed in steps of a quarter of a percentage point. The rate reached a peak of 7.5 per cent a year in 1998 and that it then fell, increased briefly, and then fell again to a low of 3.5 per cent a year in 2003. Through this period of a generally falling Bank Rate, the inflation rate was mostly on or below target and the Bank wanted to prevent it from falling further and to keep real GDP expanding and employment high.

Between 2003 and 2007, Bank Rate has been on a rising trend. The reason is that the inflation rate has moved up from below target to above target and by 2007 the inflation rate was pushing against the upper limit of a 3 per cent a year rate of increase of the CPI.

How does the Bank decide the appropriate level for Bank Rate? And how, having made that decision, does the Bank ensure that banks are supplied with the reserves they desire at the chosen Bank Rate? We'll now answer these two questions.

Figure 28.2

myeconlab

Bank Rate

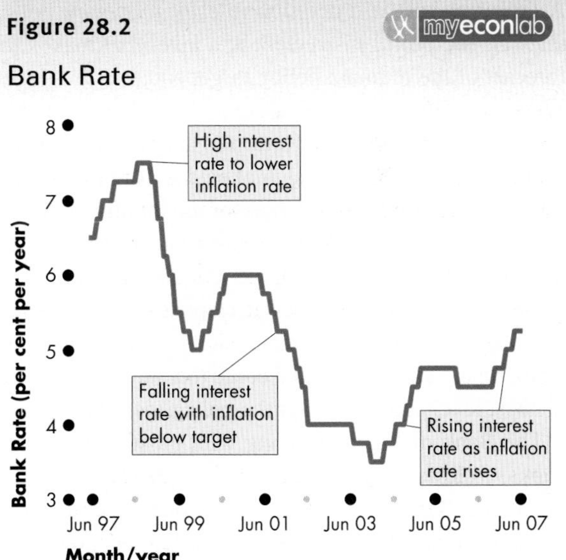

The Bank of England sets Bank Rate and then takes actions to ensure that the banking system is supplied with its desired level of reserves. When the inflation rate is above 2 per cent a year and the Bank wants to avoid going above target, it raises Bank Rate. When the inflation rate is below 2 per cent a year and the Bank wants to avoid going below target, it lowers Bank Rate.

Source of data: Bank of England.

The Bank's Decision-making Strategy

Two alternative decision-making strategies that the Bank of England might use are summarized by the terms:

- Instrument rule
- Targeting rule

Instrument Rule

An **instrument rule** is a decision rule for monetary policy that sets the policy instrument at a level that is based on the current state of the economy. The best-known instrument rule is the *Taylor rule*, in which the instrument is Bank Rate and the rule is to make Bank Rate respond by formula to the inflation rate and the output gap. (The Taylor rule is so named because it was suggested by Stanford University economist John Taylor and is widely believed to provide good inflation and employment outcomes. We examine the Taylor rule later in this chapter – see pp. 658–659.)

Targeting Rule

A **targeting rule** is a decision rule for monetary policy that sets the policy instrument at a level that makes the forecast of the ultimate policy target equal to the target. Where the ultimate policy target is the inflation rate and the instrument is Bank Rate, the targeting rule sets Bank Rate at a level that makes the forecast of the inflation rate equal to the target for the inflation rate.

To implement such a targeting rule, a central bank must gather and process a large amount of information about the economy, the way it responds to shocks and the way it responds to policy. The Central Bank must then process all this data and come to a judgement about the best level at which to set the policy instrument.

The Bank of England (along with most other central banks) follows a process that uses a targeting rule.

For the Bank of England, the process begins with an exercise that uses a model of the UK economy that you can think of as a sophisticated version of the aggregate supply–aggregate demand model (see Chapter 23). The Bank's economists provide the MPC with a variety of forecasts and scenarios running two years into the future.

All the available industry, national and international data on economic performance, financial markets and inflation expectations are reviewed, discussed and weighed in a careful deliberative process that ends with the MPC voting on the level at which to set Bank Rate.

After announcing a Bank Rate decision, the Bank engages in a public communication to explain the reasons for the MPC's decision. The Bank of England's communication exercise is extremely thorough and includes a detailed and carefully researched *Inflation Report* and press conference with the Governor. This press conference is recorded and a video placed on the Bank's website. (Take a look!)

We've now described the Bank's monetary policy instrument and the MPC's strategy for setting it. We next see how the Bank of England supplies the banking system with reserves that are consistent with its Bank Rate decision.

Supplying Bank Reserves: Open Market Operations

Once a Bank Rate decision has been made, the Bank ensures that banks are supplied with their desired reserves by instructing its bond traders to make an open market operation – to buy or sell (in a repurchase agreement) government securities from or to a commercial bank or the public. When the Bank buys securities, it pays for them with newly created reserves held by banks. When the Bank sells securities, it is paid for them with reserves held by banks. So open market operations directly influence the reserves of banks.

An Open Market Purchase

To see how an open market purchase changes bank reserves, suppose the Bank of England buys £100 million of government securities from Barclays. When this transaction is made, two things happen:

1. Barclays has £100 million fewer securities, and the Bank of England has £100 million more securities.
2. The Bank of England pays for the securities by placing £100 million in Barclay's deposit account at the Bank of England.

Figure 28.3 shows the effects of these actions on the balance sheets of the Bank of England and Barclays. Ownership of the securities passes from Barclays to the Bank of England, so Barclay's assets decrease by £100 million and the Bank of England's assets increase by £100 million, as shown by the blue arrow running from Barclays to the Bank of England.

Figure 28.3 

The Bank of England Buys Securities in the Open Market

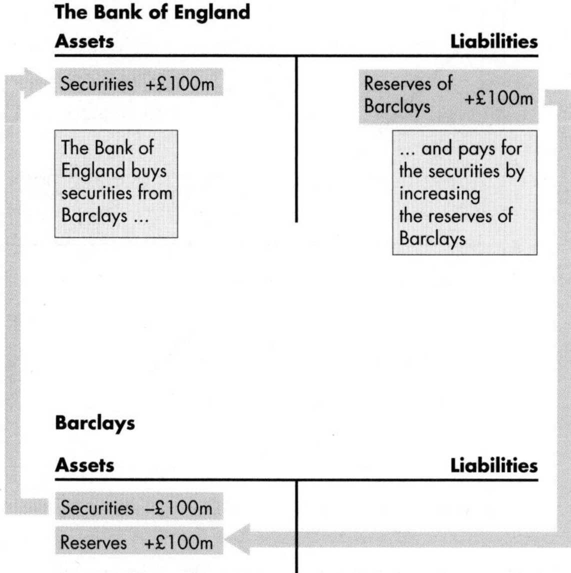

When the Bank of England buys securities in the open market, it increases bank reserves. The Bank of England's assets and liabilities increase and the selling bank's reserves increase and securities decrease.

Figure 28.4 

The Bank of England Sells Securities in the Open Market

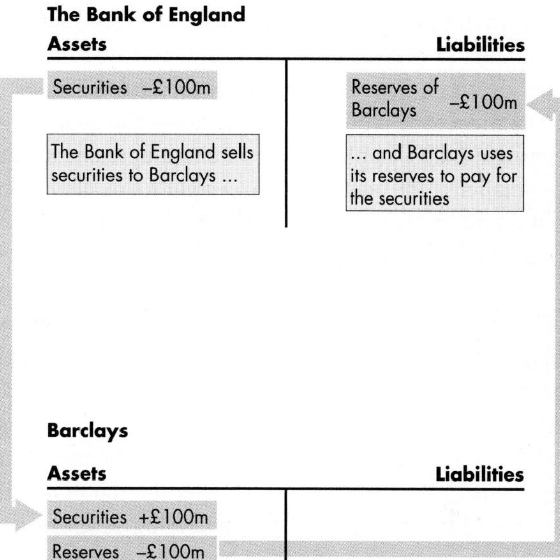

When the Bank of England sells securities in the open market, it decreases bank reserves. The Bank of England's assets and liabilities decrease and the buying bank's reserves decrease and securities increase.

The Bank of England pays for the securities by placing £100 million in Barclays' reserve account at the Bank of England, as shown by the green arrow running from the Bank of England to Barclays.

The Bank of England's assets and liabilities increase by £100 million. Barclays' total assets are unchanged: its securities are down and its reserves are up by the same amount.

An Open Market Sale

If the Bank of England *sells* £100 million of government securities to Barclays:

1 Barclays has £100 million more securities, and the Bank of England has £100 million fewer securities.

2 Barclays pays for the securities by using £100 million of its reserves deposit account at the Bank of England.

Figure 28.4 shows the effects of these actions on the balance sheets of the Bank of England and Barclays. Ownership of the securities passes from the Bank of England to Barclays, so the Bank of England's assets decrease by £100 million and Barclays' assets increase by £100 million, as shown by the blue arrow running from the Bank of England to Barclays.

Barclays uses £100 million of its reserves to pay for the securities, as the green arrow running from Barclays to the Bank of England shows.

The Bank of England's assets and liabilities decrease by £100 million. Barclays' total assets are unchanged: its securities are up and its reserves are down by the same amount.

In the examples of open market operations that we've just described, the Bank of England transacts directly with Barclays, a commercial bank. The Bank might alternatively transact with Cadburys Chocolate, a customer of Barclays. In this case, an open market purchase increases Cadburys' deposit at Barclays, and increases Barclay's reserves at the Bank of England. And an open market sale decreases Cadburys' deposit at Barclays, and decreases Barclay's reserves at the Bank of England.

Equilibrium in the Market for Reserves

Open market operations keep the interest rate in the repo market – the repo rate – in line with Bank Rate. To see how, we must look at what happens in the repo market – the market in which banks lend to and borrow from each other overnight – and in the market for bank reserves.

The higher the repo rate, the greater is the quantity of overnight loans supplied on repurchase agreements and the smaller is the quantity of overnight loans demanded in the repo market. The equilibrium repo rate balances the quantities demanded and supplied.

An equivalent way of looking at the forces that determine the repo rate is to consider the demand for and supply of bank reserves. Banks hold reserves to meet their desired reserve ratio so that they can always make payments. But reserves are costly to hold. The alternative to holding reserves is to lend them in the repo market and earn the repo rate. The higher the repo rate, the higher is the opportunity cost of holding reserves and the greater is the incentive for banks to economize on the quantity of reserves held.

So the quantity of reserves demanded by banks depends on the repo rate. The higher the repo rate, other things remaining the same, the smaller is the quantity of reserves demanded.

Figure 28.5 illustrates the market for bank reserves. The *x*-axis measures the quantity of reserves on deposit at the Bank of England, and the *y*-axis measures the repo rate. The demand for reserves is the curve labelled *RD*.

The Bank of England's open market operations determine the supply of reserves, which is shown by the supply curve *RS*. To decrease reserves, the Bank of England conducts an open market sale. To increase reserves, the Bank of England conducts an open market purchase.

Equilibrium in the market for bank reserves determines the repo rate where the quantity of reserves demanded by the commercial banks equals the quantity of reserves supplied by the Bank of England. By using open market operations, the Bank of England adjusts the supply of reserves to keep the repo rate equal to Bank Rate.

When the MPC decides to raise Bank Rate by 0.25 percentage points,[1] the Bank of England decreases the supply of reserves by selling securities on repurchase agreements. With a smaller quantity of reserves, the banks bid against each other to borrow reserves using repurchase agreements. The prices of securities fall and the repo rate rises to the new level of Bank Rate.

Similarly, when the MPC decides to lower Bank Rate by 0.25 percentage points, the Bank of England increases the supply of reserves by buying securities that others are selling on repurchase agreements. With a larger quantity of reserves, the banks are less eager to borrow reserves. The prices of securities rise and the repo rate falls to the new level of Bank Rate.

[1] When you read about interest changes in the press, you might encounter the term 25 basis points. A basis point is 100th of 1 per cent, so 25 basis points is 0.25 percentage points.

Figure 28.5 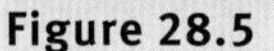 

The Market for Bank Reserves

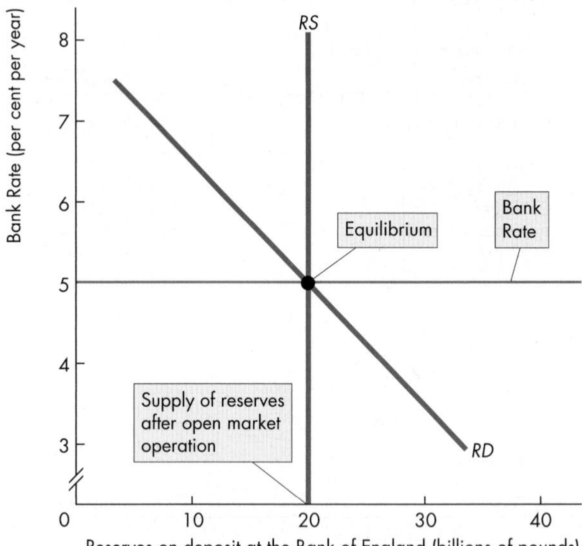

The demand curve for reserves is *RD*. The quantity of reserves demanded decreases as the repo rate rises because the repo rate is the opportunity cost of holding reserves. The supply curve of reserves is *RS*. The Bank of England uses open market operations to make the supply of reserves equal the quantity of reserves demanded (£20 billion in this case) at a repo rate equal to Bank Rate (5 per cent a year in this case).

Review Quiz

Study Plan 28.2

1. What is the Bank of England's monetary policy instrument?
2. What is the main influences on the MPC's interest rate decision?
3. What happens when the Bank of England buys or sells securities in the open market?
4. How is the repo rate determined?

Monetary Policy Transmission

You've seen that the Bank of England's goal is to keep the price level stable (keep the CPI inflation rate at 2 per cent a year) and to achieve maximum growth and employment (keep the output gap close to zero). And you've seen how the Bank can use its power to set Bank Rate at its desired level. We're now going to trace the events that follow a change in Bank Rate and see how those events lead to the ultimate policy goal. We'll begin with a quick overview of the transmission process and then look at each step a bit more closely.

Quick Overview

When the Bank of England lowers Bank Rate, other short-term interest rates and the exchange rate also fall. The quantity of money and the supply of loanable funds increase. The long-term real interest rate falls. The lower real interest rate increases consumption expenditure and investment. And the lower exchange rate makes UK exports cheaper and imports more costly. So net exports increase. Easier bank loans reinforce the effect of lower interest rates on aggregate expenditure. Aggregate demand increases, which increases real GDP and the price level relative to what they would have been. Real GDP growth and inflation speed up.

When the Bank raises Bank Rate, the sequence of events that we've just reviewed plays out but the effects are in the opposite directions.

Figure 28.6 provides a schematic summary of these ripple effects for both a cut (on the left) and a rise (on the right) in Bank Rate.

The ripple effects summarized in Figure 28.6 stretch out over a period of between one and two years but the time lags involved and the strength of each of the effects are never quite the same and are unpredictable.

The interest rate and exchange rate effects are immediate. They occur on the same day that the MPC announces its decision. Sometimes they even anticipate the decision. The effects on money and bank loans follow in a few weeks and run for a few months. Real long-term interest rates change quickly and often in anticipation of the short-term rate changes. Spending plans change and real GDP growth slows after about one year. And the inflation rate changes between one year and two years after the change in Bank Rate. But these time lags are especially hard to predict and can be longer or shorter.

We're going to look at each stage in the transmission process, starting with the interest rate effects.

Figure 28.6 myeconlab

The Ripple Effects of a Change in Bank Rate

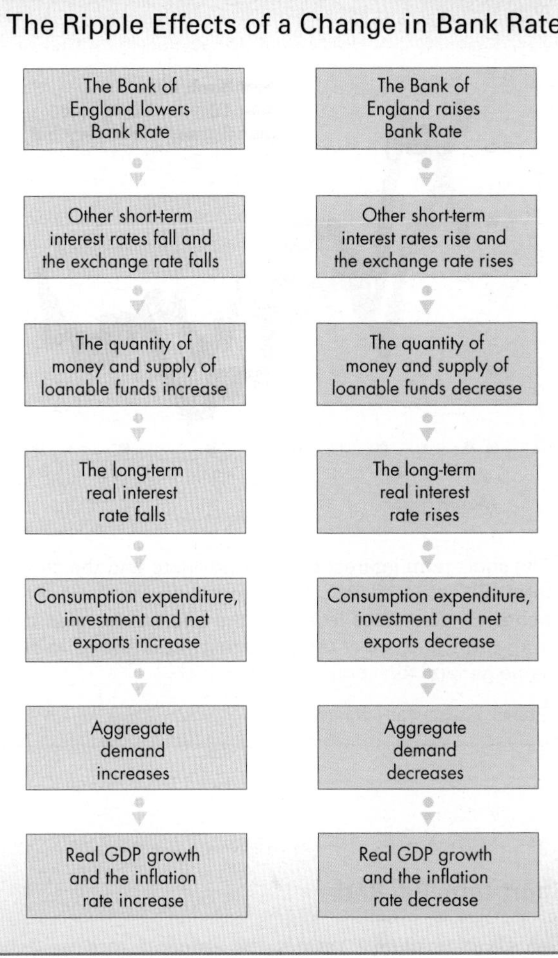

Interest Rate Changes

The first effect of a monetary policy decision by the MPC is a change in Bank Rate. Other interest rates then change. Short-term interest rate effects occur quickly and predictably. Long-term interest rate effects occur more slowly and less predictably. Figure 28.7 shows the fluctuations in three interest rates: Bank Rate, a short-term bill rate and a long-term bond rate.

Bank Rate

As soon as the MPC announces a new setting for Bank Rate, the Bank of England's bond dealers undertake the necessary open market operations to adjust reserves. There is little doubt about where the interest rate changes shown in Figure 28.7 are generated. They are driven by the Bank of England's monetary policy.

Figure 28.7 myeconlab

Three Interest Rates

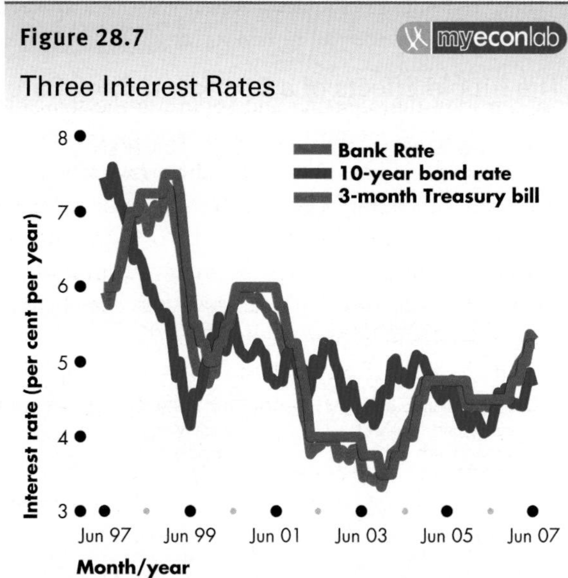

The short-term interest rates – Bank Rate and the short-term bill rate – move closely together. The long-term bond rate fluctuates less than the short-term rates but long-term and short-term interest rates move in the same general direction.

Source of data: Bank of England.

Short-term Bill Rate

The short-term bill rate is the interest rate paid by the UK government on 3-month Treasury bills. It is similar to the interest rate paid by UK businesses on short-term loans. Notice how closely the short-term bill rate follows Bank Rate. The two rates are almost identical.

A powerful substitution effect keeps short-term and long-term interest rates close. Commercial banks have a choice about how to hold their short-term liquid assets. And an overnight loan to another bank is a close substitute for short-term securities such as Treasury bills. If the interest rate on Treasury bills is higher than the repo rate, the quantity of overnight loans supplied decreases and the demand for Treasury bills increases. The price of Treasury bills rises and the interest rate falls.

Similarly, if the interest rate on Treasury bills is lower than the repo rate, the quantity of overnight loans supplied increases and the demand for Treasury bills decreases. The price of Treasury bills falls, and the interest rate on Treasury bills rises.

When the interest rate on Treasury bills is close to the repo rate, there is no incentive for a bank to switch between making an overnight loan and buying Treasury bills. Both the Treasury bill market and the repo market are in equilibrium.

The Long-term Bond Rate

The long-term bond rate is the interest rate paid on bonds issued by large corporations. It is this interest rate that businesses pay on the loans that finance their purchase of new capital and that influences their investment decisions.

Two features of the long-term bond rate stand out: it does not track closely with the short-term rates, and it fluctuates less than the short-term rates so that in some years the long-term rate exceeds the short-term rate and in other years the gap is reversed.

A dominant effect on the long-term interest rate is the long-term expected inflation rate. In 1997, just before the Bank of England began inflation targeting, the expected inflation rate was high, so the long-term bond rate was also high, and much higher than the short-term rate. In an environment of uncertain long-term inflation, long-term loans are riskier than short-term loans. To provide the incentive that brings forth a supply of long-term loans, lenders must be compensated for the additional risk. Without compensation for the additional risk, only short-term loans would be supplied.

The long-term interest rate fluctuates less than the short-term rates because it is influenced by expectations about future short-term interest rates as well as current short-term interest rates. The alternative to borrowing or lending long term is to borrow or lend using a sequence of short-term securities. If the long-term interest rate exceeds the expected average of future short-term interest rates, people will lend long term and borrow short term. The long-term interest rate will fall. If the long-term interest rate is below the expected average of future short-term interest rates, people will borrow long term and lend short term. The long-term interest rate will rise.

These market forces keep the long-term interest rate close to the expected average of future short-term interest rates. And the expected average future short-term interest rate fluctuates less than the current short-term interest rate.

Exchange Rate Fluctuations

The exchange rate responds to changes in the interest rate in the United Kingdom relative to the interest rates in other countries – *the UK interest rate differential*. We explain this influence in Chapter 33 (see pp. 733–736).

When the Bank of England raises Bank Rate, the UK interest rate differential rises and, other things remaining the same, the pound appreciates. And when the Bank lowers Bank Rate, the UK interest rate differential falls and, other things remaining the same, the pound depreciates.

Many factors other than the UK interest rate differential influence the exchange rate, so when the Bank changes Bank Rate, the exchange rate does not usually change in exactly the way it would with other things remaining the same. So while monetary policy influences the exchange rate, many other factors also make the exchange rate change.

Money and Bank Loans

The quantity of money and bank loans change when the Bank changes Bank Rate. A rise in Bank Rate decreases the quantity of money and bank loans and a fall in Bank Rate increases the quantity of money and bank loans. These changes occur for two reasons: the quantity of money supplied by the banking system changes and the quantity of money demanded by household and firms changes.

You've seen that the Bank changes the quantity of bank reserves to keep the repo rate equal to Bank Rate. A change in the quantity of bank reserves changes the monetary base, which in turn changes the quantity of deposits and loans that the banking system can create. A rise in Bank Rate decreases reserves and decreases the quantity of deposits and bank loans created; and a fall in Bank Rate increases reserves and increases the quantity of deposits and bank loans created.

The quantity of money created by the banking system must be held by households and firms. The change in the interest rate changes the quantity of money demanded. A fall in the interest rate increases the quantity of money demanded and a rise in the interest rate decreases the quantity of money demanded.

A change in the quantity of money and the supply of bank loans directly affects consumption and investment plans. With more money and easier access to loans, consumers and firms spend more. With less money and loans harder to get, consumers and firms spend less.

The Long-term Real Interest Rate

Demand and supply in the market for loanable funds determine the long-term real interest rate, which equals the long-term nominal interest rate minus the expected inflation rate. The long-term real interest rate influences expenditure decisions.

In the long run, demand and supply in the loanable funds market depend only on real forces – on saving and investment decisions. But in the short run, when the price level is not fully flexible, the supply of loanable funds is influenced by the supply of bank loans. Changes in Bank Rate change the supply of bank loans, which changes the supply of loanable funds and changes the interest rate in the loanable funds market.

A fall in Bank Rate that increases the supply of bank loans increases the supply of loanable funds and lowers the equilibrium real interest rate. A rise in Bank Rate that decreases the supply of bank loans decreases the supply of loanable funds and raises the equilibrium real interest rate.

These changes in the real interest rate, along with the other factors we've just described, change expenditure plans.

Expenditure Plans

The ripple effects that follow a change in Bank Rate change three components of aggregate expenditure:

- Consumption expenditure
- Investment
- Net exports

Consumption Expenditure

Other things remaining the same, the lower the real interest rate, the greater is the amount of consumption expenditure and the smaller is the amount of saving.

Investment

Other things remaining the same, the lower the real interest rate, the greater is the amount of investment.

Net Exports

Other things remaining the same, the lower the interest rate, the lower is the exchange rate and the greater are exports and the smaller are imports.

So eventually, a cut in Bank Rate increases aggregate expenditure and a rise in Bank Rate curtails aggregate expenditure. These changes in aggregate expenditure plans change aggregate demand, real GDP, and the price level.

Change in Aggregate Demand, Real GDP and the Price Level

The final link in the transmission chain is a change in aggregate demand and a resulting change in real GDP and the price level. By changing real GDP and the price level relative to what they would have been without a change in Bank Rate, the Bank influences its ultimate goals: the inflation rate and full employment.

The Bank Fights Recession

If inflation is low and real GDP is below potential GDP, the Bank takes actions that are designed to restore full employment. Figure 28.8 shows the effects of the Bank of England's actions, starting in the market for bank reserves and ending in the market for real GDP.

Market for Bank Reserves

In Figure 28.8(a), which shows the market for bank reserves, the MPC lowers Bank Rate from 5 per cent to 4 per cent a year. To keep the repo rate close to Bank Rate, the Bank of England buys securities and increases the supply of bank reserves from RS_0 to RS_1.

Money Market

With increased reserves, the banks create deposits by making loans and the supply of money increases. The short-term interest rate falls and the quantity of money demanded increases. In Figure 28.8(b), the increase in the supply of money shifts the supply of money curve from MS_0 to MS_1. The interest rate falls from 5 per cent to 4 per cent a year and the quantity of money increases from £1,400 billion to £1,500 billion. The interest rate in the money market and the repo rate are kept close to each other by the powerful substitution effect described on p. 650.

Loanable Funds Market

Banks create money by making loans. In the long run, an increase in the supply of bank loans is matched by a rise in the price level and the quantity of real loans is

Figure 28.8

The Bank of England Fights Recession

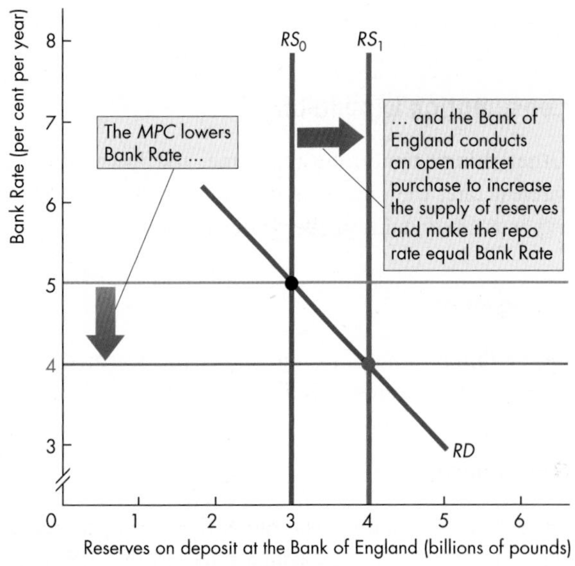

(a) The market for bank reserves

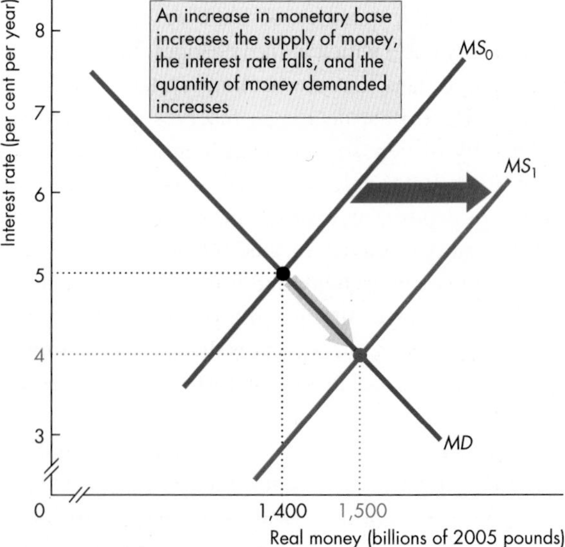

(b) Money market

In part (a), the MPC lowers Bank Rate target from 5 per cent to 4 per cent a year. To make the repo rate equal to Bank Rate, the Bank of England buys securities in an open market operation and increases the supply of reserves from RS_0 to RS_1.

In part (b), the increase in monetary base increases the supply of money from MS_0 to MS_1. The short-term interest rate falls and the quantity of money demanded increases. The short-term interest rate and Bank Rate change by similar amounts.

unchanged. But in the short run, with a sticky price level, an increase in the supply of bank loans increases the supply of (real) loanable funds.

In Figure 28.8(c), the supply of loanable funds increases and supply of loanable funds curve shifts rightward from SLF_0 to SLF_1. With the demand for loanable funds at *DLF*, the real interest rate falls from 6 per cent to 5.5 per cent a year. (Here, we assume a zero inflation rate so that the real interest rate equals the nominal interest rate.) The long-term interest rate changes by a smaller amount than the change in the short-term interest rate as described on p. 650.

The Market for Real GDP

Figure 28.8(d) shows aggregate demand for and aggregate supply of real GDP. Potential GDP is £1,300 billion, where *LAS* is located. The short-run aggregate supply curve is *SAS*, and initially, the aggregate demand curve is AD_0. Real GDP is £1,200 billion, which is less than potential GDP, so there is a recessionary gap. The Bank is reacting to this recessionary gap.

The increase in the supply of loans and the decrease in the real interest rate increase aggregate planned expenditure. (Not shown in the figure, a fall in the interest rate lowers the exchange rate, which increases net exports and also aggregate planned expenditure.) The increase in aggregate expenditure, ΔE, increases aggregate demand and also shifts the aggregate demand curve rightward to $AD_0 + \Delta E$. A multiplier process begins. The increase in expenditure increases income, which induces an increase in consumption expenditure. Aggregate demand increases further, and the aggregate demand curve eventually shifts rightward to AD_1.

The new equilibrium is at full employment. Real GDP is equal to potential GDP. The price level rises to 105 and then becomes stable at that level so after a one-time adjustment, there is price stability.

In this example, we have given the Bank a perfect hit at achieving full employment and keeping the price level stable. It is unlikely that the Bank would be able to achieve the precision of this example. A Bank Rate cut that is too little or too late leaves the economy in a recession and too big a cut sends inflation above target.

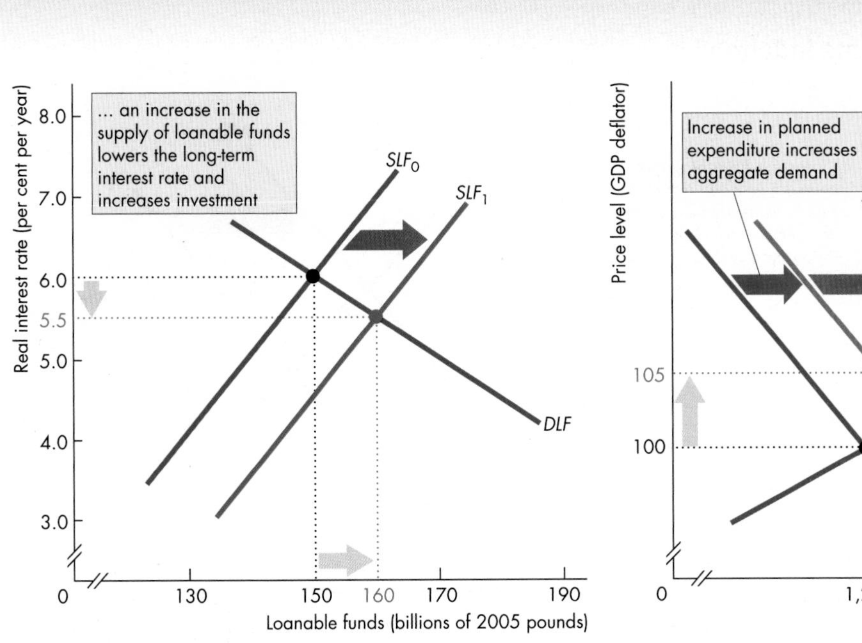

(c) The market for loanable funds

In part (c), an increase in the supply of bank loans increases the supply of loanable funds and the real interest rate falls. Aggregate planned expenditure increases.

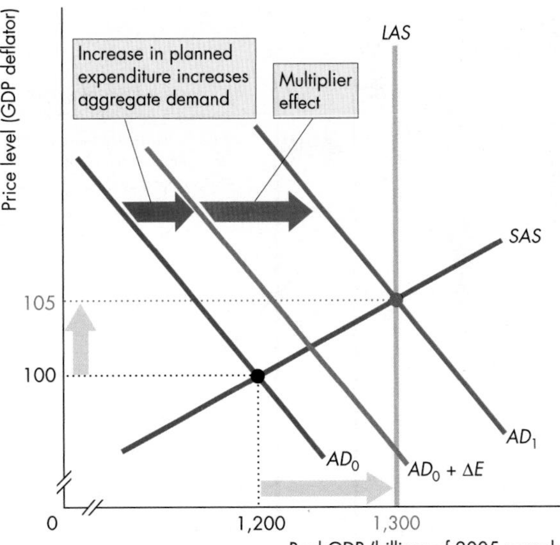

(d) Real GDP and the price level

In part (d), aggregate demand increases and the aggregate demand curve shifts to $AD_0 + \Delta E$. Eventually it shifts rightward to AD_1. Real GDP increases to potential GDP, and the price level rises.

The Bank Fights Inflation

If the inflation rate is too high and real GDP is above potential GDP, the Bank of England takes actions that are designed to lower the inflation rate and restore price stability. Figure 28.9 shows the effects of the Bank's actions starting in the market for reserves and ending in the market for real GDP.

Market for Bank Reserves

In Figure 28.9(a), which shows the market for bank reserves, the MPC raises Bank Rate from 5 per cent to 6 per cent a year. To keep the repo rate close to Bank Rate, the Bank sells securities and decreases the supply of reserves of the banking system from RS_0 to RS_1.

Money Market

With decreased reserves, the banks shrink deposits by decreasing loans and the supply of money decreases. The short-term interest rate rises and the quantity of money demanded decreases. In Figure 28.9(b), the supply of money decreases from MS_0 to MS_1, the interest rate rises from 5 per cent to 6 per cent a year and the quantity of money decreases from £1,400 billion to £1,300 billion.

Loanable Funds Market

With a decrease in reserves, banks must decrease the supply of loans. The supply of (real) loanable funds decreases, and the supply of loanable funds curve shifts leftward in Figure 28.9(c) from SLF_0 to SLF_1. With the demand for loanable funds at *DLF*, the real interest rate rises from 6 per cent to 6.5 per cent a year. (Again, we're assuming a zero inflation rate so that the real interest rate equals the nominal interest rate.)

The Market for Real GDP

Figure 28.9(d) shows aggregate demand and aggregate supply in the market for real GDP. Potential GDP and *LAS* are £1,300 billion. The short-run aggregate supply curve is *SAS* and initially, the aggregate demand is AD_0. Now, real GDP is £1,400 billion, which is greater than potential GDP, so there is an inflationary gap. The Bank is reacting to this inflationary gap.

Figure 28.9

The Bank of England Fights Inflation

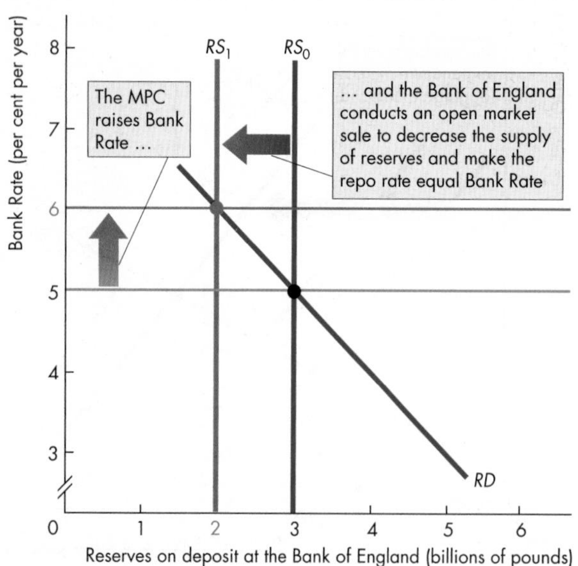

(a) The market for bank reserves

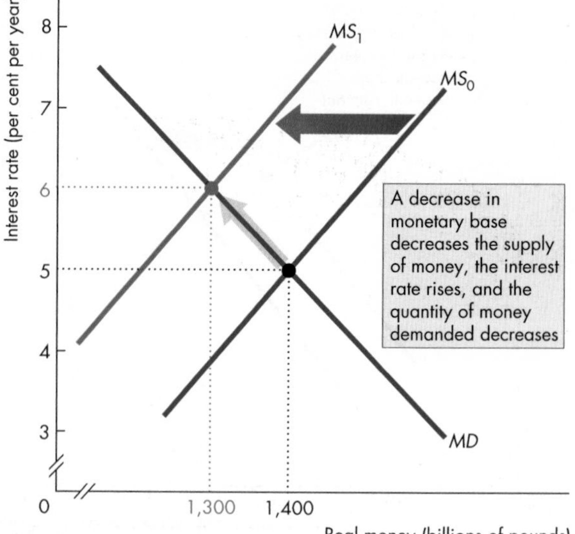

(b) Money market

In part (a), the MPC raises Bank Rate from 5 per cent to 6 per cent. To make the repo rate equal to Bank Rate the Bank of England sells securities in an open market operation to decrease the supply of reserves from RS_0 to RS_1.

In part (b), the supply of money decreases from MS_0 to MS_1, the short-term interest rate rises, and the quantity of money demanded decreases. The short-term interest rate and Bank Rate change by similar amounts.

The decrease in the supply of bank loans, and the increase in the real interest rate decrease aggregate planned expenditure. (Not shown in the figures, a rise in the interest rate raises the exchange rate, which decreases net exports and also aggregate planned expenditure.)

The decrease in aggregate expenditure, ΔE, decreases aggregate demand and the aggregate demand curve shifts to $AD_0 - \Delta E$. A multiplier process begins. The decrease in expenditure decreases income, which induces a decrease in consumption expenditure. Aggregate demand decreases further, and the aggregate demand curve eventually shifts leftward to AD_1.

The economy returns to full employment. Real GDP is equal to potential GDP. The price level falls to 105 and then becomes stable at that level so after a one-time adjustment, there is price stability.

Again, in this example, we have given the Bank a perfect hit at achieving full employment and keeping the price level stable. If the Bank raised Bank Rate by too little or too late, the economy would have remained with an inflationary gap and the inflation rate would have moved above the target. And if the Bank raised Bank Rate by too much it would push the economy from inflation to recession.

Loose Links and Long and Variable Lags

The ripple effects of monetary policy that we've just analyzed with the precision of an economic model are, in reality, very hard to predict and anticipate.

To achieve its inflation target and its additional mandate to support the government's economic policy of keeping real GDP growing at the maximum sustainable rate and maintaining full employment, the Bank needs a combination of good judgement and good luck.

Too large an interest rate cut can bring inflation, as it did during the 1970s. And too large an interest rate rise in an inflationary economy can create unemployment, as it did in 1981 and 1991.

Loose links in the chain that runs from Bank Rate to the ultimate policy goals make unwanted policy outcomes inevitable. And time lags that are both long and variable add to the Bank of England's challenges.

myeconlab

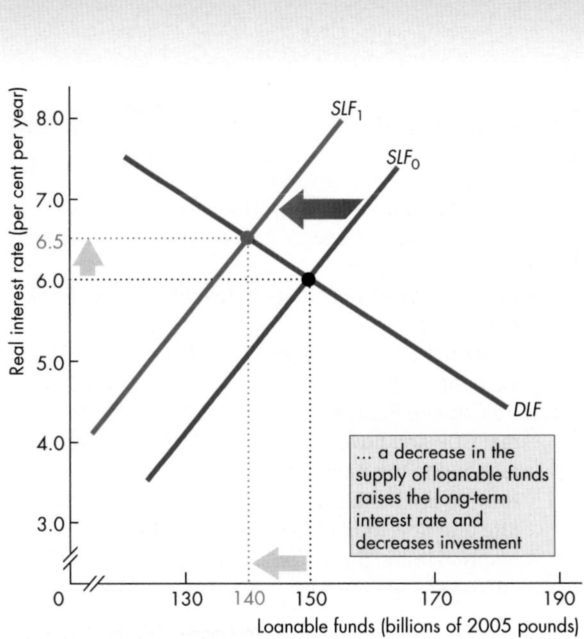

(c) The market for loanable funds

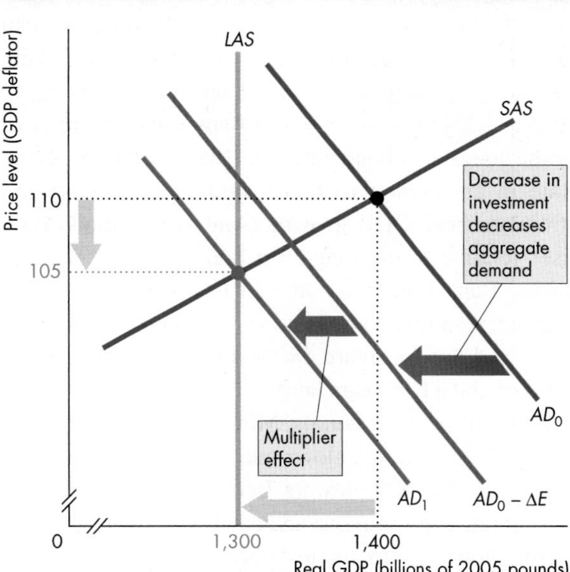

(d) Real GDP and the price level

In part (c), a decrease in the supply of bank loans decreases the supply of loanable funds and the real interest rate rises. Aggregate planned expenditure decreases.

In part (d), aggregate demand decreases and the aggregate demand curve shifts to $AD_0 - \Delta E$. Eventually it shifts leftward from AD_0 to AD_1. Real GDP decreases to potential GDP, and the price level falls.

Loose Link from Bank Rate to Spending

The real long-term interest rate that influences spending plans is linked only loosely to Bank Rate. Also, the response of the real long-term interest rate to a change in the nominal rate depends on how inflation expectations change. And the response of expenditure plans to changes in the real interest rate depend on many factors that make the response hard to predict.

Time Lags in the Adjustment Process

The Bank is especially handicapped by the fact that the monetary policy transmission process is long and drawn out. Also, the economy does not always respond in exactly the same way to a policy change. Further, many factors other than policy are constantly changing and bringing new situations to which policy must respond.

A Final Reality Check

You've studied the theory of monetary policy. Does it really work in the way we've described? It does. And Figure 28.10 provides some evidence to support this conclusion.

In Figure 28.10, the blue line shows Bank Rate that the Bank targets minus the long-term bond rate. You saw earlier (in Figure 28.7) that the short-term interest rates fluctuate more than the long-term rate. We can view the gap between the long-term bond rate and Bank Rate as a measure of how hard the Bank is trying to steer a change in course. When Bank Rate falls relative to the long-term bond rate, the Bank is cutting Bank Rate in an attempt to boost aggregate demand and stimulate real GDP growth. And when Bank Rate rises relative to the long-term bond rate, the Bank is raising Bank Rate in an attempt to decrease aggregate demand, restrain inflation and slow real GDP growth.

The red line in Figure 28.10 is the real GDP growth rate one and a half years later.

You can see that when the MPC raises Bank Rate, the real GDP growth rate slows one and a half years later. And when the MPC lowers Bank Rate, the real GDP growth rate speeds up one and a half years later.

Not shown in this figure, other things remaining the same, the inflation rate increases and decreases in line with the fluctuations in the real GDP growth rate. But the effects of an interest rate change on the inflation rate take even longer. Also, other influences on the inflation rate break the link between inflation and real GDP fluctuations.

Figure 28.10

Interest Rates and Real GDP Growth

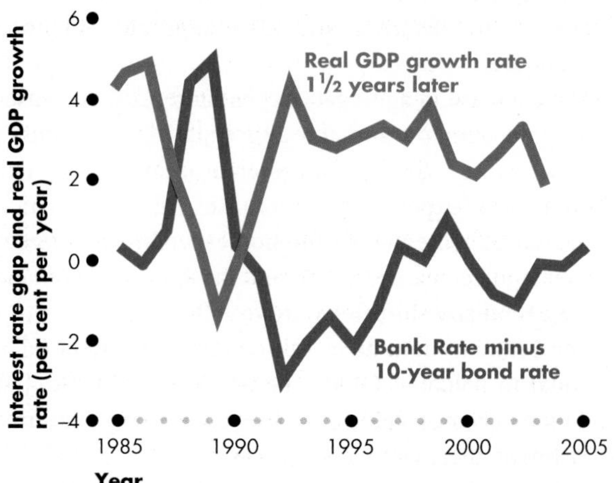

When Bank Rate rises relative to the long-term bond rates, the real GDP growth rate usually slows about one and a half years later. Similarly, when Bank Rate falls relative to the long-term bond rate, the real GDP growth rate speeds up about one and a half years later.

Sources of data: Bank of England and Office for National Statistics.

Review Quiz

Study Plan 28.3

1. Describe the channels by which monetary policy ripples through the economy and explain why each channel operates.
2. Do interest rates fluctuate in response to the Bank of England's actions?
3. How do the Bank of England's actions change the exchange rate?
4. How do the Bank of England's actions influence real GDP and how long does it take for real GDP to respond to the Bank's policy changes?
5. How do the Bank's actions influence the inflation rate and how long does it take for inflation to respond to the Bank's policy changes?

You've seen how the Bank of England conducts monetary policy and the effects of its actions. We close this chapter by looking at alternative ways in which the Bank could operate – at alternative monetary policy strategies.

Alternative Monetary Policy Strategies

So far in this chapter, we've described and analyzed the Bank of England's method of conducting monetary policy. But we haven't asked whether the Bank's strategy is the best available. The Bank has choices among alternative monetary policy strategies. What are they? And which one is the best?

We're going to end our discussion of monetary policy by examining the alternatives and explaining why the Bank of England has rejected them in favour of the interest rate strategy that we've described.

Earlier in this chapter (on p. 646), we placed all monetary policy strategies into two broad categories: *instrument rules* and *targeting rules*. And we described the Bank of England's strategy as using a *targeting rule* approach. So the Bank has rejected instrument rules. It has also rejected other possible targeting rules.

The Bank of England might have chosen any of four main alternative monetary policy strategies: Two of them are alternative targeting rules and two are instrument rules. The four alternatives are:

- Money stock targeting rule
- Exchange rate targeting rule
- Monetary base instrument rule
- Interest rate instrument rule

Money Stock Targeting Rule

As long ago as 1948, Nobel Laureate Milton Friedman proposed a targeting rule for the quantity of money. Friedman's ***k* per cent rule** makes the quantity of money grow at a rate of *k* per cent a year, where *k* equals the growth rate of potential GDP.

Friedman's idea was that by keeping the quantity of money growing at a steady (*k* per cent) rate, the inflation rate would be steady at (roughly) *k* per cent minus the real GDP growth rate, a prediction based on the quantity theory of money (see Chapter 30, pp. 700–701).

Price stability is the ultimate goal of money stock targeting. But Friedman and others who support this approach to monetary policy believe that while targeting the money stock is feasible, targeting the inflation rate is not feasible because the lags from the interest rate to the inflation target are simply too long.

Friedman's idea remained just that until the 1970s, when inflation increased to more than 20 per cent a year in the United Kingdom and above double-digits in many other major countries. In a bid to end the inflation, the Bank of England adopted the *k* per cent rule for the growth rate of the quantity of money. The inflation rate fell, but the policy was abandoned in the early 1980s. (The period from the early 1980s to 1997 when the first inflation target was adopted were years of evolution towards today's policy approach.)

Money stock targeting works when the demand for money is stable and predictable. But, as you've seen (in Chapter 27, p. 631), in the world of the 1980s and of today, technological change in the banking system has led to large and unpredictable shifts in the demand for money, which has made the use of monetary targeting unreliable.

Exchange Rate Targeting Rule

The Bank of England could, if it wished to do so, intervene in the foreign exchange market to target the exchange rate.

A fixed exchange rate is one possible exchange rate target. But with a fixed exchange rate, a country has no control over its inflation rate. The reason is that for internationally traded goods, market forces move domestic prices in line with foreign prices (see p. 738). If a computer chip costs €100 in Dublin, and if the exchange rate is €2 per £1, then the computer chip will sell for £50 (ignoring local tax differences) in London. If this price relationship didn't prevail, it would be possible to earn a profit by buying at the lower price and selling at the higher price. This trading would compete away the profit and price difference.

So with a fixed exchange rate between the pound and the euro, the prices of traded goods (and in the long run the prices of all goods and services) must rise at the same rate in the United Kingdom as they do in the Eurozone.

But the Bank of England could use a *crawling peg* (see p. 736 and p. 743) as a means of achieving an inflation target. To do so, (and continuing to use the euro as the other currency) the Bank would make the exchange rate *change* at a rate equal to the Eurozone inflation rate minus the UK target inflation rate. If the United Kingdom has an inflation target of 2 per cent a year and Eurozone has an inflation rate of 1 per cent a year, the Bank of England would make the pound depreciate at a rate of 1 per cent a year.

Some developing countries that have an inflation problem use this monetary policy strategy to lower the inflation rate. The main reason for choosing this method is that these countries don't have well-functioning financial markets in which the central bank can intervene with open market operations to influence the interest rate.

A major disadvantage of a crawling peg to target the inflation rate is that the real exchange rate often changes in unpredictable ways. The United Kingdom's real exchange rate with the Eurozone is the relative price of the GDP baskets of goods and services in the two countries. The two baskets are similar but by no means the same so the real exchange rate changes. With a crawling peg targeting the inflation rate, we would need to be able to identify changes in the real exchange rate and offset them. This task is impossible to accomplish.

Monetary Base Instrument Rule

Although the Bank of England uses open market operations to keep repo rate close to its chosen Bank Rate it could, instead, use the same open market operations to shoot for a target growth rate of the monetary base.

The idea of using a rule to hit a monetary base growth target has been suggested by Carnegie-Mellon University economist Bennet T. McCallum, and a monetary base rule bears his name.

The **McCallum rule** makes the growth rate of the monetary base respond to the long-term average growth rate of real GDP and medium-term changes in the velocity of circulation of the monetary base.

Like Friedman's *k* per cent rule, this rule is based on the quantity theory of money (see Chapter 30, pp. 700–701). McCallum's idea is that by making the monetary base grow at a rate equal to the target inflation rate plus the long-term real GDP growth rate (adjusted for changes in the demand for money), inflation will be kept close to target.

The McCallum rule shares a similar disadvantage to that of the *k* per cent rule: it relies on a stable or predicably changing demand for monetary base.

You've seen that the demand for money jumps around (see Chapter 27, p. 631) in unpredictable ways because financial innovation is constantly changing the way we use money and the composition of money. The demand for monetary base is made up of the demand for currency and the demand by commercial banks for reserves. Both components of the demand for monetary base are subject to the same amount of unpredictable change as the demand for money.

The Bank of England believes that the demand for monetary base is in fact too unstable to be a useful object to target.

Interest Rate Instrument Rule

Although the Bank of England sets an interest rate, it doesn't set it using a simple rule. Instead, the MPC members use a wide variety of indicators and place varying degrees of weight on them to come up with a best judgement about the appropriate level for the interest rate.

The idea of setting the interest rate based on a simple rule was suggested by Stanford University economist John B. Taylor, and the rule bears his name.

The **Taylor rule** sets the interest rate (Bank Rate in the United Kingdom) in response to only two indicators: the current inflation rate and the current best estimate of the output gap (real GDP minus potential GDP as a percentage of potential GDP).

When the inflation rate is on target and the output gap is zero, the Taylor rule sets the interest rate at "neutral". The neutral interest rate is the level that neither stimulates nor retards the growth rate of aggregate demand. It keeps aggregate demand on a steady course that is neither adding to nor subtracting from the current inflation rate.

Based on the average of the averages since 1997, we estimate the neutral *real* Bank Rate to be about 2.75 per cent a year. With an inflation target of 2 per cent a year, the neutral *nominal* Bank Rate is 4.75 per cent a year. (See Chapter 24, p. 545 for an explanation of the distinction and relationship between the nominal and real interest rate.)

If inflation is on target and the output gap is zero (full employment), the Taylor rule sets Bank Rate at 4.75 per cent a year. It sets Bank Rate below 4.75 per cent if the economy is below full employment and above 4.75 per cent if the economy is above full employment. The rule specifies exactly by how much the interest rate deviates from neutral with a formula.

Calling Bank Rate R, the neutral *real* Bank Rate R^*, the inflation rate p, the target inflation rate p^*, and the output gap (as a percentage of potential GDP) G, the Taylor rule says, set Bank Rate to equal:

$$R = R^* + p + 0.5(p - p^*) + 0.5G$$

In words, the Taylor rule sets Bank Rate at 2.75 per cent plus the current inflation rate, plus a half of the gap between the current inflation rate and its target, plus a half of the output gap.

Figure 28.11 shows how the MPC interest rate decisions compare with the Taylor rule. The rule would have made Bank Rate fluctuate much less than the MPC thought appropriate. Between 1997 and mid-2001,

Figure 28.11

MPC Decisions and the Taylor Rule

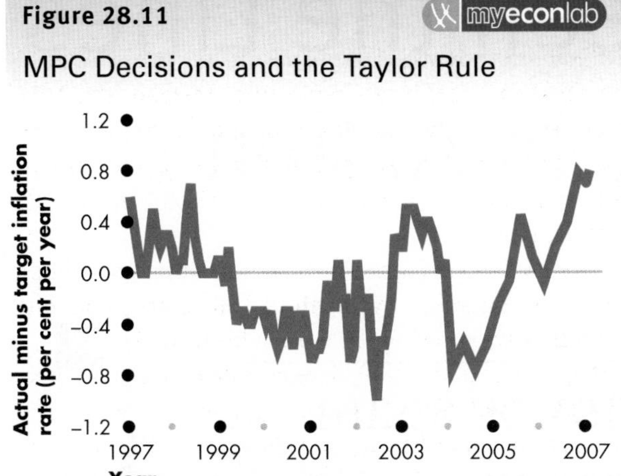

(a) Deviation from inflation target

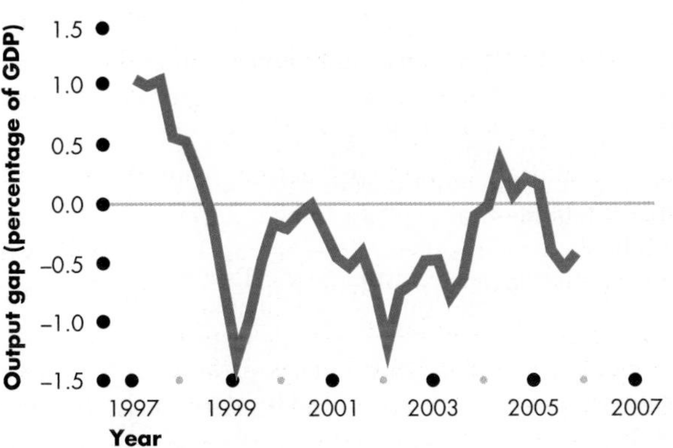

(b) Estimated output gap

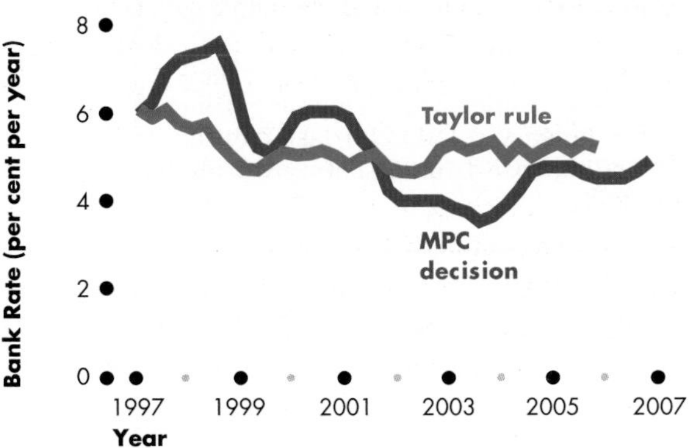

(c) MPC decisions and the Taylor Rule

The Taylor rule makes Bank Rate fluctuate less than the MPC thinks appropriate. Between 1997 and mid-2001, the Taylor rule sets Bank Rate lower than the level set by the MPC. From mid-2001 to 2006, the Taylor rule sets Bank Rate above the level set by the MPC.

Sources of data: Inflation rate, Office for National Statistics; interest rate, Bank of England; output gap, Anthony Garratt, Kevin Lee, Emi Mise and Kalvinder Shields "Real Time Representation of the UK Output Gap in the Presence of Trend Uncertainty" Birkbeck College mimeograph.

Bank Rate would have been lower than the level set by the MPC. And since mid-2001, Bank Rate based on the Taylor rule would have been higher than the level set by the MPC.

The Bank believes that because it uses much more information than just the current inflation rate and the output gap, it is able to set the interest rate more intelligently than any simple rule can set.

A problem for the Taylor rule is that the Bank needs to estimate the neutral real Bank Rate and the output gap. Both of these inputs to the rule are impossible to know exactly and are subject to estimation errors that could send the inflation rate badly off course if the rule was mechanically followed.

Why Rules?

You might be wondering why all monetary policy strategies involve *rules*. Why doesn't the Bank of England just do what seems best every day, month and year, at its discretion?

The answer is that monetary policy is about managing inflation expectations. In both financial markets and labour markets, people must make long-term commitments. So these markets work best when plans are based on correctly anticipated inflation outcomes. A well-understood monetary policy rule helps to create an environment in which inflation is easier to forecast and manage.

Review Quiz

Study Plan 28.3

1. What are the four main alternative strategies for conducting monetary policy (other than the one used by the Bank of England)?
2. What is the main objection to money stock targeting?
3. What is the main objection to exchange rate targeting?
4. What is the main objection to a rule for the growth of monetary base?
5. What is the main objection to a rule for the interest rate?

In the next chapter, we're going to explore how interactions of fiscal policy and monetary policy influence the economy. But first, take a look at *Reading Between the Lines* on pp. 660–661 and see the how the Bank of England struggled to hold inflation down during 2007.

Reading Between the Lines

Monetary Policy in Action

The Financial Times, 20 March 2007

FT

UK inflation climbs again to 2.8 per cent

Jamie Chisholm

Stronger-than-expected inflation and consumer borrowing data released on Tuesday have increased the chances of another hike in the cost of borrowing.

The pound jumped as traders reacted to news that the government's target measure of prices climbed by an annual 2.8 per cent last month and mortgage approvals, a good guide to near-term housing market activity, had their strongest-ever February.

Short sterling futures – the City's vehicle for betting on the future direction of interest – quickly gave ground, reflecting the view that the Bank of England will see such data as providing further evidence that a further tightening of monetary policy will be required to cool demand.

The Office for National Statistics said its index of consumer prices rose by 0.4 per cent between January and February, primarily nudged higher by an increase in air fares, much of which came from the chancellor's hike in passenger duty announced in December.

This took the annual inflation rate to 2.8 per cent, slightly higher than the 2.7 recorded in January and the tenth consecutive month that CPI has been above the Bank's 2 per cent target.

The annual increase in the Retail Prices Index, which includes interest payments on mortgages, jumped to 4.6 per cent, its fastest pace in more than 15 years as lenders passed on January's interest rate increase to home-owners.

Meanwhile there was further evidence that the three interest increases since last August have yet to damage the housing market.

The Building Societies Association said that mortgage approvals climbed from £4.2bn in January to £4.92bn last month. Gross lending rose from £4.06bn over the same period.

The Essence of the Story

- The February 2007 CPI inflation rate was 2.8 per cent a year compared to the Bank of England target of 2 per cent a year.
- With inflation above target, traders expect the Bank of England will raise the interest rate.
- The Office for National Statistics said that an increase in air passenger taxes that raised air fares was the primary source of the CPI jump.
- The Retail Prices Index showed inflation at 4.6 per cent a year.
- Despite previous interest rate increases, economic growth remains strong and loans for house purchase continued to grow strongly.

Economic Analysis

- The UK CPI inflation rate moved increasingly above 2 per cent a year throughout 2006 and into 2007.
- Figure 1 shows that the CPI inflation rate and Bank Rate. The inflation rate on the left axis and the Bank Rate on the right axis are aligned so that at 2 per cent inflation (the target), Bank Rate is 4.75 per cent (neutral) — see p. 658.
- You can see that Bank Rate was below neutral from mid-2005 to mid-2006 and most likely contributed to the rising inflation.
- You can also see that the Bank of England raised Bank Rate in the second half of 2006 in response to rising inflation.
- Figure 2 shows an indicator of a strongly growing economy. The left axis shows the increase in house prices and the right axis shows the growth in mortgage lending. Despite the rising Bank Rate, house prices and mortgage lending continued to grow strongly.
- Higher house prices make households feel better off, which leads to increased consumer borrowing and spending.
- In Figure 3, the UK long-run aggregate supply curve is *LAS* at potential GDP. The short-run aggregate supply curve is *SAS*.
- The Bank of England worries that in 2007, aggregate demand at AD_0 is too high and is creating an inflationary gap.
- By raising Bank Rate further, the Bank would like to shift the aggregate demand curve leftward.
- If the Bank shifts the aggregate demand curve leftward to AD_1 to eliminate the inflationary gap, inflation will stop increasing, but it will not return to 2 per cent a year.
- To lower the inflation rate back to 2 per cent a year, the Bank must shift the aggregate demand curve leftward to AD_2 where there is a recessionary gap.

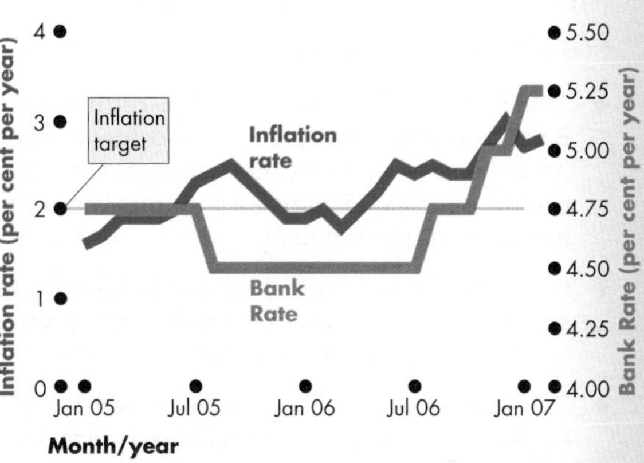

Figure 1 Inflation and Bank Rate

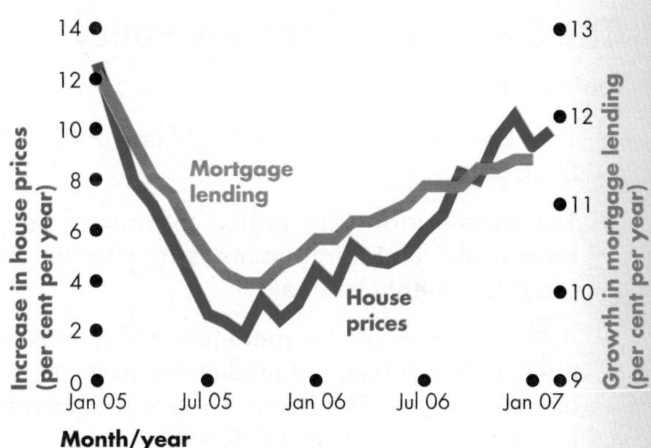

Figure 2 House price increases and the growth in mortgage lending

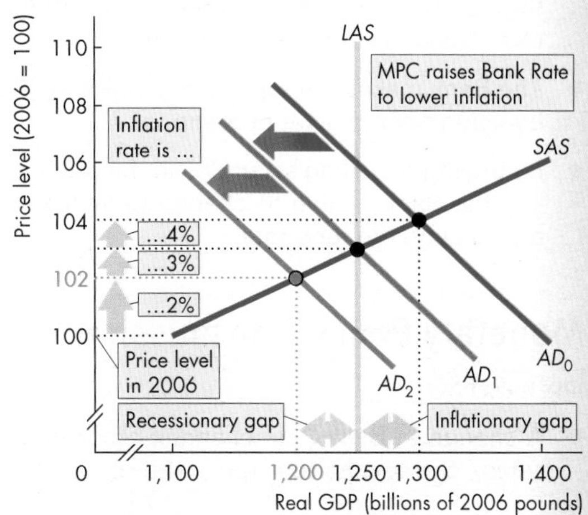

Figure 3 Aggregate supply and aggregate demand in 2007

Summary

Key Points

Monetary Policy Objectives and Framework (pp. 642–644)

- The Bank of England Act 1998 requires the Bank to use monetary policy to achieve stable prices and to support the government's economic policies of high and stable economic growth and employment.
- Each year, the Chancellor of the Exchequer specifies the Bank's remit in terms of a numerical target for the inflation rate.
- Since 2004, the Bank has been required to achieve an inflation rate measured by the CPI of 2 per cent a year.

The Conduct of Monetary Policy (pp. 645–648)

- The Bank's monetary policy instrument is Bank Rate.
- The Bank's monetary policy committee sets Bank Rate and announces any change at roughly monthly intervals.
- An instrument rule for monetary policy makes the instrument respond predictably to the state of the economy. The Bank of England does not use a mechanical instrument rule.
- A targeting rule for monetary policy sets the instrument at a level that makes the forecast of the inflation rate equal to the target inflation rate. The Bank does use such a rule.
- The Bank makes the repo rate equal Bank Rate by using open market operations.
- By buying or selling securities in the open market, the Bank is able to change bank reserves and change the repo rate.

Monetary Policy Transmission (pp. 649–656)

- A change in Bank Rate changes other interest rates, the exchange rate, the quantity of money and loans, aggregate demand and eventually real GDP and the price level.
- A change in Bank Rate changes real GDP a year to 18 months later and changes the inflation rate with an even longer time lag.

Alternative Monetary Policy Strategies (pp. 657–659)

- The main alternatives to setting Bank Rate are a money stock targeting rule, an exchange rate targeting rule, a monetary base instrument rule and an interest rate instrument rule.
- Rules dominate discretion in monetary policy because they better enable the central bank to manage inflation expectations.

Key Figures

Key Terms

Problems

Tests, Study Plan and Solutions* 

1 Compare two alternative remits for the Bank of England:

Remit *A* is to keep the inflation rate between 1 per cent and 3 per cent a year but with no requirement to keep trend inflation at 2 per cent a year.

Remit *B* is to keep the inflation rate between 1 per cent and 3 per cent a year and to keep trend inflation at 2 per cent a year.

If the Bank achieves its target and if initially the price level is 100, with remit *A*:

a What is the highest price level that might occur after 10 years?

b What is the lowest price level that might occur after 10 years?

c What is the range of uncertainty about the price level after 10 years?

d Would this type of inflation goal serve the financial markets well and provide an anchor for inflation expectations?

e With remit *B* what is the likely price level after 10 years?

f Which remit provides the greater certainty about inflation over the longer term? Which has the greater short-term certainty?

2 Bank Rate target is 4.75 per cent a year and the MPC decides to raise the rate to 5 per cent a year.

a Does the Bank buy or sell securities in the open market?

b What changes occur in the balance sheet of the Bank of England?

c What changes occur in the balance sheets of commercial banks?

d Illustrate the changes that occur in a graph of the market for bank reserves like Figure 28.5.

3 Bank Rate target is 4.75 per cent a year and the MPC decides to lower the rate to 4.5 per cent a year.

a Does the Bank buy or sell securities in the open market?

b What changes occur in the balance sheet of the Bank of England?

c What changes occur in the balance sheets of commercial banks?

d Illustrate the changes that occur in a graph of the market for bank reserves like Figure 28.5.

4 The inflation rate is 2.8 per cent and rising, real GDP is above potential and Bank Rate is 5 per cent.

a What is the most likely decision of the MPC at its next meeting?

b How does the MPC decision influence the inflation rate? Answer by tracing all the steps between a change in Bank Rate and a change in the inflation rate and describe the time lags in the monetary policy transmission process.

5 The figure shows the economy of Freezone. The aggregate demand curve is *AD*, and the short-run aggregate supply curve is SAS_A. Potential GDP is £300 billion.

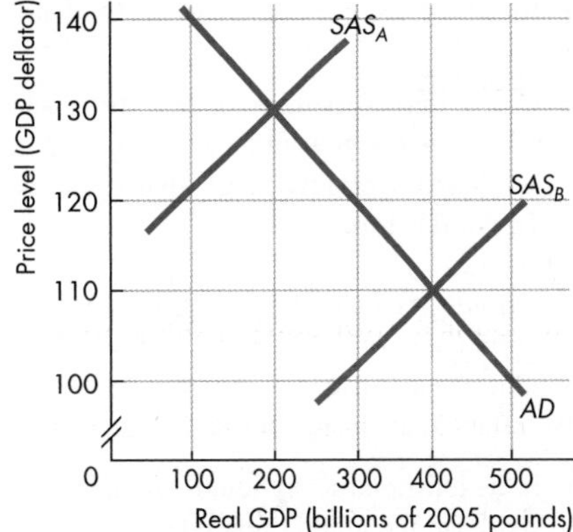

a What are the price level and real GDP?

b Does Freezone have a recession problem or an inflation problem? Why?

c What do you predict will happen in Freezone if the central bank takes no monetary policy actions?

d What monetary policy action would you advise the central bank to take and what do you predict will be the effect of that action?

6 Suppose that in Freezone, shown in problem 5, the short-run aggregate supply curve is SAS_B and potential GDP increases to £350 billion.

a What happens in Freezone if the central bank lowers the Bank Rate and buys securities on the open market?

b What happens in Freezone if the central bank increases the Bank Rate and sells securities on the open market?

c Do you recommend that the central bank lower Bank Rate and buy securities or increase Bank Rate and sell securities? Why?

* Solutions to odd-numbered problems are provided.

7 Suppose that in Freezone, shown in problem 5, the short-run aggregate supply curve is SAS_A and a drought decreases potential GDP to £250 billion.

a What happens in Freezone if the central bank lowers Bank Rate and buys securities on the open market?

b What happens in Freezone if the central bank increases the Bank Rate and sells securities on the open market?

c Do you recommend that the central bank lower Bank Rate and buy securities or increase Bank Rate and sell securities? Why?

8 Suppose that the Bank of England's Monetary Policy Committee decides to use the Taylor Rule. The United Kingdom has an inflation rate of 2.9 per cent a year and its output gap is 0.5 per cent.

a At what level does the Bank of England set Bank Rate?

b If you were a member of the MPC, what factors might make you want to set Bank Rate at a higher level or lower level than that delivered by the Taylor rule formula?

9 The South African Reserve Bank (SARB) has an inflation target of 3 per cent to 6 per cent a year and sets the South African overnight interest rate to keep the inflation rate inside this target range.

a If the inflation rate in South Africa is 4.5 per cent a year, and the neutral real rate is 3 per cent a year, what would you expect to be the overnight interest rate?

b As a member of the SARB Monetary Policy Committee, what conditions would encourage you to vote to put the overnight interest rate at 9 per cent a year or higher?

c What conditions would encourage you to vote to put the overnight interest rate at 6 per cent a year or lower?

10 The European Central Bank (ECB) targets the Eurozone inflation rate to make it remain below but close to 2 per cent a year. To pursue this goal, the ECB sets the official ECB interest rate but pays close attention to the growth rate of the quantity of money.

a Compare and contrast the monetary policy objectives of the ECB and the Bank of England.

b Compare and contrast the monetary policy strategies of the ECB and the Bank of England.

Critical Thinking

1 Study *Reading Between the Lines* on pp. 660–661 and then answer the following questions:

a What was the UK inflation rate in early 2007 and how did it compare with the target?

b Why, according to the Office for National Statistics, did the inflation rate increase? Do you think the reason offered is credible? Explain why or why not.

c What indicators suggest that the Bank of England will need to raise Bank Rate still higher during 2007?

d How did the Bank of England change Bank Rate during 2007? Do you think the decisions were good ones? Explain your answer.

2 Suppose that the United Kingdom joined the Eurozone:

a What functions would the Bank of England retain and what functions would move to the ECB?

b What would happen to the current inflation targets?

c Would this change benefit the United Kingdom?

d Would the United Kingdom incur any cost?

e Explain why you favour or oppose the United Kingdom joining the Eurozone.

3 Gordon Brown, the Chancellor of the Exchequer, tells Mervyn King, Governor of the Bank of England, to keep the interest rate stable and the quantity of money stable. The Governor asks you to draft a reply to the Chancellor explaining why the Bank is unable to do what he asks. Make your report crisp and clear so that the Chancellor is in no doubt about the impossibility of the task he has set.

Web Activities

Links to Websites

1 Visit the Bank of England website. Read the minutes of the most recent meeting of the MPC and look at the spreadsheet that shows the voting record of MPC members.

a Is the Bank trying to slow the inflation rate or speed it up? How can you tell?

b In light of the MPC's recent actions, what ripple effects do you expect over the coming months?

c Which MPC members are most concerned about inflation and which are least concerned?

CHAPTER 29

Fiscal and Monetary Interactions

After studying this chapter you will be able to:

- Explain macroeconomic equilibrium
- Explain how fiscal policy influences real GDP and the price level
- Explain how monetary policy influences real GDP and the price level
- Explain the Keynesian–monetarist debate
- Explain the effects of fiscal and monetary policy at full employment
- Explain how fiscal policy and monetary policy might be coordinated or in conflict

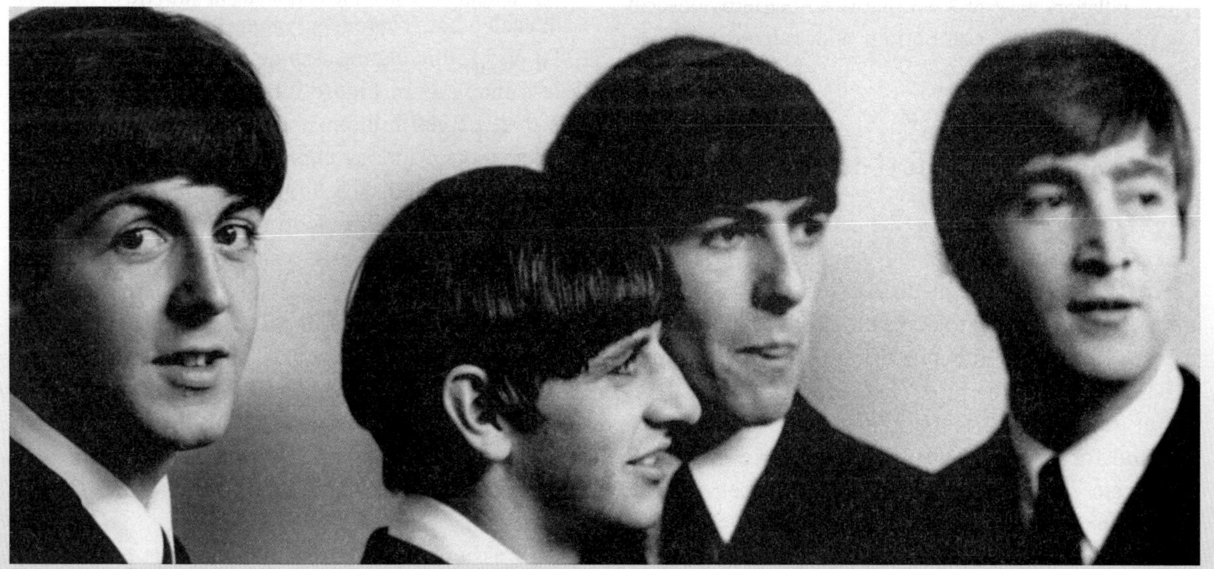

Harmony and Discord

Do fiscal and monetary policies need to be coordinated so that they work in harmony? Or can the government's fiscal policy and the Bank of England's monetary policy play their own tunes in discord? Is a tax cut just as good as an interest rate cut to get the economy growing and avoid recession? Or is one more powerful than the other? And to rein in inflation, is a tax rise just as good as an interest rate rise? Find some answers in this chapter. And at the end of the chapter, in *Reading Between the Lines*, see what the International Monetary Fund said about UK fiscal and monetary policy in 2007.

Macroeconomic Equilibrium

Your goal in this chapter is to learn how fiscal policy and monetary policy interact to influence real GDP, the price level and the inflation rate. You studied fiscal policy in Chapter 26 and monetary policy in Chapter 28. But these two accounts of the effects of policy didn't explain how fiscal and monetary policy interact. We need to know how they interact because we want to know whether we can use either on its own to achieve the same goals or whether they must be used in the correct combination.

You know that the Bank of England targets the inflation rate by setting Bank Rate. The quantity of money is a consequence of the Bank of England's interest rate decision. Despite the Bank of England's approach, we will explore fiscal and monetary policy interactions when the central bank targets the quantity of money. By doing so, we are able to review a long-running debate about policy between Keynesians and monetarists. And we are able to see the potential benefits and risks of the interest rate targeting approach favoured by the Bank of England.

To study policy effects, we ask how a given policy action changes the equilibrium. So we begin by describing macroeconomic equilibrium with a fixed target for the quantity of money.

Two Markets in Short-run Equilibrium

In a short-run equilibrium, the interest rate adjusts to make the quantity of money demanded equal to the quantity of money supplied (Chapter 27, p. 633). And the price level adjusts to make the quantity of real GDP demanded equal to the quantity of real GDP supplied (Chapter 23, pp. 518–519).

But real GDP and the price level influence the demand for money. And the interest rate influences aggregate demand. So the money market and the market for goods and services (for real GDP) are linked together.

Other things remaining the same, the greater the level of aggregate demand, the higher are real GDP and the price level. A higher real GDP means a greater demand for money; a higher price level means a smaller supply of real money; so a greater level of aggregate demand means a higher interest rate.

Aggregate demand depends on the interest rate because consumption expenditure, investment and net exports are influenced by the interest rate (see Chapter 28, p. 651). So, other things remaining the same, the lower the interest rate, the greater is the level of aggregate demand.

Only one level of aggregate demand and one interest rate are consistent with each other in macroeconomic equilibrium. Figure 29.1 describes this unique macroeconomic equilibrium.

In Figure 29.1(a), the intersection of the aggregate demand curve, *AD*, and the short-run aggregate supply curve, *SAS*, determines real GDP at £1,300 billion and the price level at 105. In Figure 29.1(b), the intersection of the demand for money curve, *MD*, and the supply of money curve, *MS*, determines the interest rate at 5 per cent a year. In Figure 29.1(c) at an interest rate of 5 per cent a year, the interest-sensitive expenditure curve, *IE*, determines the amount of interest-sensitive expenditure at £150 billion. The position of the *AD* curve depends on the quantity of money, and the demand for and supply of real money depend on the *AD* and *SAS* curves.

Simultaneous Equilibrium

The *AS–AD* equilibrium in Figure 29.1(a), the money market equilibrium in Figure 29.1(b), and interest-sensitive expenditure in Figure 29.1(c) are consistent with each other. There is no other equilibrium.

To check this claim, assume that aggregate demand is less than *AD* in Figure 29.1(a) so that real GDP is less than £1,300 billion. If this assumption is correct, the demand for money curve lies to the left of *MD* in Figure 29.1(b) and the equilibrium interest rate is less than 5 per cent a year. With an interest rate less than 5 per cent a year, interest-sensitive expenditure exceeds the £150 billion in Figure 29.1(c). If interest-sensitive expenditure exceeds £150 billion, the *AD* curve lies to the right of the one we assumed and equilibrium real GDP exceeds £1,300 billion. So if we assume that real GDP is less than £1,300 billion, equilibrium real GDP is greater than £1,300 billion. There is an inconsistency. The assumed equilibrium real GDP is too small.

Now assume that aggregate demand is greater than *AD* in Figure 29.1(a) so that real GDP exceeds £1,300 billion. If this assumption is correct, the demand for money curve lies to the right of *MD* in Figure 29.1(b) and the equilibrium interest rate exceeds 5 per cent a year. With an interest rate above 5 per cent a year, interest-sensitive expenditure is less than the £150 billion in Figure 29.1(c), in which case the equilibrium real GDP is less than £1,300 billion. There is another inconsistency. The assumed equilibrium real GDP is too large.

Figure 29.1 myeconlab

Equilibrium Real GDP, Price Level, Interest Rate and Expenditure

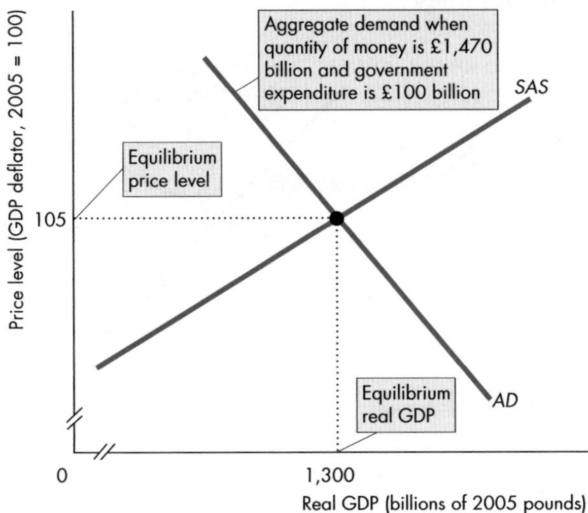

(a) Aggregate supply and aggregate demand

In part (a), the intersection of the aggregate demand curve, *AD*, and the short-run aggregate supply curve, *SAS*, determines real GDP at £1,300 billion and the price level at 105. Behind the *AD* curve, interest-sensitive expenditure is £150 billion, government expenditure is £260 billion and the rest of real GDP is £890 billion.

In part (b), when real GDP is £1,300 billion, the demand for money is *MD* and when the price level is 105, the supply of (real) money is *MS*. The intersection of the demand for money curve, *MD*, and the supply of money curve, *MS*, determines the interest rate at 5 per cent a year.

In part (c), on the *IE* curve, interest-sensitive expenditure is £150 billion at the equilibrium interest rate of 5 per cent a year.

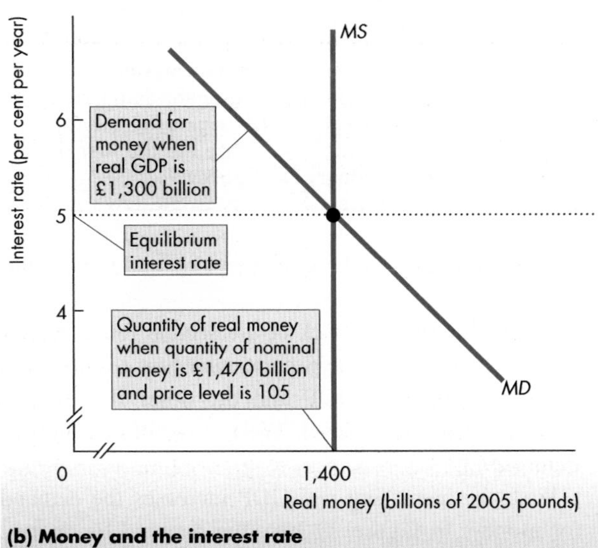

(b) Money and the interest rate

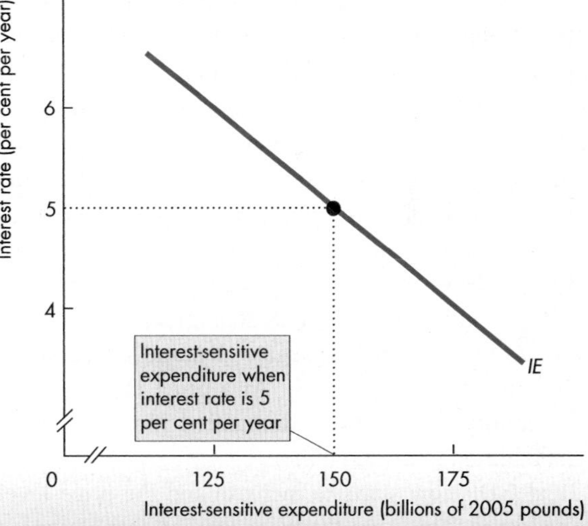

(c) Expenditure and the interest rate

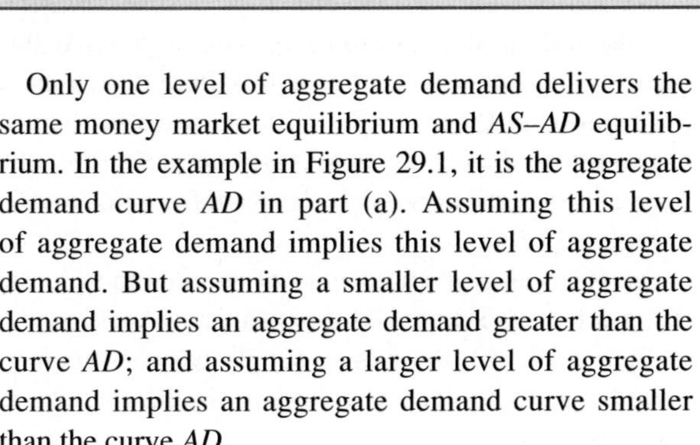
Only one level of aggregate demand delivers the same money market equilibrium and *AS–AD* equilibrium. In the example in Figure 29.1, it is the aggregate demand curve *AD* in part (a). Assuming this level of aggregate demand implies this level of aggregate demand. But assuming a smaller level of aggregate demand implies an aggregate demand greater than the curve *AD*; and assuming a larger level of aggregate demand implies an aggregate demand curve smaller than the curve *AD*.

Review Quiz

Study Plan 29.1

1 What are the links between aggregate demand, the money market and interest-sensitive expenditure at macroeconomic equilibrium?

Let's now study the effects of a change in government expenditure on real GDP and the price level.

Fiscal Policy in the Short Run

Real GDP growth is slowing, and the government is concerned that a recession is likely. So the government decides to head off the recession by using fiscal policy to stimulate aggregate demand. A fiscal policy that increases aggregate demand is called an *expansionary fiscal policy*.

The effects of an expansionary fiscal policy are similar to those of throwing a pebble into a pond. There's an initial splash followed by a series of ripples that become ever smaller. The initial splash is the "first round effect" of the fiscal policy action. The ripples are the "second round effects". You've already met the first round effects in Chapter 26, pp. 604–606, so here is a refresher.

First Round Effects of Fiscal Policy

The economy starts out in the position shown in Figure 29.1. Real GDP is £1,300 billion, the price level is 105, the interest rate is 5 per cent a year, and interest-sensitive expenditure is £150 billion. The government now increases its expenditure on goods and services by £100 billion.

Figure 29.2 shows the first round effects of this action. The increase in government expenditure has a multiplier effect because it brings an increase in induced expenditure. (You can refresh your memory of the government expenditure multiplier on pp. 598–600 of Chapter 26.) Let's assume that the multiplier is 2, so a £100 billion increase in government expenditure increases aggregate demand at a given price level by £200 billion. The aggregate demand curve shifts rightward from AD_0 to AD_1. At a price level of 105, the quantity of real GDP demanded increases from £1,300 billion to £1,500 billion.

Real GDP now starts to increase and the price level starts to rise. These are the first round effects of expansionary fiscal policy.

Figure 29.2

First Round Effects of an Expansionary Fiscal Policy

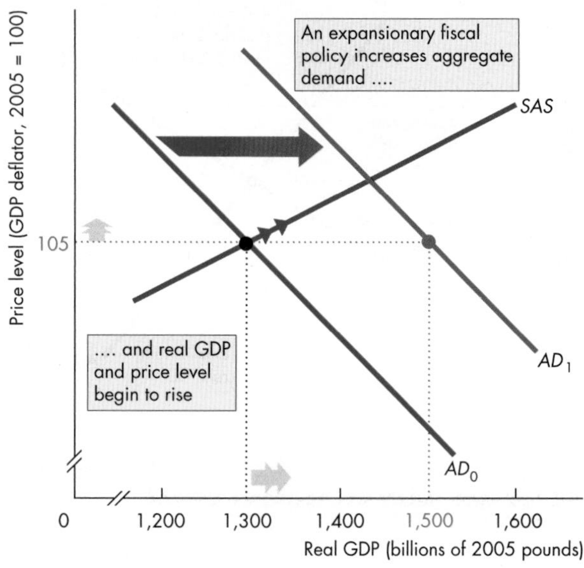

Initially, the aggregate demand curve is AD_0, real GDP is £1,300 billion and the price level is 105. A £100 billion increase in government expenditure on goods and services has a multiplier effect and increases aggregate demand by £200 billion. The aggregate demand curve shifts rightward to AD_1. Real GDP begins to increase and the price level begins to rise. These are the first round effects of an expansionary fiscal policy.

Second Round Effects of Fiscal Policy

Increasing real GDP and rising price level bring changes in the money market that creates second round effects. Through the second round, real GDP increases and the price level rises until a new macroeconomic equilibrium is reached. But to find that equilibrium and to describe the changes that result from the initial increase in government expenditure, we must keep track of further changes in the money market and in expenditure plans.

It is easier to keep track of the second round effects if we split them into two parts: one that results from the increasing real GDP and the other that results from the rising price level. We follow these effects in Figure 29.3.

First, the increasing real GDP increases the demand for money. In Figure 29.3(b), the demand for money curve shifts rightward. Eventually, it shifts to MD_1 and the interest rate rises to 6 per cent a year. At this interest rate, interest-sensitive expenditure decreases to £125 billion in Figure 29.3(c). The decrease in planned expenditure decreases aggregate demand and the aggregate demand curve shifts leftward from AD_1 to AD_2 in Figure 29.3(a).

Second, with a given quantity of nominal money, the rising price level decreases the quantity of real money. In Figure 29.3(b), the money supply curve shifts leftward from MS_0 to MS_1. The decrease in the quantity of

Figure 29.3

Second Round Effects of an Expansionary Fiscal Policy

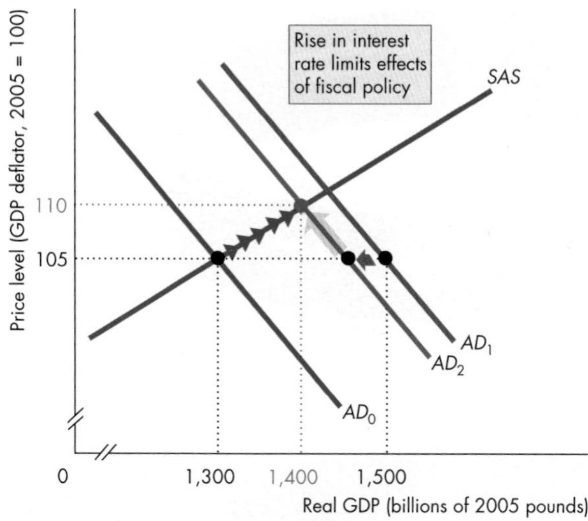

(a) Aggregate supply and aggregate demand

Initially, the demand curve for money is MD_0, the supply curve of real money is MS_0 and the interest rate is 5 per cent a year in part (b). With an interest rate of 5 per cent a year, interest-sensitive expenditure is £150 billion on the curve *IE* in part (c). With the increased government expenditure, the aggregate demand curve is AD_1 in part (a). Real GDP is increasing, and the price level is rising.

The increasing real GDP increases the demand for money and the demand for money curve shifts rightward to MD_1 in part (b). The higher interest rate decreases interest-sensitive expenditure in part (c), which decreases aggregate demand to AD_2 in part (a).

The rising price level brings a movement along the new aggregate demand curve AD_2. It does so because the rising price level decreases the supply of real money to MS_1, which in turn raises the interest rate further and decreases aggregate expenditure.

The new equilibrium occurs when real GDP has increased to £1,400 billion and the price level has risen to 110.

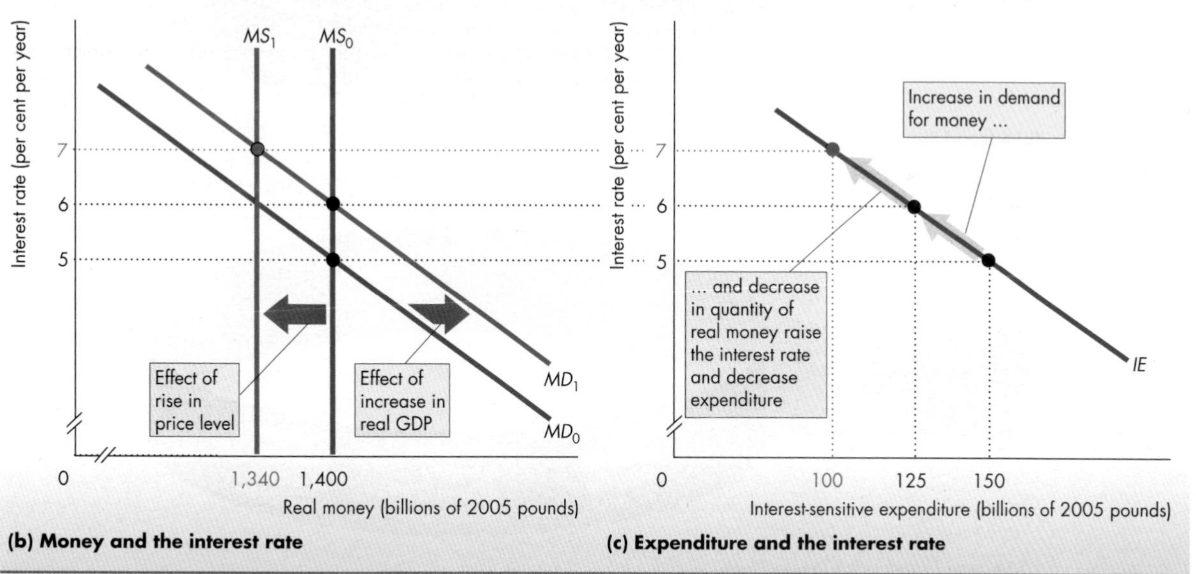

(b) Money and the interest rate

(c) Expenditure and the interest rate

real money raises the interest rate further to 7 per cent a year. In Figure 29.3(c), the higher interest rate decreases interest-sensitive expenditure to £100 billion.

Because this decrease in spending plans is induced by a rise in the price level, it decreases the quantity of real GDP demanded and is shown as a movement along the aggregate demand curve AD_2 in Figure 29.3(c).

During this second round process, real GDP is increasing and the price level is rising in a gradual movement up along the short-run aggregate supply curve as indicated by the arrows. In the new equilibrium, real GDP is £1,400 billion, the price level is 110, the interest rate is 7 per cent a year and interest-sensitive expenditure is £100 billion.

Figure 29.4

myeconlab

How the Economy Adjusts to an Expansionary Fiscal Policy

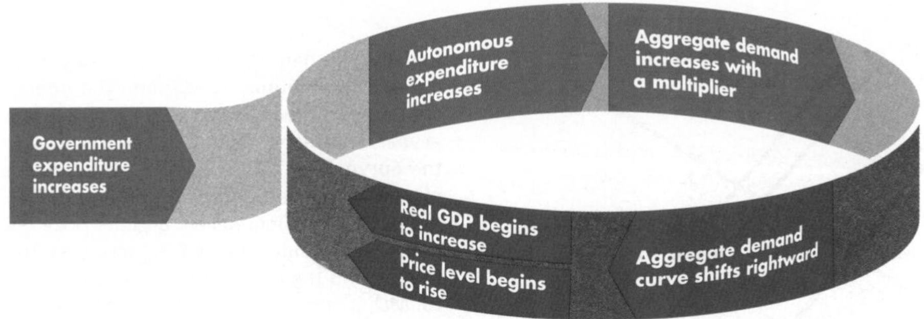

(a) First round effect of expansionary fiscal policy

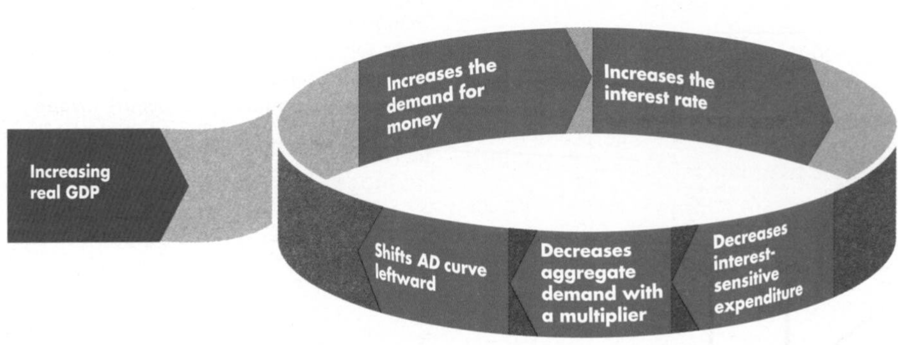

(b) Second round real GDP effect

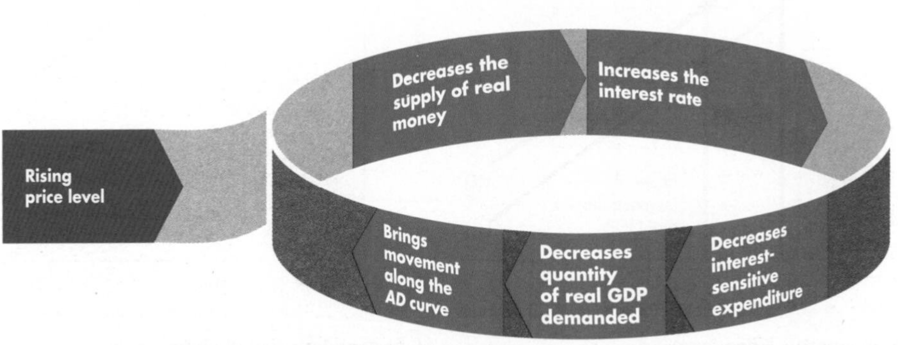

(c) Second round price level effect

Just as the initial equilibrium in Figure 29.1 was consistent, so the new equilibrium is consistent. The *AS–AD* equilibrium in Figure 29.3(a), the money market equilibrium in Figure 29.3(b) and interest-sensitive expenditure in Figure 29.3(c) are consistent with each other. And there is no other equilibrium.

Figure 29.4(a) summarizes the first round of an expansionary fiscal policy action. Figure 29.4(b) and 29.4(c) summarize the two parts of the second round adjustments as the economy responds.

Other Fiscal Policies

A change in government expenditure is only one possible fiscal policy action. Others are a change in transfer payments, such as an increase in unemployment benefits, and a change in taxes. All fiscal policy actions work by changing expenditure. But the magnitude of the initial change in expenditure differs for different fiscal actions. For example, changes in taxes and transfer payments change expenditure by smaller amounts than does a change in government expenditure. But fiscal policy actions that change autonomous expenditure by a given amount and in a given direction have similar effects on real GDP, the price level and the interest rate regardless of the initial fiscal policy action. Let's look more closely at the effect of the rise in the interest rate.

Crowding Out and Crowding In

Because an expansionary fiscal policy increases the interest rate, it decreases all the interest-sensitive components of aggregate expenditure. One of these components is investment, and the decrease in investment that results from an expansionary fiscal action is called **crowding out**.

Crowding out may be partial or complete. Partial crowding out occurs when the decrease in investment is less than the increase in government expenditure. This is the normal case – and the case we've just seen.

Complete crowding out occurs if the decrease in investment equals the initial increase in government expenditure. For complete crowding out to occur, a small change in the demand for real money must lead to a large change in the interest rate, and the change in the interest rate must lead to a large change in investment.

But another potential influence of government expenditure on investment works in the opposite direction to the crowding-out effect and is called "crowding in". **Crowding in** is the tendency for expansionary fiscal policy to *increase* investment. This effect works in three ways.

First, in a recession, an expansionary fiscal policy might create expectations of a more speedy recovery and bring an increase in expected profits. Higher expected profits might increase investment despite a higher interest rate.

Second, government expenditure might be productive and lead to more profitable business opportunities. For example, a new motorway might cut the cost of transporting a farmer's produce to a market and induce the farmer to invest in a new fleet of trucks.

Third, if an expansionary fiscal policy takes the form of a cut in taxes on business profits, firms' after-tax profits increase and firms might increase investment.

The Exchange Rate and International Crowding Out

We've seen that an expansionary fiscal policy leads to higher interest rates. But a change in interest rates also affects the exchange rate. Higher interest rates make the pound rise in value against other currencies. With interest rates higher in the United Kingdom than in the rest of the world, funds flow into the United Kingdom and people around the world demand more pounds sterling. As the pound rises in value, foreigners find UK-produced goods and services more expensive and UK residents find imports less expensive. Exports decrease and imports increase – net exports decrease.

The tendency for an expansionary fiscal policy to decrease net exports is called **international crowding out**. The decrease in net exports offsets, to some degree, the initial increase in aggregate expenditure brought about by an expansionary fiscal policy.

Review Quiz

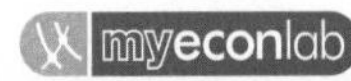

Study Plan 29.2

1. What is an expansionary fiscal policy and what are its first round effects? What is happening at the end of the first round?
2. What are the second round effects of an expansionary fiscal policy action? Describe the forces at work and the changes that occur in the interest rate, interest-sensitive expenditure, real GDP and the price level.
3. What is crowding out? How does crowding out influence the outcome of a fiscal policy action?
4. Distinguish between partial crowding out and complete crowding out.
5. What is crowding in? How does crowding in influence the outcome of a fiscal policy action?
6. How does an expansionary fiscal policy affect the exchange rate? What happens to imports and exports
7. What is international crowding out?

You've seen how the money market and the goods market interact when the government changes its fiscal policy. Next we'll study these same interactions when the Bank of England changes its monetary policy.

Monetary Policy in the Short Run

To study the effects of an expansionary monetary policy, we look at the first round effects and the second round effects, just as we did for fiscal policy. Figure 29.5 describes the economy. The quantity of real money is £1,400 billion, the interest rate is 5 per cent a year, interest-sensitive expenditure is £150 billion, real GDP is £1,300 billion and the price level is 105. With a price level of 105, the quantity of money is £1,470 billion.

First Round Effects

The Bank of England now increases the quantity of money to £2,572.5 billion. With a price level of 105, the quantity of real money increases to £2,450 billion. Figure 29.5(a) shows the immediate effect. The real money supply curve shifts rightward from MS_0 to MS_1, and the interest rate falls from 5 per cent to 1 per cent a year. The lower interest rate increases interest-sensitive expenditure to £250 billion in part (b). The increase in interest-sensitive expenditure sets off a

Figure 29.5

myeconlab

First Round Effects of an Expansionary Monetary Policy

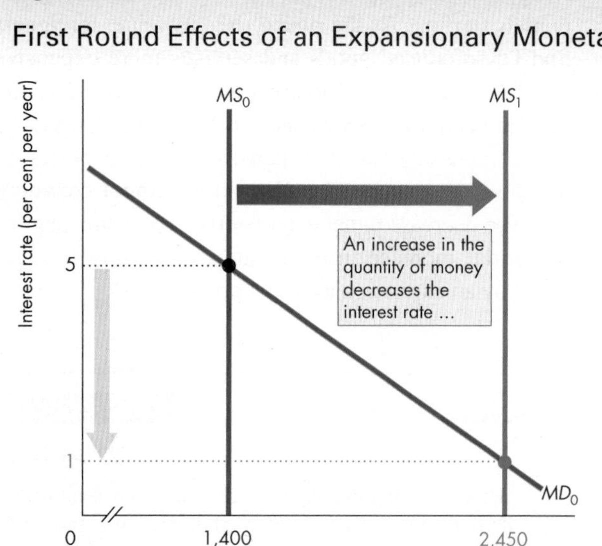

(a) Change in quantity of money

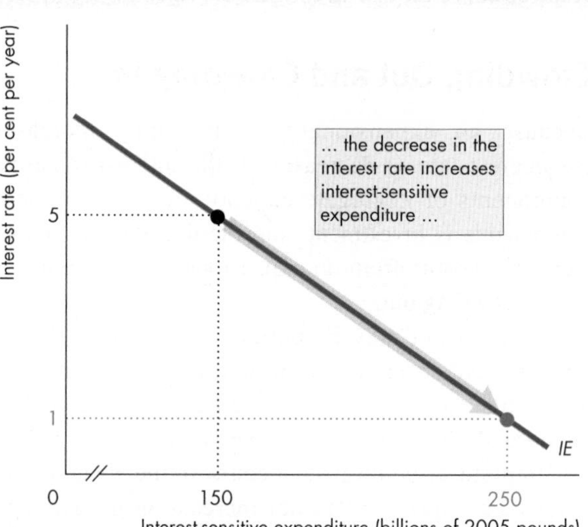

(b) Change in expenditure

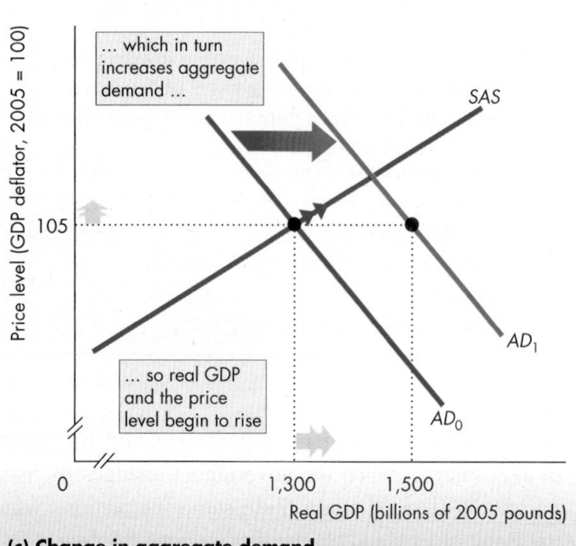

(c) Change in aggregate demand

Initially, the demand curve for real money is MD_0, the supply curve of real money is MS_0 and the interest rate is 5 per cent a year in part (a). With an interest rate of 5 per cent a year, interest-sensitive expenditure is £150 billion on the *IE* curve in part (b). The aggregate demand curve is AD_0 in part (c). Equilibrium real GDP is £1,300 billion and the price level is 105.

An increase in the quantity of money shifts the supply of real money curve rightward from MS_0 to MS_1 in part (a). The increased supply of money lowers the interest rate to 1 per cent a year and interest-sensitive expenditure increases to £250 billion in part (b). This increase in expenditure increases aggregate demand from AD_0 to AD_1 in part (c). Real GDP begins to increase and the price level begins to rise.

multiplier process and aggregate demand increases. The aggregate demand curve shifts rightward from AD_0 to AD_1 in part (c). As aggregate demand increases, real GDP and the price level begin to increase along the *SAS* curve towards a new macroeconomic equilibrium.

These are the first round effects of an expansionary monetary policy. An increase in the quantity of money decreases the interest rate and increases aggregate demand. Real GDP and the price level begin to increase. Let's now look at the second round effects.

Second Round Effects

The increasing real GDP and rising price level set off the second round, which Figure 29.6(b) illustrates. And as in the case of fiscal policy, it is best to break the second round into two parts: the consequence of increasing real GDP and the consequence of the rising price level.

The increasing real GDP increases the demand for money from MD_0 to MD_1 in Figure 29.6(a). The increased demand for money raises the interest rate to 2 per cent a year. The higher interest rate brings a

Figure 29.6

Second Round Effects of an Expansionary Monetary Policy

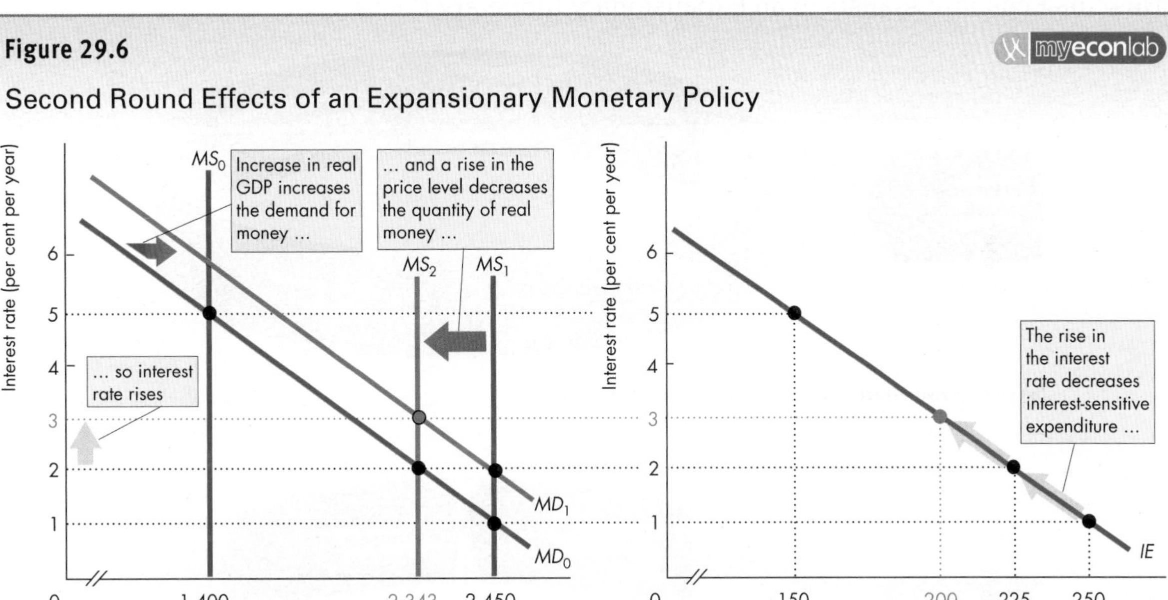

(a) Money and the interest rate

(b) Decrease in expenditure

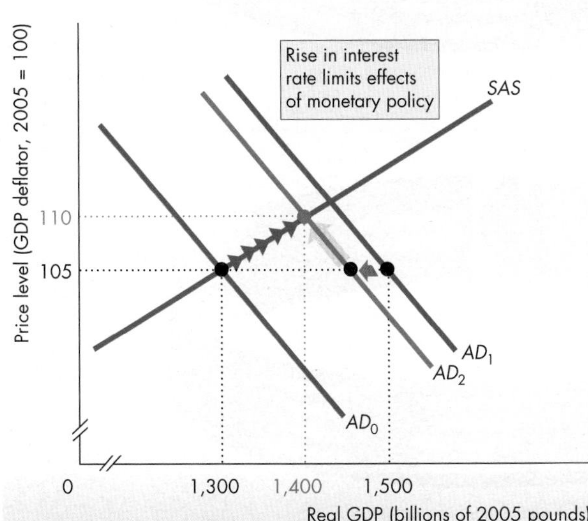

(c) Aggregate demand and aggregate supply

At the start of the second round, the demand curve for money is still MD_0 in part (a), the supply curve of real money is MS_1 and the interest rate is 1 per cent a year. With an interest rate of 1 per cent a year, interest-sensitive expenditure is £250 billion on the curve *IE* in part (b). With the increased quantity of money and expenditure, the aggregate demand curve is AD_1 in part (c). Real GDP is increasing and the price level is rising.

The increasing real GDP increases the demand for money and the demand for money curve shifts rightward from MD_0 to MD_1. The interest rate rises to 2 per cent a year. The higher interest rate decreases interest-sensitive expenditure, which decreases aggregate demand from AD_1 to AD_2 in part (c).

The rising price level brings a movement along the new *AD* curve, AD_2 because the rising price level decreases the supply of real money from MS_1 to MS_2. The interest rate rises further and expenditure decreases. The new equilibrium occurs when real GDP has increased to £1,400 billion and the price level has risen to 110.

decrease in interest-sensitive expenditure from £250 billion to £225 billion in Figure 29.6(b). And the lower level of expenditure decreases aggregate demand and shifts the aggregate demand curve leftward to AD_2 in Figure 29.6(c).

The rising price level brings a movement along the new aggregate demand curve AD_2 in Figure 29.6(c). This movement occurs because the rising price level decreases the real money supply. As the price level rises, the real money supply decreases from £2,450 billion to £2,343 billion and the money supply curve shifts leftward to MS_2 in part (a). The interest rate rises further to 3 per cent a year. And interest-sensitive expenditure decreases from £225 billion to £200 billion in part (b).

In the new short-run equilibrium, real GDP has increased to £1,400 billion, and the price level has risen

Figure 29.7

myeconlab

How the Economy Adjusts to an Expansionary Monetary Policy

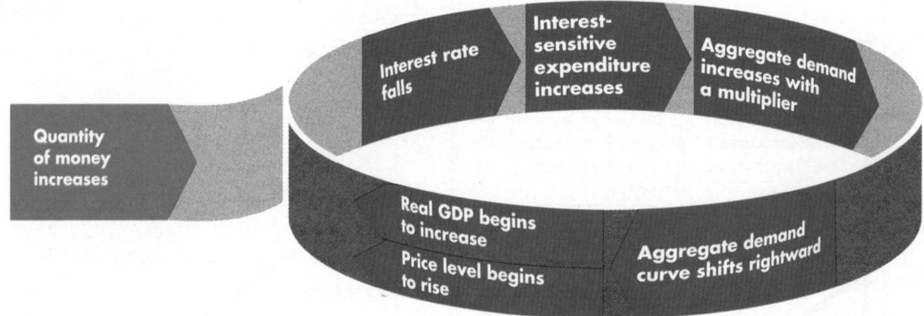

(a) First round effect of expansionary monetary policy

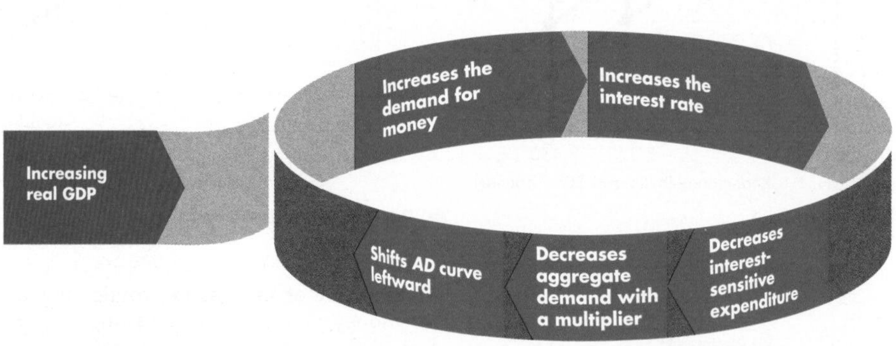

(b) Second round real GDP effect

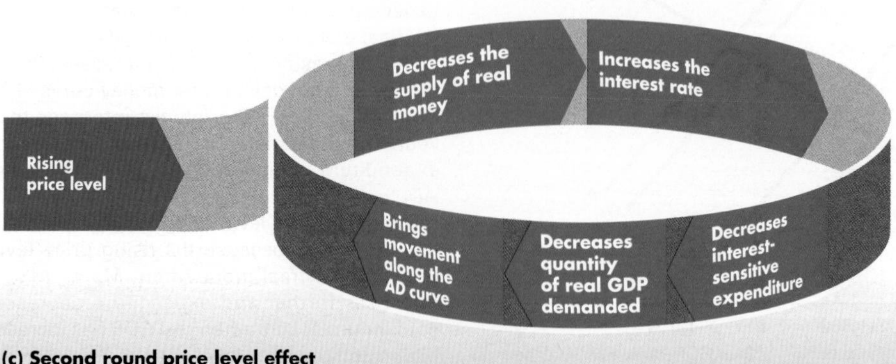

(c) Second round price level effect

to 110, where the aggregate demand curve AD_2 intersects the short-run aggregate supply curve *SAS*.

The demand for money curve is MD_1, the money supply curve is MS_2, and the interest rate is 3 per cent a year in Figure 29.6(a). With an interest rate of 3 per cent a year, interest-sensitive expenditure is £200 billion in Figure 29.6(b).

The new equilibrium is the only consistent one and is similar to that in Figure 29.1. Figure 29.7 summarizes the adjustments that occur to bring the economy to this new equilibrium.

Money and the Exchange Rate

An increase in the quantity of money lowers the interest rate. If the interest rate falls in the United Kingdom but does not fall in the Eurozone, the United States, Japan and Asia, international investors buy the now higher-yielding foreign assets and sell the relatively lower-yielding UK assets. As they make these transactions, they sell pounds. So the pound depreciates against other currencies. (This mechanism is explained in greater detail in Chapter 33, pp. 733–735.)

With a cheaper pound, foreigners face lower prices for UK-produced goods and services and people and firms in the United Kingdom face higher prices for foreign-produced goods and services. UK exports increase and UK imports decrease. UK net exports increase, and real GDP and the price level in the United Kingdom increase further.

Review Quiz

Study Plan 29.3

1 What are the first round effects of an expansionary monetary policy? What happens to the interest rate, interest-sensitive expenditure, aggregate demand, the demand for money, real GDP and the price level in the first round?
2 What are the second round effects of an expansionary monetary policy? What happens to the interest rate, interest-sensitive expenditure, aggregate demand, the demand for money, real GDP and the price level in the second round?
3 How does an expansionary monetary policy influence the exchange rate, imports and exports?

Let's now compare fiscal policy and monetary policy and see which policy is more effective.

Relative Effectiveness of Policies

We've seen that aggregate demand and real GDP are influenced by both fiscal and monetary policy. But which policy is the more potent? This question was once at the centre of a controversy among macroeconomists. Later in this section we'll look at that controversy and see how it was settled. But we begin by discovering what determines the effectiveness of fiscal policy.

Effectiveness of Fiscal Policy

The effectiveness of fiscal policy is measured by the magnitude of the increase in aggregate demand that results from a given increase in government expenditures (or decrease in taxes). The effectiveness of fiscal policy depends on the strength of the crowding-out effect. Fiscal policy is most powerful if no crowding out occurs. Fiscal policy is impotent if there is complete crowding out. And the strength of the crowding-out effect depends on two things:

1 The responsiveness of expenditure to the interest rate
2 The responsiveness of the quantity of money demanded to the interest rate

If expenditure is not very responsive to a change in the interest rate, the crowding-out effect is small. But if expenditure is highly responsive to a change in the interest rate, the crowding-out effect is large. Other things remaining the same, the smaller the responsiveness of expenditure to the interest rate, the smaller is the crowding-out effect and the bigger is the change in aggregate demand. So the less responsive expenditure is to the interest rate, the more effective is fiscal policy.

The responsiveness of the quantity of money demanded to the interest rate also affects the size of the crowding-out effect. An increase in real GDP increases the demand for money, and with no change in the supply of money, the interest rate rises. But the extent to which the interest rate rises depends on the responsiveness of the quantity of money demanded to the interest rate. Other things remaining the same, the greater the responsiveness of the quantity of money demanded to the interest rate, the smaller is the rise in the interest rate, the smaller is the crowding-out effect and the bigger is the change in aggregate demand. So the more responsive the quantity of money demanded is to the interest rate, the more effective is fiscal policy.

Effectiveness of Monetary Policy

The effectiveness of monetary policy is measured by the magnitude of the increase in aggregate demand that results from a given increase in the money supply. Like fiscal policy, the effectiveness of monetary policy depends on the responsiveness of:

1 The quantity of money demanded to the interest rate
2 Expenditure to the interest rate

The starting point for monetary policy is a change in the quantity of money that changes the interest rate. A given change in the quantity of money might bring a small change or a large change in the interest rate. Other things remaining the same, the larger the initial change in the interest rate, the more effective is monetary policy. The initial change in the interest rate will be greater, the less responsive is the quantity of money demanded to the interest rate.

But effectiveness of monetary policy also depends on how much expenditure changes. If expenditure is not very responsive to a change in the interest rate, monetary actions do not have much effect on expenditure. But if expenditure is highly responsive to a change in the interest rate, monetary actions have a large effect on aggregate expenditure. The greater the responsiveness of expenditure to the interest rate, the more effective is monetary policy.

The effectiveness of fiscal policy and monetary policy that you've just studied were once controversial. During the 1950s and 1960s, this issue lay at the heart of what was called the Keynesian–monetarist controversy. Let's look at the dispute and see how it was resolved.

The Keynesian–Monetarist Controversy

The Keynesian–monetarist controversy was an ongoing dispute in macroeconomics between two broad groups of economists. A **Keynesian** macroeconomist believes that, left alone, the economy rarely operates at full employment and that to achieve and maintain full employment, active help from fiscal policy and monetary policy is required. Keynesian views about the functioning of the economy are based on the theories of John Maynard Keynes, published in Keynes' *The General Theory of Employment, Interest and Money*. Traditionally, Keynesians assigned a low degree of importance to monetary policy and a high degree of importance to fiscal policy. Modern Keynesians assign a high degree of importance to both types of policy.

A **monetarist** is a macroeconomist who believes that most macroeconomic fluctuations are caused by fluctuations in the quantity of money and that the economy is inherently stable and requires no active government intervention. Monetarist views about the functioning of the economy are based on theories most forcefully set forth by Milton Friedman. Traditionally, monetarists assigned a low degree of importance to fiscal policy. But modern monetarists, like modern Keynesians, assign a high degree of importance to both policies.

The nature of the Keynesian–monetarist debate has changed over the years. During the 1950s and 1960s, it was a debate about the relative effectiveness of fiscal policy and monetary policy in changing aggregate demand. We can see the essence of that debate by distinguishing three views:

- Extreme Keynesianism
- Extreme monetarism
- Intermediate position

Extreme Keynesianism

The extreme Keynesian hypothesis is that a change in the quantity of money has no effect on aggregate demand and that a change in government expenditure on goods and services or taxes has a large effect on aggregate demand.

The two circumstances in which a change in the quantity of money has no effect on aggregate demand are when:

1 Expenditure is completely insensitive to the interest rate
2 The quantity of money demanded is highly sensitive to the interest rate

If expenditure is completely insensitive to the interest rate (if the *IE* curve is vertical), a change in the quantity of money changes the interest rate, but the change does not affect aggregate expenditure. Monetary policy is impotent.

If the quantity of money demanded is highly sensitive to the interest rate (if the *MD* curve is horizontal), people are willing to hold any amount of money at a given interest rate – a situation called a *liquidity trap*. With a liquidity trap, a change in the quantity of money affects only the amount of money held. It does not affect the interest rate. With an unchanged interest rate, expenditure remains constant. Monetary policy is impotent. Some people believe (incorrectly) that Japan was in a liquidity trap during the late 1990s.

Extreme Monetarism

The extreme monetarist hypothesis is that a change in government expenditure on goods and services or taxes has no effect on aggregate demand and that a change in the quantity of money has a large effect on aggregate demand. Two circumstances give rise to these predictions:

1 Expenditure is highly sensitive to the interest rate
2 The quantity of money demanded is completely insensitive to the interest rate

If an increase in government expenditure on goods and services induces an increase in the interest rate that is sufficiently large to reduce expenditure by the same amount as the initial increase in government expenditure, then fiscal policy has no effect on aggregate demand. This outcome is complete crowding out. For this result to occur, either the quantity of money demanded must be insensitive to the interest rate – a fixed amount of money is held regardless of the interest rate – or expenditure must be highly sensitive to the interest rate – any amount of expenditure will be undertaken at a given interest rate.

Intermediate Position

The intermediate position is that both fiscal policy and monetary policy affect aggregate demand. Crowding out is not complete, so fiscal policy does have an effect. There is no liquidity trap and expenditure responds to the interest rate, so monetary policy does indeed affect aggregate demand. This intermediate position is the one that now appears to be correct and is the one that we've spent most of this chapter exploring. Let's see how economists came to this conclusion.

Sorting Out the Competing Claims

The dispute among monetarists, Keynesians and those taking an intermediate position was essentially a disagreement about the magnitudes of two economic parameters:

1 The responsiveness of expenditure to the interest rate
2 The responsiveness of the quantity of money demanded to the interest rate

If expenditure is highly sensitive to the interest rate or the quantity of money demanded is barely sensitive to the interest rate, then monetary policy is powerful and fiscal policy relatively ineffective. In this case, the world looks similar to the claims of extreme monetarists. If expenditure is very insensitive to the interest rate or the quantity of money demanded is highly sensitive, then fiscal policy is powerful and monetary policy is relatively ineffective. In this case, the world looks similar to the claims of the extreme Keynesians.

By using statistical methods to study the demand for real money and expenditure and data from a wide variety of historical and national experiences, economists were able to settle this dispute. Neither extreme position is supported by the evidence. There is no liquidity trap, not even in Japan. Expenditure *is* interest sensitive. Neither the demand for money curve nor the interest-sensitive expenditure curve is vertical or horizontal, so the extreme Keynesian and extreme monetarist hypotheses are rejected.

Interest Rate and Exchange Rate Effectiveness

Although fiscal policy and monetary policy are alternative ways of changing aggregate demand, they have opposing effects on the interest rate and the exchange rate. A fiscal policy action that increases aggregate demand raises the interest rate and increases the exchange rate. A monetary policy action that increases aggregate demand lowers the interest rate and decreases the exchange rate. Because of these opposing effects on interest rates and the exchange rate, if the two policies are combined to increase aggregate demand, their separate effects on the interest rate and the exchange rate can be minimized.

Review Quiz

Study Plan 29.4

1 What two macroeconomic parameters influence the relative effectiveness of fiscal policy and monetary policy?
2 Under what circumstances is the Keynesian view correct and under what circumstances is the monetarist view correct?
3 How can fiscal policy and monetary policy be combined to increase aggregate demand yet at the same time keep the interest rate constant?

We're now going to look at expansionary fiscal and monetary policy at full employment.

Policy Actions at Full Employment

An expansionary fiscal policy or monetary policy can bring the economy to full employment. But it is often difficult to determine whether the economy is at a below full-employment equilibrium. So an expansionary fiscal policy or monetary policy might be undertaken when the economy is at full employment. What happens then? Let's answer this question starting with an expansionary fiscal policy.

Expansionary Fiscal Policy at Full Employment

Suppose the economy is at full employment and the government increases its expenditure on goods and services. All the effects that we worked out earlier in this chapter occur – except that these effects determine only a *short-run equilibrium*. That is, both the first round and second round effects of policy occur in the short run. There is a third round, which is the long-run adjustment.

Starting out at full employment, an expansionary fiscal policy will move the economy to an above full-employment equilibrium in which there is an *inflationary gap*. In the long run, the money wage rate begins to rise and short-run aggregate supply decreases. As this long-run adjustment occurs, real GDP decreases to potential GDP and the price level rises.

Figure 29.8 illustrates the combined first and second round short-run effects and the third round long-run adjustment.

In Figure 29.8, potential GDP is £1,300 billion. Real GDP equals potential GDP on aggregate demand curve AD_0 and short-run aggregate supply curve SAS_0. An expansionary fiscal policy action increases aggregate demand. The combined first round and second round effect increases aggregate demand to AD_1. Real GDP increases to £1,400 billion and the price level rises to 110. There is an inflationary gap of £100 billion.

With the economy at an above full-employment equilibrium, a shortage of labour puts upward pressure on the money wage rate, which now begins to rise. A third round of adjustment begins. The rising money wage rate decreases short-run aggregate supply and the *SAS* curve starts shifting leftward towards SAS_1.

As the short-run aggregate supply decreases, real GDP decreases and the price level rises. This process continues until the inflationary gap has been eliminated and the economy has returned to full employment. At long-run equilibrium, real GDP is £1,300 billion, which is potential GDP, and the price level is 115.

Figure 29.8 myeconlab

Fiscal Policy at Full Employment

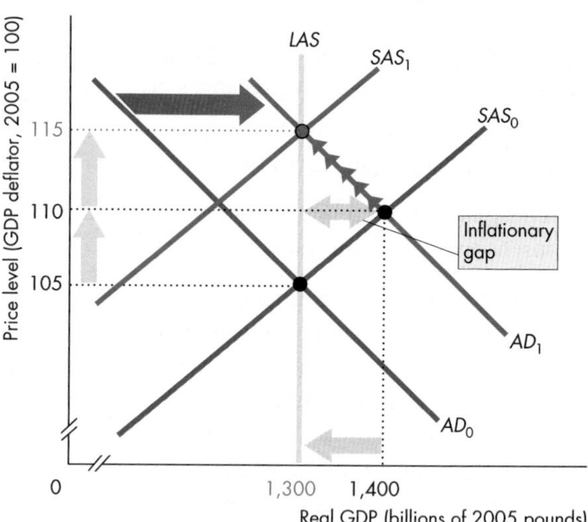

The long-run aggregate supply curve is *LAS* and initially the aggregate demand curve is AD_0 and the short-run aggregate supply curve is SAS_0. Real GDP is £1,300 billion and the price level is 105.

Changes in fiscal policy and monetary policy shift the aggregate demand curve to AD_1. At the new short-run equilibrium, real GDP is £1,400 billion and the price level is 110.

Because real GDP exceeds potential GDP, the money wage rate begins to rise and the short-run aggregate supply curve begins to shift leftward towards SAS_1. At the new long-run equilibrium, the price level is 115 and real GDP is back at its original level.

Crowding Out at Full Employment

You've just seen that when government expenditure increases when the economy is at full employment, the long-run change in real GDP is zero. The entire effect of the increase in aggregate demand is an increase in the price level. This outcome implies that at full employment, an increase in government expenditure *completely crowds out investment* or *creates an international (net exports) deficit*, or results in a combination of the two.

The easiest way to see why is to recall that aggregate expenditure, which equals consumption expenditure, *C*, plus investment, I, plus government expenditure, G, plus net exports, NX, equals real GDP. That is:

$$Y = C + I + G + NX$$

Comparing the initial situation with the outcome, real GDP has not changed. So aggregate expenditure, $C + I + G + NX$, is constant between the two situations.

But government expenditure has increased, so the sum of consumption expenditure, investment and net exports must have decreased. If net exports don't change, consumption expenditure plus investment decreases by the full amount of the increase in government expenditure. If consumption expenditure and investment don't change, net exports decrease by an amount equal to the increase in government expenditure. A decrease in net exports is an increase in our international deficit.

You've now seen that the effects of expansionary fiscal policy are extremely sensitive to the state of the economy when the policy action is taken. At less than full employment, an expansionary fiscal policy can move the economy towards full employment. At full employment, an expansionary fiscal policy raises the price level, crowds out private expenditure and creates an international deficit.

Expansionary Monetary Policy at Full Employment

Now suppose the economy is at full employment and the Bank of England increases the quantity of money. Again, all the effects that we worked out earlier in this chapter occur. But again, these effects determine only a *short-run equilibrium*. That is, the first round and second round effects of monetary policy both occur in the short run. And again, there is a third round, which is the long-run adjustment.

Starting out at full employment, an expansionary monetary policy will move the economy to an above full-employment equilibrium in which there is an *inflationary gap*. The money wage rate begins to rise, short-run aggregate supply decreases and a long-run adjustment occurs in which real GDP decreases to potential GDP and the price level rises.

Figure 29.8, which illustrates the effects of an expansionary fiscal policy when the economy is at full employment, also illustrates the effects of an expansionary monetary policy when the economy is at full employment.

In the short run, an expansionary monetary policy increases real GDP and the price level rises. But in the long run, expansionary monetary policy increases only the price level and leaves real GDP unchanged at potential GDP.

Long-run Neutrality

In the long run, a change in the quantity of money changes only the price level and leaves real GDP unchanged. The independence of real GDP from the quantity of money is an example of the long-run neutrality of money.

But long-run neutrality applies not only to real GDP but also to all real variables. The so-called **long-run neutrality** proposition is that in the long run, a change in the quantity of money changes the price level and leaves all real variables unchanged.

You can see this outcome in the case of real GDP in Figure 29.8. Because a change in the quantity of money leaves real GDP unchanged, it also leaves consumption expenditure unchanged. With no change in real GDP, the demand for money does not change. The price level rises by the same percentage as the increase in the quantity of money, so the supply of real money does not change. With no change in the demand for money and no change in the supply of real money, the interest rate does not change. And with no change in the interest rate, expenditure remains the same.

Finally, with no change in real GDP or the real interest rate, consumption expenditure, investment, government expenditure and net exports are unchanged.

Review Quiz

Study Plan 29.5

1 Contrast the short-run effects of an expansionary fiscal policy on real GDP and the price level with its long-run effects when the policy action occurs at full employment.
2 Contrast the short-run effects of an expansionary monetary policy on real GDP and the price level with its long-run effects when the policy action occurs at full employment.
3 Explain crowding out at full employment.
4 Explain the long-run neutrality of money.

You've seen how fiscal policy and monetary policy interact and contrasted the effects of each. Do fiscal and monetary policy need to be coordinated? And if they are not coordinated, do they come into conflict? Let's find the answers to these questions.

Policy Coordination and Conflict

So far, we've studied fiscal policy and monetary policy in isolation from each other. We are now going to consider what happens if the two branches of policy are coordinated and if they come into conflict.

Policy coordination occurs when the government and central bank work together to achieve a common set of goals. **Policy conflict** occurs when the government and the central bank pursue different goals and the actions of one make it harder (perhaps impossible) for the other to achieve its goals.

Policy Coordination

The basis for policy coordination is the fact that either fiscal policy or monetary policy can be used to increase aggregate demand. Starting from a position of *below full-employment equilibrium*, an increase in aggregate demand increases real GDP and decreases unemployment. If the size of the policy action is well judged, the policy action can eliminate a *recessionary gap*. Similarly, starting from a position of *above full-employment equilibrium*, a decrease in aggregate demand decreases real GDP and can, if the size of the policy action is well judged, eliminate an *inflationary gap*. Because either a fiscal policy or a monetary policy action can achieve these objectives, the two policies can (in principle) be combined to achieve the same outcome.

If either or both policies can restore full employment and eliminate inflation, why does it matter which policy is used? It matters because the two policies have different side effects – different effects on other variables about which people care. These side effects of policy work through two key variables and have:

- Interest rate effects
- Exchange rate effects

Interest Rate Effects

An expansionary fiscal policy *raises* the interest rate whereas an expansionary monetary policy *lowers* the interest rate. When the interest rate changes, investment changes, so an expansionary fiscal policy decreases investment (crowding out) whereas an expansionary monetary policy increases investment. So if an expansionary fiscal policy increases aggregate demand, consumption expenditure increases and investment decreases. But if an expansionary monetary policy increases aggregate demand, consumption expenditure and investment increase.

By coordinating fiscal policy and monetary policy and increasing aggregate demand with an appropriate combination of the two, it is possible to increase real GDP and lower unemployment with no change in the interest rate or with any desired change in the interest rate. A big dose of fiscal expansion with a small dose of monetary expansion raises the interest rate and decreases investment, whereas a small dose of fiscal expansion with a big dose of monetary expansion lowers the interest rate and increases investment.

The interest rate affects our long-term growth prospects because the growth rate of potential GDP depends on the amount of investment. The connection between investment, capital and potential GDP is explained in Chapter 24, pp. 549–550.

Exchange Rate Effects

An expansionary fiscal policy raises not only the interest rate but also the exchange rate. In contrast, an expansionary monetary policy *lowers* the exchange rate. When the exchange rate changes, net exports change. An expansionary fiscal policy decreases net exports (international crowding out), whereas an expansionary monetary policy increases net exports. So if full employment is restored by expansionary policy, net exports *decrease* with fiscal expansion and *increase* with monetary expansion.

Policy Conflict

Policy conflicts are not planned. But they can happen. When they arise, it is usually because of a divergence of the political priorities of the government and the objectives of the central bank.

Governments pay a lot of attention to employment and production over a short time horizon. They look for policies that make their re-election chances high. Central banks pay a lot of attention to price level stability and have a long time horizon. They don't have an election to worry about.

So a situation might arise in which the government wants the central bank to pursue an expansionary monetary policy but the central bank wants to keep its foot on the monetary brake. The government says that a lower interest rate and exchange rate are essential to boost investment and exports. The central bank says that the problem is with fiscal policy. Spending is too high and revenues too low. With fiscal policy too expansionary, the interest rate and the exchange rate are high and they cannot be lowered permanently by monetary policy. To lower the interest rate and give investment and exports a boost, fiscal policy must become contractionary. Only then can an expansionary monetary policy be pursued.

A further potential conflict between a government and its central bank concerns the financing of the government deficit. A government deficit can be financed by borrowing from either the general public or the central bank. If the government borrows from the general public, it must pay interest on its debt. If it borrows from the central bank, it pays interest to the bank. But the government owns the bank, so the interest comes back to the government.

But when the central bank buys government debt, it pays for the debt with a newly created monetary base. The quantity of money increases. And such finance leads to inflation. In many countries, for example in Eastern Europe, Latin America and Africa, government deficits have been financed by the central bank.

In the United Kingdom, government deficits have not been financed by the Bank of England. Indeed, the requirement for the Bank of England to achieve an inflation target along with its independence to pursue that target makes it very unlikely that a United Kingdom government would easily follow the Latin American path.

A Policy Interaction Risk

In the standard analysis of policy interaction that we've studied in this chapter, the central bank targets the quantity of money and money market equilibrium determines the interest rate. But as you learned in Chapter 28, the Bank of England conducts monetary policy by setting Bank Rate and money market equilibrium determines the quantity of money.

When a central bank targets the quantity of money, an expansionary fiscal policy action automatically raises the interest rate. It does so by increasing the demand for money. The higher interest rate moderates the effects of the expansionary fiscal policy. Aggregate demand increases and real GDP and the price level rise, but by less than they would if the interest rate were unchanged.

So when a central bank targets the interest rate rather than the quantity of money, an expansionary fiscal policy raises the interest rate only if the central bank takes an explicit action. If the central bank raises the interest rate by the amount that the market would have raised it with a given quantity of money, the outcome will be identical under the two alternative monetary policies.

But if the central bank is slow to change the interest rate, an expansionary fiscal policy might increase aggregate demand by too much. And if the central bank reacts to expansionary fiscal policy with a more aggressive increase in the interest rate, aggregate demand might increase by too little.

The key problem for monetary policy is to make a correct determination of the appropriate interest rate to accompany a change in fiscal policy. The problem is more acute when the economy is at full employment than when it is in a recession, but it is a problem in either situation.

In a recession, if the central bank raises the interest rate too little and too late, an expansionary fiscal policy could overshoot full employment and create an inflationary gap. If the central bank raises the interest rate too much and too soon, an expansionary fiscal policy could undershoot full employment and leave an unwanted recessionary gap.

At full employment, if the central bank raises the interest rate too little and too late, an expansionary fiscal policy would create an inflationary gap that would bring faster inflation, a fall in the real interest rate and a further increase in the inflationary gap. A cumulative inflation would take hold until the central bank moved the interest rate high enough to eliminate the inflationary gap. And if, at full employment, the central bank raises the interest rate too much and too soon in response to an expansionary fiscal policy, real GDP would fall below full employment and a recessionary gap would emerge. The gap would persist until the central bank lowered the interest rate.

Review Quiz

Study Plan 29.6

1. What can be achieved by coordinating fiscal policy and monetary policy?
2. What are the main sources of conflict in policy between the central bank and the government?
3. Explain what happens if the government pursues an expansionary fiscal policy while the central bank pursues a contractionary monetary policy.
4. Explain how inflation can be avoided despite a large budget deficit.

Reading Between the Lines on pp. 682–683 looks at a report by the International Monetary Fund on UK fiscal and monetary policy in 2007.

Reading Between the Lines

Fiscal and Monetary Policy Conflict

The Financial Times, 6 March 2007

FT

IMF warns Brown to rein in spending

Scheherazade Daneshku

Gordon Brown should avoid tax increases in this month's Budget and instead restrain spending to shore up the public finances, the International Monetary Fund [IMF] said yesterday. The chancellor's "credibility" in pursuing a tight spending round will be put to a "critical test" in the comprehensive spending review this summer, added the IMF. . . .

The IMF revised up economic growth to 2.9 per cent this year and 2.7 per cent in 2008, in line with Treasury projections. The economy's openness and flexibility had allowed it to benefit from globalisation but "openness may also increase exposure to downside global risks".

On the public finances, the IMF warned Mr Brown that "building the cushions needed to respond to adverse shocks should be a priority". The public spending surge of 2001–04 had led to "a sharp deterioration in the fiscal balance and rising net public debt", leaving little room for manoeuvre in the face of a global downturn.

It saw net public debt rising from 36.4 per cent of national income in 2005–06, to 39 per cent or more from 2008–09 – above Treasury forecasts. This called into question the government's ability to keep net debt below its self-imposed 40 per cent limit, said Susan Schadler, UK mission chief.

Although Mr Brown had started to rein in spending, "much remains to be done", says the report. The IMF commended "current plans to focus this consolidation on spending restraint" as "appropriate" but warned "further increases in tax rates would risk adversely affecting incentives to work and invest". . . .

The IMF welcomed the Bank of England's rate rises to 5.25 per cent, but said "additional tightening would be desirable" if wage growth accelerated or if people's expectations about the rate of inflation did not abate. . . .

The Essence of the Story

- The IMF advises the UK government to avoid raising taxes and instead restrain spending.
- The IMF raised its forecast of UK GDP growth to 2.9 per cent for 2007 and 2.7 per cent for 2008.
- UK government expenditure increased in 2001–04 and increased the budget deficit.
- Public debt increased from 36.4 per cent to 39 per cent of GDP.
- The IMF praised the Bank of England for raising the interest rate but said that a further rise would be needed if wage growth accelerated or inflation expectations did not fall.

Economic Analysis

- UK government expenditure has increased faster than economic growth and created a growing budget deficit.
- Figure 1 shows the government budget deficit. A surplus in 2000 and 2001 turned into an increasing deficit in 2002 to 2004 and the deficit persisted in 2005 and 2006.
- The IMF warns that UK fiscal policy makes the Bank of England's task of keeping the inflation rate at 2 per cent per year more difficult.
- Figure 2 shows that the interest rate fell during the period 2001 to 2003 but has risen from 2004. Monetary policy has been tightening since 2004 to counteract expansionary fiscal policy.
- Figure 3 shows the UK aggregate supply and aggregate demand curves in 2007.
- Potential GDP (and long-run aggregate supply *LAS*) was estimated to be £1,293 billion.
- The aggregate demand was AD_{07} and the short-run aggregate supply curve was SAS_{07}. Real GDP was equal to potential GDP and the price level was 106, about. The inflation rate was close to 3 per cent per year.
- With no help from monetary policy, aggregate demand would rise to AD_1 and create an inflationary gap. The inflation rate would rise.
- To achieve its inflation target, the Bank of England must raise the interest rate so that aggregate demand decreases and the aggregate demand curve shifts leftward to AD_2.
- A contractionary monetary policy must more than offset an expansionary fiscal policy. Monetary policy and fiscal policy are in conflict.
- The policy conflict will bring partial crowding out and a lower level of investment than would occur with lower government spending and a lower interest rate.

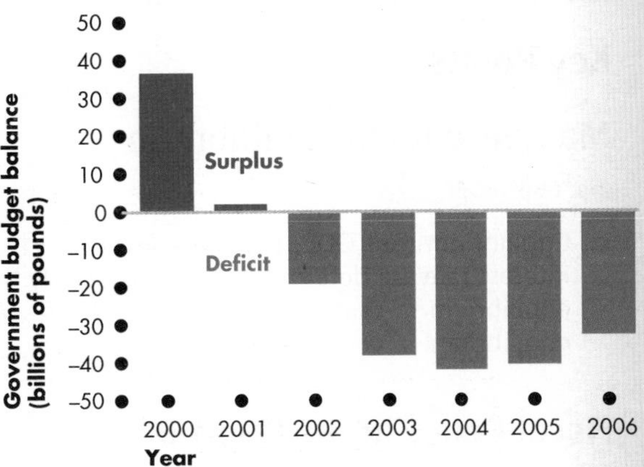

Figure 1 Government budget balance

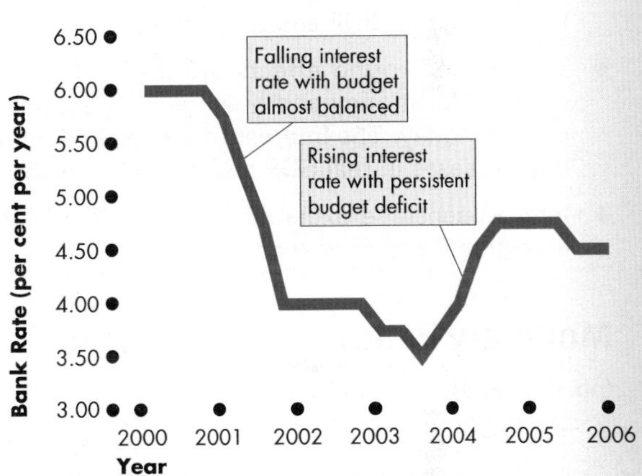

Figure 2 Bank Rate

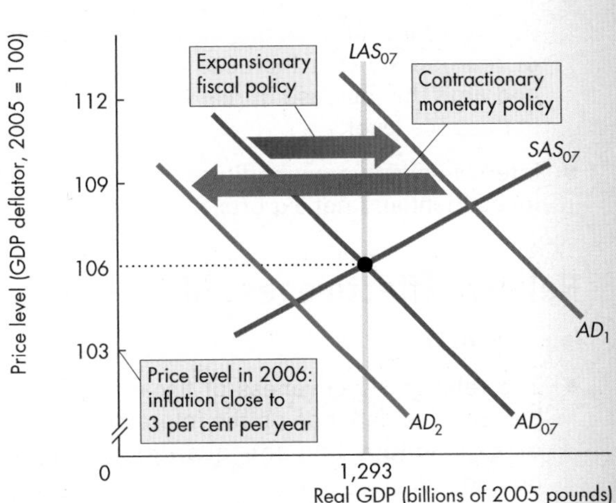

Figure 3 Aggregate supply and aggregate demand

Summary

Key Points

Macroeconomic Equilibrium

(pp. 666–667)

- Equilibrium real GDP, the price level and the interest rate are determined simultaneously by equilibrium in the money market and *AS–AD* equilibrium.

Fiscal Policy in the Short Run

(pp. 668–671)

- The first round effects of an expansionary fiscal policy are an increase in aggregate demand, increasing real GDP and a rising price level.
- The second round effects are an increasing demand for money and a decreasing quantity of real money. The interest rate rises and limit the increases in real GDP and the price level.
- Interest-sensitive expenditure, which includes investment and net exports, decreases.

Monetary Policy in the Short Run

(pp. 672–675)

- The first round effects of an expansionary monetary policy are a fall in the interest rate, an increase in aggregate demand, an increasing real GDP and a rising price level.
- The second round effects are an increasing demand for money and a decreasing quantity of real money that increase the interest rate and limit the increase in real GDP and the rise in the price level.
- Interest-sensitive expenditure, which includes investment and net exports, increases.

Relative Effectiveness of Policies

(pp. 675–677)

- The relative effectiveness of fiscal and monetary policies depends on the interest-sensitivity of expenditure and the quantity of money demanded.
- The extreme Keynesian position is that only fiscal policy affects aggregate demand. The extreme monetarist position is that only monetary policy affects aggregate demand. Neither extreme is correct.
- The mix of fiscal and monetary policy influences the composition of aggregate demand.

Policy Actions at Full Employment

(pp. 678–679)

- An expansionary fiscal policy at full employment increases real GDP and the price level in the short run but increases only the price level in the long run. Complete crowding out of investment occurs or the international deficit increases.
- An expansionary monetary policy at full employment increases real GDP and the price level in the short run but increases only the price level in the long run. Money is neutral – has no real effects – in the long run.

Policy Coordination and Conflict

(pp. 680–681)

- Policy coordination lessens fluctuations in the interest rate and the exchange rate.
- A government budget deficit can come into conflict with monetary policy to avoid inflation.

Key Figures

Key Terms

Problems

Tests, Study Plan and Solutions* 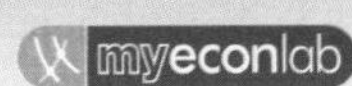

1 In the economy described in Figure 29.1, suppose the government decreases its expenditure on goods and services by £100 billion.

a Work out the first round effects.

b Explain how real GDP and the interest rate change.

c Explain the second round effects that take the economy to a new equilibrium.

2 In the economy described in Figure 29.1, suppose the government increases its expenditure on goods and services by £25 billion.

a Work out the first round effects.

b Explain how real GDP and the interest rate change.

c Explain the second round effects that take the economy to a new equilibrium.

d Compare the equilibrium in this case with the one described in this chapter on pp. 668–669. In which case is the change in the interest rate greater? Why?

3 In the economy described in Figure 29.1, suppose the Bank of England decreases the quantity of money. by £1,050 billion.

a Work out the first round effects.

b Explain how real GDP and the interest rate change.

c Explain the second round effects that take the economy to a new equilibrium.

4 In the economy described in Figure 29.1, suppose the Bank of England increases the quantity of money by £250 billion.

a Work out the first round effects.

b Explain how real GDP and the interest rate change.

c Explain the second round effects that take the economy to a new equilibrium.

d Compare the equilibrium in this case with the one described in this chapter on pp. 672–674. In which case is the change in real GDP greater? In which case is the change in the interest rate greater? Why?

5 The economies of two countries, Alpha and Beta, are identical in every way except the following: in Alpha, a change in the interest rate of 1 percentage point (e.g. from 5 per cent to 6 per cent) results in a €1 billion change in the quantity of real money demanded. In Beta, a change in the interest rate of 1 percentage point results in a €0.1 billion change in the quantity of real money demanded.

a In which economy does an increase in government expenditure on goods and services have a larger effect on real GDP?

b In which economy is the crowding-out effect weaker?

c In which economy does a change in the quantity of money have a larger effect on equilibrium real GDP?

d Which economy, if either, is closer to the Keynesian extreme and which is closer to the monetarist extreme?

6 The economy is in a recession and the government wants to increase aggregate demand, stimulate exports and increase investment. It has three policy options: an increase in government expenditure on goods and services, a decrease in taxes or an increase in the quantity of money.

a Explain the mechanisms at work under each alternative policy.

b What is the effect of each policy on the composition of aggregate demand?

c What are the short-run effects of each policy on real GDP and the price level?

d Which policy would you recommend that the government adopt? Why?

7 The economy has an inflationary gap and the government wants to decrease aggregate demand, cut exports and decrease investment. Three policy options are: a decrease in government expenditure, an increase in taxes or a decrease in the quantity of money.

a Explain the mechanisms at work under each alternative policy.

b What is the effect of each policy on the composition of aggregate demand?

c What are the short-run effects of each policy on real GDP and the price level?

d Which policy would you recommend that the government adopt? Why?

8 The economy is at full employment, but the government is disappointed with the growth rate of real GDP. It wants to increase real GDP growth by stimulating investment. At the same time, it wants to avoid an increase in the price level.

a Suggest a combination of fiscal and monetary policies that will achieve the government's objective.

* Solutions to odd-numbered problems are provided.

b Which policy would you recommend that the government adopt?

c Explain the mechanisms at work under your recommended policy.

d What is the effect of your recommended policy on the composition of aggregate demand?

e What are the short-run and long-run effects of your recommended policy on real GDP and the price level?

Critical Thinking

1 Study *Reading Between the Lines* on pp. 682–683 and then answer the following questions:

a What is happening to fiscal policy in the United Kingdom? In particular, what has happened to the budget deficit during the 2000s?

b What is the objective of the Bank of England's monetary policy?

c Was the Bank of England achieving its objective in 2007?

d How is fiscal policy influencing the Bank of England's task?

e What policy has the Bank of England taken in response to rising inflation?

f What in your opinion is the likely outcome of both the government and Bank of England policies on real GDP and inflation?

2 Norbert Walter, the respected chief economist of Deutsche Bank, noted that 2006 was a year of extraordinary effects for the German economy: "The boost from the Government's investment programme; the stimuli from temporary introduction of an accelerated depreciation scheme; the boost to sales and Germany's image from the football World Cup; and finally the effects of purchases being brought forward to beat the increase in value added tax to 19 per cent." This year, by contrast, Germany will be hit by a potentially lethal combination of higher taxes, rising interest rates and a less competitive exchange rate.

The Times, 22 February 2007.

a Was Germany's extraordinary boost in 2006 from fiscal policy, monetary policy or both?

b Were fiscal policy and monetary policy in 2006 coordinated or in conflict?

c Describe the fiscal policy and monetary policy in 2007.

d Are fiscal policy and monetary policy in 2007 coordinated or in conflict?

3 **Sarkozy warns EU to revise fiscal policy**

Nicolas Sarkozy, the frontrunner in the French presidential election campaign, on Monday urged the European Union to develop a coordinated economic strategy. . . . The EU must rethink its monetary, competition and trade policies to defend its interests. . . . Launching his latest campaign book, Mr Sarkozy argued for a reworking of European monetary policy, which he blamed for eroding the competitiveness of French industry. . . . The European Central Bank should weaken the euro to stimulate economic growth rather than focus exclusively on combating inflation.

FT.com, 3 April 2007

a Which of the policies Sarkozy suggests is part of fiscal policy?

b Which of the policies Sarkozy suggests is part of monetary policy?

c Is Sarkozy suggesting that, to stimulate growth, fiscal policy and monetary policy must be coordinated?

d If you were voting in the French election, would you vote for Sarkozy's economic plan? Explain why or why not.

Web Activities

Links to Websites

1 Visit the website of Office for National Statistics and look at the current economic conditions. On the basis of the current state of the UK economy, and in the light of what you now know about fiscal and monetary policy interaction, what do you predict would happen to real GDP and the price level:

a If the Bank of England conducted an expansionary monetary policy?

b If the Bank of England conducted a contractionary monetary policy?

c If the government conducted an expansionary fiscal policy?

d If the government conducted a contractionary fiscal policy?

e If the Bank of England conducted an expansionary monetary policy and the government conducted a contractionary fiscal policy?

f If the Bank of England conducted a contractionary monetary policy and the government conducted an expansionary fiscal policy.

Chapter 29 Appendix

The *IS–LM* Model of Aggregate Demand

After studying this appendix, you will be able to:

- **Explain the purpose and origin of the *IS–LM* model**
- **Define and derive the *IS* curve**
- **Define and derive the *LM* curve**
- **Define and derive *IS–LM* equilibrium**
- **Use the *IS–LM* model to analyze the relative effectiveness of fiscal policy and monetary policy**
- **Use the *IS–LM* model to derive the aggregate demand curve**

Purpose and Origin of the *IS–LM* Model

This appendix explains a neat way of summarizing what you've learned about aggregate demand. Before we get into the details of the *IS–LM* model, we'll examine its purpose and origin.

Purpose of the *IS–LM* Model

The purpose of the *IS–LM* model is twofold:

1 To provide a tool for analyzing fiscal policy and monetary policy

2 To derive the aggregate demand curve

In Chapter 23, you saw the importance of distinguishing between aggregate demand and the quantity of real GDP demanded at a given price level. And you learned why the aggregate demand curve slopes downward and what makes it shift.

In Chapter 25, you learned that each point on the aggregate demand curve corresponds to a point of equilibrium expenditure – a point at which the *AE* curve intersects the 45° line (Figure 25.9, p. 578). In deriving the *AD* curve, we noted that there is a different *AE* curve for each price level. The *IS–LM* model breaks the source of the shift in the *AE* curve into two parts:

1 The effect of the interest rate on spending plans

2 The effect of the price level on the interest rate

In Chapter 26, you saw how fiscal policy influences aggregate demand. Then, in Chapter 28, you saw that spending plans depend on the interest rate. The interest-sensitive expenditure curve summarizes this effect. You also saw how monetary policy influences the interest rate and spending.

Once money becomes a central part of the story about how aggregate demand is determined, things get a bit complicated. The source of the complication is that everything seems to depend on everything else! Spending plans depend on real GDP and the interest rate. In equilibrium, planned spending equals real GDP but because planned spending depends on the interest rate, we need to know how the interest rate is determined.

You've seen how the demand for money and the supply of money determine the interest rate. But the quantity of real money that people plan to hold depends on real GDP. So to determine the interest rate, that we need to determine real GDP, we need to know real GDP! We seem to be going around in a circle.

The *IS–LM* model cuts through the complexity of combining spending plans and money holding plans and shows us how both real GDP and the interest rate are determined simultaneously by equilibrium expenditure and money market equilibrium.

By using a model that simultaneously determines real GDP and the interest rate, we can see how fiscal policy and monetary policy influence both these variables. We can also see why fiscal policy and monetary policy might come into conflict and need to be coordinated.

Origin of the *IS–LM* Model

The *IS–LM* model was invented by John Hicks, of Oxford University, one of the greatest economists of the twentieth century. The model is a logically coherent clarification of the confusing prose written by John Maynard Keynes in his *General Theory of Employment, Interest and Money*. Hicks cut through the mystery of the *General Theory* and although Keynes never acknowledged that Hicks had correctly interpreted his words, almost every other economist believed that he had done so. Hicks' *IS–LM* model became the core model for macroeconomic policy analysis.

The *IS* Curve

The ***IS* curve** shows combinations of real GDP and the interest rate at which aggregate planned expenditure equals real GDP. Figure A29.1 derives the *IS* curve.

Each row of the table is an aggregate expenditure schedule. Aggregate expenditure depends on the interest rate: as the interest rate decreases aggregate expenditure increases. Part (a) shows an *AE* curve for each interest rate. For example, when the interest rate is 6 per cent a year (row *A*), the aggregate expenditure curve is AE_A. Each *AE* curve generates equilibrium expenditure. For example, on AE_A, equilibrium expenditure is £1,100 billion at point *A*.

Part (b) shows the *IS* curve – equilibrium expenditure at each interest rate. Point *A* on the *IS* curve corresponds to point *A* in part (a). It tells us that if the interest rate is 6 per cent a year, the equilibrium expenditure occurs at a real GDP of £1,100 billion. Points *B* and *C* on the *IS* curve illustrate the equilibrium expenditure at points *B* and *C* in part (a).

Figure A29.1

Aggregate Planned Expenditure and the *IS* Curve

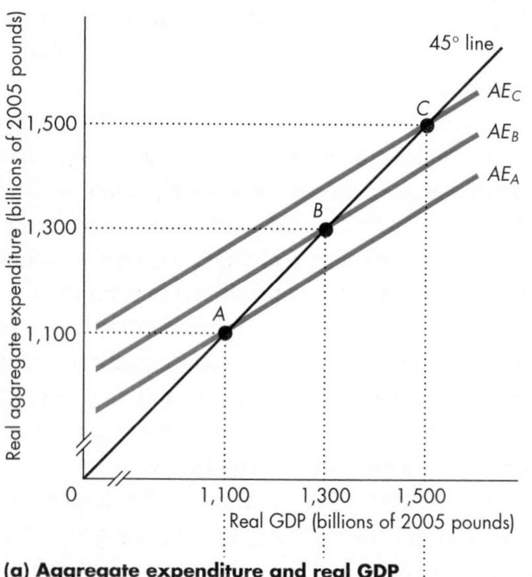

(a) Aggregate expenditure and real GDP

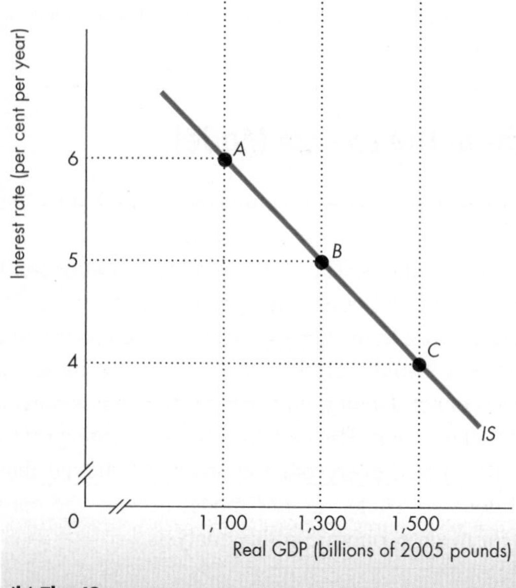

(b) The *IS* curve

The table shows aggregate planned expenditure that occurs at different combinations of the interest rate and real GDP. Each of rows *A*, *B* and *C* represents an aggregate expenditure schedule, which is plotted as the aggregate expenditure curves AE_A, AE_B and AE_C, respectively, in part (a).

Equilibrium expenditure occurs in part (a), where these *AE* curves intersect the 45° line and are marked *A*, *B* and *C*. Part (b) shows these same equilibrium positions but highlights the combinations of the interest rate and the real GDP at which they occur. The green squares show equilibrium expenditure. The line connecting these points is the *IS* curve.

	Interest rate (per cent per year)	Autonomous expenditure (billions of 2005 pounds)	Aggregate planned expenditure (billions of 2005 pounds)		
A	6	300	1,100	1,250	1,400
B	5	350	1,150	1,300	1,450
C	4	400	1,200	1,350	1,500
Induced expenditure			800	950	1,100
Real GDP (billions of 2005 pounds)			1,100	1,300	1,500

The *LM* Curve

The ***LM* curve** shows the combinations of real GDP and the interest rate at which the quantity of real money demanded equals the quantity of real money supplied. Figure A29.2 derives the *LM* curve.

Each column of the table is a demand for money schedule. The demand for money depends on real GDP: as real GDP increases the demand for money increases. Part (a) shows an *MD* curve for each real GDP. For example, when real GDP is £1,100 billion (column *D*), the demand for money curve is MD_D. Each *MD* curve generates an equilibrium interest rate. For example, on MD_D, money market equilibrium is at point *D*, where the interest rate is 4 per cent a year.

Part (b) shows the *LM* curve – equilibrium real GDP at each interest rate. Point *D* on the *LM* curve corresponds to point *D* in part (a). It tells us that if the interest rate is 4 per cent a year, the quantity of real money demanded equals the quantity supplied at a real GDP of £1,100 billion. Points *E* and *F* on the *LM* curve illustrate money market equilibrium at points *E* and *F* in part (a).

Figure A29.2

The Money Market and the *LM* Curve

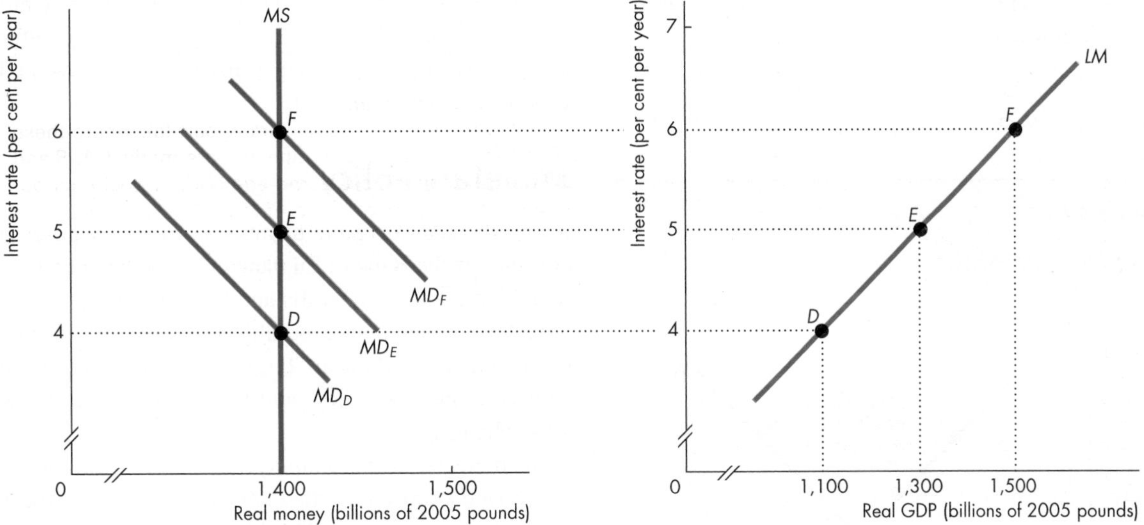

(a) Money market equilibrium

(b) The *LM* curve

Interest rate (per cent per year)	Quantity of real money demanded (billions of 2005 pounds)		
6	1,300	1,340	1,400
5	1,350	1,400	1,460
4	1,400	1,460	1,530
Real GDP	1,100	1,300	1,500
Quantity of real money (billions of 2005 pounds)	1,400	1,400	1,400
	D	E	F

The table shows the quantity of real money demanded at different combinations of the interest rate and real GDP. Money market equilibrium – equality between the quantity of real money demanded and the quantity of real money supplied – is shown by the green squares.

Each of the columns *D*, *E* and *F* represents a demand for real money schedule, plotted as the demand for real money curves MD_D, MD_E and MD_F, respectively, in part (a). Money market equilibrium occurs at points *D*, *E* and *F*. Part (b) shows these equilibrium points but highlights the combinations of the interest rate and real GDP at which they occur. The line connecting these points is the *LM* curve.

IS–LM Equilibrium

The *IS* curve and the *LM* curve determine the equilibrium interest rate and real GDP at a given price level. Figure A29.3 brings together the *IS* curve and the *LM* curve and shows the *IS–LM* equilibrium – at the intersection of the *IS* curve and *LM* curve.

At point *B* on the *IS* curve, aggregate planned expenditure equals real GDP. At point *E* on the *LM* curve, the quantity of real money demanded equals the quantity of real money supplied. At this intersection point, the equilibrium interest rate is 5 per cent a year and real GDP is £1,300 billion.

All other points are either off the *IS* curve or off the *LM* curve. At points off the *IS* curve, aggregate planned expenditure does not equal real GDP. And at points off the *LM* curve are points at which the money market is not in equilibrium.

Figure A29.3

IS–LM Equilibrium

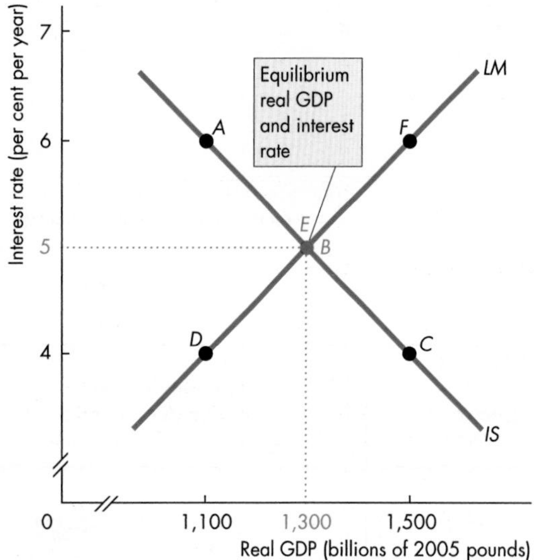

All points on the *IS* curve are points where aggregate planned expenditure equals real GDP. All points on the *LM* curve are points at which the quantity of real money demanded equals the quantity of real money supplied. The intersection of the *IS* curve and the *LM* curve determines the equilibrium interest rate and real GDP – 5 per cent a year and £1,300 billion. At this interest rate and real GDP, there is equilibrium in the goods market and the money market.

IS–LM Policy Analysis

We can use the *IS–LM* model to analyze the effects of fiscal policy and monetary policy on real GDP and the interest rate (at a given price level).

Fiscal Policy

A change in government expenditure or autonomous taxes shifts the *IS* curve, but with a given monetary policy, the *LM* curve does not change. If the government conducts an expansionary fiscal policy, the *IS* curve shifts rightward from IS_0 to IS_1 in Figure A29.4(a). The interest rate rises and real GDP increases.

The increase in real GDP is less than the shift in the *IS* curve. The reason is that the rise in the interest rate leads to a decrease in interest-sensitive expenditure, which partially offsets the increase in aggregate expenditure created by the expansionary fiscal policy – what is called *partial crowding out*.

Monetary Policy

Along the *LM* curve the quantity of money supplied is constant. If the Bank of England changes the quantity of money, the *LM* curve shifts and the interest rate adjusts to restore money market equilibrium. But other changes occur when the Bank of England conducts an expansionary monetary policy, and the *IS–LM* model shows these changes.

An increase in the quantity of money shifts the *LM* curve rightward and with a given fiscal policy, the *IS* curve does not change. The *LM* curve shifts from LM_0 to LM_1 in Figure 29.4(b). The interest rate falls and real GDP increases. Real GDP increases because the fall in the interest rate induced by the expansionary monetary policy increases the amount of interest-sensitive expenditure.

Two Extreme Cases

An extreme Keynesian outcome occurs when the *LM* curve is horizontal (LM_H), which occurs only if there is a "liquidity trap" – a situation when people are willing to hold any quantity of money at a specific interest rate. The extreme monetarist case occurs when the *LM* curve is vertical (LM_V) – the demand for money is insensitive to the interest rate.

Expansionary fiscal policy shifts the *IS* curve rightward from IS_0 to IS_1 in Figures A29.4(c) and (d). In the extreme Keynesian case, the interest rate does not

Figure A29.4

Fiscal Policy and Monetary Policy

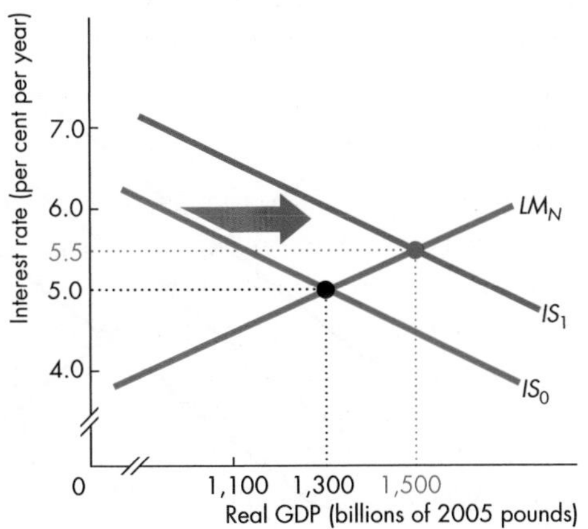

(a) Fiscal policy: normal case

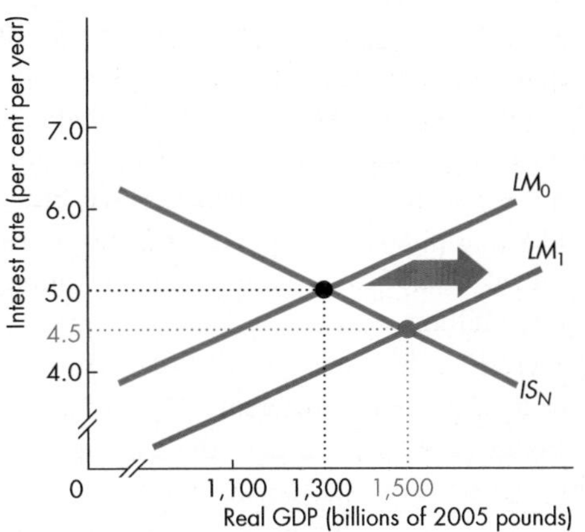

(b) Monetary policy: normal case

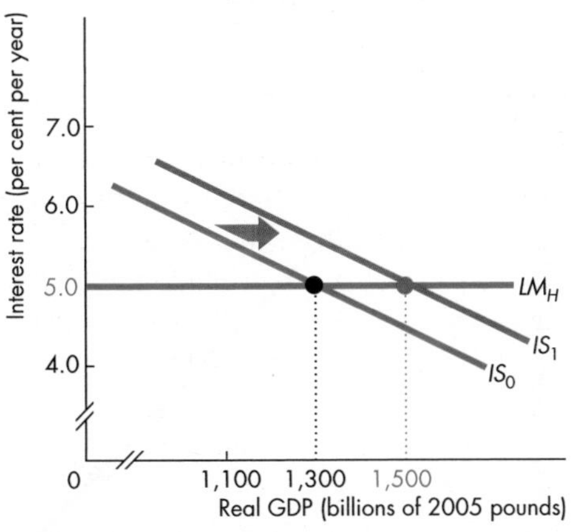

(c) Fiscal policy: maximum effect on GDP

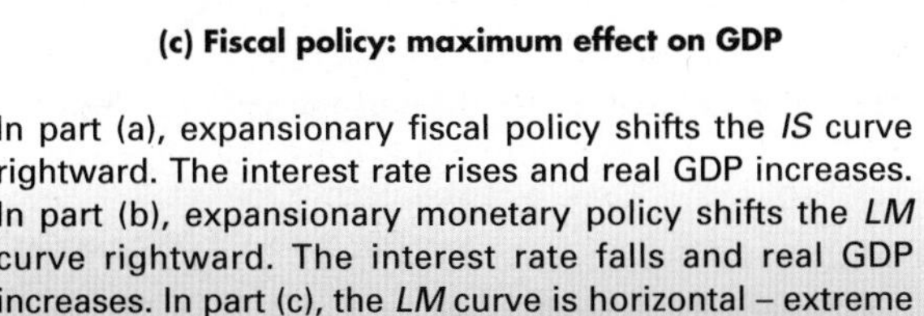

Interest rate (per cent per year)
7.0
6.0
5.0
4.0
0
LM_V
IS_1
IS_0
1,100 1,300 1,500
Real GDP (billions of 2005 pounds)

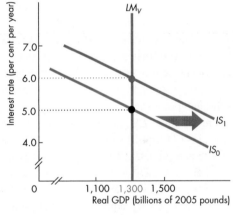

(d) Fiscal policy: no effect on GDP

In part (a), expansionary fiscal policy shifts the *IS* curve rightward. The interest rate rises and real GDP increases. In part (b), expansionary monetary policy shifts the *LM* curve rightward. The interest rate falls and real GDP increases. In part (c), the *LM* curve is horizontal – extreme Keynesian case. Expansionary fiscal policy does not change the interest rate and no crowding out occurs. In part (d), the *LM* curve is vertical – extreme monetarist case. Expansionary fiscal policy increases the interest rate and complete crowding out occurs.

change and real GDP increases by the same amount as the shift of the *IS* curve. Crowding out does not occur.

In the extreme monetarist case, the interest rate rises and real GDP does not change. The higher interest rate reduces interest-sensitive expenditure by an amount equal to the initial increase in aggregate expenditure. Complete crowding out occurs.

The extreme monetarist case shows that fiscal policy is completely ineffective and the extreme Keynesian case shows that fiscal policy is fully effective.

In contrast to fiscal policy, monetary policy is ineffective in the extreme Keynesian case. In Figure A29.4(c), the *LM* curve is horizontal, which tells us that any increase in the quantity of money is willingly held at the specific interest rate. So with a given fiscal policy (*IS* curve), an increase in the quantity of money will not lower the interest rate and real GDP remains the same.

In the extreme monetarist case, the *LM* curve is vertical, as in Figure A29.4(d). An increase in the quantity of money will shift the *LM* curve rightward. With a given fiscal policy (*IS* curve), the interest rate falls and real GDP increases.

The Aggregate Demand Curve

We can use the *IS–LM* model to derive the aggregate demand curve. In the example on pp. 688–690, the quantity of real money is £1,400 billion. Suppose that the quantity of *nominal* money is £1,470 billion and the price level is 105. If the price level was 115, the quantity of real money would be £1,278 billion (£1,470 billion divided by 115 multiplied by 100 = £1,278 billion). And if the price level was 95, the quantity of real money would be £1,547 billion.

Because there is a different quantity of real money for each price level, there is a different *LM* curve at each price level. Figure A29.5(a) illustrates the *LM* curves for the three price levels we've just considered.

The initial *LM* curve has the price level of 105. This *LM* curve is labelled LM_0 in Figure A29.5(a). When the price level is 105 and real GDP is £1,300 billion, the interest rate that achieves money market equilibrium is 6 per cent a year at point *G*. The entire *LM* curve shifts leftward to LM_1 to pass through point *G*.

When the price level is 95 and real GDP is £1,300 billion, the interest rate that achieves money market equilibrium is 4 per cent a year at point *H* in Figure A29.5(a). Again, the entire *LM* curve shifts rightward to LM_2 to pass through point *H*.

Because there are three *LM* curves in Figure A29.5, there are three *IS–LM* equilibrium points. When the price level is 105 and the *LM* curve is LM_0, equilibrium is at point *E* where real GDP is £1,300 billion and the interest rate is 5 per cent a year. When the price level is 115 and the *LM* curve is LM_1, equilibrium is at point *J* where real GDP is £1,200 billion and the interest rate is 5.5 per cent a year. And when the price level is 95 and the *LM* curve is LM_2, equilibrium is at point *K* where real GDP is £1,400 billion and the interest rate is 4.5 per cent a year.

At each price level, there is a different *IS–LM* equilibrium and a different equilibrium real GDP and interest rate. Figure A29.5(b) traces the aggregate demand curve. Notice that the price level is measured on the vertical axis of part (b) and real GDP on the horizontal axis. When the price level is 105, equilibrium real GDP is £1,300 billion (point *E*). When the price level is 115, equilibrium real GDP is £1,200 billion (point *J*). And when the price level is 95, real GDP demanded is £1,400 billion (point *K*). Each of these points corresponds to the corresponding point in part (a).

The line passing through points *J*, *E* and *K* in part (b) is the aggregate demand curve.

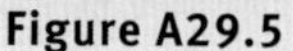
Figure A29.5

Deriving the Aggregate Demand Curve

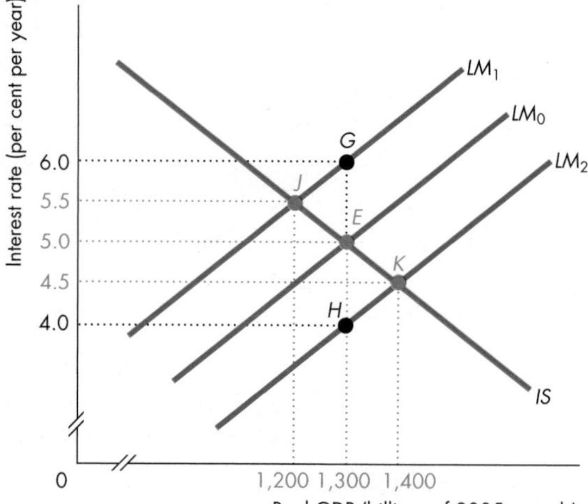

(a) IS and LM curves

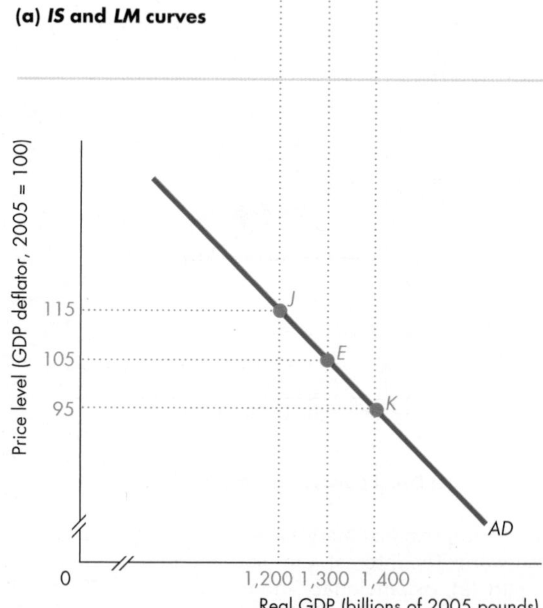

(b) Aggregate demand curve

In part (a), if the price level is 105, the *LM* curve is LM_0 and *IS–LM* equilibrium occurs at point *E*. The quantity of real GDP demanded is £1,300 billion. This combination of the price level of 105 and the quantity of real GDP demanded of £1,300 billion is point *E* on the *AD* curve in part (b).

If the price level rises to 115, the *LM* curve shifts leftward to LM_1. The *IS–LM* equilibrium occurs at point *J* and a quantity of real GDP demanded of £1,200 billion – point *J* on the *AD* curve in part (b).

If the price level falls to 95, the *LM* curve shifts rightward to LM_2. The *IS–LM* equilibrium occurs at point *K* and a quantity of real GDP demanded of £1,400 billion – point *K* on the *AD* curve in part (b).

Inflation

CHAPTER 30

After studying this chapter you will be able to:

- Distinguish between inflation and a change in the price level and between demand-pull inflation and cost-push inflation
- Explain the quantity theory of money
- Describe the effects of inflation
- Explain the short-run and long-run relationships between inflation and unemployment
- Explain the short-run and long-run relationships between inflation and interest rates

From Rome to Harare

In the dying days of the Roman Empire (at the end of the third century AD), inflation ripped away at a rate of more than 300 per cent a year. Today in Zimbabwe, the inflation rate is running at more than 1,700 per cent a year. What causes rapid inflation? What are the effects of inflation? Does inflation bring only costs and no benefits? How can inflation be controlled? You can find the answers in this chapter and, in *Reading Between the Lines* at the end of the chapter, take a close look at how Zimbabwe is struggling to contain inflation today.

Inflation: Demand-pull and Cost-push

We don't have much inflation today, but during the 1970s and the late 1980s, it was a major problem. **Inflation** is a process in which the *price level is rising* and *money is losing value*.

If the price level rises persistently, then people need more and more money to make transactions. Incomes rise, so firms must pay out more in wages and other payments to owners of factors of production.

And prices rise, so consumers must take more money with them when they go shopping. But the value of money gets smaller and smaller.

Some persistent price rises occur that are not inflation. And sometimes a jump in the price level occurs that is not inflation.

Inflation versus a Rising Relative Price

A change in *one price* is inflation. For example, suppose the price of a gallon of petrol rises by 5 per cent a year but all other prices fall slightly so that the price level remains constant. In this situation, the *relative price* of petrol *is rising* but there is no inflation. Inflation is a process in which the *price level is rising*, not the price of a single (or small number) of items.

Inflation versus a Rise in the Price Level

A one-time jump in the price level is not inflation. Instead, inflation is an ongoing *process*. Figure 30.1 illustrates this distinction. The blue line shows a one-time jump in the price level. Such a jump might occur if a broad tax such as the VAT increases. It might also occur if there is a one-time rise in the price of a widely used commodity such as oil. An economy in which the price level jumps like the blue line in the figure is not experiencing inflation. Its price level is constant most of the time.

The red line in Figure 30.1 shows a continuously rising price level. That is inflation. The steeper the rise of the price level, the faster is the inflation rate.

We calculate the inflation rate as the percentage increase in the price level and we generally measure the price level either as the Consumer Prices Index or the GDP deflator. Call the price level in the current year P_1 and the price level in the previous year P_0, then:

Figure 30.1

Inflation versus a One-time Rise in the Price Level

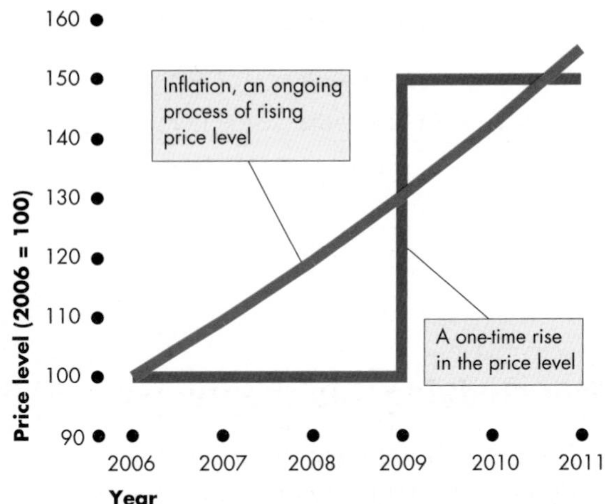

Along the red line, an economy experiences inflation because the price level rises persistently. Along the blue line, an economy experiences a one-time rise in the price level.

$$\text{Inflation rate} = \frac{P_1 - P_0}{P_0} \times 100$$

For example, if this year's price level is 111.3 and last year's price level was 106, the inflation rate is 5 per cent per year. That is:

$$\text{Inflation rate} = \frac{111.3 - 106}{106} \times 100$$

$$= 5 \text{ per cent per year}$$

This equation shows the connection between the *inflation rate* and the *price level*. For a given price level last year, the higher the price level in the current year, the higher is the inflation rate.

If the price level is *rising*, the inflation rate is *positive*. If the price level rises at a *faster* rate, the inflation rate *increases*.

Inflation can result from an aggregate-demand shock, an aggregate-supply shock or both. These two sources of impulses are called:

- Demand-pull inflation
- Cost-push inflation

We'll first study a demand-pull inflation.

Demand-pull Inflation

An inflation that results from an initial increase in aggregate demand is called **demand-pull inflation**. Such an inflation may arise from any individual factor that increases aggregate demand such as:

1 An increase in the quantity of money
2 An increase in government expenditure
3 An increase in exports

Initial Effect of an Increase in Aggregate Demand

Suppose that last year the price level was 110, real GDP was £1,300 billion and potential GDP was also £1,300 billion. Figure 30.2(a) illustrates this situation. The aggregate demand curve is AD_0, the short-run aggregate supply curve is SAS_0 and the long-run aggregate supply curve is *LAS*.

In the current year, aggregate demand increases and the aggregate demand curve shifts rightward to AD_1. Such a situation arises if, for example, the Bank of England loosens its grip on the quantity of money, the government increases its expenditure on goods and services or exports increase.

With no change in potential GDP and with no change in the money wage rate, the long-run aggregate supply curve and the short-run aggregate supply curve remain at *LAS* and SAS_0 respectively.

The price level and real GDP are determined at the point where the aggregate demand curve AD_1 intersects the short-run aggregate supply curve. The price level rises to 108 and real GDP increases above potential GDP to £1,350 billion. The economy experiences a 2.9 per cent rise in the price level (a price level of 108 compared with 105 in the previous year) and a rapid expansion of real GDP. Unemployment falls below its natural rate. The next step in the unfolding story is a rise in the money wage rate.

Money Wage Response

Real GDP cannot remain above potential GDP for ever. With unemployment below its natural rate, there is a shortage of labour. In this situation, the money wage

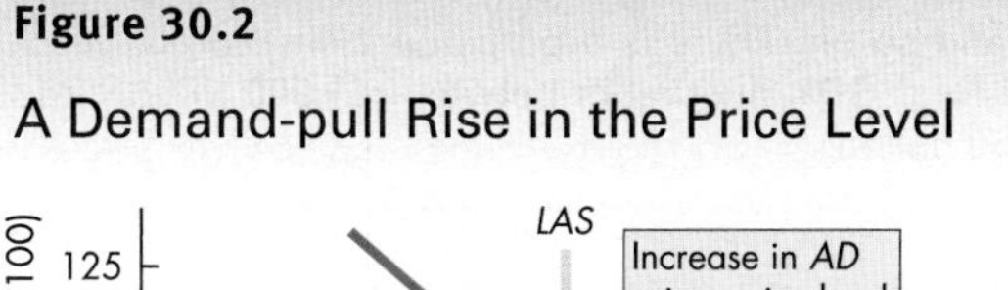

Figure 30.2

A Demand-pull Rise in the Price Level

myeconlab

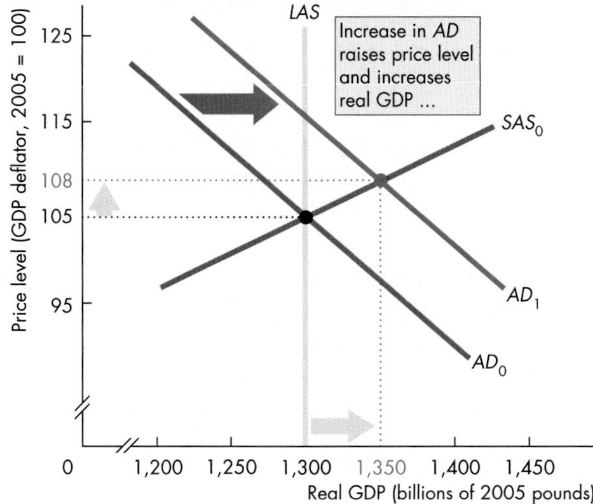

(a) Initial effect

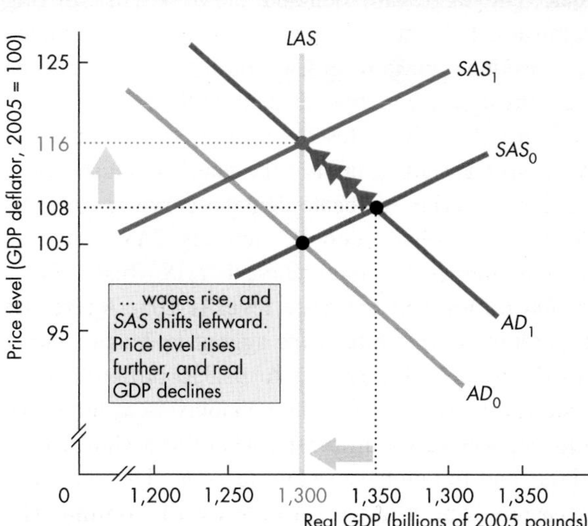

(b) The money wage adjusts

In part (a), the aggregate demand curve is AD_0, the short-run aggregate supply curve is SAS_0 and the long-run aggregate supply curve is *LAS*. The price level is 105 and real GDP is £1,300 billion, which equals potential GDP. Aggregate demand increases to AD_1. The price level rises to 108 and real GDP increases to £1,350 billion. In part (b), starting from above full employment, the money wage rate begins to rise and the short-run aggregate supply curve shifts leftward towards SAS_1. The price level rises further and real GDP returns to potential GDP.

rate begins to rise. As the money wage rate rises, the short-run aggregate supply starts to decrease and the *SAS* curve starts to shift leftward. The price level rise further and real GDP begins to decrease.

With no further change in aggregate demand – the aggregate demand curve remains at AD_1 – this process comes to an end when the short-run aggregate demand curve has shifted to SAS_1 in Figure 30.2(b). At this time, the price level has increased to 116 and real GDP has returned to potential GDP of £1,300 billion, the level from which it started.

A Demand-pull Inflation Process

The process we've just studied eventually ends when, for a given increase in aggregate demand, the money wage rate has adjusted enough to restore the real wage rate to its full-employment level. We've studied a one-time rise in the price level like that described in Figure 30.1. For inflation to proceed, aggregate demand must persistently increase.

The only way in which aggregate demand can persistently increase is if the quantity of money persistently increases. Suppose the government has a large budget deficit that it finances by selling bonds. Also suppose that the Bank of England buys these bonds. When the Bank of England buys bond, it creates more money. In this situation, aggregate demand increases year after year. The aggregate demand curve keeps shifting rightward. This persistent increase in aggregate demand puts continual upward pressure on the price level. The economy now experiences demand-pull inflation.

Figure 30.3 illustrates the process of demand-pull inflation. The starting point is the same as that shown in Figure 30.2. The aggregate demand curve is AD_0, the short-run aggregate supply curve is SAS_0, and the long-run aggregate supply curve is *LAS*. Real GDP is £1,300 billion and the price level is 105. Aggregate demand increases, shifting the aggregate demand curve to AD_1. Real GDP increases to £1,350 billion and the price level rises to 108. The economy is at an above full-employment equilibrium. There is a shortage of labour and the money wage rate rises. The short-run aggregate supply curve shifts leftward to SAS_1. The price level rises to 116 and real GDP returns to potential GDP.

But the Bank of England increases the quantity of money again and aggregate demand continues to increase. The aggregate demand curve shifts rightward to AD_2. The price level rises further to 120 and real GDP again exceeds potential GDP at £1,350 billion.

Figure 30.3 myeconlab

A Demand-pull Inflation Spiral

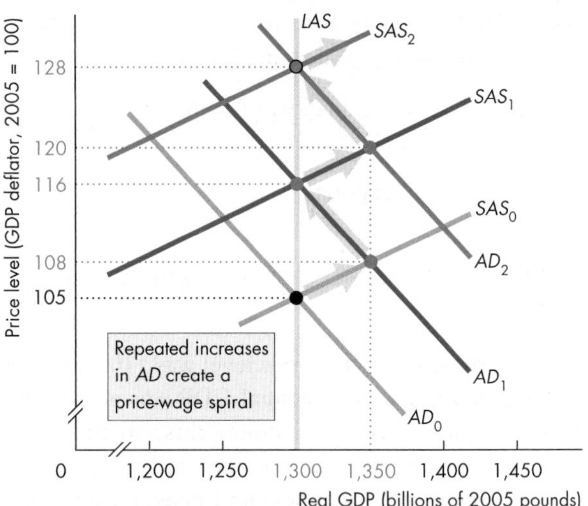

Each time the quantity of money increases, aggregate demand increases and the aggregate demand curve shifts rightward from AD_0 to AD_1 to AD_2 and so on.

Each time real GDP goes above potential GDP, the money wage rate rises and the short-run aggregate supply curve shifts leftward from SAS_0 to SAS_1 to SAS_2 and so on.

The price level rises from 105 to 108, 116, 120, 128 and so on. There is a perpetual demand-pull inflation. Real GDP fluctuates between £1,300 billion and £1,350 billion.

Yet again, the money wage rate rises and decreases short-run aggregate supply. The *SAS* curve shifts to SAS_2 and the price level rises further to 128. As the money supply continues to grow, aggregate demand increases and the price level rises in an ongoing demand-pull inflation process.

The process you have just studied generates inflation: an ongoing process of a rising price level.

Demand-pull Inflation in Hartlepool

You may better understand the inflation process that we've just described by considering what is going on in an individual part of the economy, such as a Hartlepool soft drinks factory. Initially, when aggregate demand increases, the demand for soft drinks increases and the price of soft drinks rises. Faced with a higher price, the soft drinks factory works overtime and increases production. Conditions are good for workers in Hartlepool and the soft drinks factory finds it hard to hang on to its best people. To do so it has to offer higher money wages. As money wages increase, so do the soft drinks factory's costs.

What happens next depends on what happens to aggregate demand. If aggregate demand remains unchanged, as in Figure 30.2(b), the firm's costs are increasing but the price of soft drinks is not increasing as quickly as the factory's costs. Production is scaled back. Eventually, the money wage rate and costs increase by the same percentage as the price of soft drinks. In real terms, the soft drinks factory is in the same situation as it was initially – before the increase in aggregate demand. The soft drinks factory produces the same quantity of soft drinks and employs the same amount of labour as before the increase in aggregate demand.

But if aggregate demand continues to increase, so does the demand for soft drinks and the price of lemonade rises at the same rate as the money wage rate. The soft drinks factory continues to operate above full employment and there is a persistent shortage of labour. Prices and wages chase each other upward in an unending spiral.

Demand-pull Inflation in the United Kingdom

A demand-pull inflation like the one you've just studied occurred in the United Kingdom during the 1970s.

In 1972–1973, the government pursued an expansionary monetary and fiscal policy. Its goal was to lower the unemployment rate and boost the rate of economic growth. The aggregate demand curve shifted rightward, the price level increased quickly and real GDP moved above potential GDP. The money wage rate started to rise more quickly and the short-run aggregate supply curve shifted leftward.

The Bank of England responded with a further increase in the growth rate of the quantity of money. Aggregate demand increased even more quickly and a demand-pull inflation spiral unfolded.

By the mid-1970s, the inflation rate had reached more than 20 per cent a year. Contrary to the government's goal, the growth rate of real GDP didn't increase and the unemployment rate didn't decrease. On the contrary, the late 1970s were years of extremely high unemployment and slow real GDP growth.

You've seen how demand-pull inflation arises. Let's now see how an aggregate supply shock brings cost-push inflation.

Cost-push Inflation

An inflation that results from an initial increase in costs is called **cost-push inflation**. The two main sources of increases in costs are:

1 An increase in the money wage rate
2 An increase in the money prices of raw materials

At a given price level, the higher the cost of production, the smaller is the amount that firms are willing to produce. So if the money wage rate rises or if the prices of a raw materials (for example, oil, nickel and copper) rises, firms decrease their supply of goods and services. Aggregate supply decreases and the short-run aggregate supply curve shifts leftward.[1] Let's trace the effects of such a decrease in short-run aggregate supply on the price level and real GDP.

Initial Effect of a Decrease in Aggregate Supply

Suppose that last year the price level was 105 and real GDP was £1,300 billion. Potential real GDP was also £1,300 billion. Figure 30.4 (overleaf) illustrates this situation. The aggregate demand curve was AD_0, the short-run aggregate supply curve was SAS_0 and the long-run aggregate supply curve was *LAS*.

In the current year, the world's oil producers form a price-fixing organization that strengthens their market power and increases the relative price of oil. They raise the price of oil by a large enough percentage to bring a huge decrease in short-run aggregate supply.

The short-run aggregate supply curve shifts leftward to SAS_1. The price level rises to 112, and real GDP decreases to £1,250 billion. The economy is at a below full-employment equilibrium.

This event brings a change in the relative price of oil and a one-time change in the price level, like that in Figure 30.1. It is not inflation. In fact, a supply shock *on its own* cannot cause inflation. If aggregate demand remains at AD_0, a recessionary gap eventually forces the money wage rate and all other money factor prices down and short-run aggregate supply increases. The cost-push shock brings a temporary recession but no inflation.

Something more must happen to enable a one-time aggregate supply shock, which causes a one-time rise in

[1] Some cost-push forces, such as an increase in the price of oil accompanied by a decrease in the availability of oil, can also decrease long-run aggregate supply. We'll ignore such effects here and examine cost-push factors that change only short-run aggregate supply.

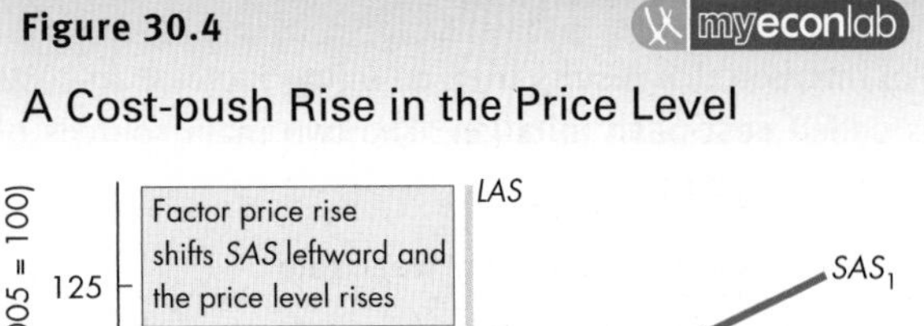

Figure 30.4

myeconlab

A Cost-push Rise in the Price Level

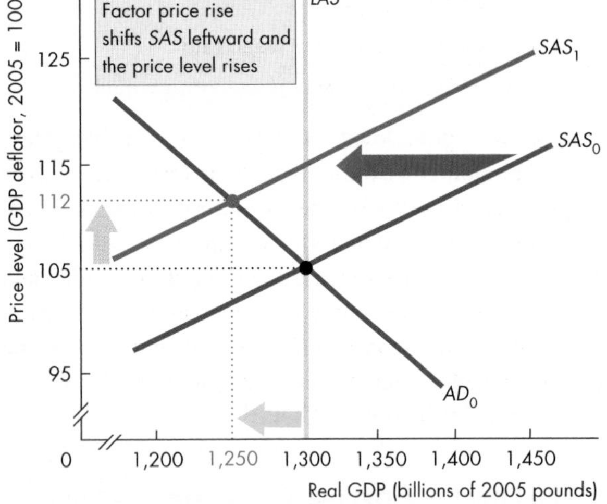

Initially, the aggregate demand curve is AD_0, the short-run aggregate supply curve is SAS_0 and the long-run aggregate supply curve is *LAS*. A decrease in aggregate supply (for example, resulting from an increase in the world price of oil) shifts the short-run aggregate supply curve to SAS_1. The economy moves to the point where the short-run aggregate supply curve SAS_1 intersects the aggregate demand curve AD_0. The price level rises to 112 and real GDP decreases to £1,250 billion. The economy experiences a one-time rise in the price level.

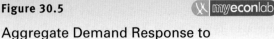

Figure 30.5

myeconlab

Aggregate Demand Response to Cost Push

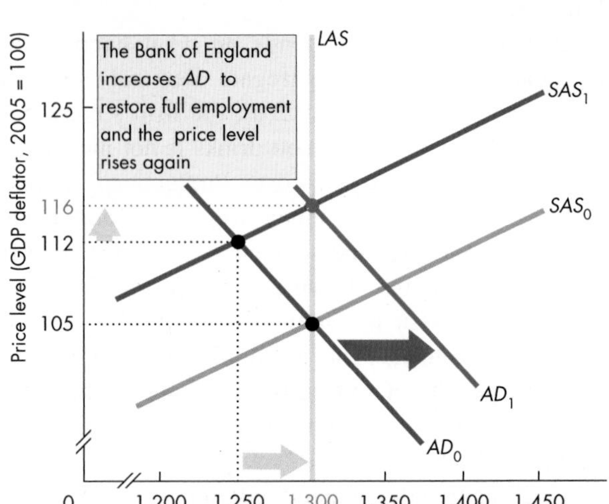

Following a cost–push increase in the price level, real GDP is below potential GDP and unemployment is above its natural rate. In this figure, real GDP is £1,250 billion and the price level is 112.

If the Bank of England responds by increasing aggregate demand to restore full employment, the aggregate demand curve shifts rightward to AD_1. The economy returns to full employment but the price level rises to 116.

the price level, to be converted into a process of ongoing inflation. That something more is a persistent increase in the quantity of money.

Aggregate Demand Response

When real GDP decreases, unemployment rises above the natural unemployment rate. In such a situation, there is usually an outcry of concern and a call for action to restore full employment. Suppose that the Bank of England increases the quantity of money. Aggregate demand increases. In Figure 30.5, the aggregate demand curve shifts rightward to AD_1. The increase in aggregate demand has restored full employment. But the price level rises to 116, a 10 per cent rise over the original price level.

The beginnings of a cost-push inflation spiral are now in place. But we still don't have cost-push inflation. A further inflationary response on the cost side is needed.

A Cost-push Inflation Process

Oil producers now see the prices of everything that they buy increasing. So they increase the price of oil again to restore its new high relative price. Figure 30.6 continues the story.

The short-run aggregate supply curve now shifts to SAS_2. The price level rises further to 124 and real GDP decreases to £1,250 billion. Unemployment increases above its natural rate. If the Bank of England responds yet again with an increase in the quantity of money, aggregate demand increases and the aggregate demand curve shifts to AD_2. The price level rises even higher – to 128 – and full employment is again restored. A cost-push inflation spiral results. But if the Bank of England does not respond, the economy remains below full employment.

You can see that the Bank of England has a dilemma. If it increases the quantity of money to restore full employment, it invites another oil price hike that will call forth another increase in the quantity of money.

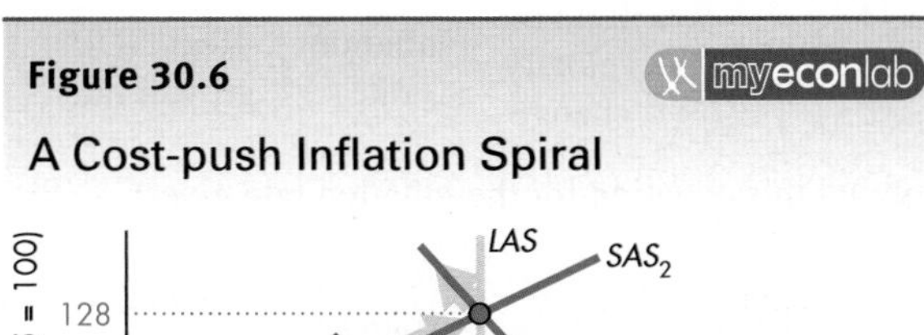

Figure 30.6

A Cost-push Inflation Spiral

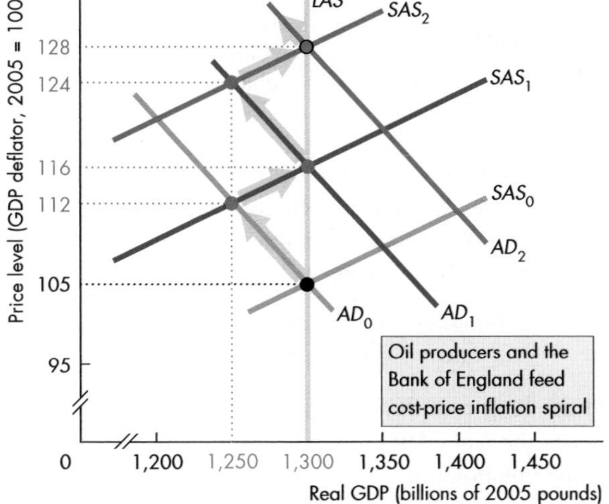

When a cost increase (for example, an increase in the world oil price) decreases short-run aggregate supply from SAS_0 to SAS_1, the price level rises to 112 and real GDP decreases to £1,250 billion. The central bank responds with an increase in the money supply that shifts the aggregate demand curve from AD_0 to AD_1. The price level rises again to 116 and real GDP returns to £1,300 billion. A further cost increase occurs, which shifts the short-run aggregate supply curve again, this time to SAS_2. Real GDP decreases again and the price level now rises to 124. The central bank responds again and the cost-push inflation spiral continues.

Inflation will rage along at a rate decided by the oil-exporting countries. If the Bank of England keeps the lid on money growth, the economy operates with a high level of unemployment.

Cost-push Inflation in Hartlepool

What is going on in the Hartlepool soft drinks factory when the economy is experiencing cost-push inflation? When the oil price increases, so do the costs of bottling soft drinks. These higher costs decrease the supply of soft drinks, increasing the price and decreasing the quantity produced. The soft drinks factory lays off some workers. This situation will persist until either the Bank of England increases aggregate demand or the price of oil falls. If the Bank of England increases aggregate demand, as it did in the United Kingdom in the mid-1970s, the demand for soft drinks increases and so does the price of soft drinks. The higher price of soft drinks brings higher profits and the factory increases its production. The soft drinks factory re-hires the laid-off workers.

Cost-push Inflation in the United Kingdom

A cost-push inflation like the one you've just studied occurred in the United Kingdom during the 1970s. In 1974 the Organization of the Petroleum Exporting Countries (OPEC) raised the price of oil fourfold. The higher oil price decreased aggregate supply, which caused the price level to rise more quickly and real GDP to shrink. The Bank of England then faced a dilemma: would it increase the quantity of money and accommodate the cost-push forces or would it keep aggregate demand growth in check by limiting money growth?

In 1975, 1976 and 1977, the Bank of England repeatedly allowed the quantity of money to grow fast and inflation proceeded rapidly. In 1979 and 1980, OPEC was again able to push oil prices higher. On that occasion, the Bank of England decided not to respond to the oil price hike with an increase in the quantity of money. The result was a recession but also, eventually, a fall in inflation.

Review Quiz

Study Plan 30.1

1. Distinguish between a rising relative price and inflation.
2. Distinguish between a one-time rise in the price level and inflation.
3. How does demand-pull inflation begin? What are the initial effects of demand-pull inflation on real GDP and the price level?
4. When real GDP exceeds potential GDP, what happens to the money wage rate and short-run aggregate supply? How do real GDP and the price level respond?
5. What must happen to create a demand-pull inflation spiral?
6. How does cost-push inflation begin? What are its initial effects on real GDP and the price level?
7. What must the Bank of England do to convert a one-time rise in the price level into a freewheeling cost-push inflation?

You've seen that inflation requires an ongoing increase in the quantity of money. The quantity theory of money explains the link between money growth and inflation.

The Quantity Theory of Money

You've seen that regardless of whether inflation originates in a demand-pull or a cost-push, to convert a one-time rise in the price level into an ongoing inflation, aggregate demand must increase. And although many factors can and do influence aggregate demand, only one factor can persistently keep aggregate demand increasing: the quantity of money. This special place of money gives rise to a special long-run theory of inflation, called the quantity theory of money.

The **quantity theory of money** is the proposition that in the long run, an increase in the quantity of money brings an equal percentage increase in the price level. The basis of the quantity theory of money is a concept known as *the velocity of circulation* and an equation called *the equation of exchange*.

The **velocity of circulation** is the average number of times a pound of money is used annually to buy the goods and services that make up GDP. GDP equals the price level (P) multiplied by real GDP (Y). That is:

$$\text{GDP} = PY$$

Call the quantity of money M. The velocity of circulation, V, is determined by the equation:

$$V = PY/M$$

For example, if GDP is £1,000 billion (PY = £1,000 billion) and the quantity of money is £250 billion, the velocity of circulation is 4. (£1,000 billion divided by £250 billion equals 4.)

From the definition of the velocity of circulation, the *equation of exchange* tells us how M, V, P and Y are connected. This equation is:

$$MV = PY$$

Given the definition of the velocity of circulation, this equation is always true – it is true by definition. The equation of exchange becomes the quantity theory of money if the quantity of money does not influence the velocity of circulation and real GDP. In this case, the equation of exchange tells us that in the long run, the price level is determined by the quantity of money. You can see why by dividing both sides of the equation by real GDP (Y). That is:

$$P = (V/Y) \times M$$

where (V/Y) is independent of M. So a change in M brings a proportional change in P.

We can also express the equation of exchange in growth rates,[2] in which form it states that:

$$\text{Money growth rate} + \text{Rate of velocity change} = \text{Inflation rate} + \text{Real GDP growth rate}$$

Solving this equation for the inflation rate gives:

$$\text{Inflation rate} = \text{Money growth rate} + \text{Rate of velocity change} - \text{Real GDP growth rate}$$

In the long run, the rate of velocity change is not influenced by the money growth rate. More strongly, in the long run, the rate of velocity change is approximately zero. With this assumption, the inflation rate in the long run is determined as:

$$\text{Inflation rate} = \text{Money growth rate} - \text{Real GDP growth rate}$$

In the long run, fluctuations in the money growth rate minus the real GDP growth rate bring equal fluctuations in the inflation rate.

Also, in the long run, with the economy at full employment, real GDP equals potential GDP, so the real GDP growth rate equals the potential GDP growth rate. This growth rate might be influenced by inflation but the influence is most likely small, and the quantity theory assumes that it is zero. So the real GDP growth rate is given and doesn't change when the money growth rate changes – inflation is correlated with money growth.

Evidence on the Quantity Theory of Money

Figure 30.7 shows two scatter diagrams of the inflation rate and the money growth rate for 134 countries in part (a) and for those countries with inflation rates below 20 per cent a year in part (b). You can see a general tendency for money growth and inflation to be correlated but the quantity theory (the red lines) does not predict inflation precisely.

Figure 30.8 summarizes some UK evidence on the quantity theory of money. The figure reveals that, on the average, as predicted by the quantity theory, the

[2] To obtain this equation, begin with

$$MV = PY$$

and then changes in these variables are related by the equation

$$\Delta MV + M\Delta V = \Delta PY + P\Delta Y$$

Divide this equation by the equation of exchange to obtain

$$\Delta M/M + \Delta V/V = \Delta P/P + \Delta Y/Y$$

The term $\Delta M/M$ is the money growth rate, $\Delta V/V$ is the rate of velocity change, $\Delta P/P$ is the inflation rate and $\Delta Y/Y$ is the growth rate of real GDP.

Figure 30.7 myeconlab

Money Growth and Inflation in the World Economy

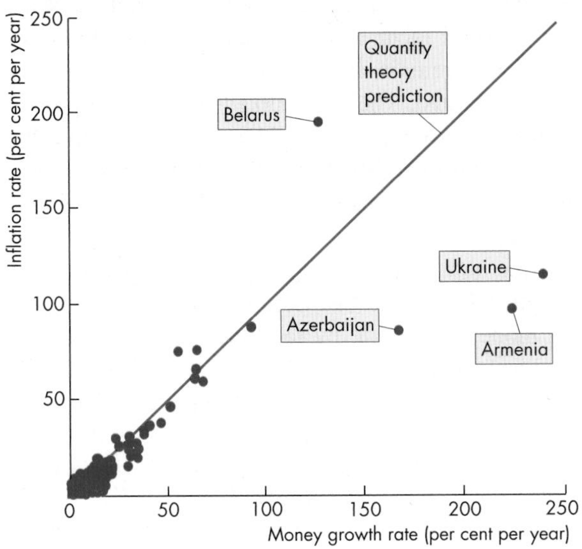

(a) 134 Countries: 1990–2005

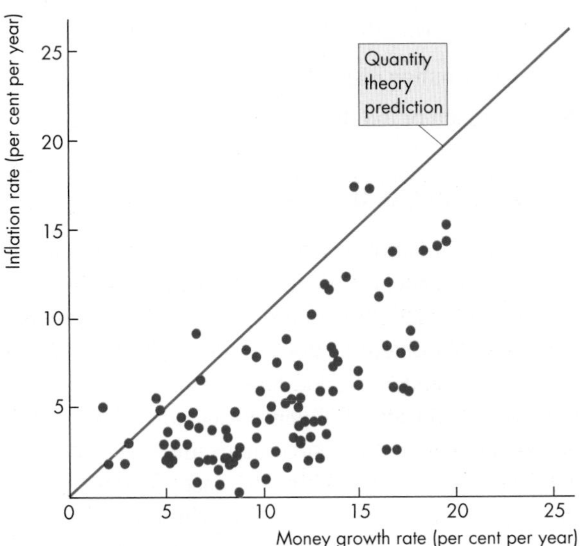

(b) 104 Lower-inflation countries: 1990–2005

Inflation and money growth in 134 countries in part (a) and low-inflation countries in part (b) show a clear positive relationship between money growth and inflation.

Sources of data: *International Financial Statistics Yearbook*, 2006 and World Economic Outlook database, International Monetary Fund, April 2006.

Figure 30.8 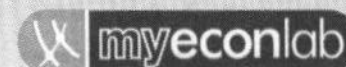

Money Growth and Inflation in the United Kingdom

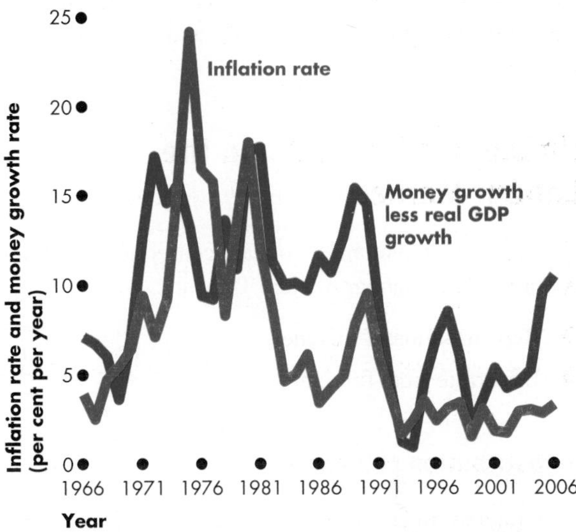

On average, the inflation rate and the money growth rate minus real GDP growth are correlated – they rise and fall together.

Sources of data: Office for National Statistics and the Bank of England.

inflation rate fluctuates in line with fluctuations in the money growth rate minus the real GDP growth rate.

The correlation between money growth and inflation isn't perfect. Nor does it tell us that money growth *causes* inflation. Money growth might cause inflation; inflation might cause money growth; or some third variable might simultaneously cause both inflation and money growth.

Review Quiz

Study Plan 30.2

1. What is the quantity theory of money?
2. What is the velocity of circulation of money and how is it calculated?
3. What is the equation of exchange? Can the equation of exchange be wrong?
4. What does the long-run historical evidence and international evidence on the relationship between money growth and inflation tell us about the quantity theory of money?

You've studied inflation and the quantity theory of money. Let's now examine the effects of inflation.

Effects of Inflation

Regardless of whether inflation is demand-pull or cost-push, the failure to *anticipate* it correctly results in unintended consequences. These unintended consequences impose costs in both labour markets and capital markets. Let's examine these costs.

Unexpected Inflation in the Labour Market

Unexpected inflation has two main consequences for the operation of the labour market. They are:

- Redistribution of income
- Departure from full employment

Redistribution of Income

Unexpected inflation redistributes income between employers and workers. Sometimes employers gain at the expense of workers and sometimes they lose. If an unexpected increase in aggregate demand increases the inflation rate, then the money wage rate will not have been set high enough. Profits will be higher than expected and real wages will buy fewer goods than expected. In this case, employers gain at the expense of workers. But if aggregate demand is expected to increase rapidly and it fails to do so, workers gain at the expense of employers. Anticipating a high inflation rate, the money wage rate is set too high and profits are squeezed. Redistributions between employers and workers create an incentive for both firms and workers to try to forecast inflation correctly.

Departures from Full Employment

Redistribution brings gains to some and losses to others. But departures from full employment impose costs on everyone. To see why, let's return to the soft drinks factory in Hartlepool. If the soft drinks factory and its workers do not anticipate inflation, but inflation occurs, the money wage rate does not rise to keep up with inflation. The real wage rate falls and the firm tries to hire more labour and increase production. But because the real wage rate has fallen, the firm has difficulty in attracting the labour it wants to employ. It pays overtime rates to its existing workforce and because it runs its factory at a faster pace, it incurs higher maintenance and parts replacement costs. But also, because the real wage rate has fallen, workers begin to quit the soft drinks factory to find jobs that pay a real wage rate closer to that prevailing before the outbreak of inflation. This labour turnover imposes additional costs on the firm. So even though its production increases, the firm incurs additional costs and its profit does not increase. The workers incur additional costs of job search and those who remain at the soft drinks factory end up feeling cheated. They've worked overtime to produce the extra output and, when they come to spend their wages, they discover that prices have increased, so their wages buy a smaller quantity of goods and services than expected.

If the soft drinks factory and its workers anticipate a high inflation rate that does not occur, they increase the money wage rate by too much and the real wage rate rises. At the higher real wage rate, the firm lays off some workers and the unemployment rate increases. Those workers who keep their jobs gain, but those who become unemployed lose. The soft drinks factory also loses because its output and profits fall.

Unexpected Inflation in the Market for Financial Capital

Unexpected inflation has two consequences for the operation of the market for financial capital. They are:

- Redistribution of income
- Too much or too little lending and borrowing

Redistribution of Income

Unexpected inflation redistributes income between borrowers and lenders. Sometimes borrowers gain at the expense of lenders; sometimes they lose. When inflation is unexpected, interest rates are not set high enough to compensate lenders for the falling value of money and borrowers gain at the expense of lenders. If inflation is expected and does not occur, interest rates will have been set too high. In this case, lenders gain at the expense of borrowers. Redistribution of income between borrowers and lenders creates an incentive for both parties to try to forecast inflation correctly.

Too Much or Too Little Lending and Borrowing

If inflation turns out to be either higher or lower than expected, the interest rate does not incorporate a correct allowance for the falling value of money and the real interest rate is either lower or higher than it otherwise would be. When the real interest rate turns out to be too low, which occurs when inflation is *higher* than expected, borrowers wish that they had borrowed more and lenders wish that they had lent less. Both groups would have made different lending and borrowing decisions with greater foresight about the inflation rate.

When the real interest rate turns out to be too high, which occurs when inflation is *lower* than expected, borrowers wish that they had borrowed less and lenders wish that they had lent more. Again, both groups would have made different lending and borrowing decisions with greater foresight about the inflation rate.

So unexpected inflation imposes costs regardless of whether the inflation turns out to be higher or lower than expected. The presence of these costs gives everyone an incentive to forecast inflation correctly. Let's see how people go about this task.

Forecasting Inflation

Inflation is difficult to forecast for two reasons. First, there are several sources of inflation – the demand-pull and cost-push sources you've just studied. Second, the speed with which a change in either aggregate demand or aggregate supply translates into a change in the price level varies. This speed of response also depends, as you will see below, on the extent to which the inflation is expected.

Because inflation is costly and difficult to forecast, people devote considerable resources to improving inflation forecasts. Some people specialize in forecasting, and others buy forecasts from specialists. The specialist forecasters are economists who work for public and private macroeconomic forecasting agencies and for banks, insurance companies, trade unions and large corporations. The returns these specialists make depend on the quality of their forecasts, so they have a strong incentive to forecast as accurately as possible. The most accurate forecast possible is the one that is based on all the relevant information available and is called a **rational expectation**.

A rational expectation is not necessarily a correct forecast. It is simply the best forecast available. It will often turn out to be wrong, but no other forecast that could have been made with the information available could be predicted to be better.

You've seen the effects of inflation when people fail to anticipate it. You've also seen why it pays to try to anticipate inflation. Let's now see what happens if inflation is correctly expected.

Expected Inflation

In the demand-pull and cost-push inflations that we studied earlier in this chapter, the money wage rate is sticky. When aggregate demand increases, either to set off a demand-pull inflation or to accommodate a cost-push inflation, the money wage rate does not change immediately. But if people correctly anticipate increases in aggregate demand, they will adjust the money wage rate so as to keep up with expected inflation.

In this case, inflation proceeds with real GDP equal to potential GDP and unemployment equal to the natural rate of unemployment. Figure 30.9 explains why. Suppose that last year the price level was 105 and real GDP was £1,300 billion, which is also potential GDP. The aggregate demand curve was AD_0, the aggregate supply curve was SAS_0 and the long-run aggregate supply curve was *LAS*.

Suppose that potential GDP does not change, so the *LAS* curve does not shift. Also suppose that aggregate demand is expected to increase and that the expected aggregate demand curve for this year is AD_1. In anticipation of the increase in aggregate demand, the money wage rate rises and the short-run aggregate supply curve shifts leftward. If the money wage rate rises by the same percentage as the price level rises, the short-run aggregate supply for next year is SAS_1.

If aggregate demand turns out to be the same as expected, the aggregate demand curve is AD_1. The short-run aggregate supply curve SAS_1 and AD_1 determine the actual price level at 116. Between last year and this year, the price level increased from 105 to 116 and the economy experienced an inflation rate of 10 per cent, the same as the inflation rate that was expected. If this expected inflation is ongoing, in the following year aggregate demand increases (as expected) and the aggregate demand curve shifts to AD_2 The money wage rate rises to reflect the anticipated inflation, and the short-run aggregate supply curve shifts to SAS_2. The price level rises by a further 10 per cent to 128.

What has caused this inflation? The immediate answer is that because people expected inflation, they increased wages and increased prices. But the expectation was correct. Aggregate demand was expected to increase and it did increase. Because aggregate demand was *expected* to increase from AD_0 to AD_1, the short-run aggregate supply curve shifted upward from SAS_0 to SAS_1. Because aggregate demand actually did increase by the amount that was expected, the actual aggregate demand curve shifted from AD_0 to AD_1. The combination

Figure 30.9

Expected Inflation

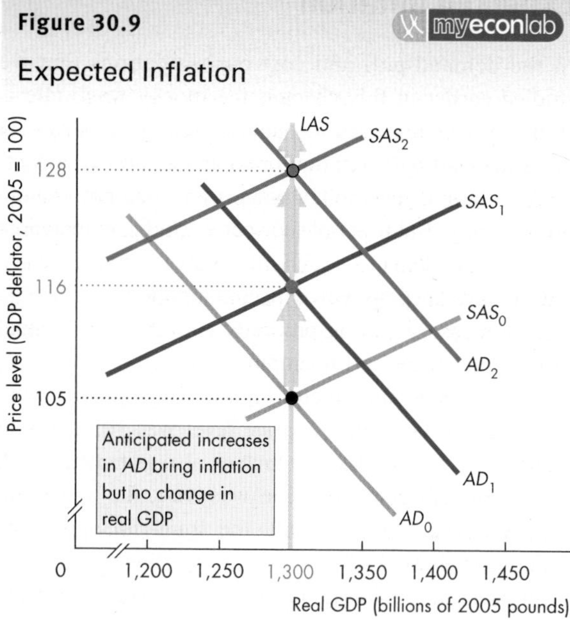

Potential real GDP is £1,300 billion. Last year, the aggregate demand curve was AD_0 and the short-run aggregate supply curve was SAS_0. The actual price level was the same as the expected price level – 105.

This year, aggregate demand is expected to increase to AD_1. The rational expectation of the price level changes from 105 to 116. As a result, the money wage rate rises and the short-run aggregate supply curve shifts to SAS_1.

If aggregate demand actually increases as expected, the actual aggregate demand curve AD_1 is the same as the expected aggregate demand curve. Real GDP is £1,300 billion and the actual price level is 116. The inflation is correctly expected.

Next year, the process continues with aggregate demand increasing as expected to AD_2 and the money wage rate rising to shift the short-run aggregate supply curve to SAS_2. Again, real GDP remains at £1,300 billion, and the price level rises, as expected, to 128.

of the expected and actual shifts of the aggregate demand curve rightward produced an increase in the price level that was expected.

Only if the forecast of aggregate demand growth is correct does the economy follow the course described in Figure 30.9. If the expected growth rate of aggregate demand is different from its actual growth rate, the expected aggregate demand curve shifts by an amount different from the actual aggregate demand curve. The inflation rate departs from its expected level and, to some extent, there is unexpected inflation.

Unexpected Inflation

When aggregate demand increases by *more* than expected, there is some unexpected inflation that looks just like demand-pull inflation that you examined earlier. Some inflation is expected and the money wage rate is set to reflect that expectation. The *SAS* curve intersects the *LAS* curve at the expected price level. Aggregate demand then increases, but by more than expected. The *AD* curve intersects the *SAS* curve at a level of real GDP that exceeds potential GDP. With real GDP above potential GDP and unemployment below the natural unemployment rate, the money wage rate rises. So the price level rises further. If aggregate demand increases again, the demand-pull spiral unwinds.

When aggregate demand increases by *less* than expected, there is some unexpected inflation that looks like cost-push inflation. Again, some inflation is expected and the money wage rate is set to reflect that expectation. The *SAS* curve intersects the *LAS* curve at that expected price level. Aggregate demand then increases, but by *less* than expected. So the *AD* curve intersects the *SAS* curve at a level of real GDP below potential GDP. Aggregate demand increases to restore full employment. But if aggregate demand is expected to increase by more than it actually does, the money wage rate again rises, short-run aggregate supply again decreases and a cost-push spiral unwinds.

We've seen that only when inflation is unexpected does real GDP depart from potential GDP. When inflation is expected, real GDP remains at potential GDP. Does this mean that an expected inflation has no costs?

The Costs of Expected Inflation

The costs of an expected inflation depend on its rate. At a moderate rate of 2 to 3 per cent a year, the cost is probably small. But as the expected inflation rate rises, so does its cost, and an expected inflation at a rapid rate is extremely costly.

Expected inflation decreases potential GDP and slows economic growth. These adverse consequences arise for three major reasons:

- Transactions costs
- Tax effects
- Increased uncertainty

Transactions Costs

The first transactions costs are known as the "shoeleather costs". These costs arise from an increase in the velocity of circulation of money and an increase in the amount of running around that people do to try to avoid incurring losses from the falling value of money.

When money loses value at a rapid expected rate, it does not function well as a store of value and people try to avoid holding money. They spend their incomes as soon as they receive them, and firms pay out incomes as soon as they receive revenue from their sales. The velocity of circulation increases. During the 1920s in Germany, when inflation reached *hyperinflation* levels (rates more than 50 per cent a month), wages were paid and spent twice in a single day!

The range of estimates of the shoeleather costs is large – from close to zero to as much as 2 per cent of GDP for a 10 per cent inflation. For a rapid inflation, these costs are much more.

The shoeleather costs are just one of several transactions costs that inflation influences. At high expected inflation rates, people seek alternatives to money as means of payment and use tokens and commodities, or even barter, all of which are less efficient than money as a means of payment. For example, in Zimbabwe in 2007, inflation in excess of 1,500 per cent a year has led people to use the South African rand. Consequently, people have to keep track of the exchange rate between the Zimbabwean dollar and the rand and engage in costly transactions in the foreign exchange market.

Because expected inflation increases transaction costs, it diverts resources from producing goods and services and decreases potential GDP.

Tax Effects

Expected inflation interacts with the tax system and creates serious distortions in incentives. Its major effect is on real interest rates. Expected inflation swells the pound returns on investments. But pound returns are taxed, so the effective tax rate rises. This effect becomes serious at even modest inflation rates.

Suppose the real interest rate is 4 per cent a year and the tax rate is 50 per cent. With no inflation, the nominal interest rate is also 4 per cent a year and 50 per cent of this rate is taxable. The real *after-tax* interest rate is 2 per cent a year (50 per cent of 4 per cent).

Now suppose the inflation rate is 4 per cent a year and the nominal interest rate is 8 per cent a year. The *after-tax* nominal rate is 4 per cent a year (50 per cent of 8 per cent). Now subtract the 4 per cent inflation rate from this amount, and you see that the *after-tax real interest rate* is zero! The true tax rate is 100 per cent.

The higher the inflation rate, the higher is the effective tax rate on income from capital. Also the higher the tax rate, the higher is the interest rate paid by borrowers and the lower is the after-tax interest rate received by lenders. With a low after-tax real interest rate, the incentive to save is weakened and the saving rate falls. With a high cost of borrowing, the amount of investment decreases. With a fall in saving and investment, the pace of capital accumulation slows and so does the long-term growth rate of real GDP.

Increased Uncertainty

When the inflation rate is high, uncertainty about the long-term inflation rate increases. Will inflation remain high for a long time or will price stability be restored? This increased uncertainty makes long-term planning difficult and gives people a shorter-term focus. Investment falls and the economic growth rate slows.

But this increased uncertainty also misallocates resources. Instead of concentrating on the activities at which they have a comparative advantage, people find it more profitable to search for ways of avoiding the losses that inflation inflicts. As a result, inventive talent that might otherwise work on productive innovations works on finding ways of profiting from the inflation instead.

The implications of inflation for economic growth have been estimated to be enormous. Peter Howitt of Brown University, building on work by Robert Barro of Harvard University, has estimated that if inflation is lowered from 3 per cent a year to zero, the growth rate of real GDP will rise by between 0.06 and 0.09 percentage points a year. These numbers might seem small, but they are growth rates. After 30 years, real GDP would be 2.3 per cent higher and the present value of all the future output would be 85 per cent of current GDP – £850 billion! In the rapid expected inflations, the costs are much greater than the numbers given here.

Review Quiz

Study Plan 30.3

1 What is a rational expectation? Are people who form rational expectations ever wrong?
2 Why do people forecast inflation and what information do they use to do so?
3 How does expected inflation occur?
4 What are the effects of a rapid expected inflation? Does expected inflation increase real GDP?

Inflation and Unemployment: The Phillips Curve

The *AS–AD* model focuses on the price level and real GDP. Knowing how these two variables change, we can work out what happens to the inflation rate and the unemployment rate. But the model does not place inflation and unemployment at the centre of the stage.

A more direct way of studying inflation and unemployment uses a relationship called the Phillips curve. The Phillips curve approach uses the same basic ideas as the *AS–AD* model, but it focuses directly on inflation and unemployment. The Phillips curve is so named because it was popularized by a New Zealand economist, A.W. Phillips, when he was working at the London School of Economics in the 1950s. A **Phillips curve** is a curve showing the relationship between inflation and unemployment. There are two time frames for Phillips curves:

- The short-run Phillips curve
- The long-run Phillips curve

The Short-run Phillips Curve

The **short-run Phillips curve** shows the relationship between inflation and unemployment, holding constant:

1 The expected inflation rate

2 The natural unemployment rate

You've just seen what determines the expected inflation rate. The natural unemployment rate and the factors that influence it are explained in Chapter 24, pp. 541–543.

Figure 30.10 shows a short-run Phillips curve, *SRPC*. Suppose that the expected inflation rate is 10 per cent a year and the natural unemployment rate is 6 per cent, point *A*. A short-run Phillips curve passes through this point. If inflation rises above its expected rate, the unemployment rate falls below its natural rate. This joint movement in the inflation rate and the unemployment rate is illustrated as a movement up the short-run Phillips curve from point *A* to point *B*. Similarly, if inflation falls below its expected rate, unemployment rises above the natural rate. In this case, there is movement down the short-run Phillips curve from point *A* to point *C*.

This negative relationship between the inflation rate and unemployment rate along the short-run Phillips curve is explained by the *AS–AD* model. Figure 30.11

Figure 30.10

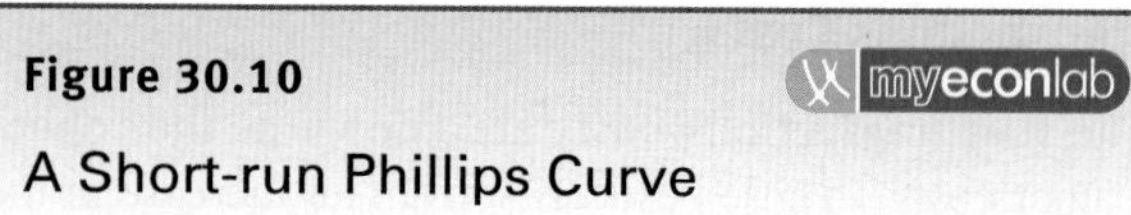

A Short-run Phillips Curve

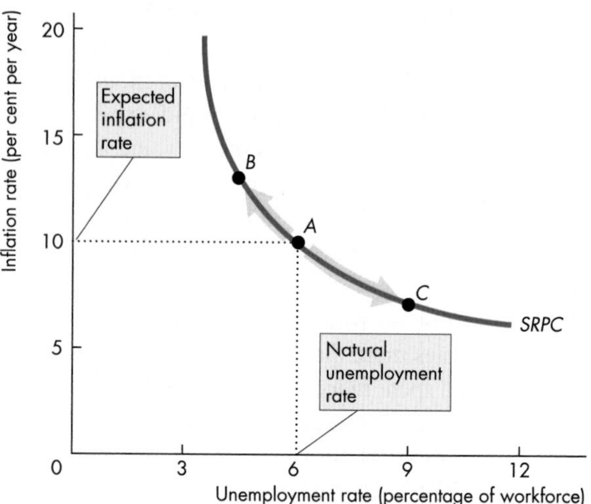

The short-run Phillips curve *SRPC* shows the relationship between the inflation rate and the unemployment rate at a given expected inflation rate and given natural unemployment rate. With an expected inflation rate of 10 per cent a year and a natural unemployment rate of 6 per cent, the short-run Phillips curve passes through point *A*.

An unexpected increase in aggregate demand lowers the unemployment rate and increases the inflation rate – a movement up the short-run Phillips curve to point *B*. An unexpected decrease in aggregate demand increases unemployment rate and lowers inflation rate – a movement down the short-run Phillips curve to point *C*.

explains the connection between the two approaches. Initially, the aggregate demand curve is AD_0, the short-run aggregate supply curve is SAS_0 and the long-run aggregate supply curve is *LAS*. Real GDP is £1,300 billion and the price level is 105. Aggregate demand is expected to increase and the aggregate demand curve is expected to shift rightward to AD_1.

In anticipation of this increase in aggregate demand, the money wage rate rises. The result is a leftward shift of the short-run aggregate supply curve from SAS_0 to SAS_1. What happens to actual inflation and real GDP depends on the *actual* change in aggregate demand.

First, suppose that aggregate demand actually increases by the amount expected, so the aggregate demand curve shifts to AD_1. The price level rises from 105 to 116, and the inflation rate is as expected 10 per cent a year. Real GDP remains at potential GDP, and unemployment remains at its natural rate – 6 per cent.

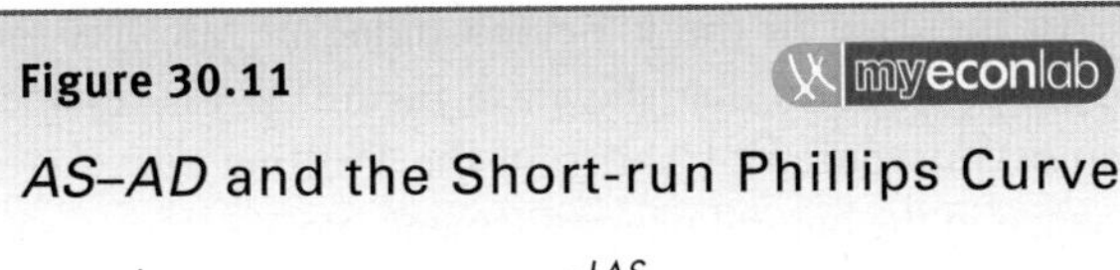

Figure 30.11

AS–AD and the Short-run Phillips Curve

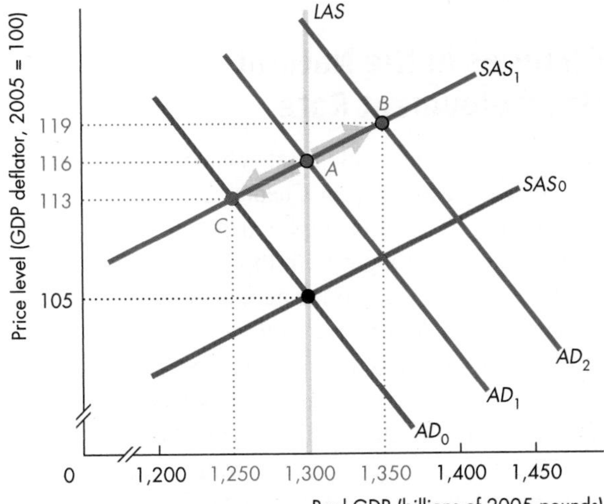

If aggregate demand is expected to increase and shift the aggregate demand curve from AD_0 to AD_1, then the money wage rate rises by an amount that shifts the short-run aggregate supply curve from SAS_0 to SAS_1. The price level rises to 116, a 10 per cent rise, and the economy is at point *A* in this figure and at point *A* on the short-run Phillips curve in Figure 30.10.

If, with the same expectations, aggregate demand increases and shifts the aggregate demand curve from AD_0 to AD_2, the price level rises to 119, a 13 per cent rise, and the economy is at point *B* in this figure and at point *B* on the short-run Phillips curve in Figure 30.10.

If, with the same expectations, aggregate demand does not change, the price level rises to 113, a 7 per cent rise, and the economy is at point *C* in this figure and at point *C* on the short-run Phillips curve in Figure 30.10.

The economy moves to point *A* in Figure 30.11 and it can equivalently be described as being at point *A* on the short-run Phillips curve in Figure 30.10.

Alternatively, suppose that aggregate demand is expected to increase to AD_1 but actually increases by more than expected to AD_2. The price level now rises to 119, a 13 per cent inflation rate. Real GDP increases above potential GDP and unemployment falls below its natural rate. We can now describe the economy as being at point *B* in Figure 30.11 or at point *B* on the short-run Phillips curve in Figure 30.10.

Finally, suppose that aggregate demand is expected to increase to AD_1 but actually remains at AD_0. The price level now rises to 113, a 7 per cent inflation rate. Real GDP falls below potential GDP and unemployment rises above its natural rate. We can now describe the economy as being at point *C* in Figure 30.11 or at point *C* on the short-run Phillips curve in Figure 30.10.

The short-run Phillips curve is like the short-run aggregate supply curve. A movement along the *SAS* curve that brings a higher price level and an increase in real GDP is equivalent to a movement along the short-run Phillips curve that brings an increase in the inflation rate and a decrease in the unemployment rate.

Similarly, a movement along the *SAS* curve that brings a lower price level and a decrease in real GDP is equivalent to a movement along the short-run Phillips curve that brings a decrease in the inflation rate and an increase in the unemployment rate.

Because the *SAS* curve and the short-run Phillips curve tell the same story, we can use either to examine the inflation rate over the business cycle. The Phillips curve version is useful because it highlights fluctuations in the unemployment rate. The *SAS* curve version is useful because it highlights the central role of the sticky money wage rate.

The Long-run Phillips Curve

The **long-run Phillips curve** is a curve that shows the relationship between inflation and unemployment, when the actual inflation rate equals the expected inflation rate. The long-run Phillips curve is vertical at the natural unemployment rate. It is shown in Figure 30.12 (overleaf) as the vertical line *LRPC*. The long-run Phillips curve tells us that any expected inflation rate is possible at the natural unemployment rate. This proposition is the same as the one you discovered in the *AS–AD* model, which predicts that when inflation is expected, real GDP equals potential GDP and unemployment is at its natural rate.

When the expected inflation rate changes, the short-run Phillips curve shifts but the long-run Phillips curve does not shift. If the expected inflation rate is 10 per cent a year, the short-run Phillips curve is $SRPC_0$. If the expected inflation rate falls to 7 per cent a year, the short-run Phillips curve shifts downward to $SRPC_1$. The distance by which the short-run Phillips curve shifts downward when the expected inflation rate falls is equal to the change in the expected inflation rate.

To see why the short-run Phillips curve shifts when the expected inflation rate changes, let's do a thought experiment. The economy is at full employment and an expected inflation rate of 10 per cent a year is raging. The central bank now begins a permanent attack on inflation by slowing the growth rate of the quantity of money. Aggregate demand growth slows and the inflation rate falls to 7 per cent a year. At first, this decrease in inflation is *un*expected, so the money wage rate continues to rise at its original rate, shifting the short-run aggregate supply curve leftward at the same pace as before. Real GDP decreases and unemployment increases. In Figure 30.12, the economy moves from point *A* to point *C* on the short-run Phillips curve $SRPC_0$.

If the actual inflation rate remains steady at 7 per cent a year, eventually this rate will come to be expected. As this happens, money wage growth slows and the short-run aggregate supply curve shifts leftward less quickly. Eventually, the short-run aggregate supply curve shifts leftward at the same pace as that at which the aggregate demand curve is shifting rightward. The actual inflation rate equals the expected inflation rate and the economy returns to full employment. Unemployment is back at its natural rate. In Figure 30.12, the short-run Phillips curve has shifted from $SRPC_0$ to $SRPC_1$ and the economy is at point *D*.

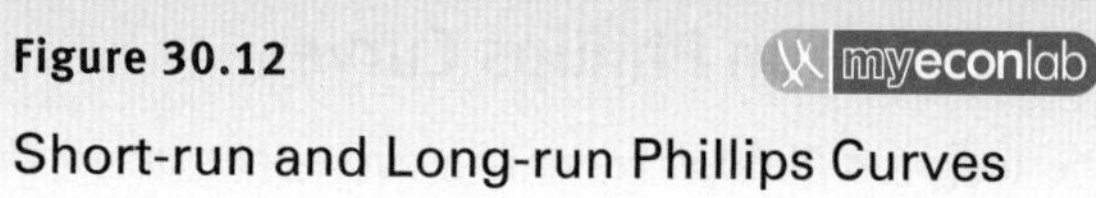

Figure 30.12 myeconlab

Short-run and Long-run Phillips Curves

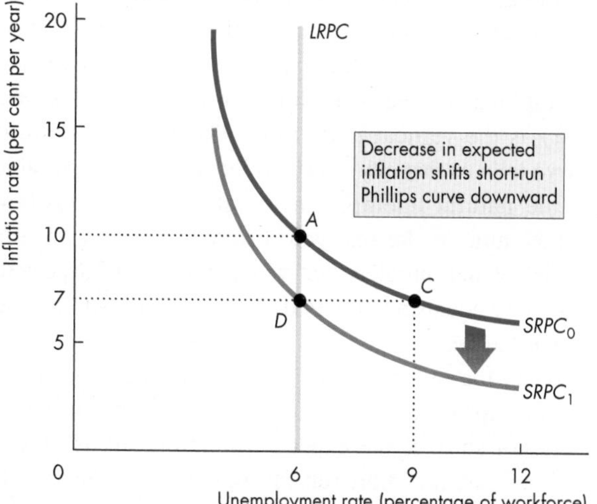

The long-run Phillips curve is *LRPC*, a vertical line at the natural unemployment rate. A fall in expected inflation shifts the short-run Phillips curve downward by the amount of the fall in the expected inflation rate. For example, when the expected inflation rate falls from 10 per cent to 7 per cent a year, the short-run Phillips curve shifts downward from $SRPC_0$ to $SRPC_1$. The new short-run Phillips curve intersects the long-run Phillips curve at the new expected inflation rate – point *D*.

With the original expected inflation rate (of 10 per cent a year), an actual inflation rate of 7 per cent a year would occur at an unemployment rate of 9 per cent, at point *C*.

An increase in the expected inflation rate has the opposite effect to that shown in Figure 20.12. Another important source of shifts in the Phillips curve is a change in the natural unemployment rate.

Changes in the Natural Unemployment Rate

The natural unemployment rate changes for many reasons that are explained in Chapter 24, pp. 541–543. A change in the natural unemployment rate shifts both the short-run and the long-run Phillips curves. Figure 30.13 illustrates such effects. If the natural unemployment rate increases from 6 per cent to 9 per cent, the long-run Phillips curve shifts from $LRPC_0$ to $LRPC_1$, and if expected inflation is constant at 10 per cent a year, the short-run Phillips curve shifts from $SRPC_0$ to $SRPC_1$. Because the expected inflation rate is constant, the short-run Phillips curve $SRPC_1$ intersects the long-run curve $LRPC_1$ (point *E*) at the same inflation rate as that at which the short-run Phillips curve $SRPC_0$ intersects the long-run curve $LRPC_0$ (point *A*).

Figure 30.13 myeconlab

A Change in the Natural Unemployment Rate

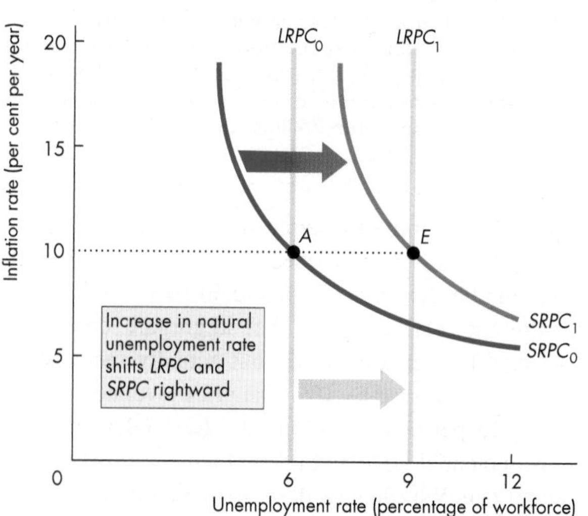

A change in the natural unemployment rate shifts both the short-run and long-run Phillips curves. Here the natural unemployment rate increases from 6 per cent to 9 per cent, and the two Phillips curves shift rightward to $SRPC_1$ and $LRPC_1$. The new Phillips curves intersect at the expected inflation rate – point *E*.

Box 30.1

Phillips Curves in the United Kingdom

When A.W. (Bill) Phillips first discovered the curve that bears his name, he was looking at data on wage inflation and unemployment between 1861 and 1957. It was hard to see the Phillips curve in the data. The scatter diagram of data covering almost 100 years was more like a snow storm than a neat inverse relationship.

Figure 1(a) continues the story that Phillips began by showing a scatter diagram of the UK inflation rate and the unemployment rate from 1960 to 2006. Each dot represents the inflation and unemployment in a particular year. We certainly cannot see a Phillips curve similar to that shown in Figure 30.10.

But we can interpret the data in terms of a shifting short-run Phillips curve like those in Figures 30.12 and 30.13. Three short-run Phillips curves appear in Figure 1(b).

During the 1960s the expected inflation rate was 2 per cent a year and the natural unemployment rate was 2 per cent at point *A*, so the short-run Phillips curve was $SRPC_0$. From the mid-1970s to the mid-1980s the expected inflation rate averaged 12.5 per cent a year and natural unemployment rate averaged 8 per cent at point *B* so the short-run Phillips curve was $SRPC_1$. During the 1990s the expected inflation rate was 2.5 per cent a year and the natural unemployment rate was 5 per cent at point *C* so the short-run Phillips curve was $SRPC_2$. All the points in the graph are on short-run Phillips curves that lie between those shown.

Figure 1

Phillips Curves in the United Kingdom

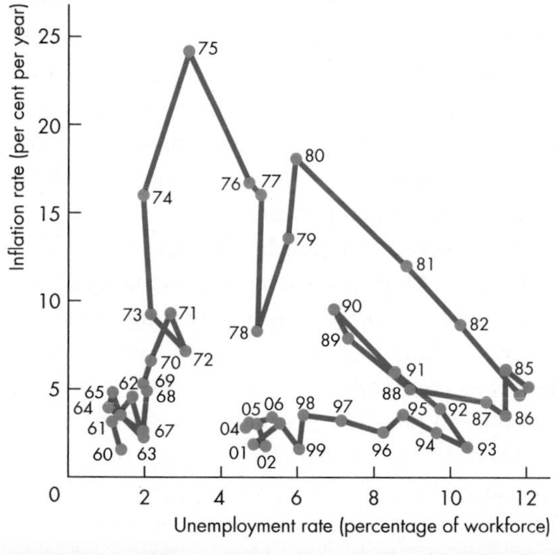

(a) Time sequence

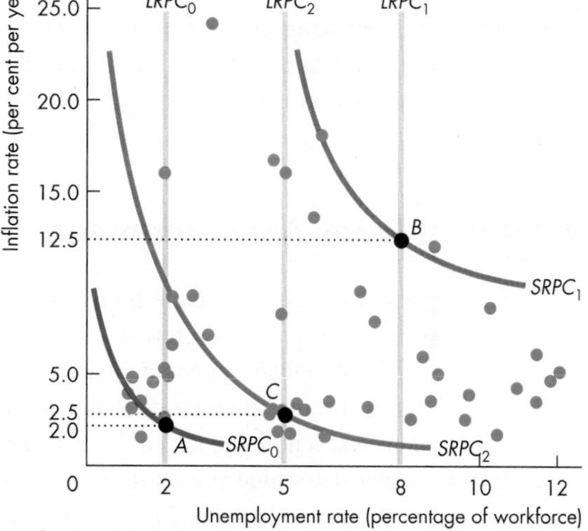

(b) Shifting Phillips curves

Source of data: Office for National Statistics.

Review Quiz

Study Plan 30.4

1. How would you use the Phillips curve to illustrate an unexpected change in the inflation rate?
2. What are the effects of an unexpected increase in the inflation rate on the unemployment rate?
3. If the expected inflation rate increases, how would the short-run and long-run Phillips curves change?
4. If the natural unemployment rate increases, what happens to the short-run and long-run Phillips curves?

So far, we've studied the effects of inflation on real GDP, real wages, employment and unemployment. We're going to conclude our investigation of the effects of inflation by looking at how inflation influences interest rates. This influence arises because inflation lowers the value of money and changes the *real* value of the amounts borrowed and repaid. As a result, inflation influences interest rates at which people are willing to borrow and lend.

Interest Rates and Inflation

Today, low-risk companies in the United Kingdom can borrow at an interest rate of less than 6 per cent a year. In contrast, even a major company that is unlikely to default on its loans pays 800 per cent a year in Zimbabwe. While companies in the United Kingdom have never paid interest rates as high as those in Zimbabwe today, they did pay around 15 per cent a year during the early 1980s. Why do interest rates fluctuate so much across countries and over time?

Part of the answer is that the real interest rate varies across countries and over time. (The *real interest rate* equals the *nominal* interest rate minus the inflation rate – see Chapter 24, p. 545.) Risk differences bring international differences in the real interest rate. Borrowers in high-risk countries pay higher interest rates than do those in low-risk countries.

But another part of the answer – a major part – is that the inflation rate varies across countries and fluctuates over time. For example, high inflation in Zimbabwe today and in the United Kingdom during the 1980s is the source of high interest rates. Box 30.2 examines the real-world relationships between the inflation rate and the interest rate.

How Interest Rates Are Determined

Demand and supply in the global loanable funds market determine the world-average *real* interest rate. The demand for and supply of loanable funds depend on the real interest rate. And the real interest rate adjusts to make borrowing plans and lending plans equal. You can think of the forces that determine the equilibrium real interest rate by using the standard demand and supply model. National real interest rates vary around the world-average real interest rate because of national differences in risk.

A *nominal* interest rate is determined by the demand for money and the quantity of money in each nation's money market. The demand for money depends on the nominal interest rate, and the quantity of money is determined by the central bank's monetary policy – the Bank of England's monetary policy in the United Kingdom. The nominal interest rate adjusts to make the quantity of money demanded equal to the quantity supplied. (Chapter 27, pp. 632–634, explains the forces that determine the equilibrium nominal interest rate.)

To see why inflation influences the nominal interest rate, think about the decisions of borrowers and lenders.

Why Inflation Influences the Nominal Interest Rate

Because the real interest rate is determined in the global capital market and nominal interest rates are determined in each nation's money market, there is no tight and mechanical link between the two interest rates. But on the average, and other things remaining the same, a 1 percentage point rise in the inflation rate leads to a 1 percentage point rise in the nominal interest rate. Why? The answer is that the financial capital market and the money market are closely interconnected. The investment, saving and demand for money decisions that people make are connected and the result is that the equilibrium nominal interest rate approximately equals the real interest rate plus the expected inflation rate.

Imagine there is no inflation and the real interest rate and nominal interest rate are 4 per cent a year. The amount that businesses and people want to borrow equals the amount that businesses and people want to lend at this real interest rate. British Petroleum (BP) is willing to pay an interest rate of 4 per cent a year to get the funds it needs to pay for its investment in new oil exploration sites. Sue, who is saving to buy a new car, and thousands of people like her, are willing to lend BP the amount it needs for its exploration work if they can get a *real* return of 4 per cent a year.

Now suppose inflation breaks out at a steady 6 per cent a year. All prices and values, including oil exploration profits and car prices, rise by 6 per cent a year. If BP was willing to pay a 4 per cent interest rate when there was no inflation, it is now willing to pay a 10 per cent interest rate. The reason is that BP's profits are rising by 6 per cent a year, owing to the 6 per cent inflation, so BP is *really* paying only 4 per cent. Similarly, if Sue was willing to lend at a 4 per cent interest rate when there was no inflation, she is now willing to lend only if she gets 10 per cent interest. The price of the car Sue is planning to buy is rising by 6 per cent a year, owing to the 6 per cent inflation, so she is *really* getting only a 4 per cent interest rate.

Because borrowers are willing to pay the higher rate and lenders are willing to lend only if they receive the higher rate, when inflation is expected the *nominal interest rate* increases by an amount equal to the expected inflation rate. The *real interest rate* remains constant. The real interest rate might change because the supply of loanable funds or the demand for loanable funds has changed for some other reason. But a change in the expected inflation rate alone does not change the real interest rate.

Box 30.2

Inflation and Interest Rates in the United Kingdom and Around the World

We can study the relationship between the inflation rate and the interest rate by looking at changes over time in a given country or across countries at a given time.

Figure 1(a) shows the relationship between the inflation rate and the nominal interest rate in the United Kingdom. The interest rate on the vertical axis is that paid by the UK government on 3-month Treasury bills. The blue line shows the relationship between the nominal interest rate and the inflation rate if the real interest rate is constant at 2.5 per cent a year. A clear relationship exists between the inflation rate and the interest rate but it is not exact.

The relationship is not exact because the real interest rate fluctuates. During the 1960s, both the inflation rate and the nominal interest rate were low. In the early 1970s, inflation began to increase, but it was not expected to increase much and not to persist. As a result, the nominal interest rate did not rise much. By the mid-1970s, there was a burst of unexpectedly high inflation. The interest rate increased but not by nearly as much as the inflation rate. During the late 1970s and early 1980s, inflation of between 15 and 20 per cent a year came to be expected. As a result, the nominal interest rate increase. Then in 1982, the inflation rate fell – at first unexpectedly. Interest rates began to fall but not nearly as quickly as the inflation rate.

Figure 1(b) shows the relationship between the inflation rate and the nominal interest rate across a number of countries. Again, you can see a strong relationship between the two variables but not a perfect relationship.

Figure 1

Inflation and the Interest Rate

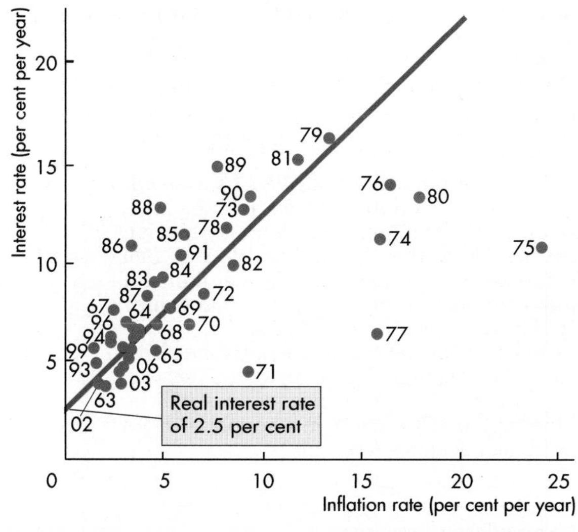

(a) United Kingdom

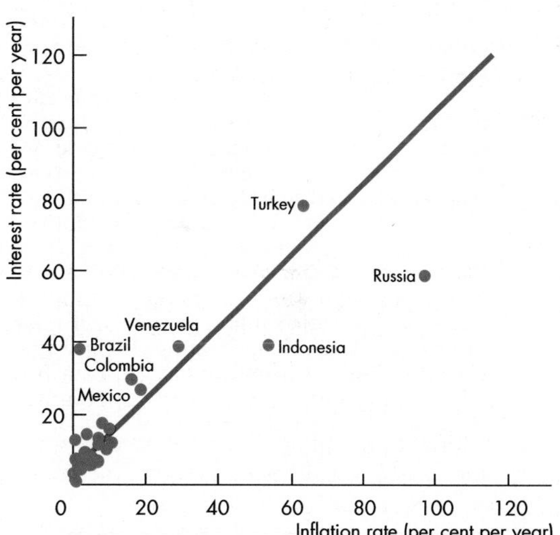

(b) Around the world

Sources of data: Office for National Statistics, Bank of England and International Monetary Fund.

Review Quiz

Study Plan 30.5

1. What is the relationship between the real interest rate, the nominal interest rate and the inflation rate?
2. Why does inflation change the nominal interest rate but not the real interest rate?

As you compete your study of inflation take a look at *Reading Between the Lines* on pp. 712–713 and see how bad inflation is today in Zimbabwe.

Your next task is to study the process of economic growth – the interaction of capital accumulation, technological change and population growth – that makes potential GDP expand.

Reading Between the Lines

Inflation in Zimbabwe

The Financial Times, 15 March 2007

FT

Zimbabwe sinks into hell of hyperinflation

Images of Morgan Tsavangirai, Zimbabwe's opposition leader, his face swollen and his head visibly wounded as he faced charges of illegal protest, testify to the deepening brutality, cynicism and desperation of President Robert Mugabe's regime. Behind that desperation is an economic chain reaction that will, unless halted soon, lead to the collapse of the Zimbabwean state and turn the country into an anarchic hell.

Zimbabwe's latest official inflation rate is 1,730 per cent. The real figure – for the median household at actual market prices – is almost certainly much higher. Price rises have accelerated sharply in recent months.

Zimbabwe has entered hyperinflation. What has happened so many times, from Weimar Germany to Zaire in the early 1990s, is happening again. As people come to expect accelerating inflation they will raise prices in anticipation, creating a spiral that feeds on itself. Chronic inflation, of a few hundred per cent per annum, can continue for years. A hyperinflation cannot.

Prices are either stabilised, or the monetary system collapses, and the economy reverts to barter and the use of foreign currency. On the monetary system rests the state: when a soldier or policeman is paid in worthless currency, he will take his gun, turn bandit and live off his fellow citizens.

Yet, a hyperinflation can be stopped easily. No outside help is needed and stabilisation at least can be achieved without much reform. All the government has to do is make a credible promise that it will not revert to the printing press and that it will balance its budget. But no government led by Mr Mugabe can make such a promise and expect to be believed.

The hyperinflation is driven by corrupt and inefficient public bodies, packed with government cronies, that demand foreign currency from the central bank to buy fuel or fertiliser from abroad. They siphon off wealth and come back for more. That is how Mr Mugabe's government works.

If the Zimbabwean state fails, if the rule of law collapses, and if an unpaid civil service drifts away, then the consequences will be catastrophic: what is lost in a couple of years could take decades to rebuild.

The Essence of the Story

- Inflation in Zimbabwe has been accelerating and in early 2007 its rate reached 1,730 per cent a year.
- If the inflation rate does not fall there is the danger that the monetary system will collapse and law and order will break down.
- Hyperinflation can be stopped by the government making a credible promise to stop printing money and that it will balance its budget.

Economic Analysis

- The news article says that Zimbabwe has entered hyperinflation. That is not strictly correct. Hyperinflation is reckoned to begin when the inflation rate passes 50 per cent a month. Zimbabwe's inflation rate was 37.8 per cent per month at the time of this news article, but rising. So hyperinflation might be just around the corner.
- Figure 1 shows Zimbabwe's inflation rate and money growth rate from 1999 to 2007.
- Figure 2 shows that real GDP growth has been negative each year between 1999 and 2007. Negative growth means that real GDP has fallen each year.
- The government controls the Reserve Bank of Zimbabwe and neither institution has a reputation for fighting inflation, so the government does not have the ability to control inflation.
- Figure 3 illustrates what has been happening in Zimbabwe using the *AS–AD* model.
- In 1999, long-run aggregate supply was LAS_{99}, short-run aggregate supply was SAS_{99} and aggregate demand was AD_{99}. Real GDP was Z$67 billion and the price level was 333.
- By 2007, rapid money growth had increased aggregate demand to AD_{07}; high inflation had increased uncertainty and decreased potential GDP to LAS_{07}; and high inflation had increased the money wage rate and decreased short-run aggregate supply to SAS_{07}. Real GDP decreased to Z$39 billion and the price level increased to 85,342,935.
- Zimbabwe's high inflation brings winners and losers.
- Corrupt officials gain by obtaining foreign currency at a low price and selling it at a high price on a black market.
- Everyone else loses because the economy reverts to barter, businesses fail, jobs are destroyed, and law and order breaks down.

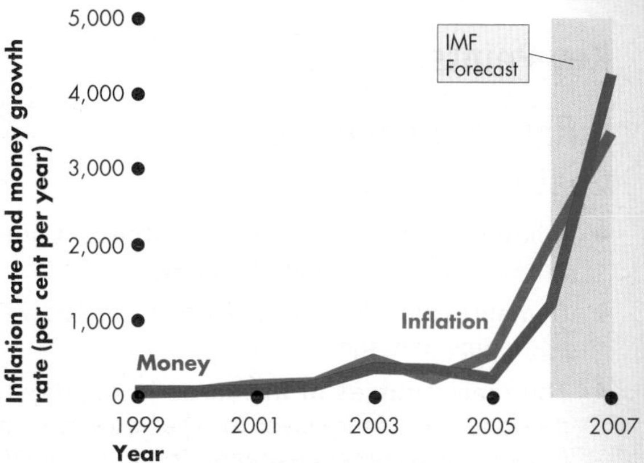

Figure 1 Inflation and money growth

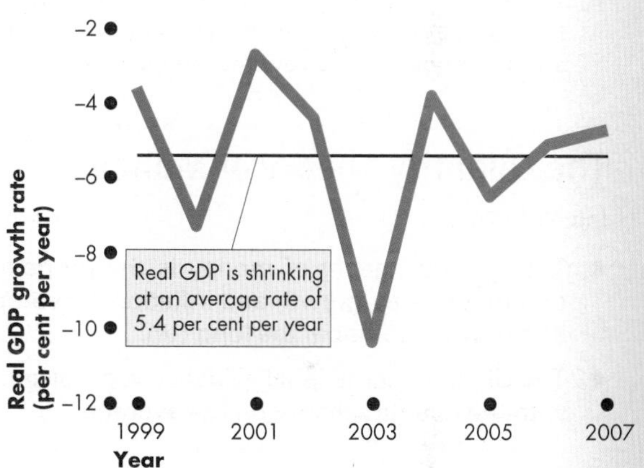

Figure 2 Real GDP negative growth

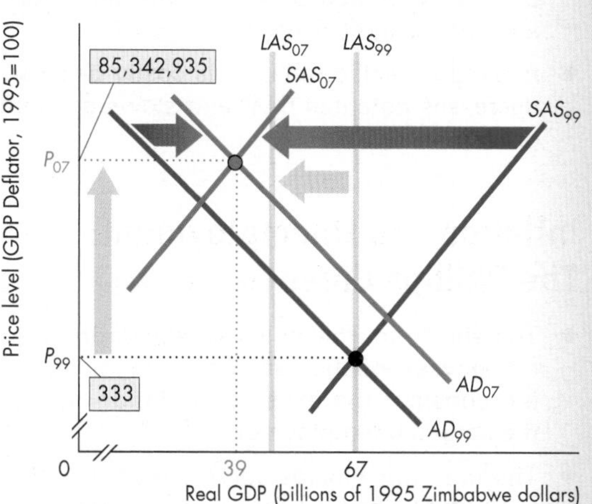

Figure 3 Aggregate supply and aggregate demand

Summary

Key Points

Inflation: Demand-pull and Cost-push (pp. 694–699)

- Inflation is a process of persistently rising prices and falling value of money.
- Demand-pull inflation arises from increasing aggregate demand.
- The main sources of increases in aggregate demand are increases in the quantity of money, government expenditure and exports.
- Cost-push inflation arises from a decrease in aggregate supply.
- The main sources of decreases in aggregate supply are increases in the money wage rate and the prices of key raw materials.

The Quantity Theory of Money (pp. 700–701)

- The quantity theory of money is the proposition that money growth and inflation move up and down together in the long run.
- The UK and international evidence is consistent with the quantity theory on the average.

Effects of Inflation (pp. 702–705)

- Inflation is costly when it is unexpected because it redistributes income and wealth and creates inefficiencies.
- A rapid expected inflation is costly because it decreases potential GDP and slows economic growth.

Inflation and Unemployment: The Phillips Curve (pp. 706–709)

- The short-run Phillips curve shows the trade-off between inflation and unemployment, holding constant the expected inflation rate and the natural unemployment rate.
- The long-run Phillips curve which is vertical, shows that when the actual inflation rate equals the expected inflation rate, the unemployment rate equals the natural unemployment rate.
- Unexpected changes in the inflation rate bring movements along the short-run Phillips curve.
- Changes in expected inflation shift the short-run Phillips curve.
- Changes in the natural unemployment rate shift both the short-run and long-run Phillips curves.

Interest Rates and Inflation (pp. 710–711)

- The higher the expected inflation rate, the higher is the nominal interest rate.
- As the expected inflation rate rises, borrowers willingly pay a higher interest rate and lenders successfully demand a higher interest rate.
- The nominal interest rate adjusts to equal the real interest rate plus the expected inflation rate.

Key Figures

Key Terms

Problems

Tests, Study Plan and Solutions* 

1 The spreadsheet provides information about the economy in Argentina. Column A is the year, Column B is real GDP in billions of 2000 pesos, and Column C is the price level.

	A	B	C
1	1993	244	97.2
2	1994	257	99.9
3	1995	250	103.1
4	1996	264	103.1
5	1997	286	102.6
6	1998	297	100.8
7	1999	297	99.0
8	2000	284	100.0
9	2001	272	98.9
10	2002	242	129.1
11	2003	263	142.7
12	2004	287	155.8

a In which years did Argentina experience inflation? In which years did it experience deflation?

b In which years did recessions occur? In which years did expansions occur?

c In which year do you expect the unemployment rate was highest? Why?

d Do these data show a relationship between unemployment and inflation in Argentina?

Use the following figure to answers problems 2, 3, 4 and 5.

2 The economy starts out on the curves AD_0 and SAS_0. Some events then occur that generate a demand-pull inflation.

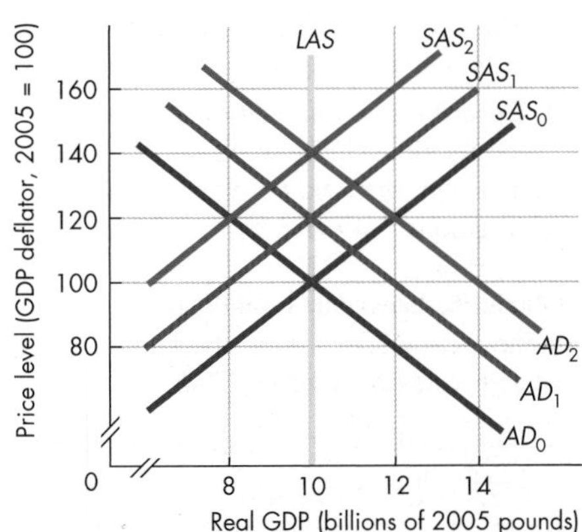

a List the events that might cause demand-pull inflation.

b Using the figure, describe the initial effects of demand-pull inflation.

c Using the figure, describe what happens as a demand-pull inflation spiral unwinds.

3 The economy starts out on the curves AD_0 and SAS_0. Some events then occur that generate a cost-push inflation.

a List the events that might cause cost-push inflation.

b Using the figure, describe the initial effects of cost-push inflation.

c Using the figure, describe what happens as a cost-push inflation spiral unwinds.

4 The economy starts out on the curves AD_0 and SAS_0. Some events then occur that generate an expected inflation.

a List the events that might cause an expected inflation.

b Using the figure, describe the initial effects of an expected inflation.

c Using the figure, describe what happens as an expected inflation proceeds.

5 Suppose that people expect deflation (a falling price level), but aggregate demand remains at AD_0.

a What happens to the short-run and long-run aggregate supply curves? (Draw some new curves if you need to.)

b Use the figure to describe the initial effects of an expected deflation.

c Use the figure to describe what happens as it becomes obvious to everyone that the expected deflation is not going to occur.

6 The Reserve Bank of New Zealand signed an agreement with the New Zealand government in which the Bank agreed to maintain inflation inside a low target range. Failure to achieve the target would result in the governor of the Bank losing his job.

a Explain how this arrangement might have influenced New Zealand's short-run Phillips curve.

b Explain how this arrangement might have influenced New Zealand's long-run Phillips curve.

7 Quantecon is a country in which the quantity theory of money operates. The country has a constant population, capital stock and technology. In year 1, real GDP was €400 million, the price level was 200, and the

* Solutions to odd-numbered problems are provided.

velocity of circulation of money was 20. In year 2, the quantity of money was 20 per cent higher than in year 1.

a What was the quantity of money in year 1?

b What was the quantity of money in year 2?

c What was the price level in year 2?

d What was the level of real GDP in year 2?

e What was the velocity of circulation in year 2?

8 An economy has an unemployment rate of 4 per cent and an inflation rate of 5 per cent a year at point *A* in the figure.

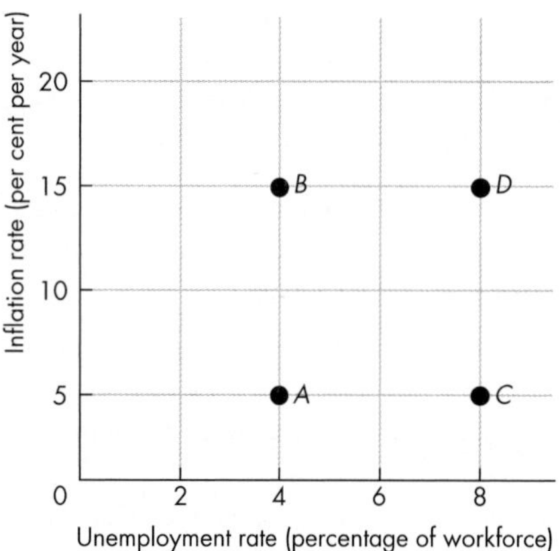

Some events then occur that move the economy in a clockwise loop from *A* to *B* to *D* to *C* and back to *A*.

a Describe the events that could create this sequence.

b Draw in the figure the sequence of the economy's short-run and long-run Phillips curves.

c Has the economy experienced demand-pull inflation, cost-push inflation, expected inflation or none of these?

Critical Thinking

1 Study *Reading Between the Lines* on pp. 712–713 and then answer the following questions.

a What is the cause of hyperinflation in Zimbabwe?

b Why might the inflation rate have increased to a higher rate than the growth rate of money? [Hint: what happened to the velocity of circulation and why?]

c Why is it hard to control inflation in Zimbabwe?

d If you were governor of the Reserve Bank of Zimbabwe, what would you do to bring inflation under control?

2 Lorenzo Bini Smaghi, of the European Central Bank in a speeech in Rome on 10 October 2005 said that monetary policy in reaction to rising oil prices can better support growth (and employment) if the primary target is price stability and if the central bank is credible in pursuing its commitment.

a What type of inflation is Lorenzo Bini Smaghi referring to?

b Use the Phillips curves to show how a primary target of price stability and the central bank crediblity will stabilize the price level and support employment in the short run.

c Use the *AS–AD* model to explain such an approach to monetary policy.

d If the ECB achieves price stability, what will determine the growth rate of the quantity of money in the long run?

Web Activities

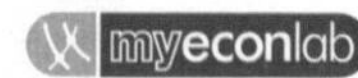

Links to Websites

1 Obtain data on the growth rate of the quantity of money and the inflation rate in the United Kingdom since 2003.

a Calculate the average growth rate of the quantity of money since 2003.

b Calculate the average inflation rate since 2003.

c Make a graph of the growth rate of the quantity of money and the inflation rate since 2003.

d Interpret your graph and explain what it tells you about the forces that generate inflation and the relationship between money growth and inflation.

2 Obtain data on the inflation rate and the unemployment rate in the United States during the 1990s and 2000s.

a Make a graph using the data you've obtained that is similar to the figure in Box 30.1.

b Describe the similarities and the differences in the relationship between inflation and unemployment in the United States and in the United Kingdom.

3 Obtain the latest data on inflation, unemployment and money growth in Japan, the United Kingdom, the United States and Canada. Then:

a Interpret the data for each country in terms of shifting Phillips curves.

b Which country do you think has the lowest expected inflation rate? Why?

CHAPTER

31

Economic Growth

After studying this chapter you will be able to:

- Define and calculate the economic growth rate and explain the implications of sustained growth
- Describe the economic growth trends in the United Kingdom and other countries and regions
- Identify the sources of economic growth
- Explain how we measure the effects of sources of economic growth and identify why the growth rate fluctuates
- Explain the theories of economic growth

Economic Miracles

In China, India and some other Asian economies, real GDP doubles in seven years. In the United Kingdom, it doubles every 25 years or so. In many African economies, real GDP barely changes from one year to the next. Why? What makes an economic miracle like the ones we see in East Asia today? Can China and India continue to expand at the current dizzying rate? Or will this growth come to an end? And if so, what kind of end: abrupt or gradual? And why do some countries stagnate? You'll find some answers in this chapter. And in *Reading Between the Lines* at the end of the chapter, you'll see how UK productivity growth stacks up against that of other large economies.

The Basics of Economic Growth

Economic growth is a sustained expansion of production possibilities measured as the increase in real GDP over a given period.

Even slow economic growth maintained over many centuries brings great wealth. That is the story of human economic growth up to the Industrial Revolution that began around 1760.

Rapid economic growth maintained over only a small number of years can transform a poor nation into a rich one. That has been the stories of Hong Kong, South Korea and Taiwan, and is the story of China, India and some other Asian economies today.

The absence of growth can condemn a nation to devastating poverty. Such has been the fate of Sierra Leone, Somalia, Zambia and much of the rest of Africa.

The goal of this chapter is to help you to understand why some economies expand rapidly and others stagnate. We'll begin by learning how to calculate the economic growth rate and by discovering the magic of sustained growth.

Calculating Growth Rates

We express the **economic growth rate** as the annual percentage change of real GDP. To calculate this growth rate, we use the formula:

$$\text{Real GDP growth rate} = \frac{\text{Real GDP in current year} - \text{Real GDP in previous year}}{\text{Real GDP in previous year}} \times 100$$

For example, if real GDP in the current year is £1,320 billion and if real GDP in the previous year was £1,200 billion, then the economic growth rate is 10 per cent.

The growth rate of real GDP tells us how rapidly the *total* economy is expanding. This measure is useful for telling us about potential changes in the balance of economic power among nations. But it does not tell us about changes in the standard of living.

The standard of living depends on **real GDP per person** (also called *per capita* real GDP), which is real GDP divided by the population. So the contribution of real GDP growth to the change in the standard of living depends on the growth rate of real GDP per person. We use the above formula to calculate this growth rate, replacing real GDP with real GDP per person.

Suppose, for example, that in the current year, when real GDP is £1,320 billion, the population is 60.6 million. Then real GDP per person is £1,320 billion divided by 60.6 million, which equals £21,782. And suppose that in the previous year, when real GDP was £1,200 billion, the population was 60 million. Then real GDP per person in that year was £1,200 billion divided by 60 million, which equals £20,000. Use these two real GDP per person values with the growth formula above to calculate the growth rate of real GDP per person. That is,

$$\text{Real GDP per person growth rate} = \frac{£21{,}782 - £20{,}000}{£20{,}000} \times 100 = 8.9 \text{ per cent}$$

The growth rate of real GDP per person can also be calculated (approximately) by subtracting the population growth rate from the real GDP growth rate. In the example you've just worked through, the growth rate of real GDP is 10 per cent. The population changes from 60 million to 60.6 million, so the population growth rate is 1 per cent. The growth rate of real GDP per person is approximately equal to 10 per cent minus 1 per cent, which equals 9 per cent.

Real GDP per person grows only if real GDP grows faster than the population grows. If the growth rate of the population exceeds the growth of real GDP, real GDP per person falls.

The Magic of Sustained Growth

Sustained growth of real GDP per person can transform a poor society into a wealthy one. The reason is that economic growth is like compound interest.

Compound Interest

Suppose that you put £100 in the bank and earn 5 per cent a year interest on it. After one year, you have £105. If you leave that £105 in the bank for another year, you earn 5 per cent interest on the original £100 and on the £5 interest that you earned last year. You are now earning interest on interest! The next year, things get even better. Then you earn 5 per cent on the original £100 and on the interest earned in the first year and the second year. You are even earning interest on the interest that you earned on the interest of the first year.

Your money in the bank is growing at a rate of 5 per cent a year. Before too many years have passed, your initial deposit of £100 will have grown to £200. But after how many years?

The answer is provided by a formula called the **Rule of 70**, which states that the number of years it takes for

Figure 31.1

The Rule of 70

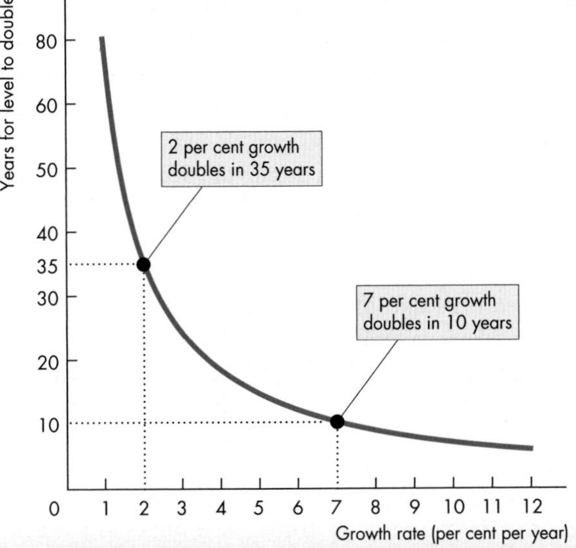

Growth rate (per cent per year)	Years for level to double
1	70.0
2	35.0
3	23.3
4	17.5
5	14.0
6	11.7
7	10.0
8	8.8
9	7.8
10	7.0
11	6.4
12	5.7

The number of years it takes for the level of a variable to double is approximately 70 divided by the annual percentage growth rate.

the level of any variable to double is approximately 70 divided by the annual percentage growth rate of the variable. Using the Rule of 70, you can now calculate how many years it takes your £100 to become £200. It is 70 divided by 5, which is 14 years.

Applying the Rule of 70

The Rule of 70 applies to any variable, so it applies to real GDP per person. Figure 31.1 shows the doubling time for growth rates of 1 per cent per year to 12 per cent per year.

You can see that real GDP per person doubles in 70 years (70 divided by 1) – an average human life span – if the growth rate is 1 per cent a year. It doubles in 35 years if the growth rate is 2 per cent a year and in just 10 years if the growth rate is 7 per cent a year.

We can use the Rule of 70 to answer other questions about economic growth. For example, in 2000, US real GDP per person was approximately 8 times that of China. China's recent growth rate of real GDP per person was 7 per cent a year. If this growth rate were maintained, how long would it take China's real GDP per person to reach that of the United States in 2000?

The answer, provided by the Rule of 70, is 30 years. China's real GDP per person doubles in 10 (70 divided by 7) years. It doubles again to 4 times its current level in another 10 years. And it doubles yet again to 8 times its current level in another 10 years. So after 30 years of growth at 7 per cent a year, China's real GDP per person is 8 times its current level and equals that of the United States in 2000. Of course, after 30 years, US real GDP per person would have increased, so China would still not have caught up to the United States.

Review Quiz

Study Plan 31.1

1 What is economic growth and how do we calculate its rate?
2 What is the relationship between the growth rate of real GDP and the growth rate of real GDP per person?
3 Use the Rule of 70 to calculate the growth rate that leads to a doubling of real GDP per person in 20 years.

You now know the basics of economic growth. Let's now review the trends in economic growth in the United Kingdom and around the world,

Economic Growth Trends

You've seen the power of economic growth to increase incomes. At a 1 per cent growth rate, it takes a human life span to double the standard of living. But at a 7 per cent growth rate, the standard of living doubles every decade. How fast is our economy growing? How fast are other economies growing? Are poor countries catching up to rich ones, or do the gaps between the rich and poor persist or even widen? Let's answer these questions.

Growth in the UK Economy

Figure 31.2 shows real GDP per person in the United Kingdom for the 150 years from 1856 to 2006. The average growth rate over this period is 1.4 per cent a year. But the economic growth rate has varied. For example, growth slowed during the 1970s to 1.4 per cent a year, down from 2.1 per cent a year during the 1960s. Growth picked up again in the 1980s and was 2.4 per cent but returned to 2.1 per cent a year in the late 1990s and 2000s.

You can see the growth slowdown of the 1970s in a longer perspective in Figure 31.2 and you can see that it is not unique. The interwar period (1919–1939) and the early years of the 1900s had even slower growth than the 1970s.

In the middle of the graph are two extraordinary events: a period of prolonged depression during the interwar years and a burst of rapid growth and higher than normal real GDP per person during the Second World War (1939–1945). The interwar depression and the Second World War growth bulge obscure changes in the long-term growth trend that occurred during those years. But between 1919 and 1953, averaging out the depression and the war, the long-term growth rate was 1.2 per cent a year.

A major goal of this chapter is to explain why our economy grows and why the long-term growth rate varies. Another goal is to explain variations in the economic growth rate across countries. Let's look at some facts about other countries' growth rates.

Figure 31.2 myeconlab

One Hundred and Fifty Years of Economic Growth in the United Kingdom

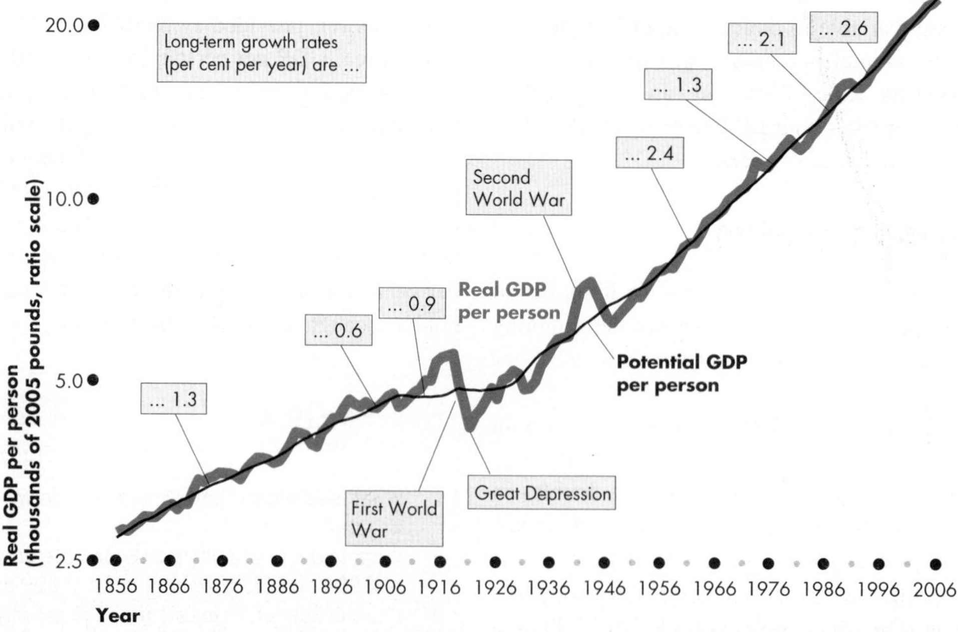

During the 150 years from 1856 to 2006, real GDP per person in the United Kingdom grew by 1.4 per cent a year, on average. The growth rate was above average during the 1950s, 1960s, 1980s and 1990s. It was below average in the 1900s, the interwar period and 1970s.

Sources of data: Charles Feinstein, *National Income Expenditure and Output of the United Kingdom 1855–1965*, Cambridge, Cambridge University Press, 1972; Office for National Statistics.

Real GDP Growth in the World Economy

Figure 31.3 shows real GDP per person in Europe Big 4 (France, Germany, Italy and the United Kingdom) and in other countries between 1960 and 2005. (The data in this figure are in 1996 US dollars.) Part (a) looks at the seven richest countries – known as the G7 nations. Among these nations, the United States has the highest real GDP per person. In 2005, Canada had the second-highest real GDP per person and Japan the third.

During the 40 years shown here, the gaps between the United States, Canada and Europe Big 4 have been constant. But starting from a long way back, Japan grew fastest. Japan caught up to Europe in 1973 and to Canada in 1990. But during the 1990s, Japan stagnated.

Many other countries are growing more slowly than, and falling farther behind, the United States. Figure 31.3(b) looks at some of these countries.

Real GDP per person in Central and South America was 28 per cent of the US level in 1960. It grew to 31 per cent of the US level by 1975 but then began to fall, and by 2005, real GDP per person in these countries had slipped to 22 per cent of the US level.

After a brief period of catch-up during the 1980s, the former Communist countries of Central Europe stagnated and fell increasingly behind the United States. More rapid growth resumed in these countries during the 1990s. Real GDP per person in Africa, the world's poorest continent, slipped from 12 per cent of the US level in 1960 to 6 per cent in 2005.

Figure 31.3 myeconlab

Economic Growth Around the World: Catch-up or Not?

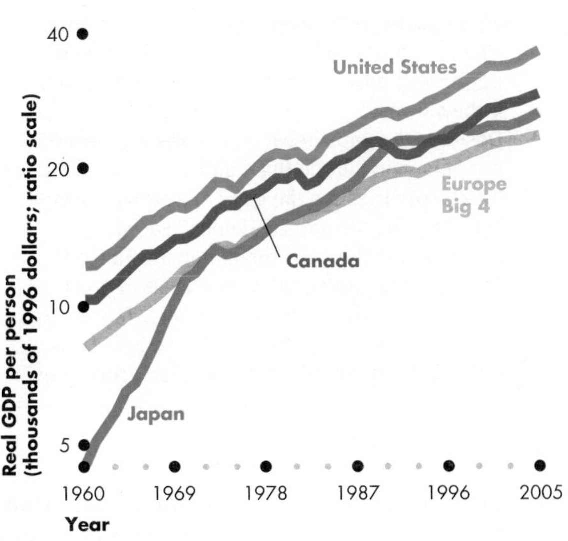

(a) Catch-up?

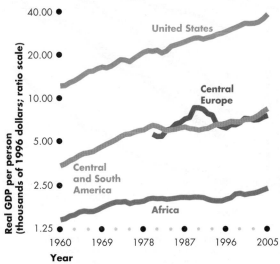

(b) No catch-up?

Real GDP per person has grown throughout the world economy. The rich industrial countries in part (a) have grown at a similar pace with the exception of Japan. Japan grew fastest before 1990 and overtook the four big countries of Europe (France, Germany, Italy and the United Kingdom) and Canada.

During the 1990s Japan stagnated.

Growth rates in the regions shown in part (b) have been lower than that of the United States and gaps between the levels of real GDP per person have widened. The gaps between the United States and Central Europe and Africa have widened most.

Sources of data: (1964–2000) Alan Heston, Robert Summers and Bettina Aten, Penn World Table Version 6.1, Center for International Comparisons at the University of Pennsylvania (CICUP), October 2002; and (2001–2004) International Monetary Fund, *World Economic Outlook*, April 2004.

A group of Asian economies provides a strong contrast to the persistent and widening gaps between the United States and other economies shown in Figure 31.3(b). Hong Kong (now part of China), South Korea, Singapore and Taiwan have experienced spectacular growth, which you can see in Figure 31.4. During the 1960s, real GDP per person in these economies averaged 31 per cent of that in the United Kingdom and 22 per cent of that in the United States. But by 2005, real GDP per person in these countries had reached 80 per cent of that in the United States and more than 100 per cent of that in the United Kingdom.

Figure 31.4 shows that China is also catching up, but from a long way behind. China's real GDP per person increased from 5 per cent of the US level in 1960 to 15 per cent in 2005.

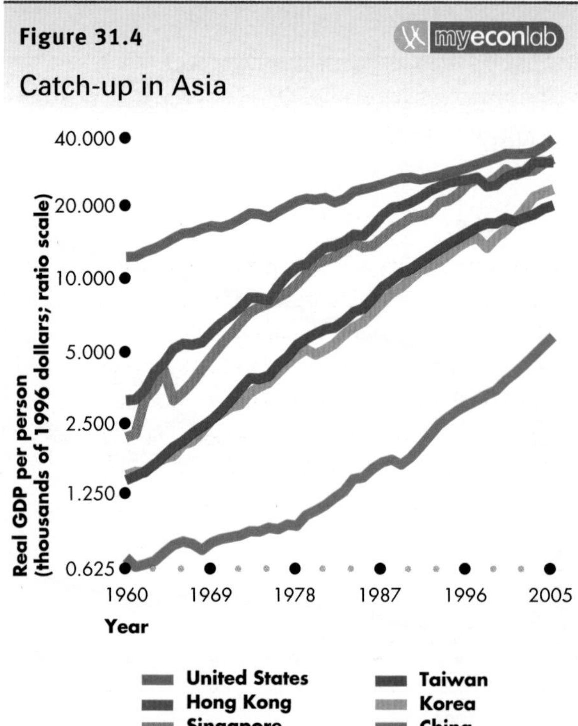

Figure 31.4

Catch-up in Asia

Catch-up has occurred in five economies in Asia. After starting out in 1960 with real GDP per person as low as 13 per cent of that in the United States, Hong Kong, Korea, Singapore, and Taiwan have substantially narrowed the gap between them and the United States. And from being a very poor developing country in 1960, China now has a real GDP per person that equals that of Hong Kong in 1965. China is growing at a rate that is enabling it to continue to catch up with the United States and other G7 countries.

Sources of data: See Figure 31.3.

The Asian economies shown in Figure 31.4 are like fast trains running on the same track at similar speeds and with a roughly constant gap between them. Hong Kong is the lead train and runs about 15 years in front of South Korea and about 40 years in front of the rest of China, which is the last train. Real GDP per person in South Korea in 2005 was similar to that of Hong Kong in 1985 and real GDP per person in China is similar to that of Hong Kong in 1965. Between 1965 and 2005, Hong Kong transformed itself from a poor developing country into one of the world's richest countries.

The rest of China is now doing what Hong Kong has done. If China continues its rapid growth, the world economy will be a dramatically different place. China has a population 200 times that of Hong Kong, more than 20 times that of the United Kingdom and more than 4 times that of the United States, so a rich China will have a huge impact on the global economy.

Review Quiz

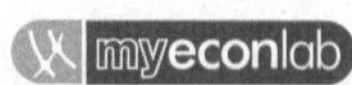

Study Plan 31.2

1. What has been the average growth rate in the United Kingdom over the past 150 years? In which period was growth the most rapid and in which was it the slowest?
2. Describe the gaps between the levels of real GDP per person in Europe Big 4 and other countries. For which countries are the gaps narrowing. For which countries are the gaps widening? For which countries are the gaps remaining unchanged?
3. Compare the growth rates and levels of real GDP per person in Hong Kong, Singapore, Taiwan, South Korea, China and the United States. How far is China behind that of the other Asian economies?

The facts about economic growth in the United Kingdom and around the world raise some big questions that we're now going to answer. We'll study the causes of economic growth in three stages. First, we'll look at the sources of economic growth and the activities that sustain it. Second, we'll learn how economists measure the relative contributions of the sources of growth – an activity called *growth accounting*. And third, we'll study three theories of economic growth that seek to explain how the influences on growth interact to determine the growth rate.

Let's begin by studying the sources of economic growth.

The Sources of Economic Growth

Most human societies have lived for centuries, and even thousands of years, with no economic growth. The key reason is that they have lacked some fundamental social institutions and arrangements that are essential preconditions for economic growth. Let's see what these preconditions are.

Real GDP grows when the quantities of the factors of production grow or when persistent advances in technology make factors of production increasingly productive. So to understand what determines the growth rate of real GDP, we must understand what determines the growth rates of the factors of production and rate of increase in their productivity. We are interested in real GDP growth because it contributes to improvements in our standard of living. But our standard of living improves only if we produce more goods and services per person. So our main concern is to understand the forces that make our labour more productive. We begin by dividing all the influences on real GDP growth into those that increase:

- Aggregate hours
- Labour productivity

Aggregate Hours

Aggregate hours are the total number of hours worked by all the people employed during a year (see Chapter 22, p. 461). We calculate aggregate hours as the number of people employed multiplied by average hours per worker. But the number of people employed equals the working-age population multiplied by the employment rate (see Chapter 22, p. 460). So aggregate hours change as a result of:

1. Working-age population growth
2. Changes in the employment rate
3. Changes in average hours per worker

Aggregate hours grow at the growth rate of the working-age population, adjusted for changes in the employment rate and changes in average hours per worker.

With steady population growth, the working-age population grows at the same rate as the total population. But in the United Kingdom in recent years, the working-age population has grown faster than the total population because of the baby boom – the surge in the birth rate during the years that followed the end of the Second World War. Through the 1960s and early 1970s, an increasing number of "babyboomers" entered the working-age group and the working-age population increased from 65 per cent of the total population in 1960 to 77 per cent in 2005.

The employment rate has increased during the past few decades as the economic activity rate has increased. There has also been a change in the composition of employment, with the male employment rate falling and the female rate rising (see Chapter 22, p. 460).

Average hours per worker have decreased as the workweek has become shorter and more people have become part-time workers (see Chapter 22, p. 461).

The combined effects of a rising economic activity rate and falling average hours per worker have kept the average hours per working-age person surprisingly constant at about 1,100 hours a year. So the growth of aggregate hours comes from population growth rather than from changes in average hours per person.

Population growth increases aggregate hours and real GDP. But to increase real GDP per person, labour must become more productive.

Labour Productivity

Labour productivity is the quantity of real GDP produced by an hour of labour. It is calculated by dividing real GDP by aggregate labour hours. For example, if real GDP is £1,000 billion and aggregate hours are 20 billion, labour productivity is £50 per hour.

When labour productivity grows, real GDP per person grows and brings a rising standard of living. The growth of labour productivity depends on three things:

- Physical capital growth
- Human capital growth
- Technological advance

These three sources of growth, which interact with each other, are the primary sources of the extraordinary growth in labour productivity during the past 200 years. Let's look at each in turn.

Physical Capital Growth

Physical capital results from saving and investment decisions. As the amount of capital per worker increases, labour productivity also increases. Labour productivity took the most dramatic upturn when the amount of capital per worker increased during the Industrial Revolution. Production processes that use hand tools can create beautiful objects, but production methods that use large amounts of capital per worker, such as car plant assembly lines and container handling equipment in the ports, are much more productive.

The accumulation of capital on farms, in textiles factories, in iron foundries and steel mills, in coal mines, on building sites, in chemical plants, in car plants, in banks and insurance companies and in retail shops and shopping malls have added incredibly to the productivity of our economy. The next time you see a film set in colonial times, look carefully at the small amount of capital. Try to imagine how productive you would be in such circumstances compared with your productivity today.

Human Capital Growth

Human capital – the accumulated skill and knowledge of human beings – is the most fundamental source of economic growth. It is a source of both increased productivity and technological advance.

The development of one of the most basic human skills – writing – was the source of some of the earliest major gains in productivity. The ability to keep written records made it possible to reap ever-larger gains from specialization and exchange. Imagine how hard it would be to do any kind of business if all the accounts, invoices and agreements existed only in people's memories.

Later, the development of mathematics laid the foundation for the eventual extension of knowledge about physical forces and chemical and biological processes. This base of scientific knowledge was the foundation for the technological advances of the Industrial Revolution 200 years ago and of today's information revolution.

But much human capital that is extremely productive is much more humble. It takes the form of millions of individuals learning and repetitively doing simple production tasks and becoming remarkably more productive in the tasks.

One carefully studied example illustrates the importance of this kind of human capital. Between 1941 and 1944 (during the Second World War), US shipyards produced some 2,500 units of a cargo ship, called the Liberty Ship, to a standardized design. In 1941, it took 1.2 million person-hours to build one ship. By 1942, it took 600,000 person-hours and, by 1943, it took only 500,000 person-hours. Not much change occurred in the capital employed during these years. But an enormous amount of human capital was accumulated. Thousands of workers and managers learned from experience and accumulated human capital that more than doubled their productivity in two years.

Technological Advance

The accumulation of physical capital and human capital has made a large contribution to economic growth. But technological change – the discovery and the application of new technologies and new goods – has made an even greater contribution.

People are many times more productive today than they were a hundred years ago. We are not more productive because we have more steam engines and horse-drawn carriages per person. Rather, it is because we have engines and transport equipment that use technologies that were unknown a hundred years ago and that are more productive than those old technologies were. Technological change makes an enormous contribution to our increased productivity. It arises from formal research and development programmes and from informal trial and error, and it involves discovering ways of getting more out of our resources.

To reap the benefits of technological change, capital must increase. Some of the most powerful and far-reaching fundamental technologies are embodied in human capital – for example, language, writing and mathematics.

But most technologies are embodied in physical capital. For example, to reap the benefits of the internal combustion engine, millions of horse-drawn carriages and horses had to be replaced by cars; to reap the benefits of computerized word processing, millions of typewriters had to be replaced by PCs and printers; and more recently, to reap the benefits of digital music, millions of Walkmans were replaced by iPods.

Figure 31.5 summarizes the sources of economic growth that we've just described. It also emphasizes that for real GDP per person to grow, real GDP growth must exceed the population growth rate.

Preconditions for Economic Growth

We began this account of the sources of economic growth by noting that for thousands of years, no growth occurred. You've seen that economic growth results from productivity growth. Why is productivity growth a relatively recent phenomenon? The reason is that early humans (like many people today) lacked the fundamental social institutions and arrangements that are essential preconditions for economic growth. We end our discussion of the sources of growth by examining its

Figure 31.5

The Sources of Economic Growth

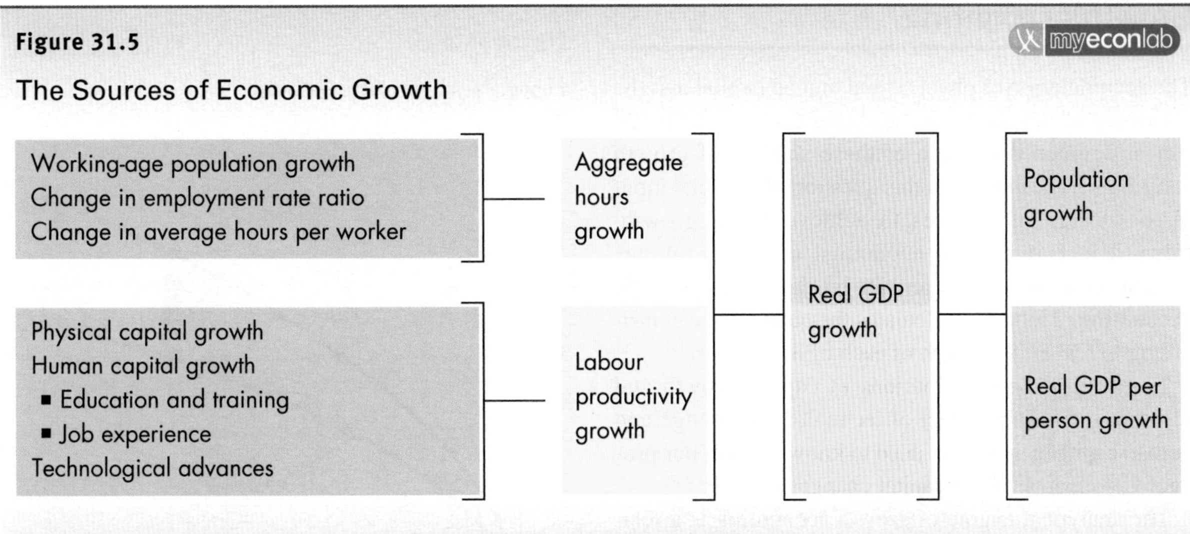

Aggregate hours growth and labour productivity growth combine to determine real GDP growth.

Real GDP per person growth depends on real GDP growth and population growth.

preconditions. The most basic precondition for economic growth is an appropriate *incentive* system. Three institutions are crucial to the creation of incentives. They are:

1 Markets
2 Property rights
3 Monetary exchange

Markets enable buyers and sellers to get information and to do business with each other, and market prices send signals to buyers and sellers that create *incentives* to increase or decrease the quantities demanded and supplied. Markets enable people to specialize and trade and to save and invest. But to work well, markets need property rights and monetary exchange.

Property rights are the social arrangements that govern the ownership, use and disposal of factors of production and goods and services. They include the right to physical property (land, buildings and capital equipment), to financial property (claims by one person against another) and to intellectual property (such as inventions). Clearly established and enforced property rights give people an assurance that a capricious government will not confiscate their income or savings.

Monetary exchange facilitates transactions of all kinds, including the orderly transfer of private property from one person to another. Property rights and monetary exchange create incentives for people to specialize and trade, to save and invest, and to discover new technologies.

No unique political system is necessary to deliver the preconditions for economic growth. Liberal democracy, founded on the fundamental principle of the rule of law, is the system that does the best job. It provides a solid base on which property rights can be established and enforced. But authoritarian political systems have sometimes provided an environment in which economic growth has occurred.

Early human societies, based on hunting and gathering, did not experience economic growth because they lacked the preconditions we've just described. Economic growth began when societies evolved the three key institutions that create incentives. But the presence of an incentive system and the institutions that create it do not guarantee that economic growth will occur. They permit economic growth but do not make it inevitable.

Review Quiz

Study Plan 31.3

1 How do physical capital growth, human capital growth and the discovery of new technologies generate economic growth?
2 Provide some examples of how human capital has created new technologies that are embodied in both human and physical capital.
3 What economic activities that lead to economic growth do markets, property rights and monetary exchange facilitate?

We've described the sources of economic growth. What are the quantitative contributions of the sources of economic growth? To answer this question, economists use growth accounting.

Growth Accounting

The accumulation of physical and human capital and the discovery of new technologies bring economic growth. But how much does each of these sources of growth contribute? The answer to this question is a crucial input in the design of policies to achieve faster growth. Edward F. Denison, an economist at the Brookings Institution, provided the answer by developing **growth accounting**, a tool that calculates the quantitative contribution to real GDP growth of each of its sources.

To identify the contributions of capital growth and separate it from the effect of technological change and human capital growth, we need to know how labour productivity changes when capital changes.

The analytical engine of growth accounting is a relationship called the productivity curve. Let's learn about this relationship and see how it is used.

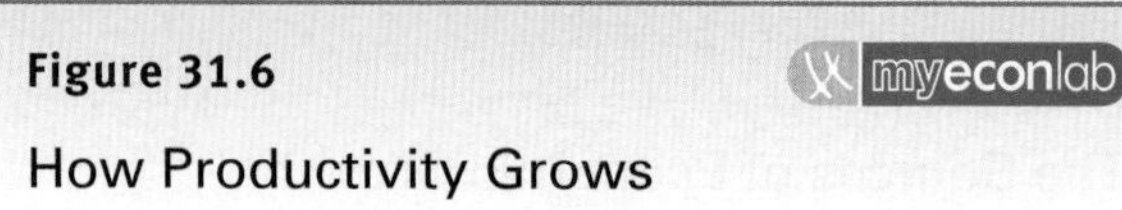

How Productivity Grows

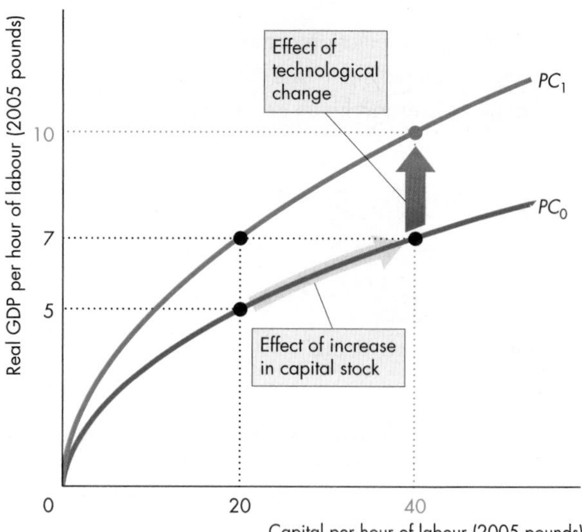

The productivity curve, *PC*, shows the effects of an increase in capital per hour of labour on productivity. Here, when capital per hour of labour increases from £20 to £40, labour productivity increases from £5 to £7 along the productivity curve PC_0.

Technological advance shifts the productivity curve upward. Here, the advance in technology shifts the productivity curve from PC_0 to PC_1. When capital per hour of labour is £40, the advance in technology increases labour productivity from £7 to £10.

The Productivity Curve

The **productivity curve** is a relationship that shows how labour productivity changes as the amount of capital per hour of labour changes with a given state of technology. Figure 31.6 illustrates the productivity curve. Capital per hour of labour is measured on the *x*-axis and labour productivity (real GDP per hour of labour) is measured on the *y*-axis. The figure shows two productivity curves – PC_0 and PC_1.

An increase in capital per hour of labour results in an increase in labour productivity, which is shown by a movement along a productivity curve. For example, on PC_0, when capital per hour of labour is £20, labour productivity is £5. On that same productivity curve, if capital per hour of labour increases to £40, labour productivity increases to £7.

Technological change increases the real GDP per hour of labour that can be produced by a given amount of capital per hour of labour. Technological change shifts the productivity curve upward. For example, if capital per hour of labour is £20 and a technological change increases labour productivity from £5 to £7, the productivity curve shifts upward from PC_0 to PC_1 in Figure 31.6.

To calculate the contributions of capital growth and technological change to productivity growth, we need to know the shape of the productivity curve. The shape of the productivity curve reflects a fundamental economic law – the law of diminishing returns. The **law of diminishing returns** states that as the quantity of one input increases with the quantities of all other inputs remaining the same, output increases but by ever smaller increments. For example, in a factory that has a given amount of capital, as more labour is hired, production increases. But each *additional* hour of labour produces less *additional* output than the previous hour produced. Two typists working with one computer type fewer than twice as many pages per day as one typist working with one computer.

Applied to capital, the law of diminishing returns states that if a given number of hours of labour use more capital (with the same technology), the *additional* output that results from the *additional* capital gets smaller as the amount of capital increases. One typist working with two computers types fewer than twice as many pages per day as one typist working with one computer. More generally, one hour of labour working with £40 of capital produces less than twice the output of one hour of labour working with £20 of capital. But how much less?

The answer is going to be different for every production process. But on the average for the economy as a whole, the answer is given by the "one-third rule" that we'll now study.

The One-third Rule

Using data on capital, labour hours and real GDP in the US economy, Robert Solow of MIT estimated the effect of capital on labour productivity. In doing so, he discovered the **one-third rule**: on average, with no change in technology, a 1 per cent increase in capital per hour of labour brings a *1/3 per cent increase* in labour productivity. The one-third rule is used to calculate the contributions of an increase in capital per hour of labour and technological change to the growth of labour productivity. Let's do such a calculation.

Suppose that capital per hour of labour grows by 3 per cent a year and labour productivity grows by 2.5 per cent a year. The one-third rule tells us that capital growth has contributed one-third of 3 per cent, which is 1 per cent, to the growth of labour productivity. The rest of the 2.5 per cent growth of labour productivity comes from technological change. That is, technological change contributed 1.5 per cent, which is the 2.5 per cent minus the 1 per cent contribution of capital growth.

Figure 31.7 myeconlab

Growth Accounting and Labour Productivity Changes

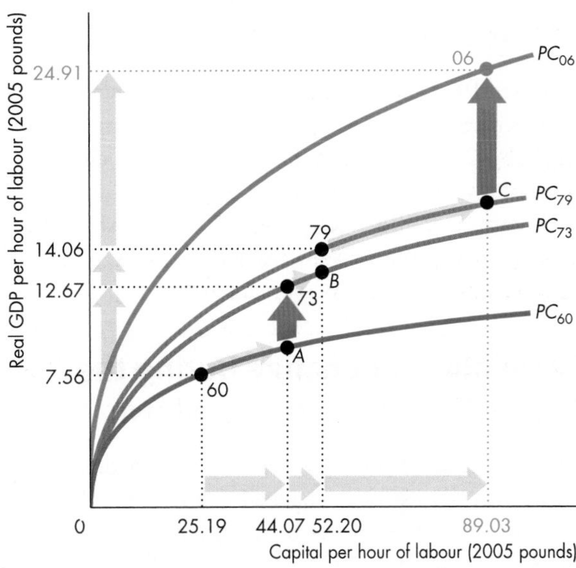

(a) The shifting productivity curve

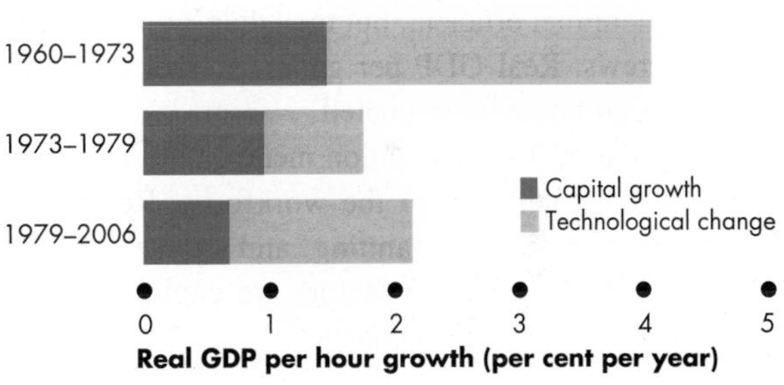

(b) The sources of growth

Labour productivity grew most quickly between 1960 and 1973 and most slowly between 1973 and 1979. Changes in the pace of technological change and human capital growth were the biggest source of fluctuations in labour productivity growth. A steady decrease in the contribution of capital accumulation slowed the productivity growth rate.

Sources of data: Office for National Statistics, and the authors' assumptions and calculations.

Accounting for the Productivity Growth Slowdown and Speed-up

We can use the one-third rule to study the UK productivity growth and productivity slowdown. Figure 31.7 tells the story, starting in 1960.

1960 to 1973

In 1960, capital per hour of labour was £25.19 (in 2005 pounds). Labour productivity was £7.56 at the point marked 60 on PC_{60} in Figure 31.7. Over the next 13 years, capital per hour grew at about 4.4 per cent a year to £44.07 and real GDP per hour increased at 4.1 per cent a year to £12.67. With no change in technology, the economy would have moved to point *A* on PC_{60}. But rapid technological change increased productivity and shifted the productivity curve upward from PC_{60} to PC_{73}. The economy moved to the point marked 73.

1973 to 1979

Between 1973 and 1979, capital per hour of labour grew at 2.9 per cent a year to £52.20 and labour productivity grew at 1.8 per cent a year to £14.07. With no change in technology, the economy would have moved to point *B* in Figure 31.7. But with almost no change in technology, the productivity curve shifted from PC_{73} to PC_{79}, an almost invisible shift, and the economy moved to the point marked 79.

The productivity growth slowdown resulted partly from slower growth in capital per hour of labour – from 4.4 per cent to 2.9 per cent a year – but mainly from a near-zero contribution of technological change.

1979 to 2006

Between 1979 and 2005, capital per hour of labour grew at 2 per cent a year to £89.03 and labour productivity grew by 2.1 per cent to £24.91. With no change in technology, the economy would have moved to point *C* in Figure 31.7. But technological change shifted the productivity curve upward from PC_{79} to PC_{06} and the economy moved to the point marked 06.

Technological Change During the Productivity Growth Slowdown

Technological change did not stop during the growth slowdown but its focus changed and to some degree it was offset by the effects of energy price shocks and industrial relations tensions.

Energy price increases in 1973–1974 and 1979 diverted research towards saving energy rather than increasing labour productivity. For example, aircraft became more fuel efficient, but they didn't operate with smaller crews. Real GDP per gallon of fuel increased but labour productivity stagnated.

During the 1970s, trade union membership increased from 45 to 59 per cent of the workforce. Restrictive labour practices, overmanning and strike activity increased. These negative factors are captured in the catch-all of "technological change".

Achieving Faster Growth

The main ways of increasing the growth rate of physical capital or human capital or the pace of technological advance are:

- Stimulate saving
- Stimulate research and development
- Target high-technology industries
- Encourage international trade
- Improve the quality of education

Stimulate Saving

Saving finances investment and investment increases the quantity of capital. So stimulating saving can increase economic growth. East Asian economies have the highest growth rates and the highest saving rates.

Stimulate Research and Development

Everyone can use the fruits of *basic* research and development efforts. For example, all biotechnology firms can use advances in gene-splicing technology. Because basic inventions can be copied, the inventor's profit is limited, and the market allocates too few resources to this activity. Governments can use public funds to finance basic research, but some mechanism is needed to allocate the funds to their highest-valued use. The universities and research councils are the main channels through which UK public funds are allocated.

Target High-technology Industries

Some people say that by providing public funds to high-technology firms and industries, a country can become the first to exploit a new technology and can earn above-average profits for a period while others are busy catching up. This strategy is risky and just as likely to use resources inefficiently as to speed growth.

Encourage International Trade

Free international trade stimulates growth by extracting all the available gains from specialization and trade. The fastest-growing nations today are those with the fastest-growing exports and imports.

Improve the Quality of Education

The free market produces too little education because education brings benefits beyond those valued by the people who receive the education. By funding basic education and by ensuring high standards in basic skills such as language, mathematics and science, governments can contribute to a nation's growth potential.

Review Quiz

Study Plan 31.4

1. Explain the one-third rule and explain how the rule is used in growth accounting to isolate the contributions of capital growth and technological change to productivity growth.
2. Explain how growth accounting can be used to provide information about the factors that contributed to the productivity growth slowdown.

Growth Theories

We've seen that real GDP grows when the quantities of labour and capital (which includes human capital) grow and when technology advances. Does this mean that the growth of labour and capital *cause* economic growth It might mean that. But there are other possibilities. *One* of these factors might be the cause of real GDP growth and the others might be the *effect*. We must try to discover how the influences on economic growth interact with each other to make some economies grow quickly and others grow slowly. And we must probe the reasons why a country's long-term growth rate sometimes speeds up and sometimes slows down.

Growth theories are designed to study the interactions among the several factors that contribute to growth and to disentangle cause and effect. They are also designed to enable us to study the way the different factors influence each other.

Growth theories are also designed to be universal. They are not theories about the growth of poor countries only or rich countries only. They are theories about why and how poor countries become rich and rich countries continue to get richer.

We're going to study three theories of economic growth, each one of which gives some insights into the process of economic growth. But none provides a definite answer to the basic questions: what causes economic growth and why do growth rates vary? Economics has some way to go before it can provide a definite answer to these most important of questions. The three growth theories we study are:

- Classical growth theory
- Neoclassical growth theory
- New growth theory

Classical Growth Theory

Classical growth theory is the view that real GDP growth is temporary and that when real GDP per person rises above the subsistence level, a population explosion eventually brings real GDP per person back to the subsistence level. Adam Smith, Thomas Robert Malthus and David Ricardo, the leading economists of the late eighteenth century and early nineteenth century, proposed this theory, but the view is most closely associated with the name of Malthus and is sometimes called the *Malthusian theory*.

Many people today are Malthusians! They say that if today's global population of 6.2 billion explodes to 11 billion by 2200, we will run out of resources and return to a primitive standard of living. We must act, say the Malthusians, to contain the population growth.

The Basic Classical Idea

To understand classical growth theory let's transport ourselves back to the world of 1710. Many of the 5.3 million people who lived in England worked on farms or on their own land and performed their tasks using simple tools and animal power. They earned about 1 shilling and 4 pence for working a 10-hour day.

Then advances in farming technology brought new types of ploughs and seeds that increased farm productivity. As farm productivity increased, farm production rose and some farm workers moved from the land to the cities, where they got work producing and selling the expanding range of farm equipment. Incomes rose and the people seemed to be prospering. But would the prosperity last? Classical growth theory says it would not.

Advances in technology – in both agriculture and industry – lead to investment in new capital, which makes labour more productive. More and more businesses start up and hire the now more productive labour. The greater demand for labour raises the real wage rate and increases employment.

At this stage, economic growth has occurred and everyone has benefited from it. Real GDP has increased and real wage rate has increased. But the classical economists believed that this new situation can't last because it will induce a population explosion.

Classical Theory of Population Growth

When the classical economists were developing their ideas about population growth, an unprecedented population explosion was under way. In Britain and other Western European countries, improvements in diet and hygiene had lowered the death rate while the birth rate remained high. For several decades, population growth was extremely rapid. For example, after being relatively stable for several centuries, the population of Britain increased by 40 per cent between 1750 and 1800 and by a further 50 per cent between 1800 and 1830. Meanwhile, an estimated 1 million people (about 20 per cent of the 1750 population) left Britain for North America and Australia before 1800, and outward migration continued on a similar scale through the nineteenth century. These facts are the empirical basis for the classical theory of population growth.

To explain the high rate of population growth, the classical economists used the idea of a **subsistence real wage rate**, which is the minimum real wage rate needed to maintain life. If the actual real wage rate is less than the subsistence real wage rate, some people cannot survive and the population decreases. In the classical theory, whenever the real wage rate exceeds the subsistence real wage rate, the population grows. But a rising population brings diminishing returns to labour. So labour productivity eventually decreases. This dismal implication led to economics being called the *dismal science*. The dismal implication is that no matter how much technological change occurs, real wage rates are always pushed back towards the subsistence level.

Classical Theory and the Productivity Curve

Figure 31.8 illustrates the classical growth theory using the productivity curve. Initially, the productivity curve is PC_0. Subsistence real GDP is £10 an hour, shown by the horizontal line in the graph. The economy starts out at point *A*, with £30 of capital per hour of labour and £10 of labour productivity, the subsistence level. Because real GDP is at the subsistence level, the population is constant.

Then a technological advance occurs, which shifts the productivity curve upward to PC_1. The economy now moves to point *B* on PC_1 and real GDP per hour of labour rises to £15. Now earning more than the subsistence wage, people have more children and live longer. The population grows.

A growing population means that labour hours grow, so capital per hour of labour falls. As capital per hour of labour falls, there is a movement down along the productivity curve PC_1. Labour productivity falls and keeps falling as long as the population grows and capital per hour of labour falls.

This process ends when labour productivity is back at the subsistence level at point *C* on productivity curve PC_1. The population stops growing and capital per hour of labour stops falling.

Repeated advances in technology play out in the same way as the advance that we've just studied. No matter how productive our economy becomes, population growth lowers capital per hour of labour and drives labour productivity towards the subsistence level. Living standards temporarily improve while the population is expanding, but when the population expansion ends, the standard of living is back at the subsistence level.

Classical Theory and Capital Accumulation

In the story you've just worked through, the total quantity of capital didn't change. Suppose that people save and invest, so capital grows. Doesn't a growing quantity of capital prevent the dismal conclusion of classical theory? It does not. *Anything* that raises labour productivity above the subsistence level triggers a population explosion that eventually wipes out the gains from greater productivity.

The dismal conclusion of classical growth theory is a direct consequence of the assumption that the population explodes if labour productivity exceeds the subsistence level. To avoid this conclusion, we need a different view of population growth.

The neoclassical growth theory that we'll now study provides a different view.

Figure 31.8 myeconlab

Classical Growth Theory

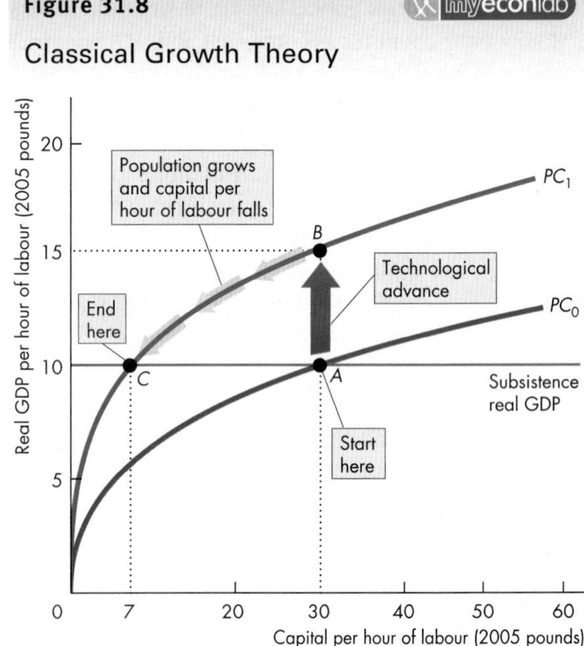

The economy starts out at point A with capital per hour of labour of £30 and labour productivity of £10 – the subsistence level – on productivity curve PC_0.

A technological advance shifts the productivity curve upward to PC_1 and the economy moves to point *B*. Labour productivity exceeds the subsistence level, so the population grows.

As the population grows, both capital and labour productivity decrease. The process ends at point *C* when labour productivity is back at its subsistence level.

Neoclassical Growth Theory

Neoclassical growth theory is the proposition that real GDP per person grows because technological change induces a level of saving and investment that makes capital per hour of labour grow. Growth ends only if technological change stops.

Robert Solow of MIT suggested the most popular version of neoclassical growth theory in the 1950s. But Frank Ramsey of Cambridge University first developed this theory in the 1920s.

Neoclassical theory's big break with its classical predecessor is its view about population growth. So we'll begin our account of neoclassical theory by examining its views about population growth.

The Neoclassical Economics of Population Growth

The population explosion of eighteenth-century Europe that created the classical theory of population eventually ended. The birth rate fell and the population growth rate became moderate. This slowdown in population growth seemed to make the classical theory less relevant. It also eventually led to the development of a modern economic theory of population growth.

The modern view is that although the population growth rate is influenced by economic factors, the influence is not a simple and mechanical one like that proposed by the classical economists. Key among the economic influences on population growth is the opportunity cost of a woman's time. As women's wage rates increase and their job opportunities expand, the opportunity cost of having children increases. Faced with a higher opportunity cost, families choose to have fewer children and the birth rate falls.

A second economic influence works on the death rate. The technological advance that brings increased productivity and increased incomes brings advances in healthcare that extend lives.

These two opposing economic forces influence the population growth rate. As incomes increase, both the birth rate and the death rate decrease. It turns out that these opposing forces almost offset each other, so the rate of population growth is independent of the rate of economic growth.

This modern view of population growth and the historical trends that support it contradict the views of the classical economists and call into question the modern doomsday conclusion that the planet will one day be swamped with too many people to feed.

Neoclassical growth theory adopts this modern view of population growth. Forces other than real GDP and its growth rate determine population growth.

Technological Change

In the neoclassical theory, the rate of technological change influences the rate of economic growth but economic growth does not influence the pace of technological change. It is assumed that technological change results from chance. When we get lucky, we have rapid technological change, and when bad luck strikes, the pace of technological advance slows.

Target Rate of Return and Saving

The key assumption in the neoclassical growth theory concerns saving. Other things remaining the same, the higher the real interest rate, the greater is the amount that people save. To decide how much to save, people compare the rate of return with a *target rate of return*. If the rate of return exceeds the target rate of return, saving is sufficient to make capital per hour of labour grow. If the target rate of return exceeds the rate of return, saving is not sufficient to maintain the current level of capital per hour of labour, so capital per hour of labour shrinks. And if the rate of return equals a target rate of return, saving is just sufficient to maintain the quantity of capital per hour of labour at its current level.

The Basic Neoclassical Idea

To understand neoclassical growth theory, imagine the world of the late 1950s, just after Robert Solow has explained his idea. Prime Minister Harold Macmillan is running a General Election campaign with the slogan "You've never had it so good." Income per person is around £6,000 a year in today's money. The population is growing at about 1 per cent a year. People are saving and investing about 20 per cent of their incomes, enough to keep the quantity of capital per hour of labour constant. Income per person is growing, but not by much.

Then technology begins to advance at a more rapid pace. The transistor revolutionizes an emerging electronics industry. New plastics revolutionize the manufacture of household appliances. Motorways begin to revolutionize road transport. Jet aeroplanes start to replace piston-engine planes and speed up air transport.

These technological advances bring new profit opportunities. Businesses expand and new businesses are created to exploit the newly available profitable technologies. Investment and saving increase. The economy enjoys new levels of prosperity and growth. But will the prosperity last? And will the growth last?

Neoclassical growth theory says that the *prosperity* will last but the *growth* will not last unless technology keeps advancing.

According to the neoclassical growth theory, the prosperity will persist because there is no classical population growth to induce lower wages.

But growth will stop if technology stops advancing, for two related reasons. First, high profit rates that result from technological change bring increased saving and capital accumulation. But second, capital accumulation eventually results in diminishing returns that lower the rate of return, and that eventually decrease saving and slow the rate of capital accumulation.

Neoclassical Theory and the Productivity Curve

Figure 31.9 illustrates the neoclassical growth theory using the productivity curve. Initially, the productivity curve is PC_0 and the economy is at point *A*, with £30 of capital per hour of labour and real GDP of £10 an hour.

The slope of the productivity curve measures the additional output that results from an additional unit of capital – the marginal product of capital or rate of return on capital. People have a target rate of return that can be illustrated by a straight line with a slope equal to the target rate of return.

At point *A* on productivity curve PC_0, the slope of the *PC* curve equals the slope of the target rate of return line. If the quantity of capital per hour of labour were less than £30, the real interest rate would exceed the target rate of return and capital per hour of labour would grow. If the quantity of capital per hour of labour were greater than £30, the rate of return would be less than the target rate of return and capital per hour of labour would shrink. But when the quantity of capital per hour of labour is £30, the rate of return equals the target rate of return and capital per hour of labour is constant.

Now a technological advance occurs that shifts the productivity curve upward to PC_1. The economy now moves to point *B* on PC_1, and labour productivity rises to £15. It is at this point in the classical theory that forces kick in to drive real GDP per hour of labour back to the subsistence level. But in the neoclassical theory, no such forces operate. Instead, at point *B*, the rate of return exceeds the target rate of return. (You can see why by comparing the slopes of PC_1 at point *B* and the target rate of return line.)

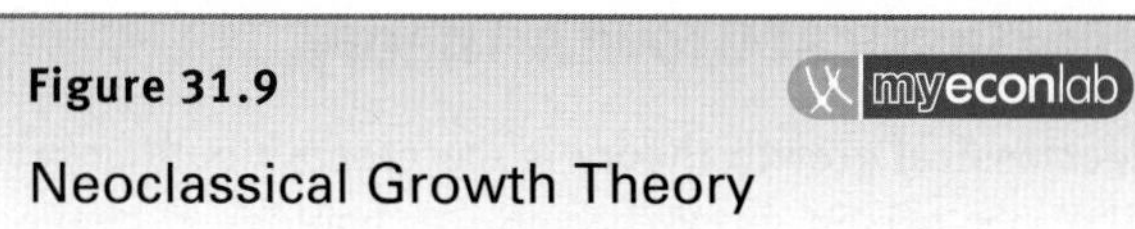

Figure 31.9

Neoclassical Growth Theory

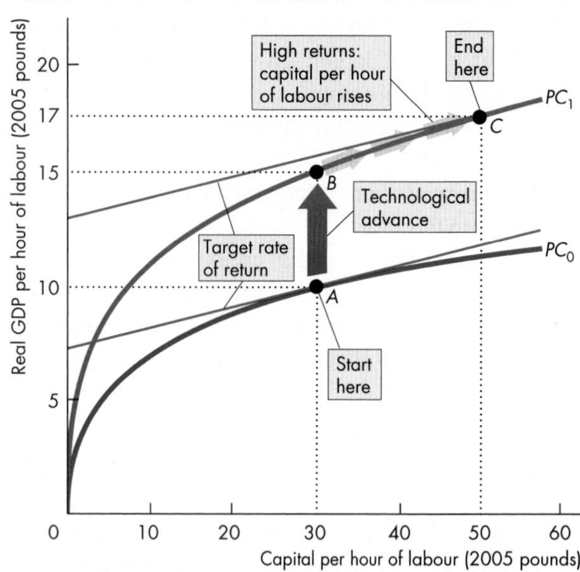

The economy starts on productivity curve PC_0 at point *A*. The slope of the productivity curve measures the rate of return, so at point *A* the rate of return equals the target rate of return.

A technological advance shifts the productivity curve upward to PC_1 and the economy moves to point *B*. The rate of return exceeds the target rate of return, and the quantity of capital per hour of labour increases – a movement up along the productivity curve PC_1. Growth ends when the rate of return again equals the target rate of return at point *C*.

With a high rate of return available, saving and investment increase and the quantity of capital per hour of labour increases. There is a movement up along the productivity curve PC_1 and labour productivity increases.

This growth process eventually ends because, as the quantity of capital per hour of labour increases, the rate of return falls. At point *C*, where the process ends, the real interest rate again equals the target rate of return.

Throughout the process you've just studied, labour productivity grows but the growth rate gradually decreases and eventually growth ends.

But if another advance in technology occurs, the process you've just seen repeats. Ongoing advances in technology constantly increase the rate of return, inducing the saving that increases capital per hour of labour. The growth process persists as long as technology advances. And the growth rate fluctuates because technological progress occurs at a variable rate.

A Problem with Neoclassical Growth Theory

All economies have access to the same technologies and capital is free to roam the globe seeking the highest available rate of return. Given these facts, neoclassical growth theory implies that growth rates and income levels per person around the globe will converge. While there is some sign of convergence among the rich countries, as Figure 31.3(a) shows, convergence is slow, and it does not appear to be imminent for all countries, as Figure 31.3(b) shows.

New growth theory attempts to overcome this shortcoming of neoclassical growth theory. It also attempts to explain how the rate of technological change is determined.

New Growth Theory

New growth theory holds that real GDP per person grows because of the choices people make in the pursuit of profit and that growth can persist indefinitely.

Paul Romer of Stanford University developed this theory during the 1980s, but the ideas go back to work by Joseph Schumpeter during the 1930s and 1940s.

The theory begins with two facts about market economies:

- Discoveries result from choices
- Discoveries bring profit and competition destroys profit

Discoveries Result from Choices

When someone discovers a new product or technique, they think of themselves as being lucky. They are right. But the pace at which new discoveries are made – at which technology advances – is not determined by chance. It depends on how many people are looking for a new way of doing something and how intensively they are looking.

Discoveries Bring Profit and Competition Destroys Profits

Profit is the spur to technological change. The forces of competition are constantly squeezing profits, so to increase profit, people constantly seek either lower-cost methods of production or new and better products for which people are willing to pay a higher price. Inventors can maintain a profit for several years by taking out a patent or a copyright. But eventually, a new discovery is copied and profits disappear.

Two further facts play a key role in the new growth theory:

- Discoveries are a public capital good
- Knowledge is capital that is not subject to diminishing returns

Discoveries Are a Public Capital Good

Economists call a good a public good when no one can be excluded from using it and when one person's use does not prevent others from using it. National defence is one example of a public good. Knowledge is another.

When, in 1992, Marc Andreesen and his friend Eric Bina developed a browser they called Mosaic, they laid the foundation for Netscape Navigator and Internet Explorer, two pieces of capital that have increased productivity unimaginably.

While patents and copyrights protect the inventors or creators of new products and production processes, and enable them to reap the returns from their innovative ideas, once a new discovery has been made, everyone can benefit from its use. And one person's use of a new discovery does not prevent others from using it. Your use of a Web browser doesn't prevent someone else from using that same browser simultaneously.

Because knowledge is a public good, as the benefits of a new discovery spread, free resources become available. These resources are free because nothing is given up when they are used. They have a zero opportunity cost. Knowledge is even more special because it is not subject to diminishing returns.

Knowledge Is Capital That Is Not Subject to Diminishing Returns

Production is subject to diminishing returns when one resource is fixed and the quantity of another resource changes. Adding labour to a fixed amount of equipment or adding equipment to a fixed amount of labour both bring diminishing marginal product – diminishing returns.

But increasing the stock of knowledge makes labour and machines more productive. Knowledge capital does not bring diminishing returns.

The fact that knowledge capital does not experience diminishing returns is the central novel proposition of the new growth theory. And the implication of this simple and appealing idea is astonishing. The new growth theory has no growth-stopping mechanism like those of the other two theories. As physical capital accumulates, the rate of return falls. But the incentive to innovate and earn a higher profit becomes stronger. So innovation occurs, which increases the rate of return. labour productivity grows indefinitely as people find new technologies that yield a higher real interest rate.

The growth rate depends on people's ability to innovate and on the rate of return. Over the years, the ability to innovate has changed. The invention of language and writing (the two most basic human capital tools) and later the development of the scientific method and the establishment of universities and research institutions brought huge increases in the rate of return. Today, a deeper understanding of genes is bringing profit in a growing biotechnology industry. And astonishing advances in computer technology are creating an explosion of profit opportunities in a wide range of information-age industries.

New Growth Theory and the Productivity Curve

Figure 31.10 illustrates new growth theory. Like Figure 31.9, which illustrates neoclassical growth theory, Figure 31.10 contains a productivity curve and a target rate of return curve, but unlike in neoclassical theory, the productivity curve in the new growth theory never stands still. The pursuit of profit means that technology is always advancing and human capital is always growing. The result is an ever upward-shifting *PC* curve. As physical capital is accumulated, diminishing returns lower its rate of return. But ever-advancing productivity counteracts this tendency and keeps the rate of return above the target rate of return curve.

Advancing technology and human capital growth keep the *PC* curve shifting upward in Figure 31.10 from PC_0 to PC_1 to PC_2 and beyond. As the productivity curve shifts upward, capital per hour of labour and labour productivity increase together along the line labelled "*Ak* line".

The new growth theory implies that although the productivity curve shows diminishing returns, if capital is interpreted more broadly as physical capital, human capital and the technologies they embody then labour productivity grows at the same rate as the growth in capital per hour of labour. Labour productivity is proportional to capital per hour of labour.

Labour productivity (real GDP per hour of labour) y is related to capital per hour of labour k by the equation:

$$y = Ak$$

In Figure 31.10, A is 1/3. When capital per hour of labour is £15, labour productivity is £5 at point *A*.

Figure 31.10

New Growth Theory

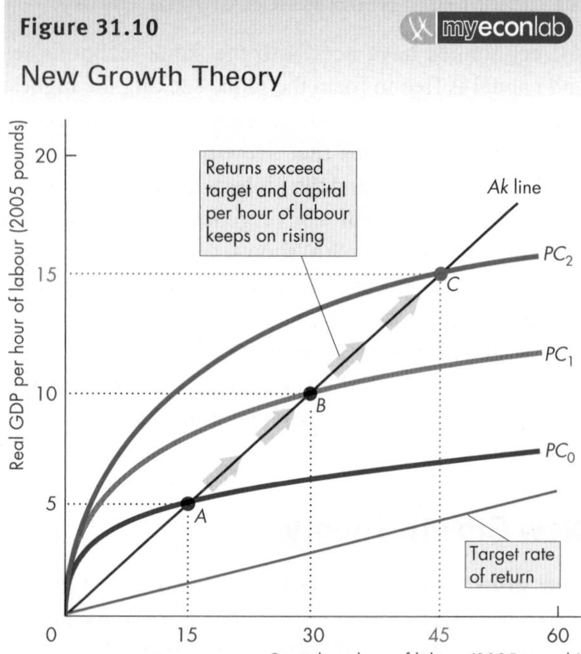

In new growth theory, economic growth results from incentives to innovate and from capital that does not experience diminishing returns. The productivity curve, *PC*, keeps shifting upward, and real GDP per hour of labour and capital per hour of labour grow along the *Ak* line.

People look for yet more profit and accumulate yet more capital. The economy expands to point *B*, with capital per hour of labour of £30 and labour productivity of £10. In pursuit of further profit, technology keeps advancing and capital per hour of labour rises to £45 with labour productivity of £15, at point *C*. Labour productivity and capital per hour of labour increase without limit.

A Perpetual Motion Economy

The new growth theory sees the economy as a perpetual motion machine, which Figure 31.11 illustrates. Insatiable wants lead us to pursue profit, innovate and create new and better products. New firms start up and old firms go out of business. As firms start up and die, jobs are created and destroyed. New and better jobs lead to more leisure and more consumption. But our insatiable wants are still there, so the process continues,

Figure 31.11

myeconlab

A Perpetual Motion Machine

Incentives
Innovation
New and better techniques
New and better products
New firms born and old firms die
New and better jobs
More leisure
More consumption goods and services
Higher standard of living
Want a higher standard of living

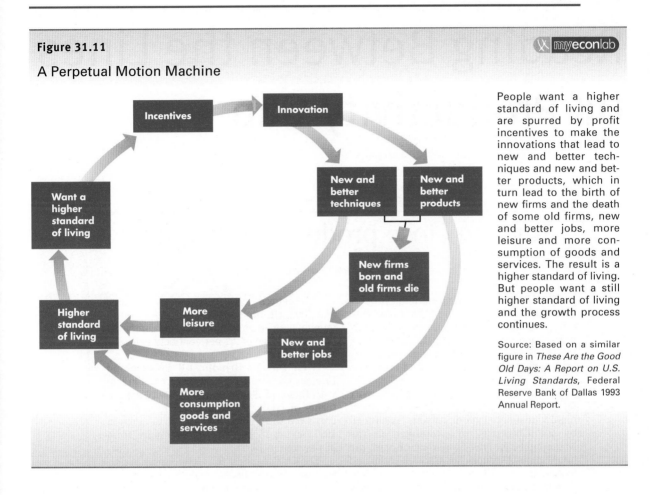

People want a higher standard of living and are spurred by profit incentives to make the innovations that lead to new and better techniques and new and better products, which in turn lead to the birth of new firms and the death of some old firms, new and better jobs, more leisure and more consumption of goods and services. The result is a higher standard of living. But people want a still higher standard of living and the growth process continues.

Source: Based on a similar figure in *These Are the Good Old Days: A Report on U.S. Living Standards*, Federal Reserve Bank of Dallas 1993 Annual Report.

going around and around a circle of wants, profits, innovation and new products.

Sorting Out the Theories

Which theory is correct? Probably none, but they all teach us something of value. The classical theory reminds us that our physical resources are limited and that with no advances in technology, we must eventually hit diminishing returns. Neoclassical theory reaches essentially the same conclusion, but not because of a population explosion. Instead, it emphasizes diminishing returns to capital and reminds us that we cannot keep growth going just by accumulating physical capital. We must also advance technology and accumulate human capital. We must become more creative in our use of scarce resources. New growth theory emphasizes the possible capacity of human resources to innovate at a pace that offsets diminishing returns.

Review Quiz

Study Plan 31.5

1. What is the central idea of classical growth theory that leads to the dismal outcome?
2. What, according to the neoclassical growth theory, is the fundamental cause of economic growth?
3. What is the key proposition of the new growth theory that makes growth persist?

Economic growth is the single most decisive factor influencing a country's living standard. But another is the extent to which the country fully employs its scarce resources. In the next chapter, we study economic fluctuations and recessions. But before embarking on this topic, take a look at *Reading Between the Lines* on pp. 736–737, which compares recent productivity levels and growth rates in four large economies.

Reading Between the Lines
UK Productivity Gap

The Financial Times, 21 March 2007

Race to close productivity gap key

Scheherazade Daneshku

. . . The UK has had a long-standing productivity gap not only with the US but also with other big European economies, principally France and Germany. In 1991, for example, the UK lagged the US, France and Germany by 30 per cent or more in terms of real gross domestic product per hour. . . .

International comparisons of productivity levels are difficult . . . [b]ut the world's most highly respected comparison, produced by the University of Groningen in the Netherlands, and the Conference Board, the international business organisation estimated in January that UK output per hour worked rose by 1.7 per cent in 2006. This was below the UK's long-run average of 2.1 per cent but was up from 1.1 per cent in 2005.

Although the UK enjoyed "steady growth" in labour productivity, it remained outside the top 10 most productive economies, according to the Conference Board.

The figures showed that between 2000 and 2006, UK productivity growth slowed to an annual average of 1.9 per cent, compared with an average of 2.1 per cent between 1987 and 2000. . . .

Even though Britain still lags behind France and Germany, it has been catching up with them. In 2005, the productivity gap, in terms of GDP per hour, with France had narrowed to 20 per cent (from 35 per cent in 1991) and to 13 per cent with Germany (from 30 per cent in 1991).

The Organisation for Economic Cooperation and Development argues that the government could do more to improve productivity growth. It has identified the following problems: relatively low general skills level, which limits the ability of the workforce to innovate and absorb new technology; complex and restrictive planning regulations and rising complexity of business.

The Essence of the Story

- In 1991, the UK labour productivity lagged that of the United States, France and Germany by 30 per cent or more, but by 2005, it lagged that of France by 20 per cent and of Germany by 13 per cent.
- UK labour productivity increased by 1.1 per cent in 2005, 1.7 per cent in 2006, 1.9 per cent on the average between 2000 and 2006 and 2.1 per cent on the average between 1987 and 2000.
- The United Kingdom is outside the top 10 on labour productivity.
- The OECD says the UK government could increase labour productivity by improving workers' general skills and simplifying business regulations.

Economic Analysis

- Labour productivity is hard to measure and compare and the measures available are approximate rather than exact.
- Economists at the University of Groningen measure labour productivity – real GDP per hour of work – using common real purchasing power parity 2006 prices and the most accurate available data on hours of labour.
- The news article discusses both the *level* and the *growth rate* of labour productivity.
- In 2006, the United Kingdom's *level* of labour productivity lagged behind that of Germany, France and the United States.
- Figure 1 shows labour productivity on the average from 2000 to 2006 for the four large economies as a percentage of the UK level. Germany is 2 per cent higher, the United States 9 per cent higher, and France 17 per cent higher.
- The United Kingdom has the lowest level of labour productivity but not the slowest growing. The United States is growing faster but Germany and France are growing more slowly.
- Figure 2 shows the growth rates of labour productivity during 2000–2006 for the four large economies.
- If the growth rates of labour productivity during 2000–2006 persist, the rankings of the level of labour productivity will change. Figure 3 shows the levels by 2020 (again as percentages of the UK level). Germany will lag the United Kingdom and the United States will have pulled level with France.
- Small differences in growth rates maintained over a number of years make big differences in levels.
- The high level of labour productivity in France has resulted from more sustained improvements in technology and human capital.
- The OECD says that the skill levels in the United Kingdom need to be improved.

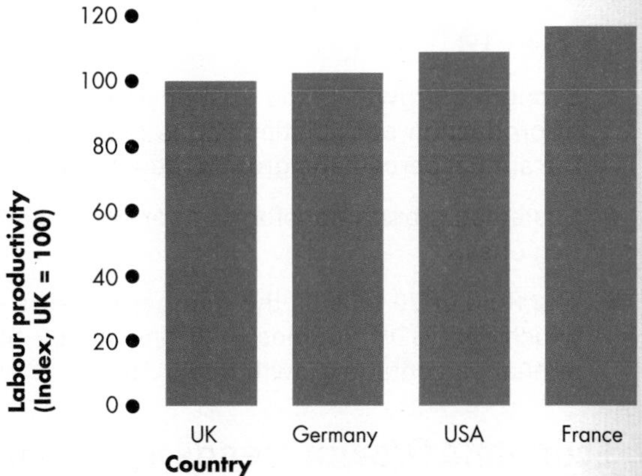

Figure 1 Productivity levels compared: 2000 to 2006 averages

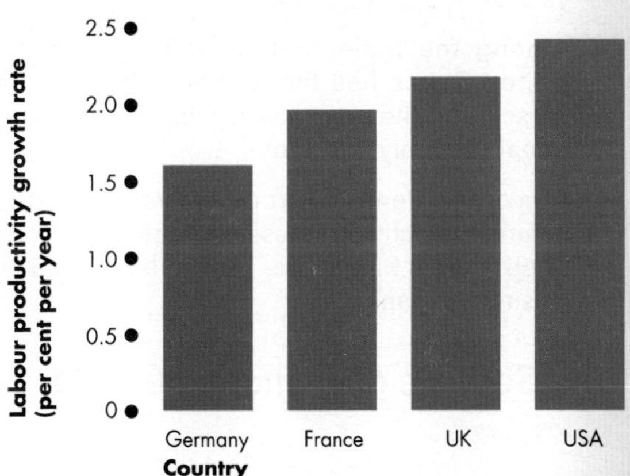

Figure 2 Productivity growth rates compared: 2000 to 2006

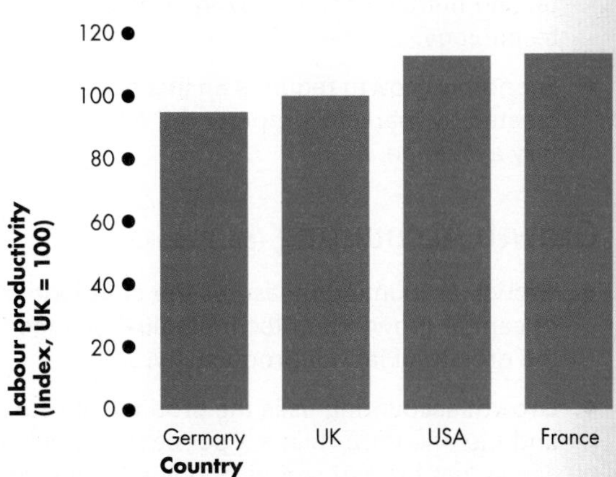

Figure 3 Productivity levels in 2020 compared at recent growth rates

Summary

Key Points

The Basics of Economic Growth

(pp. 718–719)

- Economic growth is the sustained expansion of production possibilities and is measured as the annual percentage growth rate of real GDP.
- Sustained growth transforms poor nations into rich ones.
- The Rule of 70 tells us the number of years in which real GDP doubles – 70 divided by the annual percentage growth rate.

Economic Growth Trends (pp. 720–722)

- Real GDP per person in the United Kingdom has grown at an average rate of 1.4 per cent a year over the long term.
- Among the major industrial countries, the United States has the highest real GDP per person and the gaps among the rich countries remain roughly constant.
- Africa and Central Europe are falling further behind the rich countries, whereas Hong Kong, South Korea, Singapore, Taiwan and China are closing the gaps.

The Sources of Economic Growth

(pp. 723–725)

- The sources of economic growth are increases in aggregate hours and labour productivity. Labour productivity depends on physical capital and human capital growth and advances in technology.
- Economic growth requires an incentive system created by markets, property rights and monetary exchange.

Growth Accounting (pp. 726–728)

- Growth accounting measures the contributions of capital growth and technological change to the growth of labour productivity.
- Growth accounting uses the productivity curve and the one-third rule: a 1 per cent increase in capital per hour of labour brings a 1/3 per cent increase in labour productivity.
- During the productivity growth slowdown of the 1970s, technological change made only a small contribution to real GDP growth.
- Stimulating saving and research, targeting high-technology industries, encouraging international trade and improving education might boost economic growth.

Growth Theories (pp. 729–735)

- In the classical theory, when a technological advance increases real GDP per person above the *subsistence* level, a population explosion brings diminishing returns and real GDP per person returns to the subsistence level.
- In neoclassical growth theory, when a technological advance increases saving and investment, an increase in the capital stock brings diminishing returns and eventually, without further technological change, the capital stock and real GDP per person stop growing.
- In new growth theory, growth persists indefinitely at a rate determined by decisions that lead to innovation and technological change.

Key Figures

Key Terms

Problems

Tests, Study Plan and Solutions* 

1 Japan's real GDP was 515 trillion yen in 2003 and 529 trillion yen in 2004. Japan's population was 127.7 million in 2003 and 127.9 million in 2004. Calculate:

a Japan's economic growth rate in 2004.

b The growth rate of real GDP per person in Japan in 2004.

c The approximate number of years it takes for real GDP per person in Japan to double if the 2004 economic growth rate and population growth rate are maintained.

2 If China's real GDP is growing at 9 per cent a year, its population is growing at 1 per cent a year and these growth rates continue, in what year will China's real GDP per person be twice what it is in 2006?

3 The following information has been discovered about the economy of Longland. The economy's productivity curve is:

Capital per hour of labour (2005 pounds per hour)	Real GDP per hour of labour (2005 pounds per hour)
10	3.80
20	5.70
30	7.13
40	8.31
50	9.35
60	10.29
70	11.14
80	11.94

a Does this economy conform to the one-third rule? If so, explain why. If not, explain why not and explain what rule, if any, it does conform to.

b Explain how you would do the growth accounting for this economy.

4 In Longland, described in problem 3, capital per hour of labour in 2005 was £40 and labour productivity was £8.31. In 2006, capital per hour of labour had increased to £50 and labour productivity had increased to £10.29 an hour.

a Does Longland experience diminishing returns? Explain why or why not.

b Use growth accounting to find the contribution of capital growth between 2005 and 2006 to labour productivity growth.

c Use growth accounting to find the contribution of technological change between 2005 and 2006 to labour productivity growth.

5 The following information has been discovered about the economy of Cape Despair. The subsistence real wage rate is £15 an hour. Whenever the real wage rate rises above this level the population grows, and when the real wage rate falls below this level the population decreases. The productivity curve in Cape Despair is:

Capital per hour of labour (2005 pounds per hour)	Real GDP per hour of labour (2005 pounds per hour)
20	8
40	15
60	21
80	26
100	30
120	33
140	35
160	36

Initially, the population of Cape Despair is constant and real GDP is at its subsistence level. Then a technological advance shifts the productivity curve upward by £7 at each level of capital per hour of labour.

a What is the initial capital per hour of labour and labour productivity?

b What happens to the labour productivity immediately following the technological advance?

c What happens to the population growth rate following the technological advance?

d What is the eventual quantity of capital per hour of labour in Cape Despair?

6 Martha's Island is an economy that behaves according to the neoclassical growth model. The economy has no growth, a target rate of return of 10 per cent a year and the following productivity curve:

Capital per hour of labour (2005 pounds per year)	Real GDP per hour of labour (2005 pounds per hour)
40	16
80	30
120	42
160	52
200	60
240	66
280	70
320	72

* Solutions to odd-numbered problems are provided.

a What is the initial capital per hour of labour on Martha's Island?

b What is the real GDP per hour of labour?

A technological advance shifts the productivity curve upward.

c What is the real interest rate immediately following the technological advance?

d What is the return on capital and quantity of capital per hour of labour following the technological advance?

7 Romeria is a country that behaves according to the predictions of new growth theory. The target rate is 3 per cent a year. A technological advance increases the demand for capital and raises the real interest rate to 5 per cent a year. Describe the events that happen in Romeria and contrast them with the events in Martha's Island in problem 6.

8 Explain the processes that will bring the growth of real GDP per person to a stop according to:

a Classical growth theory

b Neoclassical growth theory

c New growth theory

Critical Thinking

1 After studying *Reading Between the Lines* on pp. 736–737, answer the following questions:

a What is the distinction between the level of productivity and the growth rate of productivity and how does the United Kingdom rank among the four large economies on both measures?

b Do you believe that France has a higher level of labour productivity than the United States? Can you think of reasons that account for this fact? Can you think of reasons to explain why the data might be misleading us?

2 Write a letter to your Member of Parliament in which you set out the policies you believe the UK government must follow to speed up the growth rate of real GDP in the United Kingdom.

3 In South Africa in 2006 the growth rate of real GDP was 4.5 per cent. The population growth rate was minus 0.4 per cent.

a What was the growth rate of real GDP per person in South Africa in 2006?

b Why do you think South Africa's population growth rate is negative?

c Do you think a negative population growth rate is a problem? If so, what might be done to reverse it and make the population grow?

d If the population could be made to grow, what do you predict would happen to the growth rates of real GDP and real GDP per person? Explain your answer.

4 Is faster growth growth always a good thing? Argue the case for faster growth and the case for slower growth. Then reach a conclusion on whether growth should be increased or slowed.

5 **Make Way for India – The Next China**

. . . China . . . growing at around 9 per cent a year. . . . the one-child policy will start to reduce the size of China's working population within the next 10 years. India, by contrast, will have an increasing working population for another generation at least.

The Independent, 1 March 2006

a Given the expected population changes, do you think China or India will have the greater economic growth rate? Why?

b Would China's growth rate remain at 9 per cent a year without the restriction on its population growth rate?

c India's population growth rate is 1.6 per cent a year, and in 2005 its economic growth rate was 8 per cent a year. China's population growth rate is 0.6 per cent a year and in 2005 its economic growth rate was 9 per cent a year. In what year will real GDP per person double in each country?

Web Activities

Links to Websites

1 Visit the Penn World Table website and obtain data on real GDP per person for the United States, China, South Africa and Mexico since 1960.

a Draw a graph of the data.

b Which country has the lowest real GDP per person and which has the highest?

c Which country has experienced the fastest growth rate since 1960 and which the slowest?

d Explain why the growth rates in these four countries are ranked in the order you have discovered?

e Return to the Penn World Table website and obtain data for any four other countries that interest you. Describe and explain the patterns that you find for these countries.

The Business Cycle

CHAPTER 32

After studying this chapter you will be able to:

- Distinguish among different theories of the business cycle
- Explain the aggregate demand theories of the business cycle – Keynesian, monetarist and rational expectations
- Explain real business cycle theory
- Describe the origins of and the mechanisms at work during the 1990–1992 recession
- Describe the origins of and the mechanisms at work during the Great Depression

Must What Goes Up Always Come Down?

During the 20 years between the last two World Wars (1919–1939), the UK economy languished in a prolonged depression. From the start of the Industrial Revolution (1760), the global economy had fluctuated in what came to be called a "trade cycle". But the trend was upward. The 1920s and 1930s raised doubts that the upward path would continue. Yet while many suffered appalling economic hardship, these were years of unparalleled prosperity for others.

By the standards of the interwar years, recent economic cycles have been mild. But our economy continues to cycle in recessions and expansions around its rising trend. What causes the business cycle? That is the major question that you study in this chapter; and in *Reading Between the Lines* at the end of the chapter, you can look at China's astonishing expansion today.

Cycle Patterns, Impulses and Mechanisms

Cycles are a widespread physical phenomenon and they take several different forms. In a tennis match, the ball cycles from one side of the court to the other and back again. Every day, the earth cycles from day to night and back to day. A child on a rocking horse creates a cycle as the horse swings back and forth.

The tennis ball cycle is the simplest. It is caused by the actions of the players. The ball changes direction (at each turning point) because the racquet (an outside force) is being applied. The day–night–day cycle is the most subtle. The rotation of the earth causes this cycle. No new force is applied each day to make the sun rise and set. It happens because of the design of the objects that interact to create the cycle.

Nothing happens at a turning point (sunrise and sunset) that is any different from what is happening at other points except that the sun comes into or goes out of view. The child's rocking horse cycle is a combination of these two cases. To start the horse rocking, some outside force must be exerted (as in the tennis ball cycle). But once the horse is rocking, the to-and-fro cycle continues for some time with no further force being applied (as in the day–night–day cycle).

The rocking horse cycle eventually dies out unless the horse is pushed again, and each time the horse is pushed, the cycle temporarily becomes more severe.

The economy is a bit like all three of these examples. It can be hit by shocks (like a tennis ball) that send it in one direction or another; it can cycle indefinitely (like the turning of day into night); and it can cycle in swings that get milder until another shock sets off a new burst of bigger swings (like a rocking horse).

While none of these analogies is perfect, they all contain some insights into the business cycle. Different theories of the cycle emphasize different impulses (different tennis racquets) and different cycle mechanisms (different solar system and rocking horse designs).

Although there are several different theories of the business cycle, they all agree about one aspect of the cycle: the central role played by investment and the accumulation of capital.

The Role of Investment and Capital

Whatever the shocks are that hit the economy, they hit one crucial variable: investment. Recessions begin when investment in new capital slows down and they turn into expansions when investment speeds up. Investment and capital interact like the spinning earth and the moon to create an ongoing cycle.

In an expansion, investment proceeds at a rapid rate and the capital stock grows quickly. But rapid capital growth means that the amount of capital per hour of labour is growing. Equipped with more capital, labour becomes more productive. But the *law of diminishing returns* begins to operate. The law of diminishing returns states that as the quantity of capital increases, with the quantity of labour remaining the same, the gain in productivity from an additional unit of capital eventually diminishes. Diminishing returns to capital bring a fall in the profit rate, and with a lower profit rate the incentive to invest weakens.

As a result, investment eventually falls. When it falls by a large amount, recession begins. In a recession, investment is low and the capital stock grows slowly. In a deep recession, the capital stock might actually decrease. Slow capital growth (or even a decreasing capital stock) means that the amount of capital per hour of labour is decreasing.

With a low amount of capital per hour of labour, businesses begin to see opportunities for profitable investment and the pace of investment eventually picks up. As it does so, recession turns into expansion.

The *AS–AD* Model

Investment and capital are part of the business cycle mechanism, but they are just one part. To study the broader business cycle mechanism, we need a broader framework: the *AS–AD* model. We can use the *AS–AD* model to describe all theories of the business cycle. Theories differ in what they identify as the impulse and the cycle mechanism. But all theories can be thought of as making assumptions about the factors that make either aggregate supply or aggregate demand fluctuate and about how those assumptions interact to create a business cycle. Business cycle impulses can affect either the supply side or the demand side of the economy or both. There are no pure supply-side theories, so we classify the theories as either:

1 Aggregate demand theories
2 Real business cycle theory

We'll study the aggregate demand theories first. Then we'll study real business cycle theory, which is the more recent approach that isolates a shock that has both aggregate supply and aggregate demand effects.

Study Plan 32.1

Aggregate Demand Theories of the Business Cycle

Three types of aggregate demand theories of the business cycle have been proposed. They are:

- Keynesian theory
- Monetarist theory
- Rational expectations theory

Keynesian Theory

The **Keynesian theory of the business cycle** regards volatile expectations as the main source of economic fluctuations. This theory is distilled from Keynes' *The General Theory of Employment, Interest and Money*. We'll explore the Keynesian theory by looking at its main impulse and the mechanism that converts this impulse into a real GDP cycle.

Keynesian Impulse

The *impulse* in the Keynesian theory of the business cycle is expected future sales and profits. A change in expected future sales and profits changes the demand for new capital and changes the level of investment.

Keynes reasoned that profit expectations would be volatile because most of the events that shape the future are unknown and impossible to forecast. So, he reasoned, news or even rumours about future influences on profit (such as tax rate changes, interest rate changes, advances in technology, global economic and political events, or any of the thousands of other relevant factors) have large effects on the expected profit rate.

To emphasize the volatility and diversity of sources of changes in expected sales and profits, Keynes described these expectations as *animal spirits*.

Keynesian Cycle Mechanism

In the Keynesian theory, once a change in animal spirits has changed investment, a cycle mechanism begins to operate that has two key elements. First, the initial change in investment has a multiplier effect. The change in investment changes *aggregate* expenditure, real GDP and disposable income. The change in disposable income changes consumption expenditure and aggregate demand changes by a multiple of the initial change in investment. (Chapter 25, p. 572 and pp. 577–579 describes this mechanism in detail.) The aggregate demand curve shifts leftward in a recession and rightward in an expansion.

The second element of the Keynesian cycle mechanism is a sticky money wage rate together with a horizontal *SAS* curve. With a horizontal *SAS* curve, swings in aggregate demand translate into swings in real GDP with no changes in the price level.

Figure 32.1 illustrates the Keynesian cycle. The long-run aggregate supply curve is *LAS*, the short-run aggregate supply curve is *SAS*, and the aggregate demand curve is AD_0. Initially, the economy is at full employment (point *A*) with real GDP at £1,300 billion and the price level at 105.

A fall in animal spirits decreases investment, which decreases aggregate demand. A multiplier process decreases consumption expenditure, which decreases aggregate demand yet further. The aggregate demand

Figure 32.1 myeconlab

The Keynesian Cycle

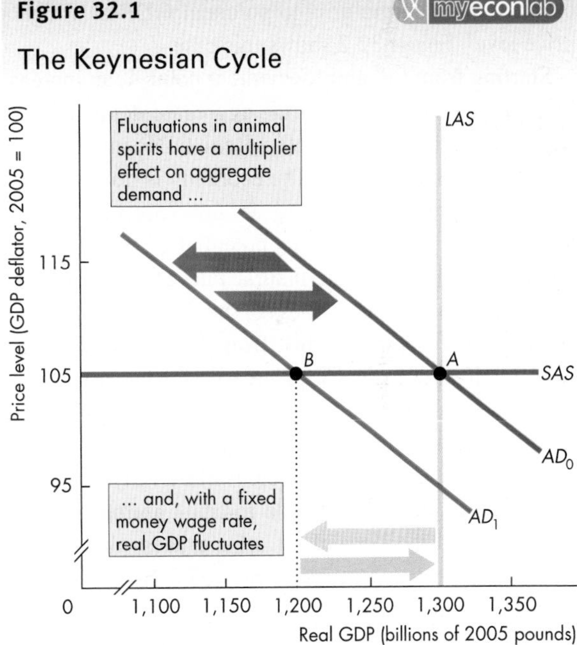

The economy is operating at point *A* at the intersection of the long-run aggregate supply curve (*LAS*), the short-run aggregate supply curve (*SAS*) and the aggregate demand curve (AD_0). A Keynesian recession begins when a fall in animal spirits decreases investment. Aggregate demand decreases and the *AD* curve shifts leftward to AD_1. With a fixed money wage rate, real GDP decreases to £1,200 billion and the price level does not change. The economy moves to point *B*. A rise in animal spirits has the opposite effect. A Keynesian expansion begins and takes the economy back to point *A*. The economy cycles by bouncing between point *A* and point *B*.

curve shifts leftward to AD_1. With a fixed money wage, real GDP decreases to £1,200 billion and the economy moves to point *B*.

Unemployment has increased and there is a surplus of labour, but the money wage rate does not fall and the economy remains at point *B* until some force moves it away.

That force is a rise in animal spirits, which increases investment. The *AD* curve shifts back to AD_0 and real GDP increases in an expansion to £1,300 billion again.

As long as real GDP remains below potential GDP (£1,300 billion in this example), the money wage rate and the price level remain constant. And real GDP cycles between points *A* and *B*.

Keynes at Above Full-employment

If animal spirits increase investment at full employment, an inflationary gap arises. Real GDP increases temporarily, but soon returns to potential GDP at a higher price level. Figure 32.2 shows this case.

Starting from full employment, at point *A*, an increase in aggregate demand shifts the aggregate demand curve rightward from AD_0 to AD_1. Real GDP increases to £1,400 billion at point *C*. The economy is now at above full-employment and there is now an inflationary gap. Once real GDP exceeds potential GDP and unemployment falls below the natural rate, the money wage rate begins to rise. As it does so, the short-run aggregate supply curve begins to shift from SAS_0 towards SAS_1. Real GDP now begins to decrease and the price level rises. The economy follows the arrows from point *C* to point *D*, the eventual long-run equilibrium.

The Keynesian business cycle is like a rally in a tennis match. It is caused by outside forces – animal spirits – that change direction and set off a process that ends at an equilibrium that must be hit again by the outside forces to disturb it.

On the downside, when aggregate demand decreases and unemployment rises, the money wage rate does not change. It is completely rigid in the downward direction. With a decrease in aggregate demand and no change in the money wage rate, the economy gets stuck in a below full-employment equilibrium. There are no natural forces operating to restore full employment. The economy remains in that situation until animal spirits are lifted and investment increases again.

On the upside, if an increase in aggregate demand creates an inflationary gap, the money wage rate rises and the price level also rises. Real GDP returns to potential GDP.

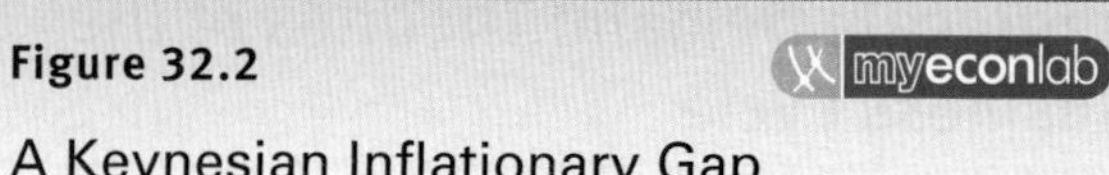

Figure 32.2

A Keynesian Inflationary Gap

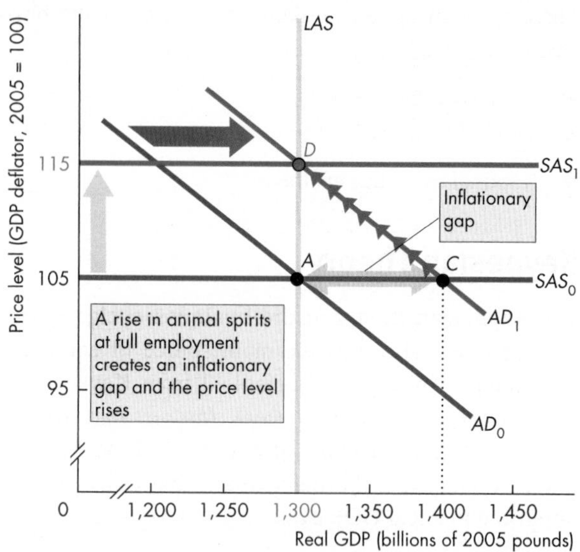

The economy is initially at full employment at point *A*. A Keynesian expansion begins when a rise in animal spirits increases investment. Aggregate demand increases and the *AD* curve shifts rightward from AD_0 to AD_1. With a fixed money wage rate, real GDP increases to £1,400 billion at point *C*.

The economy is now at above full employment and there is now an inflationary gap. The money wage rate rises and the *SAS* curve shifts from SAS_0 towards SAS_1. Real GDP decreases and the price level rises as the economy heads towards point *D*.

Monetarist Theory

The **monetarist theory of the business cycle** regards fluctuations in the quantity of money as the main source of economic fluctuations. This theory is distilled from the writings of Milton Friedman and several other economists. We'll explore the monetarist theory as we did the Keynesian theory, by looking first at its main impulse and second at the mechanism that creates a cycle in real GDP.

Monetarist Impulse

The impulse in the monetarist theory of the business cycle is the *growth rate of the quantity of money*. A speed-up in money growth brings expansion, and a slowdown in money growth brings recession. The source of the change in the growth rate of quantity of money is the monetary policy actions of the Bank of England.

Monetarist Cycle Mechanism

In the monetarist theory, once the Bank of England has changed the money growth rate, a cycle mechanism begins to operate which, like the Keynesian mechanism, first affects aggregate demand.

When the money growth rate increases, the quantity of real money in the economy increases. Interest rates fall. The foreign exchange rate also falls – the pound loses value on the foreign exchange market. These initial financial market effects begin to spill over into other markets.

Interest-sensitive expenditure, which includes investment and consumer spending on durable goods as well as exports increases. These initial increases in expenditure have a multiplier effect, just as investment has in the Keynesian theory. Through these mechanisms, a speed-up in the money growth rate shifts the aggregate demand curve rightward and brings an expansion.

Similarly, a slowdown in the money growth rate has the effects just described but in the opposite direction, which shifts the aggregate demand curve leftward to bring a recession.

The second element of the monetarist cycle mechanism is the response of aggregate supply to a change in aggregate demand. The short-run aggregate supply curve is upward-sloping. With an upward-sloping *SAS* curve, swings in aggregate demand translate into swings in both real GDP and the price level. But monetarists think that real GDP deviations from full employment are temporary in both directions.

In monetarist theory, the money wage rate is only *temporarily sticky*. When aggregate demand decreases and unemployment rises above its natural rate, the money wage rate eventually begins to fall. As the money wage rate falls, so does the price level. And after a period of adjustment, real GDP returns to potential GDP and the unemployment rate returns to the natural rate. When aggregate demand increases and unemployment falls below the natural rate, the money wage rate begins to rise. As the money wage rate rises so does the price level. And after a period of adjustment, real GDP returns to potential GDP and the unemployment rate returns to the natural rate.

Figure 32.3 illustrates the monetarist recession and recovery. The economy is initially at full employment (point *A*) on the long-run aggregate supply curve (*LAS*), the aggregate demand curve (AD_0), and the short-run aggregate supply curve (SAS_0). A slowdown in the money growth rate decreases aggregate demand and the aggregate demand curve shifts leftward to AD_1. Real GDP falls to £1,250 billion and the economy moves into recession (point *B*).

Unemployment increases and there is a surplus of labour. The money wage rate begins to fall. As the money wage rate falls, the short-run aggregate supply curve starts to shift rightward from SAS_0 to SAS_1. The price level falls and real GDP begins to expand as the economy moves to point *C*. Real GDP returns to potential GDP. Full employment is restored.

The monetarist business cycle is like a rocking horse. It needs an outside force to get it going but once going, it rocks to-and-fro (but just once). Starting from full employment, when the quantity of money decreases (or its growth rate slows), the economy cycles with a recession followed by expansion. And if the quantity of money increases (or its growth rate speeds) the economy also cycles but with an expansion followed by recession.

Figure 32.3

myeconlab

A Monetarist Recession

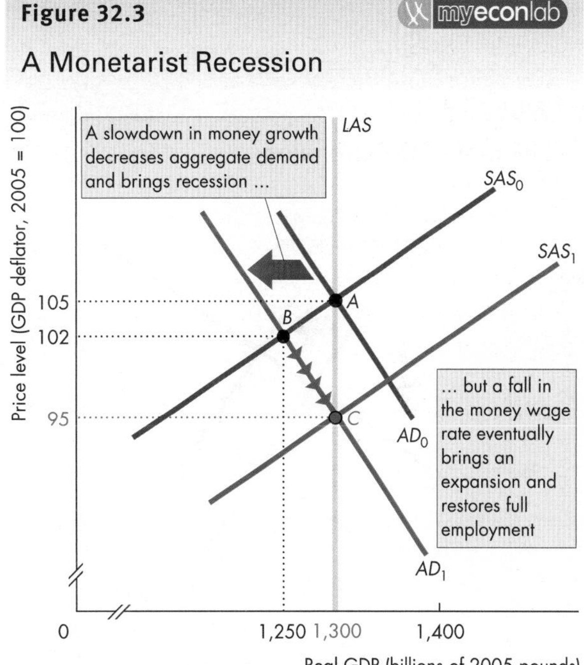

The economy is initially at full employment at point *A*. Real GDP is £1,300 billion and the price level is 105. A monetarist recession begins when a slowdown in the money growth rate decreases aggregate demand. The *AD* curve shifts leftward from AD_0 to AD_1. With a sticky money wage rate, real GDP decreases to £1,250 billion and the price level falls to 102 as the economy moves from point *A* to point *B*. With a surplus of labour, the money wage rate falls and the short-run aggregate supply curve shifts rightward from SAS_0 to SAS_1. The price level falls further and real GDP returns to potential GDP at point *C*.

Figure 32.4 shows the effects of this opposite case in which the growth rate of the quantity of money speeds up. Here, starting out at point *C*, when the growth rate of the quantity of money speeds up, aggregate demand increases and the *AD* curve shifts rightward to AD_2. Both real GDP and the price level increase as the economy moves to point *D*, where SAS_1 and AD_2 intersect.

With real GDP above potential GDP and unemployment below the natural rate, the money wage rate begins to rise. A rising money wage rate decreases short-run aggregate supply and the *SAS* curve starts to shift leftward towards SAS_2. The price level also rises and real GDP decreases. The economy moves from point *D* to point *E*, its new full-employment equilibrium.

Although monetarists think that the money wage rate will fall when real GDP is less than potential GDP – when there is a recessionary gap – they do not see this process as being a rapid one.

Figure 32.4

A Monetarist Expansion

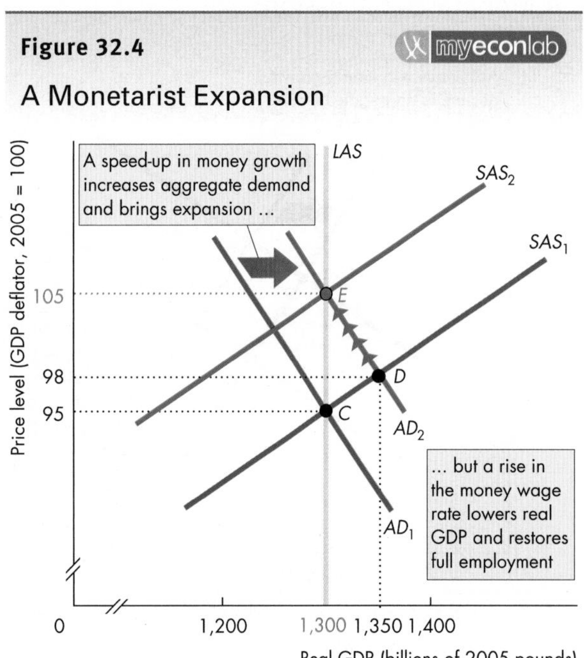

Starting at point *C*, a monetarist expansion begins when an increase in the money growth rate increases aggregate demand and shifts the *AD* curve rightward from AD_1 to AD_2. With a sticky money wage rate, real GDP increases to £1,350 billion, the price level rises to 98 and the economy moves to point *D*.

With a shortage of labour, the money wage rate rises and the *SAS* curve shifts towards SAS_2. The price level rises and real GDP decreases to potential GDP as the economy heads towards point *E*.

Rational Expectations Theories

A **rational expectation** is a forecast that is based on all the available relevant information. Rational expectations theories of the business cycle are theories based on the view that the money wage rate is determined by a rational expectation of the price level. Two distinctly different rational expectations theories of the business cycle have been proposed. A **new classical theory of the business cycle** regards *unanticipated* fluctuations in aggregate demand as the main source of economic fluctuations. This theory is based on the work of Robert E. Lucas Jr. and several other economists, including Thomas Sargent and Robert J. Barro. A different **new Keynesian theory of the business cycle** also regards *unanticipated* fluctuations in aggregate demand as the main source of economic fluctuations but it leaves room for *anticipated* fluctuations in aggregate demand to play a role. We'll explore these theories as we did the Keynesian and monetarist theories, by looking first at the main impulse and second at the cycle mechanism.

Rational Expectations Impulse

The impulse that distinguishes the rational expectations theories from the other aggregate demand theories of the business cycle is the *unanticipated change in aggregate demand*. A larger than anticipated increase in aggregate demand brings an expansion, and a smaller than anticipated increase in aggregate demand brings a recession. Any factor that influences aggregate demand – for example, fiscal policy, monetary policy or developments in the world economy that influence exports – whose change is not anticipated, can bring a change in real GDP.

Rational Expectations Cycle Mechanisms

To describe the rational expectations cycle mechanisms, we'll deal first with the new classical version. When aggregate demand decreases, if the money wage rate doesn't change, real GDP and the price level both decrease. The fall in the price level increases the *real* wage rate. Employment decreases and unemployment increases. In the new classical theory, these events occur only if the decrease in aggregate demand is not anticipated. If the decrease in aggregate demand *is* anticipated, the price level is expected to fall and both firms and workers will agree to a lower money wage rate. By doing so, they can prevent the real wage from rising and avoid an increase in the unemployment rate.

Similarly, if firms and workers anticipate an increase in aggregate demand, they expect the price level to rise and will agree to a higher money wage rate. By doing so, they can prevent the real wage from falling and avoid a fall in the unemployment rate below the natural rate.

Only fluctuations in aggregate demand that are unanticipated and not taken into account in wage contracts bring changes in real GDP. *Anticipated* changes in aggregate demand change the price level, but they leave real GDP and unemployment unchanged and do not create a business cycle.

New Keynesian economists, like new classical economists, think that the money wage rate is influenced by rational expectations of the price level. But new Keynesians emphasize the long-term nature of most wage contracts. They say that *today's* money wage rate is influenced by *yesterday's* rational expectations. These expectations, which were formed in the past, are based on old information that might now be known to be incorrect. After they have made a long-term wage agreement, both firms and workers might anticipate a change in aggregate demand, which they expect will change the price level. But because they are locked into their agreement, they are unable to change the money wage rate. So the money wage rate is sticky in the new Keynesian theory, and with a sticky money wage rate even an *anticipated* change in aggregate demand changes real GDP.

New classical economists say that long-term contracts are renegotiated when conditions change to make them outdated. So they do not regard long-term contracts as an obstacle to money wage flexibility, provided both parties to an agreement recognize the changed conditions. If both firms and workers expect the price level to change, they will change the agreed money wage rate to reflect that shared expectation. In this situation, anticipated changes in aggregate demand change the money wage rate and the price level and leave real GDP unchanged.

The distinctive feature of both versions of the rational expectations theory of the business cycle is the role of *unanticipated* changes in aggregate demand. Figure 32.5 illustrates their effect on real GDP and the price level.

Potential GDP is £1,300 billion and the long-run aggregate supply curve is *LAS*. Aggregate demand is expected to be *EAD*. Given potential GDP and *EAD*, the money wage rate is set at the level that is expected to bring full employment. At this money wage rate, the short-run aggregate supply curve is *SAS*.

Imagine that, initially, aggregate demand equals expected aggregate demand, so there is full employment. In Figure 32.5, real GDP is £1,300 billion and the price level is 105. The economy is at point *A*.

Then, unexpectedly, aggregate demand turns out to be less than expected and the aggregate demand curve shifts leftward to AD_0. Many different aggregate demand shocks, such as a slowdown in the money growth rate or a collapse of exports, could have caused this shift. A recession begins. But aggregate demand is expected to be at *EAD*, so the money wage rate doesn't change and the short-run aggregate supply curve remains at *SAS*. Real GDP decreases to £1,250 billion and the price level falls to 102. The economy moves to point *B*. Unemployment increases and there is surplus of labour.

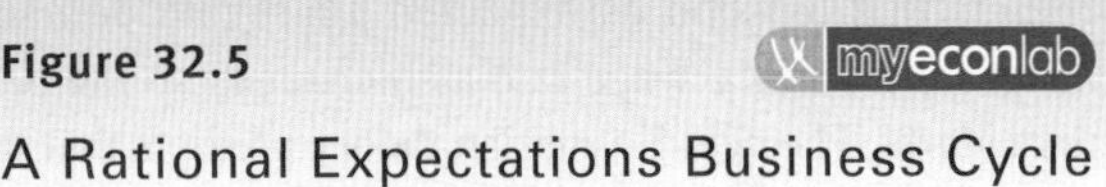

Figure 32.5

A Rational Expectations Business Cycle

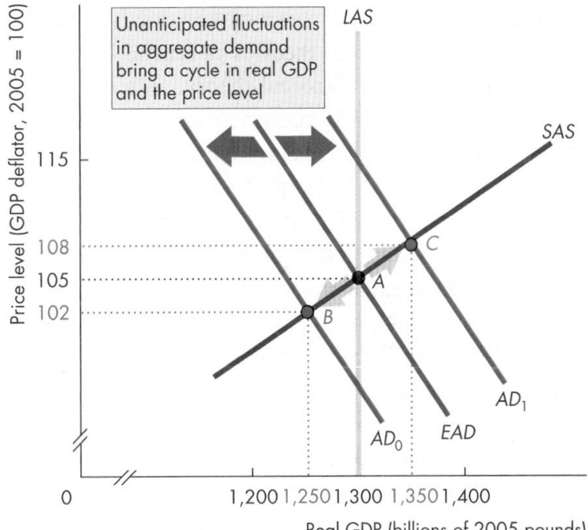

The economy is expected to be at point *A* at the intersection of the *expected* aggregate demand curve, *EAD*, the short-run aggregate supply curve, *SAS*, and the long-run aggregate supply curve, *LAS*. As long as aggregate demand is expected to be *EAD*, there is no change in the money wage rate and the *SAS* curve does not shift. A rational expectations recession begins when an unanticipated decrease in aggregate demand shifts the *AD* curve leftward to AD_0. Real GDP decreases to £1,250 billion and the price level falls to 102 as the economy moves to point *B*. A rational expectations expansion begins when an unanticipated increase in aggregate demand shifts the *AD* curve rightward to AD_1. Real GDP increases to £1,350 billion and the price level rises to 108 as the economy moves to point *C*.

A shock that takes aggregate demand to a level that exceeds *EAD* brings an expansion. The aggregate demand curve shifts rightward to AD_1. A speed-up in the money growth rate or an export boom might have increased aggregate demand. But aggregate demand is expected to be at *EAD*, so the money wage rate doesn't change and the short-run aggregate supply curve remains at *SAS*. Real GDP increases to £1,350 billion and the price level rises to 108. The economy moves to point *C*. Unemployment is below the natural rate.

Fluctuations in aggregate demand between AD_0 and AD_1 around expected aggregate demand *EAD* bring fluctuations in real GDP and the price level between points *B* and *C*.

The two versions of the rational expectations theory differ in their predictions about the effects of a change in expected aggregate demand. The new classical theory predicts that as soon as expected aggregate demand changes, the money wage rate also changes so the *SAS* curve shifts. The new Keynesian theory predicts that the money wage rate changes gradually when new contracts are made so that the *SAS* curve moves slowly. This difference between the two theories is crucial for policy. According to the new classical theory, anticipated policy actions change only the price level and have no effect on real GDP and unemployment. The reason is that when policy is expected to change, the money wage rate changes so the *SAS* curve shifts and offsets the effects of the policy action on real GDP. In contrast, in the new Keynesian theory, because money wages change only when new contracts are made, even anticipated policy actions change real GDP and can be used in an attempt to stabilize the cycle.

Like the monetarist business cycle, these rational expectations cycles are similar to rocking horses. They need an outside force to get going, but once going the economy rocks around its full-employment point. The new classical horse rocks faster and comes to rest more quickly than the new Keynesian horse.

AS–AD General Theory

All the theories of the business cycle that we've considered can be viewed as particular cases of a more general *AS–AD* theory. In this more general theory, the impulses of both the Keynesian and monetarist theories can change aggregate demand. A multiplier effect makes aggregate demand change by more than any initial change in one of its components. The money wage rate can be viewed as responding to changes in the rational expectation of the future price level. Even if the money wage rate is flexible, it will change only to the extent that price level expectations change. As a result, the money wage rate will adjust gradually.

Although in all three types of business cycle theory that we've considered, the cycle is caused by fluctuations in aggregate demand, the possibility that an occasional aggregate supply shock might occur is not ruled out by the aggregate demand theories.

A recession could occur because aggregate supply decreases. For example, a widespread drought that cuts agricultural production could cause a recession in an economy that has a large agricultural sector. But these aggregate demand theories of the business cycle regard supply shocks as rare rather than normal events. Aggregate demand fluctuations are the normal ongoing sources of fluctuations.

Review Quiz

Study Plan 32.2

1 What, according to Keynesian theory, is the main business cycle impulse?
2 What, according to Keynesian theory, are the main business cycle mechanisms? Describe the roles of *animal spirits*, the multiplier and a sticky money wage rate in this theory.
3 What, according to monetarist theory, is the main business cycle impulse?
4 What, according to monetarist theory, are the business cycle mechanisms? Describe the roles of the Bank of England and the quantity of money in this theory.
5 What, according to new classical theory and new Keynesian theory, causes the business cycle? What are the roles of rational expectations and unanticipated fluctuations in aggregate demand in these theories?
6 What are the differences between the new classical theory and the new Keynesian theory concerning the money wage rate over the business cycle?

For all their differences, the theories of the business cycle that we've just reviewed all have at their core aggregate demand fluctuations and a sticky money wage rate. A new theory of the business cycle challenges these mainstream and traditional aggregate demand theories that you've just studied. It is called the real business cycle theory. Let's take a look at this new theory of the business cycle.

Real Business Cycle Theory

The newest theory of the business cycle, known as **real business cycle theory** (or RBC theory), is that random fluctuations in the growth rate of productivity are the main source of the aggregate economic fluctuations. Further, most of the the fluctuations in the productivity growth rate result from fluctuations in the pace of technological change and the rate of human capital growth. Other potential sources of changes in the productivity growth rate are international disturbances, climate fluctuations and natural disasters.

The origins of real business cycle theory can be traced to the rational expectations revolution set off by Robert E. Lucas Jr., but the first demonstration of the power of this theory was given by two other Nobel Prize winners, Edward Prescott and Finn Kydland. Today, real business cycle theory is part of a research agenda called *dynamic general equilibrium analysis* and hundreds of young macroeconomists do research on this topic.

Like our study of the aggregate demand theories, we'll explore the RBC theory by looking first at its impulse and second at the mechanism that converts that impulse into a cycle in real GDP.

The RBC Impulse

The impulse in the RBC theory is the *growth rate of productivity that results from technological change.* Real business cycle theorists believe this impulse to be generated mainly by the process of research and development that leads to the creation and use of new technologies.

Most of the time, technological progress is steady and productivity grows at a moderate pace. But sometimes productivity growth speeds up and, occasionally, productivity *decreases* – labour becomes less productive, on average.

A period of rapid productivity growth brings a strong business cycle expansion, and a *decrease* in productivity triggers a recession.

It is easy to understand why technological change brings productivity growth. But how does it *decrease* productivity? All technological change eventually increases productivity. But if initially technological change makes a sufficient amount of existing capital (especially human capital) obsolete, productivity temporarily decreases. At such a time, more jobs are destroyed than are created and more businesses fail than start up.

To isolate the RBC theory impulse, economists use growth accounting (see Chapter 31, pp. 726–727) and

Figure 32.6

myeconlab

The Real Business Cycle Impulse

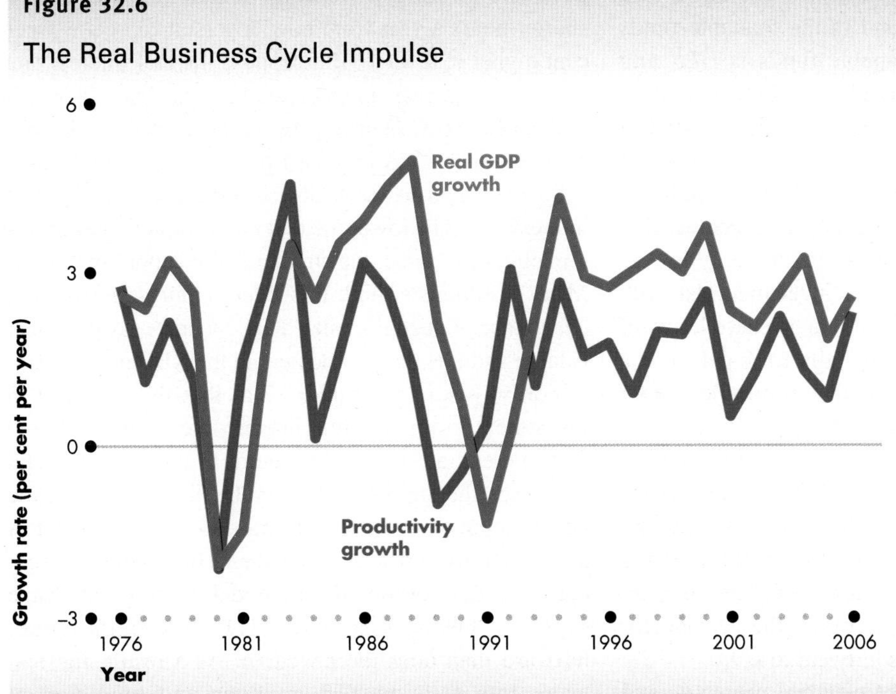

The real business cycle impulse is fluctuations in the growth rate of productivity that are caused by changes in technology. The fluctuations in productivity growth shown here are calculated by using growth accounting (the one-third rule) to remove the contribution of capital accumulation to productivity growth. Productivity fluctuations are correlated with real GDP fluctuations. Economists are not sure what the productivity variable actually measures or what causes it to fluctuate.

Sources of data: Office for National Statistics; and the authors' calculations.

Figure 32.6 shows the RBC impulse for the United Kingdom from 1976 to 2006. This figure also shows that productivity growth and real GDP fluctuations are correlated. But correlation doesn't imply causation and controversy surrounds what the RBC impulse variable actually measures.

The RBC Mechanism

Two immediate effects follow a change in productivity that get an expansion or a contraction going. They are:

1 Investment demand changes
2 Demand for labour changes

We'll study these effects and their consequences during a recession. In an expansion, they work in the opposite direction to what is described here.

Technological change makes some existing capital obsolete and temporarily decreases productivity. Firms expect their future profit rate to fall and labour productivity to fall. With lower profit expectations, firms cut back their purchases of new capital, and with lower labour productivity they plan to lay off some workers. So the initial effect of a temporary fall in productivity is a decrease in investment demand and a decrease in the demand for labour.

Figure 32.7 illustrates these two initial effects of a decrease in productivity. Part (a) shows the effect of a decrease in investment demand in the loanable funds market. The demand for loanable funds is *DLF* and the supply of loanable funds is *SLF* (both of which are explained in Chapter 24, pp. 544–548). Initially, the demand for loanable funds is DLF_0, the supply of loanable funds is *SLF*, and the equilibrium quantity of loanable funds is £150 billion at a real interest rate of 6 per cent a year. A decrease in productivity lowers the expected profit rate, decreases investment demand, and shifts the demand for loanable funds curve leftward to DLF_1. The real interest rate falls to 4 per cent a year, and the quantity of loanable funds decreases to £120 billion.

Part (b) shows the demand for labour and the supply of labour (which are explained in Chapter 24, pp. 536–539). Initially, the demand for labour curve is LD_0, the supply of labour curve is LS_0 and employment is 50 billion hours a year at a real wage rate of £17.50 an hour. The decrease in productivity decreases the demand for labour and the *LD* curve shifts leftward to LD_1.

Before we can determine the new real wage rate and employment, we need to take a ripple effect into account – the key ripple effect in RBC theory.

The Key Decision: When to Work?

According to the RBC theory, people decide *when* to work by doing a cost–benefit calculation. They compare the return from working in the current period with the *expected* return from working in a later period. You make such a comparison every day at university. Suppose your goal in this course is to get a first. To achieve this goal, you work pretty hard most of the time. But during the few days before the mid-term and final exams, you work especially hard. Why? Because you think the return from studying close to the exam is greater than the return from studying when the exam is a long time away. So during the term you hang around the Students' Union bar, go to parties, play squash and enjoy other leisure pursuits, but at exam time you work every evening and weekend.

Real business cycle theory says that workers behave like you. They work fewer hours, and sometimes zero hours, when the real wage rate is temporarily low and they work more hours when the real wage rate is temporarily high. But to compare the current wage rate with the expected future wage rate, workers must use the real interest rate. If the real interest rate is 6 per cent a year, a real wage rate of £1 an hour earned this week will become £1.06 a year from now. If the real wage rate is expected to be £1.05 an hour next year, today's wage of £1 looks good. By working longer hours now and shorter hours a year from now, a person can get a 1 per cent higher real wage. But suppose the real interest rate is 4 per cent a year. In this case, £1 earned now is worth £1.04 next year. Working fewer hours now and more next year is the way to get a 1 per cent higher real wage.

So the when-to-work decision depends on the real interest rate. The lower the real interest rate, other things remaining the same, the smaller is the supply of labour. Many economists think this *intertemporal substitution effect* to be of negligible size. RBC theorists say the effect is large and it is the key element in the RBC mechanism.

You've seen in Figure 32.7(a) that the decrease in investment lowers the real interest rate. This fall in the real interest rate lowers the return to current work and decreases the supply of labour. In Figure 32.7(b), the labour supply curve shifts leftward to LS_1. The effect of a productivity shock on the demand for labour is larger than the effect of the fall in the real interest rate on the supply of labour. That is, the *LD* curve shifts further leftward than does the *LS* curve. As a result, the real wage rate falls to £17 an hour and employment decreases to 49 billion hours. A recession has begun and is intensifying.

Figure 32.7

myeconlab

The Loanable Funds and Labour Markets in a Real Business Cycle

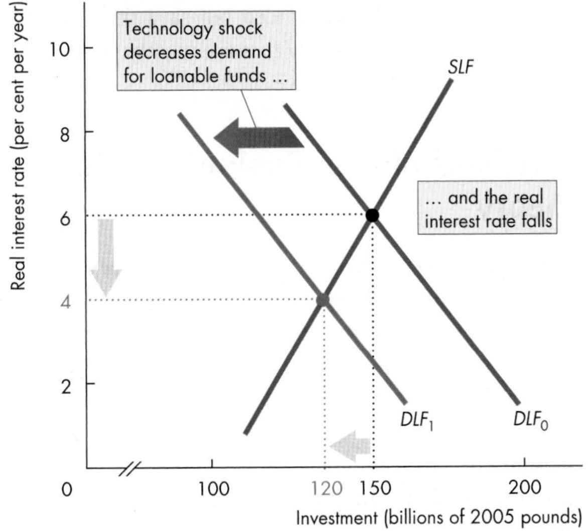

(a) Loanable funds and interest rate

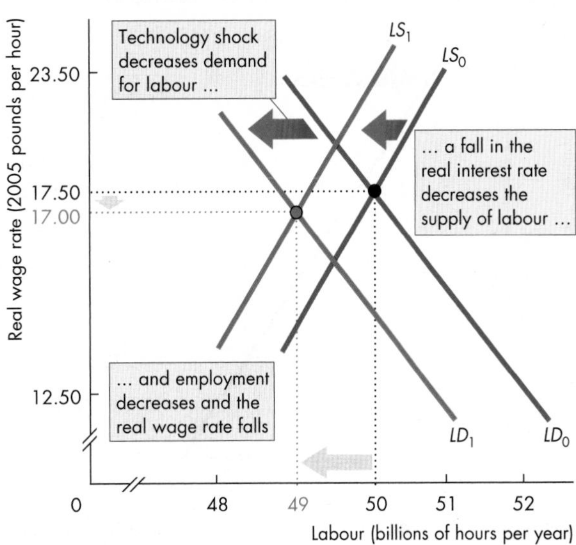

(b) Labour and wage rate

In part (a), the supply of loanable funds *SLF* and initial demand for loanable funds DLF_0 determine the real interest rate at 6 per cent a year. In part (b), the initial demand for labour, LD_0 and supply of labour, LS_0, determine the real wage rate at £17.50 an hour and employment at 50 billion hours a year.

A technological change temporarily decreases productivity, which decreases both the demand for loanable funds and the demand for labour. The demand curves shift leftward to DLF_1 and LD_1 respectively.

In part (a), the real interest rate falls to 4 per cent a year. In part (b), the fall in the real interest rate decreases the supply of labour (the when-to-work decision) and the supply curve shifts leftward to LS_1. Employment decreases to 49 billion hours, and the real wage rate falls to £17 an hour. A recession is under way.

Real GDP and the Price Level

The next part of the RBC story traces the consequences of the changes you've just seen for real GDP and the price level. With a decrease in employment, aggregate supply decreases; and with a decrease in investment demand, aggregate demand decreases. Figure 32.8 illustrates these effects, using the *AS–AD* framework. Initially, the aggregate demand curve is AD_0 and the long-run aggregate supply curve is LAS_0. The price level is 105 and real GDP is £1,300 billion. There is no short-run aggregate supply curve in this figure because in the RBC theory, the *SAS* curve has no meaning. The labour market moves relentlessly towards its equilibrium, and the money wage rate adjusts freely (either increases or decreases) to ensure that the real wage rate keeps the quantity of labour demanded equal to the quantity supplied. In RBC theory, unemployment is always at the natural rate, and the natural rate fluctuates over the business cycle because the amount of job search fluctuates.

The decrease in employment decreases total production and aggregate supply decreases. The *LAS* curve shifts leftward to LAS_1. The decrease in investment demand decreases aggregate demand and the *AD* curve shifts leftward to AD_1. The price level falls to 102, and real GDP decreases to £1,250 billion. The economy has gone through a recession.

What Happened to Money?

The name *real* business cycle theory is no accident. It reflects the central prediction of the theory: real things, not nominal or monetary things, cause the business cycle. If the quantity of money changes, aggregate demand changes. But if there is no real change – no change in the productivity or use of the factors of

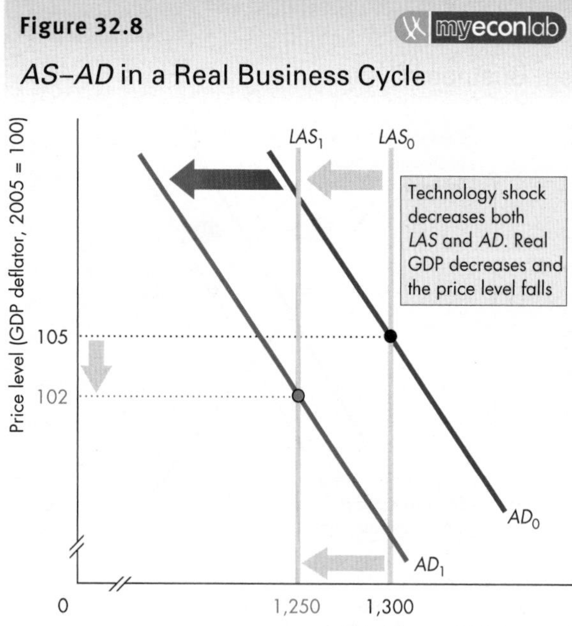

Figure 32.8

AS–AD in a Real Business Cycle

Initially, the long-run aggregate supply curve is LAS_0 and the aggregate demand curve is AD_0. Real GDP is £1,300 billion (which equals potential GDP) and the price level is 105. There is no *SAS* curve in the real business cycle theory because the money wage rate is flexible. The technological change described in Figure 32.7 temporarily decreases potential GDP and the *LAS* curve shifts leftward to LAS_1. The decrease in investment decreases aggregate demand and the *AD* curve shifts leftward to AD_1. Real GDP decreases to £1,250 billion and the price level falls to 102. The economy has gone into recession.

production, there is no change in potential GDP and the change in the quantity of money changes only the price level. In real business cycle theory, this outcome occurs because the aggregate supply curve is the *LAS* curve, which pins real GDP down at potential GDP.

According to real business cycle theory, correlation between money growth and real GDP arises from a reverse causation. A more rapid real expansion brings a faster growth rate of the quantity of money, and a slowdown in the real growth rate slows the growth rate of the quantity of money. We describe this reverse causation mechanism below.

Cycles and Growth

The shock that drives the business cycle of the RBC theory is the same as the force that generates economic growth: technological change. On average, as technology advances, productivity grows. But it grows at an uneven pace. You saw this fact when you studied growth accounting in Chapter 31. There, we focused on slow-changing trends in productivity growth. Real business cycle theory uses the same idea but says there are frequent shocks to productivity that are mostly positive but that are occasionally negative.

Criticisms of Real Business Cycle Theory

RBC theory is controversial and when economists discuss it they often generate more heat than light. Its detractors claim that its basic assumptions are just too incredible. Money wage rate *is* sticky, they claim, so to assume otherwise is at odds with a clear fact. Intertemporal substitution is too weak, they say, to account for large fluctuations in the supply of labour and employment with small changes in the real wage rate.

But what really kills the RBC story, say most economists, is an implausible impulse. Technology shocks are not capable of creating the swings in productivity that growth accounting reveals. These shocks are caused by something, they concede, but they are as likely to be caused by *changes in aggregate demand* as they are by technology. If fluctuations in productivity are caused by aggregate demand fluctuations, then the traditional aggregate demand theories are needed to explain these shocks. Fluctuations in productivity do not cause the business cycle but are caused by it!

Building on this theme, the critics point out that the so-called productivity fluctuations that growth accounting measures are correlated with changes in the growth rate of money and other indicators of changes in aggregate demand.

Defence of Real Business Cycle Theory

The defenders of RBC theory claim that the theory works. It explains the macroeconomic facts about the business cycle and is consistent with the facts about economic growth. In effect, a single theory explains *both economic growth and business cycles*. The growth accounting exercise that explains slowly changing trends also explains the more frequent business cycle swings. Its defenders also claim that RBC theory is consistent with a wide range of *microeconomic* evidence about labour supply decisions, labour demand and investment demand decisions, and information on the distribution of income between labour and capital.

RBC theorists acknowledge that money growth and the business cycle are correlated. That is, rapid money growth and expansion go together, and slow money growth and recession go together. But, they argue, causation does not run from money to real GDP as the traditional aggregate demand theories state. Instead, RBC theorists view causation as running from real GDP to money – so-called reverse causation. In a recession, the initial decrease in investment demand that lowers the real interest rate decreases the demand for bank loans and lowers the profitability of banking. So banks increase their reserves and decrease their loans. The quantity of bank deposits and hence the quantity of money decreases. This reverse causation is responsible for the correlation between money growth and real GDP according to real business cycle theory.

Defenders of real business cycle theory also argue that the RBC view is significant because it at least raises the possibility that the business cycle is efficient. The business cycle does not signal an economy that is misbehaving; it is business as usual. If this view is correct, it means that policy to smooth the cycle is misguided. Only by taking out the peaks can the troughs be smoothed out. But peaks are bursts of investment to take advantage of new technologies in a timely way. So smoothing the business cycle means delaying the benefits of new technologies.

Review Quiz

Study Plan 32.3

1 According to real business cycle theory, what causes the business cycle? What is the role of fluctuations in the rate of technological change?
2 According to real business cycle theory, how does a fall in productivity growth influence investment demand, the real interest rate, the demand for labour, the supply of labour, employment and the real wage rate?
3 According to real business cycle theory, how does a fall in productivity growth influence long-run aggregate supply, aggregate demand, real GDP and the price level?

You've now reviewed the main theories of the business cycle. Your next task is to examine some actual business cycles. In pursuing this task, we will focus on the recession phase of the business cycle. We begin by looking at the 1990–1992 recession in the United Kingdom.

The 1990–1992 Recession

In the theories of the business cycle that you've studied, recessions can be triggered by a variety of forces, some on the aggregate demand side and some on the aggregate supply side. Let's identify the shocks that triggered the 1990–1992 recession.

The Origins of the 1990–1992 Recession

Three forces were at work in United Kingdom during the early 1990s that contributed to the recession and subsequent slow growth. They were:

- Bank of England's monetary policy
- German reunification
- A slowdown in the world economy

Bank of England's Monetary Policy

The Bank of England pursued an anti-inflationary monetary policy during the early 1990s that decreased aggregate demand and contributed to the start of a recession. This anti-inflationary monetary policy was a direct consequence of the United Kingdom joining the Exchange Rate Mechanism (ERM) of the European Monetary System (EMS).

The United Kingdom joined the ERM in October 1990. The ERM is a monetary system based on pegged exchange rates. If a central bank pegs its exchange rate, it stands ready to buy its currency on the foreign exchange market when market forces push the exchange rate downward. And it stands ready to sell its currency when market forces push the exchange rate upward.[1]

Under the ERM arrangements of 1990, the exchange rate for the pound was set at 2.95 Deutschmarks (plus or minus a permitted spread around that value). To remain in the ERM, the Bank of England was required to take actions that prevented the exchange rate of the pound from moving outside the agreed range.

When the United Kingdom entered the ERM, the UK inflation rate was 10 per cent a year, which was much higher than the EU average. So the Bank of England was facing a one-way bet. It was clear to everyone that the Bank of England would have a hard time preventing the pound from falling. So speculators sold pounds and bought other currencies.

[1] You can learn more about the exchange rate in Chapter 33.

To try to convince speculators to keep holding pounds, the Bank of England increased the interest rate to a level higher than that in the rest of Europe. But the more the Bank of England resisted currency speculators by keeping the interest rate high, the stronger became the belief that devaluation could not be avoided. A game between the Bank of England and the currency speculators ensued. Like a game of "chicken", someone has to give way and be the chicken. In September 1992, the United Kingdom became the chicken and left the ERM. But by then, a lot of damage had been done.

The high interest rate lowered investment and expenditure on consumer durable goods. And with the exchange rate fixed, UK-made goods and services became increasingly more expensive in other EU countries. UK exports to other EU countries decreased. Also, other EU-made goods and services become increasingly cheaper in the United Kingdom and UK imports increased. All these changes in expenditure decreased aggregate demand in the United Kingdom.

Figure 32.9 shows the slowdown in the money growth rate and the consequences for real GDP growth.

Figure 32.9 myeconlab

M4 and Real GDP Growth: 1990–1992

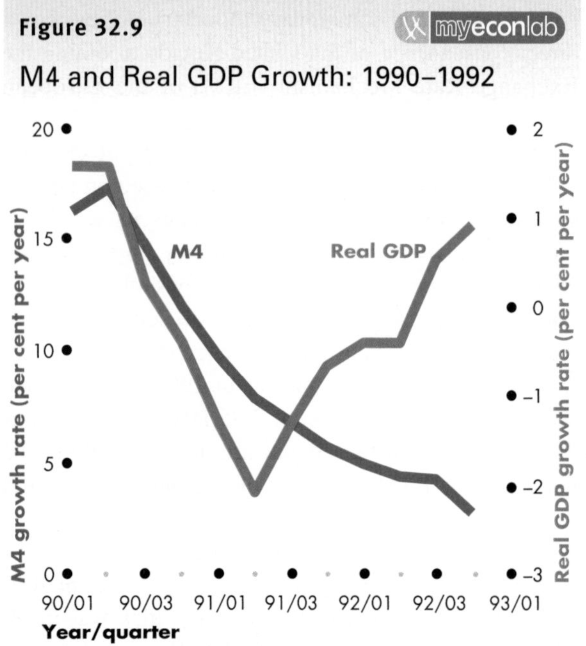

The UK entry into the ERM meant that the Bank of England had to pursue a contractionary monetary policy. The money growth rate began to slow during 1989. It slowed even further during 1990. A sharp slowdown in the money growth rate contributed to the decrease in real GDP.

Source of data: Bank of England and Office for National Statistics.

German Reunification

In November 1989, the Berlin Wall came down and in October 1990, East Germany reunited with West Germany. The cost of the reunification was large and the German government's budget went into deficit. From being a net lender in the world capital market, the new Germany began its life as a net borrower. Afraid that this budget deficit would increase the money growth rate and fuel inflation, the German central bank raised interest rates. With the Deutschmark as the anchor currency for the ERM (which means that all the other currencies in the ERM were linked to it), the rise in German interest rates meant that other members of the ERM had to raise their interest rates to maintain their fixed exchange rates. The rise in interest rates contributed to the slowdown in UK aggregate demand.

A Slowdown in the World Economy

After its longest ever period of peacetime expansion, US real GDP growth began to slow in 1989 and 1990 and the United States went into recession in mid-1990. The slowdown of the US economy brought slower growth in the US demand for the rest of the world's exports, which resulted in lower export prices and smaller export volumes. The world economic activity began to slow down.

Let's see how the events we've just described influenced the UK economy in 1991.

AS–AD in the 1990–1992 Recession

Figure 32.10 describes the effects of the various events that triggered the 1990–1992 recession. In 1990, the aggregate demand curve was AD_{90} and the short-run aggregate supply curve was SAS_{90}. Real GDP was £855 billion and the price level was 65.

The 1990–1992 recession was caused by a decrease in both aggregate demand and aggregate supply. Aggregate demand decreased initially because of the high real interest rate, the overvalued exchange rate and the slowdown in the money growth rate. These factors were soon reinforced by the slowdown in the world economy that brought a further decline in the growth of exports. The combination of these factors triggered a massive decline in investment. The resulting decrease in aggregate demand is shown in Figure 32.11 by the shift of the aggregate demand curve leftward to AD_{91}. Aggregate supply decreased because the money wage rate continued to increase throughout 1990 at a rate similar to that in 1989. This decrease in aggregate supply

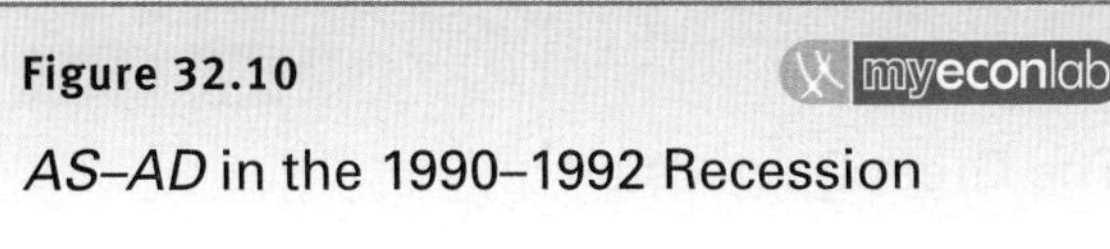

Figure 32.10

AS–AD in the 1990–1992 Recession

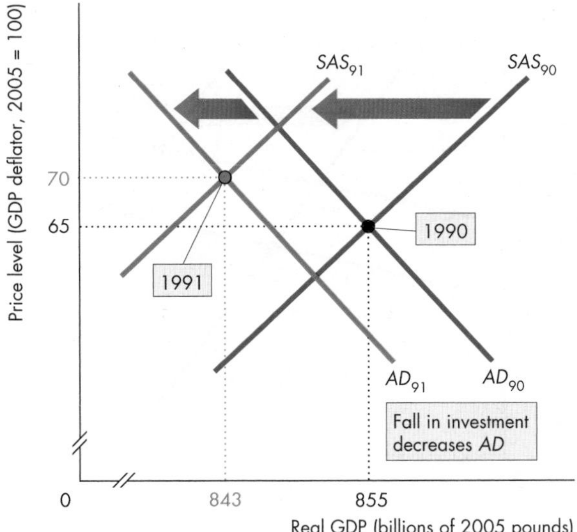

At the end of 1990, the economy was on its aggregate demand curve, AD_{90}, and its short-run aggregate supply curve, SAS_{90}, with real GDP at £855 billion and a GDP deflator of 65. The combination of a decrease in both aggregate supply and aggregate demand put the economy into recession. Real GDP decreased to £843 billion and the price level increased to 70.

Figure 32.11 myeconlab

The Labour Market in 1990–1992

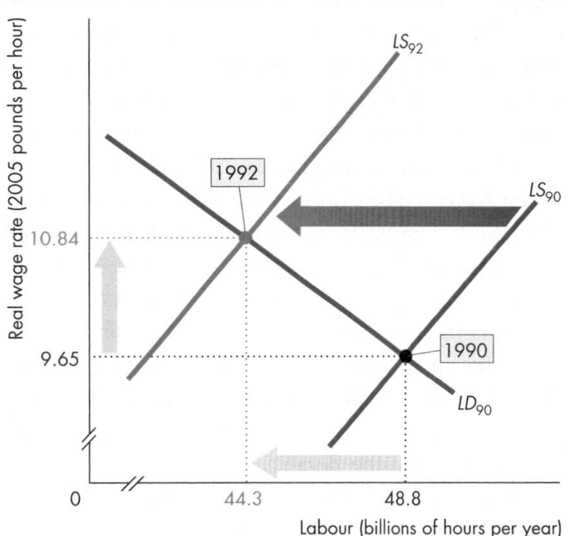

In 1990, the demand for labour was LD_{90} and the supply of labour was LS_{90}. The real wage was £9.65 an hour and employment was 48.8 billion of hours. The money wage rate continued to rise in 1991 and 1992 because people did not anticipate the fall in inflation and the *LS* curve shifted leftward to LS_{92}. The real wage rose to £10.84 an hour and employment decreased to 44.3 billion hours.

shifted the short-run aggregate supply curve leftward to SAS_{91}. (The figure does not show the long-run aggregate supply curve.)

The combined effect of the decreases in aggregate supply and aggregate demand was a decrease in real GDP to £843 billion – a 1.3 per cent decrease – and a rise in the price level to 70 – a 7.7 per cent increase.

You've seen how aggregate demand and aggregate supply changed during the 1990–1992 recession. What happened in the labour market during this recession?

The Labour Market in the 1990–1992 Recession

Figure 32.11 shows employment and the real wage rate during this period. As employment decreased in 1990, 1991 and 1992, the real wage rate increased. The money wage rate rose because people did not anticipate the slowdown in inflation. When inflation did slow down, the real wage rate increased and the quantity of labour demanded decreased.

As the expansion began in mid-1993, the demand for labour began to increase. Employment increased and the real wage rate decreased. These movements in employment and the real wage rate suggest that the forces of supply and demand do not operate smoothly in the labour market.

Review Quiz

Study Plan 32.4

1. What events triggered the 1990–1992 recession in the United Kingdom?
2. What role did external factors play and what role did UK policy play in the 1990–1992 recession?
3. What mechanisms translated the shocks into a recession?

You've seen how business cycle theory can be used to interpret the 1990–1992 recession. We'll now use business cycle theory to explain the Great Depression that engulfed the global economy during the 1930s.

The Great Depression

The late 1920s were years of economic revival in some parts of the UK economy. While the traditional industries such as coal and shipbuilding stagnated, others such as motor manufacturing were booming. New firms were created, and the capital stock of the nation expanded. At the beginning of 1929, real GDP in the United Kingdom nearly equalled potential GDP.

But as that eventful year unfolded, increasing signs of economic weakness began to appear. The most dramatic events occurred in October when the US stock market collapsed. Shares lost more than one-third of their value in two weeks. The four years that followed were years of monstrous economic depression across the world.

We'll describe the depression by using the *AS–AD* model and identify the forces that made aggregate demand and aggregate supply change.

Figure 32.12 shows the dimensions of the Great Depression. On the eve of the Great Depression in 1929, the economy was on aggregate demand curve AD_{29} and short-run aggregate supply curve SAS_{29}. Real GDP was £203 billion (2005 pounds) and the price level was 2.3 (GDP deflator, 2005 = 100).

In 1931, there was a widespread expectation that the price level would fall and the money wage rate fell. With a lower money wage rate, the short-run aggregate supply curve shifted from SAS_{29} to SAS_{31}. But increased pessimism and uncertainty decreased investment, the demand for consumer durables and international trade. Aggregate demand decreased to AD_{31}. In 1931, real GDP decreased to £191 billion and the price level fell to 2.2.

Although the Great Depression brought enormous hardship, the distribution of that hardship was uneven. At its worst point, 16 per cent of the workforce had no jobs at all. Although there were unemployment benefits and other forms of poor relief, there was a considerable level of poverty for those on the dole. But the wallets of those who kept their jobs barely noticed the Great Depression. It is true that wage rates fell. But at the same time, the price level fell by more, so real wage rates actually rose. So those who had jobs were paid a wage rate that had an increasing buying power during the Great Depression.

You can begin to appreciate the magnitude of the Great Depression if you compare it with the 1990–1992 recession. In 1991, real GDP decreased by 1.4 per cent, whereas in 1931, real GDP decreased by 5.2 per cent.

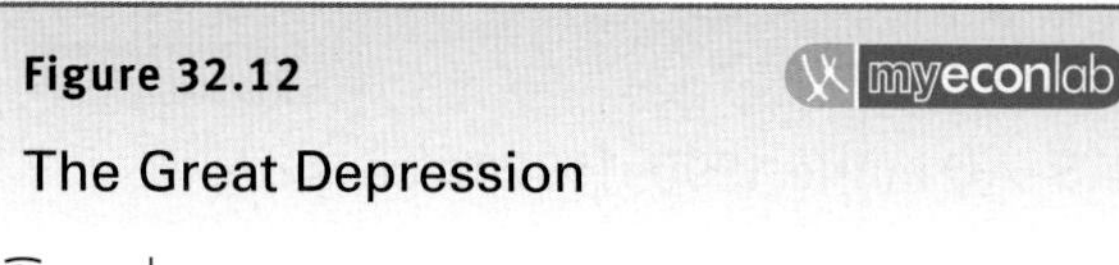

Figure 32.12

The Great Depression

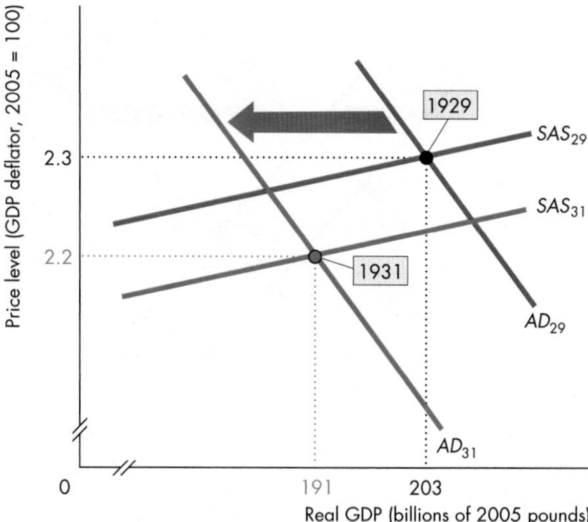

In 1929, real GDP was £203 billion and the GDP deflator was 2.3 – at the intersection of AD_{29} and SAS_{29}. Increased pessimism from a fall in world trade resulted in a drop in investment, resulting in a decrease in aggregate demand to AD_{31}. To some degree, this decrease was reflected in the labour market and the money wage rate fell, so the short-run aggregate supply curve shifted to SAS_{31}. Real GDP and the price level fell. By 1931, real GDP had fallen to £191 billion (94 per cent of its 1929 level) and the GDP deflator had fallen to 2.2 (96 per cent of its 1929 level).

Why the Great Depression Happened

The late 1920s were years of economic expansion in the world economy, but they were also years of increasing uncertainty. The main source of increased uncertainty was international. The world economy was going through tumultuous times. The patterns of world trade were changing as the United Kingdom began its period of relative economic decline and new economic powers such as Japan began to emerge. International currency fluctuations and the introduction of restrictive trade policies by many countries (see Chapter 7) further increased the uncertainty faced by firms. There was also domestic uncertainty arising from the restrictive monetary and fiscal policies followed by the government to ensure that the pound remained on the gold standard. Because prices in the United States fell, prices in the United Kingdom had to fall to maintain an exchange rate of £4.86 per pound and remain on the gold standard. So the UK expansion was good but not booming as in the United States.

In 1929, the stock market crashed and the slowdown in the world economy that followed fuelled the environment of uncertainty. It was this slowdown in the world economy which led to a drop in exports, which in turn led to a fall in income, consumer spending and investment and to the initial leftward shift of the aggregate demand curve from AD_{29} to AD_{31} in Figure 32.12.

Can It Happen Again?

We cannot be sure about anything in economics, but some features of our economy today make a Great Depression less likely. They are:

- Bank of England's role as lender of last resort
- Taxes and government spending
- Multi-income families

Bank of England's Role as Lender of Last Resort

If a bank is short of reserves, it can borrow reserves from other banks. If the entire banking system is short of reserves, banks in the United Kingdom can borrow from the Bank of England. By making reserves available (at a suitable interest rate), the Bank of England is able to make the quantity of reserves in the banking system respond flexibly to the demand for those reserves and widespread bank failures of the type that occurred in the Great Depression can be prevented.

Taxes and Government Spending

On the eve of the Great Depression, the government accounted less than 25 per cent of expenditure. Today, it accounts for 40 per cent of expenditure.

A higher level of government outlays means that when recession hits, a large component of aggregate demand does not decline.

In today's economy, government transfer payments are a particularly sensitive economic stabilizer. When the economy goes into recession and depression, more people qualify for unemployment benefits and social assistance. As a consequence, although disposable income decreases, the extent of the decrease is moderated by the existence of such programmes. Consumption expenditure, in turn, does not decline by as much as it would in the absence of such government programmes. The limited decline in consumption spending further limits the overall decrease in aggregate expenditure, thereby limiting the magnitude of an economic downturn.

Multi-income Families

At the time of the Great Depression, families with more than one wage earner were much less common than they are today. The economic activity rate in 1929 was around 45 per cent. Today, it is 75 per cent. So even if the unemployment rate increased to around 20 per cent today, 60 per cent of the adult population would actually have jobs. During the Great Depression, only 40 per cent of the adult population had work.

Multi-income families have greater security than single-income families. The chance of both (or all) income earners in a family losing their jobs simultaneously is much lower than the chance of a single earner losing work. With greater family income security, family consumption is likely to be less sensitive to fluctuations in family income that are seen as temporary. So when aggregate income falls, it does not induce an equivalent cut in consumption.

For the reasons we have just reviewed, it appears the economy has better shock-absorbing characteristics today than it had in the 1920s and 1930s. Even if there is a collapse of confidence leading to a decrease in investment, the recession mechanism that is now in place will not translate that initial shock into the large and prolonged decrease in real GDP and increase in unemployment that occurred more than 70 years ago.

Review Quiz

Study Plan 32.5

1. What events triggered the Great Depression in the United Kingdom?
2. How deep was the Great Depression compared with the 1990–1992 recession?
3. What role did the stock market crash play in the Great Depression?
4. Why are today's recessions less severe than the Great Depression?
5. Why is another Great Depression not likely?

You have now completed your study of the business cycle. In *Reading Between the Lines* on pp. 758–759, we apply some of the lessons of this chapter to explain the astonishing expansion that China is experiencing.

Your final task in your study of macroeconomics is to broaden your view and consider the international aspects of macroeconomics – the forces that determine exchange rates and make them fluctuate and the forces that determine international payments and borrowing and lending.

Reading Between the Lines

Booming China

The Financial Times, 20 October 2006

Chinese economy surges amid boom in exports

Richard McGregor

China's booming export sector has powered the Chinese economy through another quarter of above-double-digit growth, offsetting a fall in investment expansion on the back of a government campaign to rein in credit growth.

The National Bureau of Statistics said the economy expanded by 10.4 per cent in the third quarter, down from 11.3 per cent in the previous quarter but enough to ensure that growth will exceed 10 per cent for the fourth year in a row.

Growth in gross domestic product over the first three quarters was 10.7 per cent.

The rate of increase in urban investment, the prime driver of growth in recent years, sagged in the third quarter under the weight of administrative controls designed to rein in the property sector and spending by local governments.

Fixed-asset investment in urban areas rose by 23.6 per cent year-on-year in the third quarter, compared with 27.3 per cent in the nine months to September.

But Chinese exports made up for much of this slowdown, with the trade surplus rising by 26 per cent in the third quarter year-on-year. Private consumption also rose slightly.

"The government's tightening policies have been timely and effective, and the excessive growth of the national economy has started to be curbed," said Li Xiaochao, an NBS spokesman. . . .

China has used its anti-corruption campaign as a weapon to curb what it sees as reckless investment in some cities and provinces in defiance of central government's rules for project approvals.

The anti-corruption campaign may limit a resurgence in investment once the government eases its tightening campaign.

The government's belief that it has successfully managed a slight slowdown in the economy bolstered the view among many economists that it would delay further tightening measures. . . .

The Essence of the Story

- China's real GDP is growing at more than 10 per cent per year.
- This rapid real GDP growth has been driven by rapid growth in investment financed by bank loans.
- The Chinese government wants to slow real GDP growth and has used an anti-corruption programme to curb local government investment.
- The government believes its anti-corruption programme has slowed the investment growth rate.
- A slower investment growth rate has been offset by a faster export growth rate.

Economic Analysis

- Figure 1 shows the growth of China's real GDP, investment and exports. Real GDP growth has exceeded 10 per cent during 2006 and 2007.
- Investment growth decreased in 2007 because the central government limited local government spending (the so-called anti-corruption programme).
- Export growth increased to fill the gap left by slower investment growth.
- The anti-corruption policy will not keep investment growth in check. It needs to be supported by slower growth in bank loans, which in turn requires slower growth of the quantity of money.
- Figure 2 shows the money growth rate in China in 2006, a growth rate that will bring inflation if not curbed.
- The People's Bank of China has increased the interest rate and taken other measures to slow money growth. Figure 2 shows that this policy slowed the money growth rate. But the money growth rate increased in 2007.
- Figure 3 shows how a slower money growth rate might decrease the growth of aggregate demand and keep inflation in check.
- Aggregate demand in 2007 is AD_{07} and short-run aggregate supply in 2007 is SAS_{07}. Real GDP is 22.5 trillion yuan and the price level is 104 (just 4 per cent higher than in 2005).
- If potential GDP increases in 2007 at 8 per cent per year, long-run aggregate supply in 2007 will be LAS_{07} and there will be an inflationary gap.
- The goal of monetary policy and the anti-corruption programme is to slow the growth rate of aggregate demand so that the aggregate demand curve becomes AD^*.
- Real GDP in 2007 will then rise at the same rate as potential GDP and inflation will be low.

Figure 1 Real GDP, investment and exports growth

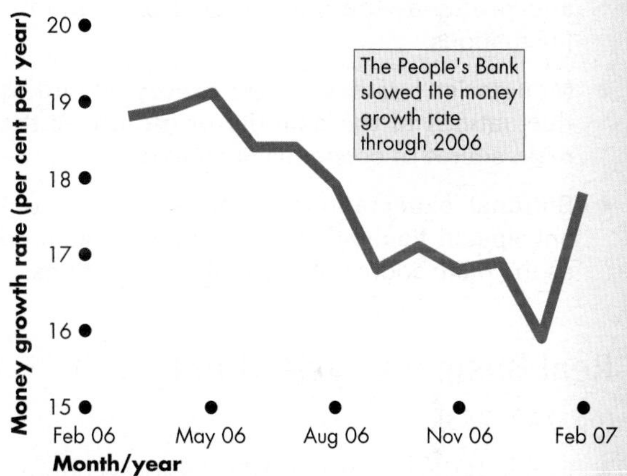

Figure 2 Money growth

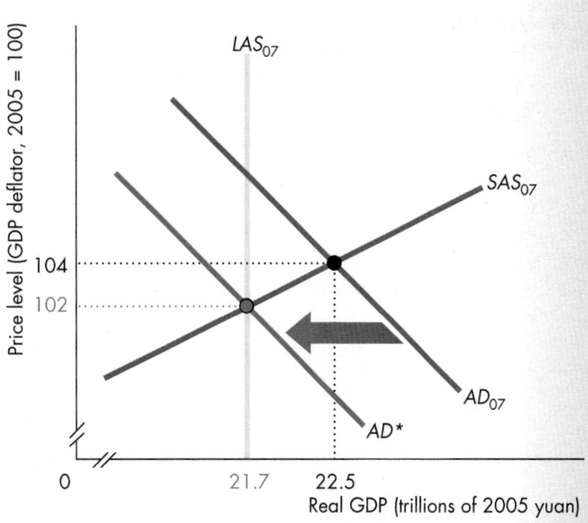

Figure 3 Aggregate supply and aggregate demand

Summary

Key Points

Cycle Patterns, Impulses and Mechanisms (p. 742)

- The economy can be hit (like a tennis ball), cycle indefinitely (like the turning of day into night), and cycle in swings that get milder until another shock hits (like a rocking horse).

Aggregate Demand Theories of the Business Cycle (pp. 743–748)

- Keynesian business cycle theory identifies volatile expectations about future sales and profits as the main source of economic fluctuations.
- Monetarist business cycle theory identifies fluctuations in the quantity of money as the main source of economic fluctuations.
- Rational expectations theories identify unanticipated fluctuations in aggregate demand as the main source of economic fluctuations.

Real Business Cycle Theory (pp. 749–753)

- In real business cycle (RBC) theory, economic fluctuations are caused by fluctuations in the influence of technological change on productivity growth.
- A temporary slowdown in the pace of technological change decreases investment demand and both the demand for labour and the supply of labour.

The 1990–1992 Recession (pp. 753–755)

- Three forces contributed to the weak performance of the UK economy in the early 1990s: the ERM, the reunification of Germany and a slowdown in the world economy.

The Great Depression (pp. 756–757)

- The Great Depression started with increased uncertainty and pessimism that brought a decrease in investment and spending.
- Increased uncertainty and pessimism also brought on the stock market crash. The crash added to the pessimistic outlook and further spending cuts occurred.

Key Figures

Key Terms

Problems

Tests, Study Plan and Solutions*

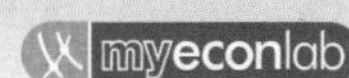

1 The figure shows the economy of Virtual Reality. When the economy is in a long-run equilibrium, it is at points B, F and J. When a recession occurs in Virtual Reality, the economy moves away from these points to one of the three other points identified in each part of the figure.

a If the Keynesian theory is the correct explanation for the recession, to which points does the economy move?

b If the monetarist theory is the correct explanation for the recession, to which points does the economy move?

c If the new classical rational expectations theory is the correct explanation for the recession, to which points does the economy move?

d If the new Keynesian rational expectations theory is the correct explanation for the recession, to which points does the economy move?

e If real business cycle theory is the correct explanation for the recession, to which points does the economy move?

2 The figure shows the economy of Vital Signs. When the economy is in a long-run equilibrium, it is at points A, E and I. When an expansion occurs in Vital Signs, the economy moves away from these points to one of the three other points identified in each part of the figure.

a If the Keynesian theory is the correct explanation for the expansion, to which points does the economy move?

b If the monetarist theory is the correct explanation for the expansion, to which points does the economy move?

c If the new classical rational expectations theory is the correct explanation for the expansion, to which points does the economy move?

d If the new Keynesian rational expectations theory is the correct explanation for the expansion, to which points does the economy move?

e If real business cycle theory is the correct explanation for the expansion, to which points does the economy move?

3 Suppose that when the recession occurs in Virtual Reality in problem 1, the economy moves to D, G and K. Which theory of the business cycle, if any, explains this outcome?

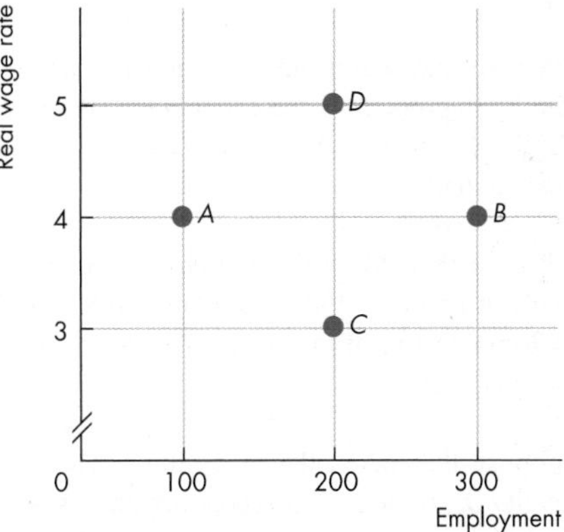

(a) Labour market

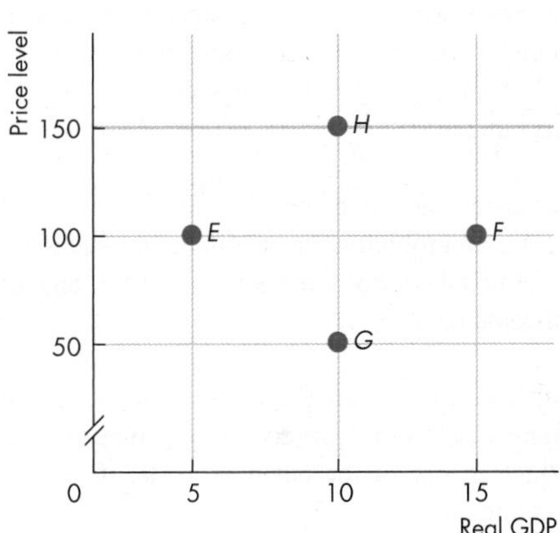

(b) *AS–AD*

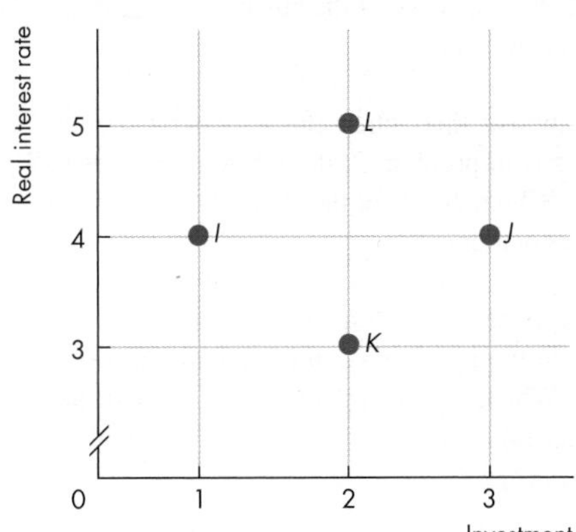

(c) Investment

* Solutions to odd-numbered problems are provided.

4 Suppose that when the expansion occurs in Vital Signs in problem 2, the economy moves to *D*, *H* and *L*. Which theory of the business cycle, if any, explains this outcome?

5 Suppose that when the recession occurs in Virtual Reality in problem 1, the economy moves to *C*, *G* and *K*. Which theory of the business cycle, if any, explains this outcome?

6 Suppose that when the expansion occurs in Vital Signs in problem 2, the economy moves to *C*, *H* and *L*. Which theory of the business cycle, if any, explains this outcome?

7 Suppose that when the recession occurs in Virtual Reality in problem 1, the economy moves to *D*, *H* and *K*. Which theory of the business cycle, if any, explains this outcome?

8 Suppose that when the expansion occurs in Vital Signs in problem 2 the economy moves to *D*, *G* and *L*. Which theory of the business cycle, if any, explains this outcome?

9 Suppose that when the recession occurs in Virtual Reality in problem 1, the economy moves to *C*, *H* and *K*. Which theory of the business cycle, if any, explains this outcome?

10 Suppose that when the expansion occurs in Vital Signs in problem 2, the economy moves to *C*, *G* and *L*. Which theory of the business cycle, if any, explains this outcome?

11 Suppose that when the recession occurs in Virtual Reality in problem 1, the economy moves to *D*, *G* and *L*. Which theory of the business cycle, if any, explains this outcome?

12 Suppose that when the expansion occurs in Vital Signs in problem 2, the economy moves to *C*, *H* and *K*. Which theory of the business cycle, if any, explains this outcome?

13 Suppose that when the recession occurs in Virtual Reality in problem 1, the economy moves to *C*, *G* and *L*. Which theory of the business cycle, if any, explains this outcome?

14 Suppose that when the expansion occurs in Vital Signs in problem 2, the economy moves to *D*, *H* and *K*. Which theory of the business cycle, if any, explains this outcome?

Critical Thinking

1 Study *Reading Between the Lines* on pp. 758–759 and then answer the following questions:

a Why has GDP growth remained high in China even though there has been a slowing in investment growth?

b What has the Chinese government done to slow the economy down? Is this policy likely to work?

c What has the central bank of China done to slow the economy down? Is this policy likely to work?

d What has been happening to the rate of growth of money in China? How is the rate of growth of money expected to affect aggregate demand in China?

e What alternative explanation can be given for the movements of real GDP in China?

Web Activities

Links to Websites

1 Obtain information about the current state of the UK economy. Then:

a List all of the features of the UK economy during the current year that you think are consistent with a pessimistic outlook for the next two years.

b List all of the features of the UK economy during the current year that you think are consistent with an optimistic outlook for the next two years.

c Describe how you think the UK economy is going to evolve over the next year or two. Explain your predictions, drawing on the pessimistic and optimistic factors that you listed in parts (a) and (b) and on your knowledge of macroeconomic theory.

International Finance

CHAPTER 33

After studying this chapter you will be able to:

- Explain how international trade is financed, describe a country's balance of payments accounts, and explain what determines the current account balance
- Describe the foreign exchange market and explain how the exchange rate is determined in alternative international monetary systems
- Describe the European Monetary Union and explain the benefits and costs of the euro

Many Monies!

The pound, the euro and US dollar are three of the world's most widely used currencies. The prices of these currencies fluctuate every day on the foreign exchange market. Why? Why don't they have stable prices?

When a country imports more than it exports, it must borrow from foreigners to cover its deficit. Today, the world's richest country, the United States, is also its biggest borrower and debtor. Why does the United States have such a big international deficit? Does it matter? What must happen to eliminate the US deficit?

Find some answers in this chapter; and in *Reading Between the Lines* apply what you learn to the situations of China and the United States today.

Financing International Trade

When Dixons, an electrical goods retail chain, imports Sony CD players, it doesn't pay for them with pounds – it uses Japanese yen. When Harrods imports Armani suits, it pays for them with euros. And when a restaurant in Tokyo buys a consignment of malt whiskey from Scotland, it uses pounds. Whenever we buy things from another country, we use the currency of that country to make the transaction. It doesn't make any difference what the item being traded is; it might be a consumer good or a capital good, a building, or even a business.

We're going to study the markets in which money – in different types of currencies – is bought and sold. But first we're going to look at the scale of international trading and borrowing and lending, and at the way in which we keep our records of these transactions. Such records are called the balance of payments accounts.

Balance of Payments Accounts

A country's **balance of payments accounts** record its international trading and its borrowing and lending. There are three balance of payments accounts:

1 Current account
2 Capital account
3 Change in reserve assets

The **current account** records the receipts from the sale of goods and services to foreigners, the payments for goods and services bought from foreigners, income and other transfers (such as foreign aid payments) received from and paid to foreigners. By far the largest items in the current account are the receipts from the sale of goods and services to foreigners (the value of exports) and the payments made for goods and services bought from foreigners (the value of imports). Net income is the earnings from foreign financial assets such as bonds and shares, and net earnings of UK workers abroad and foreign workers in the United Kingdom. Net transfers – gifts to foreigners minus gifts from foreigners – are relatively small items.

The **capital account** records all the international borrowing and lending transactions. Whereas the earnings from investments abroad are recorded in the current account, the capital account balance records the actual investments abroad and foreigners' investments in the United Kingdom. The capital account balance equals the amount that a country lends to the rest of the world minus the amount that it borrows from it.

The **change in reserve assets** shows the net increase or decrease in a country's holdings of foreign currency reserves that comes about from the official financing of the difference between the current account and the capital account balances. In practice, the change in reserve assets is an item in the capital account. It is itemized separately here so that you can see how the financing of the gap between current account and capital account adds to or subtracts from reserve assets.

Table 33.1 shows the UK balance of payments accounts in 2006. Items in the current account and capital account that provide foreign currency to the United Kingdom have a plus sign and items that cost the United Kingdom foreign currency have a minus sign. The table shows that UK imports of goods exceeded UK exports of goods in 2006 and that net trade in goods and services was a deficit of £43 billion. How do we pay for imports that exceed the value of our exports? That is, how do we pay for our current account deficit? We pay by borrowing from abroad. The capital account tells us by how much. We borrowed £690 billion but made loans of £656 billion, so our net foreign borrowing was £34 billion.

Table 33.1 myeconlab

UK Balance of Payments Accounts in 2006

	(billions of pounds)
Current account	
Exports of goods and services	370
Imports of goods and services	–424
Net income	23
Net transfers	–12
Current account balance	–43
Capital account	
Foreign investment in the United Kingdom	690
UK investment abroad	–656
Capital account balance	34
Balancing item	9
Change in reserves assets	
Increase(+)/Decrease(–) in official UK reserves	0

Source of data: Office for National Statistics, *UK Balance of Payments: The Pink Book*, 2007.

Some capital and current account transactions do not get recorded. These transactions include unidentified capital flows, illegal international trade such as the import of illegal drugs, and illegal smuggling to evade tariffs or taxes. We call the net total of all these items the *balancing item*, which in 2006 was £9 billion.

Net borrowing from abroad minus the current account deficit is the balance that is financed from official UK reserves – the government's holdings of foreign currency. In 2006, those reserves changed by less than a billion pounds (recorded as zero in Table 33.1).

The numbers in Table 33.1 give a snapshot of the balance of payments accounts in 2006. Figure 33.1 puts that snapshot into perspective by showing the balance of payments between 1990 and 2006. Because the economy grows and the price level rises, changes in the balance of payments expressed in pounds do not convey much information. To remove the influences of growth and inflation, Figure 33.1 shows the balance of payments as a percentage of nominal GDP.

As you can see, the current account balance is almost a mirror image of the capital account balance. The change in reserve assets is small compared with the balances on these other two accounts. A large current account deficit (and capital account surplus) occurred in 1990 but declined for most of the 1990s before increasing in 1999 and then decreasing again to 2003. After 2003, the current account deficit (and capital account surplus) increased again.

You will perhaps obtain a better understanding of the balance of payments accounts and the way in which they are linked together if you consider the income and expenditure, borrowing and lending, and the bank account of an individual.

Individual Analogy

An individual's current account records the income from supplying the services of factors of production and the expenditure on goods and services. Consider, for example, Joanne. She earned an income in 2003 of £25,000. Joanne has £10,000 worth of investments that earned her an income of £1,000. Joanne's current account shows an income of £26,000. Joanne spent £18,000 buying goods and services for consumption. She also bought a new house, which cost her £60,000. So Joanne's total expenditure was £78,000. The difference between her expenditure and income is £52,000 (£78,000 minus £26,000). This amount is Joanne's current account deficit.

Figure 33.1

myeconlab

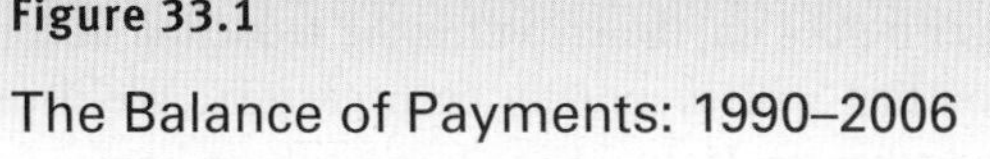

The Balance of Payments: 1990–2006

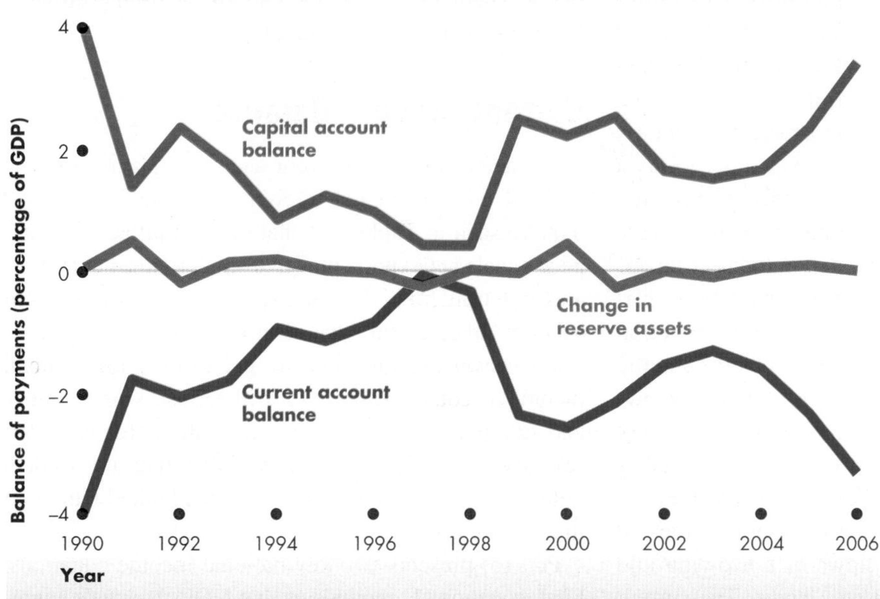

The balance of payments shows a continuous current account deficit from 1990 to 2006. The capital account balance (including the balancing item) mirrors the current account balance. When the current account balance is negative, the capital account balance is positive – we borrow from the rest of the world. Fluctuations in the change in reserve assets are usually small compared with fluctuations in the current account balance and the capital account balance.

Source of data: Office for National Statistics.

To pay for expenditure of £52,000 in excess of her income, Joanne has either to use the money that she has in the bank or to take out a loan. In fact Joanne took a mortgage of £50,000 to help buy her house. This mortgage was the only borrowing that Joanne did, so her capital account surplus was £50,000. With a current account deficit of £52,000 and a capital account surplus of £50,000, Joanne was still £2,000 short. She got that £2,000 from her own bank account. Her cash holdings decreased by £2,000.

Joanne's income from her work and investments is analogous to a country's income from its exports. Her purchases of goods and services, including her purchase of a house, are analogous to a country's imports. Joanne's mortgage – borrowing from someone else – is analogous to a country's foreign borrowing. The change in her bank account is analogous to the change in the country's reserve assets.

Borrowers and Lenders, Debtors and Creditors

A country that is borrowing more from the rest of the world than it is lending to it is called a **net borrower**. Similarly, a **net lender** is a country that is lending more to the rest of the world than it is borrowing from it. A net borrower might be going deeper into debt or might simply be reducing its net assets held in the rest of the world. The total stock of foreign investment determines whether a country is a debtor or a creditor.

A **debtor nation** is a country that during its entire history has borrowed more from the rest of the world than it has lent to it. It has a stock of outstanding debt to the rest of the world that exceeds the stock of its own claims on the rest of the world. The United Kingdom is currently a debtor nation, but for a long time it was a creditor. A **creditor nation** is a country that has invested more in the rest of the world than other countries have invested in it. The largest creditor nation today is Japan.

At the heart of the distinction between a net borrower/net lender and a debtor/creditor nation is the distinction between flows and stocks, which you have encountered many times in your study of macroeconomics. Borrowing and lending are flows – amounts borrowed or lent per unit of time. Debts are stocks – amounts owed at a point in time. The flow of borrowing and lending changes the stock of debt. But the outstanding stock of debt depends mainly on past flows of borrowing and lending, not on the current period's flows. The current period's flows determine the *change* in the stock of debt outstanding.

During the 1960s and the 1970s, the UK current account periodically swung from surplus to deficit. When the current account was a surplus, the capital account was a deficit. On the whole the United Kingdom was a net lender to the rest of the world. It was not until the late 1980s that it became a significant net borrower.

Most countries are net borrowers. But a small number of countries, which includes oil-rich Saudi Arabia and Japan, are huge net lenders.

The United Kingdom today is a small net debtor. There are many countries that are debtor nations. The United States is one. But the largest debtor nations are the capital-hungry developing countries. The international debt of these countries grew from less than one-third to more than one-half of their gross domestic product during the 1980s and created what was called the "Third World debt crisis".

Does it matter if a country is a net borrower rather than a net lender? The answer to this question depends mainly on what the net borrower is doing with the borrowed money. If borrowed money is used to finance investment that in turn is generating economic growth and higher income, borrowing is not a problem. If the borrowed money is being used to finance consumption, then higher interest payments are being incurred and, as a consequence, consumption will eventually have to be reduced. In this case, the more the borrowing and the longer it goes on, the greater is the reduction in consumption that will eventually be necessary. We'll see below whether the United Kingdom has been borrowing for investment or for consumption.

Current Account Balance

What determines the current account balance and the scale of a country's net foreign borrowing or lending? You've seen in Table 33.1 that the current account balance equals net exports plus two small items, net interest and net transfers. So net exports drives the current account balance. But what determines net exports?

To answer this question, we need to use the national income accounts. Table 33.2 will refresh your memory and summarize the necessary calculations for you. Part (a) lists the national income variables that are needed, with their symbols. Their values in the United Kingdom in 2006 are also shown.

Part (b) presents two key national income equations. First, equation (1) reminds us that GDP, Y, equals aggregate expenditure, which is the sum of consumption expenditure, C, investment, I, government expenditure on goods and services, G, and net exports (exports, X, minus imports, M). Equation (2) reminds us that aggregate income is used in three different ways. It can be consumed, saved or paid to the government in net taxes (taxes net of transfer payments). Equation (1) tells us how our expenditure generates our income. Equation (2) tells us how we dispose of that income.

Part (c) of the table looks at three balances – net exports, the government budget and the private sector. To get these balances, first subtract equation (2) from equation (1) in Table 33.2. The result is equation (3). By rearranging equation (3), we obtain a relationship for net exports that appears as equation (4) in the table.

Net exports, in equation (4), is made up of two components. The first is net taxes minus government expenditure and the second is saving minus investment. These items are the balances of the government and private sectors. Net taxes minus government expenditure on goods and services is the budget balance. If that number is positive, the government's budget is a surplus and if the number is negative, it is a deficit.

The **private sector balance** is the saving minus investment. If saving exceeds investment, the private sector has a surplus to lend to other sectors. If investment exceeds saving, the private sector hasa deficit that has to be financed by borrowing from other sectors. As you can see from our calculations, the current account deficit is equal to the sum of the other two deficits – the government's budget deficit and the private sector deficit. In the United Kingdom in 2006, the private sector had a balance of –£44 billion and the government sector had a balance of –£10 billion. The government sector balance plus the private sector balance equals net exports of –£54 billion.

Part (d) of Table 33.2 shows how investment is financed. To increase investment, either private saving or the government surplus must increase, or net exports must decrease.

The calculations that we've just performed are really nothing more than bookkeeping. We've manipulated the national income accounts and discovered that the current account deficit is just the sum of the deficits of the government and private sectors. But these calculations do reveal a fundamental fact. Our international balance of payments can change only if either our government budget balance changes or our private sector surplus or deficit changes.

We've seen that our current account deficit is equal to the sum of the government budget balance and the private sector balance. Is the private sector surplus equal to the government's budget deficit so that the current account deficit is zero? Does an increase in the government budget deficit bring an increase in the current account deficit?

You can see the answer to this question by looking at Figure 33.2 (overleaf). This figure plots the three sector balances – the government sector budget balance ($T - G$), the private sector balance ($S - I$) and the foreign sector balance ($M - X$). To remove the effects of growth and inflation, all three balances are measured as percentages of GDP.

Table 33.2 myeconlab

Sector Balances in 2006

	Symbols and equations	Billions of pounds
(a) Variables		
Gross domestic product (GDP)	Y	1,290
Consumption expenditure	C	827
Investment	I	229
Government expenditure on goods and services	G	288
Exports	X	370
Imports	M	424
Saving	S	185
Net taxes	T	278
(b) Domestic Income and Expenditure		
Aggregate expenditure	(1) $Y = C + I + G + X - M$	
Uses of income	(2) $Y = C + S + T$	
(1) minus (2)	(3) $0 = I - S + G - T + X - M$	
(c) Surpluses and Deficits		
Net exports	(4) $X - M = (T - G) + (S - I)$ $= -10 - 44 = -54$	
Government budget	(5) $T - G = 278 - 288 = -10$	
Private sector	(6) $S - I = 185 - 229 = -44$	
(d) Financing Investment		
Investment is financed by the sum of:		
Private saving,	$S = 185$	
Net government saving and	$T - G = -10$	
Net foreign saving	$M - X = 54$	
That is:	(7) $I = S + (T - G) + (M - X)$ $= 229$	

Source of data: Office for National Statistics.

The private sector was in surplus (savings greater than investment) during the 1990s and the increasing government sector deficit meant that the current account was in deficit during this period. Between 1999 and 2001, the government sector moved into surplus, but after 2001 returned to a deficit. By 2006, both the private sector and the government sector had moved into deficits so net exports moved into a larger deficit. Because the private sector balance is saving minus investment, if saving exceeds investment, a private sector surplus is lent to other sectors; and if investment exceeds saving, borrowing from other sectors finances a private sector deficit.

Is the UK Borrowing for Consumption or Investment?

We noted above that whether international borrowing is a problem or not depends on what that borrowed money is used for. Since 1990, the United Kingdom has borrowed nearly £18 billion a year, on average. Over these same years, the government sector has had an average deficit of £23 billion a year and the private sector has had an average surplus (saving minus investment has been positive) of £5 billion a year. So private sector saving has been more than sufficient to pay for investment in plant and equipment. Does the fact that foreign borrowing has financed a government deficit mean that we are borrowing to consume?

Our foreign borrowing probably has been financing public consumption to some degree. But not all government expenditure is for consumption. More than 10 per cent of government expenditure is on investment goods. But there is no sure way to divide government expenditure into a consumption component and an investment component. Some items, such as the expenditure on improved roads and bridges, are clearly investment. But what about expenditure on education and healthcare? Are these expenditures consumption or investment? A case can be made that they are investment – investment in human capital – and that they earn a rate of return at least equal to the interest rate that we pay on our foreign debt.

However, most of the foreign investment in the United Kingdom is in the private sector and is undertaken in the pursuit of the highest available profit. Foreigners diversify their lending to spread their risk. We do the same. Some of our saving is used to finance investment in firms in the United Kingdom, some is lent to the government and some is used to finance investment in other countries.

Figure 33.2 myeconlab

The Three Sector Balances

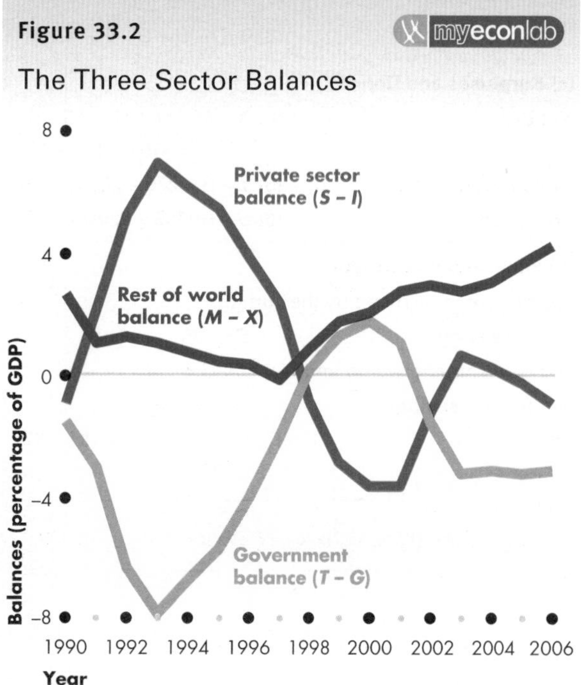

During the 1990s, the private sector was in surplus, the government sector was in deficit and the current account was in deficit. In 1999–2001, the government sector was in surplus but the private sector was in strong deficit as consumer spending boomed. By 2006, both the private sector and the government sector were in deficit and net exports moved into a larger deficit (the rest of the world moved into a larger surplus).

Sources of data: Office for National Statistics and IMF, World Economic Outlook database.

Review Quiz

Study Plan 33.1

1. When a British wine merchant buys a consignment of wine from a French vineyard, which currency gets used to make the transaction?
2. When a German manufacturer buys semi-manufactured parts from a South Wales factory, which currency gets used to make the transaction?
3. What types of transactions do we record in the balance of payments accounts?
4. What transactions does the current account record? What transactions does the capital account record? What does the change in reserves record?
5. How are the current account balance, the government sector balance and the private sector balance related?

The Foreign Exchange Market and the Exchange Rate

When we buy foreign-made goods or invest in another country, we must obtain some of that country's currency to make the transaction. When people in the rest of the world buy UK-made goods or invest in the United Kingdom, they use pounds. We get foreign currency and people in the rest of the world get pounds in the foreign exchange market. The **foreign exchange market** is the market in which the currency of one country is exchanged for the currency of another.

The foreign exchange market is made up of thousands of people: importers and exporters, banks and specialists in the buying and selling of foreign exchange called foreign exchange brokers. The market opens on Monday morning in Hong Kong. As the day advances, Singapore, Tokyo, Bahrain, Frankfurt, London, New York, Chicago and San Francisco open for trade. As the US West Coast markets close, Hong Kong is only an hour away from opening for the next day of business. The sun barely sets on the foreign exchange market. Dealers around the world are continually in contact by telephone and billions of dollars, euros and pounds change hands on any given day.

The price at which one currency exchanges for another is called a **foreign exchange rate**. For example, on 30 April 2007, one pound bought 1.47 euros and 2 US dollars.

Figure 33.3 myeconlab

Exchange Rates

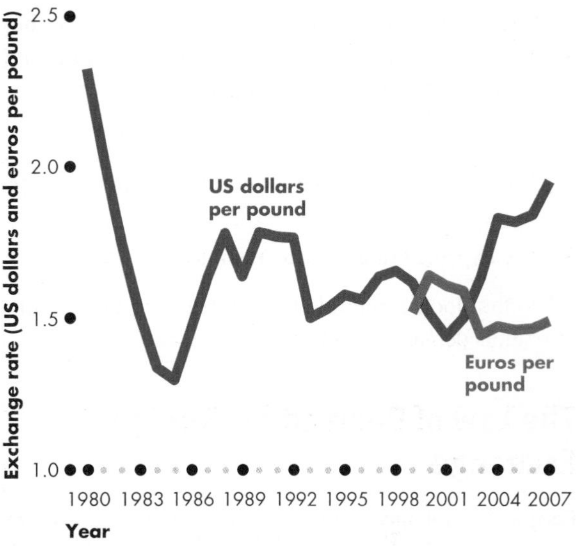

The exchange rate is the price at which two currencies can be traded. The US dollar–pound exchange rate, expressed as US dollars per pound, shows that the pound fell in value – depreciated – against the dollar between 1980 and 1985 and rose in value – appreciated – against the dollar between 1985 and 1988. Between 2001 and 2003, the pound appreciated against the US dollar and depreciated against the euro.

Source of data: Bank of England.

Exchange Rate Fluctuations

Figure 33.3 shows what happened to the exchange rate of the pound in terms of the US dollar (blue line) between 1980 and 2006 and between the pound and the euro (red line) since 1999. The pound has both depreciated and appreciated.

Currency depreciation is the fall in the value of one currency in terms of another currency. For example, in 1980, the pound was worth \$2.30. By 1985, the pound had fallen to \$1.30. The \$1.00 decrease in the value of the pound was a 43 per cent depreciation.

Currency appreciation is the rise in the value of one currency in terms of another currency. For example, when the pound rose from \$1.30 in 1985 to almost \$1.80 in 1988, it appreciated by 38 per cent.

We've just expressed the pound in terms of the US dollar. But we can express the value of the pound in terms of any currency. Figure 33.3 shows the value of the pound in terms of the euro. Sometimes, as in 2001 to 2003, the pound appreciates against the dollar and depreciates against the euro.

We can also express the exchange rate of a foreign currency in terms of the pound. When the pound depreciates against the dollar, the dollar appreciates against the pound.

Why does the pound fluctuate so much in value? Why did it depreciate sharply from 1980 to 1985? Why did it appreciate in 1986? To answer questions like these, we need to know what determines the foreign exchange rate.

The exchange rate is a price: the price of one country's money in terms of another country's money. And like all prices, demand and supply determine the exchange rate. So to understand what determines the exchange rate, we need to study demand and supply in the foreign exchange market. We'll begin on the demand side of the market.

Demand in the Foreign Exchange Market

The quantity of pounds demanded in the foreign exchange market is the amount that traders plan to buy during a given time period at a given exchange rate. This quantity depends on three main factors:

1 The exchange rate
2 The interest rate in the United Kingdom and other countries
3 The expected future exchange rate

We first look at the relationship between the quantity of pounds demanded and the exchange rate.

The Law of Demand for Foreign Exchange

People do not buy pounds because they enjoy them. The demand for pounds is a *derived demand*. People demand pounds so that they can buy UK-made goods and services (UK exports). They also demand pounds so that they can buy US assets such as bonds, shares, businesses and property. Nevertheless, the law of demand applies to pounds just as it does to anything else that people value.

Other things remaining the same, the higher the exchange rate, the smaller is the quantity of pounds demanded in the foreign exchange market. For example, if the price of the pound rises from $2.00 to $2.40 and nothing else changes, the quantity of pounds that people plan to buy in the foreign exchange market decreases. Why does the exchange rate influence the quantity of pounds demanded?

There are two separate reasons and they are related to the two sources of the derived demand for pounds:

- Exports effect
- Expected profit effect

Exports Effect

The larger the value of UK exports, the larger is the quantity of pounds demanded on the foreign exchange market. But the value of UK exports depends on the exchange rate. The lower the exchange rate, with everything else the same, the cheaper are UK-made goods and services, so the more the United Kingdom exports and the greater is the quantity of pounds demanded to pay for these exports.

Expected Profit Effect

The larger the expected profit from holding pounds, the greater is the quantity of pounds demanded in the foreign exchange market. But expected profit depends on the exchange rate. The lower the exchange rate, other things remaining the same, the larger is the expected profit from buying pounds and the greater is the quantity of pounds demanded on the foreign exchange market.

To understand this effect, suppose you think the pound will be worth $2.20 by the end of the month. If, today, a pound costs $2.00, you buy pounds today. But a person who thinks that the pound will be worth $2.00 at the end of the month does not buy pounds today.

But suppose the exchange rate falls to $1.90 per pound. Now the people who think the pound will be worth $2.00 at the end of the month buy pounds. At the lower exchange rate, more people think they can profit from buying pounds, so the quantity of pounds demanded increases.

For the two reasons we've just reviewed, other things remaining the same, when the foreign exchange rate rises, the quantity of pounds demanded decreases, and when the foreign exchange rate falls, the quantity of pounds demanded increases.

Figure 33.4 shows the demand curve for pounds in the foreign exchange market. When the foreign exchange rate rises, other things remaining the same, the quantity of pounds demanded decreases – there is a movement up along the demand curve as shown by the arrow that points upward.

When the exchange rate falls, other things remaining the same, the quantity of pounds demanded increases – there is a movement down along the demand curve as shown by the arrow that points downward.

Changes in the Demand for Pounds

A change in any influence on the number of pounds that people plan to buy in the foreign exchange market, other than a change in the exchange rate, brings a change in the demand for pounds. And a change in the demand for pounds brings a shift in the demand curve for pounds as Figure 33.5 illustrates. The forces that change the demand for pounds are:

- The interest rate in the United Kingdom and other countries
- The expected future exchange rate

Figure 33.4

The Demand for Pounds

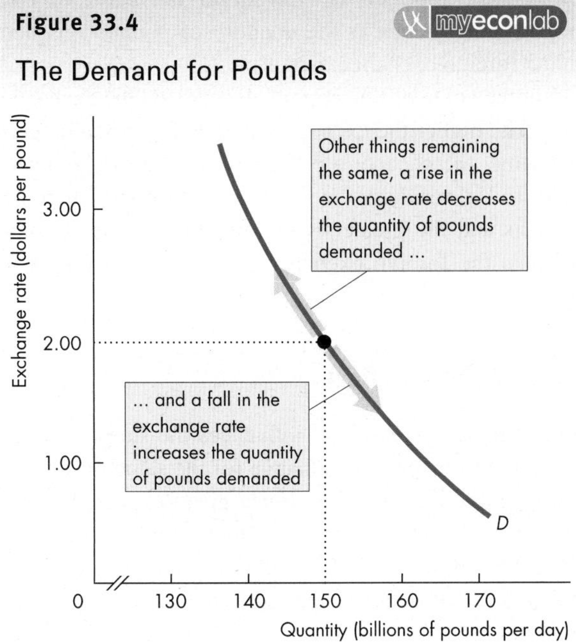

The quantity of pounds that people plan to buy depends on the exchange rate. Other things remaining the same, if the exchange rate rises, the quantity of pounds demanded decreases and there is a movement up along the demand curve for pounds. If the exchange rate falls, the quantity of pounds demanded increases and there is a movement down along the demand curve for pounds.

Figure 33.5

Changes in the Demand for Pounds

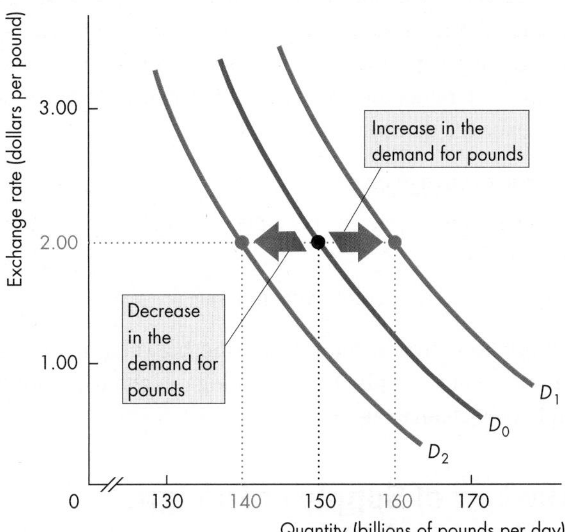

A change in any influence on the quantity of pounds that people plan to buy, other than the exchange rate, brings a change in the demand for pounds. The demand for pounds increases if the UK interest rate differential increases or the expected future exchange rate rises. The demand for pounds decreases if the UK interest rate differential decreases or the expected future exchange rate falls.

The Interest Rate in the United Kingdom and Other Countries

People buy financial assets to make a return. The higher the interest rate that people can make on UK assets compared with foreign assets, the more UK assets they buy. What matters is not the level of UK interest rates, but the UK interest rate minus the foreign interest rate, a gap that is called the **UK interest rate differential.**

If the UK interest rate rises and the foreign interest rate remains constant, the UK interest rate differential increases. The larger the UK interest rate differential, the greater is the demand for UK assets and the greater is the demand for pounds on the foreign exchange market.

The Expected Future Exchange Rate

Other things remaining the same, the higher the expected future exchange rate, the greater is the demand for pounds. To see why, suppose you are Ford's finance manager. The exchange rate is $2.00 per pound, and you think that by the end of the month, it will be $2.40 per pound. You spend $2,000 today and buy £1,000. At the end of the month, the pound is $2.40, as you predicted it would be, and you sell the £1,000. You get $2,400. You've made a profit of $400.

The higher the expected future exchange rate, other things remaining the same, the greater is the expected profit and so the greater is the demand for pounds.

Figure 33.5 summarizes the above discussion of the influences on the demand for pounds. A rise in the UK interest rate differential or a rise in the expected future exchange rate increases the demand for pounds and shifts the demand curve rightward from D_0 to D_1. A fall in the UK interest rate differential or a fall in the expected future exchange rate decreases the demand for pounds and shifts the demand curve leftward from D_0 to D_2.

Policy decisions of central banks determine the UK interest rate differential. But a large number of factors influence the expected future exchange rate. We'll review those factors after we've studied the supply side and equilibrium in the foreign exchange market.

The Supply of Pounds in the Foreign Exchange Market

The quantity of pounds supplied in the foreign exchange market is the amount that traders plan to sell during a given time period at a given exchange rate. This quantity depends on the same three main factors that influence the demand for pounds:

1 The exchange rate
2 The interest rate in the United Kingdom and other countries
3 The expected future exchange rate

Let's look first at the relationship between the quantity of pounds supplied in the foreign exchange market and the exchange rate.

The Law of Supply of Foreign Exchange

People in the United Kingdom supply pounds in the foreign exchange market when they buy other currencies. And they buy other currencies so that they can buy foreign-made goods and services (UK imports). They also supply pounds and buy foreign currencies so that they can buy foreign assets such as bonds, shares, businesses and property abroad. The law of supply applies to pounds just as it does to anything else that people plan to sell.

Other things remaining the same, the higher the exchange rate, the greater is the quantity of pounds supplied in the foreign exchange market. For example, if the price of the pound rises from $2.00 to $2.40 and nothing else changes, the quantity of pounds that people plan to sell in the foreign exchange market increases. Why does the exchange rate influence the quantity of pounds supplied?

There are two reasons, and they parallel the two reasons on the demand side of the market:

- Imports effect
- Expected profit effect

Imports Effect

The imports effect is a mirror image of the exports effect on the demand side of the foreign exchange market. The larger the value of UK imports, the larger is the quantity of foreign currency demanded to pay for these imports. And when people buy foreign currency, they supply pounds. So the larger the value of UK imports, the greater is the quantity of pounds supplied in the foreign exchange market.

But the value of UK imports depends on the exchange rate. The higher the exchange rate, with everything else the same, the cheaper are foreign-made goods and services to UK residents, so the more the United Kingdom imports and the greater is the quantity of pounds supplied in the foreign exchange market to pay for these imports.

Expected Profit Effect

The expected profit effect influences the supply side of the market for foreign exchange for the same reasons as those on the demand side. For a given expected future exchange rate, the higher the exchange rate the greater is the expected loss from holding pounds so the greater is the quantity of pounds supplied in the foreign exchange market.

For the two reasons we've just reviewed, other things remaining the same, when the foreign exchange rate rises, the quantity of pounds supplied increases and when the foreign exchange rate falls, the quantity of pounds supplied decreases.

Figure 33.6 shows the supply curve of pounds in the foreign exchange market. A change in the exchange rate brings a movement along the supply curve as shown by the arrows on supply curve *S*.

Changes in the Supply of Pounds

A change in any influence on the amount of pounds that people plan to sell in the foreign exchange market, other than a change in the exchange rate, brings a change in the supply of pounds and a shift in the supply curve of pounds. Supply either increases or decreases. These other influences parallel the other influences on demand but have exactly the opposite effects. The influences on the supply of pounds are:

- The interest rate in the United Kingdom and other countries
- The expected future exchange rate

The Interest Rate in the United Kingdom and Other Countries

The larger the UK interest rate differential, the smaller is the demand for foreign assets and the smaller is the supply of pounds on the foreign exchange market.

Figure 33.6

The Supply of Pounds

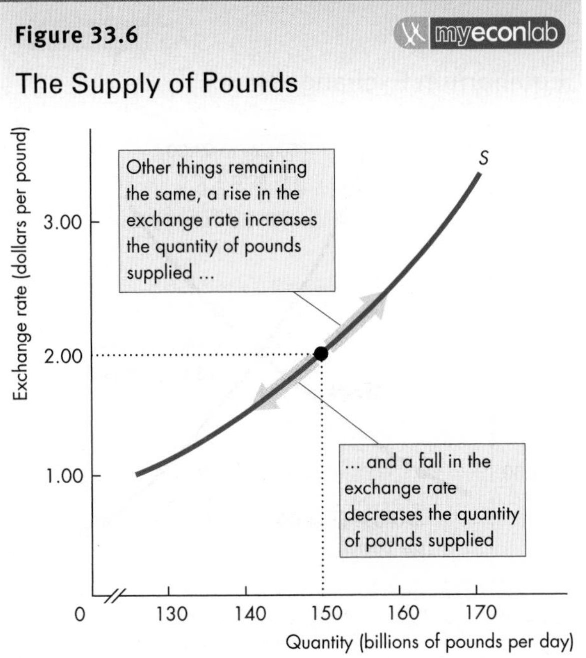

The quantity of pounds that people plan to sell depends on the exchange rate. Other things remaining the same, if the exchange rate rises, the quantity of pounds supplied increases and there is a movement up along the supply curve of pounds. If the exchange rate falls, the quantity of pounds supplied decreases and there is a movement down along the supply curve for pounds.

Figure 33.7

Changes in the Supply of Pounds

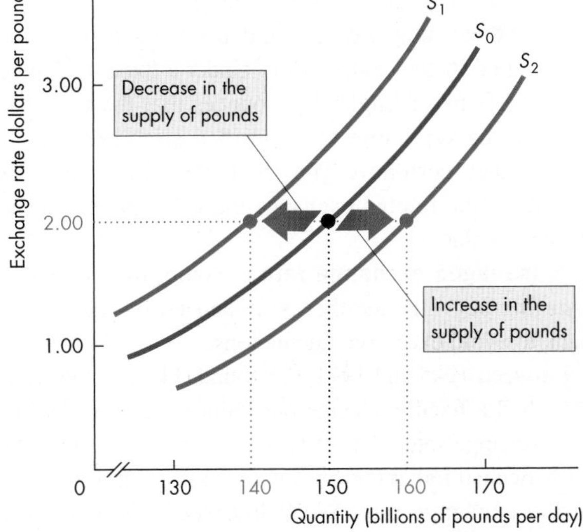

A change in any influence on the quantity of pounds that people plan to sell, other than the exchange rate, brings a change in the supply of pounds. The supply of pounds increases if the UK interest rate differential decreases or the expected future exchange rate falls. The supply of pounds decreases if the UK interest rate differential increases or the expected future exchange rate rises.

The Expected Future Exchange Rate

Other things remaining the same, the higher the expected future exchange rate, the smaller is the supply of pounds. To see why, suppose the pound is trading at \$2.00 per pound today and you think that by the end of the month, the pound will be \$2.40 per pound. You were planning on selling pounds today, but you decide to hold off and wait until the end of the month. If you supply pounds today, you get only \$2.00 per pound. But at the end of the month, if the rate is \$2.40 per pound as you predict, you'll get \$2.40 for each pound you supply. You'll make a profit of 20 per cent if you wait.

So the higher the expected future exchange rate, other things remaining the same, the smaller is the expected profit from selling pounds today and the smaller is the supply of pounds today.

Figure 33.7 summarizes the above discussion of the influences on the supply of pounds. A rise in the UK interest rate differential or a rise in the expected future exchange rate decreases the supply of pounds and shifts the supply curve leftward from S_0 to S_1.

A fall in the UK interest rate differential or a fall in the expected future exchange rate increases the supply of pounds and shifts the supply curve rightward from S_0 to S_2.

Market Equilibrium

You've now seen what determines demand and supply in the foreign exchange market and what makes demand and supply change. Our next task is to see how the exchange rate is determined.

Equilibrium in the market for pounds depends on currency traders' demand for pounds and the supply of pounds that we've just examined. It also depends on whether and how the Bank of England intervenes in the foreign exchange market. There are three possible cases to consider:

1 Flexible exchange rate
2 Fixed exchange rate
3 Managed exchange rate

A **flexible exchange rate** is one that is determined by market forces in the absence of central bank intervention. Under a flexible exchange rate, the Bank of England takes no actions in the foreign exchange market (other than to set the UK interest rate).

A **fixed exchange rate** is one that is pegged at a value determined by the central bank. Under a fixed exchange rate, the Bank of England announces that the pound is going to be kept close to a specified price in terms of some other currency. The Bank then buys or sells pounds in the foreign exchange market to maintain the declared value.

A **managed exchange rate** – sometimes called a *crawling peg* – is one that is influenced by the central bank to avoid excessive fluctuations.

Between 1945 and 1971, the pound (like most currencies) had a fixed exchange rate. Since the early 1970s, the exchange rate of most currencies has been flexible, with occasional intervention to manage fluctuations in the exchange rate. We'll first see how a flexible exchange rate is determined.

Flexible Exchange Rate Equilibrium

Figure 33.8 shows how demand and supply in the foreign exchange market determine the exchange rate. The demand curve is *D*, and the supply curve is *S*. As in all the other markets you've studied, the price (the exchange rate) acts as a regulator. If the exchange rate is too high, there is a surplus – the quantity supplied exceeds the quantity demanded. In Figure 33.8, if the exchange rate is $3.00 per pound, there is a surplus of pounds. If the exchange rate is too low, there is a shortage – the quantity supplied is less than the quantity demanded. In Figure 33.8, if the exchange rate is $1.00 per pound, there is a shortage of pounds.

At the equilibrium exchange rate, there is neither a shortage nor a surplus. The quantity supplied equals the quantity demanded. In Figure 33.8, the equilibrium exchange rate is $2.00 per pound and the equilibrium quantity is £150 billion a day.

The forces of supply and demand relentlessly pull the foreign exchange market to its equilibrium. Foreign exchange dealers are constantly looking for the best price they can get. If they are selling, they want the highest price available. If they are buying, they want the lowest price available. Information flows from dealer to dealer through the worldwide computer network and the price adjusts second by second to keep buying plans and selling plans in balance. That is, the exchange rate adjusts second by second to keep the market at its equilibrium.

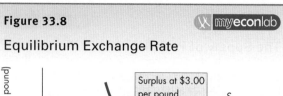

Figure 33.8 myeconlab

Equilibrium Exchange Rate

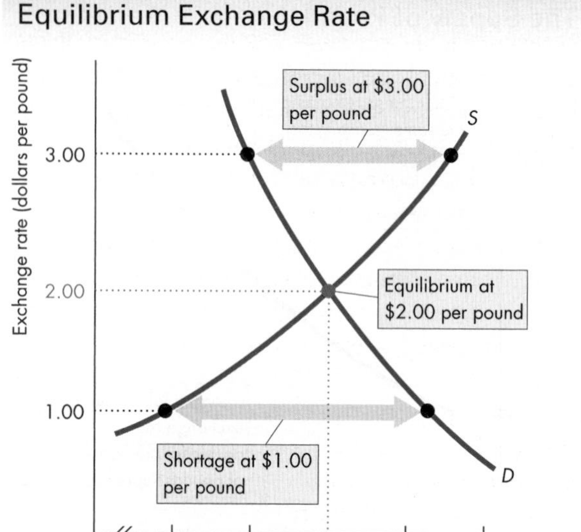

The demand curve for pounds is *D* and the supply curve is *S*. If the exchange rate is $3.00 per pound, there is a surplus of pounds and the exchange rate falls. If the exchange rate is $1.00 per pound, there is a shortage of pounds and the exchange rate rises. If the exchange rate is $2.00 per pound, there is neither a shortage nor a surplus of pounds and the exchange rate remains constant. The market is in equilibrium.

If the demand for pounds increases and the supply of pounds does not change, the exchange rate rises. If the demand for pounds decreases and the supply of pounds does not change, the exchange rate falls. Similarly, if the supply of pounds decreases and the demand for pounds does not change, the exchange rate rises. If the supply of pounds increases and the demand for pounds does not change, the exchange rate falls. These predictions about the effects of changes in demand and supply are exactly the same as those for any other market.

The demand side and supply side of the foreign exchange market have two common influences – the expected future exchange rate and the UK interest rate differential. A change in either of these factors changes *both* demand and supply and in *opposite* directions. So if the pound is expected to appreciate, the demand for pounds increases, the supply of pounds decreases and the pound does appreciate. Similarly, if the pound is expected to depreciate, the demand for pounds decreases, the supply of pounds increases and the pound does depreciate.

Intervention in the Foreign Exchange Market

Fluctuations in the exchange rate that arise from fluctuating expectations are one reason that some economists favour central bank intervention in the foreign exchange market. Let's see how this intervention works.

The Bank of England cannot avoid influencing the exchange rate because it sets the UK interest rate, which influences both demand and supply in the foreign exchange market. A rise in the UK interest rate, other interest rates remaining the same, increases the demand for pounds, decreases the supply of pounds and increases the exchange rate. A fall in the UK interest rate has the opposite effects.

But the Bank of England can intervene directly in the foreign exchange market either to fix the exchange rate or to smooth out exchange rate fluctuations.

Suppose the Bank of England wants the exchange rate to be fixed at $2.00 per pound. If the exchange rate rises above $2.00, the Bank sells pounds. If the exchange rate falls below $2.00, the Bank buys pounds. By these actions, the Bank keeps the exchange rate close to its target rate of $2.00 per pound.

Figure 33.9 shows this intervention in the foreign exchange market. The Bank of England wants to fix the pound at $2.00 per pound and takes actions to achieve that outcome.

Suppose that the demand for pounds is D_0 and the supply of pounds is S_0. The equilibrium flexible exchange rate is $1.80 per pound. At $2.00 per pound, £145 billion are demanded and £155 billion are supplied. The Bank of England must take the surplus of £10 billion off the market. The Bank uses its foreign currency reserves to buy £10 billion. The Bank's action prevents the exchange rate from falling and keeps the exchange rate at its target.

Now suppose that the demand for pounds is D_1 and the supply of pounds is S_1. The equilibrium flexible exchange rate is $2.20 per pound. At $2.00 per pound, £155 billion are demanded and £145 billion are supplied. The Bank of England must now provide enough pounds to satisfy the shortage of £10 billion. The Bank sells £10 billion in exchange for yen (or another currency). The Bank's action now prevents the exchange rate from rising above its target.

If the demand fluctuates between D_0 and D_1, the Bank can repeatedly intervene in the foreign exchange market. Sometimes the Bank buys and sometimes it sells, but on average, it neither buys nor sells.

But suppose that demand and supply change permanently to D_0 and S_0. In these circumstances, the Bank cannot maintain the exchange rate at $2.00 per pound for long. To do so, the Bank would have to use its foreign currency reserves to buy pounds *every* day. So the Bank's foreign currency reserves fall and eventually it would run out of reserves and have to abandon its attempt to fix the exchange rate.

Knowing that this outcome is inevitable, traders expect the pound to depreciate, so the demand decreases to less than D_0 and the supply increases to more than S_0, making the quantity of reserves that the Bank loses every day even larger.

Alternatively, suppose that demand and supply change permanently to D_1 and S_1. In this situation, the Bank must *sell* pounds *every* day and buy foreign currency to keep the exchange rate at $2.00 per pound.

Now, traders expect the pound to appreciate, so the demand for pounds increases to more than D_1 and supply decreases to less than S_1, making the quantity of reserves that the Bank acquires every day even larger.

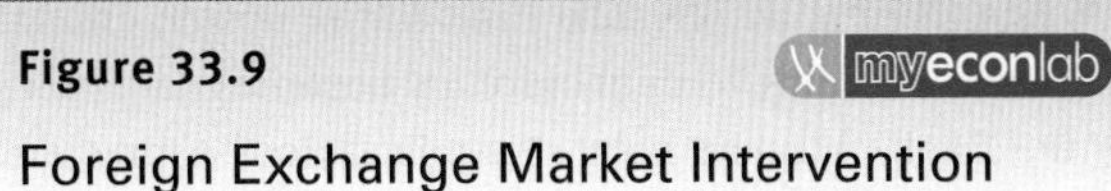

Figure 33.9

Foreign Exchange Market Intervention

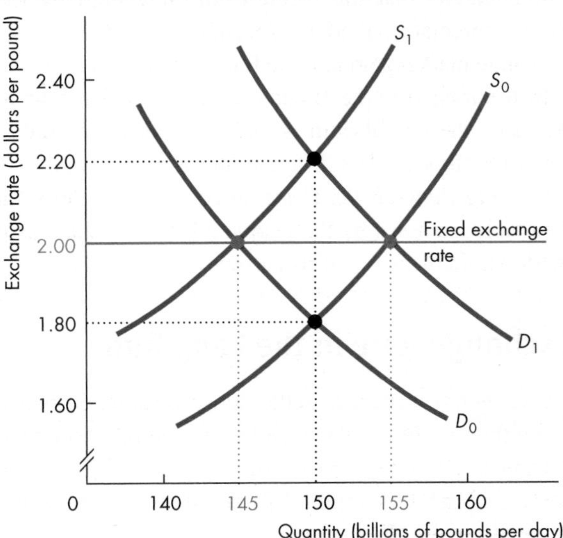

The Bank of England fixes the exchange rate at $2.00 per pound. When the demand for pounds is D_0, the supply of pounds is S_0, and the equilibrium flexible exchange rate is $1.80 per pound. At $2.00 per pound, there is a surplus of pounds, which the Bank must buy by selling foreign currency reserves. When the demand for pounds is D_1, the supply of pounds is S_1, and the equilibrium flexible exchange rate is $2.20 per pound. At $2.00 per pound, there is a shortage of pounds, which the Bank must provide by buying foreign currency.

While there is no physical limit to the upside change in reserves, holding foreign currency becomes dangerous for the Bank. At some point, the pound does appreciate, which means that the foreign currency held by the Bank depreciates. Traders (speculators) in the foreign exchange market gain and the Bank loses.

In the long run, the Bank's intervention must be to reinforce the equilibrium flexible exchange rate rather than to try to achieve a different long-run outcome.

Reading Between the Lines on pp. 780–781 looks at the challenge faced by the People's Bank of China as it tried to hold the value of its currency fixed in 2007.

Exchange Rate in the Long Run

We've seen that changes in the expected future exchange rate influence the current actual exchange rate. But what determines the expected future exchange rate? The answer is the fundamental forces that determine the value of money. They are:

- Purchasing power parity
- Interest rate parity

Purchasing Power Parity

Suppose the price of a pair of Levi jeans is £20 in London and $36 in New York. If the exchange rate is $1.80 per pound, the two monies have the same value. You can buy the jeans in London or New York for either £20 or $36 and it costs you the same in both places and monies.

This situation is called **purchasing power parity**, which means *equal value of money*. If purchasing power parity does not prevail, powerful forces go to work. To understand these forces, suppose that Levis cost £30 in London and $36 in New York and the exchange rate is still $1.80 per pound. The US dollar in New York now buys more than the pound in London.

You can spend £20 to buy $36 on the foreign exchange market and then buy a pair of Levis in New York, or you can buy a pair of Levis for £30 in London. If all (or most) prices are higher in pounds in the United Kingdom than in dollars in the United States, then people will sell pounds on the foreign exchange market and the value of the pound will fall.

Expecting the pound to fall, the demand for pounds decreases, the supply of pounds increases and the exchange rate falls. When the exchange rate has fallen to $1.20 per pound, purchasing power parity is restored. A pair of Levis now costs $36 in either London or New York in both pounds and US dollars.

Similarly, if Levis costs £10 in London and $36 in New York with an exchange rate of $1.80 per pound, the pound buys more in London than in New York. People will generally expect that the value of the pound will rise. The demand for pounds will increase, the supply of pounds will decrease and the exchange rate will rise. When the exchange rate has risen to $3.60 per pound, purchasing power parity is restored. Again a pair of Levis costs $36 in either London or New York in both pounds and US dollars.

Ultimately, the value of money is determined by the price level, which in turn is determined by aggregate supply and aggregate demand (see Chapter 23, pp. 518–519). So the deeper forces that influence the exchange rate have tentacles that spread throughout the economy. If prices in the United Kingdom rise faster than those in other countries, the pound depreciates. And if prices rise more slowly in the United Kingdom than in other countries, the pound appreciates.

Interest Rate Parity

Suppose a bank deposit in pounds in London earns 5 per cent a year and a US dollar bank deposit in New York earns 3 per cent a year. In this situation, why does anyone deposit money in New York? Why doesn't all the money flow to London? The answer is because of exchange rate expectations. Suppose people expect the pound to depreciate by 2 per cent a year. This 2 per cent depreciation must be subtracted from the 5 per cent interest to obtain the net return of 3 per cent a year that an American can earn by depositing funds in London. The two returns are equal. This situation is one of **interest rate parity**, which means *equal rates of return*.

Adjusted for risk, interest rate parity always prevails. Funds move to get the highest return available. If for a few seconds a higher return is available in London than in New York, the demand for pounds increases and the pound appreciates until interest rate parity is restored.

Review Quiz

Study Plan 33.2

1. How is the exchange rate determined?
2. How can the Bank of England influence the foreign exchange market?
3. How do changes in the expected future exchange rate influence the actual exchange rate in the flexible exchange rate system?
4. What is purchasing power parity and how does it influence exchange rate expectations?

European Monetary Union

On 1 January 1999, 11 countries formed a European Monetary Union (EMU) and irrevocably fixed the values of their currencies against the euro. Greece joined on 1 January 2001. Table 33.3 shows the exchange rates of national currencies for the 12 participating countries. As you know, membership of the EMU is a highly charged and controversial issue. Let's review the benefits and costs of the euro.

The Benefits of the Euro

Four benefits of a single currency in Europe are:

- Transparency and competition improve
- Transactions costs decrease
- Foreign exchange risk is eliminated
- Real interest rates fall

Transparency and Competition Improve

A single currency provides a single unit of account so that prices are easily compared across the entire Eurozone. A country might gain a competitive advantage by becoming more efficient, but it cannot gain an advantage by artificially lowering the prices of its exports through a depreciation of its currency.

Table 33.3 myeconlab

Euro Conversion Rates

Country	Currency unit	Units per euro
Austria	schilling	13.7603
Belgium	franc	40.3399
Finland	markka	5.94573
France	franc	6.55957
Germany	Deutschmark	1.95583
Greece	drachma	340.750
Ireland	pound	0.787564
Italy	lira	1936.27
Luxembourg	franc	40.3399
Netherlands	guilder	2.20371
Portugal	escudo	200.482
Spain	peseta	166.386

Source of data: European Central Bank.

Transactions Costs Decrease

A single currency eliminates foreign exchange transactions costs – the costs of exchanging pesetas for francs at a bank or travel agent, such as commission charges or the margin between the buy and sell exchange rates we see posted in banks and currency exchanges. The removal of these costs benefits the consumer, who knows that a euro in France buys the same as a euro in Germany.

The total benefit from eliminating the transactions costs of currency exchange has been estimated at 0.3 to 0.4 per cent of EU GDP a year.[1] For a country with an advanced banking system as in the United Kingdom, the EU Commission estimates that the benefits would be 0.1 per cent of GDP a year.

Foreign Exchange Risk Is Eliminated

With a single currency, exporters and importers no longer face foreign exchange risk. For example, Alpine Gardens, an Austrian garden company, has ordered a consignment of garden gnomes to be supplied by Britannia Gnomes Ltd, a Gloucester company, in three months' time. The contract and the price are set today, but payment will take place in three months' time. Alpine Gardens has to pay £50,000 in three months' time. To protect itself against an adverse change in the exchange rate, it pays a premium to insure against an exchange rate change.[2]

The reduction in exchange rate risk improves trade between EU countries. Cacharel, the French clothing designer can source its material from Rome or from Paris. On a strict exchange rate comparison, the Italian product is cheaper. But in the past the exchange rate between the French franc and Italian lira has fluctuated unpredictably. Cacharel doesn't want to be tied into a contract with the Italian supplier if the price in francs fluctuates with the exchange rate. Cacharel sources the material from the more expensive French supplier because the price is guaranteed but Cacharel has to charge its customers a higher price. A single currency eliminates this exchange rate risk. Cacharel can source its material from Rome, pay a lower price and pass the benefits of the lower price on to its customers. The

[1] Commission of the European Communities, "One Market, One Money: An Evaluation of the Potential Benefits and Costs of Forming an Economic and Monetary Union", *European Economy*, 44, Brussels, 1990.

[2] Alpine Gardens buys pounds in the forward market, paying a commission to the foreign currency operator which ensures the delivery of £50,000 in three months' time at an exchange rate specified today irrespective of what the exchange rate will be in three months' time.

lower price increases the quantity demanded of Cacharel clothing, which in turn increases the orders from Rome.

The removal of exchange risk means that many large companies are able to reduce their administration and financial management costs. They also no longer need to diversify their operations across borders and can consolidate them on one location.

Real Interest Rates Fall

You know that the nominal interest rate equals the real interest rate plus the expected inflation rate. In long-term bond markets, the nominal interest rate is the long-term real interest rate plus the expected long-term inflation rate plus a premium for risk. The risk premium arises from uncertainty about default and future inflation.

If the European Central Bank (ECB) delivers low inflation and develops a reputation for low inflation, its low inflation targets become credible and inflation uncertainty is reduced. A single currency and a common monetary policy governed by the ECB lead to a convergence of inflation rates and interest rates within the Eurozone. With inflation and interest rates in the Eurozone at common low levels, the risk premium and the long-term interest rate will be lower and investment greater.

Let's now look at some of the costs of the euro.

The Economic Costs of the Euro

Two costs of a single currency in Europe are:

- Shocks that need national monetary policy
- Loss of sovereignty

Shocks that Need National Monetary Policy

Many, perhaps most, economic shocks that call for a monetary policy response are country-specific shocks or shocks that affect different countries in different ways.

For example, the dismantling of the Berlin Wall had a major impact on the German economy but barely any effect on the economies of Ireland and Portugal. Also, the shock had different effects on the two parts of Germany. East German workers were less productive and earned lower wage rates than their West German counterparts. Productivity and earnings differences induced a massive reallocation and relocation of jobs and people. A common monetary policy might stimulate the economy in the East and bring inflation to the West or keep inflation in check in the West and bring prolonged recession in the East.

An oil price increase is an example of a common shock that has different effects on different economies. In Germany, an oil importer, the price rise imparts a negative aggregate supply shock and creates a current account deficit. In the United Kingdom, an oil exporter, the price rise imparts a positive supply shock and creates a current account surplus. A common monetary policy might stimulate economic activity in Germany and bring inflation to the United Kingdom or hold inflation in check in the United Kingdom and bring stagnation in Germany.

A common monetary policy is inadequate to deal with the results of country-specific shocks.

Loss of Sovereignty

In principle, fiscal policy might be used to pursue national economic policy goals. But in the case of the EMU, the Stability and Growth Pact places limits on the use of fiscal policy and replaces national freedom of action with a common regional policy.

Common regional policy enables transfers to be made from Germany and France to Italy and Spain. But a political consensus must be found to sustain such transfers. In effect, a single currency implies a political union. A loss of monetary sovereignty implies a loss of political sovereignty.

The Optimum Currency Area

When there are benefits and costs, they must be weighed against each other and an optimum outcome found. Imagine a world in which the Welsh leek and Scottish thistle exchange for each other and for the English pound at exchange rates that fluctuate every day. The United Kingdom is almost certainly better off using one currency rather than three. Is Europe better off using the euro than 12 national currencies? And why stop at Europe! Would the world be better off with one currency rather than its 200-plus currencies?

To answer these questions, we need the concept of an **optimal currency area**, a geographical area that is better served by a single currency than by several currencies. Robert Mundell, an economics professor at Columbia University in New York City, won the Nobel Prize in 1999 for his work on this topic. Mundell claimed that the key factor required for an optimal currency area is free labour mobility either across regions or between jobs.

Box 33.1

The Economic Effects of Currency Unions

Jeffrey Frankel of Harvard University and Andrew Rose of the University of California, Berkeley, have examined the change in international trade and real GDP in 200 countries or territories that have formed or joined currency unions. Their findings are remarkable.

They find that belonging to a currency union *triples* international trade with other members of the currency union and that trade does not get diverted from other areas. Instead, total trade increases. They also find strong evidence that increased international trade brings a large increase in income. Finally, they find that the gains in income come entirely from trade expansion and not from factors such as improved central bank credibility or monetary policy.

More speculatively, Frankel and Rose apply their results to hypothetical cases of countries that are currently outside currency unions joining a currency union. Of special interest are their findings about European countries joining the Eurozone. Figure 1 shows the numbers. In the United Kingdom, which falls in the middle of the pack, trade with other Eurozone members would expand by 60 per cent of real GDP and real GDP itself would expand by 20 per cent!

Figure 1

Estimated Effects of Joining the Euro

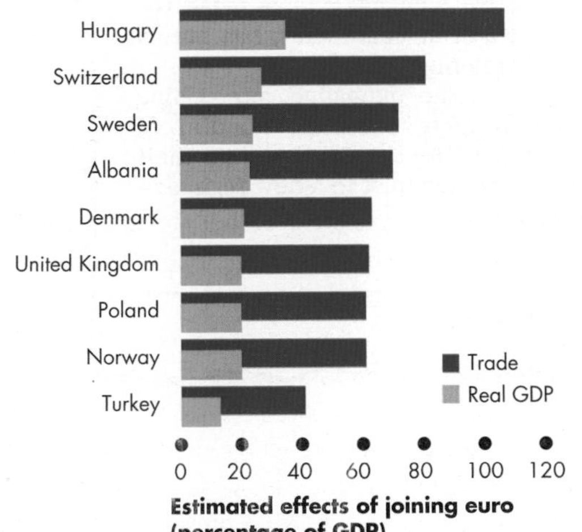

Source of data: Frankel, Jeffery A. and Rose, Andrew, "An Estimate of the Effect of Common Currencies on Trade and Income", *Quarterly Journal of Economics*, 117 No. 2, May 2002.

On this criterion, Scotland, Wales and England are better off with a single currency that they would be with an English pound, a Welsh leek and a Scottish thistle. No cultural or language barriers hamper the movement of labour. If a factory closes down in Merseyside and another opens in Clwyd, workers from Merseyside can travel to North Wales to seek employment.

Lack of regional mobility is not a problem if there is mobility between jobs. For example, if Volkswagen closes a Polo production plant in Pamplona, Spain, and opens a new plant in Wolfsburg, Germany, we would not expect former Spanish car workers to migrate to Germany – although by current EU labour laws there is nothing stopping them from doing just that. If jobless car workers in Pamplona can easily retrain and find a new job in Spain, the absence of regional labour mobility doesn't weaken the case for a single currency.

A second criterion for an optimal currency area is that regions within the area face common economic shocks. It is claimed by some economists that economies with similar industrial structures and extensive trade with each other satisfy this criterion. And it is further claimed that the Eurozone countries have sufficiently similar industrial structures and sufficiently extensive trade links to meet this criterion.

Unlike the country-specific shocks that we've just considered, common shocks can be dealt with by a common monetary policy run by a common central bank. For example, if a rise in the price of oil affected all the countries in a monetary union in the same way, the central bank could react in a way that is appropriate for all the countries in the union.

Even if a country does not share a similar industrial structure and have extensive trade links with its neighbours, some supporters of the Eurozone argue that joining a single currency area will bring convergence to a common industrial structure and stimulate trade flows. For example, each major Canadian city is closer to a major US city than it is to other Canadian cities. But there is significantly more trade among Canadian cities (using one currency) than between the closer Canadian and US cities (using two currencies).

Review Quiz

Study Plan 33.3

1 What is the EMU?
2 What are the benefits of a single currency for Europe?
3 What are the costs of a single currency for Europe?
4 What is an optimal currency area?

Reading Between the Lines

Trade Surplus and a Managed Exchange Rate in China

The Financial Times, 12 February 2007

FT

China sees strong rise in trade surplus

Richard McGregor

China's trade surplus has maintained a strong growth momentum into the new year, a trend that will ensure that Beijing's currency and monetary policies will remain under international scrutiny in 2007.

The release of the January trade figures came after the weekend meeting in Germany of G7 finance ministers, plus representatives from China, which called on Beijing to allow greater flexibility in its currency, the renminbi.

China's trade surplus reached \$25.0bn in January, up from \$9.6bn year-on-year, driven by a rise of 33 per cent in the value of exports. . . .

China's trade surplus, according to its own figures, nearly doubled in 2006 to \$177bn, and is expected to top \$200bn this year, despite recent statements from top leaders that China's trade should be "basically balanced". The trade surplus has become the primary driver both of swelling foreign reserves, which now surpass \$1,000bn, and the central bank's difficulties in keeping money supply in check.

To keep the renminbi, China's currency, stable, the central bank swaps nearly all the dollars coming into the country for the renminbi, which it then drains out of the financial system by issuing bank notes. The currency policy has a direct impact on interest rates, which are kept low by the central bank to remove incentives for more capital to flow into the country.

Washington has focused on the greenback, which has weakened against the renminbi by about 7 per cent since July 2005, but China's effective exchange rate, as measured against a basket of currencies, has barely moved in that period. . . .

In managing the exchange rate, China remains extremely cautious, mindful of the need to give local exporters and their employees time to adjust to a new regime of flexible currencies.

The Essence of the Story

- China's current account surplus is large; its foreign reserves are growing rapidly; and its currency has appreciated 7 per cent against the US dollar since mid 2005.
- The People's Bank of China, China's central bank, swaps nearly all the dollars that come into the country for renminbi and then drains the excess money out of the economy.
- But the task gets larger and more difficult as the surplus increases.

Economic Analysis

- Figure 1 shows China's current account surplus, its bilateral trade surplus with the United States, and the increase in its dollar reserves. At the end of 2006, China's reserves were $1,069 billion.
- The People's Bank of China operates a *crawling peg* to prevent the renminbi from rising too rapidly against the US dollar.
- The United States wants the renminbi to appreciate more rapidly.
- Figure 2 shows the renminbi–US dollar exchange rate, which has increased from 12 cents in July 2005 to almost 13 cents in April 2007 – a 7 per cent appreciation.
- To prevent the exchange rate from rising above its desired upper bound, the People's Bank of China supplies renminbi and buys US dollars.
- In 2006, the People's Bank accumulated $247 billion or about $677 million a *day*!
- Figure 3 shows the market for China's currency. The demand for renminbi is *D*, the supply is *S* and with a flexible exchange rate the equilibrium exchange rate would be *E*, which is greater than the upper-bound of the band in which the People's Bank buys dollars.
- Rapid growth in China's foreign currency reserves brings rapid growth of the monetary base. The People's Bank offsets the increase in money base by selling bonds to the banks. (This policy is called sterilization.)
- China wants the renminbi to appreciate slowly to prevent a large and rapid fall in the real value of its US dollar assets and to prevent a short-run loss of competitiveness in international markets.
- The United States wants the renminbi to appreciate rapidly to make China less competitive and the United States more competitive and to lower the real value of US debts to China.

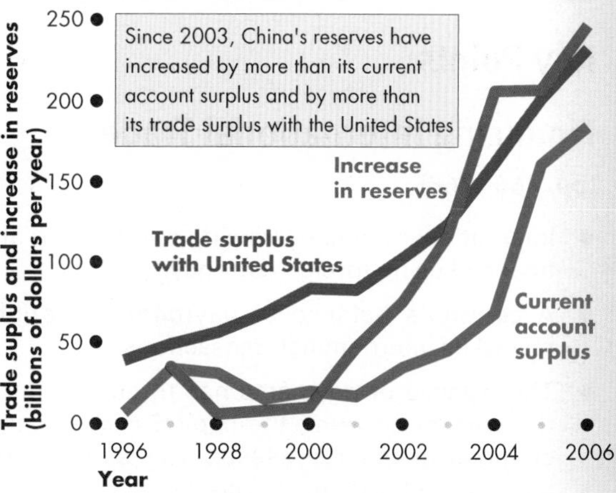

Figure 1 China's trade surplus and increase in reserves

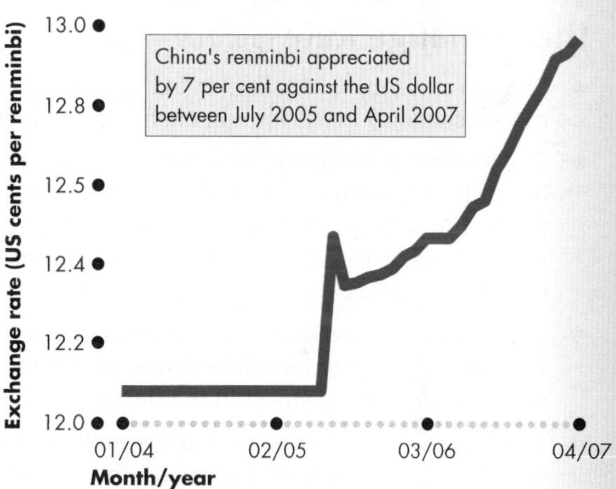

Figure 2 China's rising renminbi

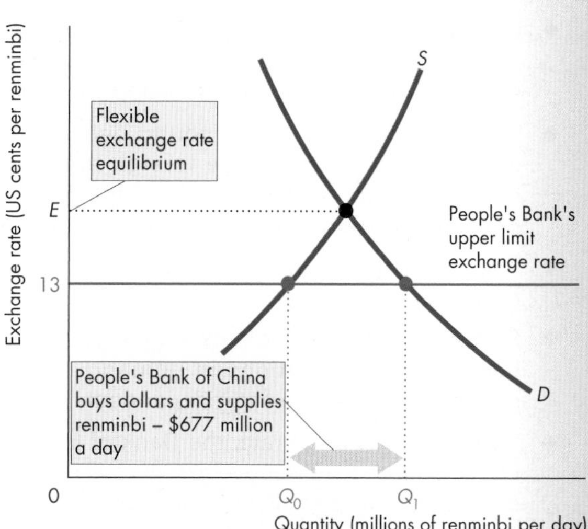

Figure 3 The People's Bank of China in the foreign exchange market

Summary

Key Points

Financing International Trade
(pp. 764–768)

- International trade, borrowing and lending are financed using foreign currency.
- A country's balance of payments accounts record its international transactions.
- The balance of payments has three accounts: the current account, the capital account and changes in reserve assets. The sum of the balances in these three accounts is zero.

The Foreign Exchange Market and the Exchange Rate (pp. 769–776)

- Foreign currency is obtained in exchange for domestic currency in the foreign exchange market.
- The lower the exchange rate, the greater is the quantity of pounds demanded in the foreign exchange market. A change in the exchange rate brings a movement along the demand curve for pounds.
- Changes in the expected future exchange rate and the UK interest rate differential change the demand for pounds and shift the demand curve.
- The lower the exchange rate, the smaller is the quantity of pounds supplied to the foreign exchange market. A change in the exchange rate brings a movement along the supply curve of pounds.
- Changes in the expected future exchange rate and the UK interest rate differential change the supply of pounds and shift the supply curve.
- The exchange rate of the pound depends on demand and supply in the foreign exchange market and on whether and how the Bank of England intervenes in the market.
- The exchange rate might be fixed or managed or flexible.
- Fluctuations in a flexible exchange rate occur because the fluctuations in demand for and supply of pounds are not independent.
- To fix the exchange rate, the Bank of England would intervene to remove any excess demand or supply and permit its holdings of foreign exchange reserves to fluctuate.

European Monetary Union
(pp. 777–779)

- The EMU came into being on 1 January 1999 with 11 countries of the European Union joining. Greece joined on 1 January 2001.
- The benefits of a single currency are greater competition, lower transactions costs, removal of exchange risk and a lower real interest rate.
- The costs of a single currency are the loss of the ability to respond to a national economic shock and the loss of sovereignty.
- An optimal currency area is one for which the benefits outweigh the costs.

Key Figures and Table

Key Terms

Problems

Tests, Study Plan and Solutions* 

1 The table give some information about the UK economy in 2003:

Item	Billions of pounds
Consumption expenditure	721
Exports of goods and services	277
Government expenditure	230
Net taxes	217
Investment 1	81
Saving	162

a Calculate the private sector balance.

b Calculate the government's budget balance.

c Calculate net exports.

d What is the relationship between the government's budget balance and net exports?

2 The table give some information about the US international transactions in 2003:

Item	Billions of US dollars
Imports of goods and services	1,487
Foreign investment in the United States	1,051
Exports of goods and services	990
US investment abroad	456
Net interest income	7
Net transfers	–68
Balancing item	–36

a Calculate the current account balance.

b Calculate the capital account balance.

c Did US official reserves increase or decrease in 2003?

d Was the United States a net borrower or a net lender in 2003? Explain your answer.

3 The US dollar exchange rate decreased from $1.30 Canadian in 2004 to $1.21 Canadian in 2005, and the US dollar exchange rate increased from 108.15 Japanese yen in 2004 to 110.11 Japanese yen in 2005.

a Did the US dollar appreciate or depreciate against of the Canadian dollar?

b Did the US dollar appreciate or depreciate against of the Japanese yen?

c What was the value of the Canadian dollar in terms of US dollars in 2004 and 2005?

d What was the value of 100 Japanese yen in terms of US dollars in 2004 and 2005?

e Did the Canadian dollar appreciate or depreciate against the US dollar in 2005?

f Did the Japanese yen appreciate or depreciate against the US dollar in 2005?

4 There is a large increase in the global demand for roses and Colombia is the biggest producer of roses. At the same time, the central bank of Colombia increases the interest rate. What happens in the foreign exchange market for Colombian pesos to:

a The demand for pesos?

b The supply of pesos?

c The quantity of pesos demanded?

d The quantity of pesos supplied?

e The exchange rate of the pesos against the US dollar?

5 In 2002 a euro deposit in a bank in Paris, France earned interest of 2.8 per cent a year and a yen deposit in Tokyo, Japan earned 0.036 per cent a year. With everything else remaining the same and adjusted for risk, what was the exchange rate expectation of the Japanese yen?

6 Suppose that the pound is trading at 1.82 US dollars per pound and that there is purchasing power parity at this exchange rate. The interest rate in the United States is 2.5 per cent a year and the interest rate in the United Kingdom is 3 per cent a year.

a Calculate the UK interest rate differential.

b What is the pound expected to be worth in terms of US dollars one year from now?

c Which country more likely has the lower inflation rate? How can you tell?

7 On 29 June 2007, you could purchase a particular laptop from an online computer store for 827.12 euros or 477.25 pounds. If the exchange rate is 1.4831 per pound. Did purchasing power parity prevail?

8 A country's currency appreciates and its holdings of foreign currency increase. What can you say about:

a The central bank's intervention in the foreign exchange market?

b The country's current account balance?

* Solutions to odd-numbered problems are provided.

9 In a country the price level is rising at a slower rate than in all other countries and the country has more rapid economic growth. The central bank does not intervene in the foreign exchange market. What can you say (and why) about:

a The exchange rate?

b The current account balance?

c The expected exchange rate?

d The interest rate differential?

e Interest rate parity?

f Purchasing power parity?

Critical Thinking

1 Study *Reading Between the Lines* on pp. 780–781 and then answer the following questions.

a What does the news article imply is the reason for China's large current account surplus and the United States' large current account deficit?

b How does the news article's explanation compare with the explanation for a current account deficit or surplus discussed in this chapter?

c How would the United States gain from a faster-rising renminbi and how would China lose?

d Would the renminbi be considered to be overvalued if China spent $200 billion a year buying US real assets such as General Motors and Microsoft stock?

e If China did spend $200 billion a year buying US real assets such as General Motors and Microsoft stock, what would happen to the prices of these assets?

f If China decided to permit the renminbi to freely find its own value on the foreign exchange market, what changes do you predict would occur in the balance of trade between China and the United States, China's real GDP growth rate, the US real GDP growth rate, and world real GDP growth?

g Do you think China should freely float the renminbi?

2 **The lesson: Buy Ruffles in Myanmar**

. . . A small bag of cheese-flavoured Ruffles potato chips is $1.69 in Japan and only 8 cents in Myanmar. A plain white T-shirt costs $16 in a mall in Cape Town, South Africa, and . . . The price of spending 1 hour at an Internet cafe inVietnam is $0.62, in China is $1.48 and in South Africa is $3.40.

The Los Angeles Times, 23 April 23 2006

Do these prices indicate that purchasing power parity-does not prevail? Why or why not?

3 The *Economist* magazine uses the price of a BigMac to determine whether a currency is undervalued or overvalued. In May 2006, the price of a Big Mac was $3.10 in New York, 10.5 yuan in Beijing and 6.30 Swiss francs in Geneva. The exchanges rates were 8.03 yuan per US dollar and 1.21 Swiss francs per US dollar.

a Was the yuan undervalued or overvalued relative to purchasing power parity?

b Was the Swiss franc undervalued or overvalued relative to purchasing power parity?

c Do you think the price of a Big Mac in different countries provides a valid test of purchasing power parity? Explain why or why not.

Web Activities

1 Get recent data on the exchange rate of your own currency (the pound, the euro, the rand or other) against the US dollar and the Japanese yen. Then:

a Use the demand and supply model of the foreign exchange market to explain the changes (or absence of changes) in the exchange rates.

b What specific events might have changed exchange rate expectations?

c What forces might have prevented the exchange rates from changing?

d What information would you need to be able to determine whether central bank intervention has prevented each exchange rate from changing by as much as it otherwise would have?

e What can you say about the US dollar-Japanese yen exchange rate? How has it changed and why?

2 Visit PACIFIC (an exchange rate service) and read the page on purchasing power parity.

a What is purchasing power parity?

b Which currencies are the most overvalued relative to the US dollar today?

c Which currencies are the most undervalued relative to the US dollar today?

d Can you offer some suggestions as to why some currencies are overvalued and some are undervalued relative to the pound?

e Do you think that the information on overvaluation and undervaluation is useful to currency speculators? Why or why not?

Glossary

Above full-employment equilibrium A macroeconomic equilibrium in which real GDP exceeds potential GDP. (p. 520)

Absolute advantage A person who is more productive than others. (p. 44)

Adverse selection The tendency for people to enter into agreements in which they can use their private information to their own advantage and to the disadvantage of the less-informed party. (p. 436)

Aggregate demand The relationship between the quantity of real GDP demanded and the price level. (p. 515)

Aggregate hours The total number of hours worked by all the people employed, both full time and part time, during a year. (p. 493)

Aggregate planned expenditure The expenditure that households, firms, governments and foreigners plan to undertake in given circumstances. It is the sum of planned consumption expenditure, planned investment, planned government expenditure on goods and services and planned exports minus planned imports. (p. 562)

Aggregate production function The relationship between the quantity of real GDP supplied and the quantities of labour and capital and the state of technology. (p. 510)

Allocative efficiency A situation in which we cannot produce more of any good without giving up some of another good that we value more highly. (p. 41)

Automatic fiscal policy A change in fiscal policy that is triggered by the state of the economy. (p. 598)

Automatic stabilizers Mechanisms that stabilize real GDP without explicit action by the government. (p. 602)

Autonomous expenditure The sum of those components of aggregate planned expenditure that do not vary with real GDP. Autonomous expenditure equals investment, government expenditure, exports and the autonomous parts of consumption expenditure and imports. (p. 569)

Autonomous taxes Taxes that do not vary with real GDP. (p. 598)

Autonomous tax multiplier The magnification effect of a change in autonomous taxes on equilibrium expenditure and real GDP. (p. 600)

Average cost pricing rule A rule that sets price to cover cost including normal profit, which means setting the price equal to average total cost. (pp. 279, 326)

Average fixed cost Total fixed cost per unit of output. (p. 220)

Average product The average product of a resource. It equals total product divided by the quantity of the resource employed. (p. 215)

Average total cost Total cost per unit of output. (p. 220)

Average variable cost Total variable cost per unit of output. (p. 220)

Balanced budget A government budget in which revenues and expenditures are equal. (p. 593)

Balanced budget multiplier The multiplier that arises from a fiscal policy action that changes *both* government expenditure and taxes by the *same* amount so that the government's budget balance remains unchanged. (p. 601)

Balance of payments accounts A country's record of international trading and its borrowing and lending. (p. 764)

Bank of England The central bank of the United Kingdom. (p. 623)

Bank Rate The Bank of England's official interest rate. (p. 624)

Barriers to entry Legal or natural constraints that protect a firm from potential competitors. (p. 264)

Barter The direct exchange of one good or service for other goods and services. (p. 618)

Below full-employment equilibrium A macroeconomic equilibrium in which potential GDP exceeds real GDP. (p. 520)

Big trade-off A trade-off between equity and efficiency. (pp. 12, 113)

Bilateral monopoly A situation in which a union (a monopoly seller) faces a monopsony buyer. (p. 390)

Black market An illegal trading arrangement in which the price exceeds the legally imposed price ceiling. (p. 123)

Budget An annual statement of the government's projected outlays and revenues during the next year together with the laws and regulations that support those outlays and revenues. (p. 592)

Budget deficit A government's budget balance that is negative – outlays exceed revenues. (p. 593)

Budget line The limits to a household's consumption choices. (p. 168)

Budget surplus A government's budget balance that is positive – revenues exceed outlays. (p. 593)

Building society A private firm licensed under the Building Societies Act 1986 to accept deposits and make loans. (p. 621)

Business cycle The periodic but irregular up-and-down movement in economic activity. (p. 452)

Capital The tools, equipment, buildings, and other constructions that businesses now use to produce goods and services. (p. 6)

Capital account A record of all international borrowing and lending transactions. (p. 764)

Capital accumulation The growth of capital resources. (p. 42)

Capital stock The total quantity of plant, equipment, buildings and inventories. (p. 544)

Capture theory A theory of regulation that states that the regulation is in the self-interest of producers. (p. 323)

Cartel A group of firms that has entered into a collusive agreement to limit output and increase prices and profits. (p. 297)

Ceteris paribus Other things being equal – all other relevant things remaining the same. (p. 15)

Chained volume measure A measure that uses the prices of two adjacent years to calculate the real GDP growth rate. (p. 478)

Change in demand A change in buyers' plans that occurs when some influence on those plans other than the price of the good changes. It is illustrated by a shift of the demand curve. (p. 60)

Change in reserve assets The net increase or decrease in a country's holdings of foreign currency reserves that comes about from the official financing of the difference between the current account and capital account balances. (p. 764)

Change in supply A change in sellers' plans that occurs when some influence on those plans other than the price of the good changes. It is illustrated by a shift of the supply curve. (p. 65)

Change in the quantity demanded A change in buyers' plans that occurs when the price of a good changes but all other influences on buyers' plans remain unchanged. It is illustrated by a movement along the demand curve. (p. 63)

Change in the quantity supplied A change in sellers' plans that occurs when the price of a good changes but all other influences on sellers' plans remain unchanged. It is illustrated by a movement along the supply curve. (p. 67)

Classical A macroeconomist who believes that the economy is self-regulating and that it is always at full employment. (p. 526)

Classical dichotomy At full employment, the forces that determine real variables are independent of those that determine nominal variables. (p. 534)

Classical growth theory A theory of economic growth based on the view that real GDP growth is temporary and that when real GDP per person increases above subsistence level, a population explosion brings real GDP back to subsistence level. (p. 729)

Classical model A model of an economy that determines the real variables – real GDP, employment and unemployment, the real wage rate, consumption, saving, investment and the real interest rate – at full employment. (p. 534)

Coase theorem The proposition that if property rights exist, only a small number of parties are involved and transactions costs are low, then private transactions are efficient. (p. 347)

Collusive agreement An agreement between two (or more) producers to restrict output, raise the price, and increase profits. (p. 302)

Command system A method of organizing production that uses a managerial hierarchy. (pp. 102, 197)

Commercial bank A private firm that is licensed by the Bank of England under the Banking Act 1987 to take deposits and make loans. (p. 621)

Common resource A resource that is rival and non-excludable. (p. 360)

Comparative advantage A person or country has a comparative advantage in an activity if that person or country can perform the activity at a lower opportunity cost than anyone else or any other country. (p. 44)

Competitive market A market that has many buyers and many sellers, so no single buyer or seller can influence the price. (p. 58)

Complement A good that is used in conjunction with another good. (p. 61)

Constant returns to scale Features of a firm's technology that lead to constant long-run average cost as output increases. When constant returns to scale are present, the *LRAC* curve is horizontal. (p. 227)

Consumer equilibrium A situation in which a consumer has allocated his or her available income in the way that, given the prices of goods and services, maximizes his or her total utility. (p. 187)

Consumer Prices Index (CPI) An index that measures the average of the prices paid by consumers for a fixed "basket" of consumer goods and services. (p. 500)

Consumer surplus The value of a good minus the price paid for it, summed over the quantity bought. (p. 105)

Consumption expenditure The total payment for consumer goods and services. (p. 471)

Consumption function The relationship between consumption expenditure and disposable income, other things remaining the same. (p. 563)

Contestable market A market in which firms can enter and leave so easily that firms in the market face competition from potential entrants. (p. 310)

Contractionary fiscal policy A decrease in government expenditure on goods and services or an increase in net taxes. (p. 605)

Cooperative equilibrium The outcome of a game in which the players make and share the monopoly profit. (p. 309)

Copyright A government-sanctioned exclusive right granted to the inventor of a good, service or productive process to produce, use and sell the invention for a given number of years. (p. 353)

Cost-push inflation An inflation that results from an initial increase in costs. (p. 697)

Creditor nation A country that during its entire history has invested more in the rest of the world than other countries have invested in it. (p. 766)

Cross elasticity of demand The responsiveness of the demand for a good to the price of a substitute or complement, other things remaining the same. It is calculated as the percentage change in the quantity demanded of the good divided by the percentage change in the price of the substitute or complement. (p. 89)

Cross-section graph A graph that shows the values of an economic variable for different groups in a population at a point in time. (p. 20)

Crowding in The tendency for expansionary fiscal policy to *increase* investment. (p. 671)

Crowding out The tendency for expansionary fiscal policy to *decrease* investment. (p. 671)

Currency The notes and coins that we use today. (p. 619)

Currency appreciation The rise in the value of one currency in terms of another currency. (p. 769)

Currency depreciation The fall in the value of one currency in terms of another currency. (p. 769)

Currency drain ratio The ratio of currency to deposits. (p. 626)

Current account A record of the receipts from the sales of goods and services to foreigners, the payments for goods and services bought from foreigners, income and other transfers received from and paid to foreigners. (pp. 461, 764)

Cyclical surplus or deficit The actual surplus or deficit minus the structural surplus or deficit. (p. 603)

Cyclical unemployment The fluctuations in unemployment over the business cycle. (p. 498)

Deadweight loss A measure of inefficiency. It is equal to the decrease in consumer surplus and producer surplus that results from an inefficient level of production. (p. 109)

Debtor nation A country that during its entire history has borrowed more from the rest of the world than it has lent to it. (p. 766)

Deflation A process in which the price level falls – a negative inflation. (p. 459)

Demand The relationship between the quantity of a good that consumers plan to buy and the price of the good when all other influences on buyers' plans remain the same. It is described by a demand schedule and illustrated by a demand curve. (p. 59)

Demand curve A curve that shows the relationship between the quantity demanded of a good and its price when all other influences on consumers' planned purchases remain the same. (p. 60)

Demand for labour The relationship between the quantity of labour demanded and the real wage rate when all other influences on firms' hiring plans remain the same. (p. 536)

Demand for loanable funds The relationship between the quantity of loanable funds demanded and the real interest rate when all other influences on borrowing plans remain the same. (p. 544)

Demand for money The relationship between the quantity of money demanded and the interest rate – the opportunity cost of holding money – when all other influences on the amount of money that people plan to hold remain the same. (p. 630)

Demand-pull inflation An inflation that results from an initial increase in aggregate demand. (p. 695)

Depreciation The decrease in the capital stock that results from wear and tear and obsolescence. (p. 473)

Deregulation The process of removing a previously imposed regulation. (p. 323)

Derived demand The demand for a factor of production, which is derived from the demand for the goods and services produced by the factor. (p. 378)

Desired reserve ratio The ratio of the reserves to deposits that banks consider prudent to hold. (p. 625)

Diminishing marginal rate of substitution The general tendency for the marginal rate of substitution to diminish as the consumer moves along an indifference curve, increasing consumption of the good on the x-axis and decreasing consumption of the good on the y-axis. (p. 172)

Diminishing marginal returns The tendency for the marginal product of an additional unit of a factor of production to be less than the marginal product of the previous unit of the factor. (p. 217)

Diminishing marginal utility The decrease in marginal utility as the quantity consumed increases. (p. 185)

Direct relationship A relationship between two variables that move in the same direction. (p. 22)

Discounting The conversion of a future amount of money to its present value. (p. 405)

Discouraged workers People who are available and willing to work but have stopped actively looking for jobs in the past four weeks. (p. 491)

Discretionary fiscal policy A policy action that is initiated by the government (Chancellor of the Exchequer in the United Kingdom). (p. 598)

Diseconomies of scale Features of a firm's technology that lead to rising long-run average cost as output increases. (p. 226)

Disposable income Aggregate income minus taxes plus transfer payments. (pp. 517, 562)

Dominant strategy equilibrium A Nash equilibrium in which the best strategy of each player is to cheat (deny) regardless of the strategy of the other player. (p. 308)

Dumping The sale by a foreign firm of exports at a lower price than the cost of production. (p. 156)

Duopoly A market structure in which two producers of a good or service compete. (p. 296)

Dynamic comparative advantage A comparative advantage that a person or country possesses as a result of having specialized in a particular activity and then, as a result of learning-by-doing, having become the producer with the lowest opportunity cost. (p. 47)

Economic activity rate The percentage of the working-age population who are economically active. (p. 491)

Economically active The people who have a job or are willing and able to take a job. (p. 490)

Economically inactive The people who do not want a job. (p. 490)

Economic depreciation The change in the market value of capital over a given period. (p. 192)

Economic efficiency A situation that occurs when the firm produces a given output at the least cost. (p. 195)

Economic growth The expansion of production possibilities that results from capital accumulation and technological change. (pp. 42, 451)

Economic growth rate The annual percentage change in real GDP. (p. 718)

Economic information Data on prices, quantities and qualities of goods and services and factors of production. (p. 435)

Economic model A description of some aspect of the economic world that includes only those features of the world that are needed for the purpose at hand. (p. 14)

Economic profit A firm's total revenue minus total cost. (p. 193)

Economic rent Any surplus – consumer surplus, producer surplus or economic profit. It is also the income received by the owner of a factor of production over and above the amount required to induce that owner to offer the factor for use. (pp. 272, 398)

Economic theory A generalization that summarizes what we think we understand about the economic choices that people make and the performance of industries and entire economies. (p. 15)

Economic welfare A comprehensive measure of the general state of economic well-being. (p. 480)

Economics The social science that studies the *choices* that individuals, businesses, governments, and entire societies make and how they cope with *scarcity* and the *incentives* that influence and reconcile those choices. (p. 4)

Economies of scale Features of a firm's technology that lead to a falling long-run average cost as output increases. (pp. 207, 226)

Economies of scope Decreases in average total cost that occur when a firm uses specialized resources to produce a range of goods and services. (p. 207)

Efficiency wage A wage rate that a firm pays above the competitive equilibrium wage rate with the aim of attracting the most productive workers. A real wage rate set above the full-employment equilibrium wage rate that balances the costs and benefits of this higher wage rate to maximize the firm's profit. (pp. 391, 543)

Efficient market A market in which the actual price embodies all currently available relevant information. Resources are sent to their highest-valued use. (p. 440)

Elastic demand Demand with a price elasticity greater than 1; other things remaining the same, the percentage change in the quantity demanded exceeds the percentage change in price. (p. 85)

Elasticity of supply The responsiveness of the quantity supplied of a good to a change in its price, other things remaining the same. (p. 92)

Employment rate The percentage of people of working age who have jobs. (p. 492)

Entrepreneurship The human resource that organizes the other three factors of production: labour, land, and capital. (p. 6)

Equilibrium expenditure The level of aggregate expenditure that occurs when aggregate planned expenditure equals real GDP. (p. 570)

Equilibrium price The price at which the quantity demanded equals the quantity supplied. (p. 68)

Equilibrium quantity The quantity bought and sold at the equilibrium price. (p. 68)

Equity Economic justice or fairness. (p. 112)

European Central Bank (ECB) The central bank of the Eurozone – the members of the European Union that use the euro as their currency. (p. 623)

Excess reserves A bank's actual reserves minus its desired reserves. (p. 625)

Excludable A good is excludable if it is possible to prevent someone from enjoying its benefits. (p. 360)

Expansion A business cycle phase between a trough and a peak – the phase in which real GDP increases. (p. 452)

Expansionary fiscal policy An increase in government expenditure on goods and services or a decrease in net taxes. (p. 605)

Expected utility The average utility arising from all possible outcomes. (p. 431)

Exports The goods and services that we sell to people in other countries. (pp. 144, 472)

External diseconomies Factors outside the control of a firm that raise the firm's costs as the industry produces a larger output. (p. 253)

External economies Factors beyond the control of a firm that lower the firm's costs as the industry produces a larger output. (p. 253)

Externality A cost or a benefit that arises from production and falls on someone other than the producer or a cost or a benefit that arises from consumption and falls on someone other than the consumer. (p. 342)

Factors of production The productive resources that businesses use to produce goods and services. (p. 5)

Final good An item that is bought by its final user during the specified time period. (p. 470)

Financial innovation Technological change and the arrival of new financial products. (p. 629)

Financial intermediary A firm that takes deposits from households and firms and makes loans to other households and firms. (p. 621)

Firm An economic unit that hires factors of production and organizes those factors to produce and sell goods and services. (pp. 47, 192)

Fiscal policy The government's attempt to influence the economy by setting and changing taxes, making transfer payments, and purchasing goods and services. (pp. 463, 517)

Five-firm concentration ratio A measure of market power that is calculated as the percentage of total revenue (the value of sales) in an industry accounted for by the five firms with the largest value of sales. (p. 202)

Fixed exchange rate A foreign exchange rate that is pegged at a value determined by the central bank. (p. 774)

Flexible exchange rate A foreign exchange rate that is determined by market forces in the absence of central bank intervention. (p. 774)

Flow A quantity per unit of time. (p. 473)

Foreign exchange market The market in which the currency of one country is exchanged for the currency of another. (p. 769)

Foreign exchange rate The price at which one currency exchanges for another. (p. 769)

Free-rider problem The absence of an incentive for people to pay for what they consume. (p. 360)

Frictional unemployment The unemployment that arises from normal labour turnover – from people entering and leaving the workforce and from the ongoing creation and destruction of jobs. (p. 497)

Full employment A situation in which all unemployment is frictional and structural, or equivalently, when there is no cyclical unemployment. (p. 498)

Full employment equilibrium A macroeconomic equilibrium in which real GDP equals potential GDP. (p. 520)

Game theory A tool that economists use to analyze strategic behaviour – behaviour that takes into account the expected behaviour of others and the recognition of mutual interdependence. (p. 300)

GDP deflator One measure of the price level, which is the average of current-year prices as a percentage of base-year prices. (p. 478)

General Agreement on Tariffs and Trade An international agreement signed in 1947 to reduce tariffs on international trade. (p. 153)

Gini coefficient The area between the line of inequality and the Lorenz curve as a percentage of the entire area beneath the line of inequality. (p. 413)

Globalization The expansion of international trade and investment. (p. 8)

Goods and services The objects that people value and produce to satisfy their wants. (p. 5)

Government budget deficit The deficit that arises when the government spends more than it collects in taxes. (p. 461)

Government budget surplus The surplus that arises when the government collects more in taxes than it spends. (p. 461)

Government debt The total amount of borrowing by the government. It equals the sum of past budget deficits minus budget surpluses minus revenue from the sale of assets. (p. 595)

Government expenditure Goods and services bought by the government. (p. 472)

Government expenditure multiplier The magnification effect of a change in government expenditure on goods and services on equilibrium expenditure and real GDP. (p. 598)

Great Depression A decade (1929–1939) of high unemployment and stagnant production throughout the world economy. (p. 450)

Gross domestic product (GDP) The market value of all the final goods and services produced within a country during a given time period – usually a year. (p. 470)

Gross investment The total amount spent on purchases of new capital and on replacing depreciated capital. (p. 473)

Growth accounting A tool that calculates the quantitative contribution to real GDP growth of each of its sources. (p. 726)

Hotelling Principle The proposition that the price of a resources is expected to rise at a rate equal to the interest rate. (p. 397)

Human capital The knowledge and skill that people obtain from education, on-the-job training, and experience. (p. 5)

Hyperinflation An inflation that exceeds 50 per cent a month. (p. 460)

Hysteresis The idea that the natural unemployment rate depends on the path of the actual unemployment rate; so where the unemployment rate ends up depends on where it has been. (p. 543)

Implicit rental rate The firm's opportunity cost of using its own capital. (p. 192)

Imports The goods and services that we buy from people in other countries. (pp. 144, 472)

Incentive A reward that encourages an action or a penalty that discourages one. (p. 4)

Incentive system A method of organizing production that uses a market-like mechanism inside the firm. (p. 197)

Income effect The effect of a change in income on consumption, other things remaining the same. (p. 176)

Income elasticity of demand The responsiveness of demand to a change in income, other things remaining the same. It is calculated as the percentage change in the quantity demanded divided by the percentage change in income. (p. 90)

Indifference curve A line that shows combinations of goods among which a consumer is indifferent. (p. 171)

Individual transferable quota (ITQ) A production limit that is assigned to an individual who is free to transfer the quota to someone else. (p. 370)

Induced expenditure The sum of the components of aggregate planned expenditure that vary with real GDP. Induced expenditure equals consumption expenditure minus imports. (p. 569)

Induced taxes Taxes that vary with real GDP. (p. 601)

Inelastic demand A demand with a price elasticity between 0 and 1; the percentage change in the quantity demanded is less than the percentage change in price. (p. 85)

Infant-industry argument The argument that a new industry must be protected to enable it to grow into a mature industry that can compete in world markets. (p. 156)

Inferior good A good for which demand decreases as income increases. (p. 61)

Inflation A process in which the price level is rising and money is losing value. (p. 694)

Inflationary gap The amount by which real GDP exceeds potential GDP. (p. 521)

Inflation rate The annual percentage change in the price level. (pp. 459, 502)

Information cost The opportunity cost of economic information – the cost of acquiring information on prices, quantities and qualities of goods and services and resources. (p. 435)

Insider–outsider theory A theory of job rationing that says that to be productive, new workers – outsiders – must receive on-the-job training from existing workers – insiders. (p. 543)

Instrument rule A decision rule for monetary policy that sets the policy instrument at a level that is based on the current state of the economy. (p. 646)

Intellectual property rights Property rights assigned to the creators of knowledge. (p. 353)

Interest The income that capital earns. (p. 6)

Interest rate parity A situation in which the rates of return on assets in different currencies are equal. (p. 776)

Intermediate good An item that is produced by one firm, bought by another firm and used as a component of a final good or service. (p. 470)

International crowding out The tendency for expansionary fiscal policy to decrease net exports. (p. 671)

Inverse relationship A relationship between variables that move in opposite directions. (p. 23)

Investment The purchase of new plant, equipment, and buildings and additions to inventories. (p. 471)

***IS* curve** A curve that shows the combinations of real GDP and the interest rate at which aggregate planned expenditure equals real GDP. (p. 688)

Isocost line A line that shows the combinations of labour and capital that can be bought for a given total cost and given factor prices. (p. 235)

Isocost map A series of isocost lines, each one of which represents a different total cost but for given prices of labour and capital. (p. 235)

Isoquant A curve that shows the different combinations of labour and capital required to produce a given quantity of output. (p. 233)

Isoquant map A series of isoquants, one for each different output level. (p. 233)

Job rationing The practice of paying a real wage rate above the equilibrium level and then rationing jobs by some method. (p. 542)

Job search The activity of looking for acceptable vacant jobs. (p. 541)

Keynesian A macroeconomist who believes that left alone, the economy would rarely operate at full employment and that to achieve full employment, active help from fiscal policy and monetary policy is required. (pp. 526, 676)

Keynesian model A model of the economy in which aggregate demand determines real GDP in the short run. (p. 562)

Keynesian theory of the business cycle A theory that regards volatile expectations as the main source of economic fluctuations. (p. 743)

***k* per cent rule** A rule that makes the quantity of money grow at a rate of *k* per cent a year, where *k* equals the growth rate of potential GDP. (p. 657)

Labour The work time and work effort that people devote to producing goods and services. (p. 5)

Labour productivity The quantity of real GDP produced per hour of labour. (pp. 549, 723)

Land The gifts of nature that we use to produce goods and services. (p. 5)

Law of demand Other things remaining the same, the higher the price of a good, the smaller is the quantity demanded; the lower the price of a good, the larger is the quantity demanded. (p. 59)

Law of diminishing marginal rate of substitution The marginal rate of substitution of labour for capital diminishes as the amount of labour increases and the amount of capital decreases. (p. 234)

Law of diminishing returns As a firm uses more of a variable input, with a given quantity of other inputs (fixed inputs), the marginal product of the variable input eventually diminishes. (pp. 217, 536, 726)

Law of supply Other things remaining the same, the higher the price of a good, the greater is the quantity supplied; the lower the price of a good, the smaller is the quantity supplied. (p. 64)

Learning-by-doing People become more productive in an activity (learn) just by repeatedly producing a particular good or service (doing). (p. 47)

Least-cost technique The combination of labour and capital that minimizes the total cost of producing a given level of output. (p. 236)

Legal monopoly A market structure in which there is one firm and entry is restricted by the granting of a public franchise, government licence, patent or copyright. (p. 264)

Limit pricing The practice of setting the price at the highest level that inflicts a loss on an entrant. (p. 311)

Linear relationship A relationship between two variables that is illustrated by a straight line. (p. 22)

***LM* curve** A curve that shows the combinations of real GDP and the interest rate at which the quantity of real money demanded equals the quantity of real money supplied. (p. 689)

Long run A period of time in which the quantities of all factors of production can be varied. (p. 214)

Long-run aggregate supply The relationship between the real GDP supplied and the price level when real GDP equals potential GDP. (p. 510)

Long-run average cost curve The relationship between the lowest attainable average total cost and output when both capital and labour are varied. (p. 225)

Long-run industry supply curve A curve that shows how the quantity supplied by an industry varies as the market price varies after all the possible adjustments have been made, including changes in plant size and the number of firms in the industry. (p. 253)

Long-run macroeconomic equilibrium A situation that occurs when real GDP equals potential GDP – the economy is on its long-run aggregate supply curve. (p. 519)

Long-run neutrality A proposition that in the long run a change in the quantity of money changes the price level and leaves real variables unchanged. (p. 679)

Long-run Phillips curve A curve that shows the relationship between inflation and unemployment when the actual inflation rate equals the expected inflation rate. (p. 707)

Lorenz curve A curve that graphs the cumulative percentage of income or wealth against the cumulative percentage of households or population. (p. 411)

M4 A measure of money that consists of currency held by the public plus bank deposits and building society deposits. (p. 619)

Macroeconomic long run A time frame that is sufficiently long for the real wage rate to have adjusted to achieve full employment: real GDP equal to potential GDP and unemployment equal to the natural unemployment rate. (p. 510)

Macroeconomics The study of the performance of the national economy and the global economy. (p. 4)

Macroeconomic short run A period during which some money prices are sticky and real GDP might be below, above or at potential GDP and unemployment might be above, below or at the natural unemployment rate. (p. 511)

Managed exchange rate An exchange rate that is influenced by the central bank to avoid excessive fluctuations – sometimes called a crawling peg. (p. 774)

Margin When a choice is changed by a small amount or by a little at a time, the choice is made at the margin. (p. 13)

Marginal benefit The benefit that a person receives from consuming one more unit of a good or service. It is measured as the maximum amount that a person is willing to pay for one more unit of the good or service. (pp. 13, 40)

Marginal benefit curve A curve that shows the relationship between the marginal benefit of a good and the quantity of that good consumed. (p. 40)

Marginal cost The opportunity cost of producing one more unit of a good or service. It is the best alternative forgone. It is calculated as the increase in total cost divided by the increase in output. (pp. 13, 39, 220)

Marginal cost pricing rule A rule that sets the price of a good or service equal to the marginal cost of producing it. (pp. 278, 325)

Marginal external benefit The benefit from an additional unit of a good or service that people other than the consumer enjoy. (p. 349)

Marginal external cost The cost of producing an additional unit of a good or service that falls on people other than the producer. (p. 345)

Marginal private benefit The benefit from an additional unit of a good or service that the consumer of that good or service receives. (p. 349)

Marginal private cost The cost of producing an additional unit of a good or service that is borne by the producer of that good or service. (p. 345)

Marginal product The increase in total product that results from a one-unit increase in the variable input, with all other inputs remaining the same. It is calculated as the increase in total product divided by the increase in the variable input employed, when the quantities of all other inputs are constant. (p. 215)

Marginal product of labour The additional real GDP produced by an additional hour of labour when all other influences on production remain the same. (p. 536)

Marginal propensity to consume The fraction of a change in disposable income that is consumed. It is calculated as the change in consumption expenditure divided by the change in disposable income. (p. 564)

Marginal propensity to import The fraction of an increase in real GDP that is spent on imports. (p. 567)

Marginal propensity to save The fraction of an increase in disposable income that is saved. It is calculated as the change in saving divided by the change in disposable income. (p. 564)

Marginal rate of substitution The rate at which a person will give up good *y* (the good measured on the *y*-axis) to get an additional unit of good *x* (the good measured on the *x*-axis) and at the same time remain indifferent (remain on the same indifference curve). (p. 172)

Marginal rate of substitution of labour for capital The increase in labour needed per unit decrease in capital to allow output to remain constant. (p. 233)

Marginal revenue The change in total revenue that results from a one-unit increase in the quantity sold. It is calculated as the change in total revenue divided by the change in quantity sold. (p. 240)

Marginal revenue product The change in total revenue that results from employing one more unit of a factor of production while the quantity of all other factors remains the same. It is calculated as the increase in total revenue divided by the increase in the quantity of the factor. (p. 380)

Marginal social benefit The marginal benefit enjoyed by society – by the consumer of a good or service (marginal private benefit) plus the marginal benefit enjoyed by others (marginal external benefit). (p. 349)

Marginal social cost The marginal cost incurred by the entire society – by the producer and by everyone else on whom the cost falls – and is the sum of marginal private cost and the marginal external cost. (p. 345)

Marginal utility The change in total utility resulting from a one-unit increase in the quantity of a good consumed. (p. 185)

Marginal utility per pound The marginal utility from a good consumed divided by its price. (p. 187)

Market Any arrangement that enables buyers and sellers to get information and to do business with each other. (p. 48)

Market failure A state in which the market does not allocate resources efficiently. (p. 320)

Market for loanable funds The market in which households, firms, governments, banks and other financial institutions borrow and lend. (p. 544)

Market power The ability to influence the market, and in particular the market price, by influencing the total quantity offered for sale. (p. 264)

McCallum rule A rule that adjusts the growth rate of the monetary base to target the inflation rate but also to take into account changes in the trend productivity growth rate and fluctuations in aggregate demand. (p. 658)

Means of payment A method of settling a debt. (p. 618)

Merger The combining of the assets of two or more firms to form a single, new firm. (p. 331)

Microeconomics The study of the choices that individuals and businesses make, the way those choices interact, and the influence governments exert on them. (p. 4)

Minimum efficient scale The smallest quantity of output at which the long-run average cost curve reaches its lowest level. (p. 227)

Minimum wage A regulation that makes the hiring of labour below a specified wage rate illegal. The lowest wage rate at which a firm may legally hire labour. (pp. 125, 543)

Monetarist A macroeconomist who believes that the economy is self-regulating and that it will normally operate at full employment, provided that monetary policy is not erratic and that the pace of money growth is kept steady. (pp. 527, 676)

Monetarist theory of the business cycle A theory that regards fluctuations in the quantity of money as the main source of economic fluctuations. (p. 744)

Monetary base The sum of the liabilities of the Bank of England plus coins issued by the Royal Mint. (p. 624)

Monetary policy The central bank conducts a nation's monetary policy by changing interest rates and adjusting the quantity of money. (pp. 463, 517)

Monetary Policy Committee The committee in the Bank of England that has the responsibility for formulating monetary policy. (p. 642)

Monetary policy instrument A variable that the central bank can directly control or closely target. (p. 645)

Money Any commodity or token that is generally acceptable as a means of payment. (pp. 48, 618)

Money multiplier The ratio of the change in the quantity of money to the change in monetary base. (p. 628)

Money price The number of pounds or euros that must be given up in exchange for a good or service. (p. 58)

Money wage rate The number of pounds (or euros) that an hour of labour earns. (p. 536)

Monopolistic competition A market structure in which a large number of firms compete by making similar but slightly different products. (pp. 201, 286)

Monopoly A market structure in which there is one firm, which produces a good or service that has no close substitute and in which the firm is protected from competition by a barrier preventing the entry of new firms. (pp. 202, 264)

Monopoly control laws Laws that regulate and prohibit monopoly and monopolistic practices. (p. 323)

Monopsony A market in which there is a single buyer. (p. 389)

Moral hazard A situation in which one of the parties to an agreement has an incentive after the agreement is made to act in a manner that brings additional benefits to himself or herself at the expense of the other party. (p. 436)

Multiplier The amount by which a change in autonomous expenditure is magnified or multiplied to determine the change in equilibrium expenditure and real GDP. (p. 572)

Nash equilibrium The outcome of a game that occurs when player A takes the best possible action given the action of player B and player B takes the best possible action given the action of player A. (p. 301)

National saving The sum of private saving (saving by households and businesses) and government saving (budget surplus). (p. 473)

Natural monopoly A monopoly is an industry in which economies of scale enable one firm to supply the entire market at the lowest possible price. (p. 264)

Natural unemployment rate of The unemployment rate when the economy is at full employment. There is no cyclical unemployment; all unemployment is frictional and structural. (p. 498)

Negative externality An externality that arises from either production or consumption and that imposes an external cost. (p. 342)

Negative relationship A relationship between variables that move in opposite directions. (p. 23)

Neoclassical growth theory A theory of economic growth that proposes that real GDP grows because technological change induces a level of saving and investment that makes capital per hour of labour grow. (p. 731)

Net borrower A country that is borrowing more from the rest of the world than it is lending to it. (p. 766)

Net exports The value of exports minus the value of imports. (pp. 144, 472)

Net investment Net increase in the capital stock – gross investment minus depreciation. (p. 473)

Net lender A country that is lending more to the rest of the world than it is borrowing from it. (p. 766)

Net present value The present value of the future flow of marginal revenue product generated by capital minus the cost of the capital. (p. 407)

Net taxes Taxes paid to governments minus transfer payments received from governments. (p. 472)

New classical A macroeconomist who holds the view that business cycle fluctuations are the efficient responses of a well-functioning market economy bombarded by shocks that arise from the uneven pace of technological change. (p. 526)

New classical theory of the business cycle A rational expectations theory of the business cycle that regards unanticipated fluctuations in aggregate demand as the main source of economic fluctuations. (p. 746)

New growth theory A theory of economic growth based on the idea that real GDP per person grows because of the choices that people make in the pursuit of ever greater profit and that growth can persist indefinitely. (p. 733)

New Keynesian A Keynesian who holds the view that not only is the money wage rate sticky but that prices of goods and services are also sticky. (p. 527)

New Keynesian theory of the business cycle A rational expectations theory of the business cycle that regards unanticipated fluctuations in aggregate demand as the main source of economic fluctuations but leaves room for anticipated demand fluctuations to play a role. (p. 746)

Nominal GDP The value of the final goods and services produced in a given year valued at the prices that prevailed in that same year. It is a more precise name for GDP. (p. 477)

Nominal interest rate The number of pounds (or euros) that a unit of capital earns. (p. 545)

Non-excludable A good is non-excludable if everyone benefits from it regardless of whether they pay for it. (p. 360)

Non-renewable natural resource A natural resource that can be used only once and that cannot be replaced once it has been used. (p. 395)

Non-rival A good is non-rival if one person's use does not decrease the quantity available for someone else. (p. 360)

Normal good A good for which demand increases as income increases. (p. 61)

Normal profit The return that an entrepreneur can expect to receive on the average. (p. 193)

Offshoring A UK firm can either produce in another country or outsource to a firm in another country. (p. 157)

Oligopoly A market structure in which a small number of firms compete. (pp. 201, 296)

One-third rule The rule that, with no change in technology, a 1 per cent increase in capital per hour of labour brings, on the average, a 1/3 of 1 per cent increase in labour productivity. (p. 727)

Open market operation The purchase or sale of government bonds by the central bank in the open market. (p. 624)

Opportunity cost The highest-valued alternative that we give up to something. (p. 12)

Optimal currency area A geographical area that is better served by a single currency than by several currencies. (p. 778)

Original income The wages, interest, rent and profit earned in factor markets and before paying income taxes. (p. 410)

Output gap Real GDP minus potential GDP. (p. 455)

Outsourcing A situation in which a firm buys finished goods, components or services from other firms. (p. 157)

Patent A government-sanctioned exclusive right granted to the inventor of a good, service or productive process to produce, use and sell the invention for a given number of years. (p. 353)

Payoff matrix A table that shows the payoffs for every possible action by each player for every possible action by each other player. (p. 300)

Perfect competition A market in which there are many firms each selling an identical product; there are many buyers; there are no restrictions on entry into the industry; firms in the industry have no advantage over potential new entrants; and firms and buyers are well informed about the price of each firm's product. (pp. 201, 240)

Perfectly elastic demand Demand with an infinite price elasticity; the quantity demanded changes by an infinitely large percentage in response to a tiny price change. (p. 85)

Perfectly inelastic demand Demand with a price elasticity of zero; the quantity demanded remains constant when the price changes. (p. 84)

Perfect price discrimination Price discrimination that extracts the entire consumer surplus. (p. 275)

Phillips curve A curve that shows a relationship between inflation and unemployment. (p. 706)

Pigovian taxes Taxes that are used as an incentive for producers to cut back on an activity that creates an external cost. (p. 348)

Policy conflict A situation in which the government and the central bank pursue different goals and the actions of one make it harder for the other to achieve its goals. (p. 680)

Policy coordination A situation in which the government and the central bank work together to achieve a common set of goals. (p. 680)

Political equilibrium The outcome that results from the choices of voters, firms, politicians and civil servants. (p. 322)

Positive externality An externality that arise from either production or consumption and that provides an external benefit. (p. 342)

Positive relationship A relationship between two variables that move in the same direction. (p. 22)

Potential GDP The quantity of real GDP at full employment – when all the economy's labour, capital, land and entrepreneurial ability are fully employed. (pp. 451, 499)

Poverty A situation in which a household's income is too low to be able to buy the quantities of food, shelter, and clothing that are deemed necessary. (p. 415)

Preferences A description of a person's likes and dislikes. (p. 40)

Present value The amount of money that, if invested today, will grow to be as large as a given future amount when the interest that it will earn is taken into account. (p. 405)

Price cap regulation A regulation that specifies the highest price that the firm is permitted to set. (p. 327)

Price ceiling A government regulation that sets the maximum price that may legally be charged. (p. 122)

Price discrimination The practice of selling different units of a good or service for different prices or of charging one customer different prices for different quantities bought. (p. 265)

Price effect The effect of a change in the price of a good on the quantity of the good consumed, other things remaining the same. (p. 175)

Price elasticity of demand A units-free measure of the responsiveness of the quantity demanded of a good to a change in its price, when all other influences on buyers' plans remain the same. (p. 82)

Price floor A regulation that makes it illegal to charge a price lower than a specified level. (p. 125)

Price level The average level of prices. (pp. 459, 478)

Price support A government guaranteed minimum price of a good. (p. 134)

Price taker A firm that cannot influence the price of the good or service it produces. (p. 240)

Principal–agent problem The problem of devising compensation rules that induce an agent to act in the best interest of a principal. (p. 197)

Principle of minimum differentiation The tendency for competitors to make themselves similar as they try to appeal to the maximum number of clients or voters. (p. 363)

Private good A good or service that is both rival and excludable. (p. 360)

Private information Information that is available to one person but is too costly for anyone else to obtain. (p. 436)

Private sector balance An amount equal to saving minus investment. (p. 767)

Privatization The sale of a government-owned enterprise to private owners. (p. 323)

Producer surplus The price of a good minus the opportunity cost of producing it, summed over the quantity sold. (p. 107)

Product differentiation Making a product slightly different from the product of a competing firm. (pp. 201, 286)

Production efficiency A situation in which the economy cannot produce more of one good without producing less of some other good. (p. 37)

Production function The relationship between real GDP and the quantity of labour when all other influences on production remain the same. (p. 535)

Production possibilities frontier The boundary between the combinations of goods and services that can be produced and the combinations that cannot. (p. 36)

Production quota An upper limit to the quantity of a good that may be produced in a specified period. (p. 134)

Productivity curve A relationship that shows how productivity changes as the amount of capital per hour of labour changes with a given state of technology. (p. 726)

Productivity growth slowdown A slowdown in the growth rate of output per hour of labour. (p. 451)

Profit The income earned by entrepreneurship. (p. 6)

Progressive income tax A tax on income at an average rate that increases with the level of income. (p. 421)

Property rights Social arrangements that govern the ownership, use and disposal of anything that people value. (pp. 48, 346)

Proportional income tax A tax on income at a constant average rate, regardless of the level of income. (p. 421)

Public good A good or service that is both non-rival and non-excludable – it can be consumed simultaneously by everyone and from which no one can be excluded. (p. 360)

Public ownership The ownership (and sometimes operation) of a firm or industry by a government or a government controlled agency. (p. 323)

Public provision The production of a good or service by a public authority that receives its revenue from the government. (p. 351)

Purchasing power parity The equal value of different monies. (p. 776)

Quantity demanded The amount of a good or service that consumers plan to buy during a given time period at a particular price. (p. 59)

Quantity supplied The amount of a good or service that producers plan to sell during a given time period at a particular price. (p. 64)

Quantity theory of money The proposition that in the long run, an increase in the quantity of money brings an equal percentage increase in the price level. (p. 700)

Quota A limit on the quantity of a good that may be imported. (p. 152)

Rate of return regulation A regulation that requires the firm to justify its price by showing that the price enables it to earn a specified target per cent return on its capital. (p. 326)

Rational expectation The most accurate forecast possible – a forecast that uses all the available information. (pp. 703, 746)

Rational ignorance The decision *not* to acquire information because the cost of doing so exceeds the expected benefit. (p. 364)

Real business cycle theory A theory that regards random fluctuations in productivity as the main source of economic fluctuations. (p. 749)

Real GDP per person Real GDP divided by the population. (p. 718)

Real gross domestic product (real GDP) The value of final goods and services produced in a given year when valued at constant prices. (p. 477)

Real income A household's income expressed as a quantity of goods that the household can afford to buy. (p. 169)

Real interest rate The quantity of goods and services that a unit of capital earns. It is the nominal interest rate adjusted for inflation and is approximately equal to the nominal interest rate minus the inflation rate. (p. 545)

Real wage rate The quantity of goods and services that an hour's work can buy. It is equal to the money wage rate divided by the price level. (pp. 493, 536)

Recession A business cycle phase in which real GDP decreases for at least two successive quarters. (p. 452)

Recessionary gap The amount by which potential GDP exceeds real GDP. (p. 520)

Reference base period The period in which the CPI is defined to be 100. (p. 500)

Regressive income tax A tax on income at an average rate that decreases with the level of income. (p. 421)

Regulation Rules administrated by a government agency to influence economic activity by determining prices, product standards and types and conditions under which new firms may enter an industry. (p. 323)

Relative price The ratio of the price of one good or service to the price of another good or service. A relative price is an opportunity cost. (pp. 58, 169)

Renewable natural resource A natural resource that can be used repeatedly without depleting what is available for future use. (p. 395)

Rent The income that land earns. (p. 6)

Rent ceiling A regulation that makes it illegal to charge a rent higher than a specified level. (p. 122)

Rent seeking The pursuit of wealth – any attempt to capture a consumer surplus, a producer surplus, or an economic profit. (p. 272)

Repo The Bank of England's loans to banks under repurchase agreements. (p. 624)

Repo rate The interest rate in the repo market. (p. 645)

Required reserve ratio The ratio of reserves to deposits that banks are required, by regulation, to hold. (p. 625)

Reservation price The highest price that a buyer is willing to pay for a good. (p. 435)

Reserve ratio The fraction of a bank's total deposits that are held in reserves. (p. 625)

Reserves Cash in a bank's vault plus its deposit at the central bank. (p. 621)

Restrictive practices Agreements between firms on prices, terms and conditions of sale and market share. (p. 331)

Retail Prices Index (RPI) An index that measures the average of the prices paid by consumers for a fixed "basket" of consumer goods and services. (p. 500)

Risk A situation in which more than one outcome might occur and the probability of each possible outcome can be estimated. (p. 430)

Risk aversion The attitude towards risk. (p. 432)

Rival A good is rival if one person's use decreases the quantity available for someone else. (p. 360)

Rule of 70 A rule that states that the number of years it takes for the level of a variable to double is approximately 70 divided by the annual percentage growth rate of the variable. (p. 718)

Saving The amount of income that households have left after they have paid their taxes and bought their consumption goods and services. (p. 472)

Saving function The relationship between saving and disposable income, other things remaining the same. (p. 563)

Scarcity Our inability to satisfy all our wants. (p. 4)

Scatter diagram A diagram that plots the value of one economic variable against the value of another. (p. 21)

Search activity The time spent looking for someone with whom to do business. (p. 123)

Self-interest The choices that you think are the best for you. (p. 7)

Short run The period of time in which the quantity of at least one factor of production is fixed and the quantities of the other factors can be varied. The fixed factor is usually capital – that is, the firm has a given plant size. (p. 214)

Short-run aggregate supply The relationship between the quantity of real GDP supplied and the price level when the money wage rate, the prices of other factors of production and potential GDP remain constant. (p. 511)

Short-run industry supply curve A curve that shows how the quantity supplied by the industry varies as the market price varies when the plant size of each firm and the number of firms in the industry remain the same. (p. 247)

Short-run macroeconomic equilibrium A situation that occurs when the quantity of real GDP demanded equals the quantity of real GDP supplied – at the point of intersection of the *AD* curve and the *SAS* curve. (p. 518)

Short-run Phillips curve A curve that shows the trade-off between inflation and unemployment when the expected inflation rate and the natural unemployment rate remain the same. (p. 706)

Shutdown point The output and price at which the firm just covers its total variable cost. In the short run, the firm is indifferent between producing the profit-maximizing output and shutting down temporarily. (p. 246)

Signal An action taken by an informed person (or firm) to send a message to uninformed people or an action taken outside a market that conveys information that can be used by that market. (pp. 294, 437)

Single-price monopoly A monopoly that must sell each unit of its output for the same price to all its customers. (p. 265)

Slope The change in the value of the variable measured on the *y*-axis divided by the change in the value of the variable measured on the *x*-axis. (p. 26)

Social interest Choices that are the best for society as a whole. (p. 7)

Social interest theory A theory that politicians supply the regulation that achieves an efficient allocation of resources. (p. 322)

Stock A quantity that exists at a point in time. (p. 473)

Strategies All the possible actions of each player in a game. (p. 300)

Structural surplus or deficit The budget balance that would occur if the economy were at full employment and real GDP were equal to potential GDP. (p. 603)

Structural unemployment The unemployment that arises when changes in technology or international competition change the skills needed to perform jobs or change the locations of jobs. (p. 498)

Subsidy A payment made by the government to a domestic producer based on the quantity produced. (pp. 133, 152, 352)

Subsistence real wage rate The minimum real wage rate needed to maintain life. (p. 730)

Substitute A good that can be used in place of another good. (p. 61)

Substitution effect The effect of a change in price of a good or service on the quantity bought when the consumer (hypothetically) remains indifferent between the original and the new consumption situations – that is, the consumer remains on the same indifference curve. (p. 177)

Sunk cost The past expenditure on a plant that has no resale value. (p. 214)

Supply The relationship between the quantity of a good that producers plan to sell and the price of the good when all other influences on sellers' plans remain the same. It is described by a supply schedule and illustrated by a supply curve. (p. 64)

Supply curve A curve that shows the relationship between the quantity supplied and the price of a good when all other influences on producers' planned sales remain the same. (p. 64)

Supply of labour The relationship between the quantity of labour supplied and the real wage rate when all other influences on work plans remain the same. (p. 538)

Supply of loanable funds The relationship between the quantity of loanable funds supplied and the real interest rate when all other influences on lending plans remain the same. (p. 546)

Supply of money The relationship between the quantity of real money supplied and the interest rate with all other influences on the amount of money that the banking system creates remaining the same. (p. 632)

Symmetry principle A requirement that people in similar situations be treated similarly. (p. 114)

Targeting rule A decision rule for monetary policy that sets the policy instrument at a level that makes the forecast of the ultimate policy target equal to the target. (p. 646)

Tariff A tax that is imposed by the importing country when an imported good crosses its international boundary. (p. 152)

Tax incidence The division of the burden of a tax between the buyer and the seller. (p. 127)

Taylor rule A rule that sets the interest rate (Bank Rate in the United Kingdom) in response to two indicators: the current inflation rate and the current best estimate of the output gap (real GDP minus potential GDP as a percentage of potential GDP). (p. 658)

Technological change The development of new goods and better ways of producing goods and services. (p. 42)

Technological efficiency A situation that occurs when the firm produces a given output by using the least amount of inputs. (p. 195)

Technology Any method of producing a good or service. (p. 194)

Time-series graph A graph that measures time (for example, months or years) on the *x*-axis and the variable or variables in which we are interested on the *y*-axis. (p. 20)

Total cost The cost of all the factors of production that a firm uses. (p. 219)

Total fixed cost The cost of the firm's fixed inputs. (p. 219)

Total product The maximum output that a given quantity of factors of production can produce. (p. 215)

Total revenue The value of a firm's sales. It is calculated as the price of the good multiplied by the quantity sold. (pp. 86, 240)

Total revenue test A method of estimating the price elasticity of demand by observing the change in total revenue that results from a change in the price, when all other influences on the quantity sold remain the same. (p. 86)

Total surplus The sum of consumer surplus and producer surplus. (pp. 108, 325)

Total utility The total benefit that a person gets from the consumption of goods and services. (p. 158)

Total variable cost The cost of all the firm's variable inputs. (p. 219)

Trade-off An exchange – giving up one thing to get something else. (p. 11)

Trades union An organized group of workers whose purpose is to increase wages and to influence other job conditions. (p. 387)

Tragedy of the commons The absence of incentives to prevent the overuse and depletion of a resource. (p. 360)

Transactions costs The costs that arise from finding someone with whom to do business, of reaching an agreement about the price and other aspects of the exchange, and of ensuring that the terms of the agreement are fulfilled. The opportunity costs of conducting a transaction. (pp. 111, 206, 347)

Trend The general tendency for a variable to move in one direction. (p. 20)

UK interest rate differential A gap equal to the UK interest rate minus the foreign interest rate. (p. 771)

Uncertainty A situation in which more than one event might occur but it is not known which one. (p. 430)

Unemployment rate The percentage of the people in the labour force who are unemployed. (pp. 457, 491)

Unit elastic demand Demand with a price elasticity of 1; the percentage change in the quantity demanded equals the percentage change in price. (p. 84)

Utilitarianism A principle that states that we should strive to achieve "the greatest happiness for the greatest number of people". (p. 112)

Utility The benefit or satisfaction that a person gets from the consumption of a good or service. (p. 185)

Utility of wealth The amount of utility that a person attaches to a given amount of wealth. (p. 430)

Velocity of circulation The average number of times a pound (or euro) of money is used annually to buy the goods and services that make up GDP. (p. 700)

Voucher A token that the government provides to households, which they can use to buy specified goods and services. (p. 352)

Wages The income that labour earns. (p. 6)

Wealth The market value of all the things that people own. (p. 473)

Workforce The sum of the people who are employed and who are unemployed. (p. 490)

Working-age population The total number of men aged 16 to 64 and women aged 16 to 59 who are not in prison, hospital or some other form of institutional care. (p. 490)

World Trade Organization An international organization that places greater obligations on its member countries to observe the GATT rules. (p. 153)

Index

Key terms and pages on which they are defined appear in **boldface**.

Publisher's Acknowledgements

We are grateful to the following for permission to reproduce copyright material:

Illustrations and tables

Figure 1.1: Data from Office of National Statistics, *Change in Gross Value Added by Industry*. Crown Copyright material is reproduced with the permission of the controller of Her Majesty's Stationery Office (HMSO) under the terms of the click-use licence; Figure 1.2: Data from Organisation for Economic Co-operation and Development, *OECD Education at a Glance: OECD Indicators 2005*. Copyright © OECD 2005; Box 7.1, Figure 1: Data from Organisation for Economic Co-operation and Development, *Agricultural Policies in OECD Countries: At a Glance – 2006 Edition*. Copyright © OECD 2006; Box 9.1, Figure 1: Data from European Commission, http://ec.europa.eu/enterprise/enterprise_policy/analysis/doc/smes_observatory_2002_report2_en.pdf. Copyright © European Communities, 2002; Box 9.2, Figure 1: Data from Office for National Statistics. Crown Copyright material is reproduced with the permission of the controller of Her Majesty's Stationery Office (HMSO) under the terms of the click-use licence; Chapter 14, Business Case Study figure: From D. Gow, and M. Milner, "Hain plays national champion", *The Guardian*, 11 May 2001. Copyright © 2001 Guardian Newspapers and Media Ltd. Reproduced by permission; Figure 15.1: Data from UK Environment Agency (www.environment-agency.gov.uk/commondata/103601/i2_airtrends_a2_dt_1158809.xls). © Environment Agency copyright and/or database right 2004. All rights reserved; Box 17.1, Figure 1: Data from Office for National Statistics, *New Earnings Survey*. Crown Copyright material is reproduced with the permission of the controller of Her Majesty's Stationery Office (HMSO) under the terms of the click-use licence; Figure 18.1: Data from Francis Jones, "The effect of taxes and benefits on household income, 2004–2005", *Economic Trends*, No. 630, May 2006. Office for National Statistics. Crown Copyright material is reproduced with the permission of the controller of Her Majesty's Stationery Office (HMSO) under the terms of the click-use licence; Figures 18.2, 18.3 and 18.5: Data from Office for National Statistics. Crown Copyright material is reproduced with the permission of the controller of Her Majesty's Stationery Office (HMSO) under the terms of the click-use licence: Figure 18.4: Data from Office for National Statistics, *Social Trends, 2006*. Crown Copyright material is reproduced with the permission of the controller of Her Majesty's Stationery Office (HMSO) under the terms of the click-use licence; Figure 18.6: Data from Office for National Statistics, *Family Spending: A Report on the 2002/2005 Family Expenditure Survey, 2006*. Crown Copyright material is reproduced with the permission of the controller of Her Majesty's Stationery Office (HMSO) under the terms of the click-use licence; Box 18.2, Figure 1: Data from European Commission, *Europe in Figures – Eurostat Yearbook 2006–07*. Eurostat Copyright © European Communities 2007. Reproduced with permission; Box 18.2, Figure 2: Data from Office for National Statistics, *Social Trends, 2006*. Crown Copyright material is reproduced with the permission of the controller of Her Majesty's Stationery Office (HMSO) under the terms of the click-use licence; Figures 20.8, 20.10, 21.3, 22.1, 22.2: Data from Office for National Statistics. Crown Copyright material is reproduced with the permission of the controller of Her Majesty's Stationery Office (HMSO) under the terms of the click-use licence; Figures 22.3, 22.4 and 22.5: Office for National Statistics, *Labour Market Trends*, June 2007. © Crown Copyright. Crown Copyright material is reproduced with the permission of the controller of Her Majesty's Stationery Office (HMSO) under the terms of the click-use licence; Figures 22.7 and 22.8: Data from Office for National Statistics, *The Labour Force Survey*. Crown Copyright material is reproduced with the permission of the controller of Her Majesty's Stationery Office (HMSO) under the terms of the click-use licence; Figure 22.9: Data from Office for National Statistics, *Labour Market Trends*, December 2003. Crown Copyright material is reproduced with the permission of the controller of Her Majesty's Stationery Office (HMSO) under the terms of the click-use licence; Figures 22.10, 22.11, 22.12, 23.14: Data from Office for National Statistics. Crown Copyright material is reproduced with the permission of the controller of Her Majesty's Stationery Office (HMSO) under the terms of the click-use licence; Box 25.1 Figure 1: Data from Office for National Statistics. Crown Copyright material is reproduced with the permission of the controller of Her Majesty's Stationery Office (HMSO) under the terms of the click-use licence; Figures 26.1, 26.2 and 26.3: HM Treasury, *Budget 2007*. Crown Copyright material is reproduced with the permission of the controller of Her Majesty's Stationery Office (HMSO) under the terms of the click-use licence; Figure 26.4: Data from HM Treasury. Crown Copyright material is reproduced with the permission of the controller of Her Majesty's Stationery Office (HMSO) under the terms of the click-use licence; Box 26.1 Figures 1, 2 and 3: Data from European Commission, *Eurostat*, (http://epp.eurostat.ec.europa.eu), 2007. Eurostat Copyright © European Communities, 2007. Reproduced with permission; Figure 26.7: Data from Office for National Statistics. Crown Copyright material is reproduced with the permission of the controller of Her Majesty's Stationery Office (HMSO) under the terms of the click-use licence; Figure 27.1: Data from Bank of England, www.bankofengland.co.uk. Reproduced by permission; Box 27.1, Figure 1: Data from European Central Bank. Copyright © European Central Bank, Frankfurt am Main, Germany. This information may be obtained free of charge from www.ecb.int; Box 27.3, Figures 1 and 2, Figures 28.2 and 28.7: Data from Bank of England, www.bankofengland.co.uk. Reproduced by permission; Box 30.1, Figure 1: Data from Office for National Statistics. Crown Copyright material is reproduced with the permission of the controller of Her Majesty's Stationery Office (HMSO) under the terms of the click-use licence; Figure 31.7: Data from Office for National Statistics. Crown Copyright material is reproduced with the permission of the controller of Her Majesty's Stationery Office (HMSO) under the terms of the click-use licence; Figure 31.11: Based on a figure in Federal Reserve Bank Dallas "These are the good old days: a report on U.S. living standards", in *Federal Reserve Bank Dallas Annual Report, 1993*. Reproduced with permission; Figures 32.6 and 33.1: Data from Office for National Statistics. Crown Copyright material is reproduced with the permission of the controller of Her Majesty's Stationery Office (HMSO) under the terms of the click-use licence; Figure 33.3: Data from Bank of England, www.bankofengland.co.uk. Reproduced by permission; Box 33.1, Figure 1: From Frankel, Jeffery A. and Rose, Andrew, "An estimate of the effect of common currencies on trade and income", *Quarterly Journal of Economics*, 117, Issue 2, May 2002. Copyright © by the President and Fellows of Harvard College and the Massachusetts Institute of Technology.

Box 6.1, Table 1: Data from European Commission, *Eurostat* (http://epp.eurostat.ec.europa.eu), 2007. Eurostat Copyright © European Communities 2007. Reproduced with permission; Box 9.1, Table 1: Data from European Commission, http://ec.europa.eu/enterprise/enterprise_policy/analysis/doc/smes_observatory_2002_report2_en.pdf. Copyright © European Communities 2002. Reproduced with permission; Box 14.1, Table 1: Data from D. Parker, "Privatization and business restructuring: change and continuity in the privatized industries", *The Review of Policy Issues*, 1994, 1(2). Reproduce with permission of the author; Box 14.2, Table 1: European Commission (http://ec.europa.eu/enterprise/). Copyright © European Communities 1995–2007. Reproduced with permission; Box 14.3, Table 1: Data from UK Department of Health. Crown Copyright material is reproduced with the permission of the controller of Her Majesty's Stationery Office (HMSO) under the terms of the click-use licence; Box 14.4, Table 1: Data from World Economic Forum, *Global Competitive Report 2006–2007*. Copyright © 2006 World Economic Forum (www.weforum.org); Tables 21.1 and 21.2: Data from Office for National Statistics, *United Kingdom National Accounts – The Blue Book 2004*, London: HMSO. Crown Copyright material is reproduced with the permission of the controller of Her Majesty's Stationery Office (HMSO) under the terms of the click-use licence; Table 26.1: HM Treasury, *Budget 2007*. Crown Copyright material is reproduced with the permission of the controller of Her Majesty's Stationery Office (HMSO) under the terms of the click-use licence; Table 27.1: Data from Bank of England, www.bankofengland.co.uk. Reproduced by permission; Table 33.1: Data from Office for National Statistics, *United Kingdom Balance of Payments – The Pink Book 2007*, London: HMSO. Crown Copyright material is reproduced with the permission of the controller of Her Majesty's Stationery Office (HMSO) under the terms of the click-use licence; Table 33.2: Data from Office for National Statistics. Crown Copyright material is reproduced with the permission of the controller of Her Majesty's Stationery Office (HMSO) under the terms of the click-use licence; Table 33.3: Data from European Central Bank. Copyright © European Central Bank, Frankfurt am Main, Germany. This information may be obtained free of charge from www.ecb.int.

Photos and cartoons

Page 1: Courtesy of Adrienne D'Ambrosio, Pearson Education, Inc.; 3: John Powell Photography / Alamy; 4: © The New Yorker Collection 1985. Frank Modell from cartoonbank.com. All rights reserved. (Published in *The New Yorker*, 2 September 1985); 14: Courtesy of PA WeatherCentre Ltd; 35: aberCPC / Alamy; 55: © Paul Almasy / Corbis; 57: Joy Skipper / Anthony Blake Photo Library, all rights reserved; 81: Harald Theissen / © imagebroker / Alamy; 101: © Tetra Images / Alamy; 109: © The New Yorker Collection 1988. Mike Twohy from cartoonbank.com. All rights reserved. (Published in *The New Yorker*, 4 July 1988); 121: © Sally and Richard Greenhill / Alamy; 143: © Lester Lefkowitz / Getty Images; 165: Jim Pickerell / © Stock Connection Blue / Alamy; 167: © David Stewart / Getty Images; 174: © The New Yorker Collection 1988. Robert Weber from cartoonbank.com. All rights reserved. (Published in *The New Yorker*, 29 February 1988); 191: Courtesy of SAP; 198: © David Austin, Financial Times; 201: Mari Tudor Jones / Pearson Education (wheat); 201: Percy Ryall / Alamy (trainers); 201: Steve Bates / BAA (aeroplanes); 201: Empics / PA (Windows XP); 213: © Terry W. Eggers / Corbis; 239: Zen Sekizawa / Getty Images; 263: Google homepage copyright © Google, Inc. and is used with permission; 276: From William Hamilton, *Voodoo Economics*, San Francisco: Chronicle Books, 1992, p. 3. © 1992 by the Chronicle Publishing Company, reprinted with permission; 285: © Justin Kase / Alamy; 317: PA Wire; 319: Walter Bibikow / © Jon Arnold Images / Alamy; 341: © Gary Parker / Science Photo Library; 359: © Durand Patrick / Corbis Sygma; 377: AP Photo / Jon Super; 409: © Rune Hellestad / Corbis; 429: Alvey & Towers; 440: © The New Yorker Collection. Aaron Bacall from cartoonbank.com. All rights reserved; 447: Courtesy of David Smith and Neil Davies; 449 top: Adrian Sherratt / Alamy; 449 bottom: © Hulton-Deustch Collection / Corbis; 469: © Kelvin Murray / Getty Images; 489: © Philip Wolmuth / Panos Pictures; 509: © Rick Doyle / Corbis; 525: © The New Yorker Collection 1991. Robert Mankoff from cartoonbank.com. All rights reserved. (Published in *The New Yorker*, 9 December 1991); 533: Kathleen Nelson / Alamy; 561: ABACA / Empics; 589: David Willis / Alamy; 591: Peter Jordan / PA Archive / PA Photos; 617: © Image Source / Alamy; 641: © Angelo Hornak / Corbis; 665: Pictorial Press Lts / Alamy; 693: Reuters / Howard Burditt; 717: © Wolfgang Kaehler / Corbis; 741: © Bettmann / Corbis; 000: Alex Segre / Alamy.

Text

Page 50: Barbara McCarthy, "Returning to college pays dividends", *The Sunday Times*, 11 March 2007. Copyright © 2007 Times Newspapers Limited. Reprinted with permission; 74: David Prosser, "Copper price rises as strike goes on at BHP's Chile mine", *The Independent*, 22 August 2006. Copyright © 2006 Independent News and Media Limited. Reprinted with permission; 96: Andrew Clennell, "Album sales hit all time high – but profits slide", *The Independent*, 18 August 2003. Copyright © 2003 Independent News and Media Limited. Reprinted with permission; 116: Somini Sengupta, "India digs deeper, but wells are drying up, and farming crisis looms", *The New York Times*, 30 September 2006. Copyright © 2006 The New York Times Company. All rights reserved. Reprinted with permission; 138: "EU sugar shake-up threatens £40m hole in profits", *The Times*, 23 June 2005. Copyright © 2005 Times Newspapers Limited. Reprinted with permission; 160: Source: Ros Davidson, "EU–China tariff war hits shoes", *The Guardian*, business section, 7 April 2006. Copyright © The Guardian News and Media Limited 2006. Reprinted with permission; 258: Anthony Fletcher, "Strawberry technology boosts UK super fruit growth", www.foodnavigator.com, 30 May 2006. Copyright © 2000–2007 Decision News Media SAS. All rights reserved. Reprinted with permission; 280: "How good is Google", *The Economist*, 30 October 2002. Copyright © The Economist Newspaper Limited 2002. Reprinted by permission; 312: "Over here, over priced, over the hill", *The Business*, 17 September 2006. Copyright © 2006 by The Business. All rights reserved. Reprinted by permission; 372: Lewis Smith and Lucy Alexander, "Surprises in the wild side of Borneo", *The Times*, 19 December 2006. Copyright © 2006 Times Newspapers Limited. Reprinted with permission; 400: David Smith, "Why the dog of high oil prices is not barking", *The Times*, 19 December 2006. Copyright © 2006 Times Newspapers Limited. Reprinted with permission; 424: David Smith, "The tax for an average lifetime: £600,000 and rising", *The Sunday Times*, 1 October 2006. Copyright © 2006 Times Newspapers Ltd. Reprinted with permission; 442: 'Grade expectations', *The Economist*, 18 March 2004. Copyright © The Economist Newspaper Limited 2004. Reprinted by permission.

We are also grateful to the Financial Times Limited for permission to reprint the following material:

Page 180: "Above-inflation rail fare increases draw protests", *Financial Times*, 2 January 2007 Copyright © 2007 The Financial Times Limited. Reprinted with permission; 354: John Aglionby, "Call for aid to fight tropical deforestation", *Financial Times*, 24 March 2007. Copyright © 2007 The Financial Times Limited. Reprinted with permission; 464: Lex Column "World economy", *Financial Times*, 12 June 2006. Copyright © 2006 The Financial Times Limited. Reprinted with permission; 484: Mure Dickie, "China revises size of economy up by 17%", *Financial Times*, 20 December 2005. Copyright © 2005 The Financial Times Limited. Reprinted with permission; 504: Jamie Chisholm, Jamie, "UK inflation accelerates as transport costs rise", *Financial Times*, 12 December 2006. Copyright © 2006 The Financial Times Limited. Reprinted with permission; 528: Jamie Chisholm, "Business investment drives UK economy forward", *Financial Times*, 24 November 2006. Copyright © 2006 The Financial Times Limited. Reprinted with permission; 556: Chris Giles, "Productivity loses steam under Labour", *Financial Times*, 23 January 2007. Copyright © 2007 The Financial Times Limited. Reprinted with permission; 582: Scheherazade Daneshkhu, "Bank see low risk as value of homes rise", *Financial Times*, 3 February 2007. Copyright © 2007 The Financial Times Limited. Reprinted with permission; 610: Haig Simonian, "Swiss canton's tax regime irks Brussels", *Financial Times*, 16 February 2007. Copyright © 2007 The Financial Times Limited. Reprinted with permission; 636: Jane Croft, "Faster payments processing on way", *Financial Times*, 16 February 2007. Copyright © 2007 The Financial Times

Limited. Reprinted with permission; 660: Jamie Chisholm, "Inflation data push up odds on rates rise", *Financial Times*, 20 March 2007. Copyright © 2007 The Financial Times Limited. Reprinted with permission; 682: Scheherazade Daneshkhu, "IMF warns Brown to rein in spending", *Financial Times*, 6 March 2007. Copyright © 2007 The Financial Times Limited. Reprinted with permission; 712: "Zimbabwe sinks into hell of hyperinflation", *Financial Times*, 15 March 2007 Copyright © 2007. The Financial Times Limited. Reprinted with permission; 736: Scheherazade Daneshkhu, "Race to close productivity gap key", *Financial Times*, 21 March 2007 Copyright © 2007. The Financial Times Limited. Reprinted with permission; 758: Richard McGregor, "Chinese economy surges amid boom in exports", *Financial Times*, 19 October 2006. Copyright © 2006. The Financial Times Limited. Reprinted with permission; 780: Richard McGregor, "Chinese sees strong rise in trade surplus", *Financial Times*, 12 February 2007. Copyright © 2007. The Financial Times Limited. Reprinted with permission.

In some instances we have been unable to trace the owners of copyright material, and we would appreciate any information that would enable us to do so.